The **Shelly Cashman** Series®

Microsoft® 365®
Access®

First Edition

Comprehensive

Sandy Cable
Jill West

Cengage

Australia • Brazil • Canada • Mexico • Singapore • United Kingdom • United States

Cengage

***The Shelly Cashman Series® Microsoft® 365® Access® Comprehensive*, First Edition**
Sandy Cable and Jill West

SVP, Product Management: Cheryl Costantini

VP, Product Management & Marketing: Thais Alencar

Senior Product Director, Portfolio Product Management: Mark Santee

Portfolio Product Director: Rita Lombard

Senior Portfolio Product Manager: Amy Savino

Senior Product Assistant: Ciara Boynton

Learning Designer: Zenya Molnar

Senior Content Manager: Anne Orgren

Digital Project Manager: Jim Vaughey

Developmental Editor: Mary-Terese Cozzola

Senior Director, Product Marketing: Danae April

Senior Marketing Manager: Mackenzie Paine

Portfolio Specialist: Matt Schiesl

Content Acquisition Analyst: Callum Panno

Production Service: Lumina Datamatics Ltd.

Senior Designer: Erin Griffin

Cover Image Source: 4Max/Shutterstock.com

Mac Users: If you're working through this product using a Mac, some of the steps may vary. Additional information for Mac users is included with the Data files for this product.

Disclaimer: This text is intended for instructional purposes only; data is fictional and does not belong to any real persons or companies.

Disclaimer: The material in this text was written using Microsoft Windows 11 and Office 365 Professional Plus and was Quality Assurance tested before the publication date. As Microsoft continually updates the Windows operating system and Office 365, your software experience may vary slightly from what is presented in the printed text.

Previous edition(s): © 2023, © 2020, © 2017

For product information and technology assistance, contact us at
Cengage Customer & Sales Support, 1-800-354-9706
or support.cengage.com.

For permission to use material from this text or product, submit all requests online at **www.copyright.com.**

Library of Congress Control Number: 2024906257

Student Edition ISBN: 978-0-357-88165-1

Loose-Leaf Edition ISBN: 978-0-357-88166-8

Cengage
5191 Natorp Boulevard
Mason, OH 45040
USA

Cengage is a leading provider of customized learning solutions. Our employees reside in nearly 40 different countries and serve digital learners in 165 countries around the world. Find your local representative at **www.cengage.com.**

To learn more about Cengage platforms and services, register or access your online learning solution, or purchase materials for your course, visit **www.cengage.com.**

Notice to the Reader

Printed at CLDPC, USA, 08-24

Brief Contents

Contents

Preface: The Shelly Cashman Series®: Microsoft® 365® & Office®

The Shelly Cashman Series® offers application-specific comprehensive print titles for Word®, Excel®, PowerPoint®, Access®, Publisher®, Outlook®, and Windows®. The modules (chapters) of the four main Microsoft® applications (Word®, Excel®, PowerPoint®, and Access®) are also offered together in each of three print titles organized by level: introductory, intermediate, and advanced. The MindTap Collection includes all of the preceding content, plus additional digital-only content for Teams®, the Mac operating system, and more.

About the Authors

Word: Misty E. Vermaat has more than 30 years of experience in the field of computer and information technology. In addition to consulting in the field, she was an Associate Professor at Purdue University Calumet, teaching or developing courses in Microsoft® Office, computer concepts, database management, systems analysis and design, and programming. Since 1990, she has led the development of the Shelly Cashman Series and has authored and co-authored numerous series textbooks, including many editions of Discovering Computers, Discovering Computers Fundamentals, Microsoft® Publisher®, and Microsoft® Word® books.

PowerPoint: Susan L. Sebok is a retired professor at South Suburban College in South Holland, Illinois, and is also a licensed attorney. Working with the leading Shelly Cashman Series® since 1993, she has co-authored several successful textbooks, including multiple versions of Discovering Computers and Microsoft® PowerPoint®. She holds both Master of Arts and Juris Doctor degrees.

Excel: Victoria Kaye brings her industry knowledge and instructor experience to Cengage Group for the Shelly Cashman Series. As an avid Excel user with Microsoft teaching experience ranging from secondary to undergraduate levels, she is thrilled to be part of the esteemed Shelly Cashman Excel Series legacy.

Dr. Mark Shellman is an instructor and Chair of the Information Technology Department at Gaston College in Dallas, North Carolina. Dr. Mark, as his students call him, prides himself on being student-centered and loves learning himself. His favorite subjects in the information technology realm include databases and programming languages. Dr. Mark has been teaching for more than 30 years and has co-authored several texts in the New Perspective series on Microsoft® Office 365 & Access®, along with a textbook on Structured Query Language.

Access: Jill West authors Cengage courses for CompTIA Cloud+, CompTIA Network+, Data Communications, Technology for Success, and the popular Shelly Cashman Series. She has taught kindergarten through college and currently teaches computer technology courses at Georgia Northwestern Technical College. Jill specializes in designing innovative, critical-thinking activities and building courses that teach popular IT certifications. She regularly presents at conferences and webinars on preparing for CompTIA certifications, teaching cloud computing and computer networking, and mentoring lifelong student learners in IT. She's a member of the 2019 inaugural cohort of Faculty Ambassadors for AWS Educate and is currently an AWS Academy Accredited Educator. Jill and her husband, Mike, live in northwest Georgia with two children at home and two off to college.

Windows 11: Steven M. Freund serves as a lead instructor of various Microsoft® Office, computer concepts, programming, and Internet technology courses throughout central Florida. An integral author for the successful Shelly Cashman Series since 2001, he has presented at the annual customer conference, the Shelly Cashman Series Institute, and other customer events. Freund has co-authored multiple editions of Discovering Computers, Mozilla Firefox, Windows® Internet Explorer, Windows® Office, and Dreamweaver books. In addition, he has written numerous successful instructor supplements. He attended the University of Central Florida.

Preface for the Instructor

Shelly Cashman's trademark step-by-step, screen-by-screen, project-based approach encourages students to expand their understanding of Office applications through hands-on experimentation and critical thinking. Module learning objectives are mapped to Microsoft Office Specialist certification objectives, reinforcing the critical skills needed for success in college and career. Other Ways boxes help users identify alternate click paths to achieve a step, while BTW sidebars offer helpful hints as readers work through projects, enabling them to make the most of Microsoft Office tools. MindTap and updated SAM (Skills Assessment Manager) online resources are also available to guide additional study to maximize results.

Shelly Cashman prepares students for success in the real world by using current and relevant scenarios that apply to everyday life and careers. It also prepares students to take the Microsoft Office Specialist (MOS) exam, which they can leverage in their careers.

Shelly Cashman is designed for students at two- and four-year schools as well as in continuing education programs. Skill levels can range from experienced — for those with a foundational understanding from prior exposure to technology — to introductory — for those using a computer or technology device for the first time.

The Shelly Cashman Series® offers application-specific comprehensive print titles for Word®, Excel®, PowerPoint®, Access®, Publisher®, Outlook®, and Windows®. The modules (chapters) of the four main Microsoft® applications (Word®, Excel®, PowerPoint®, and Access®) are also offered together in each of three print titles organized by level: introductory, intermediate, and advanced. The MindTap Collection includes all of the preceding content, plus additional digital-only content for Teams®, the Mac operating system, and more.

Market research is conducted semi-annually with both current Cengage users and those who use other learning materials. The focus of the market research is to gain insights into the user experience and overall learner needs so we can continuously evolve our content to exceed user expectations. We survey hundreds of instructors to ensure we gather information from a large and varied demographic.

New to This Edition

Shelly Cashman provides thoroughly updated coverage that reflects current Microsoft® 365® features. Narrative content has been authored using Microsoft® 365 Business Standard. Module projects incorporate career topics that apply diversity, equity, and inclusion principles and ensure accessibility. All projects, assignments, and lessons have been refreshed with authentic case scenarios that focus on practical skills and employability.

Word: New features in the Word content include the enhanced Accessibility Checker, which identifies potential accessibility issues and presents suggestions to make documents more inclusive. The Word coverage also introduces Focus mode, the updated collaboration experience, Microsoft's expanded search tool, and voice options. The Immersive Reader is covered, as is the ability to create a private document copy and use Word's screen reader.

PowerPoint: The PowerPoint content introduces the new commenting experience, which lets users display comments in contextual view or the Comments pane. The comment anchor helps reviewers identify specific slide elements with comments and place the comment bubble anywhere on the slide. With the revised search feature, users can enter a word or phrase in the Search box to find the definition. Microsoft Search also provides support articles to help perform tasks. Users can record and save a presentation that includes digital inking to capture text, drawings, and annotations, and then play back animated drawings. The Speaker Coach uses artificial intelligence (AI) to improve presentation skills by giving feedback on body language, the use of sensitive and filler words, and perceived mispronounced words.

Excel: With the Excel modules, students learn both long-standing Excel functions and tools as well as the most recent innovations. Updates to the Excel content include the new XLOOKUP and LET functions, dynamic arrays, and the Analyze Data feature. Also covered is the Accessibility Checker, which identifies issues and offers solutions to produce an accessible workbook.

Access: New features in the Access coverage include updated, real-world scenarios from a variety of industries that illustrate the relevance of Access databases in today's businesses. Completely updated projects use gapped Start and Solution files to ensure students use new, authentic files for each project from one module to the next. Module projects alternate between two sets of scenarios for expanded relevance and practicality. Further, an off-module scenario database receives updates comparable to the on-module scenario so students see similar progression in all databases. A Solutions to Critical Thinking Questions document for each module guides instructors on what to look for in student work. Critical Thinking Questions invite students to engage with the module's skills and information at a conceptual level, and to reflect on their learning, thinking processes, and the relevance of learned skills to their chosen careers.

Windows: The updates to the Windows modules reflect the changes from Windows 10 to Windows 11. New end-of-module exercises incorporate current terminology and features. Module projects have been updated with the latest Windows 11 features, including widgets, the revised Start and Search menus, and the Immersive Reader.

Organization of the Text

The *Shelly Cashman Series: Microsoft 365 & Office, First Edition* is a comprehensive introduction to Microsoft applications and is intended for students in introductory computing courses. Each application is divided into modules within the three levels — introductory, intermediate, and advanced. Each module introduces a topic through a real-world project and presents content that aligns directly with the learning objectives listed at the beginning of the module. To enable students to practice and apply skills learned, each module ends with a summary and a Consider This: Plan Ahead master planning guide that students use as they complete assignments and create projects on their own. Lastly, the end-of-module assignments are related to the top 25 industries for each application and include critical thinking questions. To increase students' confidence in their abilities, the assignments build from applying skills to experimenting beyond the module content to implementing a solution using creative thinking and problem-solving approaches.

Features of the Text

The features of the text, which are found consistently throughout all modules, are designed to aid the student in a specific way.

The projects are focused on employability based on current research and data. They use authentic case scenarios and a step-by-step approach to be as engaging, comprehensive, and easy to use as possible.

Heading levels organize topics within a module. Unique to the Shelly Cashman Series are "To-Do" heading levels for step-by-step task sequences. A To-Do head lead-in paragraph may include a **Why?** element to clarify why students are performing the steps.

To Display a Different Tab on the Ribbon

When you start Word, the ribbon displays 11 main tabs: File, Home, Insert, Draw, Design, Layout, References, Mailings, Review, View, and Help. (Note that depending on the type of computer or device you are using, the Draw tab may not appear.) The tab currently displayed is called the active tab. To display a different tab on the ribbon, you click the tab. The following step displays the View tab, that is, makes it the active tab. **Why?** When working with Word, you may need to switch tabs to access other options for working with a document or to verify settings.

Step-by-step sequences include the following features:

Q&A boxes provide troubleshooting information, equivalent touch instructions, or an additional explanation for a step.

Experiment steps encourage students to explore a feature such as the Themes gallery.

2

- If necessary, scroll to and then point to Facet in the Themes gallery to display a Live Preview of that theme applied to the document (Figure 1–37).
- **Experiment:** Point to various themes in the Themes gallery to display a Live Preview of the various themes applied to the document in the document window.

Q&A What is Live Preview?
Recall from the discussion earlier in this module that Live Preview is a feature that allows you to point to a gallery choice and see its effect in the document — without actually selecting the choice.

Can I use Live Preview on a touch screen?
Live Preview may not be available on all touch screens.

Other Ways provide additional methods to accomplish the tasks covered in specific To-Do steps.

Other Ways

1. Right-click paragraph (or if using touch, tap 'Show Context Menu' button on Mini toolbar), click Paragraph on shortcut menu, click Indents and Spacing tab (Paragraph dialog box), click Alignment arrow, click Centered, click OK
2. Click Paragraph Dialog Box Launcher (Home tab or Layout tab | Paragraph group), click Indents and Spacing tab (Paragraph dialog box), click Alignment arrow, click Centered, click OK
3. Press CTRL+E

By the Way (BTW) boxes are short marginal elements that add value for students by expanding on information in the module.

BTW

Printing Document Properties

To print document properties, click File on the ribbon to open Backstage view, click Print in Backstage view to display the Print screen, click the first button in the Settings area to display a list of options specifying what you can print, click Document Info in the list to specify you want to print the document properties instead of the actual document, and then click the Print button in the Print screen to print the document properties on the currently selected printer.

Other in-text pedagogical elements include the following:

Key terms are bold and blue in the running text. In the MindTap, each bolded key term is linked to its definition in the Master Glossary.

> Calibri and Calibri Light are **sans serif fonts**, which are fonts that do not ends of their characters. Other fonts such as Calisto MT are **serif fonts**,

Consider This is a pedagogical sidebar in the form of a question and answer that appears within the module and in the end-of-module student assignments. The question addresses conceptual or critical thinking topics, general information about the app, or other important information students should know.

> **Consider This**
>
> **How do you use the touch keyboard with a touch screen?**
>
> To display the on-screen touch keyboard, tap the Touch Keyboard button on the Windows taskbar. When finished using the touch keyboard, tap the X button on the touch keyboard to close the keyboard.

Break Point is a note to students that indicates a good place to take a break. Every module includes at least one break point.

> **Break Point:** If you want to take a break, this is a good place to do so. You can exit Word now. To resume later, start Word and continue following the steps from this location forward.

SAM Upload and Download icons are for SAM users. A SAM download icon appears next to any step where students download a data file to begin a SAM Project.

> 1
>
> • sam Click the Start button on the Windows taskbar to display the Start

A SAM upload icon appears next to any step where students submit a file to SAM for a completed SAM Project.

> 3
>
> • Click the 'Clear Search String' button to remove the search string and redisplay all objects.
>
> **Q&A** Did I have to click the button to redisplay all objects? Could I simply have erased the current string to achieve the same result?
>
> You did not have to click the button. You could have used DEL or BACKSPACE to erase the current search string.
>
> • If desired, sign out of your Microsoft account.
>
> • sam Exit Access.

Figure callouts point to important parts of a screen and include two types:

Action/navigation callouts point to commands or buttons used in the step. Action/navigation callout boxes are a different color from explanatory callouts to help students easily locate screen elements referenced in step instructions.

Explanatory callouts direct students to other significant screen elements in the figure.

1. With the text selected (shown in Figure 1–55), click the Font Size arrow (Home tab | Font group) to display the Font Size gallery.
2. Click 20 in the Font Size gallery to increase the font size of the selected text.
3. Click anywhere in the document window to remove the selection from the text (Figure 1–56).

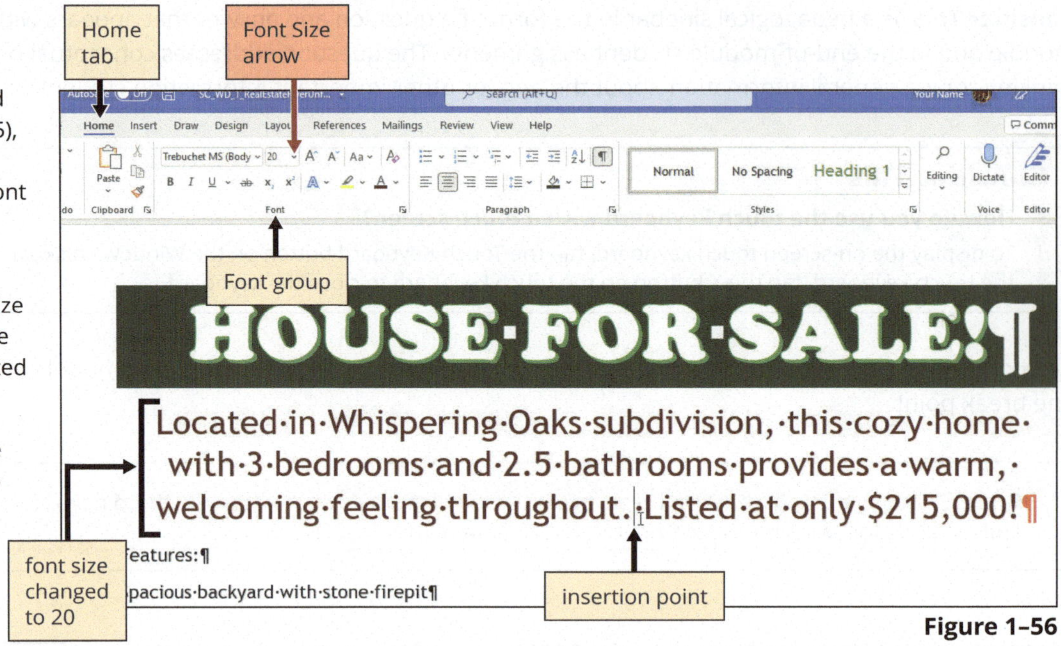

Figure 1–56

Course Solutions

Online Learning Platform: MindTap with SAM

The Shelly Cashman Series MindTap Collection, powered by SAM (Skills Assessment Manager), enables proficiency in Microsoft Office and computing concepts for your Introductory Computing courses. With a library of renowned course materials, including ready-to-assign, auto-graded learning modules, you can easily adapt your course to best prepare students for the evolving job market. In addition to an eReader that includes the full content of the printed book, The Shelly Cashman Series, First Edition MindTap course includes the following:

- SAM Textbook Projects: Follow the steps and scenarios outlined in the textbook readings; enable students to complete projects based on a real-world scenario live in Microsoft Office applications and submit them in SAM for automatic grading and feedback.
- SAM Training and Exam: Trainings teach students to complete specific skills in a simulated Microsoft application environment while exams allow students to demonstrate their proficiency (also in a simulated environment).
- SAM Projects: Students complete projects based on real-world scenarios live in Microsoft applications and submit the projects in SAM for automatic grading and feedback. SAM offers several types of projects, each with a unique purpose: 1A and 1B, critical thinking, end of module, capstone, and integration.

- Microsoft Office Specialist (MOS) resources: Training and exams are based on the Microsoft Office 365 Objective Domains for the MOS Exam and exam simulation that replicates the test-taking environment of the MOS exam for Word, Excel, Access, PowerPoint, and Outlook.

To learn more, go to: https://www.cengage.com/mindtap-collections/

Ancillary Package

Additional instructor and student resources for this product are available online. Instructor assets include an Instructor Manual, an Educator Guide, PowerPoint® slides, a Guide to Teaching Online, Solution Files, a test bank powered by Cognero®, and a Transition Guide. Student assets include data files and a glossary. Sign up or sign in at www.cengage.com to search for and access this product and its online resources. The instructor and student companion sites contain ancillary material for the full Shelly Cashman Series Collection, along with instructions on how to find specific content within the companion site.

- Instructor Manual: This guide provides additional instructional material to assist in class preparation, including module objectives, module outlines, discussion questions, and additional activities and assignments. Each outline corresponds directly with the content in the module, and additional discussion questions and activities are aligned to headings in the book.
- Educator Guide: The MindTap Educator Guide contains a detailed outline of the corresponding MindTap course, including activity types and time on task. The SAM Educator Guide explains how to use SAM functionality to maximize your course.
- PowerPoint slides: The slides may be used to guide classroom presentations, to provide to students for module review, or to print as classroom handouts. The slides align closely with the book while activities and the self-assessment align with module learning objectives and supplement the content in the book.
- Guide to Teaching Online: This guide presents technological and pedagogical considerations and suggestions for teaching the Introductory Computing course when you can't be in the same room with students.
- Solution and Answer Guide: The answers to the critical thinking questions are written by the author and correspond to critical thinking questions in the end-of-module activities.
- Solution files: These files provide solutions to all textbook projects for instructors to use to grade student work.
    - Instructors using SAM do not need solution files since projects are auto-graded within SAM.
    - Solution files are provided on the instructor companion site for instructors *not* using SAM.
- Data files: These files are provided for students to complete the projects in each module.
    - Students using SAM to complete the projects download the required data files directly from SAM.
    - Students who are *not* using SAM to complete the projects can find data files on the student companion site and within MindTap.
- Test banks: A comprehensive test bank, offered in Cognero, Word, Blackboard, Moodle, Desire2Learn, Canvas, and SAM formats, contains questions aligned with each module's learning objectives and is written by subject matter experts. Powered by Cognero, Cengage Testing is a flexible, online system that allows you to author, edit, and manage test bank content from multiple Cengage solutions and to create multiple test versions that you can deliver from your LMS, your classroom, or wherever you want.
- Transition Guide: This guide highlights all of the changes in the text and in the digital offerings from the previous edition to the current one so that instructors know what to expect.

Acknowledgments

Jill West: It's always a privilege to work with the incredible teams Cengage puts together, and this course is no exception. I've worked on many projects under the energetic and resourceful leadership of Amy Savino, whom I greatly admire and will forever be thankful for her vote of confidence in me when I needed it most. I've thoroughly enjoyed getting to know Anne Orgren, who has been our attentive and supportive content manager, providing just enough guidance exactly when needed. I can't say enough good things about MT Cozzola, developmental editor for this project. With her diversity of talents and skills, she has been a learner advocate, bringing the student's perspective to every conversation and providing synergistic insight. And I'm grateful for another opportunity to work with learning designer Zenya Molnar, who brings creative solutions to design challenges. Many other folks worked diligently behind the scenes to ensure consistency of quality, design, and innovation — their efforts are enthusiastically noted and greatly appreciated.

I owe a special thanks to my husband, Mike, for his tireless support and encouragement. And thanks to my kiddos: Winn, Sarah, Daniel, and Zack.

Victoria Kaye: Thank you for the many individuals who have made this edition possible. A text like this is not done without great effort, teamwork, and planning. Thank you to those individuals who contributed their expertise to this text, and an extra special thank you to developmental editors Barbara Clemens and MT Cozzola. Without your vast knowledge and careful consideration, this edition would not be possible. Thank you to the editorial team and their staff: Amy Savino, Senior Portfolio Product Manager; Anne Orgren, Senior Content Manager; and Zenya Molnar, Learning Designer. It is simply not possible to sum up the value of your contributions.

Getting to Know Microsoft Office Versions

Cengage is proud to bring you the next edition of Microsoft Office. This edition was designed to provide a robust learning experience that is not dependent upon a specific version of Office.

Microsoft supports several versions and editions of Office: (Refer to Table 1 below for more information)

- **Microsoft 365 (formerly known as Office 365):** A service that delivers the most up-to-date, feature-rich, modern Microsoft productivity applications direct to your device. There are several combinations of Microsoft 365 programs for business, educational, and personal use. Microsoft 365 is cloud-based, meaning it is stored, managed, and processed on a network of remote servers hosted on the Internet, rather than on local servers or personal computers. Microsoft 365 offers extra online storage and cloud-connected features, as well as updates with the latest features, fixes, and security updates. Microsoft 365 is purchased for a monthly subscription fee that keeps your software up to date with the latest features.
- **Office 2021:** The Microsoft "on-premises" version of the Office apps, available for both PCs and Macintosh computers, offered as a static, one-time purchase and outside of the subscription model. Unlike Microsoft 365, Office 2021 does not include online product updates with new features.
- **Microsoft 365 Online (formerly known as Office Online):** A free, simplified version of Microsoft web applications (Teams, Access, Word, Excel, PowerPoint, and OneNote) that lets users create and edit files collaboratively.
- **Office 365 Education:** A free subscription including Word, Excel, PowerPoint, OneNote, and now Microsoft Teams, plus additional classroom tools. Only available for students and educators at select institutions.

Table 1 Microsoft Office applications — uses and availability

Application	Use	Availability/Editions
Word	Create documents and improve your writing with intelligent assistance features.	Microsoft 365 Family, Home, Business, Office 2021, Office 365 Education
Excel	Simplify complex data into easy-to-read spreadsheets.	Microsoft 365 Personal, Home, Business, Office 2021, Office 365 Education
PowerPoint	Create presentations that stand out.	Home, Business, Office 2021, Office 365 Education
OneNote	A digital notebook for all your note-taking needs.	Home, Office 365 Education
OneDrive	Save and share your files and photos wherever you are.	Home, Business
Outlook	Manage your email, calendar, tasks, and contacts all in one place.	Home, Business
SharePoint	Create team sites to share information, files, and resources.	Business
Publisher	Create polished, professional layouts without the hassle.	Home, Business, Office 2021 (PC only)
Access	Create your own database apps easily in formats that serve your business best.	Home, Business, Office 2021 (PC only)
Teams	Bring everyone together in one place to meet, chat, call, and collaborate.	Business, Office 365 Education
Exchange	Business-class email and calendaring.	Business

Over time, the Microsoft 365 cloud interface will continuously update using its web connection, offering new application features and functions, while Office 2021 will remain static.

Because Microsoft 365 releases updates continuously, your onscreen experience may differ from what you see in this product. For example, the more advanced features and functionalities covered in this product may not be available in Microsoft 365 Online, may have updated from what you see in Office 2021, or may be from a post-publication update of Microsoft 365.

For up-to-date information on the differences between Microsoft 365, Office 2021, and Microsoft 365 Online, please visit the Microsoft Support website.

Cengage is committed to providing high-quality learning solutions for you to gain the knowledge and skills that will empower you throughout your educational and professional careers.

Thank you for using our product, and we look forward to exploring the future of Microsoft Office with you!

Using SAM Projects and Textbook Projects

SAM (Skills Assessment Manager) **Projects** allow you to actively apply the skills you learned in Microsoft Word, Excel, PowerPoint, or Access. You can also submit your work to SAM for online grading. You can use SAM Projects to become a more productive student and use these skills throughout your career.

To complete SAM Textbook Projects, please follow these steps:

SAM Textbook Projects allow you to complete a project as you follow along with the steps in the textbook. As you read the module, look for icons that indicate when you should download sam↓ your SAM Start file(s) and when to upload sam↑ your solution file to SAM for grading.

Everything you need to complete this project is provided within SAM. You can launch the eBook directly from SAM, which will allow you to take notes, highlight, and create a custom study guide, or you can use a print textbook or your mobile app. Download IOS or Download Android.

To get started, launch your SAM Project assignment from SAM, MindTap, or a link within your learning management system.

1. Step 1:
   Download Files
   - Click the "Download All" button or the individual links to download your **Start File** and **Support File(s)** (when available). You must use the SAM Start file.
   - Click the Instructions link to launch the eBook (or use the print textbook or mobile app).
   - Disregard any steps in the textbook that ask you to create a new file or to use a file from a location outside of SAM.
   - Look for the SAM Download icon sam↓ to begin working with your start file.
   - Follow the module's step-by-step instructions until you reach the SAM Upload icon sam↑.
   - Save and close the file.

2. Step 2:
   Save Work to SAM
   - Ensure you rename your project file to match the Expected File Name.
   - Upload your in-progress or completed file to SAM. You can download the file to continue working or submit it for grading in the next step.
3. Step 3:
   Submit for Grading
   - Upload your completed solution file to SAM for immediate feedback and to view the available Reports.
     - The **Graded Summary Report** provides a detailed list of project steps, your score, and feedback to aid you in revising and resubmitting the project.
     - The **Study Guide** provides your score for each project step and links to the associated training and textbook pages.
   - If additional attempts are allowed, use your reports to assist with revising and resubmitting your project.
   - To re-submit your project, download the file you saved in step 2.
   - Edit, save, and close the file, then re-upload and submit it again.

For all other SAM Projects, please follow these steps:

To get started, launch your SAM Project assignment from SAM, MindTap, or a link within your learning management system.

1. Step 1:
   Download Files
   - Click the "Download All" button or the individual links to download your **Instruction File**, **Start File**, and **Support File(s)** (when available). You must use the SAM Start file.
   - Open the Instruction file and follow the step-by-step instructions. Ensure you rename your project file to match the Expected File Name (change _1 to _2 at the end of the file name).

2. Step 2:
   Save Work to SAM
   - Upload your in-progress or completed file to SAM. You can download the file to continue working or submit it for grading in the next step.
3. Step 3:
   Submit for Grading
   - Upload the completed file to SAM for immediate feedback and to view available Reports.
     - The **Graded Summary Report** provides a detailed list of project steps, your score, and feedback to aid you in revising and resubmitting the project.
     - The **Study Guide** provides your score for each project step and links to the associated training and textbook pages.
   - If additional attempts are allowed, use your reports to assist with revising and resubmitting your project.
   - To re-submit the project, download the file saved in step 2.
   - Edit, save, and close the file, then re-upload and submit it again.

For additional tips to successfully complete your SAM Projects, please view our SAM Video Tutorials.

Databases and Database Objects: An Introduction

Objectives

After completing this module, you will be able to:

- Describe the features of the Access window
- Create a database
- Create a database using a template
- Create a table using Datasheet view
- Modify properties of a table's primary key
- Display a table's structure in Design view
- Add records to a table
- Resize a table's columns in Datasheet view
- Create a table using Design view
- Import a table
- Create a query using the Simple Query Wizard
- Run a query
- Create a form
- Create a report using the Report Wizard
- Explain special database operations

Introduction

The term **database** describes a collection of data organized in a manner that allows access, retrieval, and use of that data. Microsoft 365 Access, usually referred to as simply Access, is a database management system. A **database management system** is software that allows you to use a computer to create a database; add, change, and delete data in the database; ask and answer questions concerning the data; and create forms and reports using the data.

Project: Database Creation

Clearnet Logistics is a freight brokerage company that connects carriers with freight customers. Up until now, the tracking system has been paper-based. The two partners who run Clearnet have been using a large book to record freight loads, with each page containing specific information such as pickup and dropoff locations. Each page has slots for additional stops or detailed load information, which are made in pencil to allow for changes. Clearnet wants to computerize the tracking system with an Access database. The partners are ready to expand and need to hire an office assistant and, eventually, a tracker and another broker. To facilitate team-wide communication, they need to make the tracking system easier to use and more efficient. To accomplish that goal, the company needs computer-based record keeping.

Clearnet needs to record contact, license, and insurance information about the carriers they work with. Contact names, emails, and phone numbers for arranging loads are essential pieces of information. In addition, the team must be able to contact drivers quickly. The staff needs to record each load's driver name and mobile phone number to efficiently coordinate and track loads from shippers.

Keeping accurate load information allows for timely and accurate payments to carriers and their drivers. Each load's pickup and dropoff dates, mileage, start and end points, and agreed-upon payment terms should be recorded so that information can be easily retrieved for efficient tracking and billing. Load information should include the freight customer's billing information, which is needed to collect payments. The database should also contain each carrier's payment information for bank transfers or mailing checks.

The cost to transport each load is agreed upon before booking the load and is called the rate confirmation or "rate con" for short. This information needs to be recorded up front and then billed as loads are completed. The database system must also track locations for pickup and dropoff.

By recording all its load-tracking information in Access, Clearnet will be able to keep its data current and accurate and can analyze it for trends. Using a database will also allow Clearnet to create a variety of useful reports; for example, tracking the frequency of certain load types or areas with increased levels of transportation activity. These reports are vital for planning purposes and researching leads for more loads, carriers, and drivers.

In a **relational database**, such as those maintained by Access, a database consists of a collection of tables, each of which contains information on a specific subject. Figure 1–1 shows the database for Clearnet. It consists of five tables: the Shippers table (Figure 1–1a) contains information about the customers hiring freight transportation services, the Locations table (Figure 1–1b) contains information for pickup and dropoff locations for freight loads, the Loads table (Figure 1–1c) contains information about the transportation of loads, the Truck Type table (Figure 1–1d) contains information about the type of truck needed for the various kinds of freight, and the Carriers table (Figure 1–1e) contains a listing of the transportation companies that own and operate the trucks carrying loads.

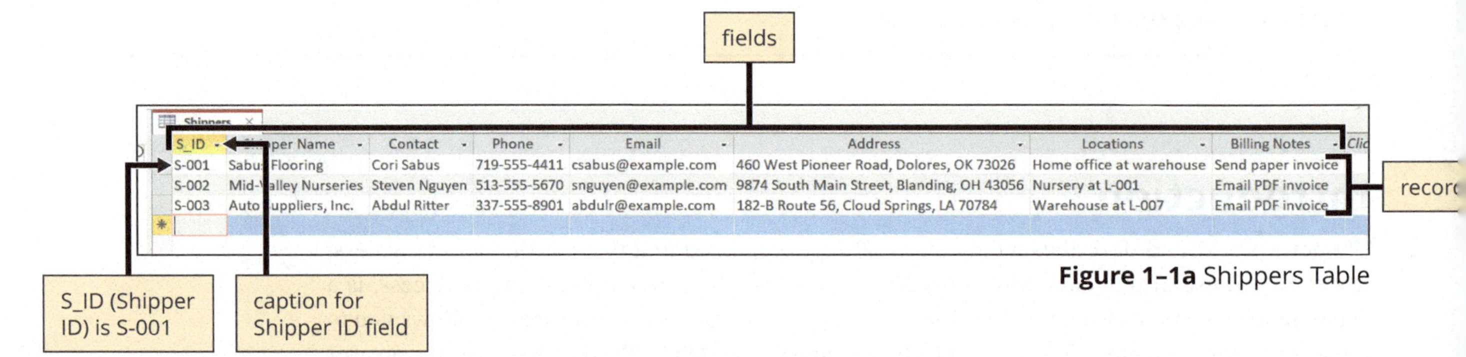

S_ID	per Name	Contact	Phone	Email	Address	Locations	Billing Notes
S-001	Sabu Flooring	Cori Sabus	719-555-4411	csabus@example.com	460 West Pioneer Road, Dolores, OK 73026	Home office at warehouse	Send paper invoice
S-002	Mid-alley Nurseries	Steven Nguyen	513-555-5670	snguyen@example.com	9874 South Main Street, Blanding, OH 43056	Nursery at L-001	Email PDF invoice
S-003	Auto uppliers, Inc.	Abdul Ritter	337-555-8901	abdulr@example.com	182-B Route 56, Cloud Springs, LA 70784	Warehouse at L-007	Email PDF invoice

Figure 1–1a Shippers Table

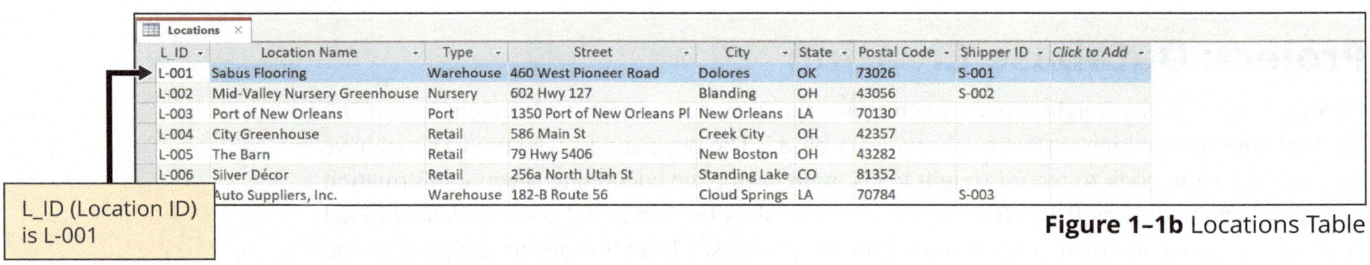

L_ID	Location Name	Type	Street	City	State	Postal Code	Shipper ID	Click to Add
L-001	Sabus Flooring	Warehouse	460 West Pioneer Road	Dolores	OK	73026	S-001	
L-002	Mid-Valley Nursery Greenhouse	Nursery	602 Hwy 127	Blanding	OH	43056	S-002	
L-003	Port of New Orleans	Port	1350 Port of New Orleans Pl	New Orleans	LA	70130		
L-004	City Greenhouse	Retail	586 Main St	Creek City	OH	42357		
L-005	The Barn	Retail	79 Hwy 5406	New Boston	OH	43282		
L-006	Silver Décor	Retail	256a North Utah St	Standing Lake	CO	81352		
	Auto Suppliers, Inc.	Warehouse	182-B Route 56	Cloud Springs	LA	70784	S-003	

Figure 1–1b Locations Table

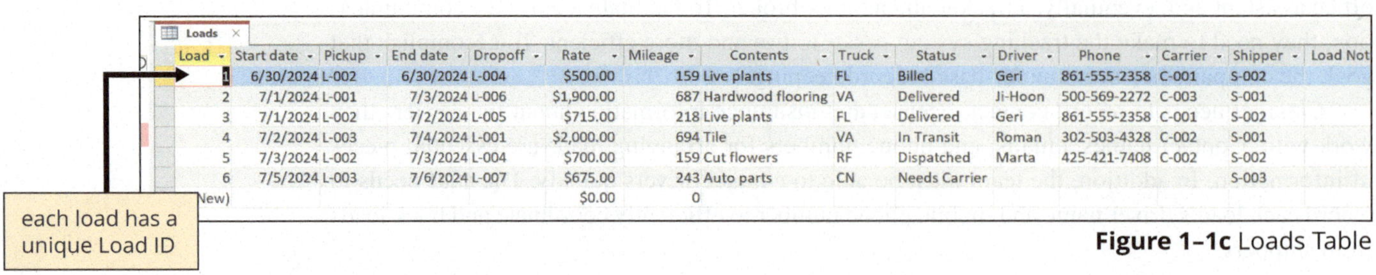

Load	Start date	Pickup	End date	Dropoff	Rate	Mileage	Contents	Truck	Status	Driver	Phone	Carrier	Shipper	Load Not
1	6/30/2024	L-002	6/30/2024	L-004	$500.00	159	Live plants	FL	Billed	Geri	861-555-2358	C-001	S-002	
2	7/1/2024	L-001	7/3/2024	L-006	$1,900.00	687	Hardwood flooring	VA	Delivered	Ji-Hoon	500-569-2272	C-003	S-001	
3	7/1/2024	L-002	7/2/2024	L-005	$715.00	218	Live plants	FL	Delivered	Geri	861-555-2358	C-001	S-002	
4	7/2/2024	L-003	7/4/2024	L-001	$2,000.00	694	Tile	VA	In Transit	Roman	302-503-4328	C-002	S-001	
5	7/3/2024	L-002	7/3/2024	L-004	$700.00	159	Cut flowers	RF	Dispatched	Marta	425-421-7408	C-002	S-002	
6	7/5/2024	L-003	7/6/2024	L-007	$675.00	243	Auto parts	CN	Needs Carrier				S-003	
New)					$0.00	0								

Figure 1–1c Loads Table

Truck Type

T_ID	Truck Type	Target Rate	Rate Notes	Click to Add
CN	Container	$2.75		
FL	Flatbed	$3.25		
HL	Heavy equipment-Long	$5.00	Distances over 500 miles	
HS	Heavy equipment-Short	$3.00	Distances under 500 miles	
PI	Premium insurance	$4.00	Premium insurance coverage for high-value loads	
RF	Reefer	$3.15	Temperature-controlled/refrigerated	
TK	Tanker	$3.00	Tanker endorsement	
VA	Dry van	$2.75	Standard trailer	
VM	Dry van-Team	$2.75	Multiple drivers	
VZ	Dry van-Hazmat	$3.15	Hazmat restrictions	
*		$0.00		

target rate for new VA (dry van) loads

Figure 1–1d Truck Type Table

Carriers

C_ID	Carrier Name	Contact	Phone	Email	Address	MC Number	USDOT	Insurance	
C-001	Williams Trucking	Marco Bailey	220-238-6682	mbailey@newmail.com	9887 Dover Rd, Searcy, AK 72210	MC01015276	1435917	Shipping Insurance, Inc.	Bank transfe
C-002	Freightliners Inc.	Teresa Gomez	435-222-4545	tgomez@newmail.com	6214 Lansing, Gainesville, UT 84511	MC00111937	2971533	Overland Insurers	Mail check to
C-003	Spotters Freight	Lata Gaspar	617-732-9888	latag@newmail.com	456 Hwy 46 S, Crestview, TN 37055	MC10011438	2297585	US Motor Group	Bank transfe
*									

Carrier ID for each carrier

Figure 1–1e Carriers Table

The rows in the tables are called **records**. A record contains information about a given person, item, or event. A row in the Shippers table, for example, contains information about a specific shipping company, such as the company's name, address, and other data.

The columns in the tables are called fields. A **field** contains a specific piece of information within a record. In the Shippers table, for example, the fourth field, Phone, contains the phone number for the main contact person at the shipping company.

The first field in the Shippers table is S_ID, which is an abbreviation for Shipper Identification. Clearnet assigns each shipper an identifying number; the Shipper ID consists of one uppercase letter followed by a three-digit number.

Each Shipper ID is unique; that is, no two shippers have the same number. Such a field is a **unique identifier**. A unique identifier, as its name suggests, is a way of uniquely identifying each record in the table. A given shipper number will appear only in a single record in the table. Only one record exists, for example, in which the Shipper ID is S-002. A unique identifier is also called a **primary key**. Thus, the Shipper ID field is the primary key for the Shippers table. This means the Shipper ID field, which has the caption S_ID, can be used to uniquely identify any record in the table. No two records can have the same value in the Shipper ID field.

The next seven fields in the Shippers table are Shipper Name, Contact, Phone, Email, Address, Locations, and Billing Notes. For example, Shipper ID S-002 is Mid-Valley Nurseries whose primary contact is Steven Nguyen. Steven can be reached at the phone number or the email address listed in the table.

Clearnet's database also contains a table called Locations. Within the Locations table, each location used for load pickup or dropoff is assigned a unique identifier called Location ID (the caption L_ID is a shortened version of this identifier). For example, Sabus Flooring's warehouse location has a Location ID of L-001. No other location has this Location ID. The location's name is indicated in the Location Name field. The location type under the Type field is recorded as Warehouse with an address in Dolores, OK. If relevant, Clearnet associates the location with the shipping company that owns it by including a field in the Locations table called Shipper ID. If the location is owned by a shipper, then the Shipper ID field in the Locations table displays a Shipper ID from the Shippers table. For instance, the L-001 warehouse is owned by a unique shipping company with the Shipper ID S-001. However, the Port of New Orleans location, which has the Location ID L-003, is not owned by a shipping company because it is used by many shippers. Therefore, it does not have information in the Shipper ID field.

BTW
Captions
You can change a field's caption, or the wording that appears as the field's name, to language that is more descriptive, shorter, or meets some other requirement.

BTW
Reserved Words
Access has several reserved words, words that have a special meaning to Access. You cannot use these reserved words as field names. For example, Name is a reserved word and could not be used on its own as a field name in the Shippers table to describe a shipping company's name. For a complete list of reserved words in Access, consult Access Help.

There are three other tables within the Clearnet database. The Loads table records each load that has been transported. Each load is assigned a Load ID, listed in the Load field. This ID is unique for each load booked through Clearnet's broker service. For example, Load ID 1 transported live plants on June 30, 2024. This load was carried on a flatbed trailer, which typically costs more than some other truck types. The target rate for flatbed freight is listed in the fourth table, Truck Type. The Truck Type table lists the types of trucks booked by Clearnet. Each truck type is assigned a unique identifier called Truck Type ID, which is a two-letter abbreviation of the truck type name. For example, Truck Type VA is a standard trailer called a dry van that does not offer any specialized equipment for transport. Therefore, this truck type costs less to hire than other truck types. Truck Type RF, which is short for reefer, provides a refrigerated truck with a controlled temperature. Because these trailers must comply with special regulations, a reefer often costs more to hire.

Finally, there is a table called Carriers that lists carriers who have hired Clearnet's brokerage service. Each carrier has a unique Carrier ID that is associated with the carrier's contact, insurance, and billing details. For example, Carrier ID C-001 is Williams Trucking, in Searcy, AK, and the primary contact is Marco Bailey. Their insurance policy is through Shipping Insurance, Inc. Payments to this carrier are made by bank transfer to their account at Liberty Bank.

Consider This

How would you find the shipper's contact information for a specific load?

Suppose a shipment of tile, Load ID 4, encounters significant delays from a hurricane, and Clearnet needs to contact the shipper to keep them informed. The broker could easily find the shipper contact's name and phone number by looking in the Loads table and then in the Shipper's table. In the Loads table, locate the affected load and read across until you come to the Shipper ID, which is S-001. Then, in the Shippers table, locate the record which has the Shipper ID S-001, and read across to find the primary contact's name and phone number.

Consider This

How would you find the pickup address for a specific load?

First, look in the Loads table to identify the specific load, and then check its Pickup location. Suppose the Load's ID is 3. Once you locate it in the table, you can read across and see that its pickup location has the ID L-002. Next, look in the Locations table for Location L-002 and find that the physical address for this location is 602 Hwy 127, Blanding, OH 43056.

Creating a Database

In Access, all the tables, reports, forms, and queries that you create are stored in a single file called a database. A database is a structure that can store information about multiple types of objects, the properties of those objects, and the relationships among the objects. The first step is to create the database that will hold your tables, reports, forms, and queries. You can start with either a blank database or a template to create a new database. If you already knew the tables and fields you wanted in your database, you would use the Blank database option in Access. If not, you can use a database template. Templates can guide you by suggesting some commonly used tables and fields in certain kinds of databases.

To Create a Database

Because you already know the tables and fields you want in the Clearnet database, you will use the Blank database option rather than a template to create the database. **Why?** The Blank database is the most efficient way to create a database for which you already know the intended data needs. The following steps create the database.

1

- Click the Windows Start button to display the Windows menu.
- Click the Access button to start Access (Figure 1–2a).

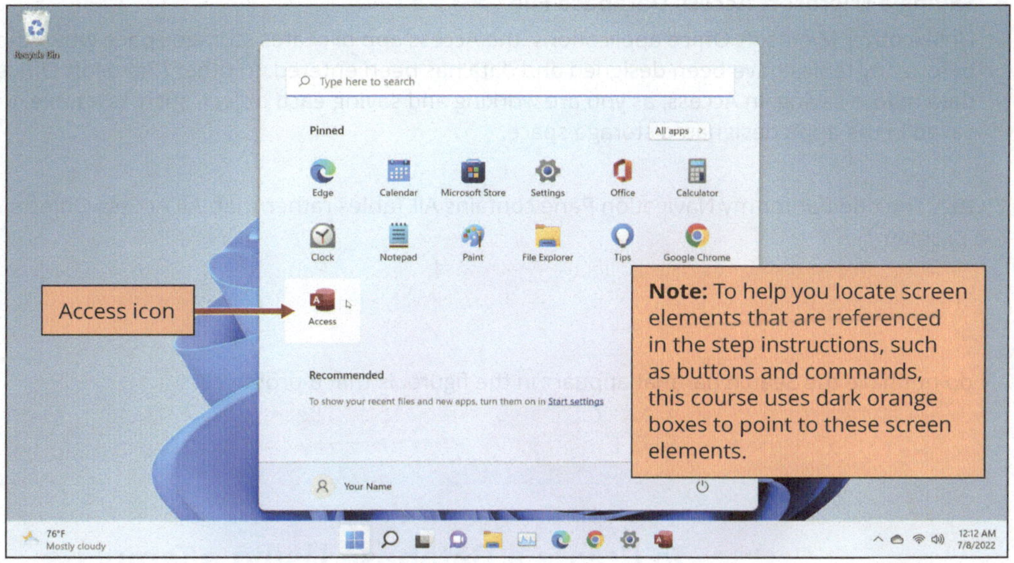

Figure 1–2a

2

- Click the Blank database button to specify the type of database to create.
- sam Type **SC_AC_01_Clearnet** in the File Name text box, and then click the Create button to create the database (Figure 1–2).

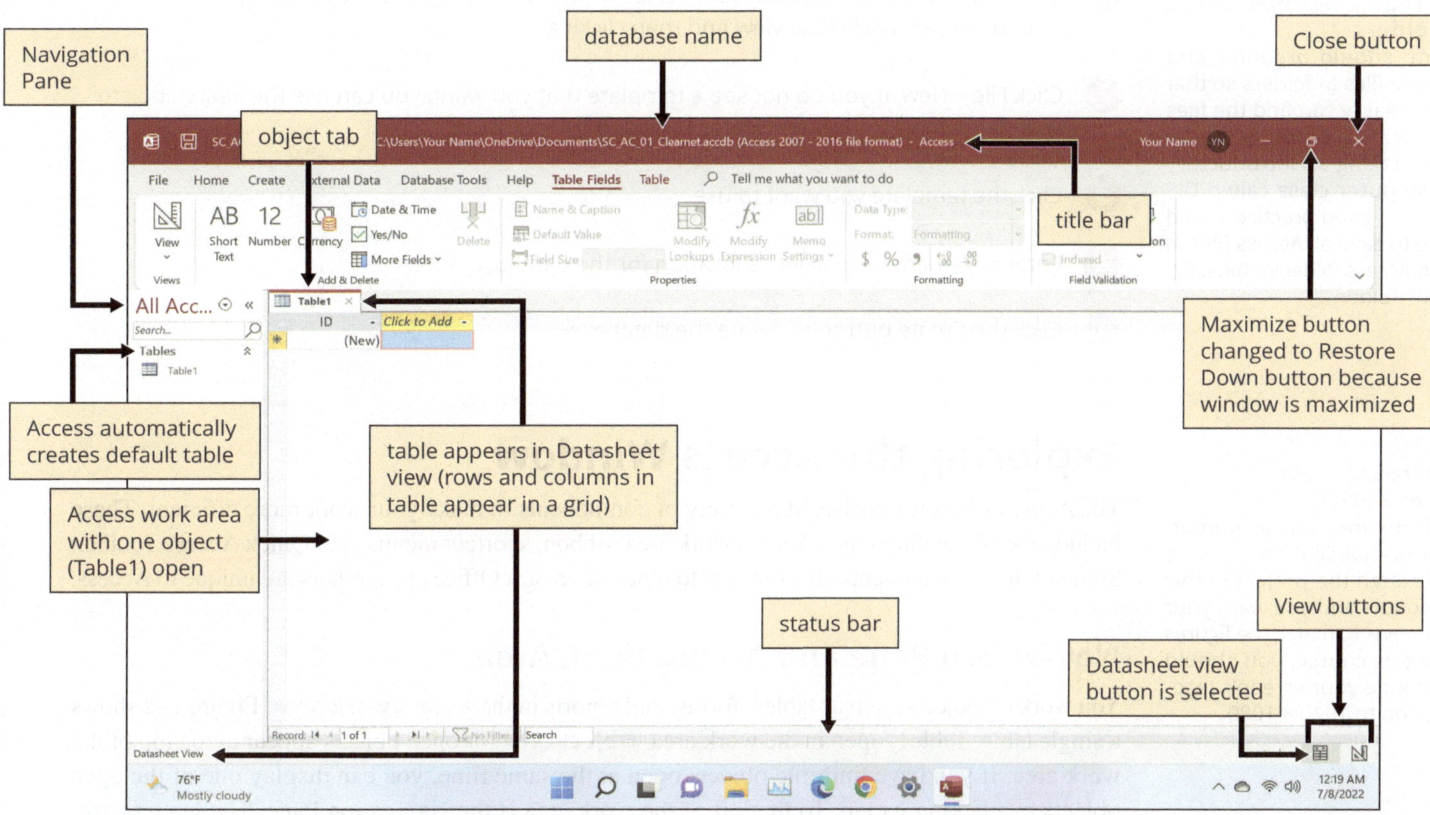

Figure 1–2

Consider This

Saving a Microsoft Access Database File

Unlike other Microsoft Office applications, the Access app allocates storage space when the database is created, even before any tables have been designed and data has been entered. In other Microsoft Office applications, you can enter data before saving. In Access, as you are working and saving each object, such as a table, the entire database is being saved in the app's designated storage space.

Q&A The title bar for my Navigation Pane contains All Tables rather than All Access Objects, as in the figure. Is that a problem?

It is not a problem. The title bar indicates how the Navigation Pane is organized. You can carry out the steps in the text with either organization. To make your screens match the ones in the text, click the Navigation Pane arrow and then click Object Type.

I do not have the Search bar that appears in the figure. Is that a problem?

It is not a problem. If your Navigation Pane does not display a Search bar and you want your screens to match the ones in the text, right-click the Navigation Pane title bar arrow to display a shortcut menu, and then click Search Bar.

To Create a Database Using a Template

Ideally, you will design your own database, create a blank database, and then create the tables you have determined that your database should contain. If you are not sure what database design you will need, you can use a template. Templates can guide you by suggesting some commonly used databases containing predesigned objects such as tables and reports. To create a database using a template, you would use the following steps.

1. If you have another database open, close it without exiting Access by clicking File on the ribbon to open Backstage view and then clicking Close.
2. Click File – New. If you do not see a template that you want, you can use the Search box to search the many online templates provided by Microsoft.
3. Click the template you want to use.
4. Enter a file name and select a location for the database.
5. Click the Create button to create the database.

BTW

Organizing Files and Folders

You should organize and store files in folders so that you easily can find the files later. For example, if you are taking an introductory computer class called CIS 101, a good practice would be to save all Access files in an Access folder within a CIS 101 folder.

BTW

Access Screen Resolution

If you are using a computer or mobile device to step through the project in this module and you want your screens to match the figures in this course, you should change your screen's resolution to 1920 × 1080.

Exploring the Access Window

The Access window consists of a variety of components to make your work more efficient. These include the Navigation Pane, Access work area, ribbon, shortcut menus, and Quick Access Toolbar. Some of these components are common to other Microsoft Office apps; others are unique to Access.

Navigation Pane and Access Work Area

You work on objects such as tables, forms, and reports in the **Access work area**. Figure 1–2 shows a single table, Table1, open in the work area. **Object tabs** for open objects appear at the top of the work area. If you have multiple objects open at the same time, you can display one of the open objects by clicking its tab. To the left of the work area is the Navigation Pane. The **Navigation Pane** contains a list of all the objects in the database. You use this pane to open an object. You can also customize the way objects are displayed in the Navigation Pane.

The **status bar**, located at the bottom of the Access window, presents information about the database object, the progress of current tasks, and the status of certain commands and keys; it also provides controls for viewing the object. As you type text or perform certain commands, various indicators might appear on the status bar. The left edge of the status bar in Figure 1–2 shows that the table object is open in **Datasheet view**. In Datasheet view, the table is represented as a collection of rows and columns called a **datasheet**. Toward the right edge are View buttons, which you can use to change the view that currently appears.

BTW
Naming Tables
Database designers typically have their own guidelines for naming tables. Some use the singular version of the object being described while others use the prefix tbl with a table name, such as tbl_students. This course uses the singular or plural version of the object (Shippers, Carriers, Loads, Locations, and Truck Type).

Determining Tables and Fields

Once you have created the database, you need to create the tables and fields that your database will contain. Before doing so, however, you need to make some decisions regarding the tables and fields.

Naming Tables and Fields

In creating your database, you must name tables, fields, and other objects. Before beginning the design process, you must understand the rules Access applies to table and field names. These rules are:

1. Names can be up to 64 characters in length.
2. Names can contain letters, digits, and spaces, as well as most common punctuation symbols.
3. Names cannot contain periods (.), exclamation points (!), accent graves (`), or square brackets ([ ]).
4. Each field in a table must have a unique name.

BTW
Multiple-Word Names
There are several ways to handle multiple-word names. You can include the space (Shipper ID), omit the space (ShipperID), or use an underscore in place of the space (Shipper_ID). Other options include using a hyphen in place of a space and/or using the same case for all letters (SHIPPER-ID or shipper-id).

It's a good idea to follow the same naming conventions throughout all of your tables and fields so that they are easier to understand and easier to remember when you need to refer to them later. The approach to naming tables and fields used in this text is to begin all names with an uppercase letter. In multiple-word names, each word begins with an uppercase letter, and there is a space between words (for example, Owner Street Address).

Determining the Primary Key

For each table, you need to determine the primary key, the unique identifier. In many cases, you will have clear choices, such as Shipper ID or Carrier ID. If you do not have a clear choice, you can use the primary key that Access creates automatically. The default ID field is an **autonumber field**, which means that Access will assign the value 1 to the first record, 2 to the second record, and so on.

BTW
Data Types
Different database management systems have different available data types. Even data types that are essentially the same can have different names. The Currency data type in Access, for example, is referred to as Money in SQL Server.

Determining Data Types for the Fields

For each field in your database, you must determine the field's **data type**, that is, the type of data that can be stored in the field. Four of the most commonly used data types in Access are:

1. **Short Text** — The field can contain any characters. A maximum number of 255 characters is allowed in a field whose data type is Short Text.
2. **Number** — The field can contain only numbers. The numbers can be either positive or negative. Fields assigned this type can be used in arithmetic operations. You usually assign fields that contain numbers but will not be used for arithmetic operations (such as postal codes) a data type of Short Text instead.
3. **Currency** — The field can contain only monetary data. The values will appear with currency symbols, such as dollar signs, commas, and decimal points, and with two digits following the decimal point. Like numeric fields, you can use currency fields in arithmetic operations. Access assigns a size to currency fields automatically.
4. **Date/Time** — The field can contain dates and/or times.

BTW
AutoNumber Fields
AutoNumber fields also are called AutoIncrement fields. In Design view, the New Values field property allows you to increment the field sequentially (Increment) or randomly (Random). The default is Increment.

Table 1–1 shows the other data types that are available in Access.

Table 1–1 Additional Data Types

Data Type	Description
Long Text	Field can store up to a gigabyte of text, although only the first 64,000 characters can be displayed.
Large Number	Field can store numeric data up to 8 bytes.
Date/Time Extended	Field can store date and time data up to 42 bytes with a longer date range and more granular fractional precision.
AutoNumber	Field can store a unique number that Access assigns to a record. Access can increment the number by 1 as each new record is added or choose random values.
Yes/No	Field can store only one of two values. The choices are Yes/No, True/False, or On/Off.
OLE Object	Field can store an OLE object, which is an image, graph, or other object linked to or embedded in the table. The object can be up to 2 GB.
Hyperlink	Field can store text that can be used as a hyperlink address to a file stored on the Internet, an intranet, a local area network (LAN), or the local computer.
Attachment	Field can contain an attached file. Images, spreadsheets, documents, charts, and other elements can be attached to this field in a record in the database. You can view and edit the attached file.
Calculated	Field is specified as a calculation based on other fields. The value is not actually stored.
Lookup Wizard	While not a data type, this option is used to define a simple or complex lookup field to draw data from another table or a value list as records are created later.

BTW
Currency Symbols
To show the symbol for the Euro (€) instead of the dollar sign, change the Format property for the field whose data type is currency. To change the default symbols for currency, change the settings in Windows.

In the Shippers table, because the Shipper ID, Shipper Name, Contact, Phone, Email, Address, Locations, and Billing Notes can all contain letters or symbols, their data types should be Short Text. The data type for Phone is Short Text instead of Number because you typically do not use phone numbers in arithmetic operations; for example, it's not common practice to add phone numbers or find an average phone number. The Shipper ID field also contains numbers, but you will not use these numbers in arithmetic operations, so its data type should be Short Text.

Similarly, in the Loads table, the data type for the Pickup, Dropoff, Contents, Truck, Status, Driver, Phone, Carrier, and Shipper fields should all be Short Text. The Pickup date and Dropoff date fields should have a data type of Date/Time. In the Truck Type table, the Target Rate contains monetary amounts, so its data type should be Currency.

For fields whose data type is Short Text, you can change the field size, that is, the maximum number of characters that can be entered in the field. If you set the field size for the Location table's State field to 2, for example, Access will not allow the user to enter more than two characters in the field. This is especially important for increasing database security and for helping ensure the data entered is correct. On the other hand, fields whose data type is Number often require you to change the field size, which is the storage space assigned to the field by Access. Table 1–2 shows the possible field sizes for Number fields.

Table 1–2 Field Sizes for Number Fields

Field Size	Description
Byte	Integer value in the range of 0 to 255
Integer	Integer value in the range of −32,768 to 32,767
Long Integer	Integer value in the range of −2,147,483,648 to 2,147,483,647
Single	Numeric values with decimal places up to 7 significant digits—requires 4 bytes of storage
Double	Numeric values with decimal places up to 15 significant digits—requires 8 bytes of storage
Replication ID	Special identifier required for replication
Decimal	Numeric values with decimal places to more accuracy than Single or Double—requires 12 bytes of storage

Consider This

What is the appropriate size for a Postal Code field?

By default, a Short Text field will allocate 255 spaces for data. However, a postal code normally would only take 9 spaces (or 10 if you include the hyphen). It is more efficient to change the Short Text field size limit to nine spaces, which accounts for the five-digit postal code followed by four numbers identifying a specific delivery route.

Creating a Table Using Datasheet View

To create a table in Access, you must define its structure. That is, you must define all the fields that make up the table and their characteristics. You must also indicate the primary key.

In Access, you can use two different views to create a table: Datasheet view and Design view. Although the main reason to use Datasheet view is to add or update records in a table, you can also use it to create a table or to later modify its structure. The other view, **Design view**, is only used to create a table or to modify the structure of a table.

As you might expect, Design view has more functionality than Datasheet view for creating a table. That is, there are certain actions that can only be performed in Design view or that are easier in Design view. One such action is choosing how new values are selected for an AutoNumber field. In this module, you will create the first table, the Shippers table, in Datasheet view. Once you have created the table in Datasheet view, you will use Design view to check (and fix as necessary) field properties such as field size and data type.

Whichever view you choose to use, before creating the table, you need to know the names and data types of the fields that will make up the table. You can also decide to enter a description for a particular field to explain important details about the field. When you select this field, this description will appear on the status bar. You might also choose to assign a **caption** to a particular field. If you assign a caption, Access will display the value you assign, rather than the field name, in datasheets and in forms. If you do not assign a caption, Access will display the field name.

BTW
Naming Files
The following characters cannot be used in a file name: question mark (?), quotation mark ("), slash (/), backslash (\ ), colon (:), asterisk (*), vertical bar (|), greater than symbol (>), and less than symbol (<).

Consider This

When would you want to use a caption?

You would use a caption whenever you wanted something other than the field name displayed. One common example is when the field name is relatively long and the data in the field is relatively short. In the Shippers table, the name of the first field is Shipper ID, but the field contains data that is only five characters long. You will change the caption for this field to S_ID, which is much shorter than Shipper ID, yet still describes the field. Doing so will enable you to greatly reduce the width of the column.

The results of these decisions for the fields in the Shippers table are shown in Table 1–3. The table also shows the data types and field sizes of the fields as well as any special properties that need to be changed. The Shipper ID short text field has a caption of S_ID, enabling the width of the Shipper ID column to be reduced in the datasheet. Other fields have captions as well to reduce redundancy in field names.

Table 1–3 Structure of Shippers Table

Field Name	Data Type	Field Size	Description and/or Caption
Shipper ID	Short Text	5	Primary Key **Description:** Unique identifier of shipping company **Caption:** S_ID
Shipper Name	Short Text	50	
Shipper Contact	Short Text	50	**Caption:** Contact
Shipper Phone	Short Text	12	**Caption:** Phone
Shipper Email	Short Text	50	**Caption:** Email
Shipper Address	Short Text	255	**Caption:** Address
Shipper Locations	Short Text	255	**Caption:** Locations
Shipper Billing Notes	Long Text		**Caption:** Billing Notes

BTW
Using Table Names in Field Names
Some database designers include a portion of a table's name in many of its field names. Field names such as Phone, Email, and Address are often used in many tables for different entities (such as listing phone numbers, email addresses, and physical addresses in both the Shippers and Carriers tables). When working with advanced database tasks, there are times when fields that all have exactly the same name but belong to different tables could be confusing to work with. Including a portion of the table's name in these field names, such as Shipper Name or Carrier Name rather than simply Name, can help minimize confusion and mistakes later.

Consider This

How do you determine the field size?

You need to determine the maximum number of characters that can be entered in the field. In some cases, the number of characters will be consistent from record to record. Field sizes of 2 for a State field and 9 for a Postal Code field are appropriate choices. In other cases, you need to determine how many characters you want to allow. In the list shown in Table 1–3, Clearnet decided that allowing 50 characters was sufficient for the name, contact, and email fields. You can change this field size later if it proves to be insufficient.

BTW

Tabbed Documents Versus Overlapping Windows

By default, Access displays database objects, such as tables, in tabbed documents instead of in overlapping windows. If your database is in overlapping windows mode, click File on the ribbon, click Options in Backstage view, click Current Database in the Access Options dialog box, and select the 'Display Document Tabs' check box and the Tabbed Documents option button. Click the OK button in the Access Options dialog box to save your changes.

To Modify the Primary Key

When you first create a database, Access automatically creates a table for you. You can immediately begin defining the fields. If, for any reason, you do not have this table or you inadvertently delete it, you can create the table by clicking Create on the ribbon and then clicking the Table button (Create tab | Tables group). In either case, you are ready to define the fields.

The following steps change the name, data type, and other properties of the first field to match the Shipper ID field in Table 1–3, which is the primary key. **Why?** Access has already created the first field as the primary key field, which it has named ID. Shipper ID is a more appropriate name.

1

- Right-click the column heading for the ID field to display a shortcut menu (Figure 1–3).

Q&A Why does my shortcut menu look different?

You may have displayed a shortcut menu for the column instead of the column heading. Be sure you right-click the column heading.

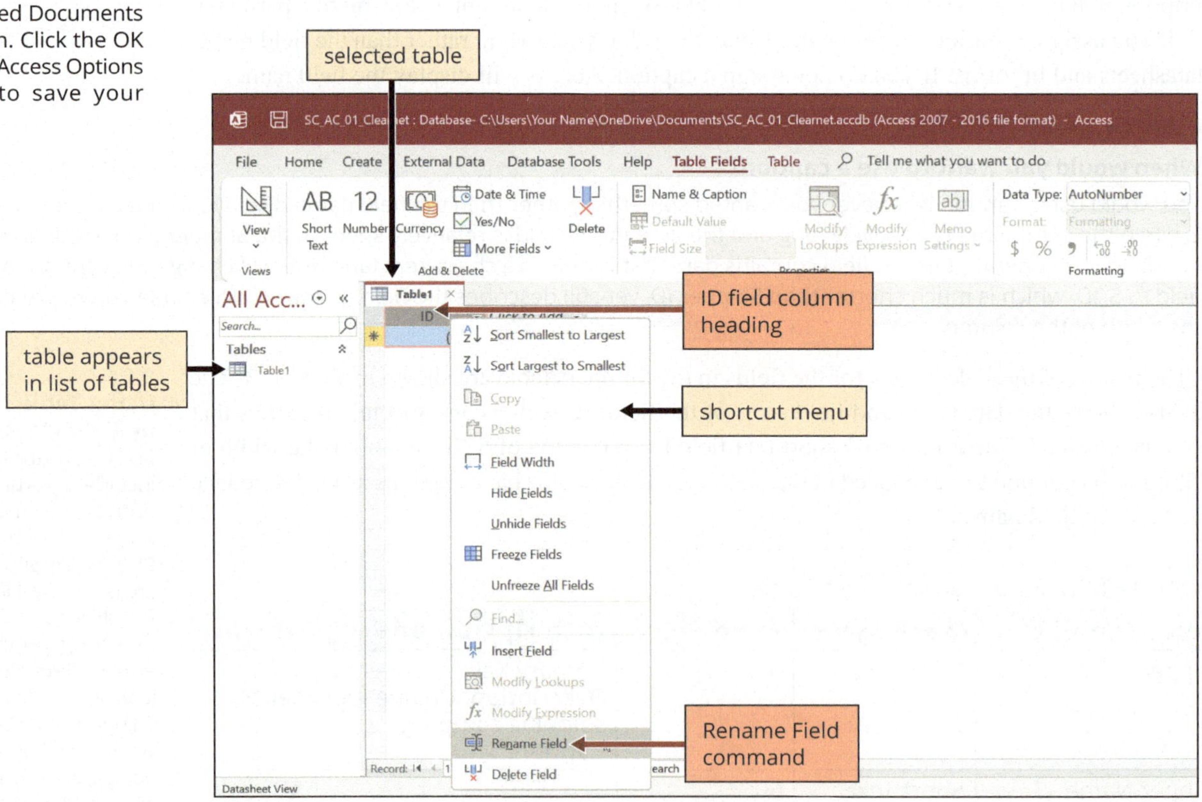

Figure 1–3

2

- Click Rename Field on the shortcut menu to highlight the current name.
- Type **Shipper ID** to assign a name to the new field.
- Click the white space immediately below the field name to complete the addition of the field (Figure 1–4).

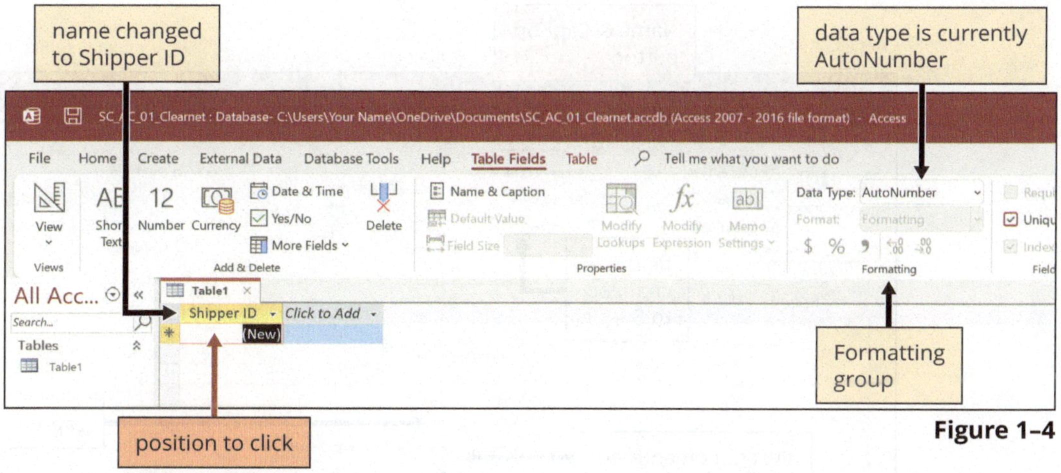

Figure 1–4

Q&A Why does the full name of the field not appear?

The default column size might not be large enough for Shipper ID, or a later field such as Shipper Billing Notes, to be displayed in its entirety. If necessary, you will address this issue in later steps.

3

- Because the data type needs to be changed from AutoNumber to Short Text, click the Data Type arrow (Table Fields tab | Formatting group) to display a menu of available data types (Figure 1–5).

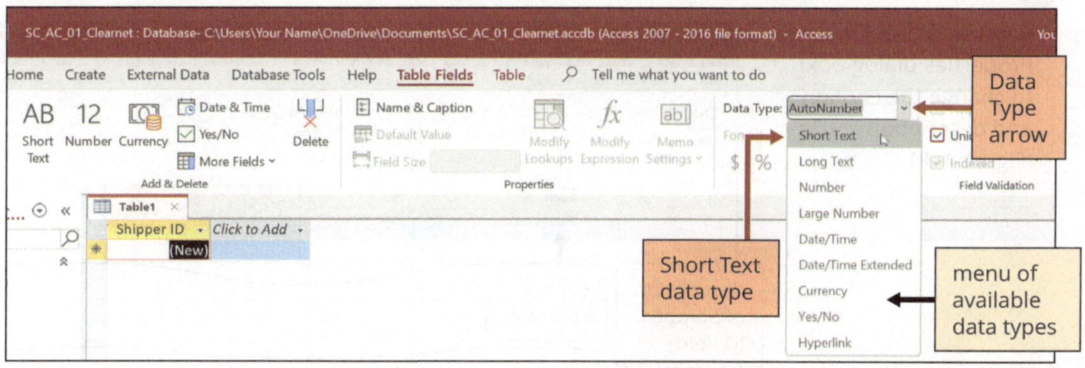

Figure 1–5

4

- Click Short Text to select the data type for the field (Figure 1–6).

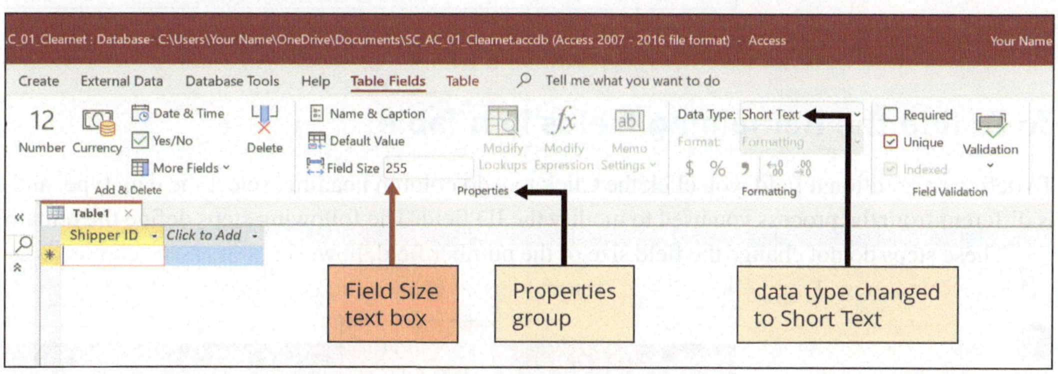

Figure 1–6

5

- Click the Field Size text box (Table Fields tab | Properties group) to select the current field size, use either DEL or BACKSPACE to erase the current field size if necessary, and then type **5** as the new field size.
- Click the Name & Caption button (Table Fields tab | Properties group) to display the Enter Field Properties dialog box.
- Click the Caption text box (Enter Field Properties dialog box), and then type **S_ID** as the caption.
- Click the Description text box, and then type **Unique identifier of shipping company** as the description (Figure 1–7).

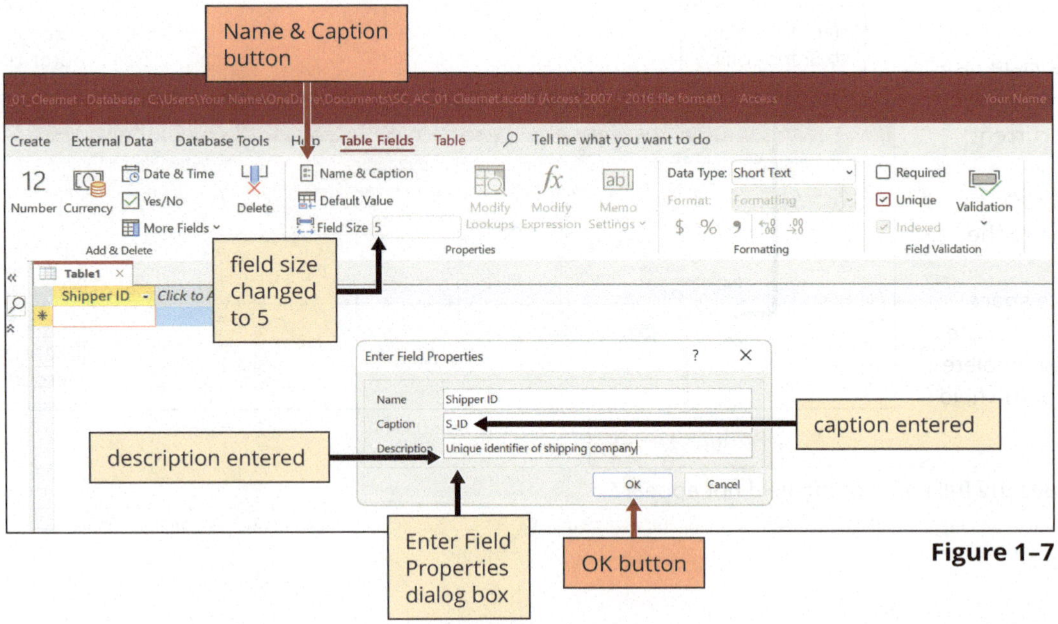

Figure 1–7

6

- Click OK (Enter Field Properties dialog box) to change the caption and description (Figure 1–8).

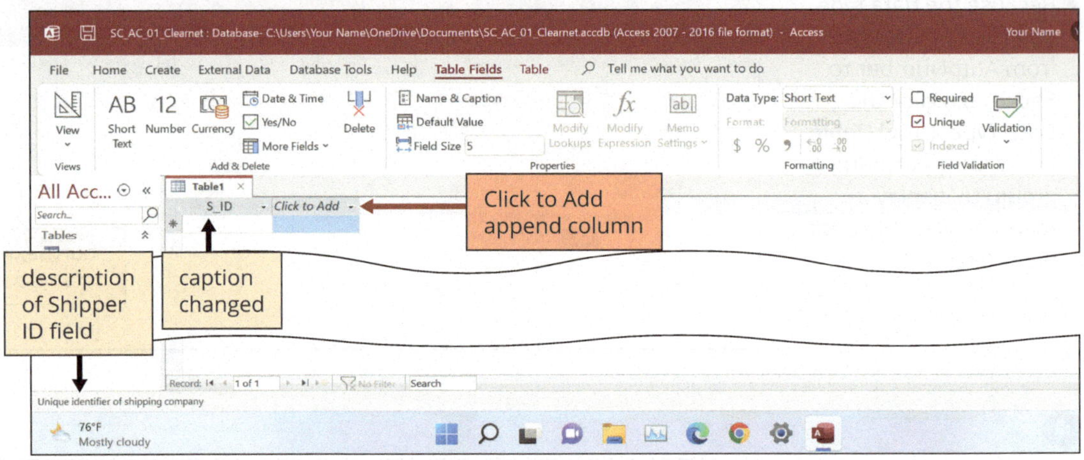

Figure 1–8

To Define the Remaining Fields in a Table

To define an additional field, you click the Click to Add column heading, select the data type, and then type the field name. This is different from the process you used to modify the ID field. The following steps define the remaining fields shown in Table 1–3.

These steps do not change the field size of the number field, however. **Why?** You can only change the field size of a number field in Design view. Later, you will use Design view to change the field size and change the format.

1

- Click the Click to Add column heading to display a menu of available data types (Figure 1–9).

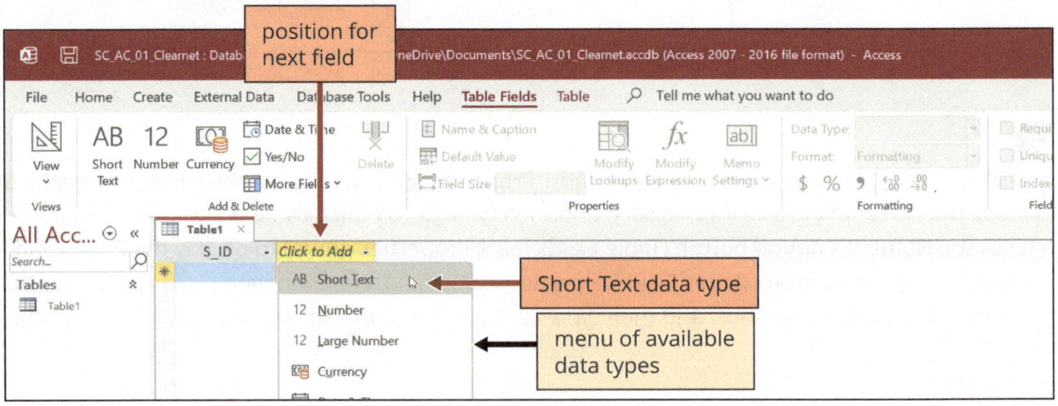

Figure 1–9

2

- Click Short Text in the menu of available data types to select the Short Text data type.
- Type **Shipper Name** to enter a field name.
- Click the blank space below the field name to complete the change of the name. Click the blank space a second time to select the field (Figure 1–10).

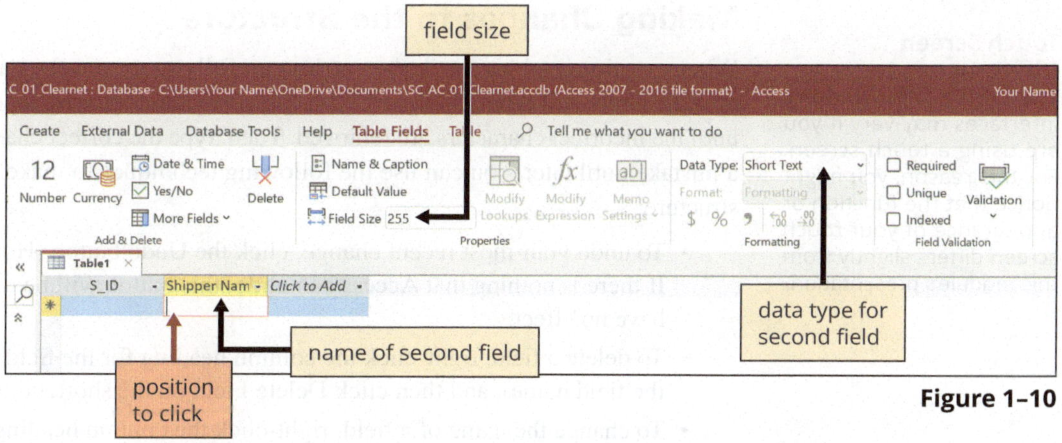

Figure 1–10

- If necessary, enlarge the field name box to display the entire name by clicking between Shipper Name and the Click to Add box. Drag the pointer, which is now a double-tipped arrow, to the right so that the entire field name of Shipper Name is visible.

Q&A After entering the field name, I realized that I selected the wrong data type. How can I correct it?
Click the Data Type arrow, and then select the correct type.

I inadvertently clicked the blank space before entering the field name. How can I correct the name?
Right-click the field name, click Rename Field on the shortcut menu, and then type the new name.

3

- Change the field size to **50** just as you changed the field size of the Shipper ID field.
- Using the same technique, add the remaining fields in the Shippers table. For the Shipper Contact, Shipper Phone, Shipper Email, Shipper Address, and Shipper Locations fields, use the Short Text data type, but change the field sizes to match Table 1–3. For the Shipper Billing Notes field, use the Long Text data type. Add Captions for the new fields as indicated in Table 1–3. Your Shippers table should look like Figure 1–11.

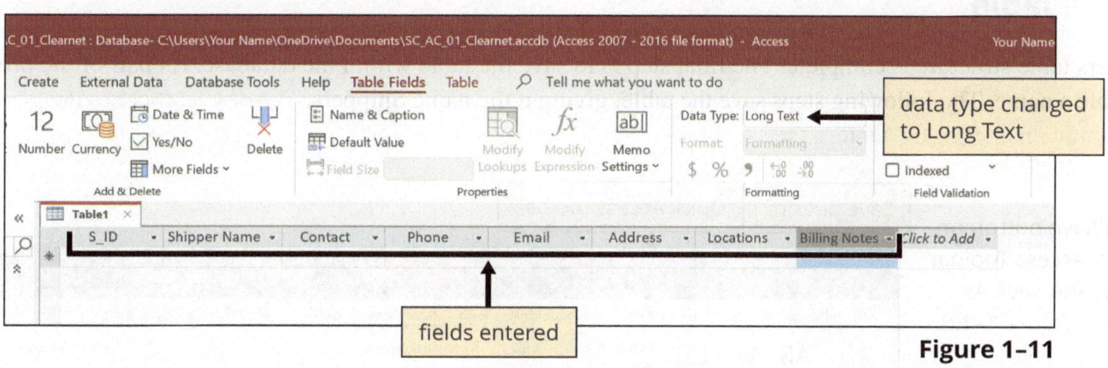

Figure 1–11

Q&A I have an extra row between the row containing the field names and the row that begins with the asterisk. What happened? Is this a problem? If so, how do I fix it?
You inadvertently added a record to the table by pressing a key. Even pressing SPACEBAR adds a record. You now have an unwanted record. To fix it, select the blank record, click the Delete button (Home tab | Records group), and then click Yes to confirm the deletion.

When I try to move on to specify another field, I get an error message indicating that the primary key cannot contain a null value. How do I correct this?
First, click the OK button to remove the error message. Next, press ESC or click the Undo button on the Home tab to undo the action. You may need to do this more than once.

BTW
Touch Screen Differences
The Office and Windows interfaces may vary if you are using a touch screen. For this reason, you might notice that the function or appearance of your touch screen differs slightly from this module's presentation.

Making Changes to the Structure

When creating a table, check the entries carefully to ensure they are correct. If you discover a mistake while still typing the entry, you can correct the error by repeatedly pressing BACKSPACE until the incorrect characters are removed. Then, type the correct characters. If you do not discover a mistake until later, you can use the following techniques to make the necessary changes to the structure:

- To undo your most recent change, click the Undo button (Home tab | Undo group). If there is nothing that Access can undo, this button will be dim, and clicking it will have no effect.
- To delete a field, right-click the column heading for the field (the position containing the field name), and then click Delete Field on the shortcut menu.
- To change the name of a field, right-click the column heading for the field, click Rename Field on the shortcut menu, and then type the desired field name.
- To insert a field as the last field, click the Click to Add column heading, click the appropriate data type on the menu of available data types, type the desired field name, and, if necessary, change the field size.
- To insert a field between existing fields, right-click the column heading for the field that will follow the new field, and then click Insert Field on the shortcut menu. Right-click the column heading for the new field, click Rename Field on the shortcut menu, and then type the desired field name.
- To move a field, click the column heading for the field to be moved to select the field, and then drag the field's black bar to the desired position.

As an alternative to these steps for correcting your table's structure, you might want to start over. To do so, click the Close button for the table, and then click the No button in the Microsoft Access dialog box. Click Create on the ribbon, and then click the Table button to create a table. You then can repeat the process you used earlier to define the fields in the table.

To Save a Table

The Shippers table structure is complete. The final step is to save the table within the database. As part of the process, you will give the table a name. The following steps save the table, giving it the name Shippers. **Why?** Clearnet has decided that Shippers is an appropriate name for the table.

1

- Click the Save button on the Quick Access Toolbar to display the Save As dialog box (Figure 1–12).

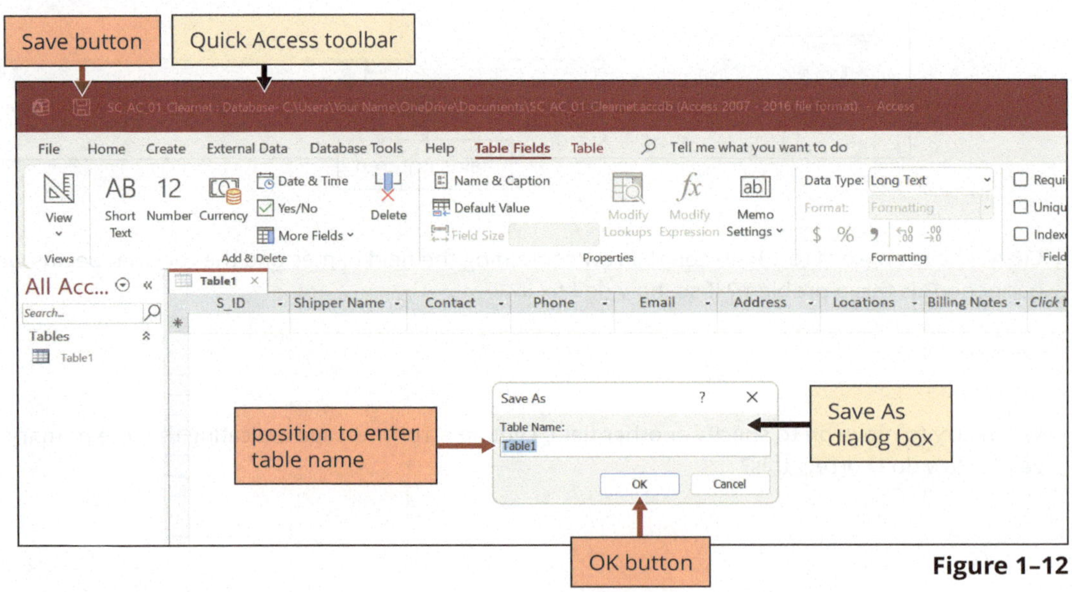

Figure 1–12

2

- Type **Shippers** to change the name assigned to the table.
- Click OK (Save As dialog box) to save the table (Figure 1–13).

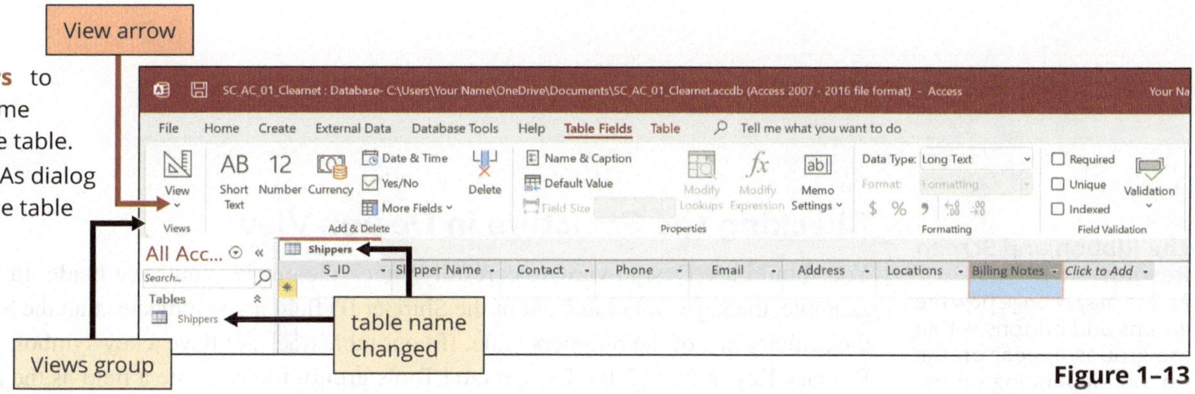

Figure 1–13

Other Ways

1. Click File on the ribbon, click Save in Backstage view to save table
2. Right-click table's tab, click Save on shortcut menu to save table
3. Press CTRL+S to save table

To View the Table in Design View

Even when creating a table in Datasheet view, Design view can be helpful. **Why?** You easily can view the fields, data types, and properties to ensure you have entered them correctly. It is also easier to determine the primary key in Design view. The following steps display the structure of the Shippers table in Design view so you can verify the design is correct.

1

- Click the View arrow (Table Fields tab | Views group) to display the View menu (Figure 1–14).

Q&A Could I just click the View button rather than the arrow?

Yes. Clicking the button is equivalent to clicking the command represented by the icon that currently appears on the button. Because the icon on the button in Figure 1–14 is for Design view, clicking the button would display the table in Design view. If you are uncertain, you can always click the arrow and select Design View from the menu.

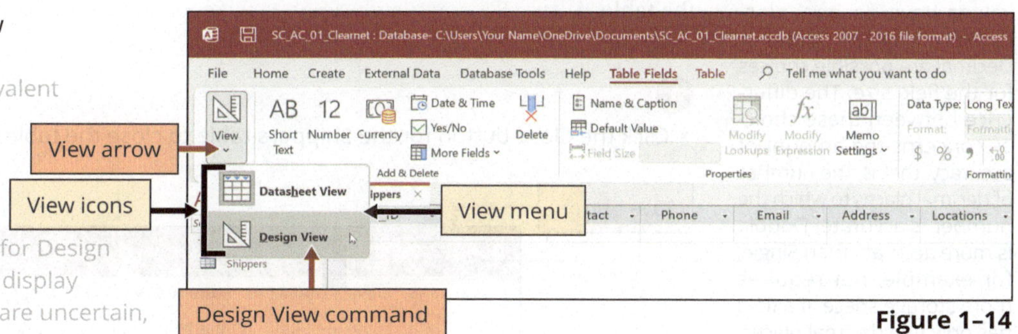

Figure 1–14

2

- Click Design View on the View menu to view the table in Design view (Figure 1–15).

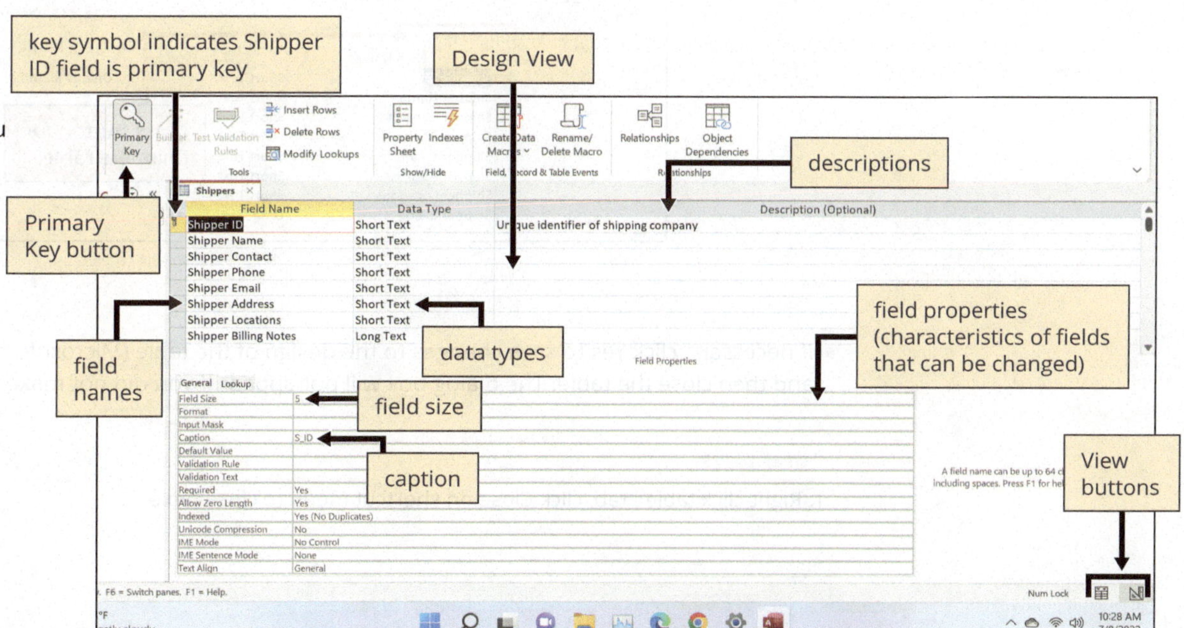

Figure 1–15

Other Ways

1. Click Design View button on status bar to view table in Design view

BTW

The Ribbon and Screen Resolution

Access may change how the groups and buttons within the groups appear on the ribbon, depending on the computer's screen resolution. Thus, your ribbon may look different from the ones in this course if you are using a screen resolution other than 1920 × 1080.

BTW

Changing a Field Size in Design View

Most field size changes can be made in either Datasheet view or Design view. However, changing the field size for Number fields can only be done in Design view. If field values have decimal places, only Single, Double, or Decimal are possible choices for the field size. The difference between these choices concerns the amount of accuracy, that is, the number of decimal places to which the number is accurate. Double is more accurate than Single, for example, but requires more storage space. If a field has only two decimal places, Single is an acceptable choice.

Checking the Structure in Design View

You should use Design view to carefully check the entries you have made. In Figure 1–15, for example, the key symbol in front of the Shipper ID field name indicates that the Shipper ID field is the primary key of the Shippers table. If your table does not have a key symbol, you can click the Primary Key button (Table Design tab | Tools group) to designate a field as the primary key. You can also check that the data type, description, field size, and caption are all correct for the first field.

For the other fields, you can see the field name, data type, and description without taking any special action. To see the field size and/or caption for a field, click the field's **row selector**, the small box to the left of the field. Clicking the row selector for the Shipper Name field, for example, displays the properties for that field in the Field Properties pane in the lower portion of the window. You then can check to see that the field size is correct. In addition, if the field has a caption, you can confirm it is correct. If you find any mistakes, you can make the necessary corrections on this screen. When you have finished, click the Save button to save your changes.

To Close the Table

Once you are sure that your entries are correct and you have saved your changes, you can close the table. *Why? Closing database objects keeps the workspace uncluttered.* The following step closes the table.

1

- Click the Close button for the Shippers table to close the table (Figure 1–16).

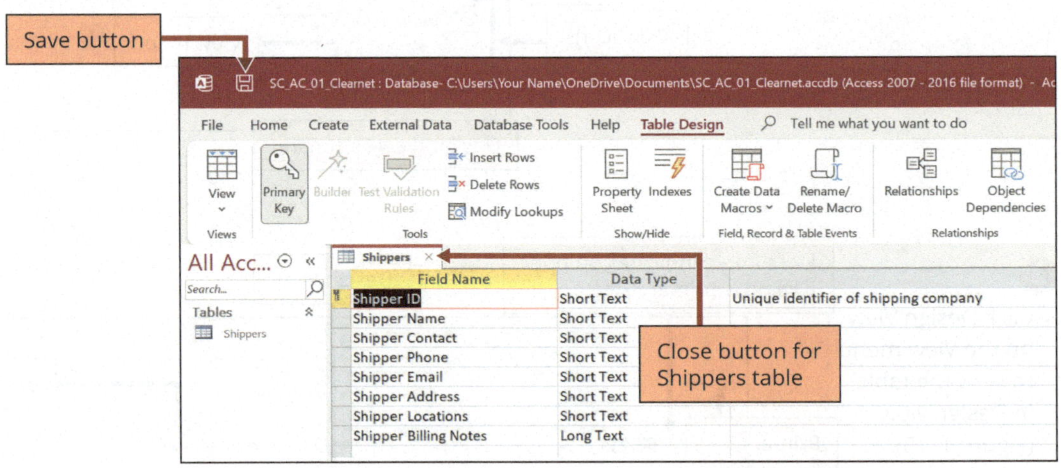

Figure 1–16

- If necessary, click Yes to save changes to the design of the table (Microsoft Access dialog box) and then close the table. The dialog box will not appear if you did not make any changes.

Other Ways

1. Right-click table's tab, click Close on shortcut menu to close table

To Add Records to a Table

Creating a table by building the structure and saving the table is the first step in the two-step process of using a table in a database. The second step is to add records to the table. To add records to a table, the table must be open. When making changes to records, you work in Datasheet view.

You often add records in phases. **Why?** You might not have enough time to add all the records in one session, or you might not have all the records currently available. The following steps open the Shippers table in Datasheet view and then add three records in the Shippers table (Figure 1–17).

S_ID	Shipper Name	Contact	Phone	Email	Address	Locations	Billing Notes
S-001	Sabus Flooring	Cori Sabus	719-555-4411	csabus@example.com	460 West Pioneer Road, Dolores, OK 73026	Home office at warehouse	Send paper invoice
S-002	Mid-Valley Nurseries	Steven Nguyen	513-555-5670	snguyen@example.com	9874 South Main Street, Blanding, OH 43056	Nursery at L-001	Email PDF invoice
S-003	Auto Suppliers, Inc.	Abdul Ritter	337-555-8901	abdulr@example.com	182-B Route 56, Cloud Springs, LA 70784	Warehouse at L-007	Email PDF invoice

Figure 1–17

1

- Right-click the Shippers table in the Navigation Pane to display the shortcut menu (Figure 1–18).

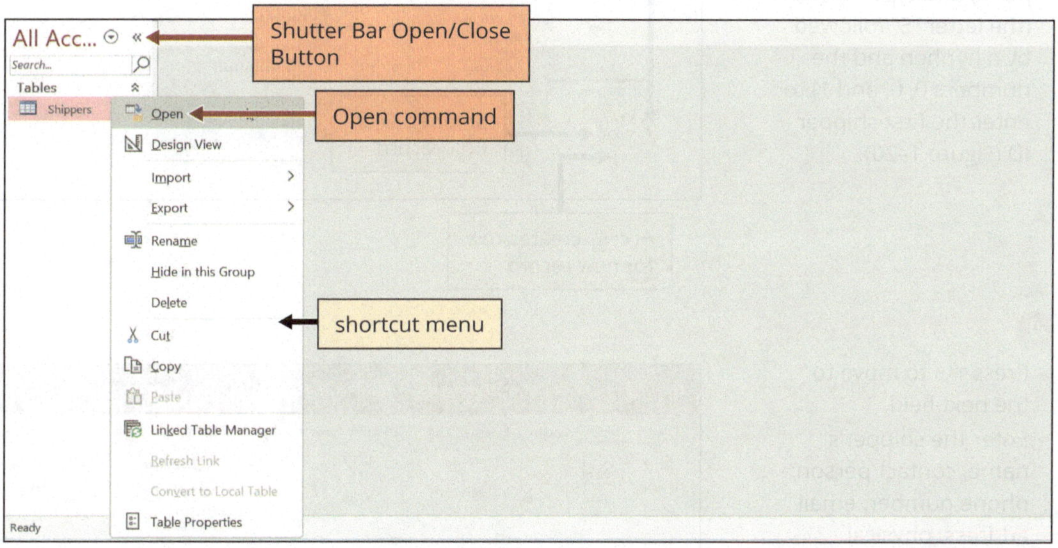

Figure 1–18

2

- Click Open on the shortcut menu to open the table in Datasheet view.
- Click the 'Shutter Bar Open/Close Button' to close the Navigation Pane (Figure 1–19).

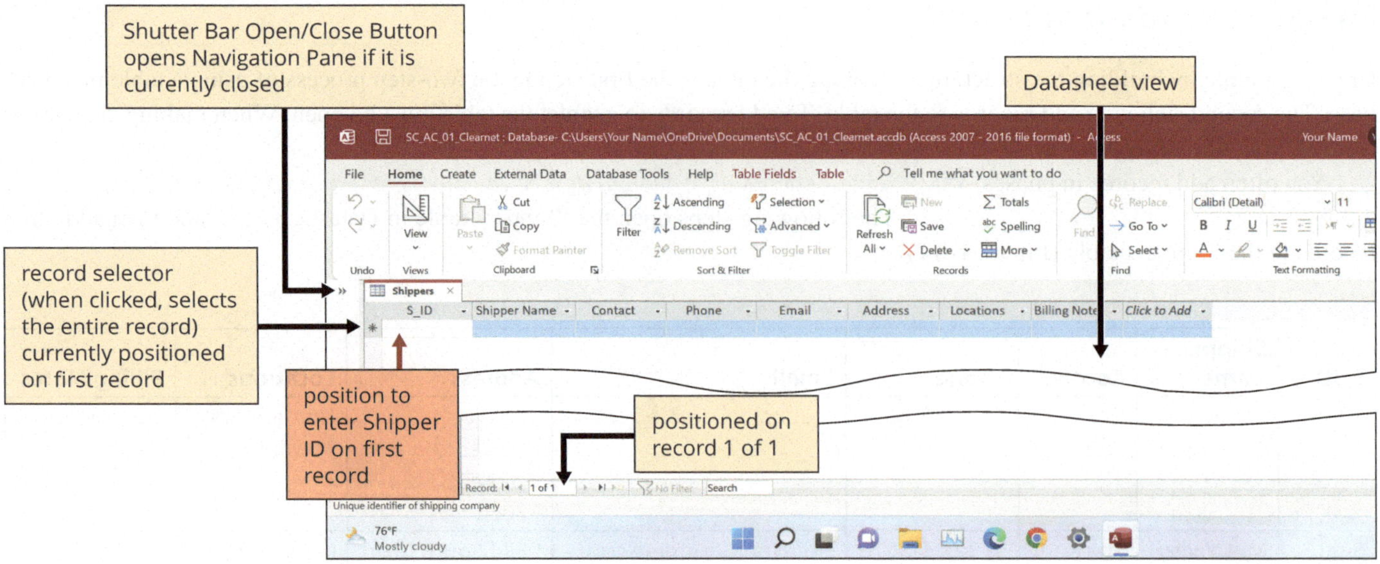

Figure 1–19

3

- Click the first row in the S_ID field if necessary to display an insertion point, and type **S-001** (the letter "S" followed by a hyphen and the numbers 0, 0, and 1) to enter the first shipper ID (Figure 1–20).

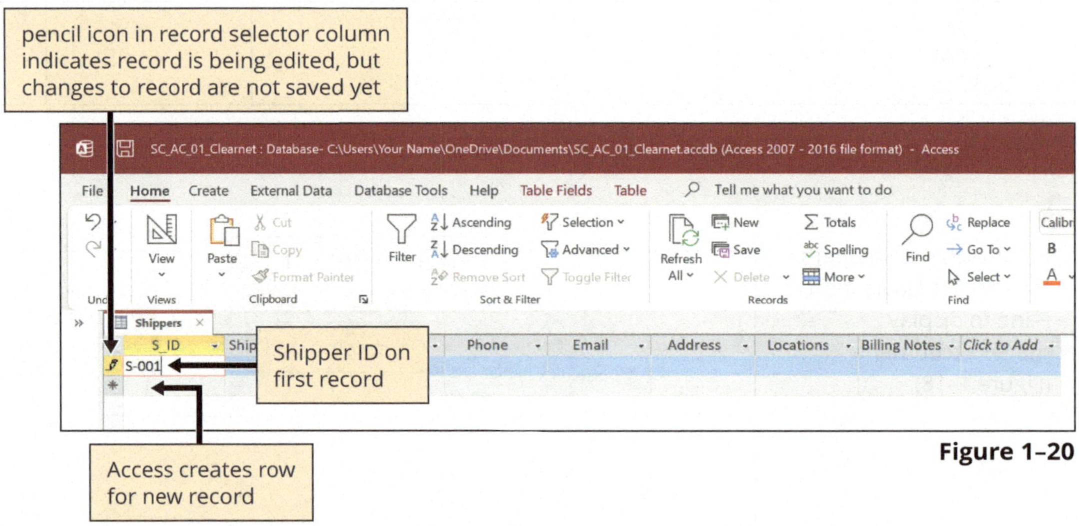

Figure 1–20

4

- Press TAB to move to the next field.
- Enter the shipper's name, contact person, phone number, email address, physical address, a list of locations, and billing notes by typing the following entries, as shown in Figure 1–21, pressing TAB after each entry: **Sabus Flooring** as the shipper's name, **Cori Sabus** as the contact person, **719-555-4411** as the contact's phone number, **csabus@example.com** as the contact's email address, **460 West Pioneer Road, Dolores, OK 73026** as the physical address, **Home office at warehouse** as the shipper's locations, and **Send paper invoice** as the billing notes.

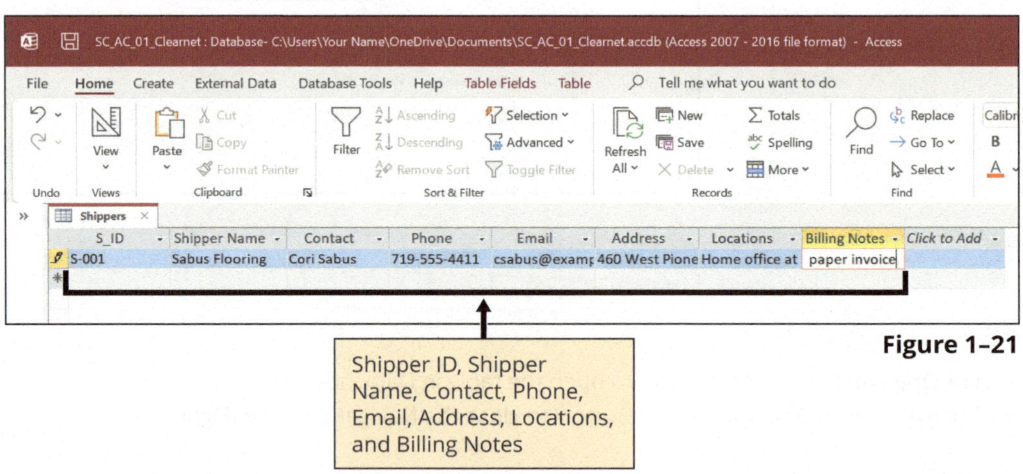

Figure 1–21

5

- Press TAB to complete the entry of the first record (Figure 1–22).

Q&A How and when do I save the record?

As soon as you have entered or modified a record and moved to another record, Access saves the original record. This is different from other applications. The rows entered in an Excel worksheet, for example, are not saved until the entire worksheet is saved.

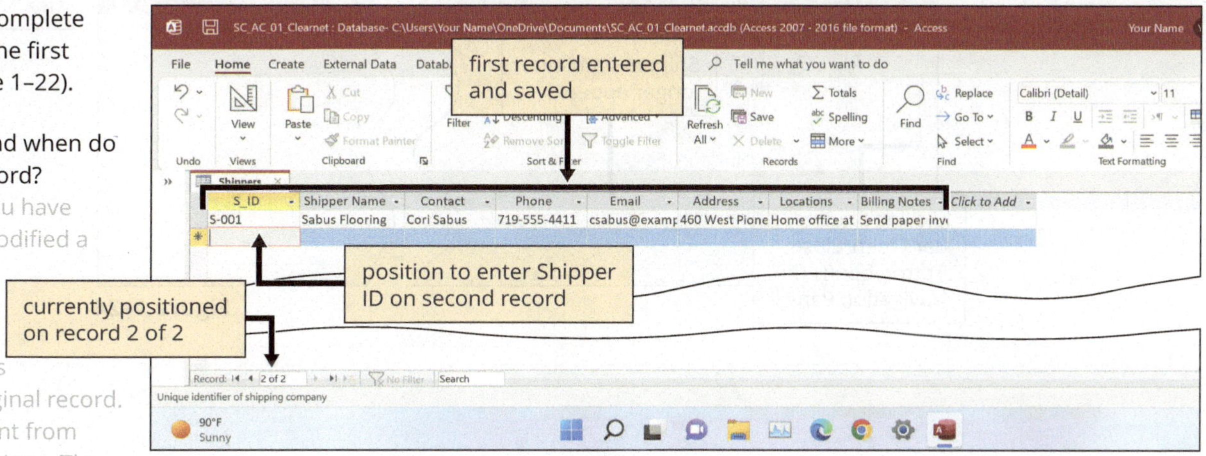

Figure 1–22

BTW

Append Row

Notice the asterisk * in the new row that is waiting for the next record to be entered. That row is called the **Append row**, the row where the next record can be added onto the table. The word append means to add onto the end of something.

6

- Use the techniques in Steps 3 through 5 to enter the data for the second and third records, referring to Figure 1–17 as needed for data to be entered (Figure 1–23).

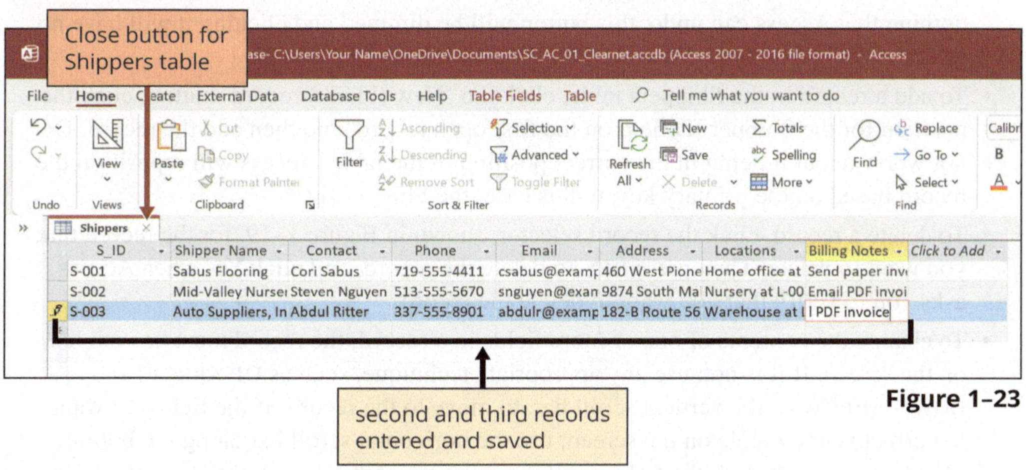

Figure 1–23

Q&A Does it matter that I entered Shipper ID S-001 after I entered Shipper ID S-002? Should the Shipper IDs be in order?

The order in which you enter the records is not important. When you close and later reopen the table, the records will be sorted in Shipper ID order, because the Shipper ID field is the primary key.

I made a mistake in entering the data. When should I fix it?

It is a good idea to fix it now, although you can fix it later as well. In any case, the following section gives you techniques you can use to make any necessary corrections. If you want to fix it now, read that section and make your corrections before proceeding to the next step.

7

- Click the Close button for the Shippers table, shown in Figure 1–23, to close the table (Figure 1–24).
- Exit Access.

Q&A Is it necessary for me to exit Access at this point?

No. The step is here for two reasons. First, you will often not be able to add all the records you need to add in one sitting. In such a case, you will add some records, and then exit Access. When you are ready to resume adding the records, you will start Access, open the table, and then continue the addition process. Second, there is a break point coming up in the module. If you want to take advantage of that break, you need to first exit Access.

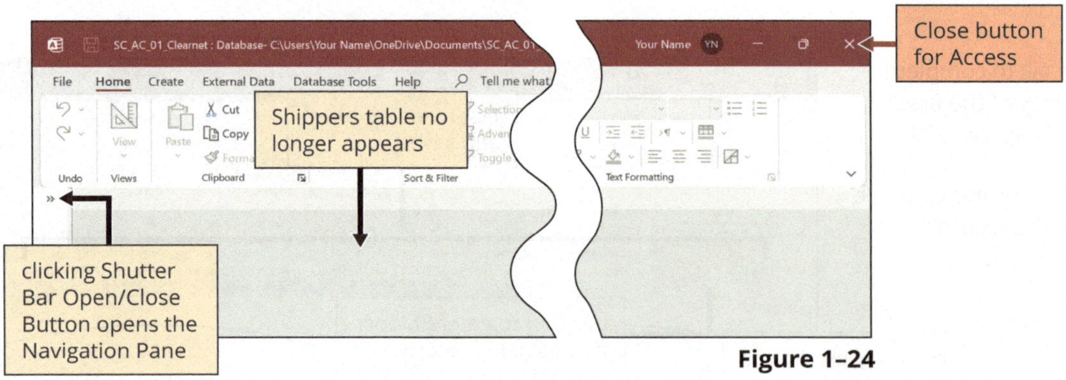

Figure 1–24

BTW
AutoCorrect Feature
The AutoCorrect feature of Access corrects common data entry errors. For example, AutoCorrect corrects two capital letters by changing the second letter to lowercase and capitalizes the first letter in the names of days. It can also correct commonly misspelled words, and you can add a custom dictionary for more assistance.

Making Changes to the Data

As you enter data in the datasheet view, check your entries carefully to ensure they are correct. If you make a mistake and discover it before you press TAB, correct it by pressing BACKSPACE until the incorrect characters are removed, and then type the correct characters. If you do not discover a mistake until later, you can use the following techniques to make the necessary corrections to the data:

- To undo your most recent change, click the Undo button on the Home tab. If there is nothing that Access can undo, this button will be dimmed and clicking it will have no effect.
- To add a record in the Shippers table, click the 'New (blank) record' button, click the position for the Shipper ID field on the first open record, and then add the record. Do not worry about it being in the correct position in the table. Access will reposition the record based on the primary key, in this case, the Shipper ID.
- To delete a record, click the record selector, shown in Figure 1–19, for the record that you want to delete. Then press DEL to delete the record, and click Yes when Access asks you to verify that you want to delete the record.
- To change the contents of one or more fields in a record, the record must be visible on the screen. If it is not, use any appropriate technique, such as UP ARROW and DOWN ARROW or the vertical scroll bar, to move to the record. If the field you want to correct is not visible on the screen, use the horizontal scroll bar along the bottom of the screen to shift all the fields until the one you want appears. If the value in the field is currently highlighted, you can simply type the new value. If you would rather edit the existing value, you must have an insertion point in the field. You can place the insertion point by clicking in the field or by pressing F2. You then can use the arrow keys, DEL, and BACKSPACE for making the correction. You can also use INS to switch between Insert and Overtype mode. When you have made the change, press TAB to move to the next field.

BTW
Spell Checking
To check the spelling in a table, Select the Home tab, Records group, Spelling.

Consider This

Duplicate Values in the Primary Key Field

When entering new records, if you inadvertently type the same value in the primary key field as another record, Access will display a dialog box saying that the changes were not successful because they would create duplicate values in the index, primary key, or relationship. To correct this problem, change the value of the primary key to a different value that has not yet been used.

If you cannot determine how to correct the data, you may find that you are "stuck" on the record, in which case Access neither allows you to move to another record nor allows you to close the table until you have made the correction. If you encounter this situation, simply press ESC. Pressing ESC will remove from the screen the record you are trying to add. You then can move to any other record, close the table, or take any other action you desire.

BTW
Other AutoCorrect Options
Using the Office AutoCorrect feature, you can create entries that will replace abbreviations with spelled-out names and phrases automatically. To specify AutoCorrect rules, click File on the ribbon to open Backstage view, click Options, and then click Proofing in the Access Options dialog box.

Break Point: If you wish to take a break, this is a good place to do so. You can exit Access now. To resume at a later time, start Access, open the database called SC_AC_01_Clearnet.accdb, and continue following the steps from this location forward.

Navigation Buttons

You will often need to update tables with new records. You can open a table that already contains data and add records using a process similar to that used to add records to an empty table. The only difference is that you place the insertion point after the last record before you enter the additional data. To position the insertion point after the last record, you can use the **Navigation buttons**, which are buttons used to move within a table, found near the lower-left corner of the screen when a table is open. It is a good habit to use the 'New (blank) record' button to select the append row. Once a table contains more records than will fit on the screen, it is easier to click the 'New (blank) record' button to move to the append row rather than scrolling to get to the row. The purpose of each Navigation button is described in Table 1–4.

BTW
Enabling Content
If the database is one that you created, or if it comes from a trusted source, you can enable the content. You should disable the content of a database if you suspect that your database might contain harmful content or damaging macros.

Table 1–4 Navigation Buttons in Datasheet View

Button	Purpose
First record	Moves to the first record in the table
Previous record	Moves to the previous record in the table
Next record	Moves to the next record in the table
Last record	Moves to the last record in the table
New (blank) record	Moves to the end of the table to a position for entering a new record in the Append row

To Resize Columns in a Datasheet

Access assigns default column sizes, which do not always provide space to display all the data in the field. In some cases, the data might appear but some of the field name is not visible. You can correct this problem by resizing the column (changing its size) in the datasheet. In some instances, you might want to reduce the size of a column. **Why?** Some fields, such as the S_ID field, are short enough that they do not require all the space on the screen that is allotted to them. Changing a column width changes the layout, or design, of a table. The following steps resize the columns in the Shippers table and save the changes to the layout.

1

- Start Access, unless it is already running.
- Open the database, SC_AC_01_Clearnet.accdb, from your hard drive, OneDrive, or other storage location (Figure 1–25). You created this database earlier in this module.
- If a Security Warning appears, click the Enable Content button.

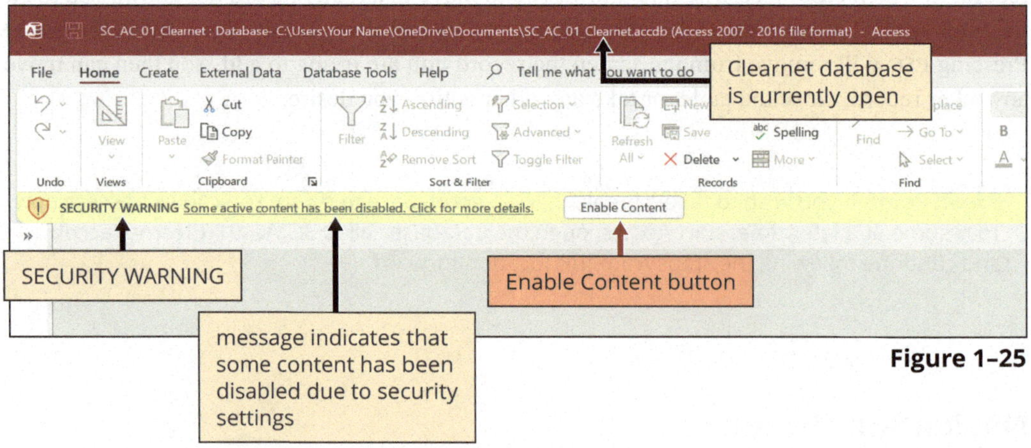

Figure 1–25

2

- If the Navigation Pane is closed, click the Shutter Bar Open/Close Button, shown in Figure 1–24, to open the Navigation Pane (Figure 1–26).

Figure 1–26

3

- Right-click the Shippers table in the Navigation Pane to display a shortcut menu.
- Click Open on the shortcut menu to open the table in Datasheet view.

Q&A Why do the records appear in a different order from how I entered them?
When you open a table, they are sorted in order based on the primary key, which may not be the order in which you entered them. In this case, the records appear in Shipper ID order.

4

- Point to the right boundary of the field selector for the Shipper Name field (Figure 1–27) so that the pointer becomes a two-headed arrow.

Q&A I am using touch and I cannot see the pointer. Is this a problem?
It is not a problem. Remember that if you are using your finger on a touch screen, you will not see the pointer.

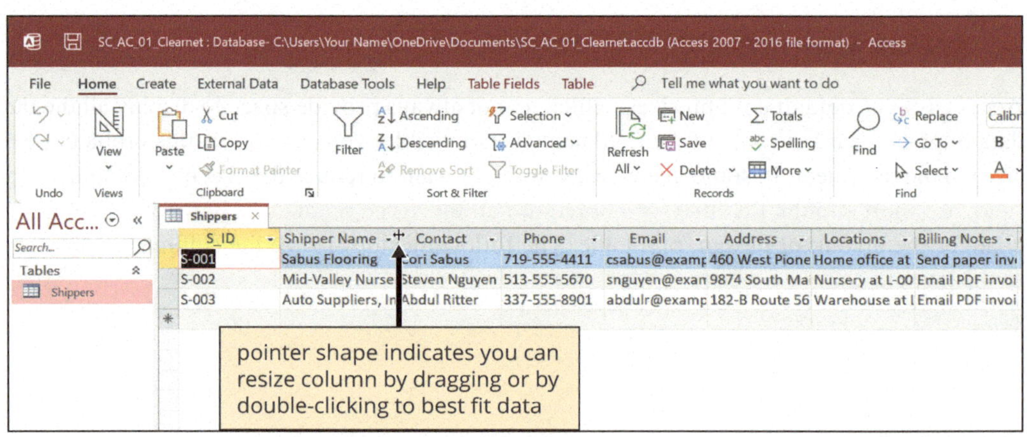

Figure 1–27

5

- Double-click the right boundary of the field selector to resize the field so that it best fits the data.
- Use the same technique to resize all the other fields to best fit the data.
- Save the changes to the layout by clicking the Save button on the Quick Access Toolbar (Figure 1–28).

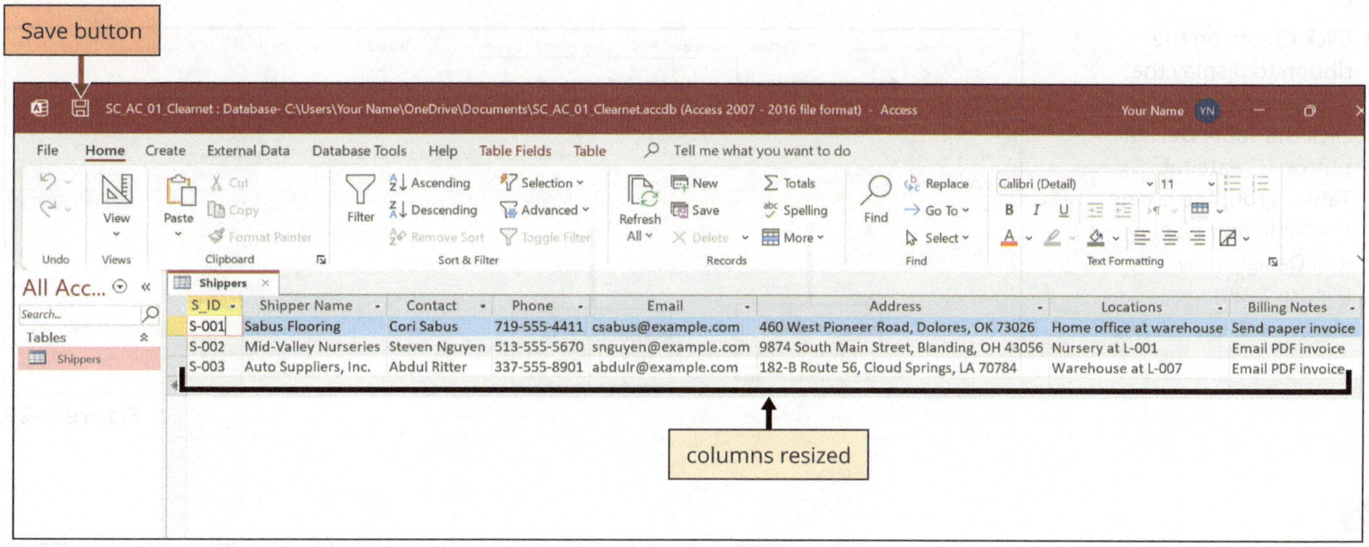

Figure 1–28

6

- Click the table's Close button (shown in Figure 1–23) to close the table.

Q&A What if I closed the table without saving the layout changes?

You would be asked if you want to save the changes.

Other Ways

1. Right-click field name, click Field Width, click Best Fit to resize field

Consider This

What is the best method for distributing database objects?

The traditional method of distributing database objects such as tables, reports, and forms uses a printer to produce a hard copy. A hard copy or printout is information that exists on a physical medium such as paper. Hard copies can be useful for the following reasons:

- Some people prefer proofreading a hard copy of a document rather than viewing it on the screen to check for errors and readability.
- Hard copies can serve as a backup reference if your storage medium is lost or becomes corrupted and you need to recreate the document. Instead of distributing a hard copy, users can distribute the document as an electronic image that mirrors the original document's appearance. The electronic image of the document can be emailed, posted on a website, or copied to a portable storage medium such as a USB flash drive. Two popular electronic image formats, sometimes called fixed formats, are PDF by Adobe Systems and XPS by Microsoft.

In Access, you can create electronic image files through the External Data tab on the ribbon. Electronic images of documents, such as PDF and XPS, can be useful for the following reasons:

- Users can view electronic images of documents without the software that created the original document (e.g., Access). Specifically, to view a PDF file, you use a program called Adobe Acrobat Reader, which can be downloaded free from Adobe's website. Similarly, to view an XPS file, you use a program called XPS Viewer, which is included in older versions of Windows and can be installed for free in newer versions of Windows.
- Sending electronic documents saves paper and printer supplies. Society encourages users to contribute to green computing, which involves reducing the electricity consumed and environmental waste generated when using computers, mobile devices, and related technologies.

To Create a Table Using Design View

The following steps use Design view to create a table. **Why?** Design view is a more efficient way to create a table than Datasheet view because you specify field name, data type, and size all in one view.

1

- Click Create on the ribbon to display the Create tab, and then click the Table Design button (Create tab | Tables group) to create the table and display it in Design view (Figure 1–29).

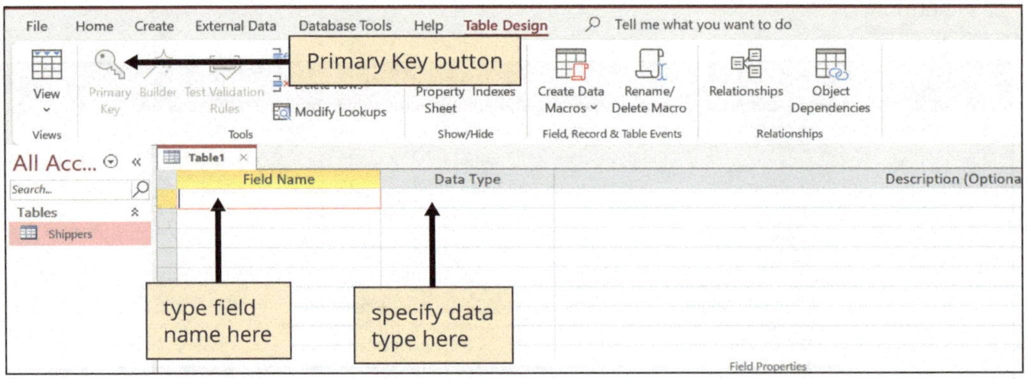

Figure 1–29

2

- Click in the empty field below Field Name if necessary to place the insertion point, and then type **Location ID** to enter the first field's name. Continue entering the data for the Locations table, as shown in Figure 1–30.

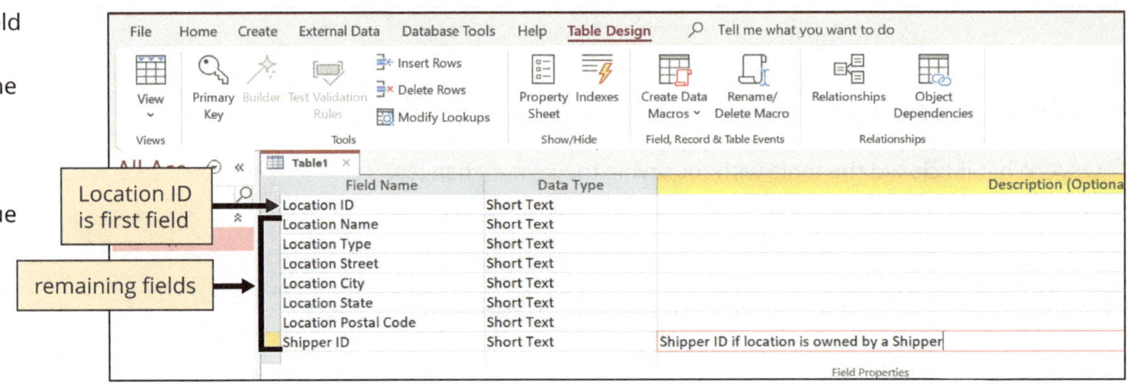

Figure 1–30

3

- Click the Location ID row selector, if necessary, and then click the Primary Key button to assign Location ID as the primary key field (Figure 1–31).

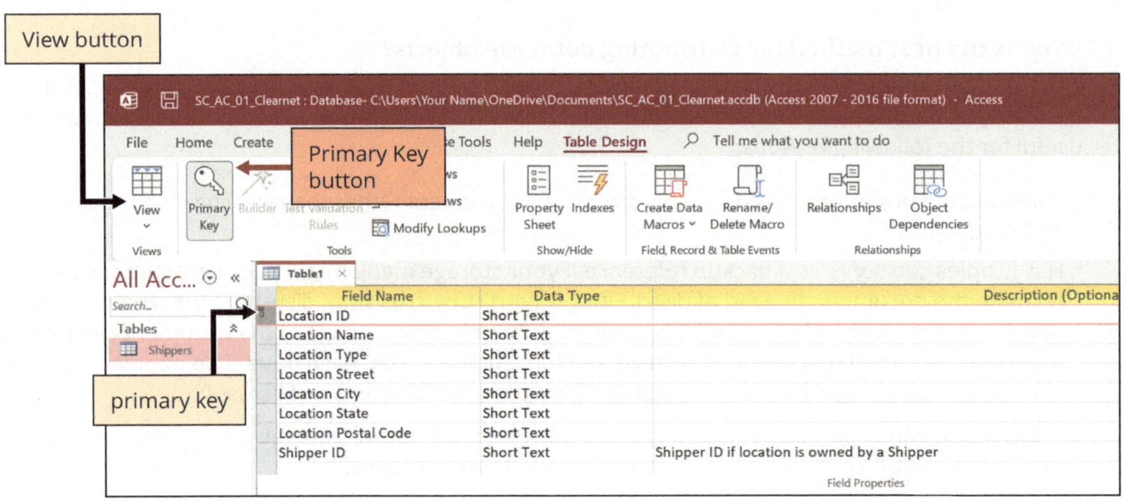

Figure 1–31

- Adjust the fields' sizes and captions as listed in Table 1–5.

Table 1–5 Structure of Locations Table

Field Name	Data Type	Field Size	Description
Location ID	Short Text	5	Primary Key **Caption:** L_ID
Location Name	Short Text	50	
Location Type	Short Text	15	**Caption:** Type
Location Street	Short Text	50	**Caption:** Street
Location City	Short Text	25	**Caption:** City
Location State	Short Text	2	**Caption:** State
Location Postal Code	Short Text	10	**Caption:** Postal Code
Shipper ID	Short Text	5	**Description:** Shipper ID if location is owned by a Shipper

- Click the Save button on the Quick Access toolbar and enter **Locations** in the text box to save the table with the name, Locations.

Q&A How do I rename a field in Design view?
In Design view, click on the end of the field you want to rename and press BACKSPACE until the name is removed. Enter the correct name.

Correcting Errors in the Structure

Whenever you create or modify a table in Design view, you should check the entries carefully to ensure they are correct. If you make a mistake and discover it before you press TAB, you can correct the error by repeatedly pressing BACKSPACE until the incorrect characters are removed. Then, type the correct characters. If you do not discover a mistake until later, you can click the entry, type the correct value, and then press ENTER. You can use the following techniques to make changes to the structure:

- If you accidentally add an extra field to the structure, select the field by clicking the row selector (the leftmost column on the row that contains the field to be deleted). Once you have selected the field, press DEL. This will remove the field from the structure.
- If you forget to include a field, select the field that will follow the one you want to add by clicking the row selector, and then press INS. The remaining fields move down one row, making room for the missing field. Make the entries for the new field in the usual manner.
- If you made the wrong field a primary key field, click the correct primary key entry for the field and then click the Primary Key button (Table Design tab | Tools group).
- To move a field, click the row selector for the field to be moved to select the field, and then drag the field to the desired position.

Click the Save button to save changes to the table's structure.

As an alternative to these steps, you might want to start over. To do so, click the Close button for the window containing the table, and then click the No button in the Microsoft Access dialog box. You then can repeat the process you used earlier to define the fields in the table.

Populating the Locations Table

Now that you have created the Locations table, you can populate the table by entering the data in Datasheet view. Populating the table means entering data into the tables.

1. Click the View button (Table Design tab | Views group) to change to Datasheet view.

2. Enter the location data, as shown in Figure 1–32.

Location							
L_ID	**Location Name**	**Type**	**Street**	**City**	**State**	**Postal Code**	**Shipper ID**
L-001	Sabus Flooring	Warehouse	460 West Pioneer Road	Dolores	OK	73026	S-001
L-002	Mid-Valley Nursery Greenhouse	Nursery	602 Hwy 127	Blanding	OH	43056	S-002
L-003	Port of New Orleans	Port	1350 Port of New Orleans Pl	New Orleans	LA	70130	
L-004	City Greenhouse	Retail	586 Main St	Creek City	OH	42357	
L-005	The Barn	Retail	79 Hwy 5406	New Boston	OH	43282	
L-006	Silver Décor	Retail	256a North Utah St	Standing Lake	CO	81352	
L-007	Auto Suppliers, Inc.	Warehouse	182-B Route 56	Cloud Springs	LA	70784	S-003

Figure 1–32

Q&A How do I type the accented é in the word Décor?
In the Locations table, type the non-accented word Decor. When you tab to the next field, Access will automatically replace the non-accented e with the accented é (called an e-acute).

To Close the Table

Now that you have completed and saved the Locations table, you can close it. The following step closes the table.

1. Click the Close button for the Locations table (Figure 1–33) to close the table.

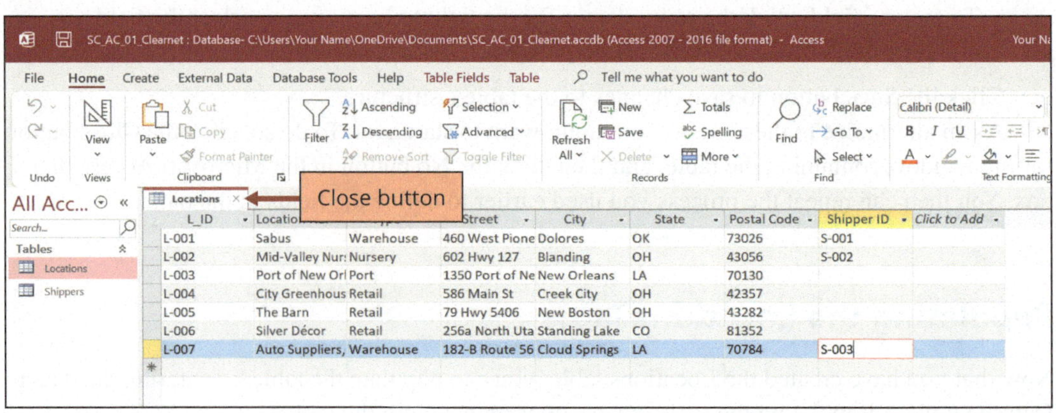

Figure 1–33

To Resize Columns in a Datasheet

You can resize the columns in the datasheet for the Locations table just as you resized the columns in the datasheet for the Shippers table. The following steps resize the columns in the Locations table to best fit the data.

1. Open the Locations table in Datasheet view.
2. Double-click the right boundary of the field selectors of each of the fields to resize the columns so that they best fit the data.
3. Save the changes to the layout by clicking the Save button on the Quick Access Toolbar.
4. Close the table.

BTW
Resizing Columns
To resize all columns in a datasheet to best fit simultaneously, select the column heading for the first column, hold down SHIFT and select the last column in the datasheet. Then, double-click the right boundary of any field selector. Click the Save button to save your changes.

Importing Additional Access Database Tables into an Existing Database

Access users frequently need to import tables that contain data into an existing database. **Why?** Organizations have data in tables that needs to be used in other databases. Importing tables ensures efficiency and accuracy. In addition to shippers and locations, Clearnet must also keep track of loads and the carriers hired to transport those loads. This information exists in another database. The following steps import three tables into the Clearnet database.

1

- Find the database file Support_AC_01_Clearnet-Extra-Tables in the Data Files and save it to the storage location specified by your instructor.
- If necessary, open your Clearnet database.
- Click External Data on the ribbon to display the External Data tab (Figure 1–34).

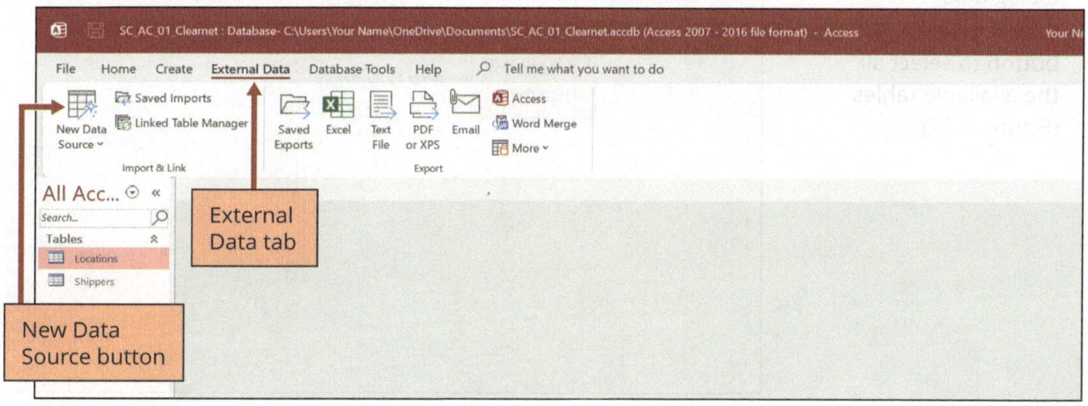

Figure 1–34

2

- Click the New Data Source button (External Data tab | Import & Link group) to open a menu.
- Point to From Database to display a menu (Figure 1–35), and then click Access to display the Get External Data – Access Database dialog box.

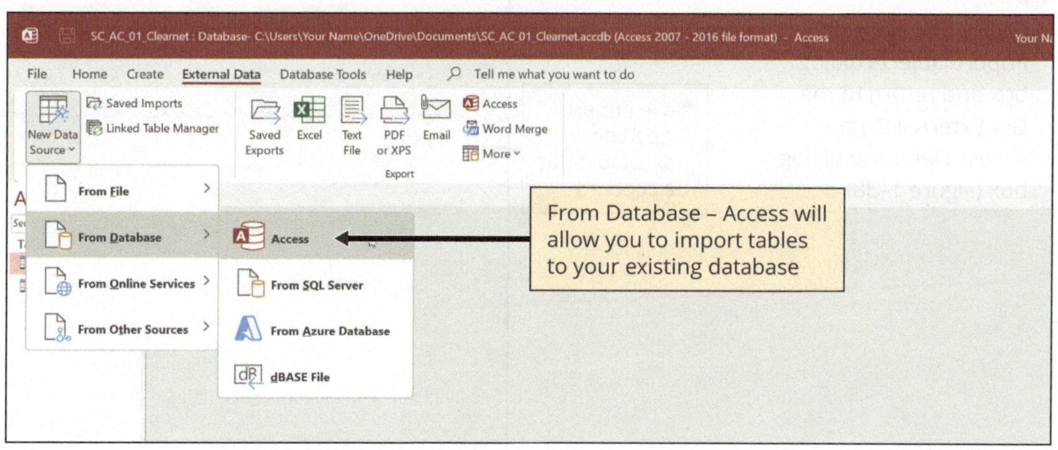

Figure 1–35

3

- Click the Browse button, navigate to the storage location for the Support_AC_01_Clearnet-Extra-Tables.accdb file, and then click Open to specify the source of the data you are importing.
- Click the 'Import tables, queries, forms, reports, macros, and modules into the current database' option button to specify how and where you want to store the data. (Figure 1–36).

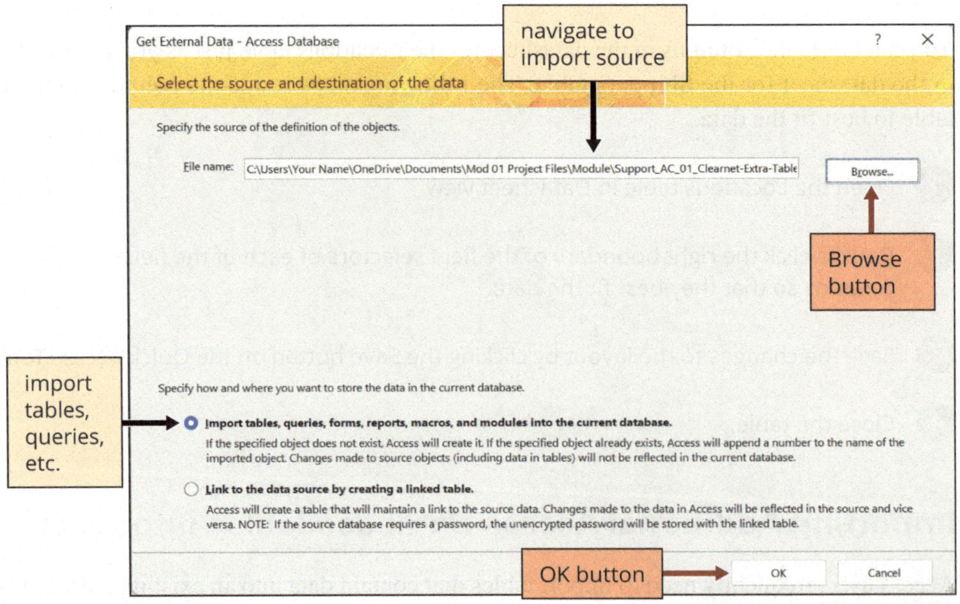

Figure 1–36

4

- Click OK to display the Import Objects dialog box.
- Click the Select All button to select all the available tables (Figure 1–37).

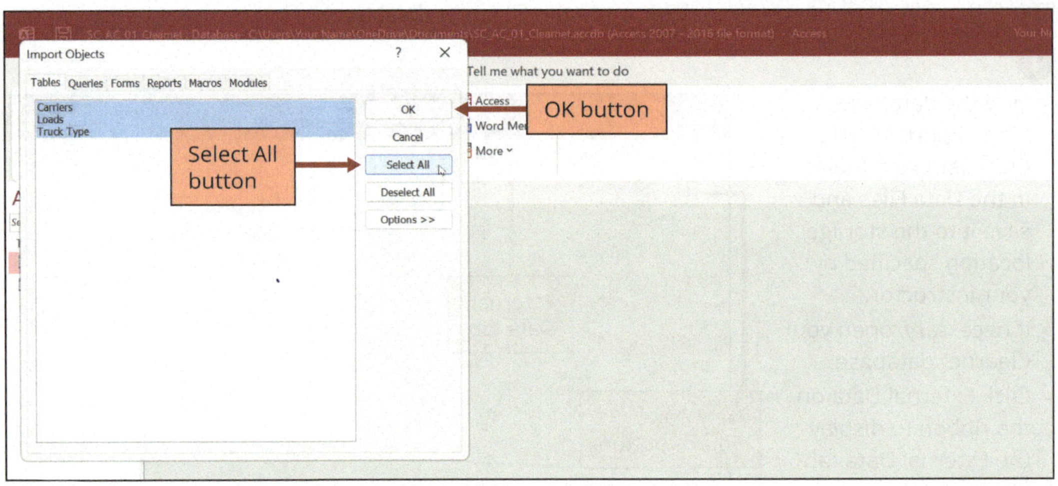

Figure 1–37

5

- Click OK to close the Import Objects dialog box and return to the Get External Data – Access Database dialog box (Figure 1–38)

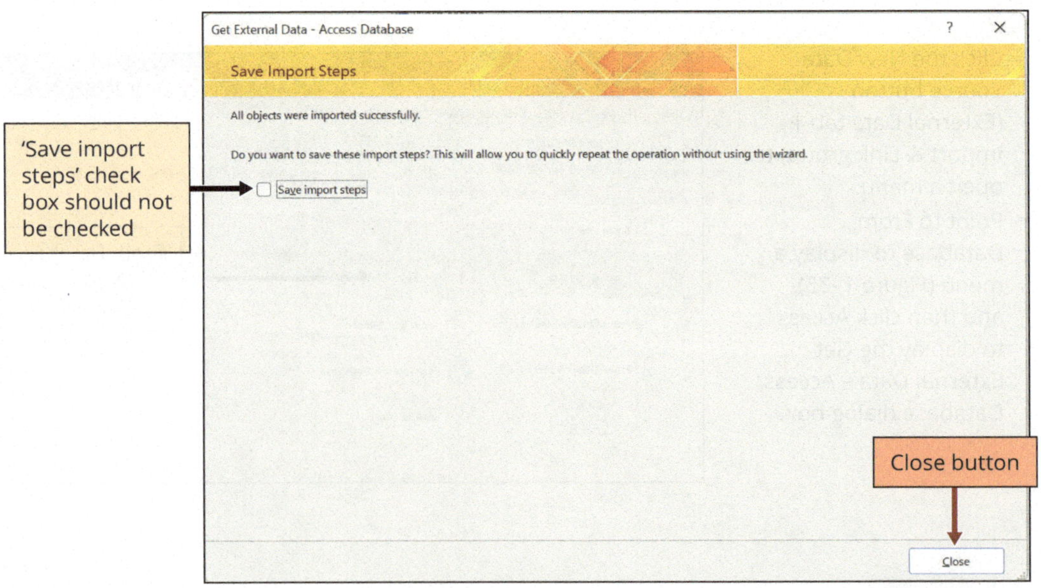

Figure 1–38

6

- Click the Close button to close the Import Objects dialog box without saving the Import steps (Figure 1–39).

Q&A Do I need to repeat this process for each table?
You have completed the import and will not repeat this import procedure in this project.

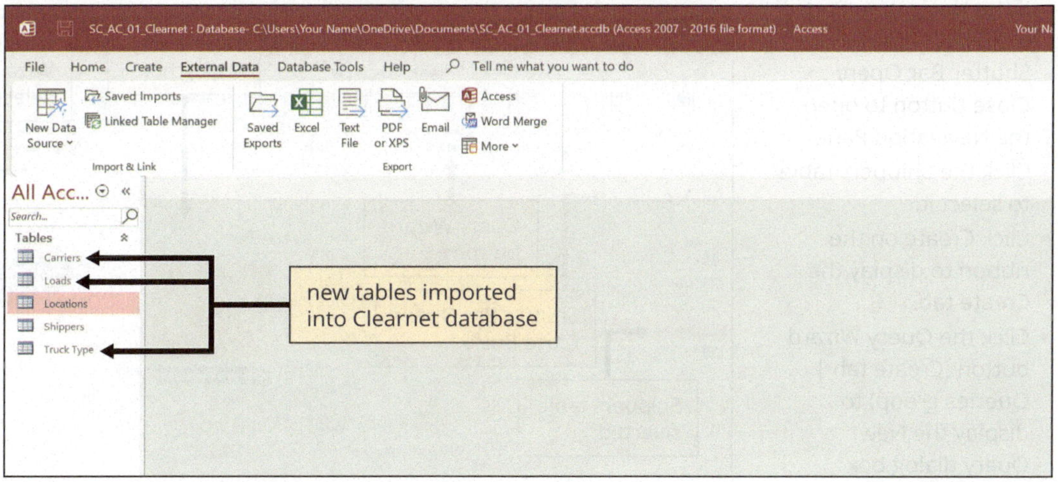

Figure 1–39

- Open the Loads table to explore its data and then close the table.

Q&A The Loads table includes a Rate field. When adding a record to the Loads table, do you need to type a dollar sign when adding data to the Rate field?
You do not need to type dollar signs or commas. In addition, because the digits to the right of the decimal point are both zeros, you do not need to type either the decimal point or the zeros.

Break Point: If you wish to take a break, this is a good place to do so. You can exit Access now. To resume at a later time, start Access, open the database called SC_AC_01_Clearnet.accdb, and continue following the steps from this location forward.

Additional Database Objects

A database contains many types of objects. Tables are the objects you use to store and manipulate data. Access supports other important types of objects as well; each object has a specific purpose that helps maximize the benefits of a database. Through queries (questions), Access makes it possible to ask complex questions concerning the data in the database and then receive instant answers. Access also allows the user to produce attractive and useful forms for viewing and updating data. Additionally, Access includes report creation tools that make it easy to produce sophisticated reports for presenting data.

BTW
Creating Queries
The Simple Query Wizard is a convenient way to create straightforward queries. It is a good method to learn about queries, although you will find that many of the queries you create require more control than the wizard provides.

Creating Queries

Queries are simply questions, the answers to which are in the database. Access contains a powerful query feature that helps you find the answers to a wide variety of questions. Once you have examined the question you want to ask to determine the fields involved in the question, you can begin creating the query. If the query involves no special sort order, restrictions, or calculations, you can use the Simple Query Wizard.

To Use the Simple Query Wizard to Create a Query

The following steps use the Simple Query Wizard to create a query that Clearnet can use to obtain a list of their shippers and create a call list for the day **Why?** The Simple Query Wizard is the quickest and easiest way to create a query. This query displays the Shipper's name, primary contact person, and their phone number and email address.

1

- If the Navigation Pane is closed, click the Shutter Bar Open/Close Button to open the Navigation Pane.
- Click the Shippers table to select it.
- Click Create on the ribbon to display the Create tab.
- Click the Query Wizard button (Create tab | Queries group) to display the New Query dialog box (Figure 1–40).

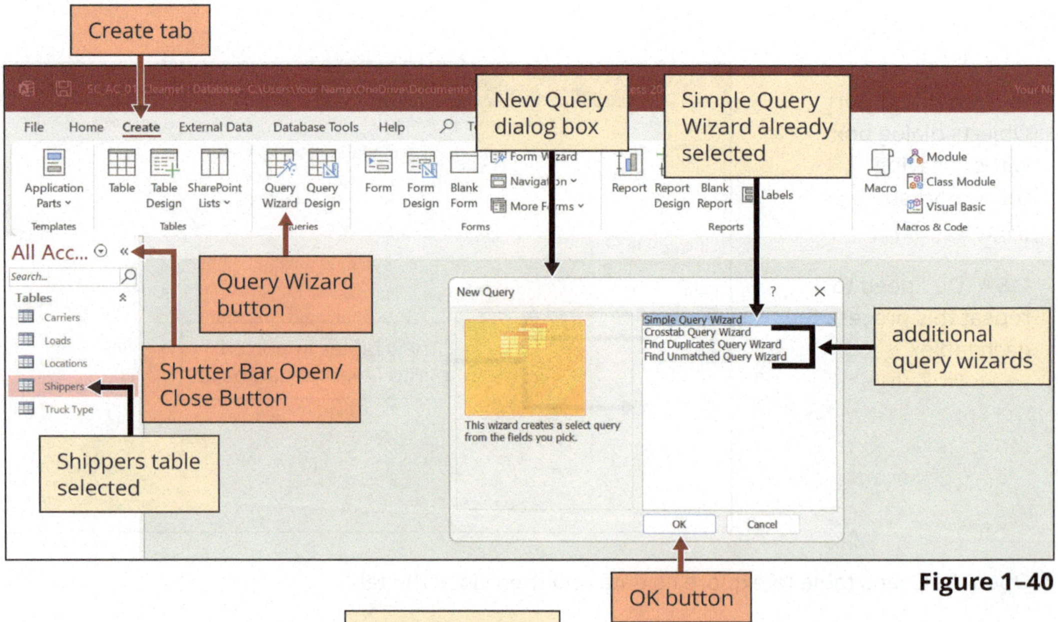

Figure 1–40

2

- Be sure Simple Query Wizard is selected, and then click OK (New Query dialog box) to display the Simple Query Wizard dialog box (Figure 1–41).

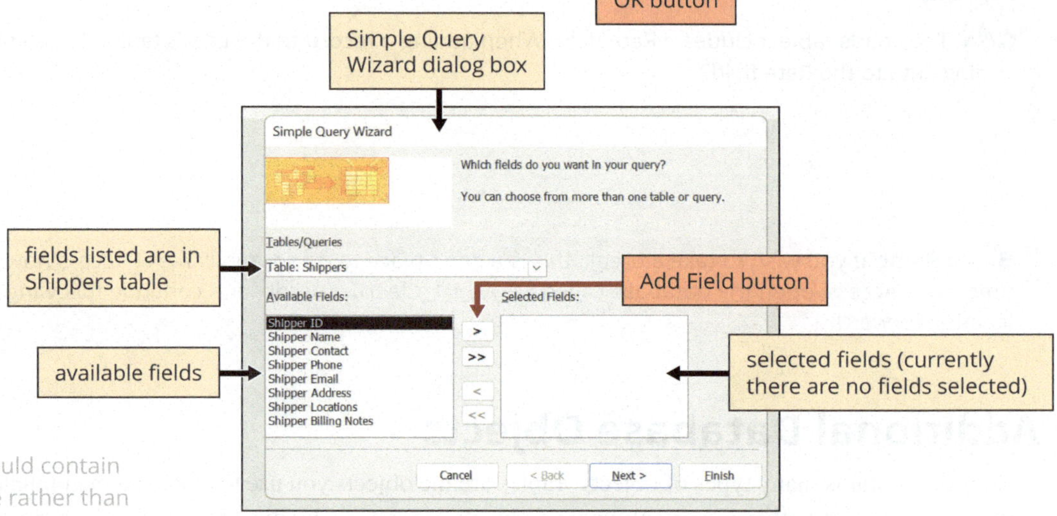

Figure 1–41

Q&A What would happen if the Carriers table were selected instead of the Shippers table?
The list of available fields would contain fields from the Carriers table rather than the Shippers table.

If the list contained Carriers table fields, how could I make it contain Shippers table fields?
Click the arrow in the Tables/Queries box, and then click the Shippers table in the list that appears.

3

- Select the Shipper Name field, and then click the Add Field button to move the field to the Selected Fields area.
- With the Shipper Contact field selected, click the Add Field button a second time to move the field to the Selected Fields area.
- Using the same technique, move the Shipper Phone and Shipper Email fields (Figure 1–42) to the query.

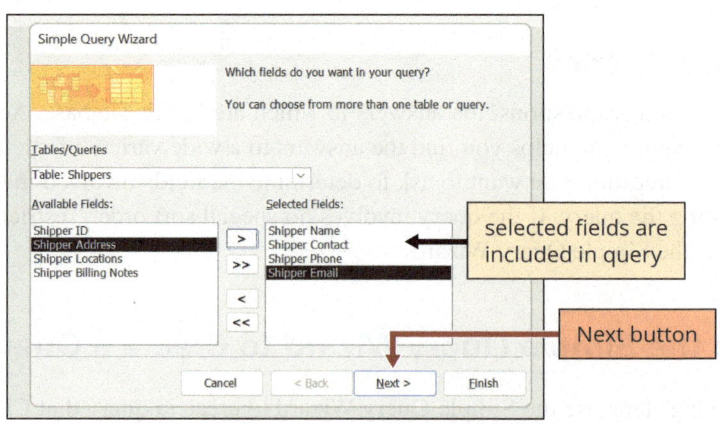

Figure 1–42

4

- Click Next to move to the next screen.
- Confirm that the title of the query is Shippers Query (Figure 1–43).

Q&A What should I do if the title is incorrect?
Click the box containing the title to produce an insertion point. Erase the current title and then type Shippers Query.

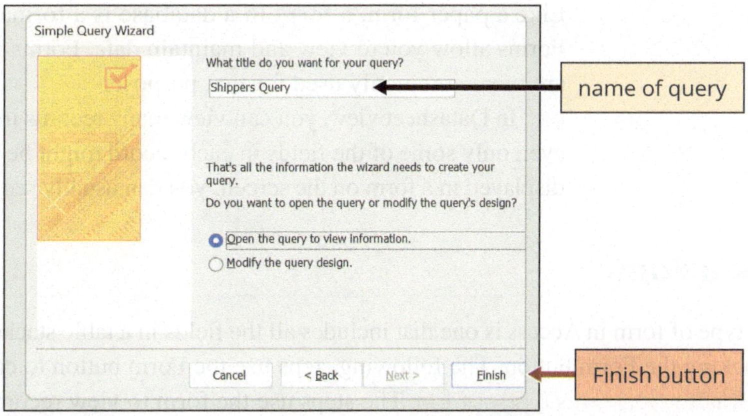

Figure 1–43

5

- Click the Finish button to create the query (Figure 1–44).
- Click the Close button for the Shippers Query to remove the query results from the screen.

Q&A If I want to use this query in the future, do I need to save the query?
Normally you would. The one exception is a query created by the wizard. The wizard automatically saves the query it creates.

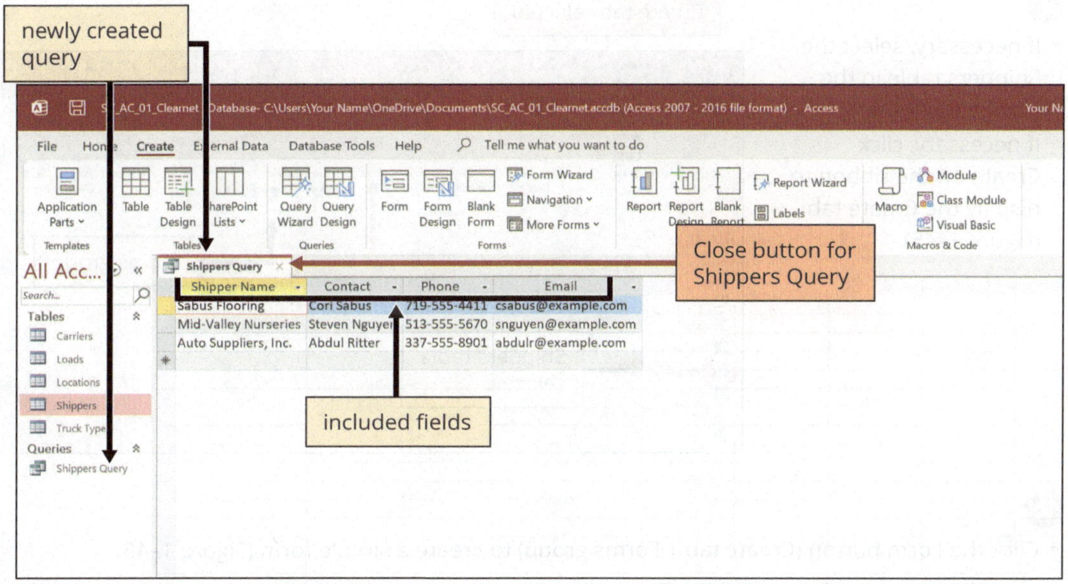

Figure 1–44

Using Queries

After you have created and saved a query, Access stores it as a database object and makes it available for use in a variety of ways:

- If you want to change the design of the query, right-click the query in the Navigation Pane and then click Design View on the shortcut menu to open the query in Design view.
- To view the results of the query from Design view, click the Run button (Query Design tab | Results group) to instruct Access to **run** the query, that is, to perform the necessary actions to produce and display the results in Datasheet view.
- To view the results of the query from the Navigation Pane, open it by right-clicking the query and clicking Open on the shortcut menu. Access automatically runs the query and displays the results in Datasheet view.

You can switch between views of a query using the View button (Home tab | Views group). Clicking the arrow in the bottom of the button produces the View button menu. You then click the desired view in the menu. The two query views you will use in this module are Datasheet view (which displays the query results) and Design view (for changing the query design). You can also click the top part of the View button; in which case, you will switch to the view identified by the icon on the button. For the most part, the icon on the button represents the view you want, so you can usually simply click the button.

Creating Forms

Like a paper form, a **form** in a database is a formatted document with fields that contain data. Forms allow you to view and maintain data. Forms can also be used to print data, though reports are more commonly used for that purpose.

In Datasheet view, you can view many records in a form at once. If there are many fields, however, only some of the fields in each record might be visible at a time. In **Form view**, where data is displayed in a form on the screen, you can usually see all the fields, but only for one record at a time.

To Create a Form

The simplest type of form in Access is one that includes all the fields in a table stacked one above the other, which can be achieved by simply clicking the Form button. The following steps use the Form button to create a form. **Why?** Using the Form button is the simplest way to create this type of form. The steps use the form to view records and then save the form.

1

- If necessary, select the Shippers table in the Navigation Pane.
- If necessary, click Create on the ribbon to display the Create tab (Figure 1–45).

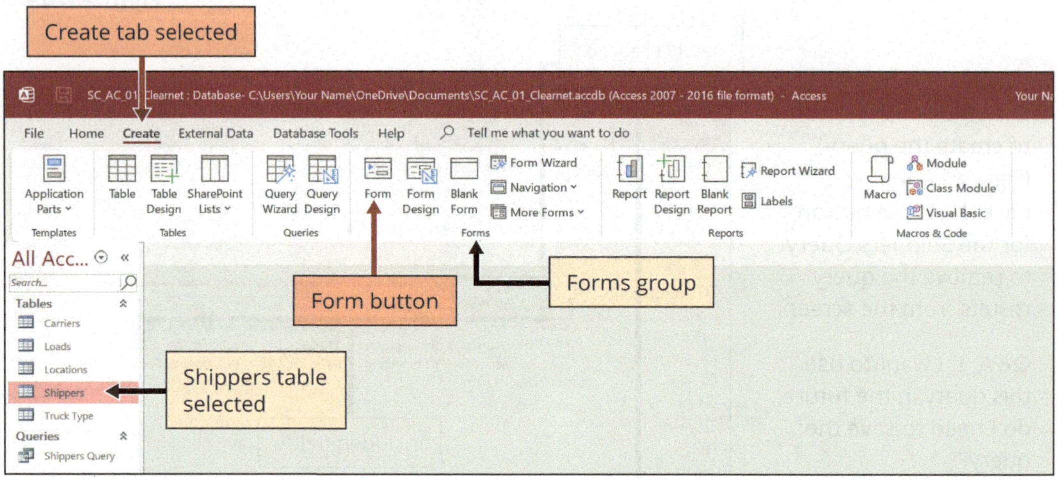

Figure 1–45

2

- Click the Form button (Create tab | Forms group) to create a simple form (Figure 1–46).

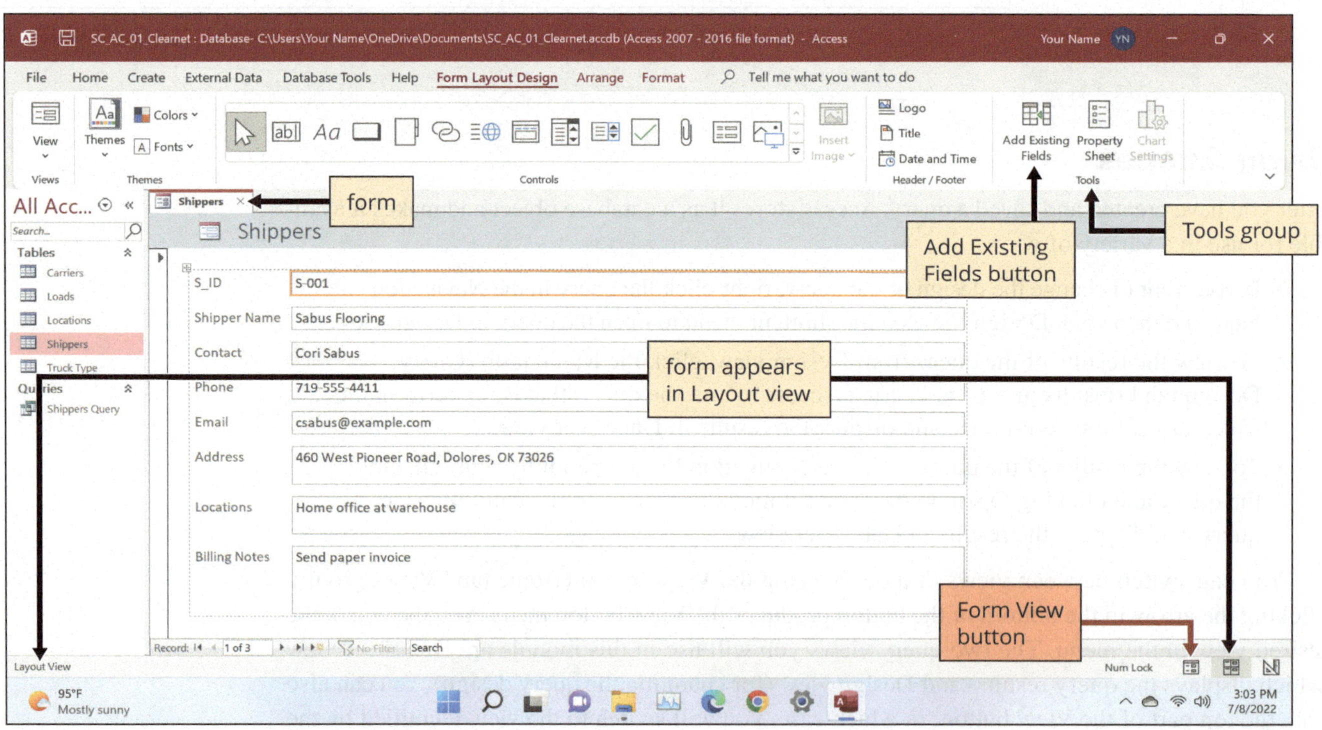

Figure 1–46

Q&A A Field list appeared on my screen. What should I do?

Click the 'Add Existing Fields' button (Form Layout Design tab | Tools group) to remove the Field list from the screen.

3

- Click the Form View button on the Access status bar to display the form in Form view rather than Layout view.

Q&A What is the difference between Layout view and Form view?
Layout view allows you to make changes to the look of the form. Form view is the view you use to examine or make changes to the data.

How can I tell which view is active?
Access identifies the current view in two ways. The left side of the status bar will list the name of the view, such as Layout view, and the current view's button will be selected on the right side of the status bar.

- Click the Next record button once to advance through the records (Figure 1–47).

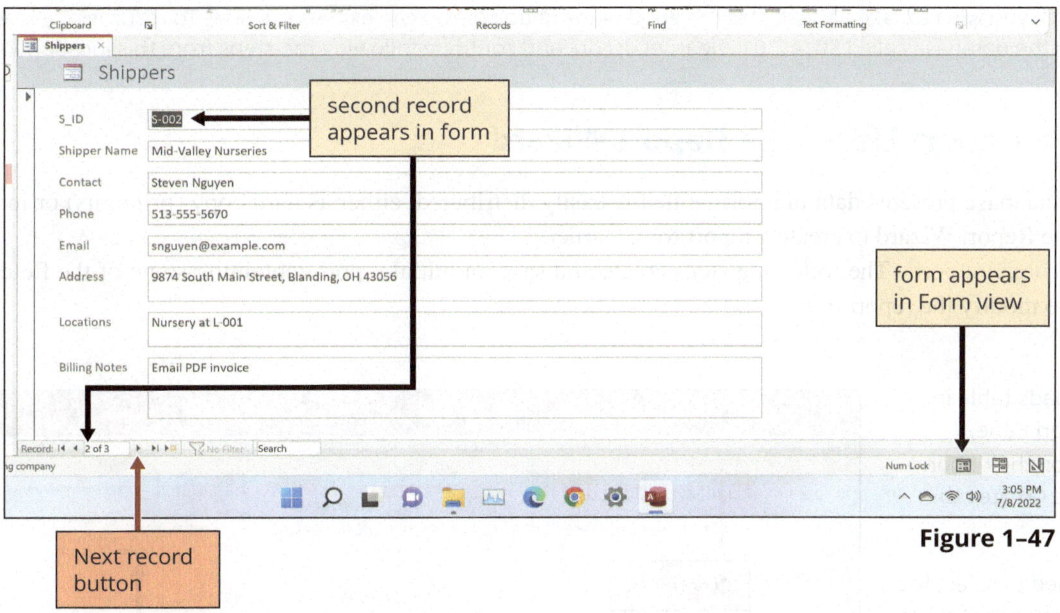

Figure 1–47

Q&A Why is the form title Shippers?
Access automatically assigns the name of the table or query used as the basis of the form or report as its title. It also automatically includes the date and time. You can change either of these later.

4

- Click the Save button on the Quick Access Toolbar to display the Save As dialog box (Figure 1–48).

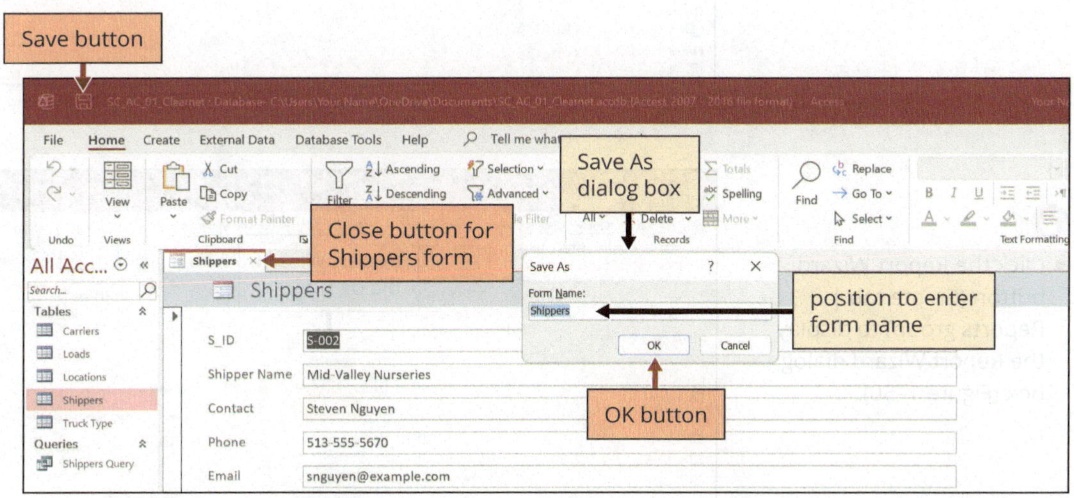

Figure 1–48

Q&A Do I have to click the Next record button before saving?
No. The only reason you were asked to click the button was so that you could experience navigation within the form.

5

- Type **Shippers Form** as the form name, and then click OK to save the form.
- Click the form's Close button to close the form.

Other Ways

1. Click View button (Home tab | Views group) to change view

Using a Form

After you have saved a form, you can use it at any time by right-clicking the form in the Navigation Pane and then clicking Open on the shortcut menu. In addition to viewing data in the form, you can also use it to enter or update data, a process that is similar to updating data using a datasheet. If you plan to use the form to enter or revise data, you must ensure you are viewing the form in Form view.

Break Point: If you wish to take a break, this is a good place to do so. You can exit Access now. To resume at a later time, start Access, open the database called SC_AC_01_Clearnet.accdb, and continue following the steps from this location forward.

To Create a Report Using the Report Wizard

A **report** in a database presents data in a format that is easily distributed, either as hard copy (printouts) or in other formats. You will use the Report Wizard to create a report for Clearnet. **Why?** Using the Report Wizard is an easy way to get started in creating professional reports. The following steps create and save an initial report containing some of the fields in the Loads table. They also modify the report title.

1

- Select the Loads table in the Navigation Pane.
- Click Create on the ribbon to display the Create tab (Figure 1–49).

Q&A Do I need to select the Loads table prior to clicking Create on the ribbon?
You do not need to select the table at that point. You do need to select a table prior to clicking the Report Wizard button, because Access will include all the fields in whichever table or query is currently selected.

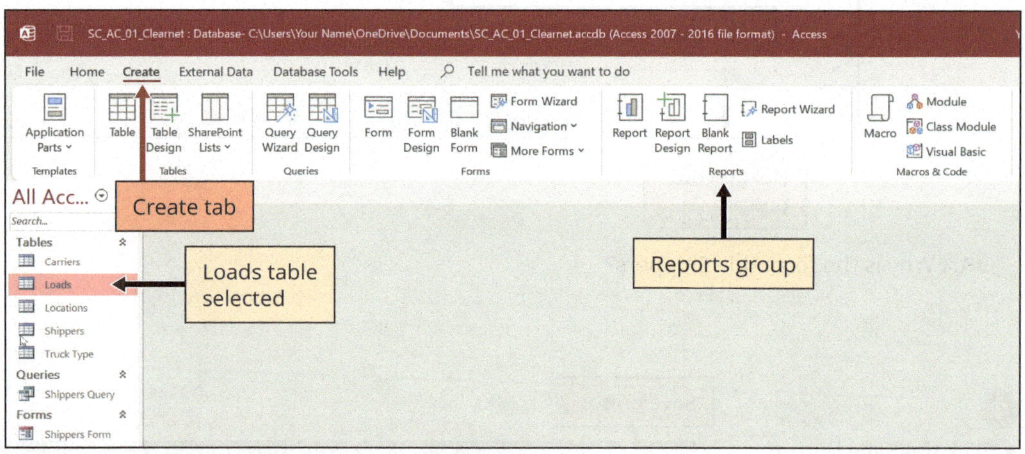

Figure 1–49

2

- Click the Report Wizard button (Create tab | Reports group) to display the Report Wizard dialog box (Figure 1–50).

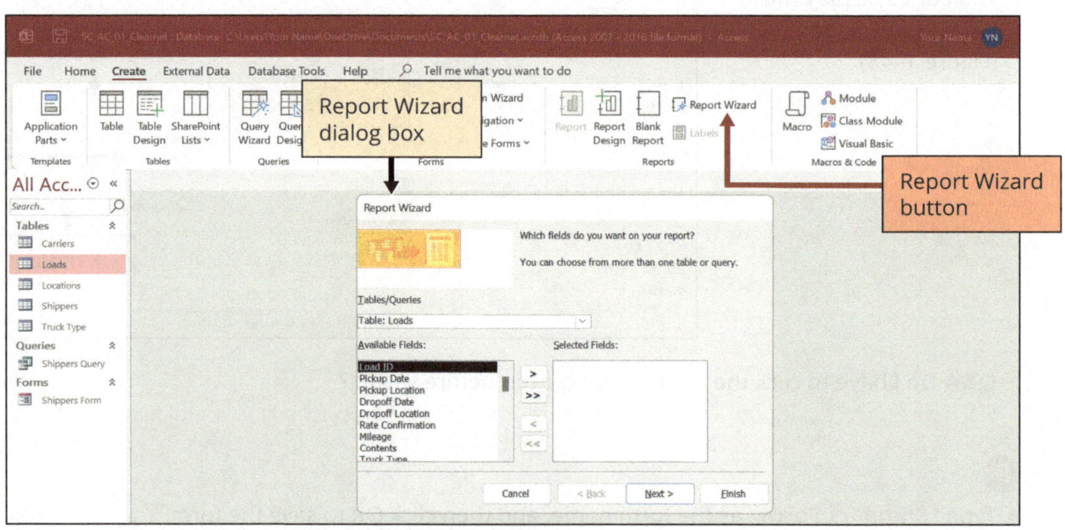

Figure 1–50

3

- In the Available Fields area, select Load ID and then click the Add Field button to add the field to the Selected Fields area.
- Click the arrow button a second time to move the Pickup Date field to the Selected Fields area.
- Move the Dropoff Date, Rate Confirmation, Truck Type, Status, and Carrier fields to the Selected Fields box (Figure 1–51).

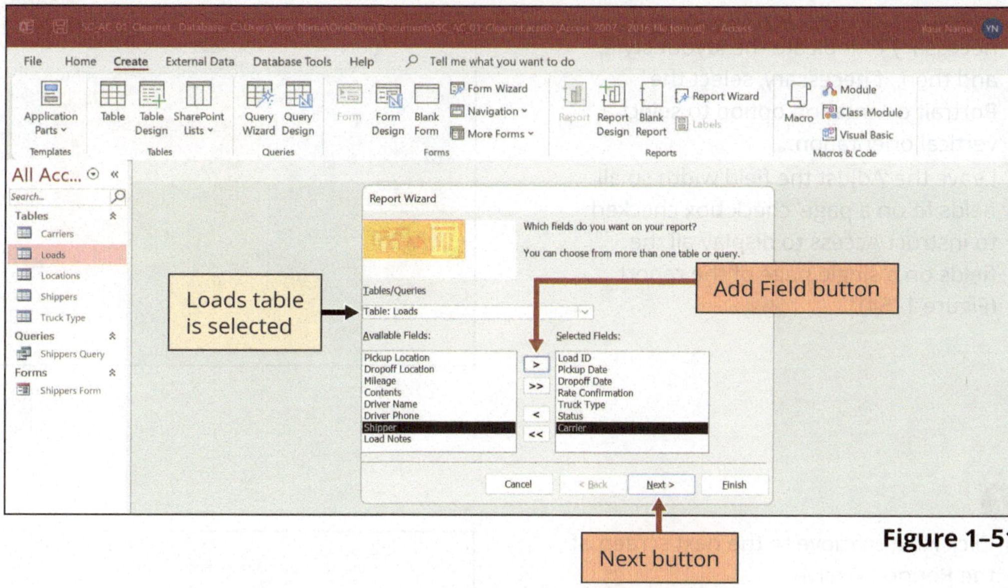

Figure 1–51

4

- Click Next, and then select Status. Click the Add Field button in the 'Do you want to add any grouping levels' area to indicate that the report will be grouped by Status (Figure 1–52).

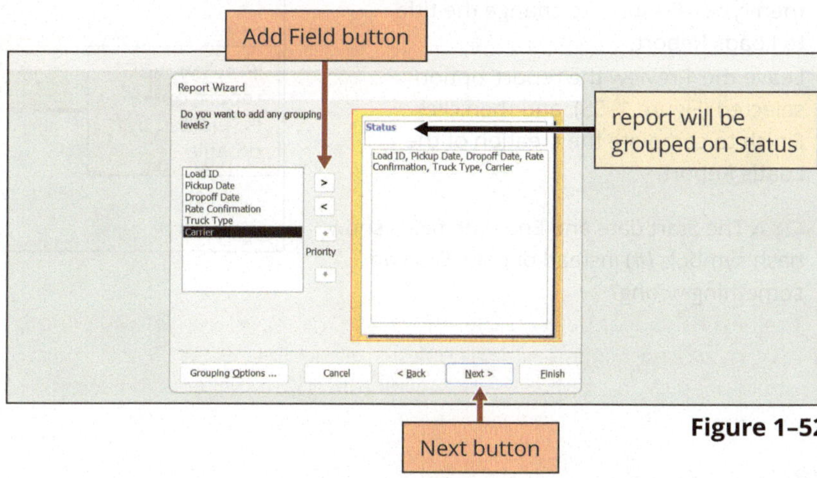

Figure 1–52

5

- Click Next to move to the next screen in the Report Wizard (Figure 1–53).

Q&A How do I correct a mistake I made in the Report Wizard?
The Report Wizard lets you click the Back button at any time to undo an action.

- Click Next again to move to the next screen without indicating a sort order or summary information for detail records.

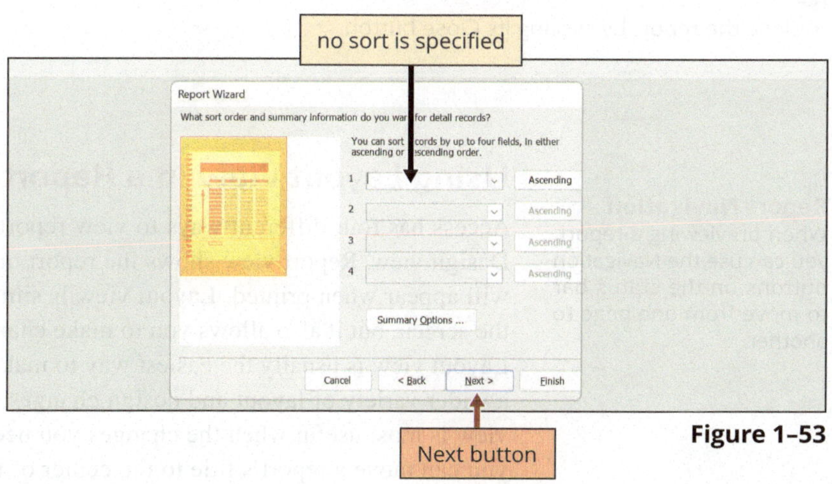

Figure 1–53

6

- Select the Stepped layout option if necessary to indicate the layout style, and then, if necessary, select the Portrait orientation option to select a vertical orientation.
- Leave the 'Adjust the field width so all fields fit on a page' check box checked to instruct Access to display all the fields on a single page of the report (Figure 1–54).

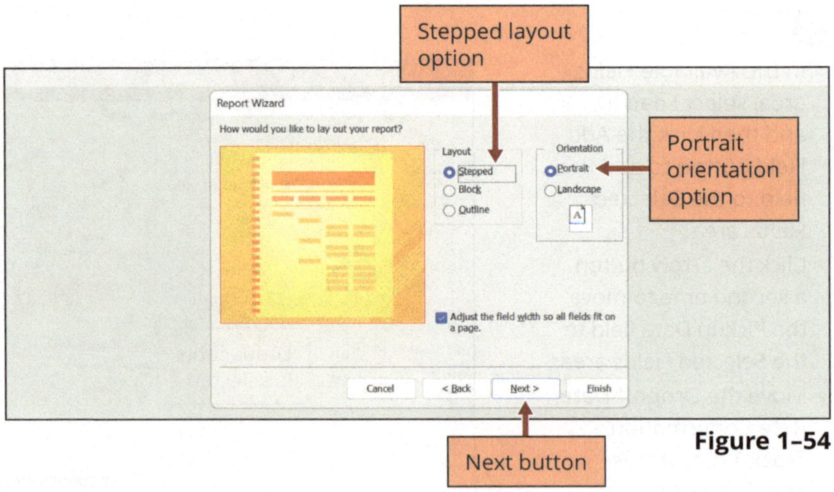

Figure 1–54

7

- Click Next to move to the next screen of the Report Wizard.
- Click to the right of the word Loads, and then type **Report** to change the title to Loads Report.
- Leave the 'Preview the report' option selected (Figure 1–55), and then click Finish to complete the creation of the Loads Report.

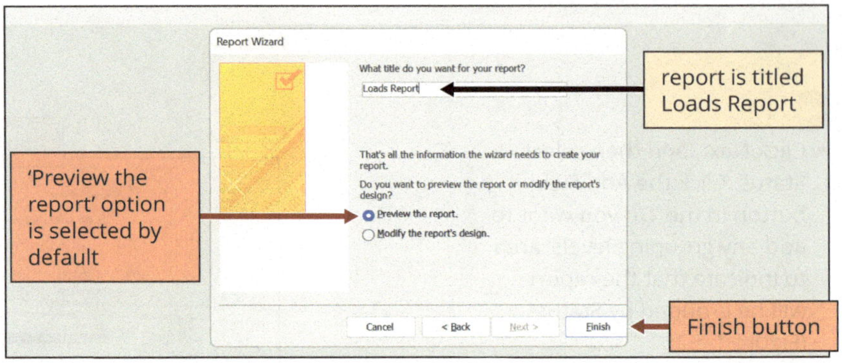

Figure 1–55

Q&A The Start date and End date fields show hash symbols (#) instead of data. Did I do something wrong?

The hashes appear because the columns in the report are not wide enough to show the entire date in each record. Rather than show a partial date, which could be misleading, Access inserts hash symbols instead. Before printing the report, you would need to adjust the size of the columns so the full date in each cell can be displayed. This skill is covered in a later module. For now, you can leave the report as is.

8

- Close the report by clicking its Close button.

BTW
Report Navigation
When previewing a report, you can use the Navigation buttons on the status bar to move from one page to another.

Using Layout View in a Report

Access has four different ways to view reports: Report view, Print Preview, Layout view, and Design view. Report view shows the report on the screen. Print Preview shows the report as it will appear when printed. Layout view is similar to Report view in that it shows the report on the screen, but it also allows you to make changes to the design and layout of the report. Using Layout view is usually the easiest way to make such changes. Design view allows you to make a wider variety of layout and design changes, but does not show you the actual report. Design view is most useful when the changes you need to make are especially complex. For example, you can move a report's title to the center of the page by dragging and dropping the label box (Figure 1–56).

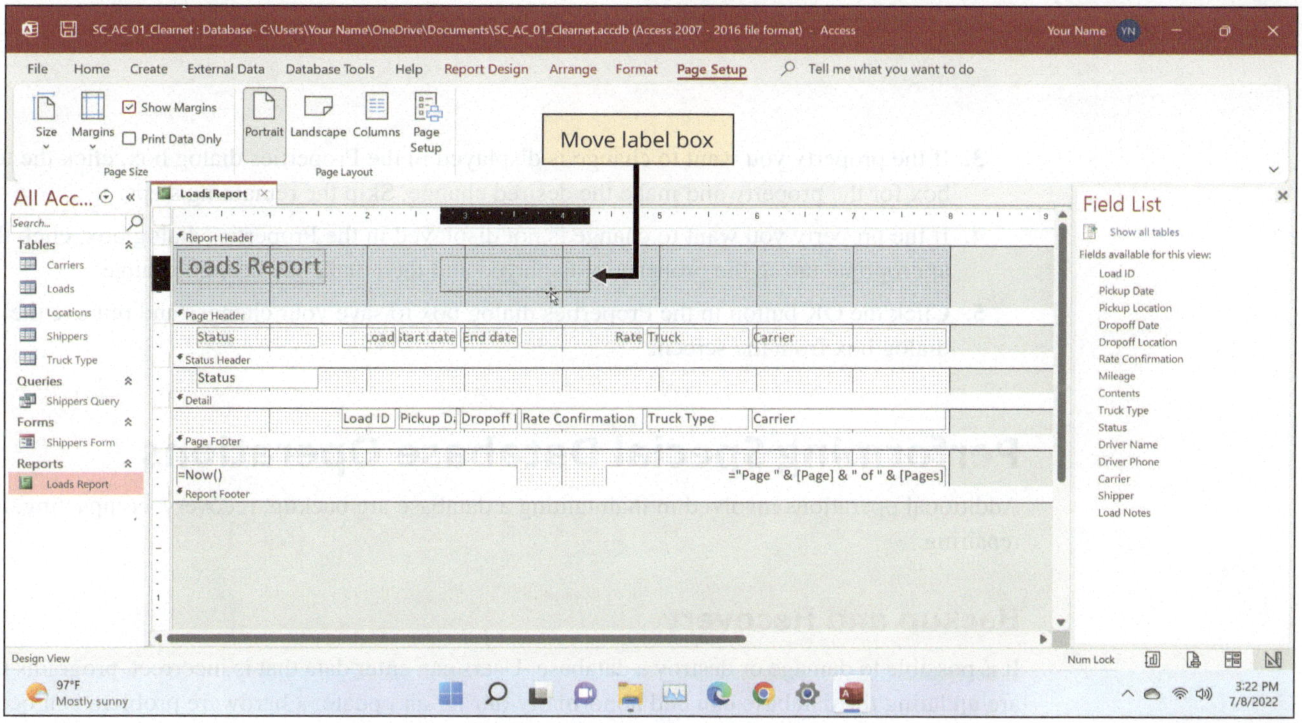

Figure 1–56

Identifying Database Properties

Access helps you organize and identify your databases by using **database properties**, which are the details about a file. Database properties, also known as **metadata**, can include such information as the project author, title, or subject. **Keywords** are words or phrases that further describe the database. For example, a class name or database topic can describe the file's purpose or content.

Five different types of database properties exist, but the more common ones used in this course are standard and automatically updated properties. **Standard properties** are associated with all Microsoft Office documents and include author, title, and subject. **Automatically updated properties** include file system properties, such as the date you create or change a file, and statistics, such as the file size.

Consider This

Why would you want to assign database properties to a database?

Database properties are valuable for a variety of reasons:

- Users can save time locating a particular file because they can view a file's database properties without opening the database.
- By creating consistent properties for files having similar content, users can better organize their databases.
- Some organizations require Access users to add database properties so that other employees can view details about these files.

To Change Database Properties

To change database properties, you would follow these steps.

1. Click File on the ribbon to open Backstage view and then, if necessary, click the Info tab in Backstage view to display the Info gallery.
2. Click the 'View and edit database properties' link in the right pane of the Info gallery to display the Clearnet Properties dialog box.

Q&A Why are some of the database properties already filled in?
The person who installed Office on your computer or network might have set or customized the properties.

3. If the property you want to change is displayed in the Properties dialog box, click the text box for the property and make the desired change. Skip the remaining steps.
4. If the property you want to change is not displayed in the Properties dialog box, click the appropriate tab so the property is displayed and then make the desired change.
5. Click the OK button in the Properties dialog box to save your changes and remove the dialog box from the screen.

Performing Special Database Operations

Additional operations involved in maintaining a database are backup, recovery, compacting, and repairing.

Backup and Recovery

It is possible to damage or destroy a database. Users can enter data that is incorrect, programs that are updating the database can end abnormally during an update, a hardware problem can occur, and so on. After any such event has occurred, the database might contain invalid data or it might be totally destroyed.

You cannot allow a situation in which data has been damaged or destroyed to go uncorrected. You must somehow return the database to a correct state. This process is called recovery; that is, you **recover** the database.

The simplest approach to recovery involves periodically making a copy of the database (called a **backup copy** or a **save copy**). This is referred to as **backing up** the database. If a problem occurs, you correct the problem by overwriting the actual database—often referred to as the **live database**—with the backup copy.

To back up the database that is currently open, you use the Back Up Database command on the Save As tab in Backstage view. In the process, Access suggests a name that is a combination of the database name and the current date. For example, if you back up the Clearnet database on October 20, 2027, Access will suggest the name, Clearnet_2027-10-20. You can change this name if you desire, although it is a good idea to use this name. Doing so will make it easy to distinguish between all the backup copies you have made to determine which is the most recent. In addition, if you discover that a critical problem occurred on October 18, 2027, you might want to go back to the most recent backup before October 18. If, for example, the database was not backed up on October 17 but was backed up on October 16, you would use Clearnet_2027-10-16.

To Back Up a Database

You would use the following steps to back up a database to a file on a hard drive, high-capacity removable disk, or other storage location.

1. Open the database to be backed up.
2. Click File on the ribbon to open Backstage view, and then click the Save As tab.
3. With Save Database As selected in the File Types area, click 'Back Up Database' in the Save Database As area, and then click the Save As button.
4. Navigate to the desired location in the Save As box. If you do not want the name Access has suggested, enter the desired name in the File name text box.
5. Click the Save button to back up the database.

Access creates a backup copy with the desired name in the desired location. Should you ever need to recover the database using this backup copy, you can simply copy it over the live version.

Compacting and Repairing a Database

As you add more data to a database, it naturally grows larger. When you delete an object (tables, queries, forms, or reports), the space previously occupied by the object does not become available for additional objects. Instead, the additional objects are given new space, that is, space that was not already allocated. To remove this empty space from the database, you must **compact** the database. The same option that compacts the database also repairs problems that might have occurred in the database.

To Compact and Repair a Database

You would use the following steps to compact and repair a database.

1. Open the database to be compacted.
2. Click File on the ribbon to open Backstage view, and then, if necessary, select the Info tab.
3. Click the 'Compact & Repair Database' button in the Info gallery to compact and repair the database.

The database now is the compacted form of the original.

Additional Operations

Additional special operations include closing a database without exiting Access and saving a database with another name. They also include deleting a table (or another object) as well as renaming an object.

When you are working in a database and you open another database from within Access, Access will automatically close the database that was previously open. Alternatively, you can open another database at the same time by opening the second database from File Explorer in Windows. Similarly, before deleting or renaming an object, you should ensure that the object has no dependent objects, that is, other objects that depend on the object you want to delete.

To Close a Database without Exiting Access

You would use the following steps to close a database without exiting Access.

1. Click File on the ribbon to open Backstage view.
2. Click Close.

To Save a Database with Another Name

To save a database with another name, you would use the following steps.

1. Click File on the ribbon to open Backstage view, and then select the Save As tab.
2. With Save Database As selected in the File Types area and Access Database selected in the Save Database As area, click the Save As button.
3. Enter a name and select a location for the new version.
4. Click the Save button.

Consider This

If you want to make a backup, could you just save the database with another name?

You could certainly do that. Using the backup procedure discussed earlier is useful because doing so automatically includes the current database name and the date in the name of the file it creates.

BTW
Access Help
At any time while using Access, you can find answers to questions and display information about various topics through Access Help. Used properly, this form of assistance can increase your productivity and reduce your frustration by minimizing the time you spend learning how to use Access.

To Delete a Table or Other Object in the Database

You would use the following steps to delete a database object.

1. Right-click the object in the Navigation Pane.
2. Click Delete on the shortcut menu.
3. Click the Yes button in the Microsoft Access dialog box.

To Rename an Object in the Database

You would use the following steps to rename a database object.

1. Right-click the object in the Navigation Pane.
2. Click Rename on the shortcut menu.
3. Type the new name and press ENTER.

To Exit Access

All the steps in this module are now complete.

1. If desired, sign out of your Microsoft account.
2. sam Exit Access.

Summary

In this module you have learned to create an Access database, create tables, add records to a database, import tables, create queries, create forms, create reports, and change database properties.

Consider This: Plan Ahead

What decisions will you need to make when creating your next database?

Use these guidelines as you complete the assignments in this module and create your own databases outside of this class.

1. Identify the information you want to record in the tables.
2. Determine the fields within those tables.
3. Determine the primary key for each table.
4. Determine the data types for the fields in the table.
5. Determine additional properties for fields.
   a. Determine if a caption is warranted.
   b. Determine if a description of the field is warranted.
   c. Determine field sizes.
   d. Determine formats.
6. Determine a storage location for the database.
7. Determine any simple queries, forms, or reports needed.

Student Assignments

Apply Your Knowledge

Reinforce the skills and apply the concepts you learned in this module.

Adding a Caption; Changing a Data Type; and Creating a Query, Form, and Report

Note: To complete this assignment, you will be required to use the Data Files. Please contact your instructor for information about accessing the Data Files.

Instructions: Start Access. Open the database, SC_AC_01-1.accdb, which is located in the Data Files folder. Enable the content. The database contains tables used to track students and counselors at City Tutoring Services. The company employs several trained and certified educational counselors to help their clients navigate their academic pursuits, from preschool through graduate school. City Tutoring has a database that keeps track of its counselors and its students. Each student is assigned to a single counselor; each counselor may be assigned many students. The database has two tables. The Students table contains data on the students who use City Tutoring. The Counselors table contains data on the educational counselors. You will add a caption; change a data type; and create a query, a form, and a report, as shown in Figure 1–57.

Perform the following tasks:

1. Save the database using the file name SC_AC_01_City-Tutoring. Enable the content.
2. Open the Counselors table in Datasheet view, and add CN # as the caption for the Counselor Number field.
3. Resize all columns to best fit the data. Save the changes to the layout of the table and close the table.
4. Open the Students table in Design view and change the data type for the Counselor Number field to Short Text. Change the field size for the field to 4 and add CN # as the caption for the Counselor Number field. Save the changes to the table and close the table.
5. Use the Simple Query Wizard to create a query for the Students table that contains the Student Number, Student Name, and Counselor Number. Use the name Students Query for the query and close the query.
6. Create a simple form for the Counselors table. Save the form and use the name Counselors for the form. Close the form.
7. Use the Report Wizard to create the report shown in Figure 1–57 for the Students table. After closing the Report Wizard, use Design View to move the report title's label box to the center of the Report Header section. Save the report as Student Counselor Report.
   If requested by your instructor, add your last name to the title of the report; that is, change the title to Student Counselor Report LastName where LastName is your actual last name. Recenter the title's label box as needed, and then re-save the report.
8. Close the report.
9. Compact and repair the database.
10. Submit the revised database (shown in Figure 1-57) in the format specified by your instructor and exit Access.
11. **Consider This:** How would you change the field name of the Street field in the Students table to Address?

Continued on next page

Student Counselor Report

Counselor Number	Student Name	Street	City
103			
	Kirk D'Elia	378 Stout Ave.	Carlton
	Heidi Croft	245 Beard St.	Kady
	Cindy Platt	178 Fletcher Rd.	Conradt
	Moss Mann	109 Fletcher Dr.	Carlton
	Carly Cohen	87 Fletcher Rd.	Conradt
120			
	Katy Cline	255 Main St.	Kady
	Irena Lam	876 Redfern Rd.	Kady
	Bob Schwartz	443 Cheddar St.	Kady

Figure 1–57

Extend Your Knowledge

Extend the skills you learned in this module and experiment with new skills. You may need to use Help to complete the assignment.

Using a Database Template to Create a Rental Properties Database

Instructions: Start Access. Access includes a variety of database templates. You can use a template to create a beginning database that can be modified to meet your specific needs. You will use a template to create a Rental Properties database. The database template includes sample tables, queries, forms, and reports. You will modify the database and create the Tenants Relationship Query shown in Figure 1–58.

Perform the following tasks:

1. Find and select the Real estate template in the template gallery.
2. Create a new database with the file name SC_AC_01_Rental-Properties.
3. Enable the content and close the Property List form.
4. If necessary, open the Navigation Pane and change the organization to Object Type.
5. Open the Tenant table in Datasheet view and delete the Attachments field in the table. The Attachments field has a paperclip as the column heading.
6. Add the field Tenant Status to the end of the table. Assign it the Short Text data type with a field size of 15.
7. Save the changes to the Tenant table and close the table.
8. Use the Simple Query Wizard to create the Tenant Status Query shown in Figure 1–58. Close the query.

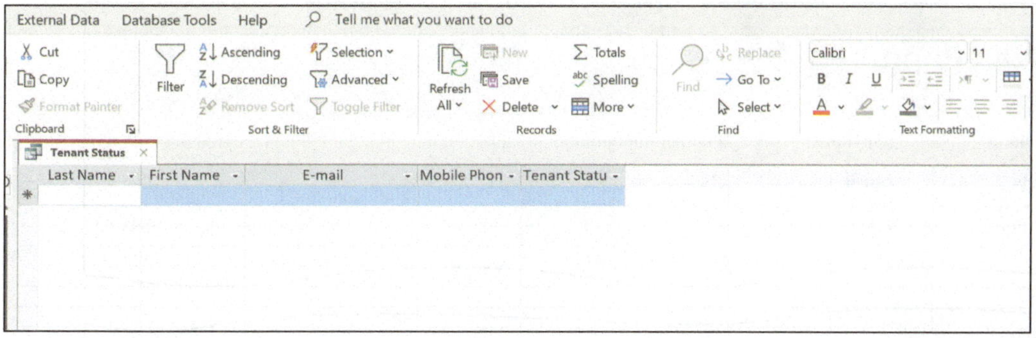

Figure 1–58

9. Open the Lease Application report in Layout view. Delete the controls containing the current date and current time in the upper-right corner of the report. Change the title of the report to Tenant Application List.
10. Save the changes to the report.
    If requested to do so by your instructor, add your first and last names to the end of the report title and save the changes to the report.
11. Submit the revised database in the format specified by your instructor.
12. a. **Consider This:** Why would you use a template instead of creating a database from scratch with just the fields you need?
    b. **Consider This:** The Attachment data type allows you to attach files to a database record. If you were using this database to keep track of tenants, what specific documents might you attach to a Tenant record?

Expand Your World

Create a solution that uses cloud or web technologies by learning and investigating on your own from general guidance.

Note: To complete this assignment, you will be required to use the Data Files. Please contact your instructor for information about accessing the Data Files.

Instructions: Start Access. Open the database called SC_AC_01-2.accdb, which is located in the Data Files folder, and enable the content. As a volunteer project, you and a few friends are creating a database for a local computer store that provides technical assistance to retirees in their homes. You want to be able to share query results and reports, so you have decided to store the items in the cloud. You are still learning Access, so you are going to create a sample query and the report shown in Figure 1–59, export the results, and save them to a cloud storage location, such as Microsoft OneDrive, Dropbox, or Google Drive.

Perform the following tasks:

1. Save the database using the filename, SC_AC_01_Solutions-IT-Support. Enable the content.
2. Use the Simple Query Wizard to create a query that includes the Client Number, First Name, Last Name, and Technician Number. Save the query as Client Query.
3. Export the Client Query as an XPS document to a cloud-based storage location of your choice. If the XPS document opens, review it and close it. You might need to activate the XPS Viewer feature in Windows to view the report. Do not save the export steps. Close the query.
4. Create the report shown in Figure 1–59. Save the report as Client Technician Report.

Continued on next page

Client Technician Report

Client Number	Last Name	First Name	Technician Number
AU10	Autley	Francis	203
BE16	Behrens	Alexa	205
DE35	Devi	Yaron	205
HE07	Heiston	Bill	203
KL12	Klingman	Cynthia	203
MA34	Marston	Libby	207
PR80	Priestly	Martin	205
SA23	Sanders	Marya	207

Figure 1–59

5. Export the Client Technician Report as a PDF document to a cloud-based storage location of your choice. You do not need to change any optimization or export settings. If the PDF opens, close it. Do not save the export steps.
   If requested to do so by your instructor, open the Technician table and change the last name and first name for Technician 203 to your last name and your first name.
6. Submit the database, query, and report files in the format specified by your instructor.
7. **Consider This:** Which cloud-based storage location did you use for this assignment and why?

In the Lab

Design and implement a solution using creative thinking and problem-solving skills.

Lab: Creating Objects for the Great Outdoors Camp Database

Note: To complete this assignment, you will be required to use the Data Files. Please contact your instructor for information about accessing the Data Files.

Problem: Great Outdoors Camp is a non-profit campground that runs several camp events each year for students ages 9 to 18. One of the administrative staff is familiar with Microsoft Access and created a database to help keep track of the various events, campers, and employees. This database tracks staff scheduling, camper enrollment, event dates, equipment storage, and cabin assignments. The database and tables have been created, but the Status field needs to be added to the Staff table. This field will identify "Seasonal" staff members, who are employed only during certain months while events are taking place. The records shown in Figure 1–60 must be added to the Staff table. Great Outdoors Camp would like to finish storing this data in a database and has asked you to help.

Perform the following tasks:

Part 1: Open the SC_AC_01-3.accdb database from the Data Files folder, and enable the content. Save the file with the name SC_AC_01_Great-Outdoors, and enable the content. Add a Status field to the Staff table. Assign an appropriate data type to hold a one-word identifier, and set the field size at 10.

Add the records shown in Figure 1–60.

Sf_ID	FullName	WorkTeam	Phone	Status
11	Otto Jensson	Instructor	7175555402	Seasonal
12	Ahmad Grady	Instructor	7175555432	Seasonal
13	Markku Twist	Instructor	7175558793	Seasonal
14	Vera Ognianov	Instructor	7175558798	Seasonal
15	Elli Rosario	Instructor	7175558789	Seasonal
16	Martyn Bell	Instructor	7175555368	Seasonal

Figure 1–60

Change the Cabins table's fields as necessary so that each is an appropriate data type and an appropriate length for the data contained in those fields. Note that you might receive a warning about validation rules; click Yes to continue. Add an appropriate caption to the CounselorName field. Save your changes.

Create a query that displays the CabinID, CounselorName, and CabinName data, and save the query using an appropriate name.

Create the report shown in Figure 1–61 for the ActivityZones table. When designing the report, remember that the caption name may differ from the field name. Save the report.

Activity Zone Assignments

Staff Name	AZ_Name	Type
Vera	Crafts	Indoor
Ahmad	Hiking	Woods
Lata	Horseback Riding	Barn
Markku	Kayaking	Lake
Maya	Survival Class	Indoor
Martyn	Swimming	Lake
Elli	Team Sports	Fields
Otto	Ziplining	Woods

Figure 1–61

If requested to do so by your instructor, change any data in the database to reflect your own personal information.

Submit the revised database in the format specified by your instructor.

Part 2: **Consider This:** The Waiver field in the Campers table is the Yes/No Data Type. Why is this appropriate?

Querying a Database

Objectives

After completing this module, you will be able to:

- Add a field to the design grid
- Use text and numeric data in criteria
- Use a wildcard in a query
- Hide a field used in a query
- Require a parameter for a query
- Use compound criteria in a query
- Sort data in query results
- Join tables in a query
- Create a report from a query
- Print a report or form
- Create a form from a query
- Export data from a query to another application
- Require a query to group or perform calculations on results
- Create crosstab queries
- Customize the Navigation Pane

Introduction

One of the primary benefits of using a database management system such as Access is having the ability to find answers to questions related to data stored in the database. When you pose a question to Access, or any other database management system, the question is called a query. A query is simply a question presented in a way that Access can process.

To find the answer to a question, you first create a corresponding query using the techniques illustrated in this module. After you have created the query, you instruct Access to run the query, that is, to perform the steps necessary to obtain the answer. Access then displays the results in Datasheet view.

In this module, you will work with a database created by a paralegal who works for the Partners Law Firm. The Partners Law Firm is owned by a group of real estate developers who also run a law firm on the side to support their main business. The paralegals are employed by the law firm, while most of the other employees work for the real estate development company. The paralegals support law firm activities, including occasional property purchases or sales, called closings, for residential and commercial properties. One of the paralegals created an Access database to help track the clients, properties, and other companies (such as mortgage companies, real estate agents, title companies, and other law firms) involved in these closings.

Project: Querying a Database

Examples of queries related to the data in the Partners database are shown in Figure 2–1. They answer questions such as which closings take place with a particular mortgage company or within a particular state. In addition to these questions, Partners paralegals also need to find information such as closing date or title company as they work, without creating a new query every time. The paralegals can use a parameter query to accomplish this task. A **parameter query** prompts you to enter a search term and then displays the results based on the search term you entered. Partners paralegals also want to summarize data in a specific way, such as by mortgage company or payoff amount, which might involve performing calculations, and they can use a crosstab query to present the data in the desired form.

In this module, you will learn how to create and use queries, including those shown in Figure 2–1.

m02q01

C_ID	Closing Date	Payoff	Payoff_MID	Loan	Purchase_MID	B_ID
C-001	4/28/2027	$246,152.28	M-001	$492,000.00	M-002	B-001
C-003	4/30/2027	$142,983.79	M-003	$325,000.00	M-002	B-003
*		$0.00		$0.00		

Figure 2–1a Closings with a Specific Mortgage Company

m02q03

Seller Name	Email	S_Agent
Riya Sumner	riyas@example.com	Laura Rosario
Alyssa Schubert	alyssa@example.com	Margary Kools
*		

Figure 2–1b Sellers Located in a Specific Area Code

m02q05

C_ID	Closing Date	B_ID
C-002	4/29/2027	B-002
C-003	4/30/2027	B-003
*		

Figure 2–1c Closings After a Specific Date

Property - State Query

P_ID	Street	City	State	Seller ID
P-001	219 Phillips St	Donahue	PA	S-001
P-002	852 Scranton Dr	Jonestown	PA	S-002
P-004	186 Alabama Hwy	Hartford	PA	S-004
P-006	87 Georgetown Rd, #2	East Barnard	PA	S-006
*				

Figure 2–1d Properties Located in a Specific State

Closings and Properties

C_ID	Closing Date	P_ID	Street	Seller ID
		P-006	87 Georgetown Rd, #2	S-006
		P-005	Route 15, Box 281	S-005
C-004	4/28/2027	P-004	186 Alabama Hwy	S-004
C-001	4/28/2027	P-001	219 Phillips St	S-001
C-002	4/29/2027	P-002	852 Scranton Dr	S-002
C-003	4/30/2027	P-003	46 Hwy 82 S	S-003
*				

Figure 2–1e Property Street Address for Each Closing Date

Creating Queries

As you learned previously, you can use queries in Access to find answers to questions about the data contained in the database. **Note:** In this module, you will save each query example. When you use a query for another task, such as to create a form or report, you will assign a specific name to a query, for example, Properties – Closings Query. In situations in which you will not use the query again, you will assign a name using a convention that includes the module number and a query number, for example, m02q01. These queries are numbered consecutively.

BTW
Select Queries
The queries you create in this module are select queries. In a select query, you retrieve data from one or more tables using criteria that you specify and display the data in a datasheet.

To Save the Partners Database with a New File Name and Add Records to the Database

With three new closings scheduled for the end of this month, the paralegals need to add records to the database prior to making queries, to ensure the queries return complete and accurate information for the month. **Why?** Databases often change over time as users add new information and adjust the structure and objects included in the database. The following steps open the Buyers, Sellers, and Properties tables and add data. Please see your instructor for information about accessing the Data Files.

1

- sam Start Access. Open the database, SC_AC_02-1.accdb, which is located in the Data Files folder. Save the file on your hard drive, OneDrive, or other storage location using the file name, **SC_AC_02_Partners**. Enable the content.
- Open the Sellers table in Datasheet view, and then click the 'Shutter Bar Open/Close Button' to close the Navigation Pane.

Q&A Is it necessary to close the Navigation Pane?
No. Closing the pane gives you more room for entering data in the table, however, so it is usually a good practice.

2

- Click the empty cell below S-003 to enter a new seller ID.
- Enter the data for seller S-004, Nadia Sutherland, as shown in Figure 2–2a.

Sellers

S_ID	Seller Name	Phone	Email	Address	S_Agent	S_Attorney	S_Payment
S-001	Riya Sumner	267-555-8368	riyas@example.com	1701 McCormick Place, Jonestown, PA 15068	Laura Rosario	Partners	Pay by check to seller
S-002	Orlando O'Keefe	215-555-1610	ookeefe@example.com	568 N Bypass, Asheville, PA 15002	Dmitri Alexander	Partners	Pay by check to seller
S-003	Alyssa Schubert	267-555-8800	alyssa@example.com	127 Main St, New Beach, NY 10046	Margary Kools	Greer & Greer	Direct deposit to NorthEast Bank
S-004	Nadia Sutherland	717-555-7028	nadias94@example.com	18603 Myrtle Ave, Corinth, PA 15025	Kelley Micheline	Partners	Pay by check to seller
S-005	Elliot Bristol	814-555-2587	eb2004@example.com	249 Scranton Dr, Jonestown, PA 15068	Jasmin Bergmann	MidTown Attorneys	Direct deposit to Main Street Bank
S-006	Robert Leonardi	814-555-8798	robleo@example.com	Route 6, Box 2780, New Beach, NY 10046	Karl Kaczka	Partners	Direct deposit to City Bank

Figure 2–2a

3

- Enter the data for the additional sellers shown in the figure.
- Resize the table columns as needed for best fit.
- Save and close the Sellers table.

4

- Click the Navigation Pane bar to open the Navigation Pane, open the Properties table in Datasheet view, and then close the Navigation Pane.
- The existing Property ID numbers do not conform with the company's naming convention. As you work with a database, you might find inconsistencies such as this one. It's a good habit to watch for these problems and fix them as you go. Change the Property ID numbers for the existing properties so they are consistent with Figure 2–2b.

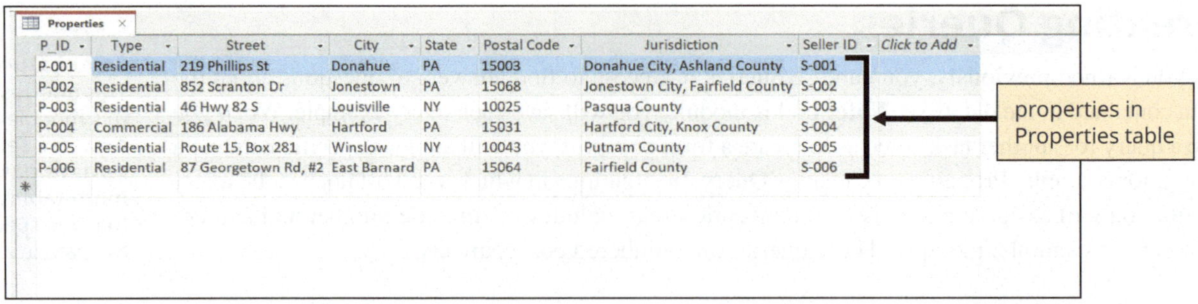

Properties

P_ID	Type	Street	City	State	Postal Code	Jurisdiction	Seller ID	Click to Add
P-001	Residential	219 Phillips St	Donahue	PA	15003	Donahue City, Ashland County	S-001	
P-002	Residential	852 Scranton Dr	Jonestown	PA	15068	Jonestown City, Fairfield County	S-002	
P-003	Residential	46 Hwy 82 S	Louisville	NY	10025	Pasqua County	S-003	
P-004	Commercial	186 Alabama Hwy	Hartford	PA	15031	Hartford City, Knox County	S-004	
P-005	Residential	Route 15, Box 281	Winslow	NY	10043	Putnam County	S-005	
P-006	Residential	87 Georgetown Rd, #2	East Barnard	PA	15064	Fairfield County	S-006	

Figure 2–2b

- Click the empty cell below P-003 to enter an ID for Property P-004 on Alabama Hwy. Enter the property's information as shown in Figure 2–2b.

5

- Enter the data for the remaining properties as shown in the figure.
- Resize the table columns as needed for best fit.
- Save and close the Properties table.

6

- Click the Navigation Pane bar to open the Navigation Pane, open the Buyers table in Datasheet view, and then close the Navigation Pane.
- Click the empty cell below B-004 to enter a new buyer's ID.
- Enter the data for Riya Sumner as shown in Figure 2–2c.

Buyers

B_ID	Buyer Name	Phone	Email	B_Agent	B_Attorney	Click to Add
B-001	Karla Breeden	878-555-4537	karlanpaul@example.com	Jasmin Bergmann	MidTown Attorneys	
B-002	Everett Moller	717-555-8047	emoller@example.com	Laura Rosario	Greer & Greer	
B-003	Celeste Alberghini	570-555-8601	celeste@example.com	Jeong-Ho Azzara	Partners	
B-004	Violet Pratt	717-555-1726	vpratt@example.com	Karl Kaczka	Greer & Greer	
B-005	Riya Sumner	267-555-8368	riyas@example.com	Laura Rosario	Partners	

Figure 2–2c

- Resize the table columns as needed for best fit.
- Save and close the Buyers table.

To Create a Query in Design View

You have already used the Simple Query Wizard to create a query. Most of the time, however, you will use Design view, which is the primary option for creating queries. **Why?** Once you have created a new query in Design view, you have more options than with the wizard and can specify fields, criteria, sorting, calculations, and so on. The following steps create a new query in Design view.

1

- Click Create on the ribbon to display the Create tab (Figure 2–3).

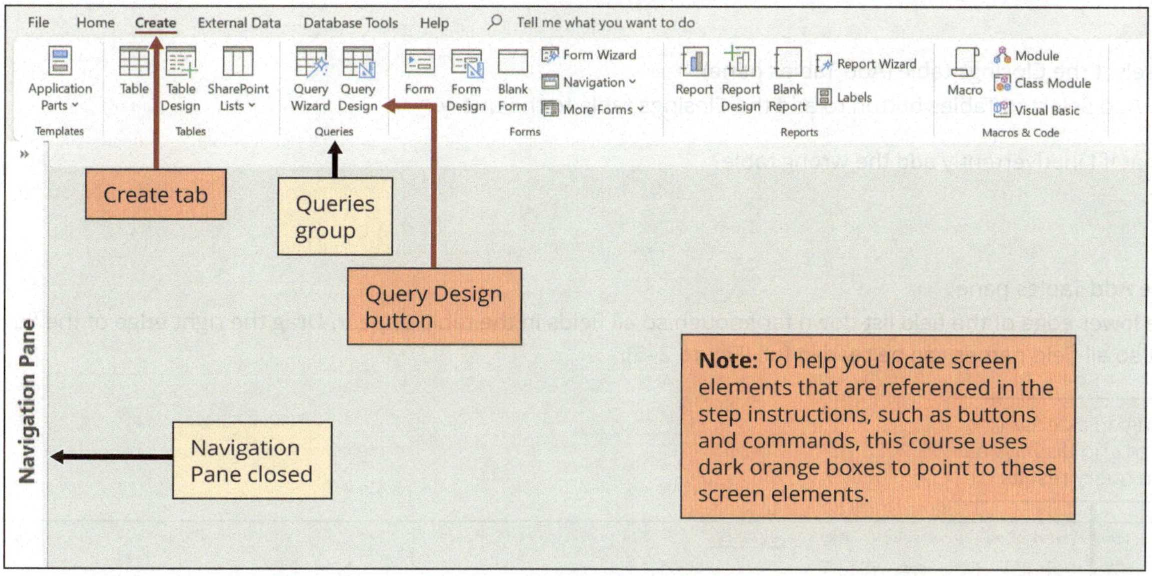

Figure 2–3

2

- Click the Query Design button (Create tab | Queries group) to create a new query (Figure 2–4).

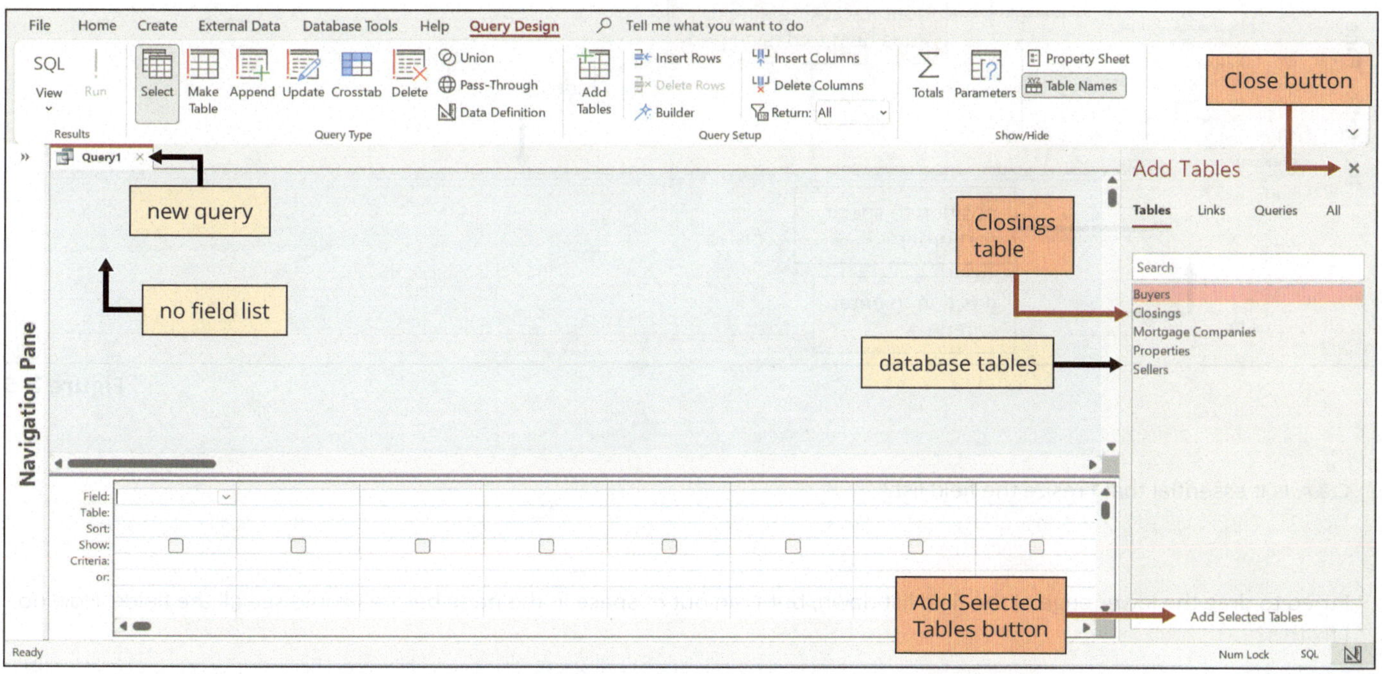

Figure 2–4

3

- Click to select the Closings table (Add Tables pane).
- Click the Add Selected Tables button to add the Closings table to the query.

Q&A What if I inadvertently add the wrong table?

Right-click the table that you added in error, and click Remove Table on the shortcut menu. You also can just close the query, indicate that you do not want to save it, and then start over.

- Close the Add Tables pane.
- Drag the lower edge of the field list down far enough so all fields in the table appear. Drag the right edge of the field list to the right so all field names can be read in full (Figure 2–5).

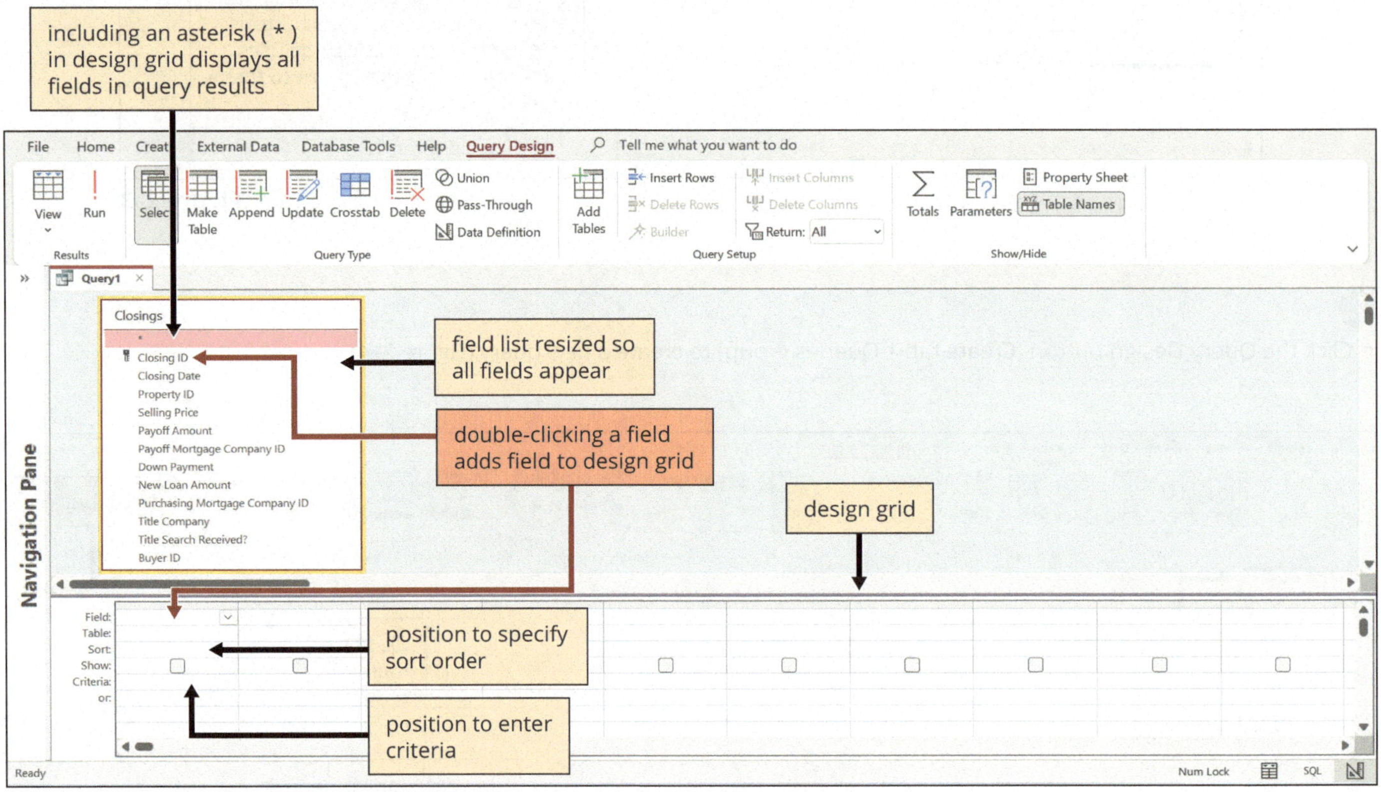

Figure 2–5

Q&A Is it essential that I resize the field list?

No. You can instead scroll through the list of fields using the scroll bar. Resizing the field list so that all fields appear is usually more convenient.

I tried to drag the lower edge of the field list down, but I ran out of space in the pane before I could see all the fields. How do I fix this?

You can resize the panes so more space is given to the field list area. Point to the thick, gray bar between the upper pane and the lower pane until you see a two-pointed arrow. Click and drag that arrow up or down to resize the panes.

Other Ways

1. Double-click table name in Add Tables pane to add it to query

To Add Fields to the Design Grid

Once you have a new query displayed in Design view, you are ready to make entries in the **design grid**, the portion of the window where you specify fields and criteria for the query. The design grid is located in the lower pane of the window. You add the fields you want included in the query to the Field row in the grid. **Why add fields to the grid?** Only the fields that appear in the design grid are included in the query results. The following steps begin creating a query that Partners Law Firm can use to obtain the closing dates, payoff information, new loan information, and information for buyers.

1

- Double-click the Closing ID field in the field list to add the field to the query's design grid.

Q&A What if I add the wrong field?
Click just above the field name in the design grid to select the column, and then press DEL to remove the field. Alternatively, you can click the arrow next to the field name and select the correct field.

2

- Double-click the Closing Date field in the field list to add the field to the query's design grid.
- Add the Payoff Amount, Payoff Mortgage Company ID, New Loan Amount, Purchasing Mortgage Company ID, and Buyer ID fields to the query's design grid (Figure 2–6).

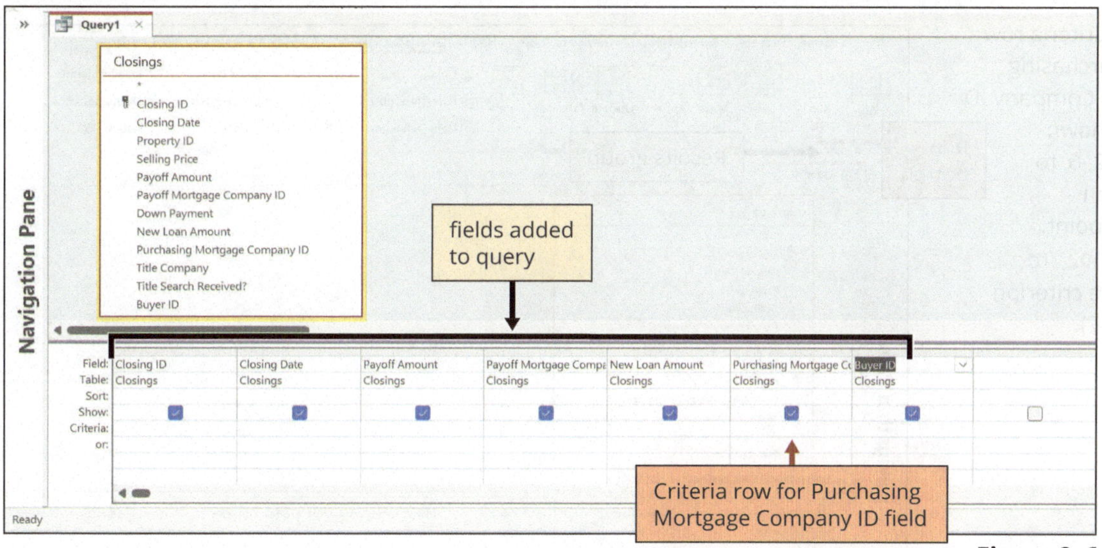

Figure 2–6

Q&A What if I want to include all fields? Do I have to add each field individually?
No. Instead of adding individual fields, you can double-click the asterisk (*) to add the asterisk to the design grid. The asterisk is a shortcut indicating all fields are to be included.

Determining Criteria

When you use queries, usually you are looking for those records that satisfy some criterion. For example, you might want to see closing dates and financial information for one of the mortgage companies. You enter criteria in the Criteria row in the design grid below the field name to which the criterion applies. For example, to find purchase closings with Cheshire Mortgage, you first must add the Purchasing Mortgage Company ID field to the design grid. For ease of typing, the mortgage companies were given ID numbers, for example, Cheshire Mortgage's ID is M-002, and Atlas Mortgage's ID is M-001. Therefore, when you enter the Mortgage ID, you will only need to type M-001 or M-002 in the Criteria row. For example, you will only need to type M-002 for Cheshire Mortgage in the Criteria row below the Purchasing Mortgage Company ID field.

BTW
Touch Screen Differences
The Office and Windows interfaces may vary if you are using a touch screen. For this reason, you might notice the function or appearance of your touch screen differs slightly from this module's presentation.

BTW
Access Screen Resolution
If you are using a computer or mobile device to step through the project in this module and you want your screens to match the figures in this course, you should change your screen's resolution to 1920 × 1080.

Running the Query

After adding the appropriate fields and defining the query's criteria, you must run the query to get the results. To view the results of the query from Design view, click the Run button to instruct Access to run the query, that is, to perform the necessary actions to produce and display the results in Datasheet view.

To Use Text Data in a Criterion

To use **text data** (data in a field whose data type is Short Text) in criteria, simply type the text in the Criteria row below the corresponding field name, just as you did previously. In Access, you typically do not need to enclose text data in quotation marks as you do in many other database management systems. **Why?** Access will enter the quotation marks automatically, so you can simply type the desired text. The following steps finish creating a query that Partners paralegals might use to obtain closing dates and financial information for closings where Cheshire Mortgage will be the buyer's new mortgage company. These steps also save the query.

1

- Click the Criteria row for the Purchasing Mortgage Company ID field, as shown in Figure 2–6, to produce an insertion point.
- Type **M-002** to specify the criterion (Figure 2–7).

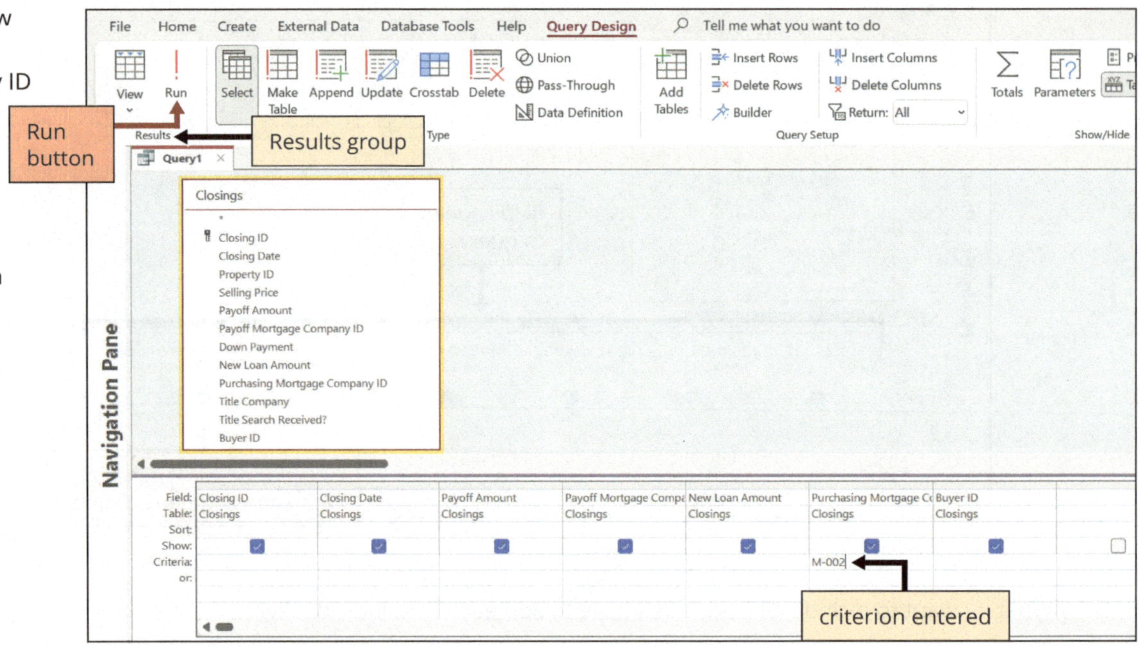

Figure 2–7

2

- Click the Run button (Query Design tab | Results group) to run the query (Figure 2–8) and display closings with new mortgages at Cheshire Mortgage.

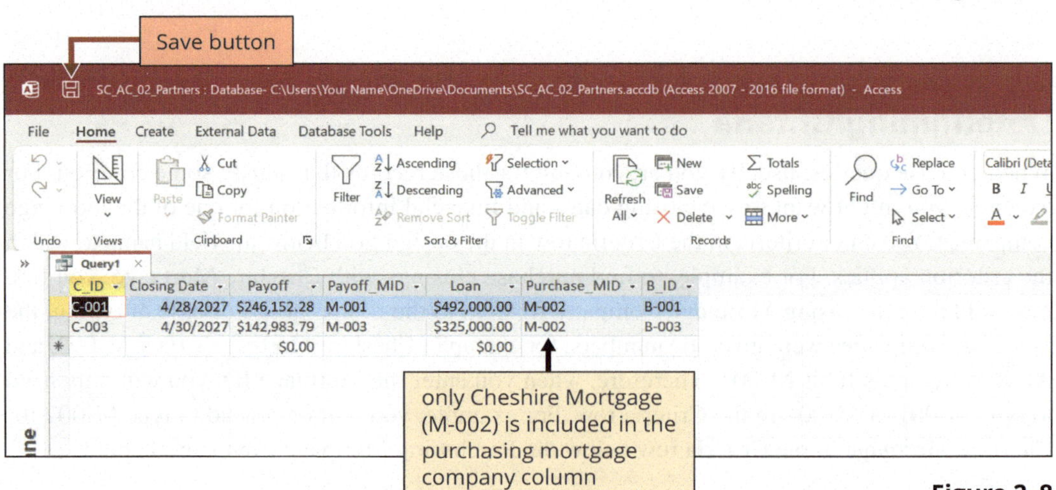

Figure 2–8

Q&A Can I also use the View button in the Results group to run the query?

Yes. You can click the View button to view the query results in Datasheet view.

My records are in a different order. Is this a problem?

No. The important thing is which records are included in the results. You will see later in this module how you can specify the order you want for situations when the order is important.

3

- Click the Save button on the Quick Access Toolbar, as shown in Figure 2–8, to display the Save As dialog box.
- Type **m02q01** as the name of the query (Figure 2–9).

Q&A Can I also save from Design view?

Yes. You can save the query when you view it in Design view just as you can save it when you view query results in Datasheet view.

I don't see the Save button on the Quick Access Toolbar. How can I save my query?

You can either click File to enter Backstage view and click Save, or you can press CTRL+S.

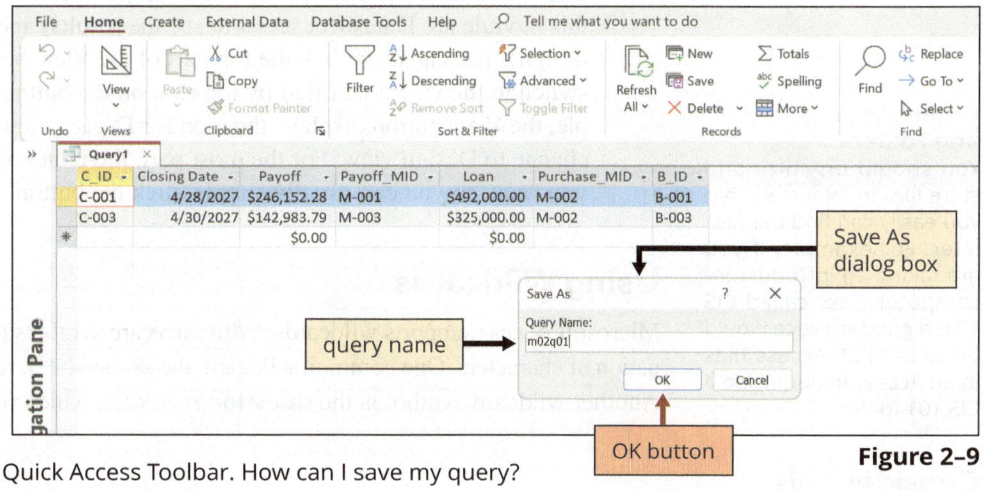

Figure 2–9

4

- Click OK (Save As dialog box) to save the query (Figure 2–10), and then close the m02q01 query.

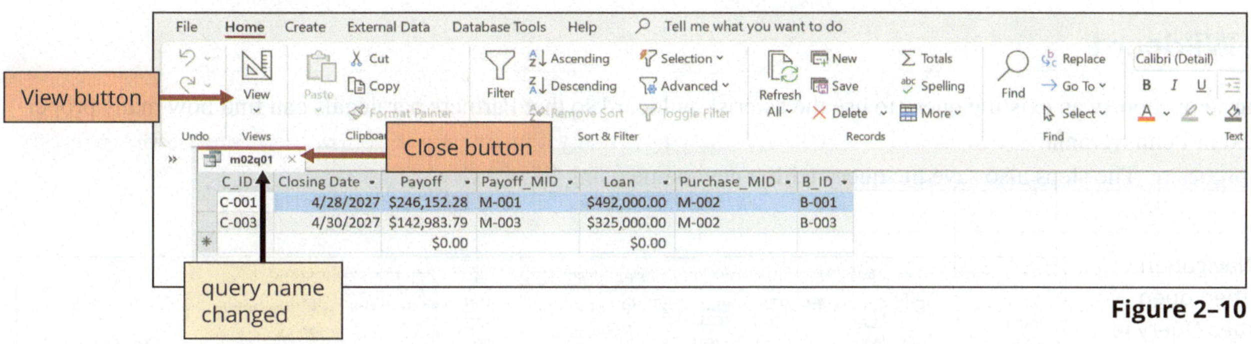

Figure 2–10

Other Ways

1. Right-click query tab, click Save on shortcut menu to save query

Using Saved Queries

After you have created and saved a query, you can use it in a variety of ways:

- To view the results of a query that is not currently open, open it by double-clicking the query in the Navigation Pane. Alternatively, you can right-click the query in the Navigation Pane and click Open on the shortcut menu.
- If you want to change the design of a query that is already open, return to Design view and make the changes.
- If you want to change the design of a query that is not currently open, right-click the query in the Navigation Pane and then click Design View on the shortcut menu to open the query in Design view.

BTW

The Ribbon and Screen Resolution

Access may change how the groups and buttons within the groups appear on the ribbon, depending on the computer or mobile device's screen resolution. Thus, your ribbon may look different from the ones in this course if you are using a screen resolution other than 1920 × 1080.

- To print the results of an open query, click File on the ribbon, click the Print tab in Backstage view, and then click Quick Print.
- To print a query without first opening it, be sure the query is selected in the Navigation Pane and click File on the ribbon, click the Print tab in Backstage view, and then click Quick Print.
- You can switch between views of a query using the View button (Home tab | Views group). Clicking the arrow at the bottom of the button produces the View button menu. You then click the desired view in the menu. The two query views you use in this module are Datasheet view (to see the results) and Design view (to change the design). You can also click the top part of the View button, in which case you will switch to the view identified by the icon on the button. In Figure 2–10, for example, the View button displays the icon for Design view, so clicking the button would change to Design view. For the most part, the icon on the button represents the view you want, so you can usually simply click the button.

BTW

Organizing Files and Folders

You should organize and store files in folders so that you easily can find the files later. For example, if you are taking an introductory computer class called CIS 101, a good practice would be to save all Access files in an Access folder inside a CIS 101 folder.

Using Wildcards

Microsoft Access supports wildcards. **Wildcards** are symbols that represent any character or combination of characters. One common wildcard, the **asterisk (*)**, represents any collection of characters. Another wildcard symbol is the **question mark (?)**, which represents any individual character.

Consider This

What does S* represent? What does T?m represent?

S* represents the letter, S, followed by any collection of characters. A search for S* might return System, So, or Superlative. T?m represents the letter, T, followed by any single character, followed by the letter, m. A search for T?m might return the names Tim or Tom.

To Use a Wildcard

The following steps modify an existing query to use the asterisk wildcard so that Partners paralegals can find how many properties are located in Pennsylvania. Why? Because you do not know how many characters will follow the P, the asterisk wildcard symbol is appropriate. The steps also save the query with a new name using Save As.

1

- Open the Navigation Pane, and then open the Properties Query in Design View.
- Click the Criteria row below the Property State field to produce an insertion point.
- If there were any existing data in the Criteria row, you would use DEL or BACKSPACE. Because there is no existing criteria, you can simply type the criteria.
- Type **P*** as the criterion (Figure 2–11).

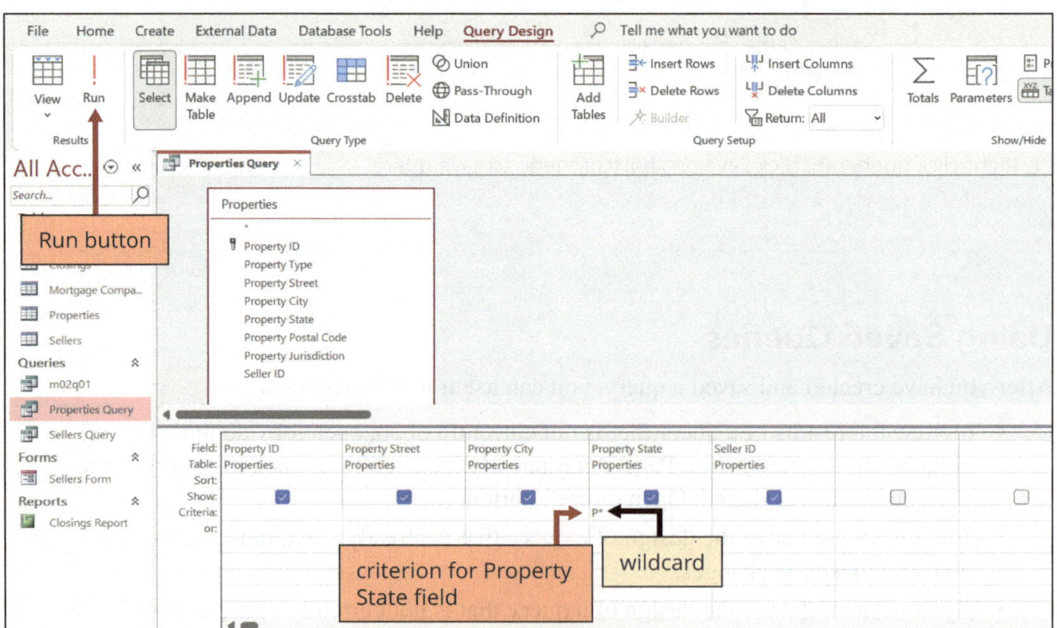

Figure 2–11

2

- Run the query by clicking the Run button (Query Design tab | Results group) (Figure 2–12).

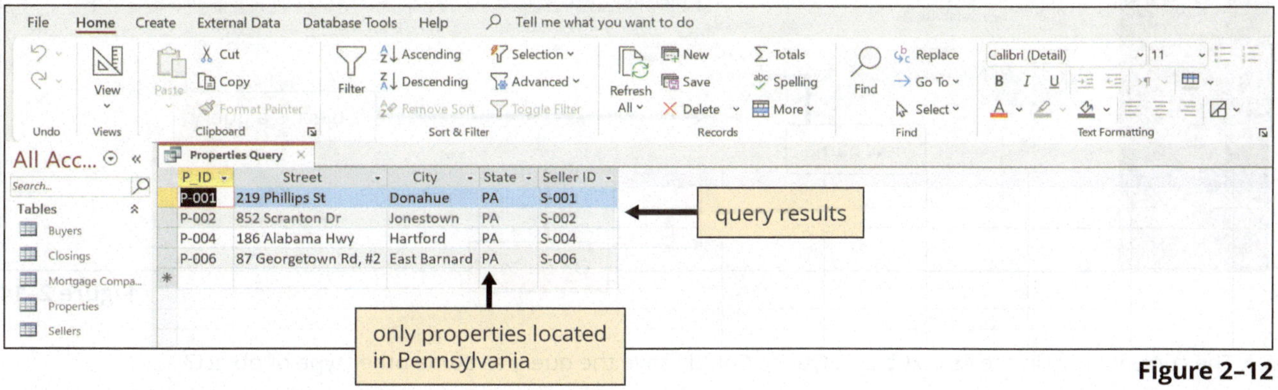

Figure 2–12

- **Experiment:** Change the letter P to lowercase in the criterion and run the query to determine whether case makes a difference when entering a wildcard.

Q&A The text I entered is now preceded by the word, Like. What happened?
Criteria that include wildcards need to be preceded by the word, Like. However, you do not have to type it; Access adds the word automatically to any criterion involving a wildcard.

3

- Click File on the ribbon to open Backstage view.
- Click the Save As tab in Backstage view to display the Save As gallery.
- Click 'Save Object As' in the File Types area (Figure 2–13).

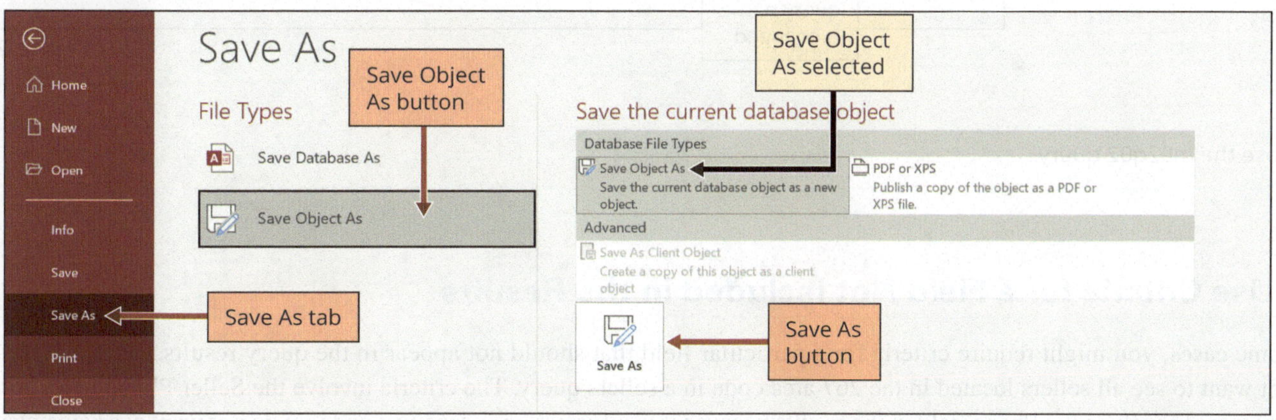

Figure 2–13

Q&A Can I just click the Save button on the Quick Access Toolbar as I did when saving the previous query?
If you clicked the Save button, you would replace the previous query with the version you just created. Because you want to save both the previous query and the new one, you need to save the new version with a different name. To do so, you must use Save Object As, which is available through Backstage view.

4

- With Save Object As selected in the File Types gallery, click the Save As button to display the Save As dialog box.
- Erase the name of the current query and type **m02q02** as the name for the saved query (Figure 2–14).

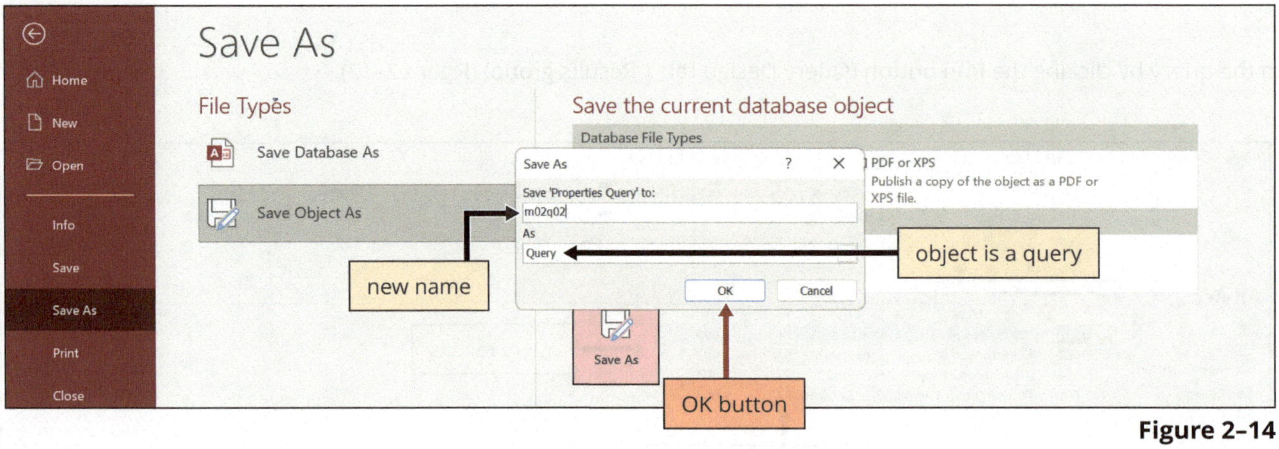

Figure 2–14

Q&A The current entry in the As text box is Query. Could I save the query as some other type of object?
Although you usually would want to save the query as another query, you can also save it as a form or report by changing the entry in the As text box. If you do, Access would create either a simple form or a simple report for the query.

5

- Click OK (Save As dialog box) to save the query with the new name and close Backstage view (Figure 2–15).

Q&A How can I tell that the query was saved with the new name?
The new name will appear on the tab.

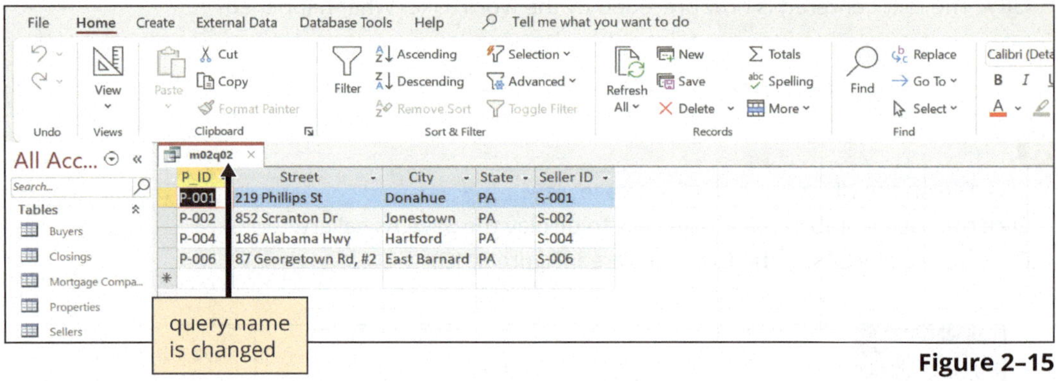

Figure 2–15

6

- Close the m02q02 query.

To Use Criteria for a Field Not Included in the Results

In some cases, you might require criteria for a particular field that should not appear in the query results. For example, you might want to see all sellers located in the 267 area code in a sellers query. The criteria involve the Seller Phone field, but you do not want to include the Phone field in the results because this information is sensitive and you do not want everyone viewing the query to see this information.

To enter a criterion for the Seller Phone field, it must be included in the design grid. Normally, it would then appear in the results. To prevent it from appearing, remove the check mark from its check box in the Show row of the grid. **Why?** A check mark in the Show check box instructs Access to show the field in the results. If you remove the check mark, you can use the field in the query without displaying it in the query results.

The following steps modify a previous query so that Partners paralegals can select only those sellers located in the 267 area code. Partners paralegals do not want the Seller Phone field to appear in the results, however. The steps also save the query with a new name.

1

- Open the Sellers Query in Design view.
- Type **267*** as the criterion for the Seller Phone field (Figure 2–16).

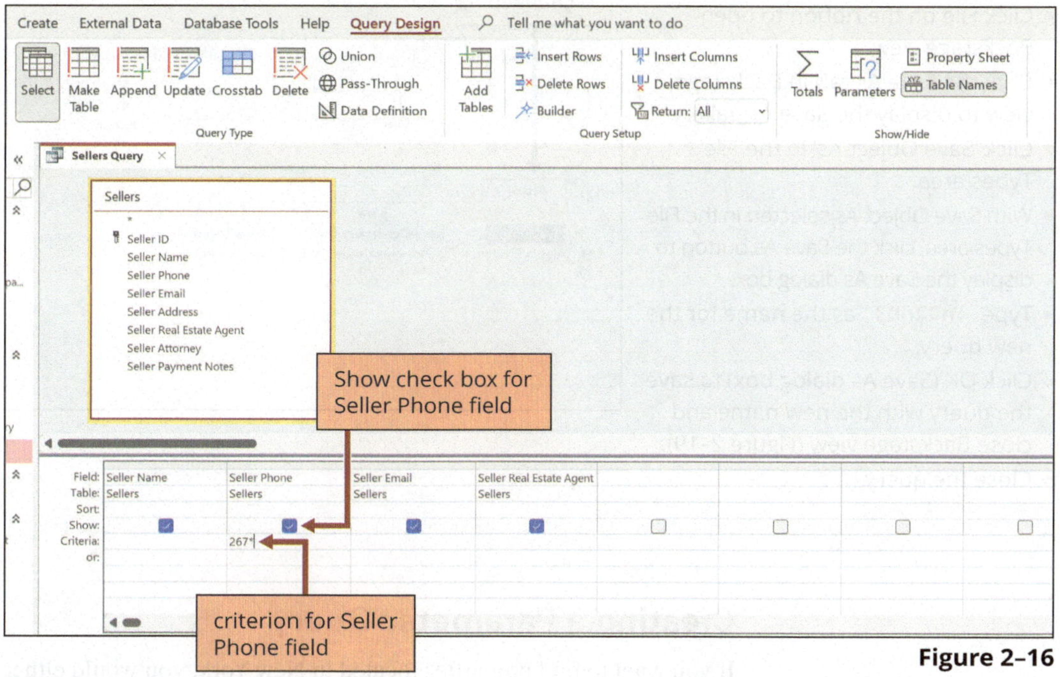

Figure 2–16

2

- Click the Show check box for the Seller Phone field to remove the check mark (Figure 2–17).

Q&A Could I have removed the check mark before entering the criterion?
Yes. The order in which you perform the two operations does not matter.

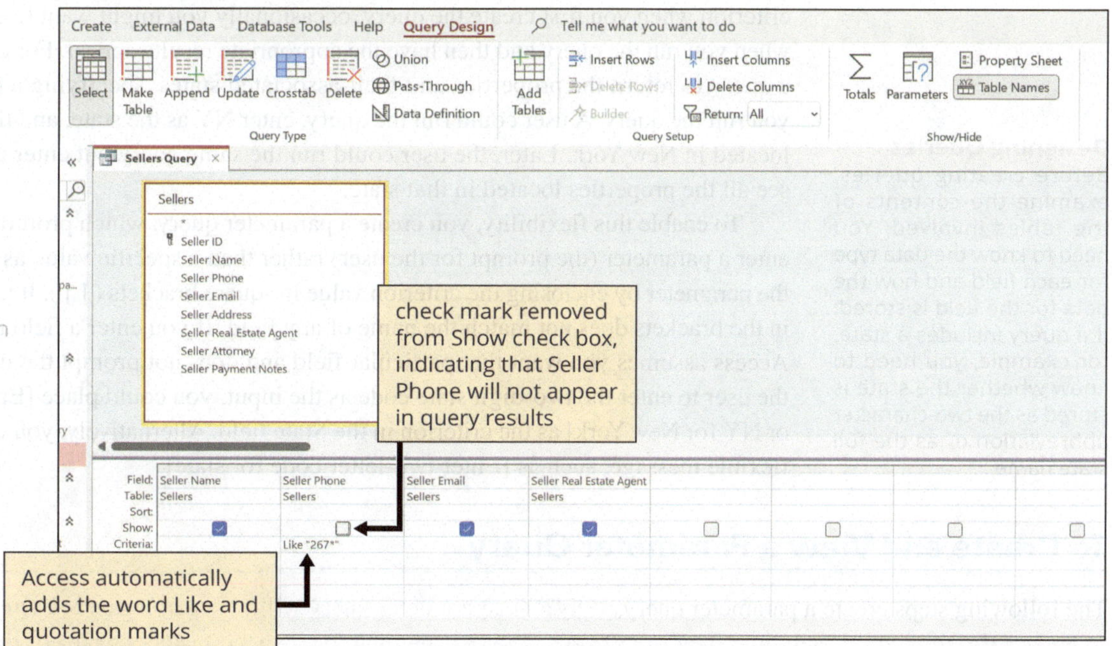

Figure 2–17

- Run the query (Figure 2–18).
- **Experiment:** Click the View button to return to Design view, enter a different area code, such as 814*, as the criterion, and run the query. Repeat this process with additional area codes, including at least one area code that is not in the database. When finished, retype the Seller Phone criteria as 267*.

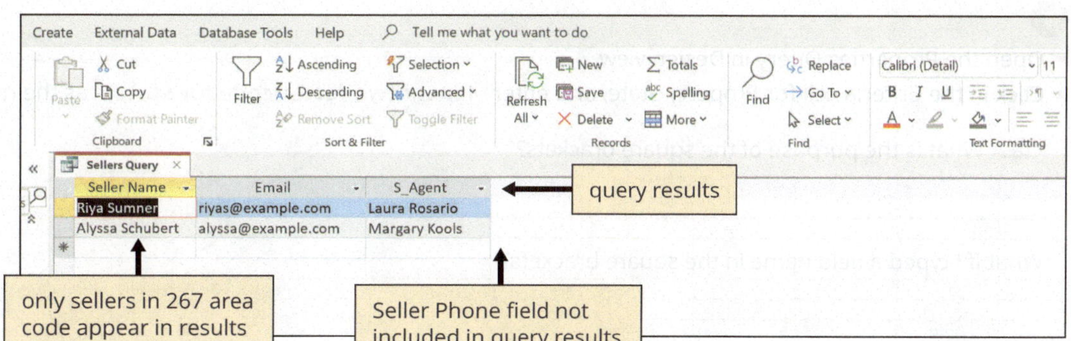

Figure 2–18

3

- Click File on the ribbon to open Backstage view.
- Click the Save As tab in Backstage view to display the Save As gallery.
- Click 'Save Object As' in the File Types area.
- With Save Object As selected in the File Types area, click the Save As button to display the Save As dialog box.
- Type **m02q03** as the name for the new query.
- Click OK (Save As dialog box) to save the query with the new name and close Backstage view (Figure 2–19).
- Close the query.

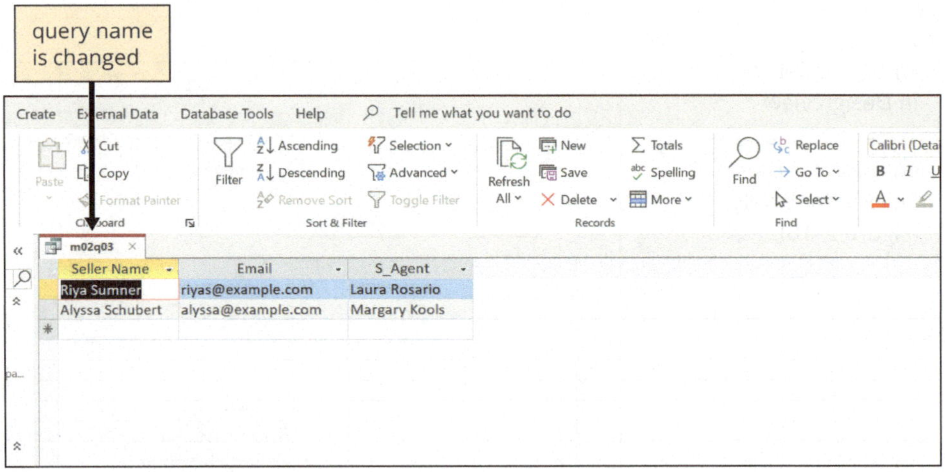

Figure 2–19

Creating a Parameter Query

If you want to find properties located in New York, you would either have to create a new query or modify the existing query by replacing P* with N* as the criterion. Rather than giving a specific criterion when you first create the query, occasionally you might want to enter part of the criterion when you run the query and then have the appropriate results appear. For example, you might want a query to return the properties and their associated states, specifying a different state each time you run the query. A user could run the query, enter NY as the state, and then see all the properties located in New York. Later, the user could run the same query but enter a different state and then see all the properties located in that state.

To enable this flexibility, you create a parameter query, which prompts the user for input. You enter a parameter (the prompt for the user) rather than a specific value as the criterion. You create the parameter by enclosing the criterion value in square brackets ([ ]). It is important that the value in the brackets does not match the name of any field. If you enter a field name in square brackets, Access assumes you want that particular field and does not prompt the user for input. To prompt the user to enter the two-digit state code as the input, you could place [Enter PA for Pennsylvania or NY for New York] as the criterion in the State field. Alternatively, you could use a shorter, more flexible message, such as [Enter two-letter code for state].

BTW
Designing Queries
Before creating queries, examine the contents of the tables involved. You need to know the data type for each field and how the data for the field is stored. If a query includes a state, for example, you need to know whether the state is stored as the two-character abbreviation or as the full state name.

To Create and View a Parameter Query

The following steps create a parameter query. **Why?** The parameter query will give paralegals at Partners Law Firm the ability to enter a different state each time they run the query rather than having a specific state as part of the criterion in the query. The steps also save the query with a new name.

1

- Open the Properties Query in Design view.
- Click in the Criteria cell for Property State, and enter **[Enter two-letter code for state]** as the new criterion (Figure 2–20).

Q&A What is the purpose of the square brackets?

The square brackets indicate that the text entered is not text that the value in the column must match. Without the brackets, Access would search for records in which the State field contains the value *Enter two-letter code for state.*

What if I typed a field name in the square brackets?

Access would simply use the value in that field. To create a parameter query, you must not use a field name in the square brackets.

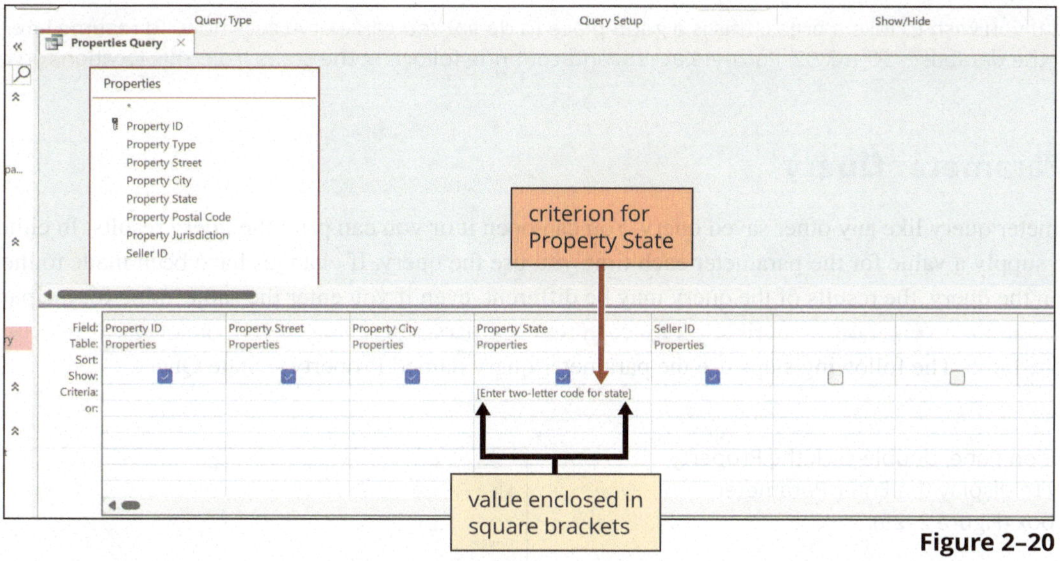

Figure 2–20

2

- Click the Run button (Query Design tab | Results group) to display the Enter Parameter Value dialog box (Figure 2–21).

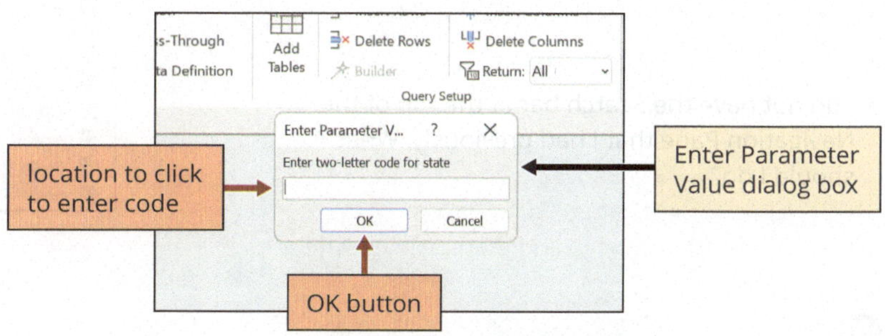

Figure 2–21

3

- Type **NY** as the parameter value in the Enter Parameter Value text box, and then click OK (Enter Parameter Value dialog box) to close the dialog box and view the query (Figure 2–22).
- **Experiment:** Try using other characters between the square brackets. In each case, run the query. When finished, change the text between the square brackets back to Enter two-letter code for state.

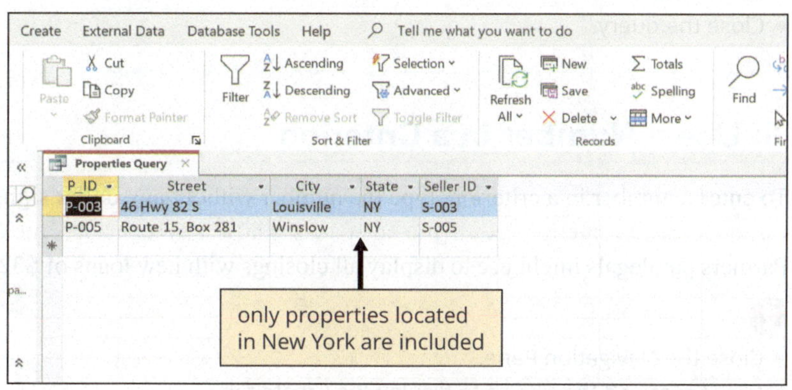

Figure 2–22

4

- Click File on the ribbon to open Backstage view.
- Click the Save As tab in Backstage view to display the Save As gallery.
- Click 'Save Object As' in the File Types area.
- With Save Object As selected in the File Types area, click the Save As button to display the Save As dialog box.
- Type **Property - State Query** as the name for the saved query.
- Click OK (Save As dialog box) to save the query with the new name.

5

- Close the Property – State Query.

Break Point: If you wish to take a break, this is a good place to do so. You can exit Access now. To resume later, start Access, open the database, SC_AC_02_Partners.accdb, and continue following the steps from this location forward.

To Use a Parameter Query

You use a parameter query like any other saved query. You can open it or you can print the query results. In either case, Access prompts you to supply a value for the parameter each time you use the query. If changes have been made to the data since the last time you ran the query, the results of the query may be different, even if you enter the same value for the parameter. **Why?** In addition to the ability to enter different field values each time the parameter query is run, the query always uses the data that is currently in the table. The following steps use the parameter query named Property – State Query.

1

- In the Navigation Pane, double-click the Property – State Query to display the Enter Parameter Value dialog box (Figure 2–23).

Q&A The title bar for my Navigation Pane contains Tables and Related Views rather than All Access Objects as it did previously. What should I do?
Click the Navigation Pane arrow, and then click 'Object Type'.

I do not have the Search bar at the top of the Navigation Pane that I had previously. What should I do?
Right-click the Navigation Pane title bar arrow to display a shortcut menu, and then click Search Bar.

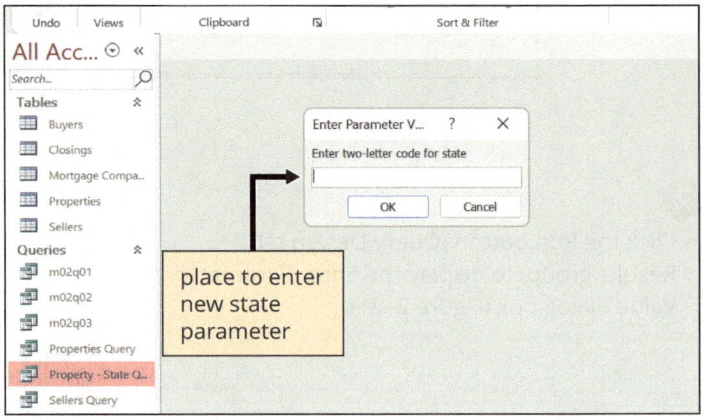

Figure 2–23

2

- Type **PA** in the Enter two-letter code for state text box, and then click OK (Enter Parameter Value dialog box) to display the results.
- Close the query.

To Use a Number in a Criterion

To enter a number in a criterion, type the number without any dollar signs or commas. **Why?** If you enter a dollar sign, Access assumes you are entering text. If you enter a comma, Access considers the criterion invalid. The following steps create a query that Partners paralegals might use to display all closings with new loans of $325,000. The steps also save the query with a new name.

1

- Close the Navigation Pane.
- Click Create on the ribbon to display the Create tab.
- Click the Query Design button (Create tab | Queries group) to create a new query.
- If necessary, click the Tables tab (Add Tables pane), and click the Closings table (Add Tables pane) to select the table.
- Click the Add Selected Tables button to add the selected table to the query.
- Close the Add Tables pane.
- Resize the field list so all fields in the list are displayed.
- In the following order, include the Closing ID, Closing Date, Purchasing Mortgage Company ID, and New Loan Amount fields in the query.

Q&A I entered the fields into the query in the wrong order. How do I fix this?
The fields will be listed in the query in the order you insert them. If you inserted fields in the wrong order, you can delete one or more fields and reinsert them in the correct order or you can move one or more fields. To move a field in the design grid, click the column selector for the field to select the field and drag it to the appropriate location.

- Type **325000** as the criterion for the New Loan Amount field (Figure 2–24).

Q&A Do I need to enter a dollar sign, comma, or decimal point?

No. Access will interpret 325000 as $325,000.00 because the data type for the New Loan Amount field is currency.

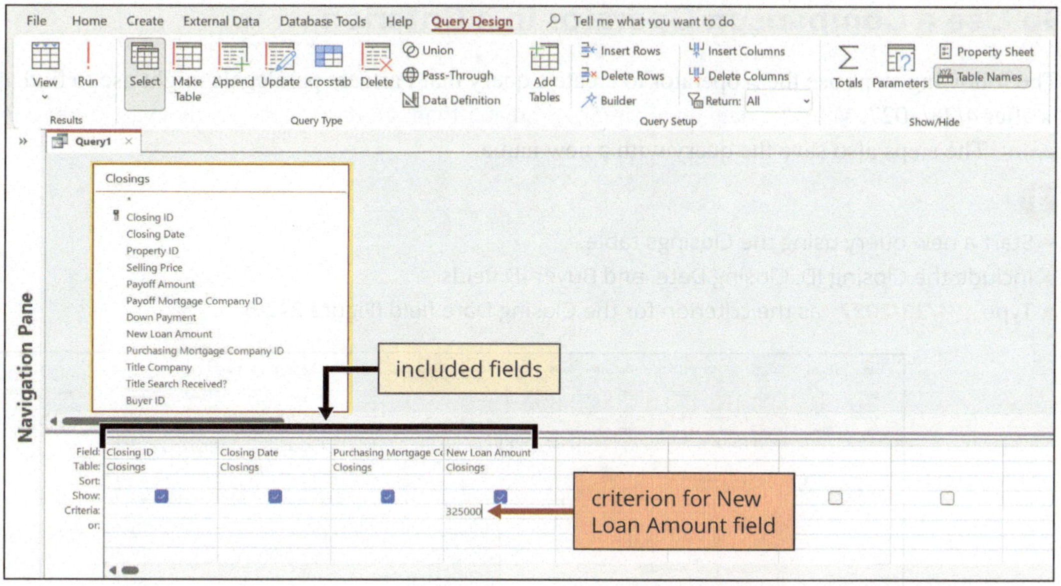

Figure 2–24

2

- Run the query (Figure 2–25).

Q&A Why did Access display the results as $325,000.00 when I only entered 325000?

Access uses the format for the field to determine how to display the result. In this case, the format indicated that Access should include the dollar sign, decimal point, and two decimal places.

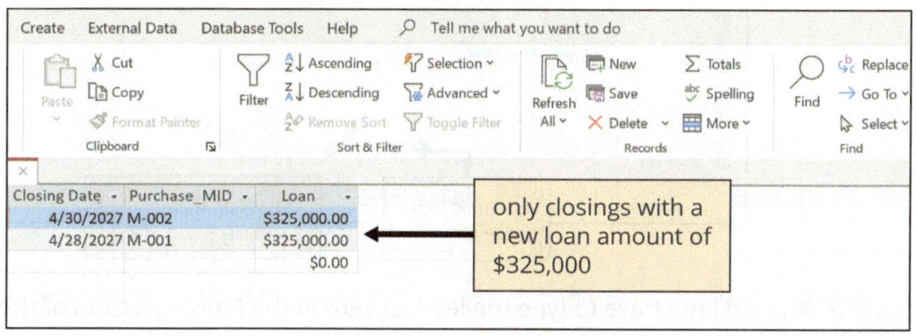

Figure 2–25

- Save the query as **m02q04**.

Q&A How do I know when to use the Save button to save a query or use Backstage view to perform a Save As?

If you are saving a new query, the simplest way is to use the Save button on the Quick Access Toolbar or press CTRL+S. If you are saving changes to a previously saved query but do not want to change the name, use the Save button. If you want to save a previously saved query with a new name, you must use Backstage view and perform a Save Object As.

- Close the query.

Comparison Operators

Unless you specify otherwise, Access assumes that the criteria you enter involves equality (exact matches). In the last query, for example, you were requesting those closings with new loan amounts of exactly $325,000. In other situations, you might want to find a range of results; for example, you could request closings whose closing date is after 4/28/2027. If you want a query to return something other than an exact match, you must enter the appropriate **comparison operator**. The comparison operators are > (greater than), < (less than), >= (greater than or equal to), <= (less than or equal to), and NOT (not equal to).

To Use a Comparison Operator in a Criterion

The following steps use the > operator to create a query that Partners paralegals might use to find all closings whose closing date is after 4/28/2027. **Why?** A date that is after, or greater than, 4/28/2027 means the date might conflict with a proposed training event. The steps also save the query with a new name.

1

- Start a new query using the Closings table.
- Include the Closing ID, Closing Date, and Buyer ID fields.
- Type **>4/28/2027** as the criterion for the Closing Date field (Figure 2–26).

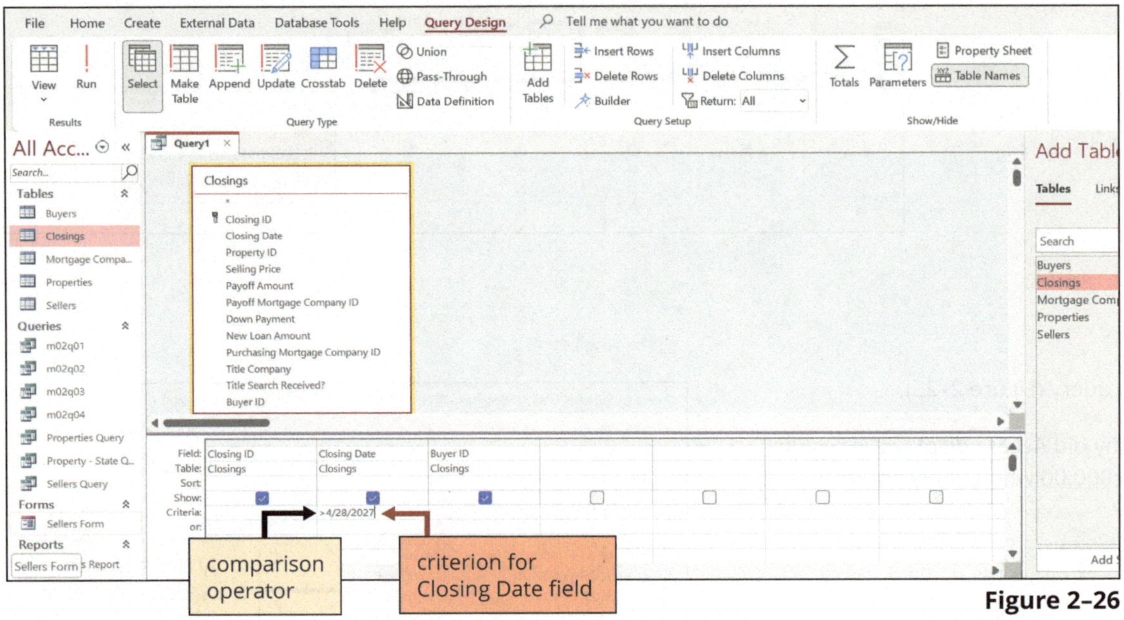

Figure 2–26

Q&A Why did I not have to type the leading zero in the Month portion of the date?
It is fine as you typed it. You also could have typed 04/28/2027. Some people often type the day or month using two digits even if the date is a single digit as the numbers 1 through 9. You also could type a leading zero for both the month and the day, such as 05/01/2027.

I noticed that Access changed >4/28/2027 to >#4/28/2027#. Why does the date now have hash signs around it?
This is the date format in Access. You usually do not have to enter the number signs because in most cases Access will insert them automatically.

2

- Run the query (Figure 2–27).
- **Experiment:** Return to Design view. Try a different criterion involving a comparison operator in the Closing Date field and run the query. When finished, return to Design view, enter the original criterion (>4/28/2027) in the Closing Date field, and run the query.

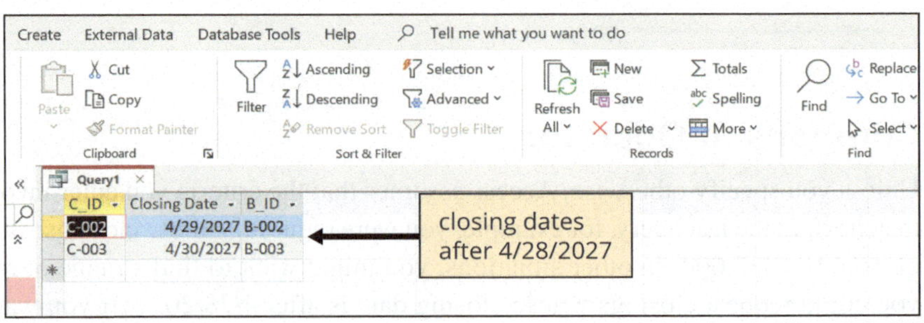

Figure 2–27

Q&A Can I use the same comparison operators with text data?
Yes. Comparison operators function the same whether you use them with number fields, currency fields, date fields, or text fields. With a text field, comparison operators use alphabetical order in making the determination.

3

- Save the query as **m02q05**.
- Close the query.

Using Compound Criteria

Often your search data must satisfy more than one criterion. This type of criterion is called a **compound criterion** and is created using the words AND or OR.

In an **AND criterion**, both individual criterion must be true in order for the compound criterion to be true. For example, an AND criterion would allow you to find closings after 4/28/2027 that are creating a new loan with the Cheshire Mortgage company.

An **OR criterion** is true if either individual criterion is true. An OR criterion would allow you to find closings after 4/28/2027 or closings that will create a loan with Cheshire Mortgage. In this case, any appointment after 4/28/2027 (regardless of mortgage company) or using Cheshire Mortgage (regardless of closing date) will be displayed.

BTW
Queries: Query-by-Example
Query-by-Example, often referred to as QBE, was a query language first proposed in the mid-1970s. In this approach, users asked questions by filling in a table on the screen. The Access approach to queries is based on Query-by-Example.

To Use a Compound Criterion Involving AND

To combine criteria with AND, place the criteria on the same row of the design grid. **Why?** Placing the criteria in the same row indicates that both criteria must be true in Access. It is important to note that sometimes when you view the results of a query, there are no records that meet the criterion entered. At this point, you might want to check to be certain the criterion was entered correctly. And, if the criterion is entered correctly, it becomes easier to trust the results even though you might have expected different results. The following steps use an AND criterion to enable Partners paralegals to find those closings with a closing date after 4/28/2027 and a new loan with Cheshire Mortgage. The steps also save the query.

1

- Start a new query using the Closings table.
- Include the Closing ID, Closing Date, Purchasing Mortgage Company ID, and Buyer ID fields.
- Type **>4/28/2027** as the criterion for the Closing Date field.
- Type **M-002** as the criterion for the Purchasing Mortgage Company ID field (Figure 2–28).

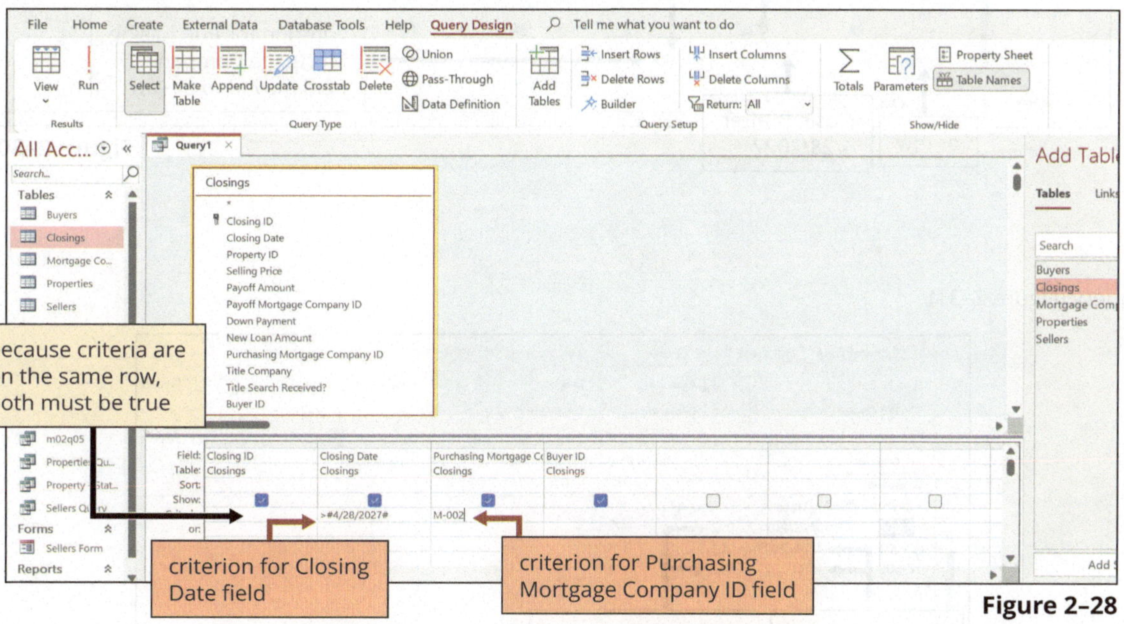

Figure 2–28

2

- Run the query (Figure 2–29) and notice that only one of the closings after 4/28/2027 will use Cheshire Mortgage.

3

- Save the query as **m02q06**. Do not close it yet.

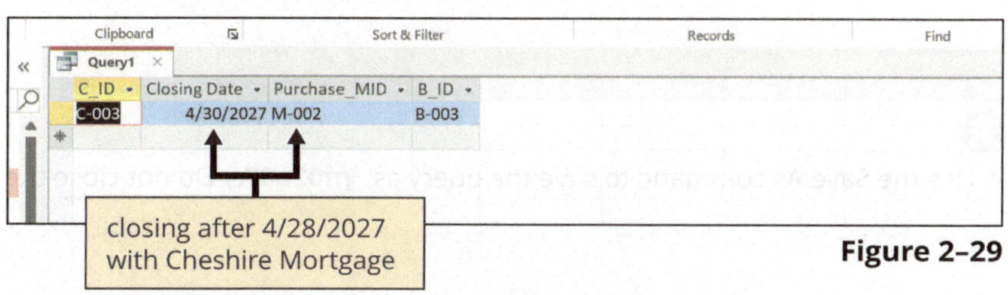

Figure 2–29

To Use a Compound Criterion Involving OR

To combine criteria with OR, each criterion must go on separate rows in the Criteria area of the grid. **Why?** Placing criteria on separate rows indicates at least one criterion must be true in Access and also shows true if both criterion are true. The following steps use an OR criterion to enable Partners paralegals to find those Closings with a Closing Date greater than 4/28/2027 or closings with new loans from Cheshire Mortgage. The steps also save the query with a new name.

1

- Return to Design view.
- In the Criteria row for the Purchasing Mortgage Company ID field, delete the existing text.
- Click the or row (the row below the Criteria row) for the Purchasing Mortgage Company ID field, and type **M-002** (Figure 2–30).

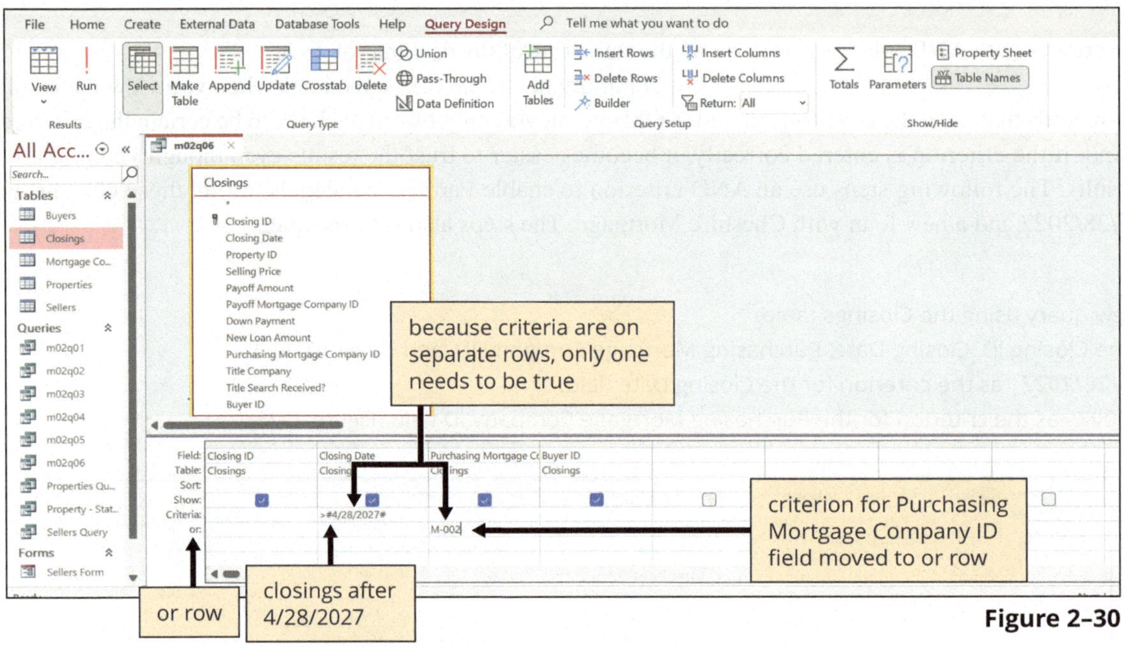

Figure 2–30

2

- Run the query (Figure 2–31).

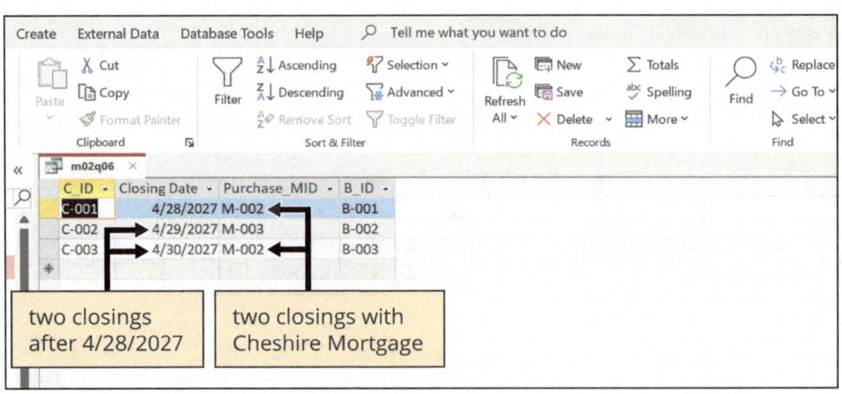

Figure 2–31

3

- Use the Save As command to save the query as **m02q07**. Do not close the query yet.

Special Criteria

You can use three special criteria in queries:

1. If you want to create a criterion involving a range of values in a single field, you can use the **AND operator**. You place the word AND between the individual conditions. For example, if you wanted to find all new loans greater than $300,000 and less than $400,000, you would enter >300000 AND <400000 as the criterion in the New Loan Amount column.
2. You can select values in a given range by using the **BETWEEN operator**. This is often an alternative to the AND operator. For example, to find all closings between 5/15/2027 and 5/31/2027, inclusive, you would enter BETWEEN 5/15/2027 AND 5/31/2027 as the criterion in the Closing Date column. This is equivalent to entering >=5/15/2027 AND <=5/31/2027.
3. You can select a list of values by using the **IN operator**. You follow the word IN with the list of values in parentheses. For example, to find the properties located in Pennsylvania (PA) or New York (NY), you would enter IN ('PA', 'NY'). Unlike when you enter a simple criterion, you must enclose text values in single quotation marks. The IN operator is like the OR operator, but it returns multiple values.

Consider This

How would you find properties located in Pennsylvania or New York without using the IN operator?

Place the text PA in the Criteria row of the State column. Place the text NY in the or row of the State column.

Sorting

In some queries, the order in which the records appear is irrelevant. All you need to be concerned about are the records that appear in the results. It does not matter which one is first or which one is last.

In other queries, however, the order can be very important. You might want to see new loan amounts arranged in ascending order (1,2,3,4,5, and so on), which is smallest to largest, or descending order (5,4,3,2,1), which is largest to smallest. Perhaps you want to see loan amounts listed by mortgage company in alphabetical order.

To order the records in a query result in a particular way, you **sort** the records. The field or fields on which the records are sorted is called the **sort key**. If you are sorting on more than one field (such as sorting by loan amount by mortgage company), the more important field (New Loan Amount) is called the **major key** (also called the **primary sort key**) and the less important field (Purchasing Mortgage Company) is called the **minor key** (also called the **secondary sort key**).

To sort in Microsoft Access, specify the sort order in the Sort row of the design grid below the field that is the sort key. If you specify more than one sort key, the sort key on the left will be the major sort key, and the one on the right will be the minor key.

BTW

Sorting Data in a Query

When sorting data in a query, the records in the underlying tables (the tables on which the query is based) are not actually rearranged. Instead, the DBMS determines the most efficient method of simply displaying the records in the requested order. The records in the underlying tables remain in their original order.

To Clear the Design Grid

Why? If the fields you want to include in the next query are different from those in the previous query, it is usually simpler to start with a clear grid, that is, one with no fields already in the design grid. You always can clear the entries in the design grid by closing the query and then starting over. A simpler approach to clearing the entries is to select all the entries and then press DEL. The following steps return to Design view and clear the design grid.

1

- If necessary, click the Design View button to display m02q07 in Design view.
- Click just above the Closing ID column heading in the grid to select the column.

Q&A I clicked above the column heading, but the column is not selected. What should I do?
You did not point to the correct location. Be sure the pointer changes into a down-pointing arrow, and then click again.

- Press and hold SHIFT and click just above the Buyer ID column heading to select all the columns (Figure 2–32).

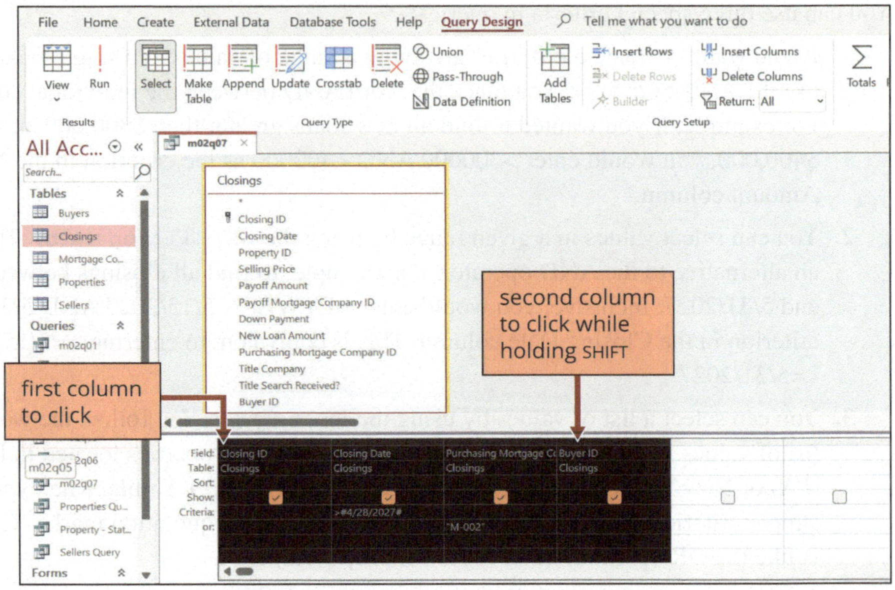

Figure 2–32

2

- Press DEL to clear the design grid.

3

- Close the query without saving these changes.

BTW
Clearing the Design Grid
You can also clear the design grid using the ribbon. To do so, click the Home tab, click the Advanced Filter Options button to display the Advanced menu (Home tab | Sort & Filter group), and then click Clear Grid on the Advanced Filter Options menu.

To Sort Data in a Query

If you determine that the query results should be sorted, you will need to specify the sort key. The following steps sort the new loan amounts in the Closings table by indicating that the New Loan Amount field is to be sorted. The steps specify Ascending sort order. **Why?** When sorting numerical data, Ascending sort order arranges the results from smallest to largest values.

1

- Create a new query in Design view based on the Closings table.
- Include the Closing ID, New Loan Amount, and Purchasing Mortgage Company ID fields in the design grid.
- Click the Sort row in the New Loan Amount field column, and then click the Sort arrow to display a menu of possible sort orders (Figure 2–33).

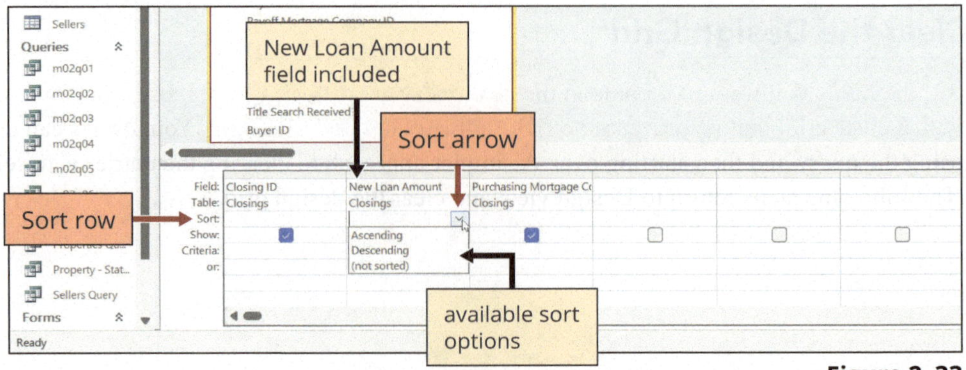

Figure 2–33

2

- Click Ascending to select the sort order (Figure 2–34).

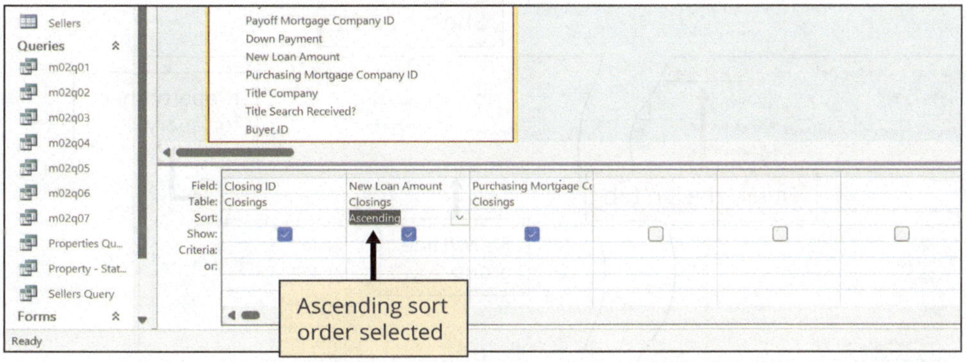

Figure 2–34

3

- Run the query (Figure 2–35) to display the loan amounts sorted in ascending order (lowest to highest).

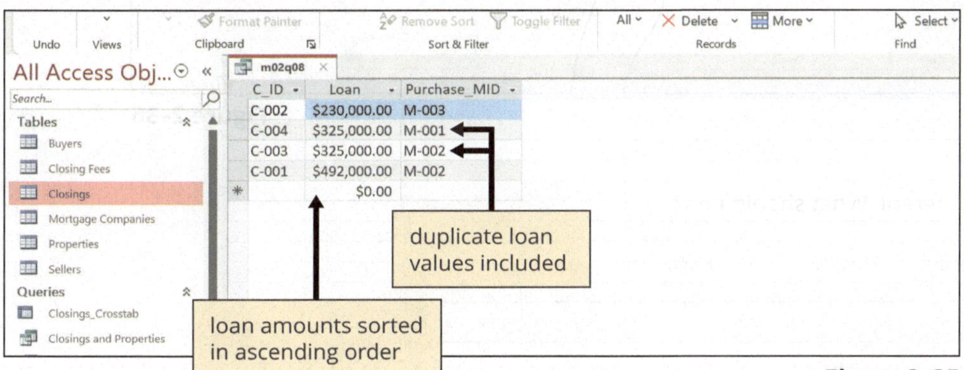

Figure 2–35

- Save the query as **m02q08**.
- **Experiment:** Return to Design view and change the sort order to Descending. Run the query. Return to Design view and change the sort order back to Ascending. Run the query.

Q&A Why do some loan amounts appear more than once?
The same loan amount is associated with multiple closings.

To Omit Duplicates

When you sort data, duplicates normally are included. In the query shown in Figure 2–35, for example, $325,000.00 appears more than once. You eliminate duplicates using the query's property sheet. A **property sheet** is a pane containing the various properties of the object. To omit duplicates, you will use the property sheet to change the Unique Values property from No to Yes.

The following steps create a query that Partners paralegals might use to obtain a sorted list of the new loan amounts in the Closings table in which each loan amount is listed only once. **Why?** Unless you wanted to know how many loan amounts are in the Closings table, the duplicates typically do not add any value. The steps also save the query with a new name.

1

- Click the Design View button to return to Design view.
- In the design grid, click just above the Closing ID field to select the field and then press DEL to remove the Closing ID field from the query.
- Similarly, delete the Purchasing Mortgage Company ID field.
- Click the second field (the empty field to the right of New Loan Amount) in the design grid to produce an insertion point.

- If necessary, click Query Design on the ribbon to display the Query Design tab.
- Click the Property Sheet button (Query Design tab | Show/Hide group) to display the property sheet (Figure 2–36).

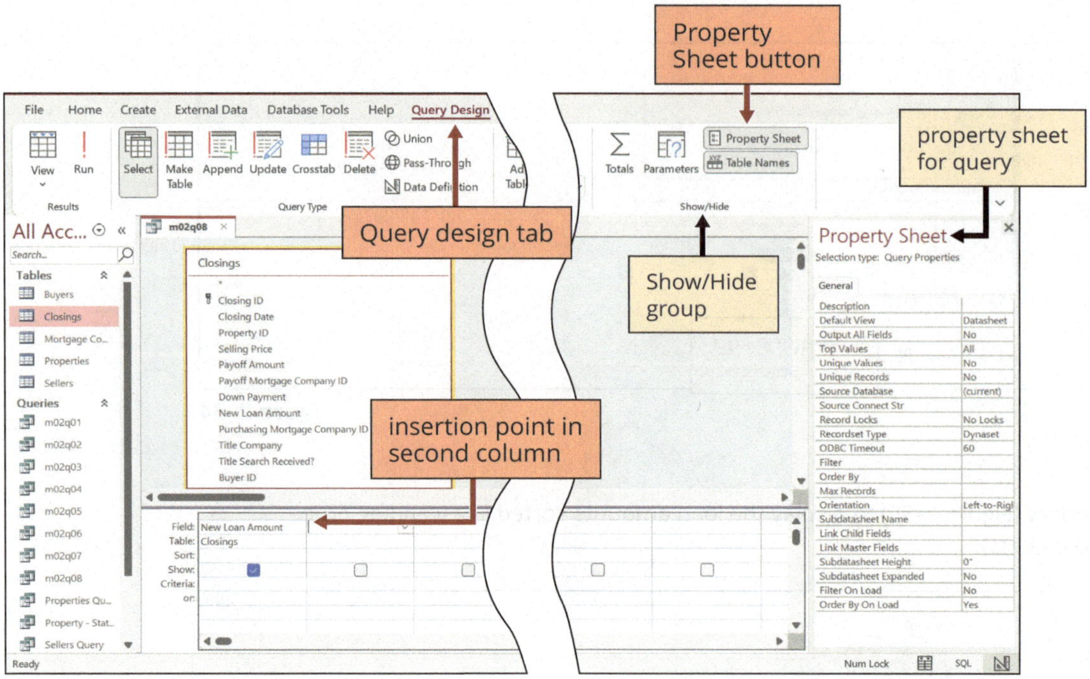

Figure 2–36

Q&A My property sheet looks different. What should I do?
If your sheet looks different, close the property sheet pane and repeat this step, making sure first to insert your insertion point in the first blank field to the right of the New Loan Amount field.

Other Ways

1. Right-click first blank field in design grid, click Properties to open Property Sheet pane

2

- Click the Unique Values property box, and then click the Unique Values arrow to display a list of available choices (Figure 2–37).

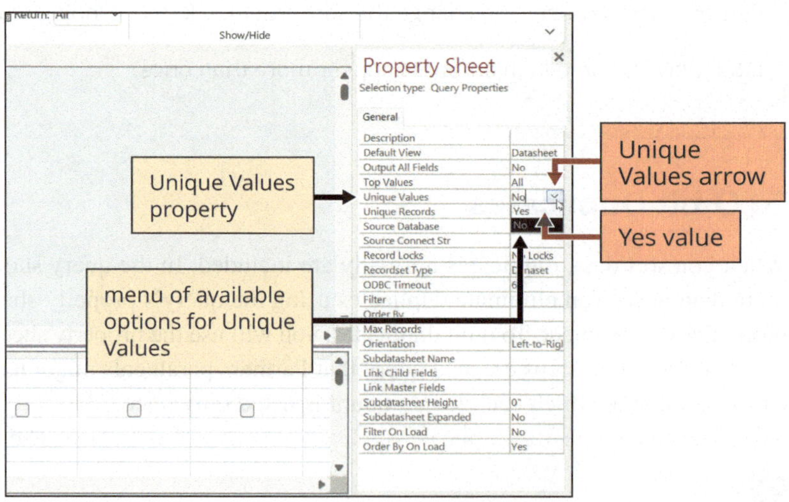

Figure 2–37

3

- Click Yes to indicate that the query will return unique values, which means that each value will appear only once in the query results.
- Close the Query Properties property sheet by clicking the Property Sheet button (Query Design tab | Show/Hide group) a second time.
- Run the query (Figure 2–38).
- Use the Save As command to save the query as **m02q09** and close the query.

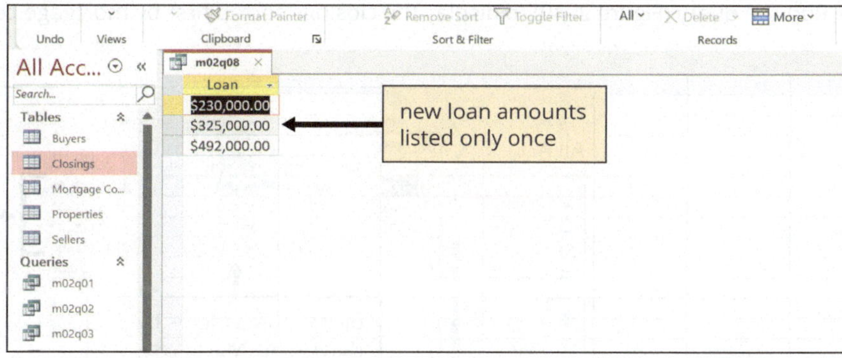

Figure 2–38

Other Ways

1. Click Close button in Property Sheet pane to close pane

To Sort on Multiple Keys

The following steps sort on multiple keys. Specifically, Partners paralegals need the data to be sorted by New Loan Amount (low to high) within Purchasing Mortgage Company ID, which means that the Purchasing Mortgage Company ID field is the major key and the New Loan Amount field is the minor key. Therefore, the steps place the Purchasing Mortgage Company ID field to the left of the New Loan Amount field. **Why?** In Access, the major key must appear to the left of the minor key. The steps also save the query.

1

- Create a new query based on the Closings table and add fields in the following order: Closing ID, Closing Date, Purchasing Mortgage Company ID, and New Loan Amount.
- Select Ascending as the sort order for both the Purchasing Mortgage Company ID field and the New Loan Amount field (Figure 2–39).

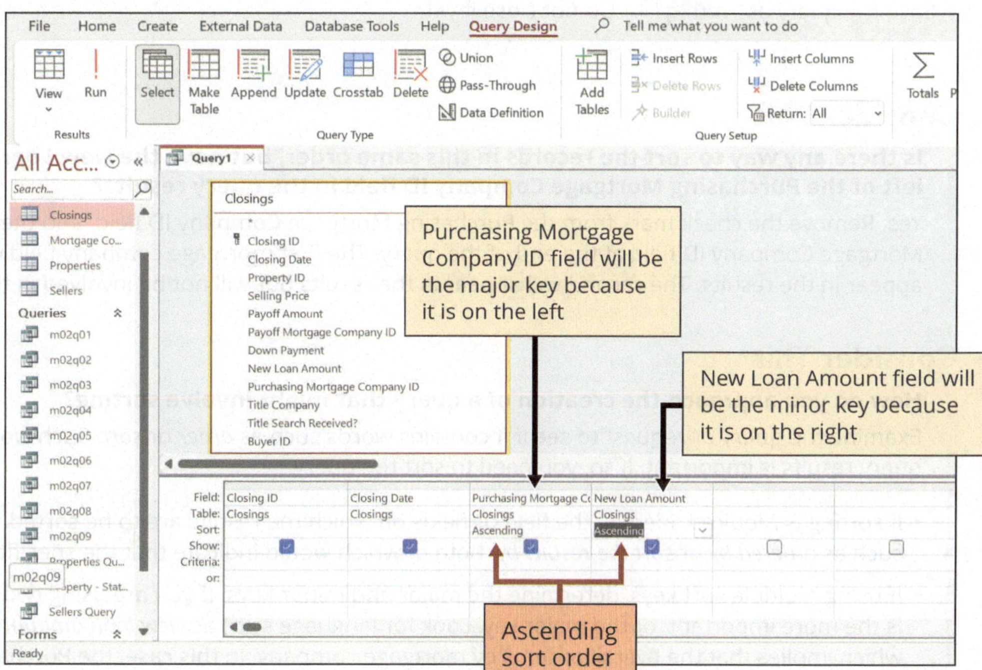

Figure 2–39

2

- Run the query (Figure 2–40) to display the closings sorted first by mortgage companies and then by new loan amount.

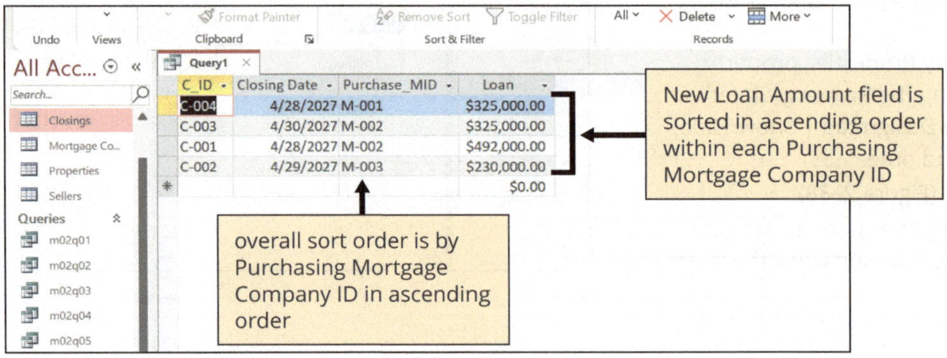

Figure 2–40

- **Experiment:** Return to Design view and try other sort combinations for the Purchasing Mortgage Company ID and New Loan Amount fields, such as Descending for the mortgage companies or Descending for the loan amounts. You might also try applying a sort order for other fields. In each case, run the query to see the effect of the changes. When finished, return the sort order to Ascending for the Purchasing Mortgage Company ID and New Loan Amount fields with no sort applied to any other field.

Q&A What if the New Loan Amount field is to the left of the Purchasing Mortgage Company ID field?
It is important to remember that the major sort key must appear to the left of the minor sort key in the design grid. If you attempted to sort by New Loan Amount within Purchasing Mortgage Company ID but placed the New Loan Amount field to the left of the Purchasing Mortgage Company ID field, your results would not accurately represent the intended sort.

3

- Save the query as **m02q10**. Do not close it yet.

Consider This

Is there any way to sort the records in this same order, but have the New Loan Amount field appear to the left of the Purchasing Mortgage Company ID field in the query results?

Yes. Remove the check mark from the Purchasing Mortgage Company ID field, and then add an additional Purchasing Mortgage Company ID field at the end of the query. The first mortgage company field will be used for sorting but will not appear in the results. The second will appear in the results but will not be involved in the sorting process.

Consider This

How do you approach the creation of a query that might involve sorting?

Examine the query or request to see if it contains words such as *order* or *sort*. Such words imply that the order of the query results is important. If so, you need to sort the query.

- If sorting is required, identify the field or fields on which the results are to be sorted. In the request, look for language such as *ordered by* or *sort the results by*, both of which would indicate that the specified field is a sort key.
- If using multiple sort keys, determine the major and minor keys. If you are using two sort keys, determine which one is the more important, or the major key. Look for language such as *view loan amounts within each mortgage company*, which implies that the overall order is by mortgage company. In this case, the Purchasing Mortgage Company ID field would be the major sort key and the New Loan Amount field would be the minor sort key.
- Determine sort order. Words such as *increasing*, *ascending*, or *low to high* imply Ascending order. Words such as *decreasing*, *descending*, or *high to low* imply Descending order. Sorting in *alphabetical order* implies Ascending order. If there were no words to imply a particular order, you would typically use Ascending.
- Examine the query or request to see if there are any special restrictions. One common restriction is to exclude duplicates. Another common restriction is to list only a certain number of records, such as the first five records.

To Create a Top-Values Query

Rather than show all the results of a query, you might want to show only a specified number of records or a percentage of records. **Why?** You might not need to see all the records, just enough to get a general idea of the results. Creating a **top-values query** allows you to restrict the number of records that appear. When you sort records, you can limit results to those records with the highest (descending sort) or lowest (ascending sort) values. To do so, first create a query that sorts the data in the desired order. Next, use the Return box on the Query Design tab to change the number of records to be included from All to the desired number or percentage.

The following steps create a query for Partners paralegals that shows only the first two records that were included in the results of the previous query. The steps also save the resulting query with a new name.

1

- Return to Design view.
- If necessary, click Query Design on the ribbon to display the Query Design tab.
- Click the Return arrow (Query Design tab | Query Setup group) to display the Return menu (Figure 2–41).

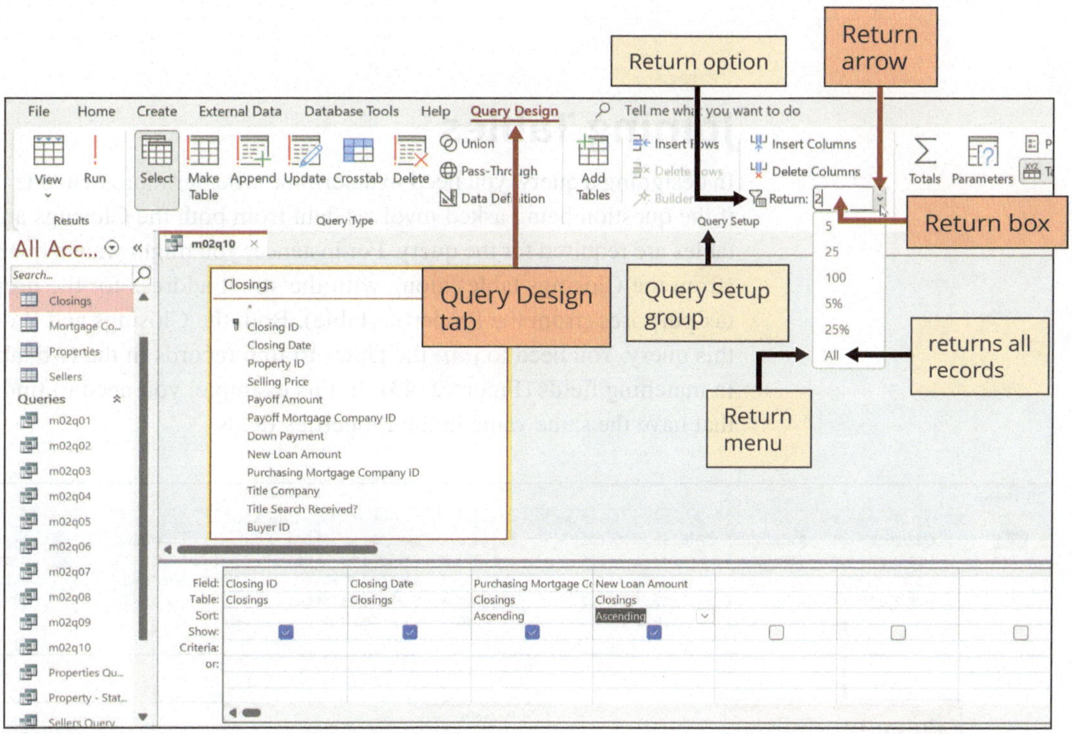

Figure 2–41

2

- Type **2** in the Return box. Access might suggest 25; delete the 5 and ensure only 2 is listed to specify that the query results should contain the first two rows.

Q&A Why does Access suggest 25 records instead of 2?
Many databases contain hundreds of records, and so requesting the top 25 records would be more useful than just the top two records. When learning how to use Access, it's easier to work with fewer records.

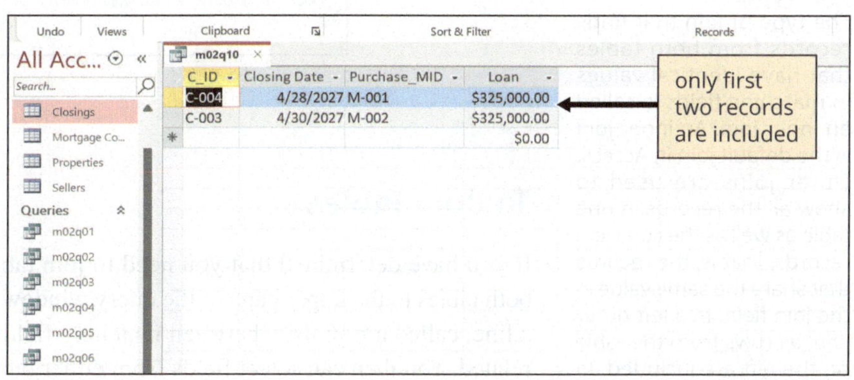

Figure 2–42

- Run the query (Figure 2–42) to display only the first two records.

3

- Use the Save As command to save the query as **m02q11**.
- Close the query.

Q&A Do I need to close the query before creating my next query?

Not necessarily. When you use a top-values query, however, it is important to change the value in the Return box back to All. If you do not change the Return value back to All, the previous value will remain in effect for later queries created from this one. Consequently, you might not get all the records you should in the next query. A good practice whenever you use a top-values query is to close the query as soon as you are done. That way, you will begin your next query from scratch, which ensures that the value is reset to All.

Joining Tables

In designing a query, you need to determine whether more than one table is required. For example, if the question being asked involves data from both the Closings and Properties tables, then both tables are required for the query. For instance, you might want a query that shows the closing dates (from the Closings table) along with the street address for the property and the jurisdiction for tax purposes (from the Properties table). Both the Closings and Properties tables are required for this query. You need to **join** the tables to find records in the two tables that have identical values in matching fields (Figure 2–43). In this example, you need to find records in the Closings table that have the same value in the Properties fields.

Closings

C_ID	Closing Date	P_ID	Price	Payoff	Payoff_MID	Down	Loan	Purchase_MID	Title Co	Title?	B_ID
C-001	4/28/2027	P-001	$568,000.00	$246,152.28	M-001	$100,000.00	$492,000.00	M-002	Records Title Co.	☑	B-001
C-002	4/29/2027	P-002	$281,000.00	$76,042.51	M-001	$25,000.00	$230,000.00	M-003	Perfect Title Co.	☑	B-002
C-003	4/30/2027	P-003	$372,000.00	$142,983.79	M-003	$60,000.00	$325,000.00	M-002	Perfect Title Co.	☐	B-003
C-004	4/28/2027	P-004	$493,000.00	$356,282.29	M-002	$175,000.00	$325,000.00	M-001	Armor Title Co.	☐	B-004
*			$0.00	$0.00		$0.00	$0.00			☐	

Properties ID field in both tables

Properties

P_ID	Type	Street	City	State	Postal Code	Jurisdiction	Seller ID
P-001	Residential	219 Phillips St	Donahue	PA	15003	Donahue City, Ashland County	S-001
P-002	Residential	852 Scranton Dr	Jonestown	PA	15068	Jonestown City, Fairfield County	S-002
P-003	Residential	46 Hwy 82 S	Louisville	NY	10025	Pasqua County	S-003
P-004	Commercial	186 Alabama Hwy	Hartford	PA	15031	Hartford City, Knox County	S-004
P-005	Residential	Route 15, Box 281	Winslow	NY	10043	Putnam County	S-005
P-006	Residential	87 Georgetown Rd, #2	East Barnard	PA	15064	Fairfield County	S-006
*							

Figure 2–43

BTW

Join Types

The type of join that finds records from both tables that have identical values in matching fields is called an inner join. An inner join is the default join in Access. Outer joins are used to show all the records in one table as well as the common records; that is, the records that share the same value in the join field. In a left outer join, all rows from the table on the left are included. In a right outer join, all rows from the table on the right are included.

To Join Tables

If you have determined that you need to join tables in a query, you first will bring field lists for both tables to the upper pane of the query window while working in Design view. Access will draw a line, called a **join line**, between matching fields in the two tables, indicating that the tables are related. You then can select fields from either table. Access joins the tables automatically.

The first step is to create a new query and add the Closings table to the query. Then, add the Properties table to the query. A join line should appear, connecting the Property ID fields in the two field lists. **Why might the join line not appear?** If the names of the matching fields differ from one table to the other, Access will not insert the line. You can insert it manually, however, by clicking one of the two matching fields and dragging the pointer to the other matching field.

The following steps create a query to display information from both the Closings table and the Properties table.

1

- Create a new query using the Closings table.
- Double-click the Properties table (Add Tables pane) to add a field list for the Properties table (Figure 2–44).

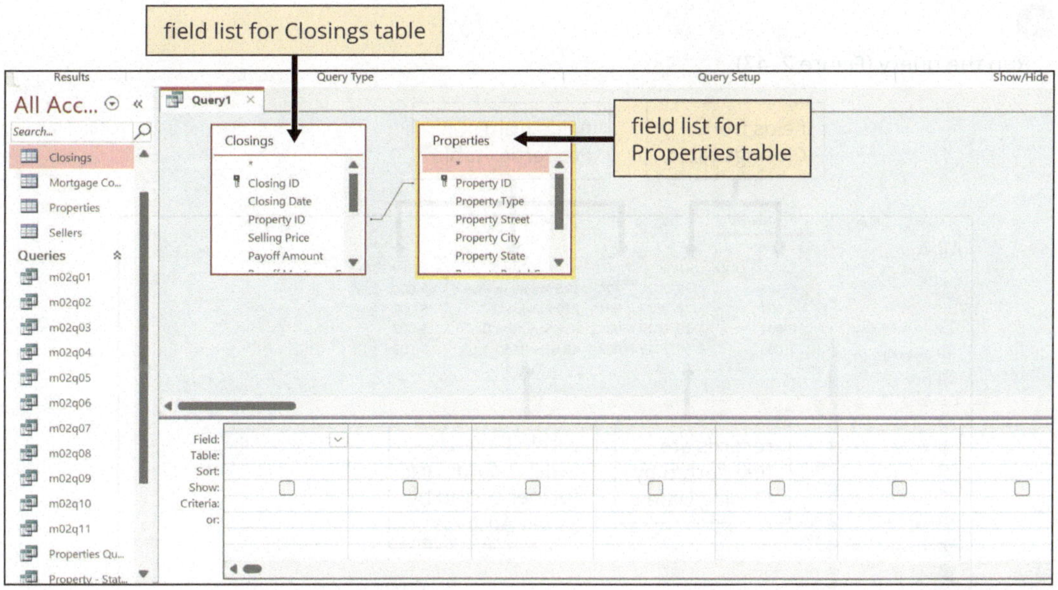

Figure 2–44

2

- Close the Add Tables pane.
- Expand the size of the two field lists so all the fields in the Closings and Properties tables appear (Figure 2–45).

Q&A I did not get a join line. What should I do?

Ensure that the names of the matching fields are the same, the data types are the same, and the matching field is the primary key in one of the two tables. If all these factors are true and you still do not have a join line, you can produce one by pointing to a matching field and dragging to the other matching field.

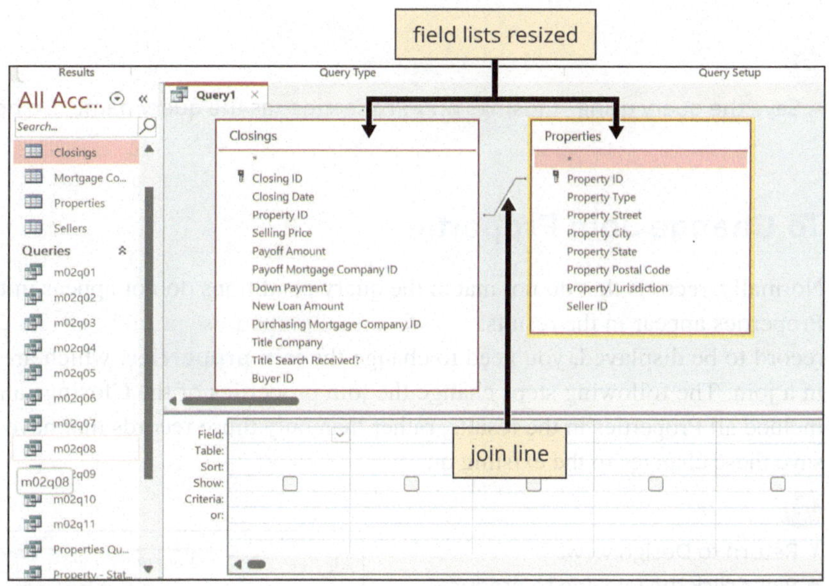

Figure 2–45

3

- In the design grid, add the Closing ID and Closing Date fields from the Closings Table, and then the Property ID, Property Street, and Seller ID fields from the Properties Table.
- Select Ascending as the sort order for both the Closing Date field and the Property Street field (Figure 2–46).

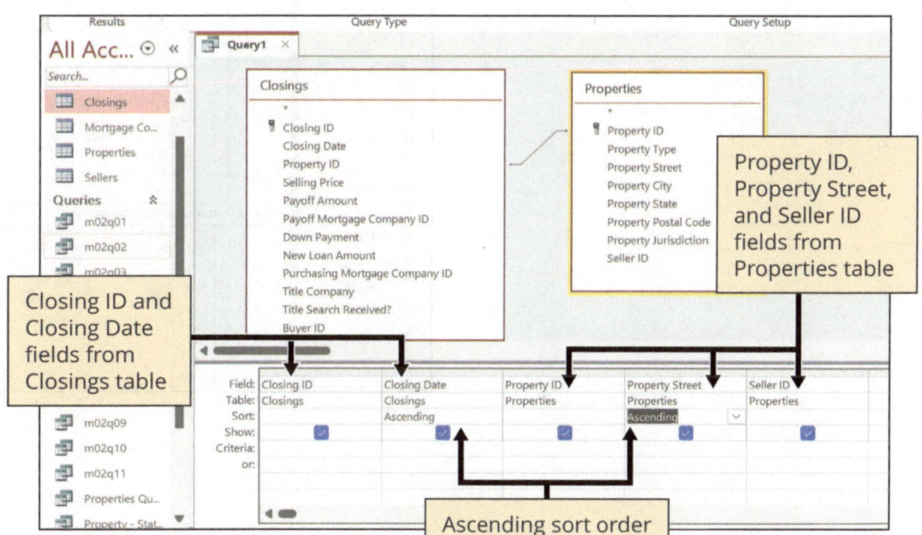

Figure 2–46

4

- Run the query (Figure 2–47).

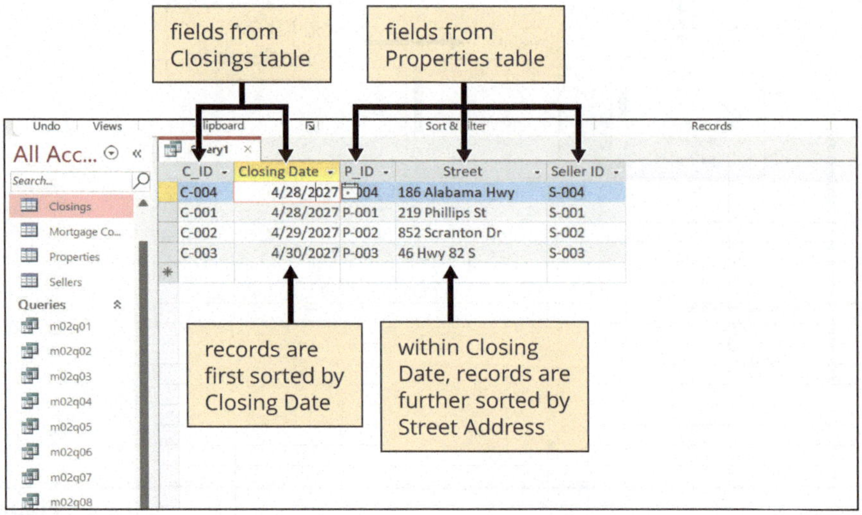

Figure 2–47

5

- Save the query using **Closings and Properties** as the query name. Do not close it yet.

BTW
Join Line
If you do not get a join line automatically, there might be a problem with one of your table designs. Open each table in Design view, and make sure that the data types are the same for the matching field in both tables and that one of the matching fields is the primary key in a table. If not, correct these errors and create the query again.

To Change Join Properties

Normally, records that do not match the query conditions do not appear in the results of a join query. For example, not all the Properties appear in the results. **Why?** Not all properties currently have a closing date associated with them. To cause such a record to be displayed, you need to change the **join properties**, which are the properties that indicate which records appear in a join. The following steps change the join properties of the Closings and Properties query so that Partners paralegals can include all Properties in the results, rather than only those records that have closing dates associated with them. The steps also save these changes to the existing query.

1

- Return to Design view.
- Right-click the join line to produce a shortcut menu (Figure 2–48).

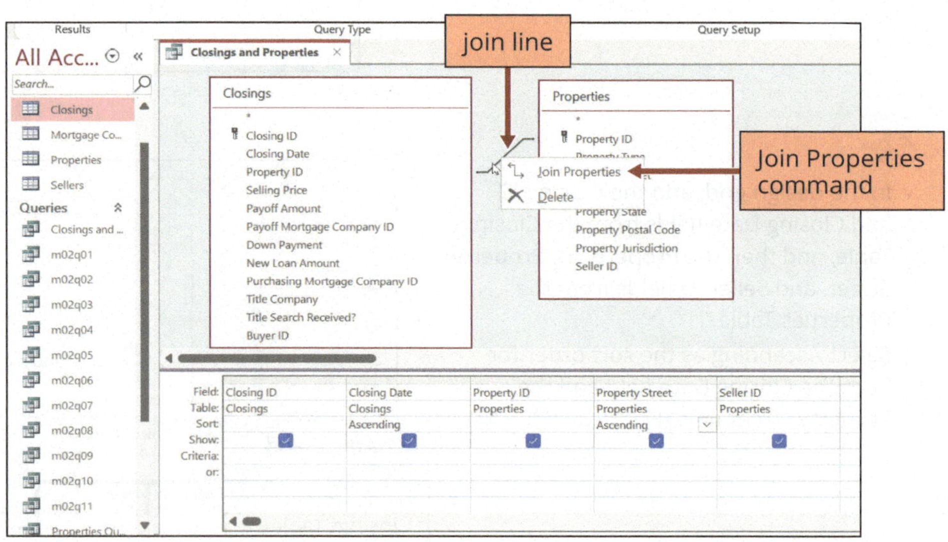

Figure 2–48

2

- Click Join Properties on the shortcut menu to display the Join Properties dialog box (Figure 2–49).

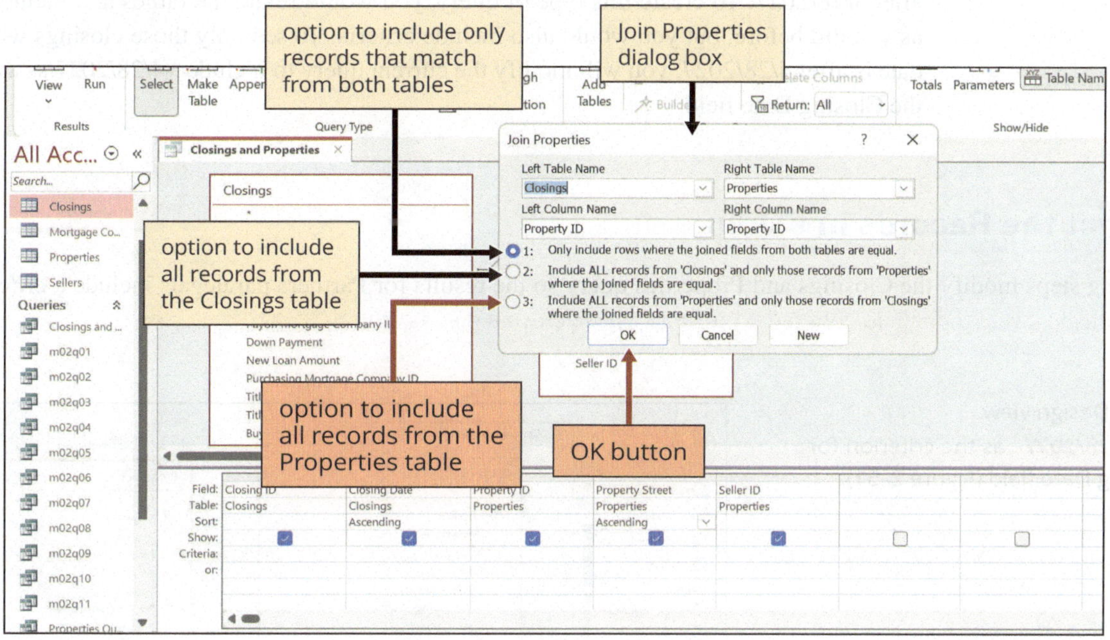

Figure 2–49

Q&A I do not see Join Properties on my shortcut menu. What should I do?
If Join Properties does not appear on your shortcut menu, you did not point to the appropriate portion of the join line. You will need to point to the middle portion and right-click again.

3

- Click option 3 (Join Properties dialog box) to include all records from the Properties table regardless of whether they match any closing dates.
- Click OK (Join Properties dialog box) to modify the join properties and close the Join Properties dialog box.
- Run the query (Figure 2–50).

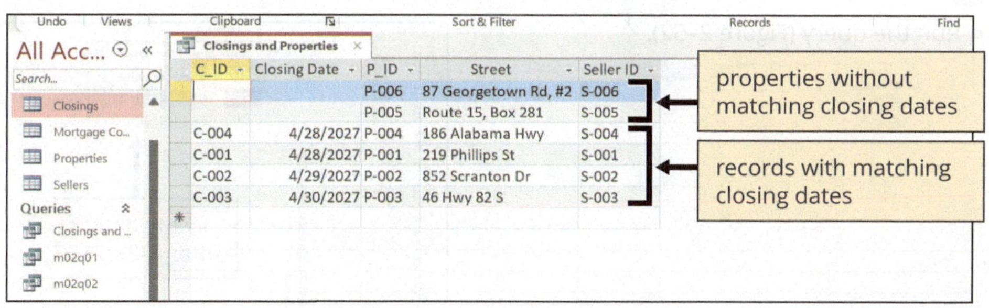

Figure 2–50

- **Experiment:** Return to Design view, change the Join properties, and select option 2. Run the query to see the effect of this option. When done, return to Design view, change the Join properties, and once again select option 3.

4

- Save the changes to the query.

Q&A I see a dialog box that asks if I want to save the query. What should I do?
Click OK to save the query.

Adding Criteria to a Join Query

Sometimes you will want to join tables, but you will not want to include all possible records. For example, the Partners paralegals need a query showing only those closings whose closing date is after 4/28/2027. To create this type of query, you would relate the tables and include fields just as you did before, but you would also include criteria. To see only those closings whose closing date is after 4/28/2027, you will modify the current query to include >4/28/2027 as a criterion for the Closing Date field.

To Restrict the Records in a Join

The following steps modify the Closings and Properties query so the results for Partners paralegals include a criterion. **Why?** Partners paralegals want to include only those closings whose closing date is after 4/28/2027.

1

- Return to Design view.
- Type **>4/28/2027** as the criterion for the Closing Date field (Figure 2–51).

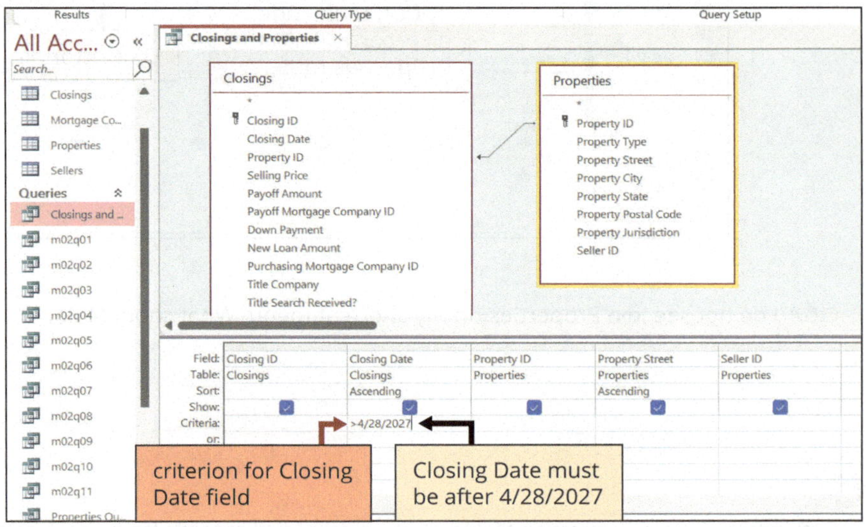

Figure 2–51

2

- Run the query (Figure 2–52).

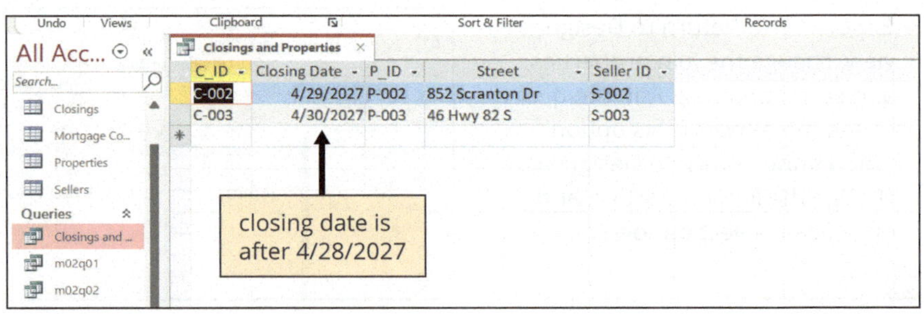

Figure 2–52

3

- Close the query.
- When asked if you want to save your changes, click No.

Q&A What would happen if I saved the changes?
The next time you used this query, you would only see closings whose closing date is after 4/28/2027.

To Create a Report from a Query

You can use queries in the creation of reports. The report in Figure 2–51 involves data from more than one table. The Closing ID and Closing Date fields are in the Closings table. The Property Type, Property Street, and Seller ID fields are from the Properties table. The Property ID field is in both tables. **Why?** The easiest way to create such a report is to base it on a query that joins the two tables. The following steps use the Report Wizard and the Closings and Properties query to create the report shown in Figure 2–53.

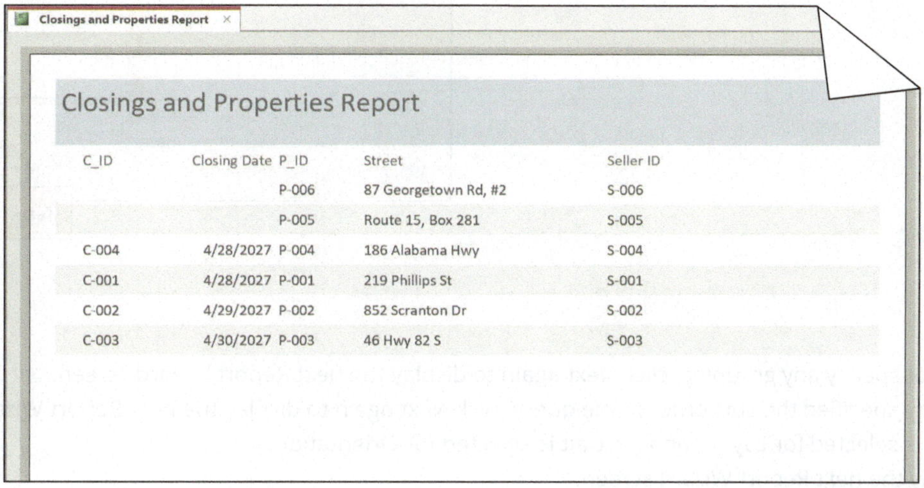

Figure 2–53

1

- Select the Closings and Properties query in the Navigation Pane.
- Click Create on the ribbon to display the Create tab.
- Click the Report Wizard button (Create tab | Reports group) to display the Report Wizard dialog box (Figure 2–54).

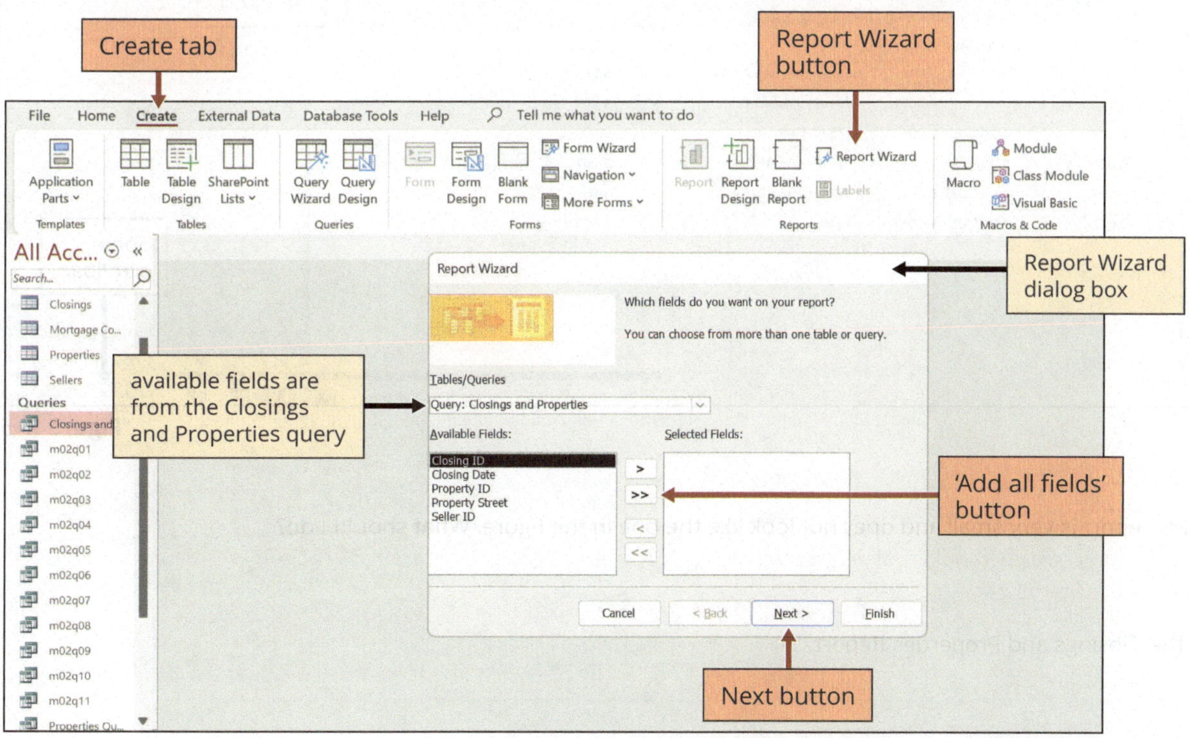

Figure 2–54

2

- Click the 'Add All Fields' button (Report Wizard dialog box) to add all the fields from the Closings and Properties query.
- Click Next to display the next Report Wizard screen (Figure 2–55).

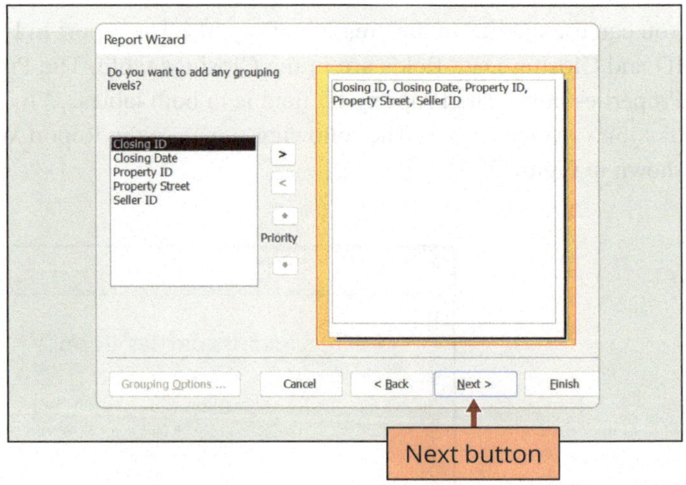

Figure 2–55

3

- Because you will not specify any grouping, click Next again to display the next Report Wizard screen.
- Because you already specified the sort order in the query, click Next again to display the next Report Wizard screen.
- Make sure Tabular is selected for Layout and Portrait is selected for Orientation.
- Click Next to display the next Report Wizard screen.
- Enter **Report** at the end of the Closings and Properties title so that Closings and Properties Report appears as the complete title.
- Click the Finish button to produce the report (Figure 2–56).

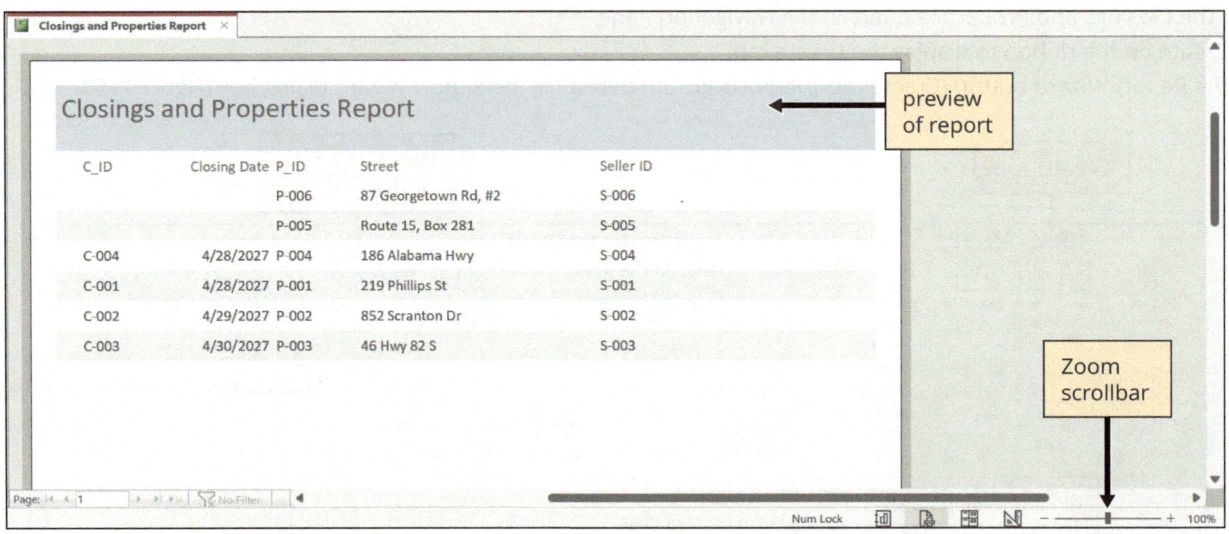

Figure 2–56

Q&A My report is very small and does not look like the one in the figure. What should I do?
Click the pointer, which should look like a magnifying glass, anywhere in the report to magnify the report or adjust the Zoom scrollbar in the Status bar.

- Close the Closings and Properties Report.

To Print a Report

Often, users will need to distribute database information in a printed format. **Why?** Partners would like to share the Closings and Properties Report with executives who prefer a hard copy. The following steps print a hard copy of the report.

1

- In the Navigation Pane, click the Closings and Properties Report to select it.
- Click File on the ribbon to open Backstage view.

2

- Click the Print tab in Backstage view to display the Print gallery.

3

- Click Print Preview to see a preview of the report before printing it and to make other changes, such as page size and page layout.
- If required by your instructor, click the Print button (Print Preview tab | Print group) to print the report. Otherwise, click Close Print Preview (Print Preview tab | Close Preview group), and then close the Closings and Properties report.

Consider This

How would you approach the creation of a query that might involve multiple tables?

- Examine the request to see if all the fields involved in the request are in one table. If the fields are in two (or more) tables, you need to join the tables.
- If joining is required, identify within the two tables the matching fields that have identical values. Look for the same column name in the two tables or for column names that are similar.
- Determine whether sorting is required. Queries that join tables often are used as the basis for a report. If this is the case, it may be necessary to sort the results. For example, the Closings and Properties Report is based on a query that joins the Closings and Properties tables. The query is sorted by Closing Date and Property Street.
- Examine the request to see if there are any special restrictions. For example, the user may only want closings scheduled after 4/28/2027.
- Examine the request to see if you only want records from both tables that have identical values in matching fields. If you want to see records in one of the tables that do not have identical values in the other table, then you need to change the join properties.

Creating a Form for a Query

You have already learned how to create a form for a table. You can also create a form for a query. Recall that a form in a database is a formatted document with fields that contain data. Forms allow you to view and maintain data. Note that changing data using a form based on a query changes the data in the underlying table.

To Create a Form for a Query

The following steps create a form, then save the form. **Why?** The form will be available for future use in viewing and maintaining the data in the query.

1

- Select the Closings and Properties query in the Navigation Pane.
- Click Create on the ribbon to display the Create tab (Figure 2–57).

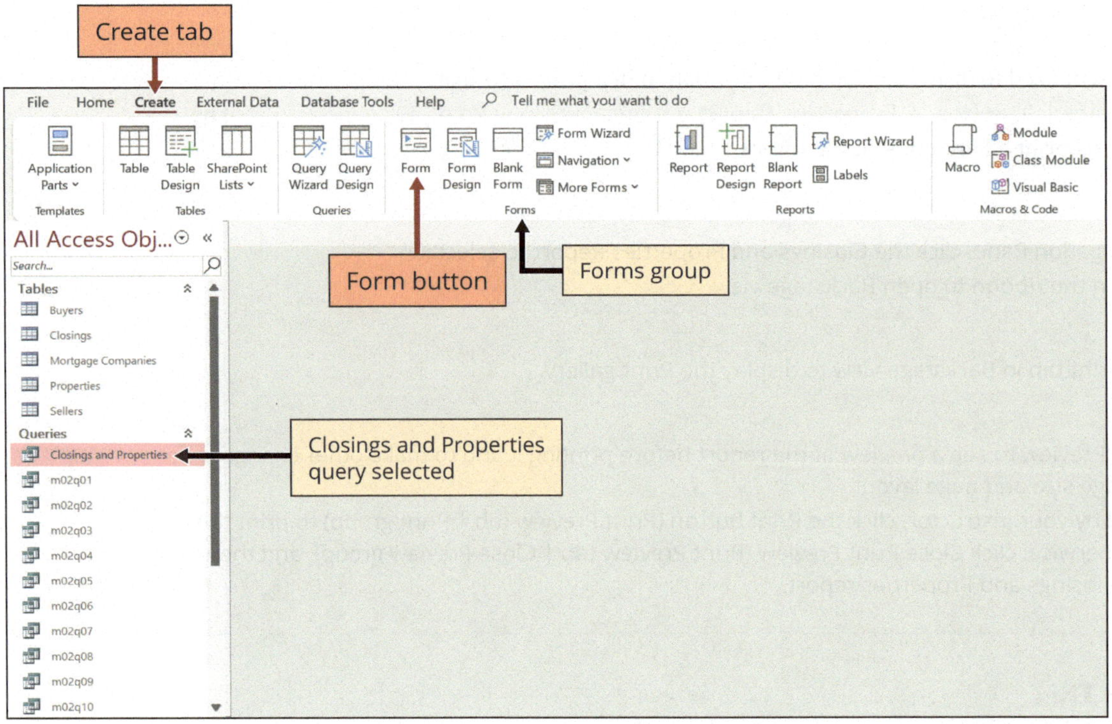

Figure 2–57

2

- Click the Form button (Create tab | Forms group) to create a simple form (Figure 2–58).

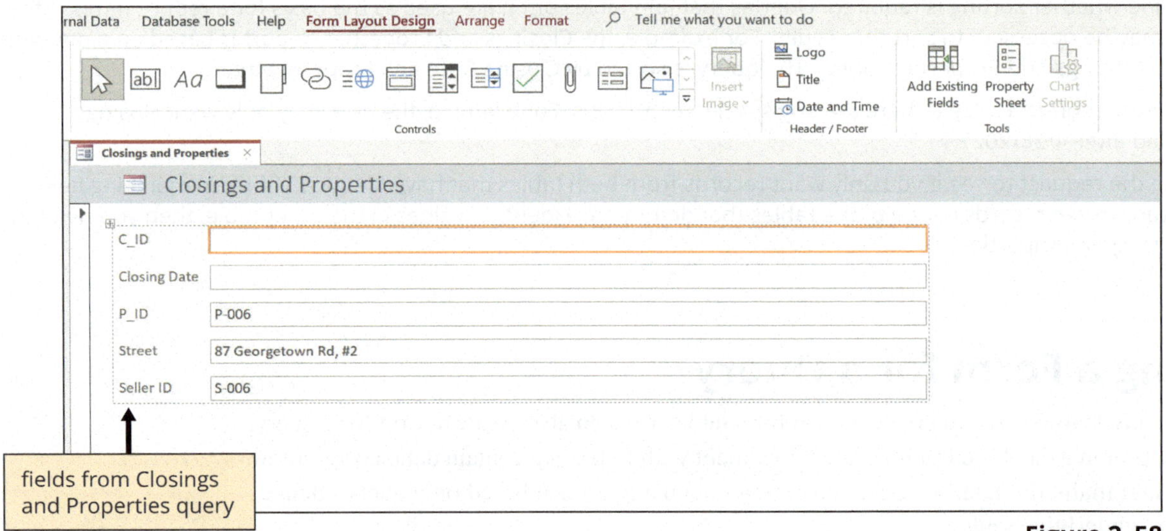

Figure 2–58

Q&A I see a field list pane also. What should I do?
Click Close for the Field List pane.

3

- Click the Save button on the Quick Access Toolbar to display the Save As dialog box.
- Enter **Form** at the end of the Closings and Properties name so that Closings and Properties Form appears as the complete name.
- Click OK to save the form.
- Close the form.

Using a Form

After you have saved a form, you can use it at any time by double-clicking the form in the Navigation Pane. If you plan to use the form to enter or edit data, you must ensure you are viewing the form in Form view.

Break Point: If you wish to take a break, this is a good place to do so. You can exit Access now. To resume later, start Access, open the database called SC_AC_02_Partners.accdb, and continue following the steps from this location forward.

Exporting Data from Access to Other Applications

You can **export**, or copy, tables or queries from an Access database so that another application (for example, Excel or Word) can use the data. The application that will receive the data determines the export process to be used. You can export to text files in a variety of formats. For applications to which you cannot directly export data, you often can export an appropriately formatted text file that the other application can import. Figure 2–59 shows the workbook produced by exporting the Closings and Properties query to Excel. The columns in the workbook have been resized to best fit the data.

BTW
Exporting Data
You frequently need to export data so that it can be used in other applications and by other users in an organization. For example, the Accounting department might require financial data in an Excel format to perform certain financial functions. Legal might require a list of buyer or seller names and property addresses in Word or rich text format (RTF) for filing documents at the appropriate courthouse.

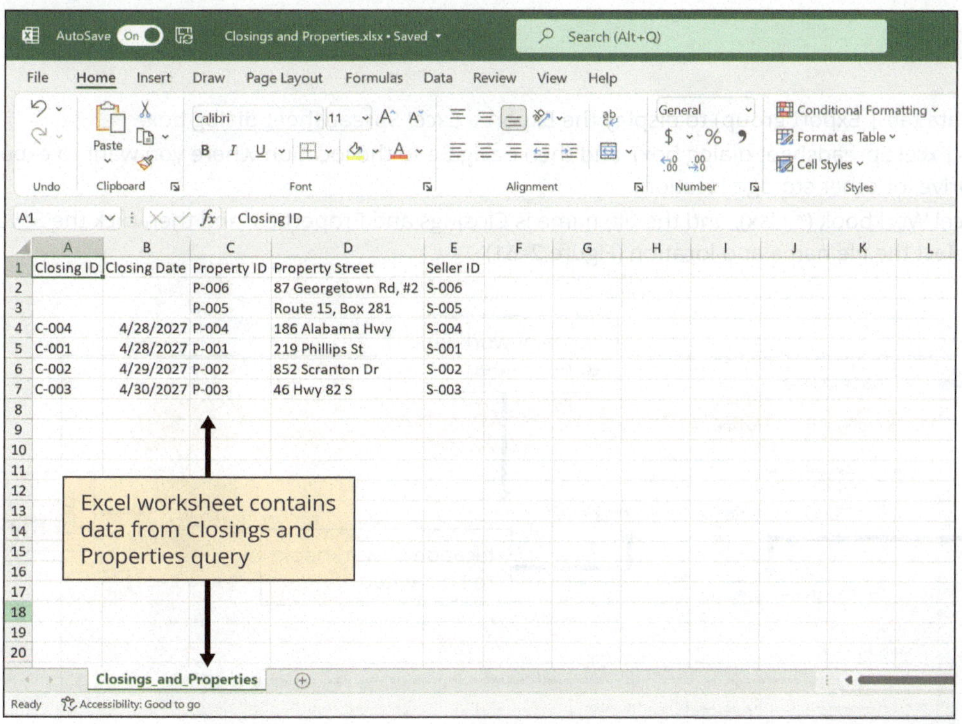

Figure 2–59

To Export Data to Excel

For Partners paralegals to make the Closings and Properties query available to Excel users, they need to export the data. To export data to Excel, select the table or query to be exported and then click the Excel button in the Export group on the External Data tab. The following steps export the Closings and Properties query to Excel and save the export steps. Why save the export steps? By saving the export steps, you could easily repeat the export process whenever you like without going through all the steps. You can then use the saved steps to export data in the future by clicking the Saved Exports button (External Data tab | Export group) and then selecting the steps you saved.

1

- If necessary, click the Closings and Properties query in the Navigation Pane to select it.
- Click External Data on the ribbon to display the External Data tab (Figure 2–60).

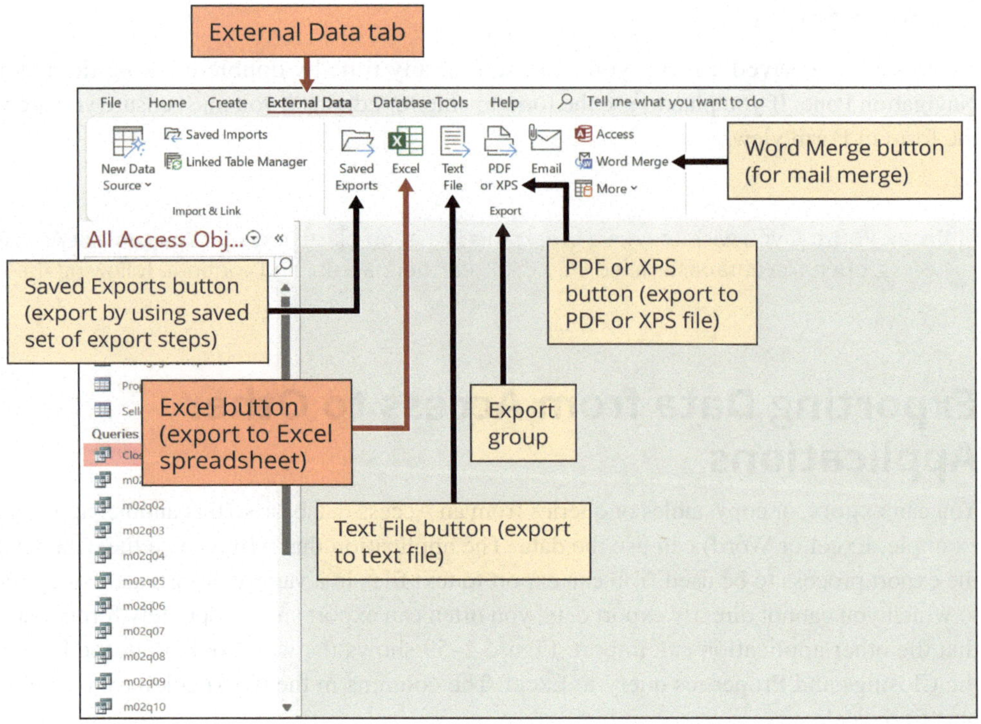

Figure 2–60

2

- Click the Excel button (External Data tab | Export group) to display the Export – Excel Spreadsheet dialog box.
- Click the Browse button (Export – Excel Spreadsheet dialog box), and then navigate to the location where you want to export the query (your hard drive, OneDrive, or other storage location).
- Confirm that the file format is Excel Workbook (*.xlsx), and the file name is Closings and Properties, and then click the Save button (File Save dialog box) to select the file name and location (Figure 2–61).

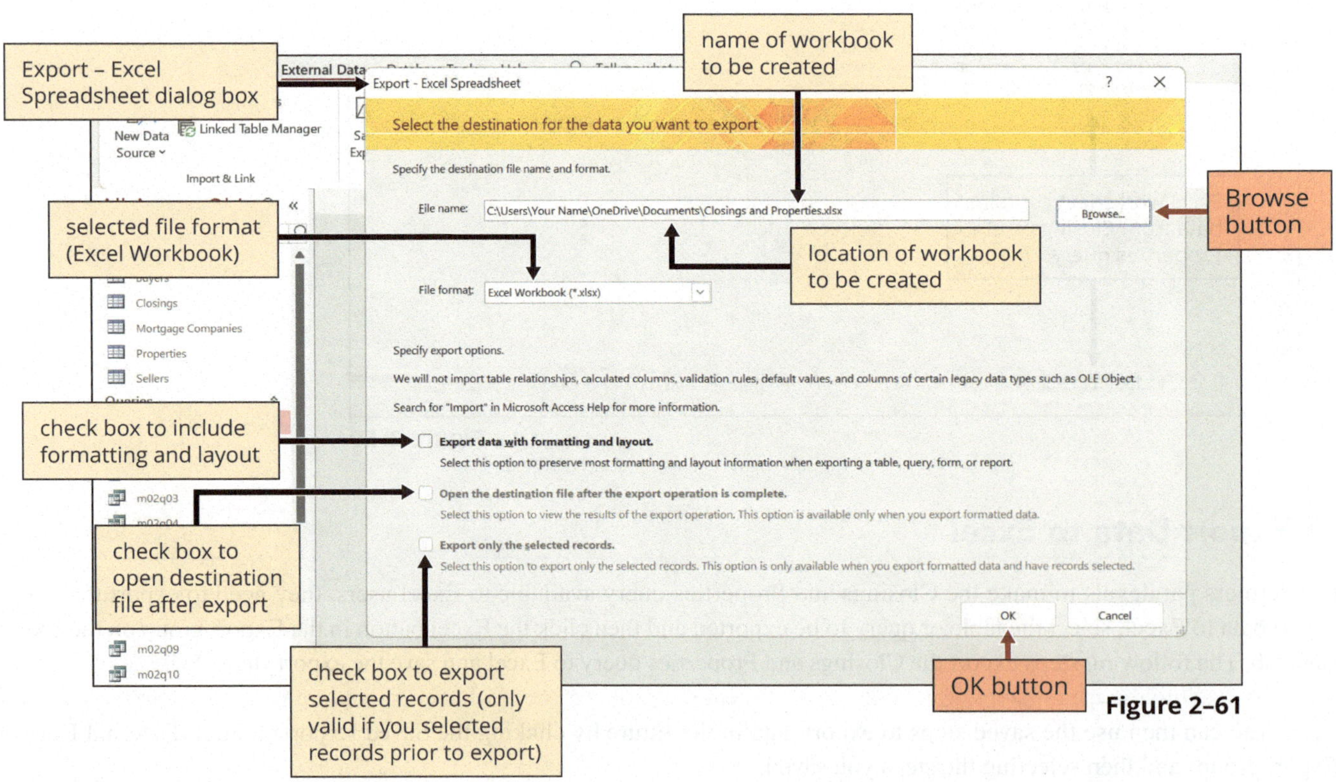

Figure 2–61

Q&A Did I need to browse?

No. You could type the appropriate file path location.

Could I change the name of the file?

You could change it. Simply replace the current file name with the one you want.

What if the file I want to export already exists?

Access will indicate that the file already exists and ask if you want to replace it. If you click Yes, the file you export will replace the old file. If you click No, you must either change the name of the export file, change its location, or cancel the process.

3

- Click OK (Export – Excel Spreadsheet dialog box) to export the data (Figure 2–62).

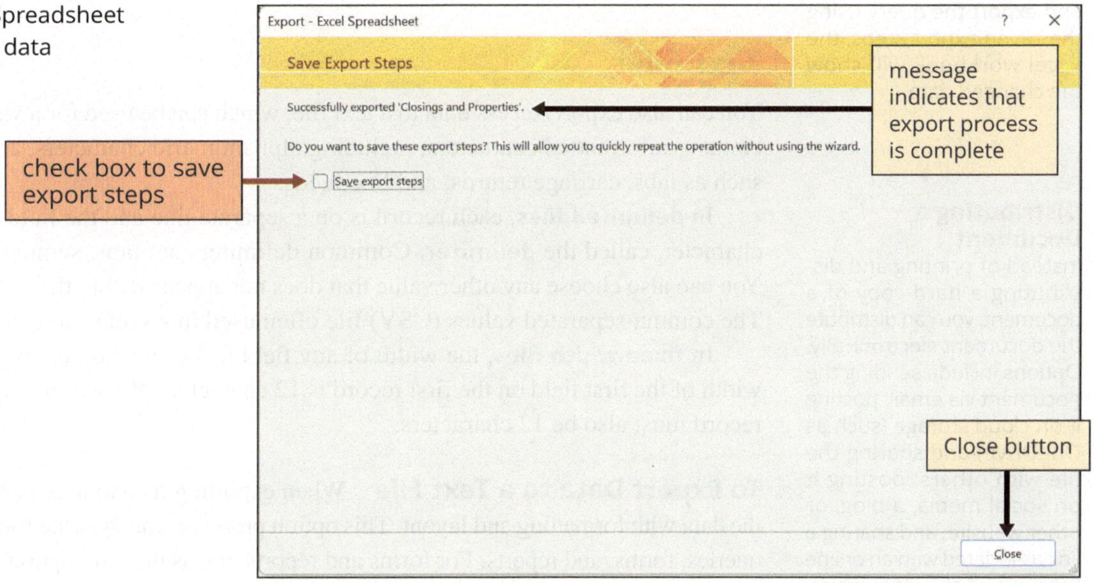

Figure 2–62

4

- Click the 'Save export steps' check box (Export – Excel Spreadsheet dialog box) and then click the Save Export button that appears (Figure 2–63).

Q&A How could I reuse the export steps?

You can use these steps to export data in the future by clicking the Saved Exports button (External Data tab | Export group) and then selecting the steps you saved.

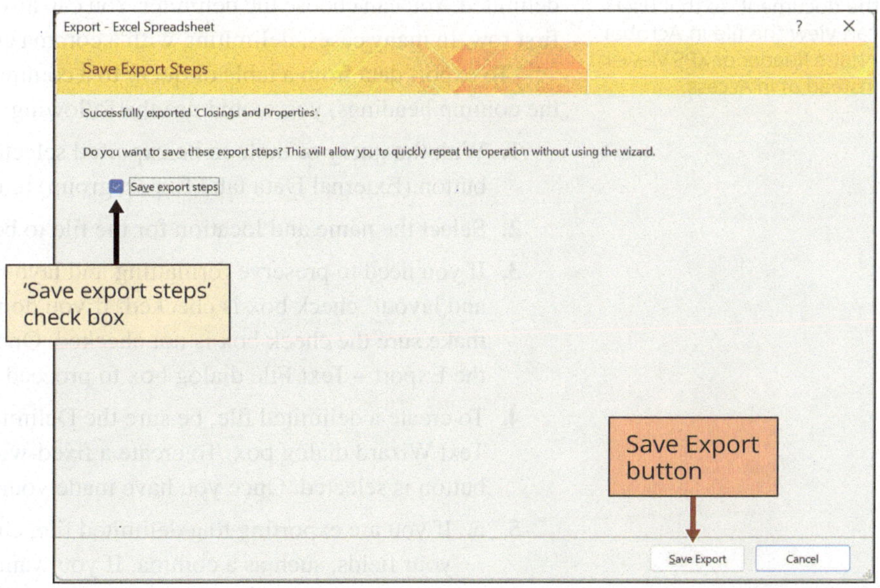

Figure 2–63

Other Ways

1. Right-click database object in Navigation Pane, point to Export, choose export format to export object

BTW
Saving Export Steps
Because query results are based on the data in the underlying tables, a change to an underlying table would result in a new query result. For example, if the closing date for a property changed from 4/28/2027 to 4/30/2027, the change would be made in the Closings table. If you run the Closings and Properties query again and export the query using the saved export steps, the Excel workbook will show the changed date.

BTW
Distributing a Document
Instead of printing and distributing a hard copy of a document, you can distribute the document electronically. Options include sending the document via email; posting it on cloud storage (such as OneDrive) and sharing the file with others; posting it on social media, a blog, or other website; and sharing a link associated with an online location of the document. You also can create and share a PDF or XPS image of the document, so that users can view the file in Acrobat Adobe Reader or XPS Viewer instead of in Access.

To Export Data to Word It is not possible to export data from Access to the standard Word format. It is possible, however, to export the data as an RTF file, which Word can open. To export data from a query or table to an RTF file, you would use the following steps.

1. With the query or table to be exported selected in the Navigation Pane, click the More button (External Data tab | Export group) and then click Word on the More menu to display the Export – RTF File dialog box.
2. Navigate to the location in which to save the file and assign a file name.
3. Click the Save button, and then click OK to export the data.
4. Save the export steps if you want, or simply click Close in the Export – RTF File dialog box to close the dialog box without saving the export steps.

Text Files

You can also export Access data to a text file, which can be used for a variety of purposes. Text files contain unformatted characters, including alphanumeric characters, and some special characters, such as tabs, carriage returns, and line feeds.

In **delimited files**, each record is on a separate line and the fields are separated by a special character, called the **delimiter**. Common delimiters are tabs, semicolons, commas, and spaces. You can also choose any other value that does not appear within the field contents as the delimiter. The comma-separated values (CSV) file often used in Excel is an example of a delimited file.

In **fixed-width files**, the width of any field is the same on every record. For example, if the width of the first field on the first record is 12 characters, the width of the first field on every other record must also be 12 characters.

To Export Data to a Text File When exporting data to a text file, you can choose to export the data with formatting and layout. This option preserves much of the formatting and layout in tables, queries, forms, and reports. For forms and reports, this is the only option for exporting to a text file.

If you do not need to preserve the formatting, you can choose either delimited or fixed-width as the format for the exported file. The most common option, especially if formatting is not an issue, is delimited. You can choose the delimiter. You can also choose whether to include field names on the first row. In many cases, delimiting with a comma and including the field names is a good choice.

To export data from a table or query to a comma-delimited file in which the first row contains the column headings, you would use the following steps.

1. With the query or table to be exported selected in the Navigation Pane, click the Text File button (External Data tab | Export group) to display the Export – Text File dialog box.
2. Select the name and location for the file to be created.
3. If you need to preserve formatting and layout, be sure the 'Export data with formatting and layout' check box is checked. If you do not need to preserve formatting and layout, make sure the check box is not checked. Once you have made your selection, click OK in the Export – Text File dialog box to proceed to the Export Text Wizard.
4. To create a delimited file, be sure the Delimited option button is selected in the Export Text Wizard dialog box. To create a fixed-width file, be sure the Fixed Width option button is selected. Once you have made your selection, click the Next button.
5. a. If you are exporting to a delimited file, choose the delimiter that you want to separate your fields, such as a comma. If you want to include field names on the first row, click the 'Include Field Names on First Row' check box. If you want to select a text qualifier, select it in the Text Qualifier list. When you have made your selections, click the Next button.

   b. If you are exporting to a fixed-width file, review the position of the vertical lines that separate your fields. If any lines are not positioned correctly, follow the directions on the screen to reposition them. When you have finished, click the Next button.

6. Click the Finish button to export the data.
7. Save the export steps if you want, or simply click Close in the Export – Text File dialog box to close the dialog box without saving the export steps.

To Import a Table

Partners Law Firm requires additional data to be able to run some of its required queries. As you learned previously, you can import data from external sources. The following steps import the Closing Fees table from the Partners Extra Tables database.

1

- Open the database, Support_AC_02_Partners-Extra-Tables.accdb, which is located in the Data Files folder. Enable the content. View the Closing Fees table to see what information is included. Close the Closing Fees table, and close the Extra Tables database.

2

- In the Partners database, click the 'New Data Source button' (External Data tab | Import & Link group).
- Click From Database in the New Data Source menu, and then click Access to display the Get External Data - Access Database dialog box.

3

- Click the Browse button and navigate to your storage location for the file, Support_AC_02_Partners-Extra-Tables.accdb.
- Select Support_AC_02_Partners-Extra-Tables.accdb, and then click the Open button to select this database as the data source.

4

- If necessary, click the 'Import tables, queries, forms, reports, macros, and modules into the current database' option to indicate how and where to store the data in the current database.
- Click OK to display the Import Objects dialog box.

5

- If necessary, click the Tables tab (Import Objects dialog box).
- Select the Closing Fees table to indicate the object to import, and then click OK to import the table.

6

- Close the Get External Data - Access Database dialog box without saving the import steps.
- Confirm the Closing Fees table is now listed as a table object in the Navigation Pane.

Calculations

If a special calculation is required for a query, you need to determine whether the calculation is an **individual record calculation** (for example, adding the values in two fields for one record) or a **group calculation** (for example, finding the total of the values in a particular field on all the records).

Partners paralegals might want to know the total real estate commissions assigned in the Closing Fees table (for the buying and selling agents) for each closing. This would seem to pose a problem because the table does not include a field for total cost. You can calculate it, however, because the total amount is equal to the sum of both listed commissions. A field that can be computed from other fields is called a **calculated field** or a **computed field** and is not usually included in the table. Including it introduces the possibility for errors in the table. If the value in the field does not happen to match the results of the calculation, the data is inconsistent. A calculated field is an individual record calculation because each calculation only involves fields in a single record.

Partners paralegals might also want to calculate the average attorney fees for all closings. This type of calculation is called a group calculation because each calculation involves groups of records. A group calculation can apply to all records from the source table or to only a subset of records.

To Use a Calculated Field in a Query

If you need a calculated field in a query, you enter a name (also called an alias) for the calculated field, a colon, and then the calculation in one of the columns in the Field row of the query's design grid. Any fields included in the expression must be enclosed in square brackets ([ ]). For example, for the total amount, you will type Total Cost:[Quantity]*[Cost] as the expression.

You can use addition (+), subtraction (-), multiplication (*), or division (/) in calculations. If you have multiple calculations in an expression, you can include parentheses to indicate which calculations should be done first.

You can type the expression directly into the Field row in Design view. The preferred method, however, is to select the column in the Field row and then use the Zoom command on its shortcut menu. When Access displays the Zoom dialog box, you can enter the expression. **Why use the Zoom command?** You will not be able to see the entire entry in the Field row, because the space available is not large enough.

The following steps create a query that Partners paralegals will be able to use to obtain total real estate commissions for each closing, by adding the selling agent's commission and the buying agent's commission, which is a calculated field.

1

- Create a query using the Closing Fees table.
- Add the Settlement Sheet ID, Closing ID, Selling Agent Commission, and Buying Agent Commission fields to the query.
- Right-click the Field row in the first empty column in the design grid to display a shortcut menu (Figure 2–64).

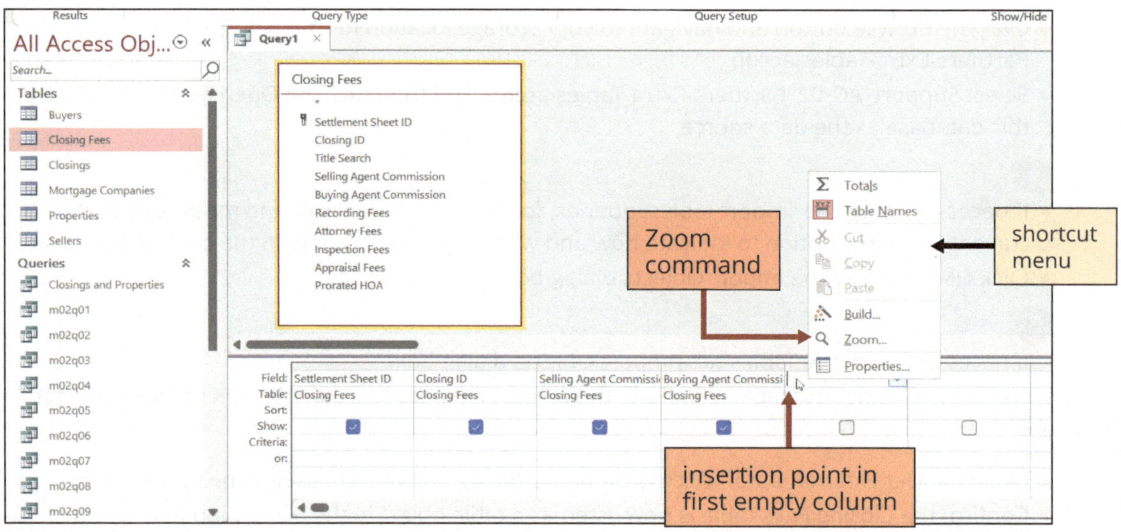

Figure 2–64

2

- Click Zoom on the shortcut menu to display the Zoom dialog box.
- Type **Total Commission:[Selling Agent Commission]+[Buying Agent Commission]** in the Zoom dialog box (Figure 2–65) to enter the expression.

Q&A Do I always need to put square brackets around field names?

If the field name does not contain spaces, square brackets are technically not required. It is a good practice, however, to get in the habit of using the brackets in field calculations.

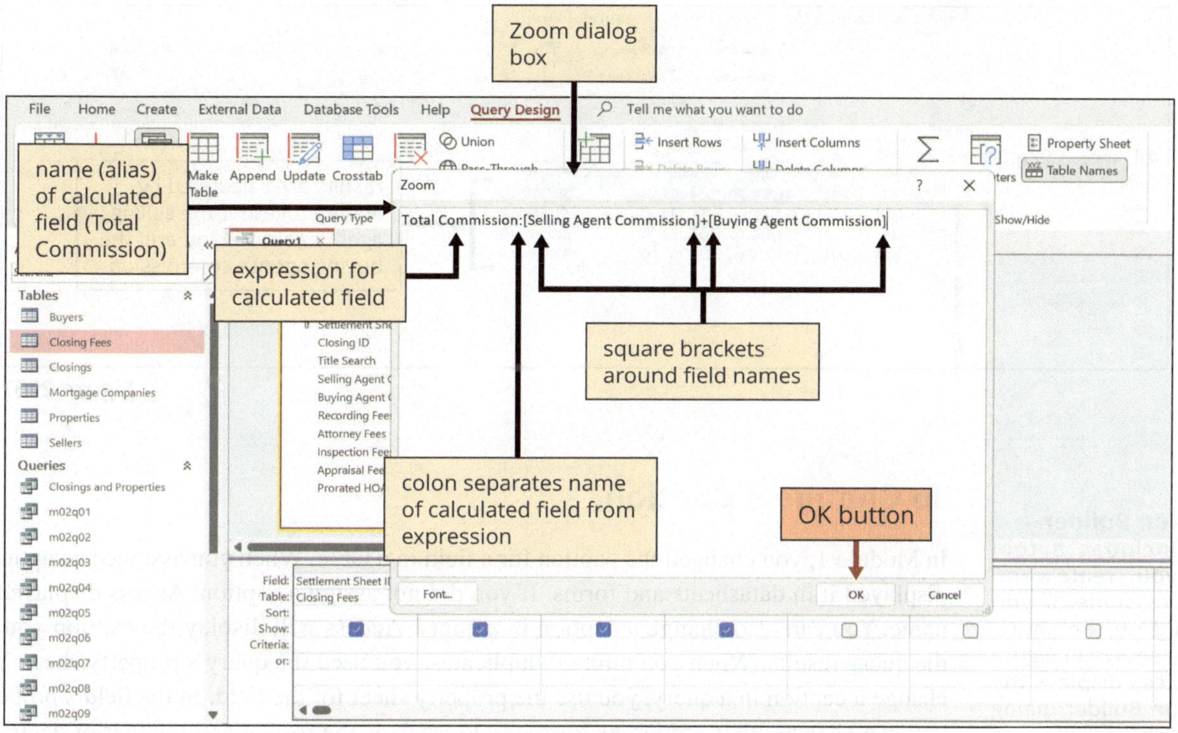

Figure 2–65

Other Ways

1. Press SHIFT+F2 to display Zoom dialog box

3

- Click OK (Zoom dialog box) to complete the expression and close the dialog box.
- Resize the Total Commission column to see all the content (Figure 2–66).

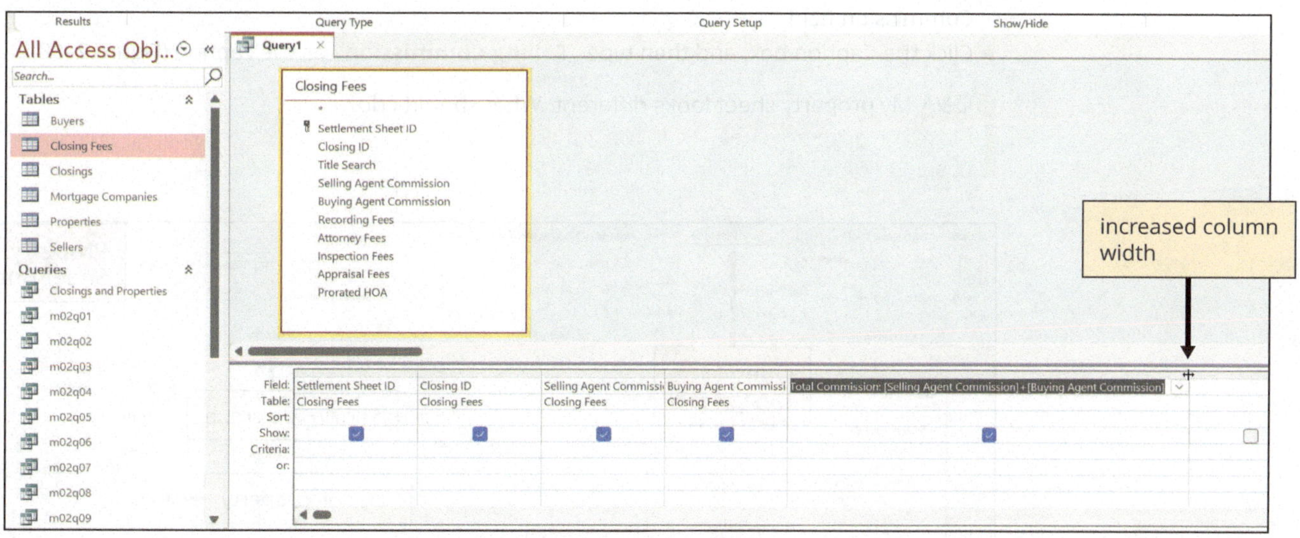

Figure 2–66

- Run the query to see the calculated results for the new Total Commission field.
- Resize all columns for best fit (Figure 2–67).
- **Experiment:** Return to Design view and try other expressions. In at least one case, omit the Total Commission and the colon. In at least one case, intentionally misspell a field name. In each case, run the query to see the effect of your changes. When finished, re-enter the original expression.

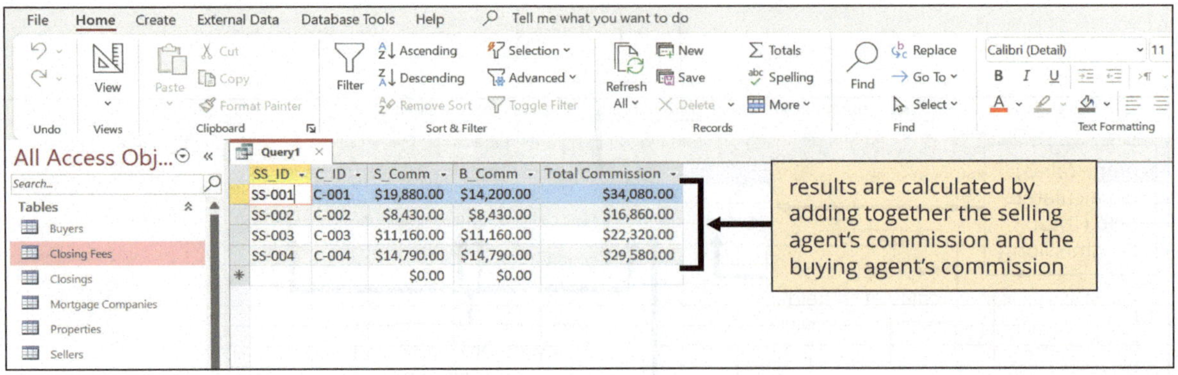

Figure 2–67

BTW

Expression Builder

Access includes a tool to help you create complex expressions. If you click Build on the shortcut menu shown in Figure 2–64, Access displays the Expression Builder dialog box, which includes an expression box, operator buttons, and expression elements. You can type parts of the expression directly and paste operator buttons and expression elements into the box. You also can use functions in expressions.

To Change a Caption

In Module 1, you changed the caption for a field in a table. When you assigned a caption, Access displayed it in datasheets and forms. If you did not assign a caption, Access displayed the field name. You can also change a caption in a query. Access will display the caption you assign in the query results. When you omitted duplicates, you used the query's property sheet. When you change a caption in a query, you use the property sheet for the field. In the field's property sheet, you can change other properties for the field, such as the format and number of decimal places. The following steps change the caption of each commission field to better identify which agent is being paid. *Why? These changes give more descriptive, yet very readable, column headings for the fields.* The steps also save the query with a new name.

1

- Return to Design view.
- If necessary, click Query Design on the ribbon to display the Query Design tab.
- Click the Selling Agent Commission field in the design grid, and then click the Property Sheet button (Query Design tab | Show/Hide group) to display the properties for the Selling Agent Commission field.
- Click the Caption box, and then type **Selling Commission** as the caption (Figure 2–68).

Q&A My property sheet looks different. What should I do?

Close the property sheet and repeat this step, making sure to select the correct field in the design grid before clicking the Property Sheet button.

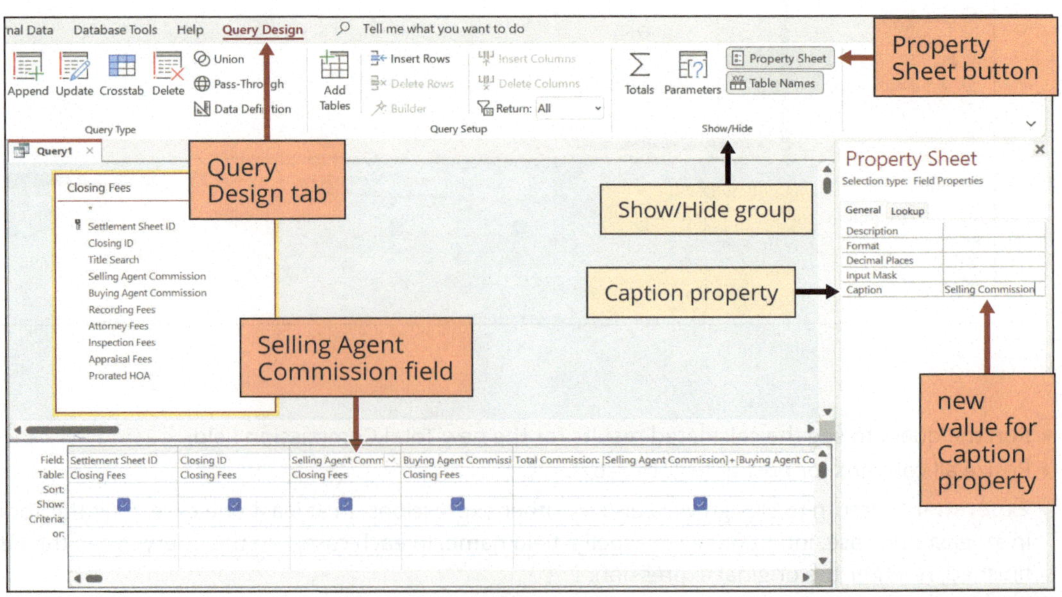

Figure 2–68

2

- Click the Buying Agent Commission field in the design grid to view its properties in the Property Sheet.
- Click the Caption box, and then type **Buying Commission** as the caption.
- Close the Property Sheet by clicking the Property Sheet button a second time.
- Run the query.
- Resize the query columns for best fit (Figure 2–69).

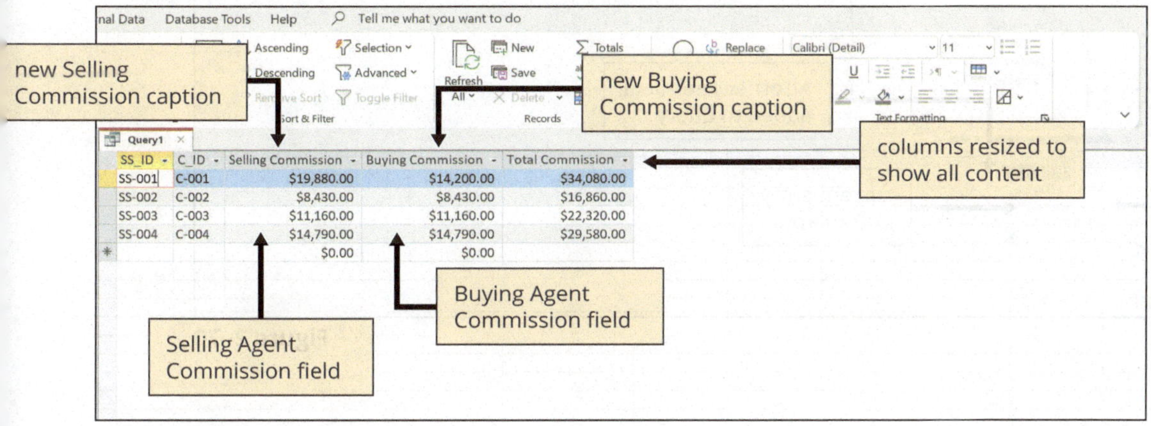

Figure 2–69

3

- Save the query as **m02q13**.
- Close the query.

Other Ways

1. Right-click field in design grid, click Properties to open Property Sheet pane

To Calculate Statistics

For group calculations, Microsoft Access supports several built-in statistics: COUNT (count of the number of records), SUM (total), AVG (average), MAX (largest value), MIN (smallest value), STDEV (standard deviation), VAR (variance), FIRST (first value), and LAST (last value). These statistics are called aggregate functions. An **aggregate function** is a function that performs some mathematical function against a group of records. To use an aggregate function in a query, you include it in the Total row in the design grid. In order to do so, you must first include the Total row by clicking the Totals button on the Design tab. **Why?** The Total row usually does not appear in the grid. Statistical calculations are performed regularly in Access queries by some, but not all learners. So, the process for these calculations requires extra steps.

The following steps create a new query for the Closing Fees table. The steps include the Total row in the design grid, and then calculate the average cost for all attorney fees.

1

- Create a new query using the Closing Fees table.
- Click the Totals button (Query Design tab | Show/Hide group) to include the Total row in the design grid.
- Add the Attorney Fees field to the query (Figure 2–70).

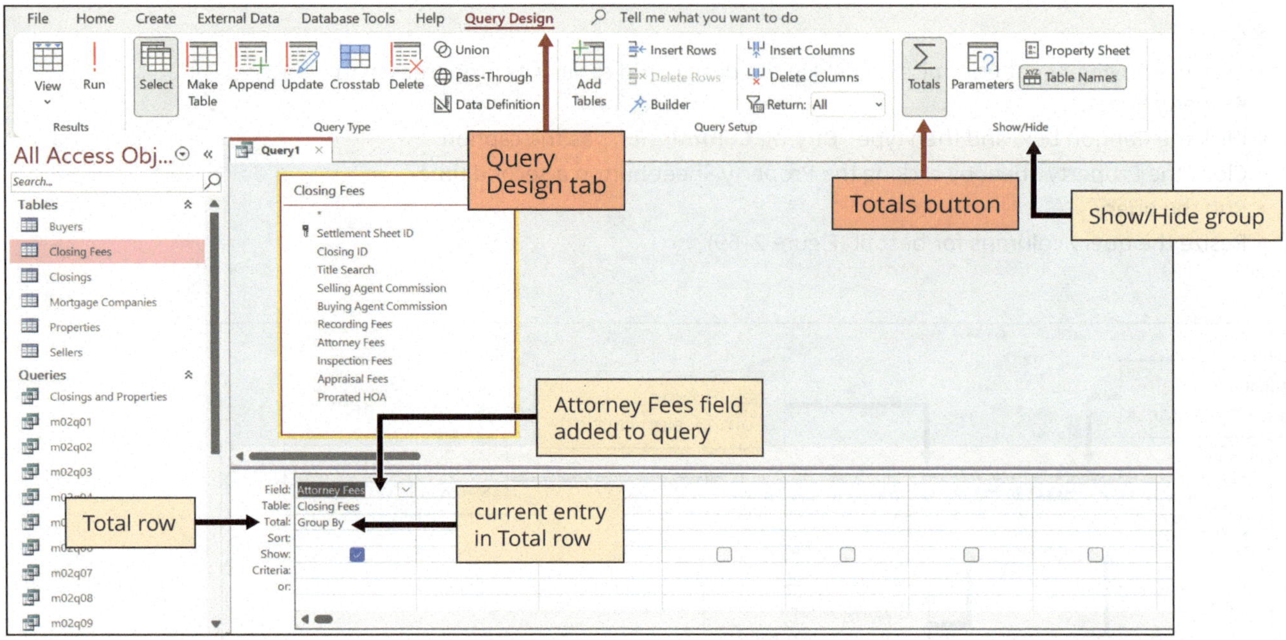

Figure 2–70

2

- Click the Total row in the Attorney Fees column to display the Total arrow.
- Click the Total arrow to display the Total list (Figure 2–71).

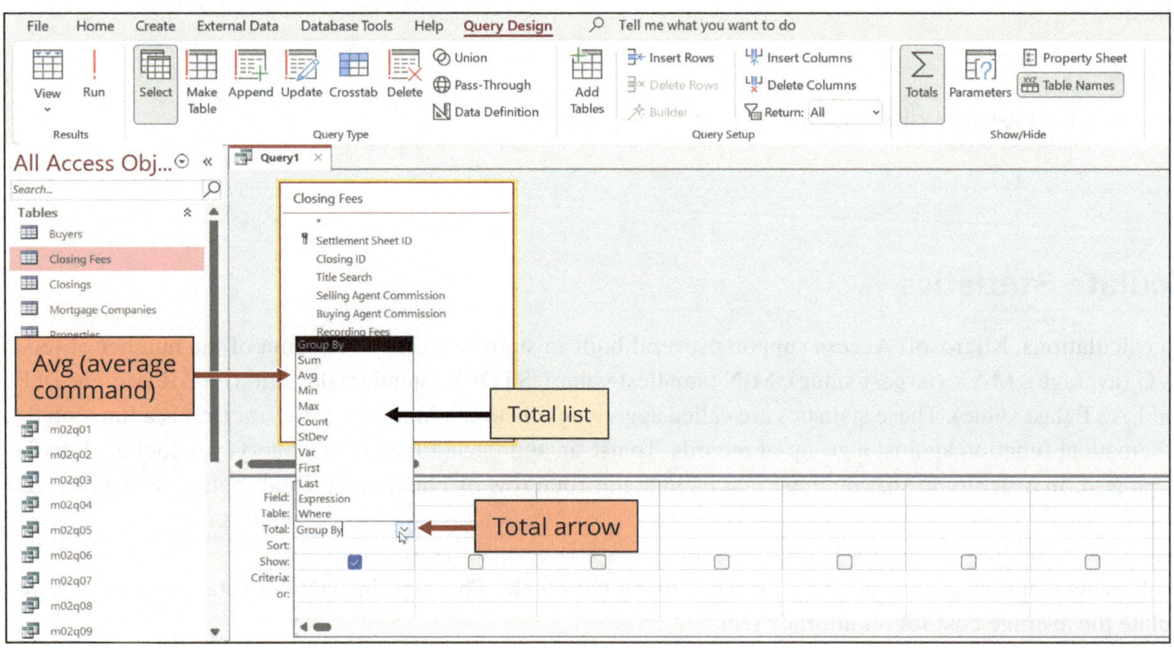

Figure 2–71

3

- Click Avg to select the calculation that Access is to perform (Figure 2–72).
- Run the query (Figure 2–73).
- **Experiment:** Return to Design view and try other aggregate functions. In each case, run the query to see the effect of your selection. When finished, select Avg once again.

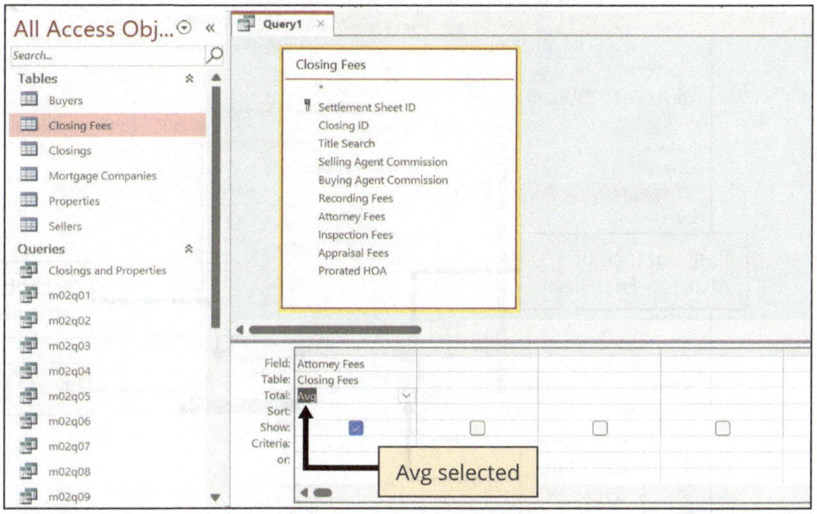

Figure 2–72

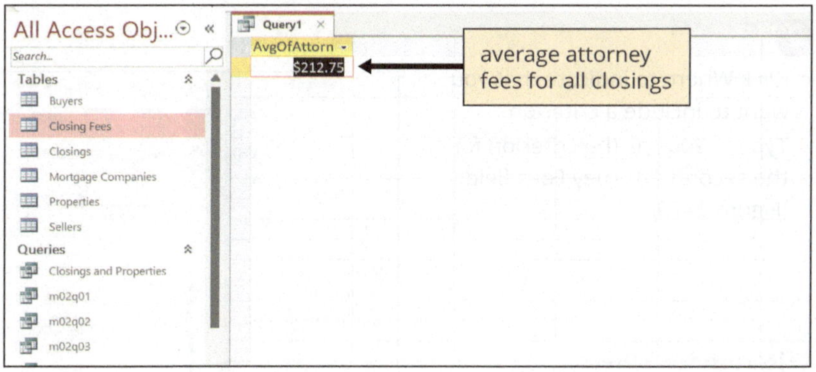

Figure 2–73

To Use Criteria in Calculating Statistics

Sometimes calculating statistics for all the records in the table is appropriate. In other cases, however, you will need to calculate the statistics for only those records that satisfy certain criteria. Notice in the previous query that the average is skewed lower than it should be because one of the clients is a family member and is paying a lower-than-normal fee. **Why?** Including a criterion that only includes records where the attorney fee is more than $200 will yield a more accurate result. To enter a criterion in a field, first you select Where as the entry in the Total row for the field, and then enter the criterion in the Criteria row. Access uses the word, Where, to indicate that you will enter a criterion. The following steps use this technique to calculate the average attorney fees where the fee is more than $200. The steps also save the query.

1

- Return to Design view.
- Include the Attorney Fees field again, this time in the second column in the design grid. The Attorney Fees field will be listed twice in the design grid.
- Click the Total row in the second Attorney Fees column.
- Click the Total arrow in the second Attorney Fees column to display the Total list (Figure 2–74).

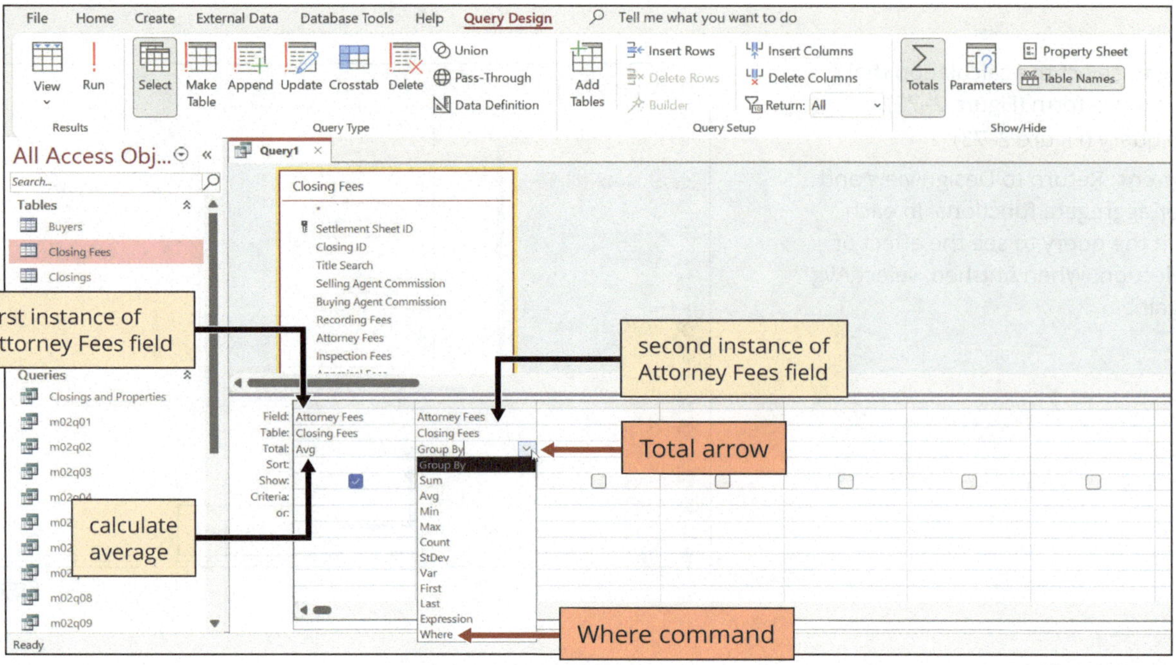

Figure 2–74

2

- Click Where to indicate that you want to include a criterion.
- Type **>200** as the criterion for the second Attorney Fees field (Figure 2–75).

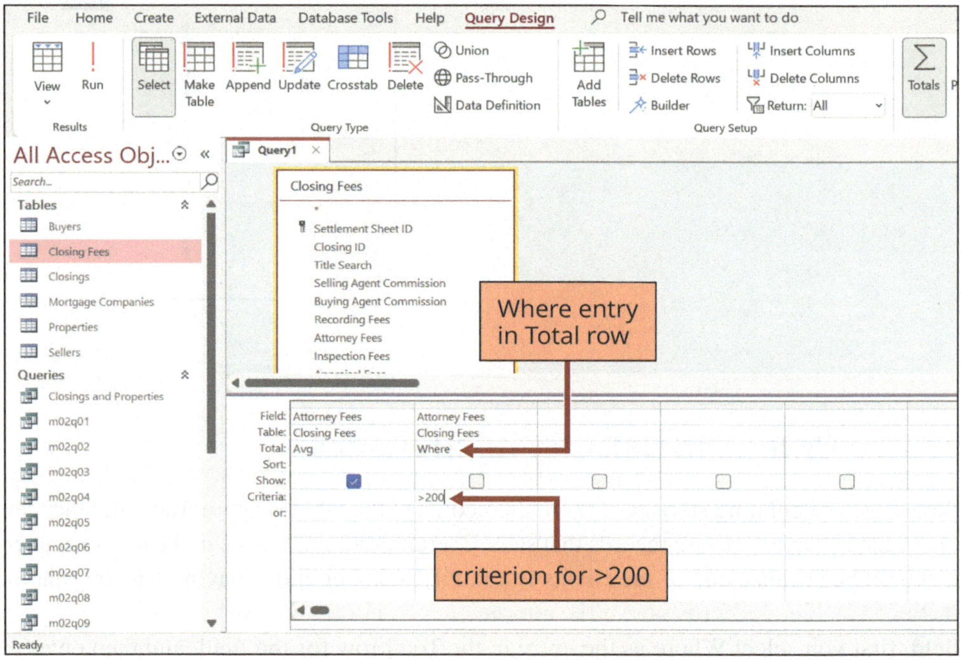

Figure 2–75

BTW

Criterion for Where

Access treats the criterion for the Where object just as it would for any criterion in a field. For example, you could also use a wildcard rather than spelling out the entire criterion, such as Part* for Partners Law Firm. Access recognizes and utilizes the wildcard to find the desired result.

3

- Run the query (Figure 2–76) to display the average attorney fees where the fee is more than $200.

4

- Save the query as **m02q14**.
- Close the query.

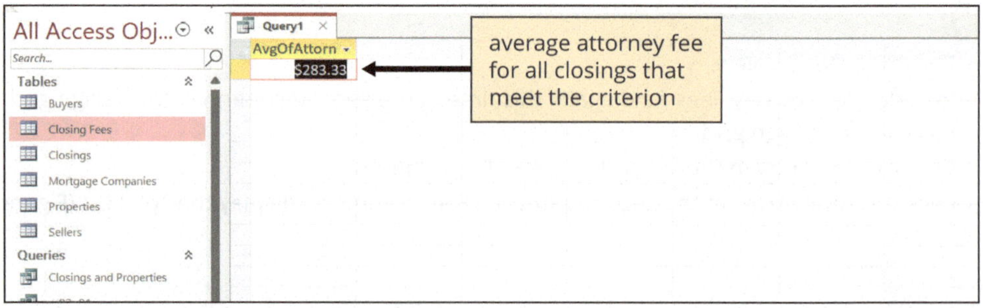

Figure 2–76

To Use Grouping

Statistics are often used in combination with grouping; that is, statistics are calculated for groups of records. For example, Partners paralegals could calculate the average new loan amount for each mortgage company, which would require the average for the mortgage company specified in the criteria. **Grouping** means creating groups of records that share some common characteristic. In grouping new loans by mortgage company, for example, the new loans with Atlas Mortgage would form one group, the new loans with Cheshire Mortgage would form a second group, and the new loans with County Mortgage would form a third group. The calculations are then made for each group. To indicate grouping in Access, select Group By as the entry in the Total row for the field to be used for grouping. Even though the entry indicates Group By, the mortgage companies will appear individually. **Why?** Access needs to know the field that you want to review the averages on, and it indicates this by the text Group By. Group By does not mean that it will group together all the mortgage companies, it just refers to looking at that particular group.

The following steps create a query that calculates the average new loan amount with each mortgage company involved in closings with Partners Law Firm. The steps also save the query.

1

- Create a query using the Closings table.
- Add the New Loan Amount and Purchasing Mortgage Company ID fields to the query.
- Click the Totals button (Query Design tab | Show/Hide group) to include the Total row in the design grid.
- Select Avg as the calculation in the Total row for the New Loan Amount field (Figure 2–77).

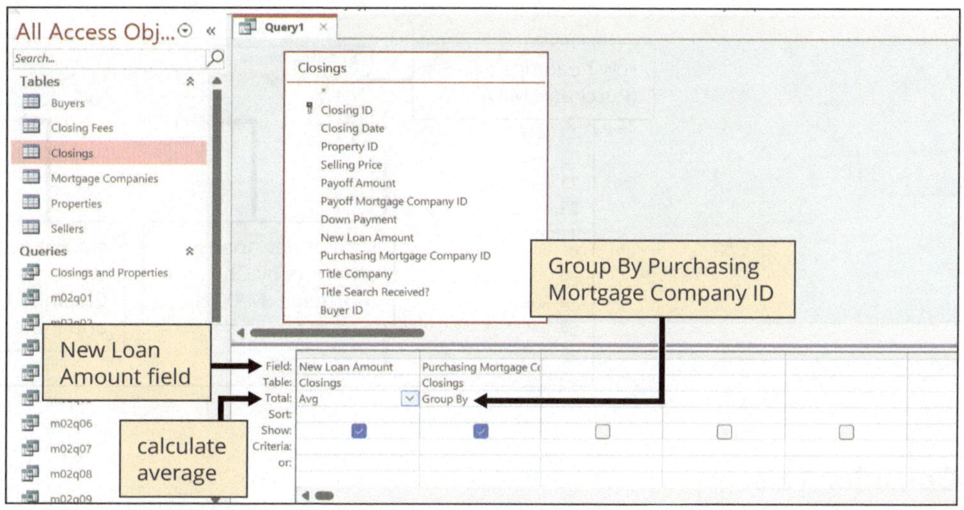

Figure 2–77

Q&A Why was it not necessary to change the entry in the Total row for the Purchasing Mortgage Company ID field?

Group By, which is the initial entry in the Total row when you add a field, is correct. Thus, you did not need to change the entry.

2

- Run the query (Figure 2–78).

3

- Save the query as **m02q15**.
- Close the query.

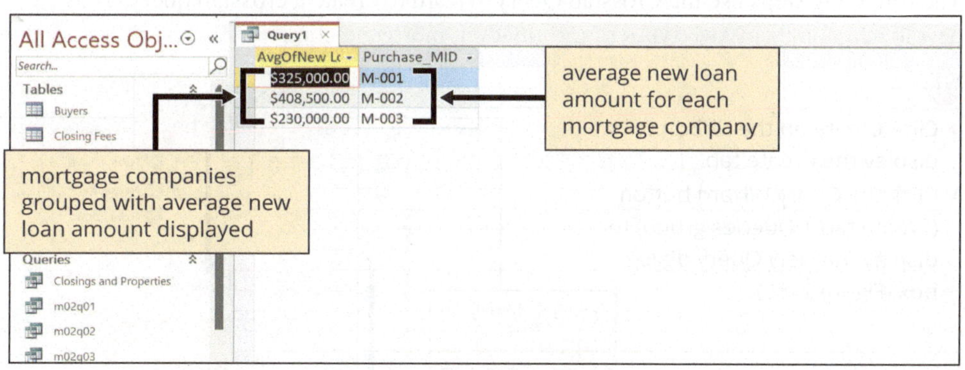

Figure 2–78

Crosstab Queries

A **crosstab query**, or simply, crosstab, calculates a statistic (for example, sum, average, or count) for data that is grouped by two different types of information. One of the types will appear down the side of the resulting datasheet, and the other will appear across the top. Crosstab queries are useful for summarizing data by category or group.

For example, if a query must summarize the sum of new loan amounts grouped by both mortgage company and title company, you could have mortgage company IDs as the row headings—that is, down the side. You could have title companies as the column headings—that is, across the top. The entries within the datasheet represent the total of new loan amounts. Figure 2–79 shows a crosstab in which the total of new loan amounts is grouped by both mortgage company ID and title company, with mortgage company IDs down the left side and title company names across the top. For example, the entry in the row labeled M-002 and in the column labeled Perfect Title represents the total of the new loan amounts by all closings using Perfect Title and Cheshire Mortgage (M-002).

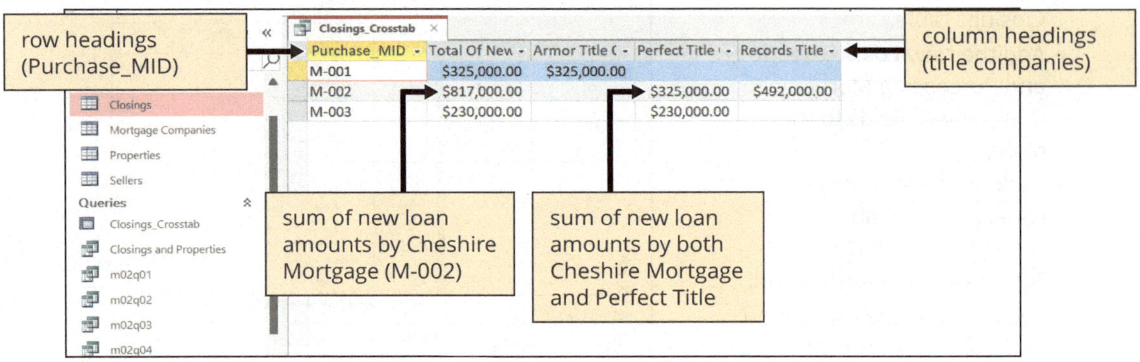

Figure 2–79

Consider This

How do you know when to use a crosstab query?

If data is to be grouped by two different types of information, you can use a crosstab query. You will need to identify the two types of information. One of the types will form the row headings and the other will form the column headings in the query results.

To Create a Crosstab Query

The following steps use the Crosstab Query Wizard to create a crosstab query. **Why?** Partners paralegals want to group data on new loan amounts by two types of information: mortgage company ID and title company.

1

- Click Create on the ribbon to display the Create tab.
- Click the Query Wizard button (Create tab | Queries group) to display the New Query dialog box (Figure 2–80).

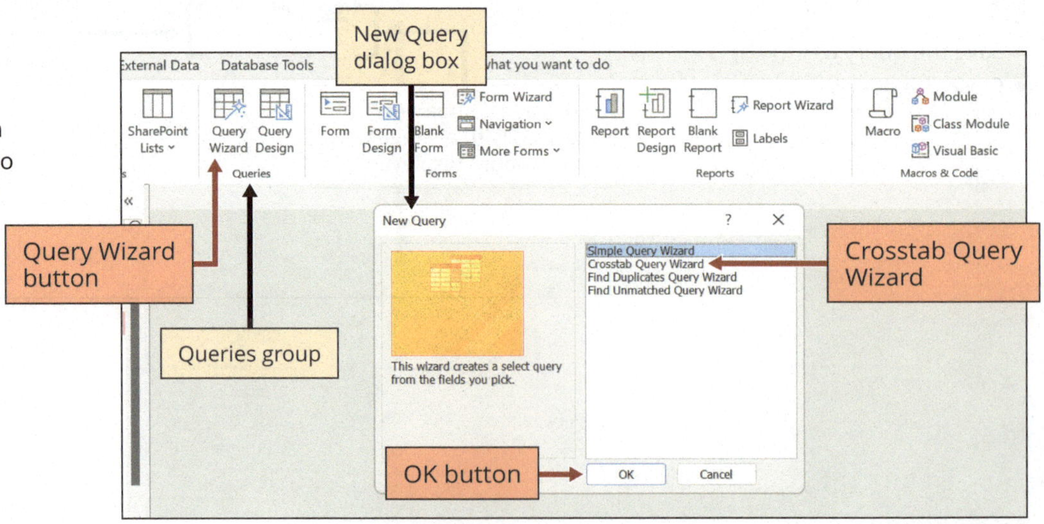

Figure 2–80

2

- Click Crosstab Query Wizard (New Query dialog box).
- Click OK to display the Crosstab Query Wizard dialog box (Figure 2–81).

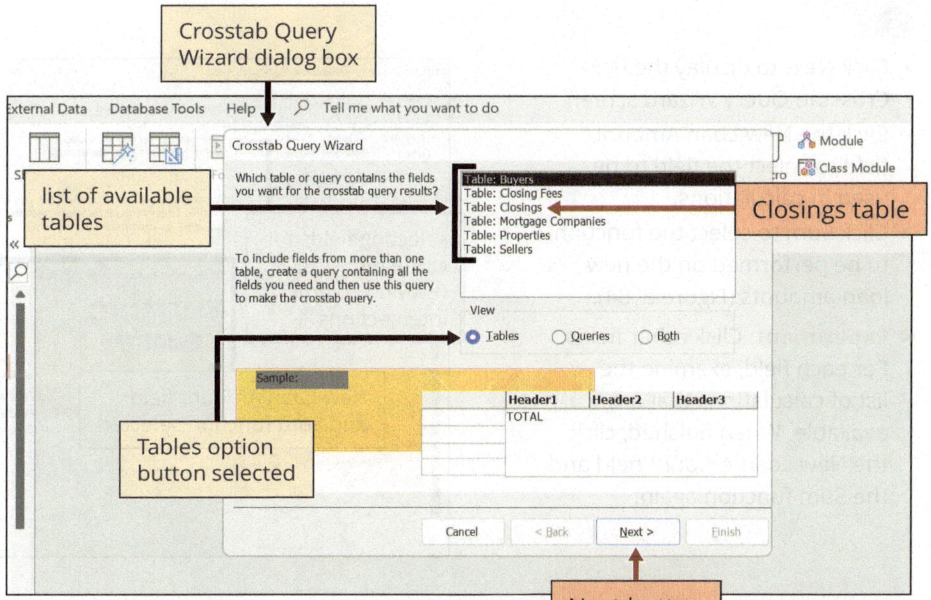

Figure 2–81

3

- With the Tables option button selected, click Table: Closings to select the Closings table, and then click the Next button to display the next Crosstab Query Wizard screen.
- Click the Purchasing Mortgage Company ID field, and then click the Add Field button to select the Purchasing Mortgage Company ID field for row headings (Figure 2–82).

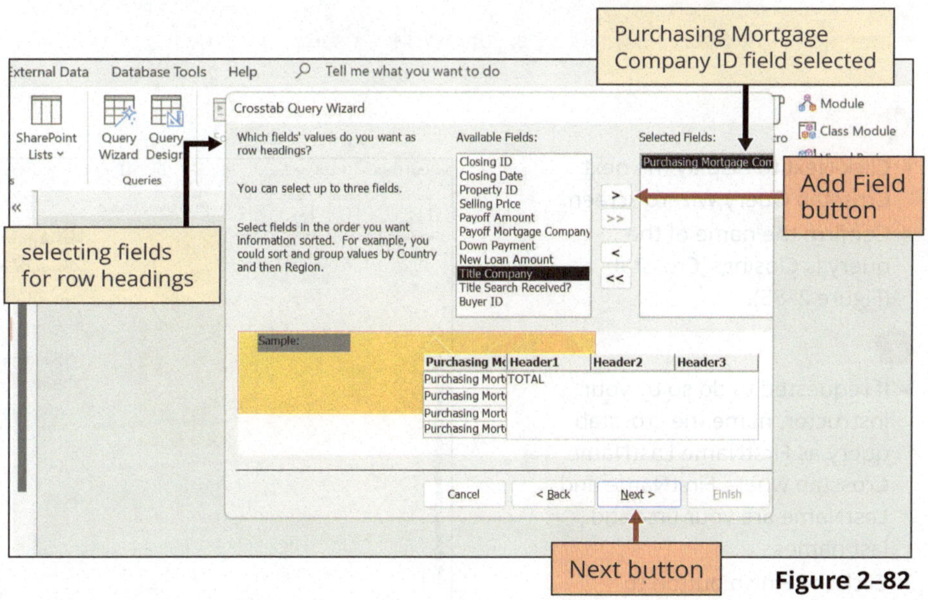

Figure 2–82

4

- Click the Next button to display the next Crosstab Query Wizard screen.
- Click the Title Company field to select the field for column headings (Figure 2–83).

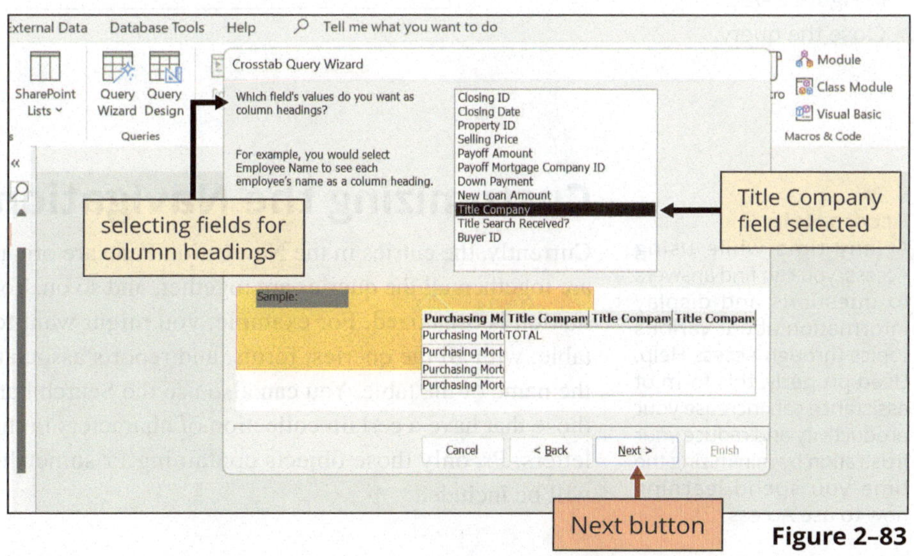

Figure 2–83

5

- Click Next to display the next Crosstab Query Wizard screen.
- Click the New Loan Amount field to select the field to be used in calculations.
- Click Sum to select the function to be performed on the new loan amounts (Figure 2–84).
- **Experiment:** Click other fields. For each field, examine the list of calculations that are available. When finished, click the New Loan Amount field and the Sum function again.

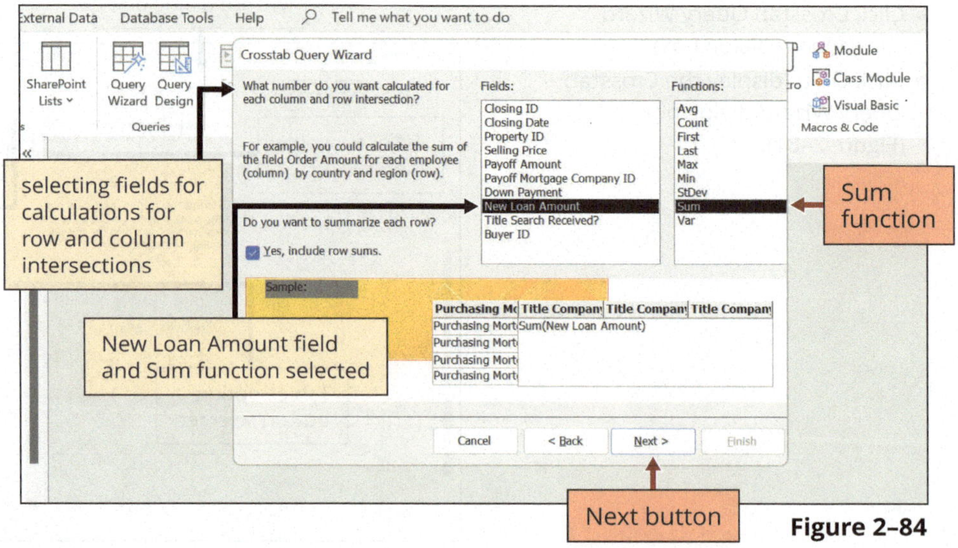

Figure 2–84

Q&A My list of functions is different. What did I do wrong?
Either you clicked the wrong field, or the New Loan Amount field has the wrong data type. For example, if you mistakenly assigned it the Short Text data type, you would not see Sum in the list of available calculations.

6

- Click Next to display the next Crosstab Query Wizard screen.
- Confirm the name of the query is Closings_Crosstab (Figure 2–85).

7

- If requested to do so by your instructor, name the crosstab query as FirstName LastName Crosstab where FirstName and LastName are your first and last names.
- Click the Finish button to produce the crosstab shown in Figure 2–79.
- Close the query.

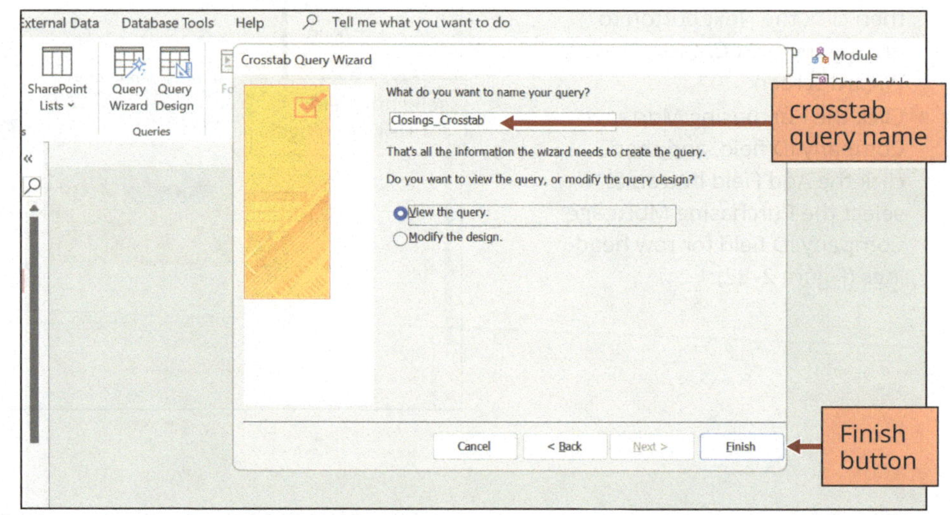

Figure 2–85

BTW
Access Help
At any time while using Access, you can find answers to questions and display information about various topics through Access Help. Used properly, this form of assistance can increase your productivity and reduce your frustration by minimizing the time you spend learning how to use Access.

Customizing the Navigation Pane

Currently, the entries in the Navigation Pane are organized by object type. That is, all the tables are together, all the queries are together, and so on. You might want to change the way the information is organized. For example, you might want to have the Navigation Pane organized by table, with all the queries, forms, and reports associated with a particular table appearing after the name of the table. You can also use the Search bar to restrict the objects that appear to only those that have a certain collection of characters in their name. For example, if you entered the letters, Pr, only those objects containing Pr somewhere within the name (such as Properties) will be included.

To Customize the Navigation Pane

The following steps change the organization of the Navigation Pane. They also use the Search bar to restrict the objects that appear. **Why?** Using the Search bar, you can reduce the number of objects that appear in the Navigation Pane and just show the ones in which you are interested.

1

- If necessary, click the 'Shutter Bar Open/Close Button' to open the Navigation Pane.
- Click the Navigation Pane arrow to display the Navigation Pane menu and then click 'Tables and Related Views' to organize the Navigation Pane by table rather than by object type (Figure 2–86).

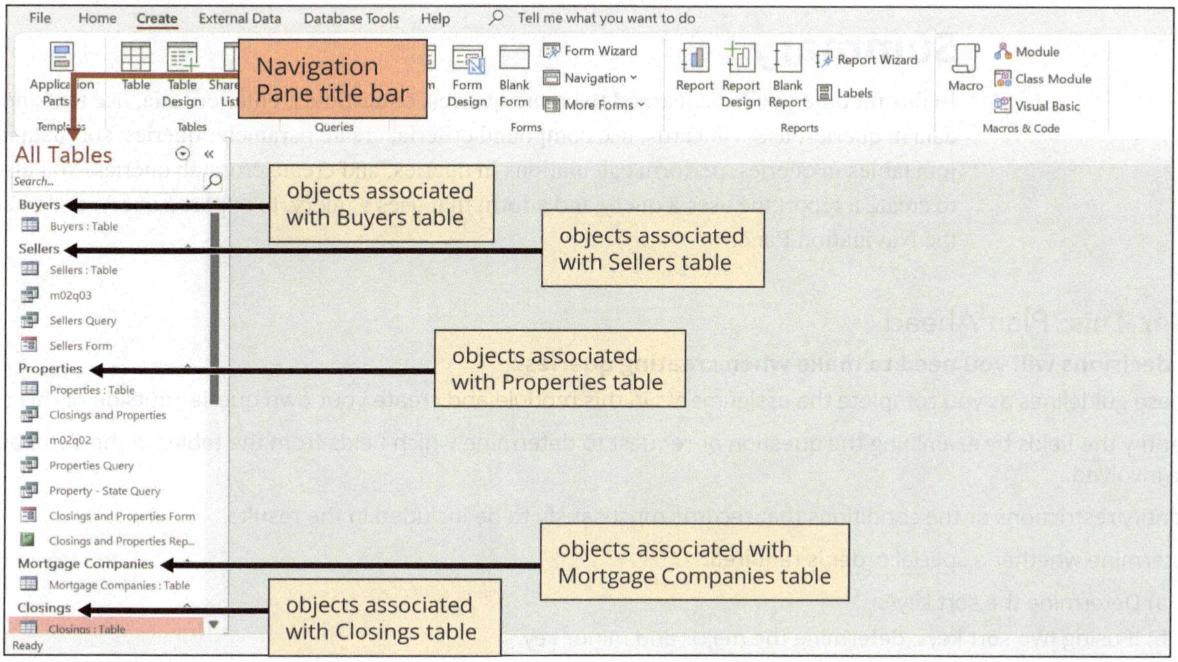

Figure 2–86

2

- Click the Navigation Pane arrow to display the Navigation Pane menu.
- Click Object Type to once again organize the Navigation Pane by object type.
- **Experiment:** Select different Navigate To Category options to see the effect of the option. With each option you select, select different Filter By Group options to see the effect of the filtering. When you have finished experimenting, select 'Object Type' for the Navigate To Category option and 'All Access Objects' for the Filter By Group option.
- If the Search bar does not appear, right-click the Navigation Pane and click Search Bar on the shortcut menu.
- Click in the Search box to produce an insertion point.
- Type **pr** as the search string to restrict the objects displayed to only those containing the desired string (Figure 2–87).

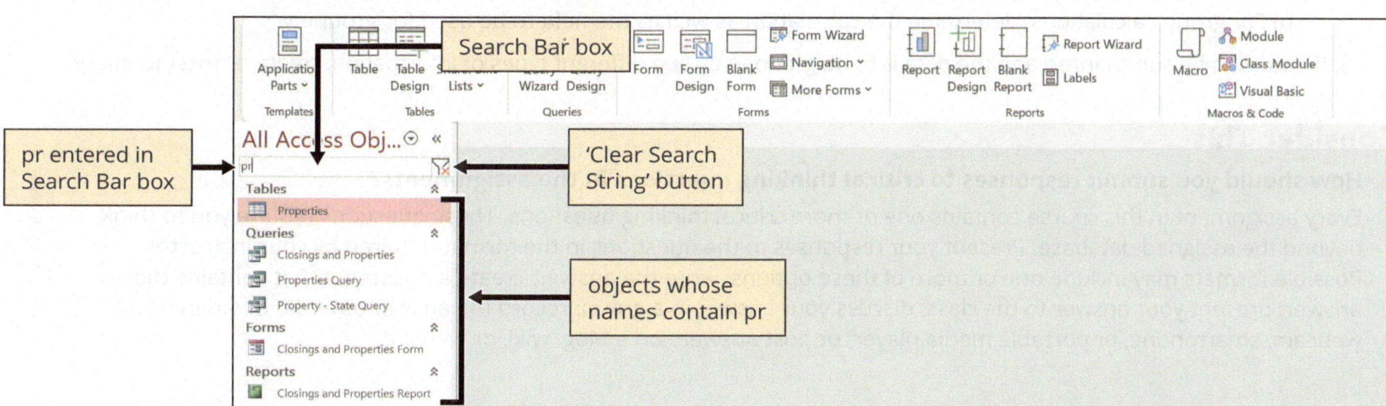

Figure 2–87

3

- Click the 'Clear Search String' button to remove the search string and redisplay all objects.

Q&A Did I have to click the button to redisplay all objects? Could I simply have erased the current string to achieve the same result?
You did not have to click the button. You could have used DEL or BACKSPACE to erase the current search string.

- If desired, sign out of your Microsoft account.
- sam Exit Access.

Summary

In this module you have learned to create queries, enter fields, enter criteria, use text and numeric data in queries, use wildcards, use compound criteria, create parameter queries, sort data in queries, join tables in queries, perform calculations in queries, and create crosstab queries. You also learned to create a report the uses a query and a form that uses a query, to export a query, and to customize the Navigation Pane.

Consider This: Plan Ahead

What decisions will you need to make when creating queries?

Use these guidelines as you complete the assignments in this module and create your own queries outside of this class.

1. Identify the fields by examining the question or request to determine which fields from the tables in the database are involved.
2. Identify restrictions or the conditions that records must satisfy to be included in the results.
3. Determine whether a special order is required.
   a) Determine the sort key(s).
   b) If using two sort keys, determine the major and minor key.
   c) Determine sort order. If there are no words to imply a particular order, you would typically use Ascending sort order.
   d) Determine restrictions, such as excluding duplicates.
4. Determine whether more than one table is required.
   a) Determine which tables to include.
   b) Determine the matching fields.
   c) Determine whether sorting is required.
   d) Determine restrictions.
   e) Determine join properties.
5. Determine whether calculations are required.
   a) For individual record calculations, determine the calculation and a name for the calculated field.
   b) For group calculations, determine the calculation as well as the field to be used for grouping.
6. If data is to be summarized and the data is to be grouped by two different types of information, create a crosstab query.

Consider This

How should you submit responses to critical thinking questions in the assignments?

Every assignment in this course contains one or more critical thinking questions. These questions require you to think beyond the assigned database. Present your responses to the questions in the format required by your instructor. Possible formats may include one or more of these options: write the answer; create a document that contains the answer; present your answer to the class; discuss your answer in a group; record the answer as audio or video using a webcam, smartphone, or portable media player; or post answers on a blog, wiki, or website.

Student Assignments

Apply Your Knowledge

Reinforce the skills and apply the concepts you learned in this module.

Using Wildcards in a Query, Creating a Parameter Query, Joining Tables, and Creating a Report

Note: To complete this assignment, you will be required to use the Data Files. Please contact your instructor for information about accessing the Data Files.

Instructions: Start Access. Open the database, SC_AC_02-2.accdb, which is located in the Data Files folder. Enable the content. The database was created by the new project manager at Build It Construction. Before she was hired, the owners kept a "mental list" of which subcontractor was hired for each construction project. When the new project manager started work, she realized this was inefficient and allowed for many mistakes, miscommunications, and delayed projects. She created a small database with a table for job sites, a table for subcontractors, and a query to produce a checklist she can use to track communications throughout each work week. The project manager has exported some payment information from another system. She needs you to add this data to her database. You will import the Accounting table, create some queries with this information, and create a report.

Perform the following tasks:

1. Save the database using the file name, SC_AC_02-Construction. Enable the content.
2. Import the Accounting table from the Support_AC_02_Construction-Extra-Tables.accdb database. Do not save the import steps.
3. Create a query using the Accounting table and add the SC # (stands for Subcontractor Number), Subcontractor Name, Amount Paid, and JS # (stands for Job Site Number) fields to the design grid. Sort the records in descending order by Amount Paid. Add a criterion for the JS # field that allows the user to enter a different job site number each time the query is run. Run the query and enter 112 as the job site number to test the query. Save the query as Apply 2 Step 3 Query. Close the query.
4. Create another query for the Accounting table and add the SC #, Subcontractor Name, and Current Due fields to the design grid. Add a criterion to find all subcontractors whose current due amount is less than $500. Run the query and then save it as Apply 2 Step 4 Query. Close the query.
5. Create a query that joins the Job Sites and Subcontractors tables. Add the Job Site Number, Owner, and City fields from the Job Sites table and the Subcontractor Number and Subcontractor Name fields from the Subcontractors table to the design grid. Sort the records in ascending order by Subcontractor Number and Job Site Number. Run the query and save it as Job Site-Subcontractor Query. **Note:** If any error messages appear, check the field types of the fields in the query tables and make changes as necessary. Close the query.
6. Create the report shown in Figure 2–88. The report uses the Job Site-Subcontractor Query.

   If requested to do so by your instructor, rename the Job Site-Subcontractor Report in the Navigation Pane as LastName-Subcontractor Report where LastName is your last name.
7. Submit the revised database, including all objects shown in the Navigation Pane in Figure 2–88, in the format specified by your instructor.

Continued on next page

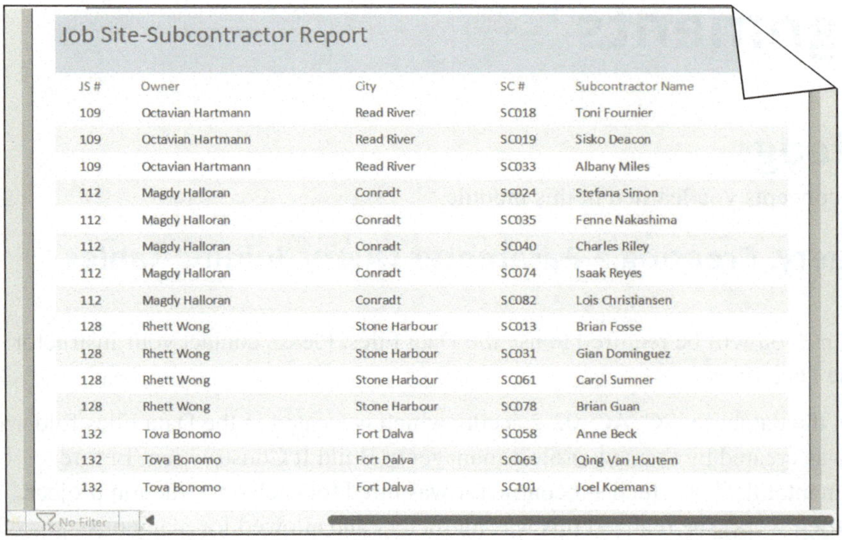

Job Site-Subcontractor Report

JS #	Owner	City	SC #	Subcontractor Name
109	Octavian Hartmann	Read River	SC018	Toni Fournier
109	Octavian Hartmann	Read River	SC019	Sisko Deacon
109	Octavian Hartmann	Read River	SC033	Albany Miles
112	Magdy Halloran	Conradt	SC024	Stefana Simon
112	Magdy Halloran	Conradt	SC035	Fenne Nakashima
112	Magdy Halloran	Conradt	SC040	Charles Riley
112	Magdy Halloran	Conradt	SC074	Isaak Reyes
112	Magdy Halloran	Conradt	SC082	Lois Christiansen
128	Rhett Wong	Stone Harbour	SC013	Brian Fosse
128	Rhett Wong	Stone Harbour	SC031	Gian Dominguez
128	Rhett Wong	Stone Harbour	SC061	Carol Sumner
128	Rhett Wong	Stone Harbour	SC078	Brian Guan
132	Tova Bonomo	Fort Dalva	SC058	Anne Beck
132	Tova Bonomo	Fort Dalva	SC063	Qing Van Houtem
132	Tova Bonomo	Fort Dalva	SC101	Joel Koemans

Figure 2–88

8. **Consider This:** What criteria would you enter in a query using the Mobile Phone field if you wanted to find all subcontractors whose phone numbers begin with the area code 405?

Extend Your Knowledge

Extend the skills you learned in this module and experiment with new skills. You may need to use Help to complete the assignment.

Creating Queries Using Criteria and Exporting a Query

Note: To complete this assignment, you will be required to use the Data Files. Please contact your instructor for information about accessing the Data Files.

Instructions: Start Access. Open the database, SC_AC_02-3.accdb, which is located in the Data Files folder, and enable the content. The Asset Management database provides a lending library database structure for lending out equipment to employees in various departments. You will enter some initial data, create a query, enter data in a form, and export a report.

Perform the following tasks:

1. Save the database using the file name, SC_AC_02_IT-Assets. Enable the content.
2. Enter the asset information shown in Figure 2–89 into the Assets List that appears when the database is opened.

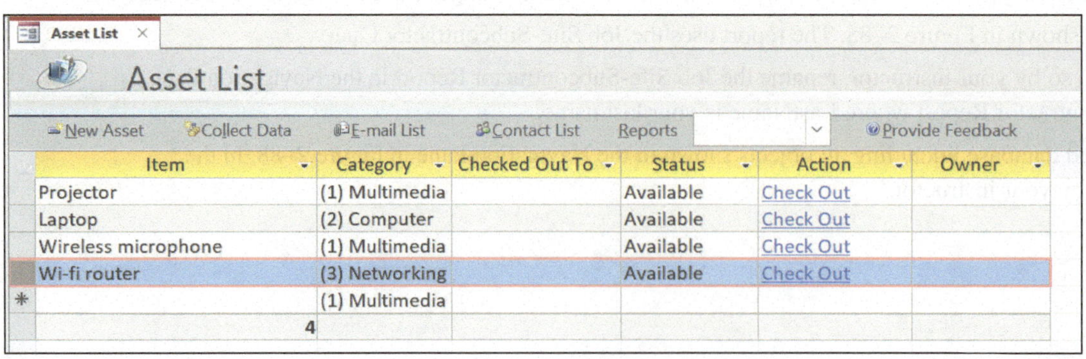

Item	Category	Checked Out To	Status	Action	Owner
Projector	(1) Multimedia		Available	Check Out	
Laptop	(2) Computer		Available	Check Out	
Wireless microphone	(1) Multimedia		Available	Check Out	
Wi-fi router	(3) Networking		Available	Check Out	
	(1) Multimedia				
4					

Figure 2–89

3. Enter the contact information shown in Figure 2–90 into the Contacts table.

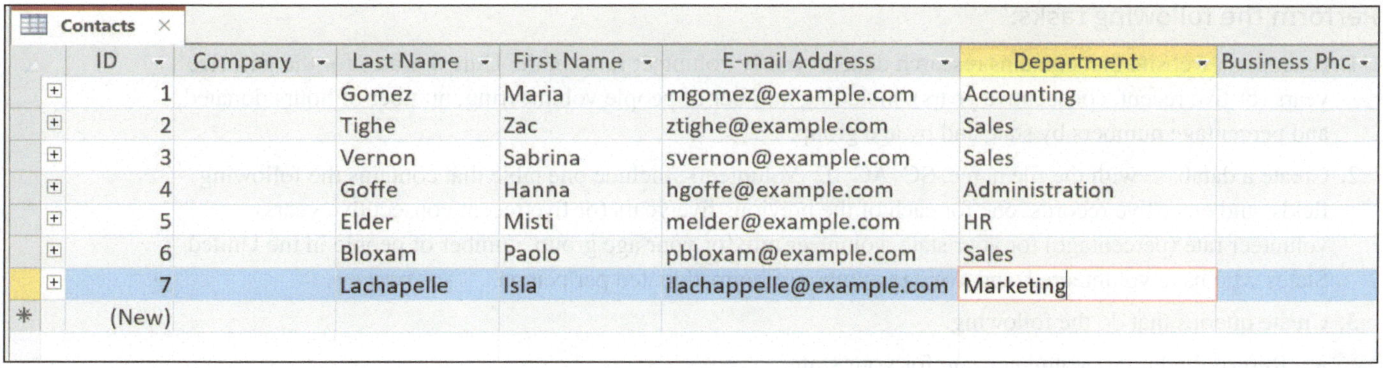

Contacts

ID	Company	Last Name	First Name	E-mail Address	Department	Business Phc
1		Gomez	Maria	mgomez@example.com	Accounting	
2		Tighe	Zac	ztighe@example.com	Sales	
3		Vernon	Sabrina	svernon@example.com	Sales	
4		Goffe	Hanna	hgoffe@example.com	Administration	
5		Elder	Misti	melder@example.com	HR	
6		Bloxam	Paolo	pbloxam@example.com	Sales	
7		Lachapelle	Isla	ilachappelle@example.com	Marketing	
(New)						

Figure 2–90

4. Create a query to find all Assets in the "(1) Multimedia" category. Include the ID, Item, and Category fields. Save the query as Extend 2 Step 4 Query.
5. Enter information for Tyron Black into the Contact Details form, as shown in Figure 2–91.

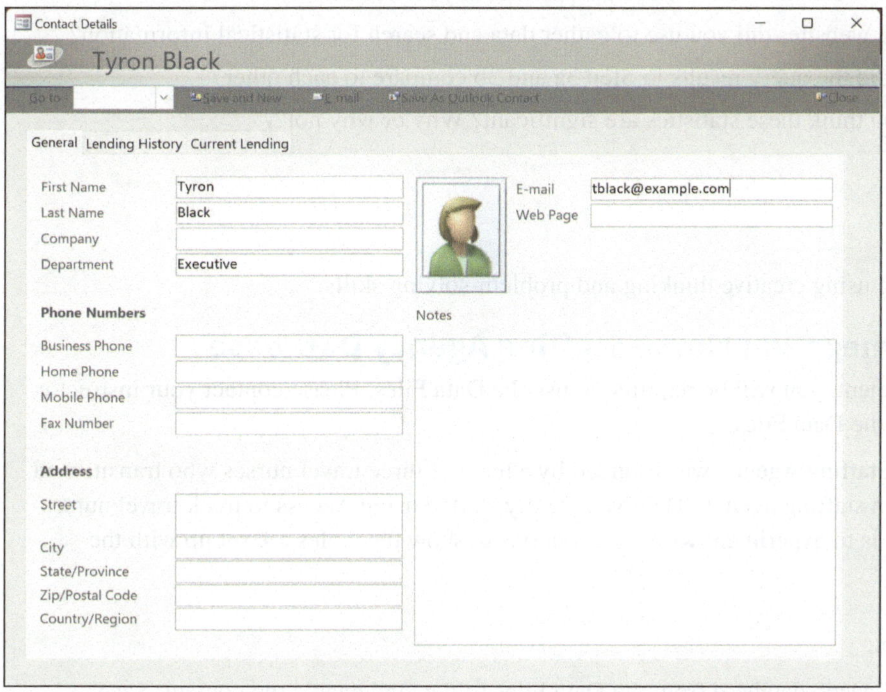

Figure 2–91

6. Open the All Assets report and delete the date and time from the upper-right corner of the report.
7. Export the report as a Word file named All Assets List and save the export steps.
8. Submit the database and the exported RTF file in the format specified by your instructor.
9. **Consider This:** How would you alter the query in Step 4 so it shows assets that are *not* in the Multimedia category?

Expand Your World

Create a solution, which uses cloud and web technologies, by learning and investigating on your own from general guidance.

Instructions: Start Access. You are taking a sociology course and the instructor would like you to gather some statistics and query the statistics on the rates of volunteer hours donated by various groups of people.

Continued on next page

Perform the following tasks:

1. Examine a website that contains research data on yearly volunteer rates in the United States for the past five years (or five recent, consecutive years), including number of people volunteering, number of hours donated, and percentage numbers by state and by age group.
2. Create a database with the file name, SC_AC_02_Volunteers. Include one table that contains the following fields, and enter five records, one for each of the previous five years (or five recent consecutive years): volunteer rate (percentage) for your state, volunteer rate for your age group, number of people in the United States who have volunteered, and average number of hours donated per person.
3. Create queries that do the following:
   a. Return the largest volunteer rate for your state.
   b. Return the largest volunteer rate for your age group.
   c. Calculate the difference between the largest volunteer rate in your state and the lowest volunteer rate in your state over the past five years.
4. Submit the database in the format specified by your instructor.
5. Use an Internet search engine to find three volunteer opportunities in your community.
6. a. **Consider This:** Which websites did you use to gather data and search for statistical information?
   b. **Consider This:** How did the query results in Step 3a and 3b compare to each other?
   c. **Consider This:** Do you think these statistics are significant? Why or why not?

In the Lab

Design and implement a solution using creative thinking and problem-solving skills.

Lab: Querying the Homegrown Nurse Staffing Agency Database

Note: To complete this assignment, you will be required to use the Data Files. Please contact your instructor for information about accessing the Data Files.

Problem: Homegrown Nurse Staffing Agency was founded by a team of three travel nurses who transitioned to building and running their own staffing agency. They've recently started using Access to track travel nurses and their assignments. Your task is to experiment with some queries to show the tables are set up with the needed information.

Perform the following tasks:

Part 1: Open the SC_AC_02-4.accdb database from the Data Files folder, and enable the content. Save the file with the name SC_AC_02_Travel-Nurses, and enable the content. Use the concepts and techniques presented in this module to create queries for the following.

a) Create a new query called Assignments - Facilities Query that joins the Assignments and Facilities tables and shows travelers assigned to each facility. In the query, include Assignment ID and Facility ID from the Assignments table, Facility Name and Facility Type from the Facilities table, and then Traveler ID from the Assignments table. Sort in Ascending order by Facility ID.

b) Create a new query that finds the Traveler ID, Name, License, and Availability for travelers with an SD license only. Name the query SD Travelers Query.

c) Create a new query that finds all apartment-style housing. Include the Housing ID and Location ID fields without showing the Housing Type in the query results, and name the query Apartments Query.

d) Find all assignments that include housing reimbursement. Include the Assignment ID, Facility ID, Traveler ID, and Reimbursements fields. The result should appear as shown in Figure 2–92. Name the query Assignments with Housing Query.

A_ID	Facility	Traveler	Reimbursements
A-001	F-001	T-001	Housing, update license
A-002	F-005	T-002	Housing, travel
A-005	F-004	T-007	Housing
A-006	F-003	T-005	Housing+meals
A-007	F-002	T-010	Housing+meals, travel
A-010	F-004	T-013	Housing+meals, travel
A-011	F-006		Housing

Assignments with Housing Query

Figure 2–92

Submit your database in the format specified by your instructor.

Part 2: **Consider This:** You made several decisions while creating the queries in this assignment. What was the rationale behind your decisions? How would you modify the query in Part 1.d to include assignments with travel reimbursement? How would you further modify the query to sort the query results by highest bill rates without showing bill rate information in the results?

Maintaining a Database

Objectives

After completing this module, you will be able to:

- Create a split form
- Add records using a form
- Search for a record
- Delete a record
- Filter records in a table
- Add a lookup, multivalued, or calculated field to a table
- Use an action query to add, change, or delete records
- Specify validation rules, default values, and formats
- Use a lookup field
- Include a Total row in a datasheet
- Format a datasheet
- Include a multivalued field in query results
- Create a relationship between tables
- Use a subdatasheet
- Explain how to handle data inconsistency

Introduction

Once you have created a database and loaded it with data, you must maintain it. **Database maintenance** means modifying the data to keep it up to date by adding new records, changing the data for existing records, and deleting records. Updating can include mass updates or mass deletions (i.e., updates to, or deletions of, many records at the same time).

Database maintenance can also involve the need to **restructure** the database periodically. Restructuring can include adding new fields to a table, changing the characteristics of existing fields, and removing existing fields. Restructuring also includes the creation of validation rules and referential integrity. Validation rules ensure the validity of the data in the database, whereas referential integrity ensures the validity of the relationships between entities. Maintaining a database can also include filtering records. This process ensures only the records that satisfy some criterion appear when viewing and updating the data in a table. Changing the appearance of a datasheet is also a maintenance activity.

BTW
Organizing Files and Folders
You should organize and store files in folders so that you easily can find the files later. For example, if you are taking an introductory computer class called CIS 101, a good practice would be to save all Access files in an Access folder in a CIS 101 folder.

Project: Maintaining a Database

Clearnet Logistics faces the task of keeping its database up to date. As the company takes on new shippers and carriers, it will need to add new records, make changes to existing records, and delete records. Clearnet is also planning to hire a third shipping agent, and the owners believe they can track loads and payments better by changing the structure of the database to categorize the loads according to which agent arranges each load. The company will do this first by adding an Agent field to the Loads table. Further, Clearnet would like to adjust its database to handle multiple pickup or dropoff locations for a single load. Because loads might involve more than one pickup or dropoff location, the pickup and dropoff fields will each be a multivalued field, which is a field that can store multiple values or entries. Along with these changes, Clearnet wants to change the appearance of a datasheet when displaying data.

Clearnet also would like the ability to make mass updates, that is, to update or delete many records in a single operation. It wants rules that limit users to entering only valid, or appropriate, data into the database. Clearnet also wants to ensure that the database cannot contain a load that is not associated with a specific shipper.

Figure 3–1 summarizes some of the various types of activities involved in maintaining the Clearnet database.

Figure 3–1

BTW
The Ribbon and Screen Resolution
Access may change how the groups and buttons within the groups appear on the ribbon, depending on the computer or mobile device's screen resolution. Thus, your ribbon may look different from the ones in this course if you are using a screen resolution other than 1920 x 1080.

Updating Records

Keeping the data in a database current requires updating records in three ways: adding new records, changing the data in existing records, and deleting existing records. You can add records to a database using Datasheet view, and as you add records, the records appear on the screen in a datasheet. The data looks like a table. When you need to add additional records, you can use the same techniques.

You can use a simple form to view records. You can also use a **split form**, which is a form that allows you to simultaneously view both the simple form and Datasheet views of the data. You can use either portion of a split form to add or update records. To add new records, change existing records, or delete records, you use the same techniques you used in Datasheet view.

To Save the Clearnet Database with a New File Name and Create a Split Form

The following steps create a split form. **Why?** With a split form, you have the advantage of seeing a single record in a form while simultaneously viewing several records in a datasheet.

1

- sam Start Access. Open the database, SC_AC_03-1.accdb, which is located in the Data Files folder. Save the file on your hard disk, OneDrive, or other storage location using the file name, **SC_AC_03_Clearnet**. Enable the content.
- Open the Navigation Pane if it is currently closed.
- If necessary, click the Loads table in the Navigation Pane to select it.

- Click Create on the ribbon to display the Create tab.
- Click the More Forms button (Create tab | Forms group) to display the More Forms menu (Figure 3–2).

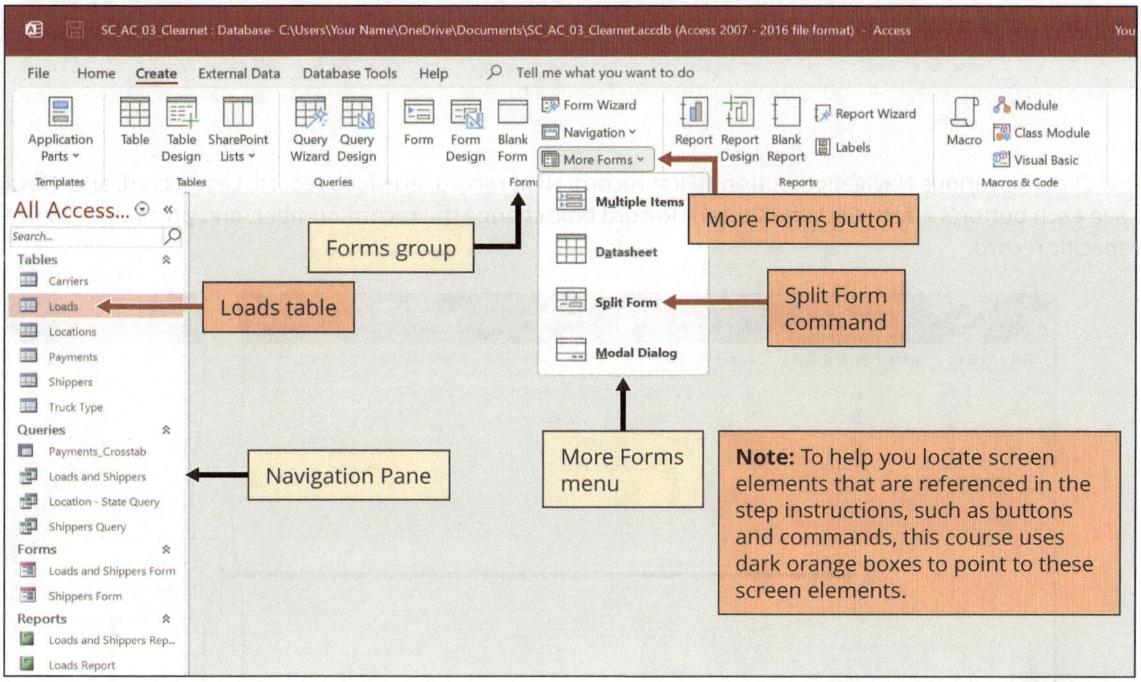

Figure 3–2

2

- Click Split Form to create a split form based on the Loads table.
- Close the Navigation Pane (Figure 3–3).

Q&A Is the form automatically saved?

No. You will take specific actions later to save the form.

A field list pane appeared when I created the form. What should I do?

Click the 'Add Existing Fields' button (Form Layout Design tab | Tools group) to close the field list.

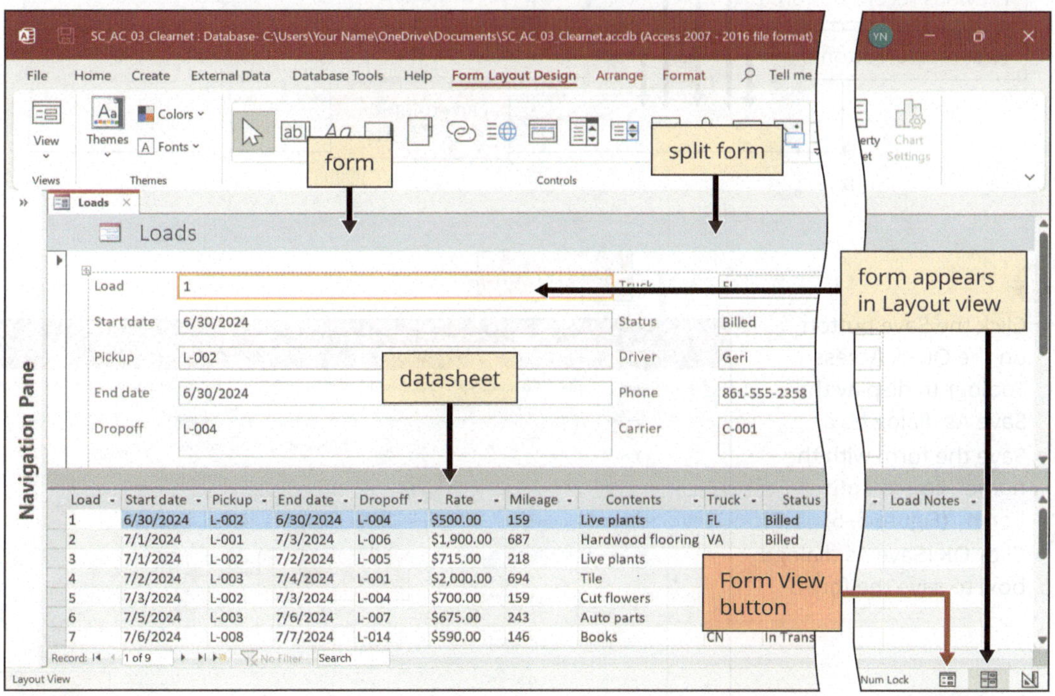

Figure 3–3

3

- Click the Form View button on the Access status bar to display the form in Form view rather than Layout view (Figure 3–4).

Q&A What is the difference between Form view and Layout view?
Form view is the view you use to view, enter, and update data. Layout view is the view you use to make design changes to the form while viewing a preview of those changes. It shows you the form with data in it so you can immediately see the effects of any design changes you make, but it is not intended to be used to enter and update data.

- **Experiment:** Click the various Navigation buttons (First record, Next record, Previous record, Last record, and 'New (blank) record') to see each button's effect. Click the Current Record box, change the record number, and press ENTER to see how to move to a specific record.

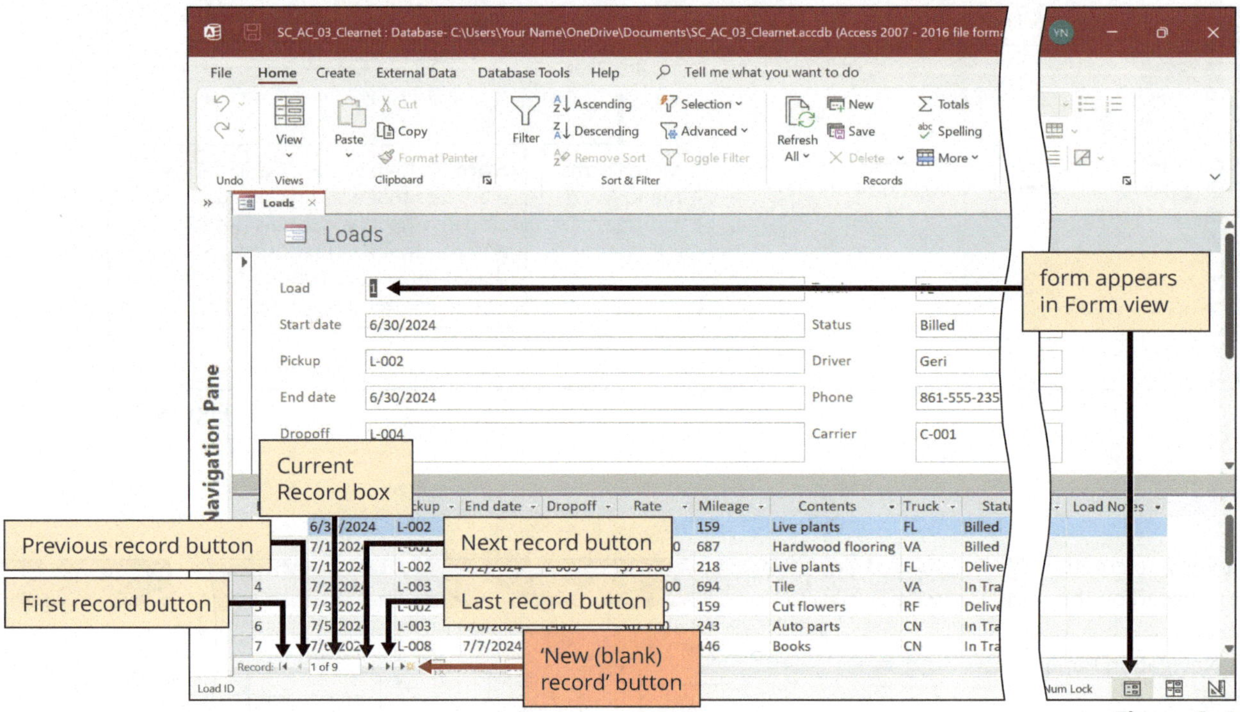

Figure 3–4

4

- Click the Save button on the Quick Access Toolbar to display the Save As dialog box.
- Save the form with the name **Loads Split Form** (Figure 3–5).
- Click OK (Save As dialog box) to save the form.

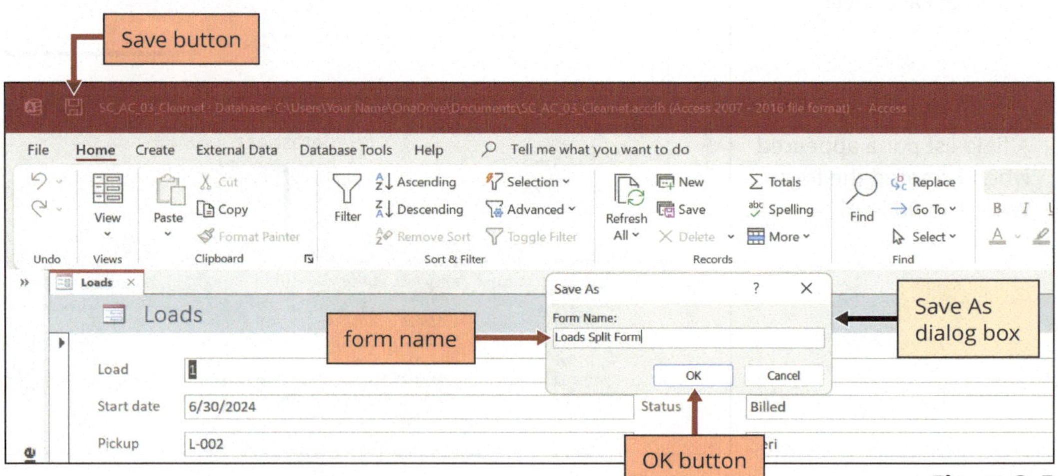

Figure 3–5

Other Ways

1. Right-click form's tab, click Form View on shortcut menu to change view

To Use a Form to Add Records

Once a form or split form is open in Form view, you can add records using the same techniques you used to add records in Datasheet view. In a split form, the changes you make on the form are automatically made on the datasheet. You do not need to take any special action. The following steps use the split form that you just created to add records. **Why?** With a split form, as you add a record, you can immediately see the effect of the addition on the datasheet.

1

- Click the 'New (blank) record' button on the Navigation bar to enter a new record, and then type the data for the new record, as shown in Figure 3–6, keeping in mind that the ID field is an autonumber and will appear automatically when typing in a new record. Press TAB after typing the data in each field. Note that pressing tab after typing the data for the final field (Load Notes) will complete the entry of the record.
- Click the Save button on the Quick Access Toolbar to save the form.
- Close the form.

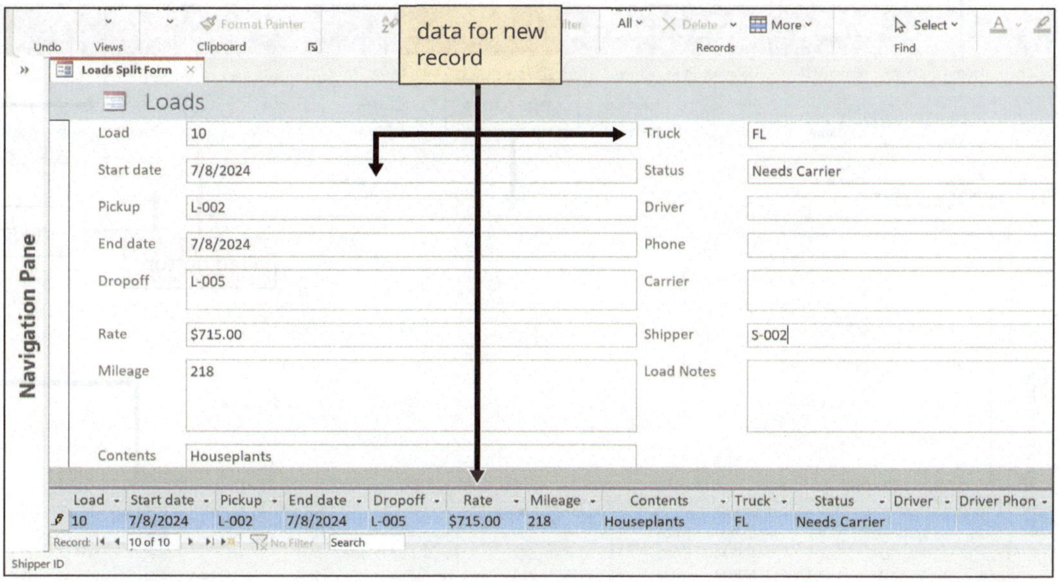

Figure 3–6

Other Ways

1. Click New button (Home tab | Records group) to create new record
2. Press CTRL+PLUS SIGN (+) to create new record

To Search for a Record

In a database environment, **searching** means looking for records that satisfy some criterion. Looking for a load driven by Roman is an example of searching. Running a query is another way of searching. In a query, Access must locate those records that satisfy one or more criteria.

You can perform a search in Form view or Datasheet view without creating a query. The following steps search for Roman's loads. **Why?** You want to locate the record quickly so you can update this load's status.

1

- Open the Navigation Pane.
- Right-click Loads Split Form to display a shortcut menu, and then click Open on the shortcut menu to open the form in Form view.
- Click the Driver field in the datasheet portion of the split form.

Q&A I see both Layout view and Design view in the shortcut menu, but no option for Form view. Which command gives me Form view?

The Open command opens the form in Form view.

- Close the Navigation Pane (Figure 3–7).

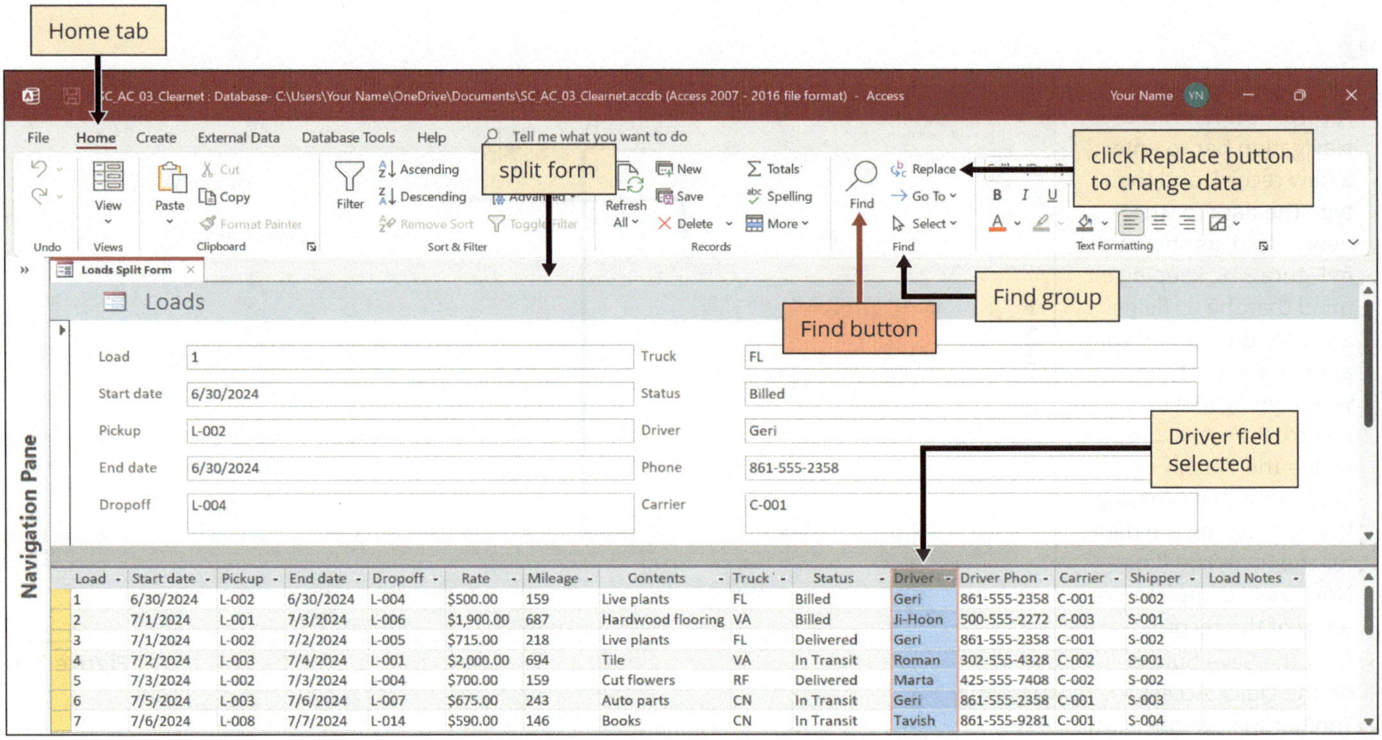

Figure 3–7

2

- Click the Find button (Home tab | Find group) to display the Find and Replace dialog box.
- Type **Roman** in the Find What text box (Find and Replace dialog box), and then click the Find Next button to find Roman's in-transit load and display the record in the form (Figure 3–8).

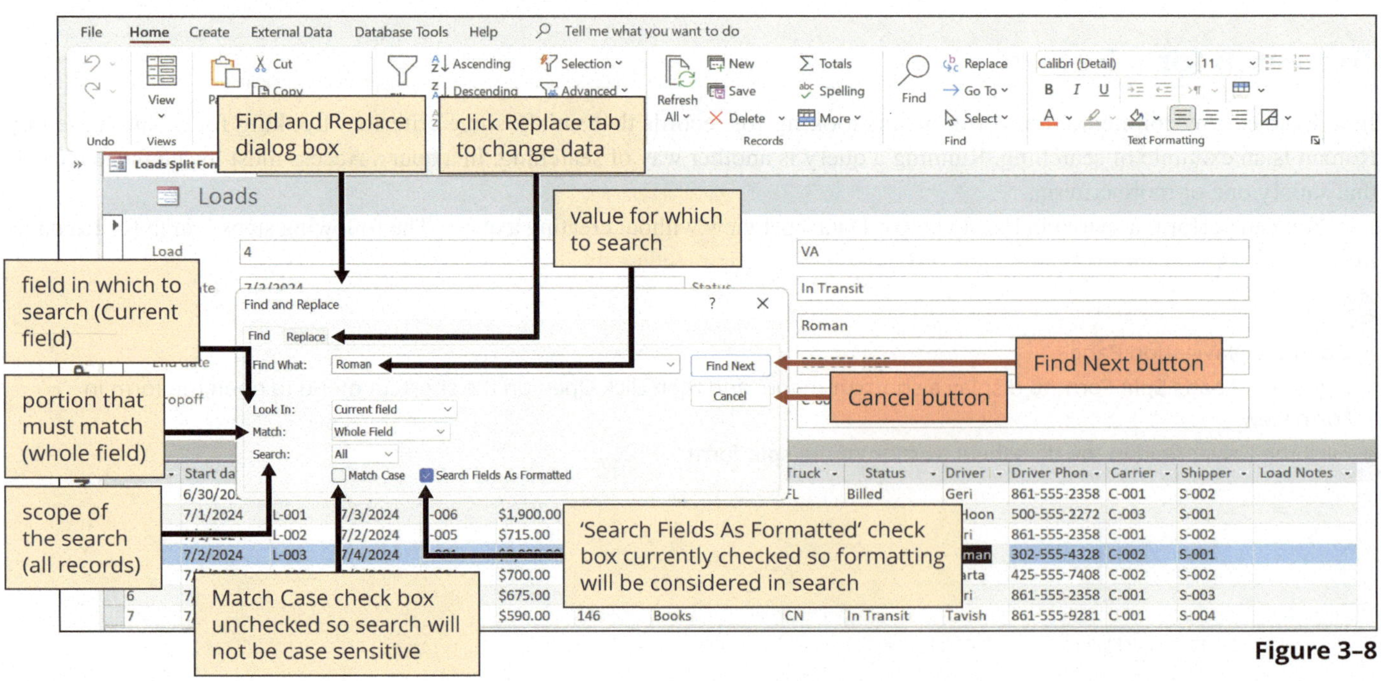

Figure 3–8

Q&A My search didn't find any records. How can I fix this?
By default, the search parameters are configured to only look in the current field, not all fields. Make sure you select the Driver field in either portion of the split form before doing the search. Also confirm your search term is typed correctly.

Why does the button in the dialog box read Find Next, rather than simply Find?
In some cases, after locating a record that satisfies a criterion, you might need to find the next record that satisfies the same criterion. For example, you might want to find the next load that is scheduled after the driver's current load is delivered; or, if the first load was already delivered, you might then want to find that driver's load that is still in transit. To do so, click the Find Next button. You will not need to retype the value each time.

3

- Click Cancel (Find and Replace dialog box) to remove the dialog box from the screen.

Q&A Can I find records using this method in both Datasheet view and Form view?
Yes. You use the same process to find (and replace) records whether you are viewing the data with a split form, in Datasheet view, or in Form view.

Other Ways

1. Press CTRL+F to search for text

Consider This

Can you replace one value with another using the Find and Replace dialog box?

Yes. Either click the Replace button (Home tab | Find group) or click the Replace tab in the Find and Replace dialog box. You then can enter both the value to find and the new value.

To Update the Contents of a Record

The following step uses Form view to change a load's status. **Why? Roman has successfully delivered his load.** After locating the record to be changed, select the field to be changed by clicking the field. You can also press TAB repeatedly until the desired field is selected. Then make the appropriate changes. (Clicking the field automatically produces an insertion point. If you use TAB, you will need to press F2 to produce an insertion point.)

1

- Click in the Status field in the form portion of the split form for Load 4 immediately to the right of the In Transit text.
- Backspace and replace In Transit with **Delivered**.
- Press TAB to complete the change and move to the next field (Figure 3–9).

Q&A Could I have changed the contents of the field in the datasheet portion of the split form?
Yes. You first need to ensure the record to be changed appears in the datasheet. You then can change the value just as in the form.

Do I need to save my change?
No. Once you move to another record or close this form, the change to the name is saved automatically.

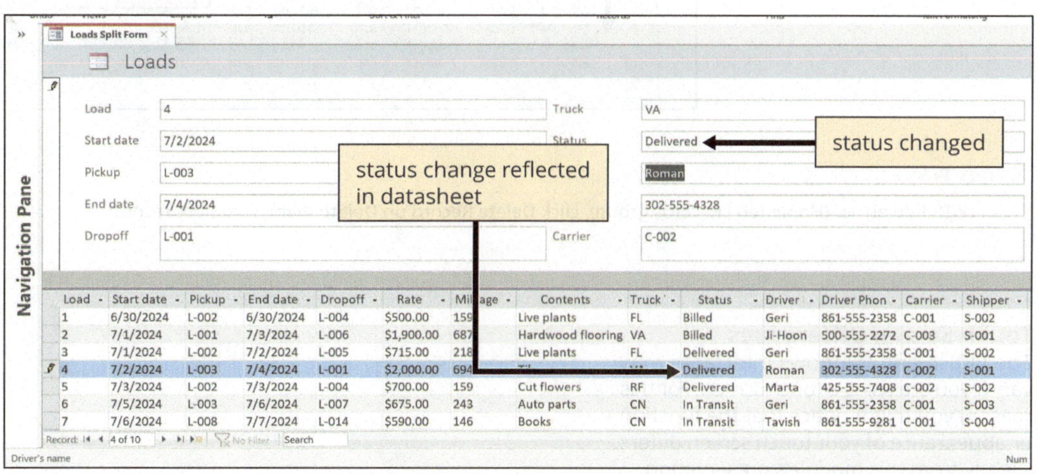

Figure 3–9

To Delete a Record

When records are no longer needed, you should delete them (remove them) from the table. The following steps delete Load 8, which was to deliver raw milk to a food processing factory. **Why?** The farm's refrigeration unit for this load failed, ruining the milk, so the record can be deleted.

1

- With the Loads Split Form still open, click the record selector in the datasheet portion of the form for Load 8, coming from pickup location L-011 on 7/7/2024 to select the record (Figure 3–10).

Q&A This technique works in the datasheet portion. How do I select the record in the form portion?
With the desired record appearing in the form, click the record selector (the triangle in front of the record) to select the entire record.

What do I do if the record I want to delete does not appear on the screen?
First search for the record you want to delete using the Find and Replace dialog box.

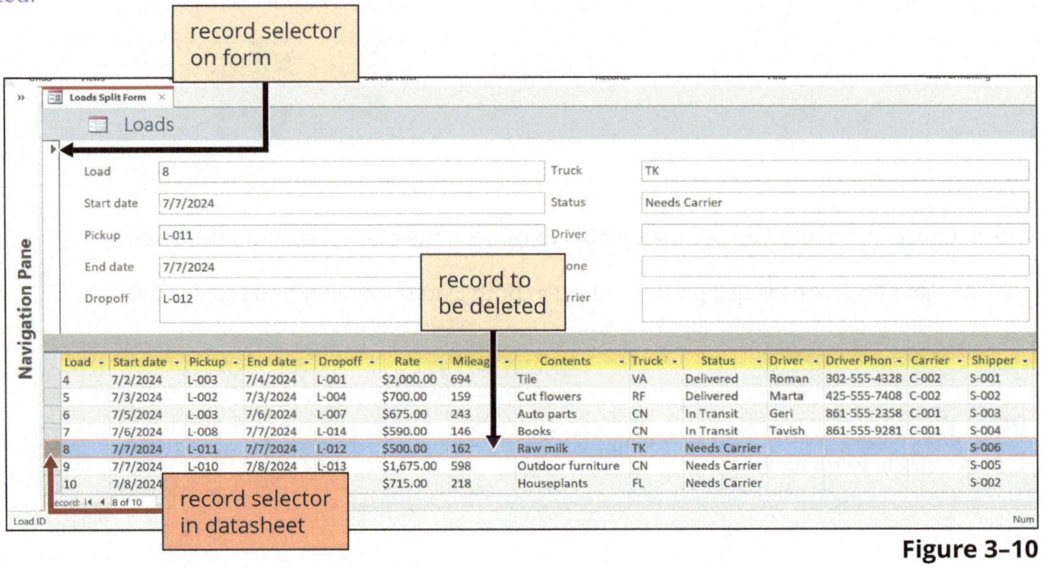

Figure 3–10

2

- Press DEL to delete the record (Figure 3–11).

3

- Click Yes to complete the deletion.
- Save and close the Loads Split Form.

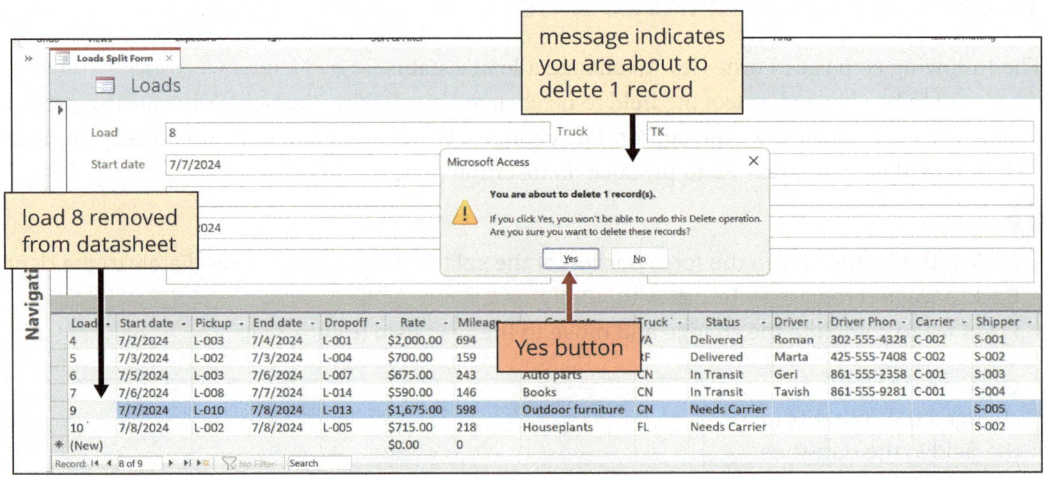

Figure 3–11

Other Ways

1. Click Delete arrow (Home tab | Records group), click Delete Record on Delete menu to delete record

BTW
Touch Screen Differences
The Office and Windows interfaces may vary if you are using a touch screen. For this reason, you might notice that the function or appearance of your touch screen differs slightly from this module's presentation.

Filtering Records

You can use the Find button in either Datasheet view or Form view to locate a record quickly that satisfies some criterion (for example, the ID 2). However, using these approaches show all records, not just the record or records that satisfy the criterion. To have only the record or records that satisfy the criterion appear, use a **filter**. Four types of filters are available: Filter By Selection, Common Filters, Filter By Form, and Advanced Filter/Sort. You can use a filter in either Datasheet view or Form view.

BTW
Using the Find Button
You can use the Find button (Home tab | Find group) to search for records in datasheets, forms, query results, and reports.

To Use Filter By Selection

To use Filter By Selection, you give Access an example of the data you want by selecting the data within the table. You then choose the option you want on the Selection menu. The following steps use Filter By Selection in Datasheet view to display only the records for loads in transit. *Why? Filter By Selection is appropriate for displaying these records and is the simplest type of filter.*

1

- Open the Navigation Pane.
- Open the Loads table in Datasheet view, and then close the Navigation Pane.
- Click the Status field on Load 6 (the sixth record) to specify In Transit as the desired status for the filter (Figure 3–12).

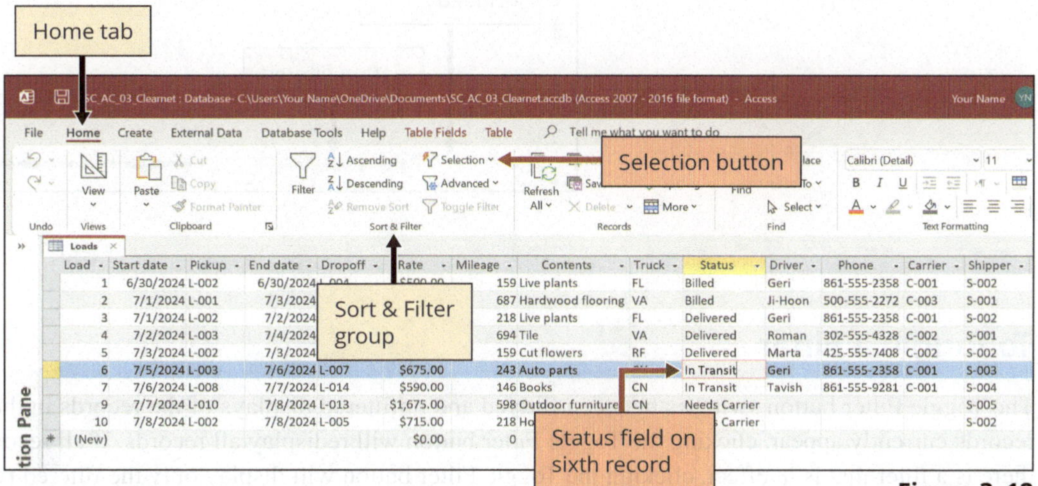

Figure 3–12

Q&A Could I have selected the Status field on another record where the status is also In Transit to select the same status?
Yes. It does not matter which record you select, as long as the status is In Transit.

2

- Click the Selection button (Home tab | Sort & Filter group) to display the Selection menu (Figure 3–13).

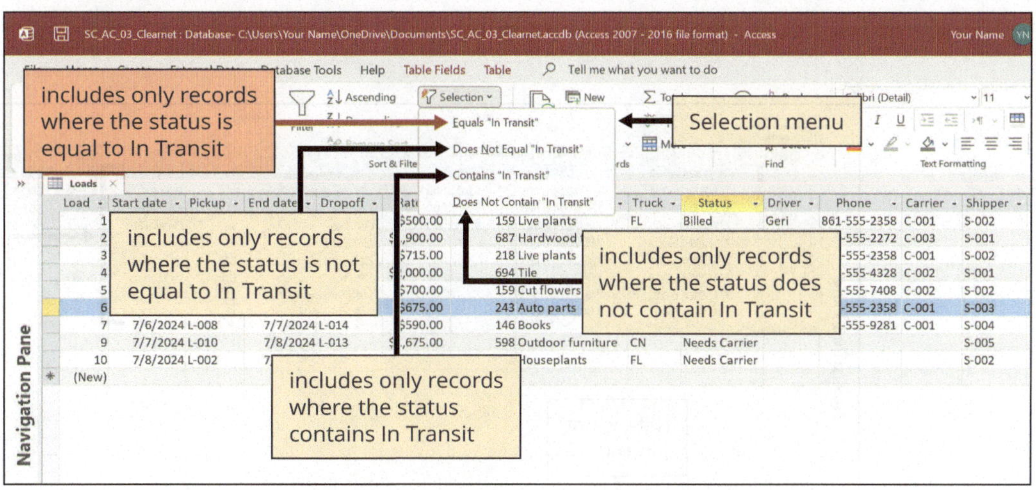

Figure 3–13

3

- Click 'Equals "In Transit"' to select only those loads whose status is In Transit (Figure 3–14).

Q&A Can I also filter in Form view?
Yes. Filtering works the same whether you are viewing the data with a split form, in Datasheet view, or in Form view.

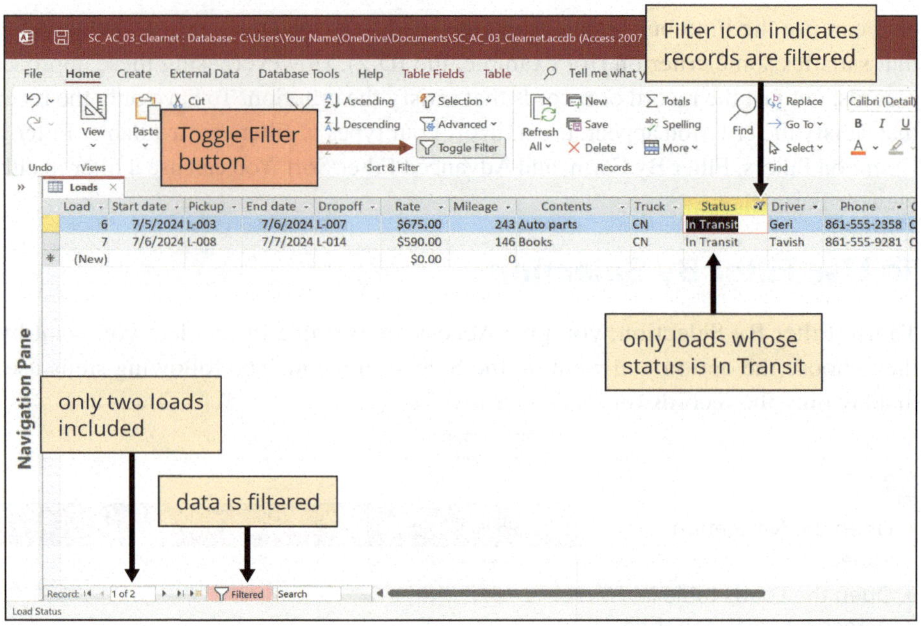

Figure 3–14

To Toggle a Filter

The Toggle Filter button switches between filtered and unfiltered displays of the records in the table. That is, if only filtered records currently appear, clicking the Toggle Filter button will redisplay all records. If all records are currently displayed and there is a filter that is in effect, clicking the Toggle Filter button will display only the filtered records. If no filter is active, the Toggle Filter button will be dimmed, so clicking it would have no effect.

The following step toggles the filter. **Why?** Clearnet wants to once again view all the records.

1

- Click the Toggle Filter button (Home tab | Sort & Filter group) to toggle the filter and redisplay all records (Figure 3–15).

Q&A Does this action clear the filter?
No. The filter is still in place. If you click the Toggle Filter button a second time, you will again see only the filtered records using the previously configured filter.

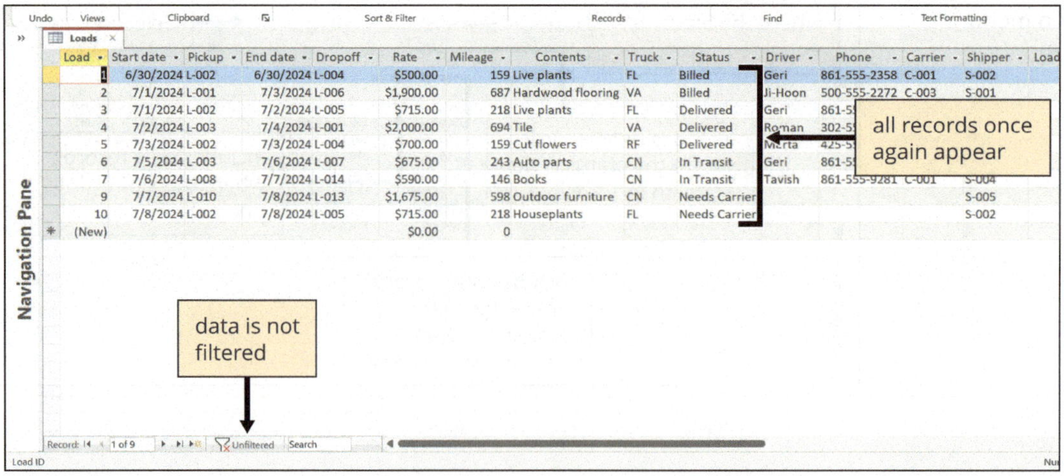

Figure 3–15

To Clear a Filter

Once you have finished using a filter, you can clear (remove) the filter. After doing so, you no longer will be able to use the filter by clicking the Toggle Filter button. The following steps clear the filter.

1 Click the Advanced button (Home tab | Sort & Filter group) to display the Advanced menu (Figure 3–16).

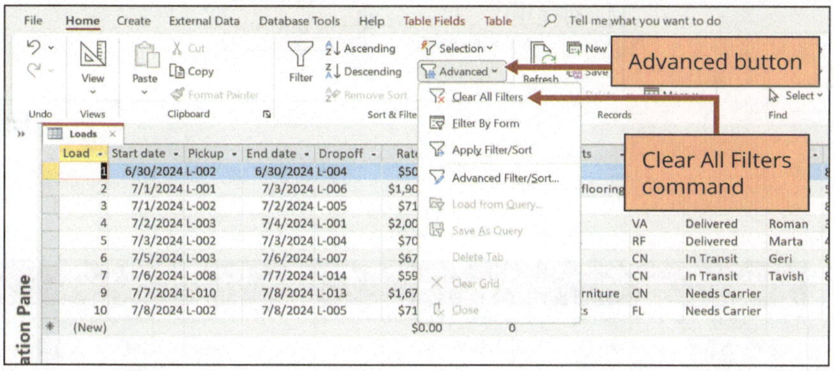

Figure 3–16

2 Click Clear All Filters on the Advanced menu. Leave the Loads table open for now.

BTW
Access Screen Resolution
If you are using a computer or mobile device to step through the project in this module and you want your screens to match the figures in this course, you should change your screen's resolution to 1920 x 1080.

To Use a Common Filter

Suppose you have determined you want to look at locations whose city begins with the letter B. In this case, Filter By Selection would not be appropriate. None of the options within Filter By Selection would support this type of criterion. You can filter individual fields by clicking the arrow to the right of the field name and using one of the **common filters** that are available for the field. **Why?** Access includes a collection of filters that perform common filtering tasks; you can modify a common filter by customizing it for the specific field. The following steps customize a common filter to include only those locations whose city begins with B.

1

- Open the Navigation Pane.
- Open the Locations table in Datasheet view, and then close the Navigation Pane.
- Click the City arrow to display the common filter menu.
- Point to the Text Filters command to display the custom text filters (Figure 3–17).

Q&A If I wanted certain cities included, could I use the check boxes?

Yes. Be sure the cities you want are the only ones checked.

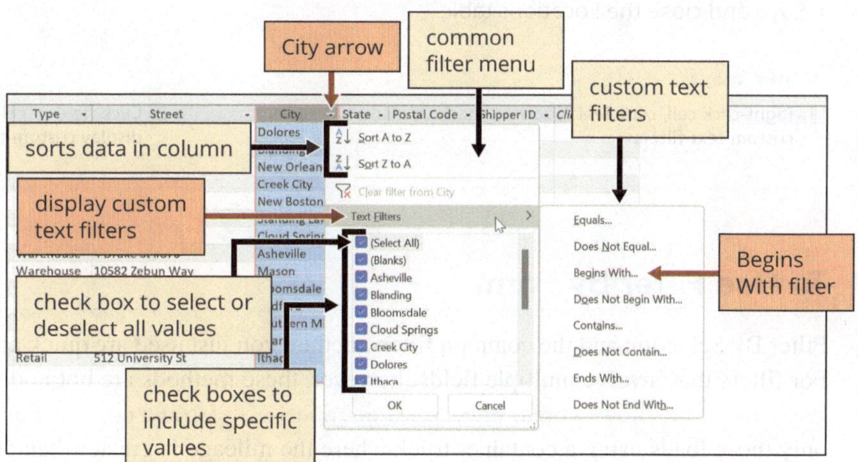

Figure 3–17

2

- Click Begins With to display the Custom Filter dialog box.
- Type **B** as the City begins with value (Figure 3–18).

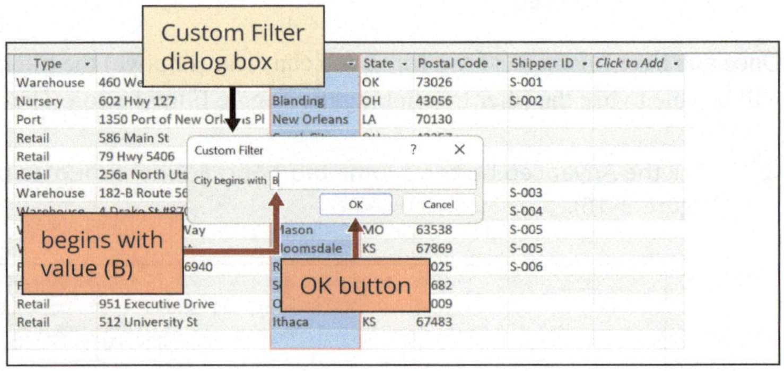

Figure 3–18

3

- Click the OK button to filter the records (Figure 3–19).
- **Experiment:** Try other options in the common filter menu to see their effects. When done, once again select those accounts whose city begins with B.

Q&A Can I use the same technique in Form view?

In Form view, you would need to click the field and then click the Filter button to display the Common Filter menu. The rest of the process is the same.

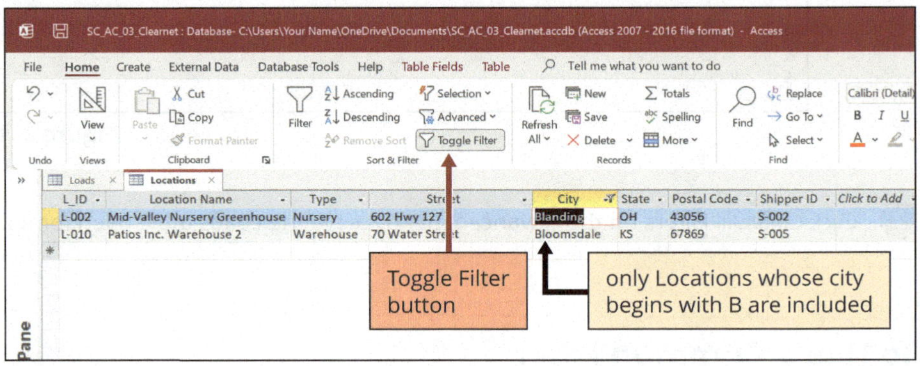

Figure 3–19

4

- Click the Toggle Filter button (Home tab | Sort & Filter group) to toggle the filter and redisplay all records.
- Save and close the Locations table.

Other Ways

1. Right-click cell, click Text Filters on shortcut menu to display custom text filters
2. Click field or cell, click Filter button (Home tab | Sort & Filter group) to display custom text filters

To Use Filter By Form

Filter By Selection and the common filters method you just used are quick and easy ways to filter by the value in a single field. For filters that involve multiple fields, however, these methods are not appropriate, so you would use Filter By Form. **Why?** Filter By Form allows you to filter based on multiple fields and criteria. For example, Filter By Form would allow you to find only those loads using a container truck where the mileage is greater than 500 miles. The following steps use Filter By Form to restrict the records that appear.

1

- With the Loads table tab active, click the Advanced button (Home tab | Sort & Filter group) to display the Advanced menu (Figure 3–20).

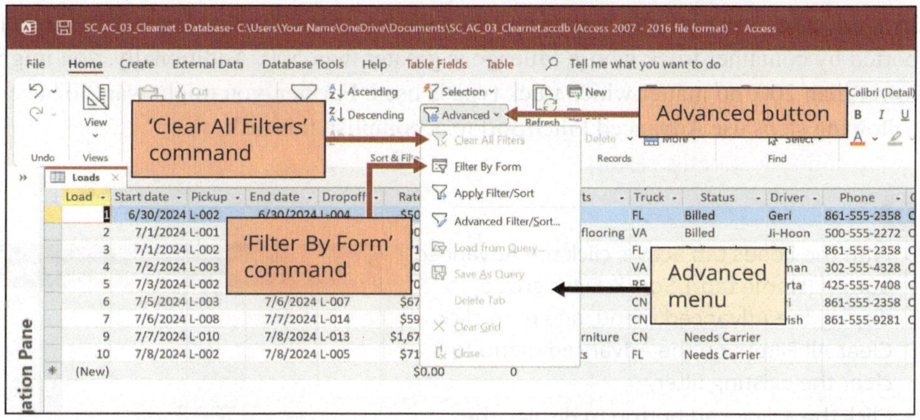

Figure 3–20

2

- If necessary, clear the existing filter by clicking Clear All Filters on the Advanced menu. Then click the Advanced button again to display the Advanced menu a second time.
- Click Filter By Form on the Advanced menu.
- Click the blank row below the Mileage field, and then type **>500** to display loads with a mileage more than 500 miles.
- Click the blank row in the Truck field, click the arrow that appears, and then choose 'CN' from the menu to enter a criterion for the Truck field (Figure 3–21).

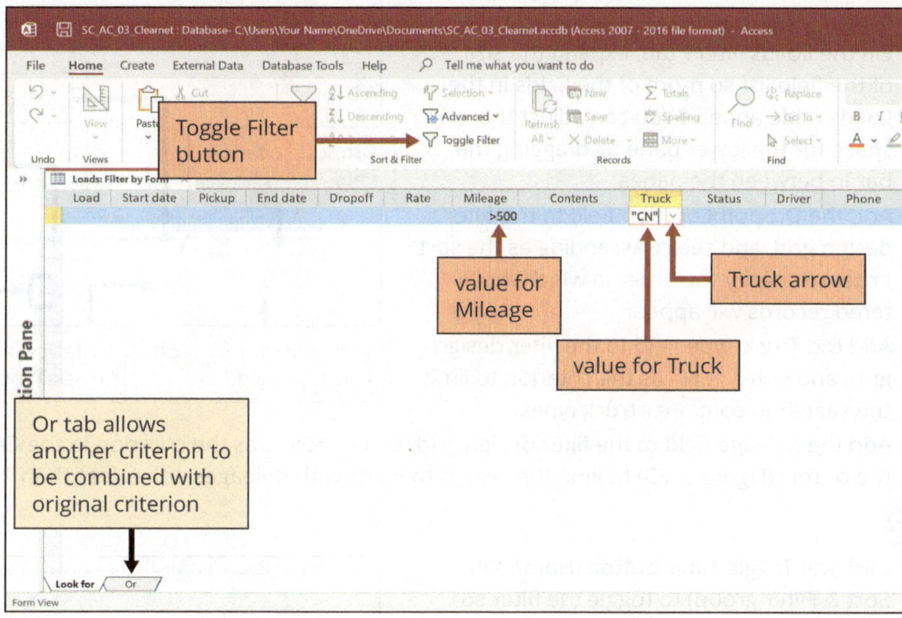

Figure 3–21

Q&A Could I have clicked the arrow in the Mileage field and then made a selection, rather than typing a criterion?

No. Because your criterion involves something other than equality, you need to type the criterion rather than selecting from a list.

Is there any difference in the process if I am viewing a table in Form view rather than in Datasheet view?

In Form view, you will make your entries in a form rather than a datasheet. Otherwise, the process is the same.

3

- Click the Toggle Filter button (Home tab | Sort & Filter group) to apply the filter (Figure 3–22).
- **Experiment:** Select Filter By Form again and enter different criteria. In each case, toggle the filter to see the effect of your selection. When done, once again select those loads whose truck type is CN and whose mileage is >500.

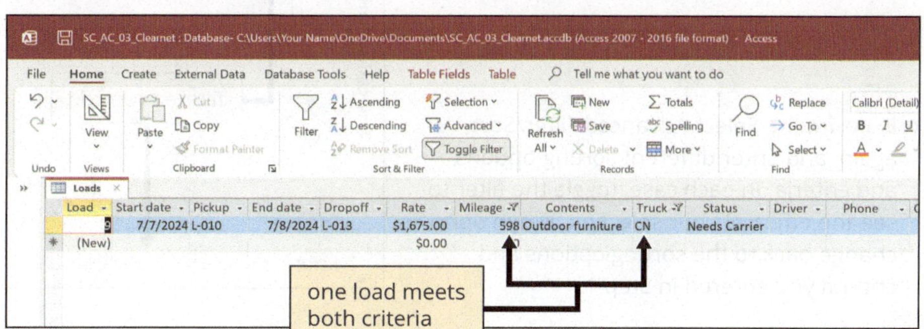

Figure 3–22

Other Ways

1. Click the Advanced button (Home tab | Sort & Filter group), click Apply Filter/Sort on Advanced menu to see filter results

To Use Advanced Filter/Sort

In some cases, your criteria will be too complex even for Filter By Form. You might decide you want to include any load transported by container truck whose Mileage is greater than 500. Additionally, you might want to include any load with a mileage lower than 200, no matter which truck type is used. Further, you might want to have the results sorted by dropoff location. The following steps use Advanced Filter/Sort to accomplish this task. **Why?** Advanced Filter/Sort supports complex criteria as well as the ability to sort the results.

1

- With the Loads tab active, click the Advanced button (Home tab | Sort & Filter group) to display the Advanced menu, and then click Clear All Filters on the Advanced menu to clear the existing filter.
- Click the Advanced button to display the Advanced menu a second time.
- Click Advanced Filter/Sort on the Advanced menu.
- On the LoadsFilter1 tab, expand the size of the field list so more of the fields in the Loads table appear. You can adjust the space for the lower pane by dragging the bar in between the panes.
- Add the Dropoff Location field to the filter design grid, and select Ascending as the sort order to specify the order in which the filtered records will appear.
- Add the Truck Type field to the filter design grid, and enter **CN** as the criterion to limit the search to container truck types.
- Add the Mileage field to the filter design grid. Enter **>500** as the criterion in the Criteria row and **<200** as the criterion in the or row (Figure 3–23) to limit the search to loads with mileages either less than 200 or greater than 500.

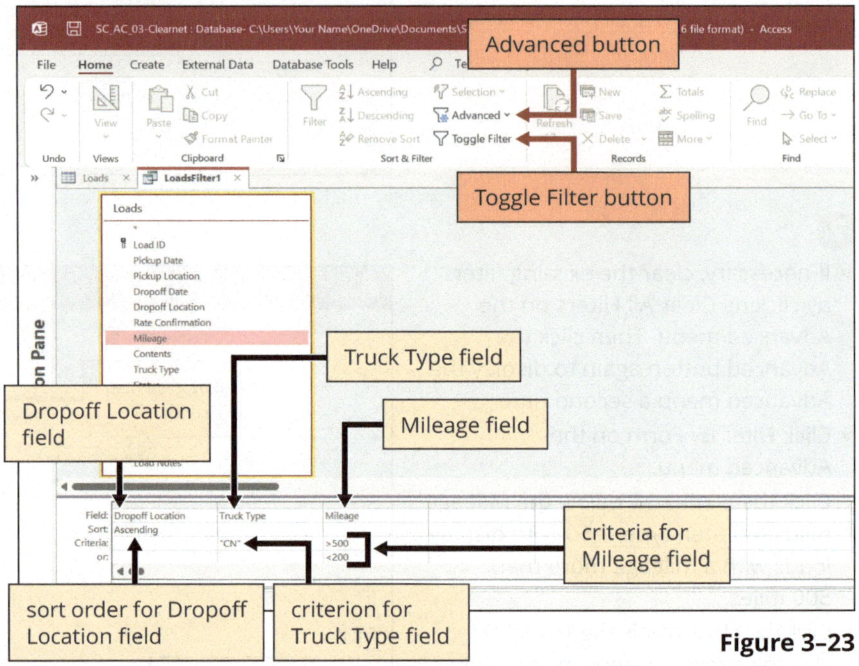

Figure 3–23

2

- Click the Toggle Filter button (Home tab | Sort & Filter group) to toggle the filter so that only records that satisfy the criteria will appear (Figure 3–24).

Q&A Why are these particular records included in the filter results?

Record 9 is included because the Truck Type is CN for container *and* the mileage is greater than 500. The other records are included because their mileages are less than 200.

- **Experiment:** Select Advanced Filter/Sort again, and enter different sorting options and criteria. In each case, toggle the filter to see the effect of your selection. When done, change back to the sorting options and criteria you entered in Step 1.

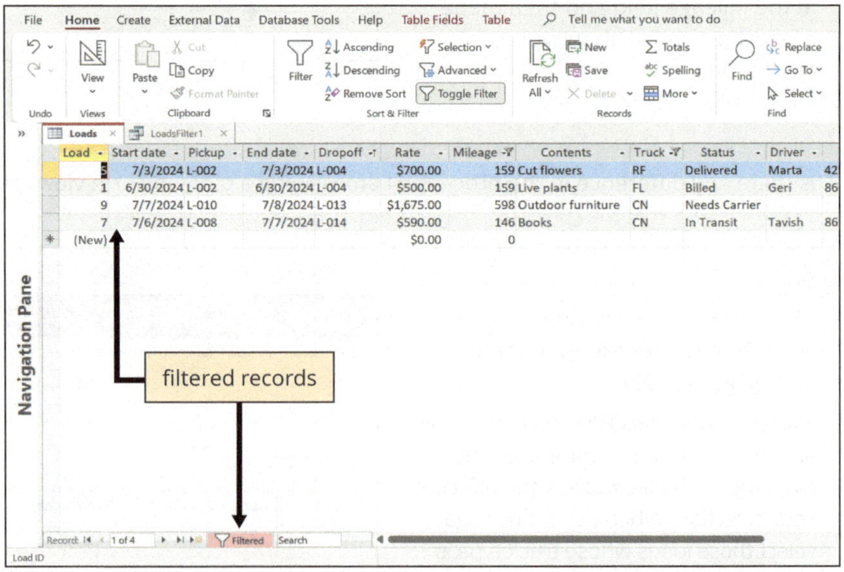

Figure 3–24

3

- Close the Loads table. When asked if you want to save your changes, click the No button.

Q&A Shouldn't I have cleared all filters before closing the table?

If you are closing a table and not saving the changes, it is not necessary to clear the filter. No filter will be active when you next open the table.

Filters and Queries

Now that you are familiar with how filters work, you might notice similarities between filters and queries. Both objects are used to locate data that meets specific criteria. Filters and queries are related in three ways.

1. You can apply a filter to the results of a query just as you can apply a filter to a table.
2. Once you create a filter using Advanced Filter/Sort, you can save the filter settings as a query by using the Save as Query command on the Advanced menu.
3. You can restore filter settings that you previously saved in a query by using the Load from Query command on the Advanced menu.

BTW
Using Wildcards in Filters
Both the question mark (?) and the asterisk (*) wildcards can be used in filters created using Advanced Filter/Sort.

Consider This

How do you determine whether to use a query or a filter?

The following guidelines apply to this decision.

- If you think that you will frequently want to display records that satisfy this exact criterion, you should consider creating a query whose results contain only the records that satisfy the criterion. To display those records in the future, simply open the query.
- If you are viewing data in a datasheet or form and decide you want to restrict the records to be included, it is easier to create a filter than a query. You can create and use the filter while you are viewing the data.
- If you have created a filter that you would like to be able to use again, you can save the filter as a query.

Consider This

Once you have decided to use a filter, how do you determine which type of filter to use?

- If your criterion for filtering is that the value in a particular field matches or does not match a certain specific value, you can use Filter By Selection.
- If your criterion only involves a single field but is more complex (for example, the criterion specifies that the value in the field begins with a certain collection of letters), you can use a common filter.
- If your criterion involves more than one field, use Filter By Form.
- If your criteria involve more than a single And or Or statement, or if your filter involves sorting, you will probably find it simpler to use Advanced Filter/Sort.

Break Point: If you wish to take a break, this is a good place to do so. You can quit Access now. To resume at a later time, start Access, open the database called SC_AC_03_Clearnet.accdb, and continue following the steps from this location forward.

Changing the Database Structure

When you initially create a database, you define its **structure**; that is, you assign names and data types to all the fields. In many cases, the structure you first define will not continue to be appropriate as you use the database.

Perhaps a field currently in the table is no longer necessary. If no one ever uses a particular field, it is not needed in the table. Because it is occupying space and serving no useful purpose, you should remove it from the table. You would also need to delete the field from any forms, reports, or queries that include it.

More commonly, an organization will find that it needs to add data that was not anticipated at the time the database was first designed. The organization's own requirements may have changed. In addition, outside regulations that the organization must satisfy may change as well. Either case requires the addition of fields to an existing table.

Datasheet and Design View

Although you can make some changes to the database structure in Datasheet view, it is usually easier and better to make these changes in Design view. The following steps compare your options within each view for various tasks. You will often think you can complete a structure change in Datasheet view but then find the one change necessitates other changes. And then these other changes can only be made in Design view. Therefore, it's a good idea to develop the habit of using Design view for database structure changes.

BTW
Changing Data Types
It is possible to change the data type for a field that already contains data. Before doing so, you should consider the effect on other database objects, such as forms, queries, and reports. For example, you could convert a Short Text field to a Long Text field if you find that you do not have enough space to store the data that you need. You also could convert a Number field to a Currency field or vice versa.

Note that you cannot change a field's data type to AutoNumber once data has been added anywhere in the table.

To Change a Field's Data Type, Properties, and Primary Key

A field in one of your tables might need a change of its data type and properties; for example, a data type might have been set that prevents users from including the field in calculations. To make a change to the data type and properties of a field, you would use the following steps.

1. Open the table in Design view.
2. Next to the field name, click the box under Data Type.
3. Choose the correct data type from the menu.
4. A description of the field may be added under the Description column.
5. If necessary, change the field size in the Field Properties General tab in the lower pane.
6. To change the key field, select the new key field by clicking in the gray box to the left of the field name. On the ribbon, click Primary Key (Table Design tab | Tools group).
7. When you close the table, you will be prompted to save the changes. Select Yes.

To Change a Field's Properties in Datasheet View

Alternatively, some of these changes may be done in Datasheet view. To use Datasheet view to change a field's name, caption, or data type, you would use the following steps.

1. Open the table in Datasheet view.
2. Select the desired field and click the Table Fields tab.
3. Click Name & Caption (Table Fields tab | Properties group), and set a caption and description for the field.
4. In the Formatting group, you can set a data type.

To Delete a Field in Design View

If a field in one of your tables is no longer needed, you should delete the field. For example, it might not serve a useful purpose, or it might have been included by mistake. To delete a field, you would use the following steps.

1. Open the table in Design view.
2. Click the row selector for the field to be deleted.
3. Press DEL.
4. When Access displays the dialog box requesting confirmation that you want to delete the field, click Yes.

To Delete a Field in Datasheet View

1. In Datasheet view, right-click the field and then click Delete Field.

To Move a Field in Design View

If you decide you would rather have a field in one of your tables in a different position in the table, you can move it. To move a field, you would use the following steps.

1. Open the table in Design view.
2. Click the row selector for the field to be moved.

3. Drag the field to the desired position.
4. Release the mouse button to place the field in the new position.

To Move a Field in Datasheet View

If you are working in Datasheet view and want to move a field, you would use the following steps.

1. In Datasheet view, select the field to be moved.
2. Drag the field to the desired position.
3. Release the mouse button to place the field in the new position.

To Change a Number Field Size in Design View

Most field size changes can be made in either Datasheet view or Design view. However, changing the field size for Number fields, such as the Mileage field, is best done in Design view to access the full list of options. This is because number fields can carry qualitatively different types of data. Consider that the values in the Mileage field do not need any decimal places and will never exceed a few thousand miles for loads in North America. Integer, Long Integer, or Single field sizes could all meet these requirements. One difference between these options concerns the amount of storage space required. For example, the Integer field size requires 2 bytes of storage space per record per field. Long Integer, in contrast, requires 4 bytes of storage space per entry, as does Single. Double can store up to 15 significant digits but requires 8 bytes of storage space per entry.

Another difference between these field sizes is the degree of accuracy if decimal places are needed, that is, the number of decimal places to which the number is accurate. For example, Double is more accurate than Single by allowing more decimal places (15 significant digits versus 7 significant digits); however, Double requires more storage space.

Because the mileage values in this table are not tracked to any decimal places, Integer is the best choice, providing sufficient digits while minimizing required storage space in the database. The following steps change the field size of the Mileage field to Integer, the format to Fixed, and the number of decimal places to 0, along with extending those changes to any form or report that uses this field. **Why change the format and number of decimal places?** Changing the format and number ensures that each value will appear with no decimal places.

1

- Open the Navigation Pane, open the Loads table in Design view, and then close the Navigation Pane.
- If necessary, click the vertical scroll bar to display the Mileage field, and then click the row selector for the Mileage field to select the field (Figure 3–25).

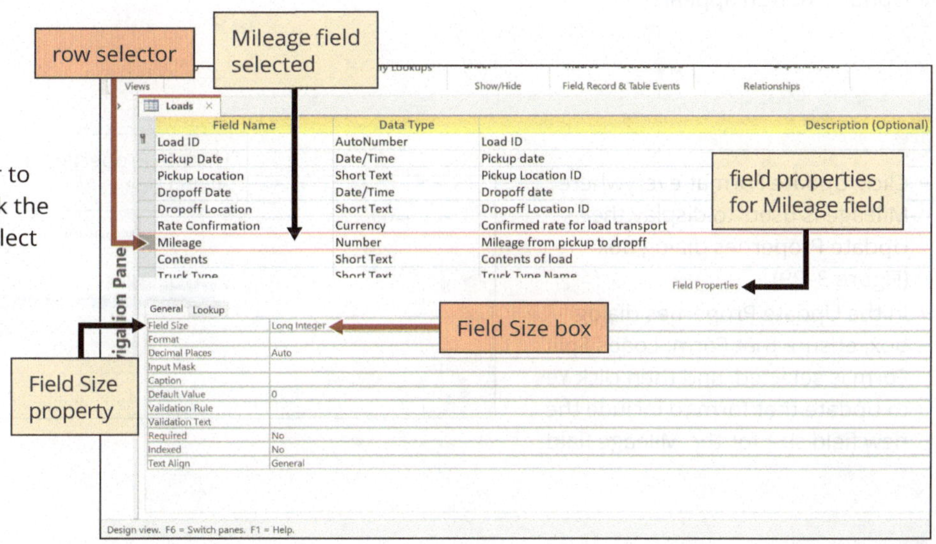

Figure 3–25

2

- Click the Field Size box to display the Field Size arrow.
- Click the Field Size arrow to display the Field Size menu (Figure 3–26).

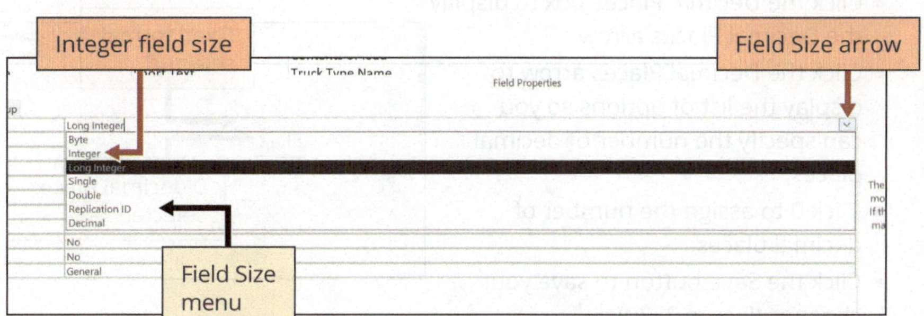

Figure 3–26

Q&A What would happen if I left the field size set to Long Integer?

If the field size is Long Integer, Single, Double, or Decimal, the database will set aside much more space for that field than is needed. For example, using Long Integer, a value of 100 would be stored as 0000000100, using ten digits. With Integer, a value of 100 is stored as 00100, using only five digits.

3

- Click Integer to select the smaller field size.
- Click the Format box to display the Format arrow.
- Click the Format arrow to display the Format menu (Figure 3–27).

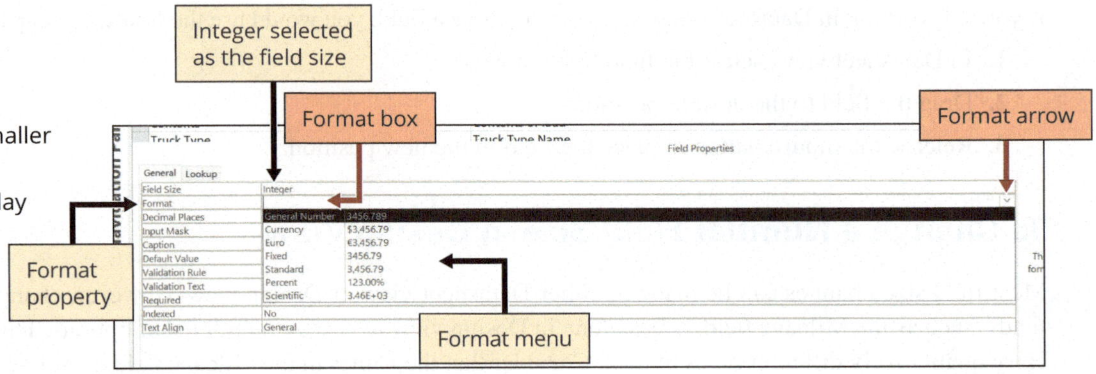

Figure 3–27

4

- Click Fixed to select fixed as the format.
- Click the 'Property Update Options' button to display the options for updating the property of this field to any form or report that uses this field (Figure 3–28).

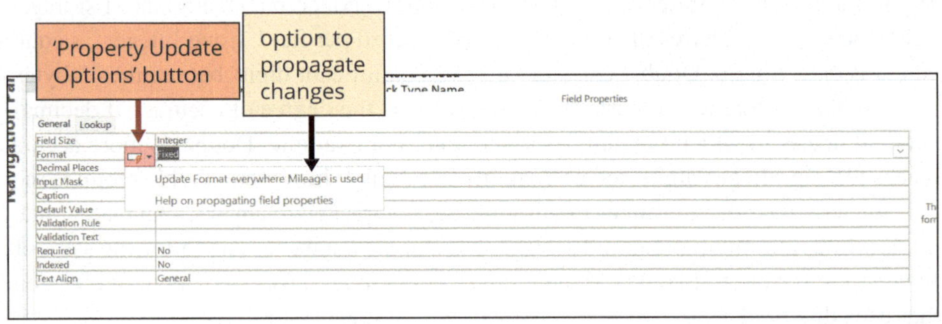

Figure 3–28

Q&A Why did the 'Property Update Options' button appear?

You changed the number of digits used to store the number data. The 'Property Update Options' button offers a quick way of making the same change everywhere Mileage appears.

5

- Click 'Update Format everywhere Mileage is used' to display the Update Properties dialog box (Figure 3–29).
- In the Update Properties dialog box, ensure that Form: Loads Split Form is selected, and then click Yes to update that form to include the new field size for the Mileage field.

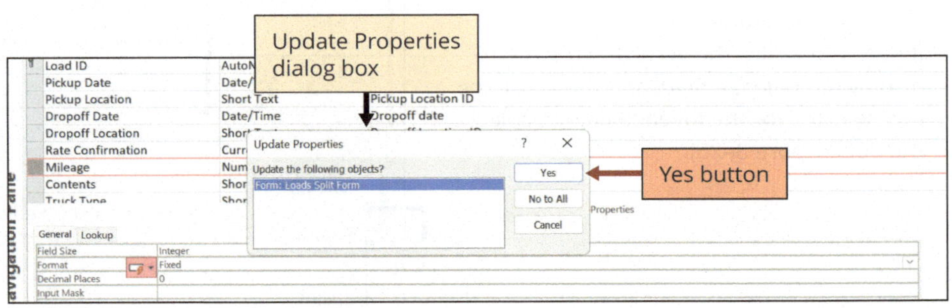

Figure 3–29

6

- Click the Decimal Places box to display the Decimal Places arrow.
- Click the Decimal Places arrow to display the list of options so you can specify the number of decimal places.
- Click 0 to assign the number of decimal places.
- Click the Save button to save your changes (Figure 3–30).

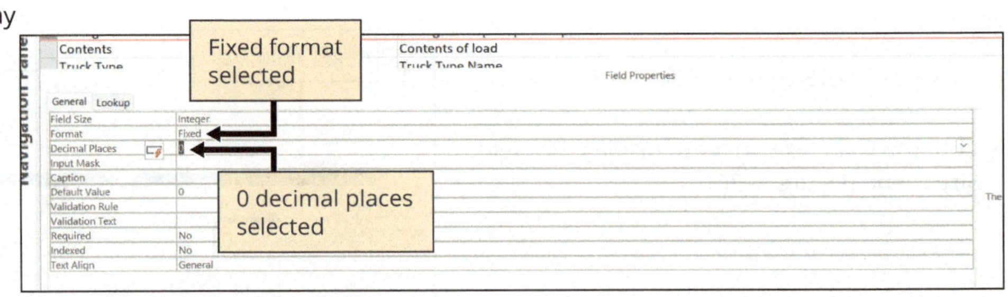

Figure 3–30

To Change the Format of a Number Field in Datasheet View

Although the field size of number formatted fields cannot be changed in Datasheet view, the format of a number field can be changed in Datasheet view. The number format can be General Number, Currency, Euro, Fixed, Standard, Percent, or Scientific. To change the format of a number field in the datasheet, you would use the following steps.

1. Open the table in Datasheet view.
2. Select the field that you want to change.
3. Click the Format arrow (Table Fields tab | Formatting group) to display the Format menu, and then select the desired number format.

To Add a New Field

Clearnet has recently hired a new agent. The owners realized their database needs to track which agent arranges each load so they can properly assign commissions. You can add fields to a table in a database. The following step adds the Agent field to the Loads table immediately after the Load Notes field. **Why?** Clearnet has decided that it can track agents with an additional field, Agent, in the Loads table. The possible values for Agent are Emery, Ariel, or Becka.

1

- With the Loads table still open in Design view, click the Field Name column in the blank row below the Load Notes field to produce an insertion point.
- Type **Agent** as the field name and then press TAB to move to the data type space.

To Create a Lookup Field

A **lookup field** allows the user to select from a list of values when updating the contents of the field. The following steps make the Agent field a lookup field. **Why?** The Agent field has only three possible values, making lookup field an appropriate data type for this field.

1

- Click the Data Type arrow to display the menu of available data types (Figure 3–31).

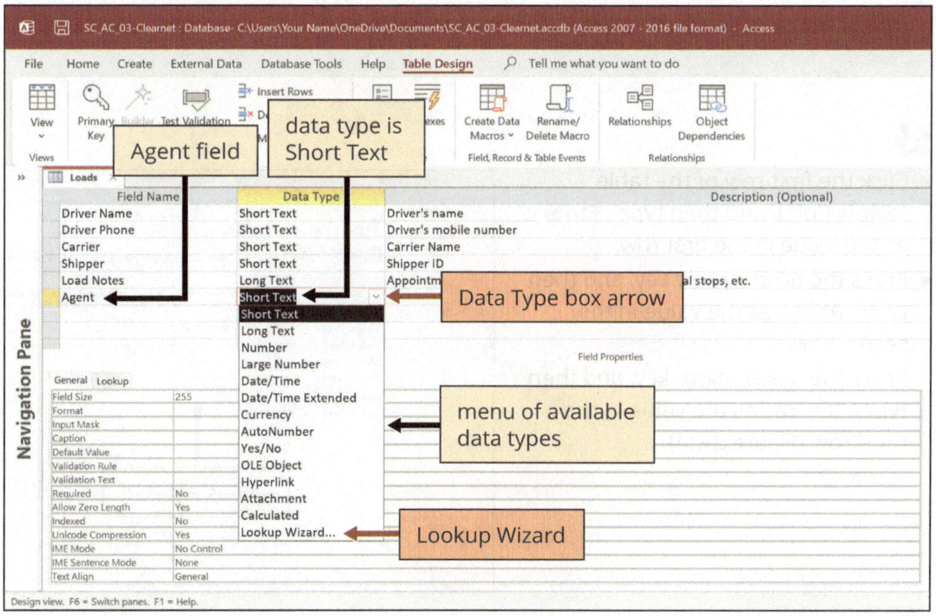

Figure 3–31

2

- Click Lookup Wizard, and then click the 'I will type in the values that I want.' option button (Lookup Wizard dialog box) to indicate that you will list the values (Figure 3–32).

Q&A When would I use the other option button?
You would use the other option button if the items to be entered in this field were found in another table or query.

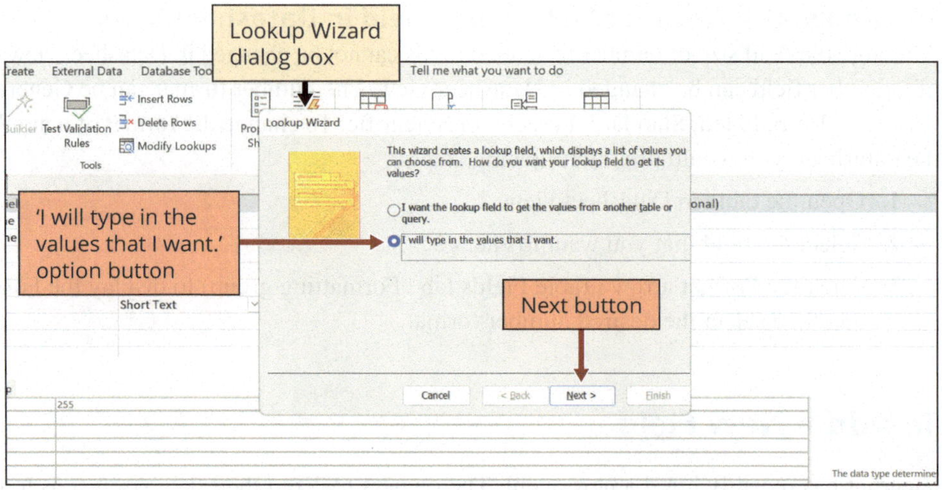

Figure 3–32

3

- Click the Next button to display the next Lookup Wizard screen (Figure 3–33).

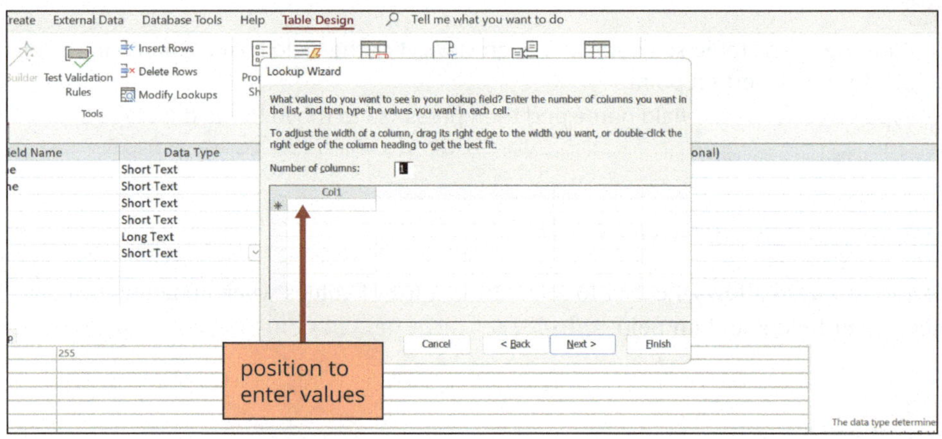

Figure 3–33

4

- Click the first row of the table (below Col1), and then type **Emery** as the value in the first row.
- Press the DOWN ARROW key, and then type **Ariel** as the value in the second row.
- Press the DOWN ARROW key, and then type **Becka** as the value in the third row (Figure 3–34).

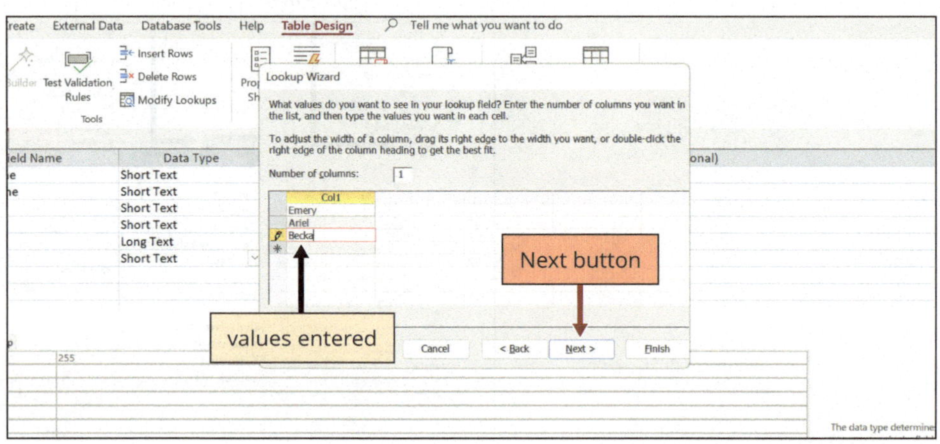

Figure 3–34

5

- Click the Next button to display the next Lookup Wizard screen.
- Ensure Agent is entered as the label for the lookup field and that the Allow Multiple Values check box is NOT checked (Figure 3–35).

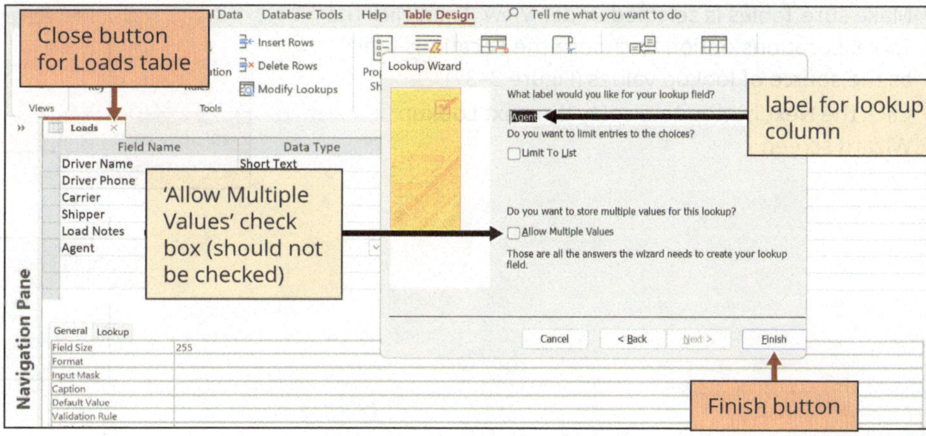

Figure 3–35

Q&A What is the purpose of the Limit To List check box?
With a lookup field, users can select from the list of values, in which case they can only select items in the list. They can also type their entry, in which case they are not necessarily limited to items in the list. If you check the Limit To List check box, users will be limited to items in the list, even if they type their entry. You will accomplish this same restriction later in this module with a validation rule, so you do not need to check this box.

6

- Click Finish to complete the definition of the lookup field.
- Save and close the table.

Q&A Why does the data type for the Agent field still show Short Text?
The data type is still Short Text because the values entered in the wizard were entered as text.

Why did I not change the field size for the Agent field?
You could have changed the field size to something like 10 or 15, but it is not necessary. When you create a lookup field and indicate specific values for the field, you automatically restrict the field size.

To Add a Multivalued Field

Normally, fields contain only a single value. In Access, it is possible to have **multivalued fields**, that is, fields that can contain more than one value. Clearnet wants to use such a field to store load pickup and dropoff locations. Occasionally, a shipper needs a truck to pick up items at two different locations or deliver to multiple locations. Allowing multiple locations for pickup or dropoff will provide more flexibility in record-keeping that will more accurately represent the reality of a truck's trip. Additionally, Clearnet would like to pull these available values from the Location ID field in the Locations table. This way, the Lookup field list in the Loads table will not need to be manually updated as new locations are added to the database.

BTW
Multivalued Fields
Do not use multivalued fields if you eventually plan to move your data to another relational database management system, such as SQL Server. SQL Server and other relational DBMSs do not support multivalued fields.

Creating a multivalued field uses the same process as creating a lookup field, with the exception that you check the Allow Multiple Values check box. In this case, you will also have the lookup field get values from another table instead of typing the available values. The following steps change two Short Text fields to multivalued fields that get possible values from another table.

1

- Open the Loads table in Design view.

2

- Click the Data Type arrow to display the menu of available data types for the Pickup Location field, and then click Lookup Wizard in the menu of available data types to start the Lookup Wizard.
- Make sure the 'I want the lookup field to get the values from another table or query.' option button is selected (Figure 3–36).
- Click the Next button to display the next Lookup Wizard screen.

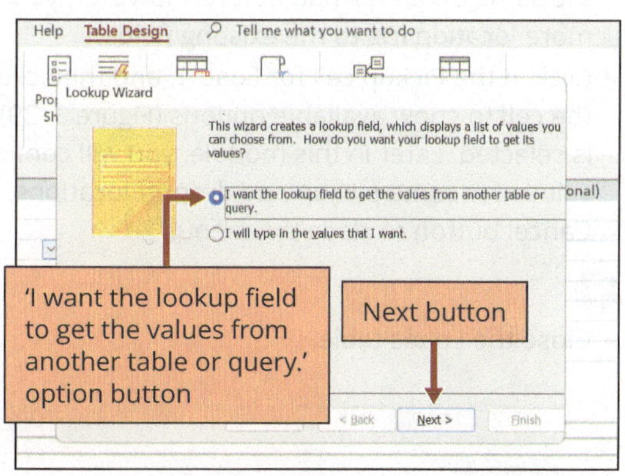

Figure 3–36

3

- Make sure Tables is selected under View. Then click the Table: Locations option to choose the Locations table as the source of lookup values (Figure 3–37).
- Click the Next button to display the next Lookup Wizard screen.

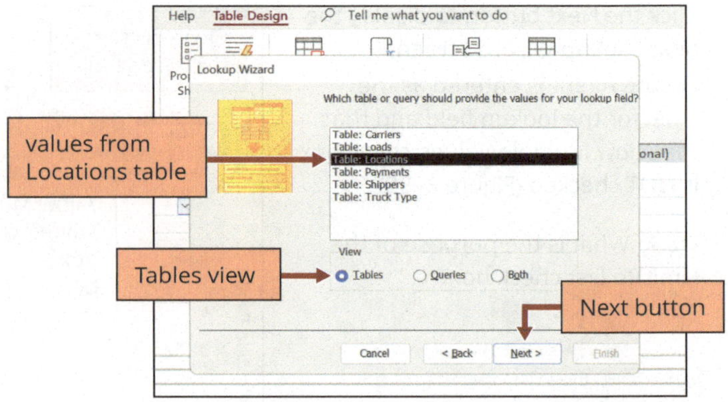

Figure 3–37

4

- Make sure Location ID is selected under Available Fields, and then click the Select Field button (Figure 3–38).
- Click the Next button to display the next Lookup Wizard screen.

5

- You will not configure a sort order for lookup values, so click the Next button to display the next Lookup Wizard screen.
- You will not change the column width, so click the Next button to display the next Lookup Wizard screen.

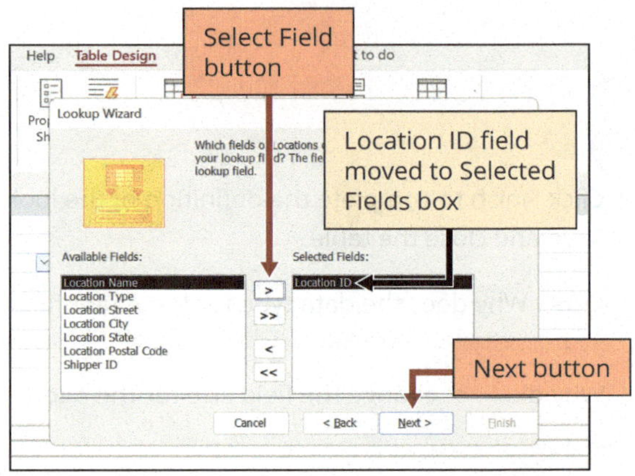

Figure 3–38

6

- Ensure that Pickup Location is entered as the label for the lookup field.
- Click the Allow Multiple Values check box to allow the user to enter multiple values.
- Click the Finish button to complete the definition of the Lookup Wizard field.
- You will see a warning to confirm you want to make the change because you will not be able to undo the change once saved. Click the Yes button.
- You will see a warning saying you must save the table to create the relationship between the tables for the lookup field. Click the Yes button.

7

- Repeat Steps 2 through 6 for the Dropoff Location field in the Loads table, ensuring that the label for this field is Dropoff Location.

8

- Switch to Datasheet view. The Pickup and Dropoff fields contain the same data they had before. However, you now can also add more location IDs to the existing fields.
- Click in the Pickup cell for Load 1, and then click the arrow for the cell to show available options (Figure 3–39). Currently, L-002 is selected. Later in this module, you will configure multiple values for some pickup and dropoff locations. For now, click the Cancel button to close the menu.

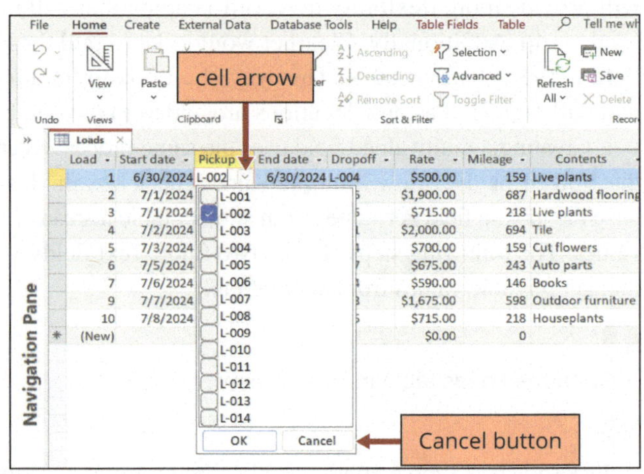

Figure 3–39

9

- Close the Loads table.

To Modify Single Valued or Multivalued Lookup Fields

At some point, you might want to change the list of choices in a lookup field. If you needed to modify a single value or multivalued lookup field, you would use the following steps.

1. Open the table in Design view and select the field to be modified.
2. Click the Lookup tab in the Field Properties pane.
3. Change the list in the Row Source property to the desired list of values.

To Add a Calculated Field

As you learned in Module 2, a field that can be computed from other fields is called a calculated field or a computed field. You can create a calculated field in a query. In Access 2019 and later versions, it is also possible to include a calculated field in a table. Users will not be able to update this field. **Why?** Access will automatically perform the necessary calculation and display the correct value whenever you display or use this field in any way. The following steps add to the Payments table a field that calculates the remainder of the payment due to the Carrier after the Agent Commission and Brokerage Fees are removed.

1

- Open the Payments table in Design view.
- Right-click the row selector for the Carrier Payment Status field (Figure 3–40), and then click Insert Rows on the shortcut menu to insert a blank row above the selected field.
- Type **Carrier Payment** as the field name, and then press TAB.
- Click the Data Type arrow to display the menu of available data types (Figure 3–41).

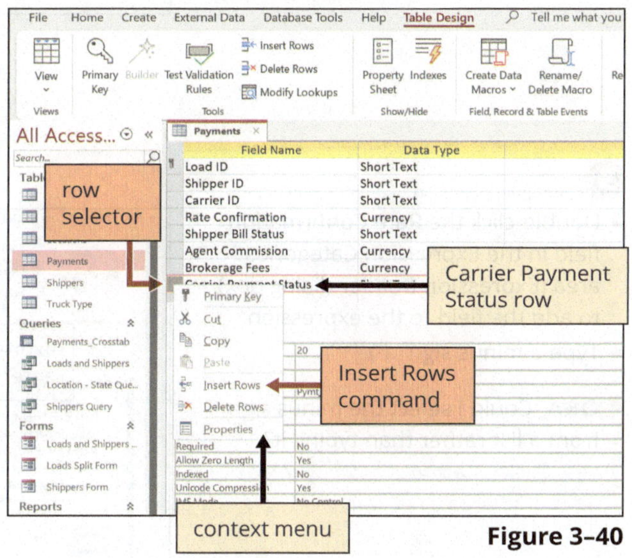

Figure 3–40

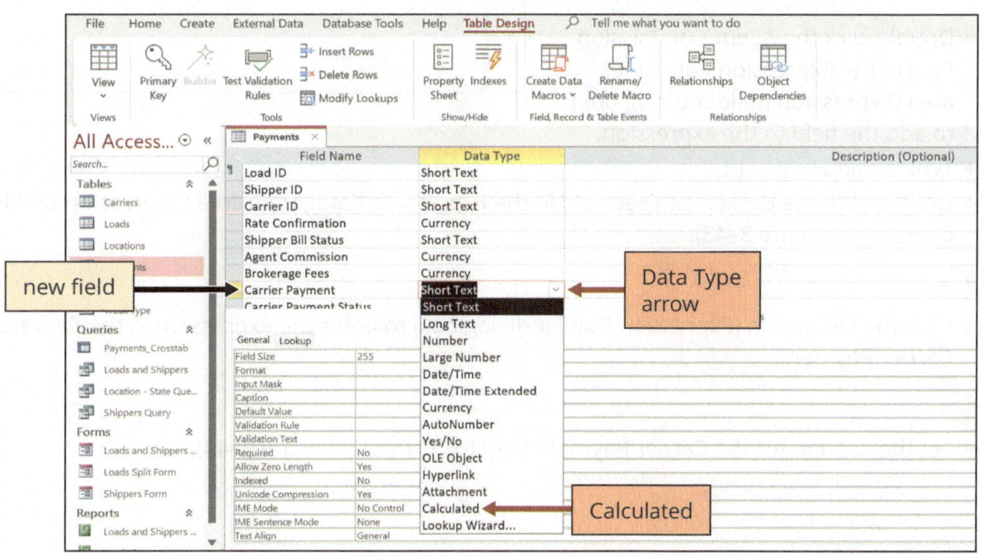

Figure 3–41

2

- Click Calculated to select the Calculated data type and display the Expression Builder dialog box (Figure 3–42).

Q&A I do not have the list of fields in the Expression Categories area. What should I do?
Click Payments in the Expression Elements area.

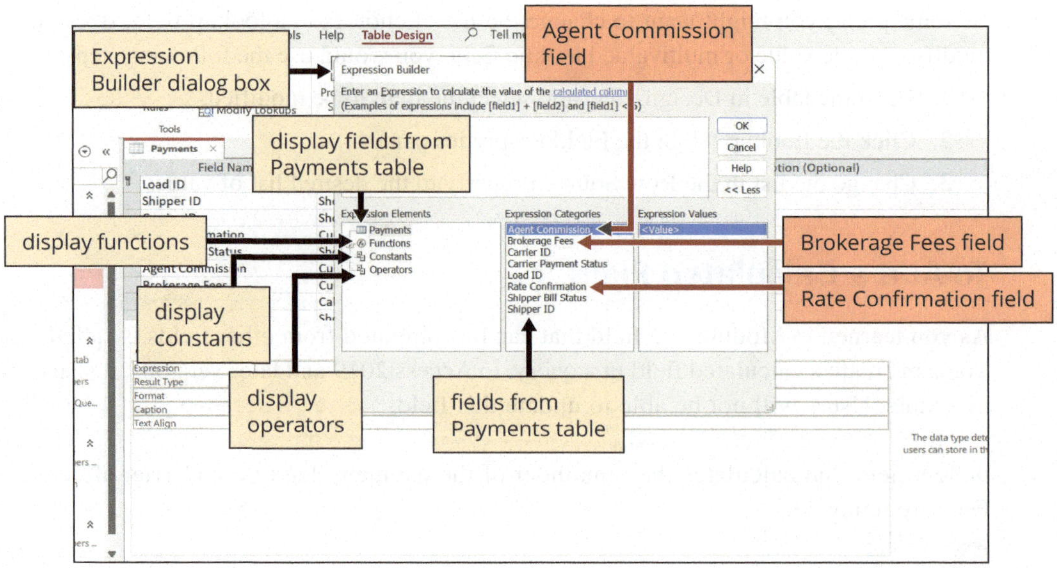

Figure 3–42

3

- Double-click the Rate Confirmation field in the Expression Categories area (Expression Builder dialog box) to add the field to the expression.
- Type a minus sign (-).

Q&A Could I select the minus sign from a list rather than typing it?
Yes. Click Operators in the Expression Elements area to display available operators, and then double-click the minus sign.

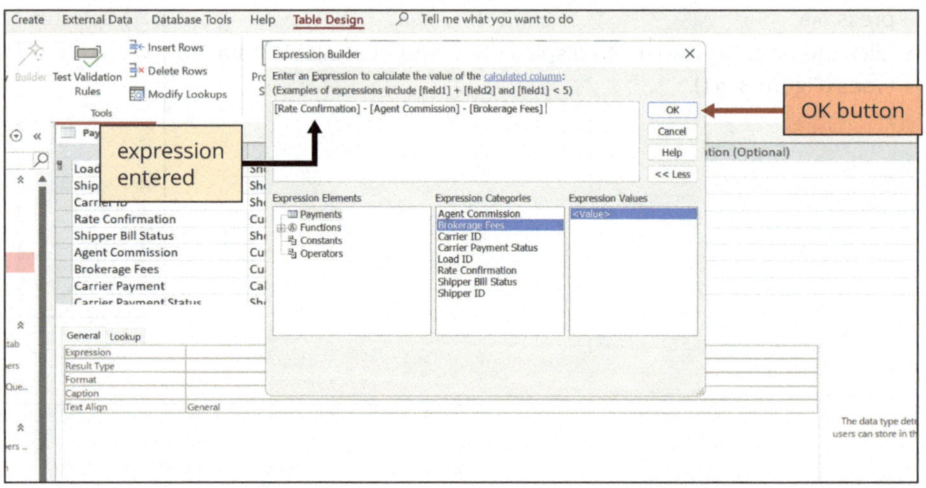

Figure 3–43

- Double-click the Agent Commission field in the Expression Categories area (Expression Builder dialog box) to add the field to the expression.
- Type a minus sign (-).
- Double-click the Brokerage Fees field in the Expression Categories area (Expression Builder dialog box) to add the field to the expression (Figure 3–43).

4

- Click the OK button (Expression Builder dialog box) to enter the expression in the Expression property of the Carrier Payment.

5

- Set the caption for the Carrier Payment field to **C_Pymt** (Figure 3–44).

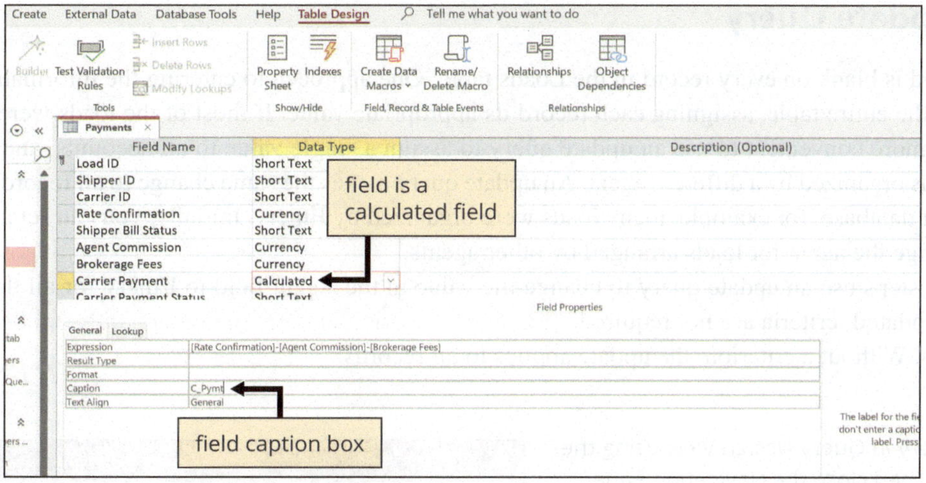

Figure 3–44

6

- Click the Save button on the Quick Access Toolbar to save the changes.
- Switch to Datasheet view to see the calculated amounts. Adjust the C_Pymt column size to the best fit.
- Save and close the table.

Q&A Could I have typed the expression in the Expression Builder dialog box rather than selecting the fields from a list?

Yes. You can use whichever technique you find more convenient.

Earlier, when I entered a calculated field in a query, I typed the expression in the Zoom dialog box. Could I have used the Expression Builder then instead?

Yes. To do so, you would click Build rather than Zoom on the shortcut menu.

Could I make a calculated field in the Datasheet view of a table?

Yes. To do so, open the table in Datasheet view, click the Click to Add arrow in the rightmost blank field space, select Calculated Field, and then indicate the type of data you want in that calculated field. Access displays the Expression Builder, where you can complete the calculated field.

Can I modify the calculated field in Design view?

Yes. In Design view, select the calculated field. In the Field Properties pane, click the General tab, if necessary, and click to the right of the Expression for the calculated field. Click the small box with three dots to open the Expression Builder dialog box.

Mass Changes

In some cases, rather than making individual changes to records, you will want to make mass changes. That is, you will want to add, change, or delete many records in a single operation. You can do this with action queries. Unlike select queries, which simply present data in specific ways, an **action query** adds, deletes, or changes data in a table. An **update query** allows you to make the same change to all records satisfying some criterion. If you omit the criterion, you will make the same changes to all records in the table. A **delete query** allows you to delete all the records satisfying some criterion. You can add the results of a query to an existing table by using an **append query**. You also can add the query results to a new table by using a **make-table query**.

BTW
Database Backup
If you are making mass changes to a database, be sure to back up the database prior to doing the updates.

To Use an Update Query

The new Agent field is blank on every record in the Loads table. One approach to entering the information for the field would be to step through the entire table, assigning each record its appropriate value. If most of the loads were arranged by the same agent, it would be more convenient to use an update query to assign a single value to all accounts, and then update the agent name for those loads organized by a different agent. An update query makes the same change to all records satisfying a criterion.

In the Clearnet database, for example, many loads were organized by Emery. Initially, you can set all the values to Emery. Later, you can change the agent for loads arranged by other agents.

The following steps use an update query to change the value in the Agent field to Emery for all the records. Because all records are to be updated, criteria are not required. **Why?** If a criterion is used, the update only applies to those records that satisfy the criterion. Without a criterion, the update applies to all records.

1

- Create a new query in Query Design View using the Loads table, and then close the Navigation Pane and the Add Tables pane. Resize the fields list as desired.
- Click the Update button (Query Design tab | Query Type group) to specify an update query.
- Double-click the Agent field to add the field to the query design grid.
- Click the Update To row in the first column of the design grid, and then type **Emery** as the new value (Figure 3–45).

Q&A If I change my mind and do not want an update query, how can I change the query back to a select query?

Click the Select button (Query Design tab | Query Type group).

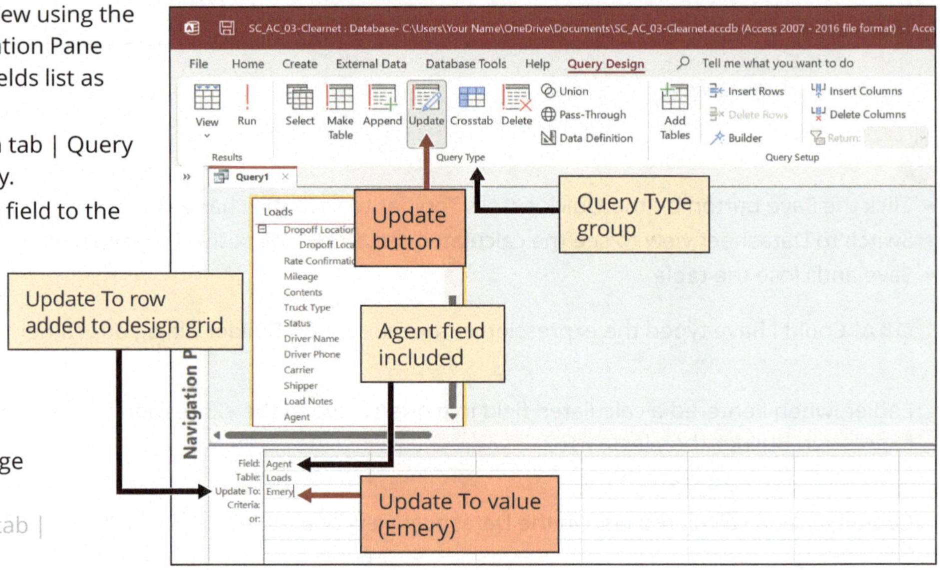

Figure 3–45

2

- Click the Run button (Query Design tab | Results group) to run the query and update the records (Figure 3–46).

Q&A The dialog box did not appear on my screen when I ran the query. What happened?

If the dialog box did not appear, it means that you did not click the Enable Content button when you first opened the database. Close the database, open it again, and enable the content. Then, create and run the query again.

- Click the Yes button to make the changes. Leave the query open for now.
- Open the Navigation Pane, and open the Loads table in Datasheet view to confirm all the updates were made correctly. Then close the Loads table.

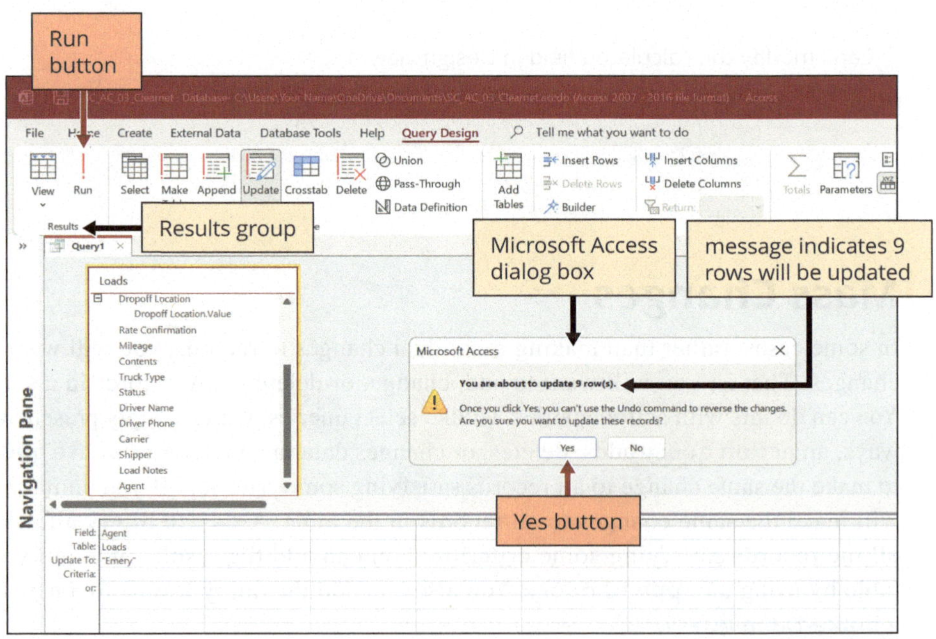

Figure 3–46

- **Experiment:** Create an update query to change the account type to MC. Enter a criterion to restrict the records to be updated, such as loads for Shipper S-001, and then run the query. Open the table to view your changes. When finished, create and run an update query to change the agent name to Emery on all records.
- Close the query. Because you do not need to use this update query again, do not save the query.

Other Ways

1. Right-click any open area in upper pane, click the Query Type arrow on shortcut menu, click Update Query on Query Type submenu to choose Update query type

To Use a Delete Query

In some cases, you might need to delete several records at a time. If, for example, Clearnet no longer dealt with loads being delivered to locations in Colorado (CO), the locations with this value in the State field could be deleted from the Clearnet database. Instead of deleting these accounts individually, which could be very time-consuming in a large database, you can delete them in one operation by using a delete query, which is a query that deletes all the records satisfying the criteria entered in the query. To create a delete query, you would use the following steps.

1. Create a query for the table containing the records to be deleted.
2. In Design view, indicate the fields and criteria that will specify the records to delete.
3. Click the Delete button (Query Design tab | Query Type group).
4. Click the Run button (Query Design tab | Results group) to run the query.
5. When Access indicates the number of records to be deleted, click the Yes button.

BTW
Viewing Records before Updating
You can view records affected by an update query before running the query. To do so, use the Select button to convert the query to a select query, add any additional fields that would help you identify the records, and then view the results. Make any necessary corrections to the query in Design view. When you are satisfied, use the Update button to once again convert the query to an update query.

To Use an Append Query

An append query adds a group of records from one table, called the Source table, to the end of another table, called the Destination table. For example, suppose that Clearnet acquires some new shippers; these new shippers are accompanied by a related database. To avoid entering all this information manually, you can append it to the Shippers table in the Clearnet database using the append query. To create an append query, you would use the following steps.

1. Create a select query for the Source table.
2. In Design view, indicate the fields to include, and then enter any necessary criteria.
3. View the select query results to be sure you have specified the correct data, and then return to Design view.
4. Click the Append button (Query Design tab | Query Type group).
5. When Access displays the Append dialog box, specify the name of the Destination table and its location. The Destination table might be in the same database or in a different one. When you're ready, click the OK button (Append dialog box).
6. Run the query by clicking the Run button (Query Design tab | Results group).
7. When Access indicates the number of records to be appended, click the OK button.

BTW
Delete Queries
If you do not specify any criteria in a delete query, Access will delete all the records in the table.

To Use a Make-Table Query

In some cases, you might want to create a new table that contains only records from an existing table. If so, use a make-table query to add the records to a new table. To create a make-table query, you would use the following steps.

1. Create a select query for the Source table.
2. In Design view, indicate the fields to include, and then enter any necessary criteria.
3. View the query results to be sure you have specified the correct data, and then return to Design view.
4. Click the Make Table button (Query Design tab | Query Type group).

BTW
Archive Tables
You can use a make-table query to create an archive table. An archive table is a table that contains data that is no longer used in operations but that might still be needed by the organization.

5. When Access displays the Make Table dialog box, specify the name of the Destination table and its location. The Destination table might be in the same database or in a different one. When you're ready, click the OK button (Make Table dialog box).
6. Run the query by clicking the Run button (Query Design tab | Results group).
7. When Access indicates the number of records to be inserted, click the OK button.

Break Point: If you wish to take a break, this is a good place to do so. You can quit Access now. To resume at a later time, start Access, open the database called SC_AC_03_Clearnet.accdb, and continue following the steps from this location forward.

BTW
Using the BETWEEN Operator in Validation Rules
You can use the BETWEEN operator to specify a range of values. For example, to specify that entries in the Mileage field must be between 0 and 3,000, type BETWEEN 0 and 3000 as the rule.

Validation Rules

You now have created, loaded, queried, and updated a database. Nothing you have done so far, however, restricts users to entering only valid data, that is, data that follows the rules established for data in the database. An example of such a rule would be that agents can only be Emery, Ariel, or Becka. To ensure the entry of valid data, you create **validation rules**, or rules that a user must follow when entering the data. When the database contains validation rules, Access prevents users from entering data that does not follow the rules. You can also specify **validation text**, which is the message that appears if a user attempts to violate the validation rule.

Validation rules can indicate a **required field**, a field in which the user *must* enter data; failing to enter data into a required field generates an error. Validation rules can also restrict a user's entry to a certain **range of values**; for example, the values in the Mileage field must be between 0 and 3,000; including a practical limit like this for the data in that field helps prevent errors in data entry. Alternatively, rules can specify a **default value**, that is, a value that Access will display on the screen in a particular field before the user begins adding a record. To make data entry of account numbers more convenient for the user, you can also have lowercase letters appear automatically as uppercase letters. Finally, validation rules can specify a collection of acceptable values.

BTW
Using Wildcards in Validation Rules
You can include wildcards in validation rules. For example, if you enter the expression, like T?, in the validation rule for the State field, the only valid entries for the field will be TN or TX. However, erroneous data also could be entered, such as TE or TA.

To Change a Field Size

The Field Size property for text fields represents the maximum number of characters a user can enter in the field. For example, the default field size for the Postal Code field in the Locations table was 255, but a user would never enter a postal code that long. Currently, the field is set to be 10 characters, which allows for a 5-digit postal code, a hyphen, and four route digits in that field. Occasionally, you will find that the field size that seemed appropriate when you first created a table is no longer appropriate. In the Locations table, the Postal Code field needs to be adjusted to fit 20 characters, in case there is a foreign postal code that is longer than the postal code plus four. To allow this longer postal code in the table, you need to change the field size for the Location Postal Code field. The following steps change the field size for the Location Postal Code field from 10 to 20.

1

- Open the Locations table in Design view and close the Navigation Pane.
- Select the Location Postal Code field by clicking its row selector.
- Click the Field Size property to select it, delete the current entry (10), and then type **20** as the new field size.

2

- Save and close the table.

To Specify a Required Field

To specify that a field is to be required, change the value for the Required property from No to Yes. The following step specifies that the Agent field in the Loads table is a required field. **Why?** Users will not be able to leave the Agent field blank when entering or editing records.

1

- Open the Navigation Pane, open the Loads table in Design view, and then close the Navigation Pane.
- Scroll down and select the Agent field by clicking its row selector.
- Click the Required property box in the Field Properties pane, and then click the arrow that appears.
- Click Yes in the list to make Agent a required field (Figure 3–47).

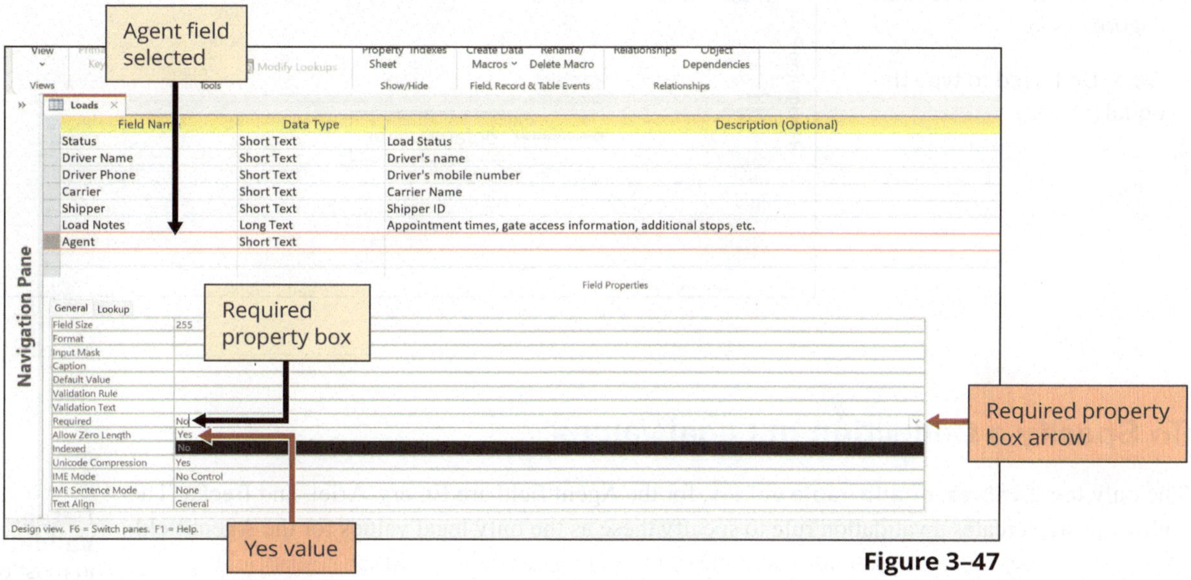

Figure 3–47

To Specify a Range

The following step specifies that entries in the Mileage field must be greater than 0 and less than 3,001. To indicate this range, the criterion specifies that the Mileage amount must be both > 0 (greater than 0) and <= 3000 (less than or equal to 3,000). **Why?** Combining these two criteria with the word, and, is logically equivalent to being between 0 and 3,001.

1

- Select the Mileage field by clicking its row selector, click the Validation Rule property box to produce an insertion point, and then type **>0 and <=3000** as the rule.
- Click the Validation Text property box to produce an insertion point, and then type **Must be greater than 0 and at most 3,000** as the text (Figure 3–48).

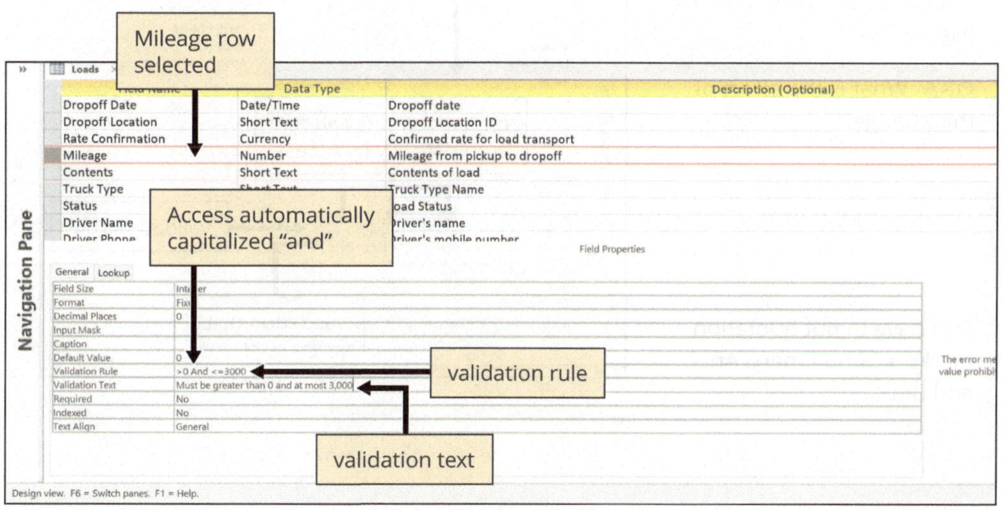

Figure 3–48

Q&A What is the effect of this change?

Users will now be prohibited from entering a Mileage amount that is either less than or equal to 0 or greater than 3,000 when they add records or change the value in the Mileage field.

To Specify a Default Value

To specify a default value, enter the value in the Default Value property box. The following step specifies Emery as the default value for the Agent field. **Why?** Emery is currently the only full-time agent, and so arranges the majority of loads. By making Emery's name the default value, if a user does not enter an Agent, the agent value will be Emery.

1

- Select the Agent field, click the Default Value property box to produce an insertion point, and then type **=Emery** as the value (Figure 3–49).

Q&A Do I need to type the equal (=) sign?
No. You could enter just Emery as the default value.

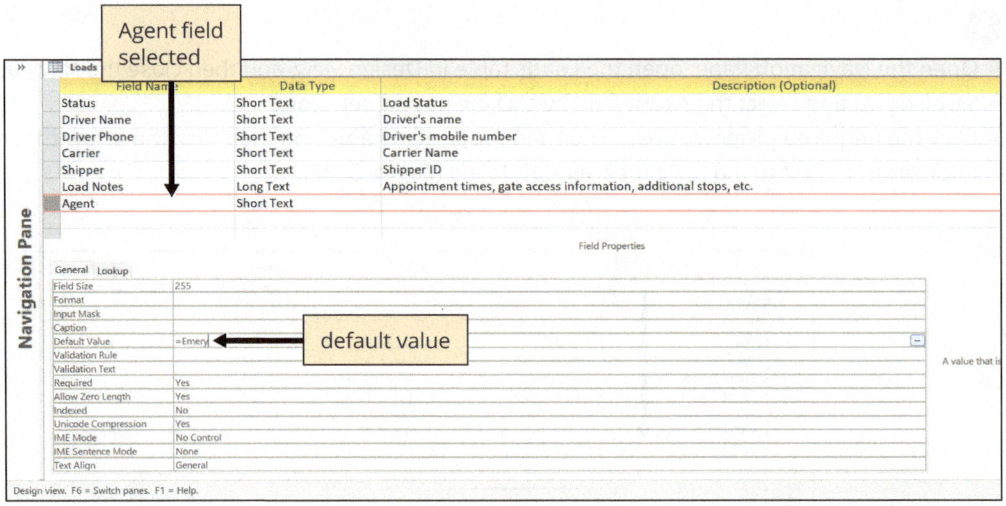

Figure 3–49

To Specify a Collection of Legal Values

The only **legal values**, or **allowable values**, for the Agent field are Emery, Ariel, and Becka. The following step creates a validation rule to specify these as the only legal values for the Agent field. **Why?** The validation rule prohibits users from entering any other value in the Agent field.

BTW
Database Design: Validation
In most organizations, decisions about what is valid and what is invalid data are made during the requirements-gathering process and the database design process.

1

- With the Agent field selected, click the Validation Rule property box to produce an insertion point and then type **=Emery or =Ariel or =Becka** as the validation rule.
- Click the Validation Text property box, and then type **Must be Emery, Ariel, or Becka** as the validation text (Figure 3–50).

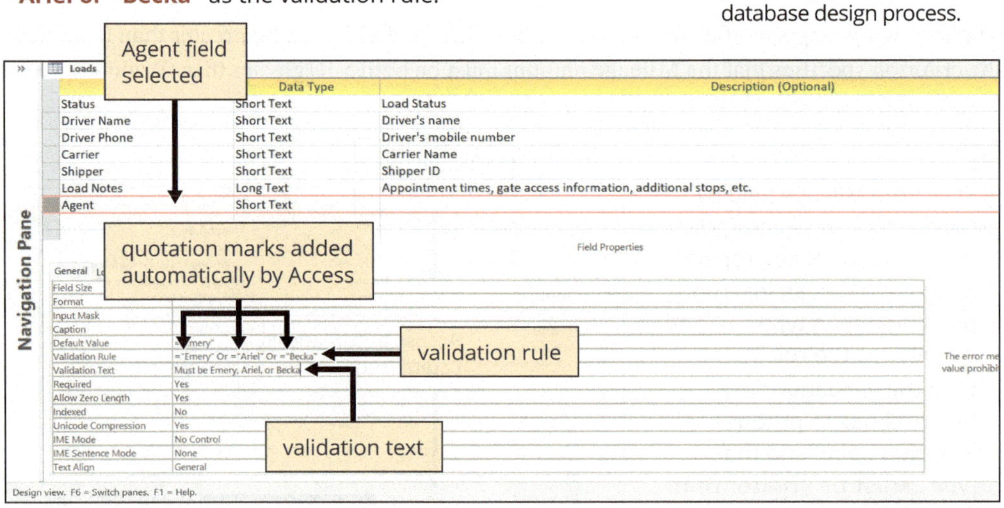

Figure 3–50

Q&A What is the effect of this change?
Users will now only be allowed to enter Emery, Ariel, or Becka in the Agent field when they add records or make changes to this field.

Do I have to put quotation marks around Emery, Ariel, and Becka?
No, you can just type =Emery or =Ariel or =Becka. Access automatically will put quotation marks around the product types and capitalize both instances of the word, or.

To Save the Validation Rules, Default Values, and Formats

The following steps save the validation rules, default values, and formats.

1

- Click the Save button on the Quick Access Toolbar to save the changes (Figure 3–51).

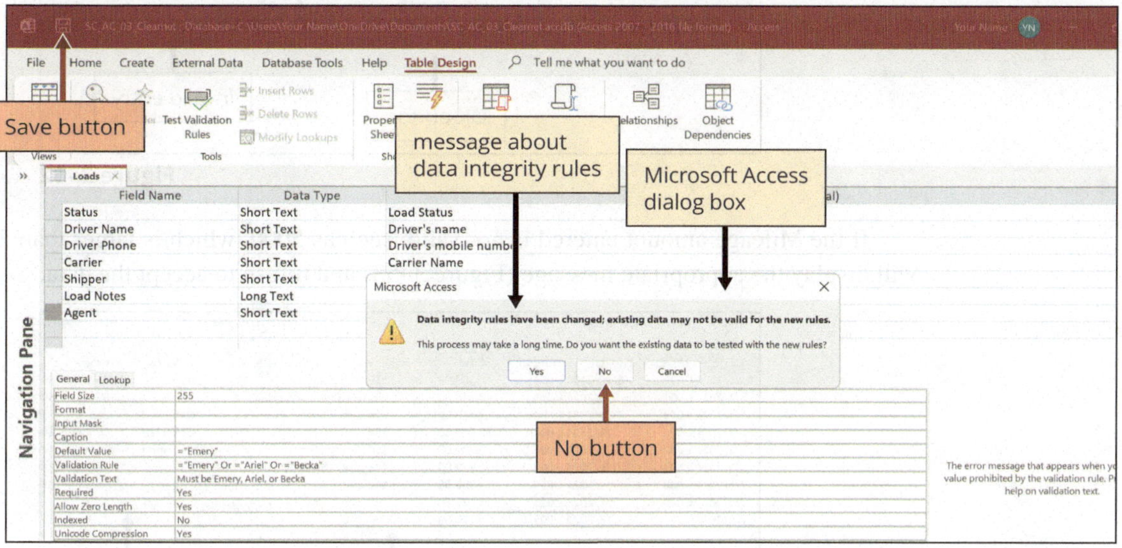

Figure 3–51

2

- If a Microsoft Access dialog box appears, click No to save the changes without testing current data.

Q&A When would you want to test current data?
If you have any doubts about the validity of the current data, you should be sure to test the data before saving changes.

3

- Close the Loads table.

Q&A Can I set validation rules, validation text, and properties in Datasheet view?
Yes, in Datasheet view, select the field and display the Table Fields tab. Click the Default Value button (Table Fields tab | Properties group) to open the Expression Builder. In the Properties group, you can also modify lookups. In the Field Validation group, you can set validation.

Updating a Table That Contains Validation Rules

Now that the Clearnet database contains validation rules, Access restricts the user to entering data that is valid and is formatted correctly. If a user enters a number that is out of the required range, for example, or enters a value that is not one of the permitted choices, Access displays an error message in the form of a dialog box. The user cannot update the database until the error is corrected.

If the Agent name entered is not valid, such as Kirsten, which is not one of the three names you specified, Access will display the text message you specified (Figure 3–52) and prevent the data from being entered into the database.

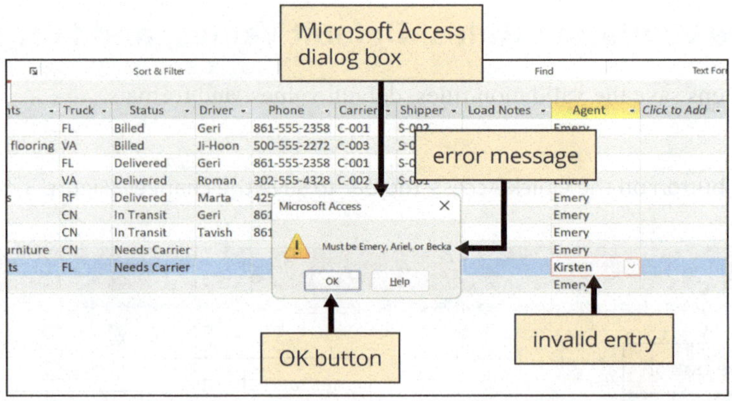

Figure 3–52

If the Mileage amount entered is not valid, such as 5000, which is larger than 3000, Access will display the appropriate message (Figure 3–53) and refuse to accept the data.

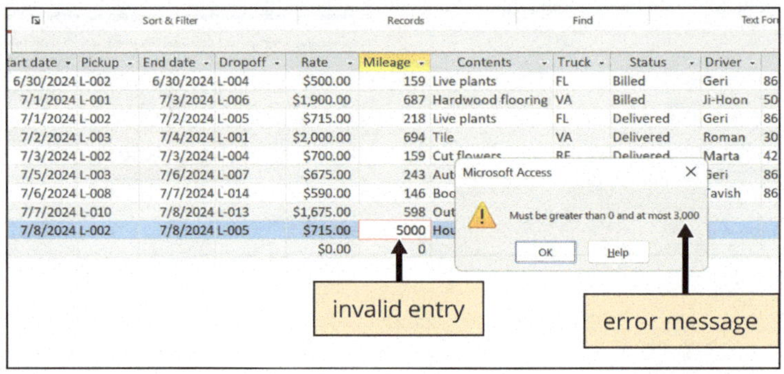

Figure 3–53

If a required field contains no data, Access indicates this by displaying an error message as soon as you attempt to leave the record (Figure 3–54). The field must contain a valid entry before Access will move to a different record, even if you did not specify validation text.

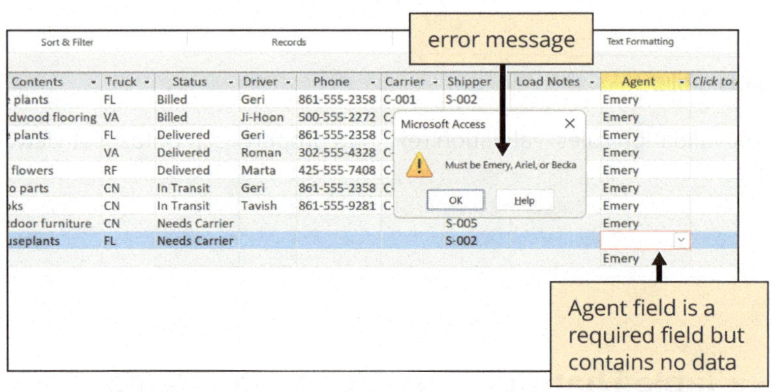

Figure 3–54

Consider This

When entering invalid data into a field with a validation rule, is it possible that you could not enter the data correctly? What would cause this? If it happens, what should you do?

If you cannot remember the validation rule you created or if you created the rule incorrectly, you might not be able to enter the data. In such a case, you will be unable to leave the field or close the table because you have entered data into a field that violates the validation rule.

If this happens, first try again to type an acceptable entry. If this does not work, repeatedly press BACKSPACE to erase the contents of the field, and then try to leave the field. If you are unsuccessful using this procedure, press ESC until the record is removed from the screen. The record will not be added to the database.

Should the need arise to take this drastic action, you probably have a faulty validation rule. Use the techniques of the previous sections to correct the existing validation rules for the field.

Making Additional Changes to the Database

Now that you have changed the structure and created validation rules, there are additional changes to be made to the database. You will use both the lookup and multivalued lookup fields to change the contents of the fields. You will also update both the form and the report to reflect the changes in the table.

To Use a Lookup Field

Earlier, in the Loads table, you changed all the entries in the Agent field to Emery. You have created a rule to ensure that only legitimate values (Emery, Ariel, or Becka) can be entered in the field. You also made Agent a lookup field. **Why?** You can make changes to a lookup field for individual records by simply clicking the field to be changed, clicking the arrow that appears in the field, and then selecting the desired value from the list. The following steps change the incorrect Agent values to the correct values.

1

- Open the Navigation Pane, open the Loads table in Datasheet view, and then close the Navigation Pane.
- Click in the Agent field on the third record (ID 3) to display an arrow.
- Click the arrow to display the drop-down list of available choices for the Agent field (Figure 3–55).

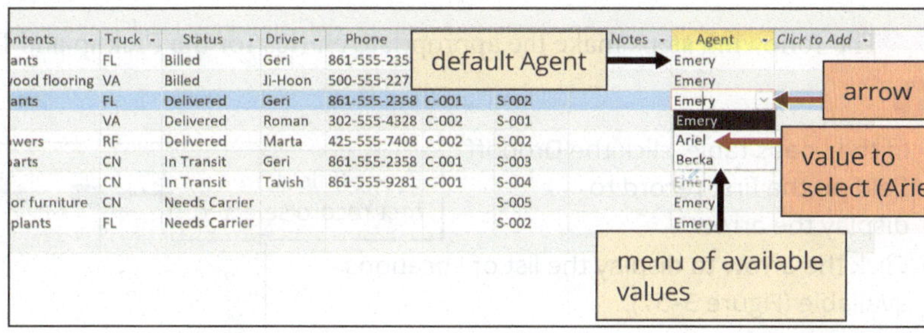

Figure 3–55

Q&A I got the drop-down list as soon as I clicked. I did not need to click the arrow. What happened?
If you click in the position where the arrow would appear, you will get the drop-down list. If you click anywhere else, you would need to click the arrow.

2

- Click Ariel to change the value.

Q&A Could I type the value instead of selecting it from the list?
Yes. Once you have either deleted the previous value or selected the entire previous value, you can begin typing. You do not have to type the full entry. When you begin with the letter, A, for example, Access will automatically suggest the full name.

3

- In a similar fashion, change the values on Loads 5 and 6 to Ariel, and change the value on Load 9 to Becka. Make sure the Agent field values match those shown in Figure 3–56.

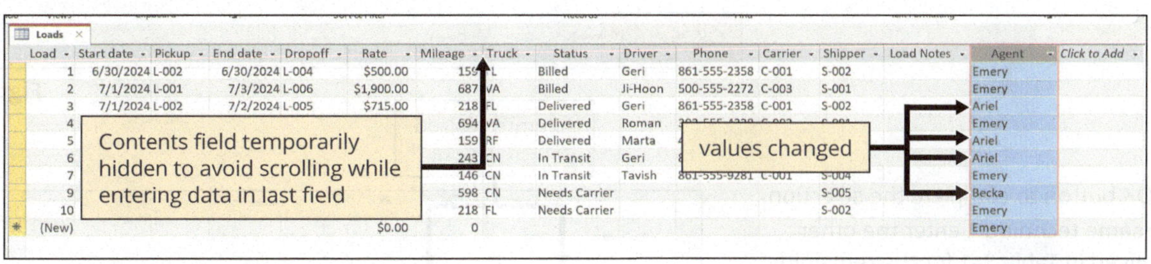

Figure 3–56

Q&A It's awkward scrolling back and forth on the table to choose the correct Load ID, and then choose the correct value in the Agent column. Is there a way to see both these columns at once?
Yes. You can temporarily hide some of the unneeded columns, and then unhide them when you're finished. To hide a column, right-click the column header (such as Contents) and click Hide Fields. When you're finished entering data, unhide all hidden fields by right-clicking any visible column header and selecting the check box for each hidden field (Unhide Columns dialog box), and then click Close.

To Use a Multivalued Lookup Field

Using a multivalued lookup field is similar to using a regular lookup field. The difference is that when you display the list, the entries are all preceded by check boxes. **Why?** Having the check boxes allows you to make multiple selections. You check all the entries that you want. Table 3–1 shows the appropriate entries for the loads with more than one pickup or dropoff location. As indicated in the table, only a few loads include multiple pickup or dropoff locations.

Table 3–1 Multivalued Pickup and Dropoff Locations

Load ID	Pickup Locations	Dropoff Locations
2	L-001	L-005, L-006
3	L-002	L-004, L-005
9	L-009, L-010	L-013

The following steps make the appropriate entries for the Pickup and Dropoff fields in the Loads table.

1

- In the Loads table, click the Dropoff field on the first record to display the arrow.
- Click the arrow to display the list of Locations available (Figure 3–57).

Q&A What if there were too many locations to fit?

Access would automatically include a scroll bar that you could use to scroll through all the choices.

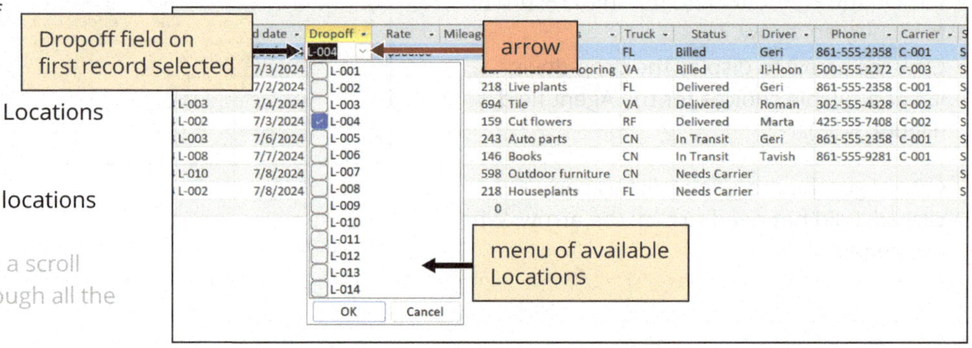

Figure 3–57

2

- Click the L-005 check box to select the additional dropoff location for the second load; Location L-004 has already been selected (Figure 3–58).

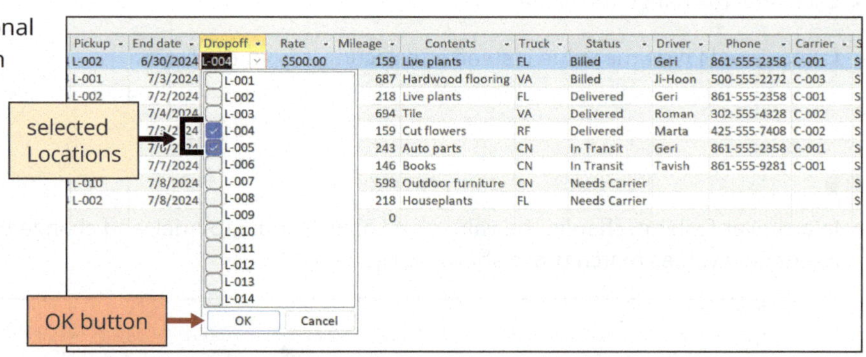

Figure 3–58

3

- Click the OK button to complete the selection.
- Using the same technique, enter the other locations given in Table 3–1 for the remaining accounts.
- Double-click the right boundary of the field selector for the Pickup field to resize the column so that it best fits the data. Repeat for the Dropoff field (Figure 3–59).

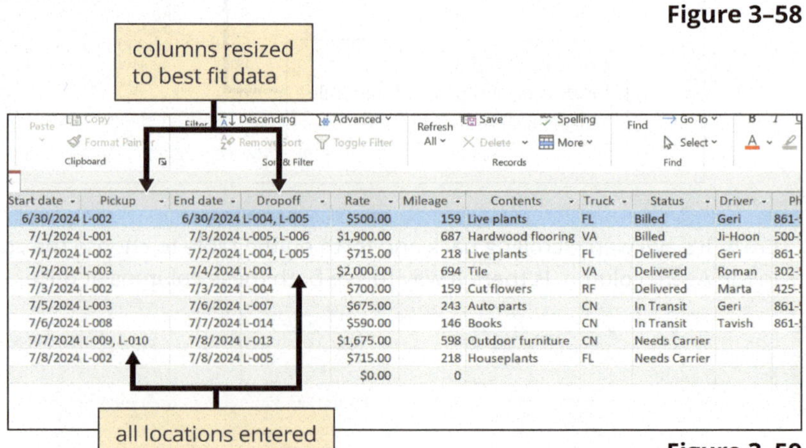

Figure 3–59

4

- Save the changes to the layout and close the Loads table.

Q&A What if I closed the table without saving the layout changes?
You would be asked if you want to save the changes.

Changing the Appearance of a Datasheet

You can change the appearance of a datasheet in a variety of ways. You can include totals in the datasheet. You can also change the appearance of gridlines or the text colors and font.

To Include Totals in a Datasheet

The following steps first include an extra row, called the Total row, in the datasheet for the Payments table. Note that this is not a calculated field. **Why?** It is possible to include totals and other statistics at the bottom of a datasheet in the Total row. The steps then display the total amount of money collected for all loads.

1

- Open the Navigation Pane, open the Payments table in Datasheet view, and then close the Navigation Pane.
- Click the Totals button (Home tab | Records group) to include the Total row in the datasheet. Note that a blank row for the next new record will remain above the Total row.
- Click the Total row in the RateCon column to display an arrow.
- Click the arrow to display a menu of available calculations (Figure 3–60).

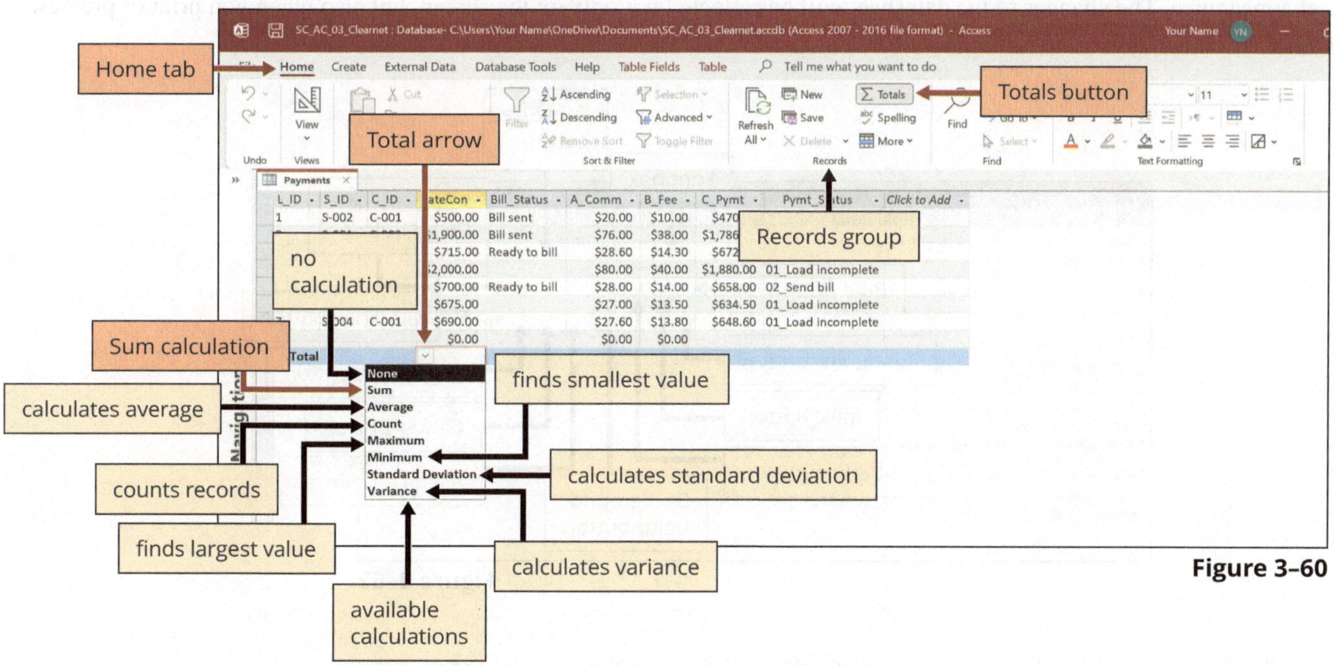

Figure 3–60

Q&A Can I also create a totals row in a query?
Yes, you can create a totals row in the Datasheet view of a query just like you did in the Datasheet view of the table.

Will I always get the same list?
No. You will only get the items that are applicable to the type of data in the column. You cannot calculate the sum of text data, for example.

2

- Click Sum to calculate the total of the RateCon amounts.
- Resize the RateCon column to best fit the total amount (Figure 3–61), if necessary.
- **Experiment:** Experiment with other statistics for the RateCon column and for other columns. When finished, once again select Sum for the RateCon column and clear any other statistics in other columns on the Total row.

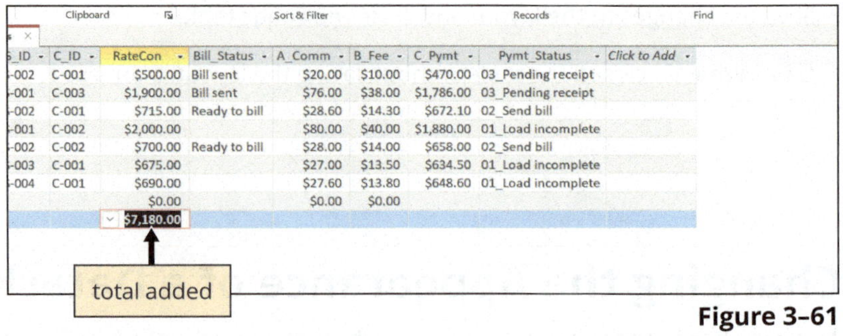

Figure 3–61

To Remove Totals from a Datasheet

If you no longer want the totals to appear as part of the datasheet, you can remove the Total row. The following step removes the Total row.

1

- Click the Totals button (Home tab | Records group), which is shown in Figure 3–60, to remove the Total row from the datasheet.

To Change Gridlines in a Datasheet

Figure 3–62 shows the various buttons, located in the Text Formatting group on the Home tab, that are available to change the datasheet appearance. The changes to the datasheet will be reflected not only on the screen, but also when you print or preview the datasheet.

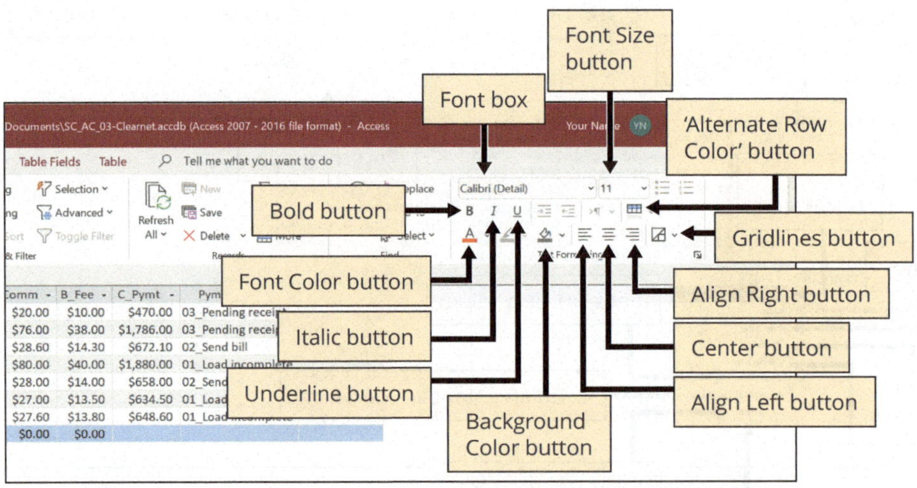

Figure 3–62

The following steps change the datasheet so that only horizontal gridlines are included. **Why?** You might prefer the appearance of the datasheet with only horizontal gridlines.

1

- With the Payments table open in Datasheet view, click the datasheet selector, which is the box in the upper-left corner of the datasheet, to select the entire datasheet (Figure 3–63).

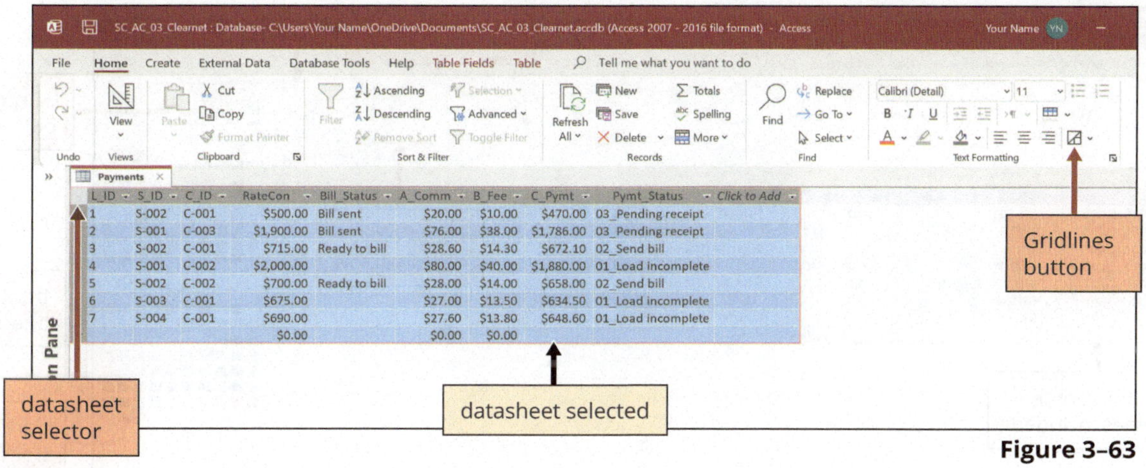

Figure 3–63

2

- Click the Gridlines button (Home tab | Text Formatting group) to display the Gridlines gallery (Figure 3–64).

Q&A Does it matter whether I click the button or the arrow?

In this case, it does not matter. Either action will display the gallery.

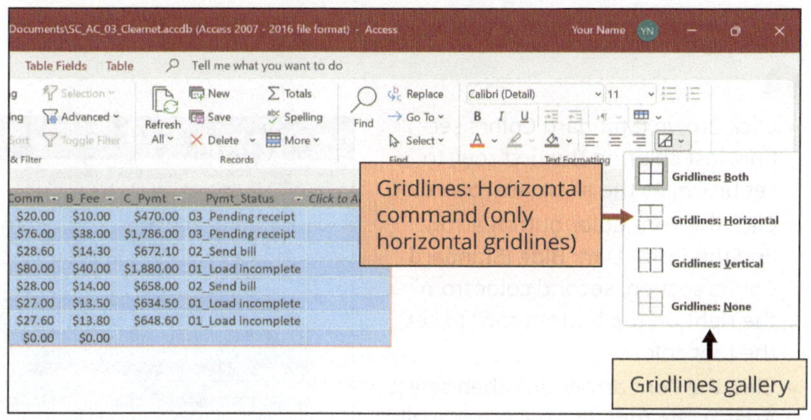

Figure 3–64

3

- Click Gridlines: Horizontal in the Gridlines gallery to include only horizontal gridlines.
- **Experiment:** Experiment with other gridline options. When finished, once again select horizontal gridlines.

To Change the Colors and Font in a Datasheet

You can also modify the appearance of the datasheet by changing the colors and the font. The following steps change the Alternate Fill color, a color that appears on every other row in the datasheet. **Why?** Having rows appear in alternate colors is an attractive way to visually separate the rows. The steps also change the font color, the font, and the font size.

1

- With the datasheet for the Payments table selected, click the Alternate Row Color button arrow (Home tab | Text Formatting group) to display the color palette (Figure 3–65).

Q&A Does it matter whether I click the button or the arrow?

Yes. Clicking the arrow produces a color palette. Clicking the button applies the currently selected color. When in doubt, you should click the arrow.

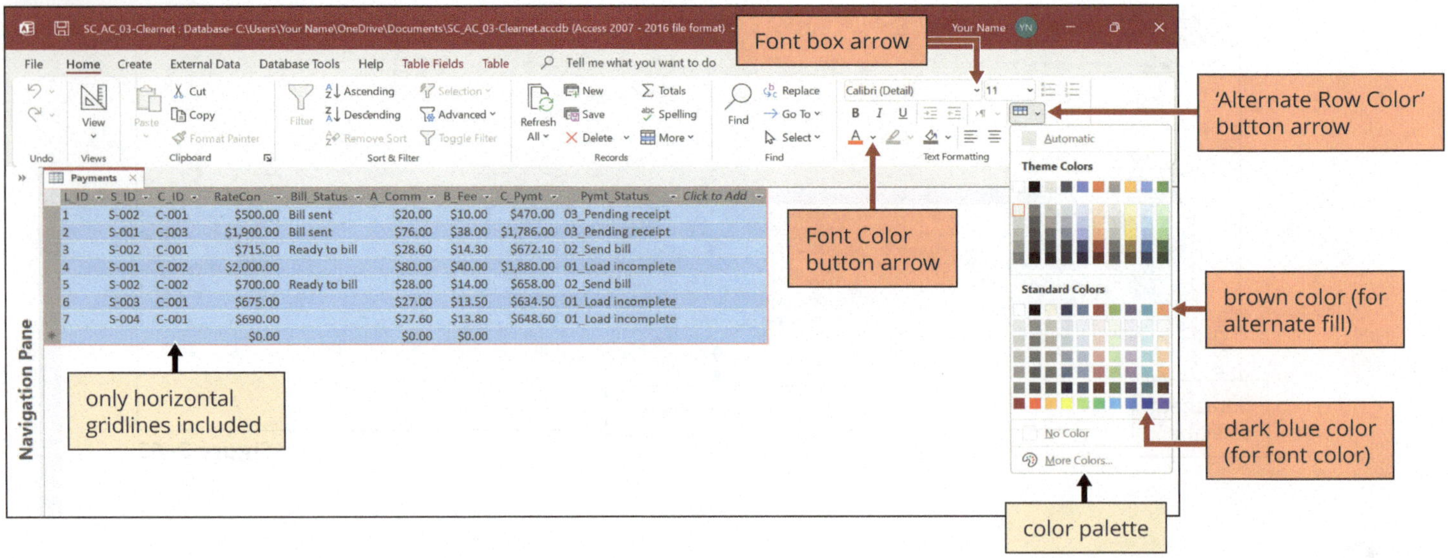

Figure 3–65

2

- Click Brown (Standard Colors section, last color on the first row) to set brown as the alternate row color.
- Click the Font Color button arrow, and then click Dark Blue (Standard Colors section, second color from the right on the bottom row) to set the font color.
- Click the Font arrow, and then select Arial as the font. (If Arial is not available, select any font of your choice.)
- Click the Font Size arrow and select 10 as the font size (Figure 3–66).

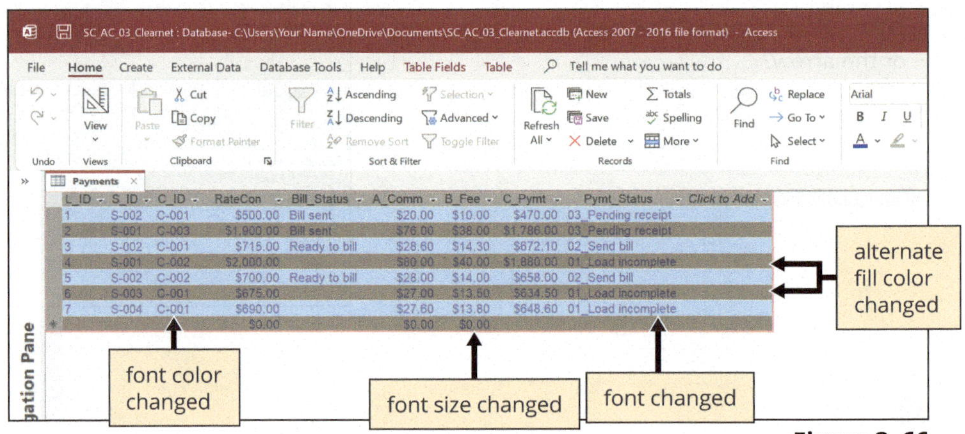

Figure 3–66

Q&A Does the order in which I make these selections make a difference?

No. You could have made these selections in any order.

- **Experiment:** Experiment with other colors, fonts, and font sizes. When finished, return to the options selected in these steps.

BTW

Microsoft Office Color Palettes

Microsoft Office color palettes are often divided into two main sections: Theme Colors and Standard Colors. In Access, the listed theme colors are based on the selected theme for the active object. The colors in the first row of theme colors each have a name, such as Blue or Gold, and a statement of their intended use, such as Background 1, Text 1, or Accent 2. You can see this name if you are using a mouse and hover your cursor over each color. For most devices, a screen tip will appear showing the color's name.

The colors in the rows immediately below the first row offer shades of these theme colors. The first row of shades is the lightest with the colors labeled by percentage of intensity, such as Lighter 80% or Darker 5%. Each row going lower gets darker and is named progressively according to the change of shading, such as Lighter 60%, Lighter 40%, and so on.

The standard colors are common to all themes but might vary according to color palette, screen resolution, Office version, etc. Screen resolution might also affect the location of the standard colors within the color palette. Standard colors also have names, such as Medium Gray or Dark Blue.

Most of the lower rows in the Standard Colors section are numbered according to shade, such as Medium Gray 1, Medium Gray 2, and so on. The bottom row provides colors that are more widely consistent across color palettes, use cases, and applications. These colors also have names, such as Dark Red and Dark Blue. Note that a color on one row with the same name as a color on another row is not necessarily the same color, such as the two Dark Blue colors in the Standard Colors section. When needing to choose a color from a color palette, read the instructions carefully and check figures when provided to help you select the correct color.

Using the Datasheet Formatting Dialog Box

As an alternative to using the individual buttons, you can click the Datasheet Formatting dialog box launcher, which is the arrow at the lower-right corner of the Text Formatting group, to display the Datasheet Formatting dialog box (Figure 3–67). You can use the various options within the dialog box to make changes to the datasheet format. Once you are finished, click the OK button to apply your changes.

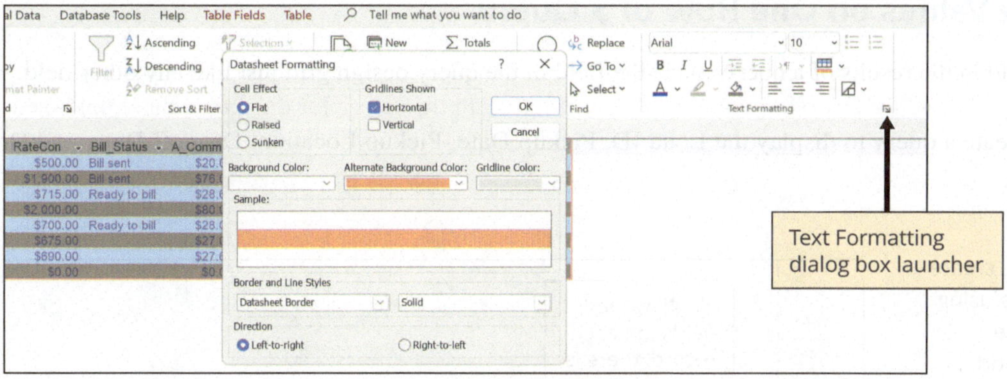

Figure 3–67

Q&A Can I also format my datasheet in other ways?
There are many other formatting options for your table in Datasheet view. You can select all the records as shown in Figure 3–63 by clicking the datasheet selector. Then you can bold, underline, or italicize your font (Home tab | Text Formatting group). Additionally, you can set the background color and align the data.

To Close the Datasheet without Saving the Format Changes

The following step closes the datasheet without saving the changes to the format. Because the changes are not saved, the next time you open the Account Manager table in Datasheet view it will appear in the original format. If you had saved the changes, the changes would be reflected in its appearance.

1

- Close the Payments table.
- Click the No button in the Microsoft Access dialog box when asked if you want to save your changes.

Q&A I like some of the formatting changes made to this table. Why are these changes not being saved?
When using formatting elements in tables, it's best practice to use the same or similar formatting for all tables in the database. Spending the time needed to make that many formatting changes in this project is not necessary.

Consider This

What kind of decisions should I make in determining whether to change the format of a datasheet?

- You'll need to ask yourself a series of questions to help determine which format changes are needed. For example, consider the following questions.
- Would totals or other calculations be useful in the datasheet? If so, include the Total row and select the appropriate computations.
- Would another gridline style make the datasheet more useful? If so, change to the desired gridlines.
- Would alternating colors in the rows make them easier to read? If so, change the alternate fill color.
- Would a different font and/or font color make the text stand out better? If so, change the font color and/or the font.
- Is the font size appropriate? Can you see enough data at one time on the screen and yet have the data be readable? If not, change the font size to an appropriate value.
- Is the column spacing appropriate? Are some columns wider than they need to be? Do some columns not display all the data? Change the column sizes as necessary.

As a general guideline, once you have decided on a particular look for a datasheet, all datasheets in the database should have the same look, unless there is a compelling reason for a datasheet to differ.

Multivalued Fields in Queries

You can use multivalued fields in queries in the same way you use other fields in queries. You can choose to display the multiple values either on a single row or on multiple rows in the query results.

To Include Multiple Values on One Row of a Query

To include a multivalued field in the results of a query, place the field in the query design grid just like any other field. **Why?** *When you treat the multivalued field like any other field, the results will list all the values for the multivalued field on a single row.* The following steps create a query to display the Load ID, Pickup Date, Pickup Location, Dropoff Date, and Dropoff Location for the Loads table.

1

- Open the Navigation Pane, create a query for the Loads table using Design view, and then close the Navigation Pane and Add Tables pane.
- Include the Load ID, Pickup Date, Pickup Location, Dropoff Date, and Dropoff Location fields in the query (Figure 3–68).

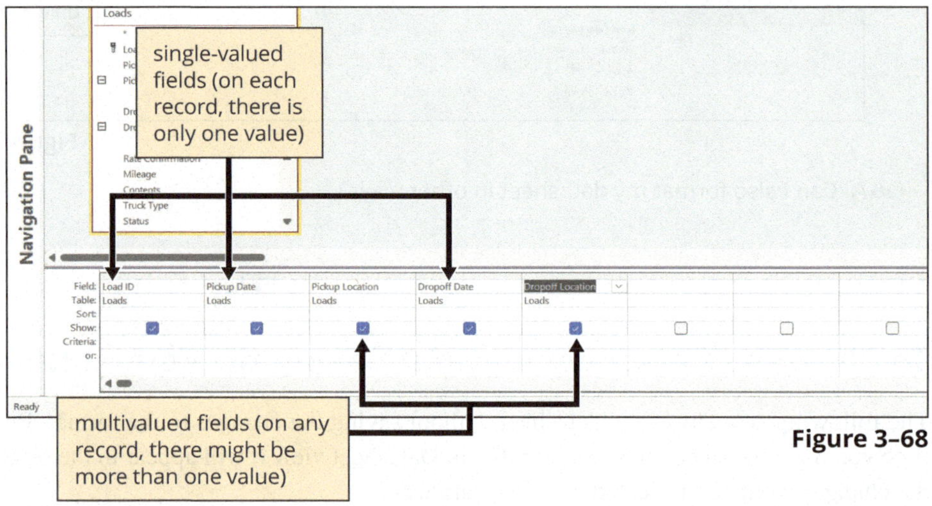

Figure 3–68

2

- Run the query and view the results (Figure 3–69).

Q&A Can I include criteria for a multivalued field?

Yes. You can include criteria for a multivalued field.

- Save the query as **m03q01**. Leave it open for now.

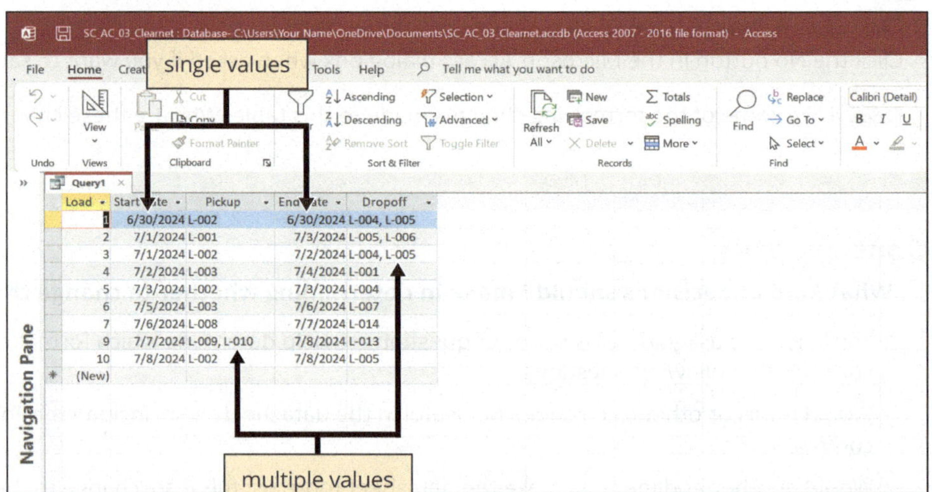

Figure 3–69

To Include Multiple Values on Multiple Rows of a Query

You might want to see the multiple pickup or dropoff locations for a load on separate rows rather than on a single row. **Why?** *Each row in the results will focus on one specific location.* To do so, you need to use the Value property of the Pickup and Dropoff fields by following the name of each field with a period and then the word, Value. The following steps use the Value property to display each location on a separate row.

1

- In the query, switch back to Design view and ensure that the Load ID, Pickup Date, Pickup Location, Dropoff Date, and Dropoff Location fields are included in the design grid.
- In the design grid, click the Pickup Location field name to produce an insertion point, press END to move the insertion point to the end of the field name, and then type a period (**.**).

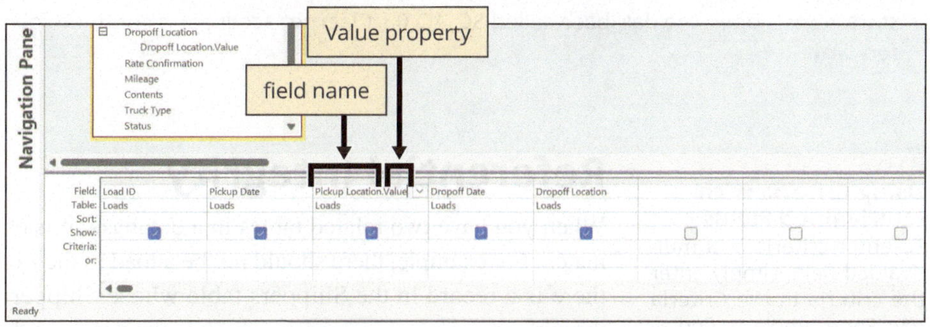

Figure 3–70

- If the word, Value, does not automatically appear after the period, type the word **Value** after the period following the word, Location, to use the Value property (Figure 3–70). You might need to press END again to see if the word, Value, was automatically inserted, or resize the column.

Q&A I do not see the word, Value. Did I do something wrong?

No. There is not enough room to display the entire name. If you want to see it without using the navigation buttons on your keyboard, you can point to the right boundary of the column selector and then either drag or double-click to resize the column.

I see Pickup Location.Value as a field in the Loads table's field list. Could I have deleted the Pickup Location field from the design grid and added the Pickup Location.Value field?

Yes. Either approach is fine.

2

- In the design grid, click the Dropoff Location field to produce an insertion point, press END to move the insertion point to the end of the field name, and then type a period (**.**).
- If the word, Value, does not automatically appear after the period, type the word **Value** after the period following the word, Location, to use the Value property. You might need to press END again to see if the word, Value, was automatically inserted.

3

- Run the query and view the results, resizing the Loads.Pickup Location.Value field and the Loads.Dropoff Location.Value field to display the entire heading for each column (Figure 3–71).

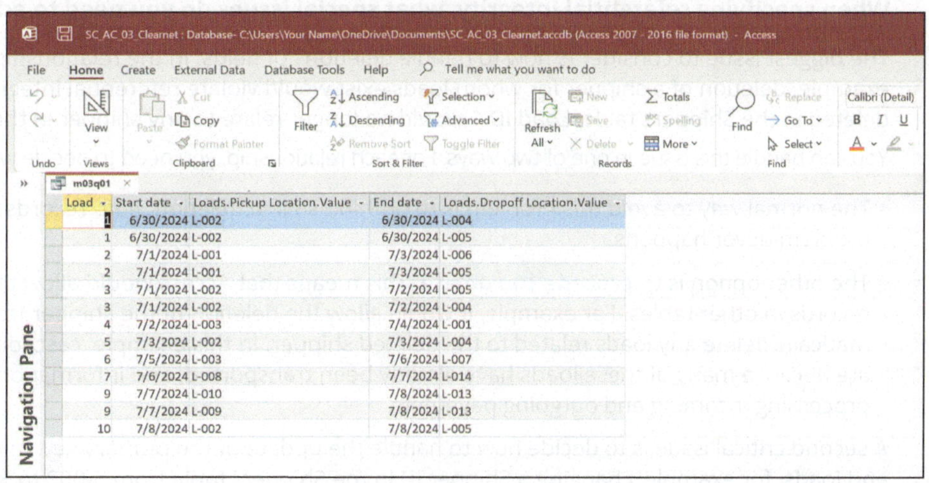

Figure 3–71

Q&A Can I now include criteria for the multivalued field?

Yes. You could enter a criterion just like in any other query.

Could I sort the rows by Start date or End date?

Yes. Select Ascending as the sort order just as you have done in other queries.

4

- Use the Save Object As operation to save the query as a new object in the database named **m03q02**.
- Close the query.

Break Point: If you wish to take a break, this is a good place to do so. You can quit Access now. To resume at a later time, start Access, open the database called SC_AC_03_Clearnet.accdb, and continue following the steps from this location forward.

BTW
Using Criteria with Multivalued Fields
To enter criteria in a multivalued field, simply enter the criteria in the Criteria row. For example, to find all loads being delivered to location L-005 in the Loads table, enter L-005 in the Criteria row under Dropoff Location.

Referential Integrity

When you have two related tables in a database, it is essential that the data in the common fields match. For example, there should not be a load in the Loads table whose shipper ID is S-002 unless there is a record in the Shippers table whose Shipper ID is S-002. This restriction is enforced through **referential integrity**, which is the property that ensures the value in a foreign key must match that of another table's primary key.

A **foreign key** is a field in one table whose values are required to match the *primary key* of another table. In the Loads table, the Shipper ID field is a foreign key that must match the primary key of the Shippers table; that is, the Shipper ID for any load must exist as a Shipper ID currently in the Shippers table. A load whose Shipper ID is L-009, for example, should not be stored in the Loads table because no such shipper currently exists in the Shippers table.

In Access, to specify referential integrity, you must explicitly define a relationship between the tables by using the Relationships button. As part of the process of defining the relationship, you indicate that Access is to enforce referential integrity. Access then prohibits any updates to the database that would violate referential integrity.

The type of relationship between two tables specified by the Relationships command is referred to as a **one-to-many relationship**. This means that *one* record in the first table is related to, or matches, *many* records in the second table, but each record in the second table is related to only *one* record in the first. In the Clearnet database, for example, a one-to-many relationship exists between the Shippers table and the Loads table. *One* shipper is associated with *many* loads, but each load is associated with only one shipper. In general, the table containing the foreign key will be the *many* part of the relationship.

Consider This

When specifying referential integrity, what special issues do you need to address?

The biggest issue to consider is how to handle deletions of fields. In the relationship between shippers and loads, for example, deletion of a shipper for whom loads exist would violate referential integrity. Specifically, if Shipper S-002 is deleted in the Shippers table, Load ID 1 would no longer relate to any shipper in the Shippers table.

You can handle this issue in one of two ways. For each relationship, you need to decide which of these approaches is appropriate.

- The normal way to avoid this problem is to prohibit such a deletion. If no records can be deleted in either table, the problem never happens.
- The other option is to **cascade the delete**. This means that Access would allow the deletion but then delete all related records in other tables. For example, it would allow the deletion of the shipper from the Shippers table but then automatically delete any loads related to the deleted shipper. In this example, cascading the delete would not be appropriate because many of these loads have already been transported, and information from those loads must be kept for processing incoming and outgoing payments.

A second critical issue is to decide how to handle the update of the primary key. In the relationship between shippers and loads, for example, changing a Shipper ID in the Shippers table from S-002 to S-009 would cause a problem because some records in the Loads table are related to Shipper ID S-002. These loads no longer would relate to any shipper.

You can handle this issue in one of two ways. For each relationship, you need to decide which of these approaches is appropriate.

- The normal way to avoid this problem is to prohibit this type of update. If primary key fields can't be changed, relationships remain intact across tables.
- The other option is to **cascade the update**. This means to allow the change, but make the corresponding change in the foreign key on all related records. In the relationship between shippers and loads, for example, Access would allow the update but then automatically make the corresponding change for any load where the Shipper ID is S-002. It would change the Shipper ID for those loads to S-009.

To Specify Referential Integrity

The following steps use the Relationships button on the Database Tools tab to specify referential integrity by explicitly indicating a relationship between the Shippers and Loads tables. The steps also ensure that updates will cascade, but that deletes will not. **Why?** This combination of configurations allows sufficient flexibility for updating records as information changes, while not allowing deletions of records in the Shippers table. By indicating a relationship between tables, and specifying that updates will cascade, it will be possible to change the Shipper ID for a shipper, and the same change will automatically be made for all loads related to that shipper. By not specifying that deletes will cascade, it will not be possible to delete any shipper who has loads in the database.

1

- Click Database Tools on the ribbon to display the Database Tools tab. (Figure 3–72).

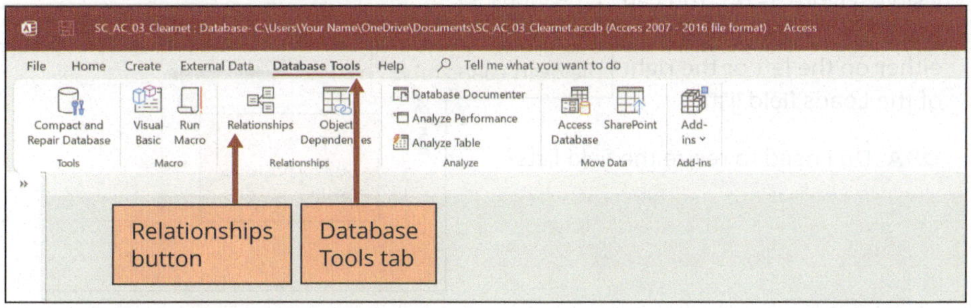

Figure 3–72

2

- Click the Relationships button (Database Tools tab | Relationships group) to open the Relationships window and display the Add Tables pane. If the Add Tables pane does not open automatically, click the Add Tables button (Relationships Design tab | Relationships group). If necessary, click the Tables tab (Add Tables pane) to see the list of tables (Figure 3–73).

Q&A The field lists in the Relationships area are spread out, and I can't see all the field lists at one time. How can I fix this?
Drag the field list boxes as desired to position the boxes in a way you can see all the lists at one time. However, keep the boxes in the same order from left to right. Resize the field list boxes as desired so you can see all the fields listed within each box.

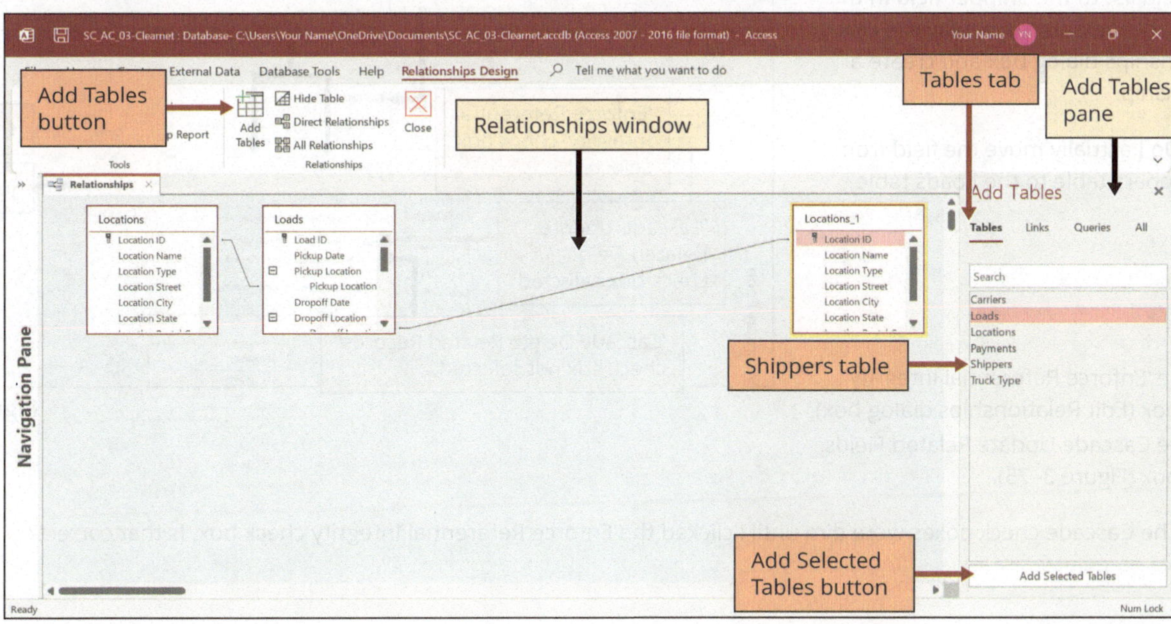

Figure 3–73

3

- Click the Shippers table (Add Tables pane), and then click the Add Selected Tables button to add a field list for the Shippers table to the Relationships window.
- Close the Add Tables pane.
- Reposition and resize the field lists in the Relationships window so all fields are visible (Figure 3–74). You can place the Shippers field list either on the left or the right of the Loads field list.

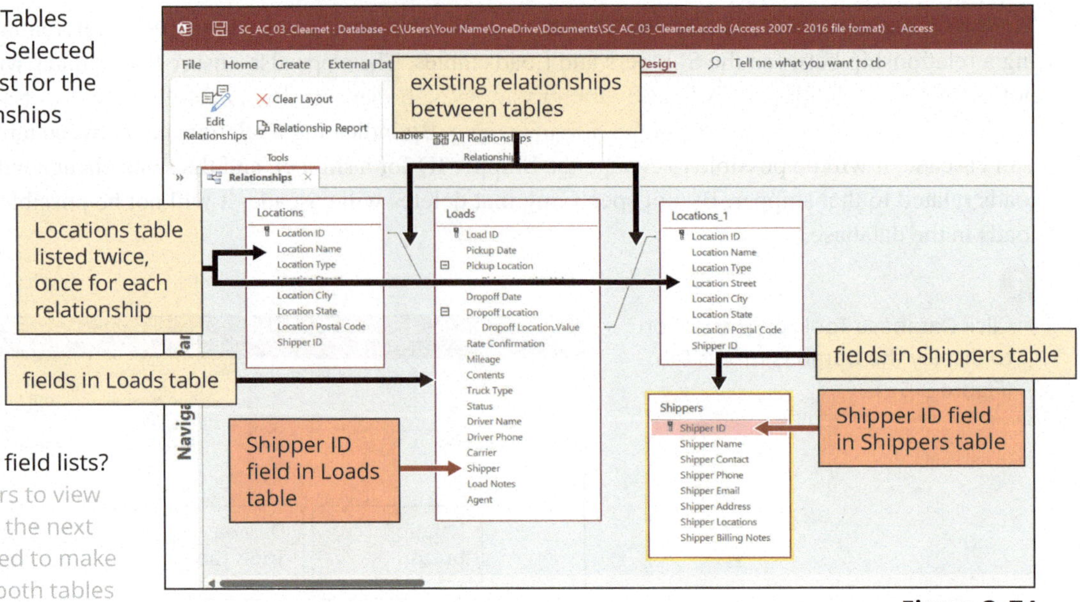

Figure 3–74

Q&A Do I need to resize the field lists?
No. You can use the scroll bars to view the fields. Before completing the next step, however, you would need to make sure the Shipper ID fields in both tables appear on the screen. Note that, in the Loads table, the Shipper ID field is called Shipper.

The Shipper ID field in the Loads table only says Shipper, not Shipper ID. Is that a problem?
No. When the Loads table was created, the Shipper ID field was given a shortened name, which was sufficient to identify its purpose in the context of the Loads table. So long as the data types match and the field contains the correct data, you can still create the relationship.

4

- Drag the Shipper ID field in the Shippers table field list to the Shipper field in the Loads table field list to display the Edit Relationships dialog box and create a relationship.

Q&A Do I actually move the field from the Shippers table to the Loads table?
No. The pointer will change shape to indicate you are in the process of dragging, but the field itself does not move.

- Click the 'Enforce Referential Integrity' check box (Edit Relationships dialog box).
- Click the Cascade Update Related Fields check box (Figure 3–75).

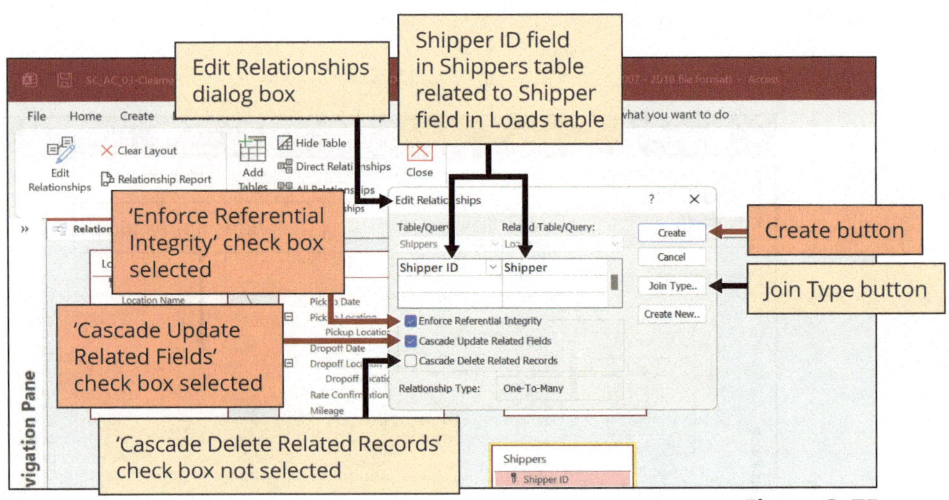

Figure 3–75

Q&A The Cascade check boxes were dim until I clicked the Enforce Referential Integrity check box. Is that correct?
Yes. Until you have chosen to enforce referential integrity, the cascade options are not applicable.

5

- Click the Create button (Edit Relationships dialog box) to complete the creation of the relationship (Figure 3–76).

Q&A What is the symbol at the lower end of the join line?

It is the mathematical symbol for infinity. It is used here to denote the "many" end of the relationship.

Can I print a copy of the relationship?

Yes. Click the Relationship Report button (Relationships Design tab | Tools group) to produce a report of the relationship. You can print the report. You can also save it as a report in the database for future use. If you do not want to save it, close the report after you have printed it and do not save the changes.

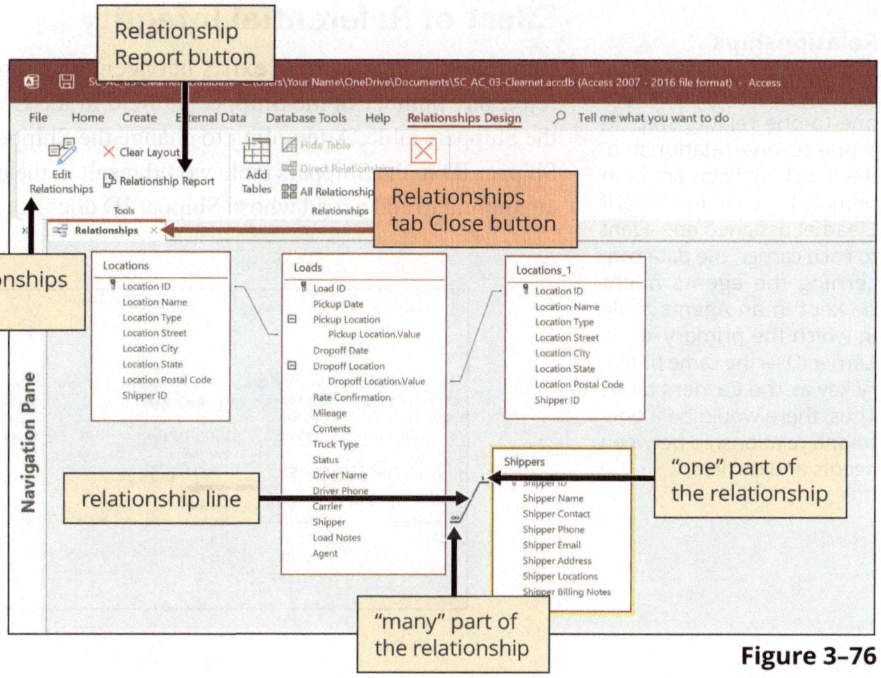

Figure 3–76

6

- Click the Save button on the Quick Access Toolbar to save the relationship you created.
- Click the Close button on the Relationships tab (the X next to the tab name) to close the Relationships window.

Q&A What is the purpose of saving the relationship?

The relationship ensures that the data has referential integrity.

Can I later modify the relationship if I want to change it in some way?

Yes. Click Database Tools on the ribbon to display the Database Tools tab, and then click the Relationships button (Database Tools tab | Relationships group) to open the Relationships window. To add another table, click the Add Tables button on the Relationships Design tab. To remove a table, click the Hide Table button. To edit a relationship, select the relationship and click the Edit Relationships button.

BTW
Exporting a Relationship Report
You also can export a relationship report. To export a report as a PDF or XPS file, right-click the report in the Navigation Pane, click Export on the shortcut menu, and then click PDF or XPS as the file type.

Consider This

Can I change the join type as I can in queries?

Yes. Click the Join Type button in the Edit Relationships dialog box. Click option button 1 to create an INNER join, that is, a join in which only records with matching values in the join fields appear in the result. Click option button 2 to create a LEFT join, that is, a join that includes all records from the left-hand table, but only records from the right-hand table that have matching values in the join fields. Click option button 3 to create a RIGHT join, that is, a join that includes all records from the right-hand table, but only records from the left-hand table that have matching values in the join fields.

Other Ways

1. Click Close button on Relationships Design tab to close Relationships window

BTW
Relationships
You also can use the Relationships window to specify a one-to-one relationship. In a one-to-one relationship, the matching fields are both primary keys. For example, if Clearnet assigned one agent to each carrier, the data concerning the agents might be kept in an Agents table in which the primary key is Carrier ID — the same primary key as the Carriers table. Thus, there would be a one-to-one relationship between agents and carriers.

Effect of Referential Integrity

Referential integrity now exists between the Shippers and the Loads tables. Access now will reject any number in the Shipper ID field in the Loads table that does not match a Shipper ID in the Shippers table. Attempting to change the Shipper ID for a load to one that does not match any Shipper ID in the Shippers table would result in the error message shown in Figure 3–77. Similarly, attempting to add a load whose Shipper ID does not match would produce the same error message.

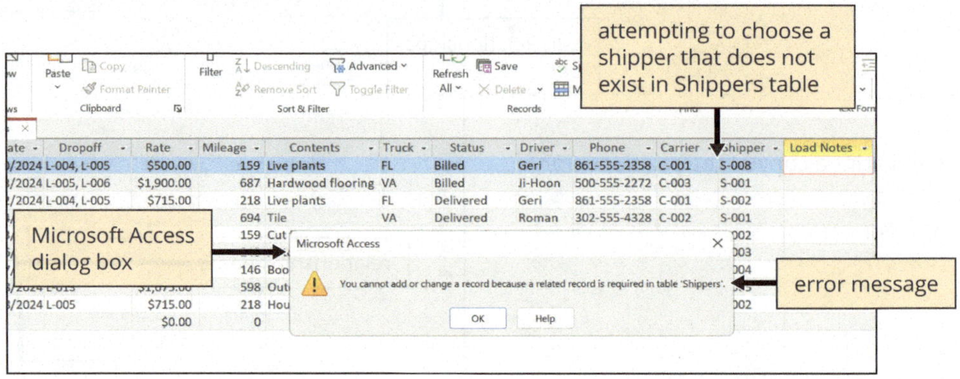

Figure 3–77

Access also will reject the deletion of a Shipper ID for whom related loads exist. Attempting to delete Shipper ID S-002 from the Shippers table, for example, would result in the message shown in Figure 3–78.

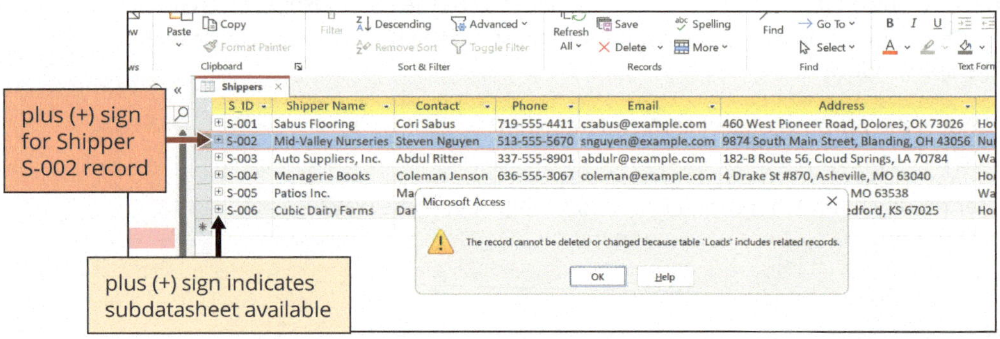

Figure 3–78

Access would, however, allow the change of a Shipper ID in the Shippers table. It would then automatically make the corresponding change to the Shipper ID for all the loads related to that shipper. For example, if you changed a Shipper ID in the Shippers table from S-002 to S-009, the Shipper ID S-009 would appear in the Shipper ID field for loads whose Shipper ID had been S-002.

To Use a Subdatasheet

One consequence of the tables being explicitly related is that a shipper's loads can appear below the Shipper ID in a **subdatasheet**. Because the two tables are joined by a common field, the data for the loads belonging to the shipper can be embedded within that particular shipper's record. **Why is a subdatasheet useful?** A subdatasheet is useful when you want to review or edit data in joined or related tables. The availability of such a subdatasheet is indicated by a plus sign that appears in front of the rows in the Shippers table. The following steps display the subdatasheet for Shipper S-002.

1

- Open the Navigation Pane, open the Shippers table in Datasheet view, and then close the Navigation Pane.

2

- Click the plus sign in front of the row for Shipper ID S-002 to display the subdatasheet (Figure 3–79).

Q&A How do I hide the subdatasheet when I no longer want it to appear?
When you clicked the plus sign, it changed to a minus sign. Click the minus sign to collapse the subdatasheet.

- **Experiment:** Display subdatasheets for other owners. Display more than one subdatasheet at a time. Remove the subdatasheets from the screen.

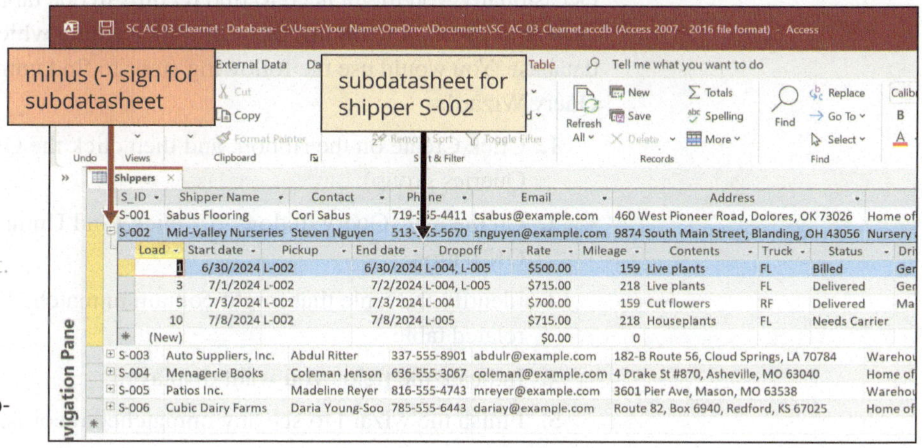

Figure 3–79

Q&A How do I remove a subdatasheet?
Open the table. With the subdatasheet closed, click the More button (Home tab | Records Group) to display a menu. Select Subdatasheet, Remove.

3

If requested by your instructor, replace the city and state for Shipper ID S-001 with your city and state.

- Close the Shippers table.
- Click the No button (Microsoft Access dialog box) when asked if you want to save your changes.

Handling Data Inconsistency

In many organizations, databases evolve and change over time. One department might create a database for its own internal use. Employees in another department might decide they need their own database containing much of the same information. For example, the Purchasing department of an organization might create a database of products that it buys, and the Receiving department might create a database of products that it receives. Each department is keeping track of the same products. When the organization eventually merges the databases, they might discover inconsistencies and duplication. The Find Duplicates Query Wizard and the Find Unmatched Query Wizard can assist in clearing the resulting database of duplication and errors.

To Find Duplicate Records

One reason to include a primary key for a table is to eliminate duplicate records. A possibility still exists, however, that duplicate records can get into your database. You would use the following steps to find duplicate records using the Find Duplicates Query Wizard.

1. Click Create on the ribbon, and then click the Query Wizard button (Create tab | Queries group).
2. On the New Query dialog box, click Find Duplicates Query Wizard and then click the OK button.
3. Identify the table and field or fields that might contain duplicate information.
4. Indicate any other fields you want displayed.
5. Finish the wizard to see any duplicate records.

To Find Unmatched Records

Occasionally, you might need to find records in one table that have no matching records in another table. For example, you might want to determine which shippers currently have no loads in the database. You would use the following steps to find unmatched records using the Find Unmatched Query Wizard.

1. Click Create on the ribbon, and then click the Query Wizard button (Create tab | Queries group).
2. On the New Query dialog box, click Find Unmatched Query Wizard and then click the OK button.
3. Identify the table that might contain unmatched records, and then identify the related table.
4. Indicate the fields you want displayed.
5. Finish the wizard to see any unmatched records.

Sorting Records

Normally, Access sequences the records in the Shippers table by Shipper ID when listing them because the Shipper ID field is the table's primary key. You can change this order, if desired.

To Use the Ascending Button to Sort Records

To change the order in which records appear, use the Ascending or Descending buttons. Either button reorders the records based on the field in which the insertion point is located. The following steps sort the records by Shipper Name in alphabetical order using the Ascending button. **Why?** Using the Ascending button is the quickest and easiest way to order records.

1

- Open the Navigation Pane, open the Shippers table in Datasheet view, and then close the Navigation Pane.
- Click the Shipper Name field on the first record to select the field (Figure 3–80).

Q&A Did I have to click the field on the first record?

No. Any other record would have worked as well.

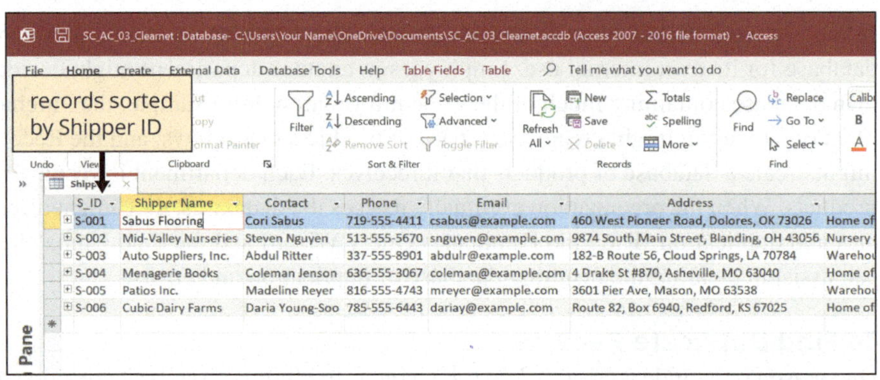

Figure 3–80

2

- Click the Ascending button (Home tab | Sort & Filter group) to sort the records by Shipper Name (Figure 3–81).

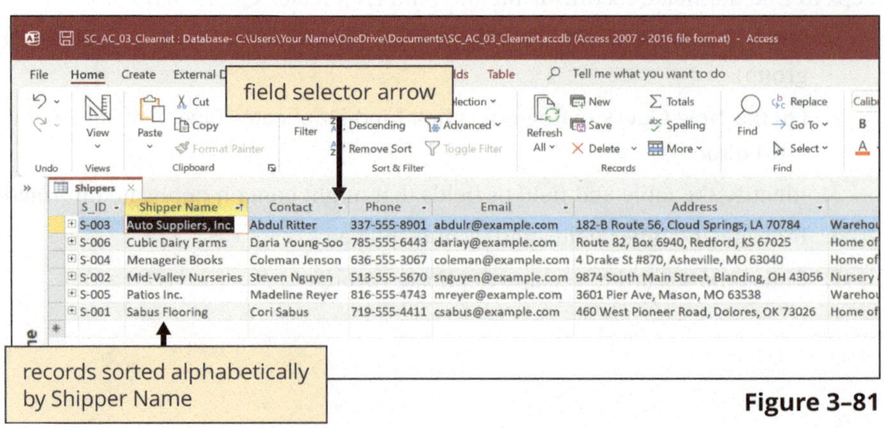

Figure 3–81

3

- Close the Shippers table.
- Click the No button (Microsoft Access dialog box) when asked if you want to save your changes.

Q&A What would happen if I saved the changes?

The next time you open the table, the records will be sorted by Shipper Name.

- If desired, sign out of your Microsoft account.
- **sam** Exit Access.

Other Ways

1. Right-click field name, click Sort A to Z (for ascending) or Sort Z to A (for descending) to sort records
2. Click field selector arrow, click Sort A to Z or Sort Z to A to sort records

To Use the Ascending Button to Sort Records on Multiple Fields

Just as you are able to sort the answer to a query on multiple fields, you can also sort the data that appears in a datasheet on multiple fields. To do so, the major and minor keys must be next to each other in the datasheet with the major key on the left. If this is not the case, you can drag the columns into the correct position. Instead of dragging, however, usually it will be easier to use a query that has the data sorted in the desired order.

To sort on a combination of fields where the major key is just to the left of the minor key, you would use the following steps.

1. Click the field selector at the top of the major key column to select the entire column.
2. Hold down SHIFT and then click the field selector for the minor key column to select both columns.
3. Click the Ascending button to sort the records.

BTW

Modifying Table Properties

You can change the properties of a table by opening the table in Design view and then clicking the Property Sheet button (Table Design tab | Show/Hide group). This opens the Property Sheet pane on the right side of the screen. To display the records in a table in an order other than primary key (the default sort order), use the Order By property. For example, to display the Payments table automatically in Carrier ID order, change the Order By property setting to Payments.Carrier ID in the property box, close the property sheet, and save the change to the table design. When you open the Payments table in Datasheet view, the records will be sorted in Carrier ID order.

Summary

In this module you have learned how to create a split form, use a form to add records to a table, search for records, delete records, filter records, change the database structure, create and use lookup fields, create and use multivalued fields, create calculated fields, make mass changes, create validation rules, change the appearance of a datasheet, specify referential integrity, and use subdatasheets.

BTW

Access Help

At any time while using Access, you can find answers to questions and display information about various topics through Access Help. Used properly, this form of assistance can increase your productivity and reduce your frustrations by minimizing the time you spend learning how to use Access.

Consider This: Plan Ahead

What decisions will you need to make when maintaining your own databases?

Use these guidelines as you complete the assignments in this module and maintain your own databases outside of this class.

1. Determine when it is necessary to add, change, or delete records in a database.
2. Determine whether you should filter records.
   a) If your criterion for filtering is that the value in a particular field matches or does not match a certain specific value, use Filter By Selection.
   b) If your criterion only involves a single field but is more complex, use a common filter.
   c) If your criterion involves more than one field, use Filter By Form.
   d) If your criterion involves more than a single And or Or, or if it involves sorting, use Advanced Filter/Sort.
3. Determine whether additional fields are necessary or whether existing fields should be deleted.
4. Determine whether validation rules, default values, and formats are necessary.
   a) Can you improve the accuracy of the data entry process by enforcing data validation?
   b) What values are allowed for a particular field?
   c) Are there some fields in which one particular value is used more than another?
   d) Should some fields be required for each record?
   e) Are there some fields for which special formats would be appropriate?
5. Determine whether changes to the format of a datasheet are desirable.
   a) Would totals or other calculations be useful in the datasheet?
   b) Would different gridlines make the datasheet easier to read?
   c) Would alternating colors in the rows make them easier to read?
   d) Would a different font and/or font color make the text stand out better?
   e) Is the font size appropriate?
   f) Is the column spacing appropriate?
6. Identify related tables to implement relationships between the tables.
   a) Is there a one-to-many relationship between the tables?
   b) If so, which table is the one table?
   c) Which table is the many table?
7. When specifying referential integrity, address deletion and update policies.
   a) Decide how to handle deletions. Should deletion be prohibited or should the delete cascade?
   b) Decide how to handle the update of the primary key. Should the update be prohibited or should the update cascade?

Consider This

How should you submit solutions to critical thinking questions in the assignments?

Every assignment in this course contains one or more critical thinking questions. These questions require you to think beyond the assigned database. Present your responses to the questions in the format required by your instructor. Possible formats may include one or more of these options: write the answer; create a document that contains the answer; present your answer to the class; discuss your answer in a group; record the answer as audio or video using a webcam, smartphone, or portable media player; or post answers on a blog, wiki, or website.

Student Assignments

Apply Your Knowledge

Reinforce the skills and apply the concepts you learned in this module.

Adding Lookup Fields, Specifying Validation Rules, Updating Records, Updating Reports, and Creating Relationships

Note: To complete this assignment, you will be required to use the Data Files. Please contact your instructor for information about accessing the Data Files.

Instructions: Start Access. Open the database, SC_AC_03-2.accdb, which is located in the Data Files folder. Enable the content.

Perform the following tasks:

1. Save the database using the file name, SC_AC_03_City-Tutoring. Enable the content.
2. Open the Students table in Design view.
3. Add a single-valued Lookup field called Student Type to the Students table. The field should be inserted after the Counselor Number field. The field will contain data on the type of student. The student types are GR (meaning grade school), HS (meaning high school), HE (meaning higher education), and AE (meaning adult education). Save the changes to the Students table.
4. Create the following validation rules for the Students table.
   a. Specify the legal values GR, HS, HE, and AE for the Student Type field. Enter **Must be GR, HS, HE, or AE** as the validation text.
   b. Make the Student Name field a required field.
5. Save the changes and close the table. You do not need to test the current data.
6. Create an update query for the Students table. Change all the entries in the Student Type field to GR. Run the query and save it as Student Type Update Query, and then close the query.
7. Update the following records in the Students table, and then close the table:
   a. Change the student type for students BB35, CC25, CP03, and YD45 to HS.
   b. Change the student type for students MM01 and PS67 to AE.
8. Create a split form for the Students table. Save the form as Students Split Form.
9. Open the Students Split Form in Form view, find student HN23, and change the student's name from Henry Niemer to Henry Neimer. Close the form.
10. Establish referential integrity between the Counselors table (the one table) and the Students table (the many table). Display the Add tables pane if necessary and add the appropriate tables. Cascade the update but not the delete. Save the relationship and close the Relationships tab.
    If requested to do so by your instructor, rename the Students Split Form as Split Form for First Name Last Name, where First Name Last Name is your name.
11. Submit the revised database in the format specified by your instructor.
12. **Consider This:** The values in the Student Type field are currently in the order GR, HS, HE, and AE. How would you reorder the values to GR, HS, AE, and HE in the Student Type list?

Extend Your Knowledge

Extend the skills you learned in this module and experiment with new skills. You may need to use Help to complete the assignment.

Creating Action Queries, Changing Table Properties, and Adding Totals to a Datasheet

Note: To complete this assignment, you will be required to use the Data Files. Please contact your instructor for information about accessing the Data Files.

Instructions: Start Access. Open the database, SC_AC_03-3.accdb, which is located in the Data Files folder. A physical therapy clinic in Lebanon, Arizona, is being sold to another clinic in a nearby town. The office staff need to do some database maintenance by finding duplicate records and finding unmatched records.

Perform the following tasks:

1. Save the database using the file name, SC_AC_03_Physical-Therapy. Enable the content.
2. Create a make-table query to create the Potential Clients table in the Physical Therapists database shown in Figure 3–82. Run the query and save it as Make Table Query.

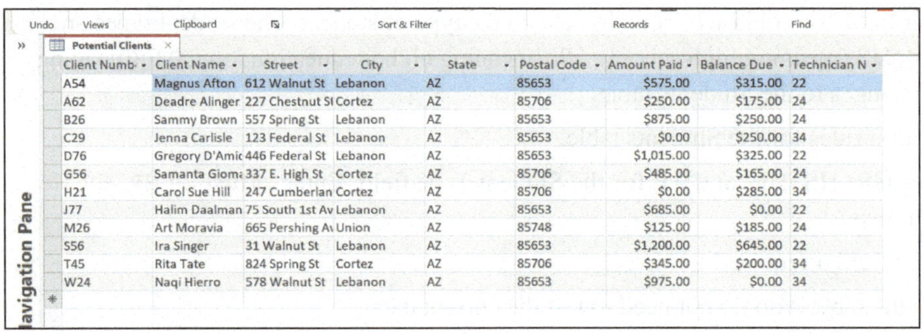

Client Numb	Client Name	Street	City	State	Postal Code	Amount Paid	Balance Due	Technician N
A54	Magnus Afton	612 Walnut St	Lebanon	AZ	85653	$575.00	$315.00	22
A62	Deadre Alinger	227 Chestnut St	Cortez	AZ	85706	$250.00	$175.00	24
B26	Sammy Brown	557 Spring St	Lebanon	AZ	85653	$875.00	$250.00	24
C29	Jenna Carlisle	123 Federal St	Lebanon	AZ	85653	$0.00	$250.00	34
D76	Gregory D'Amic	446 Federal St	Lebanon	AZ	85653	$1,015.00	$325.00	22
G56	Samanta Giom	337 E. High St	Cortez	AZ	85706	$485.00	$165.00	24
H21	Carol Sue Hill	247 Cumberlan	Cortez	AZ	85706	$0.00	$285.00	34
J77	Halim Daalman	75 South 1st Av	Lebanon	AZ	85653	$685.00	$0.00	22
M26	Art Moravia	665 Pershing A	Union	AZ	85748	$125.00	$185.00	24
S56	Ira Singer	31 Walnut St	Lebanon	AZ	85653	$1,200.00	$645.00	22
T45	Rita Tate	824 Spring St	Cortez	AZ	85706	$345.00	$200.00	34
W24	Naqi Hierro	578 Walnut St	Lebanon	AZ	85653	$975.00	$0.00	34

Figure 3–82

3. Open the Potential Clients table and select the datasheet. Change the font to Arial with a font size of 10. Resize the columns to best fit the data. Save the changes to the table and close the table.
4. Open the Technician table and add the Totals row to the table. Calculate the average hourly rate and the sum of Earnings YTD. Save the changes to the table layout and close the table.
5. Use the Find Duplicates Query Wizard to find duplicate information in the City field of the Client table. Include the Client Name in the query. Save the query as City Duplicates Query and close the query.
6. Use the Find Unmatched Query Wizard to find all records in the Technician table that do not match records in the Client table. Technician Number is the common field in both tables. Include the Technician Number, Last Name, and First Name in the query. Save the query as Technician Unmatched Query and close the query.
   If requested to do so by your instructor, change the client name in the Client table for client number S56 to First Name Last Name, where First Name Last Name is your name. If your name is longer than the space allowed, simply enter as much as you can.
7. Submit the revised database in the format specified by your instructor.
8. **Consider This:** What differences, if any, are there between the Client table and the Potential Clients table you created with the make-table query?

Expand Your World

Create a solution, which uses cloud and web technologies, by learning and investigating on your own from general guidance.

Note: To complete this assignment, you will be required to use the Data Files. Please contact your instructor for information about accessing the Data Files.

Instructions: Start Access. Open the database, SC_AC_03-4.accdb, which is located in the Data Files folder, and enable the content. Solutions IT Support wants to ensure that all Clients are matched with Technicians. The database needs a relationship created to ensure this matching. Your boss wants a copy of the report of this relationship.

Perform the following tasks:

1. Save the database using the file name, SC_AC_03_Solutions-IT-Support. Enable the content.
2. Create a relationship between the Client table and the Technician table using an appropriate field for this task. Enforce referential integrity and Cascade Update Related Fields.
3. Create a relationship report for the relationship and save the report as First Name Last Name Relationship Report where First Name Last Name is your name.
4. Export the report as a PDF file to a cloud-based storage location of your choice. Do not save the export steps. Close the report and the Relationships tab.
5. Research the web to find how diagrams depict a one-to-many relationship for a relational database. (**Hint:** Use your favorite search engine and enter keywords such as ERD diagram, entity-relationship diagram, or one-to-many relationship.)
6. Create your own graphic using a drawing tool, such as app.diagrams.net. Your diagram should illustrate the one-to-many relationship between the Client table and the Technician table. Export the image as a .png or .jpg file.
7. Submit the revised database, the PDF report, and the relationship diagram in the format specified by your instructor.
8. a. **Consider This:** Which cloud-based storage location did you use?
   b. **Consider This:** How did you locate your diagram samples?
   c. **Consider This:** Which app did you use to create your diagram?

In the Lab

Design and implement a solution using creative thinking and problem-solving skills.

Lab: Maintaining the Great Outdoors Database

Note: To complete this assignment, you will be required to use the Data Files. Please contact your instructor for information about accessing the Data Files.

Problem: Great Outdoors Camp needs to make some updates to their database to track Camper payments and remove campers who haven't made a payment before a certain date. Additionally, campground counselors want to organize some backup plans for when one of them needs to cover for another. One of the staff has also asked you to add some validation rules to ensure required information is included when campers or counselors are entered into the database.

Continued on next page

Perform the following tasks:

Part 1: Open the SC_AC_03-5.accdb database from the Data Files folder. Save the file with the name SC_AC_03_Great-Outdoors, and enable the content. Use the concepts and techniques presented in this module to modify the database according to the following requirements:

1. Import the Camper Payments table from the Support_AC_03_Great-Outdoors-Extra-Tables.accdb database. Do not save the import steps.
2. The accountant in charge of camper payments has asked for a calculated field that will add the amount campers have paid plus their balance due to determine their total fees (paid fees + unpaid fees = total fees), which will help with budgeting for the season. Create this calculated field in the appropriate table.
3. Create rules for the Counselors table that require information in the Counselor FirstName and LastName fields for every record. You do not need to test the data.
4. Using Filter By Form, delete all the records where any camper's amount paid is zero and the balance due is greater than zero. Save and close the table.
5. Camp staff have decided they need to know who can oversee which activities in case any instructors are out sick. They would like an additional multivalued lookup field, Activities, added to the Staff table. These activities will include items from the ActivityZones table in addition to alternative activities that are not usually scheduled but can be used when needed. As you create the field, refer to Table 3–2, which lists the Activities to be added to the list of lookup values.

Table 3–2 Activity Abbreviations and Descriptions

Abbreviations	Names
CRFT	Crafts
HKG	Hiking
HRSB	Horseback Riding
KYK	Kayaking
SRVL	Survival Class
SWM	Swimming
ZPLN	Ziplining
PING	Ping-Pong
SOC	Soccer
TGFB	Tag Football

6. Change the Activities field size to 50.
7. Add the data shown in Table 3–3 to the Staff table for the Activities field. Resize the field to best fit.

Table 3–3

Staff ID	First Name	Last Name	Activities
14	Vera	Ognianov	CRFT, PING
12	Ahmad	Grady	HKG
3	Lata	Gaspar	HRSB
13	Markku	Twist	KYK, SWM
2	Maya	Dillard	SRVL, CRFT
16	Martyn	Bell	SWM, KYK
11	Otto	Jensson	ZPLN
15	Elli	Rosario	SOC, TGFB

8. In the Counselors table, find the record for Co_ID 78978, and change the Co_ID to 78797.
If requested to do so by your instructor, in the Campers table, change the last name for Camper ID 34872 to your last name. If your last name is longer than 15 characters, simply enter as much as you can.

9. In the Enrollments table, change the Camper ID field to Short Text with a field size of 20.

10. a. Establish referential integrity between the Campers table (the one table) and the Enrollments table (the many table). Cascade the update but not the delete.

    b. **Consider This:** Why do you think you get an error message?

    c. Fix the problem, and then create the relationship.

Submit the revised database in the format specified by your instructor.

Part 2: **Consider This:** The Activities field currently has 10 values. If Great Outdoors Campground picked up another sport, such as fishing, how would you add FSH to the Activities field list? You added a calculated field in the Camper Payments table. Do the results of the calculated field actually exist in the database? Are there any issues that you need to consider when you create a calculated field?

Creating Reports and Forms

Objectives

After completing this module, you will be able to:

- Organize data in a report by grouping and sorting
- Include calculated controls in a report or form
- Format a control
- Filter records in a report
- Create a report from multiple tables
- Create a report using Layout view
- Describe options to apply a theme to a report or form
- Create a summary report
- Create a form using the Form Wizard
- Apply a control layout
- Include special items on a report or form to enhance its design
- Move a control
- Add a field to a report or form
- Use the Advanced filter/sort tool
- Prepare mailing labels

Introduction

One of the advantages to maintaining data in a database is the ability to present the data in attractive reports and forms that highlight certain information. Reports present data in an organized format that is usually printed. The data can come from one or more tables. On the other hand, you usually view forms on the screen, although you can print them. In addition to viewing data, you can also use forms to update data. That is, you can use forms to add records, delete records, or change records. Like reports, the data in the form can come from one or more tables.

This module shows how to create reports and forms by creating two reports and a form. There are several ways to create both reports and forms. One approach is to use the Report or Form Wizard. You can also use either Layout view or Design view to create or modify a report or form. In this module, you will use Layout view for this purpose. In later modules, you will learn how to use Design view. You will also use the Label Wizard to produce mailing labels.

Project: Reports and Forms

The paralegals at Partners Law Firm are now able to better keep track of their closings information and to target the needs of the practice by using its database. Partners paralegals hope to improve their closing preparation processes further by using custom reports that meet the practice's specific needs. They also need to create some reports in response to requests from the Accounting Department. Figure 4–1 shows the Closings and Properties report, which is a modified version of an existing report. The report features grouping. That is, the report shown in Figure 4–1 groups records by state. There are two separate groups, one each for the two states, Pennsylvania and New York, where properties are located. The appropriate state name appears above each group. The total of the Payoff Amount field just for the properties within each group (called a **subtotal**) appears below the group. Further below, at the end of the report, is the grand total of the same field for all the properties. This report contains conditional formatting.

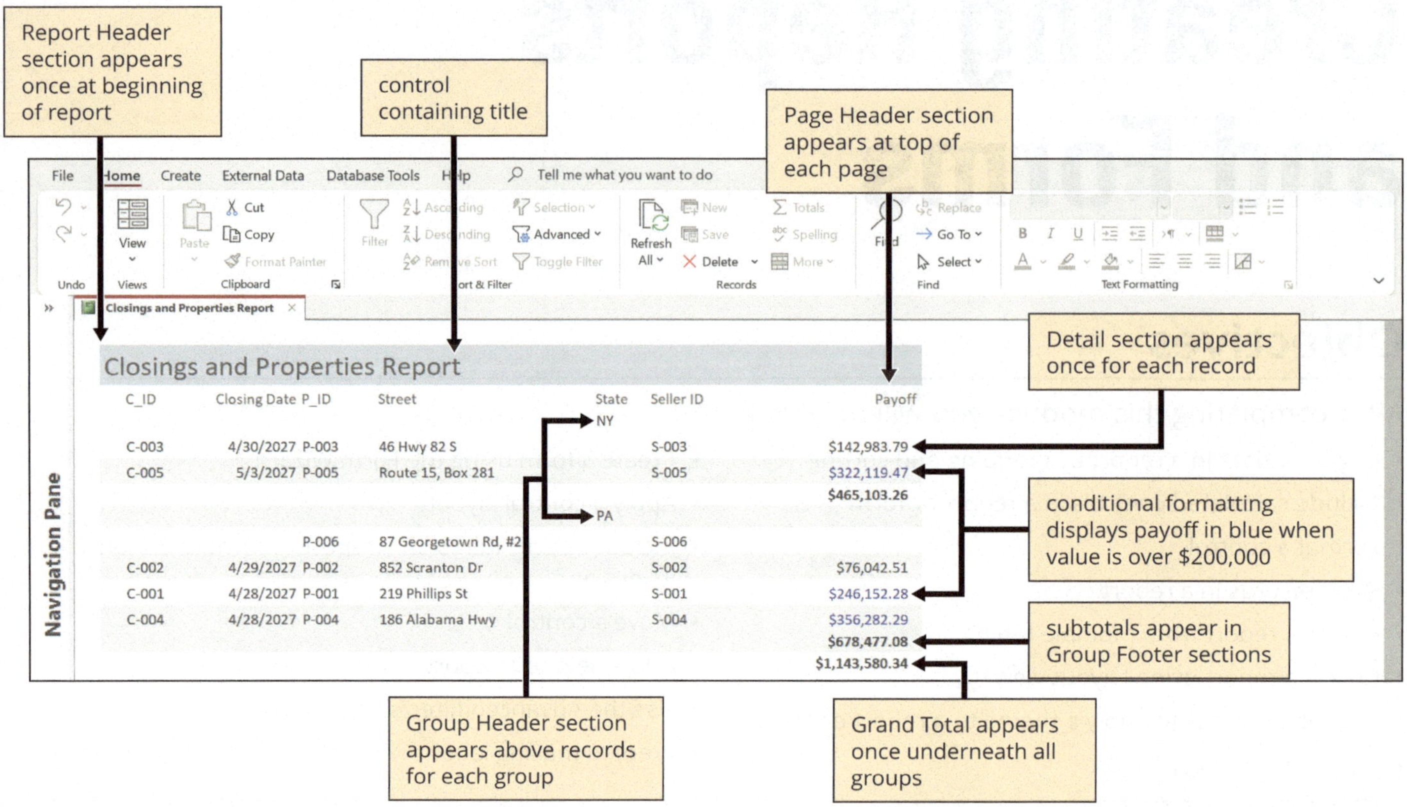

Figure 4–1a Closings and Properties Report

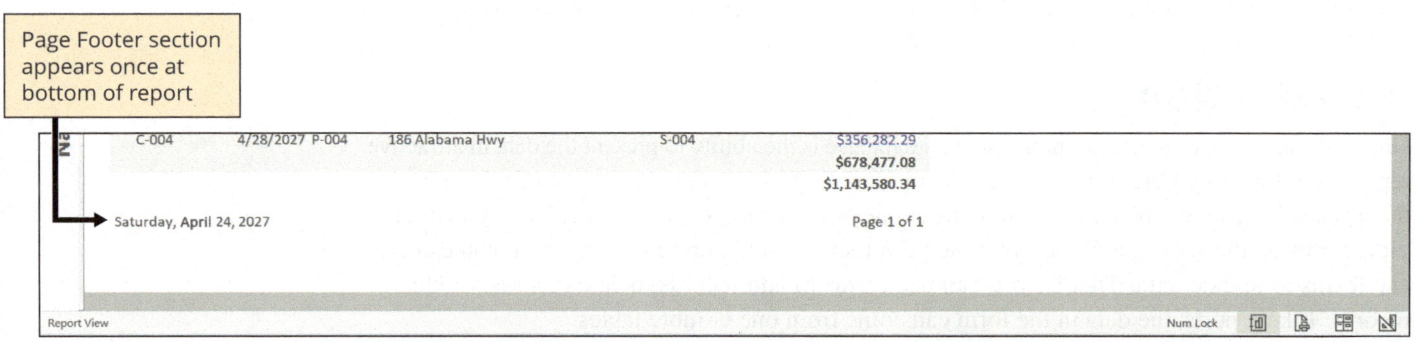

Figure 4–1b Closings and Properties Report

BTW
Consider Your Audience
Always design reports and forms with your audience in mind. Make your reports and forms accessible to individuals who may have problems with colorblindness or reduced vision.

Figure 4–2 shows the second report. This report encompasses data from the Sellers, Properties, Closings, and Closing Fees tables. Like the report in Figure 4–1, the data is grouped, although this time it is grouped by the month of the closing date. Not only does the closing date appear in each group, but each group's subtotal of agent commissions appears as well.

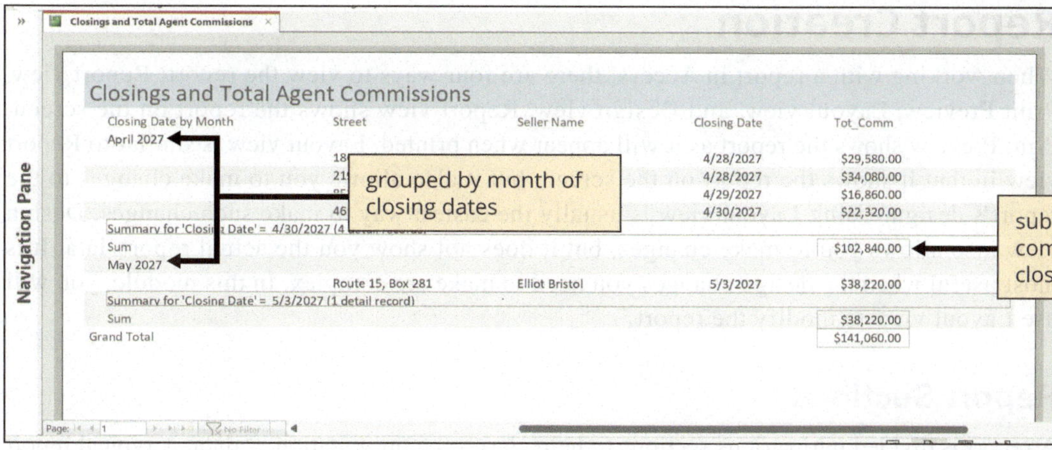

Figure 4–2

Partners paralegals also want to improve the process of updating data by using a custom form, as shown in Figure 4–3. The form has a title, but unlike the form you can create by clicking the Form button, this form does not contain all the fields in the Mortgage Companies table. In addition, the fields are in a different order than in the table. For this form, Partners paralegals like the appearance of including the fields in a stacked layout.

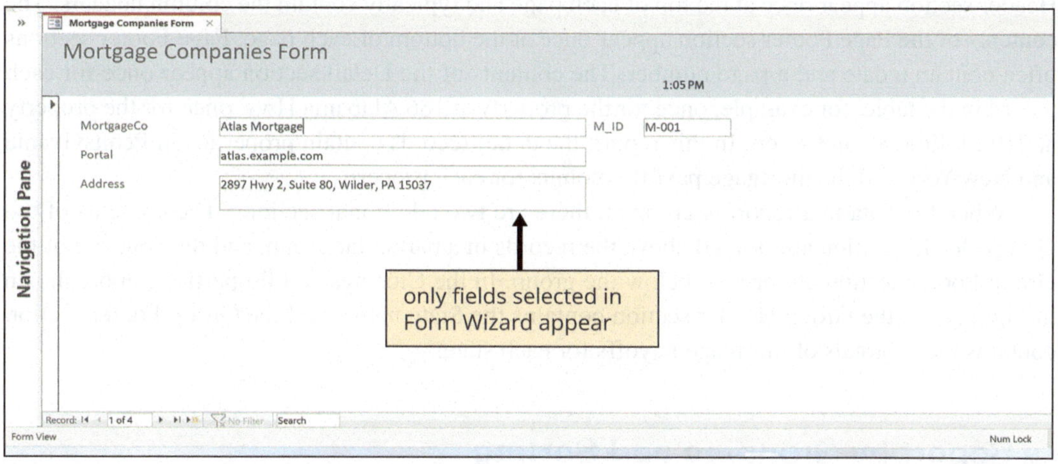

Figure 4–3

Partners also wants to be able to produce mailing labels for new property owners. These labels must align correctly with the particular labels Partners uses and must be sorted by postal code (Figure 4–4).

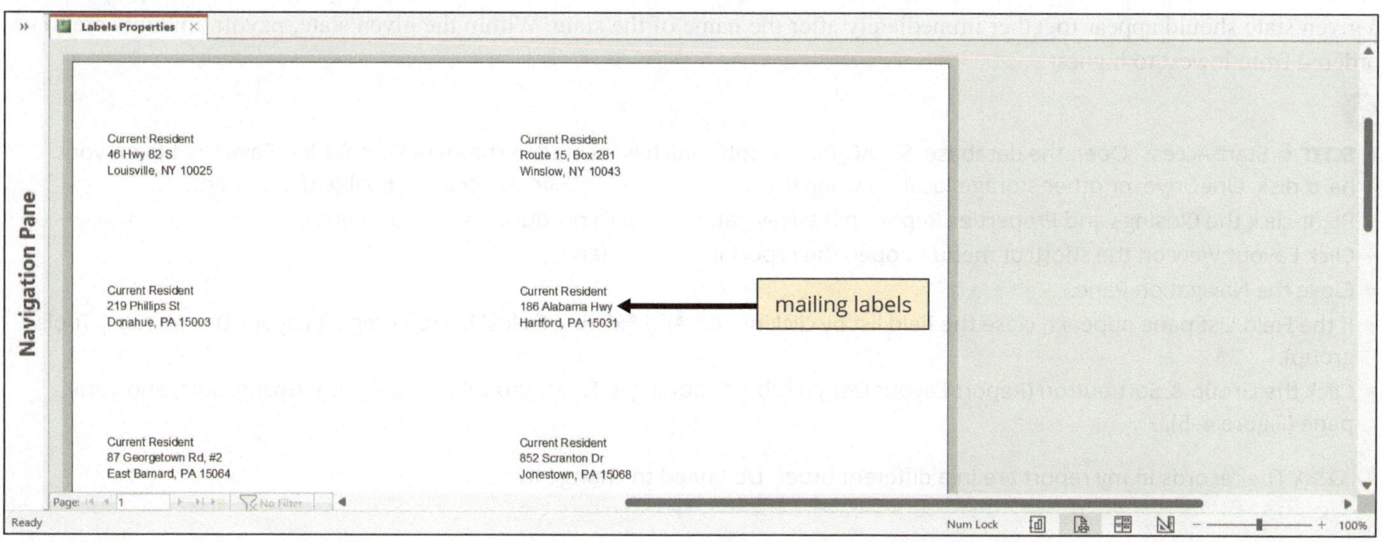

Figure 4–4

BTW
The Ribbon and Screen Resolution
Access may change how the groups and buttons within the groups appear on the ribbon, depending on the computer or mobile device's screen resolution. Thus, your ribbon may look different from the ones in this course if you are using a screen resolution other than 1920 x 1080.

BTW
Touch Screen Differences
The Office and Windows interfaces may vary if you are using a touch screen. For this reason, you might notice that the function or appearance of your touch screen differs slightly from this module's presentation.

BTW
Enabling the Content
For each of the databases you use in this module, you will need to enable the content.

Report Creation

When working with a report in Access, there are four ways to view the report: Report view, Print Preview, Layout view, and Design view. Report view shows the report on the screen. Print Preview shows the report as it will appear when printed. Layout view is similar to Report view in that it shows the report on the screen, but it also allows you to make changes to the report's design. Using Layout view is usually the easiest way to make such changes. Design view also allows you to make changes, but it does not show you the actual report data. It is most useful when the design changes you need to make are complex. In this module, you will use Layout view to modify the report.

Report Sections

A report is divided into various sections to help clarify the presentation of data. A typical report consists of a Report Header section, Page Header section, Detail section, Page Footer section, and Report Footer section, as shown earlier in Figure 4–1.

The contents of the Report Header section appear once at the beginning of the report. In the Closings and Properties Report, the report title is in the Report Header section. The contents of the Report Footer section appear once at the end of the report. In the Closings and Properties Report, the Report Footer section contains the grand totals of Payoff amounts. The contents of the Page Header section appear once at the top of each page and typically contain the column headers. The contents of the Page Footer section appear once at the bottom of each page; Page Footer sections often contain a date and a page number. The contents of the Detail section appear once for each record in the table; for example, once for the property at 186 Alabama Hwy, once for the property at 219 Phillips St, and so on. In this report, the detail records contain properties in Pennsylvania and New York and the mortgage payoff amounts for each property.

When the data in a report is grouped, there are two additional sections. The contents of the Group Header section are printed above the records in a particular group, and the contents of the Group Footer section are printed below the group. In the Closings and Properties Report shown in Figure 4–1, the Group Header section contains the State name, and the Group Footer section contains the subtotals of mortgage payoffs for each state.

To Organize Data in a Report by Grouping and Sorting

In Layout view of the report, you can specify both grouping and sorting by using the Group & Sort button on the Design tab. The following steps open the Closings and Properties Report in Layout view and then specify both grouping and sorting in the report. **Why?** Partners paralegals have determined that the records in the report should be grouped by state and sorted by payoff amount to produce a report requested by the Accounting department. That is, all the mortgage payoff amounts for properties in a given state should appear together immediately after the name of the state. Within the given state, payoff amounts are to be ordered from lowest to highest.

1

- sam Start Access. Open the database, SC_AC_04-1.accdb, which is located in the Data Files folder. Save the file on your hard disk, OneDrive, or other storage location using the file name, **SC_AC_04_Partners**. Enable the content.
- Right-click the Closings and Properties Report in the Navigation Pane to produce a shortcut menu.
- Click Layout View on the shortcut menu to open the report in Layout view.
- Close the Navigation Pane.
- If the Field List pane appears, close the field list by clicking the 'Add Existing Fields' button (Report Layout Design tab | Tools group).
- Click the Group & Sort button (Report Layout Design tab | Grouping & Totals group) to display the Group, Sort, and Total pane (Figure 4–5).

Q&A The records in my report are in a different order. Do I need to change it?
No. You will change the order of the records in the following steps.

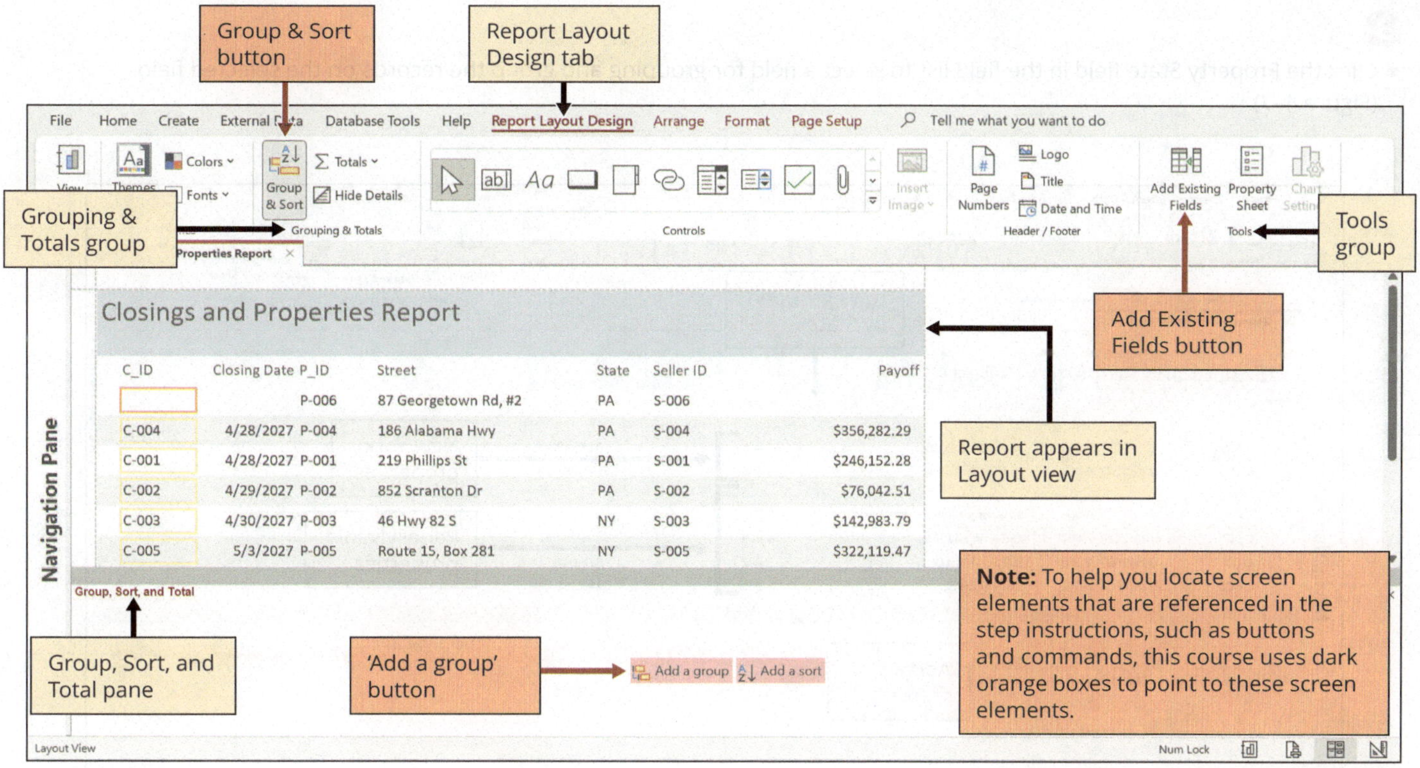

Figure 4–5

2

- Click the 'Add a group' button to add a group and display a field list (Figure 4–6).

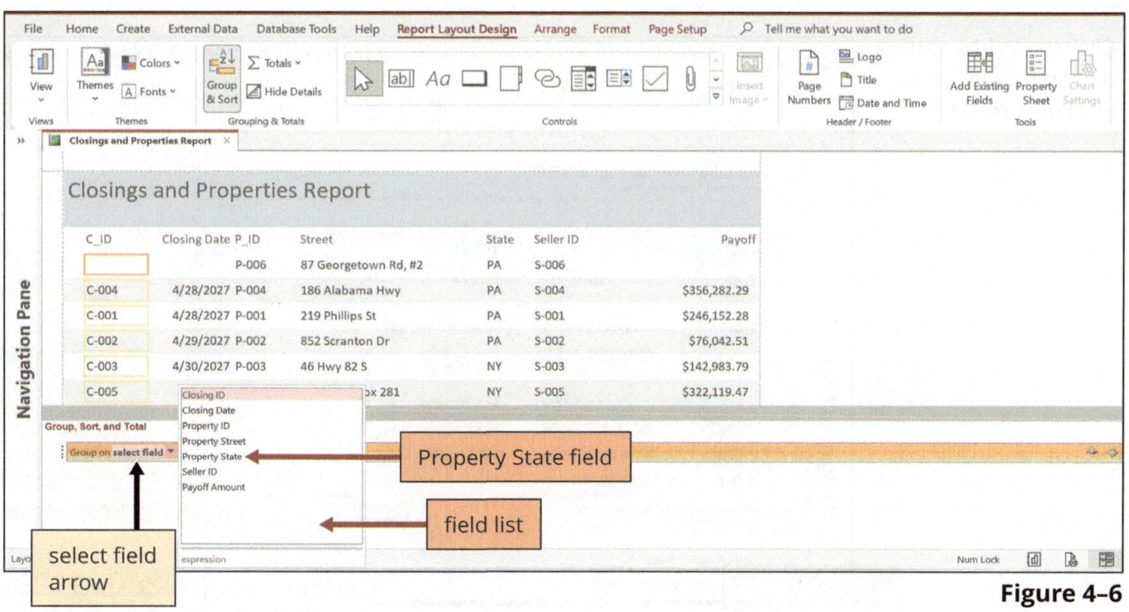

Figure 4–6

3

- Click the Property State field in the field list to select a field for grouping and group the records on the selected field (Figure 4–7).

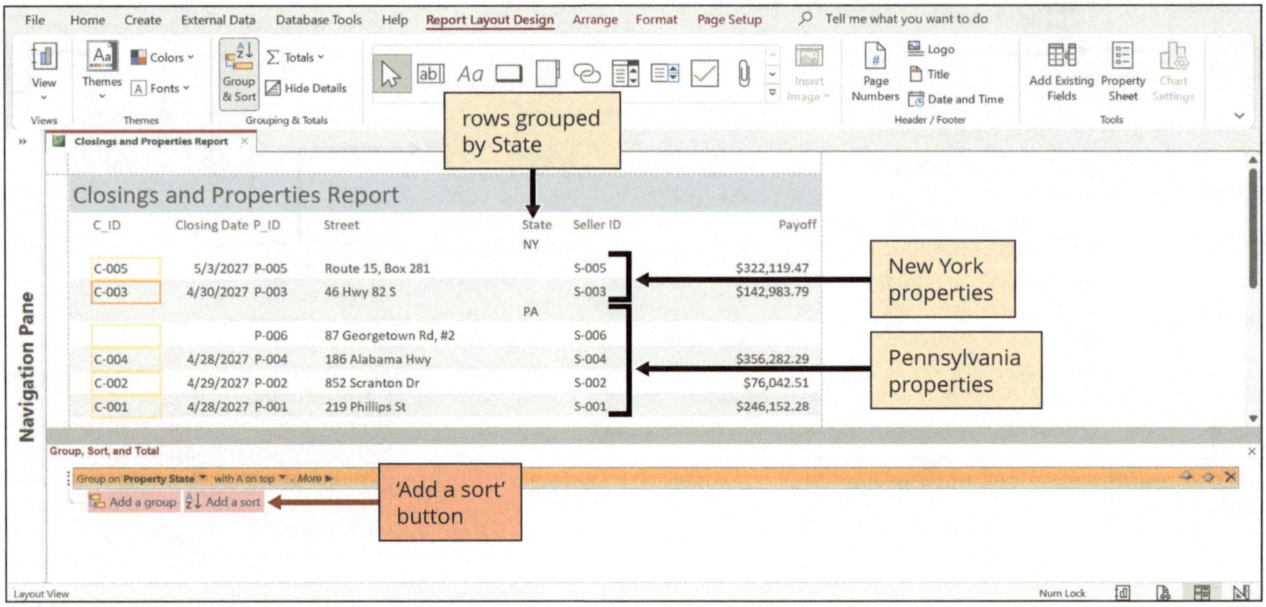

Figure 4–7

4

Click the 'Add a sort' button to add a sort level (Figure 4–8).

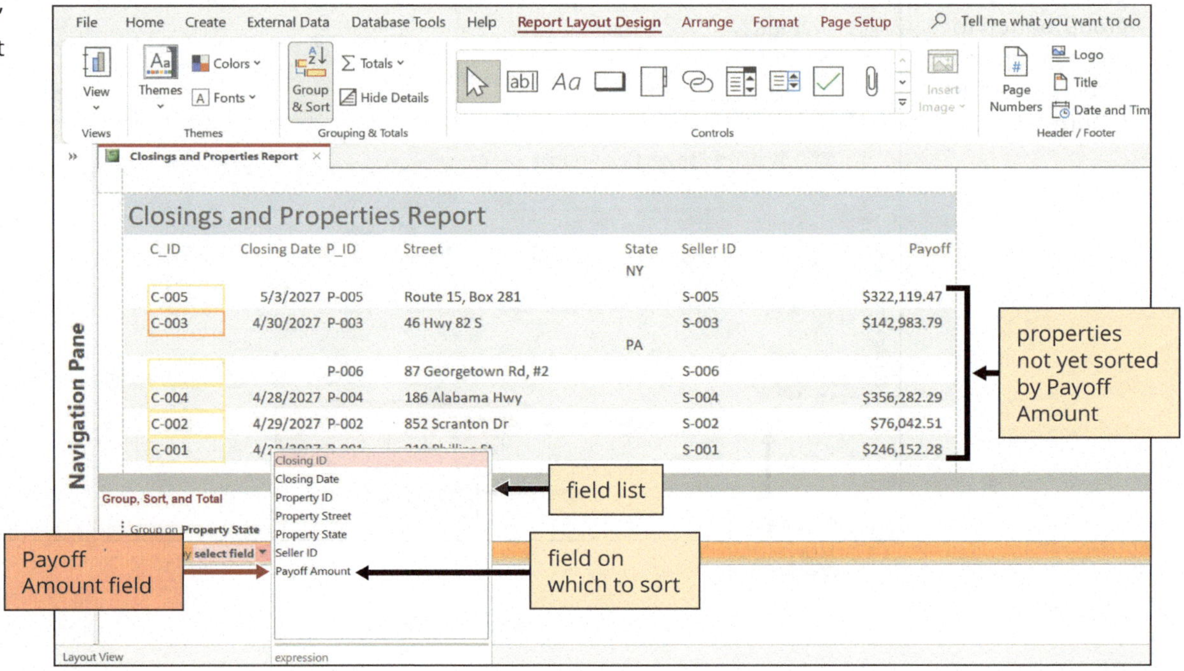

Figure 4–8

5

- Click the Payoff Amount field in the field list to specify the field on which the records in each group will be sorted (Figure 4–9).

Q&A I thought the report would be sorted by State, because I chose to group on that field. What is the effect of choosing to sort by Payoff Amount?

This second sort takes place within groups. You are specifying that within the list of the same State, the rows will be ordered by Payoff Amount.

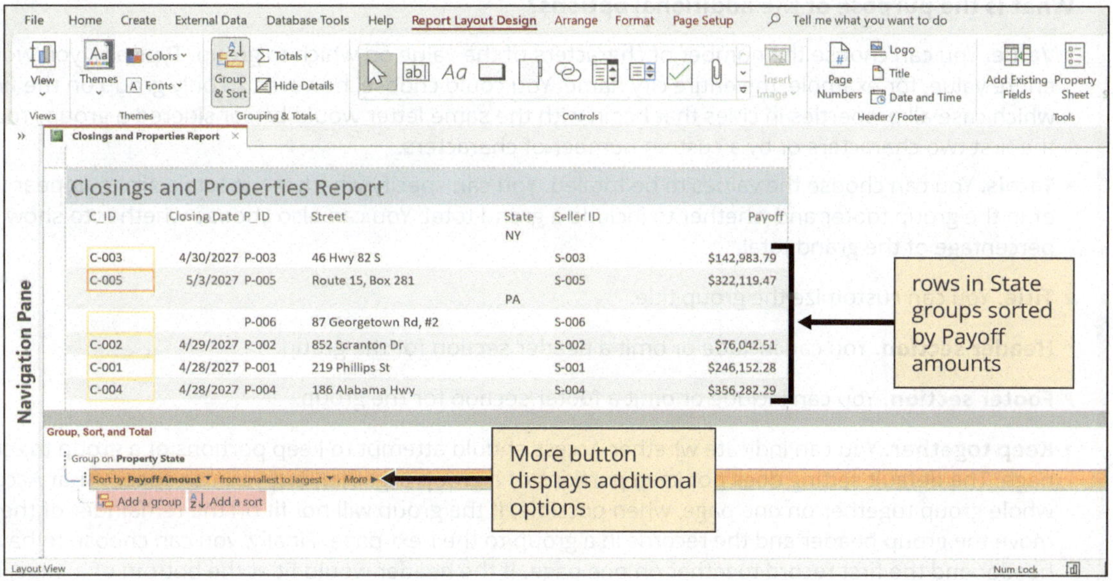

Figure 4–9

Other Ways

1. Right-click column header for field, click Group On (field name) to add grouping

Grouping and Sorting Options

For both grouping and sorting, you can click the More button to specify additional options (Figure 4–10).

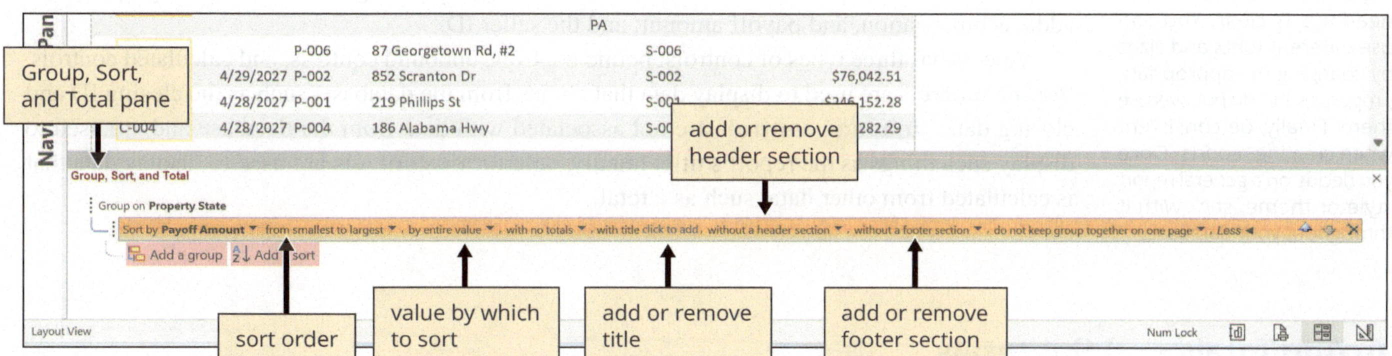

Figure 4–10

Consider This

What is the purpose of the additional options?

- **Value.** You can choose the number of characters of the value on which to group. Typically, you would group by the entire value, for example, the entire city name. You could choose, however, to only group on the first character, in which case all properties in cities that begin with the same letter would be considered a group. You could also group by the first two characters or by a custom number of characters.
- **Totals.** You can choose the values to be totaled. You can specify whether the totals are to appear in the group header or in the group footer and whether to include a grand total. You can also choose whether to show group totals as a percentage of the grand total.
- **Title.** You can customize the group title.
- **Header section.** You can include or omit a header section for the group.
- **Footer section.** You can include or omit a footer section for the group.
- **Keep together.** You can indicate whether Access should attempt to keep portions of a group together on the same page. The default setting does not keep portions of a group together, but you can specify that Access should keep a whole group together on one page, when possible. If the group will not fit on the remainder of the page, Access will move the group header and the records in a group to the next page. Finally, you can choose to have Access keep the header and the first record together on one page. If the header would fit at the bottom of a page, but there would not be room for the first record, Access will move the header to the next page.

BTW
Grouping
You should allow sufficient white space between groups. If you feel the amount is insufficient, you can add more space by enlarging the group header or group footer.

BTW
Report Design Considerations
The purpose of any report is to present specific information. Make sure the meaning of the row and column headings is clear. You can use different fonts and sizes by changing the appropriate properties, but do not overuse them. Finally, be consistent when creating reports. Once you decide on a general report style or theme, stick with it throughout your database.

Report Controls

The various objects on a report are called **controls**. You can manipulate these controls to modify their location and appearance. The report title, column headers, contents of various fields, subtotals, and so on are all contained in controls. When working in Layout view, as you will do in this module, Access handles details concerning placement, sizing, and format of these controls for you automatically. When working in Design view, you will see and manipulate the controls. Even when working in Layout view, however, it is useful to understand the concepts of controls.

The report shown in Figure 4–1 has a control containing the title, Closings and Properties Report. The report also includes controls containing each column header (C_ID, Closing Date, P_ID, Street, State, Seller ID, and Payoff). A control in the Group Header section displays the state name.

In the finished report, there are two controls in the Group Footer section: One control displays the subtotal of Payoff Amounts and a second displays the total of Payoff Amounts for all the groups. The Detail section has controls containing the closing ID and date; the property ID, address information, and payoff amount; and the seller ID.

Access has three types of controls: bound controls, unbound controls, and calculated controls. **Bound controls** are used to display data that comes from the database, such as the closing ID and closing date. **Unbound controls** are not associated with data from the database and are used to display such things as the report's title. Finally, **calculated controls** are used to display data that is calculated from other data, such as a total.

To Add Totals and Subtotals

To add totals or other statistics, use the Totals button on the Design tab. You then select from a menu of aggregate functions, which are functions that perform some mathematical function against a group of records. The available aggregate functions, or calculations, are Sum (total), Average, Count Records, Count Values, Max (largest value), Min (smallest value), Standard Deviation, and Variance. Because the report is grouped, each group will have a subtotal, that is, a total for just the records in the group. At the end of the report, there will be a **grand total**, that is, a total for all records.

The following steps specify totals for the Payoff Amount field. **Why?** Along with grouping data in this report, Partners accountants have also requested that subtotals and a grand total of the Payoff Amount field be included in the report.

1

- Click any record in the Payoff field, and then click the Totals button (Report Layout Design tab | Grouping & Totals group) to display the list of available calculations (Figure 4–11).

Q&A Can I click the column header?

Yes, you can try to click the column header, but if you are unable to select the field, click the Payoff field on any record. If you click the column header and the Totals button does not become available, you will need to click a Payoff field in a record.

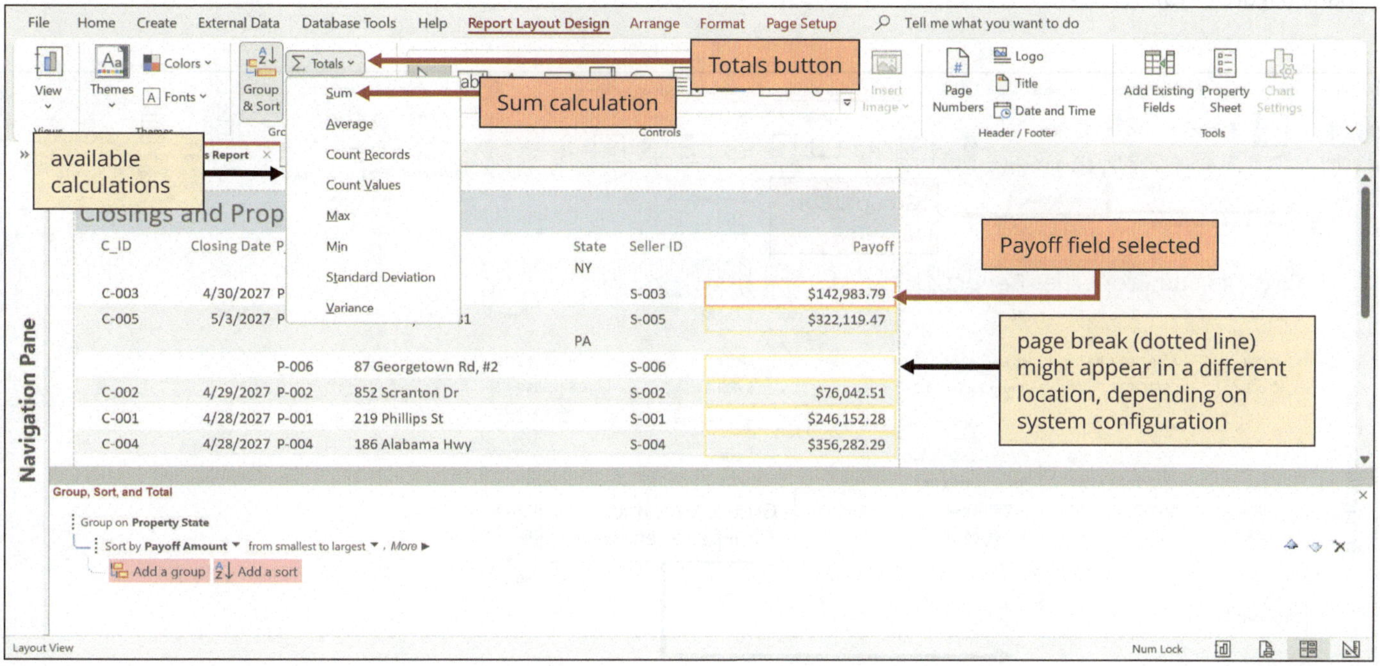

Figure 4–11

2

- Click Sum to calculate the sum of the Payoff values.
- If the subtotal does not appear completely, click the subtotal control and then drag the lower boundary of the control to the approximate position shown in Figure 4–12.

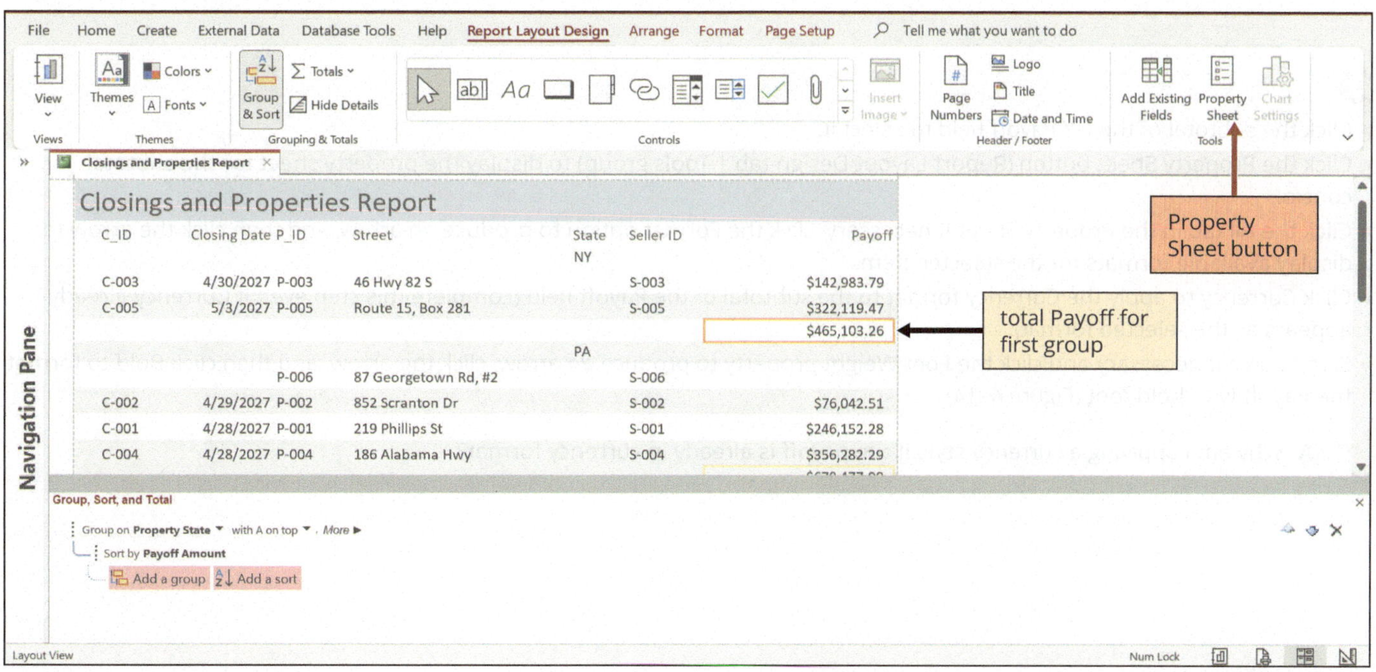

Figure 4–12

Q&A I moved the control rather than resizing it. What did I do wrong?

You dragged the control rather than dragging its lower boundary. Click the Undo button (Home tab | Undo group) to undo your change and then drag again, making sure you are pointing to the control's lower boundary.

3

- Click the Group & Sort button (Report Layout Design tab | Grouping & Totals group) to remove the Group, Sort, and Total pane (Figure 4–13).

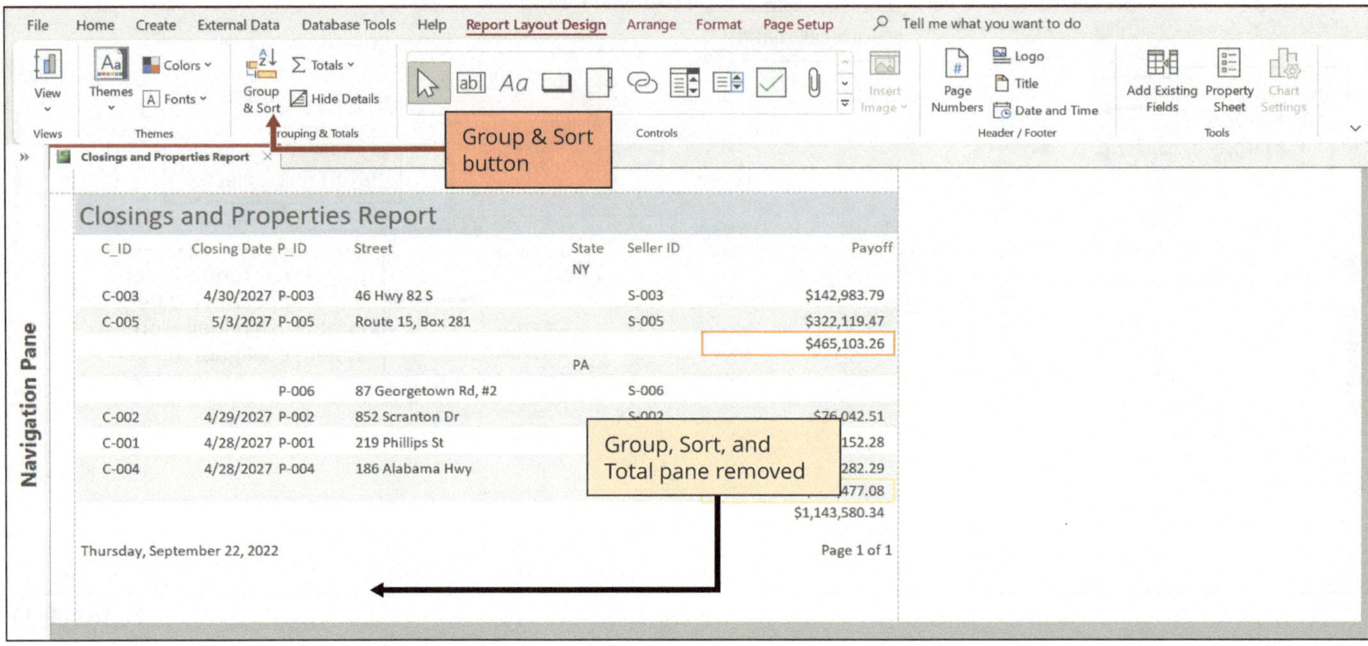

Figure 4–13

Q&A Do I need to remove the Group, Sort, and Total pane?

No. Doing so provides more room on the screen for the report, however. You can easily display the pane whenever you need it by clicking the Group & Sort button again.

4

- Click the subtotal of the NY Payoff field to select it.
- Click the Property Sheet button (Report Layout Design tab | Tools group) to display the property sheet for the subtotal control.
- Click the All tab in the Property Sheet if necessary, click the Format option to produce an arrow, and then click the arrow to display available formats for the selected item.
- Click Currency to apply the Currency format to the subtotal of the Payoff field (complete this step even if Currency already appears as the selected format).
- Scroll down if necessary and click the Font Weight property to produce an arrow, click the arrow, and then click Bold to format the Payoff with bold font (Figure 4–14)

Q&A Why am I applying a currency style if the payoff is already in currency format?

Access contains many options for currency. Confirming and applying the correct format will ensure the format is correct even if you make other changes to the report.

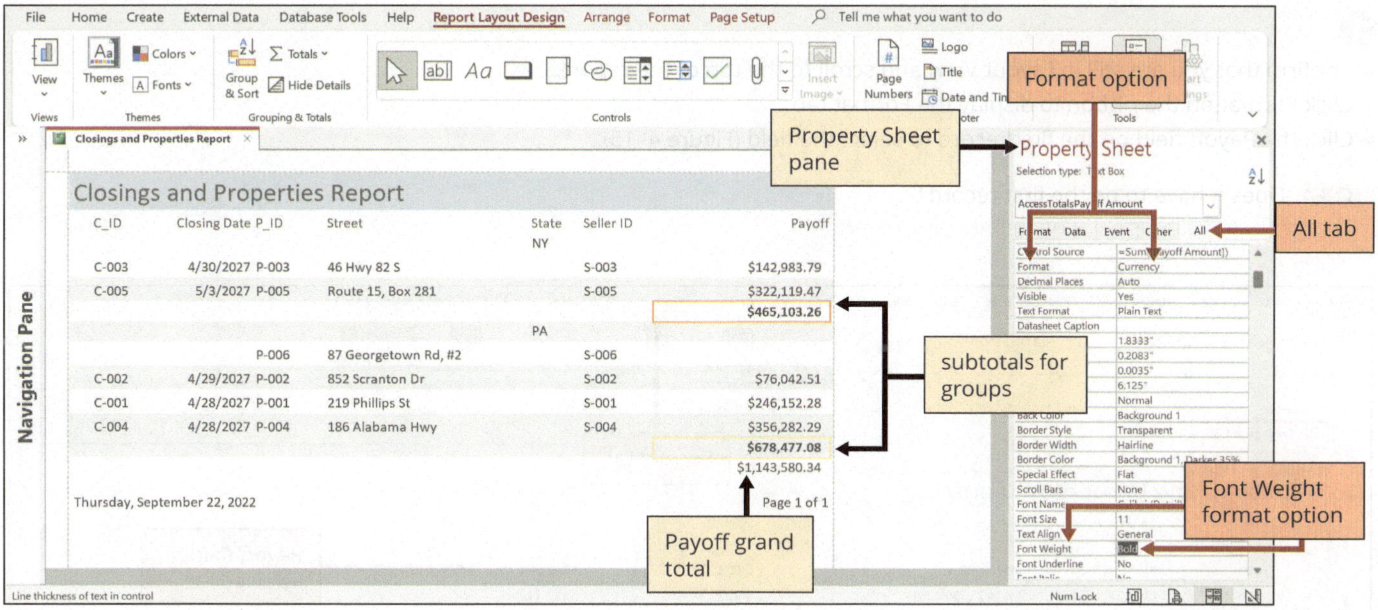

Figure 4–14

5

- Scroll to the bottom of the report and use the same technique to change the format for the grand total of Payoff to Currency and Bold.
- If necessary, drag the grand total control's lower boundary so the numbers are completely visible.
- Click the Property Sheet button (Report Layout Design tab | Tools group) to close the property sheet.
- Click Save to save your changes to the report.

Other Ways

1. Click 'Close Grouping Dialog Box' button in upper-right corner of Group, Sort, and Total pane to close pane

Consider This

How do you determine the organization of the report or form?

Determine various details concerning how the data in your report or form is to be organized.

Determine sort order. Is there a special order in which the records should appear?

Determine grouping. Should the records be grouped in some fashion? If so, what should appear before the records in a group? If, for example, records are grouped by city, the name of the city should probably appear before the group. What should appear after the group? For example, does the report include some fields for which subtotals should be calculated? If so, the subtotals would come after the group. Determine whether you need multiple levels of grouping.

To Conditionally Format Controls

Conditional formatting is special formatting that is applied to values that satisfy some criterion. Partners paralegals have decided to apply conditional formatting to the Payoff field. **Why?** They would like to emphasize values in the Payoff field that are greater than or equal to $200,000.00 by changing the font color to blue. By emphasizing the payoff amounts are equal to or higher in cost than $200,000, they can review the higher payoff amounts that may carry additional tax implications. The following steps conditionally format the Payoff field by specifying a **rule** stating that if the values in the field are greater than or equal to $200,000.00, such values will be formatted in blue.

1

- Confirm that you are still in Layout View and scroll to the top of the report.
- Click Format on the ribbon to display the Format tab.
- Click the Payoff field on the first record to select the field (Figure 4–15).

Q&A Does it have to be the first record?

No. You could click the Payoff field on any record.

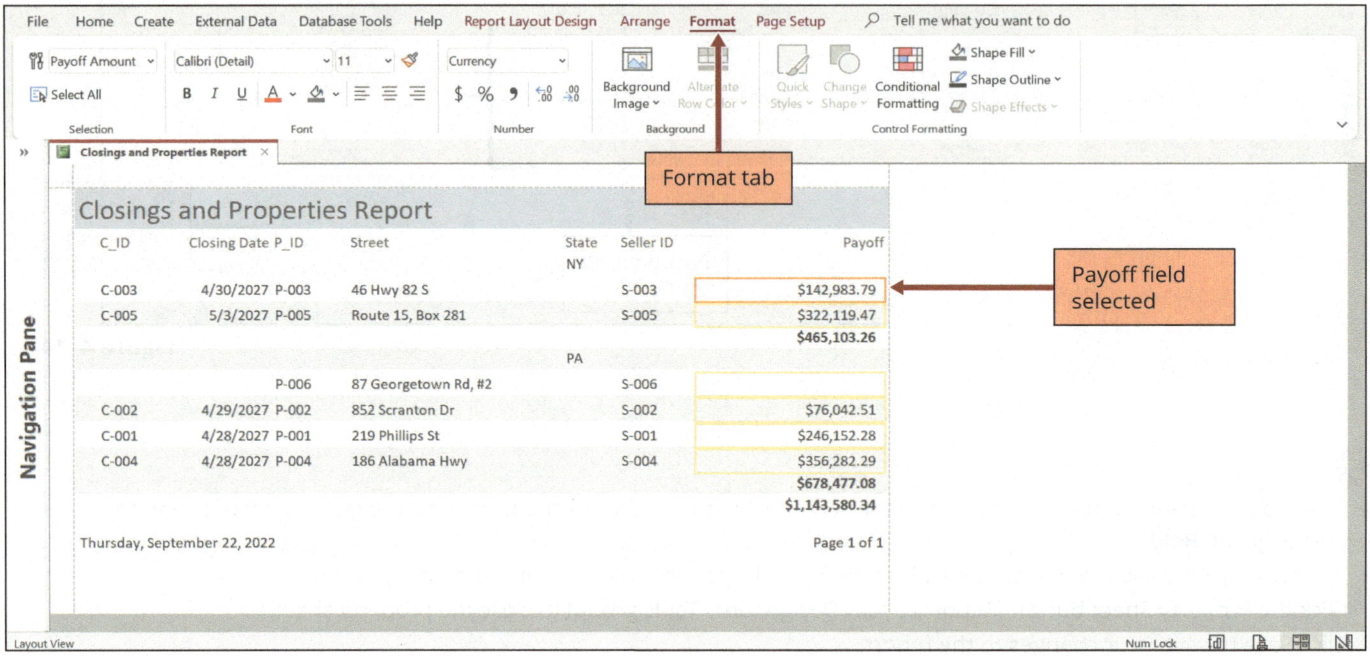

Figure 4–15

2

- Click the Conditional Formatting button (Format tab | Control Formatting group) to display the Conditional Formatting Rules Manager dialog box (Figure 4–16).

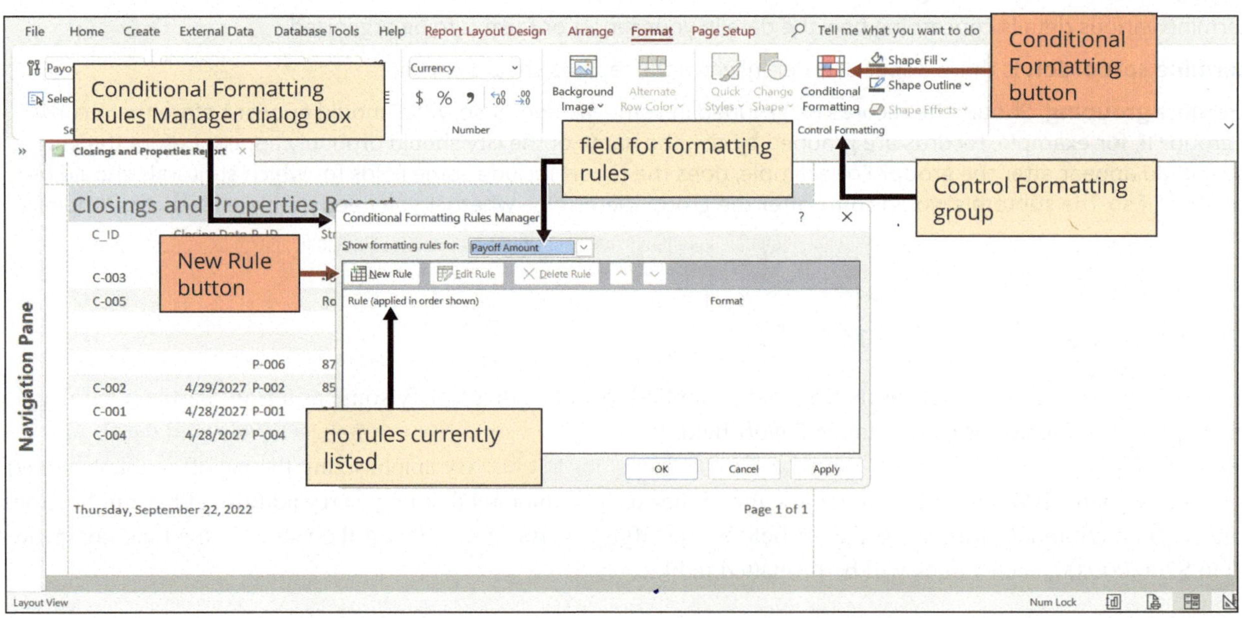

Figure 4–16

3

- Click the New Rule button (Conditional Formatting Rules Manager dialog box) to display the New Formatting Rule dialog box (Figure 4–17).

Q&A I see there are two boxes to enter numbers. I only have one number to enter, 200000. Am I on the right screen?
Yes. Next, you will change the comparison operator from "between" to "greater than or equal to." Once you have done so, Access will display only one box for entering a number.

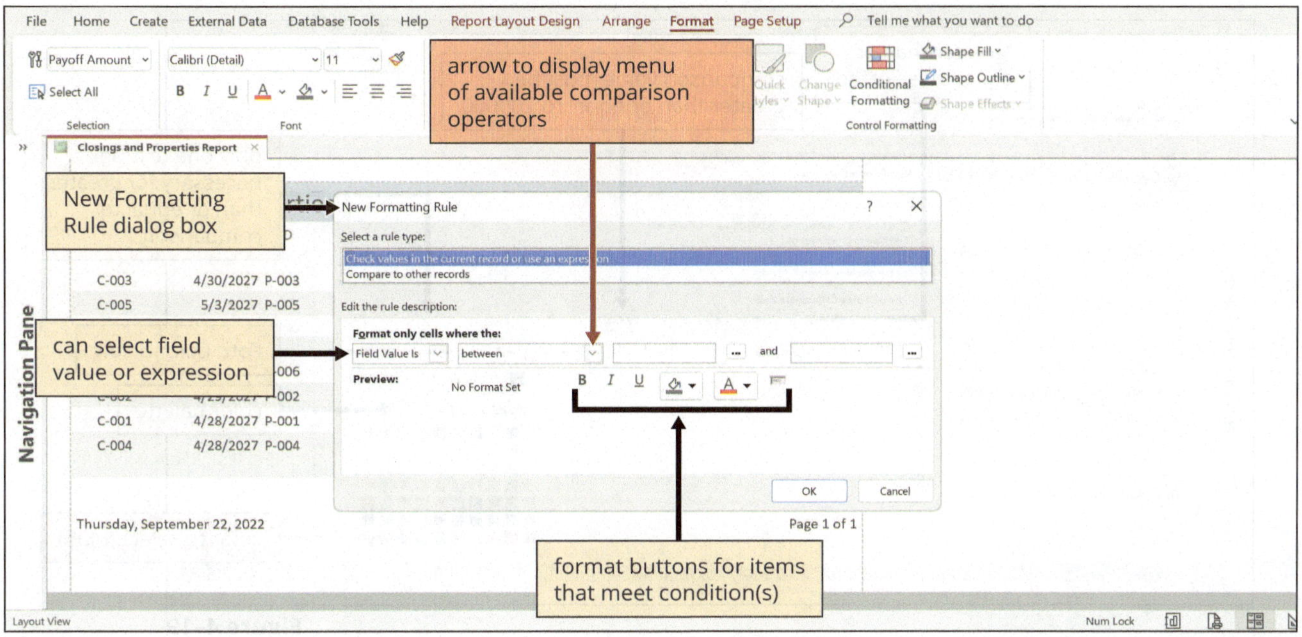

Figure 4–17

4

- Click the arrow to display the list of available comparison operators (New Formatting Rule dialog box) (Figure 4–18).

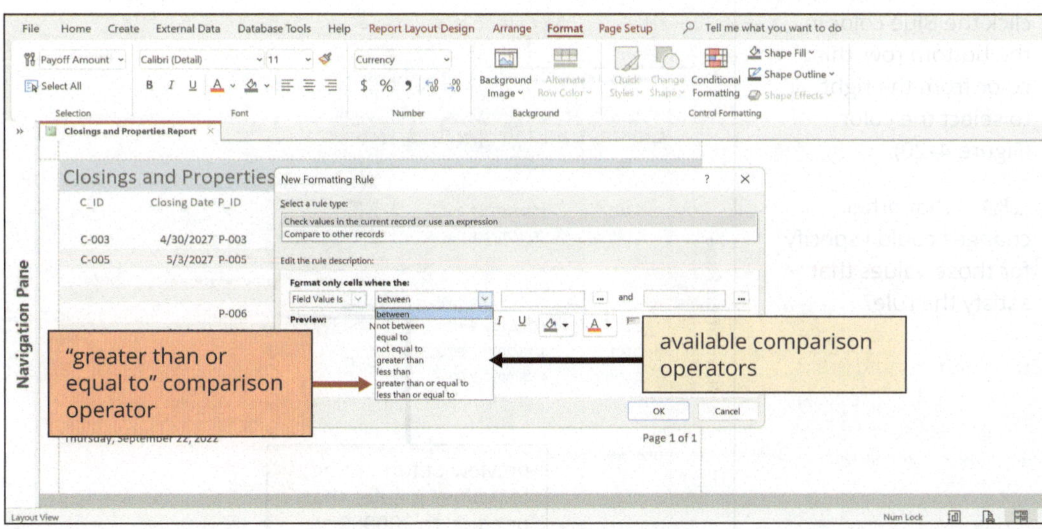

Figure 4–18

5

- Click "greater than or equal to" to select the comparison operator.
- Click the box for the comparison value, and then type **200000** as the comparison value.
- Click the Font Color arrow (New Formatting Rule dialog box) to display a color palette (Figure 4–19).

Q&A What is the effect of selecting this comparison operator and entering this number?
Values in the field that are greater than or equal to 200000 satisfy this rule. Any formatting that you now specify will apply to those values and no others.

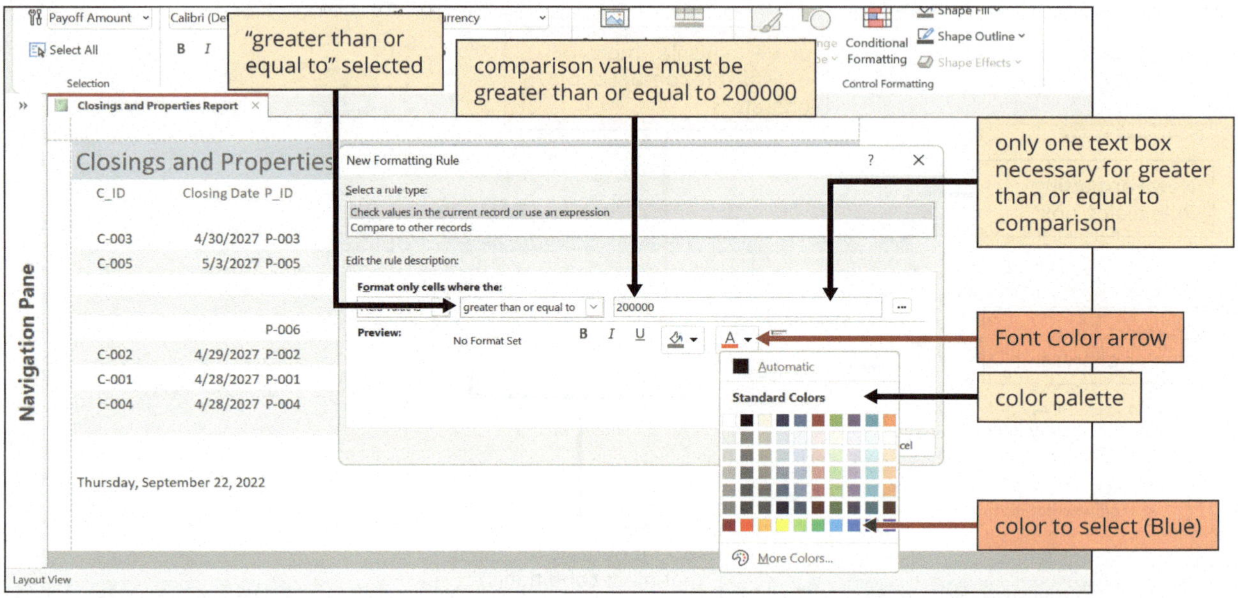

Figure 4–19

6

- On the color palette, click the Blue color in the bottom row, third color from the right to select the color (Figure 4–20).

Q&A What other changes could I specify for those values that satisfy the rule?
You could specify that the value is bold, italic, and/or underlined. You could also specify a background color.

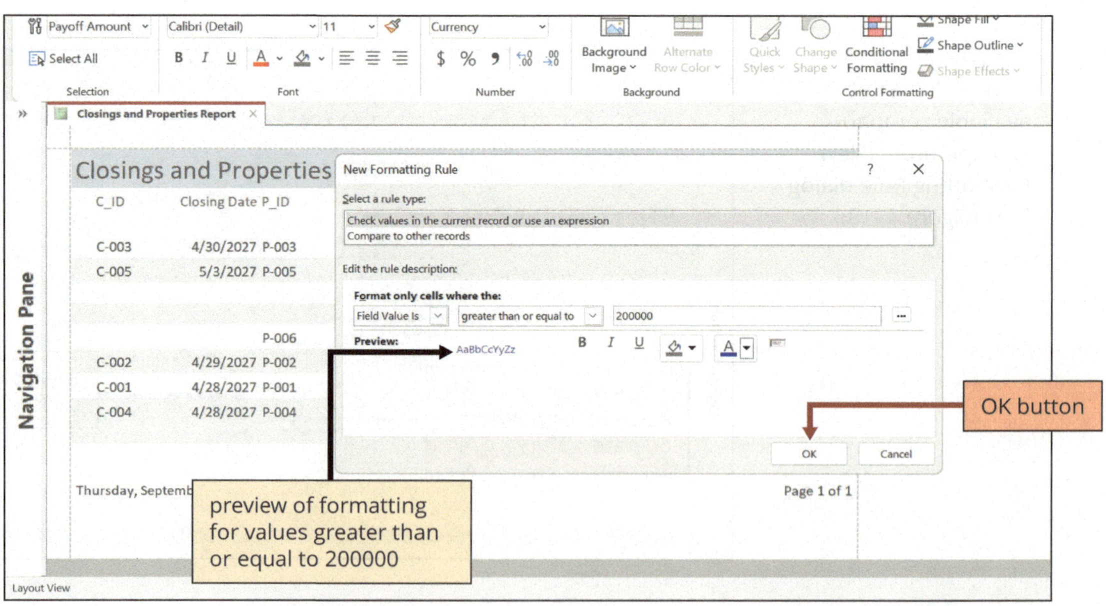

Figure 4–20

7

- Click OK (New Formatting Rule dialog box) to enter the rule (Figure 4–21).

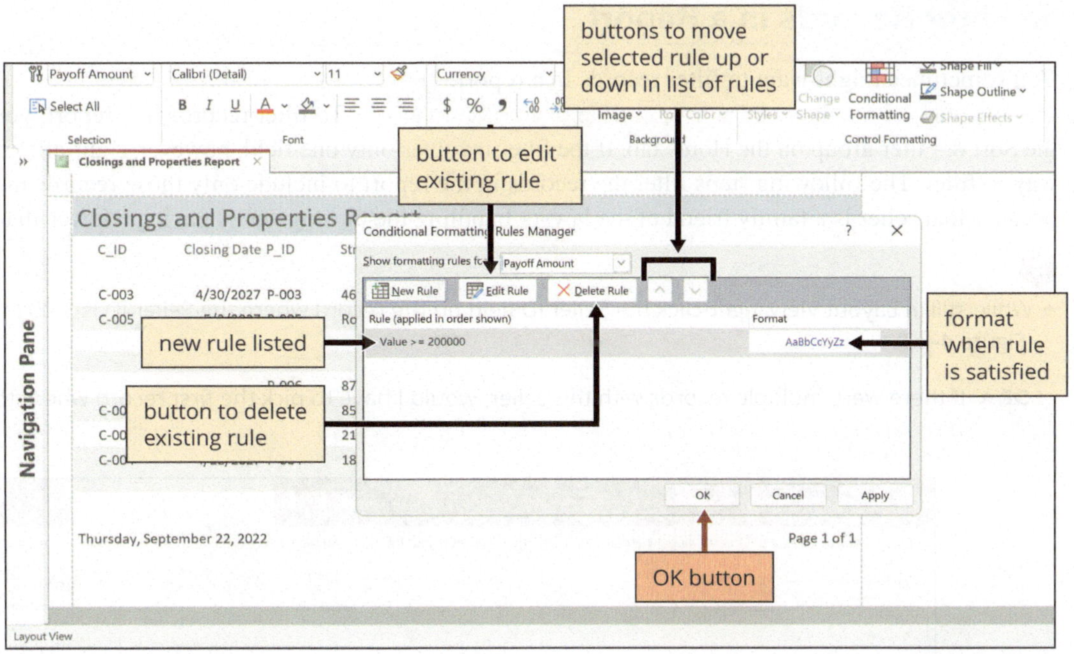

Figure 4–21

Q&A What if I have more than one rule?
The rules are applied in the order in which they appear in the dialog box. If a value satisfies the first rule, the specified formatting will apply, and no further rules will be tested. If not, the value will be tested against the second rule. If it satisfies the rule, the formatting for the second rule would apply. If not, the value would be tested against the third rule, and so on.

Can I change this conditional formatting later?
Yes. Select the field for which you had applied conditional formatting on any record, click the Conditional Formatting button (Format tab | Control Formatting group), click the rule you want to change, click the Edit Rule button, and then make the necessary changes. You can also delete the selected rule by clicking the Delete Rule button, or move the selected rule by clicking the Move Up or Move Down buttons.

8

- Click OK (Conditional Formatting Rules Manager dialog box) to complete the entry of the conditional formatting rules and apply the rule (Figure 4–22).

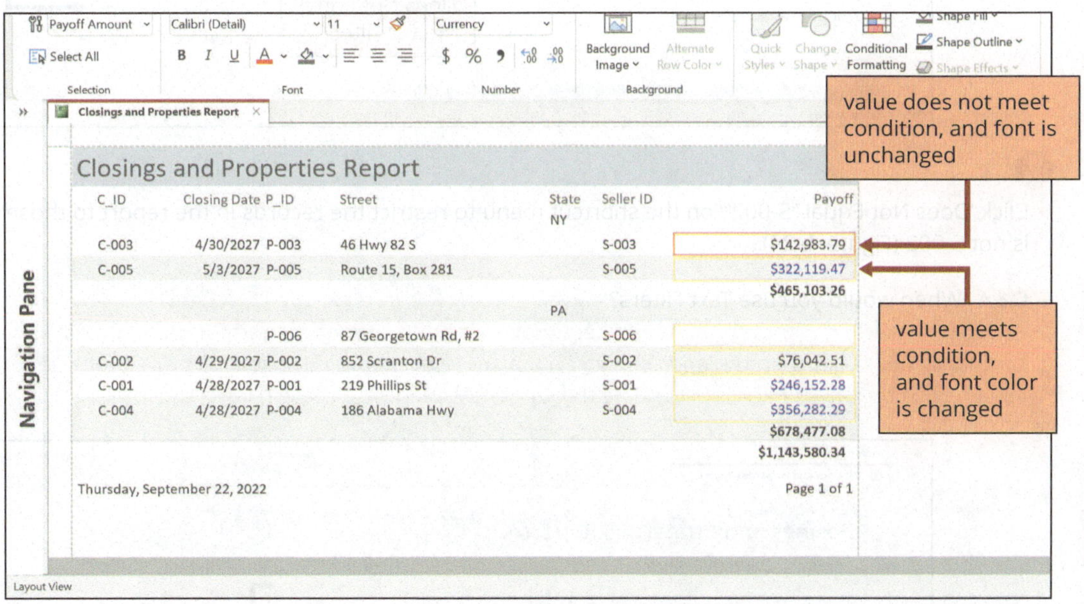

Figure 4–22

9

- Click Save on the Quick Access Toolbar to save your changes to the report.
- **Experiment:** After saving your changes, experiment with different rules. Add a second rule that changes the format for any current due amount that is greater than or equal to $350,000 to a different color to see the effect of multiple rules. Change the order of rules to see the effect of a different order. When you have finished, delete any additional rules you have added so the report contains only the one rule you created earlier.

To Filter Records in a Report

You sometimes might want to filter records in a report. **Why?** You might want to include in a report only those records that satisfy some criterion and be able to change that criterion easily. To filter records in a report, you can use the filter buttons in the Sort & Filter group on the Home tab. If the filter involves only one field, however, right-clicking the field provides a simple way to filter. The following steps filter the records in the report to include only those records in which the seller is not S-002 because that seller is a family friend of the lawyer handling the closing and is paying a lower-than-standard fee.

1

- While still in Layout View, right-click the Seller ID field on the record where the Seller ID is S-002 to display a shortcut menu (Figure 4–23).

Q&A If there were multiple records with this seller, would I have to pick the first record where the value is S-002?

No. You could pick any record on which the Seller ID value is S-002.

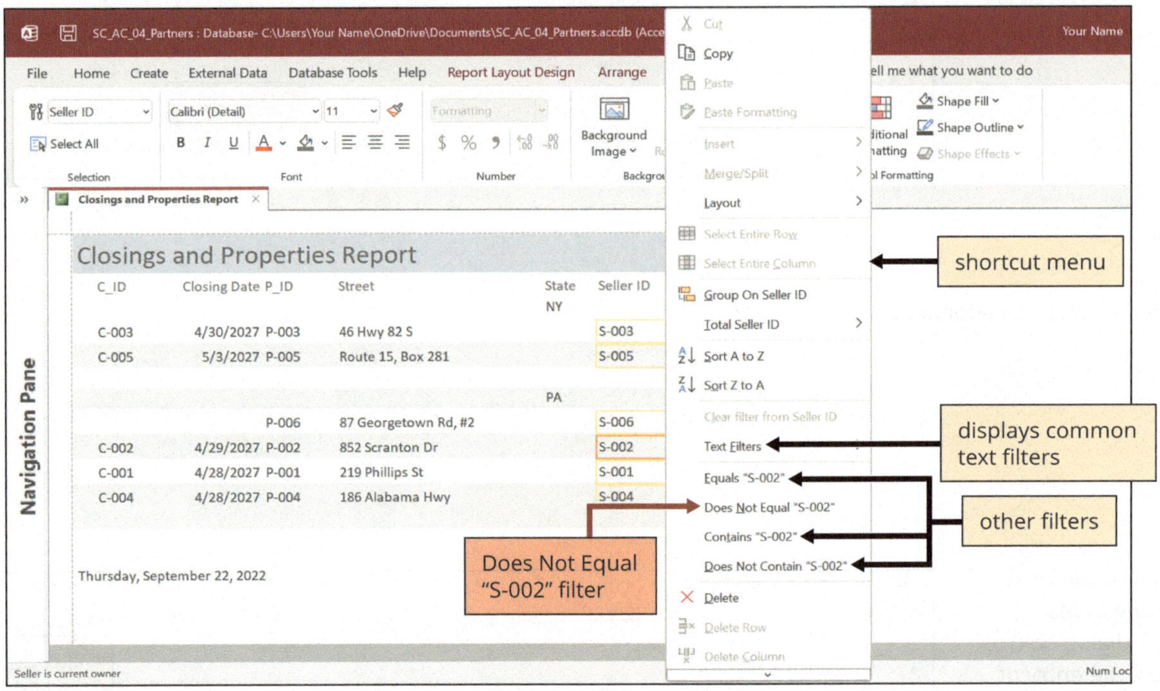

Figure 4–23

2

- Click 'Does Not Equal "S-002"' on the shortcut menu to restrict the records in the report to those on which the Seller ID value is not S-002 (Figure 4–24).

Q&A When would you use Text Filters?

You would use Text Filters if you need filters that are not on the main shortcut menu or if you need the ability to enter specific values other than the ones shown on the shortcut menu. If those filters are insufficient for your needs, you can use Advanced Filter/Sort, which is accessible through the Advanced button (Home tab | Sort & Filter group).

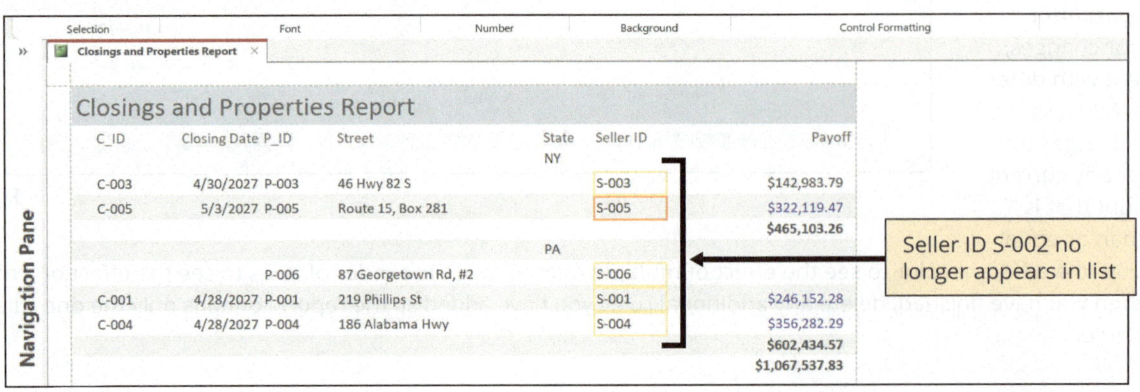

Figure 4–24

Other Ways

1. Click Selection button (Home tab | Sort & Filter group) to apply filter

To Clear a Report Filter

The following steps clear the filter on the Seller ID field. **Why?** When you no longer want the records to be filtered, you clear the filter so all records are again included.

1

- On the first record, right-click the Seller ID field to display a shortcut menu (Figure 4–25).

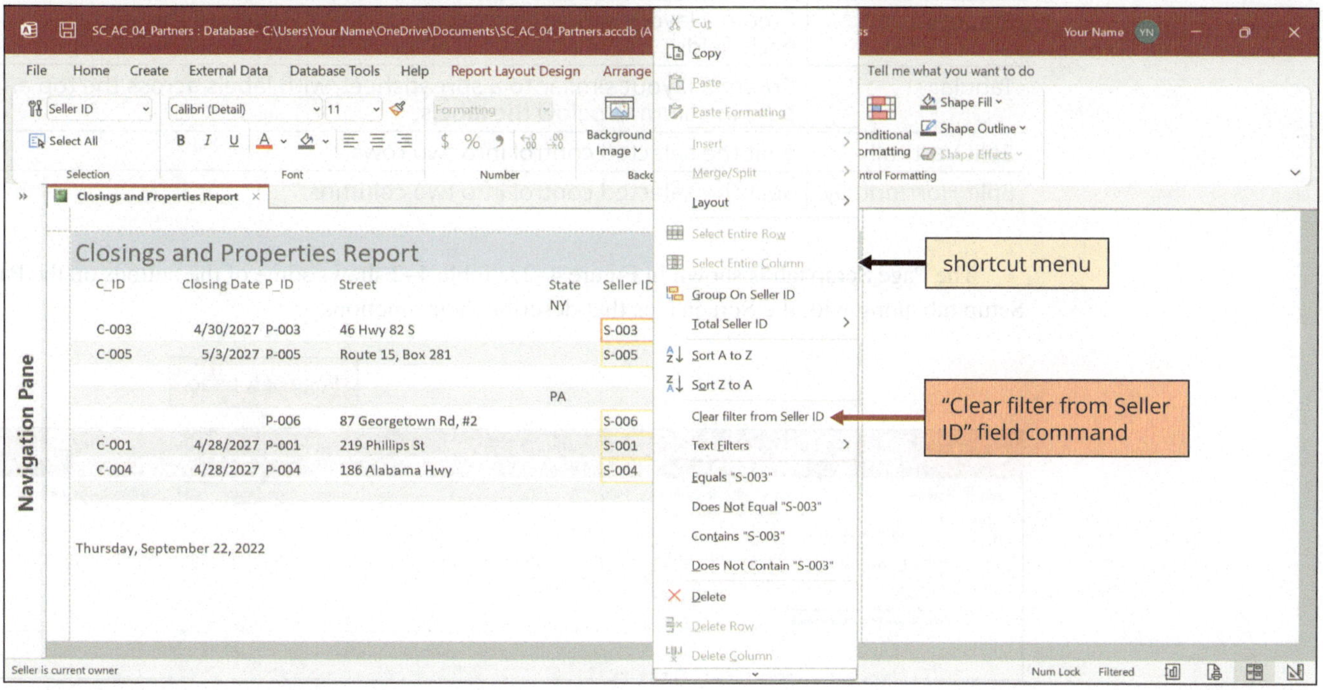

Figure 4–25

Q&A Did I have to pick the first record?
No. You could pick the Seller ID field on any record.

- Click 'Clear filter from Seller ID' on the shortcut menu to clear the filter and redisplay all records.
- **Experiment:** Try other filters on the shortcut menu for the Seller ID field to see their effect. When you are done with each, clear the filter.
- Save your work.
- Close the Closings and Properties Report.

Other Ways

1. Click Advanced button (Home tab | Sort & Filter group) to clear filter.

The Arrange and Page Setup Tabs

When working on a report in Layout view, you can make additional layout changes by using the Arrange and/or Page Setup tabs. The Arrange tab is shown in Figure 4–26. Table 4–1 shows some of the buttons on the Arrange tab along with the ScreenTips that describe their functions.

BTW
Using the Arrange Tab
Because the commands located on the Arrange tab are actions associated with previously selected controls, be sure to select the desired control or controls first.

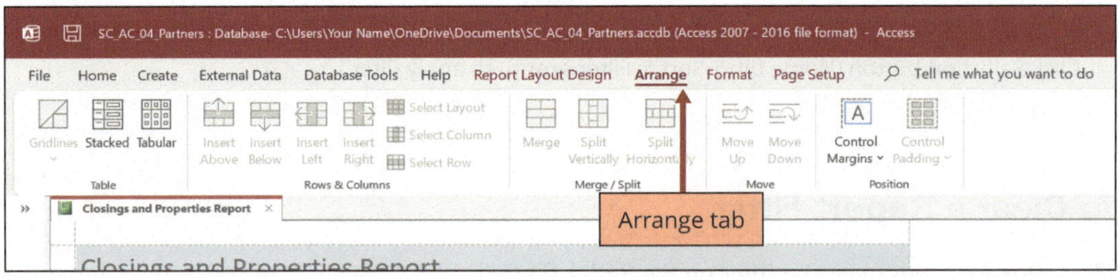

Figure 4–26

Table 4–1 Arrange Tab

Button	ScreenTip
Stacked	Create a layout similar to a paper form, with labels to the left of each field.
Tabular	Create a layout similar to a spreadsheet, with labels across the top and data in columns below the labels.
Split Vertically	Split the selected control into two rows.
Split Horizontally	Split the selected control into two columns.

The Page Setup tab is shown in Figure 4–27. Table 4–2 shows some of the buttons on the Page Setup tab along with the ScreenTips that describe their functions.

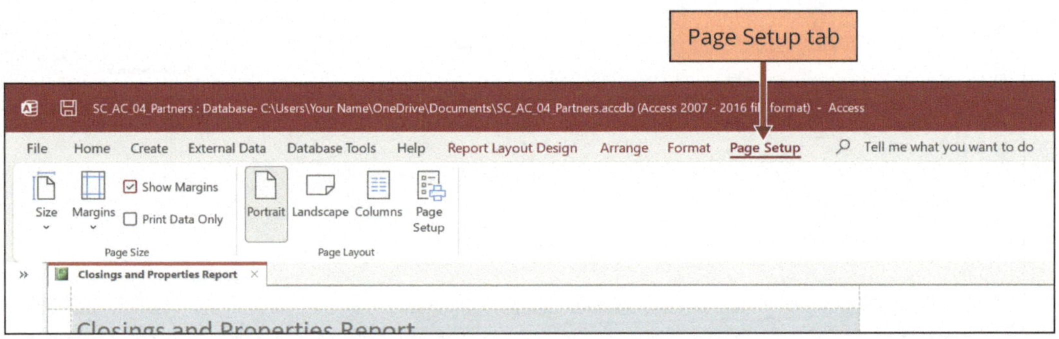

Figure 4–27

Table 4–2 Page Setup Tab

Button	ScreenTip
Size	Choose a paper size for your document.
Margins	Set the margin sizes for the entire document or the current section. Choose from several commonly-used margin formats, or customize your own.
Portrait	Change to portrait orientation.
Landscape	Change to landscape orientation.
Page Setup	Don't see what you're looking for? Check out the full set of page formatting options.

BTW

Distributing a Document

Instead of printing and distributing a hard copy of a document, you can distribute the document electronically. Options include sending the document via email; posting it on cloud storage (such as OneDrive) and sharing the file with others; posting it on a social networking site, blog, or other website; and sharing a link associated with an online location of the document. You can also create and share a PDF or XPS image of the document, so that users can view the file in Acrobat Reader or XPS Viewer instead of in Access.

To Print a Report

If you wanted to print your report, you would use the following steps.

1. With the report selected in the Navigation Pane, click File on the ribbon to open the Backstage view.
2. Click Print tab in Backstage view to display the Print gallery.
3. Click the Quick Print button to print the report.

Q&A How can I print multiple copies of my report?

Click File on the ribbon to open Backstage view. Click the Print tab, click Print in the Print gallery to display the Print dialog box, increase the number in the Number of Copies box, and then click OK (Print dialog box).

Break Point: If you wish to take a break, this is a good place to do so. You can quit Access now. To resume at a later time, start Access, open the database called SC_AC_04_Partners.accdb, and continue following the steps from this location forward.

BTW

Searching for Records in a Report

You can use the Find button to search for records in a report. To do so, open the report in Report view or Layout view and select the field in the report on which to search. Click the Find button (Home tab | Find group) to display the Find dialog box. Type the desired value on which to search in the Find What text box (Find dialog box), and then click the Find Next button.

Multiple-Table Reports

Sometimes you will create reports that require data from more than one table. You can use the Report Wizard to create a report based on multiple tables just as you can use it to create reports based on single tables or queries. The following steps use the Report Wizard to create a report that includes fields from the Sellers, Properties, Closings, and Closing Fees tables.

To Create a Report that Involves Multiple Tables

Currently, there are two existing relationships, one between the Closings table and Mortgage Companies table and another between the Closings table and the Properties table. To produce the report currently needed by the managers, you will need to add relationships for the Sellers and Closing Fees tables. **Why?** Partners paralegals need a report that shows detailed agent commission information and that includes the Property Street, Seller Name, Closing Date, and Total Agent Commission information from existing tables.

Before starting to create reports from multiple tables, it is always a good idea to check the current relationships between tables and add any necessary relationships to the tables. The Closings table will be the basis for much of the information in the report needed by Partners paralegals. The following steps review the existing relationships and add the necessary tables to the Relationships window.

1

- Click the Database Tools tab, and then click the Relationships button to open the Relationships window (Figure 4–28).

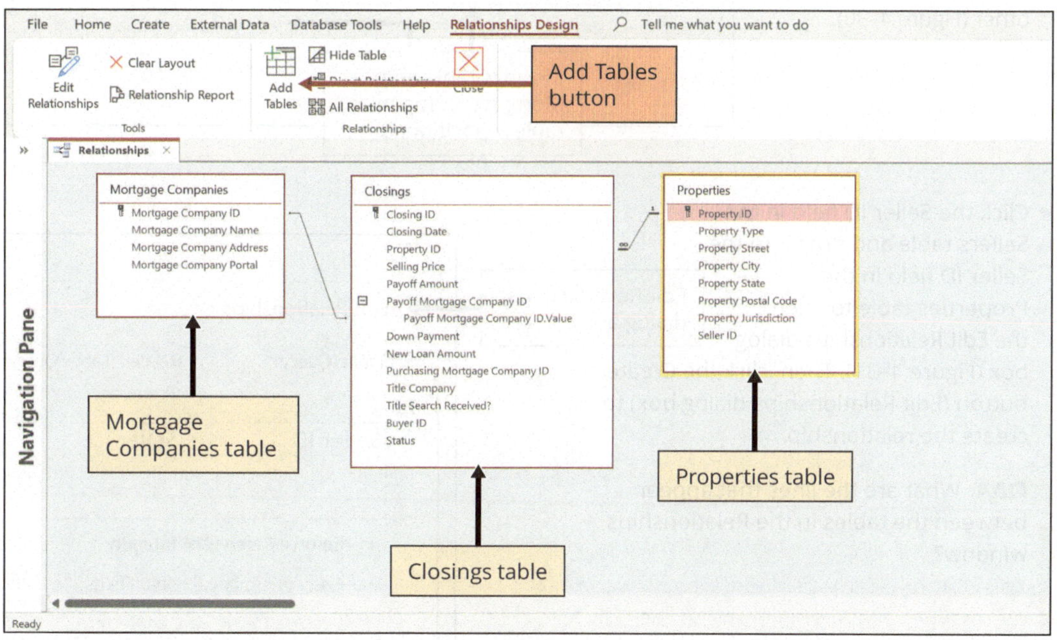

Figure 4–28

2

- Click the Add Tables button to view available tables in the Add Tables pane.
- Click the Sellers table and then click the Add Selected Tables button to add this table to the Relationships window (Figure 4–29).

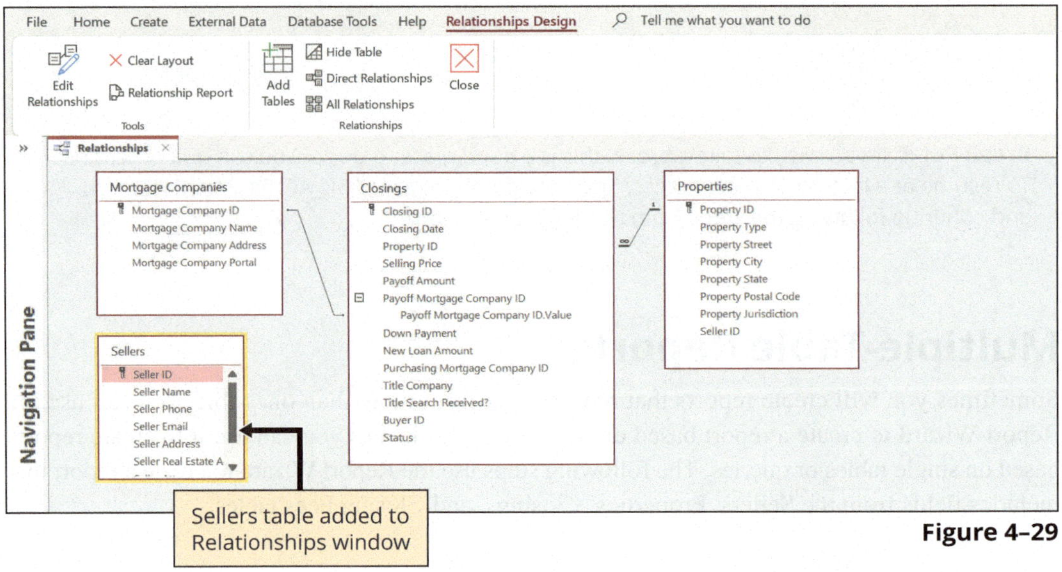

Figure 4–29

3

- Adjust the positions and sizes of the tables so you can see the Seller ID field in the Sellers table and the Seller ID field in the Properties table. It might also be easier to create the relationship if the Sellers and Properties tables are positioned next to each other (Figure 4–30).

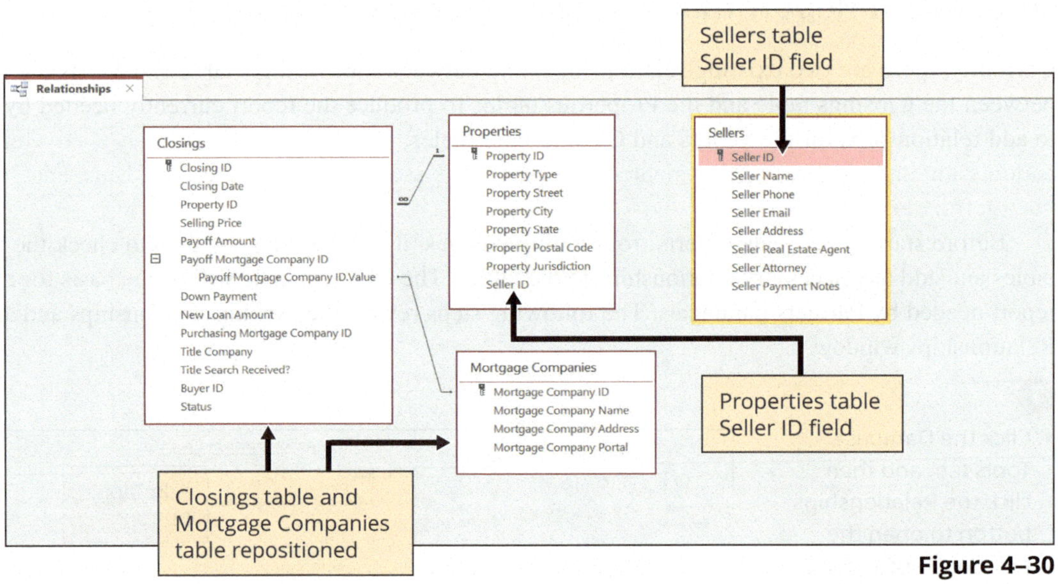

Figure 4–30

- Click the Seller ID field in the Sellers table and drag it to the Seller ID field in the Properties table to open the Edit Relationships dialog box (Figure 4–31). Then, click the Create button (Edit Relationships dialog box) to create the relationship.

Q&A What are the lines that appear between the tables in the Relationships window?

The lines depict the relationships between tables. The relationship between the Properties and Sellers tables is based on the Seller ID field. A relationship also exists between the Property ID field in the Properties table and the Property ID field in the Closings table.

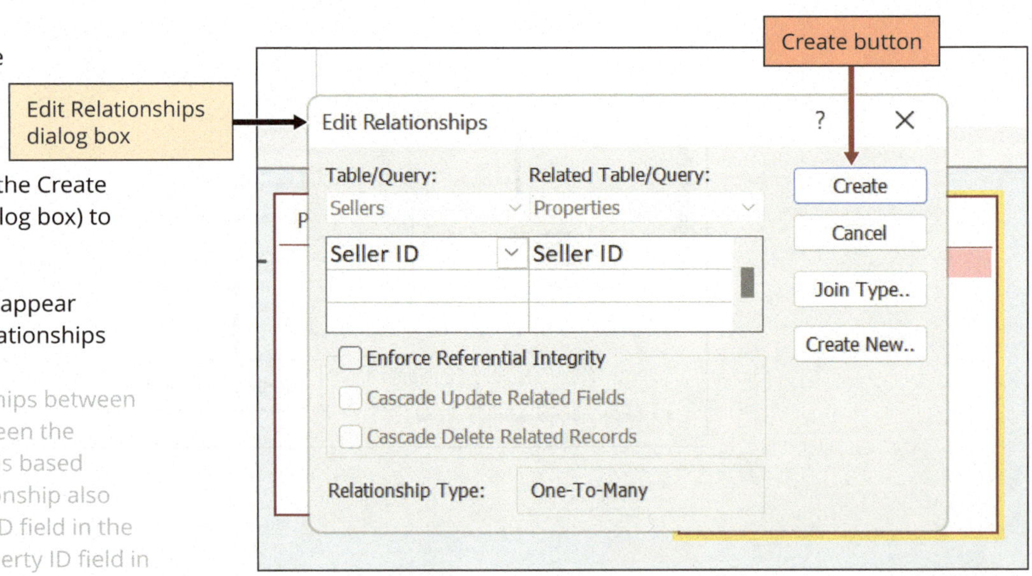

Figure 4–31

4

- Click the Closing Fees table in the Add Tables pane, and click the Add Selected Tables button to add the table to the Relationship window. Resize and reposition the tables as desired so the Closing Fees table is positioned near the Closing table (Figure 4–32).
- Click the Closing ID field in the Closing Fees table and drag it to the Closing ID field in the Closings table to open the Edit Relationships dialog box. Click the Create button to create the relationship, which will enable you to view fees in the report.

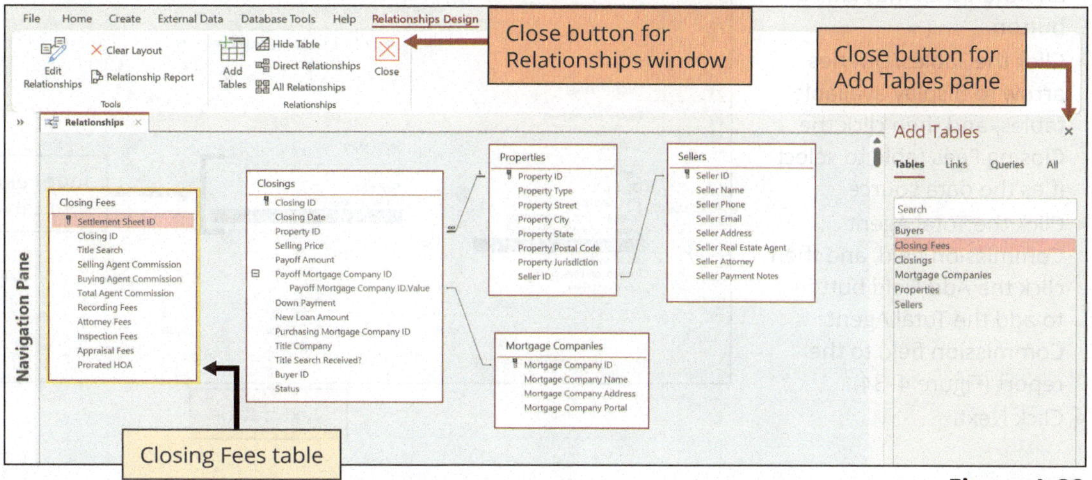

Figure 4–32

Q&A How does Access relate the Closings and Mortgage Companies tables?

Access recognizes there is a relationship between the Payoff Mortgage Company ID.Value field in the Closings table and the Mortgage Company ID field in the Mortgage Companies table. Mortgage Company ID and Payoff Mortgage Company ID.Value are displayed on two lines in the Closings table for the same field because this field was previously updated to a multivalued lookup field that displays the field on multiple lines.

5

- Click Save on the Quick Access Toolbar to save your changes.
- Click the Close button on the Add Tables pane.
- Click the Close button (Relationships Design tab | Relationships group) to close the Relationships window.

6

- Open the Navigation Pane if it is currently closed, and then select the Properties table.
- Click Create on the ribbon to display the Create tab.
- Click the Report Wizard button (Create tab | Reports group) to open the Report Wizard.
- Click the Property Street field, and then click the Add Field button to add the street information to the report (Figure 4–33).

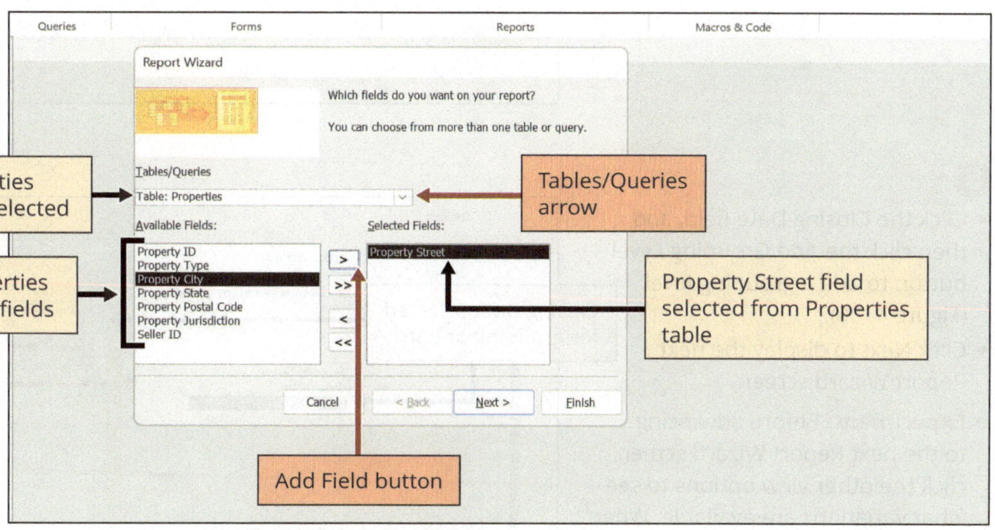

Figure 4–33

7

- Click the Tables/Queries arrow to display available tables and then click Table: Sellers to select the Sellers table as the data source.
- Click the Seller Name field and then click the Add Field button.
- Click the Tables/Queries arrow to display available tables, and then click the Closings table to select it as the data source.

- Click the Closing Date field, and then click the Add Field button
- Click the Tables/Queries arrow to display available tables, and then click the Closing Fees table to select it as the data source.
- Click the Total Agent Commission field, and then click the Add Field button to add the Total Agent Commission field to the report (Figure 4–34).
- Click Next.

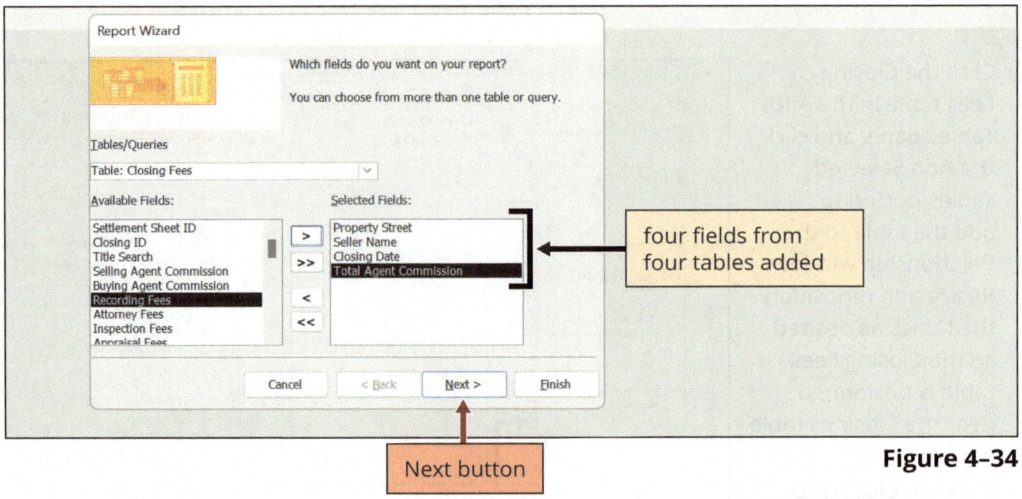

Figure 4–34

8

- For the most efficient layout of the included information, click the 'by Closing Fees' option (Figure 4–35).
- Click Next.

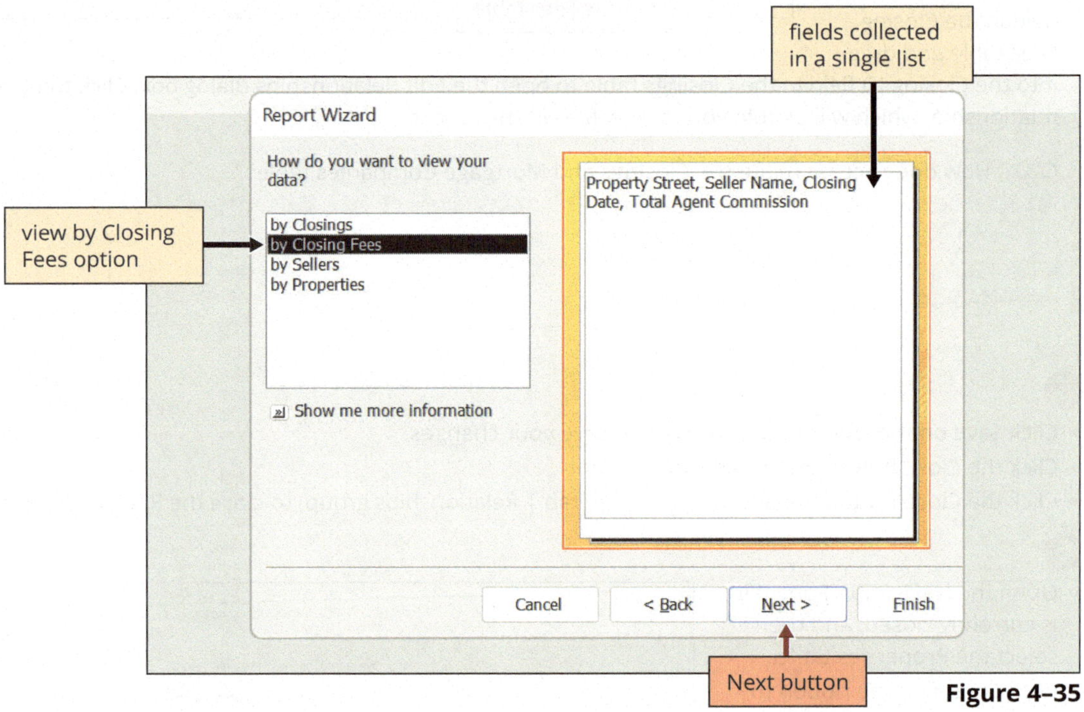

Figure 4–35

9

- Click the Closing Date field, and then click the Add Grouping Level button to add a grouping level (Figure 4–36).
- Click Next to display the next Report Wizard screen.
- **Experiment:** Before advancing to the next Report Wizard screen, click the other view options to see what variations are available. When you're ready, again select the 'by Closing Fees' option.

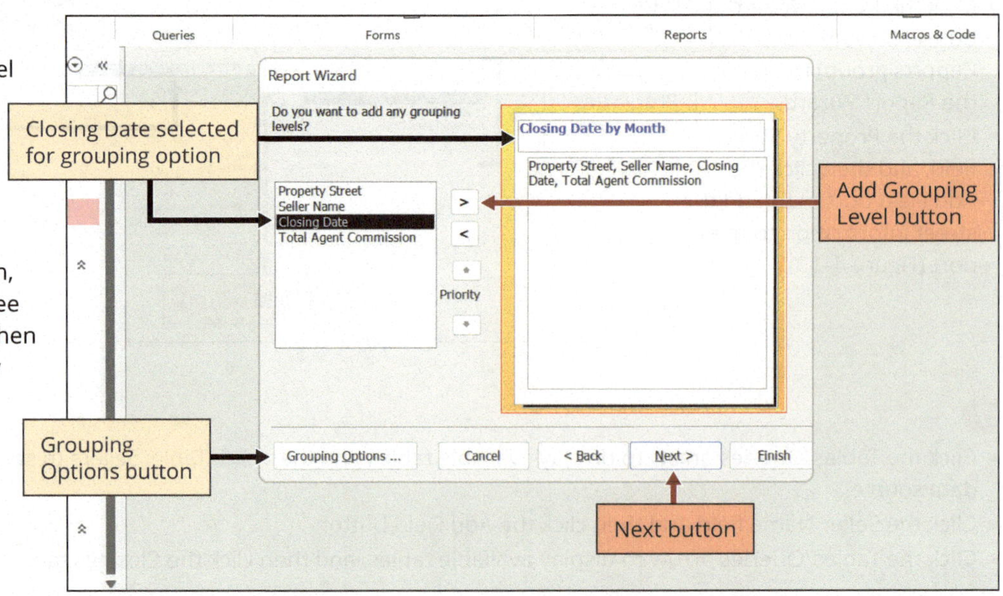

Figure 4–36

10

- Click the Summary Options button to display the Summary Options dialog box.
- Click the Sum check box to calculate the sum of Total Agent Commissions.
- If necessary, click the Detail and Summary option button to select it (Figure 4–37).
- Click OK (Summary Options dialog box) to close the Summary Options dialog box.
- Click Next to display the next Report Wizard screen.

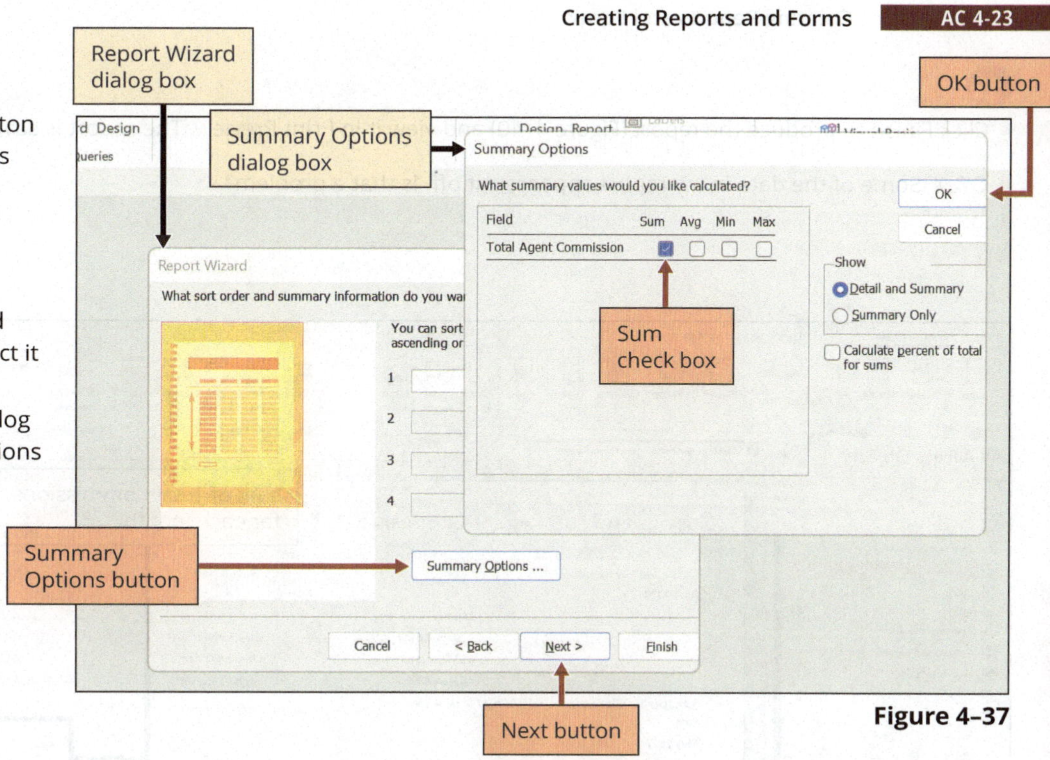

Figure 4–37

11

- Confirm that Stepped layout is selected, and then click the Landscape option button to select landscape orientation (Figure 4–38).
- Click Next to display the next Report Wizard screen.

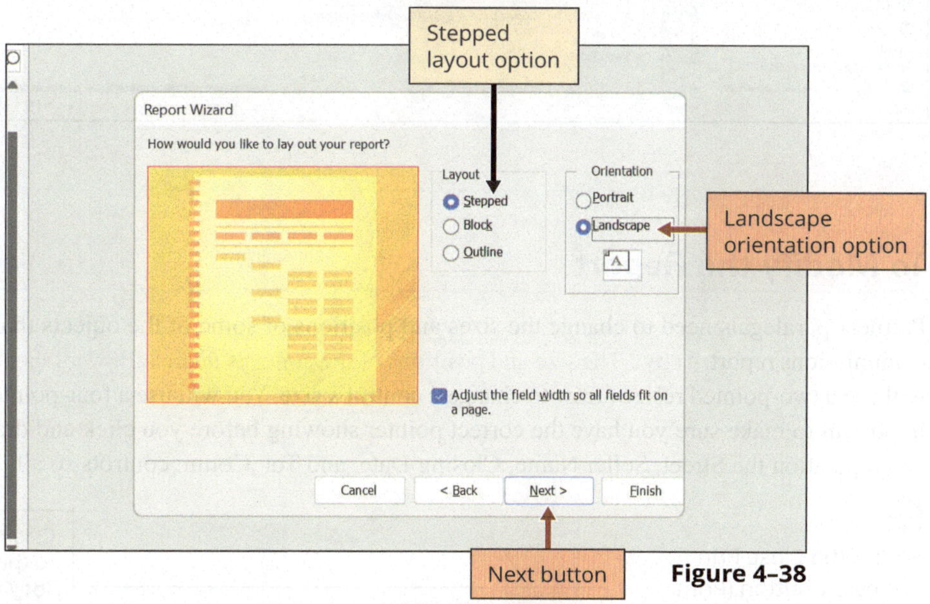

Figure 4–38

12

- Click the text box for the title, delete any existing text, and then type **Closings and Total Agent Commissions** as the title (Figure 4–39).

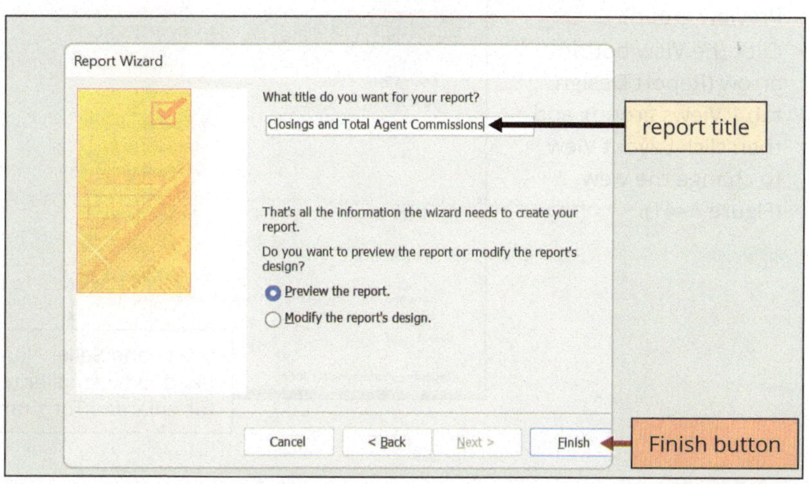

Figure 4–39

13

- Click Finish to produce the report (Figure 4–40) and view it in Print Preview. The report is saved automatically.

Q&A Some of the data in my report appears cut off. Is that a problem?

No. It's common for some data to appear cut off when you first produce a report. You will resolve this issue when you modify the report.

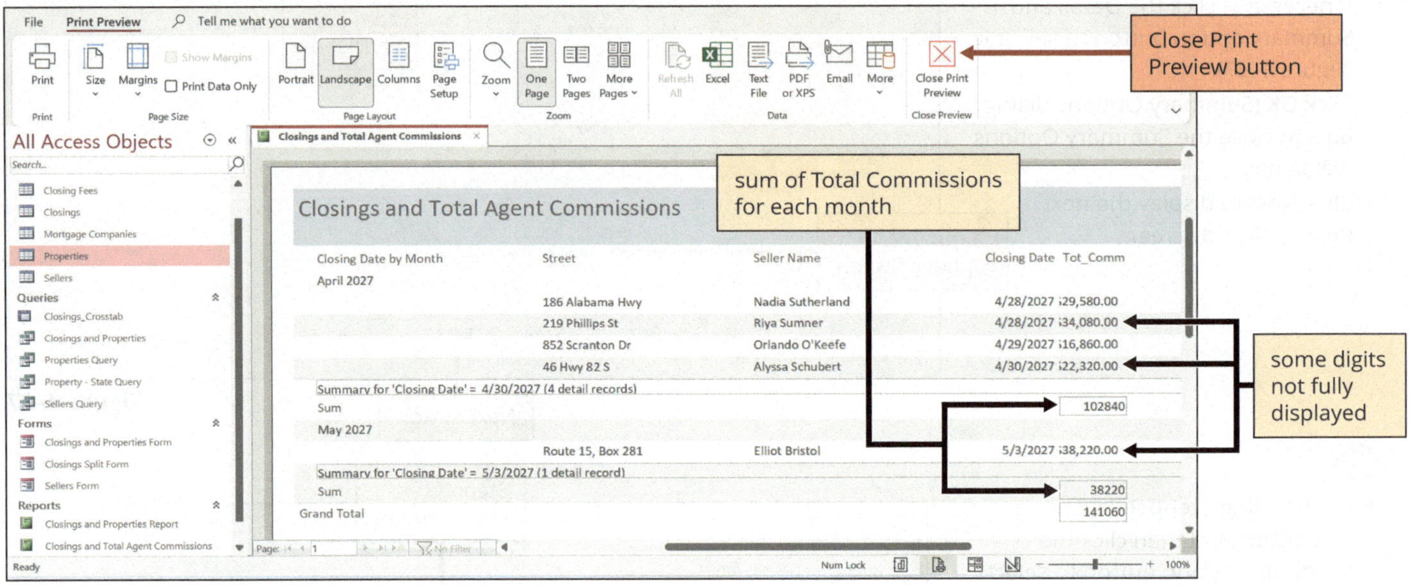

Figure 4–40

To Modify the Report

Partners paralegals need to change the sizes and positions of some of the objects that appear in the Closings and Total Agent Commissions report. **Why?** The size and positions of the controls do not allow all the data to appear in some of the controls. You will use a two-pointed resize arrow to change a control's size. You will use a four-pointed move arrow to reposition a control. It's important to make sure you have the correct pointer showing before you click and drag the pointer. The following steps resize and reposition the Street, Seller Name, Closing Date, and Tot_Comm controls so all the data is visible.

1

- Click the Close Print Preview button (Print Preview tab | Close Preview group).
- Click the View button arrow (Report Design tab | Views group), and then click Layout View to change the view (Figure 4–41).

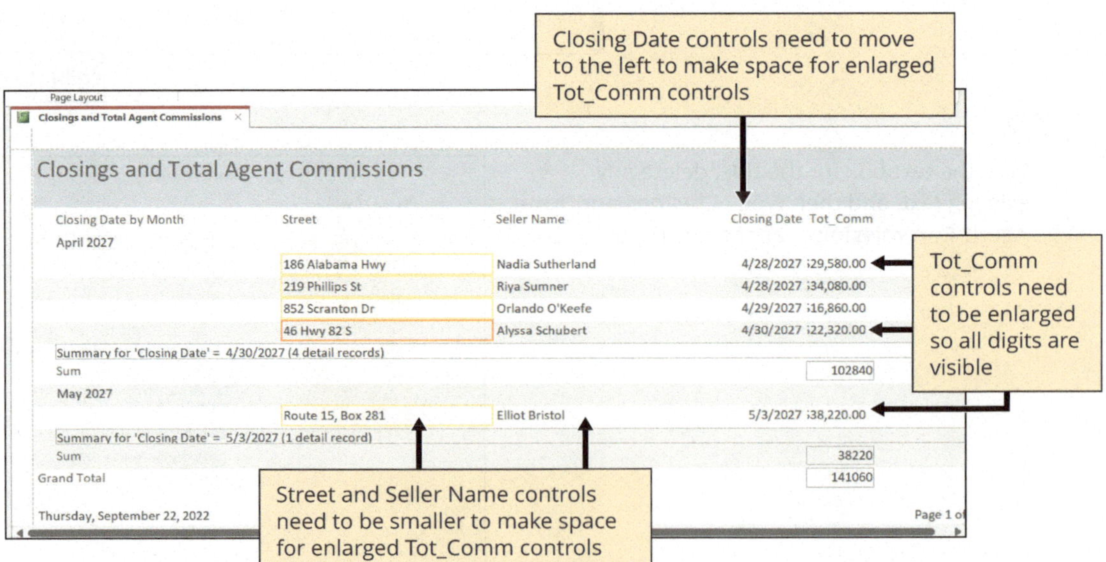

Figure 4–41

2

- Click the Street control under the Street heading to select it.
- Point to the right border of the Street control until the pointer becomes a double-pointed arrow (Figure 4–42). Then, drag the pointer to the left to make the control smaller.

3

- Using the process you followed in Step 2, decrease the size of the Seller Name control.

4

- Click the Seller Name heading. While holding SHIFT on your keyboard, click the Seller Name control to select both the heading and the data field controls at the same time.
- Point to the Seller Name control until the pointer becomes a four-pointed arrow (Figure 4–43). Then, drag the pointer to the left to move the Seller Name column closer to the Street column.

5

- Using the process you followed in Step 4, move the Closing Date control closer to the Seller Name control.

6

- Click the Tot_Comm control, point to the left border of the control until you see the two-pointed arrow, and then drag the border to the left to increase the control's size so all the digits are displayed (see Figure 4–44).

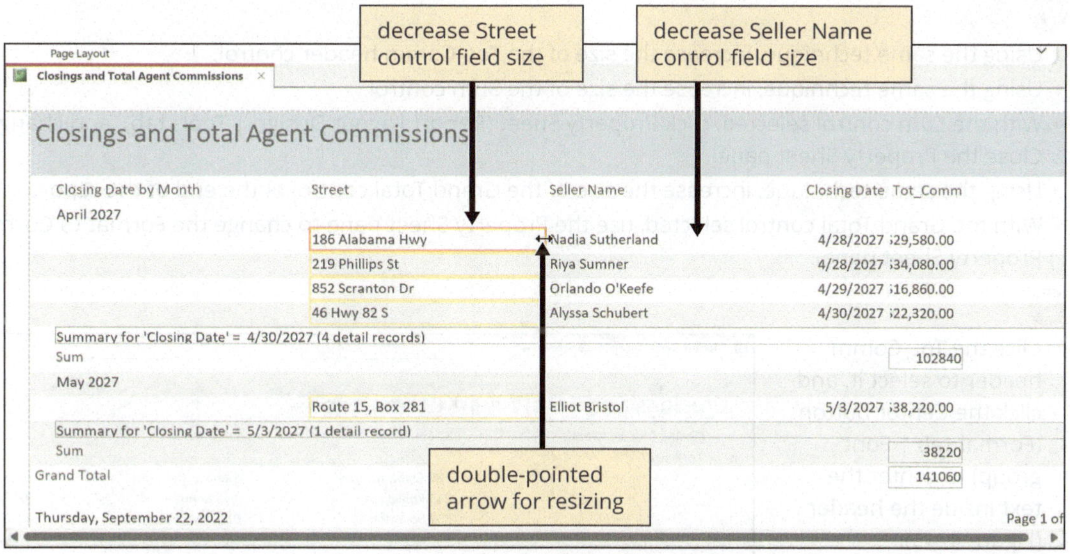

Figure 4–42

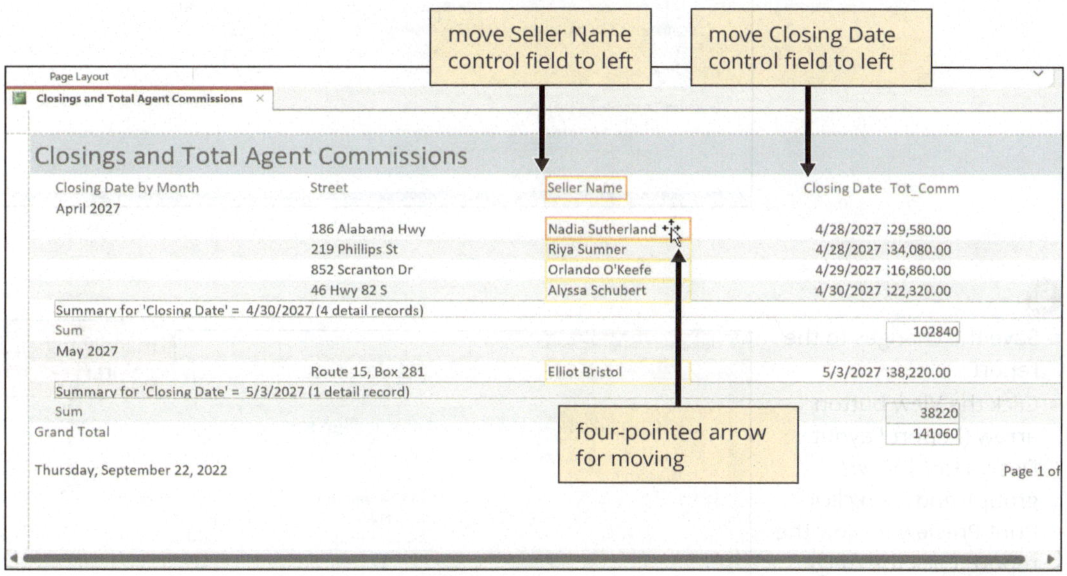

Figure 4–43

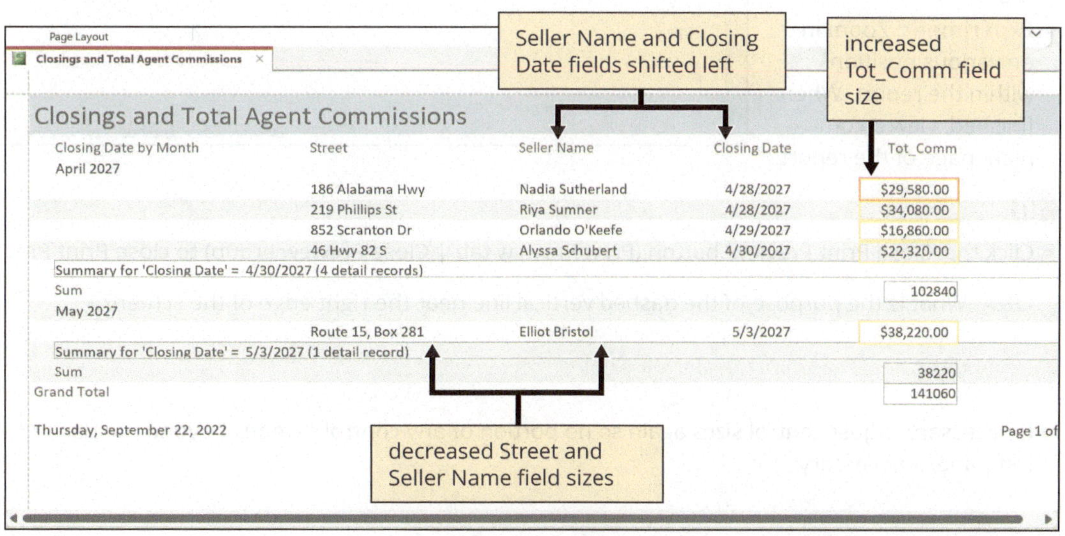

Figure 4–44

7

- Using the same technique, increase the size of the Tot_Comm header control.
- Using the same technique, increase the size of the Sum control.
- With the Sum control selected, click Property Sheet (Report Layout Design | Tools tab), and change the Format to Currency. Close the Property Sheet pane.
- Using the same technique, increase the size of the Grand Total control at the end of the report.
- With the Grand Total control selected, use the Property Sheet pane to change the Format to Currency, and then close the Property Sheet pane.

8

- Click the Tot_Comm header to select it, and click the Center button (Format tab | Font group) to center the text inside the header (Figure 4–45).

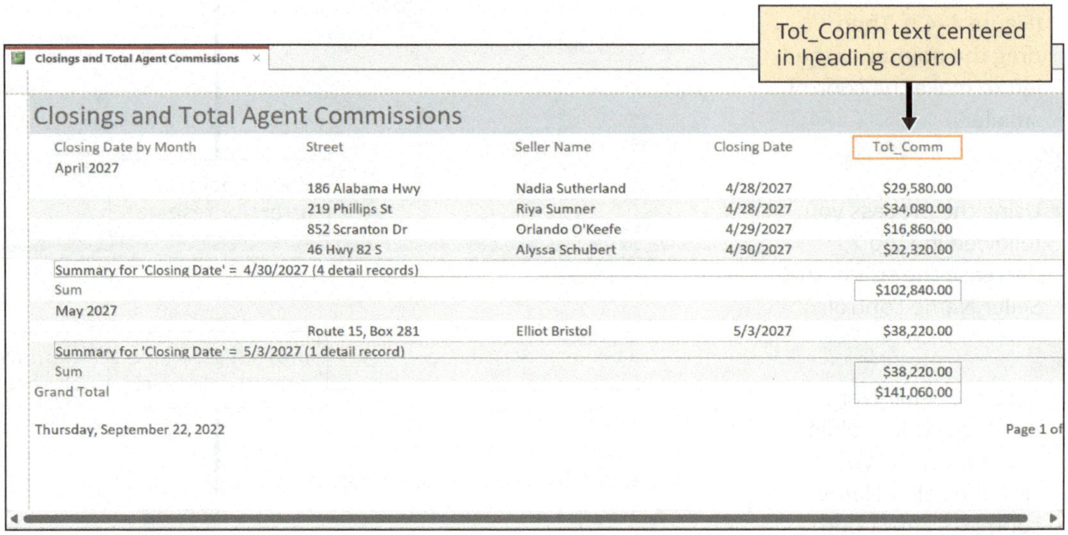

Figure 4–45

9

- Save the changes to the report.
- Click the View button arrow (Report Layout Design tab | Views group), and then click Print Preview to view the report. Click the magnifying glass pointer to view more of the report (Figure 4–46).
- **Experiment:** Zoom in on various positions within the report. When finished, view a complete page of the report.

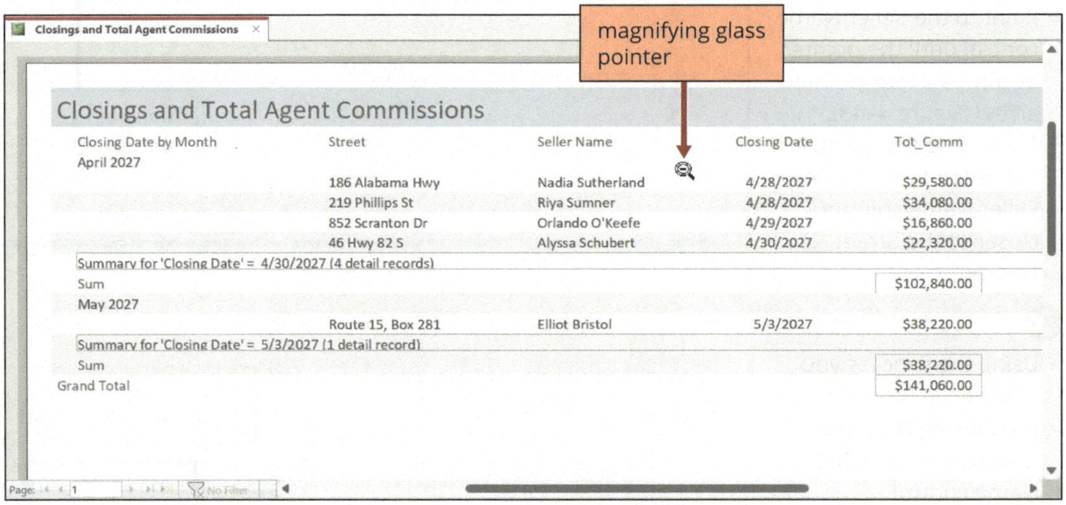

Figure 4–46

10

- Click the 'Close Print Preview' button (Print Preview tab | Close Preview group) to close Print Preview.

Q&A What is the purpose of the dashed vertical line near the right edge of the screen?

The line shows the right border of the amount of the report that will print on one page. If any portion of the report extends beyond the line, the report might not print correctly.

- If necessary, adjust control sizes again so no portion of any control extends beyond the dashed vertical line. Close the Field List pane, if necessary.

Q&A Do I have to resize all the controls that begin with the word, Summary, individually?
No. When you resize one of them, the others will all be resized the same amount automatically.

- Ensure the Page Number control is visible in the lower-right corner of the report. Click the Page Number control to select it, and then drag it to the left, if necessary, so no portion of the control extends beyond the dashed line. For more precise positioning, with the Page Number control selected, use the arrow keys on your keyboard.
- Save your work and close the report.

Consider This

How do you determine the tables and fields that contain the data needed for the report?

First, you need to know the requirements for the report. Precisely what data is the report intended to convey? Once you understand those requirements, follow these guidelines:

- **Examine the requirements for the report to determine the tables.** Do the requirements only relate to data in a single table, or does the data come from multiple tables? What is the relationship between the tables?
- **Examine the requirements for the report to determine the fields necessary.** Look for all the data items specified for the report. Each should correspond to a field in a table or be able to be computed from fields in a table. This information gives you the list of fields to include.
- **Determine the order of the fields.** Examine the requirements to determine the order in which the fields should appear. Be logical and consistent in your ordering. For example, in an address, the city should come before the state and the state should come before the postal code, unless there is some compelling reason for another order.

Creating a Report in Layout View

You can use the Report button to create a report that automatically contains all the fields in a table. You then can delete the unwanted fields so the resulting report contains only the desired fields. At that point, you can use Layout view to modify the report and produce the report you want.

You can also use Layout view to create single- or multiple-table reports from scratch. To do so, you first create a blank report and display a field list for the table containing the first fields you want to include on the report.

There are times when you might want to create a report that has multiple columns. For example, a phone list with employee names and phone numbers could be printed in multiple columns. To do so, create the report using Layout view or Design view and then click the Page Setup tab, click the Columns button, enter the number of columns, select the desired column layout, and then click OK.

Next you would drag any fields you want from the table onto the report in the order you want them to appear. You would then change the size of the controls as you did previously by clicking the control, pointing to the edge of the selected control, and dragging to the desired size.

If the report involves a second table, you display the fields from the second table in the field list and then drag the fields from the second table onto the report in the desired order.

When you create a report in Layout view, the report does not automatically contain a title, but you can add one by clicking the Title button (Report Layout Design tab | Header / Footer group). Once you have added the title, you can type whatever title you want for the report.

BTW
Adding a Second Table to a Report
If the report involves a second table, display the fields in the second table, and then drag the fields from the second table onto the report in the desired order.

To Create a Report in Layout View by Creating a Blank Report

Partners paralegals need an additional report that shows information related to closings and their fees. The paralegals want to create the report in Layout view. **Why?** Layout view works best when you need to change the look and feel of a report because you can rearrange fields and change their sizes. The following steps create a report in Layout view.

1

- Click Create on the ribbon to display the Create tab.
- Click the Blank Report button (Create tab | Reports group) to create a blank report. If necessary, close the Navigation Pane.
- If the Field List pane does not appear, display it by clicking the 'Add Existing Fields' button (Report Layout Design tab | Tools group) (Figure 4–47).

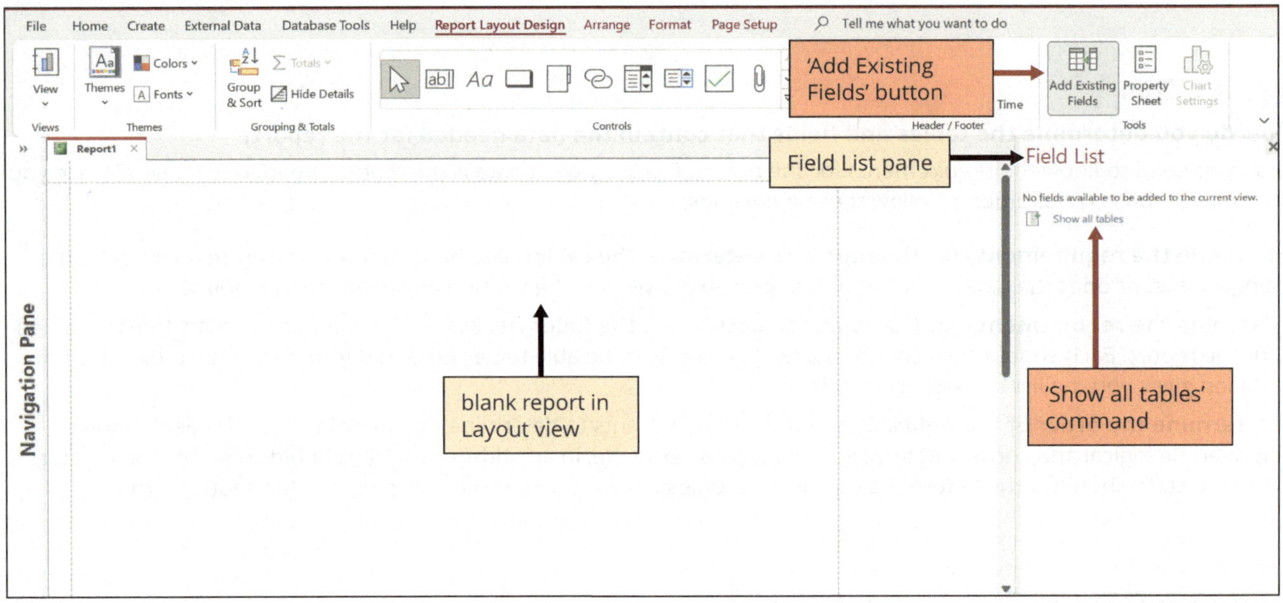

Figure 4–47

2

- If the tables do not appear in the field list, click 'Show all tables.'
- Click the plus sign (+) next to the Closing Fees table name to display its fields in the Field List pane (Figure 4–48).
- Drag the Closing ID, Title Search, Total Agent Commission, Recording Fees, Attorney Fees, Inspection Fees, Appraisal Fees, and Prorated HOA fields from the Field List pane to the report, positioning the fields as shown in Figure 4–49.

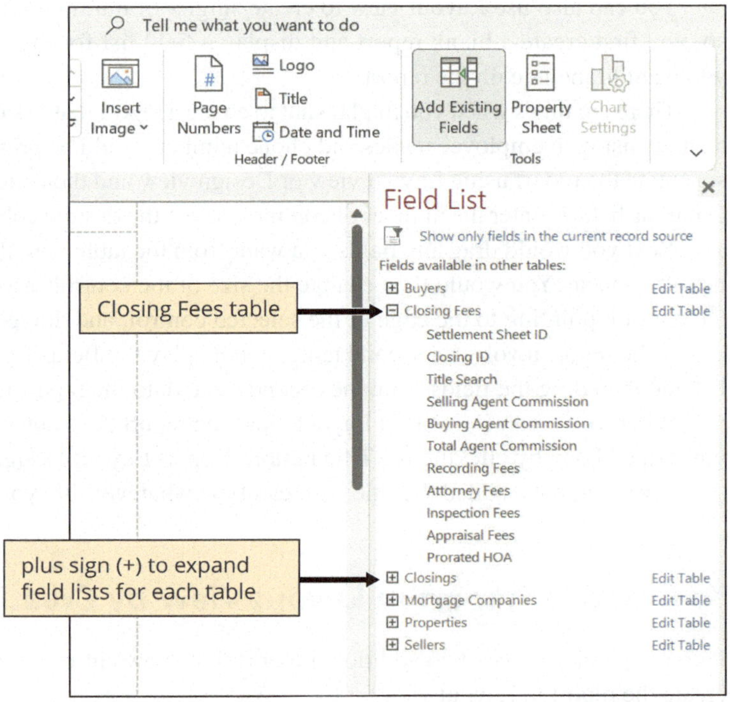

Figure 4–48

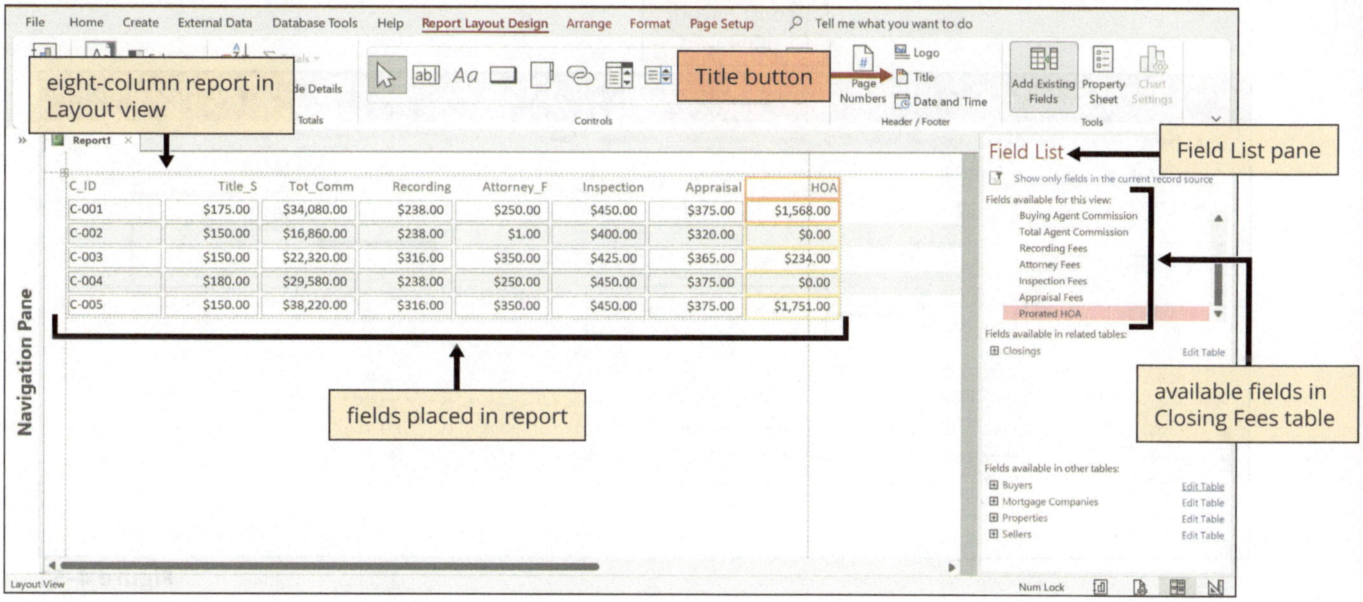

Figure 4–49

3

- Close the Field List pane.
- To fit all the columns on the same page, click the Landscape button (Page Setup tab | Page Layout group), which sets a wider page orientation (Figure 4–50).

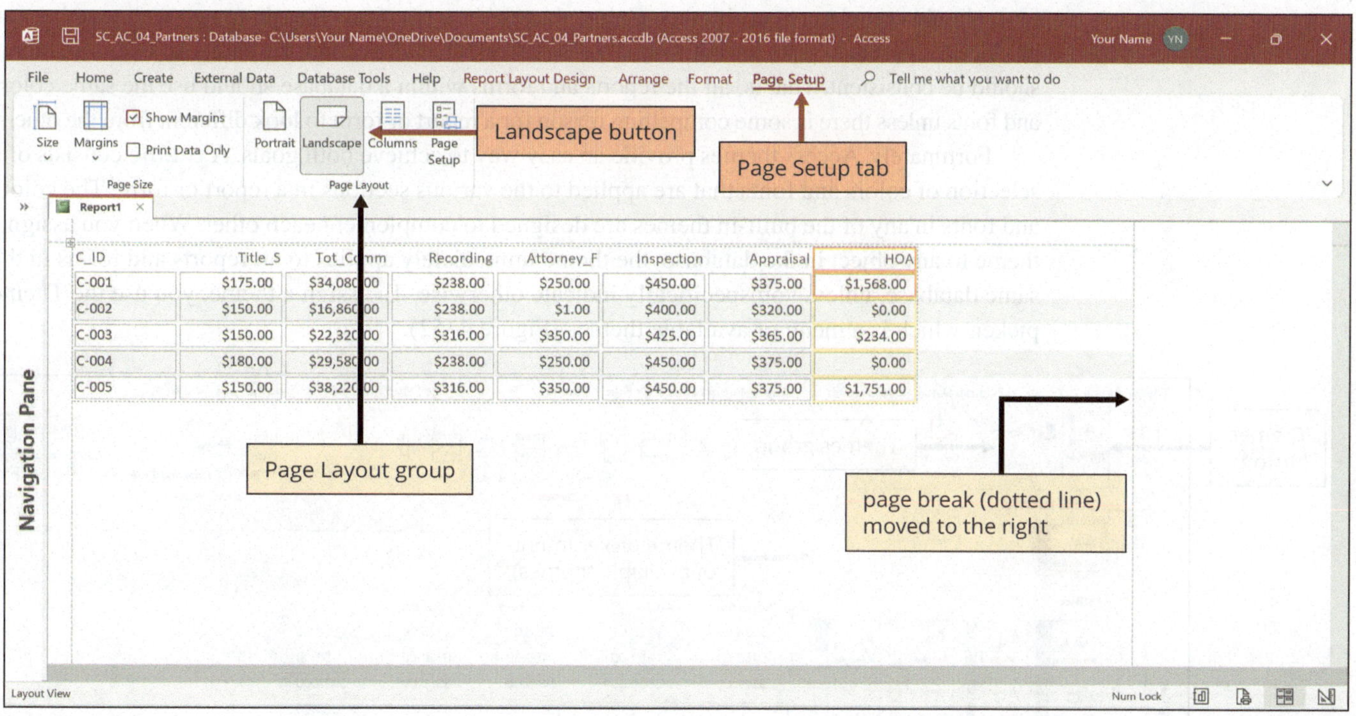

Figure 4–50

4

- To add a report title, click the Title button (Report Layout Design tab | Header / Footer group) and then type **Closing Fees Report** (Figure 4–51).
- Save the report as **Closing Fees Report**, and then close the report.

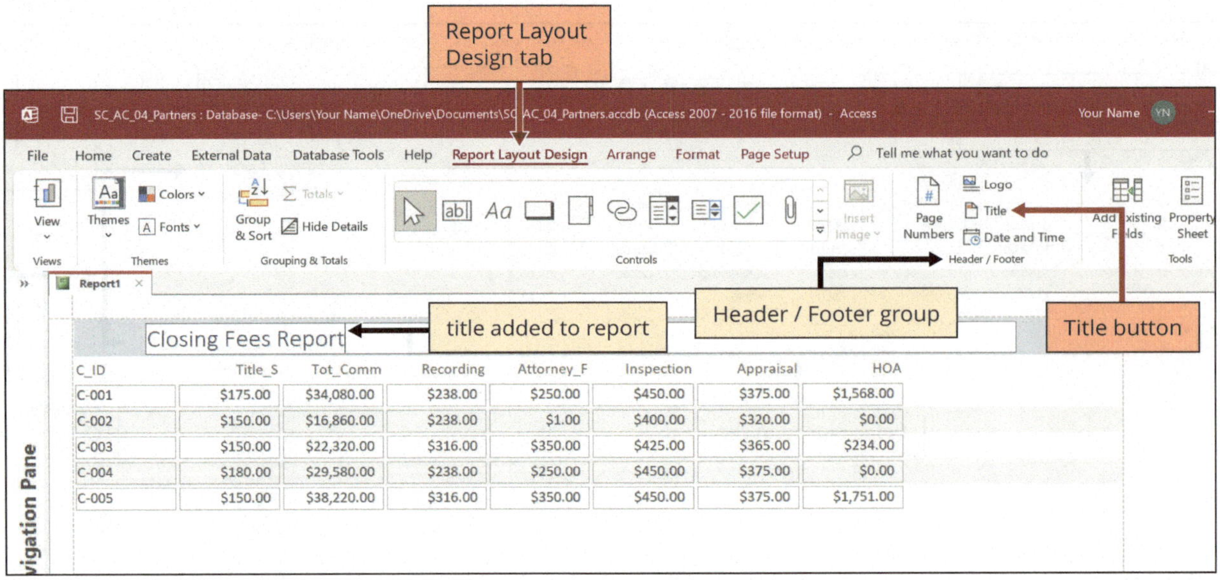

Figure 4–51

Using Themes

The most important characteristic of a report or form is that it presents the desired data in a useful arrangement. Another important characteristic, however, is the general appearance of the form. The colors and fonts that you use in the various sections of a report or form contribute to this look. You should keep in mind two important goals when assigning colors and fonts. First, the various colors and fonts should complement each other. Colors that clash or two fonts that do not go well together can produce a report that looks unprofessional or is difficult to read. Second, the choice of colors and fonts should be consistent. That is, all the reports and forms within a database should use the same colors and fonts unless there is some compelling reason for a report or form to look different from the others.

Fortunately, Access themes provide an easy way to achieve both goals. A **theme** consists of a selection of colors and fonts that are applied to the various sections in a report or form. The colors and fonts in any of the built-in themes are designed to complement each other. When you assign a theme to any object in the database, the theme immediately applies to all reports and forms in the same database, unless you specifically indicate otherwise. To assign a theme, you use the Theme picker, which is a menu of available themes (Figure 4–52).

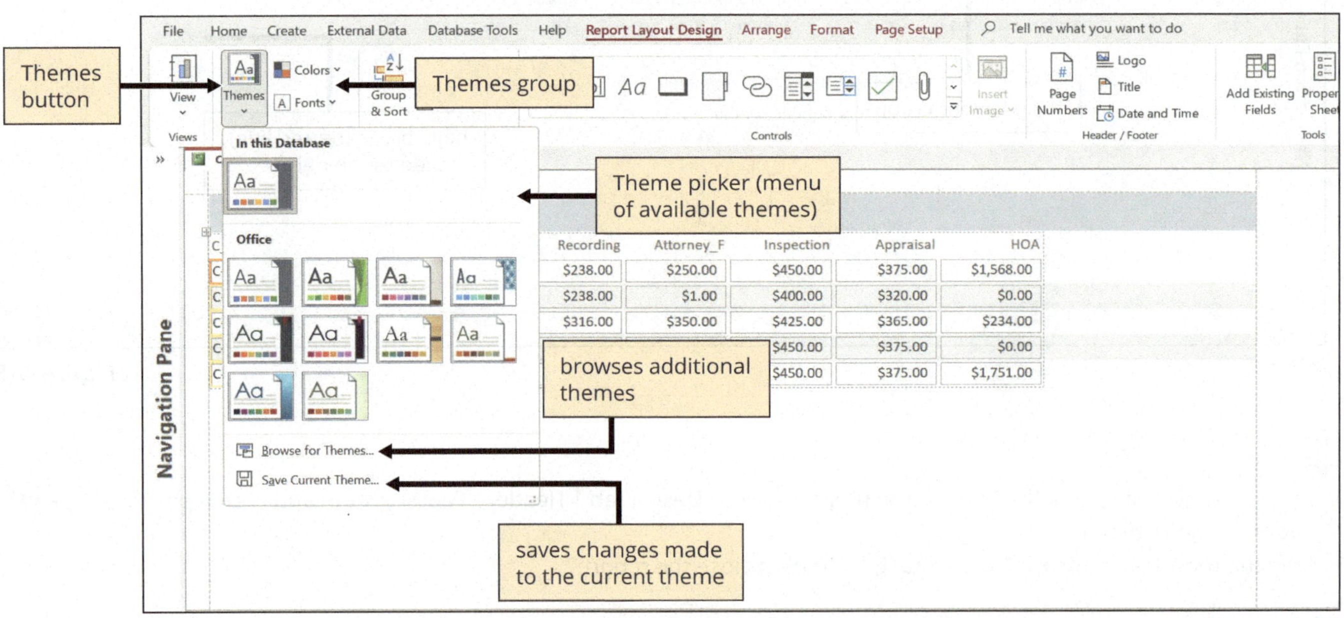

Figure 4–52

If you point to any theme in the Theme picker, you will see a ScreenTip giving the name of the theme. When you select a theme, the colors and fonts represented by that theme will immediately be applied to all reports and forms. If you later decide that you would prefer a different theme, you can change the theme for all the objects in the database by repeating the process with a different theme.

You can also use the Browse for Themes command to browse for themes that are not listed as part of a standard Access installation but are available for download. You can also create your own customized theme by specifying a combination of fonts and colors and using the Save Current Theme command to save your combination. If, after selecting a theme using the Themes button, you do not like the colors in the current theme, you can change the theme's colors. Click the Colors button (Report Layout Design tab | Themes group) (Figure 4–53), and then select an alternative color scheme.

BTW
Using Themes
Office themes are designed to enhance an organization's brand identity. Many organizations consistently use themes, styles, and color schemes to visually assist in identifying their products and/or services.

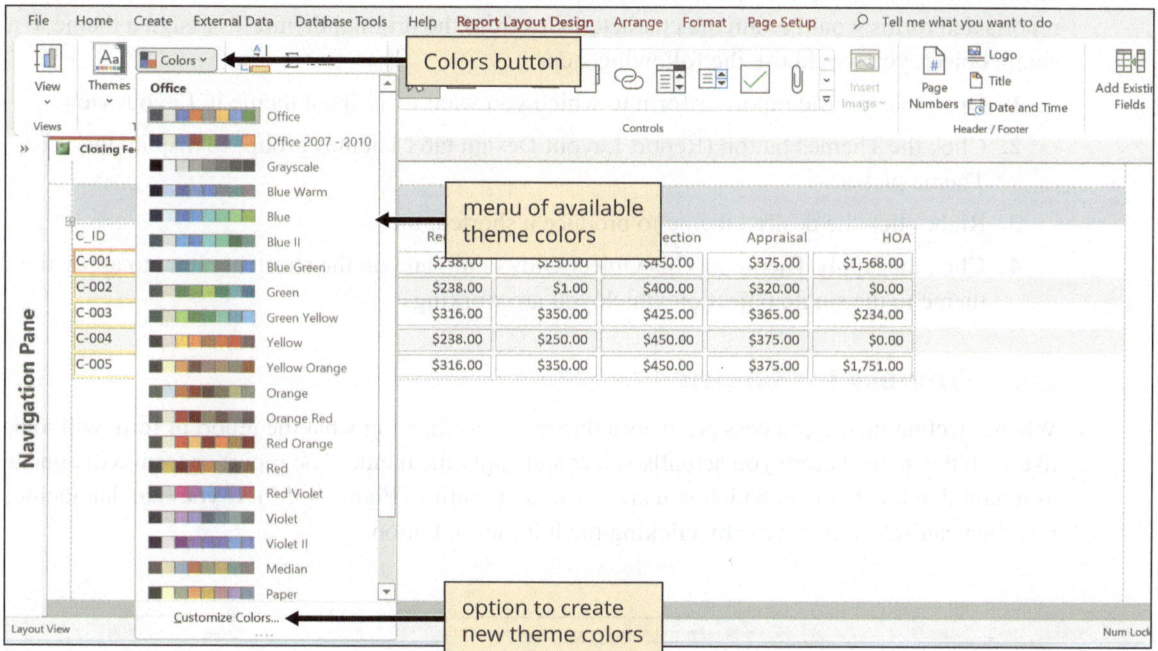

Figure 4–53

Similarly, if you do not like the fonts in the current theme, you can click the Fonts button (Report Layout Design tab | Themes group) (Figure 4–54). You then can select an alternative font for the theme.

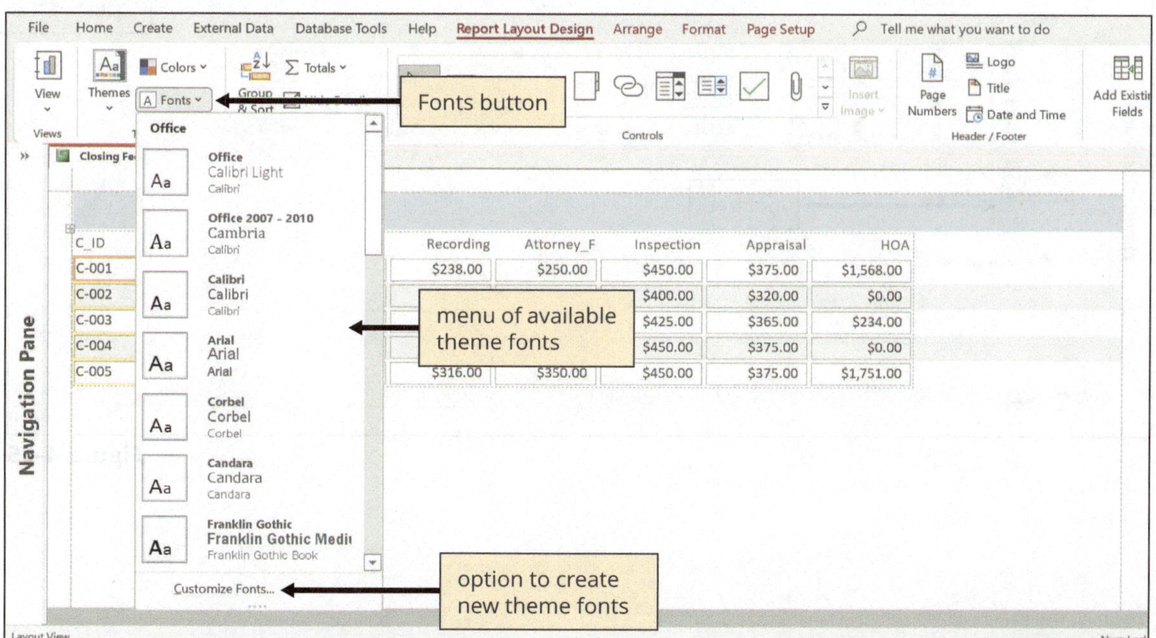

Figure 4–54

To Assign a Theme to All Objects

To assign a theme, it is easiest to use Layout view. You can use Design view as well, but it is easier to see the result of picking a theme when you are viewing the report or form in Layout view. To assign a theme to all reports and forms, you would use the following steps.

1. Open any report or form in Layout view.
2. Click the Themes button (Report Layout Design tab | Themes group) to display the Theme picker.
3. Click the desired theme.

To Assign a Theme to a Single Object

In some cases, you might only want to apply a theme to the current report or form, while all other reports and forms would retain the characteristics from the original theme. To assign a theme to a single object, you would use the following steps.

1. Open the specific report or form to which you want to assign a theme in Layout view.
2. Click the Themes button (Report Layout Design tab | Themes group) to display the Theme picker.
3. Right-click the desired theme to produce a shortcut menu.
4. Click the Apply Theme to This Object Only command on the shortcut menu to apply the theme to the single object on which you are working.

Live Preview for Themes

When selecting themes, Access provides a **live preview** showing what the report or form will look like with the theme before you actually select and apply the theme. The report or form will appear as it would in the theme to which you are currently pointing (Figure 4–55). If you like that theme, you then can select the theme by clicking the left mouse button.

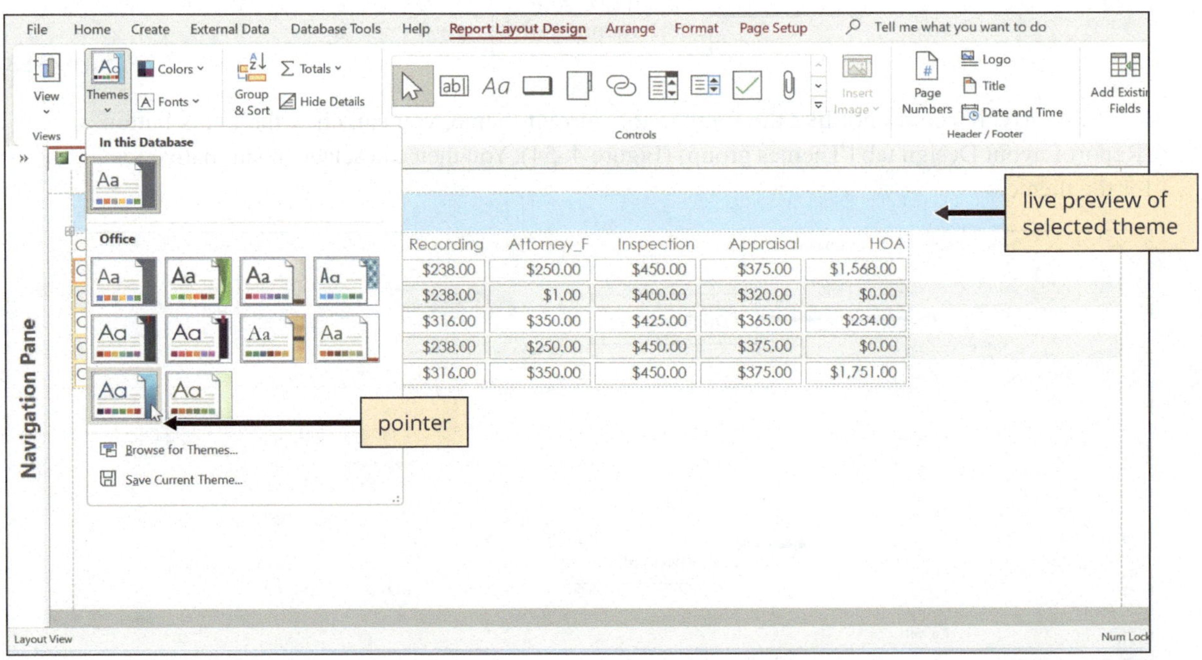

Figure 4–55

To Create a Summary Report

A report that includes group calculations such as subtotals, but does not include the individual detail lines, is called a **summary report**. **Why?** You might need a report that only shows the overall group calculations, but not all the records. The following steps hide the detail lines in the Closings and Properties Report, thus creating a summary report.

1

- Open the Navigation Pane, open the Closings and Properties Report in Layout view, and then close the Navigation Pane.
- Click the Hide Details button (Report Layout Design tab | Grouping & Totals group) to hide the details in the report (Figure 4–56).

Q&A How can I see the details once I have hidden them?
Click the Hide Details button a second time.

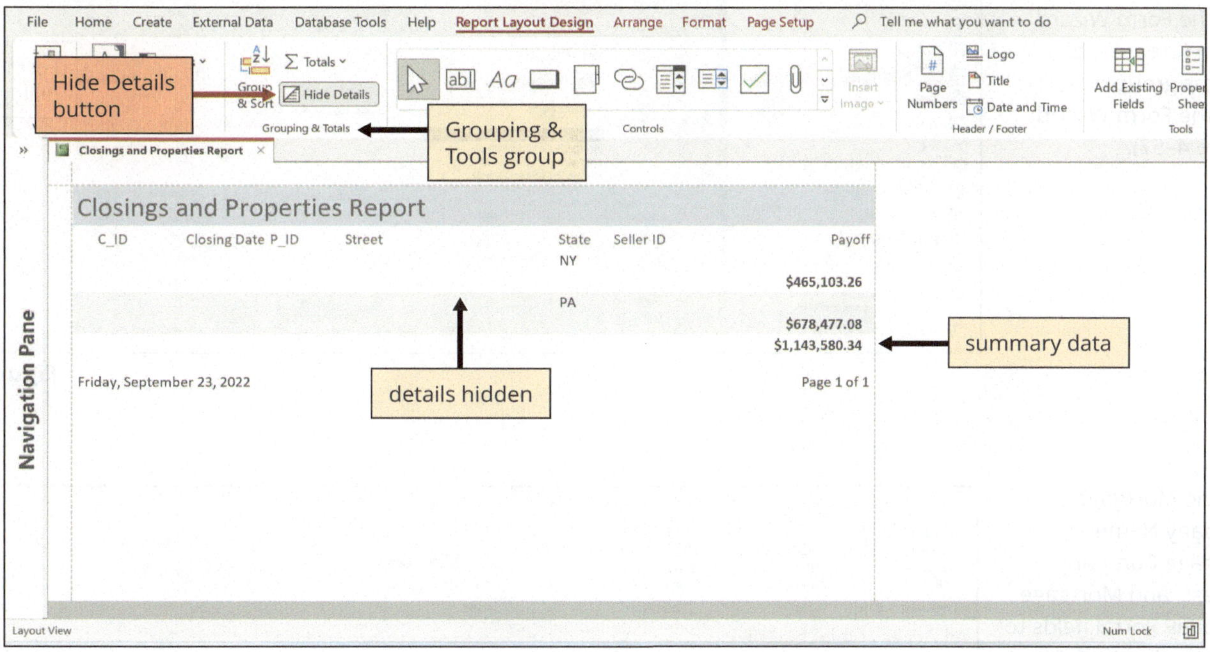

Figure 4–56

- Close the report without saving your changes.

Q&A What would happen if I saved the report?
The next time you viewed the report, the details would still be hidden. If that happened and you wanted to show all the details, you would click the Hide Details button a second time.

Break Point: If you wish to take a break, this is a good place to do so. You can quit Access now. To resume at a later time, start Access, open the database called SC_AC_04_Partners.accdb, and continue following the steps from this location forward.

Form Creation

You can create a simple form consisting of all the fields in the Mortgage Companies table using the Form button (Create tab | Forms group). To create more customized forms, you can use the Form Wizard. Once you have used the Form Wizard to create a form, you can modify that form in either Layout view or Design view.

BTW
Summary Reports
You can create a summary report in either Layout view or Design view.

To Use the Form Wizard to Create a Form

The following steps use the Form Wizard to create an initial version of the Mortgage Companies Form. **Why?** Using the Form Wizard is the easiest way to create this form. The initial version will contain the Mortgage Company Name, Address, and Portal fields.

1

- Open the Navigation Pane and select the Mortgage Companies table.
- Click Create on the ribbon to display the Create tab.
- Click the Form Wizard button (Create tab | Forms group) to start the Form Wizard (Figure 4–57).

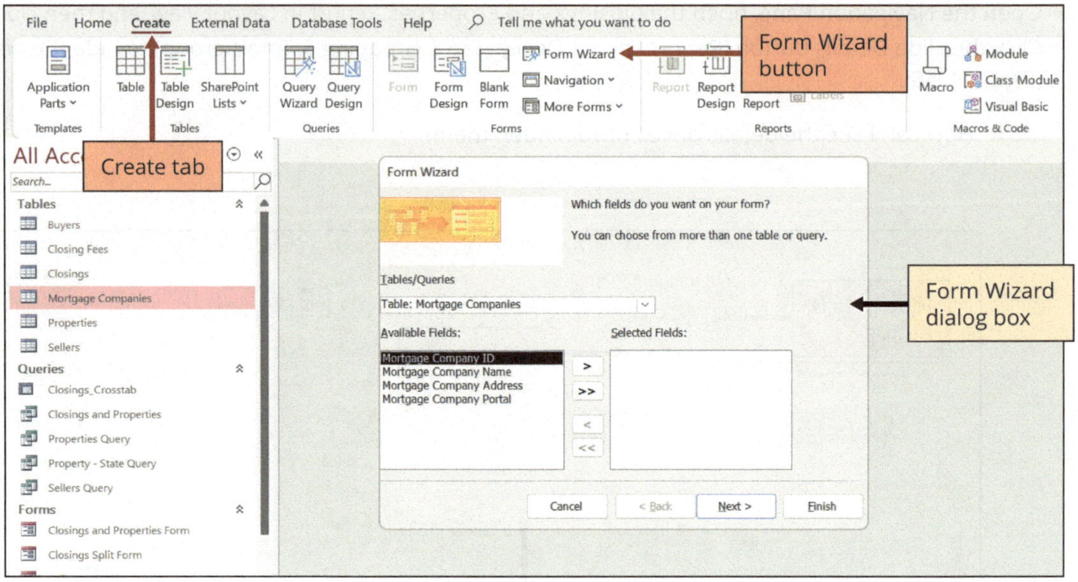

Figure 4–57

2

- Add the Mortgage Company Name, Mortgage Company Address, and Mortgage Company Portal fields to the form (Figure 4–58).

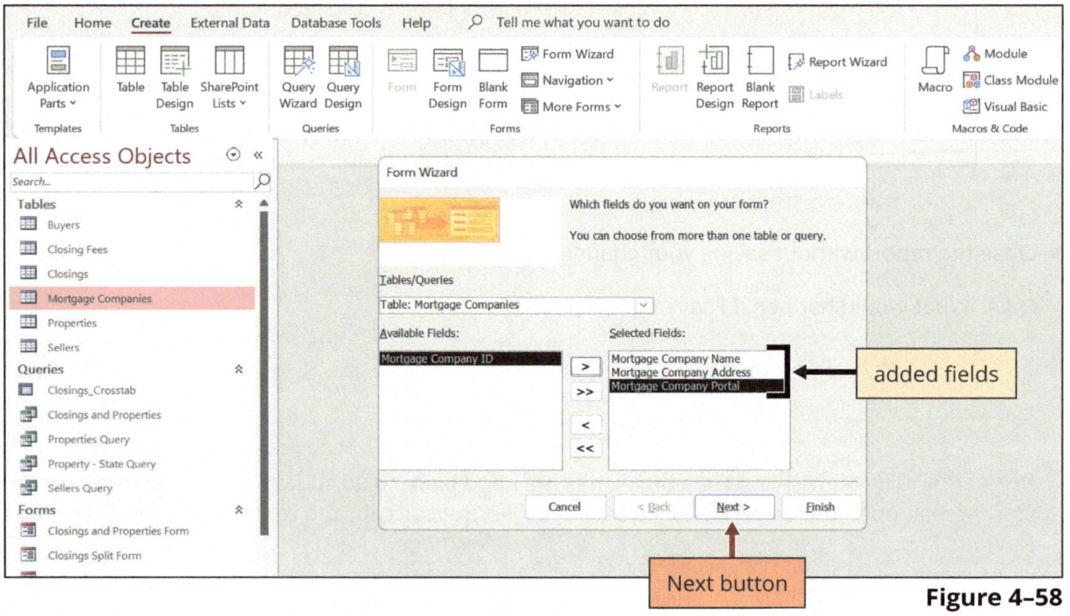

Figure 4–58

3

- Click Next to display the next Form Wizard screen (Figure 4–59).
- Be sure the Columnar layout is selected, and then click Next to display the next Form Wizard screen.

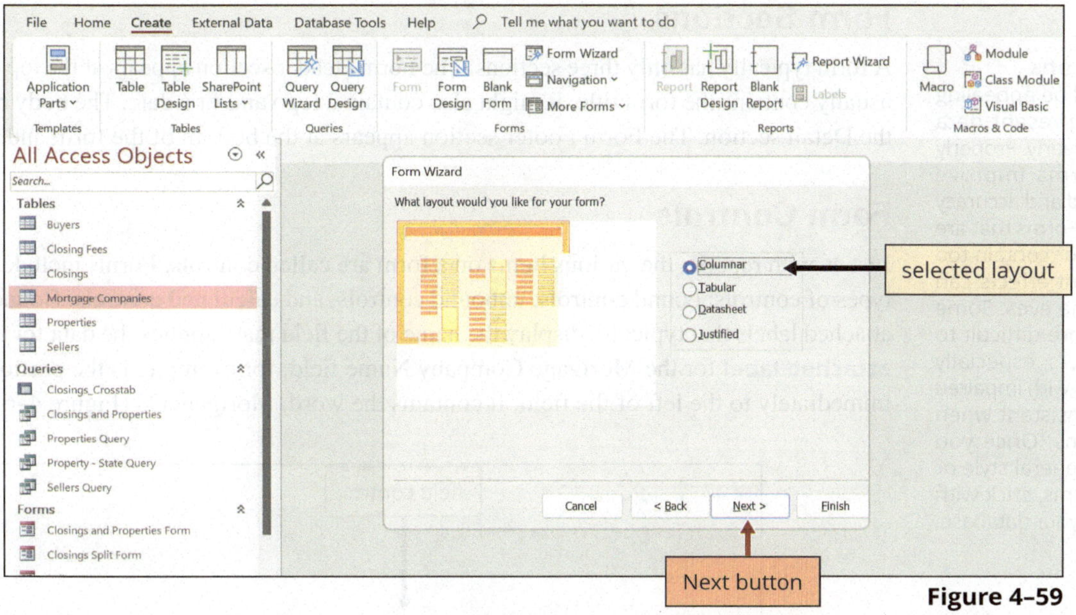

Figure 4–59

4

- Click in the Title text box at the end of the existing text and type **Form** so the title reads, Mortgage Companies Form (Figure 4–60).

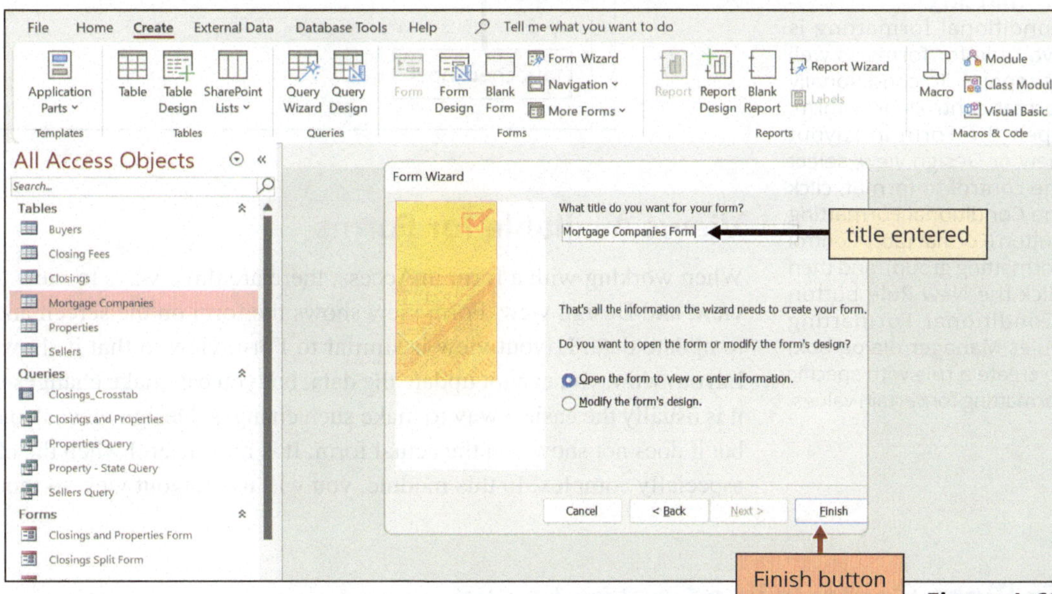

Figure 4–60

5

- Click Finish to complete and display the form (Figure 4–61).
- Click the form's Close button to close the Mortgage Companies Form.

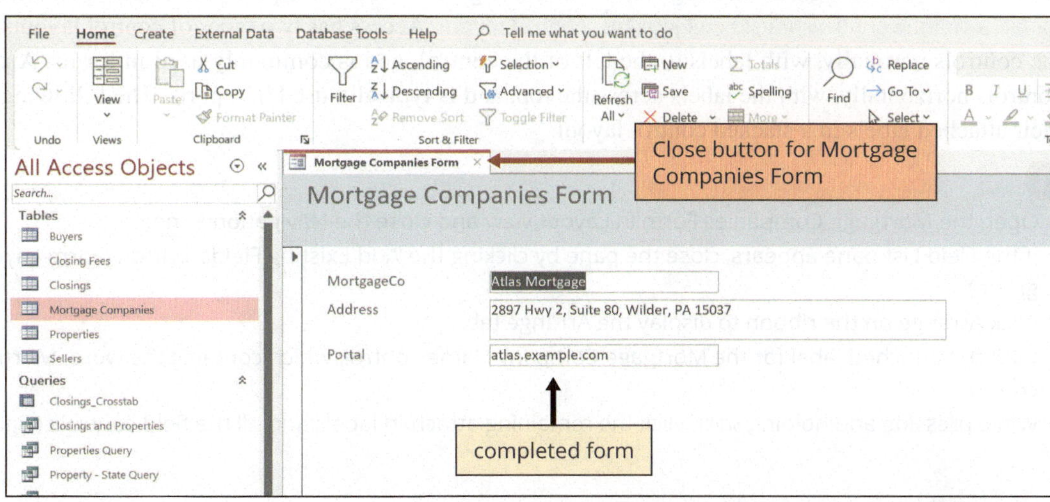

Figure 4–61

BTW
Form Design Considerations
Forms should be appealing visually and present data logically and clearly. Properly designed forms improve both the speed and accuracy of data entry. Forms that are too cluttered or contain too many different effects can be hard on the eyes. Some colors are more difficult to see than others, especially for individuals with impaired vision. Be consistent when creating forms. Once you decide on a general style or theme for forms, stick with it throughout your database.

BTW
Conditional Formatting
Conditional formatting is available for forms as well as reports. To conditionally format controls on a form, open the Form in Layout view or Design view, select the control to format, click the Conditional Formatting button (Format tab | Control Formatting group), and then click the New Rule button (Conditional Formatting Rules Manager dialog box) to create a rule with specific formatting for certain values.

Form Sections

A form typically has only three sections. The Form Header section appears at the top of the form and usually contains the form title. It might also contain a logo and/or a date. The body of the form is in the Detail section. The Form Footer section appears at the bottom of the form and is often empty.

Form Controls

Just as with reports, the various items on a form are called controls. Forms include the same three types of controls: bound controls, unbound controls, and calculated controls. Bound controls have attached labels that typically display the name of the field that supplies the data for the control. The **attached label** for the Mortgage Company Name field, for example, is the portion of the screen immediately to the left of the field. It contains the word, MortgageCo (Figure 4–62).

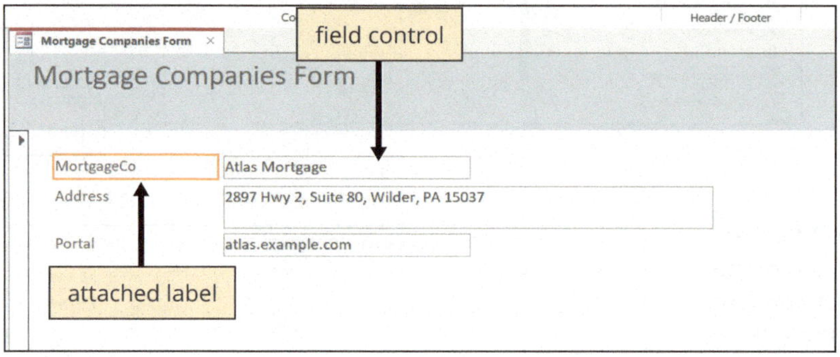

Figure 4–62

Views Available for Forms

When working with a form in Access, there are three ways to view the form: Form view, Layout view, and Design view. Form view shows the form on the screen and allows you to use the form to update data. Layout view is similar to Form view in that it shows the form on the screen. In Layout view, you cannot update the data, but you can make changes to the layout of the form, and it is usually the easiest way to make such changes. Design view also allows you to make changes, but it does not show you the actual form. It is most useful when the changes you need to make are especially complex. In this module, you will use Layout view to modify the form.

To Place Controls in a Control Layout

A **control layout** is a guide that aligns the controls to give the form or report a uniform appearance. **Why?** To use Layout view with a form, the controls must be placed in a control layout. Access has two types of control layouts. A **stacked layout** arranges the controls vertically, with labels to the left of the control, and is commonly used in forms. A **tabular layout** arranges the controls horizontally, with the labels across the top, and is typically used in reports. The following steps place the controls and their attached labels in a stacked control layout.

1

- Open the Mortgage Companies Form in Layout view and close the Navigation Pane.
- If the Field List pane appears, close the pane by clicking the 'Add Existing Fields' button (Form Layout Design tab | Tools group).
- Click Arrange on the ribbon to display the Arrange tab.
- Click the attached label for the Mortgage Company Name control, which contains the word, MortgageCo, to select the control.
- While pressing and holding SHIFT, click the remaining attached labels and all the field controls (Figure 4–63).

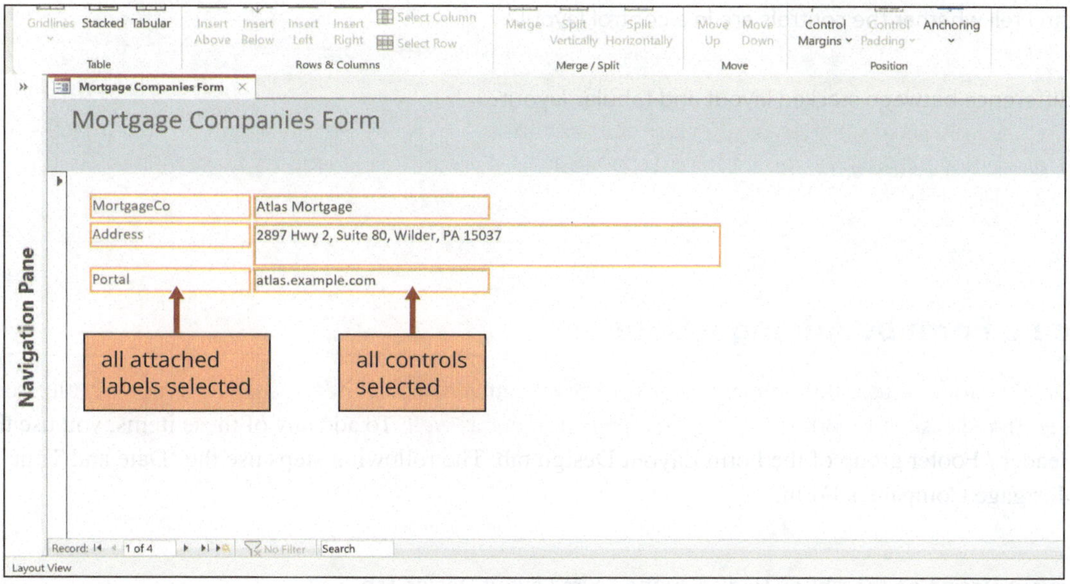

Figure 4–63

Q&A Why did I have to hold SHIFT when I clicked the remaining labels and controls?
If you did not hold SHIFT, you would only select one control at a time. The other controls no longer would be selected. Holding SHIFT allows you to select multiple labels and controls at one time.

Did I have to select the attached labels and controls in a particular order?
No. As long as you selected all controls, the order in which you selected them does not matter.

When I clicked some of the controls, they moved so they are no longer aligned as well as they are in the figure. What should I do?
You do not have to worry about it. Once you complete the next step, they will once again be aligned properly.

Is there a faster way to select all the attached labels and controls?
Yes. You could instead press CTRL + A to select all the items, and then hold SHIFT while clicking the title control in the header to deselect it.

2

- Click the Stacked button (Arrange tab | Table group) to place the controls in a stacked layout (Figure 4–64).

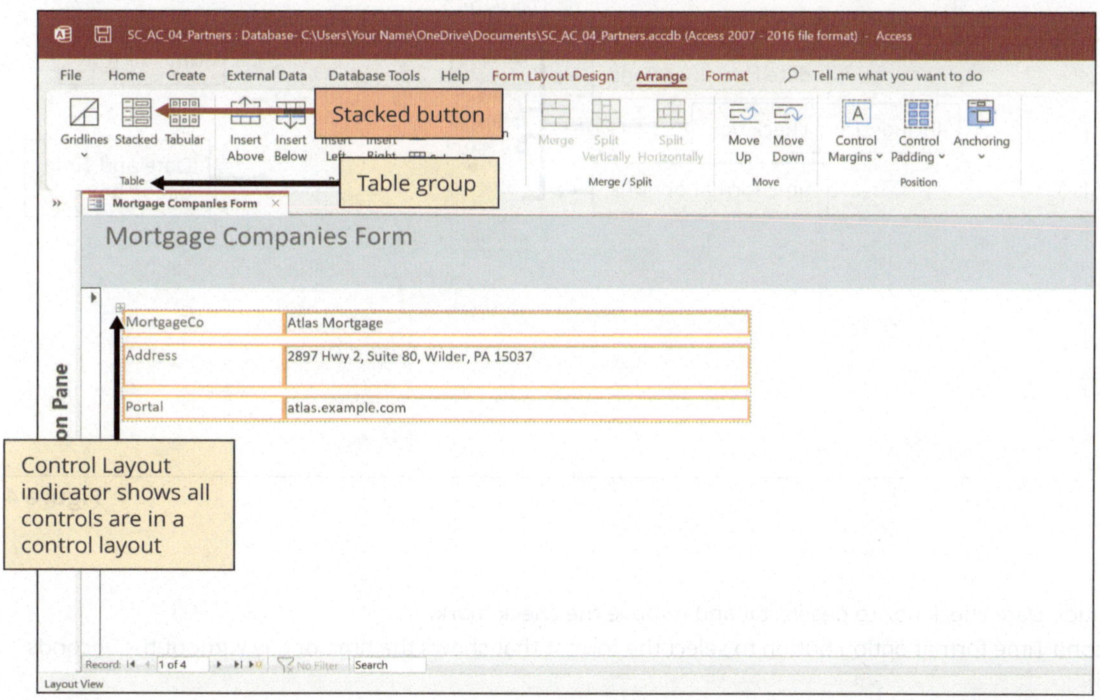

Figure 4–64

Q&A How can I tell whether the controls are in a control layout?

Look for the Control Layout indicator in the upper-left corner of the control layout.

What is the difference between stacked layout and tabular layout?

In a stacked layout, which is more often used in forms, the controls are placed vertically with the labels to the left of the controls. In a tabular layout, which is more often used in reports, the controls are placed horizontally with the labels above the controls.

To Enhance a Form by Adding a Date

Why? To enhance the look or usability of a report or form, you can add special items, such as a logo or title. You can also add the date and time. In the case of reports, you can add a page number as well. To add any of these items, you use the appropriate button in the Header / Footer group of the Form Layout Design tab. The following steps use the 'Date and Time' button to add a time to the Mortgage Companies Form.

1

- Click Form Layout Design on the ribbon to display the Form Layout Design tab.
- Click the 'Date and Time' button (Form Layout Design tab | Header / Footer group) to display the Date and Time dialog box (Figure 4–65).

Q&A What is the purpose of the various check boxes and option buttons?

If the Include Date check box is checked, you must pick a date format from the three options underneath the check box. If it is not checked, the options will be dimmed. If the Include Time check box is checked, you must pick a time format from the three options underneath the check box. If it is not checked, the options will be dimmed.

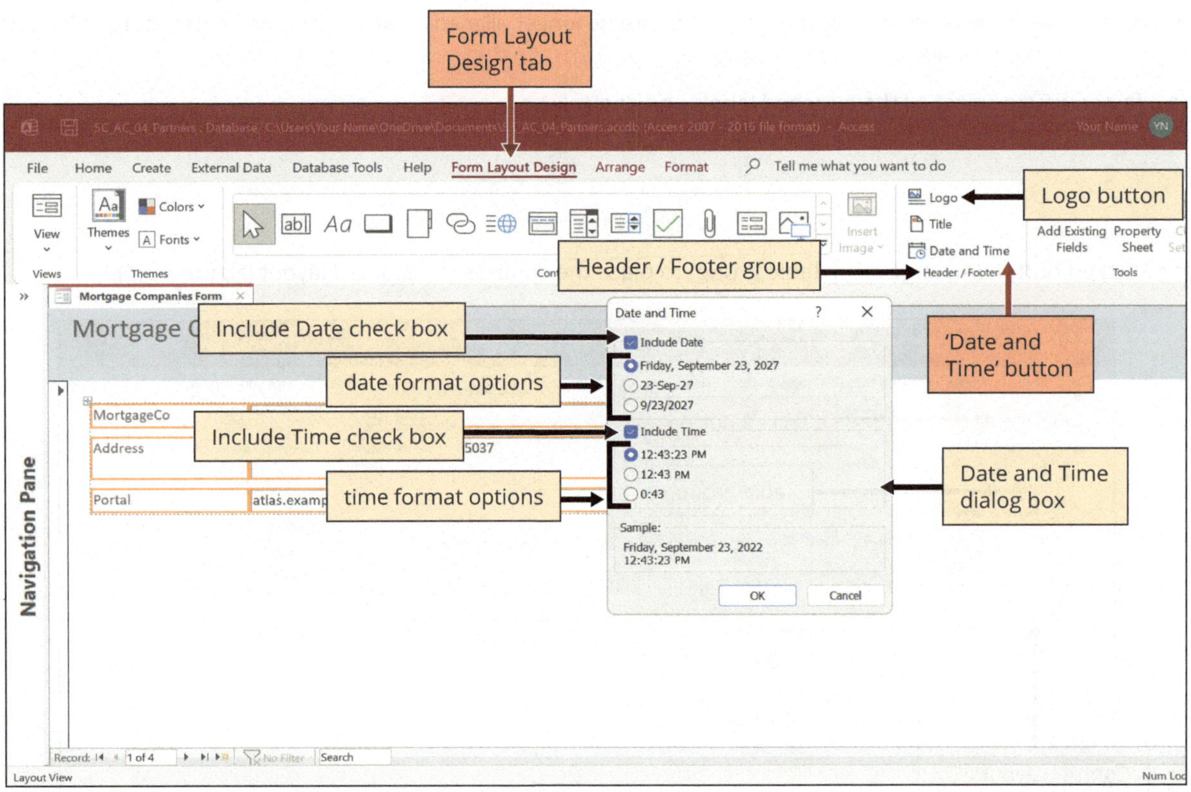

Figure 4–65

2

- Click the Include Date check box to deselect it and remove the check mark.
- Click the second Time format option button to select the format that shows the time of day without the seconds (Figure 4–66).

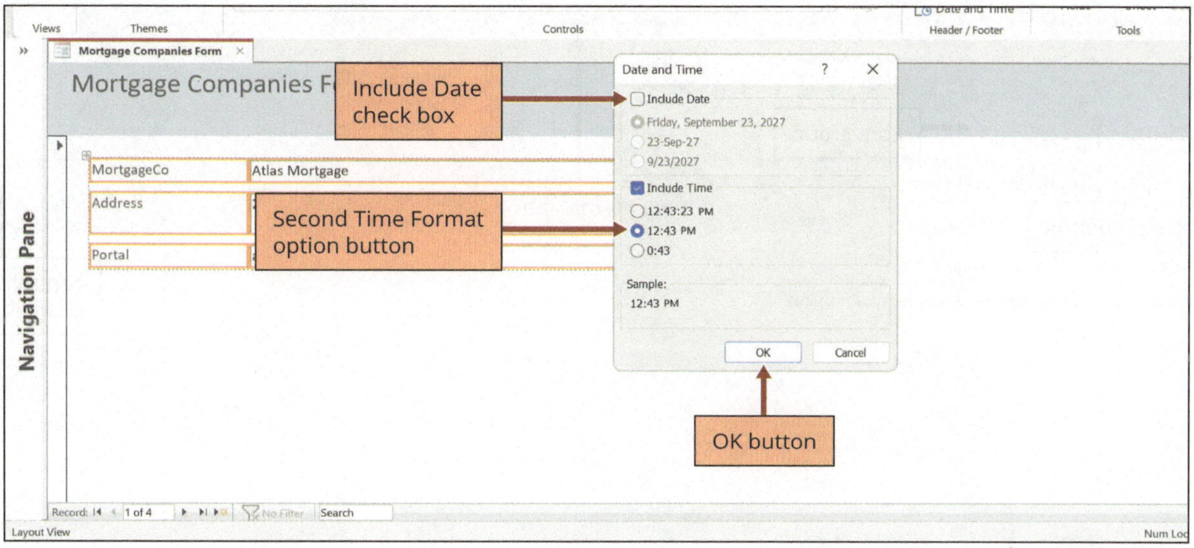

Figure 4–66

3

- Click OK (Date and Time dialog box) to add the time to the form (Figure 4–67).

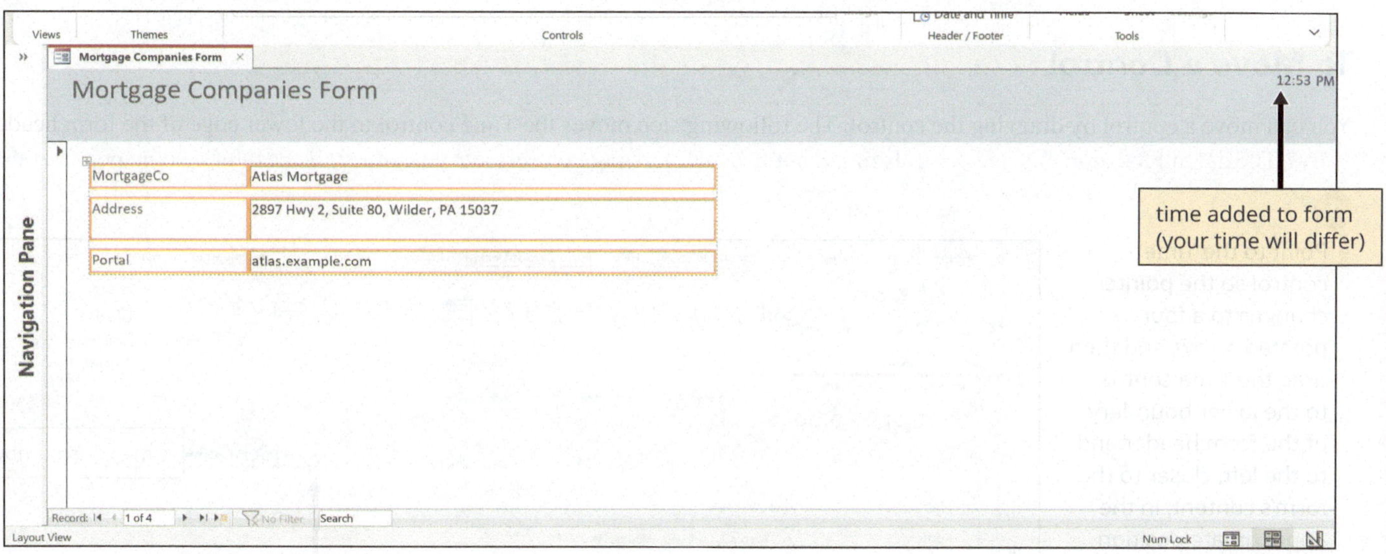

Figure 4–67

To Change the Format of a Control

You can change the format of a control by clicking the control and then clicking the appropriate button on the Format tab. The following step uses this technique to bold the time. **Why?** Formatting controls on a form lets you visually emphasize certain controls.

1

- Click the Time control to select it.
- Click Format on the ribbon to display the Format tab.
- Click the Bold button (Format tab | Font group) to bold the time (Figure 4–68).

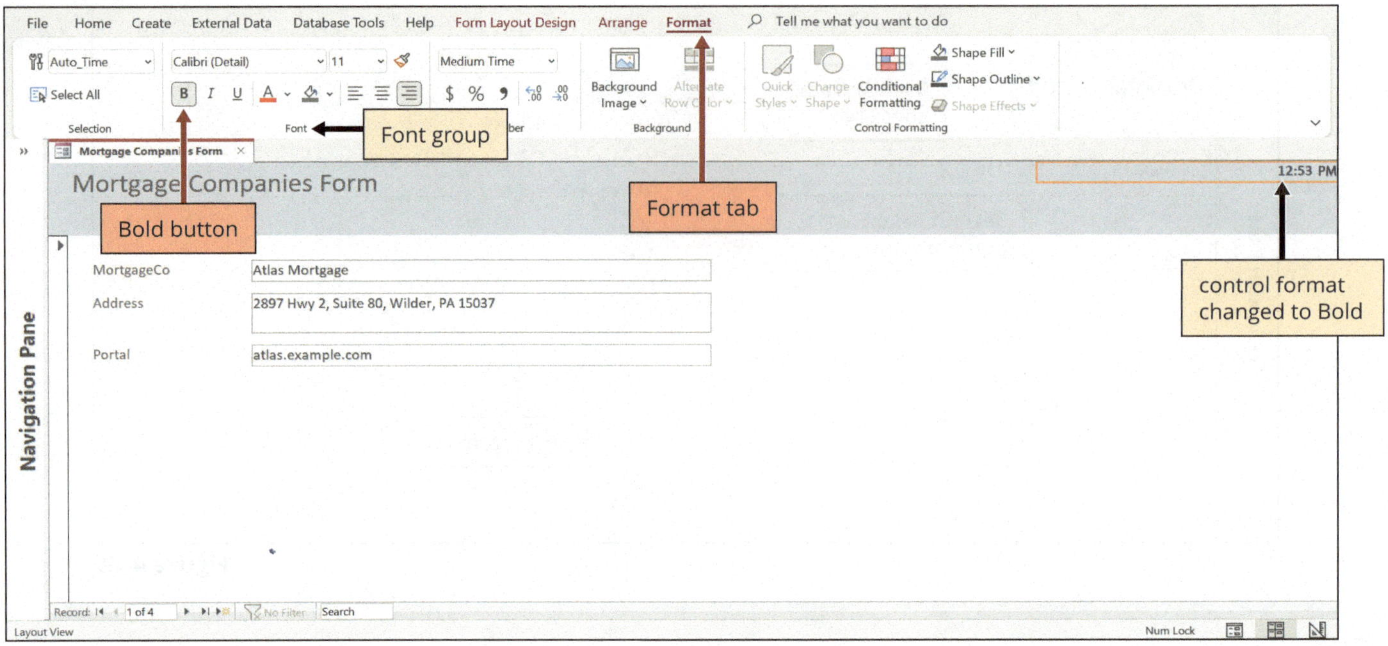

Figure 4–68

To Move a Control

You can move a control by dragging the control. The following step moves the Time control to the lower edge of the form header. **Why?** The default location of some controls might not be ideal; moving controls lets you adjust the design to your specifications.

1

- Point to the Time control so the pointer changes to a four-pointed arrow, and then drag the Time control to the lower boundary of the form header and to the left, closer to the form's content, in the approximate position shown in Figure 4–69.
- Save your changes to the form. Do not close it yet.

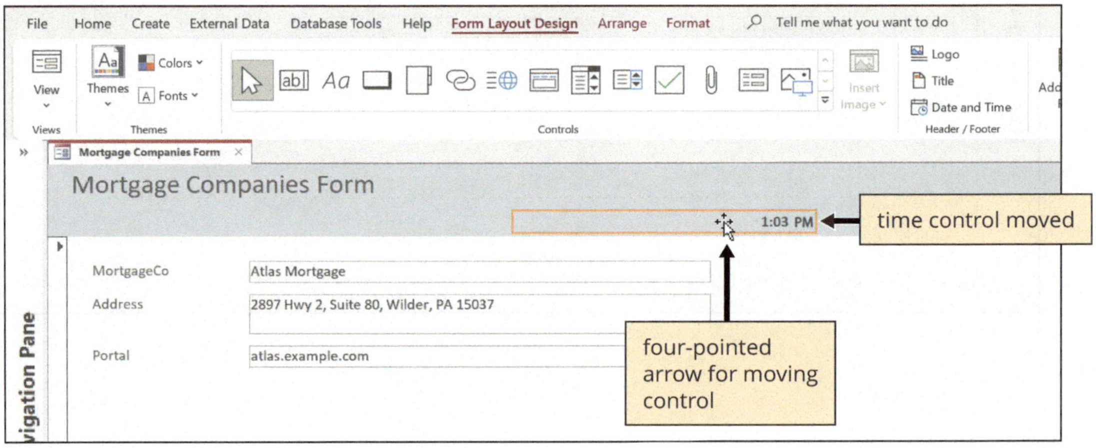

Figure 4–69

Q&A I moved my pointer a little bit and it became a two-pointed arrow. Can I still drag the pointer?

If you drag when the pointer is a two-pointed arrow, you will resize the control. To move the control, it must be a four-pointed arrow.

Could I drag other objects as well? For example, could I drag the title to the center of the form header?

Yes. Be sure you are pointing at the object and the pointer is a four-pointed arrow. You then can drag the object to the desired location.

To Move Controls in a Control Layout

Just as you moved the Time control in the previous section, you can move any control within a control layout by dragging the control to the location you want. As you move it, a line will indicate the position where the control will be placed when you release the mouse button or your finger. You can move more than one control in the same operation by selecting multiple controls prior to moving them.

The following steps move a control in the Mortgage Companies Form. These steps will move the Mortgage Company Portal field so it follows the Mortgage Company Name field. **Why?** The web portal is the primary means used to interact with mortgage company documents and resources, and this field would be quicker to access when listed directly below the Mortgage Company Name, which is called MortgageCo in the form.

1

- With the Mortgage Companies Form in Layout view, click the label for the Portal field to select it.
- While holding SHIFT, click the control for the Portal field to select both the field and its label (Figure 4–70).

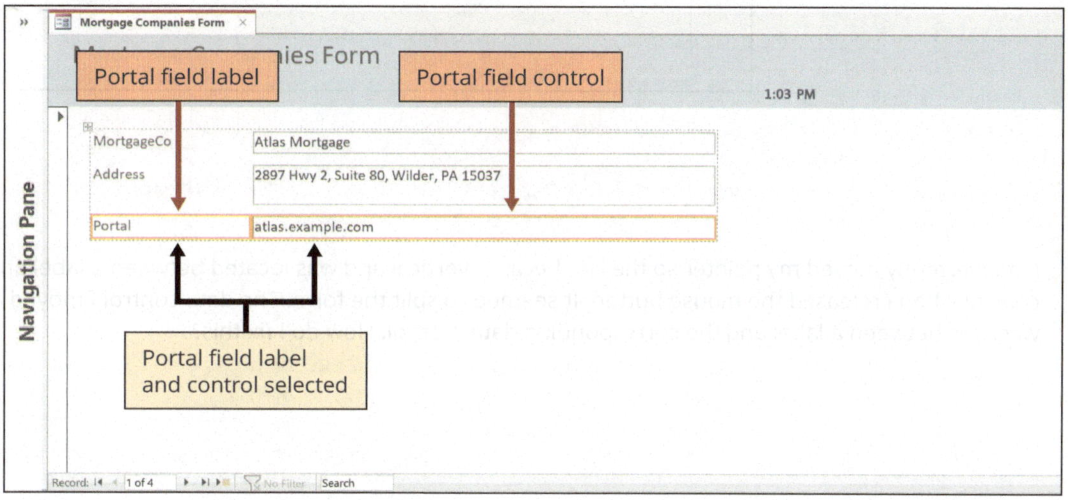

Figure 4–70

2

- Using the four-pointed, move arrow, drag the field straight up to the position of the red line shown in Figure 4–71; the red line appears as you move the field to its new location.

Q&A What is the purpose of the line by the pointer?
It shows you where the field will be positioned once you release it.

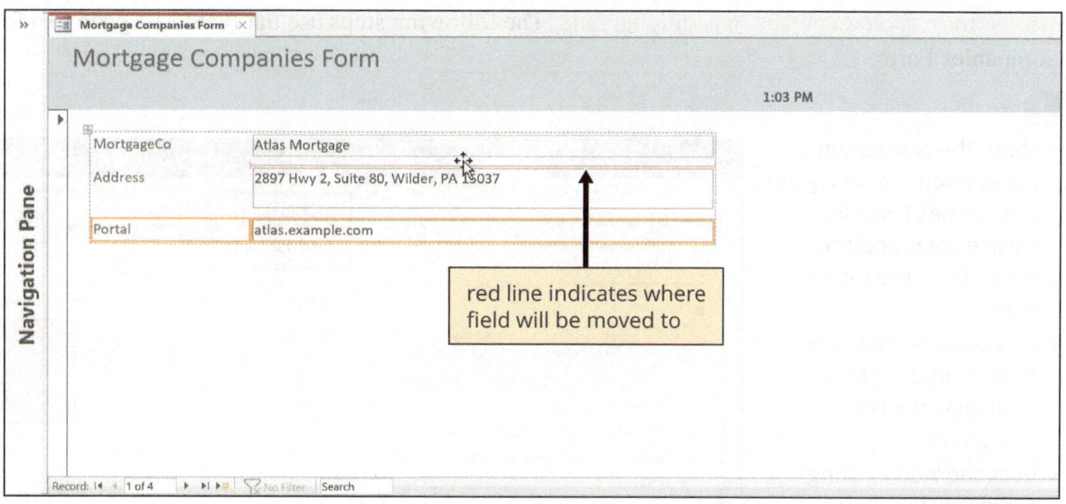

Figure 4–71

3

- Release the mouse button or your finger to complete the movement of the field (Figure 4–72).
- Save and close the Mortgage Companies Form.

Q&A I inadvertently dragged the label instead of the data control and dropped it under the MortgageCo data control. The label I moved is now in the data controls column, and the data control I moved is in a new column to the right. How do I fix this?

You can try to move it back where it was, but that can be tricky. The easiest way is to use the Undo button (Home tab | Undo group) to undo your change, or press CTRL + Z to undo. Then, try again, making sure to release the mouse button only when the red line is correctly positioned.

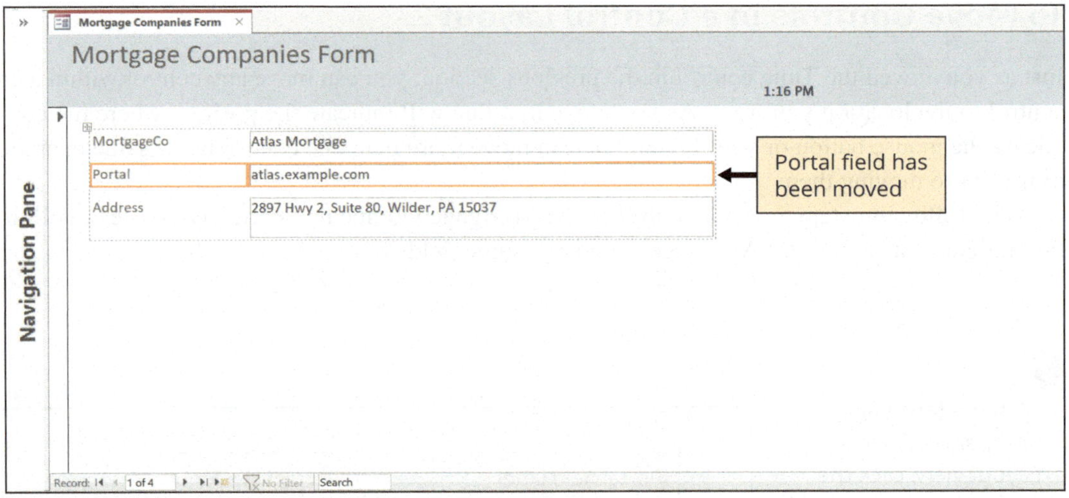

Figure 4–72

I inadvertently moved my pointer so the line became vertical and was located between a label and the corresponding data control when I released the mouse button. It seemed to split the form. The data control I moved appears right where the line was. It is between a label and the corresponding data control. How do I fix this?

Use the Undo button (Home tab | Undo group) to undo your change, or press CTRL + Z to undo. Then, try again, making sure to release the mouse button only when the red line is correctly positioned.

To Add a Field

After reviewing the Mortgage Companies Form, management decided that ID fields would help keep information straight between multiple tables, forms, and reports. **Why?** Just as with a report, once you have created an initial form, you might decide that the form should contain an additional field. The following steps use the Field List pane to add the ID field to the Mortgage Companies Form.

1

- Open the Navigation Pane, open the Mortgage Companies Form in Design view, and then close the Navigation Pane.
- If necessary, click Form Design on the ribbon to display the Form Design tab.
- Click the 'Add Existing Fields' button (Form Design tab | Tools group) to display the Field List pane (Figure 4–73).

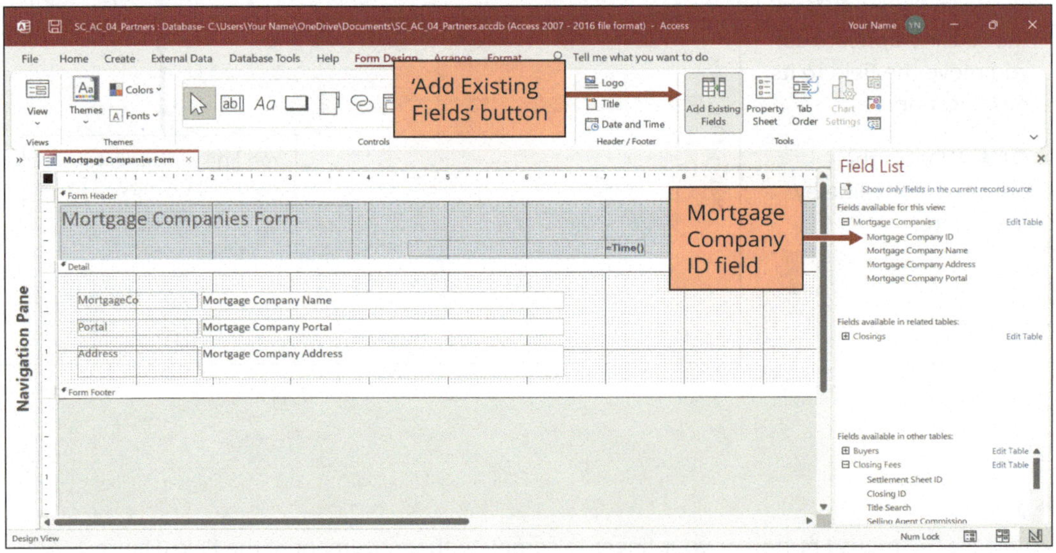

Figure 4–73

2

- Point to the Mortgage Company ID field in the field list, and then drag the pointer to the position shown in Figure 4–74.

Q&A Does the position of the ID field have to be exact?

The exact position is not critical at this time as long as the field is in the general position shown in the figure.

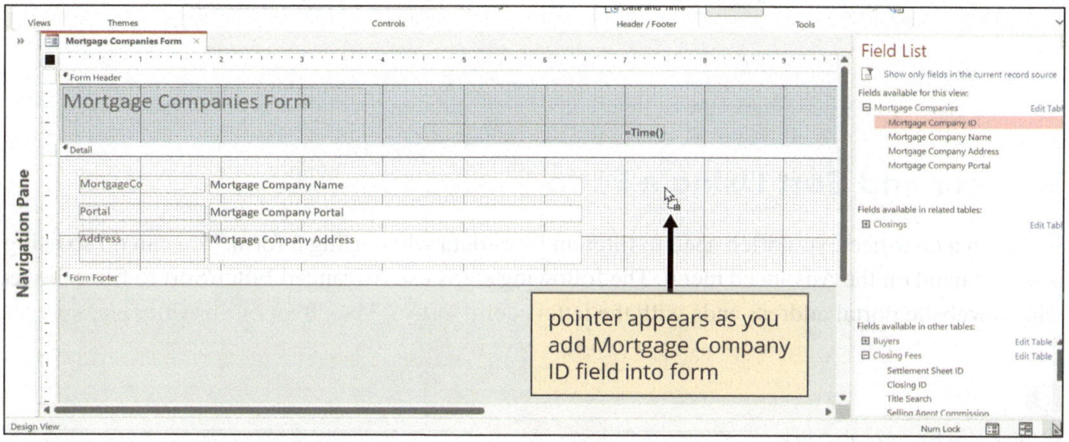

Figure 4–74

3

- Release the mouse button or your finger to place the field (Figure 4–75).

Q&A What if I make a mistake?

Just as when you are modifying a report, you can delete the field by clicking the field and then pressing DEL and then try again. Alternatively, you can move the field by dragging it to the correct position.

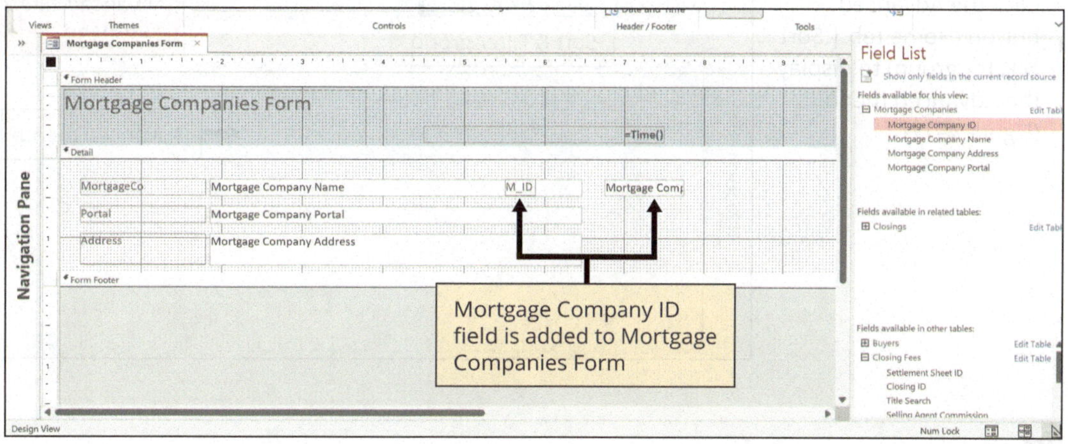

Figure 4–75

4

- Click the 'Add Existing Fields' button (Form Design tab | Tools group) to remove the Field List pane.
- Click the Mortgage Company Name field to select it.
- Use the two-pointed, resize arrow to reduce the size of the column holding the other controls so the Mortgage Company Name control does not overlap the M_ID label (Figure 4–76). This will give you sufficient space to position both the Mortgage Company Name field and the M_ID field on the same page, even though you cannot see the page borders at this time. Resize and reposition the Mortgage Company ID control as needed to fit the space as shown in Figure 4-76.
- Save your changes to the form. Do not close it yet.

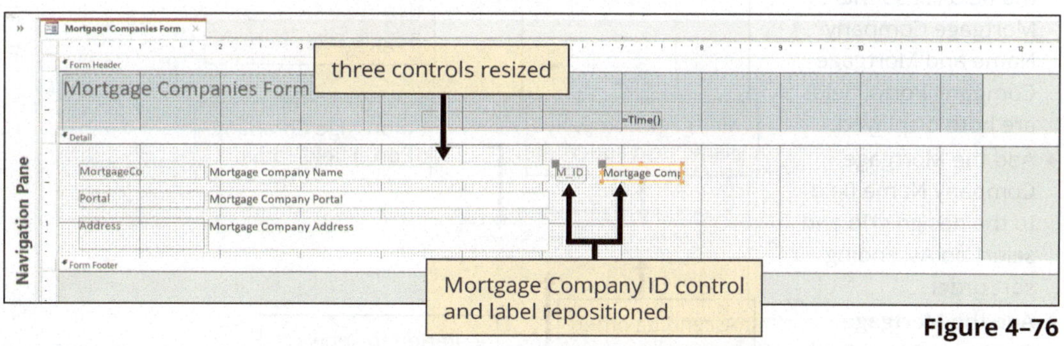

Figure 4–76

Q&A In the figure, it looks like the M_ID label is closer to the Mortgage Company ID control than it is on my screen. How do I match my screen to the figure?
When you select the Mortgage Company ID control or its label, gray boxes appear over each component. You can drag one of these gray boxes to change the distance between the control and its label.

To Filter and Sort Using a Form

Just as in a datasheet, you often need to filter and sort data when using a form. You can do so using Advanced Filter/Sort, which is a command on the Advanced menu. The following steps use Advanced Filter/Sort to filter the records to mortgage companies whose website portal address ends with the letters com. **Why?** The effect of this filter and sort is that you use the form to view only those mortgage companies using a .com website.

1

- Click the Home tab, click the View button arrow, and then select Layout View to change the view.
- Click the Advanced button (Home tab | Sort & Filter group) to display the Advanced menu (Figure 4–77).

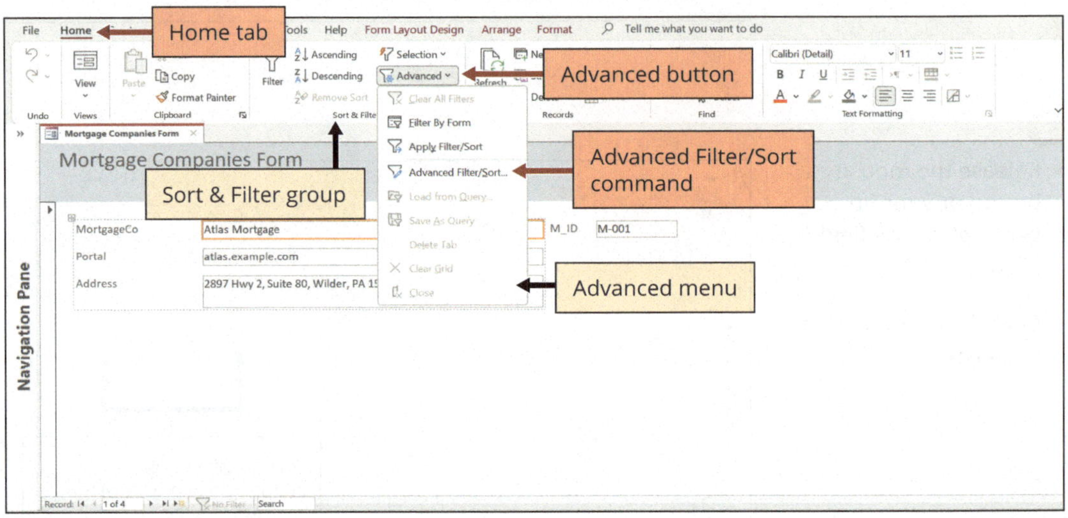

Figure 4–77

2

- Click Advanced Filter/Sort on the Advanced menu.
- If necessary, resize the field list so the Mortgage Company Name and Mortgage Company Portal fields are both displayed.
- Add the Mortgage Company Name field to the design grid and select an Ascending sort order.
- Add the Mortgage Company Portal field and type ***com** as the criterion for the Mortgage Company Portal field (Figure 4–78).

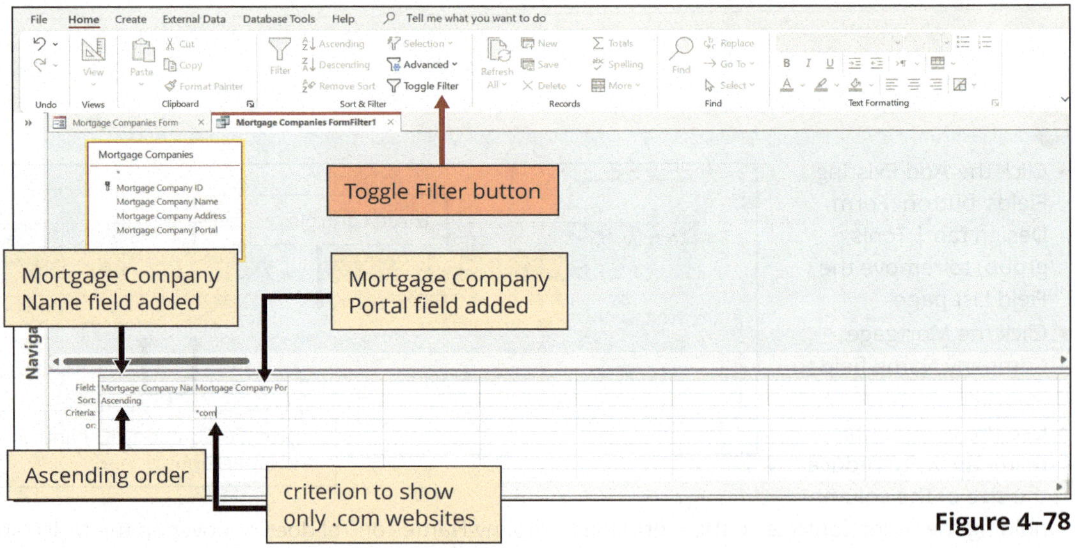

Figure 4–78

3

- Click the Toggle Filter button (Home tab | Sort & Filter group) to filter the records (Figure 4–79).

Q&A I can only see one record at a time in the form. How can I see which records are included?
You need to scroll through the records using the arrows in the Navigation bar.

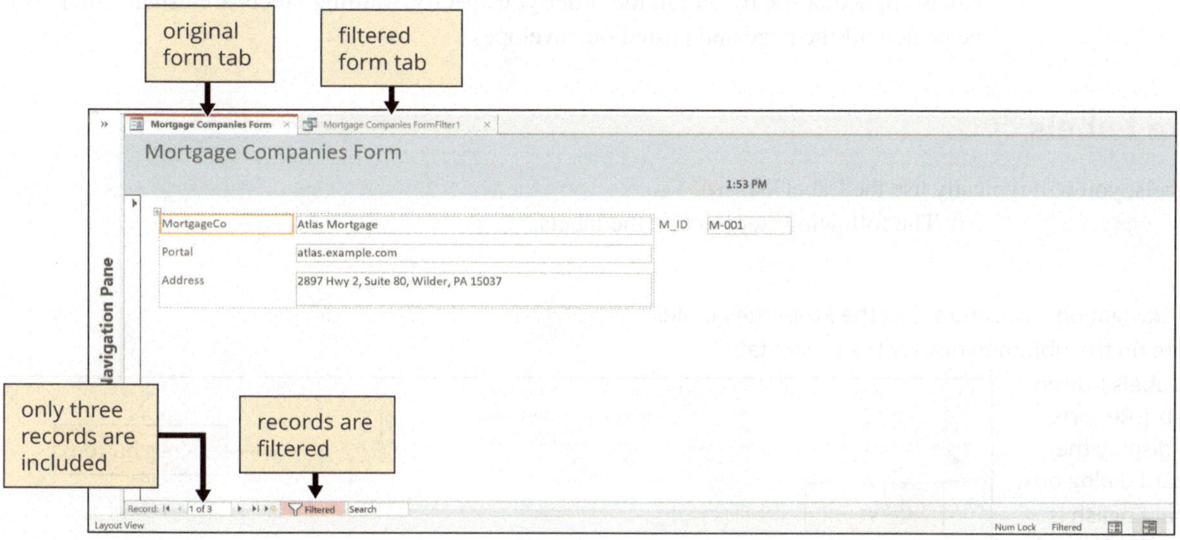

Figure 4–79

To Clear a Form Filter

When you no longer want the records to be filtered, you clear the filter. The following steps clear the current filter for the Mortgage Companies Form.

1

- Click the Advanced button (Home tab | Sort & Filter group) to display the Advanced menu.
- Click Clear All Filters on the Advanced menu to clear the filter.

2

- Save your work and close the form.

The Arrange Tab

Forms, like reports, have an Arrange tab that you can use to modify the form's layout. However, the Page Setup tab is not available for forms. The buttons on the Arrange tab and the functions of those buttons are just like the ones described in Table 4–1.

To Print a Form

You can print all records, a range of records, or a selected record of a form by selecting the appropriate print range. To print the selected record, the form must be open. To print all records or a range of records, you can simply highlight the form in the Navigation Pane. To print a specific record in a form, you would use the following steps.

1. Be sure the desired form is open and the desired record is selected.
2. Click File on the ribbon to open Backstage view.
3. Click the Print tab in Backstage view to display the Print gallery.
4. Click the Print button to display the Print dialog box.
5. Click the Selected Record(s) option button in the Print Range section, and then click OK.

BTW
Printing Forms
To change the page setup and page layout options for a form, such as adjusting margins and changing the orientation, use the Print Preview window. To open the Print Preview window for a form, click File on the ribbon, click Print, and then click Print Preview.

Mailing Labels

Organizations need to send all kinds of correspondence—such as invoices, letters, reports, and surveys—to accounts, customers, and other business partners on a regular basis. Using preprinted mailing labels eliminates much of the manual labor involved in preparing mailings. In Access, mailing labels are a special type of report. When this report prints, the data appears on the mailing labels aligned correctly and in the order you specify. Mailing labels are usually stickers that can be peeled off the page and pasted on envelopes.

To Create Labels

To create labels, you will typically use the Label Wizard. **Why?** Using the wizard, you can specify the type and dimensions, the font, and the content of the label. The following steps create the labels.

1

- Open the Navigation Pane and select the Properties table.
- Click Create on the ribbon to display the Create tab.
- Click the Labels button (Create tab | Reports group) to display the Label Wizard dialog box.
- Ensure that English is selected as the Unit of Measure and that Avery is selected in the Filter by manufacturer box.
- If necessary, scroll through the product numbers until C2163 appears, and then click C2163 in the Product number list to select the specific type of labels (Figure 4–80).

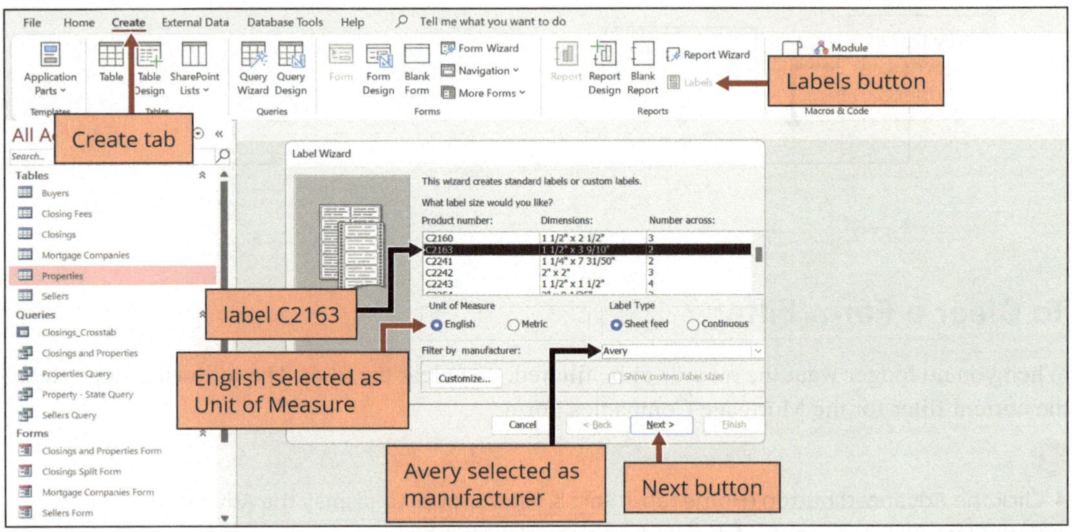

Figure 4–80

2

- Click Next (Figure 4–81).

Q&A What font characteristics could I change with this screen?
You could change the font, the font size, the font weight, and/or the font color. You could also specify italic or underline.

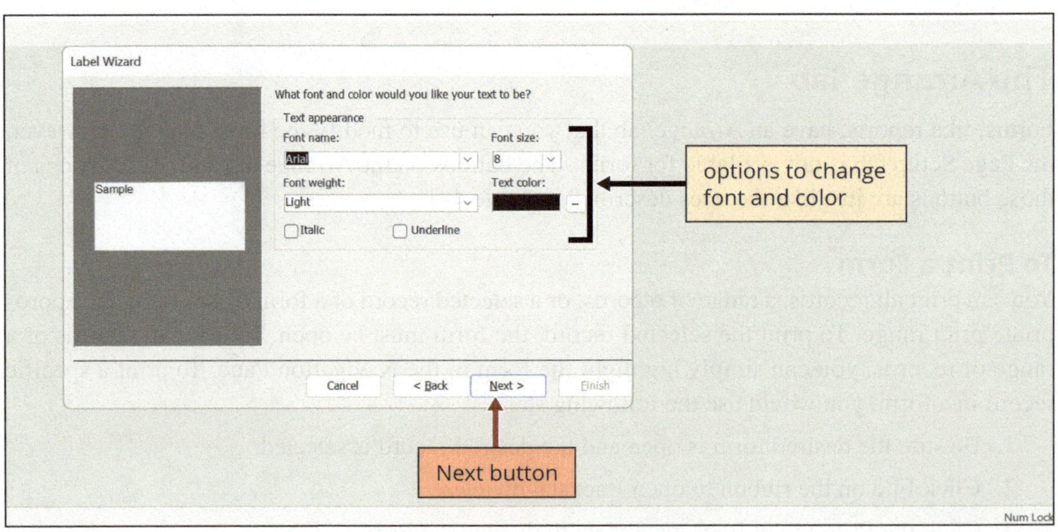

Figure 4–81

3

- Click Next to accept the default font and color settings.
- In the Prototype label section, type **Current Resident** on the first line (Figure 4–82).

Q&A What should I do if I make a mistake?

You can erase the contents of any line in the label by clicking in the line to produce an insertion point and then using DEL or BACKSPACE to erase the current contents. You then can add the correct text by typing or the correct field by clicking the field and then clicking the Add Field button.

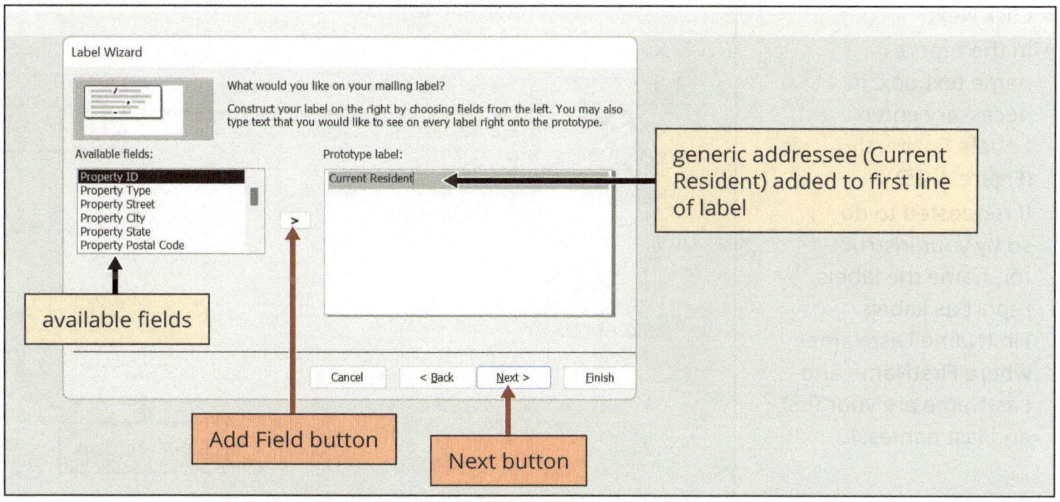

Figure 4–82

4

- Click the second line of the label, click the Property Street field, and then click the Add Field button.
- Click the third line of the label.
- Add the Property City field, type a comma (**,**), press the SPACEBAR, add the Property State field, press the SPACEBAR, and then add the Property Postal Code field (Figure 4–83).

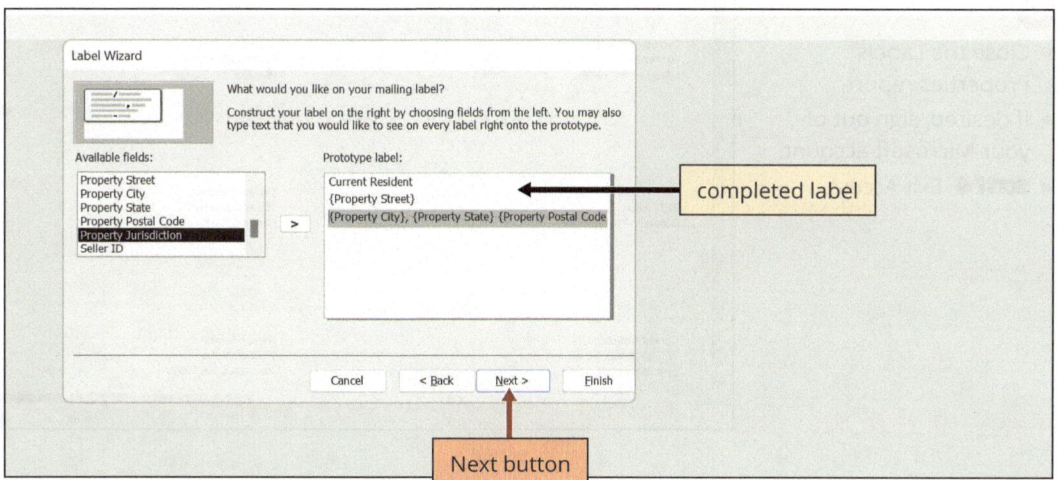

Figure 4–83

5

- Because you have now added all the necessary fields to the label, click Next.
- Select the Property Postal Code field as the field to sort by, and then click the Add Field button (Figure 4–84).

Q&A Why am I sorting by postal code?

When you need to do a bulk mailing, that is, send a large number of items using a special postage rate, businesses that provide mailing services often require that the mail be sorted in postal code order.

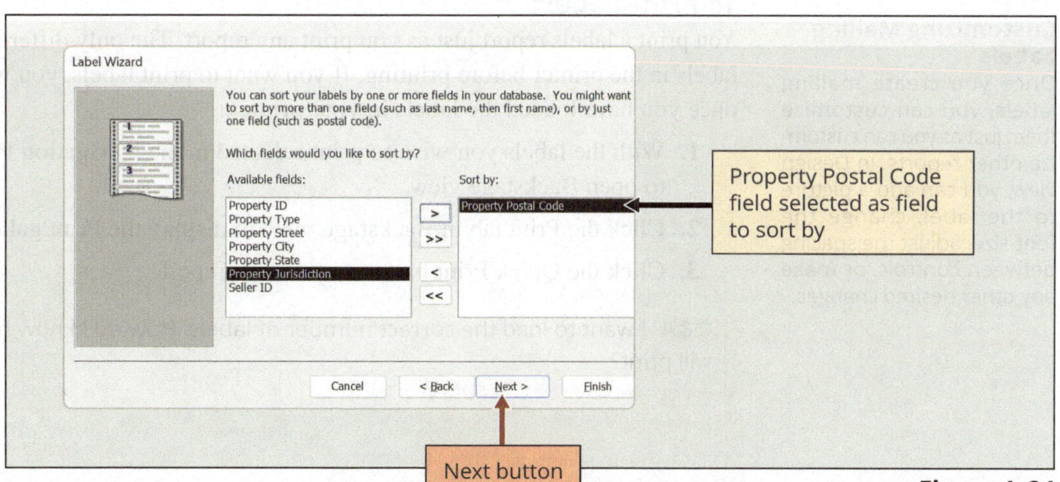

Figure 4–84

6

- Click Next.
- In the report name text box, if necessary enter **Labels Properties** (Figure 4–85).
  If requested to do so by your instructor, name the labels report as Labels FirstName LastName where FirstName and LastName are your first and last names.

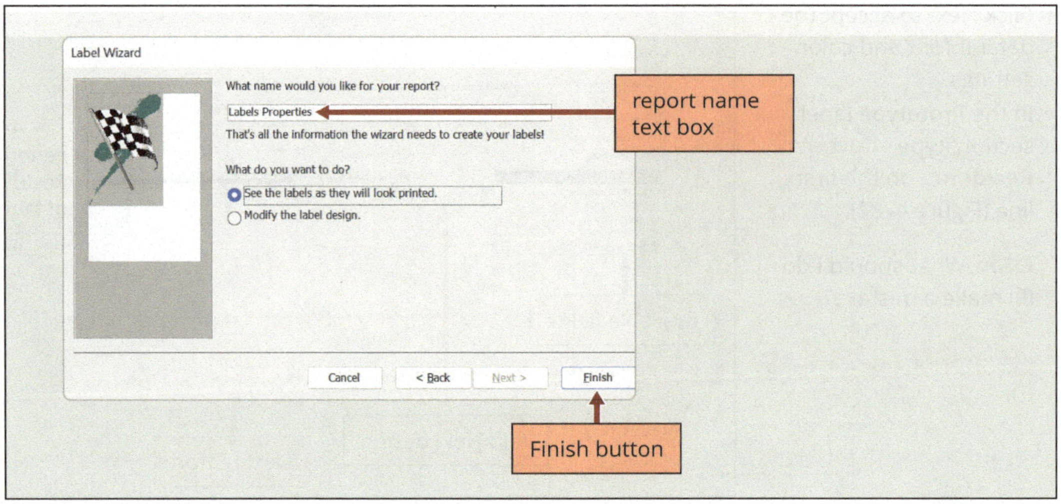

Figure 4–85

7

- Click Finish to complete the labels (Figure 4–86).

8

- Close the Labels Properties report.
- If desired, sign out of your Microsoft account.
- **sam** Exit Access.

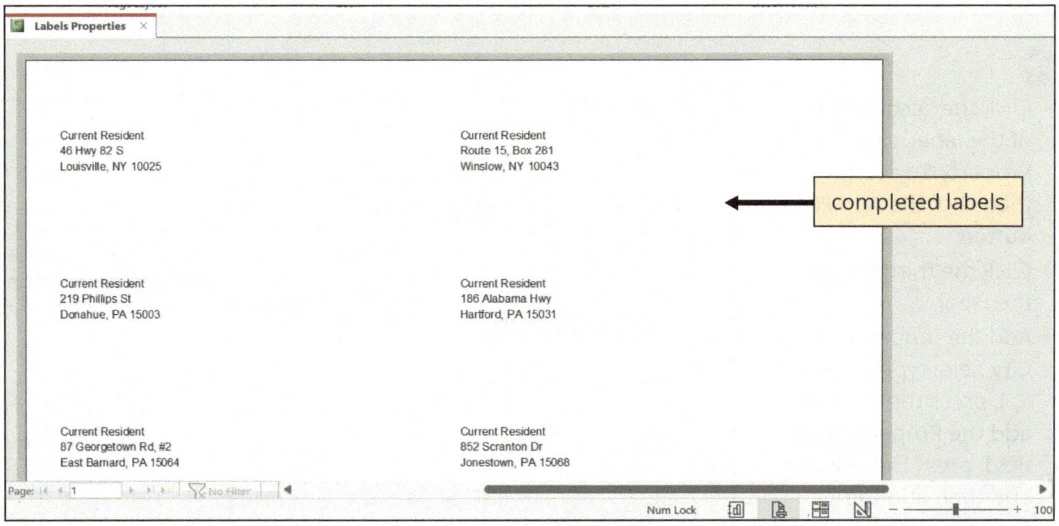

Figure 4–86

BTW

Customizing Mailing Labels

Once you create mailing labels, you can customize them just as you can customize other reports. In Design view, you can add a picture to the label, change the font size, adjust the spacing between controls, or make any other desired changes.

To Print Labels

You print a labels report just as you print any report. The only difference is that you must load the labels in the printer before printing. If you want to print labels, you would use the following steps once you have loaded the labels in your printer.

1. With the labels you wish to print selected in the Navigation Pane, click File on the ribbon to open Backstage view.
2. Click the Print tab in Backstage view to display the Print gallery.
3. Click the Quick Print button to print the report.

Q&A I want to load the correct number of labels. How do I know how many pages of labels will print?

If you are unsure how many pages of labels will print, open the label report in Print Preview first. Use the Navigation buttons in the status bar of the Print Preview window to determine how many pages of labels will print.

Summary

In this module you have learned to use wizards to create reports and forms, modify the layout of reports and forms using Layout view, group and sort in a report, add totals to a report, conditionally format controls, filter records in reports and forms, resize and move controls, add fields to reports and forms, create a stacked layout for a form, add a date/time, move controls in a control layout, apply themes, and create mailing labels.

Consider This: Plan Ahead

What decisions will you need to make when creating your own reports and forms?

Use these guidelines as you complete the assignments in this module and create your own reports and forms outside of this class.

1. Determine whether the data should be presented in a report or a form.
   a. Do you intend to print the data? If so, a report would be the appropriate choice.
   b. Do you intend to view the data on the screen, or will the user update data? If so, a form would be the appropriate choice.
2. Determine the intended audience for the report or form.
   a. Who will use the report or form?
   b. Will the report or form be used by individuals external to the organization? For example, many government agencies require reports from organizations. If so, government regulations will dictate the report requirements. If the report is for internal use, the user will have specific requirements based on the intended use.
   c. Adding unnecessary data to a report or form can make the form or report unreadable. Include only data necessary for the intended use.
   d. What level of detail should the report or form contain? Reports used in day-to-day operations need more detail than weekly or monthly reports requested by management.
3. Determine the tables that contain the data needed for the report or form.
   a. Is all the data found in a single table?
   b. Does the data come from multiple related tables?
4. Determine the fields that should appear on the report or form.
5. Determine the organization of the report or form.
   a. In what order should the fields appear?
   b. How should they be arranged?
   c. Should the records in a report be grouped in some way?
   d. Are any calculations required?
   e. Should the report be used to simply summarize data?
   f. Should the data for the report or form be filtered in some way?
6. Determine the format of the report or form.
   a. What information should be in the report or form header?
   b. Do you want a title and date?
   c. Do you want a logo?
   d. What information should be in the body of the report or form?
   e. Is any conditional formatting required?
   f. What style should be applied to the report or form? In other words, determine the visual characteristics that the various portions of the report or form should have.
   g. Is it appropriate to apply a theme to the reports, forms, and other objects in the database?
7. Review the report or form after it has been in operation to determine whether any changes are necessary.
   a. Is the order of the fields still appropriate?
   b. Are any additional fields required?

8. For mailing labels, determine the contents, order, and type of label.
    a. What fields should appear on the label?
    b. How should the fields be arranged?
    c. Is there a certain order (for example, by postal code) in which the labels should be printed?
    d. Who is the manufacturer of the labels and what is the style number for the labels?
    e. What are the dimensions for each label?
    f. How many labels print across a page?

Consider This

How should you submit solutions to critical thinking questions in the assignments?

Every assignment in this course contains one or more critical thinking questions. These questions require you to think beyond the assigned database. Present your responses to the questions in the format required by your instructor. Possible formats may include one or more of these options: write the answer; create a document that contains the answer; present your answer to the class; discuss your answer in a group; record the answer as audio or video using a webcam, smartphone, or portable media player; or post answers on a blog, wiki, or website.

Student Assignments

Apply Your Knowledge

Reinforce the skills and apply the concepts you learned in this module.

Creating Two Reports and a Form

Note: To complete this assignment, you will be required to use the Data Files. Please contact your instructor for information about accessing the Data Files.

Instructions: Start Access. Open the database, SC_AC_04-2.accdb, which is located in the Data Files folder. Enable the content.

Perform the following tasks:

1. Save the database using the file name, SC_AC_04_Construction. Enable the content.
2. Use the Report Wizard to create a report from the Accounting table that shows how much money is due to subcontractors. Group the report by Job Site number and sort the report by Current Due in Ascending order. Add subtotals and a total to the Current Due field. Save the report as Subcontractors with Current Due Amounts. Adjust control sizes, positions, and text alignment as needed so all data is visible. Your finished report should look like Figure 4–87.

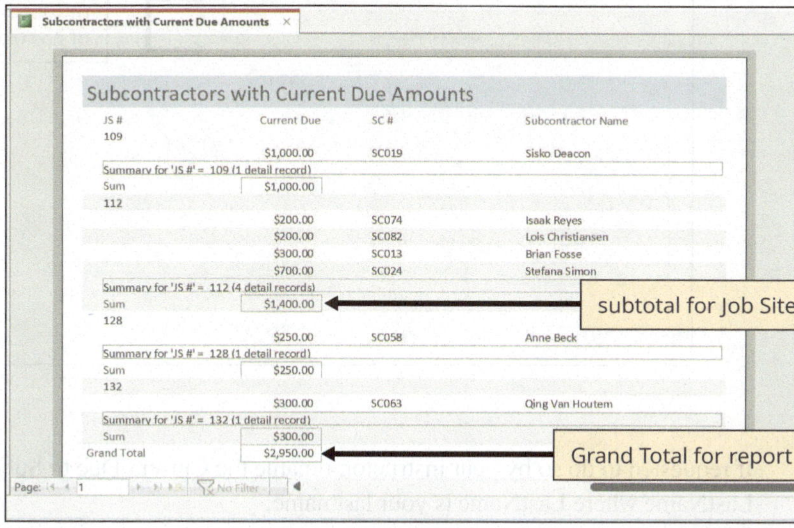

Figure 4–87

3. Create a report that counts the number of subcontractors for each Job Site. Group the report by Job Site Number and use the title Count of Subcontractors by Job Site. Modify the design to include a count of the subcontractors within each job site. Adjust control sizes and positions as needed so your finished report looks like Figure 4–88. Save the report.

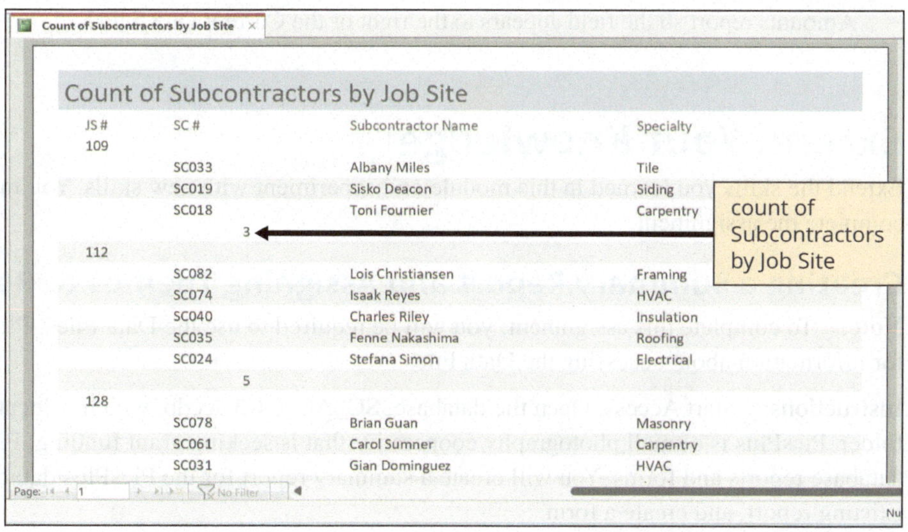

Figure 4–88

Continued on next page

4. Use the Form Wizard to create the Current Due to Subcontractor form shown in Figure 4–89. The form has a columnar layout and includes the current date. Bold the date control, change the Alignment to Align Left, and reposition the date control as shown in Figure 4–89. Decrease the size of the SC# and Subcontractor Name controls so they reflect the appropriate size for these fields. Use Figure 4–89 for reference. Save the form.

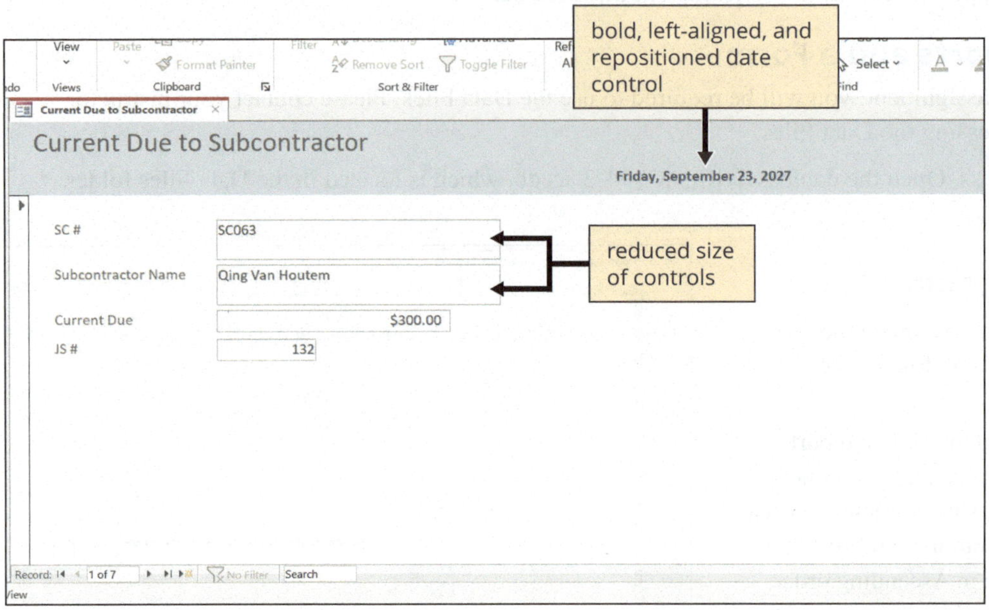

Figure 4–89

If requested to do so by your instructor, rename the Current Due to Subcontractor form as Current Due with LastName where LastName is your last name.

5. Submit the revised database in the format specified by your instructor.
6. **Consider This:** How would you add the Amount Paid field to the Subcontractors with Current Due Amounts report so the field appears to the right of the Current Due field?

Extend Your Knowledge

Extend the skills you learned in this module and experiment with new skills. You may need to use Help to complete the assignment.

Creating a Summary Report and Assigning Themes to Reports and Forms

Note: To complete this assignment, you will be required to use the Data Files. Please contact your instructor for information about accessing the Data Files.

Instructions: Start Access. Open the database, SC_AC_04-3.accdb, which is located in the Data Files folder. PicsPlus is a small photography cooperative that is seeking grant funding. PicsPlus needs to update its database reports and forms. You will create a summary report for the PicsPlus database, assign a theme to an existing report, and create a form.

Perform the following tasks:

1. Save the database using the file name, SC_AC_04_PicsPlus. Enable the content.
2. Use the Report Wizard to create the summary report shown in Figure 4–90. View the data by Photographer and sort by Client Name. Sum the Balance Due field for the Summary option. Save your report as Photographer Balances Summary Report. Apply the Gallery theme and resave it.

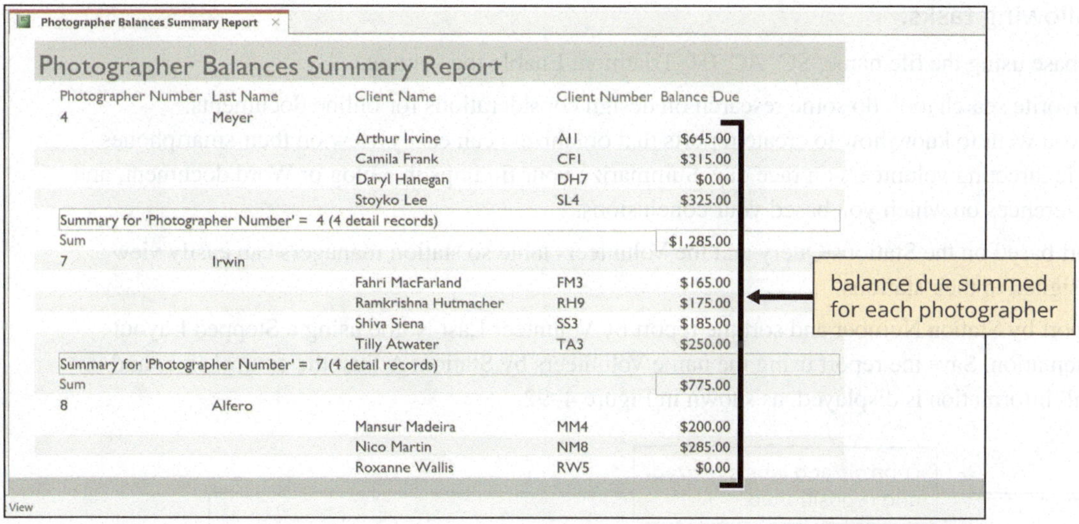

Figure 4–90

3. Create the Photographer Form shown in Figure 4–91, taking note of the included fields and the order they're listed. The form has a Columnar control layout. Use the Property Sheet to change the Caption of the Photographer Number label. Apply the Slice theme to this object only. Save the changes to the form.

Figure 4–91

If requested to do so by your instructor, open the Photographer Form in Form view and change the first name and last name for Tech# 7 to your first and last names.

4. Submit the revised database in the format specified by your instructor.
5. **Consider This:** How would you change the theme font for the Photographer Form to Arial?

Expand Your World

Create a solution, which uses cloud and web technologies, by learning and investigating on your own from general guidance.

Note: To complete this assignment, you will be required to use the Data Files. Please contact your instructor for information about accessing the Data Files.

Instructions: Start Access. Open the database, SC_AC_04-4.accdb, which is located in the Data Files folder, and enable the content. Organizers for a fundraising triathlon need to provide a list to all stations showing which volunteers are assigned where. The organizers have asked you to create a report that documents these relationships. Organizers need to view this report during their final planning meeting and on the morning of the event as volunteers arrive and check in.

Continued on next page

Perform the following tasks:

1. Save the database using the file name, SC_AC_04_Triathlon. Enable the content.
2. Using your favorite search tool, do some research on design considerations for online documents. Specifically, you want to know how to create reports that organizers can easily view on their smartphones or tablets while directing volunteers on race day. Summarize your findings in a blog or Word document, and include the references on which you based your conclusions.
3. Create a report based on the Stations Query and the Volunteers table so station managers can easily view volunteers assigned to their stations.
4. Group the report by Station Number and sort the report by Volunteer Last Name using a Stepped Layout in Portrait orientation. Save the report using the name Volunteers by Station. Adjust the control sizes and positions so all information is displayed, as shown in Figure 4–92.

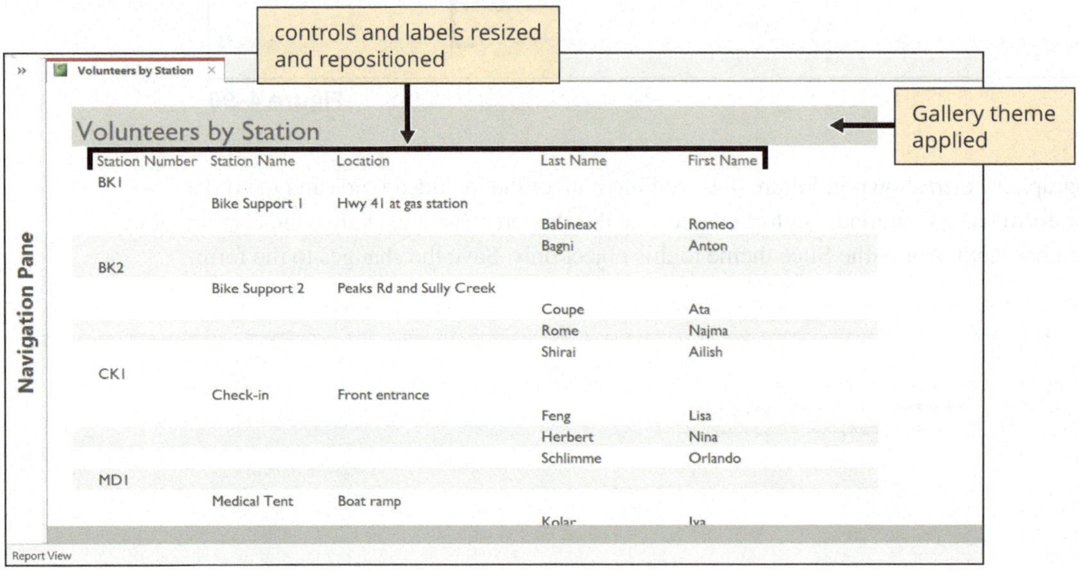

Figure 4–92

5. Add the Gallery theme to the Volunteers by Station report. Remove the Date field from the report and save the revised report with the new changes.
6. After completing the report, submit the revised database and the blog Word document you created in Step 2. Submit the files in the format specified by your instructor.
7. **Consider This:** After researching design considerations for reports, what changes to the Volunteers by Station report design would you suggest? Why do you think these changes would make the report more user friendly for station managers on race day?

In the Lab

Design and implement a solution using creative thinking and problem-solving skills.

Lab: Updating Reports and Forms in the Homegrown Nurse Staffing Agency Database

Note: To complete this assignment, you will be required to use the Data Files. Please contact your instructor for information about accessing the Data Files.

Problem: Homegrown Nurse Staffing Agency is growing and needs some data from its database to help attract more nursing professionals willing to travel. Your task is to create one report showing relevant information about recent assignments and another report with housing information for placing travelers with upcoming assignments. You also need to create a form that shows travelers who are available now for assignments.

Perform the following tasks:

Part 1: Open the SC_AC_04-5.accdb database from the Data Files folder. Save the file with the name, SC_AC_04_Travel-Nurses, and enable the content. Use the concepts and techniques presented in this module to create reports and forms so the data is easily viewed and understood.

a. The office manager wants to see assignment ID number, specialty, and term for all travel assignments. She also wants to be able to quickly see which assignments offer bill rates of $40,000 or more and an overall average of all assignment bill rates. Using a Tabular layout, create a report called Assignment Bill Rates that does not contain grouping. Include sorting, formatting, and a calculation that will produce a report similar to that shown in Figure 4–93.

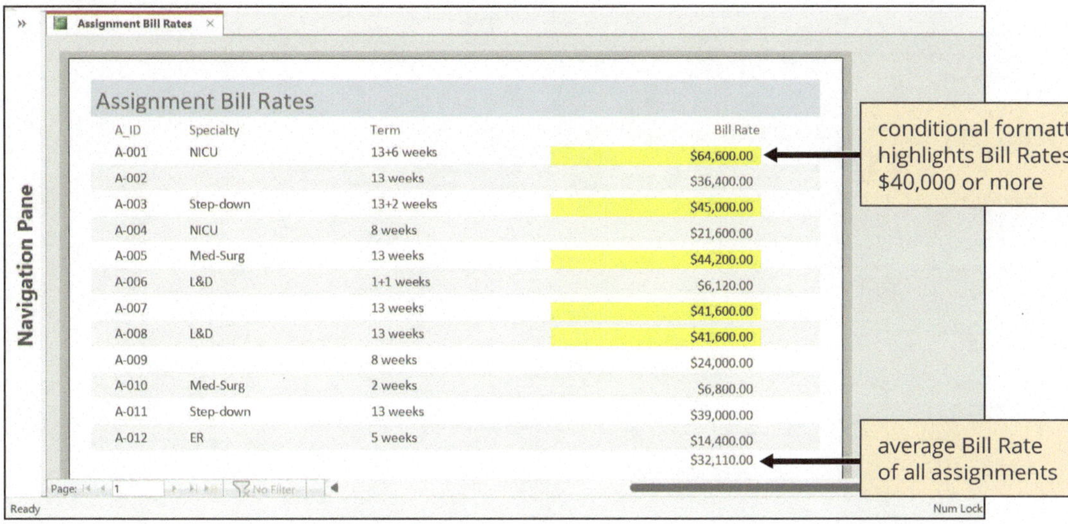

Figure 4–93

b. Create a one-page report that includes all fields in the Housing table. Apply grouping and sorting as shown in Figure 4–94. Adjust the size and position of the controls as necessary.

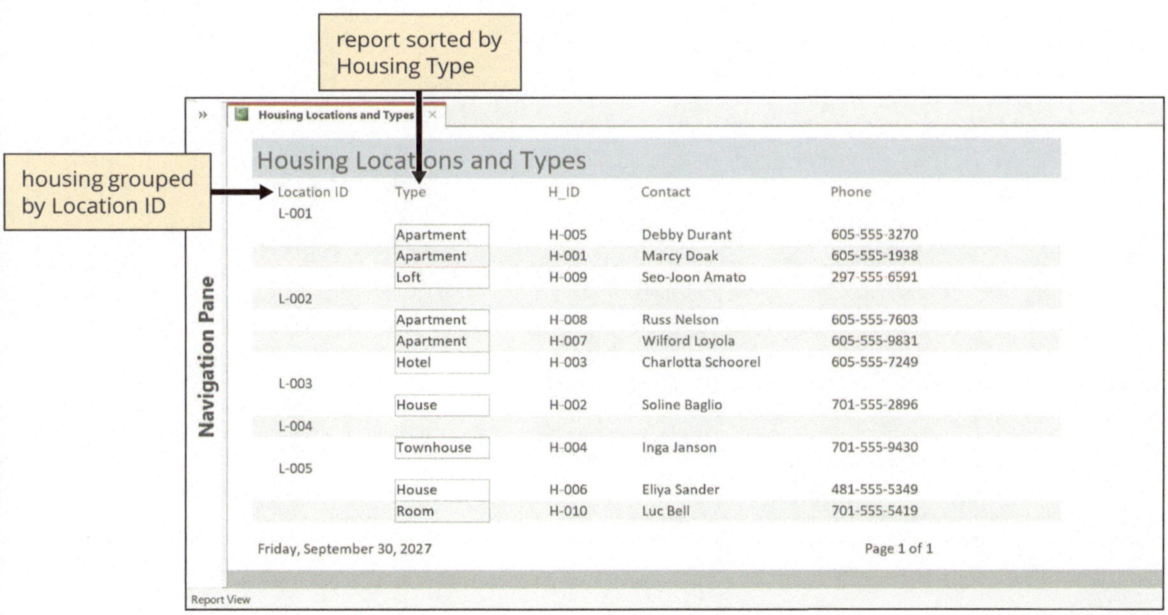

Figure 4–94

Continued on next page

c. Create a form for the Travelers table that includes each travel nurse's name, ID, license, phone number, and availability. While using this form to update traveler availability, office staff occasionally need to apply a filter to display all travelers who are currently available (that is, listed as available at any time) and sort the results in descending order by Traveler ID. Save the form as Filtered Traveler Availability. Reopen the form and confirm that your saved filter can be applied using the Toggle Filter button.

Submit your assignment in the format specified by your instructor.

Part 2: Consider This: You made several decisions while creating these reports and forms, including conditionally formatting values and applying grouping, sorting, and filtering. What was the rationale behind your decisions? How did you apply the filter and sort to the Filtered Traveler Availability Form? Why? What other options are available?

Multiple-Table Forms

Objectives

After completing this module, you will be able to:

- Use Yes/No, Long Text, and Attachment fields in a form
- Apply an input mask
- Enter data of various types
- Enter a file in an attachment field
- Create a form using Design view
- Create a form with a subform
- Modify subform and form design
- Modify a label in a form
- Enhance the appearance of a form title
- Set the tab stop sequence in a form
- Use a form to view data and attachments
- View object dependencies
- Use Date/Time, Long Text, and Yes/No fields in a query
- Explain how to include a datasheet on a form
- Explain how to create a multiple-table form

Introduction

When creating a form, you often need to incorporate data from more than one table. To accomplish this, it's important that the tables have an existing relationship that indicates the field connecting the tables and the type of relationship, such as one-to-many. This type of relationship identifies the table on the "one" side of the relationship and the table on the "many" side of the relationship. On the "one" side, a single record in the table relates to many records in the table on the "many" side. You might also need to add fields that can contain special data types, such as photos or other graphics, documents, or other attachments. These fields, then, can appear in queries that draw information from the relevant tables.

Project: Multiple-Table Forms

Clearnet uses its database to keep records about carriers and loads. The owners are in the process of contracting with some specialty carriers to handle complicated loads. The increase in complexity means that Clearnet needs to maintain additional data on its carriers. With this data, the team can promote the new carrier capabilities. They also want to include each carrier's available truck types as well as photos of the drivers. Additionally, Clearnet wants to connect the new carriers' online resources, such as a payment portal, and other documentation from the carriers, such as a bill of lading template. A bill of lading is required for each load, and sometimes carriers provide this documentation for their loads. These files are separate from the database; some are maintained in Word and others as PDFs. Clearnet would like a way to attach these files to the corresponding carrier's record in the database. Finally, Clearnet wants to adjust the Phone Number field in the Carriers table. Users should type only the digits in the phone number and then have Access format

BTW
Touch Screen Differences
The Office and Windows interfaces may vary if you are using a touch screen. For this reason, you might notice that the function or appearance of your touch screen differs slightly from this module's presentation.

BTW
Touch and Pointers
Remember that if you are using your finger on a touch screen, you will not see the pointer.

the number appropriately. For example, if the user enters 8255553455, Access will format the number as (825) 555–3455.

After the proposed fields have been added to the database, Clearnet wants users to be able to use a form that incorporates the Carriers and Loads tables and includes the newly added fields as well as some of the existing fields in the Carriers table. The form should also include the Carrier ID, the Carrier name, contact person, phone number, and list of drivers. Clearnet would like to see multiple loads for each carrier on the screen at the same time (Figure 5–1). The database should allow users to scroll through all the loads and see the start date, end date, rate confirmation, mileage, and truck type. At any time, the carrier's documentation can be opened for viewing. Finally, Clearnet will need queries that use the new fields and provide easy access to the data held in the new attachment fields.

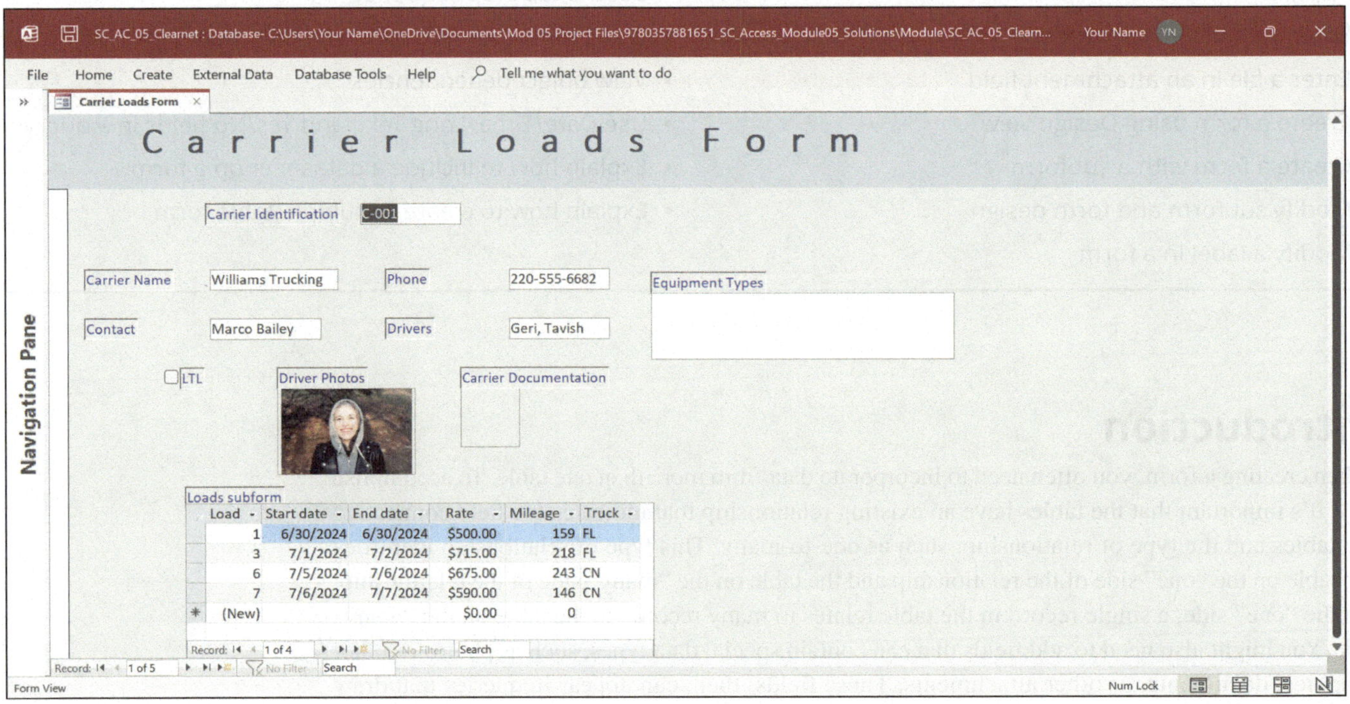

Marivi Pazos/Unsplash

Figure 5–1

BTW
The Ribbon and Screen Resolution
Access may change how the groups and buttons within the groups appear on the ribbon, depending on the computer's screen resolution. Thus, your ribbon might look different from the ones in this course if you are using a screen resolution other than 1920 × 1080.

BTW
OLE Object Fields
OLE Object fields can store video clips, sound, and other objects from Windows-based apps.

Adding Special Fields

Having analyzed its requirements, Clearnet management has identified a need for some new fields for the Carriers table. They need an LTL (Less than a Load) field, which indicates whether a carrier handles shipments that are less than a full truckload; this field's data type will be Yes/No. They need an Equipment Type field that identifies each carrier's available truck types, which will be a Long Text field. The Carrier Documentation field, which must be able to contain multiple attachments for each carrier, will be an Attachment field. The Driver Photos field is the only field whose data type is uncertain—the data type could be either OLE Object, which can contain objects created by a variety of applications, or Attachment. An OLE Object (Object Linking and Embedding Object) creates a bitmap of the image file, which can result in very large files, so Clearnet has decided to use the Attachment data type for greater efficiency.

Clearnet wants to assist users in entering the correct format for a phone number, so the field will use an input mask. An **input mask** specifies how data is to be entered and how it will appear. For example, an input mask can indicate that a phone number has parentheses around the first three digits and a hyphen between the sixth and seventh digits.

The form shown in Figure 5–1 contains two attachment fields, the Driver Photos field and the Carrier Documentation field. When viewed as a table, these both appear as paper clips, not as the actual attachment. However, when the table's attachment fields are displayed in a form, you can view the photo itself and an icon of the document, in this case, a Word file.

BTW
Long Text Fields
Long Text fields can store up to a gigabyte of text. If you need to keep a historical record of changes to a Long Text field, set the value for the Append Only property to Yes. To use formatting such as bold and underline in a Long Text field, set the value for the Text Format property to Rich Text.

To Add Fields with New Data Types to a Table

You add the new fields to the Carriers table by modifying the design of the table and inserting the fields at the appropriate position in the table structure. The following steps add the LTL (Less than a Load), Equipment Types, Driver Photos, and Carrier Documentation fields to the Carriers table. **Why?** These new fields will track required information as the business continues to grow.

1

- Start Access. Open the database, SC_AC_05-1.accdb, which is located in the Data Files folder. Save the file on your hard disk, OneDrive, or other storage location using the file name, **SC_AC_05_Clearnet**. Enable the content and open the Navigation Pane, if necessary.
- Right-click the Carriers table to display a shortcut menu (Figure 5–2).

BTW
Adding Captions to Attachment Fields
You can add a caption to an Attachment field. To add a caption in Design view, use the Caption property box.

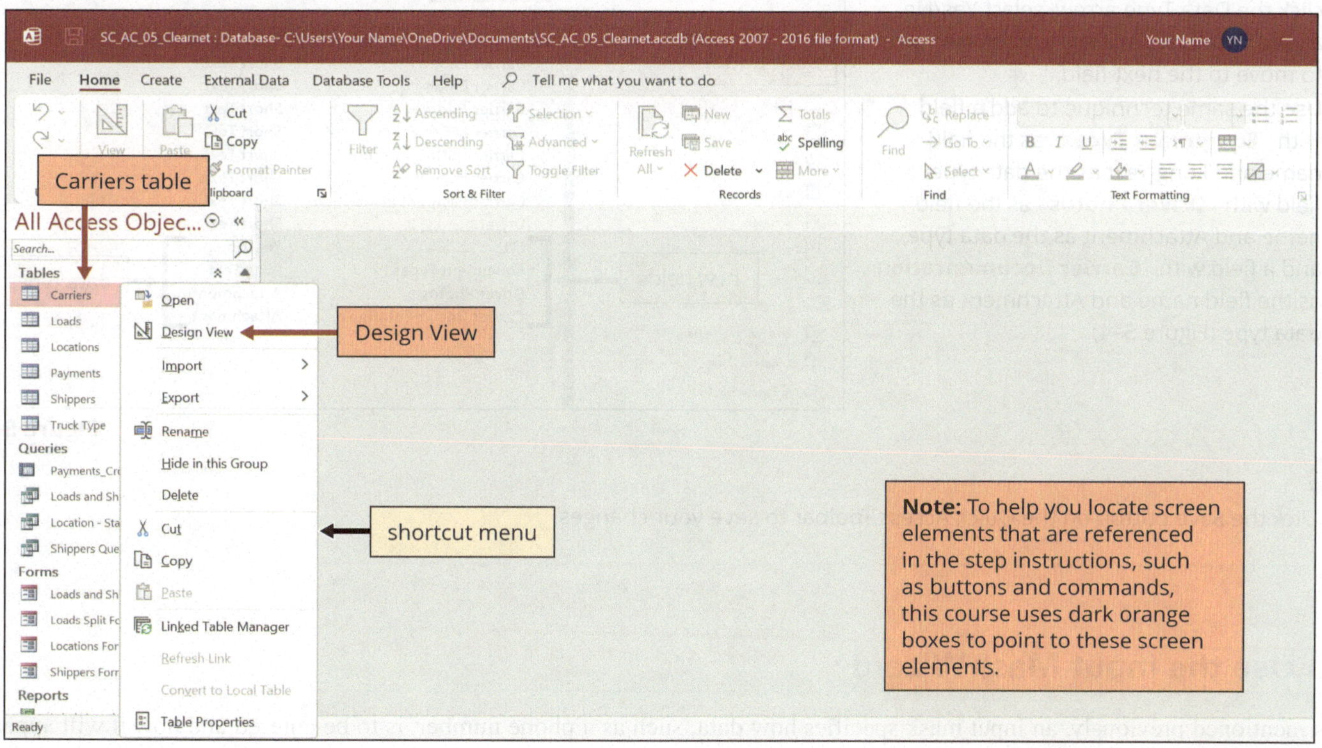

Figure 5–2

2

- Click Design View on the shortcut menu to open the table in Design view (Figure 5–3).

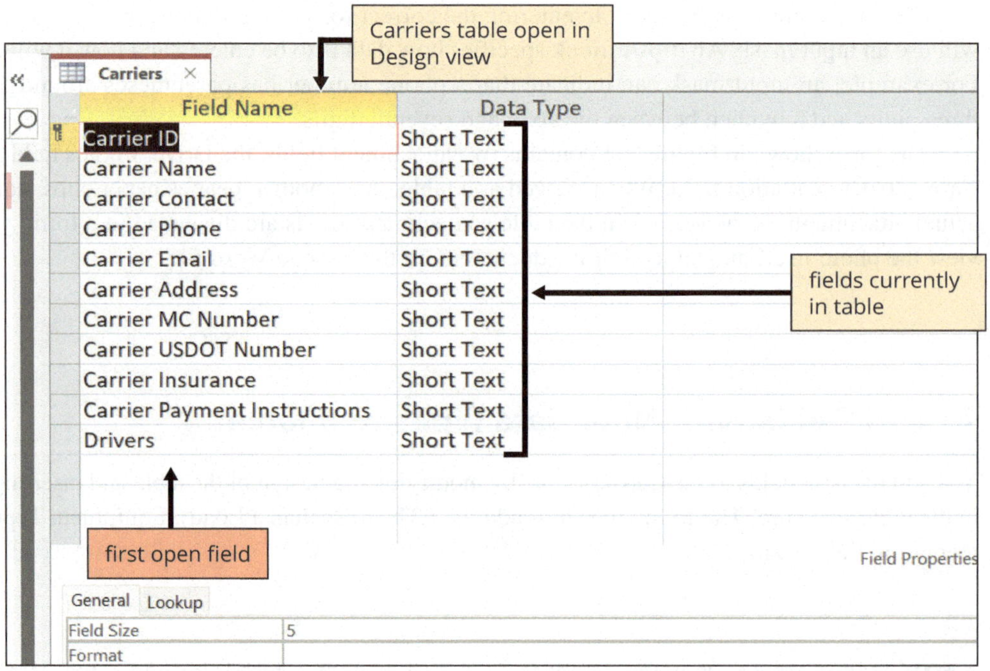

Figure 5–3

3

- Click the first open field to select the position for the first additional field.
- Type **LTL** as the field name, press TAB, click the Data Type arrow, select Yes/No as the data type, and then press TAB twice to move to the next field.
- Use the same technique to add a field with **Equipment Types** as the field name and Long Text as the data type, a field with **Driver Photos** as the field name and Attachment as the data type, and a field with **Carrier Documentation** as the field name and Attachment as the data type (Figure 5–4).

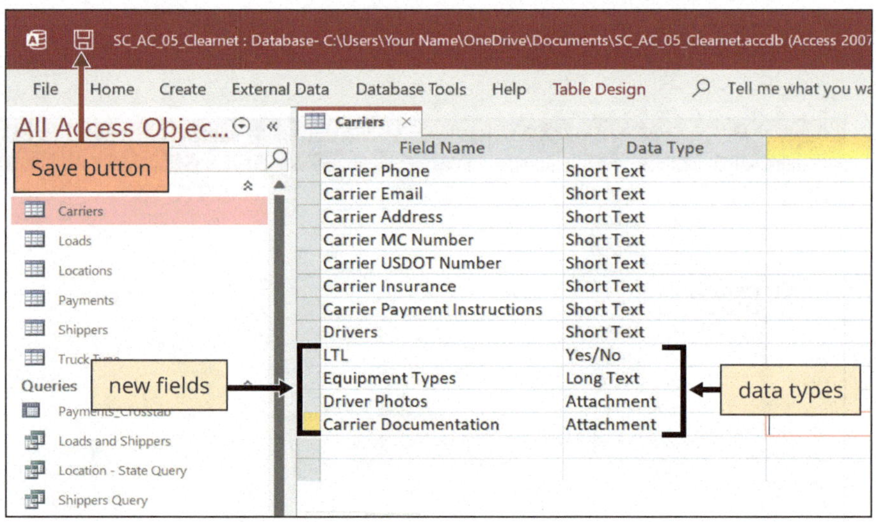

Figure 5–4

4

- Click the Save button on the Quick Access Toolbar to save your changes.

To Use the Input Mask Wizard

As mentioned previously, an input mask specifies how data, such as a phone number, is to be entered and how it will appear. You can enter an input mask directly, but you will use the Input Mask Wizard. **Why?** The wizard assists you in the creation of the input mask by allowing you to select from a list of the most frequently used input masks.

To use the Input Mask Wizard, select the Input Mask property in the field's property sheet and then select the Build button. The following steps use the Input Mask Wizard to specify how the carriers' phone numbers are to appear.

1

- Click the Carrier Phone field.
- Click the Input Mask property box (Figure 5–5).

Q&A Do I need to change the data type?
No. Short Text is the appropriate data type for a Phone Number field.

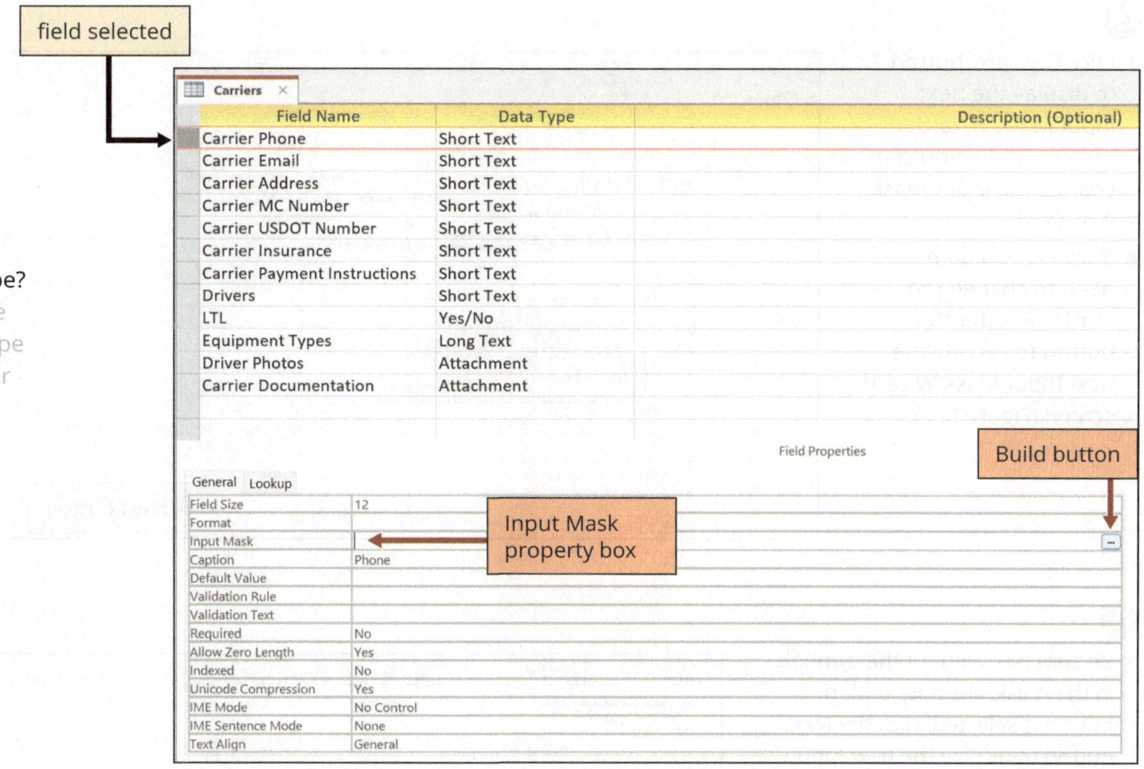

Figure 5–5

2

- Click the Build button to use a wizard to enter the input mask.
- If a dialog box appears asking you to save the table, click Yes. (If a dialog box displays a message that the Input Mask Wizard is not installed, check with your instructor before proceeding with the following steps.)
- Ensure that Phone Number is selected (Figure 5–6).

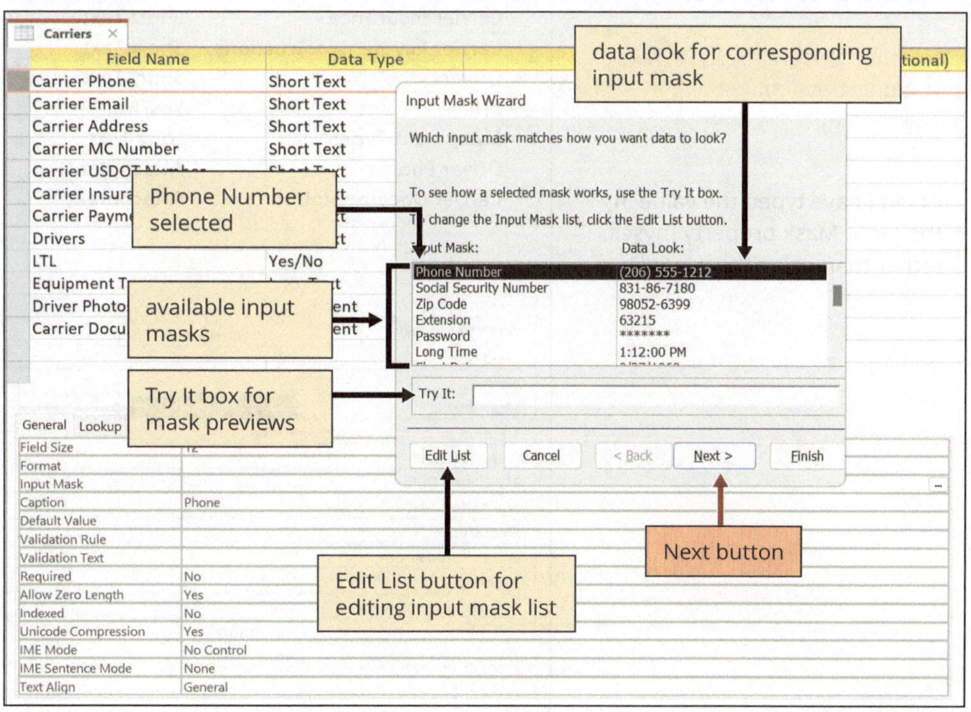

Figure 5–6

- **Experiment:** Click different input masks and enter data in the Try It text box to see the effect of the selected mask. When you are done, click the Phone Number input mask.

3

- Click the Next button to display the next Input Mask Wizard screen, where you can change the input mask, if desired.
- Because you do not need to change the mask, click the Next button to display the next Input Mask Wizard screen (Figure 5–7).

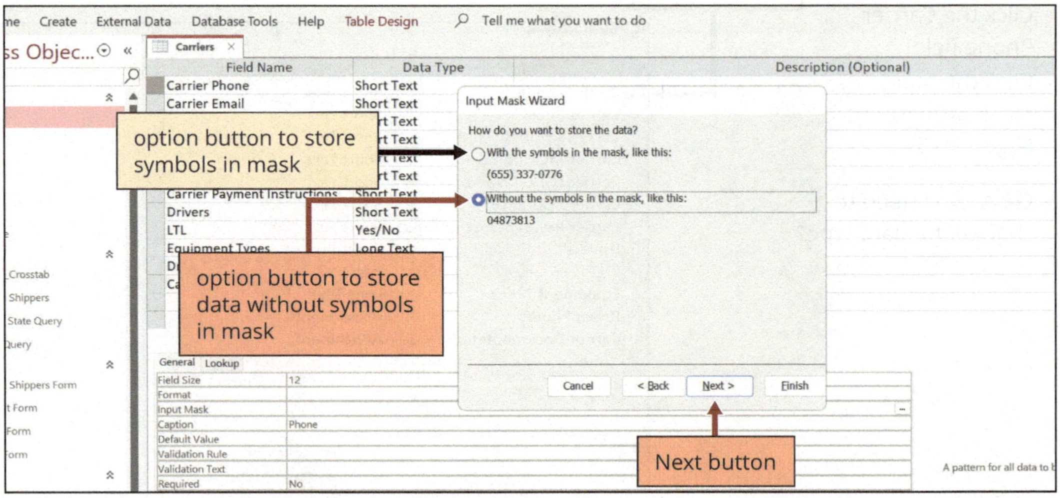

Figure 5–7

4

- Be sure the 'Without the symbols in the mask, like this:' option button is selected, click the Next button to display the next Input Mask Wizard screen, and then click the Finish button (Figure 5–8).

Q&A Why does the data type not change to Input Mask?

The data type of the Phone Number field is still Short Text. The only thing that changed is one of the field properties, the Input Mask property.

Could I have typed the value in the Input Mask property myself, rather than using the wizard?

Yes. Input masks can be complex, however, so it is usually easier and safer to use the wizard.

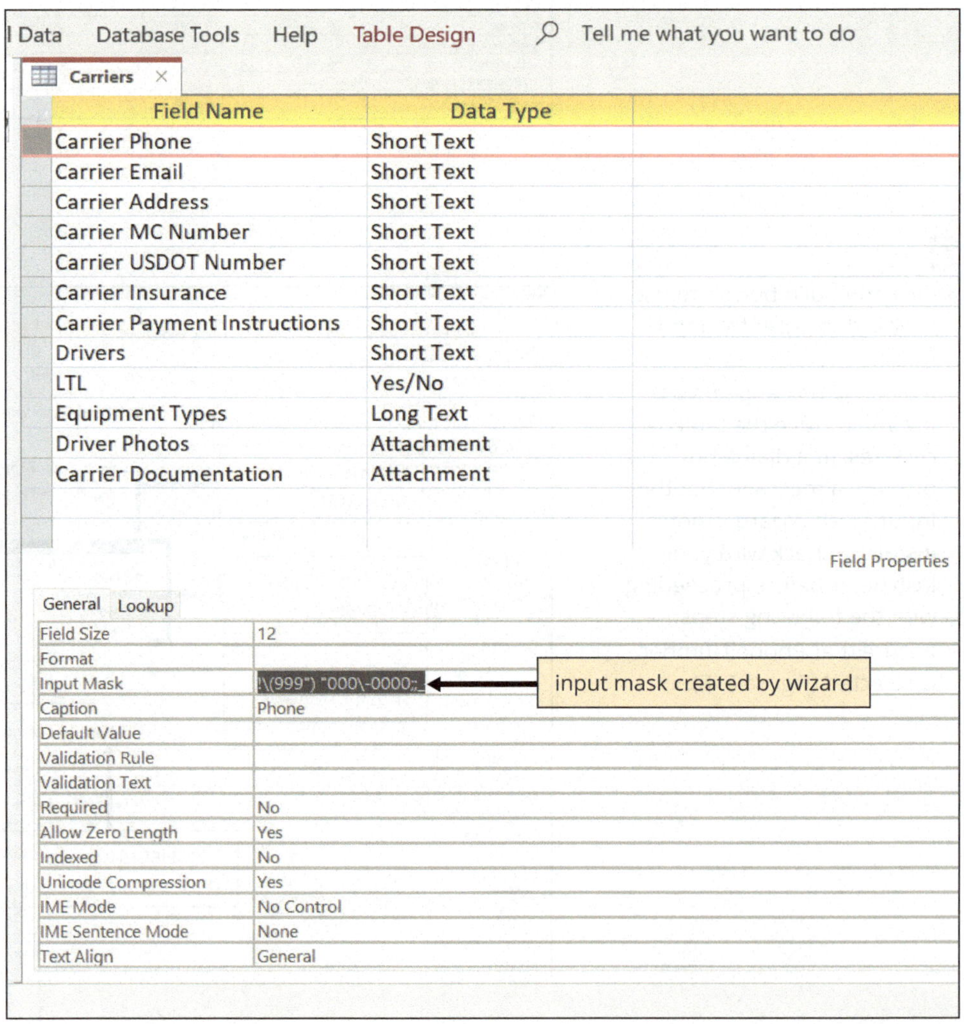

Figure 5–8

5

- Save the Carriers table.

Adding Fields in Datasheet View

Previously you added fields to a table using Design view. You can also add fields in Datasheet view. One way to do so is to use the Add & Delete group on the Table Fields tab (Figure 5–9). Select the field that precedes the position where you want to add the new field, and then click the appropriate button. You can click the Short Text button to add a Short Text field, the Number button to add a Number field, the Currency button to add a Currency field, and so on. Alternatively, you can click the More Fields button to display the Data Type gallery. You then can click a data type in the gallery to add a field with that type.

The gallery provides more options for ways to display various types of data. For example, if you click the Check Box version of a Yes/No field, the field will be displayed as a check box, which is the common way to display such a field. If instead you click the Yes/No version of a Yes/No field, the value in the field will be displayed as either the word, Yes, or the word, No.

If you scroll down in the Data Type gallery, you will find a Quick Start section. The commands in this section give you quick ways of adding some common types of fields. For example, clicking Address in the Quick Start section immediately adds several fields: Address, City, State Province, ZIP Postal, and Country Region. Clicking Start and End Dates immediately adds both a Start Date field and an End Date field.

In Datasheet view, you can rename fields by right-clicking the field name, clicking Rename Field on the shortcut menu, and then typing the new name. Delete a field by clicking the field and then clicking the Delete button (Table Fields tab | Add & Delete group). Move a field from one location to another by dragging the field.

BTW

Input Mask Characters

When you create an input mask, Access adds several characters. These characters control the literal values that appear when you enter data. For example, the first backslash in the input mask in Figure 5–8 displays the opening parenthesis. The double quotation marks direct Access to display the closing parenthesis and a space. The second backslash directs Access to display the hyphen that separates the first and second part of the phone number.

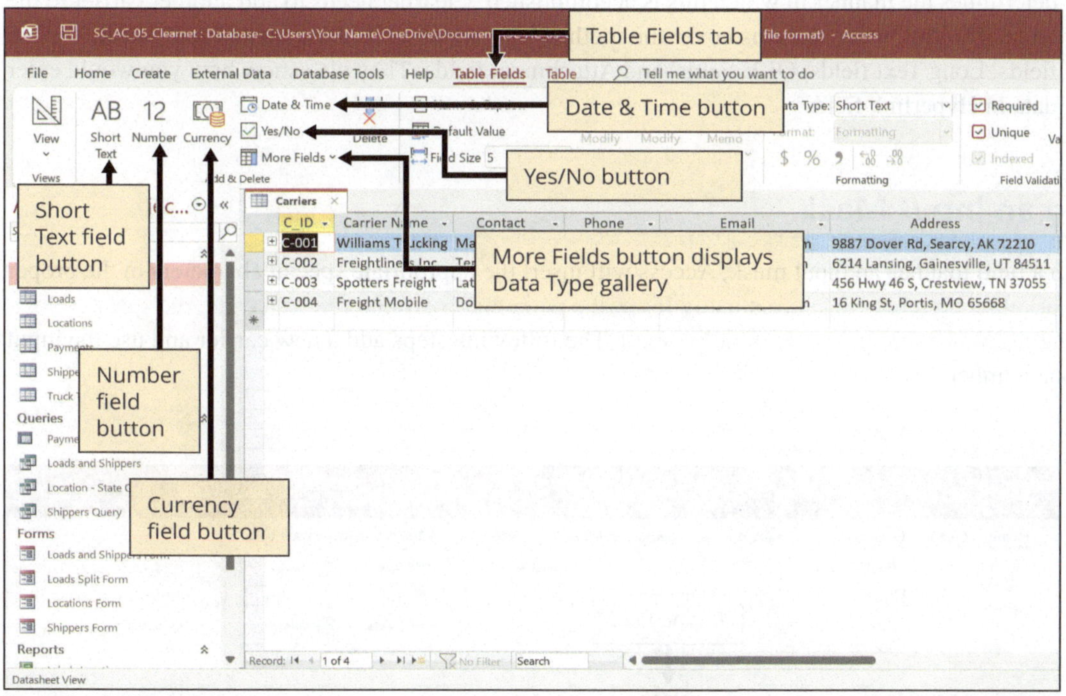

Figure 5–9

Consider This

How do you determine if fields need special data types or an input mask?

- **Determine whether an input mask is appropriate.** Sometimes the data in the field should be displayed in a special way, for example, with parentheses and a hyphen like a phone number, or separated into three groups of digits like a Social Security number. If so, should Access assist the user in entering the data in the right format? For example, by including an input mask in a field, Access can automatically insert the parentheses and a hyphen when a user enters phone number digits.

- **Determine whether the Yes/No data type is appropriate.** A field is a good candidate for the Yes/No data type if the only possible field values are Yes or No, True or False, or On or Off.
- **Determine whether the Long Text data type is appropriate.** A field that contains text that is variable in length and potentially very long is an appropriate use of the Long Text data type. If you want to use special text effects, such as bold and italic, you can assign the field the Long Text data type and change the value of the field's Text Format property from Plain Text to Rich Text. You can also collect history on the changes to a Long Text field by changing the value of the field's Append Only property from No to Yes. If you do so, when you right-click the field and click Show Column History on the shortcut menu, you will see a record of all changes made to the field.
- **Determine whether the Attachment data type or the OLE Object data type is appropriate for an image, such as a photo or artwork.** Does the field contain an image? Does it contain an object created by other applications that support **OLE (Object Linking and Embedding)**? Is your storage space limited? If storage space is limited, you should use the Attachment data type.
- **Determine whether the Attachment data type is appropriate for documents.** Will the field contain one or more attachments that were created in other applications? If so, the Attachment data type is appropriate. It allows you to store multiple attachments on each record. You can view and manipulate these attachments in their original application.
- **Determine whether the Hyperlink data type is appropriate.** A field with the hyperlink data type contains a hyperlink, that is, a link to another location such as a webpage or a file. Will the field contain an email address, links to other Office documents, or links to webpages? If so, Hyperlink is appropriate.

Updating the New Fields

After adding the new fields to the table, the next task is to enter data into the fields. The data type determines the manner in which this is accomplished. Clearnet needs to add another carrier to the table. The following sections cover the methods for updating fields with an input mask, Yes/No fields, Long Text fields, OLE fields, and Attachment fields. They also show how you would enter data in Hyperlink fields.

To Enter Data Using an Input Mask

When you are entering data in a field that has an input mask, Access will insert the appropriate special characters in the proper positions. **Why?** The input mask directs Access to automatically insert the parentheses around the area code, the space following the second parenthesis, and the hyphen in the Phone Number field. The following steps add a new carrier and use the input mask to add the carrier's phone number.

1

- Change the Carriers table to Datasheet view, and close the Navigation Pane.
- Click on the first blank row in the C_ID field and type **C-005**.
- Press TAB to move to the next field. Enter **Truck-n-Go Inc.** for the Carrier Name and **Filipa Martinez** for the Contact.
- Press TAB to move to the beginning of the Phone field on the new record and display an insertion point in the field (Figure 5–10).

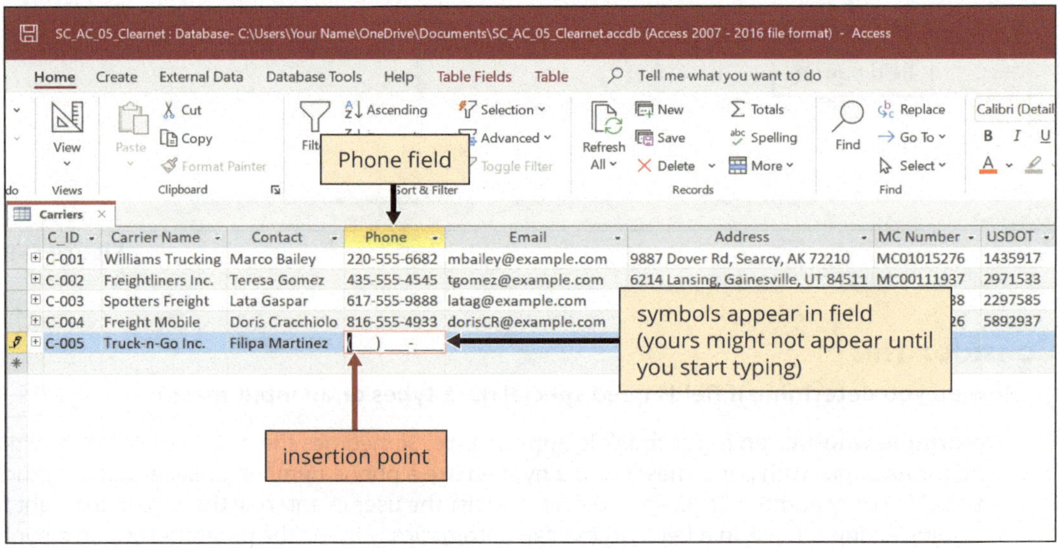

Figure 5–10

Q&A Do I need to click at the beginning of the field for the phone numbers?

Yes. If you do not, the data will not be entered correctly.

I do not see the parentheses and hyphen as shown in the figure. Did I do something wrong?

You might not see the symbols upon entering the field. Regardless, as soon as you start typing in the field, the symbols should appear.

2

- Type **8165552442** as the phone number (Figure 5–11).

BTW

Input Mask on New Records

When you place an input mask on a field with existing data, only new records added from this point on will adhere to that input mask.

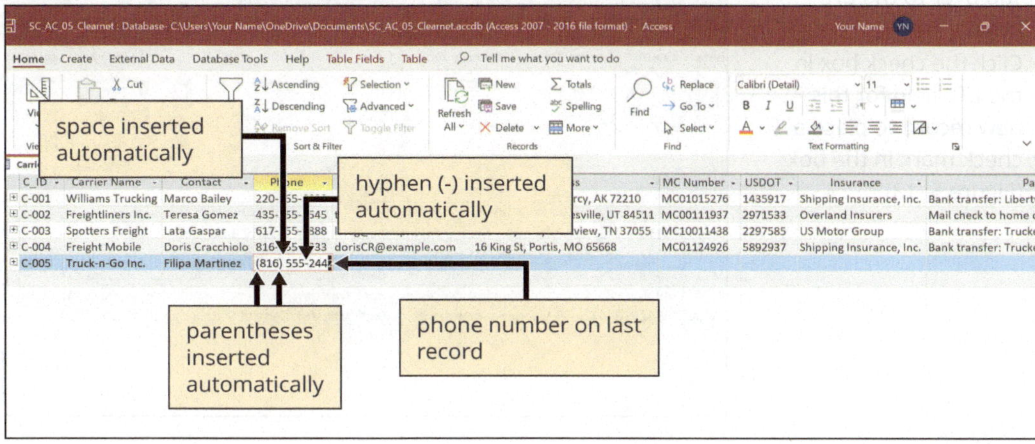

Figure 5–11

3

- Using TAB, enter the information provided in Table 5–1 for the next several fields (Figure 5–12).

Table 5–1 Data for New Record in Carriers Table

Field Name	Data
Email	**filipam@example.com**
Address	**Rt 59, Box 8822, Empire, MO 63044**
MC Number	**MC00102942**
USDOT	**3448229**
Insurance	**Overland Insurers**
Payment Instructions	**Bank transfer: Central State, account #2283-573-14**
Drivers	**Erika**

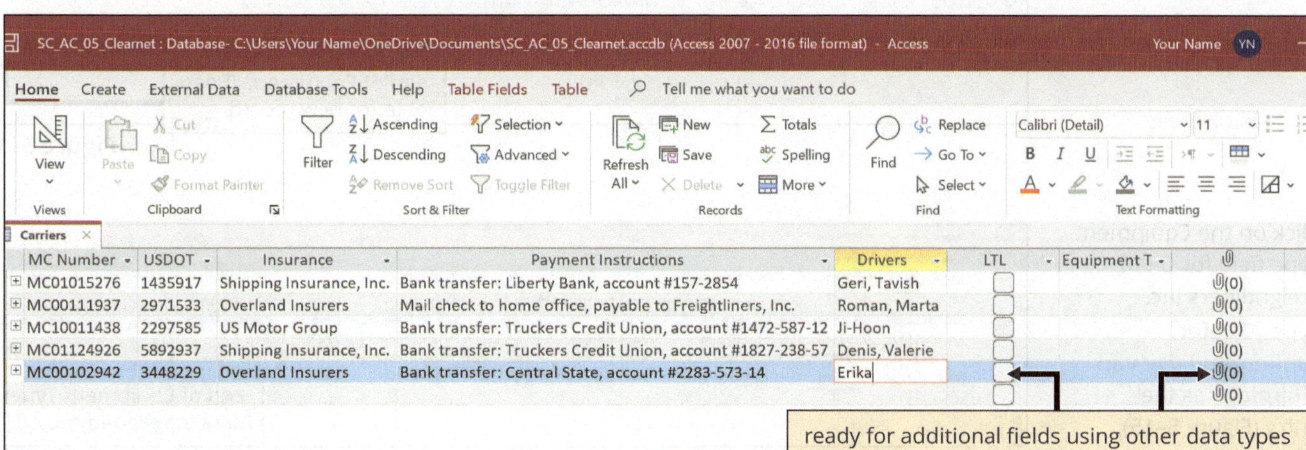

Figure 5–12

To Enter Data in Yes/No Fields

Fields that are Yes/No fields contain check boxes. To set the value to Yes, place a check mark in the check box. **Why?** A check mark indicates the value is Yes, or True. To set a value to No (False), leave the check box blank. The following step sets the value of the LTL field, a Yes/No field, to Yes for the new carrier. The other carriers do not accept LTL loads.

1

- Tab over to the LTL field.
- Click the check box in the LTL field for this new record to place a check mark in the box (Figure 5–13).

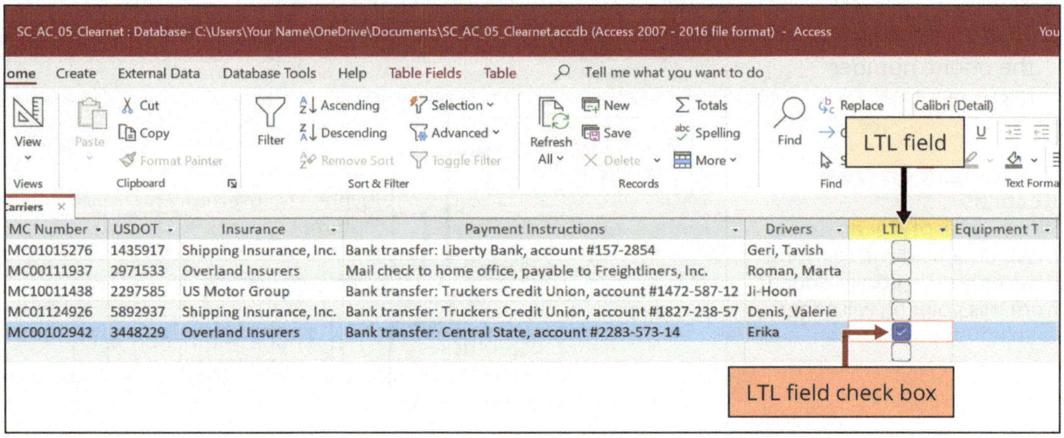

Figure 5–13

To Enter Data in Long Text Fields

To update a long text field, simply type the data in the field. You will later change the spacing to allow more room for the text. **Why?** With the current row and column spacing on the screen, only a small portion of the text will appear. The following steps enter the new carrier's available equipment types and similar information for another carrier.

1

- Press TAB to move to the Equipment Type field.
- For the new record, type **Container, reefer, and dry van shipping** as the entry (Figure 5–14), and press TAB. Recall that in shipping, reefer means refrigerated.

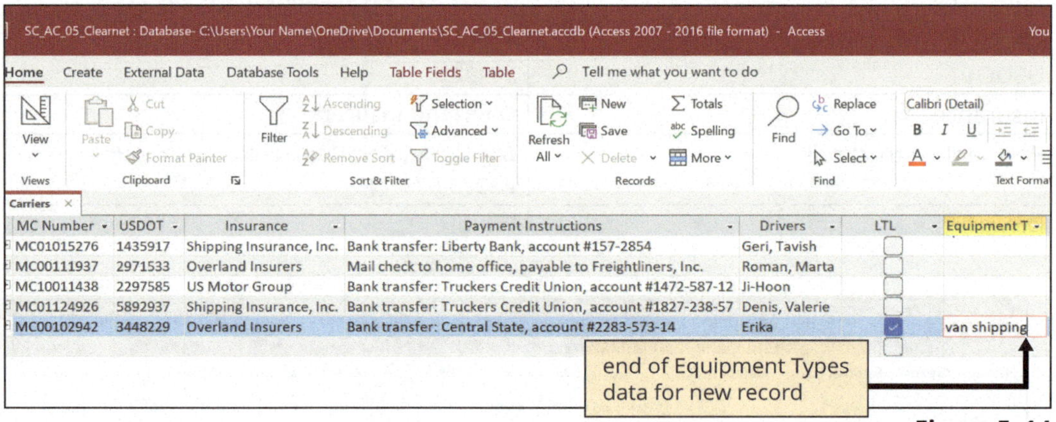

Figure 5–14

2

- Click on the Equipment Type field for C-002, Freightliners Inc.
- Type **Reefer, tanker, and dry van shipping** as the entry (Figure 5–15), and press TAB.

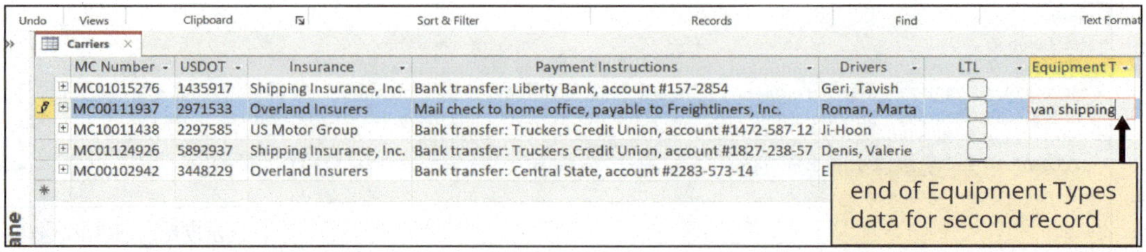

Figure 5–15

To Change the Row and Column Size

Only a small portion of the Equipment Type data appears in the datasheet. To allow more of the information to appear, you can expand the size of the rows and the columns. You can change the size of a column by using the field selector. The **field selector** is the bar containing the field name. To change the size of a row, you use a record's record selector.

The following steps resize the column containing the Equipment Type field, the reformatted Phone field, and the rows of the table. **Why?** Resizing the columns and the rows allows all data in these fields to appear.

1

- Double-click the right border of the Phone field's selector when you see the resize arrow, to autofit the column width (Figure 5–16).

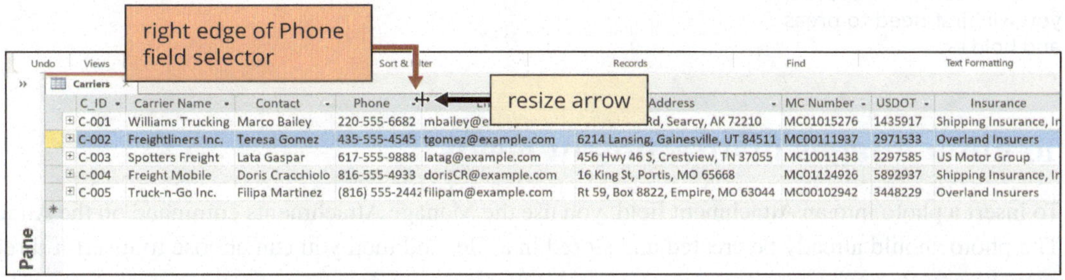

Figure 5–16

2

- Scroll a little past the Equipment Type field, and then drag the right edge of the field selector for the Equipment Type field to the right to resize the column to the approximate size shown in Figure 5–17.

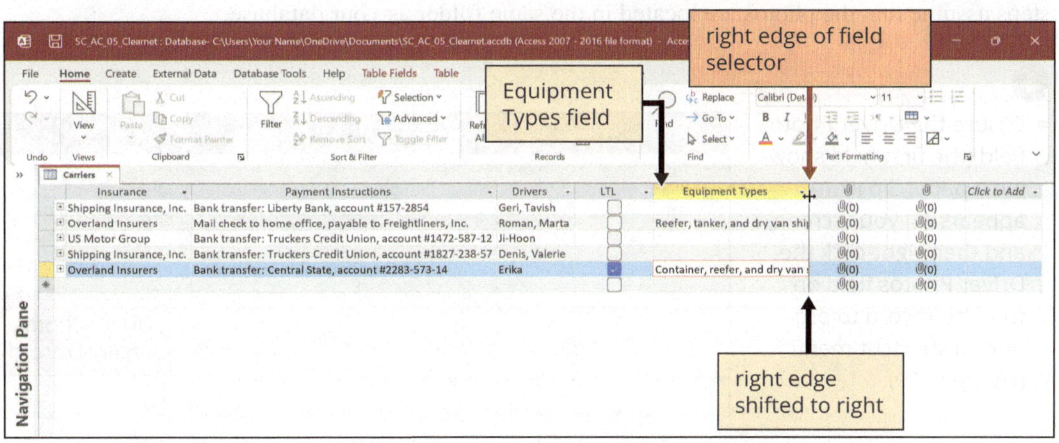

Figure 5–17

3

- Drag the lower edge of any record selector to approximately the position shown in Figure 5–18.

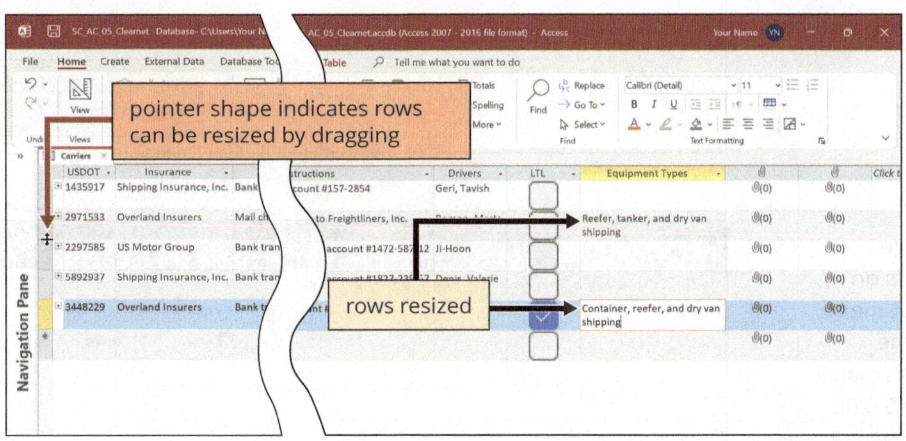

Figure 5–18

Q&A Can rows be different sizes?

No. Access formats all rows in a table to be the same size.

Other Ways

1. Right-click record selector, click Row Height to change row spacing
2. Right-click field selector, click Field Width to change column size

BTW

Entering Data in Long Text Fields

You also can enter data in a long text field using the Zoom dialog box. To do so, click the long text field and then press SHIFT+F2 to open the Zoom dialog box. Note that, on some keyboards, you will first need to press and hold FN.

Undoing Changes to Row Height and Column Width

If you later find that the changes you made to the row height or the column width are no longer appropriate, you can undo them. To undo changes to the row height, right-click the row selector, click Row Height on the shortcut menu, and then click the Standard Height check box (Row Height dialog box). To undo changes to the column width, right-click the field selector, click Field Width on the shortcut menu, and then click the Standard Width check box (Column Width dialog box).

To Enter Images in Attachment Fields

To insert a photo into an Attachment field, you use the Manage Attachments command on the Attachment field's shortcut menu. The photo should already be created and stored in a file, and then you can choose to insert it directly from the file. **Why?** The Manage Attachments command makes it easy to attach a photo to a field rather than using an OLE object field. The OLE object field requires Access to open a compatible application before you can view the photo.

The following steps insert photos into the Driver Photos field. The photos will appear as paper clips in the datasheet. The steps assume that the photos are located in the same folder as your database.

1

- Ensure the Driver Photos field (the first field showing a paperclip icon) appears on your screen, and then right-click the Driver Photos field on the fifth record to produce a shortcut menu (Figure 5–19).

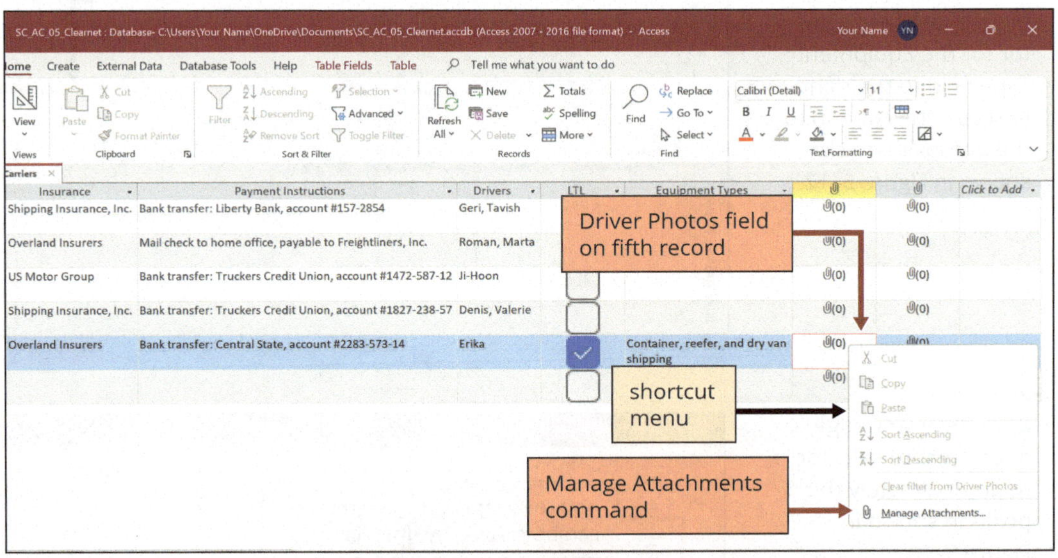

Figure 5–19

2

- Click Manage Attachments on the shortcut menu to display the Attachments dialog box (Figure 5–20).

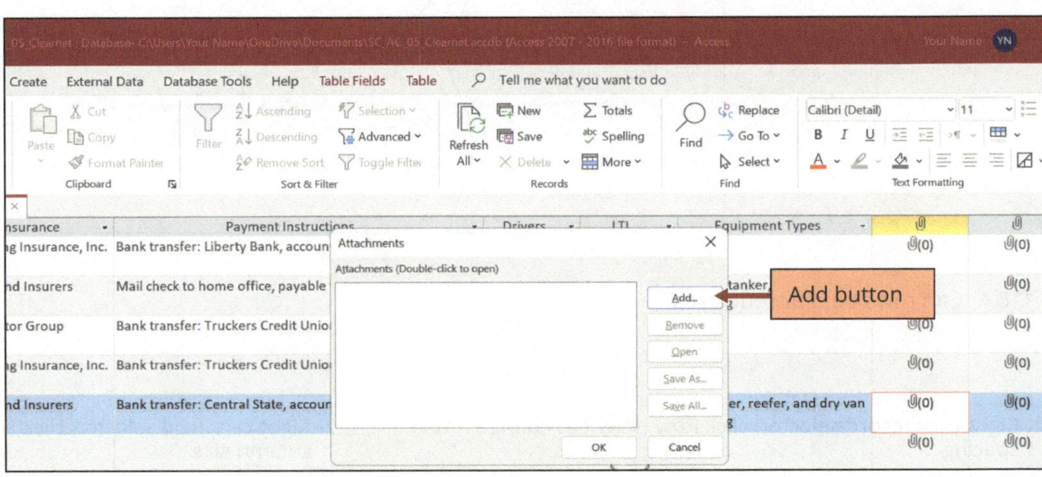

Figure 5–20

3

- Click the Add button.

Q&A Unlike the figure, my window is maximized. Does that make a difference?
No. The same steps will work in either case.

- Navigate to the photo file for Erika, Support_AC_05_Erika.jpg, click to select it, and then click Open (Figure 5–21).

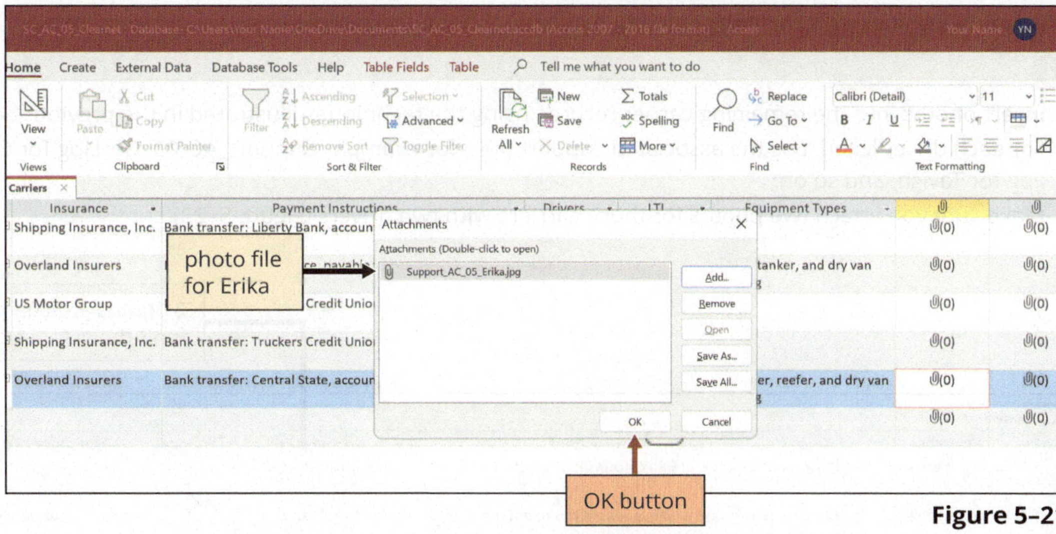

Figure 5–21

4

- Click the OK button to attach the photo (Figure 5–22).

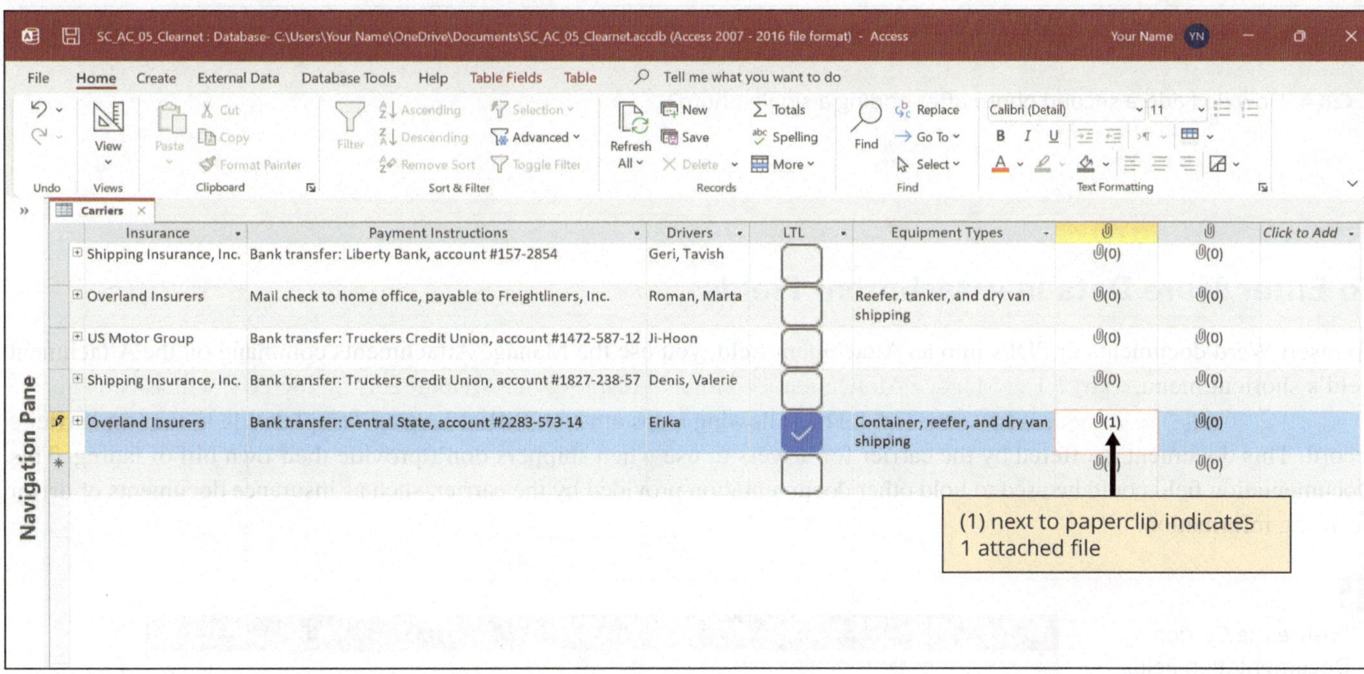

Figure 5–22

Q&A I do not see the photo. I just see the paper clip. Is that correct?
Yes. You will see the actual photo when you use this field in a form.

To Insert the Remaining Photos

The following step adds the remaining photos to the other Carrier records.

1

- Insert photos into the remaining carrier records using the techniques illustrated in the previous set of steps.
- For each driver listed, use the associated support file—for example, Support_AC_05_Geri.jpg for Geri, Support_AC_05_Tavish .jpg for Tavish, and so on.
- Make sure you attach two photos for those carriers with two drivers (Figure 5–23).

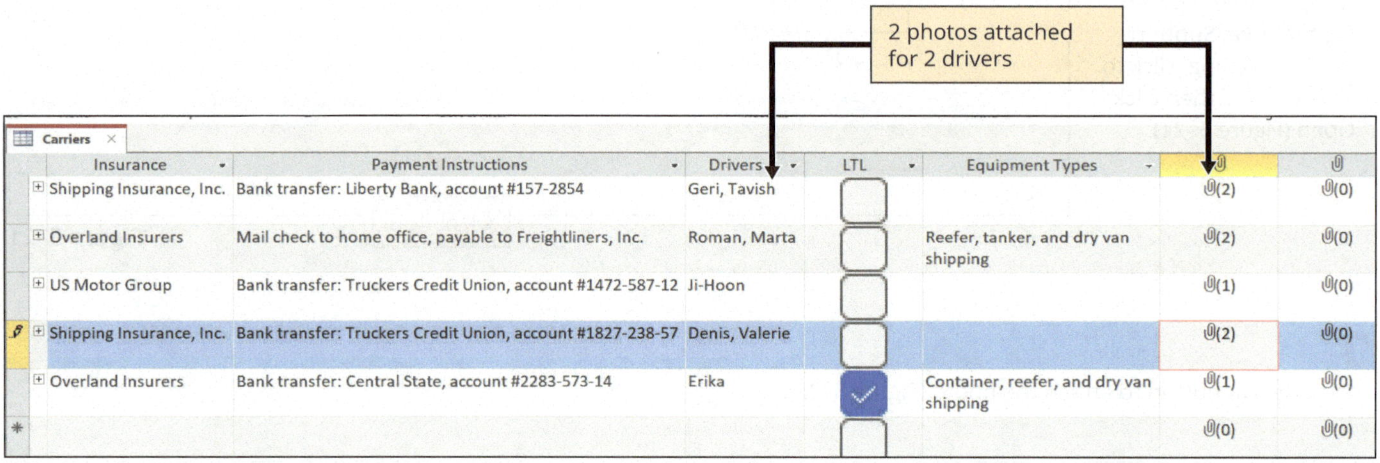

Figure 5–23

Q&A How do I add a second photo after adding a single photo?

Before closing the Attachments dialog box for that record, click the Add button again. Choose the second photo, and then click the Open button (Choose File dialog box). After the second photo is added, click the OK button (Attachments dialog box).

To Enter More Data in Attachment Fields

To insert Word documents or PDFs into an Attachment field, you use the Manage Attachments command on the Attachment field's shortcut menu. **Why?** The Manage Attachments command displays the Attachments dialog box, which you can use to attach as many files as necessary to the field. The following steps attach a Bill of Lading Template file to the last carrier's record. This document is offered by the carrier for drivers to use when shippers don't provide their own bill of lading. This Documentation field could be used to hold other documentation provided by the carrier, such as insurance documents or driver licensing information.

1

- Ensure the Carrier Documentation field, the second field that displays a paper clip in the field selector, appears on your screen, and then right-click the Carrier Documentation field on the fifth carrier record to produce a shortcut menu (Figure 5–24).

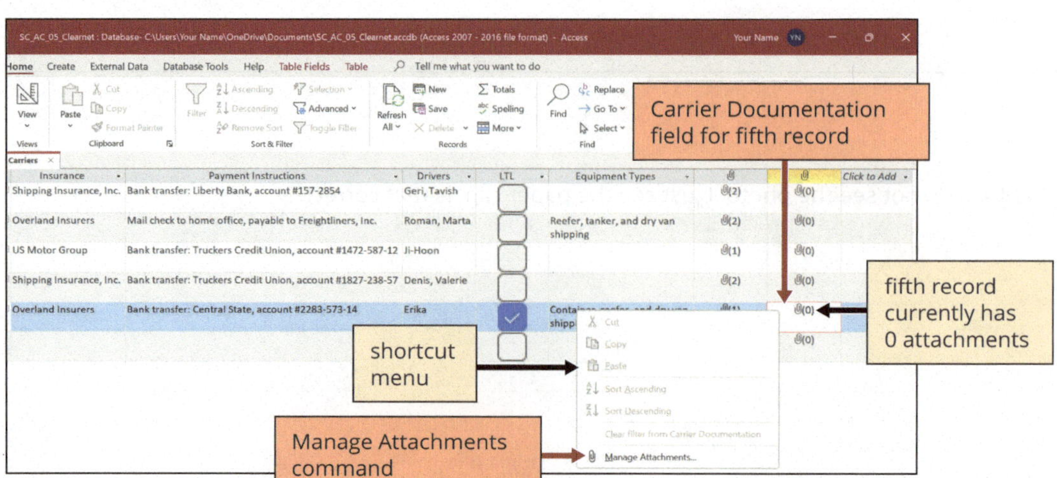

Figure 5–24

2

- Click Manage Attachments on the shortcut menu to display the Attachments dialog box (Figure 5–25).

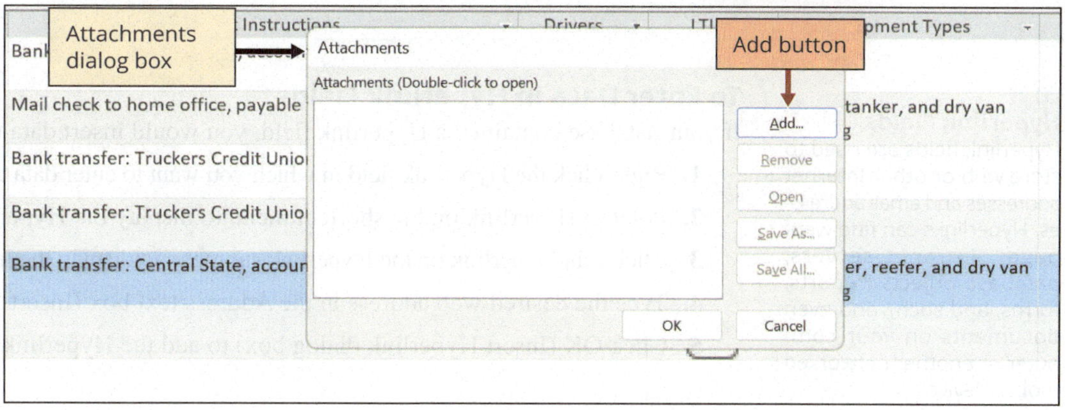

Figure 5–25

3

- Click Add (Attachments dialog box) to display the Choose File dialog box, where you can add an attachment.
- Navigate to the location containing your attachment files.
- Click Support_AC_05_Bill-of-Lading-Template.docx, which is a Word file, and then click the Open button (Choose File dialog box) to attach the file (Figure 5–26).

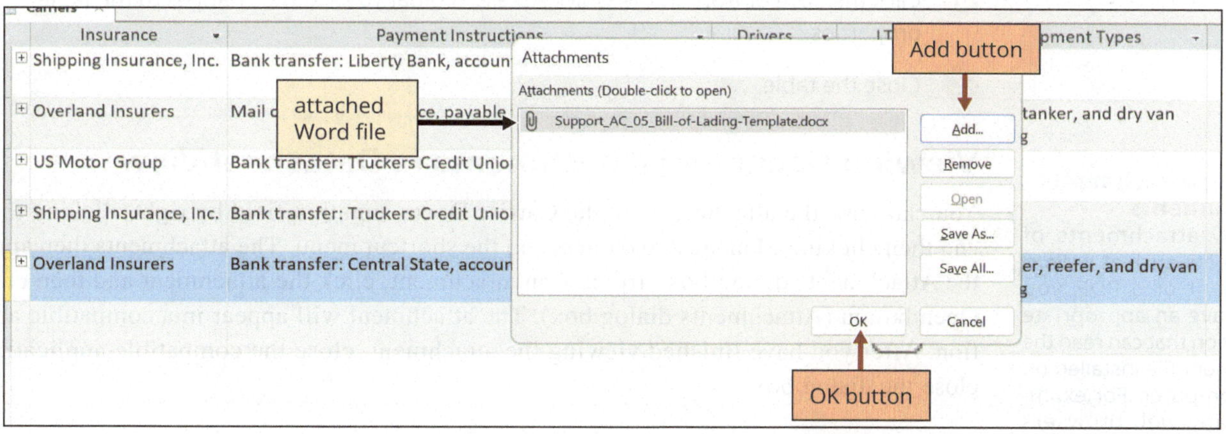

Figure 5–26

4

- Click OK (Attachments dialog box) to close the Attachments dialog box (Figure 5–27). The other carriers have no new attachments at this time.

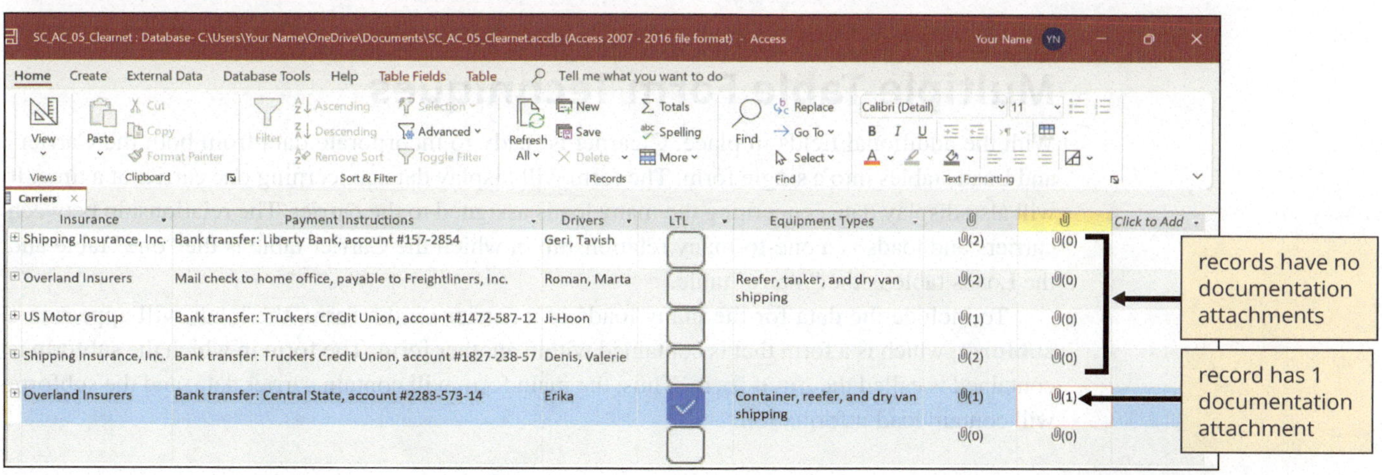

Figure 5–27

Q&A If I had more than one document to add to a load's record, could I attach multiple files in this one Attachment field?
Yes, you can attach multiple files to a single Attachment field.

BTW
Hyperlink Fields
Hyperlink fields are used to store web or other Internet addresses and email addresses. Hyperlinks can find webpages, intranet servers, database objects (reports, forms, and such), and even documents on your computer or another networked mobile device.

To Enter Data in Hyperlink Fields

If your database contained a Hyperlink field, you would insert data using the following steps.

1. Right-click the Hyperlink field in which you want to enter data to display a shortcut menu.
2. Point to Hyperlink on the shortcut menu to display the Hyperlink submenu.
3. Click Edit Hyperlink on the Hyperlink submenu to display the Insert Hyperlink dialog box.
4. Type the desired web address in the Address text box (Insert Hyperlink dialog box).
5. Click OK (Insert Hyperlink dialog box) to add the Hyperlink.

To Save the Properties

The row and column spacing are table properties. When changing any table properties, the changes apply only as long as the table is active *unless they are saved*. Once you have saved them, they will apply every time you open the table.

The following steps first save the properties and then close the table.

1. Click the Save button on the Quick Access Toolbar to save the changes to the table properties.
2. Close the table.

BTW
Viewing Attachments of Documents
To view attachments of documents, such as a Word document or a PDF, you must have an appropriate application that can read the attachment file installed on your computer. For example, many web browsers can open and read PDF files.

Viewing Document Attachments in Datasheet View

You can view the attachments in the Carrier Documentation field by right-clicking the field and then clicking Manage Attachments on the shortcut menu. The attachments then appear in the Attachments dialog box. To view an attachment, click the attachment and then click the Open button (Attachments dialog box). The attachment will appear in a compatible application. After you have finished viewing the attachment, close the compatible application and close the dialog box.

Break Point: If you wish to take a break, this is a good place to do so. You can quit Access now. To resume at a later time, start Access, open the database called SC_AC_05_Clearnet.accdb, and continue following the steps from this location forward.

Multiple-Table Form Techniques

With the additional fields in place, Clearnet is ready to incorporate data from both the Carriers and Loads tables into a single form. The form will display data concerning one carrier at a time. It will also display data concerning the many loads assigned to the carrier. The relationship between carriers and loads is a one-to-many relationship in which the Carrier table is the "one" table and the Loads table is the "many" table.

To include the data for the many loads of a carrier on the form, the loads will appear in a **subform**, which is a form that is contained within another form. The form in which the subform is contained is called the **main form**. Thus, the main form will contain carrier data, and the subform will contain load information.

Consider This

When a form includes data from multiple tables, how do you relate the tables?
Once you determine that you need data from more than one table, you need to determine the main table and its relationship to any other table.

- **Determine the main table the form is intended to view and/or update.** You need to identify the purpose of the form and the table it is mainly intended to show, which is the *main* table.
- **Determine how the additional table should fit into the form.** If the additional table is the "many" part of the relationship, the data should probably be in a subform or datasheet. If the additional table is the "one" part of the relationship, the data should probably simply appear as fields on the form.

To Create a Form in Design View

You can create a form in Design view. **Why?** Design view gives you increased flexibility in laying out a form by using a blank design on which you place objects in the precise locations you want. The following steps create a form in Design view.

1

- Open the Navigation Pane and be sure the Carriers table is selected.
- Click Create on the ribbon to display the Create tab (Figure 5–28).

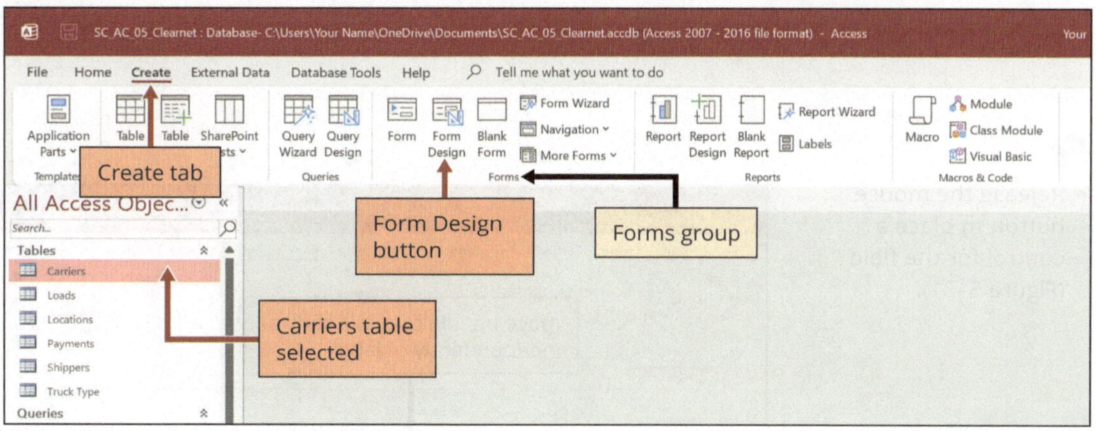

Figure 5–28

2

- Click the Form Design button (Create tab | Forms group) to create a new form in Design view.
- Close the Navigation Pane.
- If necessary, click the 'Add Existing Fields' button (Form Design tab | Tools group) to display the Field List pane (Figure 5–29). If you do not see the tables listed, click 'Show all tables'. (Your list might show all fields in the Carriers table.)

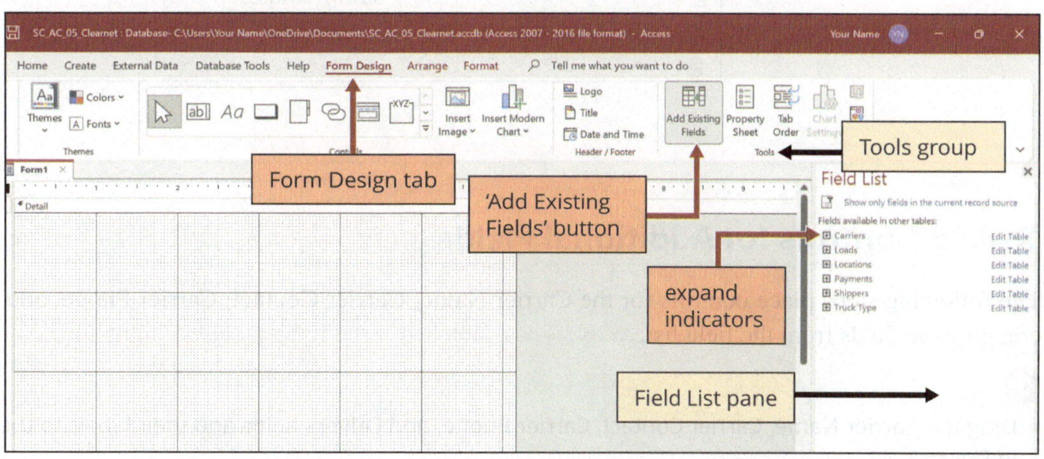

Figure 5–29

To Add a Control for a Field to the Form

To place a control for a field on a form, drag the field from the field list to the desired position. The following steps place the Carrier ID field on the form. **Why?** Dragging is the easiest way to place a field on a form.

1

- If necessary, click the expand indicator for the Carriers table to display the fields in the table. Drag the Carrier ID field in the field list for the Carriers table to the approximate position shown in Figure 5–30.

Q&A Do I have to be exact?
No. Just be sure you are in the same general location.

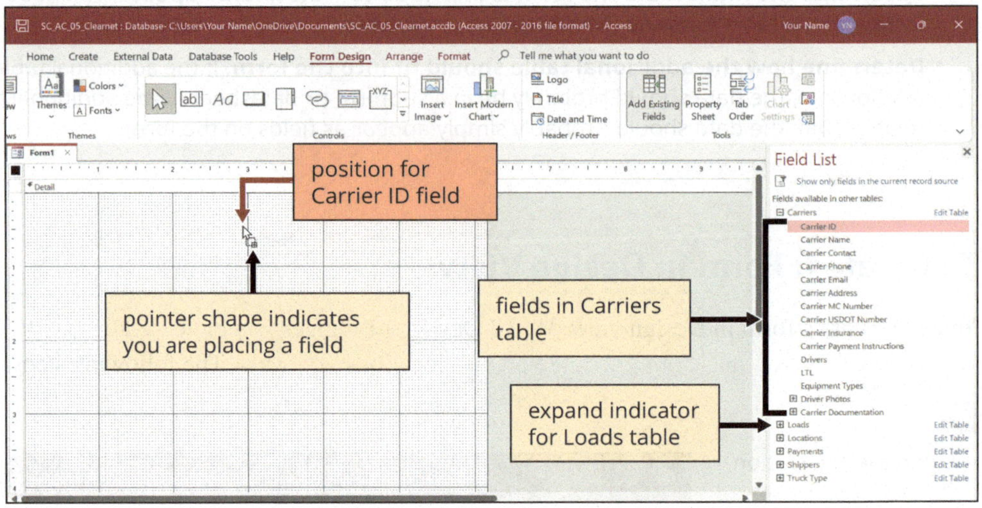

Figure 5–30

2

- Release the mouse button to place a control for the field (Figure 5–31).

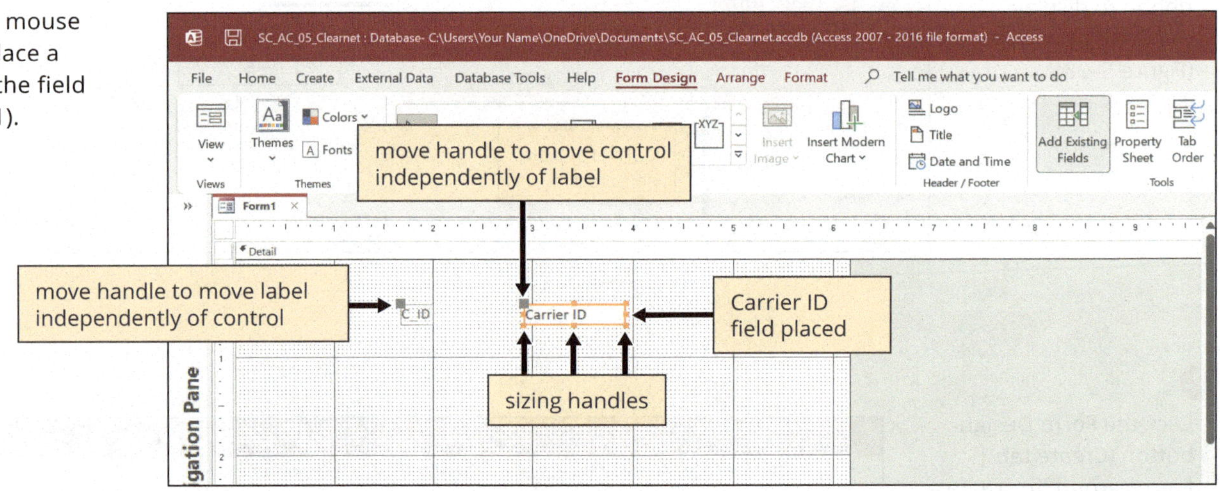

Figure 5–31

To Add Controls for Additional Fields

The following steps place controls for the Carrier Name, Carrier Contact, Carrier Phone, and Drivers fields on the form by dragging the fields from the field list. **Why?** These fields all need to be included in the form.

1

- Drag the Carrier Name, Carrier Contact, Carrier Phone, and Drivers fields and their labels to the approximate positions shown in Figure 5–32.

Q&A Do I have to align them precisely?
You can, but you do not need to. In the next steps, you will instruct Access to align the fields properly.

What if I drag the wrong field from the field list? Can I delete the control?
Yes. With the control selected, press DEL.

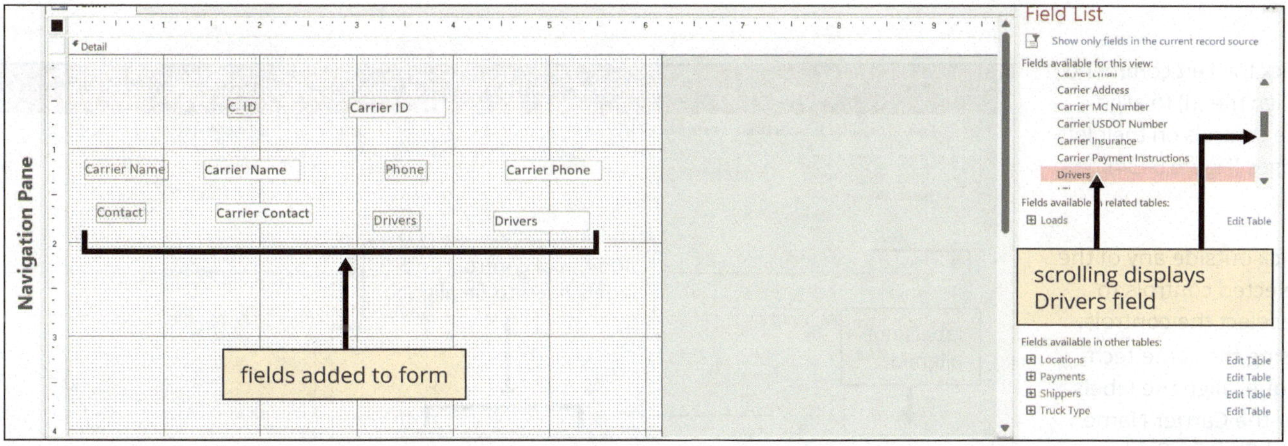

Figure 5–32

To Align Controls on the Left

To ensure that a group of controls is aligned properly with each other, select all the affected controls, and then use the appropriate alignment button on the Arrange tab. **Why?** Often, you will want form controls to be aligned in some fashion. For example, the controls might be aligned so their right edges are even with each other. In another case, controls might be aligned so their top edges are even.

You can use one of two methods to select multiple controls. One way is to use a ruler. If you click a position on the horizontal ruler, you will select all the controls for which a portion of the control is under that position on the ruler. Similarly, if you click a position on the vertical ruler, you will select all the controls for which a portion of the control is to the right of that position on the ruler.

The second way to select multiple controls is to select the first control by clicking it. Then, select all the other controls by holding down SHIFT while clicking each additional control.

The following steps select the Carrier Name, Carrier Contact, Carrier Phone, and Drivers controls and then align them so their left edges line up.

1

- Click the Carrier Name control (the one with the white box, not the label that shows the dotted background in the box) to select the control.
- Press and hold SHIFT and click the Carrier Contact control to select an additional control.

Q&A I selected the wrong collection of fields. How can I start over?

Simply begin the process again by clicking outside all controls to deselect fields, and then make sure you do not hold SHIFT down when you select the first field.

- Click Arrange on the ribbon to display the Arrange tab.
- Click the Align button (Arrange tab | Sizing & Ordering group) to display the Align menu (Figure 5–33).

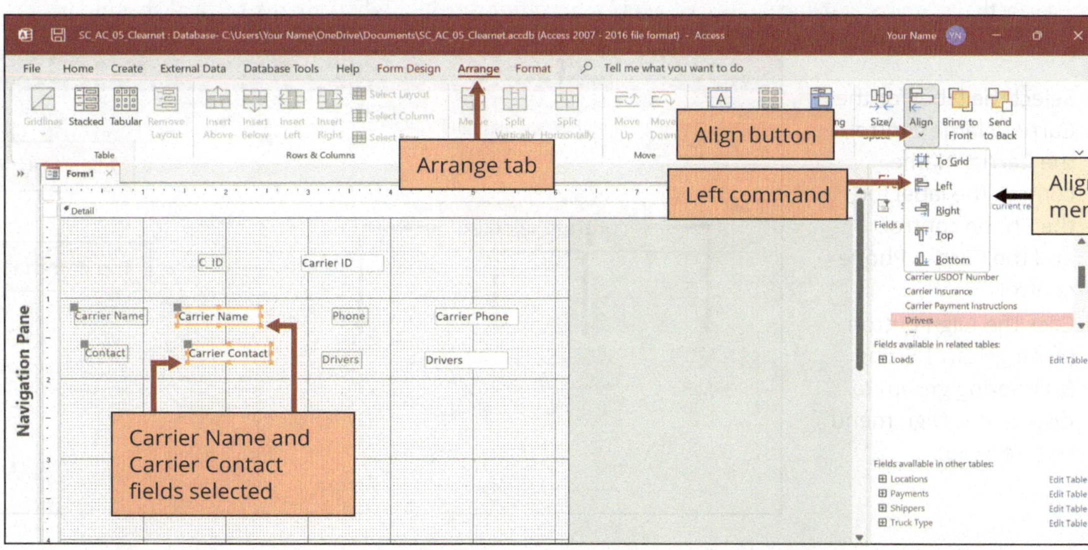

Figure 5–33

2

- Click the Left command (Align menu) to align the controls on their left edges (Figure 5–34).

3

- Click outside any of the selected controls to deselect the controls.
- Using the same technique, align the labels for the Carrier Name and Contact fields on their left edges.
- Using the same technique, align the Carrier Phone and Drivers fields on their left edges.
- Using the same technique, align the labels for the Phone and Drivers fields on their left edges.

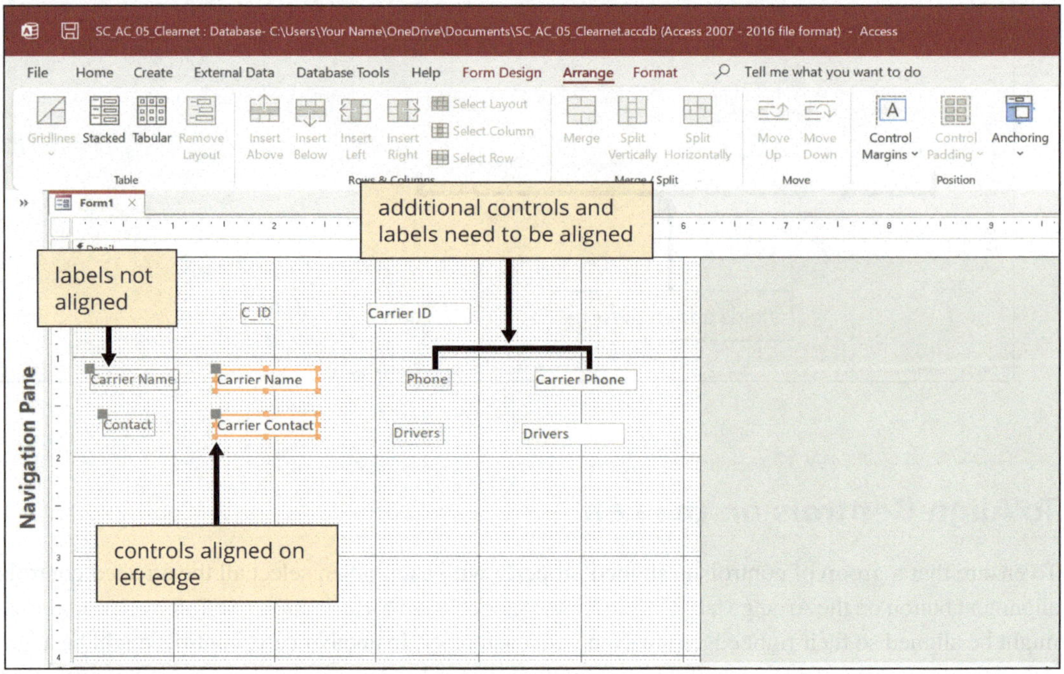

Figure 5–34

Q&A When I try to align the controls, some of them overlap others and aren't spaced out well. How can I fix this?
Before automatically aligning the controls, make sure they're spaced far enough apart that they will not overlap once they are aligned. You can also reposition each field control separately from its label control by using the gray move handle before performing the automatic alignment.

Other Ways

1. Right-click selected controls, point to Align, and choose an alignment to align controls

To Align Controls on the Top and Adjust Vertical Spacing

The following steps align each row of controls so they are aligned on their top edges. Once these controls are aligned, you adjust the vertical spacing so the same amount of space separates each row of controls. **Why?** Aligning the top edges of controls improves the neatness and appearance of a form. In addition, you might want the vertical spacing between controls to be the same.

1

- Select the label for the Carrier Name control, the Carrier Name control, the label for the Phone control, and the Carrier Phone control.
- Click the Align button (Arrange tab | Sizing & Ordering group) to display the Align menu (Figure 5–35).

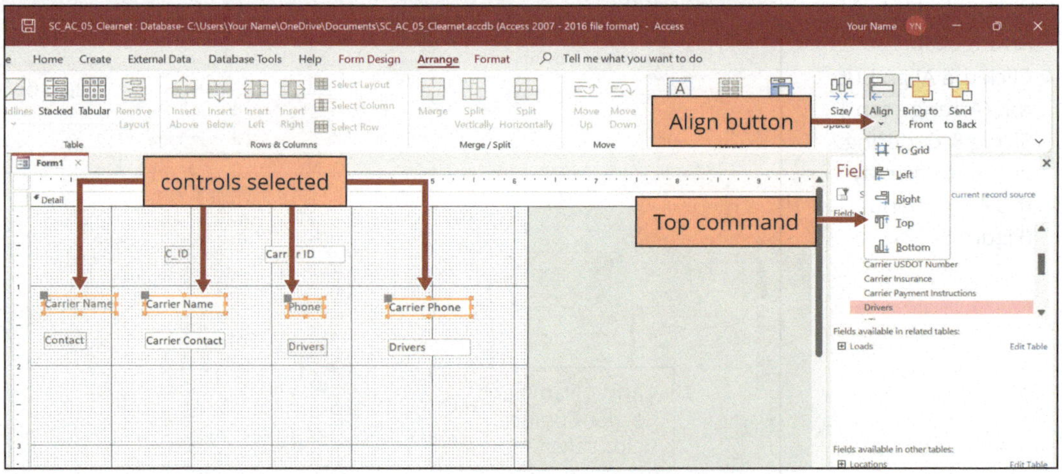

Figure 5–35

2

- Click the Top command on the Align menu to align the controls on the top.
- Select the Carrier Contact and Drivers fields and their labels, and then align the controls to the top.
- Click outside any of the selected controls to deselect the controls.
- Select the four fields, Carrier Name, Carrier Contact, Carrier Phone, and Drivers.
- Click the Size/Space button (Arrange tab | Sizing & Ordering group) to display the Size/Space menu (Figure 5–36).

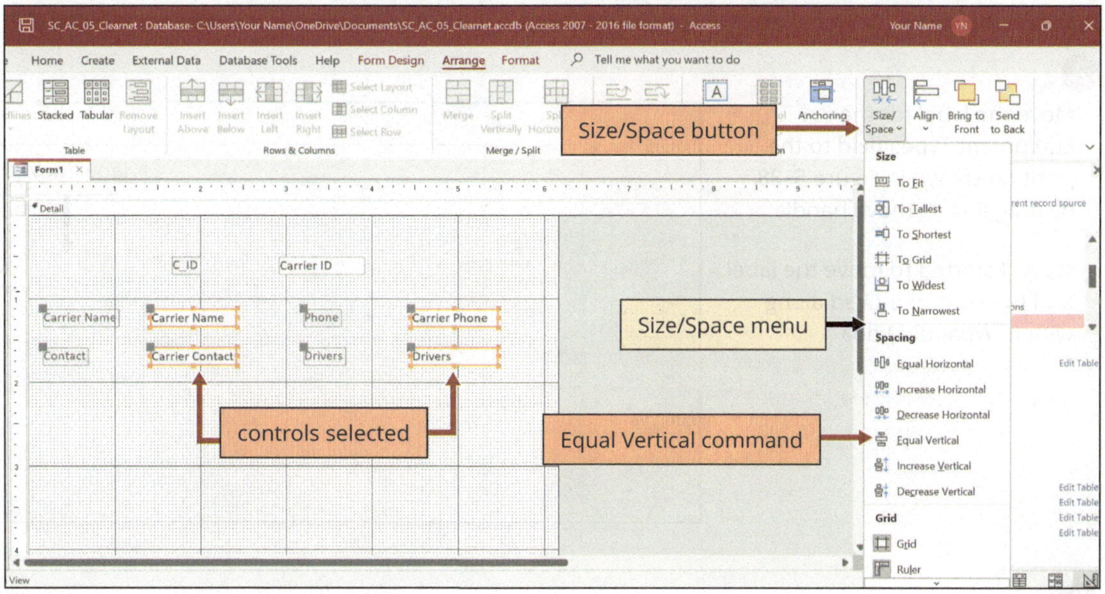

Figure 5–36

Q&A Do I need to select the labels too?

No. If you select the control and adjust its vertical spacing, its label's vertical position will also be adjusted.

3

- Click Equal Vertical (Size/Space menu) to specify the spacing.

Q&A What is the purpose of the other commands on the Size/Space menu?

You can adjust the spacing to fit the available space. You can adjust the space to match the tallest, shortest, widest, or narrowest section. You can adjust the space to match the closest grid points. You can specify equal horizontal spacing. Finally, you can increase or decrease either the vertical or the horizontal spacing.

- Click outside the controls to deselect the controls.
- Because it is a good idea to save the form before continuing, click the Save button on the Quick Access Toolbar.
- Type **Carrier Loads Form** as the name of the form, and then click OK to save the form.

To Add Controls for the Remaining Fields

The following steps place the attached labels and controls for the LTL, Equipment Types, Driver Photos, and Documentation fields in the desired positions. **Why?** Controls for these fields are to be included in the completed form.

1

- Drag the controls for the LTL and Equipment Types fields from the field list to the approximate positions shown in Figure 5–37.

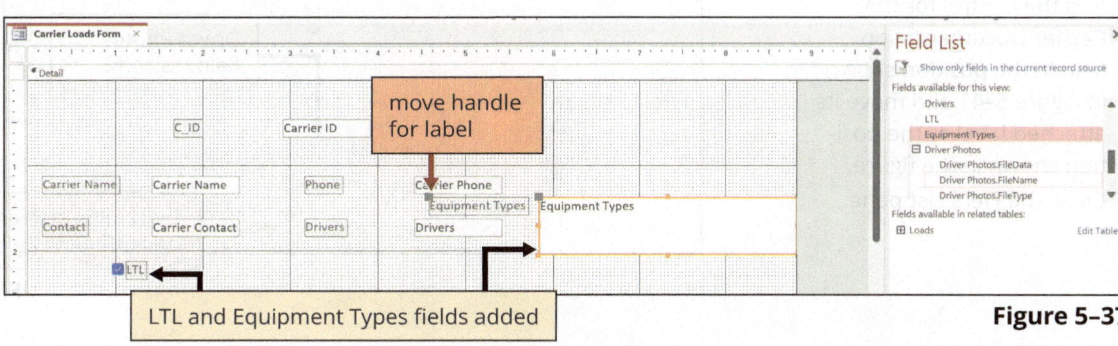

Figure 5–37

Q&A Is there enough space on the form to add the Equipment Types field?
Yes. The size of the form will expand as you drag the field to the form.

2

- Move the label for the Equipment Types field to the position shown in Figure 5–38 by dragging its move handle.

Q&A I started to move the label and the control moved along with it. What did I do?
You were not pointing at the handle to move the label independently of the control. Make sure you are pointing to the little box in the upper-left corner of the label.

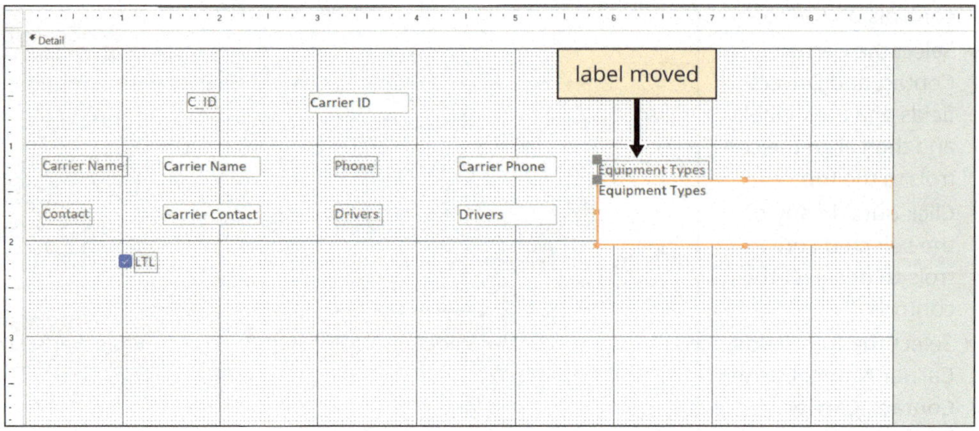

Figure 5–38

3

- Using the same techniques, add the control for the Driver Photos field to the approximate position shown in Figure 5–39, and move and resize its label to match the size and position shown in the figure.

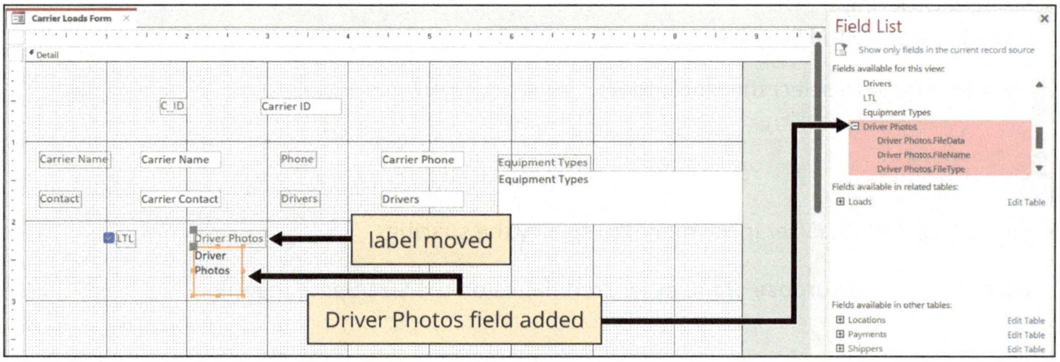

Figure 5–39

Q&A My Driver Photos label is next to the field, not above it as shown in the figure. Is that a problem?
You can use the move handle in the upper-left corner of the Driver Photos label to move it. Its position does not have to be precise. You will further rearrange the labels later in the module.

4

- Click the control for the Driver Photos field and drag the lower-right corner to the approximate position shown in Figure 5–40 to resize the control.
- Add the control for the Carrier Documentation field in the position shown in Figure 5–41 and move its attached label to the position shown in the figure.
- Close the Field List pane.

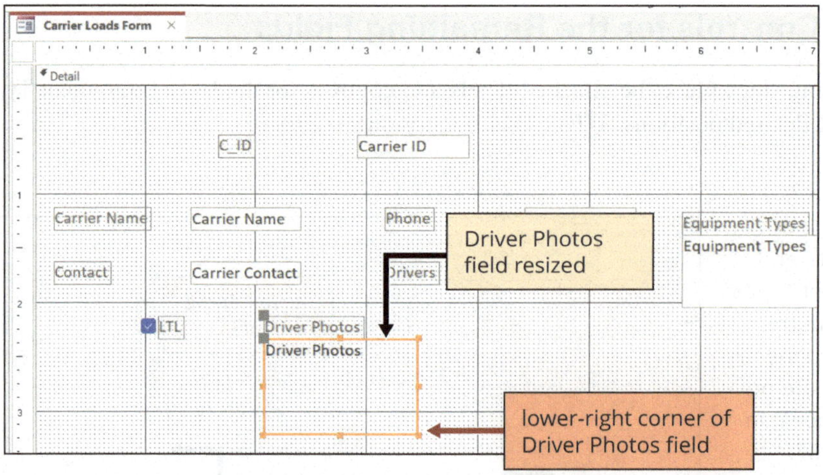

Figure 5–40

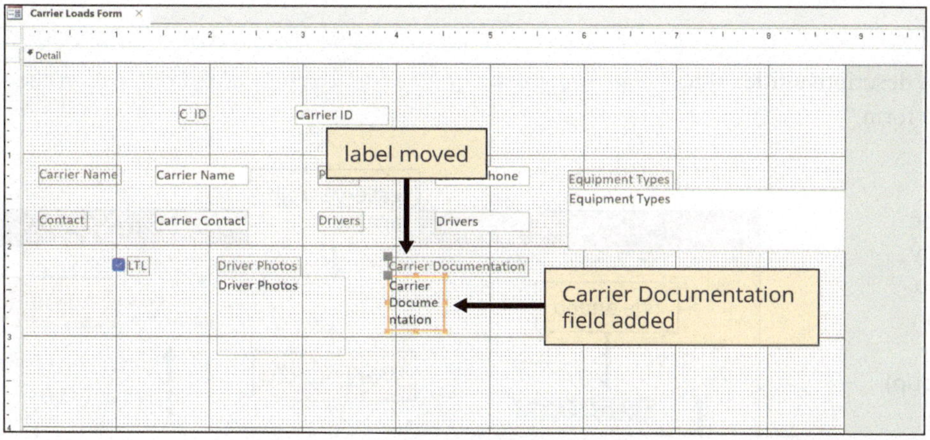

Figure 5–41

To Use a Shortcut Menu to Change the Fill/Back Color

You can use the Background Color button on the Format tab to change the background color of a form. You can also use a shortcut menu. The following steps use a shortcut menu to change the background color of the form to gray. **Why?** Using a shortcut menu is a simple way to change the background color.

1

- Right-click in the approximate position shown in Figure 5–42 to produce a shortcut menu.

Q&A Does it matter where I right-click?

You can right-click anywhere on the form as long as your pointer is not on or inside any controls.

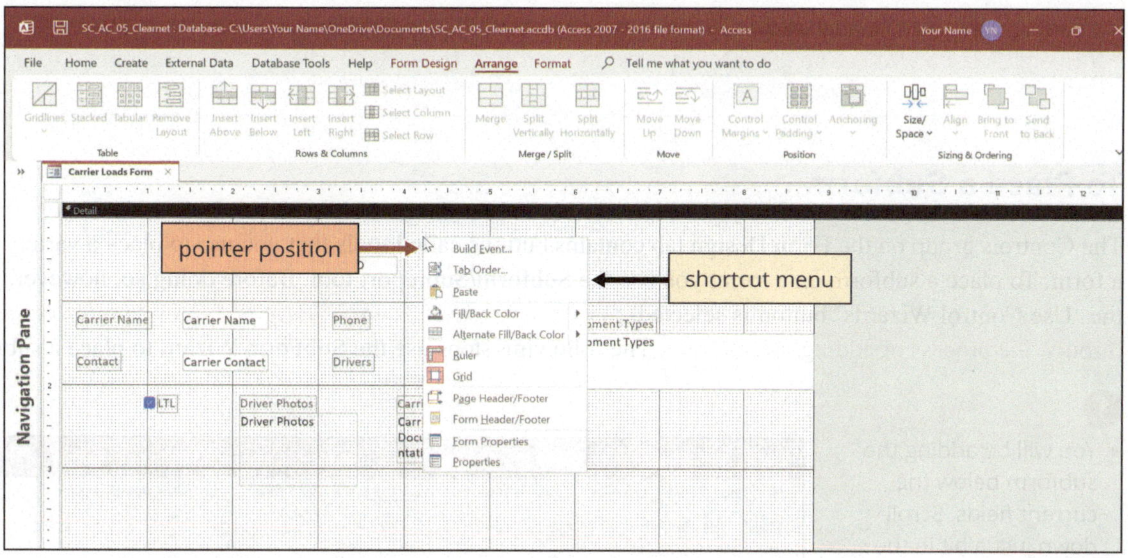

Figure 5–42

2

- Point to the Fill/Back Color arrow on the shortcut menu to display a color palette (Figure 5–43).

3

- Click the light gray color (row 2, column 1) shown in Figure 5–43 to change the fill/back color to light gray.

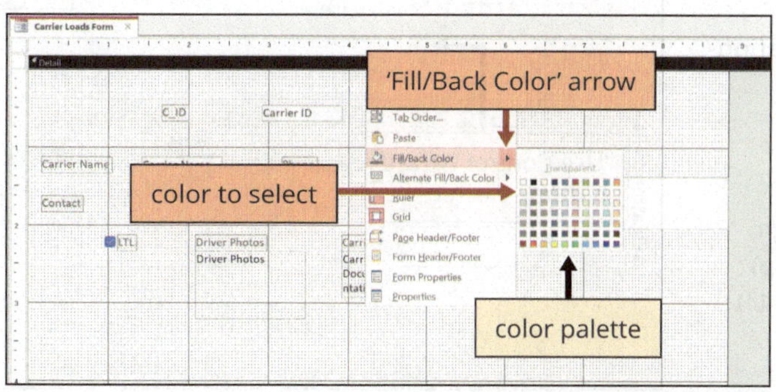

Figure 5–43

To Add a Title

A form should have a descriptive title. **Why?** The title gives a concise description of the purpose of the form. The following step adds a title to the form.

1

- Click Form Design on the ribbon to display the Form Design tab.
- Click the Title button (Form Design tab | Header / Footer group) to add a title to the form (Figure 5–44).

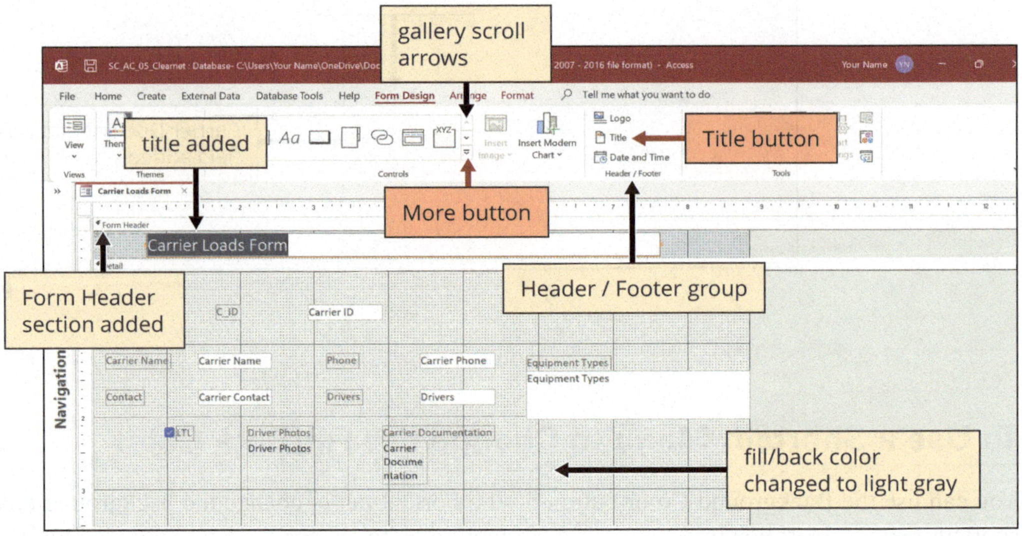

Figure 5–44

Q&A Can I change this title if I want something different?

Yes. You can change it as you would any other text. For the purposes of this project, however, you will leave the title as it is.

Why is there a new section?

The form title belongs in the Form Header section. When you clicked the Title button, Access added the Form Header section automatically and placed the title control in it.

Could I add a Form Header section without having to click the Title button?

Yes. Right-click anywhere on the form background and click Form Header/Footer on the shortcut menu.

To Place a Subform

The Controls group on the Form Design tab contains buttons called tools that you use to place a variety of types of controls on a form. To place a subform on a form, you use the Subform/Subreport tool. Before doing so, however, you should ensure that the 'Use Control Wizards' button is selected. **Why?** If the 'Use Control Wizards' button is selected, a wizard will guide you through the process of adding the subform. The following steps use the SubForm Wizard to place a subform.

1

- You will be adding the subform below the current fields. Scroll down just a bit in the form so you have space below the Driver Photos and Carrier Documentation controls.

2

- Click the More button (Form Design tab | Controls group) (shown in Figure 5–44) to display a gallery of available tools (Figure 5–45).

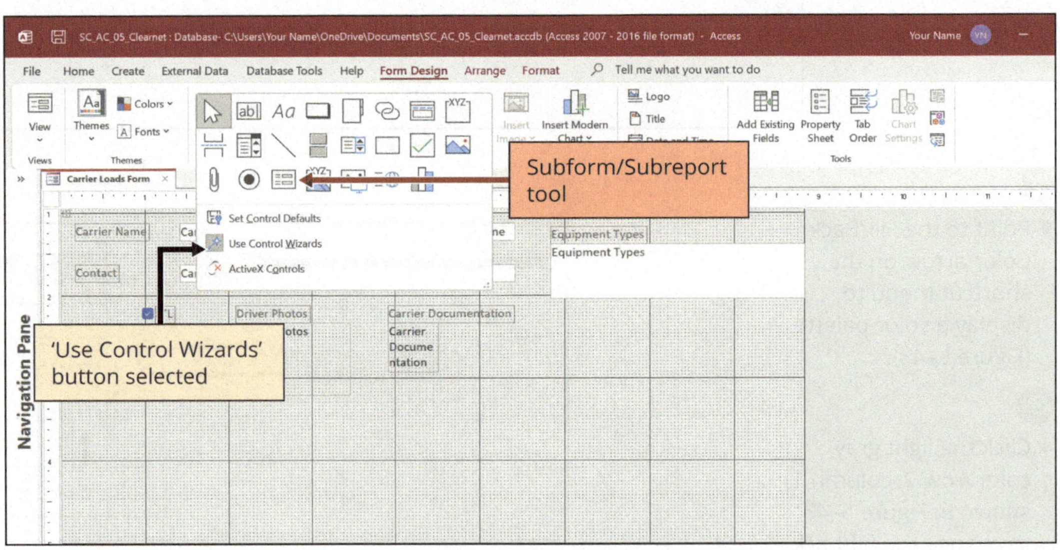

Figure 5–45

3

- Be sure the 'Use Control Wizards' button is selected, click the Subform/ Subreport tool on the Form Design tab, and then move the pointer to the approximate position shown in Figure 5–46.

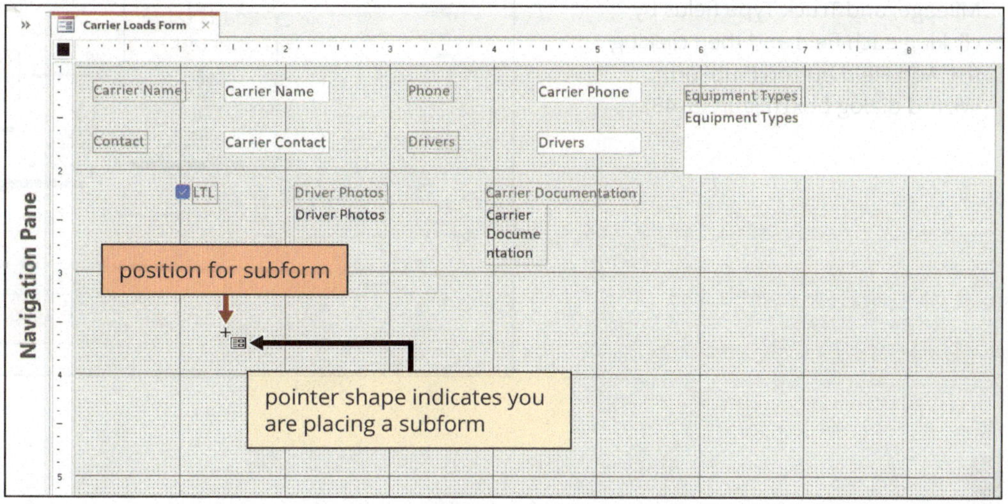

Figure 5–46

Q&A How can I tell whether the 'Use Control Wizards' button is selected?
The icon for the 'Use Control Wizards' button will be highlighted, as shown in Figure 5–45. If it is not, click the 'Use Control Wizards' button to select it, and then click the More button again and click the Subform/Subreport tool.

4

- Click the position shown in Figure 5–46 to place the subform and open the SubForm Wizard.
- Ensure the 'Use existing Tables and Queries' option button is selected (SubForm Wizard dialog box) (Figure 5–47).

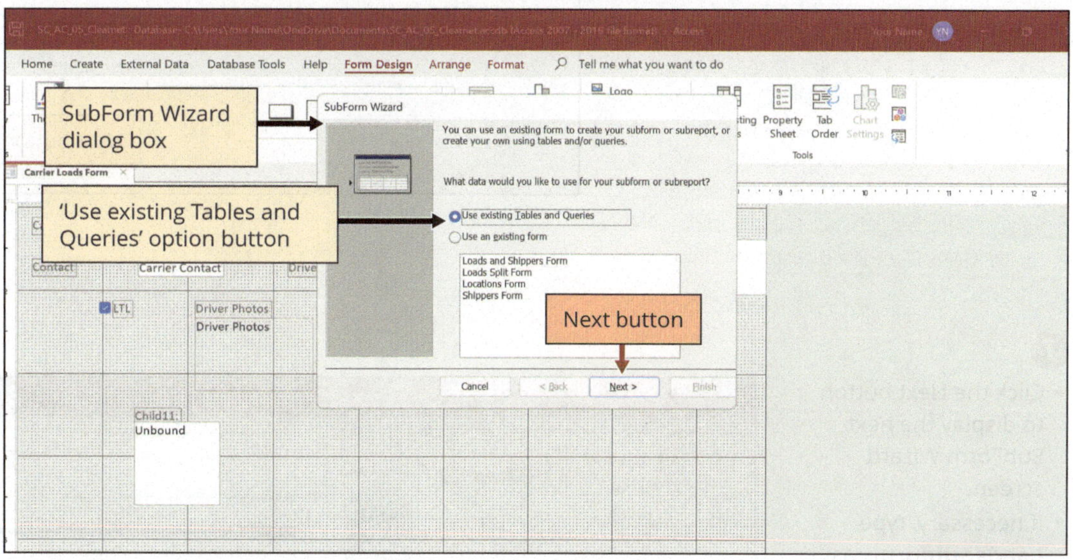

Figure 5–47

Q&A My control is placed on the screen, but no wizard appeared. What should I do?
Press DEL to delete the control you placed. Ensure the 'Use Control Wizards' button is selected, as described previously, and then try Steps 3 and 4 again.

5

- Click the Next button to display the next SubForm Wizard screen.
- If the Loads table is not already selected, click the Tables/Queries arrow, and then click Table: Loads to select it as the table that contains the fields for the subform.

- Add the Load ID, Pickup Date, Dropoff Date, Rate Confirmation, Mileage, and Truck Type fields by clicking each field and then clicking the Add Field button (SubForm Wizard dialog box) (Figure 5–48).

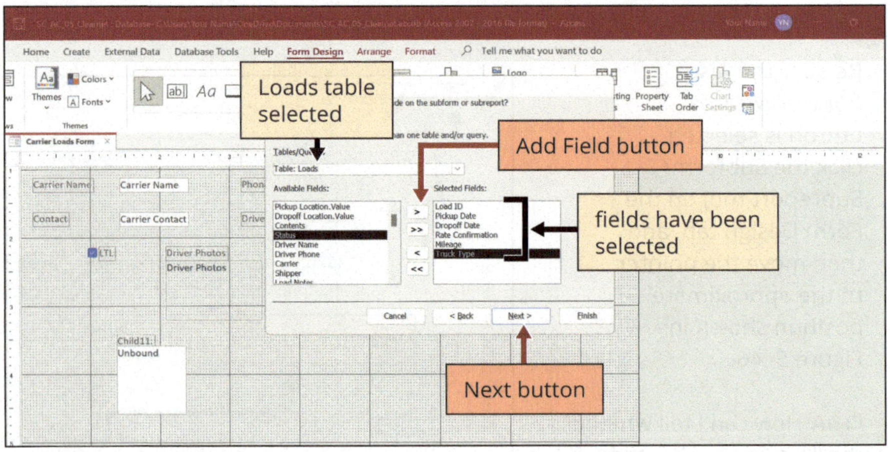

Figure 5–48

6

- Click Next to display the next SubForm Wizard screen.
- Be sure the 'Choose from a list.' option button is selected (Figure 5–49).

Q&A Why do I use this option?

Most of the time, Access will have determined the appropriate fields to link the subform and the main form and placed an entry specifying those fields in the list. By choosing from the list, you can take advantage of the information that Access has created for you. The other option is to define your own, in which case you would need to specify the appropriate fields.

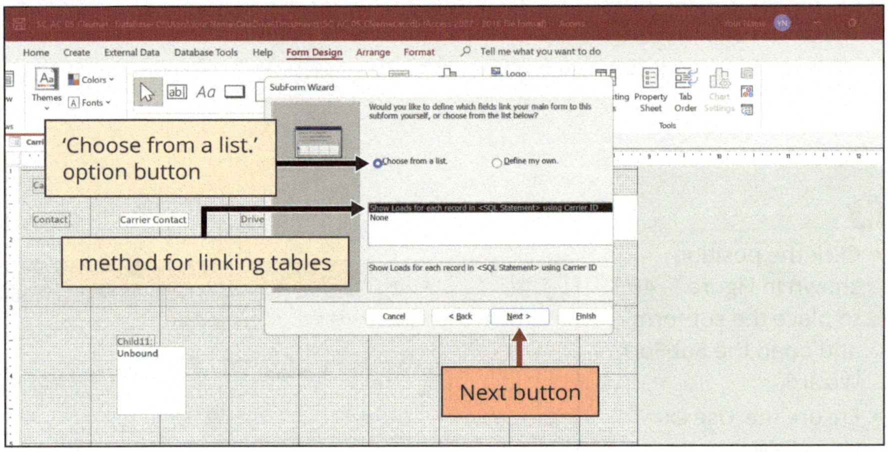

Figure 5–49

7

- Click the Next button to display the next SubForm Wizard screen.
- If necessary, type **Loads subform** as the name of the subform (Figure 5–50).

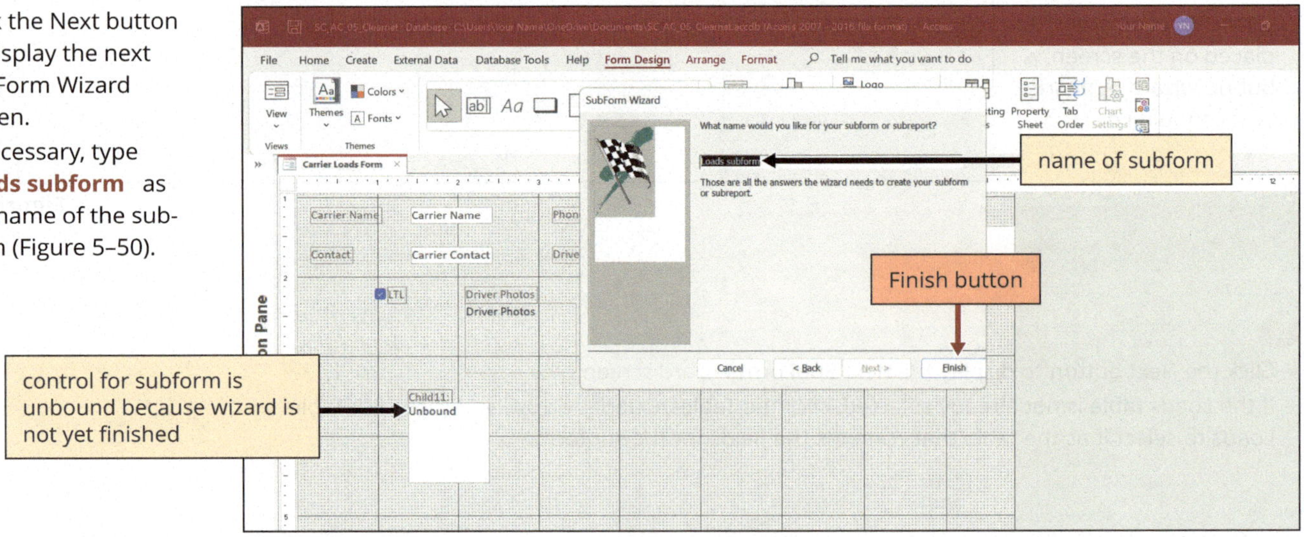

Figure 5–50

8

- Click the Finish button to place the subform.
- If necessary, shift the subform control and nearby controls to best use the space without any overlapping of controls and so subform fits above the Form Footer section (Figure 5–51).

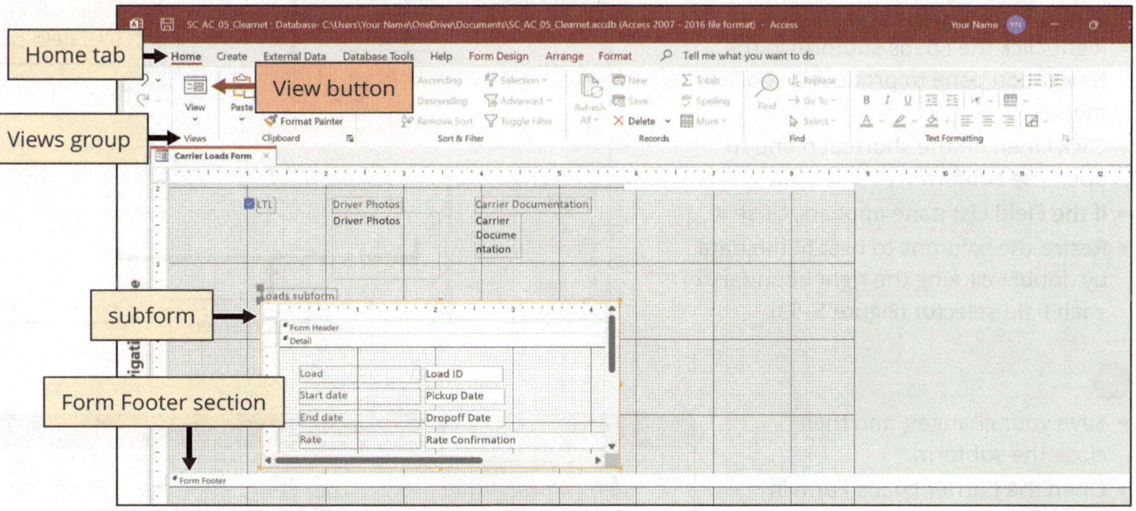

Figure 5–51

9

- Click the View button (Home tab | Views group) to choose Form view, and then navigate to the fifth record (Figure 5–52).

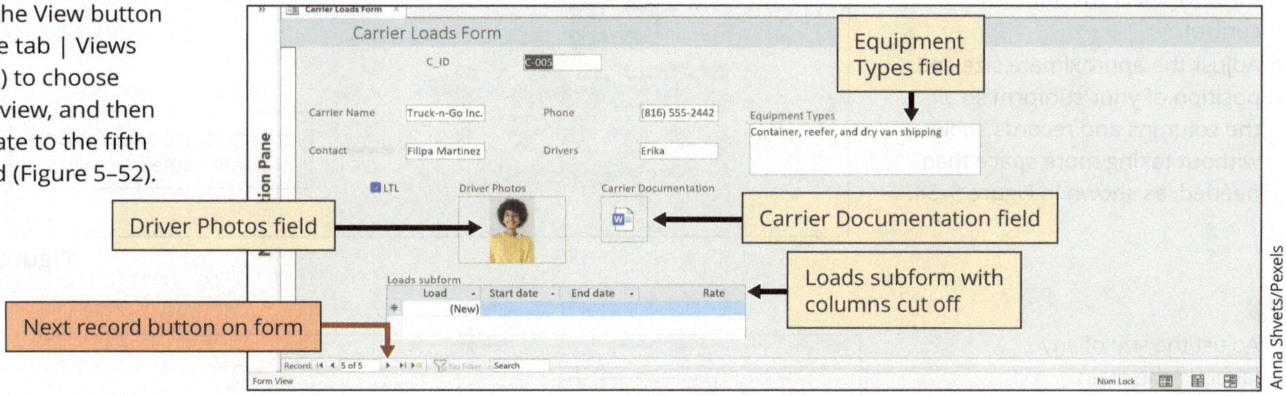

Figure 5–52

Q&A Everything looks good except the subform. I do not see all the fields I should see. What should I do?
You need to modify the subform, which you will do in the upcoming steps.

10

- Save and then close the form.

Break Point: If you wish to take a break, this is a good place to do so. You can quit Access now. To resume at a later time, start Access, open the database called SC_AC_05_Clearnet.accdb, and continue following the steps from this location forward.

To Modify a Subform and Move the Picture

The next task is to resize the columns in the subform, which appear on the form in Datasheet view. The subform exists as a separate object in the database; it is stored independently of the main form. The following steps open the subform and then resize the columns. **Why?** The column sizes need to be adjusted so the data is displayed correctly. The steps then view the form and, finally, move and resize the picture.

1

- Open the Navigation Pane.
- Right-click the Loads subform in the Navigation pane to produce a shortcut menu.
- Click Open on the shortcut menu to open the subform.
- If the Field List pane appears, close it.
- Resize the columns to best fit the data by double-clicking the right boundary of each field selector (Figure 5–53).

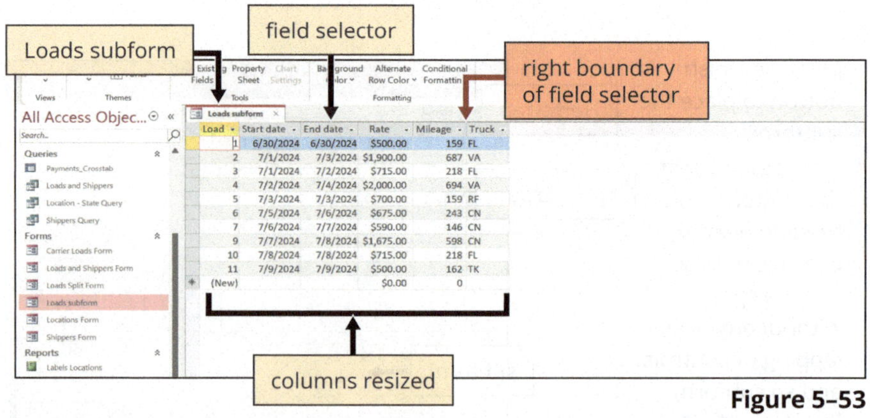

Figure 5–53

2

- Save your changes, and then close the subform.
- Open the Carrier Loads Form in Layout view, and then close the Navigation Pane.
- Click any boundary of the subform to select the subform control.
- Adjust the approximate size and position of your subform so all the columns and records show without taking more space than needed, as shown in Figure 5–54.

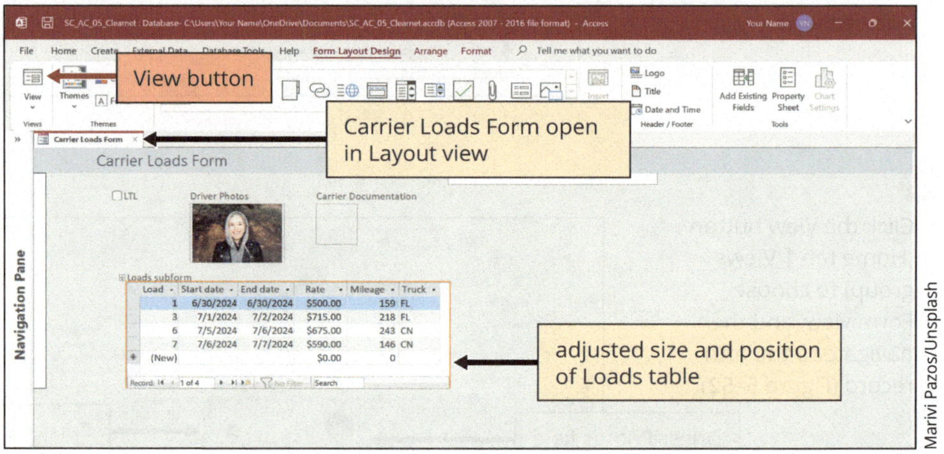

Figure 5–54

3

- Adjust the size of any labels in the main form whose names are obscured, such as increasing the width of the Carrier Name control. Navigate through the other carrier records to confirm the field controls are big enough for all data in all records.
- Click the View button (Form Layout Design tab | Views group) to view the form in Form view (Figure 5–55).

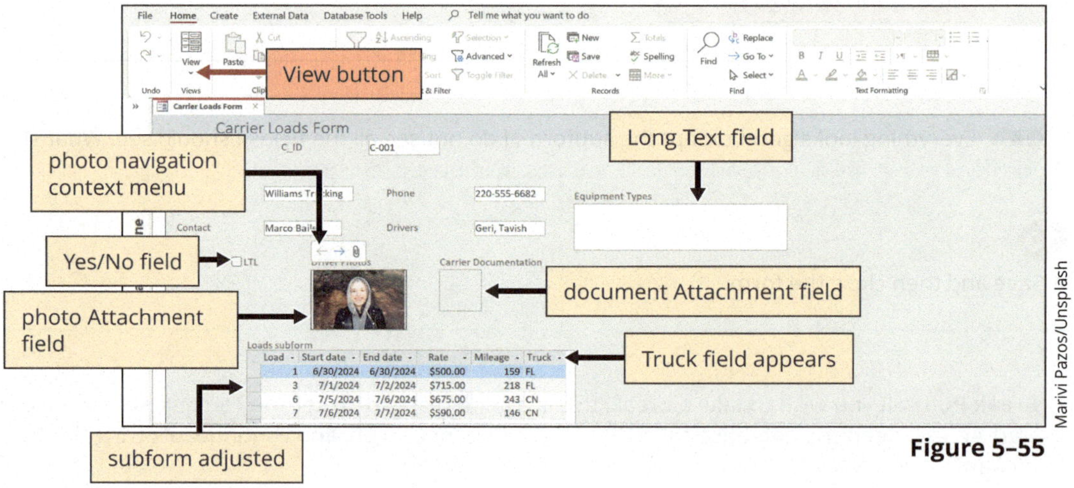

Figure 5–55

Q&A Could I have clicked the View arrow and then clicked Form View?

Yes. You can always use the arrow to see all view options. If the icon for the view you want appears on the face of the View button, however, you can just click the button.

The photo seems to be a slightly different size from the one in Figure 5–55. How do I fix this?

You can move and also resize the photo.

I know many of these carrier records contain more than one driver photo, but I only see one driver's photo on each record. How can I see the other photos?

You can toggle between all the photos for each carrier. Click the Driver Photos control to select it. A context menu appears above the photo (Figure 5–55). Click the blue navigation buttons to scroll to the right or left and see other photos, if available.

How can I tell if the new size and location are correct for the photo and for other controls?
View the form. If you are not satisfied with the size or location of any control, return to Design view or Layout view and make the necessary adjustments. Repeat the process until you are satisfied. You may have to allow a small amount of white on the borders of the photo. You will learn about some options you can use to adjust the specific look of the photo later in this module.

Consider This

Is there any way to determine the way images fit within the control?

Yes. Access determines the portion of an image that appears as well as the way it appears using the **size mode** property. The three size modes are as follows:

Clip: This size mode displays only a portion of the image that will fit in the space allocated to it.

Stretch: This size mode expands or shrinks the image to fit the precise space allocated on the screen. For photographs, usually this is not a good choice because fitting a photograph to the allocated space can distort the image, giving it a stretched appearance.

Zoom: This size mode does the best job of fitting the image to the allocated space without changing the look of the image. The entire image will appear and be proportioned correctly. Some white space may be visible either above or to the right of the image, however.

To Change a Label

Labels can be changed in a form to be more descriptive. **Why?** The form has enough room to display more than the entire field name, so adding extra information adds clarity. The following steps change the contents of the label from C_ID to Carrier Identification.

1

- Switch to Design view.
- Click the C_ID label to select it.
- Click the label a second time to produce an insertion point.
- Delete the existing text (C_ID), and then type **Carrier Identification** as the new label (Figure 5–56).

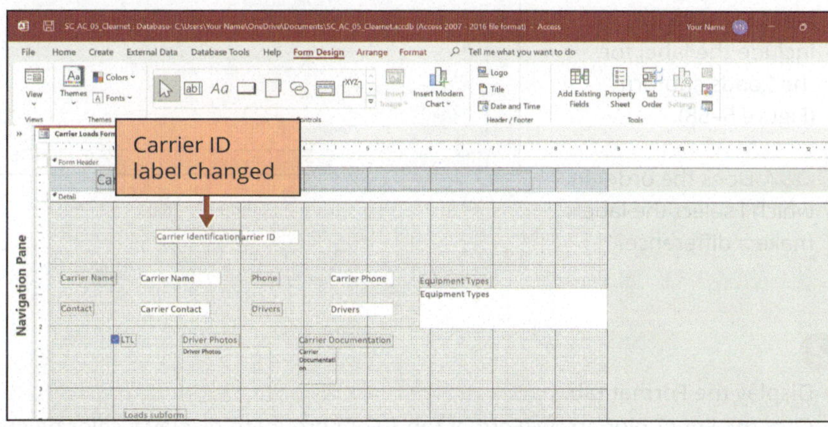

Figure 5–56

2

- Click outside the label to deselect it.
- Click the label to select it.
- Drag the move handle in the upper-left corner of the label control to move the label to the approximate position shown in Figure 5–57.

Q&A Why did I need to deselect the label and then select it again?
With the insertion point appearing in the label, you could not move the label. By deselecting it and then selecting it again, the label will be selected, but there will be no insertion point.

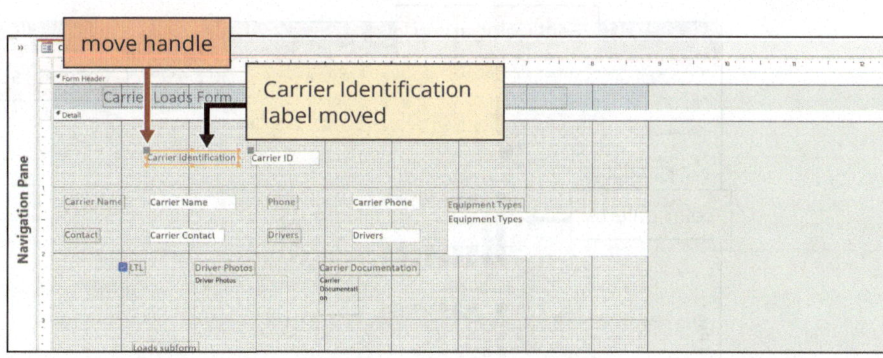

Figure 5–57

3

- Save your changes.

BTW
Moving Controls
When you are dragging a label or control, you might need to make very small movements. You can use the arrow keys on the keyboard to make fine adjustments to control placement.

To Change the Size Mode

Currently, the size mode for the Driver Photos should be Zoom, which is appropriate. If it were not and you wanted to change it, you would use the following steps.

1. Click the control containing the picture, and then click the Property Sheet button (Form Design tab | Tools group) to display the control's property sheet.
2. Click the Picture Size Mode property, and then click the Picture Size Mode property arrow.
3. Click Zoom, and then close the property sheet by clicking its Close button.

To Change Label Effects and Colors

Access allows you to change many of the characteristics of the labels in the form. You can change the border style and color, the background color, the font, and the font size. You can also apply special label effects, such as raised or sunken. The following steps change the font color of the labels and add special effects. **Why?** Modifying the appearance of the labels improves the appearance of the form.

1

- Click the Carrier Identification label to select it, if necessary.
- Select each of the remaining labels by holding down SHIFT while clicking each label. Be sure to include the label for the Loads subform (Figure 5–58).

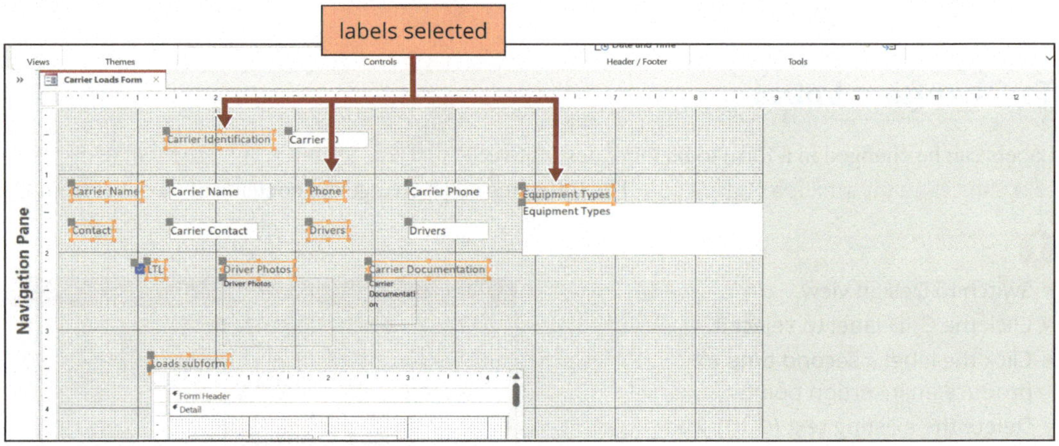

Figure 5–58

Q&A Does the order in which I select the labels make a difference?
No. The only thing that is important is that all label controls are selected when you are done.

2

- Display the Format tab.
- Click the Font Color arrow (Format tab | Font group) to display a color palette (Figure 5–59).

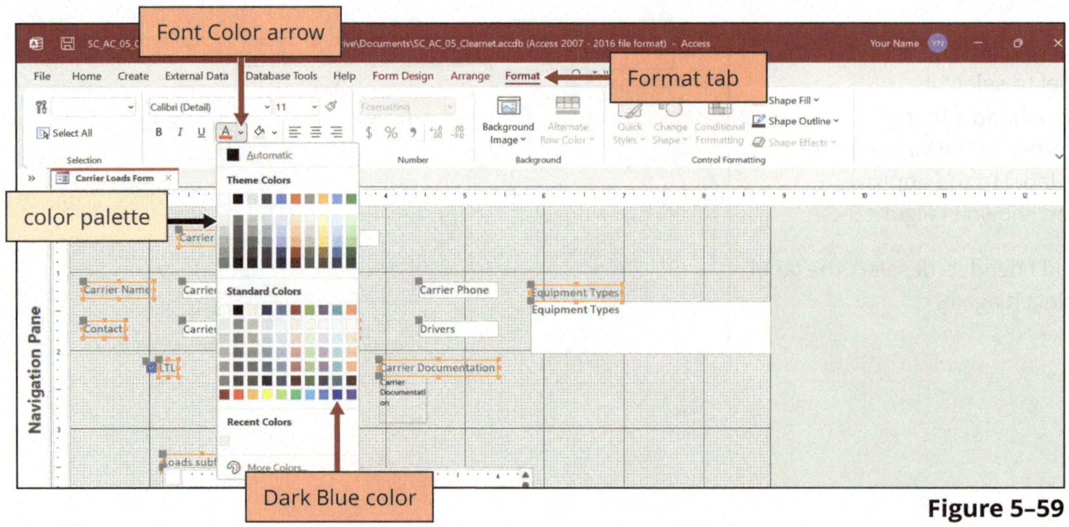

Figure 5–59

3

- In the Standard Colors section, click Dark Blue (bottom row, second position from the right) to change the font color for the labels.
- **Experiment:** Try other colors by clicking the Font Color arrow and then clicking other colors to see which colors you think would be good choices for the font. View the form to see the effect of your choice, and then return to Design view. When done, select the Dark Blue color.
- Display the Form Design tab.
- Click the Property Sheet button (Form Design tab | Tools group) to display the property sheet for the selected labels. Make sure the All tab is selected.
- Click the Border Style property box to display the Border Style property arrow, and then click the arrow to display a menu of border styles (Figure 5–60).

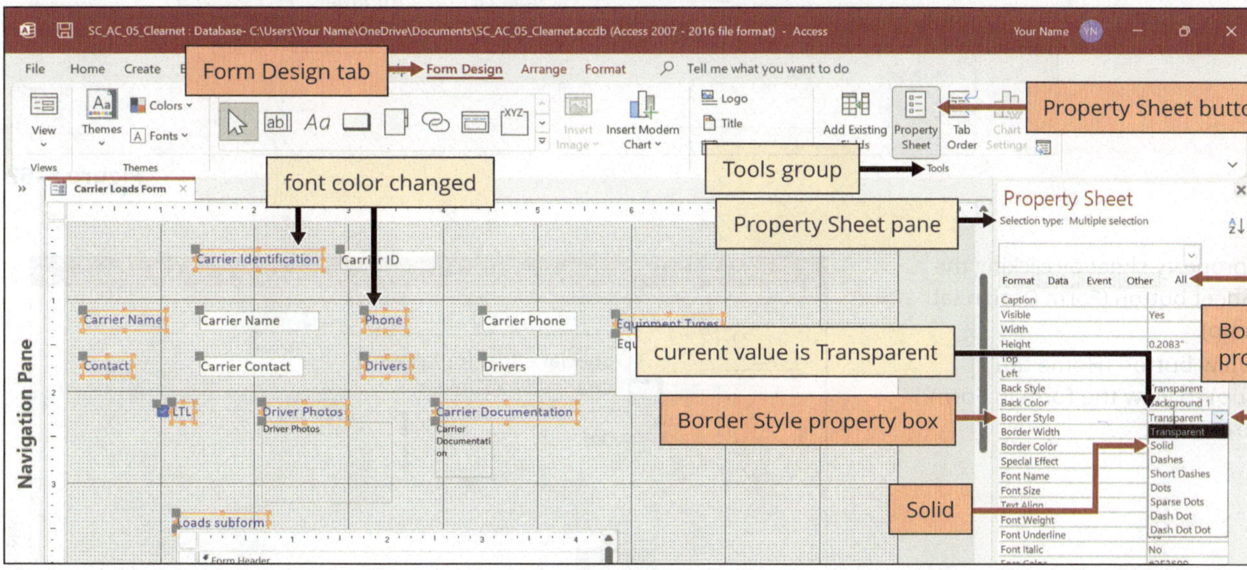

Figure 5–60

Q&A The Property Sheet pane is too small to display the property arrow. Can I change the size of the pane?

Yes. Point to the left border of the Property Sheet pane so that the pointer changes to a two-pointed arrow. You then can drag to adjust the size.

4

- Click Solid in the menu of border styles to select a border style.
- Click the Border Width property box to display the Border Width property arrow, and then click the arrow to display a menu of border widths.
- Click 3 pt to change the border width to 3 points.
- Click the Special Effect property box to display the Special Effect property arrow, and then click the arrow to display a menu of special effects (Figure 5–61).

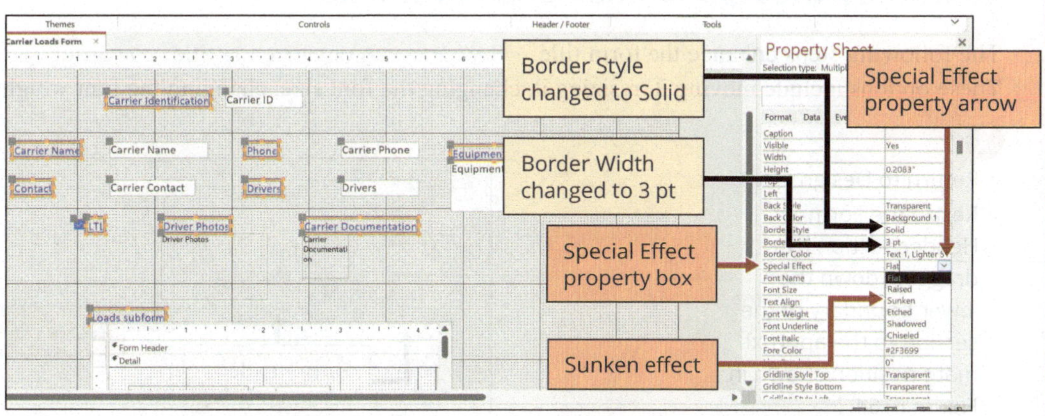

Figure 5–61

5

- Click Sunken in the menu of special effects to select this special effect (Figure 5–62).
- **Experiment:** Try other special effects. In each case, view the form to see the special effect you selected, and then return to Design view. When you are done, select Sunken for the Special Effect property.

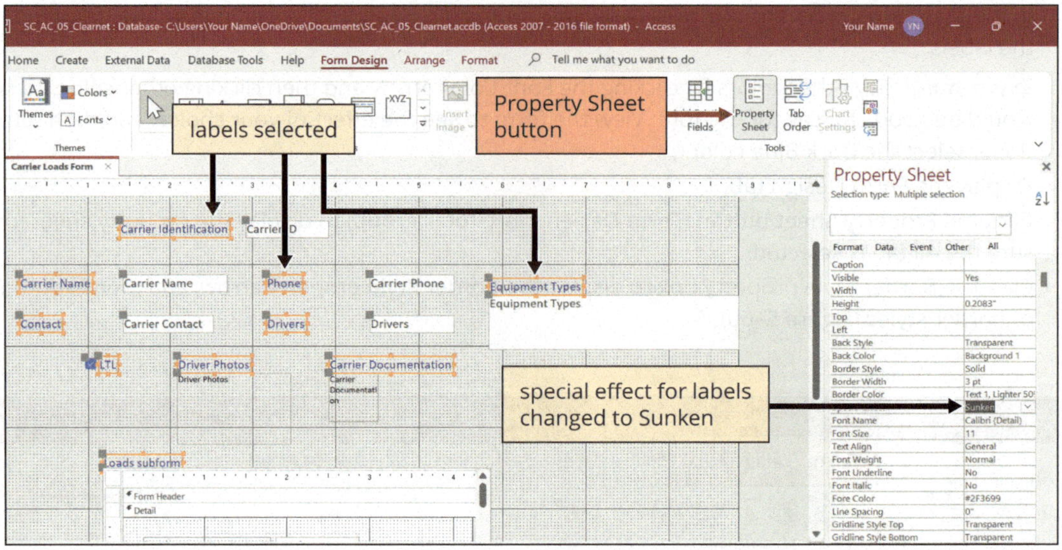

Figure 5–62

6

- Close the property sheet by clicking the Property Sheet button (Form Design tab | Tools group).
- Click the View button (Home tab | Views group) to view the form in Form view (Figure 5–63).

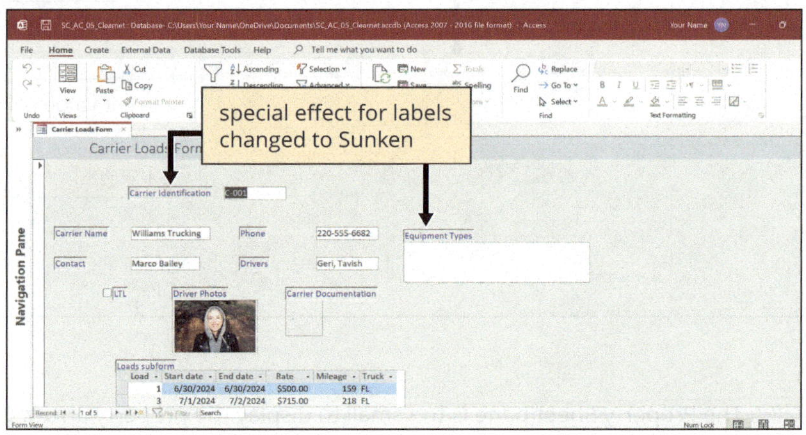

Marivi Pazos/Unsplash

Figure 5–63

To Modify the Appearance of a Form Title

The following steps enhance the form title. **Why?** You can enhance the title in a variety of ways by changing its appearance. These options include moving it, resizing it, changing the font size, changing the font weight, and changing the alignment.

1

- Return to Design view.
- Resize the Form Header section by dragging down the lower boundary of the section to the approximate position shown in Figure 5–64.

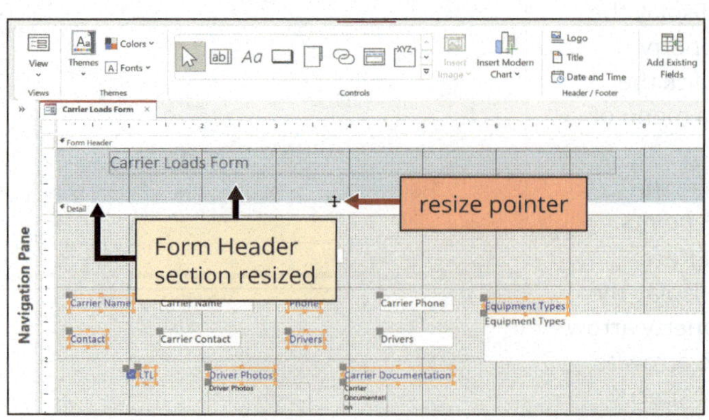

Figure 5–64

2

- Click the control containing the form title to select it.
- Drag the lower-right sizing handle to resize the control to the approximate size shown in Figure 5–65.

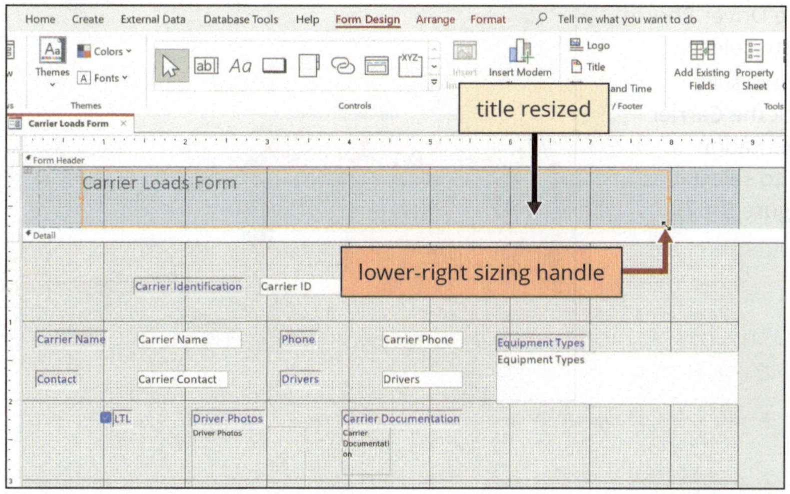

Figure 5–65

3

- Click the Property Sheet button (Form Design tab | Tools group) to display the control's property sheet.
- Click the Font Size property box, click the Font Size property arrow, and then click 28 to change the font size.
- In a similar fashion, change the Text Align property value to Distribute and the Font Weight property value to Semi-bold (Figure 5–66).

4

- Close the property sheet.

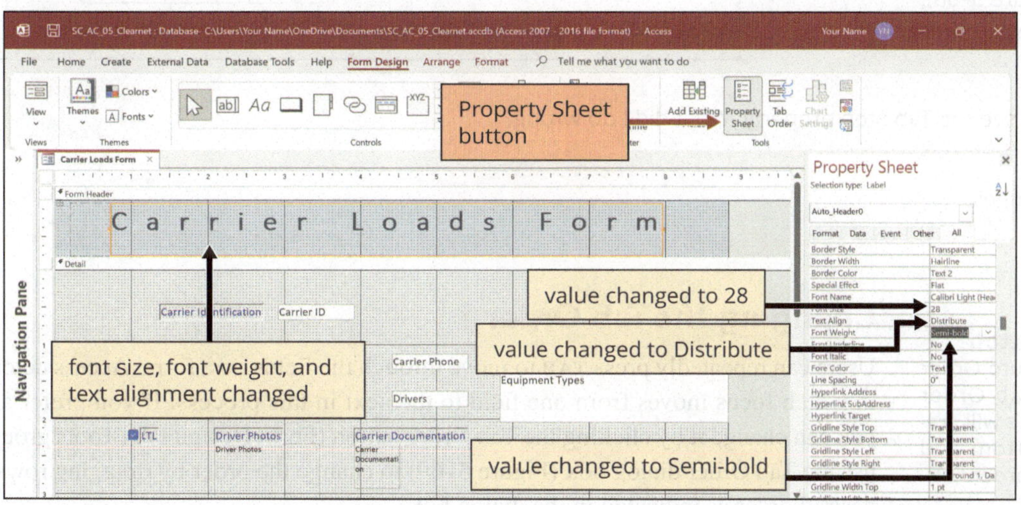

Figure 5–66

Other Ways

1. Enter font size value in Font Size box to set font size

To Change a Tab Stop

Users can repeatedly press TAB to move through the controls on the form; however, they should bypass the Driver Photos and Documentation controls because users do not enter data into these fields. To omit these controls from the tab stop sequence, the following steps change the value of the Tab Stop property for the controls from Yes to No. **Why?** Changing the Tab Stop property for these fields to No removes them from the Tab Stop sequence.

1

- Click the Driver Photos control to select it.
- Hold down SHIFT and click the Carrier Documentation control to select it as well (Figure 5–67).

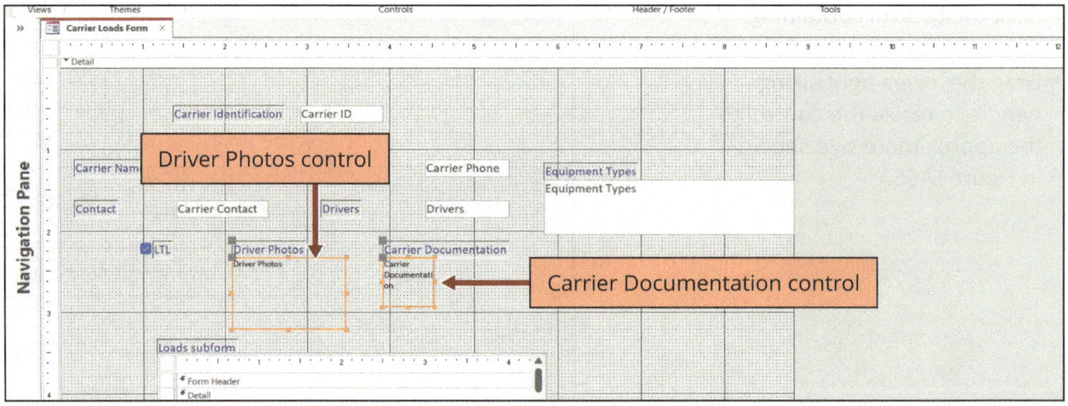

Figure 5–67

2

- Click the Property Sheet button (Form Design tab | Tools group) to display the property sheet.
- Make sure the All tab (Property Sheet) is selected, scroll down until the Tab Stop property appears, click the Tab Stop property, click the Tab Stop property arrow, and then click No to instruct Access to skip the Driver Photos and Carrier Documentation fields in the tab sequence (Figure 5–68).
- Close the property sheet.

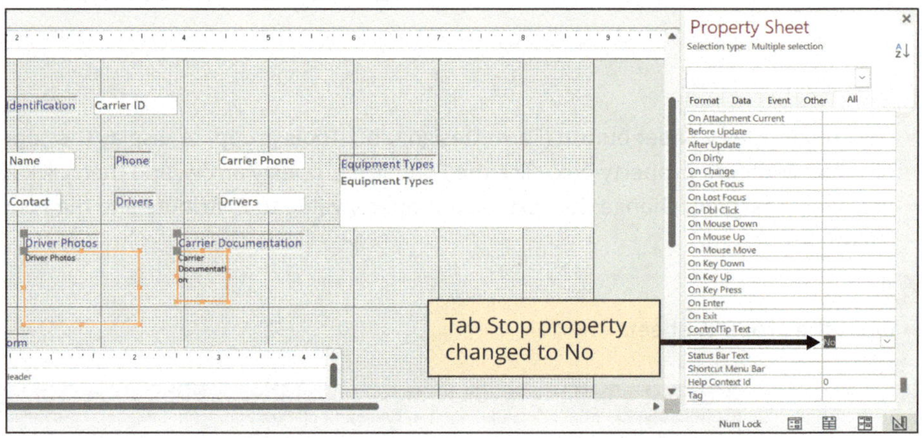

Figure 5–68

Q&A I do not see the Tab Stop property. What did I do wrong?
You clicked the controls for the labels, not the field controls.

- Save your changes.

BTW
Auto Order Button
If you click the Auto Order button in the Tab Order dialog box, Access will create a top-to-bottom and left-to-right tab order.

Changing the Tab Order

Users can repeatedly press TAB to move through the fields on a form. Access determines the order in which focus moves from one field to the next in this process. If you prefer a different order, you can change it by clicking the Tab Order button (Form Design tab | Tools group). You then can use the Tab Order dialog box (Figure 5–69) to change the order by dragging rows (fields) to their desired order as indicated in the dialog box.

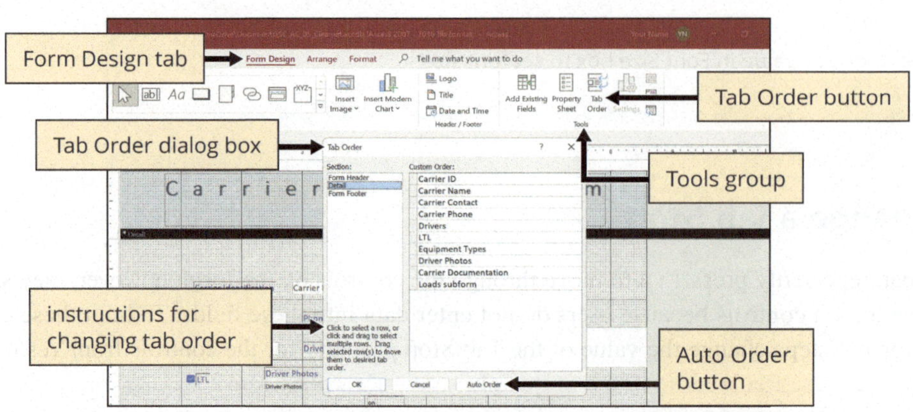

Figure 5–69

To Use the Form

The form gives you flexibility in selecting both carriers and their loads. **Why?** You can use the Navigation buttons at the bottom of the screen to move among carriers. You can use the Navigation buttons in the subform to move among the loads currently shown on the screen. The following steps use the form to display the desired data.

1

- Click the View button (Form Design tab | Views group) to view the form in Form view.
- In the form, navigate to the fifth record, Truck-n-Go Inc.
- Right-click the Carrier Documentation field to display a shortcut menu (Figure 5–70).

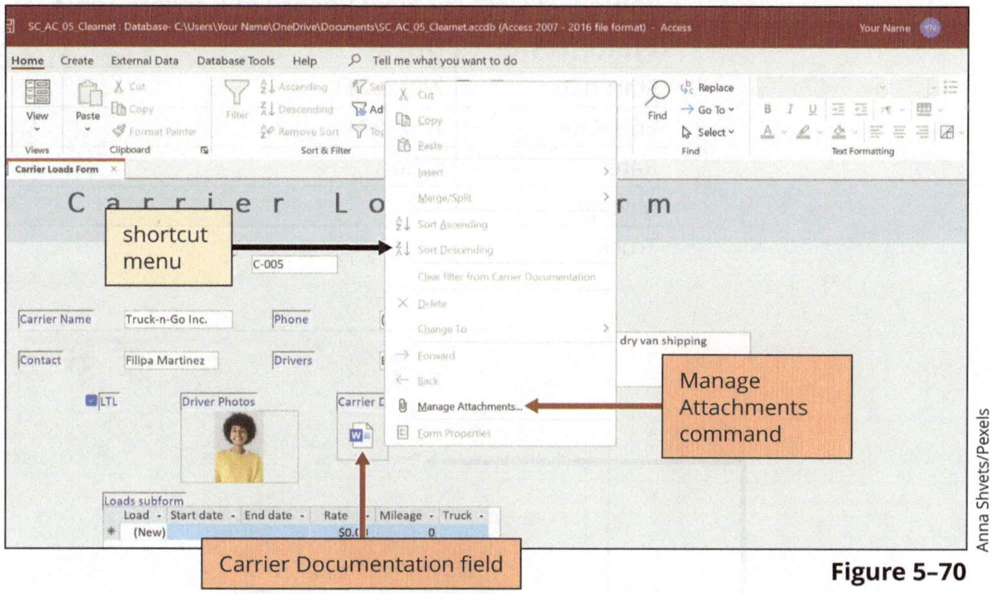

Figure 5–70

2

- Click the Manage Attachments command on the shortcut menu to display the Attachments dialog box (Figure 5–71).

Q&A How do I use this dialog box?

Select an attachment and click the Open button to view the attachment in a compatible application. Click the Add button to add a new attachment or the Remove button to remove the selected attachment. By clicking the Save As button, you can save the selected attachment as a file in whatever location you specify. You can save all attachments at once by clicking the Save All button.

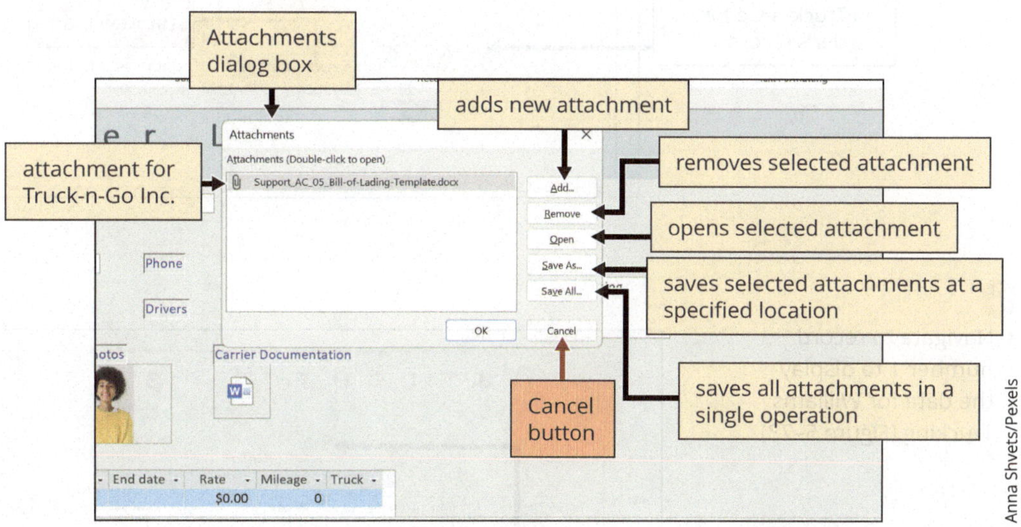

Figure 5–71

- **Experiment:** If you have a compatible application, such as Microsoft Word, Word Online, Google Docs, or Apple Pages, click the Open button to open and view the attachment. When finished, close the compatible application.

Other Ways

1. Double-click Attachments control to open an attachment

3

- Click the Cancel button to close the Attachments dialog box.
- In the Loads subform, click the Start date field next to the word, "(New)", to enter a new load.
- Enter the data listed in Table 5–2, pressing TAB to move from column to column (Figure 5–72). After completing the record, press TAB once to move to the next row.

Table 5–2 Data for New Record in Carriers Table

Field Name	Data
Start date	**7/9/2024**
End date	**7/9/2024**
Rate	**1200**
Mileage	**371**
Truck	**RF**

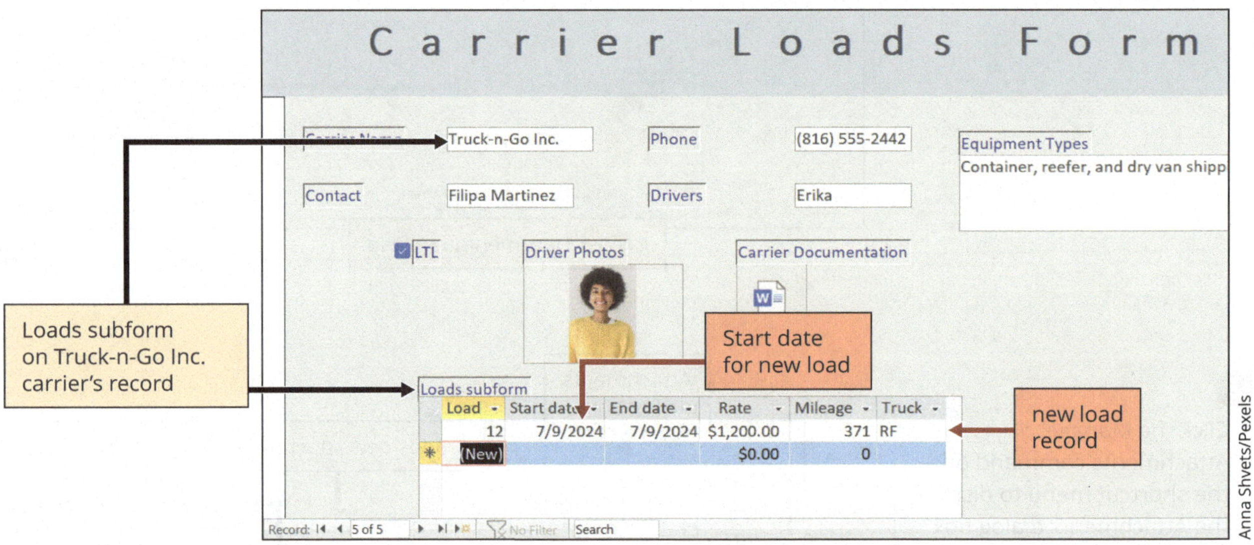

Figure 5–72

4

- Navigate to record number 1 to display the data for Williams Trucking (Figure 5–73).

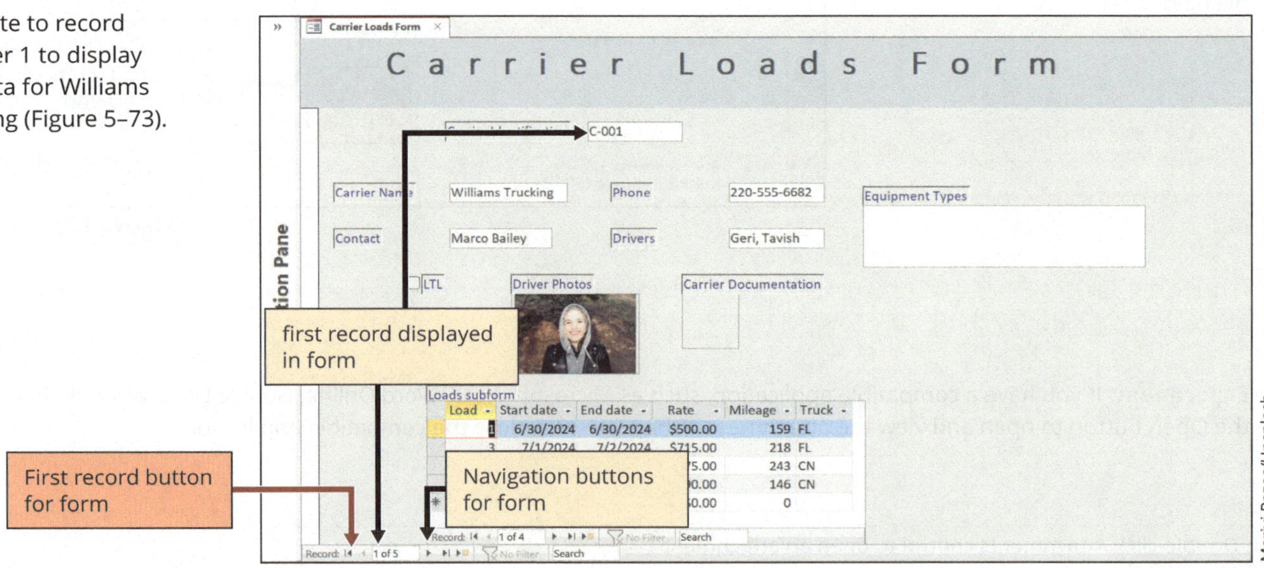

Figure 5–73

5

- Click the subform's Next record button once to highlight the carrier's load on 7/1/2024 (Figure 5–74).

6

- Close the form. If you are prompted to save your changes, click Yes.

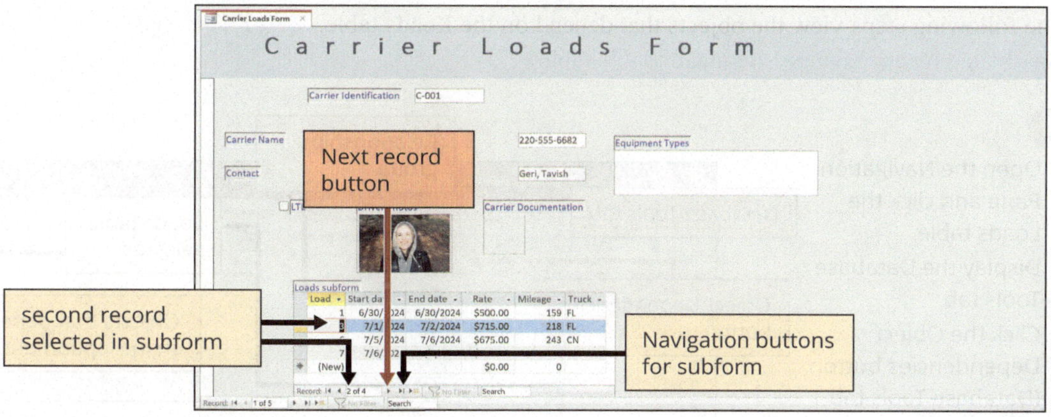

Figure 5–74

Navigation in the Form

The previous steps illustrated ways you work with a main form and subform. Clicking the Navigation buttons for the main form moves to a different carrier. Clicking the Navigation buttons for the subform moves to different loads of the carrier that currently appears in the main form. The following are other navigation actions you can take within the form:

1. To move from the last field in the main form to the first field in the subform, press TAB. To move back to the last field in the main form, press SHIFT+TAB.
2. To move from any field in the subform to the first field in the next record's main form, press CTRL+TAB.
3. To switch from the main form to the subform using touch or the mouse, click anywhere in the subform. To switch back to the main form, click any control in the main form. Clicking the background of the main form will not cause the switch to occur.

BTW
Navigation
To go to a specific record in the main form, enter the record number in the Current Record box for the main form. To go to a specific record in the subform, enter the record number in the Current Record box for the subform.

Break Point: If you wish to take a break, this is a good place to do so. You can quit Access now. To resume at a later time, start Access, open the database called SC_AC_05_Clearnet.accdb, and continue following the steps from this location forward.

Object Dependencies

In Access, some objects depend on other objects. For example, a report depends on the table or query on which it is based. That is, a change to the structure of the table or query could affect the report, so in that sense the report depends on the table or query. If you delete a field from the table, for instance, any report based on that table that uses the deleted field would no longer be valid.

You can view information on dependencies between database objects. Viewing a list of objects that depend on a specific object helps in the maintenance of a database and avoids errors when changes are made to the objects involved in the dependency. For example, many items, such as queries and forms, use data from the Loads table and thus depend on the Loads table. By clicking the Object Dependencies button, you can see what items are based on the object. You also can see the items on which the object depends.

If you are unfamiliar with a database, viewing object dependencies can help you better understand the structure of the database. Viewing object dependencies is especially useful after you have made changes to the structure of tables. If you know which reports, forms, and queries depend on a table, you will be better able to make changes to a table without negatively affecting the related database objects.

To View Object Dependencies

The following steps view the objects that depend on the Loads table. **Why?** The objects that depend on the Loads table might be affected by any change you make to this table.

1

- Open the Navigation Pane and click the Loads table.
- Display the Database Tools tab.
- Click the Object Dependencies button (Database Tools tab | Relationships group) to display the Object Dependencies pane.

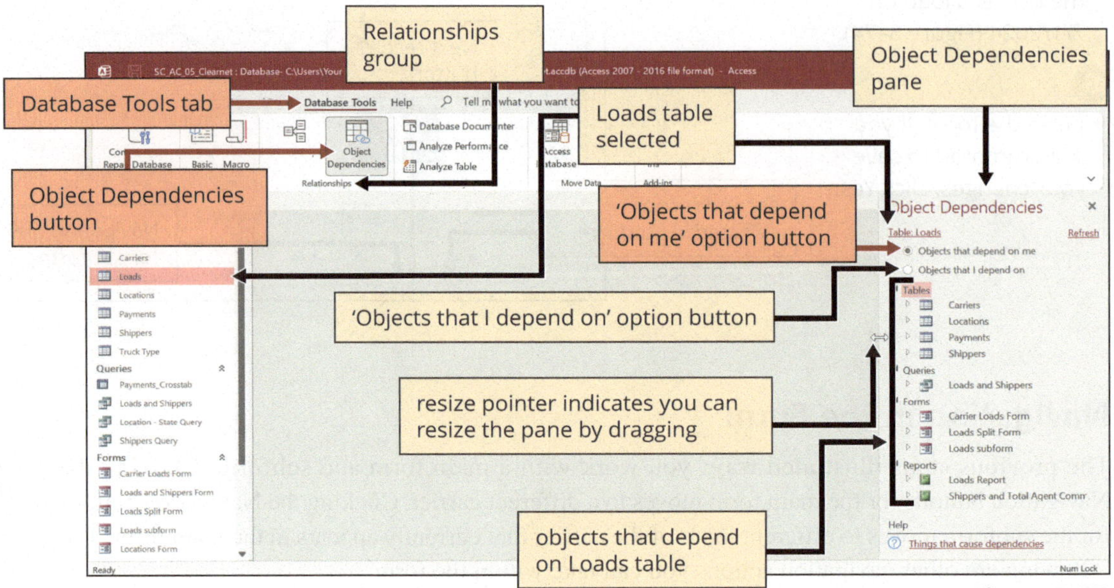

Figure 5–75

Q&A The Object Dependencies pane is squished on the side of my screen. How do I make it bigger?
Point to the left edge of the Object Dependencies pane until you see a two-pointed resize arrow. Press and drag the resize pointer to the left to enlarge the pane.

- If necessary, click the 'Objects that depend on me' option button to select it (Figure 5–75). The 'me' in this case is the selected object, the Loads table.
- **Experiment:** Click the 'Objects that I depend on' option button to see the objects on which the Loads table depends. Then try both options for other objects in the database.

2

- Close the Object Dependencies pane by clicking the Object Dependencies button (Database Tools tab | Relationships group) a second time.

BTW
Date Fields in Queries
To test for the current date in a query, type Date() in the Criteria row of the appropriate column. Typing <Date() in the Criteria row for the Dropoff Date, for example, finds those carriers who are scheduled to drop off a load today.

BTW
Long Text Fields in Queries
When you query long text fields, consider alternative spellings and phrases. For example, Computer Science also can be referenced as CS.

Date/Time, Long Text, and Yes/No Fields in Queries

By specifying load dates using Date/Time fields, Clearnet can run queries to find carriers' loads before or after a certain date. Similarly, management can search for carriers with specific equipment by adding Long Text and Yes/No fields.

To use Date/Time fields in queries, you simply type the dates, including the slashes. To search for records with a specific date, you must type the date. You also can use comparison operators. To find all the appointments whose date is after June 1, 2024, for example, you would type >6/1/2024 as the criterion.

You can also use Long Text fields in queries by searching for records that contain a specific word or phrase in the Long Text field. To do so, you use wildcards. For example, to find all the carriers who have the word, reefer, somewhere in the Equipment Types field, you type *reefer* as the criterion. The asterisk at the beginning indicates that any characters can appear before the word, reefer. The asterisk at the end indicates that any characters can appear after the word, reefer.

To use Yes/No fields in queries, type the word, Yes, or the word, No, as the criterion. The following steps create and run queries that use Date/Time, Long Text, and Yes/No fields.

To Use Date/Time, Long Text, and Yes/No Fields in a Query

The following steps use Date/Time, Long Text, and Yes/No fields in queries to search for carriers and loads that meet specific criteria. **Why?** Clearnet wants to find carrier loads dropped off after 7/3/2024; who have the word, reefer, in their equipment type field; or who accept LTL loads.

1

- Create a query for the Carriers and Loads tables and include the Carrier Name, Dropoff Date, Equipment Types, and LTL fields in the query (Figure 5–76).

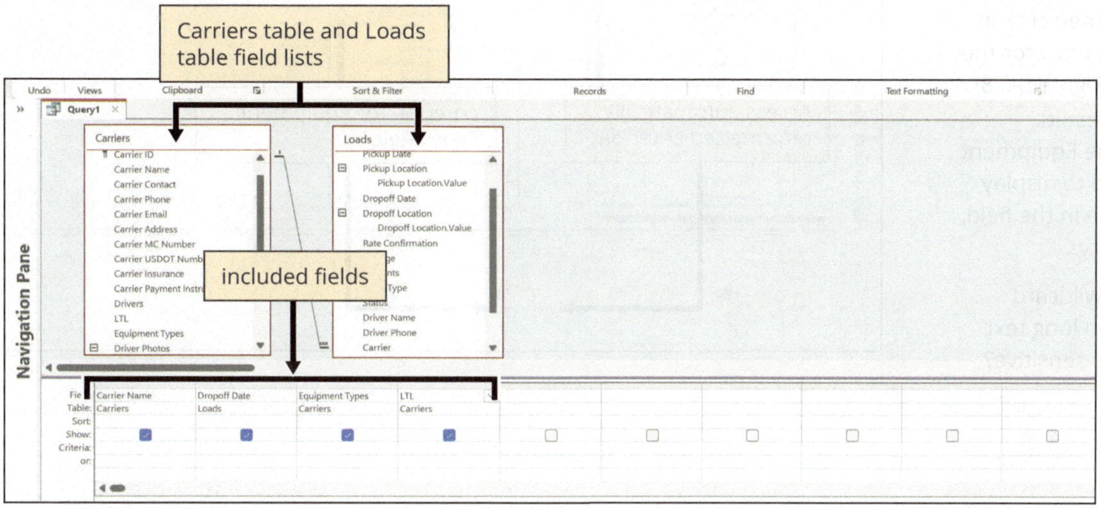

Figure 5–76

2

- Click the Criteria row under the Dropoff Date field, type **>7/3/2024** as the criterion, and then click in the Criteria row for the Equipment Types field (Figure 5–77).
- View the results.

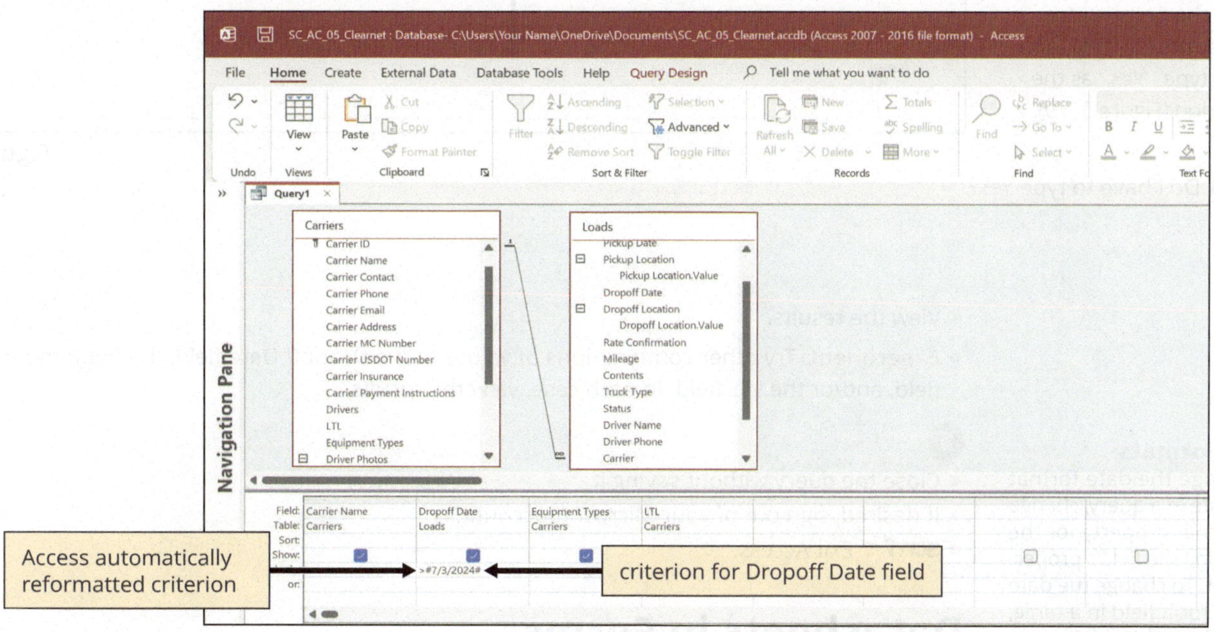

Figure 5–77

Q&A Why does the date have hash signs (#) around it?
This is the date format in Access. Access reformats the date appropriately when you click another Criteria cell.

3

- Click the View button to return to Design view.
- Erase the criterion in the Dropoff Date field.
- Click the Criteria row under the Equipment Types field, type ***reefer*** as the criterion, and then click in the Criteria row for the LTL field (Figure 5–78).
- View the results. Expand the Equipment Types field to display all the data in the field, if necessary.

Q&A Are wildcard searches in long text fields case-sensitive?
No.

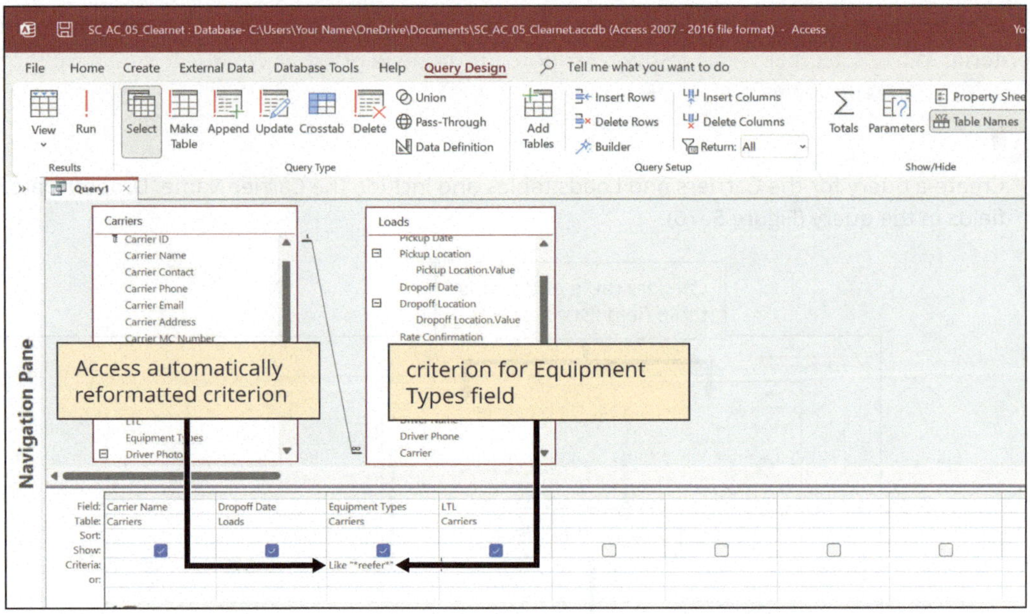

Figure 5–78

4

- Click the View button to return to Design view.
- Erase the criterion in the Equipment Types field.
- Click the Criteria row under the LTL field, and then type **Yes** as the criterion (Figure 5–79).

Q&A Do I have to type Yes?
You could also type True.

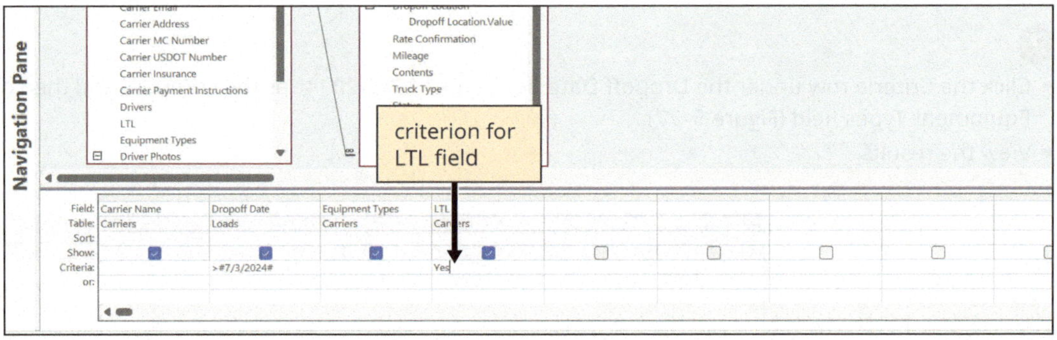

Figure 5–79

- View the results.
- **Experiment:** Try other combinations of values in the Dropoff Date field, the Equipment Types field, and/or the LTL field. In each case, view the results.

5

- Close the query without saving it.
- If desired, sign out of your Microsoft account.
- sam Exit Access.

BTW
Date Formats
To change the date format for a date in a query, change the format property for the field using the field's property sheet. To change the date format for a field in a table, open the table in Design view and change the format property for the field.

Datasheets in Forms

Subforms are not available in forms created in Layout view, but you can achieve similar functionality to subforms by including datasheets. Like subforms, datasheets contain data for the "many" table in the relationship.

Creating a Simple Form with a Datasheet

If you create a simple form for a table that is the "one" table in a one-to-many relationship, Access automatically includes the "many" table in a datasheet within the form. If you create a simple form for the Carriers table, for example, Access will include the Loads table in a datasheet within the form, as in Figure 5–80. The loads in the datasheet will be the loads of the carrier currently on the screen, in this case, Williams Trucking.

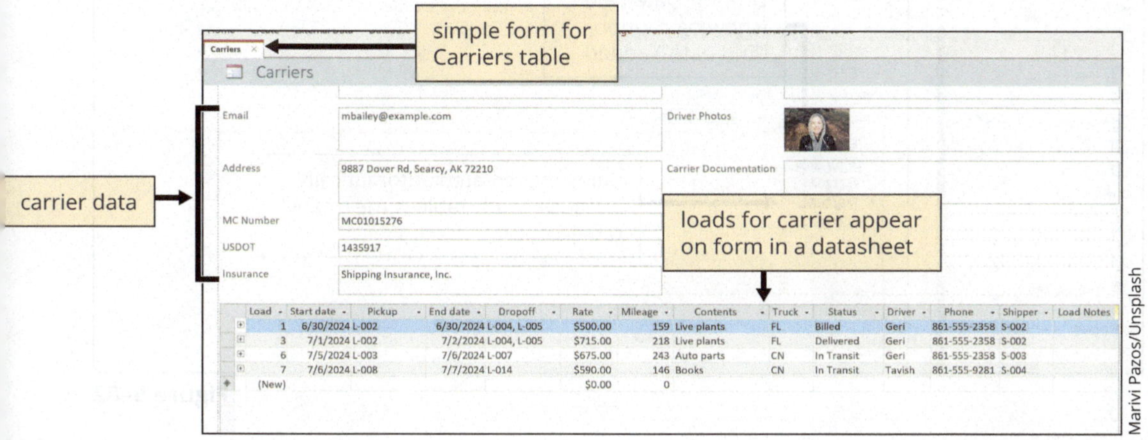

Figure 5–80

To Create a Simple Form with a Datasheet

To create a simple form with a datasheet, you would use the following steps.

1. Select the table in the Navigation Pane that is the "one" part of a one-to-many relationship.
2. Display the Create tab.
3. Click the Form button (Create tab | Forms group).

Creating a Form with a Datasheet in Layout View

You can create a form with a datasheet in Layout view. To create a form based on the Carriers table that includes the loads records, which are stored in the Loads table, you would first use the field list to add the required fields from the "one" table. In Figure 5–81, fields from the Carriers table have been added to the form.

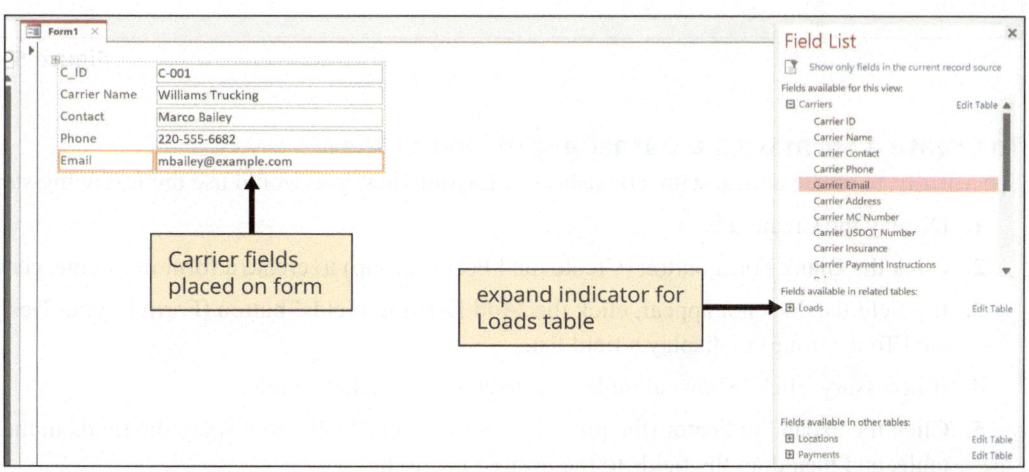

Figure 5–81

BTW

Distributing a Document

Instead of printing and distributing a hard copy of a document, you can distribute the document electronically. Options include sending the document via email; posting it on cloud storage (such as OneDrive) and sharing the file with others; posting it on a social networking site, blog, or other website; and sharing a link associated with an online location of the document. You also can create and share a PDF or XPS image of the document, so that users can view the file in Acrobat Reader or XPS Viewer instead of in Access.

BTW

Placing Fields on a Datasheet

Be sure to select the datasheet before adding additional fields to it. When dragging a field from the field list to the datasheet, drag the field to the right boundary of the previous field. The pointer will change to show that you are placing a control and you will see a vertical line.

Next, you would use the field list to add a single field from the "many" table, as shown in Figure 5–82, in which the Dropoff Date field has been added. Access will automatically create a datasheet containing this field.

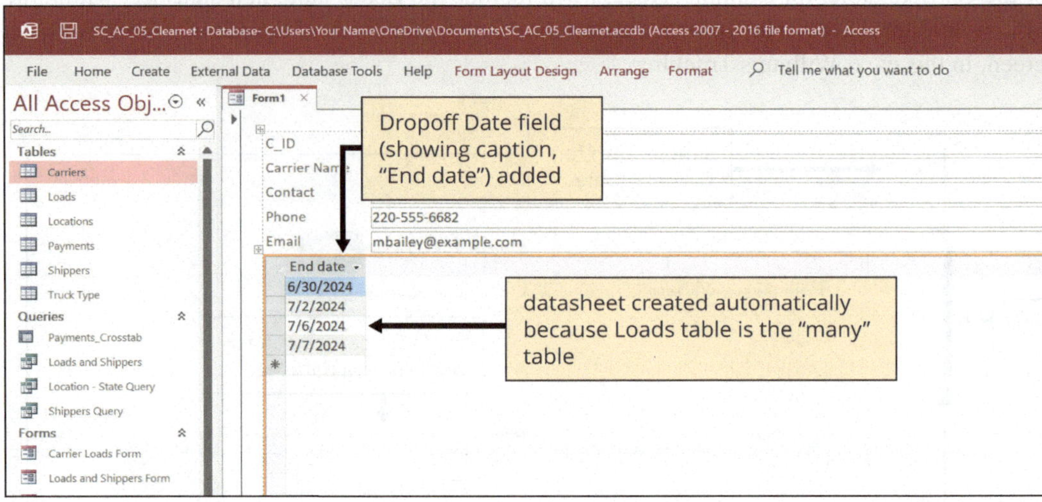

Figure 5–82

Finally, you would click the datasheet to select it and then use the field list to add the other fields from the "many" table that you want to include in the form, as shown in Figure 5–83.

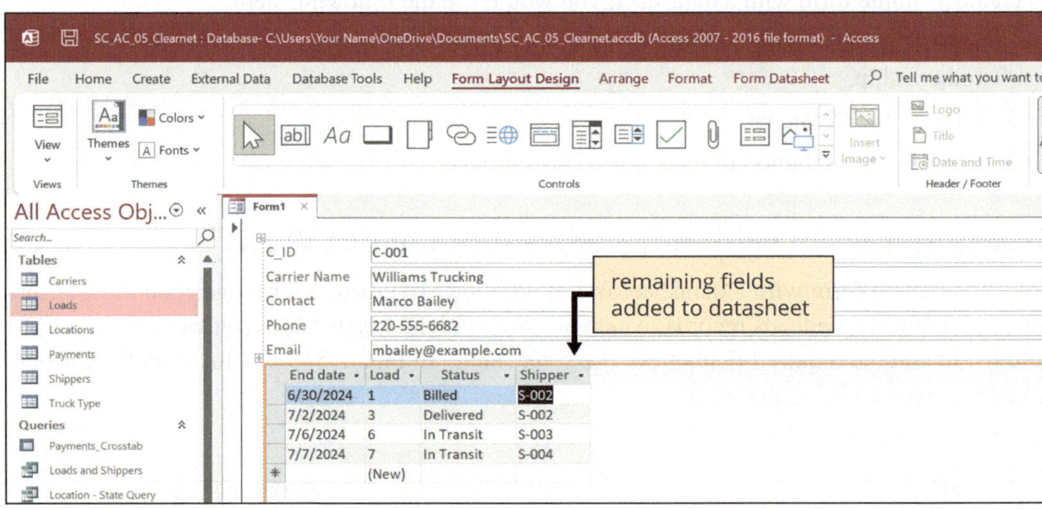

Figure 5–83

To Create a Form with a Datasheet in Layout View

Specifically, to create a form with a datasheet in Layout view, you would use the following steps.

1. Display the Create tab.
2. Click the Blank Form button (Create tab | Forms group) to create a form in Layout view.
3. If a field list does not appear, click the 'Add Existing Fields' button (Form Layout Design tab | Tools group) to display a field list.
4. If necessary, click 'Show all tables' to display the available tables.
5. Click the expand indicator (the plus sign) for the "one" table to display the fields in the table, and then drag the fields to the desired positions.

6. Click the expand indicator for the "many" table and drag the first field for the datasheet onto the form to create the datasheet.
7. Select the datasheet and drag the remaining fields for the datasheet from the field list to the desired locations in the datasheet.

Consider This

Can you modify the form so the complete labels for the carrier fields appear?

Yes. Click any of the labels for the carrier fields to select the label, and then click the Select Column button (Arrange tab | Rows & Columns group) to select all the labels. You can then drag the right boundary of any of the labels to resize all the labels simultaneously.

Creating a Multiple-Table Form Based on the Many Table

All the forms discussed so far in this module were based on the "one" table, in this case, the Carriers table. The records from the "many" table were included in a subform. You can also create a multiple-table form based on the "many" table, in this case, the Loads table. Such a form is shown in Figure 5–84.

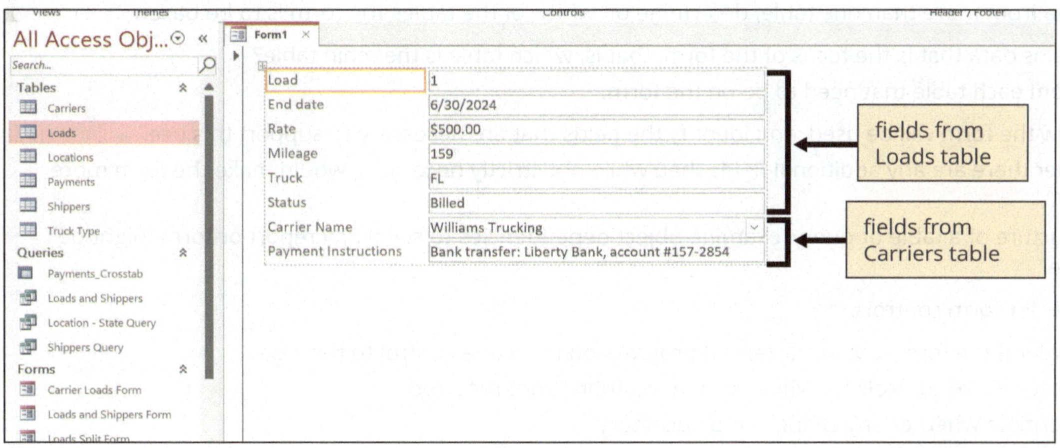

Figure 5–84

In this form, the Load, End date, Rate, Mileage, Truck, and Status fields are from the Loads table. The Carrier Name and Payment Instructions fields are found in the Carriers table and are included in the form to help identify the carrier whose load is appearing in the upper fields.

To Create a Multiple-Table Form Based on the Many Table

To create a multiple-table form based on the "many" table, you would use the following steps.

1. Click the Blank Form button (Create tab | Forms group) to create a form in Layout view.
2. If a field list does not appear, click the 'Add Existing Fields' button on the Design tab to display a field list.
3. Drag the fields for the "many" table to the desired positions.
4. Drag the fields for the "one" table to the desired positions.

Summary

In this module you have learned to use Yes/No, Long Text, and Attachment data types; create and use an input mask; create a form and add a subform; enhance the look of the controls on a form; change tab order and stops; use a form with a subform; create queries involving Yes/No, Date/Time, and Long Text fields; view object dependencies; and create forms containing datasheets in Layout view.

Consider This: Plan Ahead

What decisions will you need to make when creating your own forms?

Use these guidelines as you complete the assignments in this module and create your own forms outside of this class.

1. Determine the purpose of the fields to see if they need special data types.
    a. If the field only contains values such as Yes and No or True and False, it should have Yes/No as the data type.
    b. If the field contains an extended description, it should have Long Text as the data type.
    c. If the field contains a picture and you need to conserve storage space, its data type should be Attachment.
    d. If the field contains attached files, its data type should be Attachment.
2. Determine whether the form requires data from more than one table.
3. If the form requires data from more than one table, determine the relationship between the tables.
    a. Identify one-to-many relationships.
    b. For each relationship, identify the "one" table and the "many" table.
4. If the form requires data from more than one table, determine on which of the tables the form is to be based.
    a. Which table contains data that is the focus of the form, that is, which table is the main table?
5. Determine the fields from each table that need to be on the form.
    a. Decide exactly how the form will be used, and identify the fields that are necessary to support this use.
    b. Determine whether there are any additional fields that, while not strictly necessary, would make the form more functional.
6. When changing the structure of a table or query, examine object dependencies to see if any report or form might be impacted by the change.
7. Determine the tab order for form controls.
    a. Change the tab order if the form requires a certain progression from one control to the next.
    b. Remove tab stops for those controls for which form navigation is not required.
8. Review the form to determine whether any changes are necessary.
    a. Are there visual changes, such as different colors or a larger font, that would make the form easier to use?
    b. Does the form have a similar look to other forms in the database?
    c. Does the form conform to the organization's standards?

Consider This

How should you submit solutions to critical thinking questions in the assignments?

Every assignment in this course contains one or more critical thinking questions. These questions require you to think beyond the assigned database. Present your responses to the questions in the format required by your instructor. Possible formats may include one or more of these options: write the answer; create a document that contains the answer; present your answer to the class; discuss your answer in a group; record the answer as audio or video using a webcam, smartphone, or portable media player; or post answers on a blog, wiki, or website.

Student Assignments

Apply Your Knowledge

Reinforce the skills and apply the concepts you learned in this module.

Adding Phone Number, Yes/No, Long Text, and Picture Attachment Fields, Using an Input Mask Wizard, and Querying Long Text Fields

Note: To complete this assignment, you will be required to use the Data Files. Please contact your instructor for information about accessing the Data Files.

Instructions: Start Access. Open the database, SC_AC_05-2.accdb, which is located in the Data Files folder. Enable the content.

Perform the following tasks:

1. Save the database using the file name, SC_AC_05_City-Tutoring. Enable the content. Open the Counselors table in Design view.
2. Add the Phone Number, CPR Certification, Other Skills, and Photo fields to the Counselors table structure, as shown in Figure 5–85. Create an input mask for the new Phone Number field. When building the mask, instruct Access to store the phone number data without symbols. CPR Certification is a field that indicates whether the counselor has completed a CPR (Cardiopulmonary Resuscitation) and first aid training course and passed the course exam.

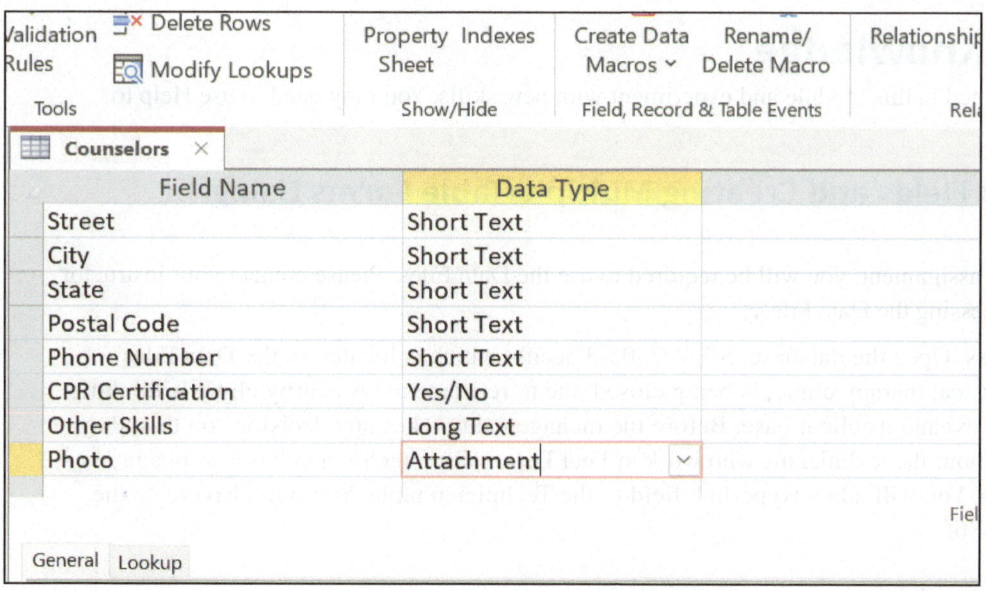

Figure 5–85

Continued on next page

3. Add the data shown in Table 5–3 to the Counselors table. Adjust the row and column spacing to best fit the data. Save the changes to the layout of the table.

Table 5–3 Data for Counselors Table

Counselor Number	Phone Number	CPR Certification	Other Skills	Photo
103	(615) 555-4648	Yes	Taught high school math for 10 years	Support_AC_05_Enrique.jpg
110	(931) 555-9105	Yes	Has a bachelor's degree in biology	Support_AC_05_Rachel.jpg
114	(423) 555-8589	No	Worked as an accountant for 4 years	Support_AC_05_Chou.jpg
120	(931) 555-5498	No	Working on a bachelor's degree in English	Support_AC_05_Chris.jpg

4. If requested to do so by your instructor, change the phone number for counselor number 103 to your phone number.
5. Query the Counselors table to find all counselors who have CPR Certification. Include the Counselor Number, Last Name, First Name, and Phone Number fields in the query result. Save the query as Apply 5 Step 5 Query.
6. Query the Counselors table to find all counselors with a bachelor's degree or pursuing a bachelor's degree who have completed the CPR Certification. Also include the Counselor Number, Last Name, and First Name fields in the query result. Save the query as Apply 5 Step 6 Query.
7. Submit the revised database in the format specified by your instructor.
8. **Consider This:** What value did you enter in the criteria row for the CPR Certification field in the query in Step 5 above? Could you have entered the criteria differently? If yes, then how else could you enter the criteria to find the information?

Extend Your Knowledge

Extend the skills you learned in this module and experiment with new skills. You may need to use Help to complete the assignment.

Adding Hyperlink Fields and Creating Multiple-Table Forms Using Layout View

Note: To complete this assignment, you will be required to use the Data Files. Please contact your instructor for information about accessing the Data Files.

Instructions: Start Access. Open the database, SC_AC_05-3.accdb, which is located in the Data Files folder. Feel Better, a physical therapy clinic, is being closed due to retirements. A nearby clinic is thinking of buying the practice to expand its client base. Before the management makes any decisions on this, they need more information about the technicians who work at Feel Better. Each technician has a webpage about their qualifications. You will add a Hyperlink field to the Technician table. You will also create the form shown in Figure 5–86.

Perform the following tasks:

1. Save the database using the file name, SC_AC_05_Physical-Therapists. Enable the content. Open the Technician table in Design view and add a field with the Hyperlink data type. Insert the field after the Earnings YTD field. Use Website as the name of the field.
2. Switch to Datasheet view and add data for the Website field to the first record. Use your school's URL as the data. If necessary, resize the column so the complete URL is displayed. Close the table.
3. If requested to do so by your instructor, enter your name as the technician name for the first record of the Technician table.

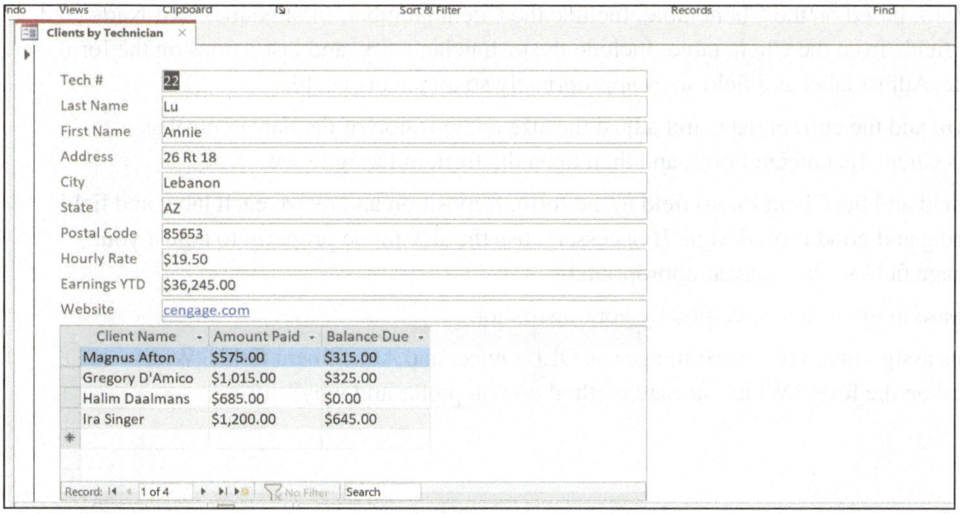

Figure 5–86

4. Use Layout view to create the new multiple-table form shown in Figure 5–86. The Client table appears as a subform in the form. The Technician table is the "one" table in the form. Use Clients by Technician as the form name.
5. Submit the revised database in the format specified by your instructor.
6. **Consider This:** How would you add a required field for an email address to the Technician table?

Expand Your World

Create a solution, which uses cloud and web technologies, by learning and investigating on your own from general guidance.

Note: To complete this assignment, you will be required to use the Data Files. Please contact your instructor for information about accessing the Data Files.

Instructions: Start Access. Open the database, SC_AC_05-4.accdb, which is located in the Data Files folder, and enable the content. This file is a database of clients and technicians. To understand the difference between Attachment and OLE Object data types, you will add one of each of these fields to the Clients table. Then, you will insert images that you download from the Internet. Finally, you will create a multiple-table form for the database.

Perform the following tasks:

1. Access any website containing royalty-free images and search the images to find four different photos of computers and related devices. As a suggestion, you might choose a desktop, laptop, printer, and gaming device.
2. Save these images to a storage location of your choice.
3. Save the database using the file name, SC_AC_05_Solutions-IT-Support. Enable the content. Open the Client table in Design view. Add a Device Image field with an OLE Object data type. Add a Client Photo field with an Attachment data type. Assign the caption, Photo, to the Client Photo field. The fields should appear after the Technician Number field.
4. Use the techniques shown in the module to add the photos of computers and other devices to the Device Image field. Reuse the 4 images as needed throughout the records. Add photos of yourself, your friends, or family members as attachments to the Client Photo field.

Continued on next page

5. Create a multiple-table form based on the Client table. Include the Client Number, First Name, Last Name, and Technician Number fields from the Client table. Include the technician's first and last names on the form from the Technician table. Adjust label and field sizes appropriately so all data is visible.
6. Include a title for the form and the current date, and adjust the size and position of the date control as needed. Save the form as Client Technician Form, and then open the form in Design view.
7. Add the Device Image field and the Client Photo field to the form. Reposition and resize each label and field as needed for clean spacing and good form design. If necessary, use the size mode property to adjust your images in the Device Image field so they appear appropriately.
8. Submit the revised database in the format specified by your instructor.
9. **Consider This:** In this assignment you stored images as OLE Object and Attachment fields. What differences did you notice on the form? Which storage method do you prefer and why?

In the Lab

Design and implement a solution using creative thinking and problem-solving skills.

Lab: Adding Fields and Creating Multiple-Table Forms for the Great Outdoors Database

Note: To complete this assignment, you will be required to use the Data Files. Please contact your instructor for information about accessing the Data Files.

Problem: The Great Outdoors staff would like you to add some fields to the Counselors table. They would also like to create a form for the Cabins table that shows the counselor assigned to each cabin and the camper enrollments for each cabin.

Perform the following tasks:

Part 1: Open the SC_AC_05-5.accdb database from the Data Files folder. Save the file with the name, SC_AC_05_Great-Outdoors, and enable the content. Use the concepts and techniques presented in this module to perform each of the following tasks.

a. For the Counselors table, add a photo field using the Attachment data type and a notes field using the Long Text data type.

b. For the counselor pictures, use your own photos. For the notes field, add the notes shown in Table 5–4. Make sure all data appears in the datasheet.

Table 5–4 Data for Counselors Table

Counselor ID	Notes
17893	Plays high school basketball
18797	Working on bachelor's in P.E.
18798	Camp counselor for 3 years
18990	Coached Little League baseball
78797	Ran track in high school
78979	Chess champion
79798	Camp alumnus
79879	Camp alumnus
82374	Plays high school volleyball
83329	Plays high school football
83648	Mother of a camper
85114	Played in college band
86718	Competitive video gamer

c. Form a relationship between the Enrollments table and the Cabins table on the field containing the cabin identification number in each table. Enforce referential integrity, and cascade updates. Form a relationship between the Cabins table and the Counselors table on the Cabin ID and Cabin fields, respectively. Enforce referential integrity, and cascade updates.

d. Create a Cabin Counselor Form for the Cabins table that is similar in design to the form shown in Figure 5–1. On the form, include the CabinID, CabinName, Min Campers, and Max Campers from the Cabins table, and include the First Name, Last Name, Photo, and Notes fields from the Counselors table. The subform should display the ID, Camper ID, and Camper First Name fields from the Enrollments table. Customize the form by adding special effects to controls and labels and by changing the background color of the form. Add a title and the current date to the form header.

e. Create a query that lists all cabin IDs and cabin names where the cabin offers a minimum of at least 5 campers and an assigned counselor has been involved in high school sports. Name the query Lab 5 Query 1.

Submit your assignment in the format specified by your instructor.

Part 2: **Consider This:** You made several decisions while adding the fields and creating the form and query for this assignment. What was the rationale behind your decisions? For example, how did you decide on layout details for the fields on the form? And how did you choose the criteria for the query? As you consider the functionality of the Counselors table, what additional fields would you add to this table to best reflect counselor experience levels and their preferences for the type and number of students they host in their cabins?

Advanced Report Techniques

Objectives

After completing this module, you will be able to:

- Import data to a table
- Enforce referential integrity in a table relationship
- Identify a query as a report's record source
- Use the Expression Builder
- Create a report using Design view
- Modify a label in a report
- Add a text box to a report
- Check a report's design using Print Preview
- Modify grouping of a report's controls
- Update multiple report controls
- Include a subreport in a report
- Modify section properties in a report
- Modify content and design of a report header or footer
- Include a calculation in a report
- Modify a report's page setup characteristics

Introduction

Previously you created forms and reports in Layout view for simpler designs, and you created forms in Design view for more complex configuration options. Design view offers extensive options for formatting, layout, functionality, and built-in logic. As you will see in this module, in Design view, you can set a control to expand its size automatically when the data held in that control needs more space. You can also group controls in sections according to the type of data being displayed and how much detail is required, or according to the type of calculations you want performed.

In this module, you will create two reports in Design view. Both reports feature grouping and sorting. The first report contains a subreport, which is a report that is contained within another report. The subreport contains data from a query and is related to data in the main report. The second report uses aggregate functions to calculate subtotals and totals. It also uses a function to calculate a value where the actual calculation will vary from record to record depending on whether a given criterion is true.

Project: Creating Detailed Reports

Partners Law Firm paralegals want a summary list of properties and the buyers for each property. This list should be available as an Access report and will have the name Buyers and Account Information Summary List. For each buyer, the report will include buyer, property, and closing information, even if the firm's client was instead the seller. In addition to offering its closing services, Partners offers workshops designed to educate buyers on various aspects of retirement planning. Data on workshop participation is stored in the database. To help Partners gauge the effectiveness of these workshops, the report should also list any workshops the buyers are enrolled in.

The Buyers and Account Information Summary List report is shown in Figure 6–1a. The report is organized by Buyer ID, with the data for each Buyer ID beginning on a new page. The buyer data includes the Buyer ID, buyer name, street address, attorney, closing date, property jurisdiction, and property location. For each workshop the buyer is taking, the report lists the workshop code, description, total hours the workshop requires, hours already spent, and hours remaining.

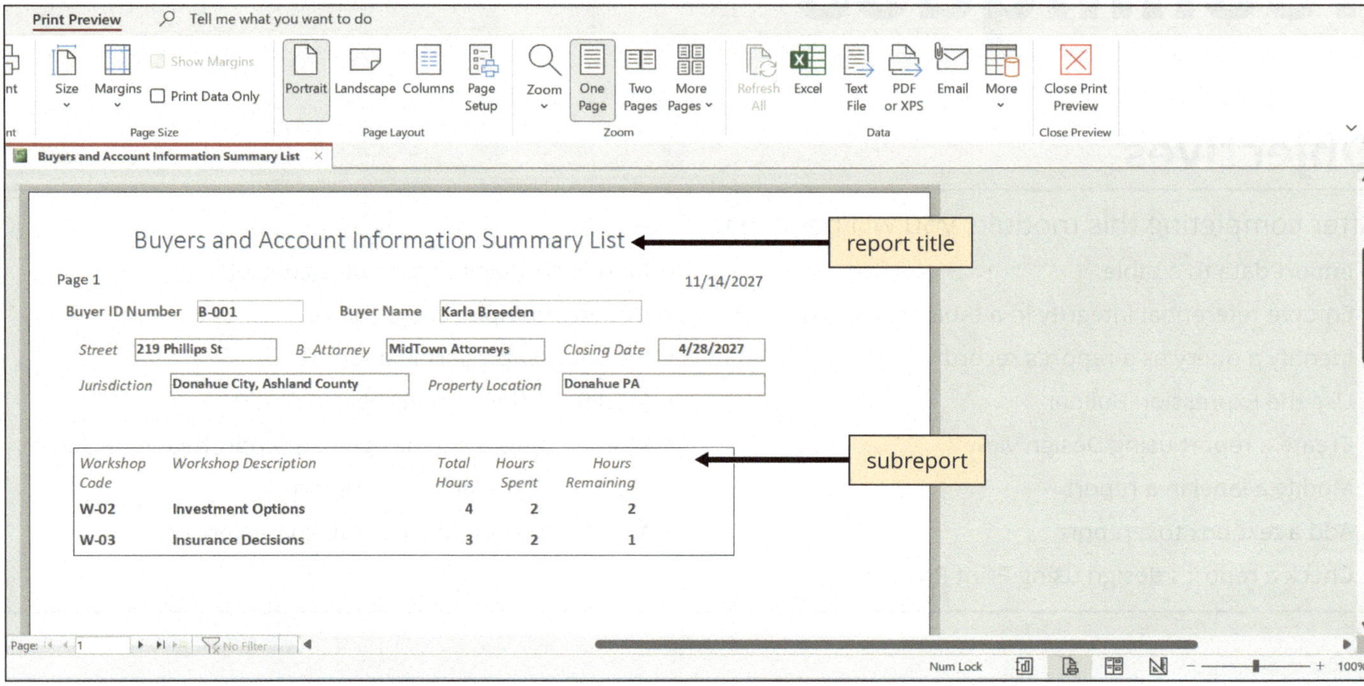

Figure 6–1a

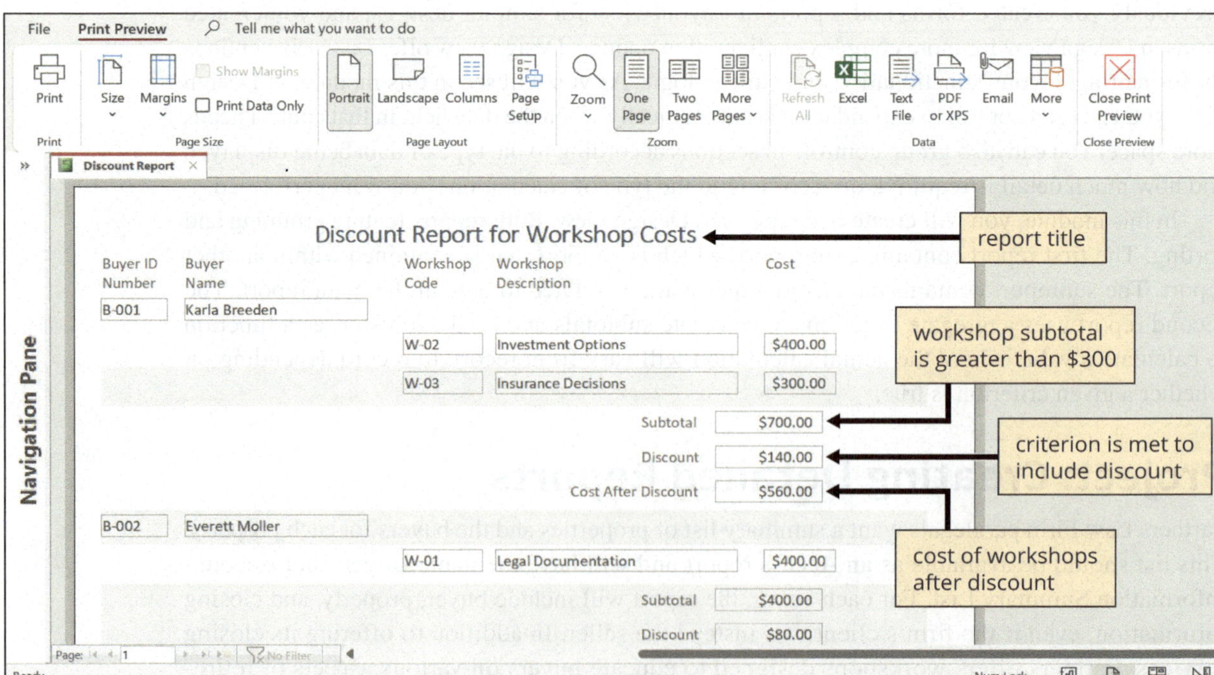

Figure 6–1b

To attract new clients and reward current clients, Partners Law Firm is considering offering a discount to clients who spend more than a certain amount on workshops. To assist in determining the discount, Partners paralegals need a report like the one shown in Figure 6–1b. The report groups clients by Buyer ID. It includes a subtotal of the workshop costs for that client. In addition, the report includes a discounted cost for the workshops, if the total workshop cost for that client is more than $300. Finally, it shows the cost of the workshops less the discount amount.

Additional Tables

Partners has recently teamed up with other local businesses, such as an insurance agency and an investment agency, to present workshops on various aspects of retirement planning. Partners paralegals would like to incorporate this workshop data into the Partners database.

Before creating the reports, you need to create two additional tables for the Partners database. The first table, Workshops, is shown in Table 6–1a. As described in Table 6–1a, each workshop has a code and a description. The table also includes the duration of the workshop in total hours and in increments, or standard time blocks in which the workshop is scheduled. Table 6–1b contains the specific workshops that Partners and the other workshop team members offer to their clients. The first row, for example, indicates that workshop W-01 is called Legal Documentation. It is typically offered in four total hours, organized into two-hour increments.

Table 6–1a Structure of Workshops Table

Field Name	Data Type	Field Size	Description
Workshop Code	Short Text	4	Primary Key
Workshop Description	Short Text	50	
Hours	Number	Integer	
Increments	Number	Integer	
Cost	Currency	n/a	

Table 6–1b Workshops Table

Workshop Code	Workshop Description	Hours	Increments	Cost
W-01	Legal Documentation	4	2	$400
W-02	Investment Options	4	2	$400
W-03	Insurance Decisions	3	1	$300
W-04	Budgeting For and In Retirement	3	1	$300
W-05	End-of-Life Decisions	2	1	$200

The second table, Workshop Enrollments, is described in Table 6–2a and contains a buyer ID, a workshop code, the total number of hours the workshop is scheduled for the buyer, and the number of hours already spent by the buyer in the workshop. Because each combination of Buyer and Workshop needs to be a uniquely identified record, you will create a combined primary key for this table. Shortly you will see why a combined primary key is a more effective approach for this table than if you instead used a single ID field as the primary key.

Table 6–2a Structure of Workshop Enrollments Table

Field Name	Data Type	Field Size	Description
Buyer ID	Short Text	5	Part of Primary Key
Workshop Code	Short Text	4	Part of Primary Key
Total Hours	Number	Integer	
Hours Spent	Number	Integer	

BTW
The Ribbon and Screen Resolution
Access may change how the groups and buttons within the groups appear on the ribbon, depending on the computer's screen resolution. Thus, your ribbon may look different from the ones in this course if you are using a screen resolution other than 1920 x 1080.

BTW
Touch Screen Differences
The Office and Windows interfaces may vary if you are using a touch screen. For this reason, you might notice the function or appearance of your touch screen differs slightly from this module's presentation.

BTW
Touch and Pointers
Remember that if you are using your finger on a touch screen, you will not see the pointer.

BTW
Enabling the Content
For each of the databases you use in this module, you will need to enable the content.

BTW
AutoNumber Field as Primary Key
When you create a table in Datasheet view, Access automatically creates an ID field with the AutoNumber data type as the primary key field. As you add records to the table, Access increments the ID field so each record will have a unique value in the field. AutoNumber fields are useful when there is no data field in a table that is a suitable primary key.

Table 6–2b gives the data for the Workshop Enrollments table. For example, the first record shows that Buyer ID B-001 is currently scheduled for the workshop W-02 (Investment Options). The workshop includes four hours of instructional time, and the buyer has so far spent two hours in class.

Table 6–2b Workshop Enrollments Table

Buyer ID	Workshop Code	Total Hours	Hours Spent
B-001	W-02	4	2
B-001	W-03	3	2
B-002	W-01	4	1
B-003	W-02	4	1
B-005	W-03	3	1
B-004	W-04	3	2
B-002	W-02	4	0

If you examine the data in Table 6–2b, you see the Buyer ID field cannot be the primary key for the Workshop Enrollments table. The first and second records, for example, both have a Buyer ID of B-001. The Workshop Code field also cannot be the primary key. The first, fourth, and seventh records have the same workshop code. This is why a combined primary key is needed for this table. Buyer IDs can be duplicated as buyers enroll in multiple workshops, and Workshop Codes can be duplicated as multiple buyers enroll in the same workshop. However, the combination of a single buyer with a single workshop creates a unique record. Therefore, the combination of the Buyer ID and the Workshop Code can, together, represent a unique enrollment.

To Create the New Tables

You will use Design view to create the new tables. The steps to create the new tables are similar to the steps you used previously to add fields to an existing table and to define primary keys. The only difference is the way you specify a primary key. **Why?** *In the Workshop Enrollments table, the primary key consists of more than one field, which requires a slightly different process.* To specify a primary key containing more than one field, you must select both fields that make up the primary key by clicking the row selector for the first field, and then press and hold CTRL while clicking the row selector for the second field. Once the fields are selected, you can use the Primary Key button to indicate the primary key consists of both fields. The following steps create the tables in Design view.

1

- **sam** Start Access. Open the database, SC_AC_06-1.accdb, which is located in the Data Files folder. Save the file to your hard disk, OneDrive, or other storage location using the file name, **SC_AC_06_Partners**. Enable the content.
- If necessary, close the Navigation Pane.
- Display the Create tab (Figure 6–2).

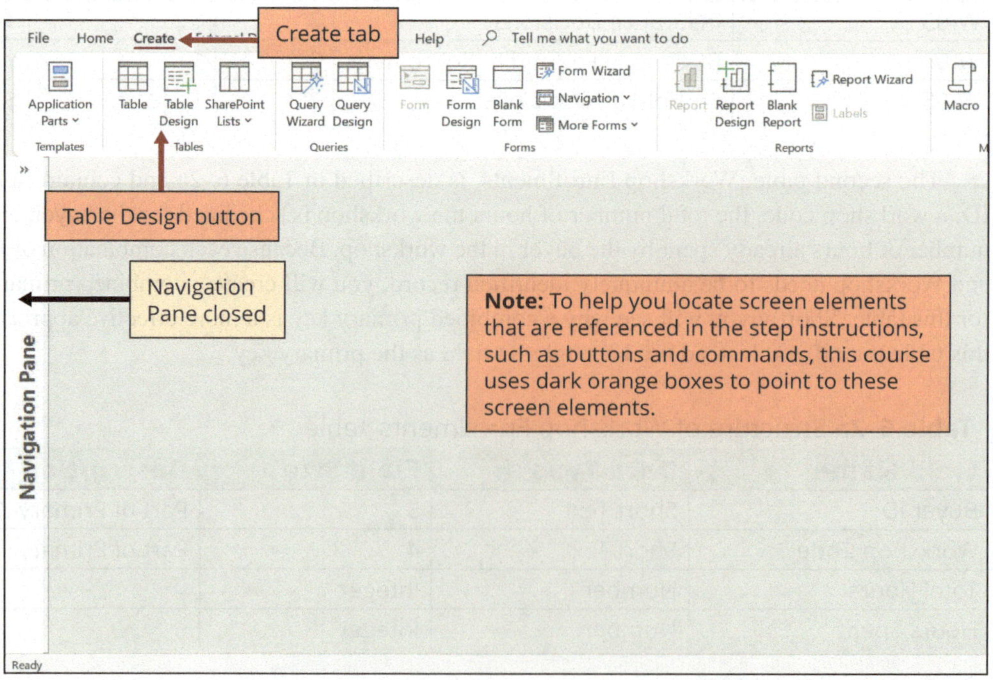

Figure 6–2

2

- Click the Table Design button (Create tab | Tables group) to create a table in Design view.
- Enter the information for the fields in the Workshop table as indicated in Table 6–1a, making Workshop Code the primary key, and specifying the indicated field sizes.
- Save the table using the name **Workshops** and close the table.

3

- Display the Create tab and then click the Table Design button (Create tab | Tables group) to create a second table in Design view.
- Enter the information for the fields in the Workshop Enrollments table as indicated in Table 6–2a. You will designate the primary key in Step 4.

4

- Click the row selector for the Buyer ID field.
- Hold down CTRL and then click the row selector for the Workshop Code field so both fields are selected.
- Click the Primary Key button (Table Design tab | Tools group) to select the combination of the two fields as the primary key (Figure 6–3).

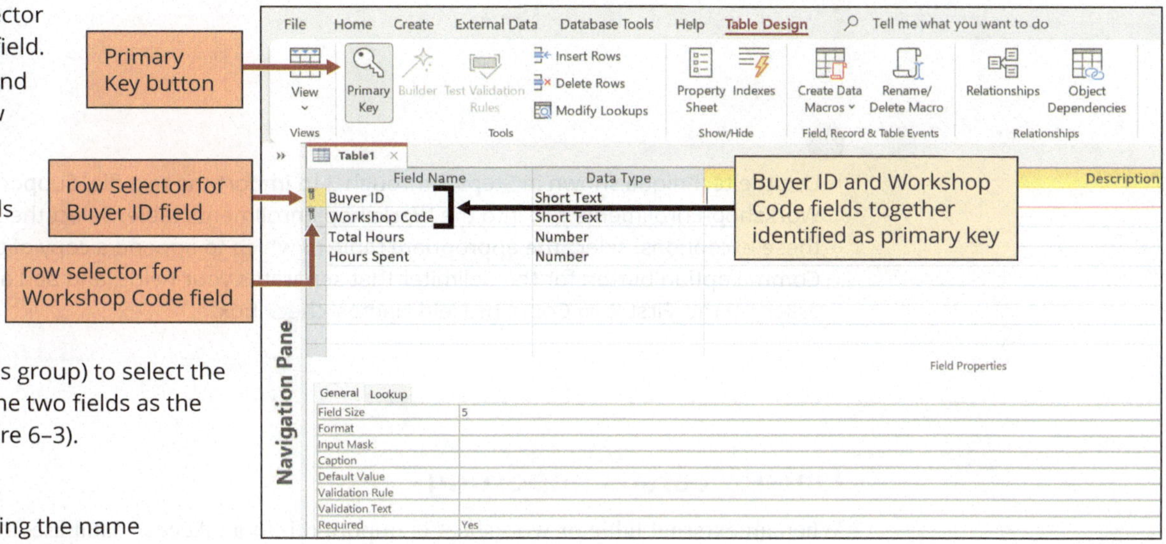

Figure 6–3

5

- Save the table using the name **Workshop Enrollments** and close the table.

Q&A I realized I designated the wrong fields as the primary key. How can I correct the primary key?
Click any field that currently participates in the primary key, and then click the Primary Key button to remove the primary key designation. You then can specify the correct primary key.

To Import the Data

Now that the tables have been created, you need to add data to them. You could enter the data manually, or, if the data is already in electronic form, you could import the data. The data for the Workshops and Workshop Enrollments tables is included in the Data Files. The files are text files formatted as delimited files. The Workshops data is in a tab-delimited text (.txt) file, and the Workshop Enrollments data is in a comma-separated values (.csv) file, which is also a delimited text file. The following steps import the data for both tables.

BTW
Copying the Structure of a Table
If you want to create a table that has a structure similar to that of an existing table, you can copy the structure of the table only. Select the table in the Navigation Pane and click Copy, and then click Paste. In the Paste Table As dialog box, type the new table name and click the Structure Only option button. Then click the OK button. To modify the new table, open it in Design view.

1

- With the Partners database open, click the External Data tab, click the New Data Source button (External Data tab | Import & Link group), point to From File, and then click Text File to display the Get External Data – Text File dialog box.

2

- Click the Browse button (Get External Data – Text File dialog box), and then navigate to the location containing the text file for the Workshops table as specified by your instructor.

- Click the file, Support_AC_06_Workshops.txt, and then click Open.
- If necessary, click the 'Append a copy of the records to the table' option button, select the Workshops table from the list, and then click OK.

3

- With the Delimited option button selected, click Next.
- With the Tab option button selected, click the 'First Row Contains Field Names' check box, click Next, and then click Finish.
- Click the Close button to close the Get External Data – Text File dialog box without saving the import steps.

Q&A I got an error message after I clicked the Finish button that indicated there were errors. The data was not imported. What should I do?
First, click the Cancel button to terminate the process. Then, review the structure of the table in Design view to ensure the field names are all spelled correctly and the data types are correct. Correct any errors you find, save your work, and then repeat the steps to import the data.

4

- Use the technique shown in Steps 1 through 3 to import the text file, Support_AC_06_Workshop-Enrollments.csv, into the Workshop Enrollments table. Select the same options with these exceptions: select the appropriate table to which to append a copy of the file, select the Comma option button for the delimiter that separates your fields, and add a check mark if necessary in the 'First Row Contains Field Names' check box.

Linking versus Importing

When an external table or worksheet is imported into an Access database, a copy of the data is placed in a table in the database. The original data still exists, just as it did before, but no further connection exists between the source file and the data in the database. Changes to the original data do not affect the data in the database. Likewise, changes in the database do not affect the original data.

It is also possible to link data stored in a variety of formats to Access databases. To do so, you would select the 'Link to the data source by creating a linked table' option button when importing data, rather than the 'Import the source data into a new table in the current database' or 'Append a copy of the records to the table' option buttons. With linking, the connection is maintained; changes made to the data in the external table or worksheet affect the Access table.

To identify that a table is linked to other data, Access displays an arrow in front of the table in the Navigation Pane. In addition, an icon is displayed in front of the name that indicates the type of file to which the data is linked. For example, an Excel icon in front of the name indicates the table is linked to an Excel worksheet.

BTW
Linking
Two of the primary reasons to link data from another program to Access are to use the query and report features of Access. When you link an Access database to data in another application, all changes to the data must be made in the source application. For example, if you link an Excel workbook to an Access database, you cannot edit the linked table in Access. You must make all changes to the data in Excel.

To Modify Linked Tables

After you link tables between a worksheet and a database or between two databases, you can modify many of the linked table's features. To rename the linked table, set view properties, and set links between tables in queries, you would use the following steps.

1. Click the 'Linked Table Manager' button (External Data tab | Import & Link group) to update the links.
2. Select the linked table for which you want to update the links.
3. Click the OK button.

To Relate the New Tables

The following steps relate, or create a relationship between, the tables. **Why?** The new tables need to be related to the existing tables in the Partners database. The Buyers and Workshop Enrollments tables are related through the Buyer ID field that exists in both tables. The Workshops and Workshop Enrollments tables are related through the Workshop Code fields in both tables.

1

- Display the Database Tools tab.
- Click the Relationships button (Database Tools tab | Relationships group) to open the Relationships window (Figure 6–4).

Q&A I only see one table; did I do something wrong?
Click the All Relationships button to display all the tables in relationships.

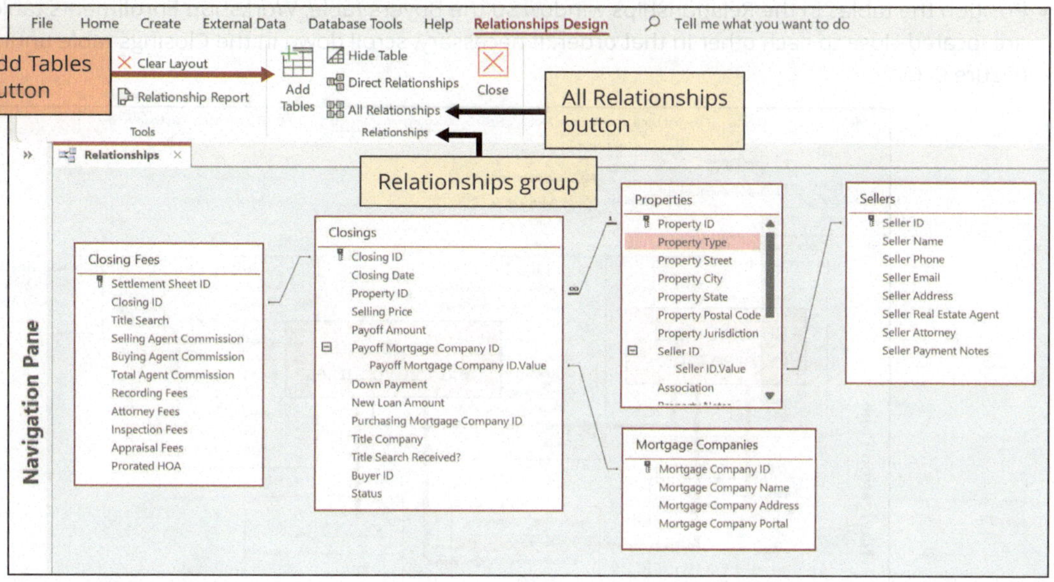

Figure 6–4

2

- Click the Add Tables button (Relationships Design tab | Relationships group) to display the Add Tables pane (Figure 6–5).

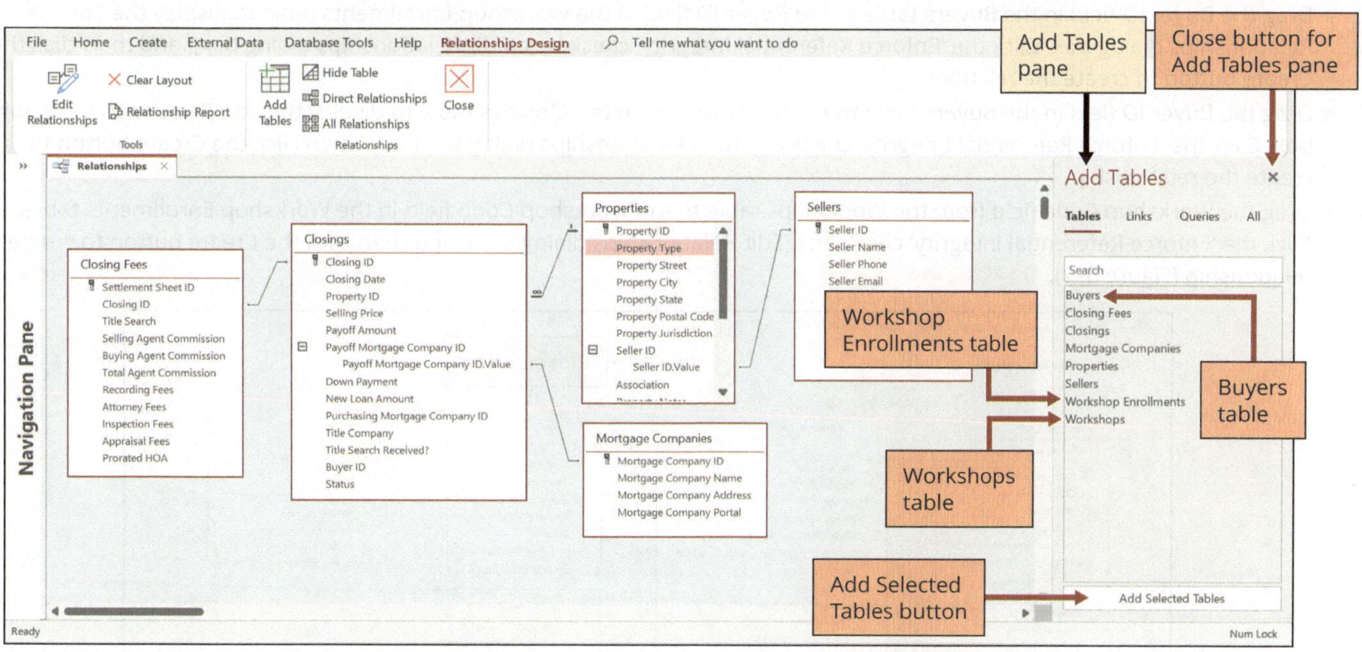

Figure 6–5

3

- Click the Workshop Enrollments table, press and hold CTRL, click the Workshops table, and then click the Buyers table to select all three tables. Click the Add Selected Tables button (Add Tables pane) to add the three tables to the Relationships window.
- Click Close to close the Add Tables pane.

Q&A I cannot see all the tables in the Relationships window; some are obscured.

Drag the tables to other locations in the Relationships window for easier viewing.

I cannot see the Workshop Enrollments table. Should I repeat the step?

If you cannot see the table, it likely is behind the Add Tables pane. You do not need to repeat the step.

4

- Position the tables in the Relationships window so the Buyers table, Workshop Enrollments table, and Workshops table are located close to each other in that order. If necessary, scroll down in the Closings table until you see the Buyer ID field (Figure 6–6).

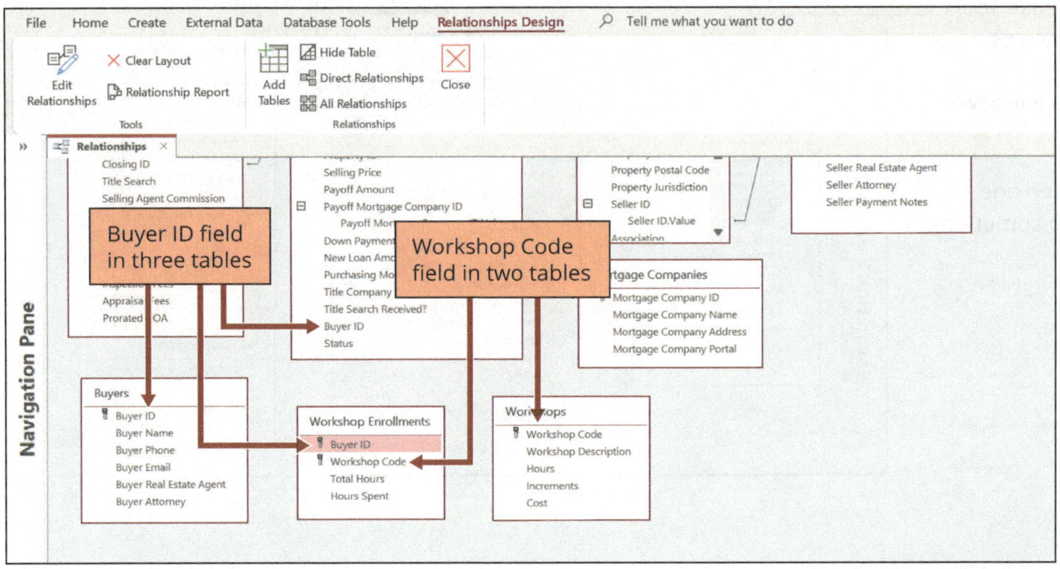

Figure 6–6

- Drag the Buyer ID field in the Buyers table to the Buyer ID field in the Workshop Enrollments table to display the Edit Relationships dialog box. Click the 'Enforce Referential Integrity' check box (Edit Relationships dialog box), and then click the Create button to create the relationship.
- Drag the Buyer ID field in the Buyers table to the Buyer ID field in the Closings table to display the Edit Relationships dialog box. Click the 'Enforce Referential Integrity' check box (Edit Relationships dialog box), and then click the Create button to create the relationship.
- Drag the Workshop Code field from the Workshops table to the Workshop Code field in the Workshop Enrollments table. Click the 'Enforce Referential Integrity' check box (Edit Relationships dialog box), and then click the Create button to create the relationship (Figure 6–7).

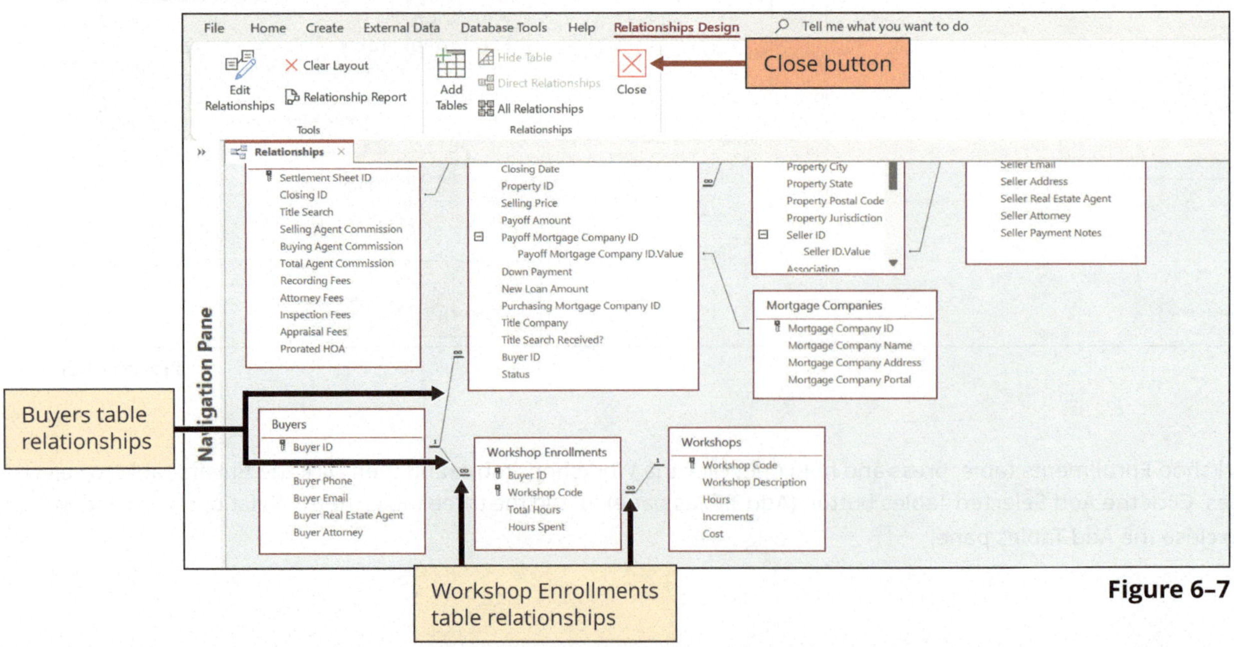

Figure 6–7

5

- Save the changes and then click the Close button (Relationships Design tab | Relationships group).

Creating Reports in Design View

Previously, you have used both Layout view and the Report Wizard to create reports. However, you can create a report in Design view. You can also use Design view to modify a report you previously created. When you create a report in Design view, you must place all the fields in the desired locations. You must also specify any sorting or grouping that is required.

Whether you use the wizard or simply use Design view to create a report, you must determine on which table or query to base the report. If you decide to base the report on a query, you must first create the query, unless it already exists.

BTW
Invalid Relationships
If Access will not allow you to create a relationship and enforce referential integrity, it could be because the two matching fields do not have the same data type. Open the tables in Design view and check the data types and field sizes. You should also check to be sure you do not have a foreign key value in the "many" table that does not match the primary key value in the "one" table. To do this, create a Find Unmatched Query using the Query Wizard to find the unmatched records in the "many" table.

To Create a Query for the Report

To create the two reports needed by Partners paralegals, it is more convenient to build each report from a query because each report will need to pull data from multiple tables. These two queries for the two reports do not yet exist, so you will need to create them. The first query relates buyers and their account information. The buyer account information consists of closing dates, properties purchased, property jurisdictions, and closing attorneys. The second query relates workshops and workshop enrollments. The following steps create the Buyers and Account Information query.

BTW
Many-to-Many Relationships
There is a many-to-many relationship between the Buyers table and the Workshops table. To implement a many-to-many relationship in a relational database management system such as Access, you create a third table, often called a junction or intersection table, that has as its primary key the combination of the primary keys of each of the tables involved in the many-to-many relationship. The primary key of the Workshop Enrollments table is the combination of the Buyer ID and the Workshop Code fields.

1

- Display the Create tab, and then click the Query Design button (Create tab | Queries group) to create a new query.

2

- Click the Buyers table (Add Tables pane).
- While holding CTRL, click the Closings table, and then click the Properties table.
- Release CTRL and click the Add Selected Tables button (Add Tables pane).
- Close the Add Tables pane by clicking its Close button, reposition the field lists as desired, and resize the field lists to display as many fields as possible.

Q&A Why must I use CTRL here instead of SHIFT to select the tables?
Holding SHIFT selects the first table clicked, the next table clicked, and all tables appearing in the list between them. Holding CTRL selects exactly the tables clicked and no other tables.

3

- In the Buyers table, double-click the Buyer ID, Buyer Name, and Buyer Attorney fields to display them in the design grid.
- In the Closings table, double-click the Closing Date field to display it in the design grid.
- In the Properties table, double-click the Property Street, Property City, Property State, and Property Jurisdiction fields to display them in the design grid.
- Select Sort in Ascending Order on the Closing Date field.

4

- Run the query to view the results.
- Scroll through the fields to make sure you have included all the necessary fields. If you have omitted a field, return to Design view and add it (Figure 6–8).

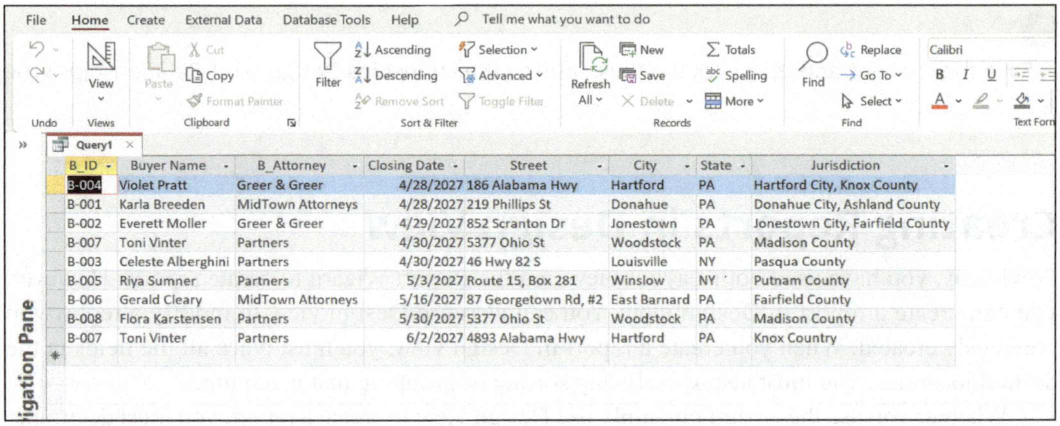

Figure 6–8

5

- Click the Save button on the Quick Access Toolbar to save the query, type **Buyers and Account Information** as the name of the query, and then click OK.
- Close the query.

To Create an Additional Query for the Report Using Expression Builder

The following steps create the Workshop Enrollments and Workshops query, which includes a calculated field for hours remaining in each buyer's current workshops, that is, the total number of hours minus the hours the buyer has spent in each offering. **Why?** Partners paralegals need to include in the Buyers and Account Information Summary List report the number of hours that remain in a workshop offering.

1

- Display the Create tab and then click the Query Design button (Create tab | Queries group) to create a new query.
- Use CTRL to select the Buyers table, Workshop Enrollments table, and Workshops table.
- Click the Add Selected Tables button, and then close the Add Tables pane.

2

- In the Buyers table, double-click the Buyer ID and Buyer Name fields to add the fields to the design grid.
- In the Workshop Enrollments table, double-click the Workshop Code field to add the field to the design grid.
- In the Workshops table, double-click the Workshop Description and Cost fields to add the fields to the design grid.
- In the Workshop Enrollments table, double-click the Total Hours and Hours Spent fields to add the fields to the design grid.

3

- Click in the top cell in the Field row of the first open column in the design grid to select it.
- Click the Builder button (Query Design tab | Query Setup group) to display the Expression Builder dialog box (Figure 6–9).

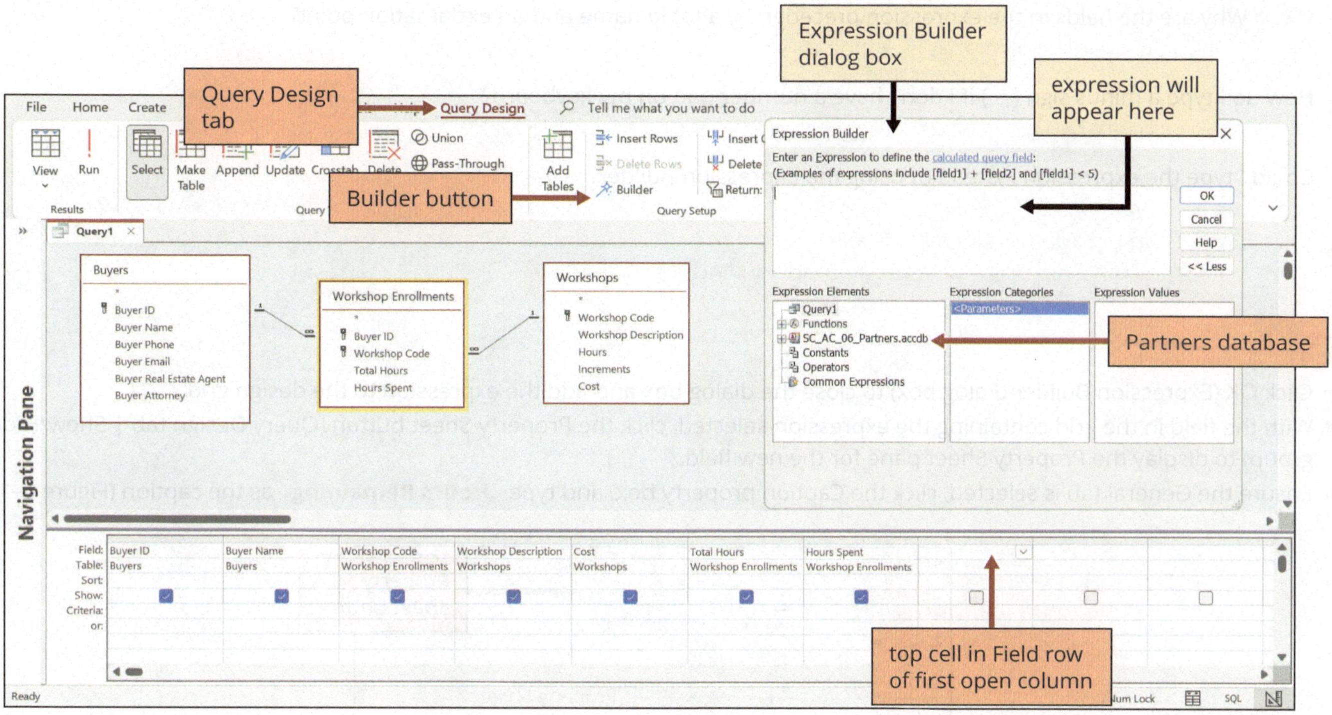

Figure 6–9

Other Ways

1. Right-click field in grid, click Build to open Expression Builder

4

- Double-click the Partners database in the Expression Elements section to display the categories of objects within the Partners database, and then double-click Tables to display a list of tables.
- Click the Workshop Enrollments table to select it.
- Double-click the Total Hours field to add it to the expression.
- Type a minus sign (–) to add it to the expression.
- Double-click the Hours Spent field to add it to the expression (Figure 6–10).

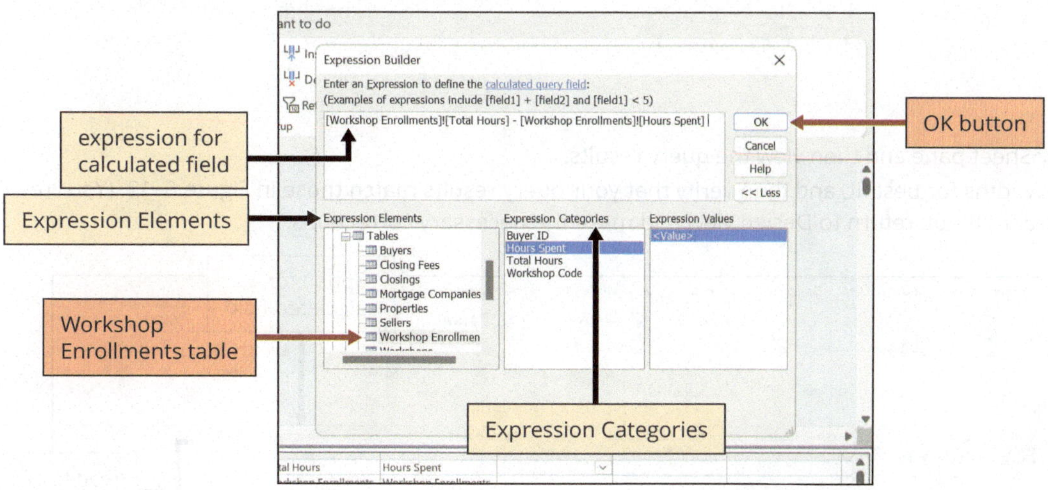

Figure 6–10

Q&A Why are the fields in the expression preceded by a table name and an exclamation point?

This notation qualifies the field; that is, it indicates to which table the field belongs.

How do I type a minus sign (–) if I don't have a number pad on my keyboard?

You can type a hyphen instead, which Access will interpret as a minus sign.

Could I type the expression instead of using the Expression Builder?

Yes. You could type it directly into the design grid. You could also right-click the column and click Zoom to allow you to type the expression in the Zoom dialog box. Finally, you could use the Expression Builder, but simply type the expression rather than clicking any buttons. Use whichever method you find most convenient.

5

- Click OK (Expression Builder dialog box) to close the dialog box and add the expression to the design grid.
- With the field in the grid containing the expression selected, click the Property Sheet button (Query Design tab | Show/Hide group) to display the Property Sheet pane for the new field.
- Ensure the General tab is selected, click the Caption property box, and type **Hours Remaining** as the caption (Figure 6–11).

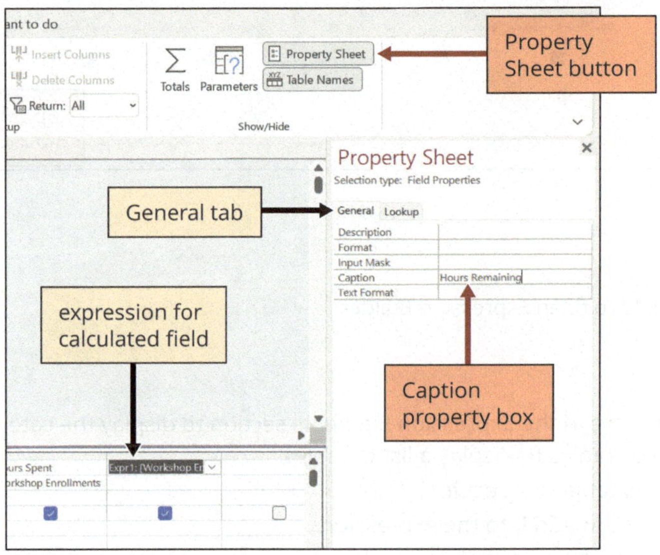

Figure 6–11

Q&A I do not have a Caption property in my property sheet. What went wrong? What should I do?

You either inadvertently clicked a different location in the grid, or you have not yet completed entering the expression. The easiest way to ensure you have done both is to click any other column in the grid and then click the column with the expression.

6

- Close the Property Sheet pane and then view the query results.
- Adjust the column widths for best fit, and then verify that your query results match those in Figure 6–12. (Your results might be in a different order.) If not, return to Design view and make the necessary corrections.

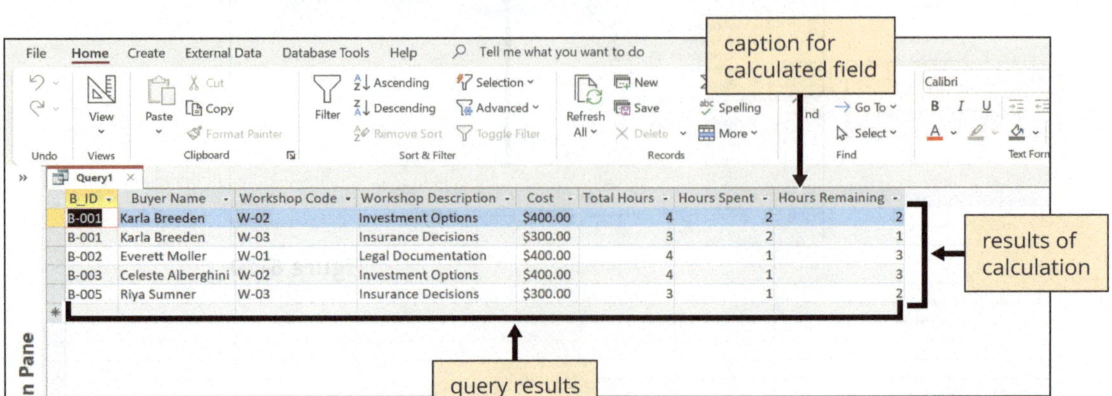

Figure 6–12

7

- Save the query as **Workshop Enrollments and Workshops**.
- Close the query.

Consider This

How do you determine the tables and fields for the report?

If you determine that data should be presented as a report, you then need to determine which tables and fields contain the data for the report.

- **Examine the requirements for the report in general to determine the tables.** Do the requirements only relate to data in a single table, or does the data come from multiple tables? Is the data in a query, or could you create a query that contains some or all the fields necessary for the report?
- **Examine the specific requirements for the report to determine the fields necessary.** Look for all the data items that are specified for the report. Each item should correspond to a field in a table, or it should be able to be computed from a field or fields in a table. This information gives you the list of fields to include in the query.
- **Determine the order of the fields.** Examine the requirements to determine the order in which the fields should appear. Be logical and consistent in your ordering. For example, in an address, the city should come before the state, and the state should come before the postal code, unless there is some compelling reason for another order.

What decisions do you make in determining the organization of the report?

- **Determine sort order.** Is there a special order in which the records should appear?
- **Determine grouping.** Should the records be grouped in some fashion? If so, what information should appear before the records in a group? If, for example, buyers are grouped by property ID number, the ID number of the property should probably appear before the group. Should the property address also appear? What should appear after the group? For example, are there some fields for which subtotals should be calculated? If so, the subtotals would come after the group.
- **Determine whether to include a subreport.** Rather than use grouping, you can include a subreport, as shown in the Buyers and Account Information Summary List in Figure 6–1a. The data concerning workshop enrollments for the buyers could have been presented by grouping the workshop enrollments' data by Buyer ID. The headings currently in the subreport would have appeared in the group header. Instead, it is presented in a subreport. Subreports, which are reports in their own right, offer more flexibility in formatting than using group headers and footers. More importantly, in the Buyers and Account Information Summary List, some buyers do not have any workshop enrollments. If this information were presented using grouping, the group header would still appear for these buyers, cluttering the report. With a subreport, buyers that have no workshop enrollments do not appear.

To Create an Initial Report in Design View

Creating from scratch the report shown in Figure 6–1a involves creating the initial report in Design view, adding the subreport, modifying the subreport separately from the main report, and then making the final modifications to the main report. When you want to create a report from scratch, you use Design view rather than the Report Wizard. Why? The Report Wizard is suitable for simple, customized reports. Using the Report Design screen, you can make advanced design changes, such as adding subreports. The following steps create the initial version of the Buyers and Account Information Summary List and select the **record source** for the report, that is, the table or query that will furnish the data for the report. The steps then specify sorting and grouping for the report.

1

- Display the Create tab.
- Click the Report Design button (Create tab | Reports group) to create a report in Design view.
- Ensure the selector for the entire report, the box in the upper-left corner of the report, contains a black square, which indicates the report is selected (Figure 6–13).

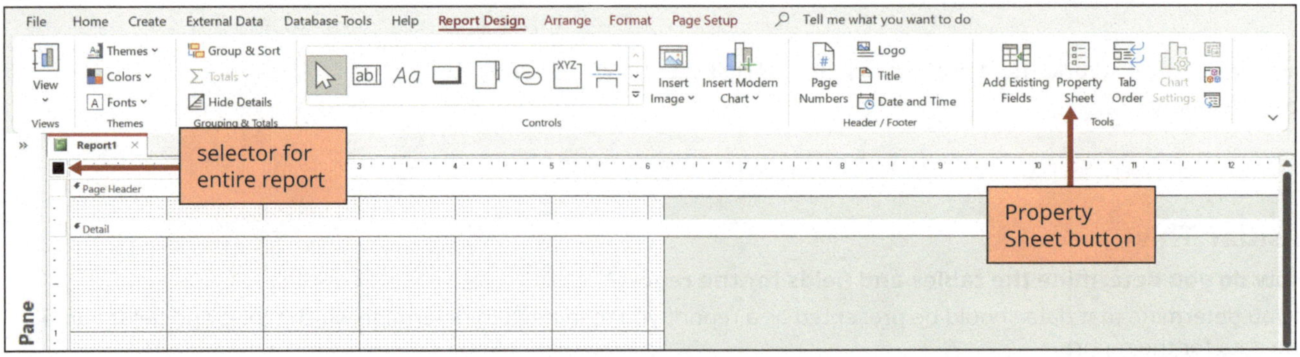

Figure 6–13

- Click the Property Sheet button (Report Design tab | Tools group) to display the Property Sheet pane.
- Drag the left border of the Property Sheet pane to increase its width.
- With the All tab (Property Sheet pane) selected, click the Record Source property box arrow to display the list of available tables and queries (Figure 6–14).

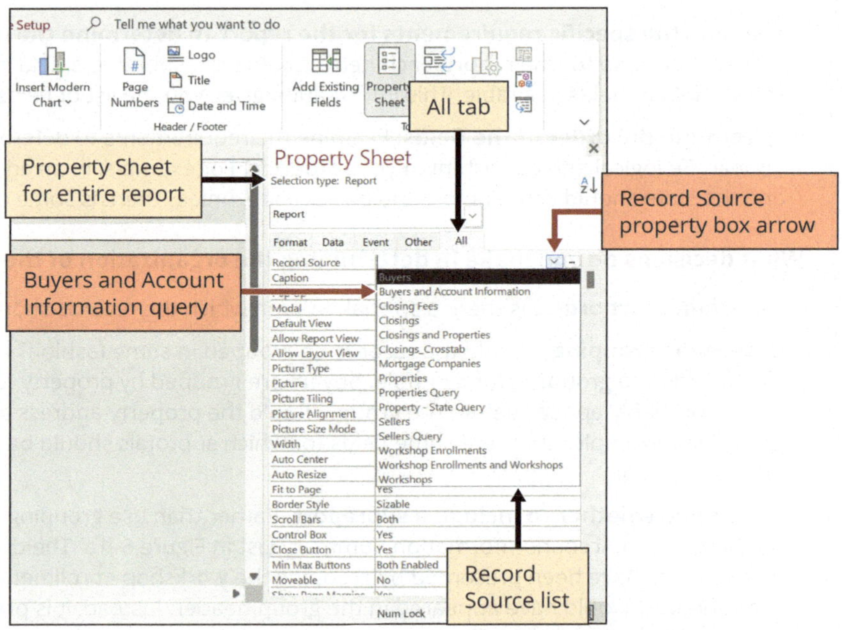

Figure 6–14

Q&A Can I move the Property Sheet pane?

Yes, you can move the Property Sheet pane by dragging its title bar. If you want to place the Property Sheet pane back in its original position, drag the pane to the right edge of your screen so it pops back into place.

Can I increase the size of the Record Sources list?

Yes, you can change the width of the portion of the pane used for the Record Source list by dragging the dividing line between the property names and the property boxes.

2

- Click the Buyers and Account Information query to select the query as the record source for the report.
- Close the Property Sheet pane.

To Group and Sort

In Design view of the report, you can specify both grouping and sorting by using the Group & Sort button on the Report Design tab, just as you did in Layout view. The following steps specify both grouping and sorting in the report. **Why?** Partners paralegals have determined the records in the report should be grouped by Buyer ID. That is, all the information of a given buyer should appear together. Within the account information of a given buyer, they have determined that closings are to be ordered by closing date.

1

- Click the Group & Sort button (Report Design tab | Grouping & Totals group) to display the Group, Sort, and Total pane (Figure 6–15).

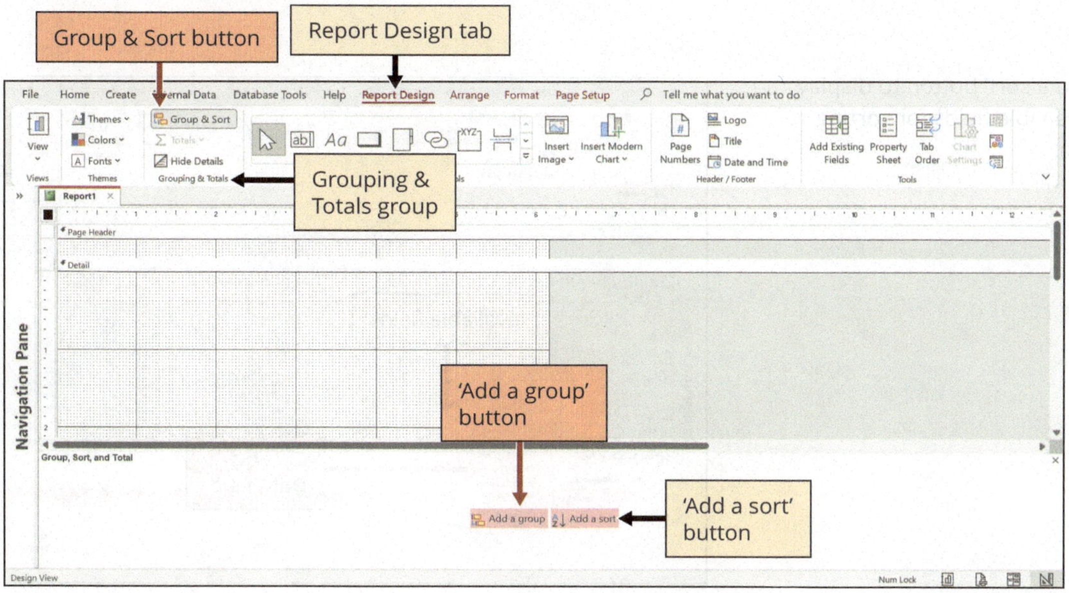

Figure 6–15

Other Ways

1. Right-click any open area of report, click Sorting & Grouping to open Group, Sort, and Total pane

2

- Click the 'Add a group' button to display the list of available fields for grouping (Figure 6–16).

Q&A The list of fields disappeared before I had a chance to select a field. What should I do?

Click the 'select field' arrow to once again display the list of fields.

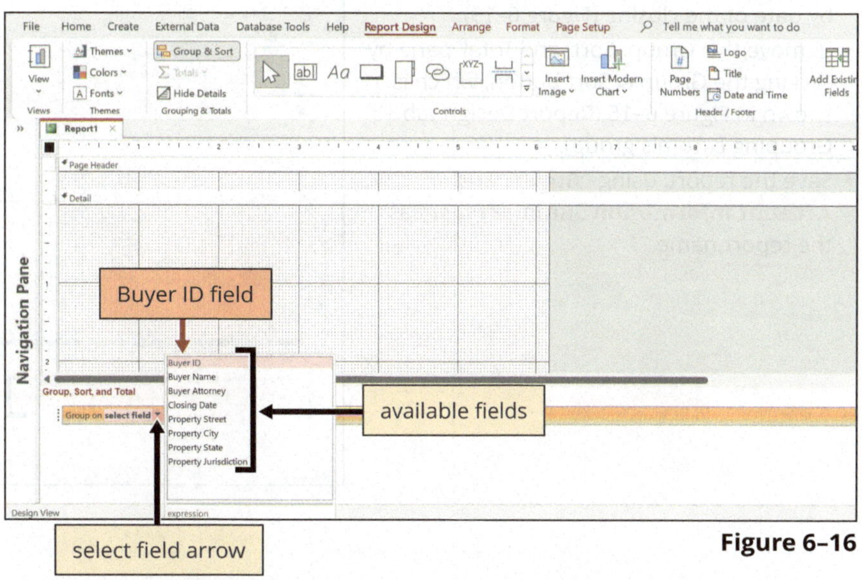

Figure 6–16

3

- Click the Buyer ID field to group by buyer ID number (Figure 6–17).

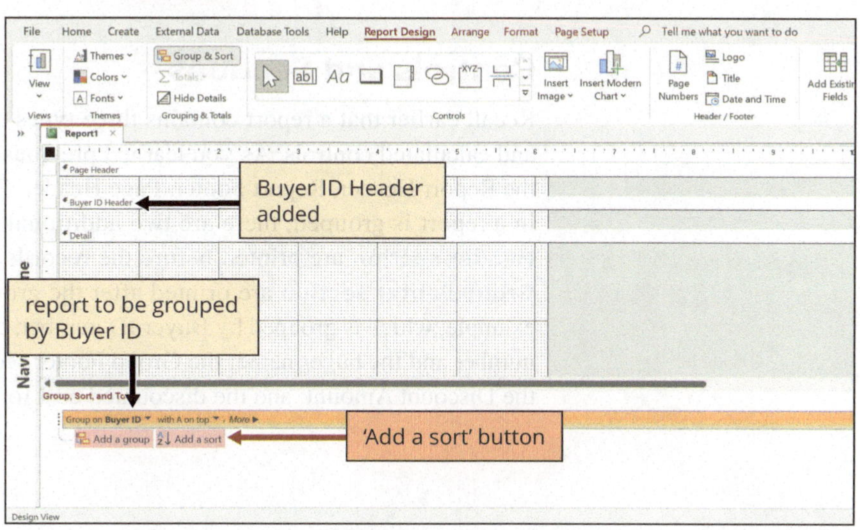

Figure 6–17

4

- Click the 'Add a sort' button to display the list of available fields for sorting (Figure 6–18).

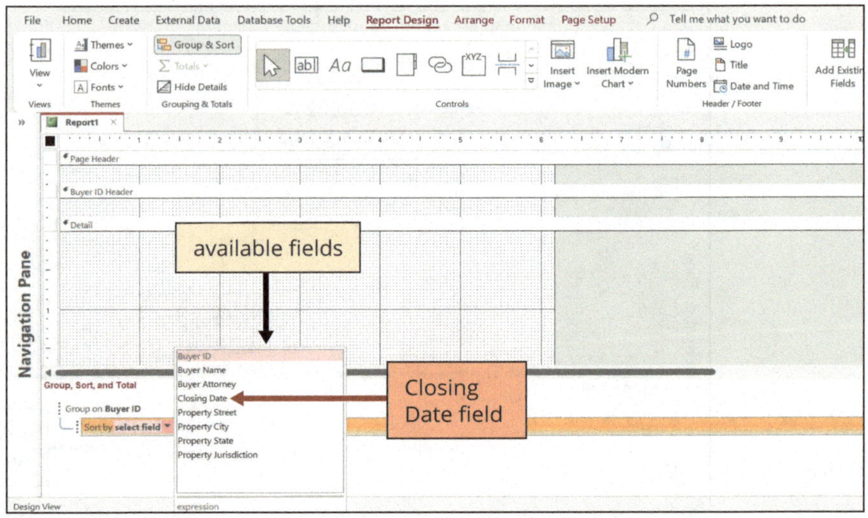

Figure 6–18

5

- Click the Closing Date field to sort closings by date of the closing (Figure 6–19).
- Remove the 'Group, Sort, and Total' pane by clicking the Group & Sort button, which is shown in Figure 6–15 (Report Design tab | Grouping & Totals group).
- Save the report, using **Buyers and Account Information Summary List** as the report name.

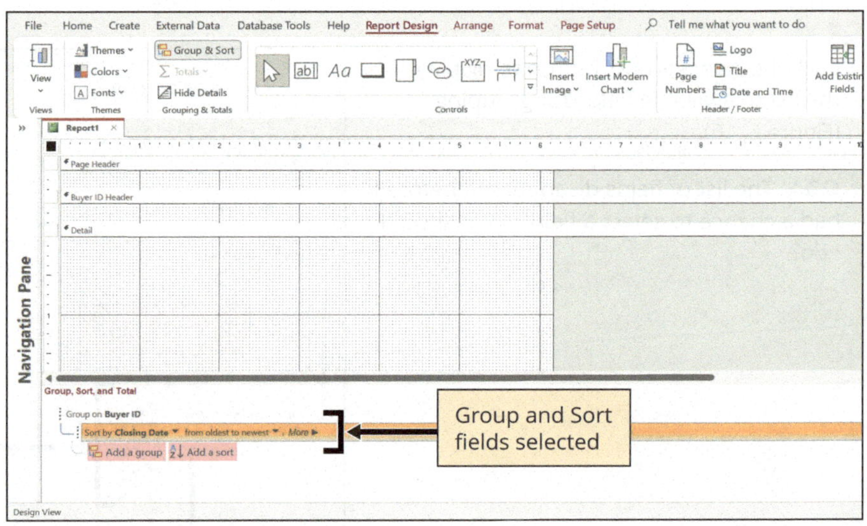

Figure 6–19

Controls and Sections

Recall earlier that a report contains three types of controls: bound controls, unbound controls, and calculated controls. As you learned previously, reports contain standard sections, including the Report Header, Report Footer, Page Header, Page Footer, and Detail sections. When the data in a report is grouped, there are two additional possible sections. The contents of the **Group Header section** are printed before the records in a particular group, and the contents of the **Group Footer section** are printed after the group. In the Discount Report (Figure 6–1b), for example, which is grouped by Buyer ID number, the Group Header section contains the Buyer ID number and the buyer name; the Group Footer section contains subtotals of the Workshop Costs, the Discount Amount, and the discounted cost for all workshops for that buyer.

To Add Fields to the Report in Design View

Why? Once you have determined the fields that are necessary for the report, you need to add them to the report design. You can add the fields to the report by dragging them from the field list to the appropriate position on the report. The following steps add the fields to the report.

1

- Click the 'Add Existing Fields' button (Report Design tab | Tools group) to display a field list.
- Drag the Buyer ID field to the approximate position shown in Figure 6–20. (The pointer shape appears as an arrow with a plus sign as you drag a field.)

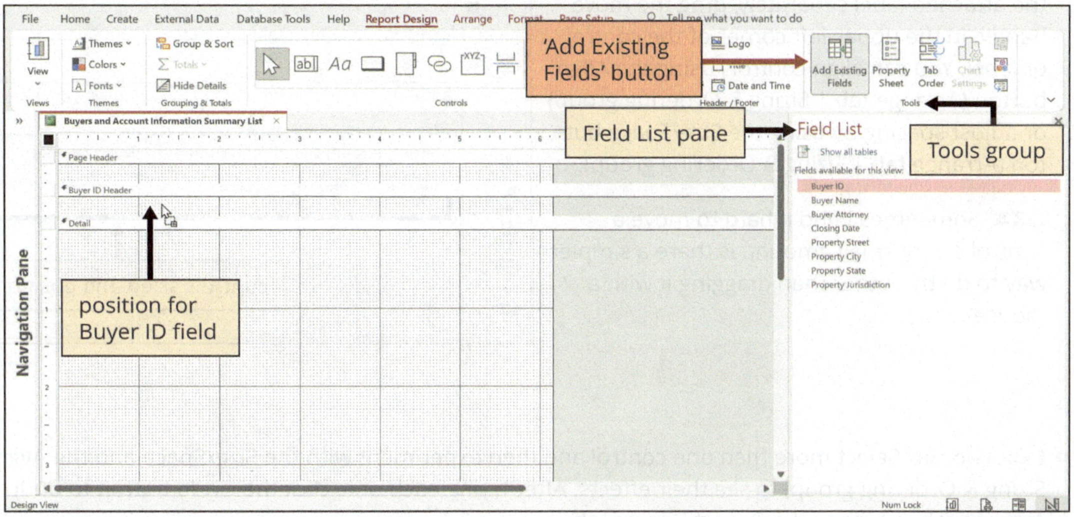

Figure 6–20

Q&A My field list does not look like the one in the figure. It has several tables listed, and at the top it has 'Show only fields in the current record source.' The figure has 'Show all tables.' What should I do?

Click the 'Show only fields in the current record source' link. Your field list should then match the one in the figure.

2

- Release the mouse button to place the field.
- Using the same technique, drag the Buyer Name field to the Buyer ID Header section.
- Place additional fields in the report Details section (Figure 6–21).

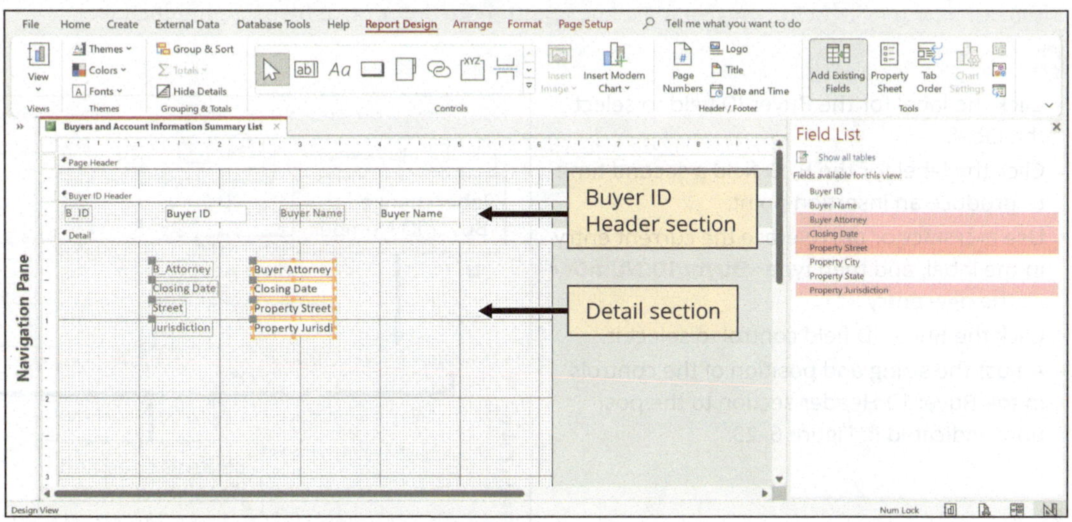

Figure 6–21

Q&A Could I drag several fields from the field list at once?

Yes. You can select multiple fields by selecting the first field, holding down the CTRL key, and selecting the additional fields. Once you have selected multiple fields, you can drag them all at once. How you choose to select fields and drag them onto the report is a matter of personal preference.

3

- Close the Field List pane.
- Adjust the positions and sizes of the labels and controls to those shown in Figure 6–22. If any field is not in the correct position, drag it to its correct location. To move the control or the attached label separately, drag the move handle in the upper-left corner of the control or label. You can align controls using the Align button (Arrange tab | Sizing & Ordering group) or adjust spacing by using the Size/Space button (Arrange tab | Sizing & Ordering group).

Q&A Sometimes I find it hard to move a control a very small amount. Is there a simpler way to do this other than dragging it with a mouse?

Yes. Once you have selected the control, you can use the arrow keys to move the control a very small amount in the desired direction.

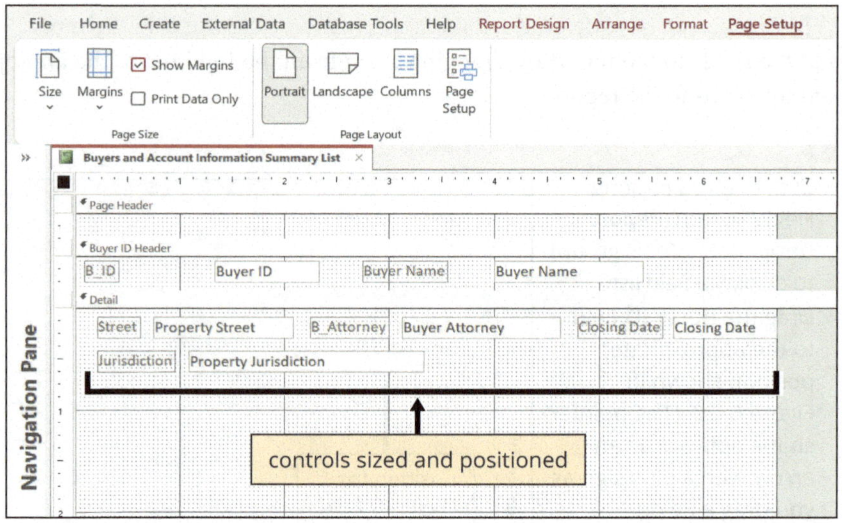

Figure 6–22

- **Experiment:** Select more than one control and then experiment with the Size/Space and the Align buttons (Arrange tab | Sizing & Ordering group) to see their effects. After trying each one, click the Undo button to undo the change. If you used the Arrange tab, return to the Report Design tab.

To Change Labels

The label for the Buyer ID field currently contains the caption B_ID for that field. The following step changes the contents of the label for the Buyer ID field from B_ID to Buyer ID Number. **Why?** Because there is plenty of room on the report to display a longer name for the field, you can make the report more descriptive by changing the label.

1

- Click the label for the Buyer ID field to select the label.
- Click the label for the B_ID field a second time to produce an insertion point.
- Use BACKSPACE or DEL to erase the current entry in the label, and then type **Buyer ID Number** as the new entry.
- Click the Buyer ID field control to select it.
- Adjust the sizing and position of the controls in the Buyer ID Header section to the positions indicated in Figure 6–23.

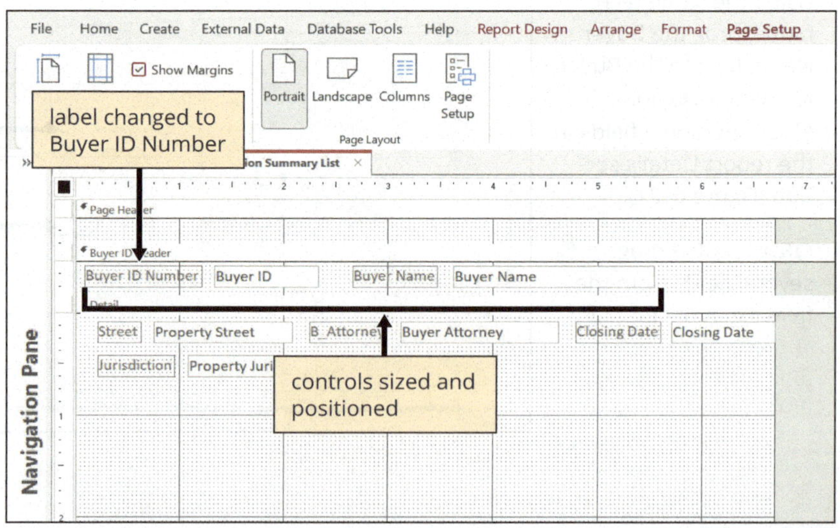

Figure 6–23

Using Other Tools in the Controls Group

Previously, you used the Subform/Subreport tool within the Controls group on the Design tab to place special controls on a form. The Controls group has additional tools available that can be used with forms and reports. A description of the additional tools appears in Table 6–3.

Table 6–3 Additional Tools in the Controls Group

Tool	Description
Select	Select to be able to size, move, or edit existing controls. If you click another tool and want to cancel the effect of the tool before using it, you can click the Select tool.
Text Box	Create a text box for entering, editing, and displaying data. You can also bind the text box to a field in the underlying table or query.
Label	Create a label, which is a box containing text that cannot be edited and is independent of other controls, such as a title.
Button	Create a command button.
Tab Control	Create a tab control, which contains a series of tabbed pages. Each tabbed page can contain its own controls.
Link	Insert a hyperlink to an existing file, web page, database object, or email address.
Option Group	Create an option group, which is a rectangle containing a collection of option buttons. To select an option, you click the corresponding option button.
Insert or Remove Page Break	Insert or remove a physical page break (typically in a report).
Combo Box	Create a combo box, which is a combination of a text box and a list box.
Line	Draw a line on a form or report.
Toggle Button	Add a toggle button. With a toggle button, a user can make a Yes/No selection by clicking the button. The button either appears to be pressed (for Yes) or not pressed (for No).
List Box	Create a list box, a box that allows the user to select from a list of options.
Rectangle	Create a rectangle.
Check Box	Insert a check box. With a check box a user can make multiple Yes/No selections.
Unbound Object Frame	Insert an OLE object (for example, a graph, picture, sound file, or video) that is not contained in a field in a table within the database.
Attachment	Insert a field to hold attached files, such as images, documents, or presentation slides.
Option Button	Insert an option button. With an option button, a user can make a single Yes/No selection from among a collection of at least two choices.
Subform/Subreport	Create a subform (a form contained within another form) or a subreport (a report contained within another report).
Bound Object Frame	Insert an OLE object (for example, a graph, picture, sound file, or video) that is contained in a field in a table within the database.
Image	Insert a frame into which you can insert a graphic. The graphic will be the same for all records.
Chart	Create a chart.

To Add Text Boxes

You can place a text box in a report or form by using the Text Box tool in the Controls group on the Design tab. The text box consists of a control that is initially unbound and an attached label. The next step is to update the **control source**, which is the source of data for the control. You can do so by entering the expression in the text box or by updating the Control Source property in the property sheet with the expression.

Once you have updated the control source property with the expression, the control becomes a calculated control. If the expression is just a single field (for example, =[Cost]), the control would be a bound control. **Why?** The control is bound (tied) to the corresponding field. The process of converting an unbound control to a bound control is called **binding**. Expressions can also be arithmetic operations: for example, calculating the sum of Cost and Current Due. Many times, you need to **concatenate**, or combine, two or more text data items into a single expression; the process is called **concatenation**. To concatenate text data, you use the **ampersand (&) operator**. For example, the expression =[Property City] & ' ' & [Property State] indicates the concatenation of a city name, a single blank space, and a state name.

BTW

Drop Down Controls

Drop-down boxes can be combo boxes or list boxes. To add a combo box to a report, click the Combo Box tool from the Controls gallery (Report Design tab | Controls group), move the pointer to the desired location, and click the position to place the combo box. Follow the directions in the Combo Box Wizard dialog box to specify the options and values for the combo box. To add a list box to a report, click the List Box tool from the Controls gallery (Report Design tab | Controls group) and follow the steps described above for a combo box.

The following steps add text boxes and create calculated controls. Remember that controls can be resized by clicking the control to select it and then dragging the edge of the control to the desired size.

1

- Click the Text Box tool (Report Design tab | Controls group) and move the pointer to the approximate position shown in Figure 6–24 in the Detail section.

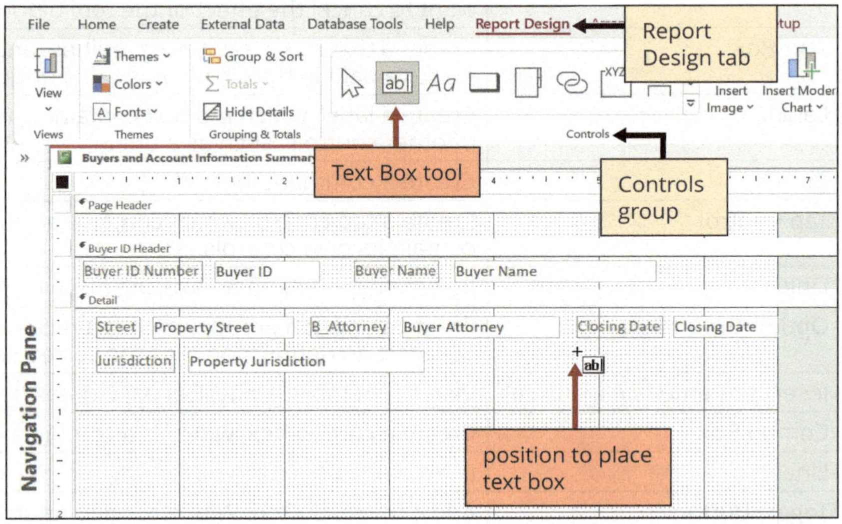

Figure 6–24

BTW

Default Names for Controls

Because each control has properties associated with it, Access assigns a default name to each new control. The default name includes a control identifier and a number. For example, if you create a text box on a report, the default name could be Text32. You should change the default name to something meaningful to make it easier to remember the purpose of the control.

2

- Click the position shown in Figure 6–24 to place a text box on the report (Figure 6–25). Reposition it if necessary so neither the text box nor its label overlap other controls.

Q&A My text box overlaps an object already on the screen. Is that a problem?

You can move and/or resize your text box to the desired location and size. You also can continue to make adjustments to the text box's size and position as other changes are made to the report.

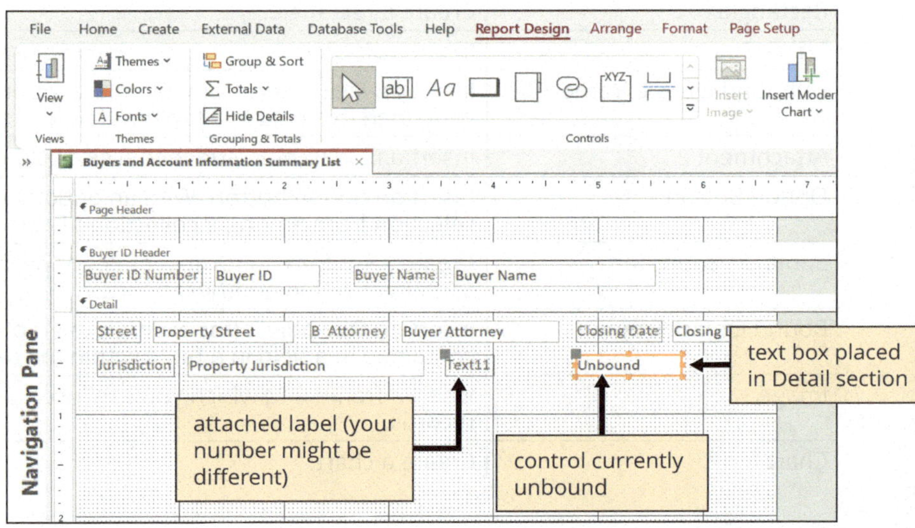

Figure 6–25

3

- Click in the text box to produce an insertion point (Figure 6–26).

Q&A I inadvertently clicked somewhere else, so the text box was no longer selected. When I clicked the text box a second time, it was selected, but there was no insertion point. What should I do?

Click the text box again to produce the insertion point.

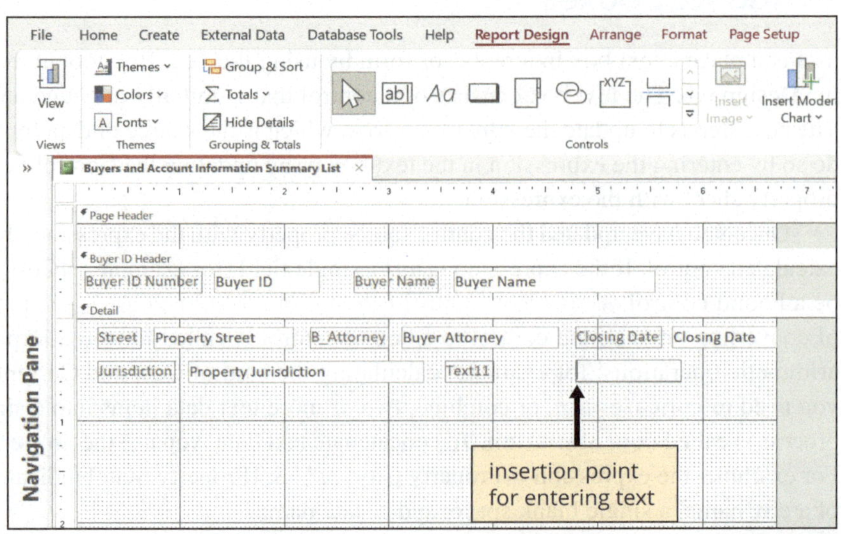

Figure 6–26

4

- In the text box, type **=[Property City] & ' ' & [Property State]** to display the name of the property city, followed by a space, and then the name of the property state.

Q&A Could I use the Expression Builder instead of typing the expression?

Yes. Click the Property Sheet button and then click the Build button, which contains three dots, next to the Control Source property.

Do I need to use single quotes (')?

No. You could also use double quotes (").

- Click in the text box label to select the label, and then click the label a second time to produce an insertion point (Figure 6–27).

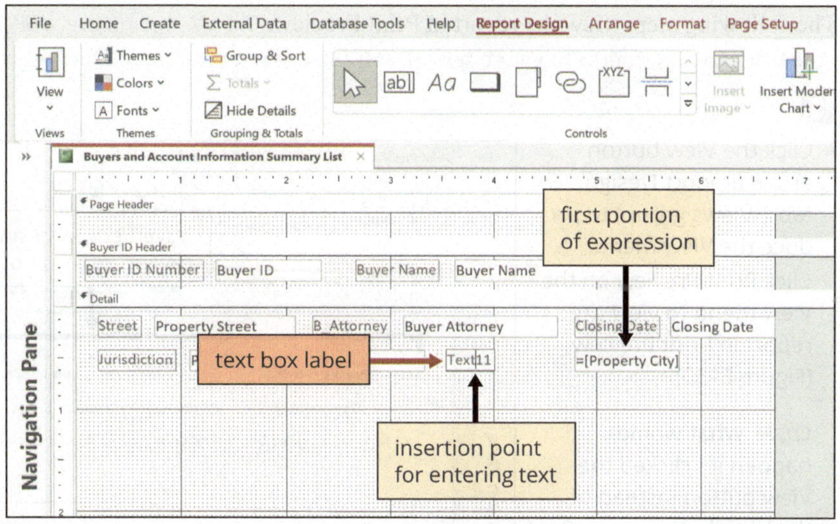

Figure 6–27

5

- Use BACKSPACE or DEL to erase the current entry in the label, and then type **Property Location** as the new entry.
- Click outside the label to deselect it, and then drag the label to the position shown in the figure by dragging the Move handle in the upper-left corner of the label (Figure 6–28).

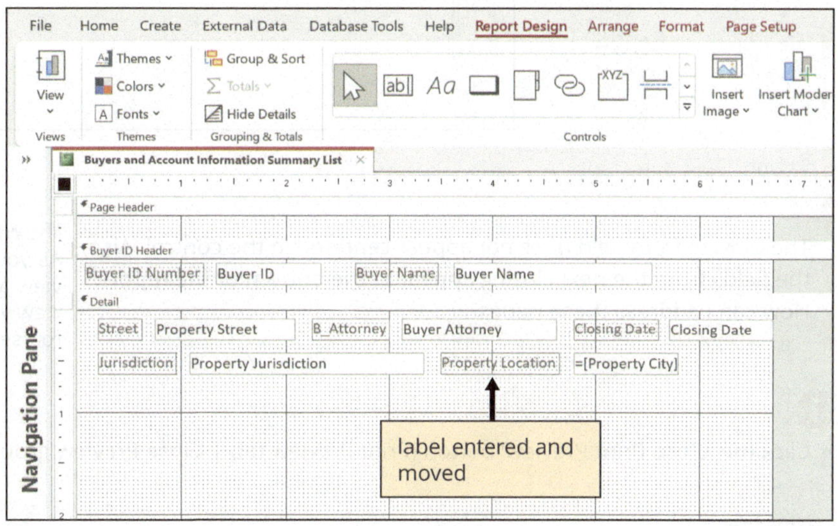

Figure 6–28

6

- Resize the text box control to display more of the expression (Figure 6–29).

7

- Save the report.

Q&A My label is not in the correct position. What should I do?

Click outside the label to deselect it, click the label to select it, and then use its move handle to drag it to the desired position.

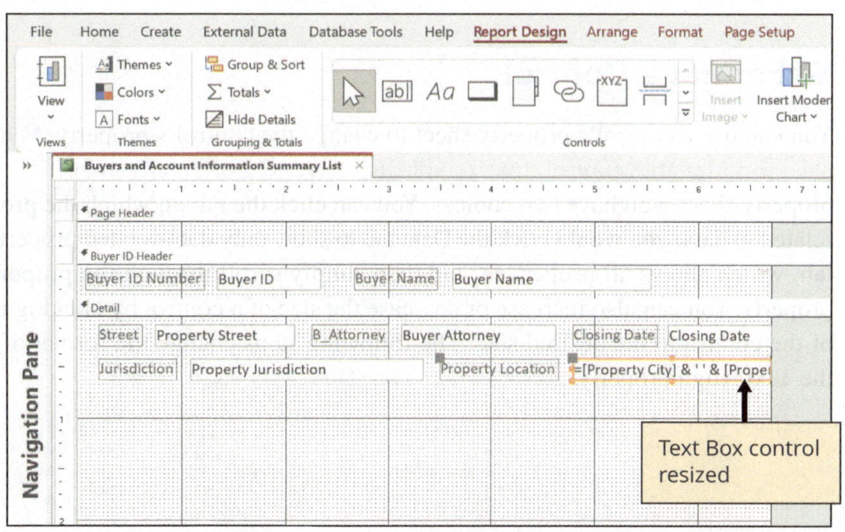

Figure 6–29

To View the Report in Print Preview

The following steps view the report in Print Preview. **Why?** As you are working on a report in Design view, it is useful to periodically view the report to gauge how it will look containing data. One way to do so is to use Print Preview.

1

- Click the View button arrow (Report Design tab | Views group) to produce the View menu.
- Click Print Preview on the View menu to view the report in Print Preview (Figure 6–30).

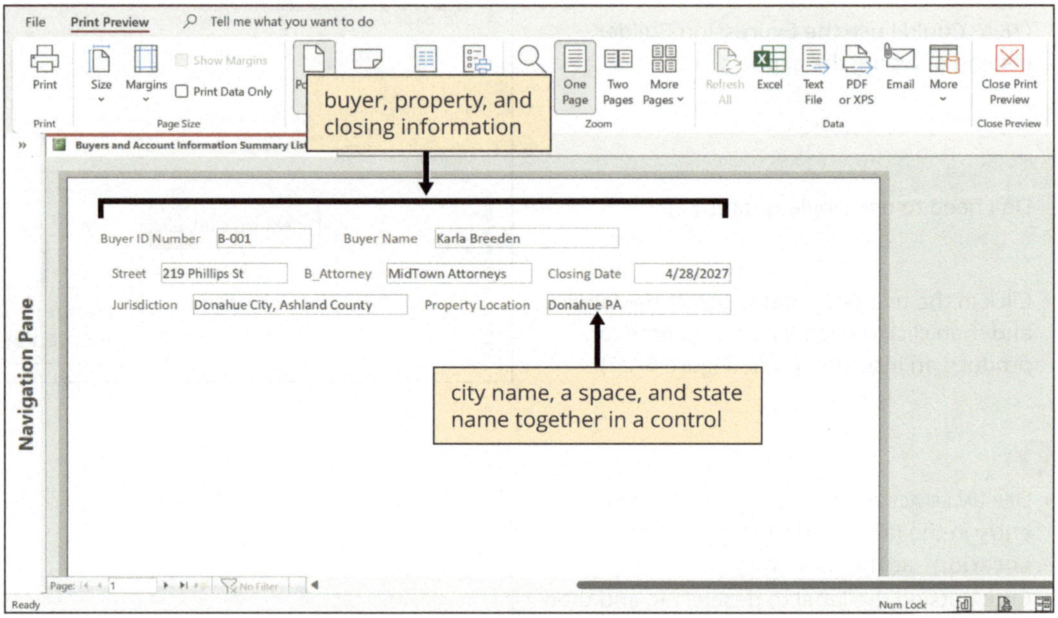

Figure 6–30

Q&A What would happen if I clicked the View button instead of the View button arrow?
The icon on the View button is the icon for Report View, so you would view the results in Report view. This is another useful way to view a report, but compared with Print Preview, Report view does not give as accurate a picture of how the final, printed report will look.

The Closing Date field does not appear centered in the control. Also, the fields from the next closing appear at the bottom of the report. How can I address these issues?
You will address these issues in the next sections.

BTW
Viewing Report Modifications
As you work through this module, switch between Design view and either Report view or Print Preview frequently to view your changes. An easy way to switch back and forth is to use the different view buttons on the status bar.

2

- Click the 'Close Print Preview' button (Print Preview tab | Close Preview group) to return to Design view.

Other Ways

1. Click Print Preview button on status bar to open Print Preview

To Format a Control

You can use a control's property sheet to change the control's property. **Why?** When you add controls to a report, you often need to format the control, for example, to add a bold or an alignment format. If a property does not appear in the control's property sheet, you have two choices. You can click the tab on which the property is located. For example, if it were a control related to data, you would click the Data tab to show only data-related properties. Many people, however, prefer to click the All tab, which shows all properties, and then simply scroll through the properties, if necessary, until locating the appropriate property. You can also increase or decrease the size of a control by clicking the control to select it and then dragging the edge of the control to the desired size. The following steps change the format of the Closing Date control to Center by changing the Text Align property.

1

- Click the Closing Date control to select it, and then click the Property Sheet button (Report Design tab | Tools group) to display the Property Sheet pane.
- If necessary, click the All tab (Figure 6–31).

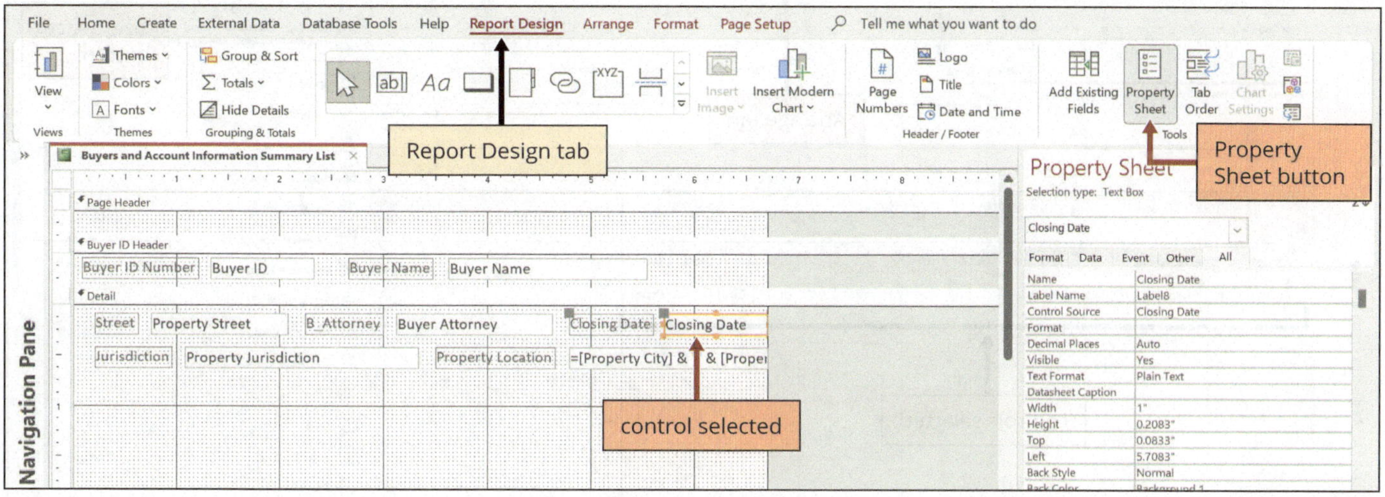

Figure 6–31

Other Ways

1. Right-click control, click Properties to open Property Sheet pane

- **Experiment:** Click the other tabs in the property sheet to see the types of properties on each tab. When finished, once again click the All tab.

2

- Click the Text Align property box (Property Sheet pane), click the arrow that appears, and then click Center to select Center as the control's alignment.
- Close the Property Sheet pane.
- Preview the report using Print Preview to see the effect of the property changes.
- Click the 'Close Print Preview' button (Print Preview tab | Close Preview group) to return to Design view.

To Group Controls

The following steps group the controls within the Detail section. **Why?** If your report contains a collection of controls that you will frequently want to format in the same way, you can simplify the process of selecting all the controls by grouping them. Once they are grouped, selecting any control in the group automatically selects all the controls in the group. You can then apply the desired change to all the controls.

1

- Click the Property Street control to select it.

Q&A Do I click the field control with the white background or the label control with the transparent background?
Click the field control with the white background.

- While holding SHIFT, click all the other field controls (not the label controls) in the Detail section to select them.

Q&A Does it matter in which order I select the other field controls?
No. It is only important that you select all the field controls in the Detail section, but do not select the label controls.

- Display the Arrange tab.
- Click the Size/Space button (Arrange tab | Sizing & Ordering group) to display the Size/Space menu, and then scroll to the bottom of that menu (Figure 6–32).

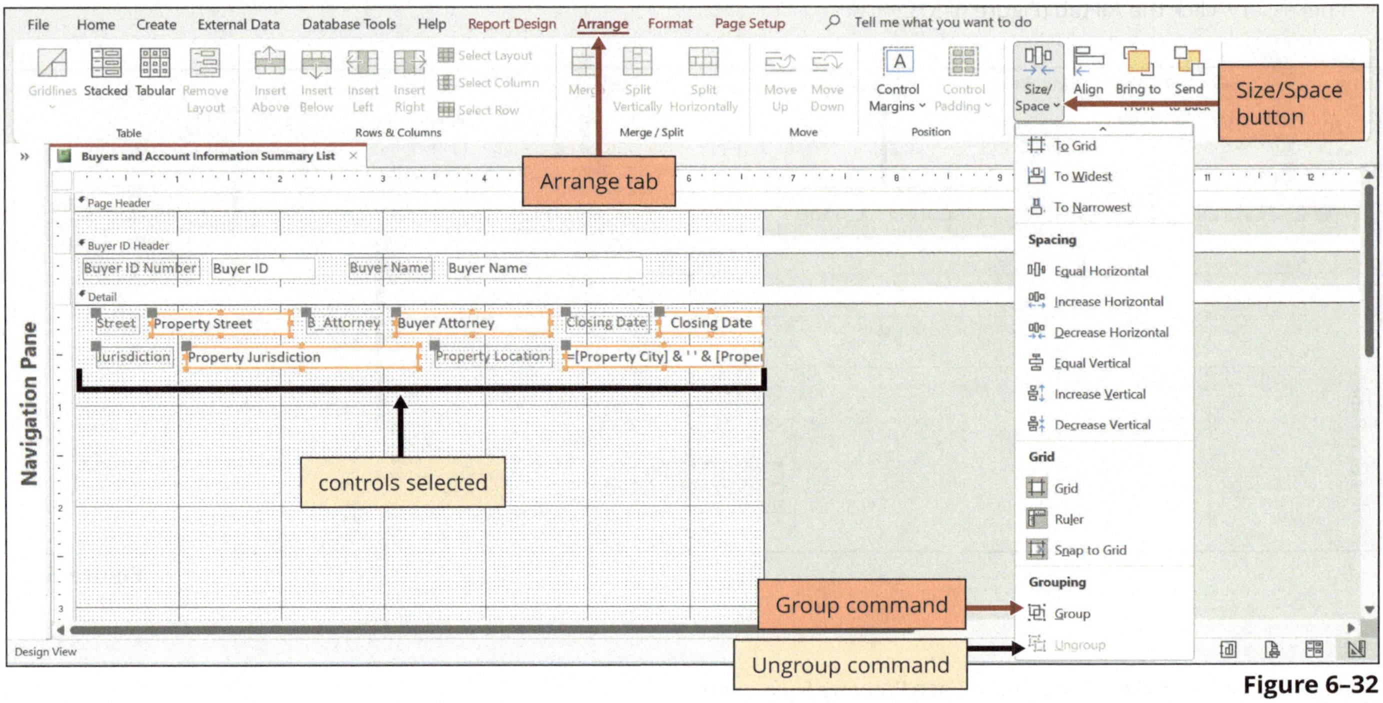

Figure 6–32

2

- Click Group on the Size/Space button menu to group the controls.
- Click outside the controls to deselect the group.

Q&A What if I make a mistake and group the wrong collection of controls?
Ungroup the controls using the following steps, and then group the correct collection of controls.

To Ungroup Controls

If you no longer need to simultaneously modify all the controls you have placed in a group, you can ungroup the controls. To do so, you would use the following steps.

1. Click any of the controls in a group to select the entire group.
2. Display the Arrange tab.
3. Click the Size/Space button (Arrange tab | Sizing & Ordering group) to display the Size/Space button menu.
4. Click the Ungroup button on the Size/Space button menu to ungroup the controls.

Consider This

Can you group controls in forms?

Yes. The process is identical to the process of grouping controls in reports.

To Modify Grouped Controls

To modify grouped controls, click any control in the group to select the entire group. **Why?** Any change you make then affects all controls in the group. The following steps bold the controls in the group, resize them, and then change the border style.

1

- Click any one of the grouped controls to select the group.
- Display the Format tab.
- Click the Bold button (Format tab | Font group) to bold all the controls in the group (Figure 6–33).

Q&A How do I change only one control in the group?

Double-click the control to select just the one control and not the entire group. You then can make any change you want to that control.

Do I need to use the Property Street field to select the group or could I use another field?

Any field in the group will work.

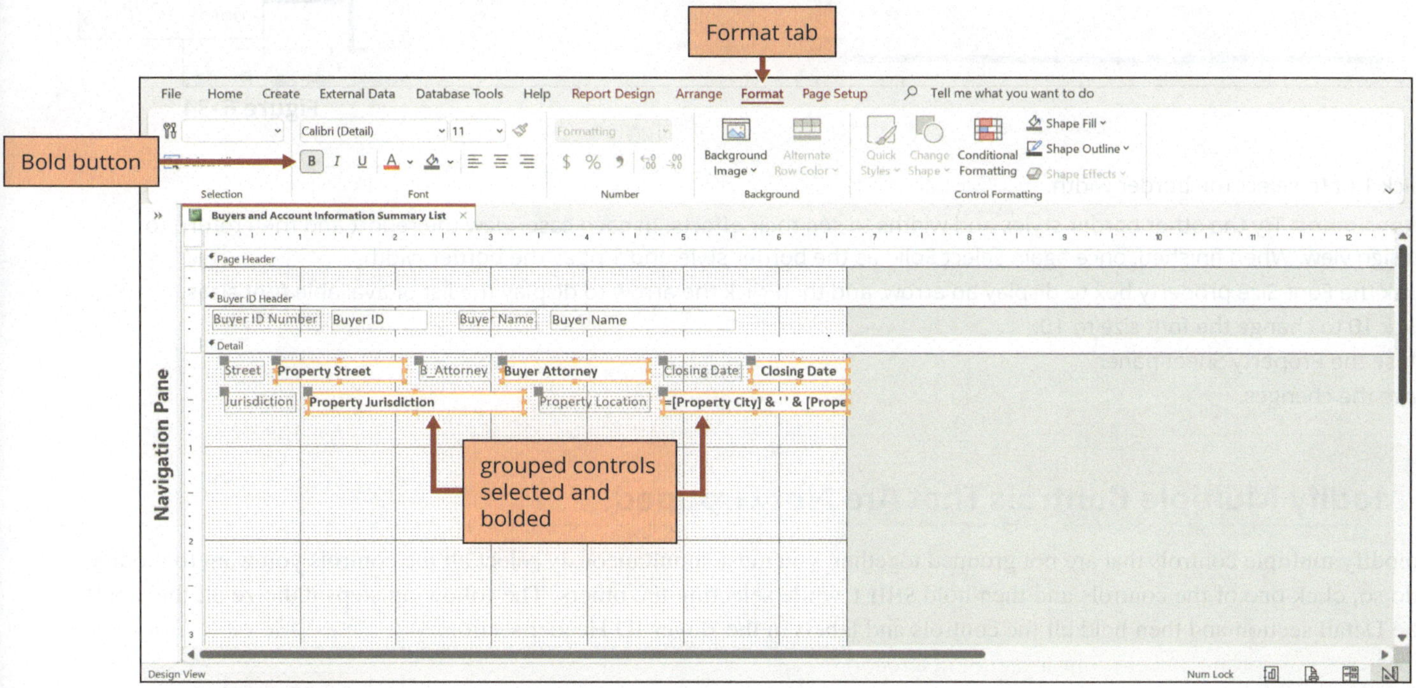

Figure 6–33

2

- Display the Report Design tab, and then click the Property Sheet button (Report Design tab | Tools group) to display the property sheet for the grouped controls.
- With the All tab (Property Sheet pane) selected, ensure the Border Style property is set to Solid. If it is not, click the Border Style property box to display an arrow, click the arrow to display the list of available border styles, and click Solid.
- Click the Border Width property box to display an arrow, and then click the arrow to display the list of available border widths (Figure 6–34).

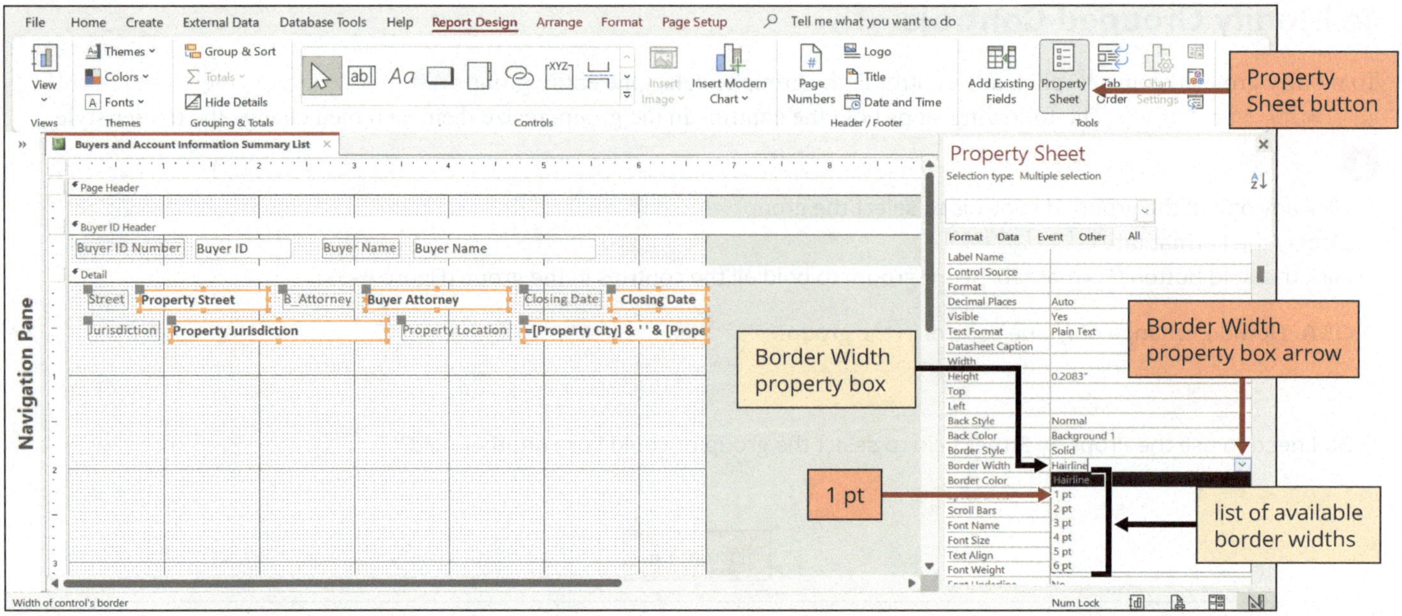

Figure 6–34

3

- Click 1 pt to select the border width.
- **Experiment:** Try the other border styles and widths to see their effects. In each case, view the report and then return to Design view. When finished, once again select Solid as the border style and 1 pt as the border width.
- Click the Font Size property box to display an arrow, and then click the arrow to display the list of available font sizes.
- Click 10 to change the font size to 10.
- Close the Property Sheet pane.
- Save the changes.

To Modify Multiple Controls That Are Not Grouped

To modify multiple controls that are not grouped together, you must simultaneously select all the controls you want to modify. To do so, click one of the controls and then hold SHIFT while selecting the others. The following steps italicize all the labels in the Detail section and then bold all the controls and labels in the Buyer ID Header section. **Why?** Text formatting makes it easier to visually group pieces of information in a report.

1

- Click the label (the control with the transparent background) for the Street control to select it.
- While pressing SHIFT, click the labels for all the other controls in the Detail section to select them.
- Display the Format tab.
- Click the Italic button (Format tab | Font group) to italicize the labels (Figure 6–35).

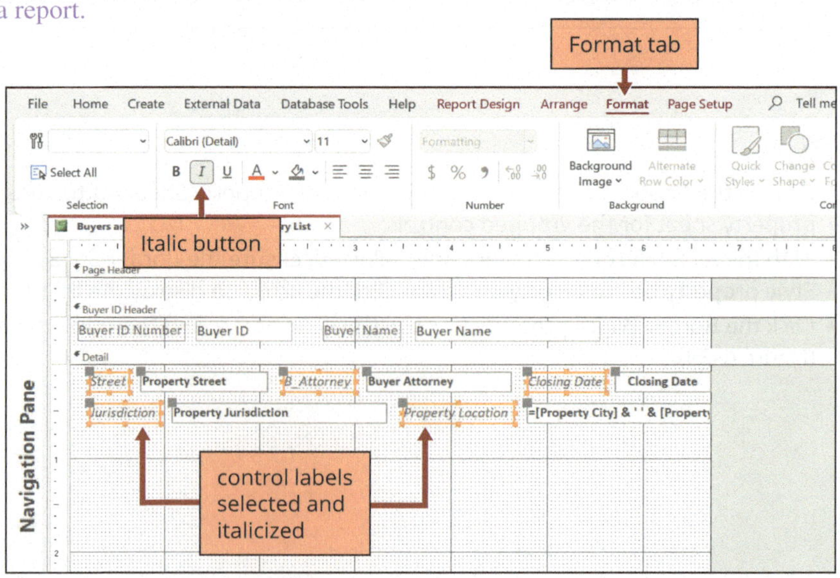

Figure 6–35

2

- Click in the vertical ruler to the left of the Buyer ID control to select all the controls in the Buyer ID Header section.

Q&A What exactly is selected when I click in the vertical ruler?
If you picture a horizontal line through the point you clicked, any control that intersects that horizontal line is selected.

- Use the buttons on the Arrange tab to align the controls on the top, if necessary.
- Display the Format tab, and then click the Bold button (Format tab | Font group) to bold all the selected controls (Figure 6–36).

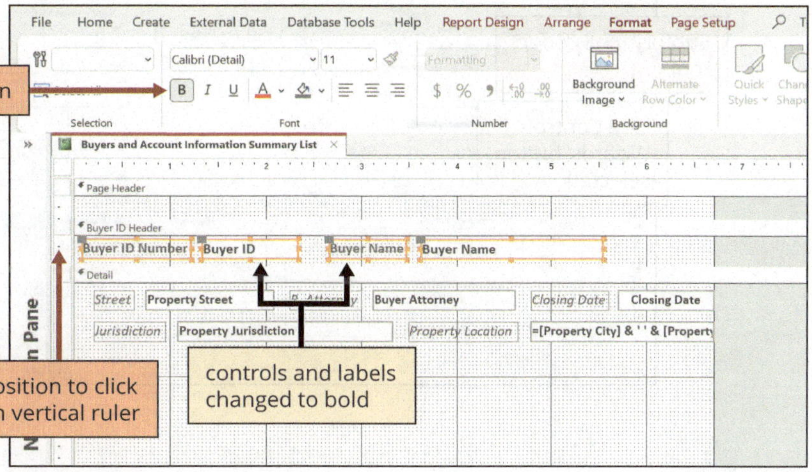

Figure 6–36

3

- View the report in Print Preview and then make any necessary adjustments.
- Close Print Preview and save the report.

Undoing and Saving

Remember that if you make a mistake, you can often correct it by clicking the Undo button on the Home tab. Clicking the Undo button usually will reverse your most recent change. You can also click the Undo button more than once to reverse multiple changes.

You should save your work frequently. That way, if you have problems that the Undo button will not fix, you can close the report without saving it and open it again. The report will be in exactly the state it was in the last time you saved it.

To Add a Subreport

To add a subreport to a report, you use the Subform/Subreport tool on the Report Design tab. The following steps add a subreport to display the workshop data, after first ensuring the 'Use Control Wizards' button is selected. **Why?** Provided the 'Use Control Wizards' button is selected, a wizard will guide you through the process of adding the subreport.

1

- If necessary, switch to Design view, and then display the Report Design tab.
- Click the More button, which is shown in Figure 6–37a (Report Design tab | Controls group), to display a gallery of available tools (Figure 6–37b).

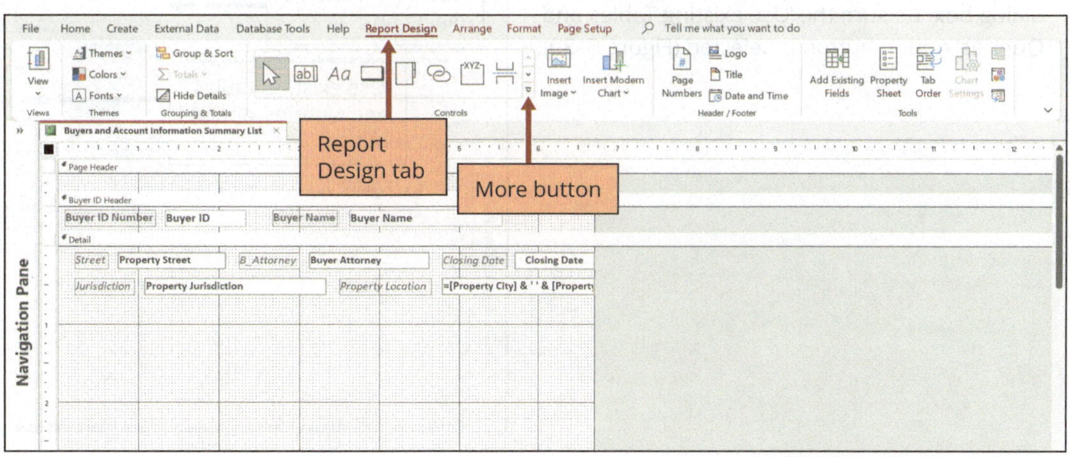

Figure 6–37a More Button

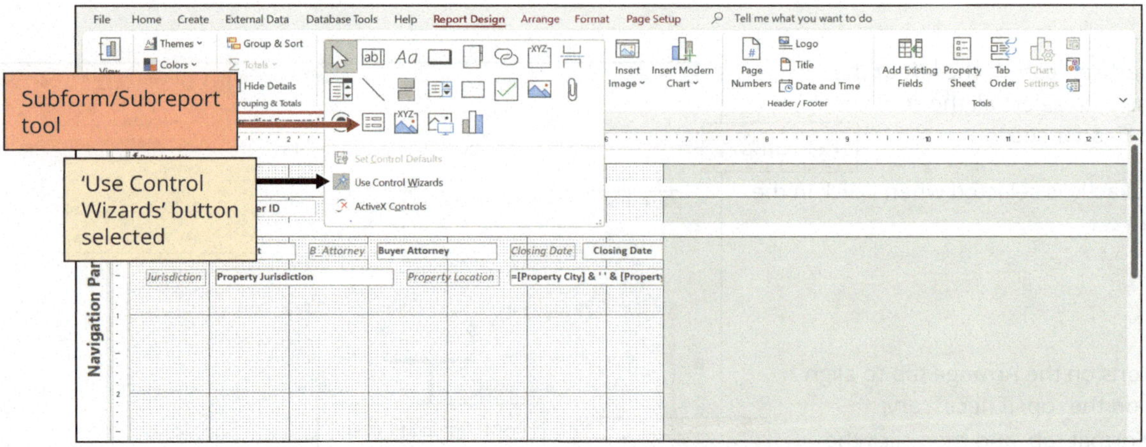

Figure 6–37b Design Tools Gallery

2

- Be sure the 'Use Control Wizards' button is selected, click the Subform/Subreport tool, and then move the pointer, which has changed to a plus sign with a subreport, to the approximate position shown in Figure 6–38.

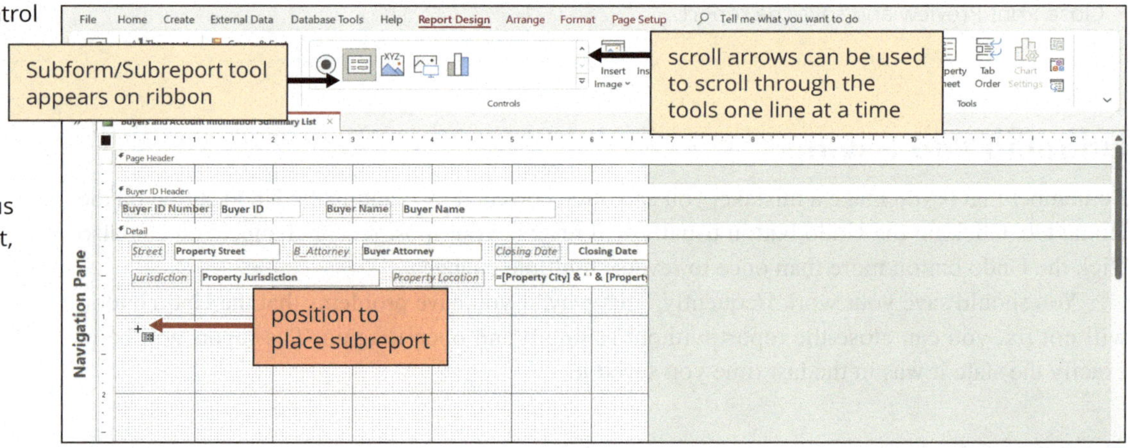

Figure 6–38

3

- Click the position shown in Figure 6–38 to place the subreport and display the SubReport Wizard dialog box. Be sure the 'Use existing Tables and Queries' option button is selected (Figure 6–39).

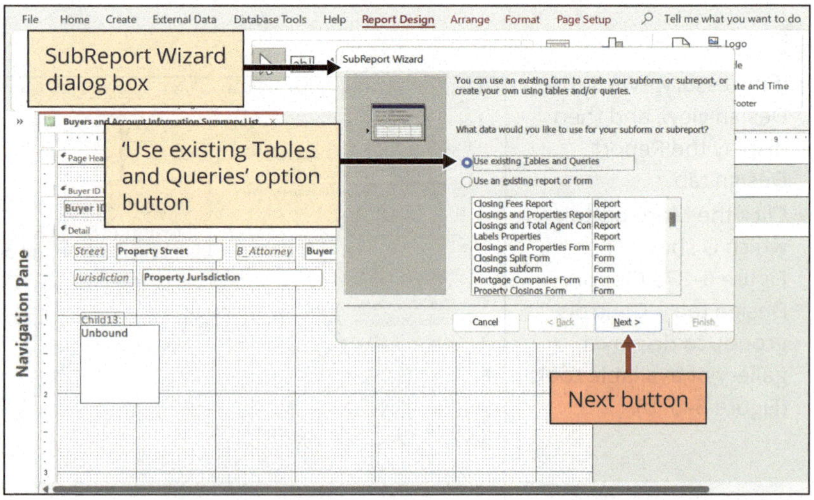

Figure 6–39

4

- Click the Next button.
- Click the Tables/Queries box arrow to display a list of the available tables and queries.
- Scroll down and click Query: Workshop Enrollments and Workshops to specify this query as the data source, and then click the 'Add All Fields' button to select all the fields in the query and add them to the subreport (Figure 6–40).

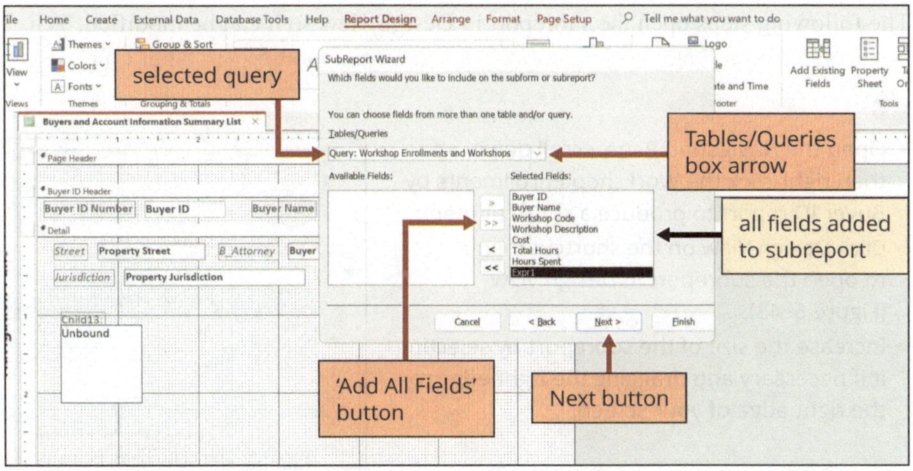

Figure 6–40

5

- Click the Next button and then ensure the 'Choose from a list.' option button is selected. If necessary, click 'Show Workshop Enrollments and Workshops for each record in Buyers and Account Information using Buyer ID.' (Figure 6–41).

Q&A What is the purpose of this dialog box?

You use this dialog box to indicate the fields that link the main report (referred to as a "form") to the subreport (referred to as a "subform"). If the fields have the same name, as they often will, you can simply select 'Choose from a list' and then accept the selection Access already has made.

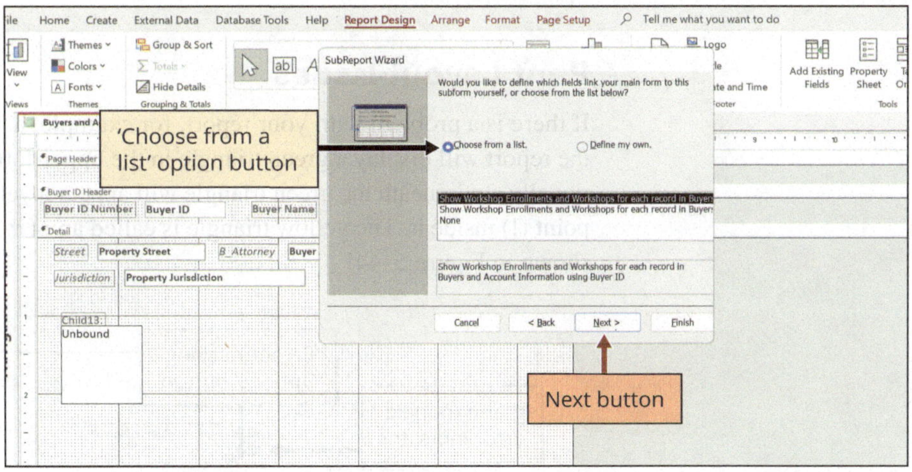

Figure 6–41

6

- Click the Next button, change the subreport name to **Workshop Enrollments by Buyer ID** and then click the Finish button to add the subreport to the Buyers and Account Information Summary List report (Figure 6–42).

7

- Click outside the subreport to deselect it.
- Save your changes.
- Close the report.

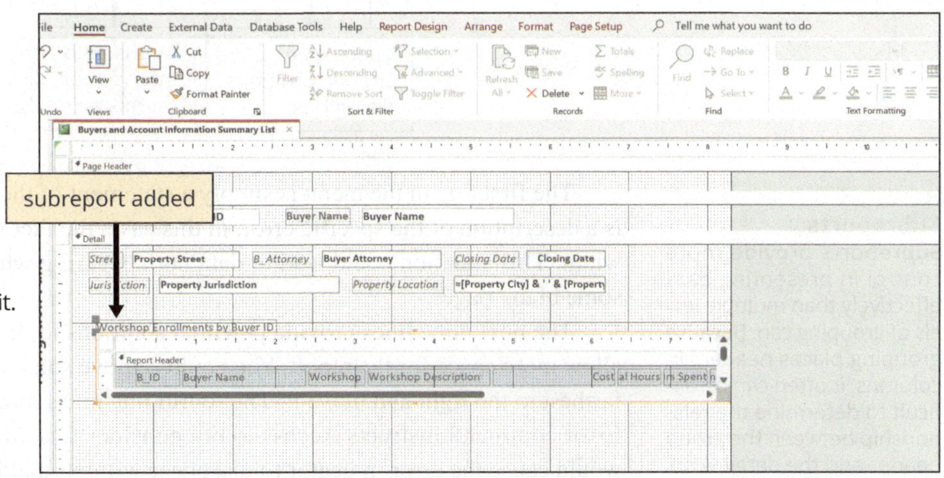

Figure 6–42

Break Point: If you wish to take a break, this is a good place to do so. You can quit Access now. To resume at a later time, start Access, open the database called SC_AC_06_Partners.accdb, and continue following the steps from this location forward.

To Open the Subreport in Design View

The following steps open the subreport in Design view so it can be modified. **Why?** The subreport appears as a separate report in the Navigation Pane. You can modify it just as you modify any other report.

1

- Open the Navigation Pane, scroll down, and then right-click the Workshop Enrollments by Buyer ID report to produce a shortcut menu.
- Click Design View on the shortcut menu to open the subreport in Design view (Figure 6–43).
- Increase the size of the subreport by selecting it if necessary and dragging the right edge to the right edge of your screen.

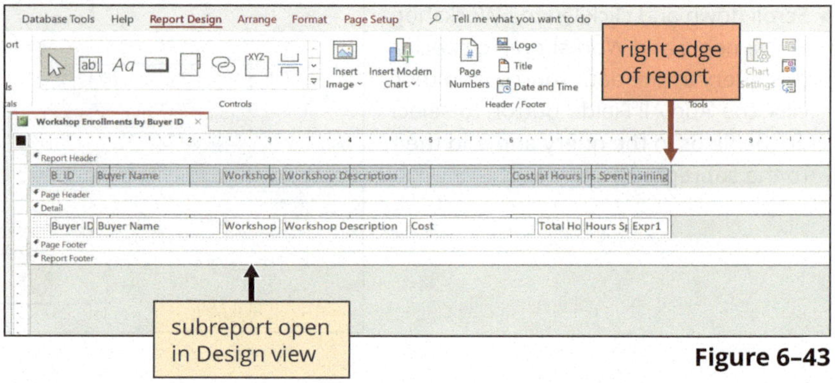

Figure 6–43

Print Layout Issues

If there is a problem with your report, for example, a report that is too wide for the printed page, the report will display a green triangle in the upper-left corner of the report selector button. Additionally, underneath the green triangle will appear a yellow triangular symbol with an exclamation point (!) inside it. The yellow triangle is called an **error indicator**. Clicking it produces the menu shown in Figure 6–44.

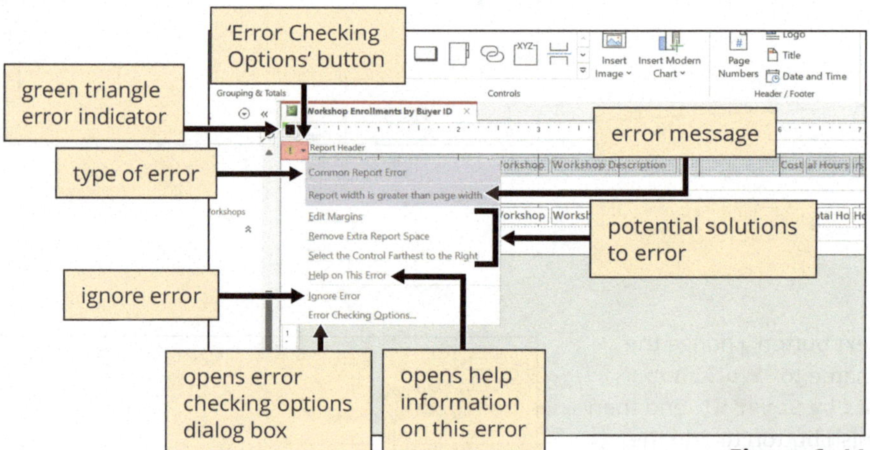

Figure 6–44

BTW
Subreports
Subreports provide more control in presenting data effectively than multiple levels of grouping can. Because grouping places headers in columns, it often can be difficult to determine the relationship between the group header and the detail. Also, you might want to present subreports side by side. You cannot do this with grouping.

The first line in the menu is simply a statement of the type of error that occurred. The second is a description of the specific error, in this case, the fact the report width is greater than the page width. This situation could lead to data not appearing where you expect it to, as well as printing some blank pages.

The next three lines provide potential solutions to the error. You could change the margins to allow more space for the report. You could remove some extra space. You could select the control farthest to the right and move it. The fourth line gives more detailed help on the error. The Ignore Error command instructs Access to not consider this situation an error. Selecting Ignore Error would cause the error indicator to disappear without making any changes. The final line displays the Error Checking Options dialog box, where you can make other changes.

Later in this module, you will fix the problem by changing the width of the report, so you do not need to take any action at this time.

To Modify the Controls in the Subreport

The query used to create the subreport contains three fields not needed for this report. The fields are needed in the query for another report, but they should not be listed in this subreport. The following steps modify the subreport by deleting the Buyer ID, Buyer Name, and Cost controls and revising the appearance of the column headings. **Why?** Because the Buyer ID appears in the main report, it does not need to be duplicated in the subreport.

1

- Close the Navigation Pane.
- Click the Buyer ID control in the Detail section to select the control. While holding SHIFT, click the Buyer Name control and the Cost control in the Detail section, and then click the Buyer ID control, the Buyer Name control, and the Cost control in the Report Header section to select all six controls.
- With six controls selected, press DEL to delete the controls.

2

- Break the heading for the Total Hours column over two lines by clicking in front of the word, Hours, to produce an insertion point and then pressing SHIFT+ENTER to move the second word to a second line.
- Break the headings for the Hours Spent and Hours Remaining columns over two lines using the same technique.
- Adjust the sizes and placement of the labels in the Report Header section to match those shown in Figure 6–45.
- Change the sizes and positions of the controls in the Detail section to match those in the figure by selecting the controls and dragging the sizing handles and by using the alignment controls (Arrange tab | Sizing & Ordering group).

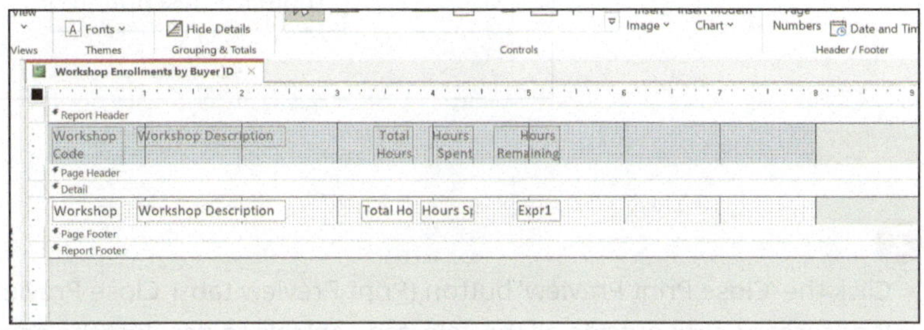

Figure 6–45

Q&A Why does Expr1 appear in the Detail section under the Hours Remaining label?
Expr1 indicates that Hours Remaining is a calculated control.

Consider This

How can you adjust fields where some of the entries are too long to fit in the available space?

This problem can be addressed in several ways.

1. Move the controls to allow more space between controls. Then, drag the appropriate handles on the controls that need to be expanded to enlarge them.
2. Use the Font Size property to select a smaller font size. This will allow more data to fit in the same space.
3. Use the Can Grow property. By changing the value of this property from No to Yes, the data can be spread over two lines, thus allowing all the data to print. Access will split data at natural break points, such as commas, spaces, and hyphens.

To Change the Can Grow Property

The third suggested approach to handling entries that are too long is the easiest to use and also produces a very readable report. The following steps change the Can Grow property for the Workshop Description field. **Why?** Changing the Can Grow property allows Access to optimize the size of fields in reports.

1

- Click the View button arrow (Report Design tab | Views group), and then click Print Preview to preview the report (Figure 6–46). If an error message appears indicating the report is too wide, click OK.

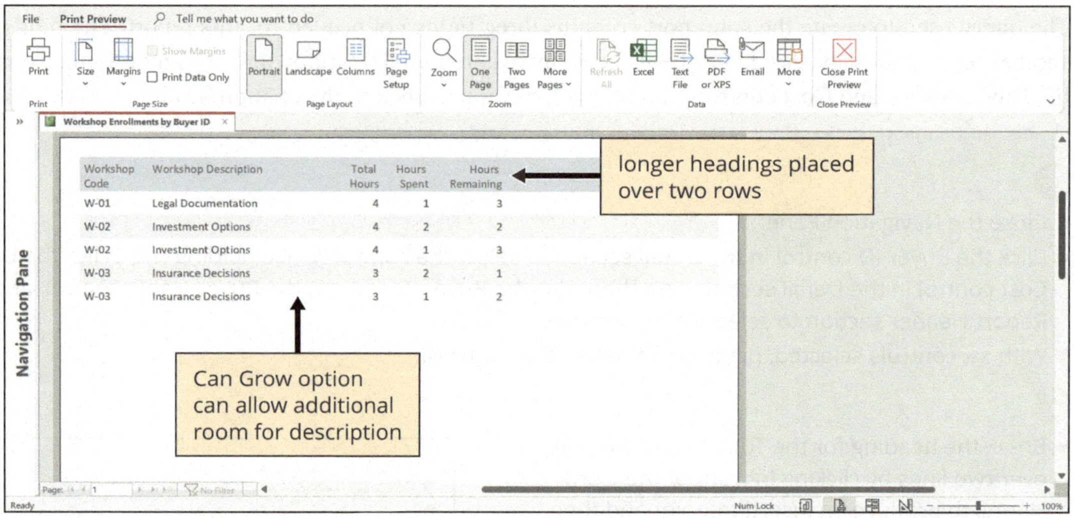

Figure 6–46

2

- Click the 'Close Print Preview' button (Print Preview tab | Close Preview group) to return to Design view.
- If necessary, click outside all the selected controls to deselect the controls.
- Click the Workshop Description control in the Detail section to select it.
- Click the Property Sheet button (Report Design tab | Tools group) to display the Property Sheet pane.
- With the All tab selected, scroll down until the Can Grow property appears, click the Can Grow property box to display the property arrow, and then click the Can Grow property box arrow to display the list of possible values for the Can Grow property (Figure 6–47).

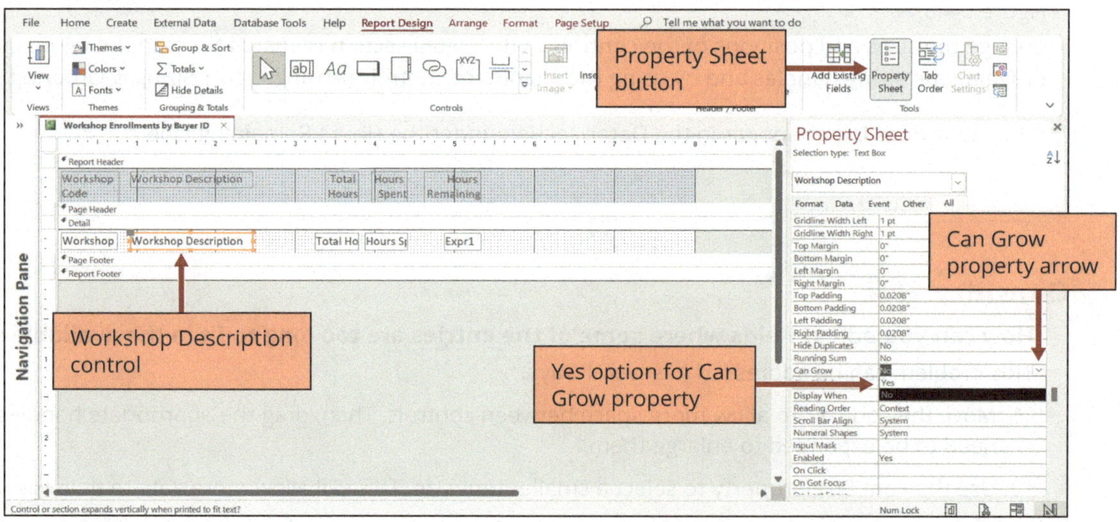

Figure 6–47

Q&A What is the effect of the Can Shrink property?

If the value of the Can Shrink property is set to Yes, Access will remove blank lines that occur when the field is empty.

3

- Click Yes in the list to allow the Workshop Description control to grow as needed.
- Close the Property Sheet pane.

To Change the Appearance of the Controls in the Subreport

Why? Partners paralegals prefer certain formatting for the subreport controls. The following steps change the controls in the Detail section to bold and the controls in the Report Header section to italic. They also change the background color in the Report Header section to white.

1

- Drag the right boundary of the subreport to the approximate position shown in Figure 6–48. The error indicator should disappear.

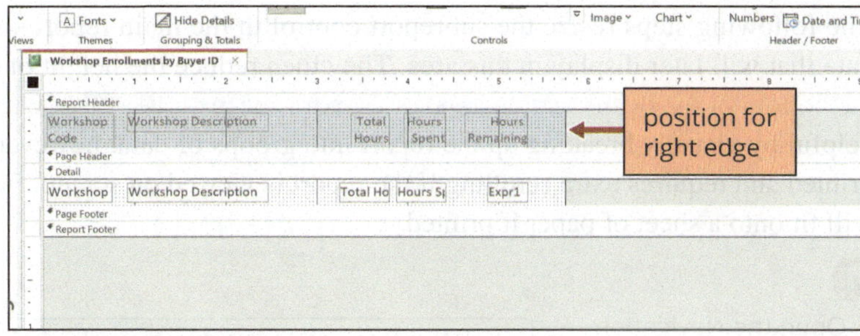

Figure 6–48

2

- Display the Format tab.
- Click the vertical ruler to the left of the controls in the Detail section to select the controls in that section, and then click the Bold button (Format tab | Font group) to bold the controls.
- Click the ruler to the left of the controls in the Report Header section to select the controls in that section, and then click the Italic button (Format tab | Font group) to italicize the controls.
- Click the title bar for the Report Header to select the header without selecting any of the controls in the header.
- Click the Background Color button arrow (Format tab | Font group) to display a color palette (Figure 6–49).

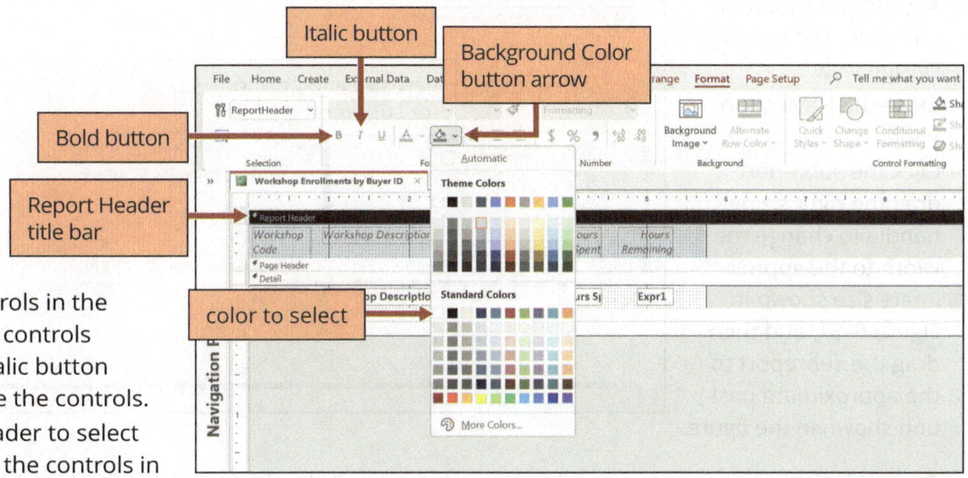

Figure 6–49

3

- Click White in the first row, first column of the Standard Colors to change the background color to white (Figure 6–50).

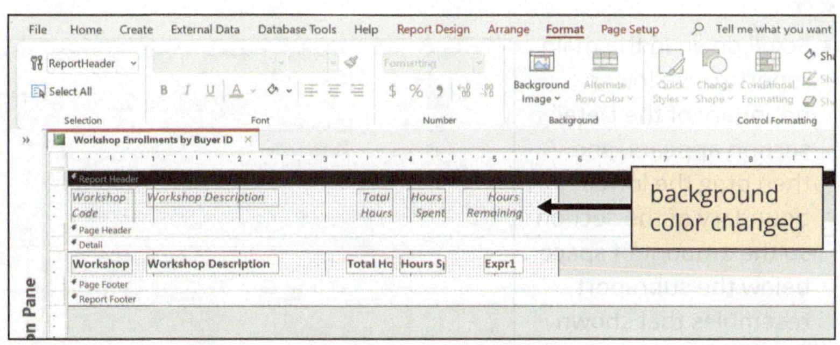

Figure 6–50

Q&A What is the difference between clicking a color in the Theme colors and clicking a color in the Standard Colors?

The theme colors are specific to the currently selected theme. The first column, for example, represents "background 1," one of the selected background colors in the theme. The various entries in the column represent different intensities of the color at the top of the column. The colors would be different if a different theme were selected. If you select one of the theme colors and a different theme is selected in the future, the color you selected would change to the color in the same location. On the other hand, if you select a standard color, a change of theme would have no effect on the color.

- Save the changes, and then close the subreport.

To Resize the Subreport and the Report in Design View

The following steps resize the subreport control in the main report so the control for the subreport will appropriately fit the data that will later display in this area. They then reduce the height of the detail section. **Why?** Any additional white space at the bottom of the detail section appears as extra space at the end of each detail line in the final report. Some extra space can be helpful by visually breaking up the report into groups of data; however, too much extra space just wastes paper if the report is printed and requires extra scrolling if the report is viewed on screen. Finally, the steps reduce the width of the main report so it will fit onto a sheet of paper if printed.

1

- Open the Navigation Pane.
- Open the Buyers and Account Information Summary List report in Design view.
- Close the Navigation Pane.
- Click the subreport, drag the right sizing handle to change the width to the approximate size shown in Figure 6–51, and then drag the subreport to the approximate position shown in the figure.

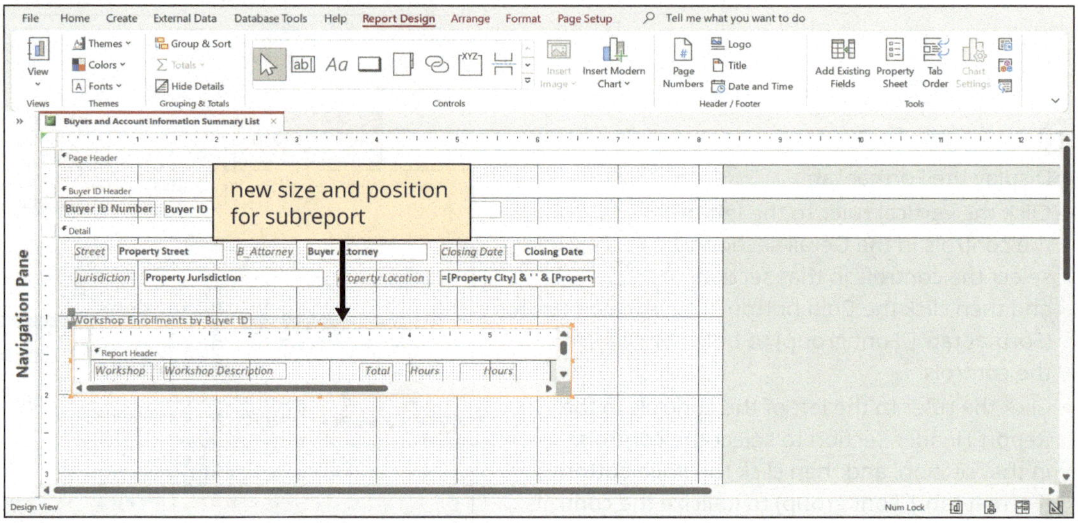

Figure 6–51

Q&A Why is the subreport so small from top to bottom? Shouldn't all the controls inside the subreport appear as well?
The rulers in the subreport control take up a lot of space in Design view that will later be used to display the subreport's data in Report view or Print Preview. Considering the data that will eventually be displayed in this area, the subreport does not need to be any taller. You can check that the subreport is tall enough without being too tall by switching to Report view or Print Preview as you make changes to the sizes and positions of all controls.

2

- Scroll down in the main report so the lower boundary of the Detail section appears, and then drag the lower boundary of the section so the amount of space below the subreport resembles that shown in Figure 6–52.

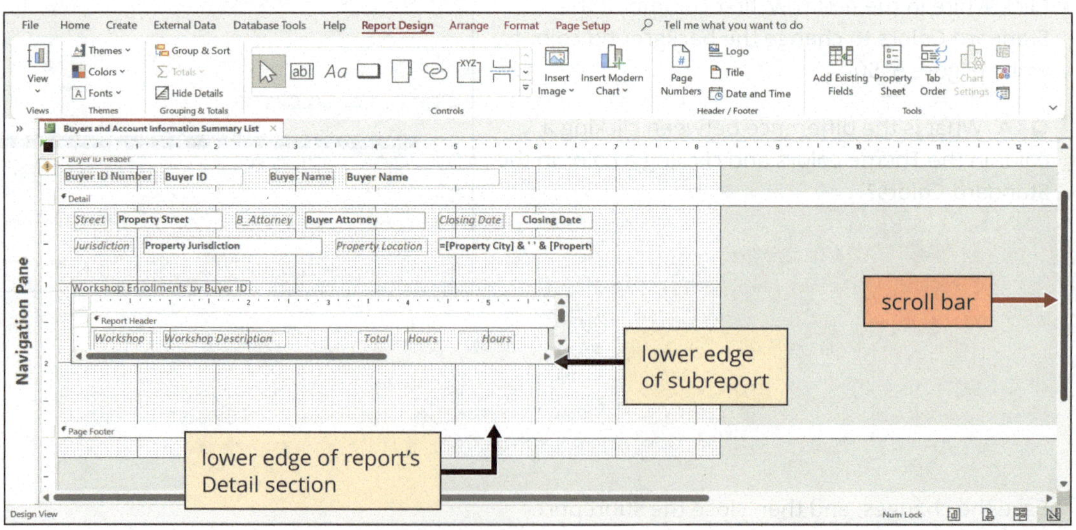

Figure 6–52

Q&A I scrolled down to see the lower boundary of the Detail section, and the controls are no longer on the screen. What is the easiest way to drag the boundary when the position to which I want to drag it is not visible?
You do not need to see the location to drag to it. As you get close to the top of the visible portion of the screen, Access will automatically scroll. You might find it easier, however, to drag the boundary near the top of the visible portion of the report, use the scroll bar to scroll up, and then drag some more. You might have to scroll more than once.

3

- Click the label for the subreport (the label that reads Workshop Enrollments by Buyer ID), and then press DEL to delete the label.
- Resize the report by dragging its right border to the location shown in Figure 6–53.

Q&A How does a report become the wrong size?
When you move a control and a portion of the control extends into the area to the right of the right boundary of the report, the report will be resized. The new, larger size will remain even if you move the control back to the left. Thus, it is possible that your report has a larger size than it did before. If this is the case, you need to drag the right boundary to resize the report.

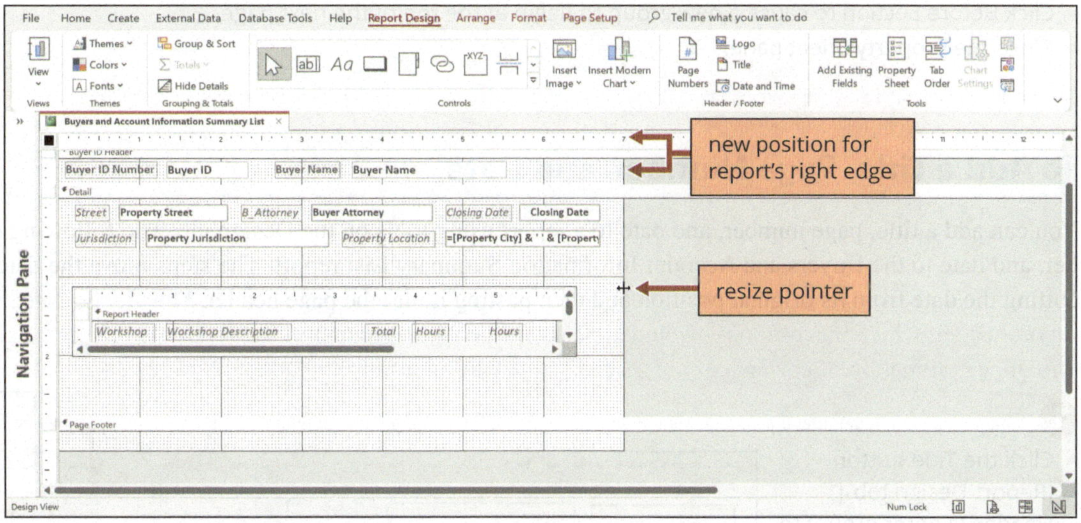

Figure 6–53

To Modify Section Properties

The following steps make two modifications to the Buyer ID Header section. The first modification, which causes the contents of the Group Header section to appear at the top of each page, changes the Repeat Section property to Yes. **Why?** Without this change, the Buyer ID and name would only appear at the beginning of each buyer's account information. If the list of account information occupies more than one page, it would not be apparent on subsequent pages which buyer ID is associated with that information. The second modification changes the Force New Page property to Before Section, causing each section to begin at the top of a page.

1

- Click the Buyer ID Header bar to select the header, and then click the Property Sheet button (Report Design tab | Tools group) to display the Property Sheet pane.
- With the All tab selected, click the Repeat Section property box, click the arrow that appears, and then click Yes to cause the contents of the group header to appear at the top of each page of the report.
- Click the Force New Page property box, and then click the arrow that appears to display the menu of possible values (Figure 6–54).

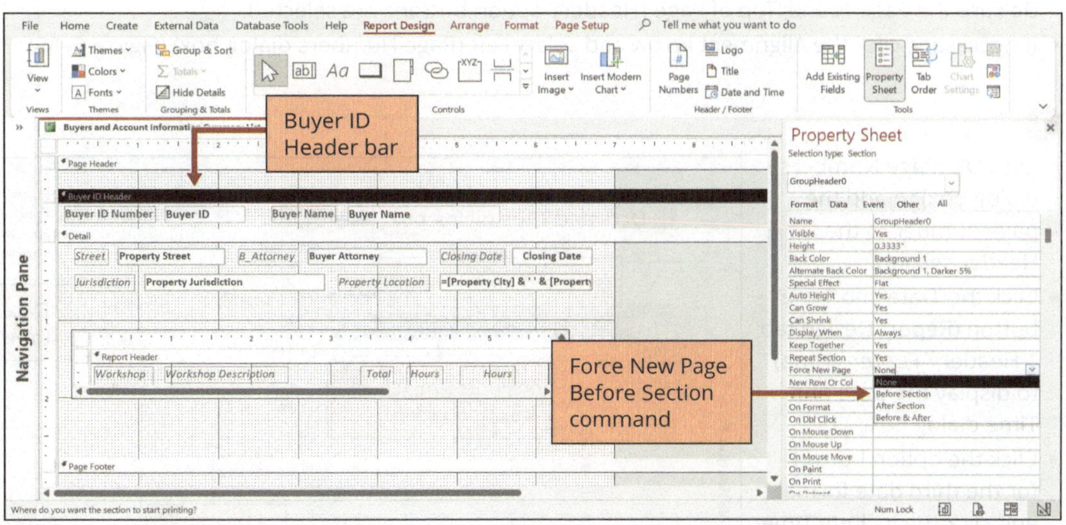

Figure 6–54

2

- Click Before Section to cause a new group to begin at the top of the next page.
- Close the Property Sheet pane.

To Add a Title, Page Number, and Date

You can add a title, page number, and date to a report using tools on the Design tab. The following steps add a title, page number, and date to the Buyers and Account Information Summary List report. The steps move the date to the page header by first cutting the date from its original position and then pasting it into the page header. **Why?** The date is automatically added to the report header, which means it only would appear once at the beginning of the report. If it is in the page header instead, the date will appear at the top of each page.

1

- Click the Title button (Report Design tab | Header / Footer group) to add a title.

Q&A The title is the same as the name of the report object. Can I change the report title without changing the name of the report object in the database?

Yes. The report title is a label, and you can change it using any of the techniques that you used for changing column headings and other labels.

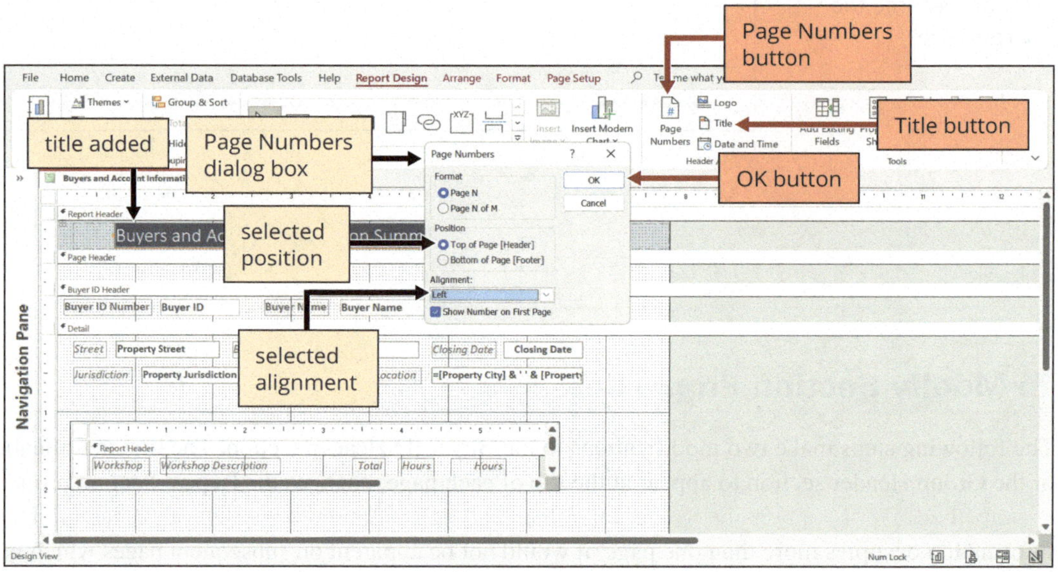

Figure 6–55

- Click the Page Numbers button (Report Design tab | Header / Footer group) to display the Page Numbers dialog box.
- Be sure the Page N and 'Top of Page [Header]' option buttons are selected.
- If necessary, click the Alignment arrow and select Left (Page Numbers dialog box) (Figure 6–55).

2

- Click OK (Page Numbers dialog box) to add the page number to the Header section.
- Click the 'Date and Time' button (Report Design tab | Header / Footer group) to display the Date and Time dialog box.
- Click the option button for the third date format and click the Include Time check box to remove the check mark (Figure 6–56).

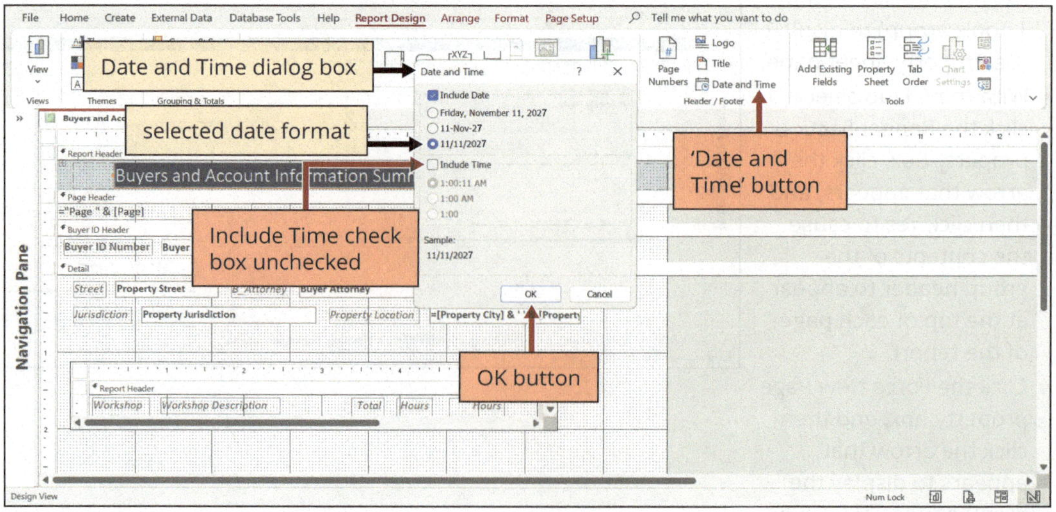

Figure 6–56

3

- Click the OK button (Date and Time dialog box) to add the date to the Report Header.
- Display the Home tab.
- If the Date control is not selected, click the Date control to select it (Figure 6–57).

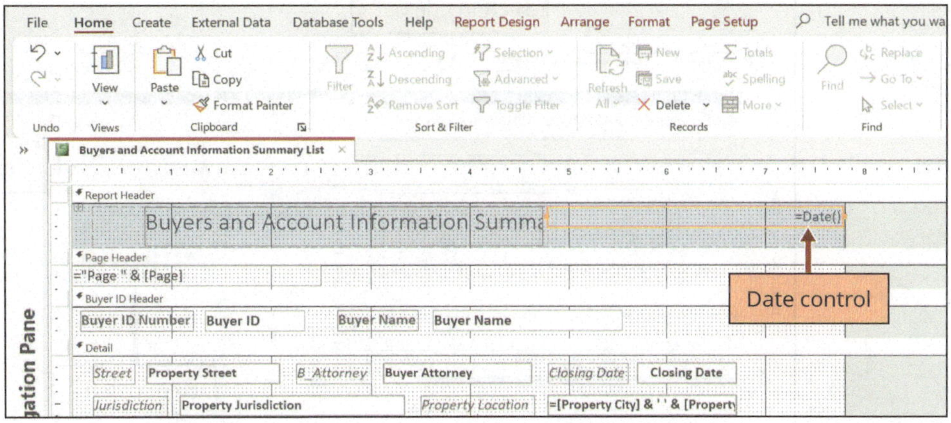

Figure 6–57

4

- With the control containing the date selected, click the Cut button (Home tab | Clipboard group) to cut the date, click the title bar for the Page Header to select the page header, and then click the Paste button (Home tab | Clipboard group) to paste the Date control at the beginning of the page header.

Q&A When I click the Cut button, the control disappears, but the Paste button grays out and won't work. How can I fix this?

You might have an error in your Access installation and should consider reinstalling Access. In the meantime, you can work around this limitation by copying the control instead of cutting it, and then the Paste button should still work. Make sure to delete the original control from the section where you intended to cut it from.

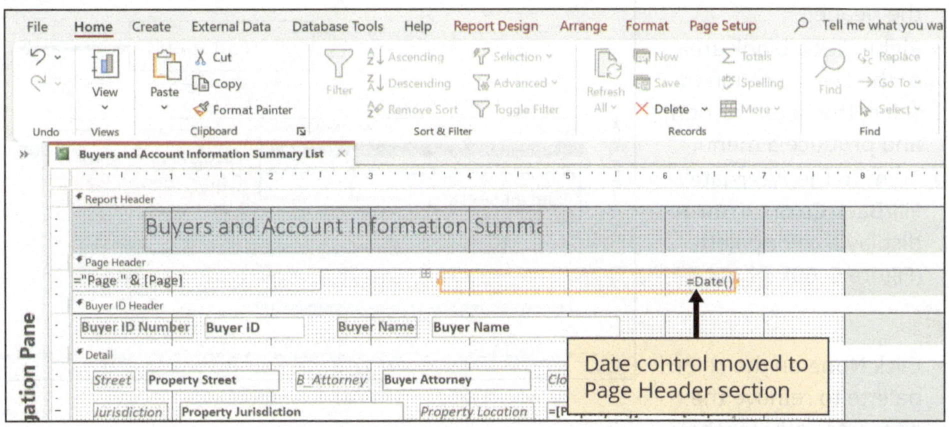

Figure 6–58

- Drag the Date control, which is currently sitting on top of the Page Number control, to the position shown in Figure 6–58.

To Remove the Header Background Color and the Alternate Color

The report header currently has a blue background, which is not what Partners paralegals want. In addition, the report has alternate colors, as you saw in Figure 6–46. An **alternate color** is a color different from the main color that appears on every other line in a datasheet or report. Using alternate colors can sometimes make a datasheet or report more readable but is not always desirable.

The following steps first remove the color from the report header. They then remove the alternate colors from the various sections in the report, starting with the Detail section. **Why?** Access automatically assigns alternate colors within the report. In reports with multiple sections, the alternate colors can be confusing. If you do not want these alternate colors, you must remove them.

1

- Right-click the title bar for the Report Header to select the header without selecting any of the controls in the header and to produce a menu.
- Point to the 'Fill/Back Color' arrow to display a color palette (Figure 6–59).

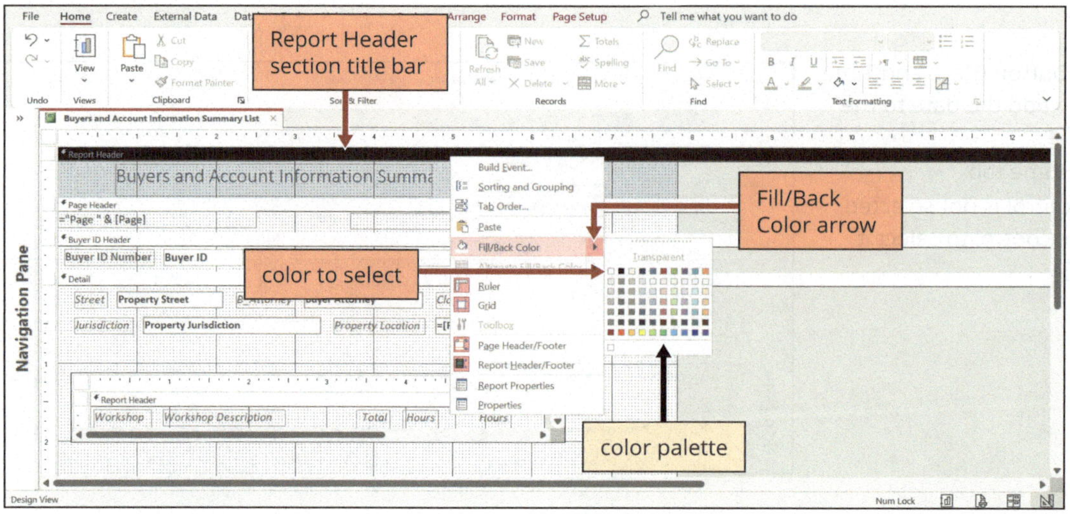

Figure 6–59

2

- Click White in the first row, first column of the color palette to change the background color for the header.
- Right-click a blank area of the Detail section to select the detail section and produce a menu.
- Point to the 'Alternate Fill/Back Color' arrow to display a color palette (Figure 6–60).

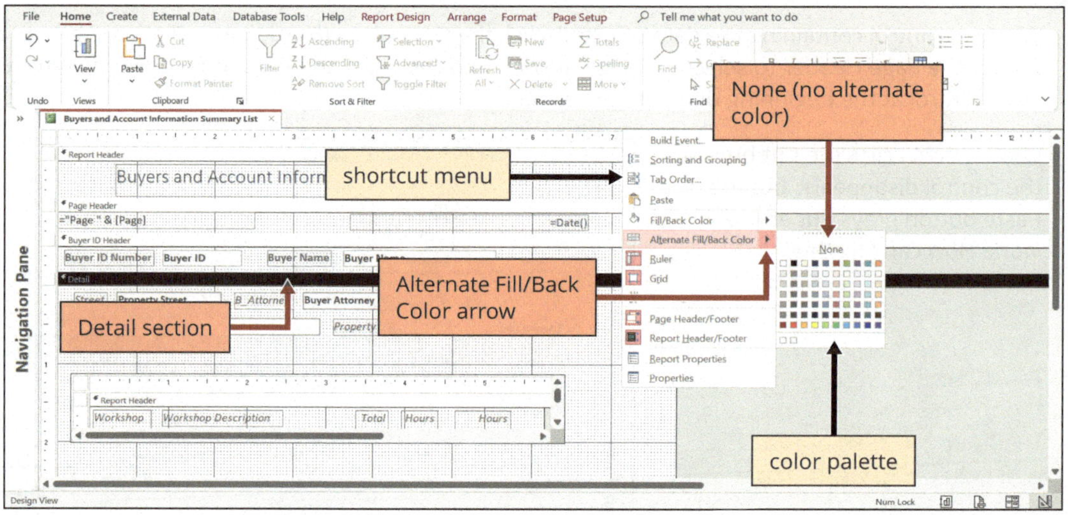

Figure 6–60

3

- Click None on the color palette to remove the alternate color for the Detail section.
- Save the report.

4

- To open the subreport in Design view from the report, click the subreport control, and then click the 'Subreport in New Window' button (Report Design tab | Tools group) (Figure 6–61).

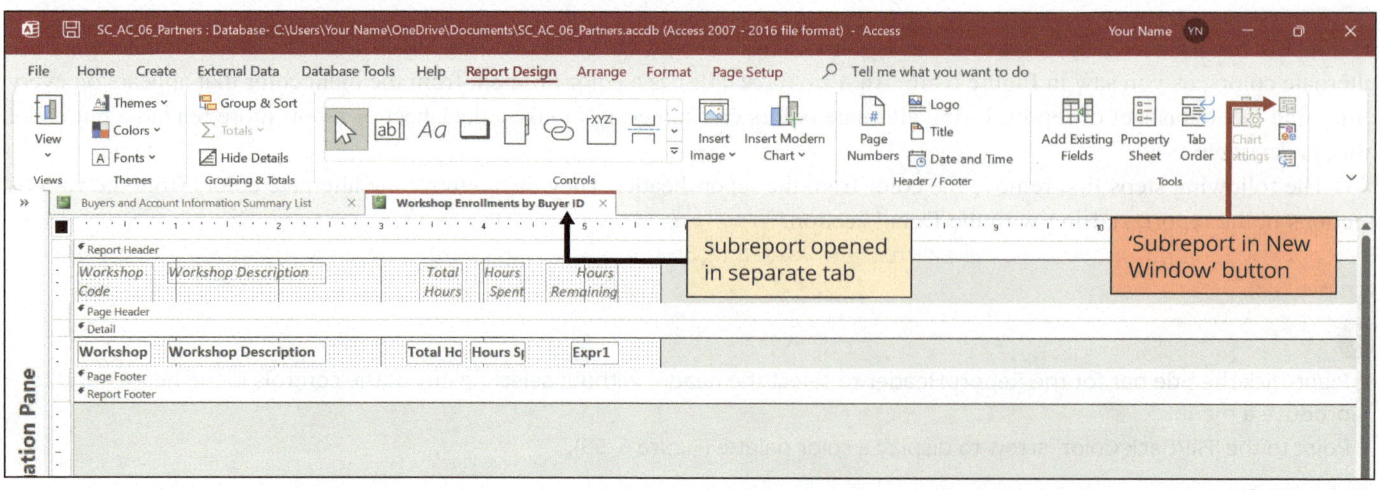

Figure 6–61

- Remove the header background color and the alternate color from the subreport using similar techniques as the changes you just made to the main report.
- Save and close the subreport.
- View the report in Print Preview (Figure 6–62).
- Close Print Preview, and then save and close the report.

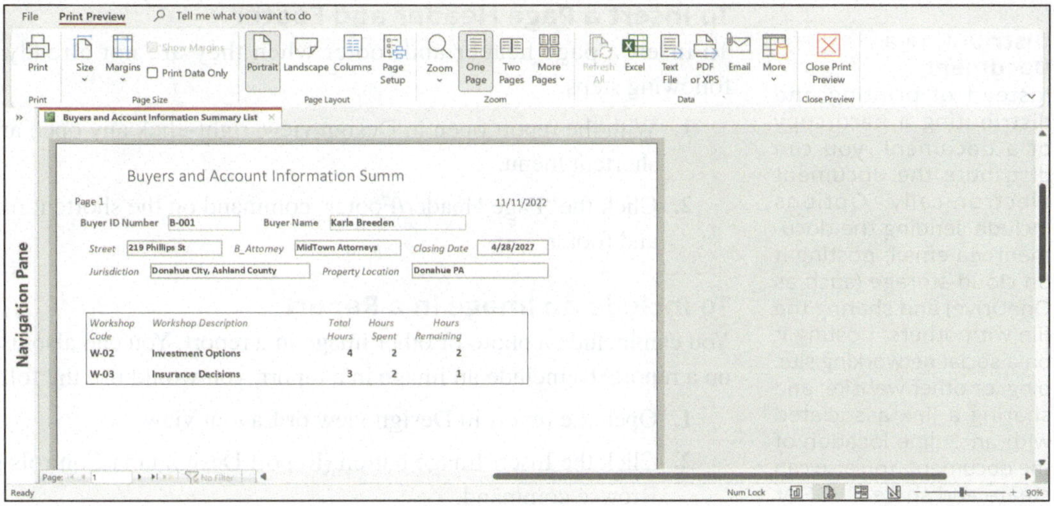

Figure 6–62

Q&A How can I be sure I removed all the background colors where needed?

View the report in Print Preview to check no color appears in the report.

Headers and Footers

Access gives you some options for including or omitting headers and footers in your reports. They go together, so if you have a report header, you will also have a report footer. If you do not want one of the sections to appear, you can shrink its size so there is no room for any content, or you can remove the header and footer from your report altogether. If you later decide you want to include them, you once again can add them. You have similar options with page headers and page footers.

To Remove a Report Header and Footer

To remove a report header and footer, you would use the following steps.

1. With the report open in Design view, right-click any open area of the report to produce a shortcut menu.
2. Click the 'Report Header/Footer' command on the shortcut menu to remove the report header and footer.
3. If the Microsoft Access dialog box appears, asking if it is acceptable to delete any controls in the section, click Yes.

To Remove a Page Header and Footer

To remove a page header and footer, you would use the following steps.

1. With the report open in Design view, right-click any open area of the report to produce a shortcut menu.
2. Click the 'Page Header/Footer' command on the shortcut menu to remove the page header and footer.
3. If the Microsoft Access dialog box appears, asking if it is acceptable to delete any controls in the section, click Yes.

To Insert a Report Header and Footer

To insert a report header and footer when they are not already present, you would use the following steps.

1. With the report open in Design view, right-click any open area of the report to produce a shortcut menu.
2. Click the 'Report Header/Footer' command on the shortcut menu to insert a report header and footer.

BTW

Report Title Placement

You also can place a report title in a page header. One advantage of doing so is that the title will then print on each page of the report.

BTW

Page Breaks

You can force a page break to occur at a particular position in a report by adding a page break control to the report. To do so, click the Insert Page Break tool from the Controls gallery (Report Design tab | Controls group), move the pointer to the desired position, and click the position to place the page break.

BTW

White Space

In page layout and report design, white space is the space on a printed page that is left unmarked. This includes margins, spacing between records, and space around graphics. Not enough white space can make a report look cluttered and can be difficult to read. Too much white space wastes paper. Thoughtful use of white space can make a report more visually appealing and easier to interpret.

BTW
Distributing a Document
Instead of printing and distributing a hard copy of a document, you can distribute the document electronically. Options include sending the document via email; posting it on cloud storage (such as OneDrive) and sharing the file with others; posting it on a social networking site, blog, or other website; and sharing a link associated with an online location of the document. You also can create and share a PDF or XPS image of the document, so that users can view the file in Acrobat Reader or XPS Viewer instead of in Access.

To Insert a Page Header and Footer

To insert a page header and footer when they are not already present, you would use the following steps.

1. With the report open in Design view, right-click any open area of the report to produce a shortcut menu.
2. Click the 'Page Header/Footer' command on the shortcut menu to insert a page header and footer.

To Include an Image in a Report

You can include a photo or other image in a report. You can also use an image as the background on a report. To include an image in a report, you would use the following steps.

1. Open the report in Design view or Layout view.
2. Click the Insert Image button (Report Design tab | Controls group), and then click the Browse command.
3. Select the desired image and click OK.
4. Click the desired location to add the image to the report.

To Use an Image as Background for a Report

To include an image as a background for a report, you would use the following steps.

1. Open the report in Design view or Layout view.
2. Click anywhere in the report, click the Background Image button (Format tab | Background group), and then click the Browse command.
3. Select the desired image for the background and click OK.

To Publish a Report

You can make a report available as an external document by publishing the report as either a PDF or an XPS file. To do so, you would use the following steps.

1. Select the report to be published in the Navigation Pane.
2. Display the External Data tab.
3. Click the PDF or XPS button (External Data tab | Export group) to display the Publish as PDF or XPS dialog box.
4. Select the appropriate Save as type (either PDF or XPS).
5. Select either 'Standard (publishing online and printing)' or 'Minimum size (publishing online).'
6. If you want to publish only a range of pages, click the Options button, select the desired range, and click OK.
7. Click the Publish button to publish the report in the desired format.
8. If you want to save the export steps, click the 'Save export steps' check box (Expert – PDF dialog box), and then click the Save Export button. If not, click the Close button.

Break Point: If you wish to take a break, this is a good place to do so. You can quit Access now. To resume at a later time, start Access, open the database called SC_AC_06_Partners.accdb, and continue following the steps from this location forward.

Creating a Second Report

Partners would also like a report that groups accounts by Buyer ID and Workshop Costs. The report should include subtotals and a discount amount based on the total cost of workshops for each buyer. Finally, it should show the combined cost of the workshops less the discount. The discount amount is based on the total workshop cost. Buyers taking workshops in excess of $300 will receive a 20 percent discount on all workshops, and buyers taking workshops totaling $300 or less will not receive a discount.

BTW
Graphs
You can add graphs, called charts, to a report using the Chart tool. To add a chart to a report, click the Chart tool, move the pointer to the desired location, and click the position to place the chart. Follow the directions in the Chart Wizard dialog box to specify the data source for the chart, the values for the chart, and the chart type.

To Create a Second Report

The following steps create the Discount Report, select the record source, and specify grouping and sorting options.

1

- If necessary, close the Navigation Pane.
- Display the Create tab and then click the Report Design button (Create tab | Reports group) to create a report in Design view.

2

- Ensure the selector for the entire report, which is the box in the upper-left corner of the report, contains a black square indicating it is selected, and then click the Property Sheet button (Report Design tab | Tools group) to display the Property Sheet pane.

3

- With the All tab selected, click the Record Source property box arrow, and then click the Workshop Enrollments and Workshops query to select the query as the record source for the report.
- Close the Property Sheet pane.

4

- Click the Group & Sort button (Report Design tab | Grouping & Totals group) to display the 'Group, Sort, and Total' pane.
- Click the 'Add a group' button to display the list of available fields for grouping, and then click the Buyer ID field to group by Buyer ID. When you add a group, a header will appear above each Buyer ID. However, you also need a group footer.

5

- On the 'Group on Buyer ID' row (Group, Sort, and Total pane), click More.
- Click the arrow next to 'without a footer section' to display the options for the Buyer ID section footer.
- Click 'with a footer section' to add a Buyer ID section footer to the report.

6

- Click the 'Add a sort' button to display the list of available fields for sorting, and then click the Workshop Code field to sort workshops by the workshop code.
- Remove the 'Group, Sort, and Total' pane by clicking the Group & Sort button (Report Design tab | Grouping & Totals group).

7

- Save the report as **Discount Report** but do not close it yet.

Q&A Why save it at this point?

You do not have to save it at this point. It is a good idea to save often, however. Doing so will give you a convenient point from which to restart if you have problems. If you have problems, you could close the report without saving it. When you reopen the report, it will be in the state it was in when you last saved it.

To Add and Move Fields in a Report

As with the previous reports, you can add a field to the report by dragging the field from the field list. After adding a field to a report, you can adjust the placement of the field's label, separating it from the control to which it is attached by dragging the move handle in its upper-left corner. This technique does not work, however, if you want to drag the attached label to a section different from the section where the control is placed. If you want the label to be in a different section, you must select the label, cut the label, select the section to which you want to move the label, and then paste the label. You then can move the label to the desired location.

The following steps add the Buyer ID field to the Buyer ID Header section, and then they move the Buyer ID label to the Page Header section. **Why?** The label should appear at the top of each page, rather than in the group header.

1

- Click the 'Add Existing Fields' button (Report Design tab | Tools group) to display a field list. (Figure 6–63).

Q&A My field list displays 'Show only fields in the current record source,' not 'Show all tables,' as in the figure. What should I do?
Click the 'Show only fields in the current record source' link at the top of the field list to display only those fields in the Workshop Enrollments and Workshops query.

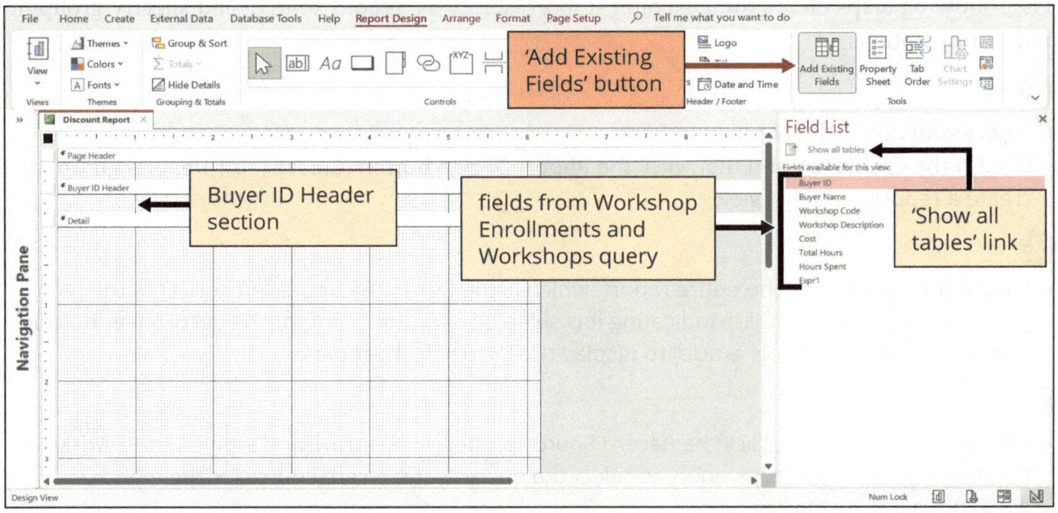

Figure 6–63

2

- Drag the Buyer ID field to the approximate position shown in Figure 6–64.

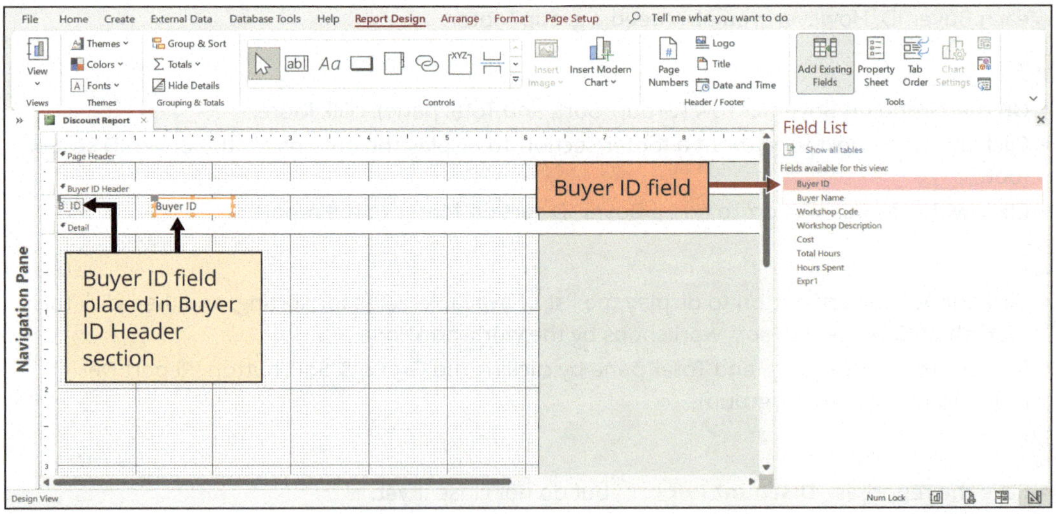

Figure 6–64

3

- Click the label for the Buyer ID control to select it (Figure 6–65).

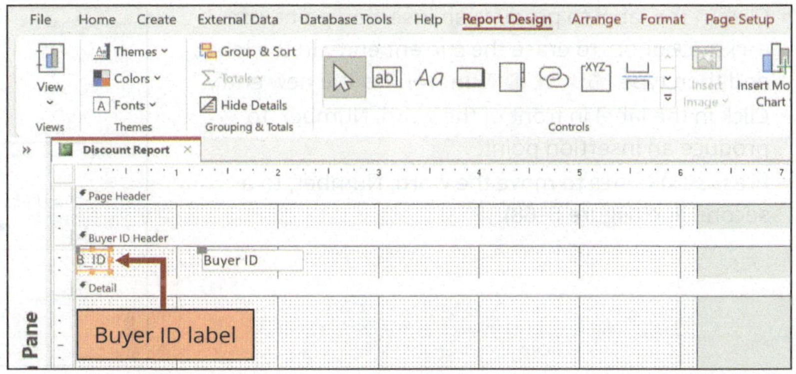

Figure 6–65

4

- Display the Home tab.
- Click the Cut button (Home tab | Clipboard group) to cut the label.
- Click the Page Header bar to select the page header (Figure 6–66).

Q&A Do I have to click the bar, or could I click somewhere else within the section?
You could also click within the section. Clicking the bar is usually safer, however. If you click in a section intending to select the section, but click within one of the controls in the section, you will select the control rather than the section. Clicking the bar always selects the section.

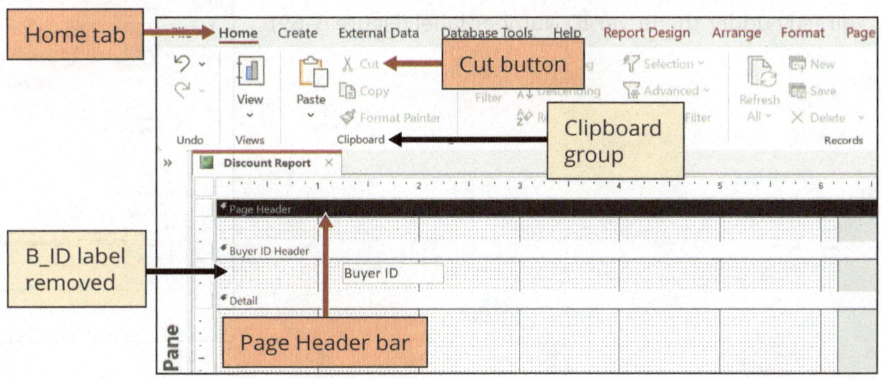

Figure 6–66

5

- Click the Paste button (Home tab | Clipboard group) to paste the label in the Page Header section (Figure 6–67).

Q&A When would I want to click the Paste button arrow rather than just the button?
Clicking the arrow displays the Paste button menu, which includes the Paste command and two additional commands. Paste Special allows you to paste data into different formats. Paste Append, which is available if you have cut or copied a record, allows you to paste the record to a table with a similar structure. If you want the simple Paste command, you can just click the button.

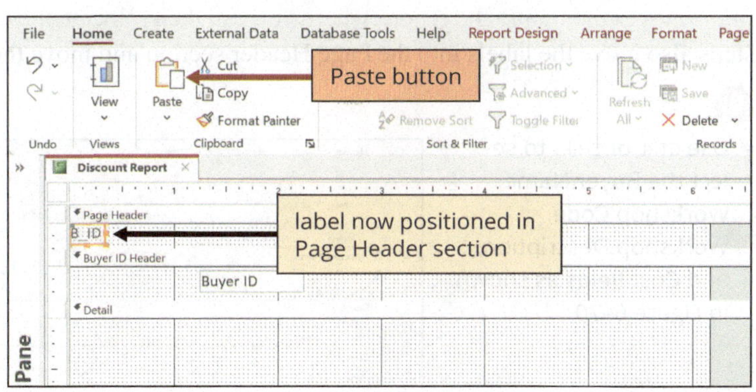

Figure 6–67

6

- Click in the label to produce an insertion point, use BACKSPACE or DEL to erase the current entry in the label, and then type **Buyer ID Number** as the new entry.
- Click in the label in front of the word, Number, to produce an insertion point.
- Press SHIFT+ENTER to move the word, Number, to a second line (Figure 6–68).

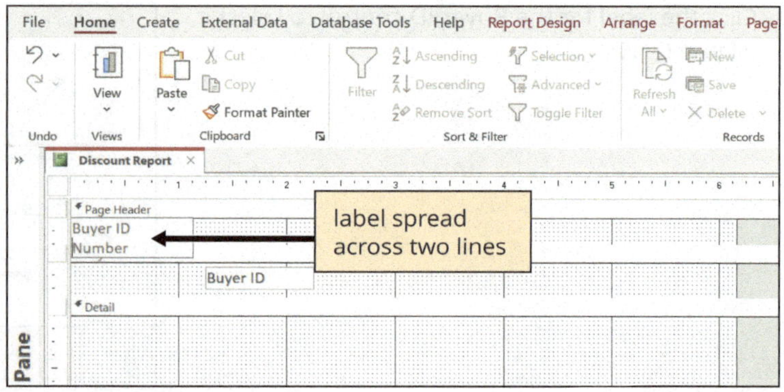

Figure 6–68

7

- Move the Buyer ID control to the left edge of the report, directly under the Buyer ID Number label (Figure 6–69).

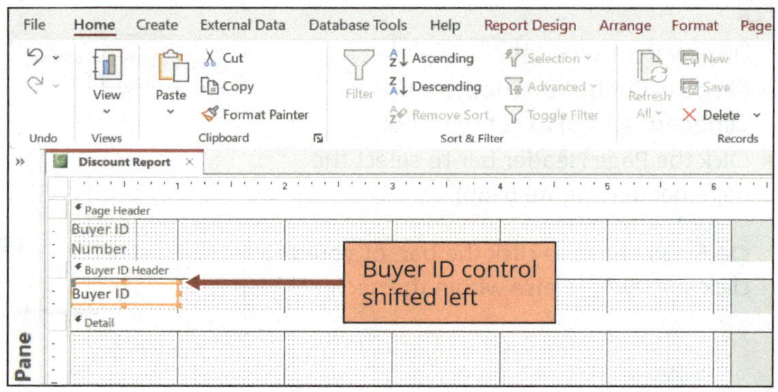

Figure 6–69

To Add the Remaining Fields

The following steps add all the remaining fields for the report by dragging them into the Detail section. **Why?** Dragging the fields moves them onto the report, where you can then relocate the controls and labels individually to the desired locations. The steps also move the labels into the Page Header section and move the controls containing the fields to the appropriate locations.

1

- Use CTRL or SHIFT to select the Buyer Name, Workshop Code, Workshop Description, and Cost fields as shown in Figure 6–70.

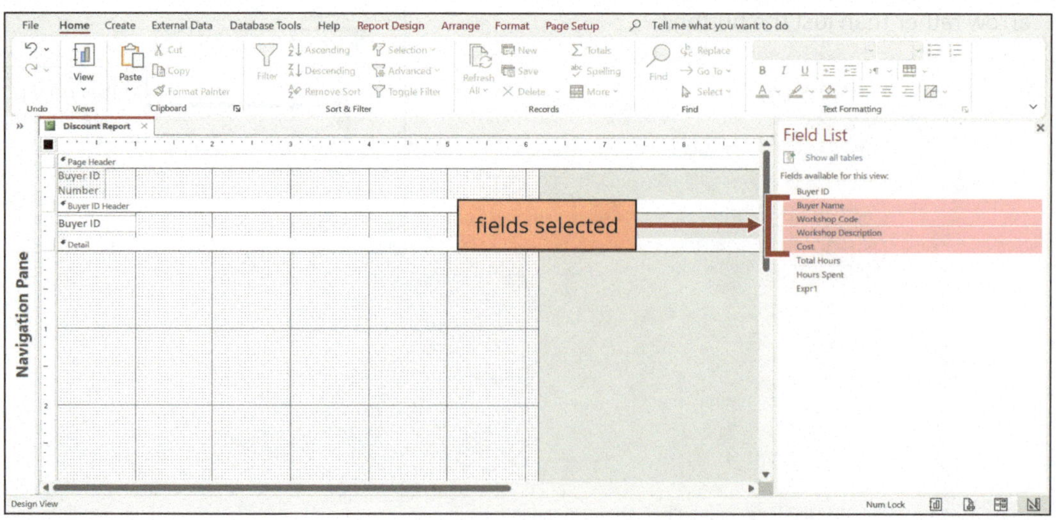

Figure 6–70

- Drag the Buyer Name, Workshop Code, Workshop Description, and Cost fields into the Detail section and close the Field List pane (Figure 6–71).

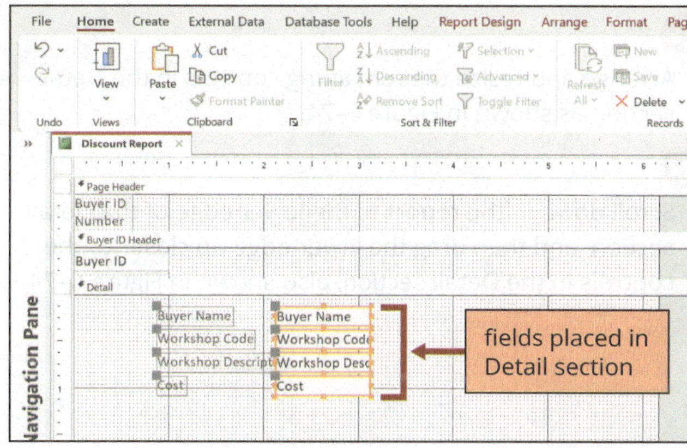

Figure 6–71

2

- One at a time, move the Buyer Name, Workshop Code, Workshop Description, and Cost label controls to the Page Header section, resize them, and break each label into two lines where appropriate (Figure 6–72).

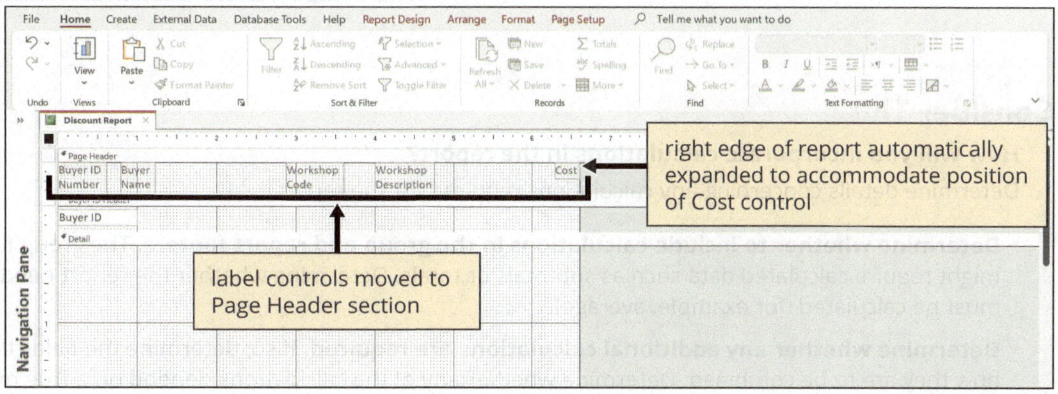

Figure 6–72

Q&A When I paste the label, it is always placed at the left edge, superimposing the Buyer ID label control. Can I change where Access places it?

Unfortunately, when you paste to a different section, Access places the control at the left edge. You will need to drag each control to its proper location after pasting it into the Page Header section.

How can I place the control accurately when there are no gridlines?

When you click the position for the control, Access will automatically expand the grid. You can then adjust the control using the grid.

Can I automatically cause controls to be aligned to the grid?

Yes. Click the Size/Space button (Arrange tab | Sizing & Ordering group), and then click Snap to Grid on the Size/Space menu. From that point on, any controls you add will be automatically aligned to the grid.

3

- Move and resize the Buyer Name control to its approximate position in the Buyer ID Header section, resizing the Buyer ID control as needed to fit the space (Figure 6–73).

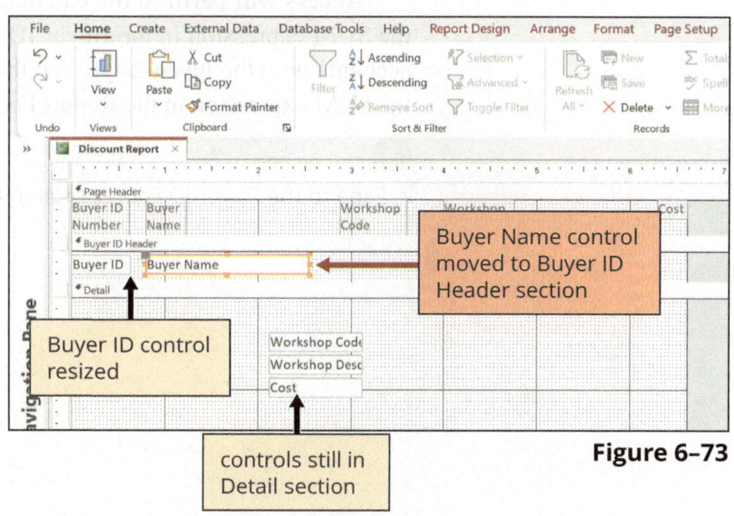

Figure 6–73

4

- Arrange and resize the remaining controls in the Detail section as shown in Figure 6–74.

5

- Scroll down in the report to the lower edge of the Detail section, and then drag the lower edge up closer to the controls in the Detail section, also shown in Figure 6–74.

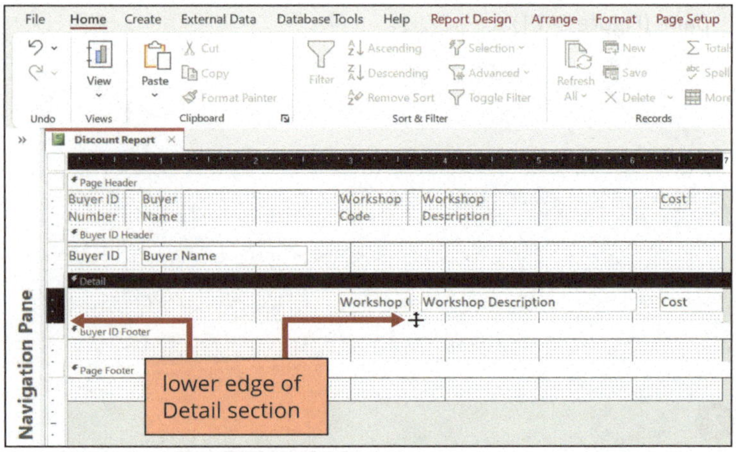

Figure 6–74

Consider This

How will you incorporate calculations in the report?

Determine details concerning any calculations required for the report.

- **Determine whether to include calculations in the group and report footers.** The group footers or report footers might require calculated data such as subtotals or totals. Determine whether the report needs other statistics that must be calculated (for example, average).
- **Determine whether any additional calculations are required.** If so, determine the fields that are involved and how they are to be combined. Determine whether any of the calculations depend on a true or false statement for a criterion, in which case the calculations are conditional.

BTW

Arguments

An argument is a piece of data on which a function operates. For example, in the expression =SUM([Cost]), Cost is the argument because the SUM function will calculate the total of Cost.

Totals and Subtotals

To add totals or other statistics to a footer, add a text box control. You can use any of the aggregate functions in a text box: COUNT, SUM, AVG (average), MAX (largest value), MIN (smallest value), STDEV (standard deviation), VAR (variance), FIRST, and LAST. To use a function, type an equal (=) sign, followed by the function name. You then include a set of parentheses containing the item for which you want to perform the calculation. If the item name contains spaces, such as Annual Total, you must enclose it in square brackets. For example, to calculate the sum of values of a field named Annual Total, the expression would be =SUM([Annual Total]).

Access will perform the calculation for the appropriate collection of records. If you enter the SUM expression in the Buyer ID Footer section, Access will only calculate the subtotal for accounts with the given Buyer ID; that is, it will calculate the appropriate subtotal. If you enter the SUM expression in the Report Footer section, Access will calculate the total for all accounts.

1

- Expand the Buyer ID Footer section by dragging the lower edge down (Figure 6–75).

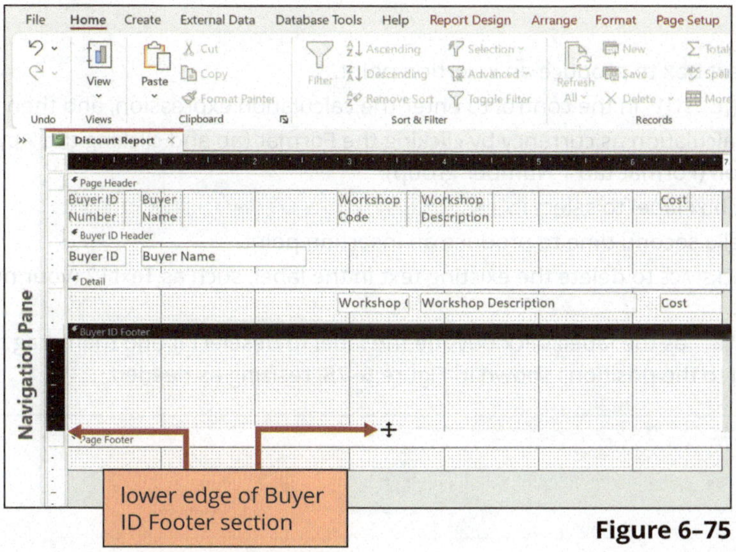

Figure 6–75

2

- Click the Text Box tool (Report Design tab | Controls group), and then point to the position shown in Figure 6–76.

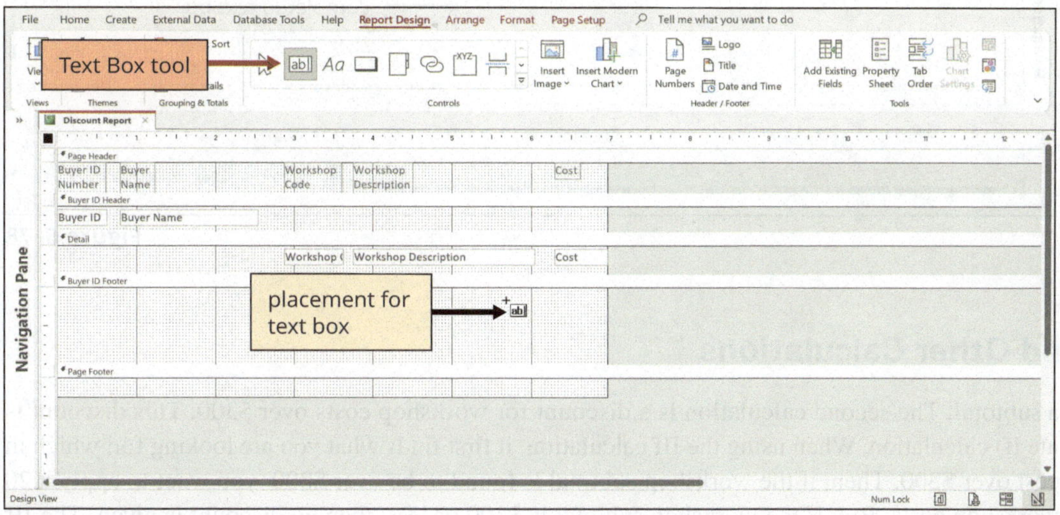

Figure 6–76

3

- Click the position shown in Figure 6–76 to place a text box (Figure 6–77).

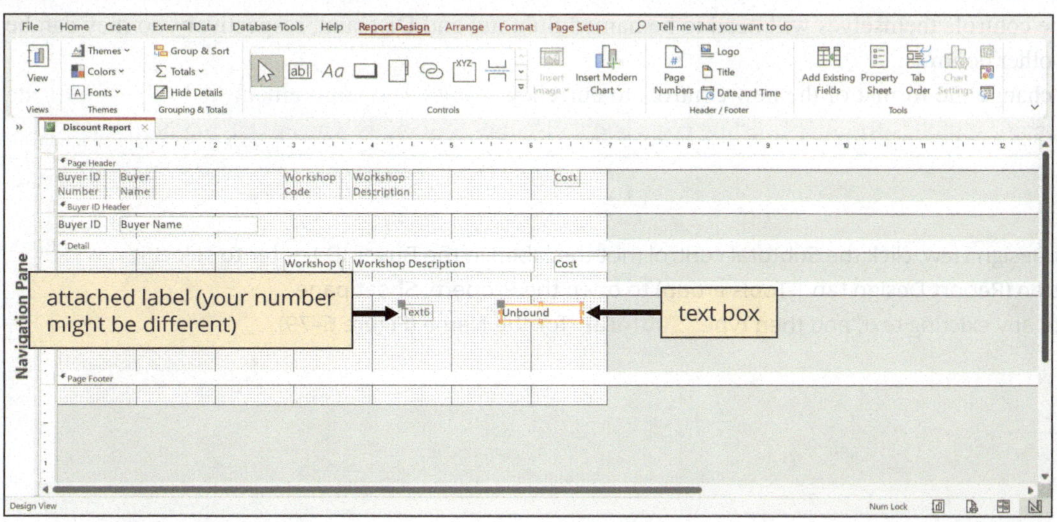

Figure 6–77

4

- Click in the text box to produce an insertion point.
- Type **=Sum([Cost])** in the control to enter the calculation expression, and then press ENTER.
- Format the calculation as currency by clicking the Format tab and clicking the 'Apply Currency Format' button (Format tab | Number group).
- Click the text box label to select it.
- Click the label a second time to produce an insertion point.
- Use DEL or BACKSPACE to delete the existing text in the label, such as Text12 (your number might be different).
- Type **Subtotal** as the label. Click outside the label to deselect it and then drag the control and the label to the positions shown in Figure 6–78, resizing as needed.

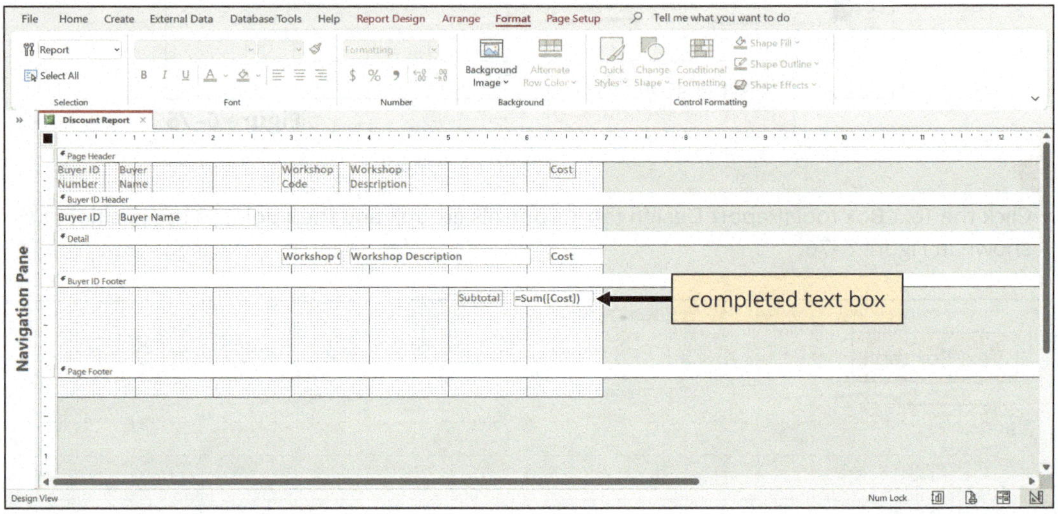

Figure 6–78

To Add Subtotals and Other Calculations

The preceding steps created a subtotal. The second calculation is a discount for workshop costs over $300. This discount is applied using the IIf (Immediate If) calculation. When using the IIf calculation, it first finds what you are looking for, which in this case is a total workshop cost over $300. Then, if the workshop subtotal is found to be over $300, you want to apply a 20 percent (.20) discount to the workshop costs. But, if the workshop subtotal is $300 or less, then no discount is given. The IIf calculation for this example would be entered manually in a control as follows: =IIf([subtotal]>300,[subtotal]*0.2,0) Notice that the subtotal field needs to be in square brackets. Also, note that there are commas after each part of the calculation. The results of the subtotal and the IIf calculations will both be displayed in the Buyer ID Footer section with the control labels Subtotal and Discount. Additionally, the controls themselves will need to be named Subtotal and Discount, respectively, so they can be referenced in calculations for other controls.

The following steps also change the format of the new controls to currency. **Why?** The requirements at Partners indicate the Discount Report should contain subtotals for the workshop costs and a discount for clients who are paying more than $300 for their workshop costs.

1

- With the Discount Report in Design view, click the Subtotal control (not the label) in the Buyer ID Footer to select it.
- Click the Property Sheet button (Report Design tab | Tools group) to open the Property Sheet pane.
- Click in the Name box, delete any existing text, and then type **Subtotal** for the Name (Figure 6–79).

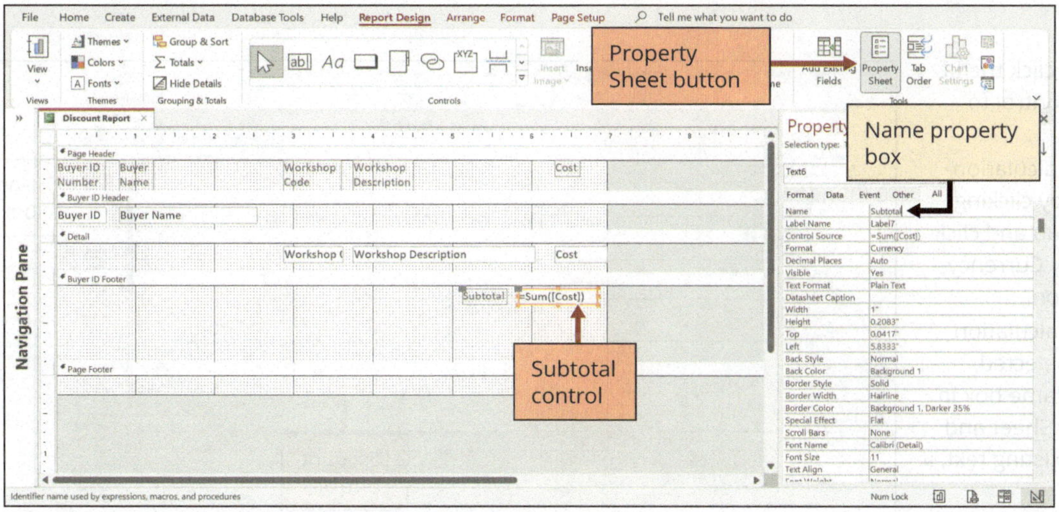

Figure 6–79

2

- Click the Text Box tool (Report Design tab | Controls group), and then click the position in the Buyer ID Footer section shown in Figure 6–80.

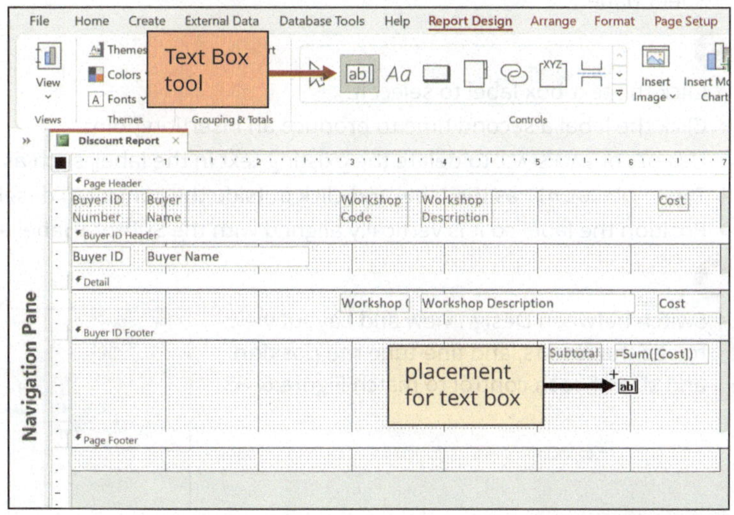

Figure 6–80

3

- Click the text box to produce an insertion point.
- Type **=IIf([Subtotal]>300,[Subtotal]*0.2,0)** in the control to enter the expression calculation, and then press ENTER (Figure 6–81).

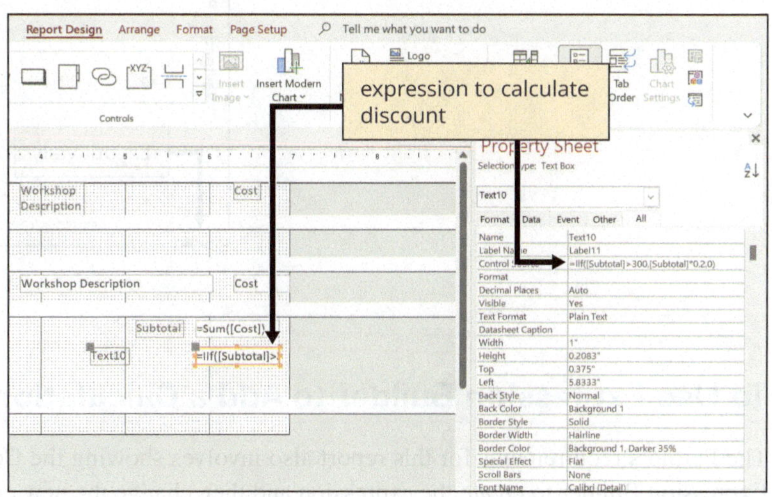

Figure 6–81

4

- If necessary, click the IIf calculation control to select it.
- Format the calculation as currency by clicking the Format tab and clicking the 'Apply Currency Format' button.
- With the IIf calculation control still selected, click in the Name box in the Property Sheet and delete any existing text, if necessary.
- Type **Discount** for the Name (Figure 6–82), and then close the Property Sheet pane.

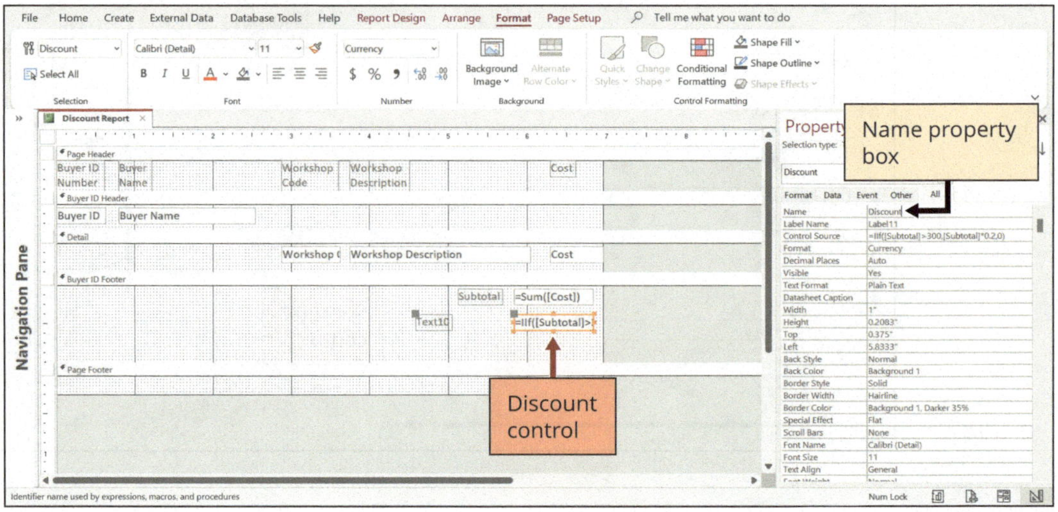

Figure 6–82

5

- Click the text box label to select it.
- Click the label a second time to produce an insertion point.
- Use DEL or BACKSPACE to delete the existing text in the label, such as Text18 (your number might be different).
- Type **Discount** as the label and click outside the control to deselect it.
- Position the label so it is vertically aligned with the Subtotal label and horizontally aligned with the Discount control.

6

- Switch between Design view and Layout view to see the results, and fine-tune the position and size of each control to match Figure 6–83.

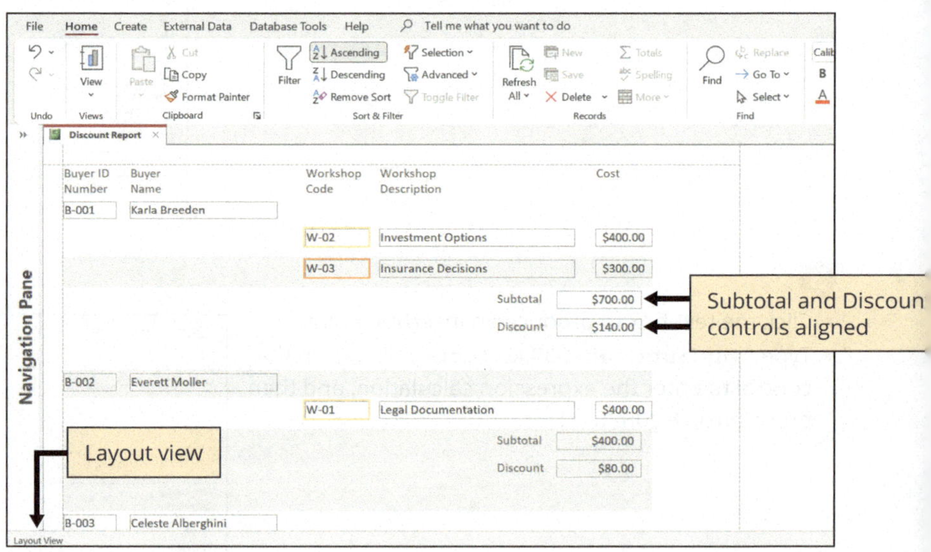

Figure 6–83

To Use Expression Builder to Add a Calculation

The Partners requirements for this report also involves showing the Cost subtotal less the Discount amount. These steps use Expression Builder to create the expression and then change the new control's properties. **Why?** Expression Builder is a convenient way to include a calculation.

1

- If necessary, return to Design view.
- Click the Text Box tool (Report Design tab | Controls group), and then click in the approximate position in the Buyer ID Footer section to place the control for the calculation (Figure 6–84).

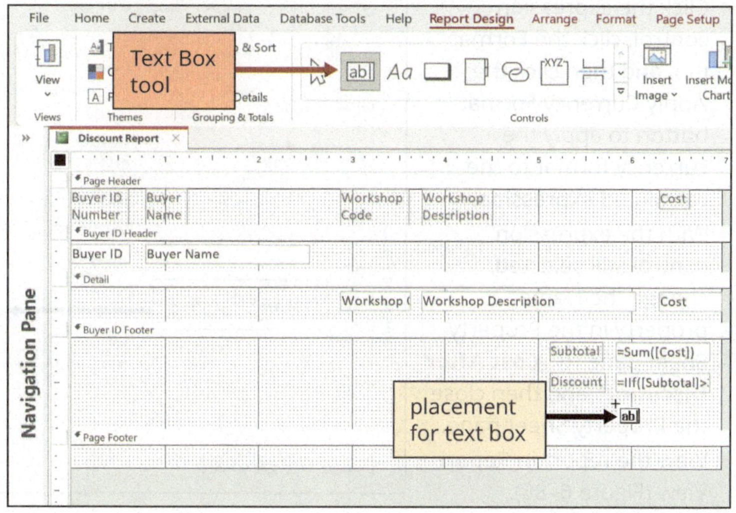

Figure 6–84

2

- Click the text box control, and then open the Property Sheet pane.
- On the All tab, click the Control Source property, and then click the Build button to display the Expression Builder dialog box.
- Type an equal sign (**=**) in the Expression Builder box.
- Click Discount Report in the Expression Elements category in the first column.
- Scroll down in the second column so that Subtotal appears, and then double-click the Subtotal control in the second column.
- Type a minus sign (**–**), scroll in the second column so that Discount appears, and then double-click the Discount control to add it to the expression (Figure 6–85).

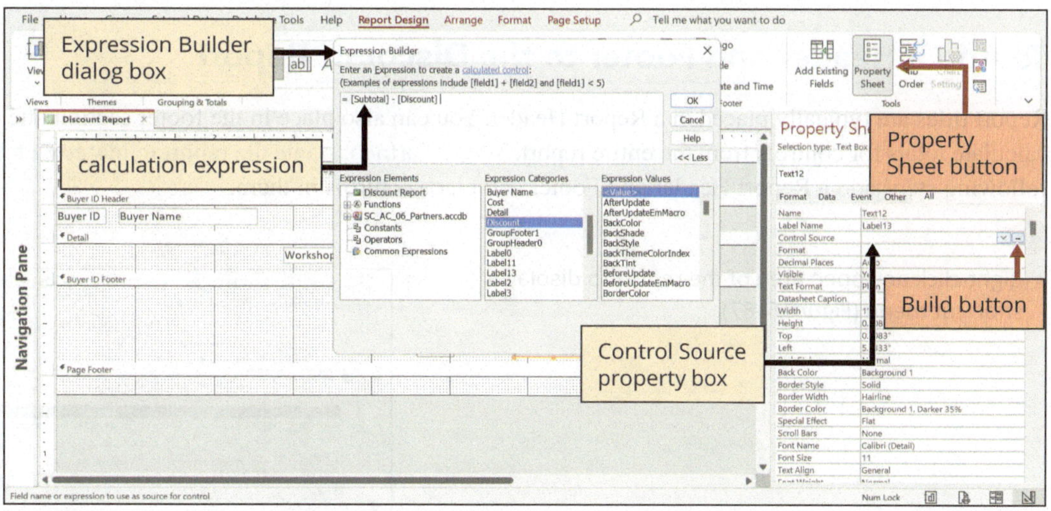

Figure 6–85

Q&A Why did I choose Control Source instead of Record Source?

You use Record Source to select the source of the records in a report, usually a table or a query. You use the Control Source property to specify the source of data for the control. This allows you to bind an expression or field to a control.

Are there other ways I could enter the expression?

Yes. You could just type the whole expression. On the other hand, you could select the function just as in these steps, and, when entering each argument, you could select the fields from the list of fields and click the desired operators.

3

- Click OK to close the Expression Builder dialog box.
- Click the label for the expression control, and then click the label for the expression control a second time to produce an insertion point.
- Use BACKSPACE or DEL to erase the current entry in the label, and then type **Cost After Discount** as the new entry.
- Use the move handle to reposition the label control as needed so it does not overlap the expression control.

4

- Click the expression control, click the Format tab, and then click the 'Apply Currency Format' button to apply the currency format to the calculated expression.
- With the expression control still selected, change the Name property in the Property Sheet pane to **Cost After Discount** and then close the Property Sheet pane.
- View the report in Report View (Figure 6–86).

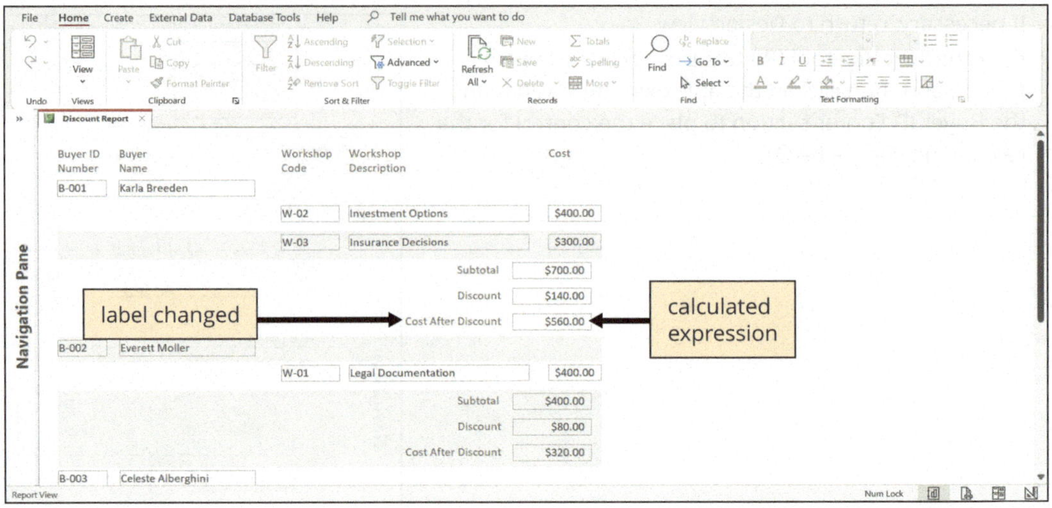

Figure 6–86

5

- Return to Design view and save your changes.

To Add a Header and Footer to the Discount Report

Report titles are typically placed in a Report Header. You can also place in the footer section one or more calculation fields that calculate totals for controls from the entire report. *Why? Partners wants the report to include a total for all workshop costs.* The following steps add a Report Header and Footer and place controls in them.

1

- Right-click any open area of the report to display a shortcut menu (Figure 6–87).

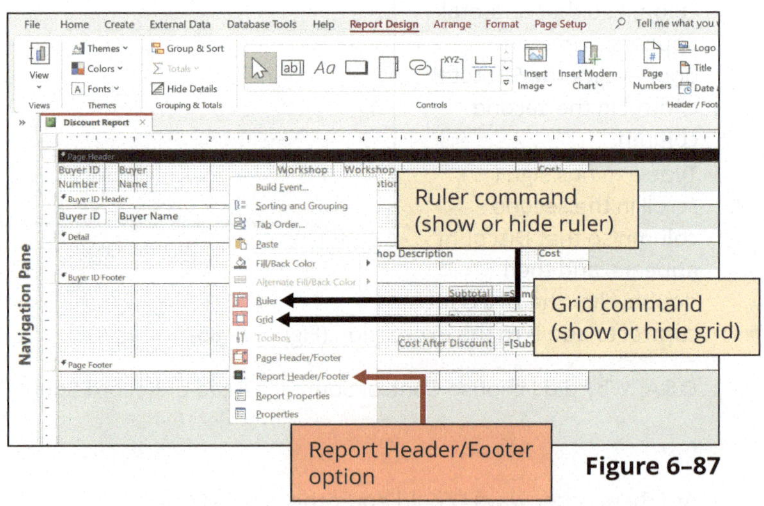

Figure 6–87

2

- Click 'Report Header/Footer' to display the Report Header and Footer sections.
- Click the Subtotal control in the Buyer ID Footer section to select the control and its label.
- Display the Home tab.
- Click the Copy button (Home tab | Clipboard group) to copy the selected controls to the Clipboard.
- Click the Report Footer bar to select the footer, and then click the Paste button (Home tab | Clipboard group) to paste a copy of the controls into the report footer (Figure 6–88).

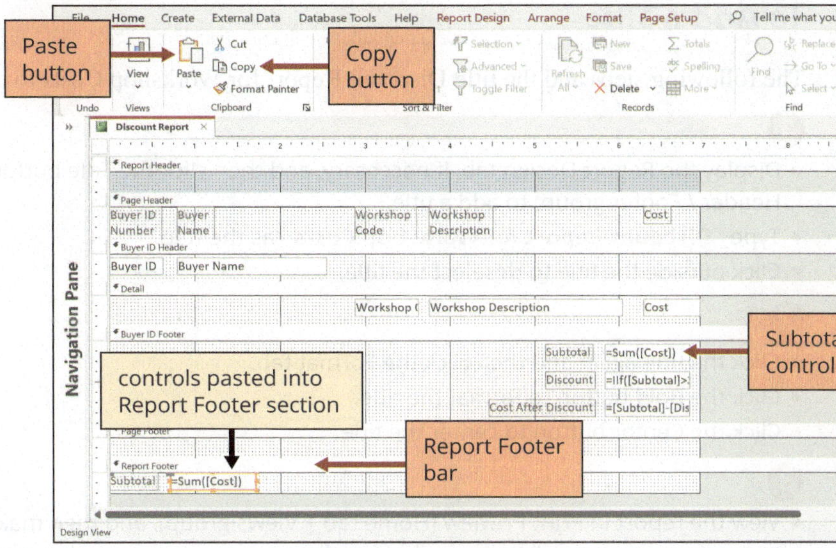

Figure 6–88

3

- Click the label in the Report Footer section to select the label, and then click a second time to produce an insertion point.
- Use BACKSPACE or DEL to erase the current contents, type **Total** to change the label, and then move the label and control to the positions shown in Figure 6–89.

4

- View your changes in Layout view, and then return to Design view and save the report.

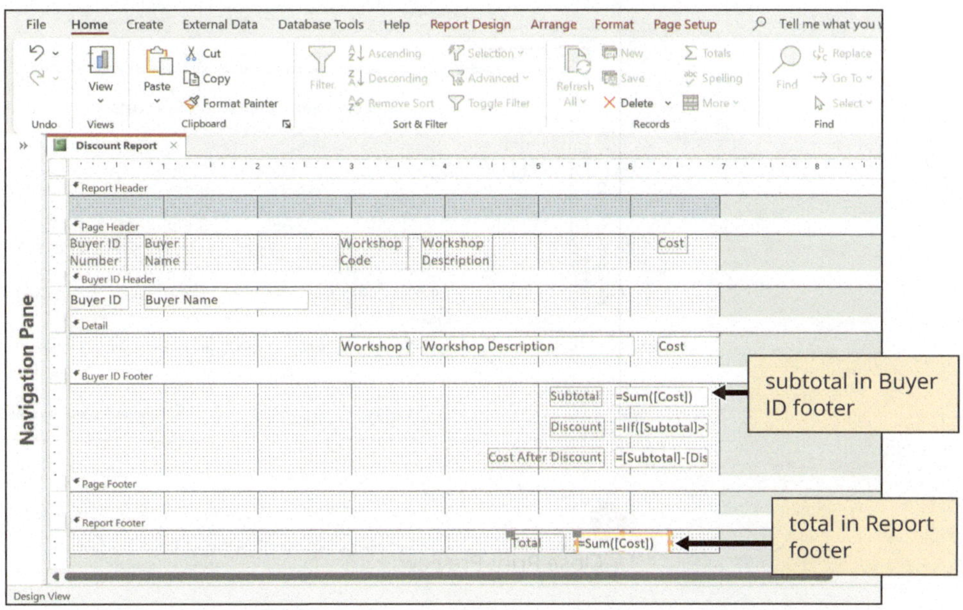

Figure 6–89

To Remove the Color from the Report Header

The following step removes the color from the Report Header section by changing the background color for the header to white.

1

- Right-click the report header to produce a menu.
- Point to the 'Fill/Back Color' arrow on the shortcut menu to display a color palette.
- Click White in the first row, first column to change the background color to white.

To Add a Title

The following steps add the title Discount Report for Workshop Costs to the report.

1

- Display the Report Design tab, if necessary, and then click the Title button (Report Design tab | Header / Footer group) to add a title.
- Type **Discount Report for Workshop Costs** as the title.
- Click outside the title to deselect the title.

2

- Click the title again and then click the Format tab.
- Click the Bold button to format the title.
- Click the Center button to center the title.

3

- View the report in Print Preview (Home tab | Views group), and then make any further adjustments to controls so all text is visible for all records and all controls are neatly aligned and organized, as shown in Figure 6–90.

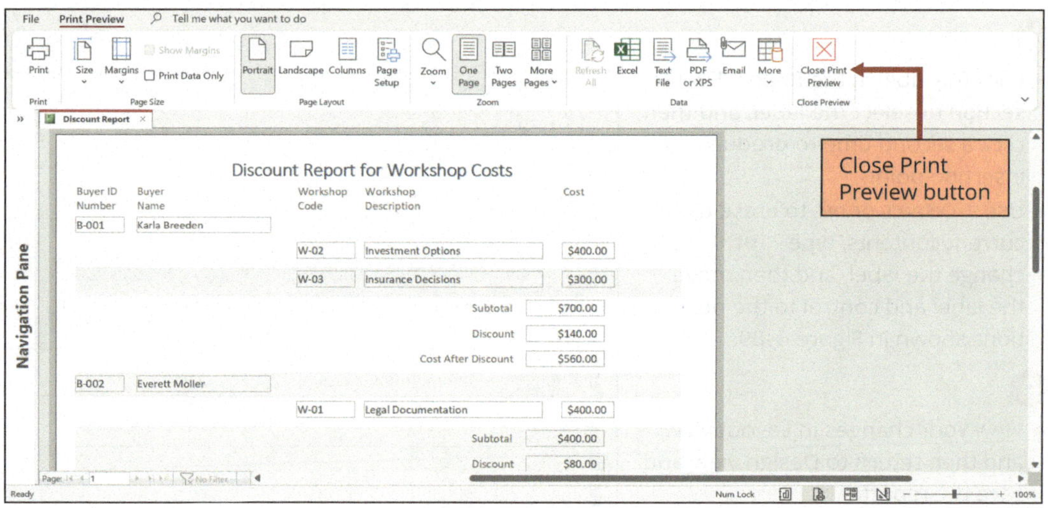

Figure 6–90

4

- Close Print Preview.

Obtaining Help on Functions

There are many functions included in Access that are available for a variety of purposes. To see the list of functions, display the Expression Builder. (See Figure 6–85 for one way to display the Expression Builder.) Double-click Functions in the first column and then click Built-In Functions. You can then scroll through the entire list of functions in the third column. Alternatively, you can click a function category in the second column, in which case the third column will only contain the functions in that category. To obtain detailed help on a function, highlight the function in the third column and click the Help button. The Help information presented will show the syntax of the function, that is, the specific rule for how you must type the function and any arguments. It will give you general comments on the function as well as examples illustrating the use of the function.

Page Setup Tab

You can use the buttons on the Page Setup tab to change margins, orientation, and other page setup characteristics of the report (Figure 6–91a). If you click the Margins button, you can choose from among some predefined margins or set your own custom margins (Figure 6–91b). If you click the Columns button, you will see the Page Setup dialog box with the Columns tab selected (Figure 6–91c). You can use this tab to specify multiple columns in a report as well as column spacing. You can specify orientation by clicking the Page tab (Figure 6–91d). You can also select paper size, paper source, and printer using this tab. Back on the ribbon, if you click the Page Setup button, you will see the Page Setup dialog box with the Print Options tab selected (Figure 6–91e). You can use this tab to specify custom margins.

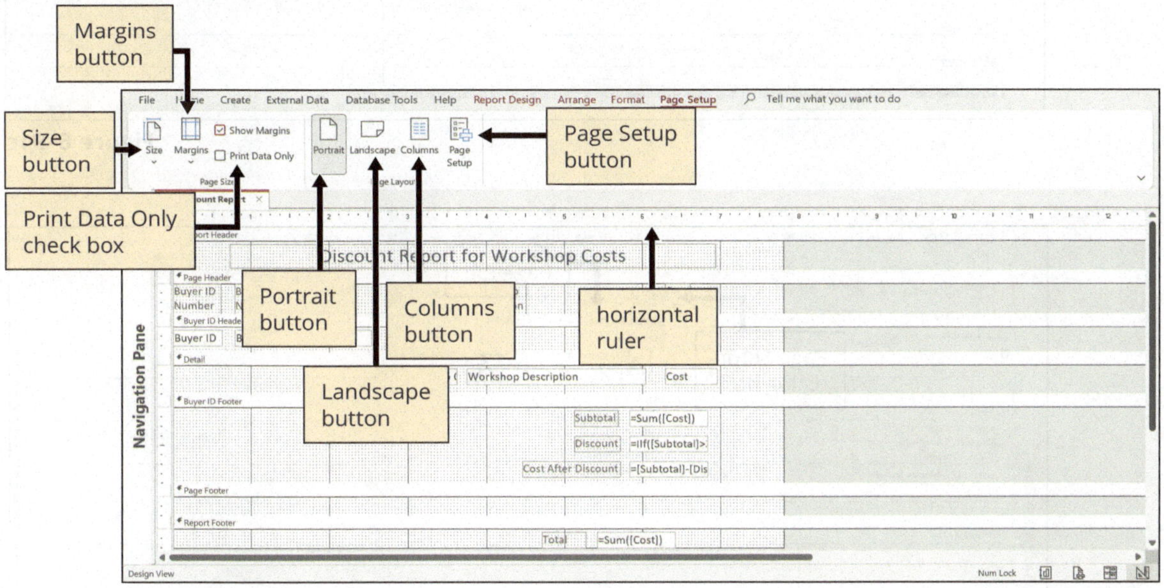

Figure 6–91a

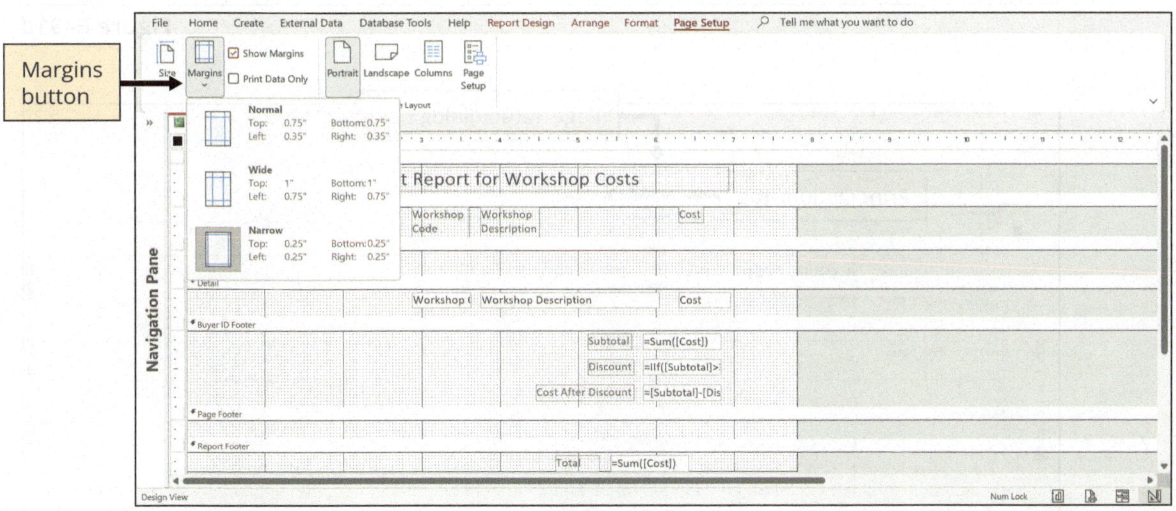

Figure 6–91b

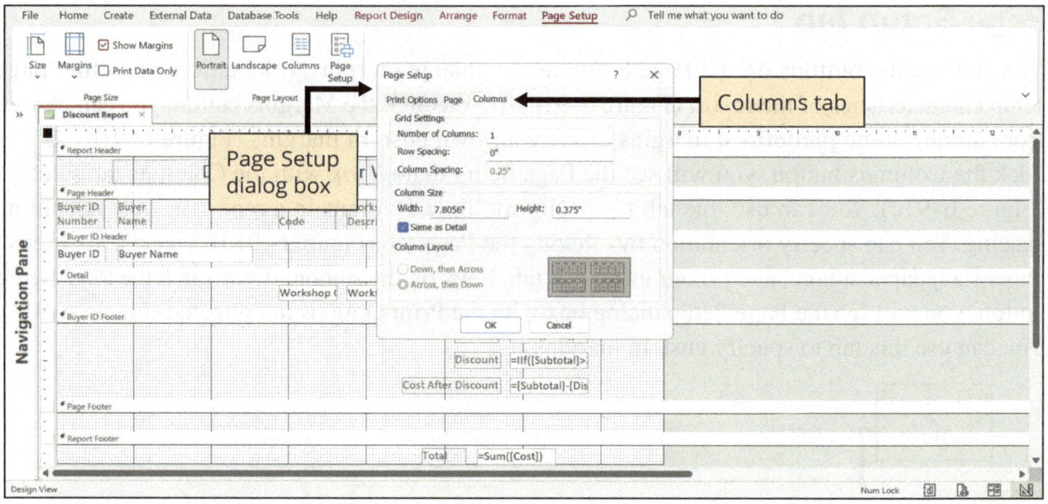

Figure 6–91c

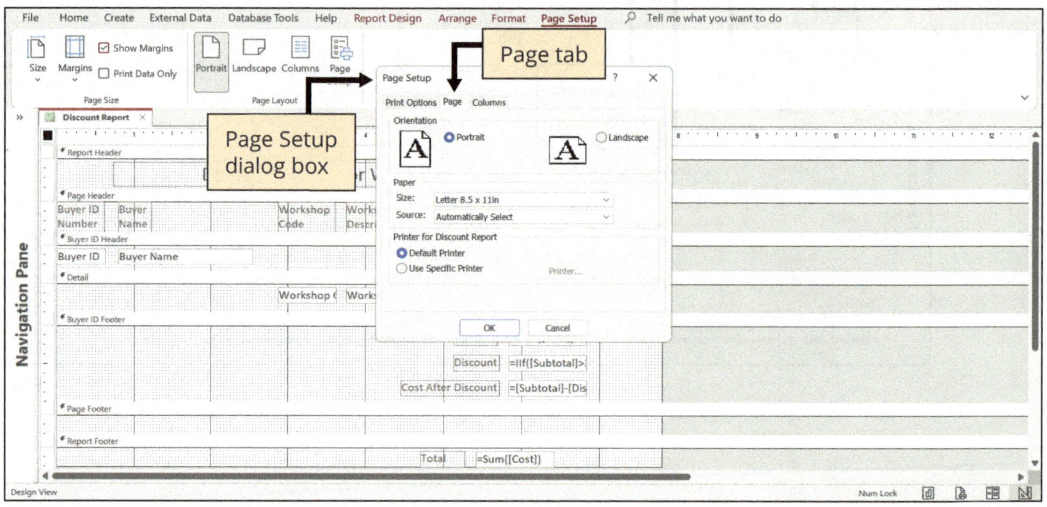

Figure 6–91d

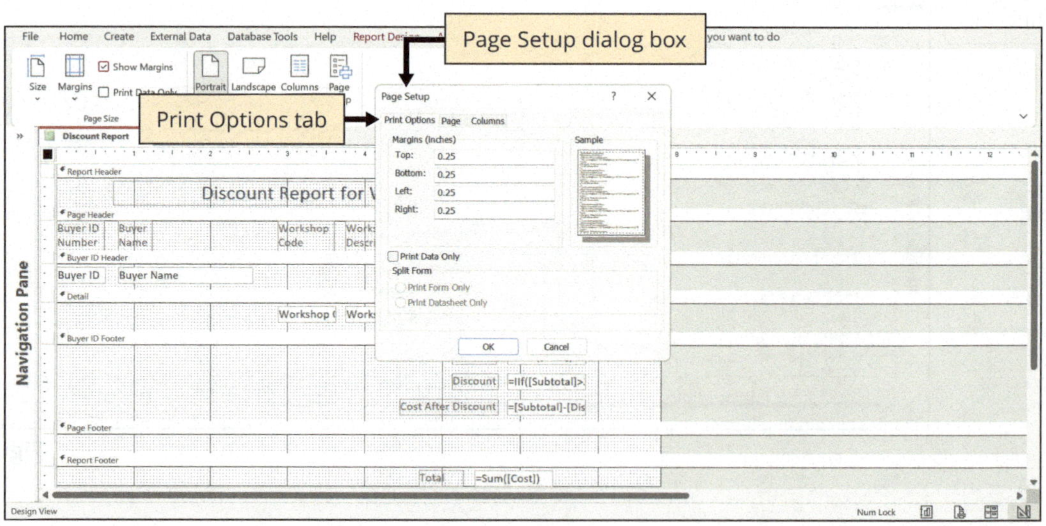

Figure 6–91e

To Change the Report Margins

Looking at the horizontal ruler in Figure 6–91a, you will notice the report width is nearly 8 inches. Because the report will probably print on standard 8½" × 11" paper, an 8-inch report with 1-inch margins on the left and right would result in a 10-inch width, which will not fit. To allow the report to fit on the page, you could change the orientation from Portrait to Landscape or you could reduce the margins. There are two ways to change the margins. You can click the Margins button on the Page Setup tab and then select one of the predefined options. If you want more control, you can click the Page Setup button to display the Page Setup dialog box. You can then specify your own margins, change the orientation, and also specify multiple columns if you want a multicolumn report.

The following step uses the Margins button to confirm Narrow margins is selected, as this option will provide the most printable space on the page.

1

- Display the Page Setup tab.
- Click the Margins button (Page Setup tab | Page Size group).
- If necessary, click Narrow to specify the Narrow margin option.

Fine-Tuning a Report

When you have finished a report, you should review several of its pages in Print Preview to make sure the layout is precisely what you want. You might find that you need to increase the size of a control, which you can do by selecting the control and dragging the appropriate sizing handle. You might decide to add a control, which you could do by using the appropriate tool in the Controls group or by dragging a field from the field list.

In both cases, if the control is located between other controls, you have a potential problem. You might not have enough space between the other controls to increase the size or to add an additional control. If the control is part of a control layout that you had when you modified earlier reports in Layout view, you can resize controls or add new fields, and the remaining fields automatically adjust for the change. In Design view with individual controls, you must make any necessary adjustments manually.

To Make Room for Resizing or Adding Controls

To make room for resizing a control or for adding controls, you would use the following steps.

1. Select all controls to the right of the control you want to resize, or to the right of the position where you want to add another control.
2. Drag any of the selected controls to the right to make room for the change.

To Save and Close a Report

Now that you have completed your work on your report, you should save the report and close it. The following steps first save your work on the report and then close the report.

1

- If instructed to do so by your instructor, change the title of the Discount Report to LastName Report where LastName is your last name.
- Click the Save button on the Quick Access Toolbar to save your work.
- Close the Discount Report.

2

- If desired, sign out of your Microsoft account.
- sam Exit Access.

Summary

In this module, you have learned to create and relate additional tables; create queries for a report; create reports in Design view; add fields and text boxes to a report; format controls; group and ungroup controls; modify multiple controls; add and modify a subreport; modify section properties; add a title, page number, and date; add subtotals; use a function in a text box; and publish a report.

Consider This: Plan Ahead

What decisions will you need to make when creating your own reports?

Use these guidelines as you complete the assignments in this module and create your own reports outside of this class.

1. Determine the intended audience and purpose of the report.
   a. Identify the user or users of the report and determine how they will use it.
   b. Specify the necessary data and level of detail to include in the report.
2. Determine the source of data for the report.
   a. Determine whether all the data is in a single table or whether it comes from multiple related tables.
3. Determine whether the data is stored in a query.
   a. You might need to create multiple versions of a report for a query where the criterion for a field changes, in which case, you would use a parameter query and enter the criterion when you run the report.
   b. If the data comes from multiple related tables, you might want to create a query and use the query as a source of data.
4. Determine the fields that belong on the report.
   a. Identify the data items that are needed by the user of the report.
5. Determine the organization of the report.
   a. The report might be enhanced by displaying the fields in a particular order and arranged in a certain way.
   b. Should the records in the report be grouped in some way?
   c. Should the report contain any subreports?
6. Determine any calculations required for the report.
   a. Should the report contain totals or subtotals?
   b. Are there any special calculations?
   c. Are there any calculations that involve criteria?
7. Determine the format and style of the report.
   a. What information should be in the report heading?
   b. Do you want a title and date?
   c. Do you want special background colors or alternate colors?
   d. Should the report contain an image?
   e. What should be in the body of the report?

Consider This

How should you submit solutions to critical thinking questions in the assignments?

Every assignment in this course contains one or more critical thinking questions. These questions require you to think beyond the assigned database. Present your responses to the questions in the format required by your instructor. Possible formats may include one or more of these options: write the answer; create a document that contains the answer; present your answer to the class; discuss your answer in a group; record the answer as audio or video using a webcam, smartphone, or portable media player; or post answers on a blog, wiki, or website.

Student Assignments

Apply Your Knowledge

Reinforce the skills and apply the concepts you learned in this module.

Creating a Report with a Subreport

Note: To complete this assignment, you will be required to use the Data Files. Please contact your instructor for information about accessing the Data Files.

Instructions: Start Access. Open the database, SC_AC_06-2.accdb, which is located in the Data Files folder. Enable the content.

Perform the following tasks:

1. Save the database using the file name, SC_AC_06_Construction. Enable the content.
2. In the Relationships window, delete the existing relationship between the Job Sites table and the Subcontractors table. Add the Accounting table to the window.
3. Create a one-to-many relationship (enforce referential integrity) between the Subcontractors table and the Accounting table using the Subcontractor Number field in both tables. Create a second one-to-many relationship (enforce referential integrity) between the Job Sites table and the Accounting table using the Job Site Number field in both tables. Save the relationships and close the Relationships window.
4. Create a query that joins the Subcontractors and Accounting tables. Include the Subcontractor Number, Subcontractor Name, and Specialty fields from the Subcontractors table. Include the Pymt ID, Amount Paid, Current Due, and JS # fields from the Accounting table. Sort the results by Subcontractor Number in Ascending order. Save the query as Subcontractors and Accounting. Run the query to confirm it shows all seven records from the Accounting table in the results, and then save and close the query.
5. Create the report shown in Figure 6–92. The report uses the Subcontractors and Accounting query as the basis for the main report and the Job Sites table as the basis for the subreport. Group by Subcontractor Number and sort by JS #. When stepping through the SubReport Wizard, link the subform to the main form using the job site number field on each side of the connection. Use the name Subcontractors and Job Sites Summary List for the report. The report title has a Text Align property value of Center. The Border Width property for the detail controls is 1 pt and the subreport name is Job Sites subreport. The report is similar in style to the Buyers and Account Information Summary List shown in Figure 6–1a.

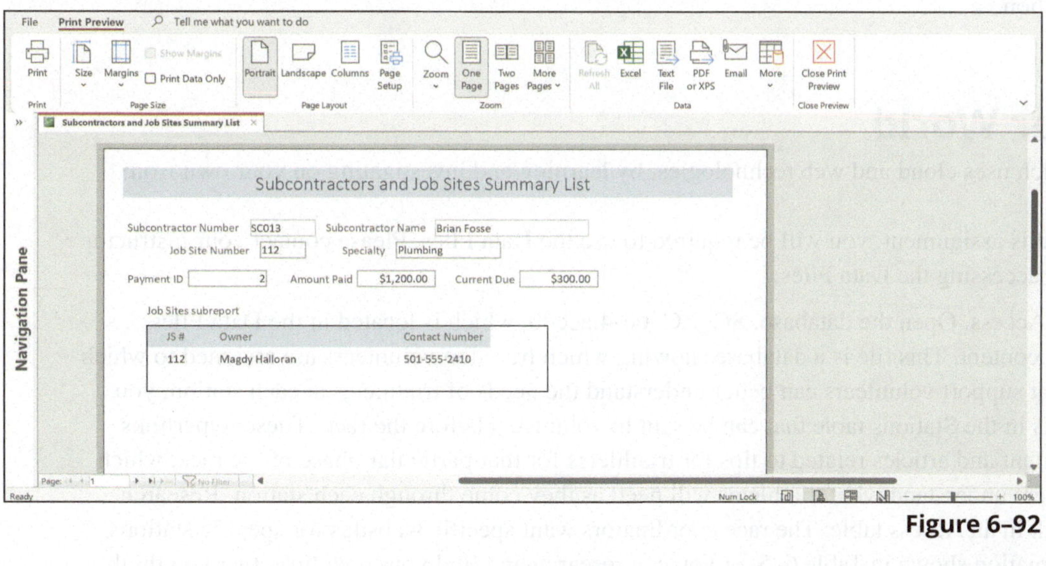

Figure 6–92

Continued on next page

6. If requested to do so by your instructor, change the title for the report to First Name Last Name Summary List where First Name and Last Name are your first and last names.
7. Submit the revised database in the format specified by your instructor.
8. **Consider This:** How would you change the font weight of the report title to bold?

Extend Your Knowledge

Extend the skills you learned in this module and experiment with new skills. You may need to use Help to complete the assignment.

Modifying Reports

Note: To complete this assignment, you will be required to use the Data Files. Please contact your instructor for information about accessing the Data Files.

Instructions: Start Access. Open the database, SC_AC_06-3.accdb, which is located in the Data Files folder. PicsPlus is a small photography cooperative that is seeking grant funding. As part of the grant application process, PicsPlus needs to make some design changes to a report in its database.

Perform the following tasks:

1. Save the database using the file name, SC_AC_06_PicsPlus. Enable the content.
2. Open the Photographer Balances Summary Report in Design view. Insert a date field (such as 14-Nov-27) in the report header. If necessary, arrange the date so it aligns with the right edge of the report.
3. Change the report title to Revised Photographer Balances Summary Report. Change the report header background to white. Use the Property Sheet to change the font of the title text to Calibri with a font weight of semi-bold. Make sure the entire title is visible and the title is left-aligned in the Report Header section.
4. Add a label to the report footer section. The label should contain text to indicate the end of the report, for example, End of Report or similar text.
5. Use conditional formatting to format the sum for each record with the Green 3 background color for all records where the value is equal to or greater than $1,000.00.
6. If requested to do so by your instructor, open the Photographer table and add your name to the table.
7. Submit the revised database in the format specified by your instructor.
8. **Consider This:** Do you think the borders surrounding the controls enhance or detract from the appearance of the Photographer Balances Summary Report? What other design changes would you suggest? Explain your position.

Expand Your World

Create a solution, which uses cloud and web technologies, by learning and investigating on your own from general guidance.

Note: To complete this assignment, you will be required to use the Data Files. Please contact your instructor for information about accessing the Data Files.

Instructions: Start Access. Open the database, SC_AC_06-4.accdb, which is located in the Data Files folder, and enable the content. This file is a database showing which triathlon volunteers are assigned to which support station. So that support volunteers can better understand the needs of triathletes at each station, you want to add hyperlinks in the Stations table that can be sent to volunteers before the race. These hyperlinks should connect to content and articles related to tips for triathletes for that particular phase of the race, which will also help volunteers understand what triathletes will need as they come through each station. Research how to add a hyperlink in an Access table. The race coordinators want specific websites for specific stations. You can use the information shown in Table 6–5, or you can research and find your own links that you think would be helpful for volunteers at each station. After placing the hyperlinks in the Stations table, add the hyperlink field to the Volunteers Stations Report.

Perform the following tasks:

1. Search the web to find how to add a hyperlink in an Access table and also in a report that was created previously.
2. Save the database using the file name, SC_AC_06_Triathlon. Enable the content. Create a new field with the Hyperlink Data Type called Information in the Stations table. Add the websites shown in Table 6–5 in the new field for the station indicated; alternatively, find another website for each station that would be helpful for volunteers at each station and add those websites instead.

Table 6–5 Stations and Associated Hyperlinks

Station Number	Suggested Hyperlink
BK1 and BK2	https://www.trigirl.co.uk/beginners/top-5-cycling-tips-for-beginner-triathletes/
RN1 and RN2	https://www.trainingpeaks.com/blog/five-steps-run-faster-triathlon/
SW1	https://www.formswim.com/blogs/all/triathlon-swimming-strokes

3. Open the Volunteers Stations Report in Design view and delete any alternate background color in the report.
4. Add the hyperlink field to the Volunteers Stations Report.
5. Review the report in Report view and verify the accuracy of the website hyperlinks.
6. Save your changes.
7. Submit the revised database in the format specified by your instructor.
8. **Consider This:** What steps did you select to create a hyperlink? What source did you use to learn this information? Justify your selection of the source.

In the Lab

Design and implement a solution using creative thinking and problem-solving skills.

Lab: Creating a Report for the Homegrown Nurse Staffing Agency Database

Note: To complete this assignment, you will be required to use the Data Files. Please contact your instructor for information about accessing the Data Files.

Problem: From time to time, equipment needs to be updated or replaced. Team managers, coaches, and administrators want to keep track of the changes as part of the database.

Perform the following tasks:

Part 1: Open the SC_AC_06-5.accdb database from the Data Files folder. Save the file with the name, SC_AC_06_Travel-Nurses, and enable the content. Use the concepts and techniques presented in this module to perform each of the following tasks. The agency needs to create a report to help track payments by traveler and assignment.

1. Create a query that includes fields from the Travelers table and the Assignments table (these tables are joined in a one-to-many relationship). Include the Traveler ID and Traveler Name fields from the Travelers table. Include the Assignment ID, Assignment Pay Rate, and Assignment Reimbursements fields from the Assignments table. Sort in Ascending order on Traveler ID. Save the query as Travelers and Pay Rates.

Continued on next page

2. Create the report shown in Figure 6–93. The report uses the Travelers and Pay Rates query as the basis for the main report and the Traveler Payments table as the basis for the subreport. Use the name Travelers and Payments Summary List as the name for the report and the name Traveler Payments as the name for the subreport. Change the Text Align property for the title to Center.

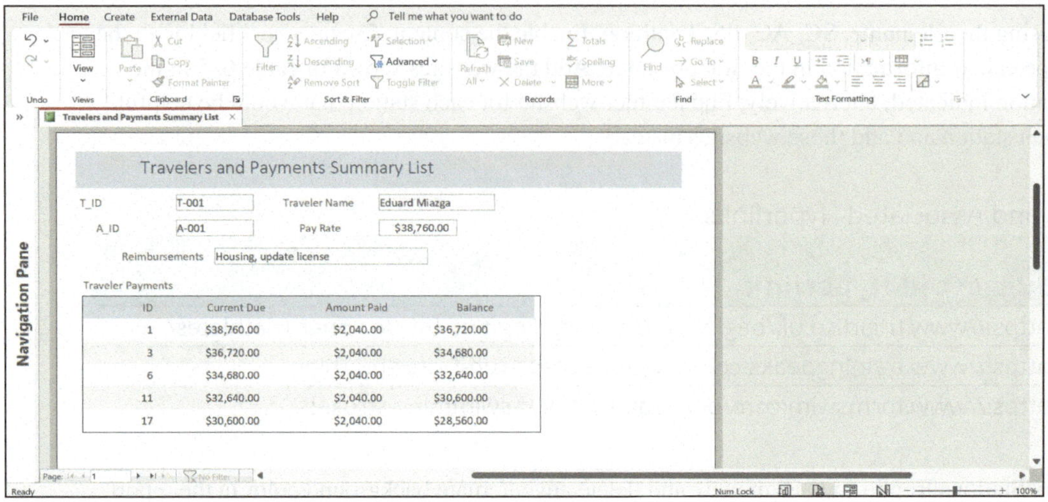

Figure 6–93

3. The page number and current date appear in the report footer section. Change the Can Grow property for the Traveler Name field to Yes.
4. If instructed to do so by your instructor, add a label to the report footer with your first and last name.
5. **Consider This:** Adding a subreport can provide quick reference to other database information. What are your thoughts about using the Traveler Payments table for the subreport? Do you think it is helpful or would you use another table or some other object in the subreport?

Submit your assignment in the format specified by instructor.

Part 2: Consider This: You made several decisions, such as creating a query, creating and modifying a report, and adding a subreport control. What was the rationale behind your decisions? Would you add any additional fields to this table?

Advanced Form Techniques

Objectives

After completing this module, you will be able to:

- Add a combo box that selects values
- Apply formatting characteristics with the Format Painter
- Modify content and design of a header or footer
- Insert an image in a form
- Add a command button to a form
- Add a combo box for searching
- Add a rectangle shape
- Modify a button's actions in a form
- Modify VBA (Visual Basic for Applications) code
- Add concatenated fields to a form
- Use tab controls to create a multipage form
- Insert a chart
- Modify a chart type
- Format a chart

Introduction

In other modules, you created basic forms using the Form Wizard, and you created more complex forms using Design view. In this module, you continue learning advanced design and formatting techniques for when you are working with forms. With the proper tools, forms can provide a valuable means of interacting with data in the database. You will create two new forms that include elements to increase functionality and display different types of information. The first form contains two combo boxes, one for selecting data from a related table and one for finding a record on the form. It also contains command buttons to accomplish various tasks.

The second form you will create is a **multipage form**, which is a form that contains more than one page of information. The form contains a tab control that allows you to access two different pages. Clicking the first tab displays a page containing a subform. Clicking the second tab displays a page containing two charts.

Project: Advanced Form Techniques

Clearnet wants two additional forms to use with its Carriers and Loads tables. The first form, Loads View and Update Form (Figure 7–1a), contains fields from the Loads table. The form has five command buttons: Next Record, Previous Record, Add Record, Delete Record, and Close Form. Clicking any of these buttons causes the action indicated on the button to occur.

The form also contains combo boxes for the Carrier and Shipper fields, which assists users in viewing who is involved in the load (Figure 7–1b).

To assist users in finding an account when they know the load number, the form also includes a combo box they can use for record navigation (Figure 7–1c). This combo box allows users to enter the load number in one of two ways: they can either type the number in the text field, or they can click the arrow to display a list and then select the load they want. Access will then locate the account and display that load's data in the form (Figure 7–1d).

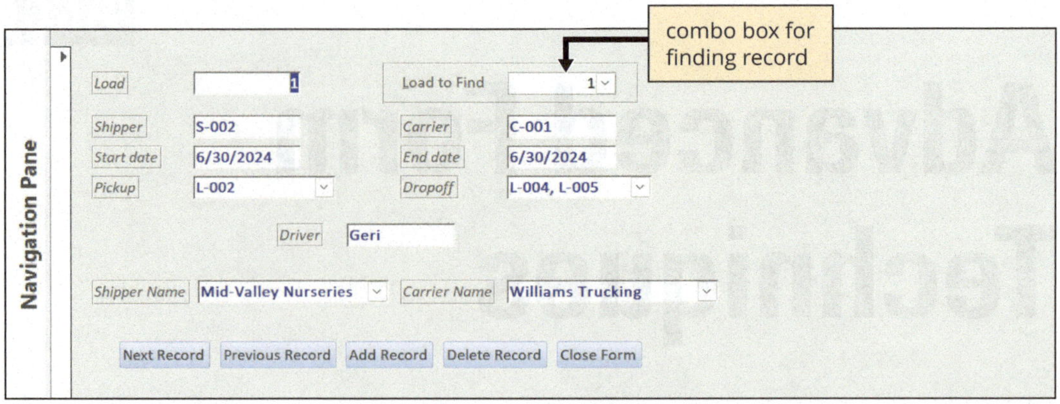

Figure 7–1a Loads View and Update Form

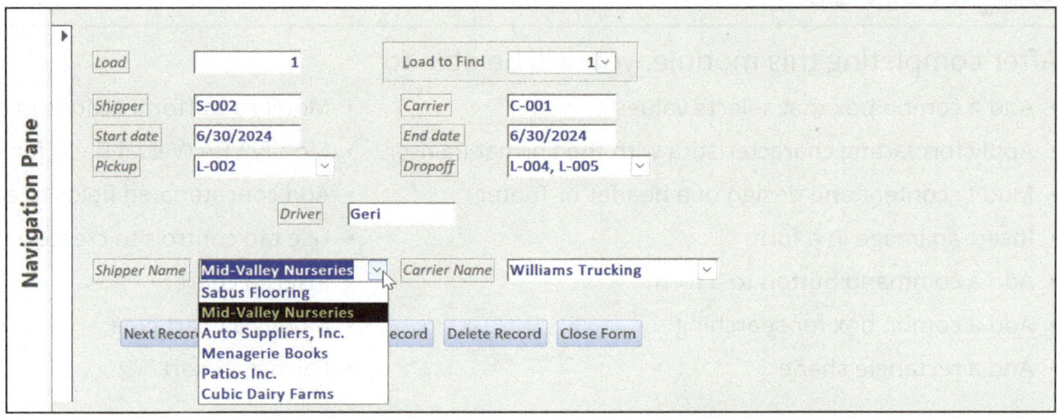

Figure 7–1b Shipper Combo Box

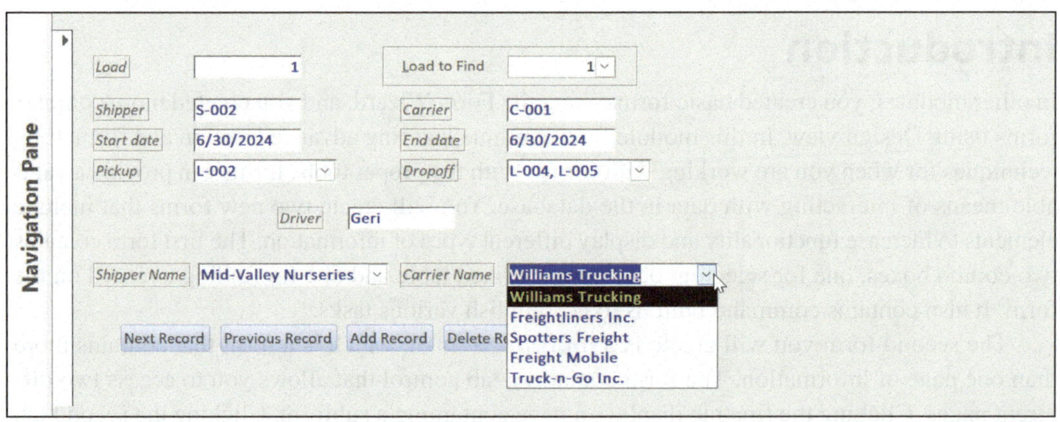

Figure 7–1c Carrier Combo Box

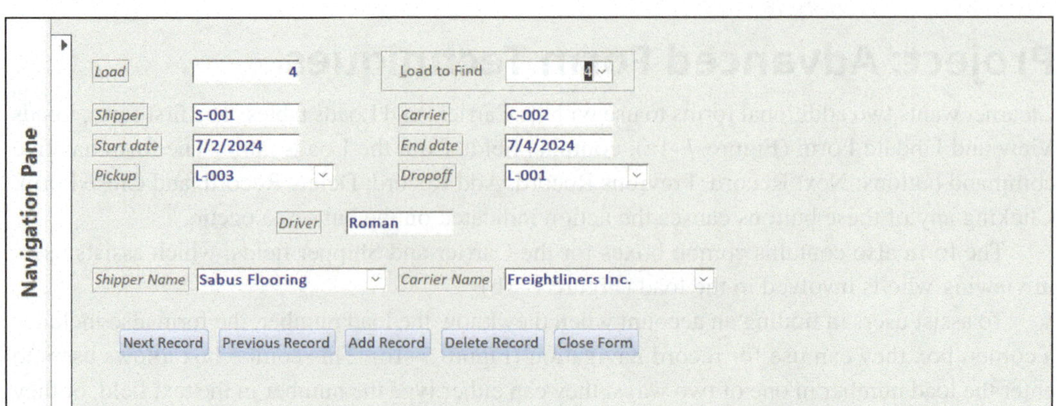

Figure 7–1d Load Data

BTW

Drop-Down Boxes

Combo boxes also are called drop-down boxes because a list drops down when you click the combo box arrow. This is one of the primary differences between a combo box and a list box (which is a different type of control). The list box displays the list all the time, and you cannot type a different value into a list box. You simply click the value that you want from the list. With a combo box, however, the drop-down list only appears when you click the arrow, and you have the option of typing a different value into the box.

For the second new form, Clearnet needs a multipage form that lists the payments by shipper. Each of the two pages that make up the form is displayed in its own tab. Selecting the first tab, the one labeled Datasheet, displays a subform listing information about rate confirmations and agent commissions for each shipper (Figure 7–2a).

Selecting the other tab, the one labeled Charts, displays two charts that illustrate data about the shipper's rate cons and agent commissions for each load (Figure 7–2b). In the pie chart, the slices of the pie represent the sum of rate confirmations for each bill status. They are color-coded, and the legend at the bottom indicates the meaning of the various colors. The size of the pie slice gives a visual representation of the portion of rate confirmations with that bill status. The chart also includes specific percentages. If you look at the purple slice in the Rate Confirmation Statuses chart, for example, you see the color represents Bill Sent statuses. This slice signifies 58 percent of the total. The columns in the second chart represent the amount of agent commission earned for each load sent by that shipper. Over time, this chart would start to show trends of agent commissions with each shipper.

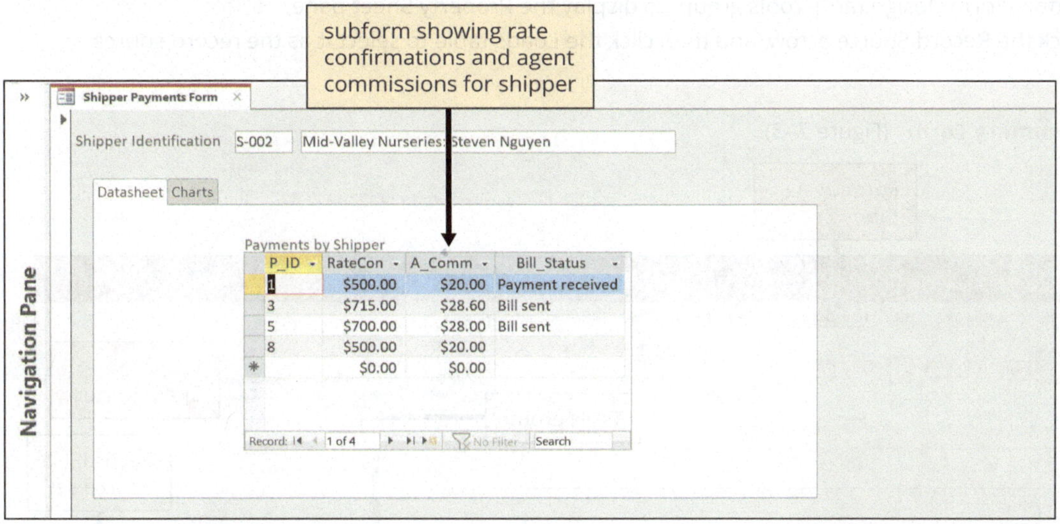

Figure 7–2a Datasheet

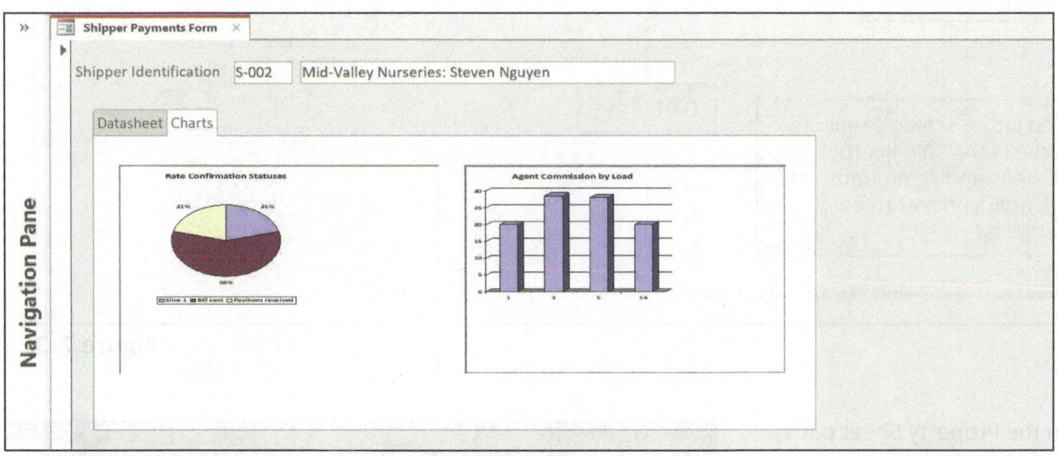

Figure 7–2b Charts

Creating a Form with Combo Boxes and Command Buttons

After planning a form, you might decide that including features such as combo boxes and command buttons will make the form easier to use. You can include such items while modifying the form in Design view.

BTW
Enabling the Content
For each of the databases you use in this module, you will need to enable the content.

To Create a Form in Design View

As you have previously learned, Access provides several ways to create a form, including tools such as the Form Wizard and the Form button. The following steps create a form in Design view. **Why?** Creating a form in Design view gives you the most flexibility in laying out the form. You will be presented with a blank design on which to place objects.

1

- **sam** Start Access. Open the database, SC_AC_07-1.accdb, which is located in the Data Files folder. Save the file to your hard disk, One Drive, or other storage location using the file name, **SC_AC_07_Clearnet**. Enable the content.
- Display the Create tab.
- Click the Form Design button (Create tab | Forms group) to create a new form in Design view.
- Close the Navigation Pane.

2

- Ensure the form selector, the box in the upper-left corner of the form, is selected.
- Click the Property Sheet button (Form Design tab | Tools group) to display the Property Sheet pane.
- With the All tab selected, click the Record Source arrow, and then click the Loads table to select it as the record source.

3

- Save the form as **Loads Summary Form** (Figure 7–3).

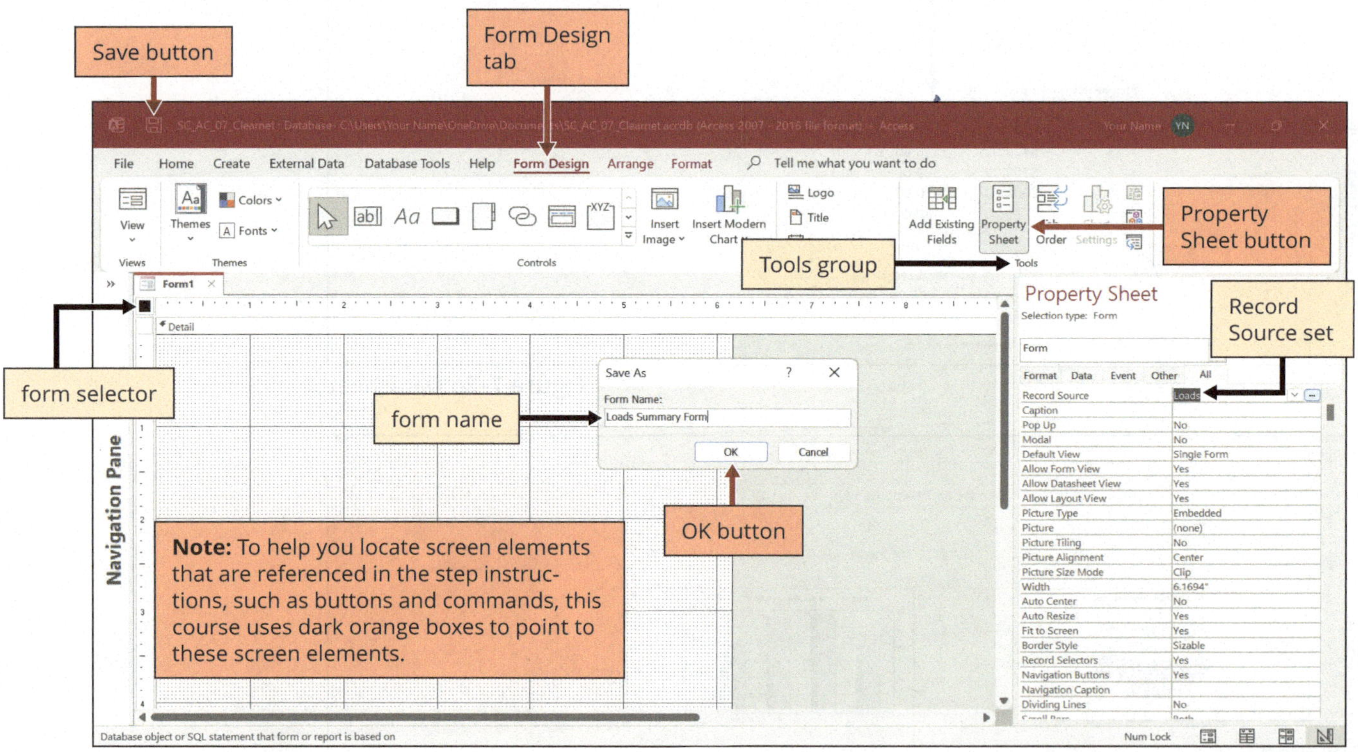

Figure 7–3

4

- Click the Caption property in the Property Sheet pane, and then type **Loads View and Update Form** as the new caption.
- Close the Property Sheet pane.
- Click the 'Add Existing Fields' button (Form Design tab | Tools group) to display the Field List pane (Figure 7–4).

Q&A Why does the name on the tab not change to the new caption, Loads View and Update Form?

The name on the tab will change to the new caption in Form view. In Design view, you still see the name of the form object.

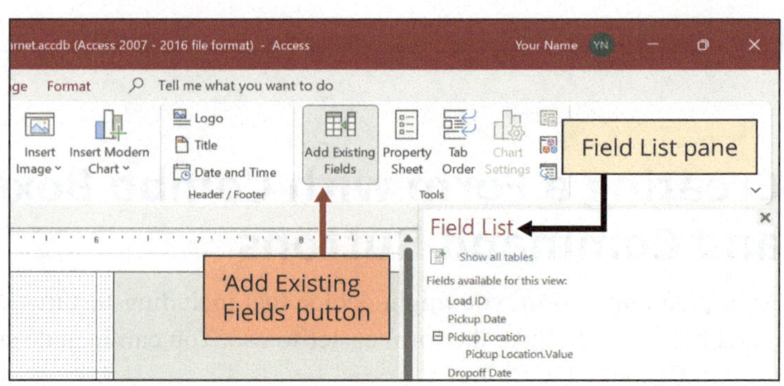

Figure 7–4

To Add Fields to the Form Design

After deciding which fields to add to the Loads View and Update Form, you can place them on the form by dragging the fields from the field list to the desired position. The following steps first display only the fields in the Loads table in the Field List pane, and then place the appropriate fields on the form.

1

- If necessary, click the 'Show only fields in the current record source' link at the top of the Field List pane to change the link to 'Show all tables' so the pane displays only the fields in the Loads table.
- Drag the Load ID field from the Field List pane to the top-left area of the form and adjust the location as necessary to match Figure 7–5.

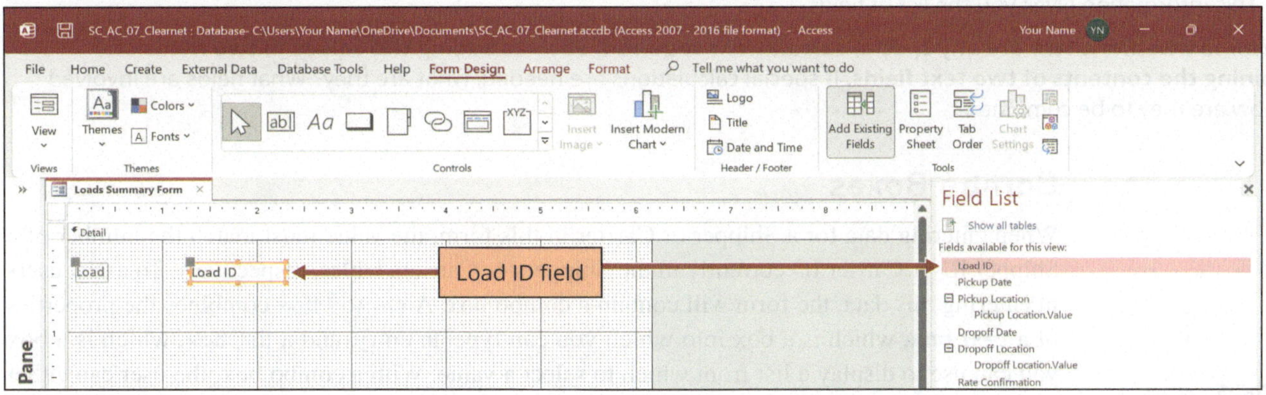

Figure 7–5

2

- Use CTRL to select the Pickup Date, Pickup Location, Dropoff Date, Dropoff Location, Driver Name, Carrier, and Shipper fields in the Field List pane.
- Drag the selected fields to a position below the Load ID field.
- Close the Field List pane, and reposition the fields and their labels to the approximate positions shown in Figure 7–6. If controls for any of the fields are not aligned properly, align them by dragging them to the desired location or by using the alignment buttons on the Arrange tab.

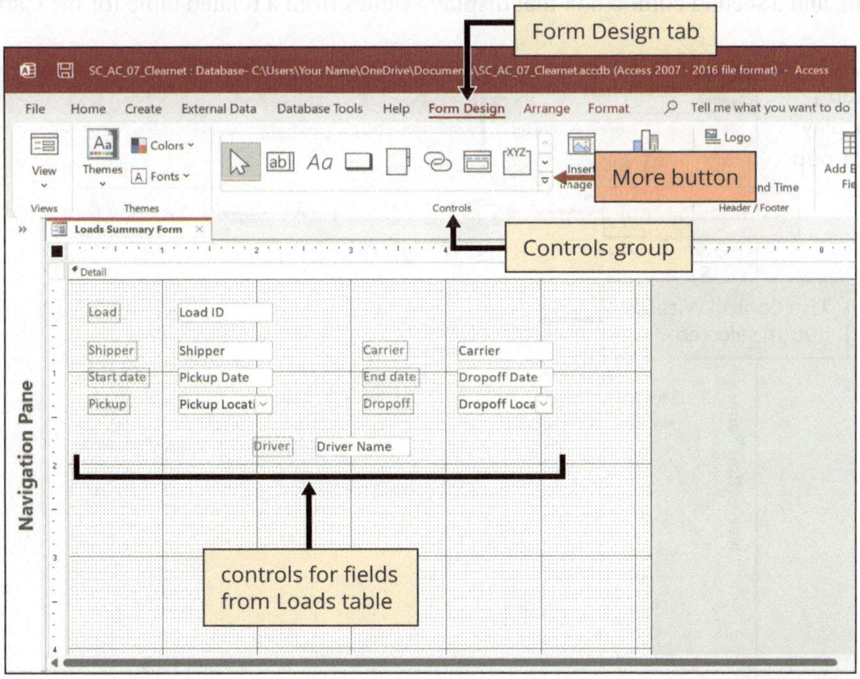

Figure 7–6

BTW

The Ribbon and Screen Resolution

Access may change how the groups and buttons within the groups appear on the ribbon, depending on the computer's screen resolution. Thus, your ribbon might look different from the ones in this course if you are using a screen resolution other than 1920 x 1080.

BTW

Touch Screen Differences

The Office and Windows interfaces may vary if you are using a touch screen. For this reason, you might notice the function or appearance of your touch screen differs slightly from this module's presentation.

Q&A I added a field twice by mistake. Can I delete the control?
Yes, select the control and press DEL.

Consider This

How do you decide on the contents of a form?

To design and create forms, follow these general guidelines:

- **Determine the fields that belong on the form.** If you determine that data should be presented as a form, you then need to determine which tables and fields contain the data for the form.
- **Examine the requirements for the form in general to determine the tables.** Do the requirements only relate to data in a single table, or does the data come from multiple tables? How are the tables related?
- **Examine the specific requirements for the form to determine the fields necessary.** Look for all the data items that are specified for the form. Each item should correspond to a field in a table or be able to be computed from a field in a table. This information gives you the list of fields.
- **Determine whether there are any special calculations required, such as adding the values in two fields or combining the contents of two text fields.** If special calculations are needed, what are they? What fields are involved and how are they to be combined?

Combo Boxes

When entering data for a Shipper or Carrier in this form, the value must match the number of a Shipper ID or Carrier ID currently in the Shippers or Carriers tables, respectively. To assist users in entering this data, the form will contain a combo box. A **combo box** combines the properties of a **text box**, which is a box into which you can type an entry, and a **list box**, which is a box you can use to display a list from which to select a value. With a combo box, the user can either type the data or click the combo box arrow to display a drop-down list of possible values and then select an item from the list.

BTW
Combo Boxes
You also can create combo boxes for reports.

To Add a Combo Box That Selects Values

If you have determined that a combo box displaying values from a related table would be useful on your form, you can add the combo box to a form using the Combo Box tool in the Controls group on the Form Design tab. **Why?** A combo box that allows the user to select a value from a list is a convenient way to enter data. Before adding the combo box, you should make sure the 'Use Control Wizards' button is selected. The following steps place on the form one combo box that displays values from a related table for the Shipper field, and a second combo box that displays values from a related table for the Carrier field.

1

- Click the More button (Form Design tab | Controls group) (see Figure 7–6) to display all the available tools in the Controls group (Figure 7–7).

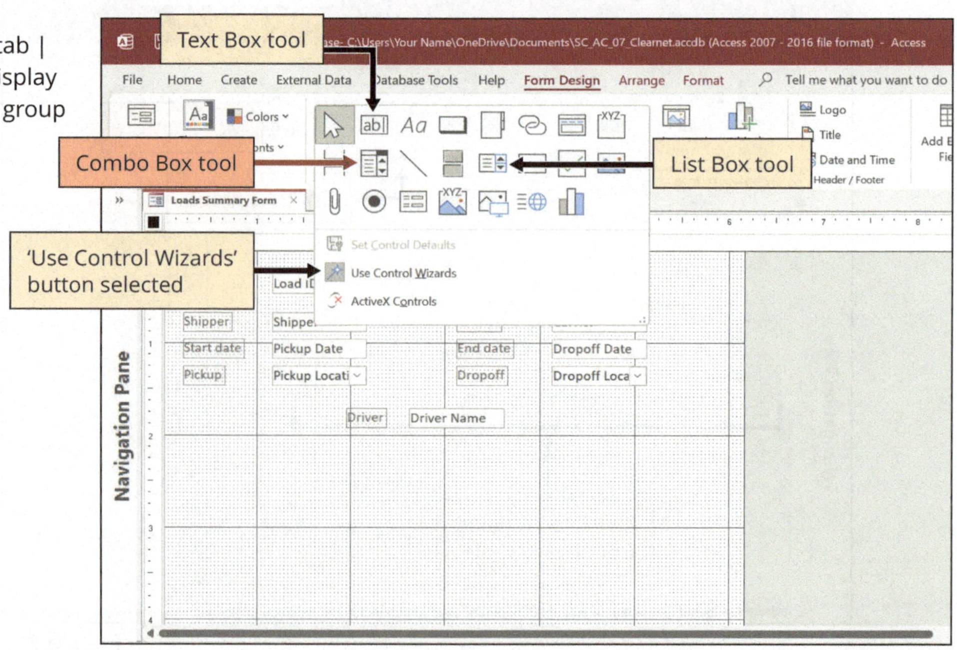

Figure 7–7

2

- With the 'Use Control Wizards' button in the Controls group on the Form Design tab selected, click the Combo Box tool (Form Design tab | Controls group), and then move the pointer, whose shape has changed to a small plus (+) symbol accompanied by a combo box, to the position shown in Figure 7–8.

BTW
Touch and Pointers
Remember that if you are using your finger on a touch screen, you will not see the pointer.

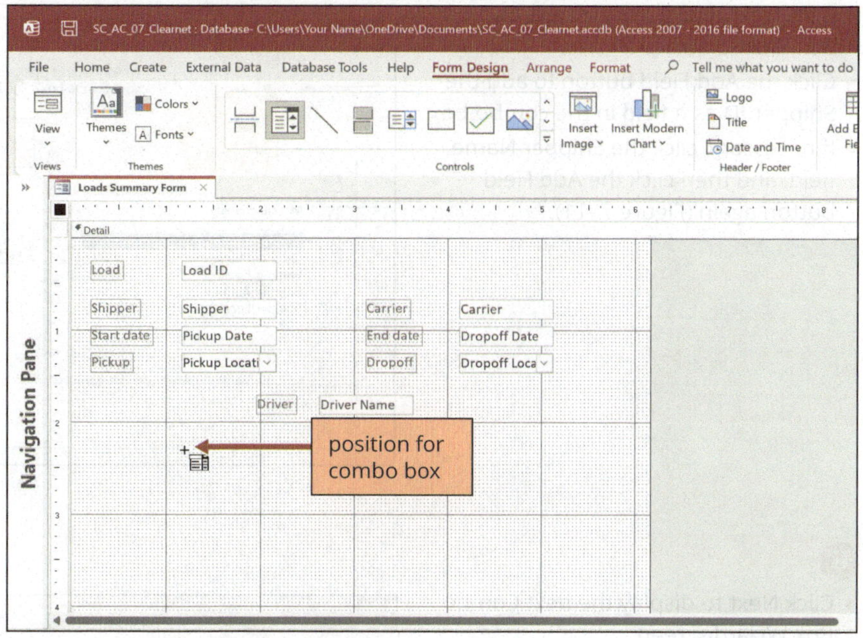

Figure 7–8

3

- Click the position shown in Figure 7–8 to place a combo box and display the Combo Box Wizard dialog box.
- If necessary, in the Combo Box Wizard dialog box, click the 'I want the combo box to get the values from another table or query.' option button (Figure 7–9).

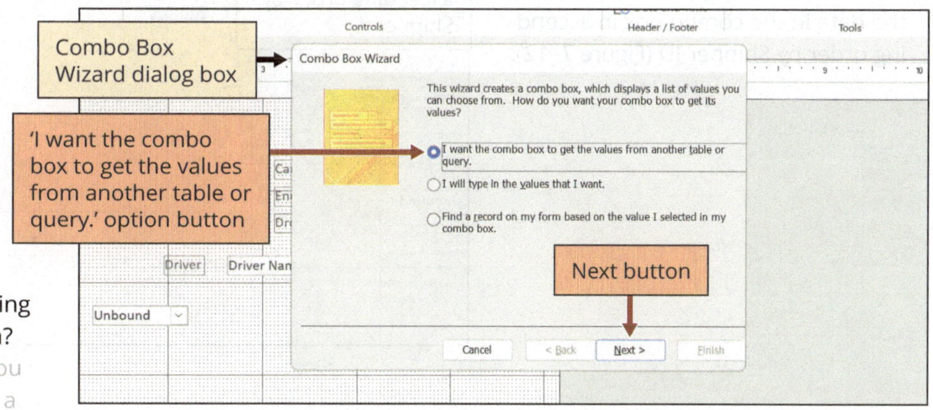

Figure 7–9

Q&A Why did I receive a security warning when I placed a combo box in the form?
Depending on your security settings, you might receive a warning when creating a combo box. Click the Open button to allow the Combo Box Wizard to initiate.

What is the purpose of the other options on the first screen in the Combo Box Wizard dialog box?
Use the second option if you want to type a list from which the user will choose. Use the third option if you want to use the combo box to search for a record. You will use this third option later in this module.

4

- Click Next, and then, with the Tables option button selected in the View area, click Table: Shippers (Figure 7–10) in the list of tables to specify that the combo box values will come from the Shippers table.

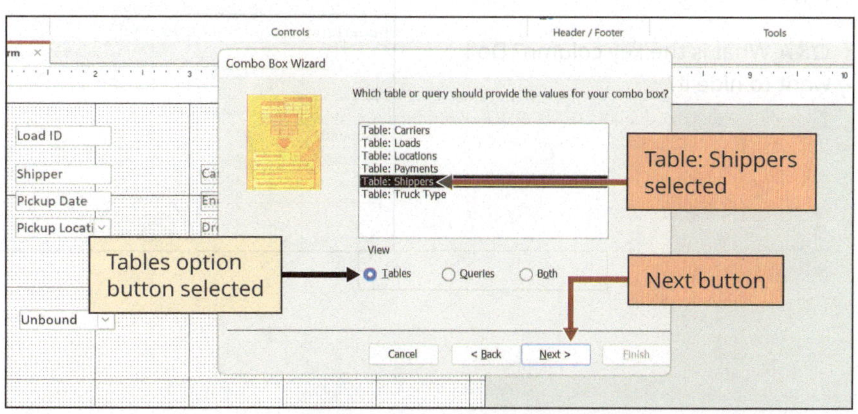

Figure 7–10

5

- Click Next to display the next Combo Box Wizard screen.
- Click the Add Field button to add the Shipper ID as a field in the combo box.
- If necessary, click the Shipper Name field, and then click the Add Field button again (Figure 7–11).

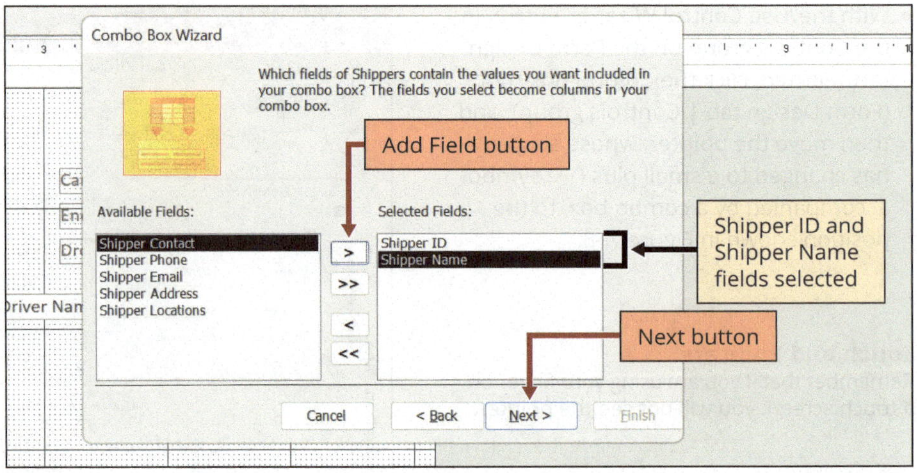

Figure 7–11

6

- Click Next to display the next Combo Box Wizard screen.
- Click the arrow in the first text box, and then select the Shipper ID field to sort the data in the combo box in ascending order by Shipper ID (Figure 7–12).

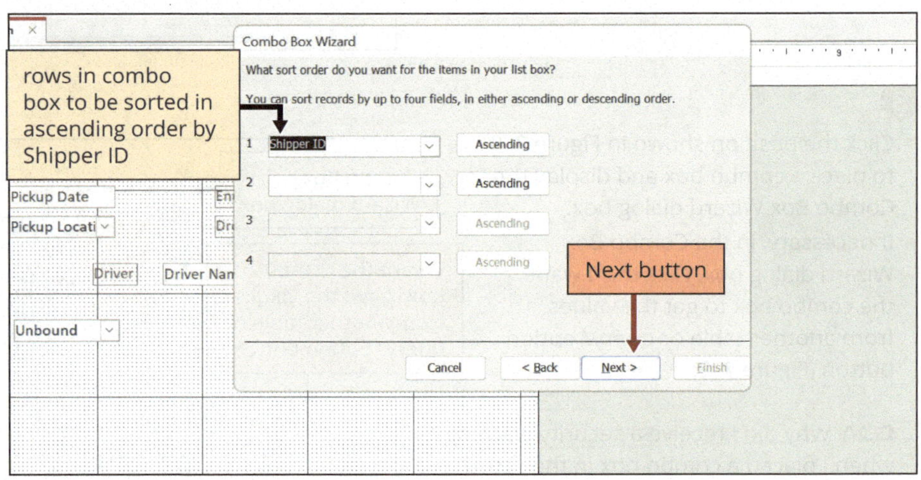

Figure 7–12

7

- Click Next to display the next Combo Box Wizard screen.
- Double-click the right edge of the Shipper Name column to autofit the column so all data is visible (Figure 7–13).

Q&A What is the key column? Do I want to hide it?

The key column would be the Shipper ID, which is the column that identifies a shipper name. Because the purpose of this combo box is to display the shipper's name, you want the Shipper IDs to be hidden.

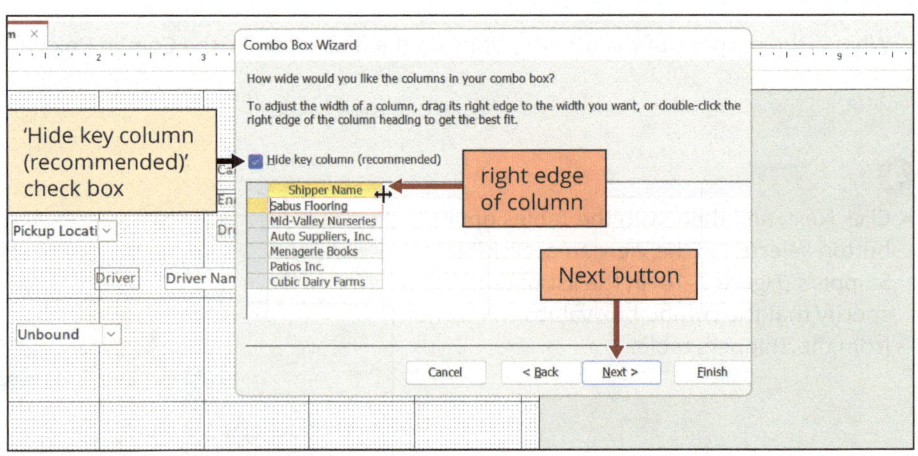

Figure 7–13

8

- Click Next to display the next Combo Box Wizard screen.
- Click the 'Store that value in this field:' option button.
- Because you want the value the user selects to be stored in the Shipper field in the Loads table, click the 'Store that value in this field:' box arrow, and then click Shipper (Figure 7–14).

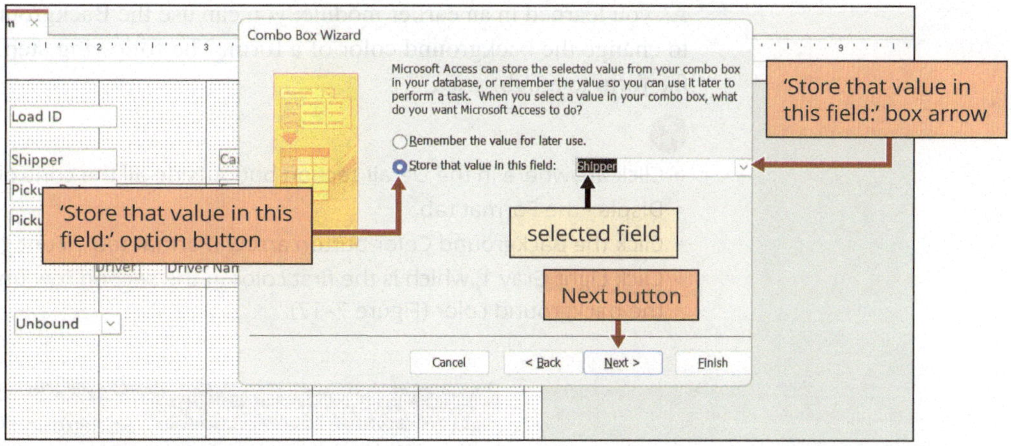

Figure 7–14

9

- Click Next to display the next Combo Box Wizard screen.
- Type **Shipper Name** as the label for the combo box, and then click the Finish button to place the combo box.

Q&A Could I change the label to something else?
Yes. If you prefer a different label, you could change it.

- Reposition and resize the Shipper Name control and label by dragging their move handles to match the sizes and positions shown in Figure 7–15.

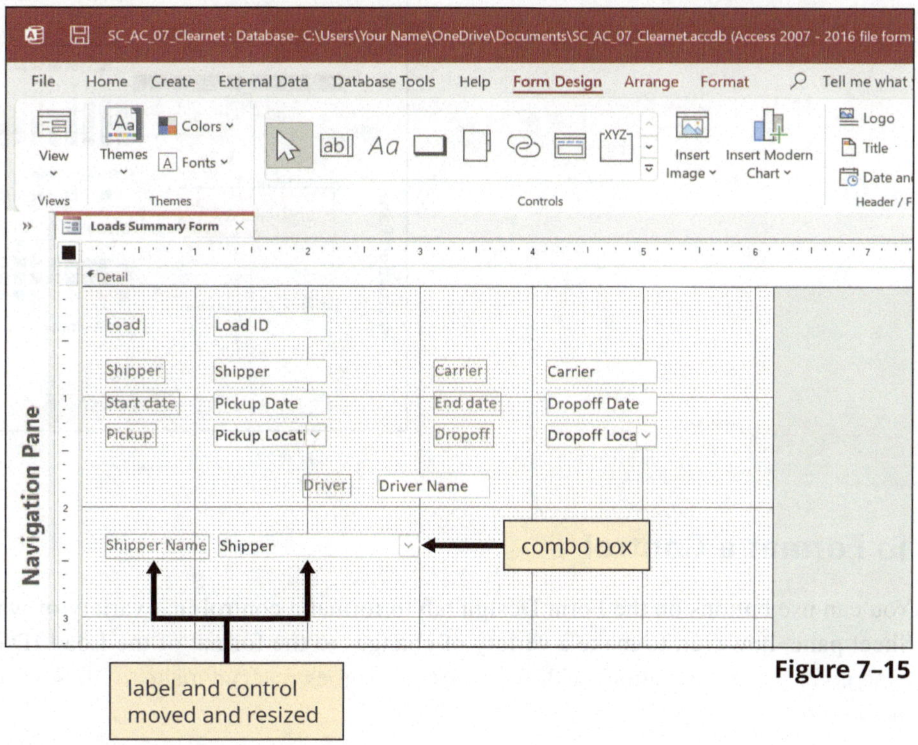

Figure 7–15

10

- Repeat steps 1–9 for the Carrier Name field from the Carriers table, with the following differences: select the Carriers table to provide the data for the combo box, type **Carrier Name** as the label for the Carrier Name combo box, and store the value in the Carrier field of the Loads table.
- Reposition and resize the combo box and label to match Figure 7–16.

11

- Save your changes to the form.

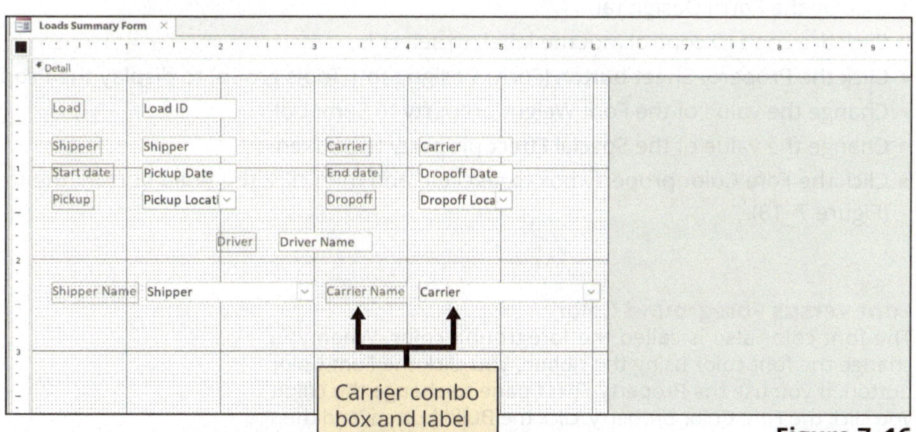

Figure 7–16

To Use the Background Color Button

As you learned in an earlier module, you can use the Background Color button on the Format tab to change the background color of a form. The following step changes the background color of the form to a light gray.

1

- Click anywhere in the Detail section but outside all the controls to select the section.
- Display the Format tab.
- Click the Background Color button arrow (Format tab | Font group) to display a color palette.
- Click Light Gray 1, which is the first color in the second row under Standard Colors, to change the background color (Figure 7–17).

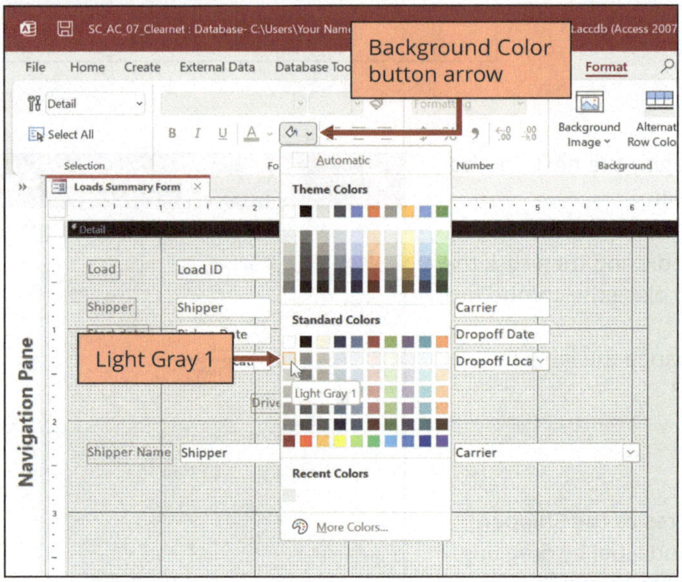

Figure 7–17

To Format a Control

You can use buttons on the Form Design tab to format a control in a variety of ways. The following steps use the Property Sheet pane, however, to make a variety of changes to the format of the Load ID control. **Why?** Using the Property Sheet pane gives you more options with the types of changes you can make to the form controls than you have with simply using the buttons.

1

- Display the Form Design tab.
- Click the Load ID control (not the label) to select it.
- Click the Property Sheet button (Form Design tab | Tools group) to display the Property Sheet pane.
- Change the value of the Font Weight property to Semi-bold.
- Change the value of the Special Effect property to Sunken.
- Click the Fore Color property box to select it, and then click the Build button (the three dots) to display a color palette (Figure 7–18).

BTW

Font versus Foreground Color

The font color also is called the foreground color. When you change the font color using the ribbon, you click the Font Color button. If you use the Property Sheet pane to change the color, you click the Fore Color property, click the Build button, and then click the desired color.

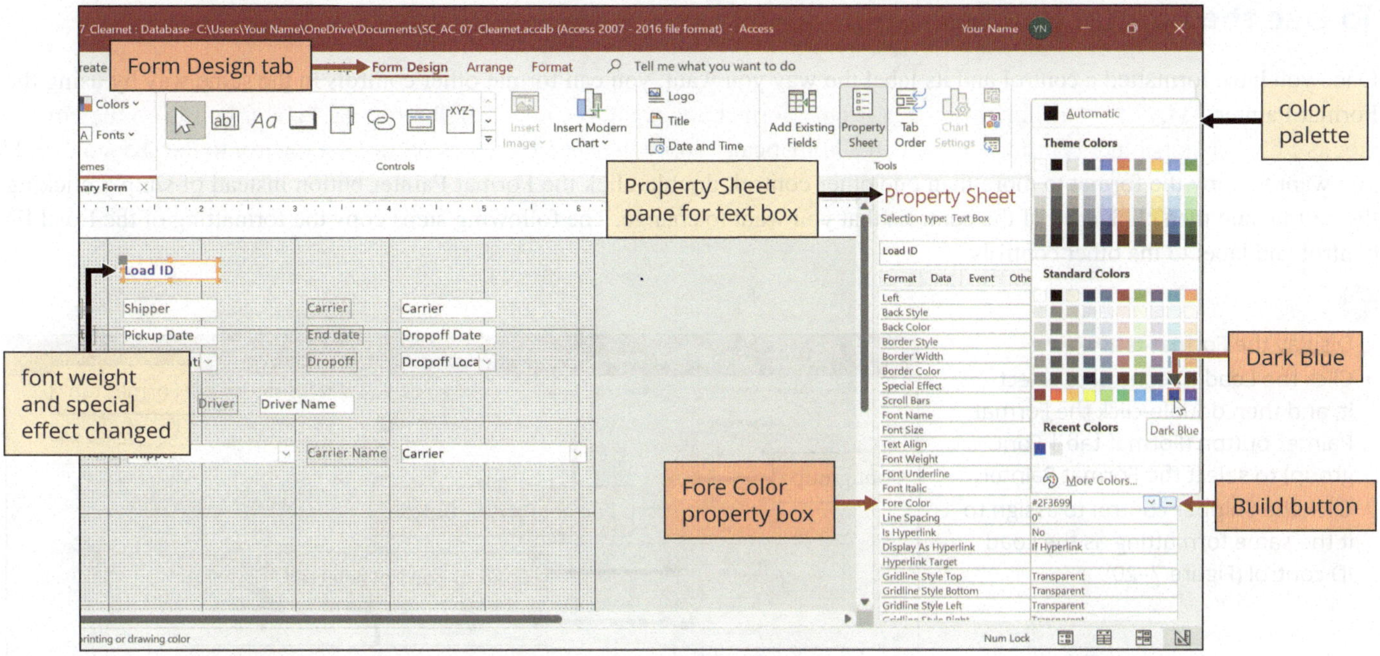

Figure 7–18

2

- Click Dark Blue (the second color from the right in the bottom row under Standard Colors) to select it as the fore color, which is the font color.

3

- Click the label for the Load ID field to select it.
- Change the value of the Font Italic property to Yes.
- Change the value of the Special Effect property to Etched (Figure 7–19).

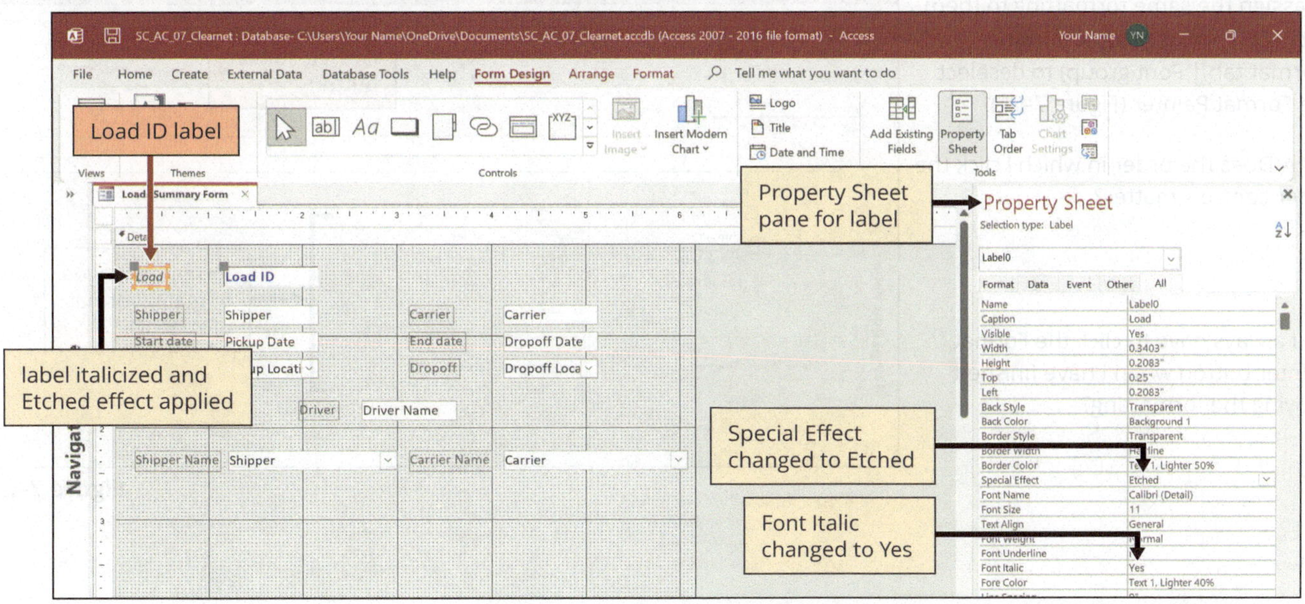

Figure 7–19

4

- Close the Property Sheet pane.

Q&A Should I not have closed the Property Sheet pane before selecting a different control?
You could have, but it is not necessary. The Property Sheet pane displayed on the screen always applies to the currently selected control or group of controls.

To Use the Format Painter

Once you have formatted a control and its label the way you want, you can format other controls in the same way by using the Format Painter. **Why?** If you click the control whose format you want to copy, click the Format Painter button on the Format tab, and then click another control, Access will automatically apply the characteristics of the first control to the second one. If you want to copy the format to more than one other control, double-click the Format Painter button instead of simply clicking the button, and then click each of the controls that you want to change. The following steps copy the formatting of the Load ID control and label to the other controls.

1

- Display the Format tab.
- Click the Load ID control to select it, and then double-click the Format Painter button (Format tab | Font group) to select the Format Painter.
- Click the Shipper control to assign to it the same formatting as the Load ID control (Figure 7–20).

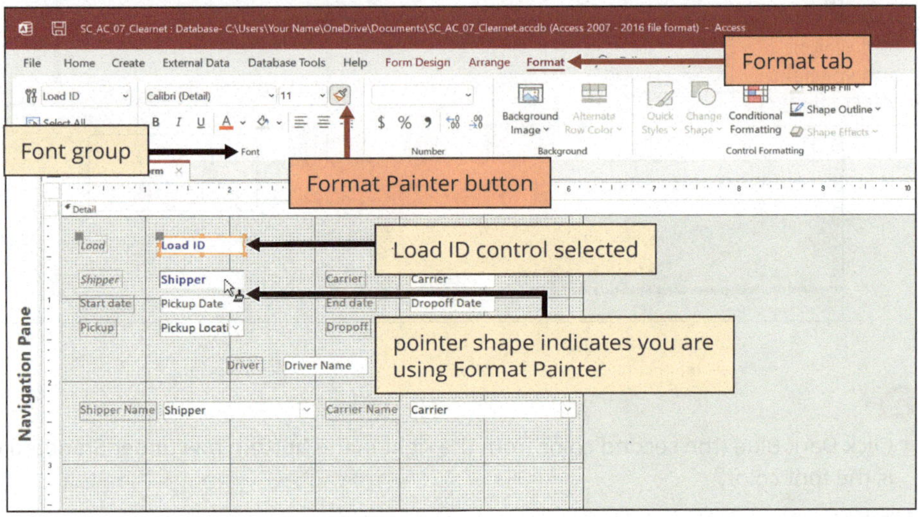

Figure 7–20

2

- Click all the other controls on the form to assign the same formatting to them.
- Click the Format Painter button (Format tab | Font group) to deselect the Format Painter (Figure 7–21).

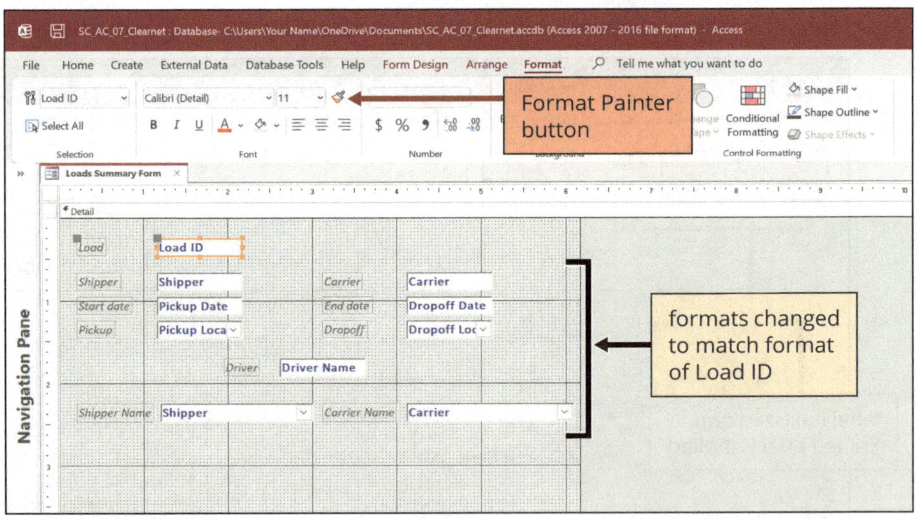

Figure 7–21

Q&A Does the order in which I click the other controls matter?

No. The only thing that is important is to click all the controls whose formatting you want to change.

Do I always have to click the Format Painter button when I have finished copying the formatting?

If you double-clicked the Format Painter button to enable you to copy the formatting to multiple controls, you need to click the Format Painter button again to turn off the copying or press ESC on your keyboard. If you single-clicked the Format Painter button to enable you to copy the formatting to a single control, you do not need to click the button again. As soon as you copy the formatting to a single control, the copying will be turned off.

3

- Save your changes to the form.

To View the Form

The following steps view the form in Form view and then return to Design view. **Why?** As you are working on the design of a form, it is a good idea to periodically view the form in Form view to see the effects of your changes.

1

- Display the Form Design tab.
- Click the View button (Form Design tab | Views group) to view the form in Form view.
- As needed, return to Design view, adjust the controls to display the entire field for each control, and then again check the design in Form view (Figure 7–22).

Q&A Why did I have to change from the Format tab to the Design tab?
The Format tab does not have a View button. Alternatively, you could use the view buttons in the status bar.

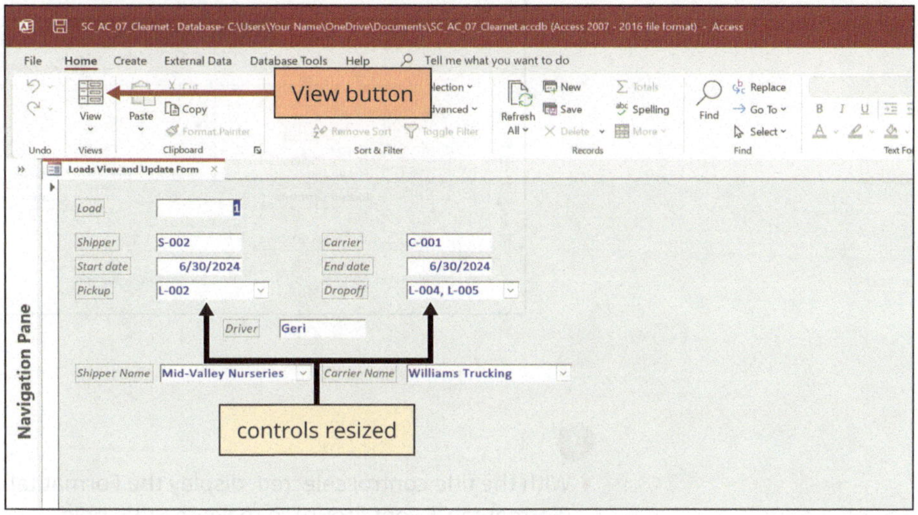

Figure 7–22

2

- Click the View button arrow (Home tab | Views group) to produce the View button menu.
- Click Design View on the View menu to return to Design view.

Q&A Could I simply click the View button to return to Design view?
No. When in Form view, the icon on the View button is the one for Layout view. Clicking the button would show you the form in Layout view, but you are working on the form in Design view.

Other Ways

1. Click Form View button on status bar to change to Form view
2. Click Design View button on status bar to change to Design view

To Add a Title and Expand the Form Header Section

The following steps insert the Form Header and Form Footer sections, and then add a title to the Form Header section. They also expand the Form Header section.

1

- Click the Title button (Form Design tab | Header / Footer group) to add a Form Header section and to add a control for the title to the Form Header section.

2

- Drag the lower boundary of the Form Header section down to the approximate position shown in Figure 7–23.

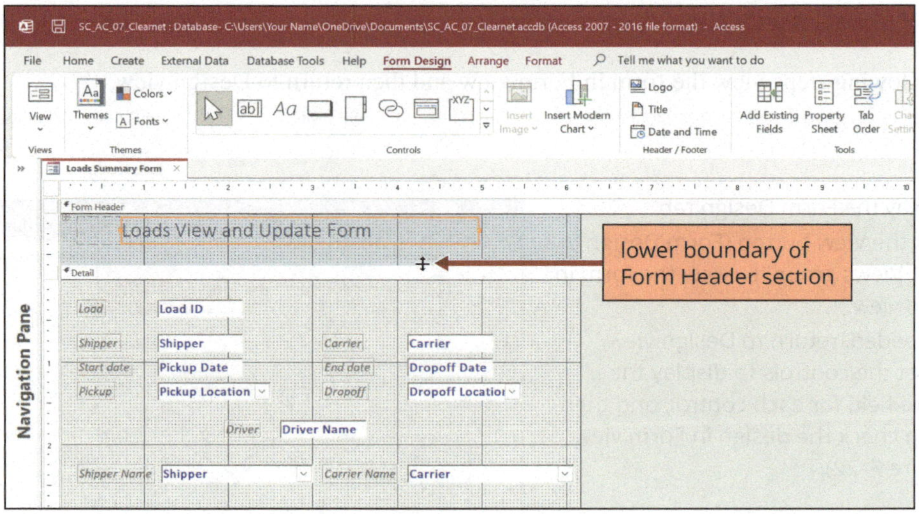

Figure 7–23

3

- With the title control selected, display the Format tab, and then click the Bold button (Format tab | Font group) to make the title bold.

To Change the Background Color of the Form Header

The background color of the form header in the form in Figure 7–1 is the same as the rest of the form. The following steps change the background color of the form header appropriately.

1

- Click anywhere in the Form Header section but outside the control to select the section.

2

- Click the Background Color button arrow (Format tab | Font group) to display a color palette.
- Click Light Gray 1, the first color in the second row under Standard Colors, to change the background color.

3

- Save your changes to the form.

Headers and Footers

Just as with reports, you have control over whether your forms contain a form header and footer. They go together, so if you have a form header, you will also have a form footer. If you do not want the header and footer sections to appear, you can shrink the size so there is no room for any content. You can also remove the sections from your form altogether. If you later decide you want to include them, you can once again add them. You have similar options with page headers and page footers, although typically page headers and page footers are only used with reports. If you had a very long form that spanned several pages on the screen, you might choose to use page headers and footers, but it is not common to do so.

To Remove a Form Header and Footer

To remove a form header and footer, you would use the following steps.

1. With the form open in Design view, right-click any open area of the form to produce a shortcut menu.

2. Click the Form Header/Footer command on the shortcut menu to remove the form header and footer.
3. If the Microsoft Access dialog box appears, asking if it is acceptable to delete any controls in the section, click Yes.

To Remove a Page Header and Footer

To remove a page header and footer, you would use the following steps.

1. With the form open in Design view, right-click any open area of the form to produce a shortcut menu.
2. Click the Page Header/Footer command on the shortcut menu to remove the page header and footer.
3. If the Microsoft Access dialog box appears, asking if it is acceptable to delete any controls in the section, click Yes.

To Insert a Form Header and Footer

To insert a form header and footer, you would use the following steps.

1. With the form open in Design view, right-click any open area of the form to produce a shortcut menu.
2. Click the Form Header/Footer command on the shortcut menu to insert a form header and footer.

To Insert a Page Header and Footer

To insert a page header and footer, you would use the following steps.

1. With the form open in Design view, right-click any open area of the form to produce a shortcut menu.
2. Click the Page Header/Footer command on the shortcut menu to insert a page header and footer.

Images

You can include an image such as a photo in a form. You can also use an image as the background for a form or as a logo.

To Include an Image in a Form

To include an image in a form, you would use the following steps.

1. Open the form in Design view or Layout view.
2. Click the Insert Image button (Form Design tab | Controls group), and then click the Browse command.
3. Select the desired image.
4. Click the desired location to add the image to the form.

To Use an Image as Background for a Form

To include an image as background for a form, you would use the following steps.

1. Open the form in Design view or Layout view.
2. Click anywhere in the form, click the Background Image button (Format tab | Background group), and then click the Browse command.
3. Select the desired image for the background.

To Add a Logo to a Form

To include an image as a logo for a form, you would use the following steps.

1. Open the form in Design view or Layout view.
2. Click anywhere in the form, and then click the Logo button (Form Design tab | Header / Footer group).
3. Select the desired image for the logo.

Break Point: If you wish to take a break, this is a good place to do so. You can quit Access now. To resume at a later time, start Access, open the database called SC_AC_07_Clearnet.accdb, open the Loads Summary Form in Design view, and continue following the steps from this location forward.

BTW
Record Order
When you use the Next Record button to move through the records, recall that the records are in order by Load ID, which is the primary key, and not in alphabetical order.

Command Buttons

Command buttons are buttons placed on a form that users can click to carry out specific actions. To add command buttons, you use the Button tool in the Controls group on the Form Design tab. When using the series of Command Button Wizard dialog boxes, you indicate the action that should be taken when the command button is clicked, for example, go to the next record. Within the Command Button Wizard, Access includes several categories of commonly used actions.

Consider This

When would you include command buttons in your form?

You can make certain actions more convenient for users by including command buttons. Buttons can carry out record navigation actions (for example, go to the next record), record operation actions (for example, add a record), form operation actions (for example, close a form), report operation actions (for example, print a report), application actions (for example, quit application), and some miscellaneous actions (for example, run a macro).

To Add Command Buttons to a Form

You might find that you can improve the functionality of your form by adding command buttons. **Why?** Command buttons enable users to accomplish tasks with a single click. Before adding the buttons, you should make sure the 'Use Control Wizards' button is selected.

In the Record Navigation action category, you will select the Go To Next Record action for one of the command buttons. From the same category, you will select the Go To Previous Record action for another. Other buttons will use the Add New Record and the Delete Record actions from the Record Operations category. The Close Form button will use the Close Form action from the Form Operations category.

The following steps add command buttons to move to the next record, move to the previous record, add a record, delete a record, and close the form.

1

- Scroll down a bit in the Loads Summary Form so you can see more of the space below the last fields in the Detail section.
- If necessary, display the Form Design tab, click the More button in the Controls gallery, and then ensure the 'Use Control Wizards' button is selected.
- Click the Button tool (Form Design tab | Controls group), and then move the pointer to the approximate position shown in Figure 7–24.

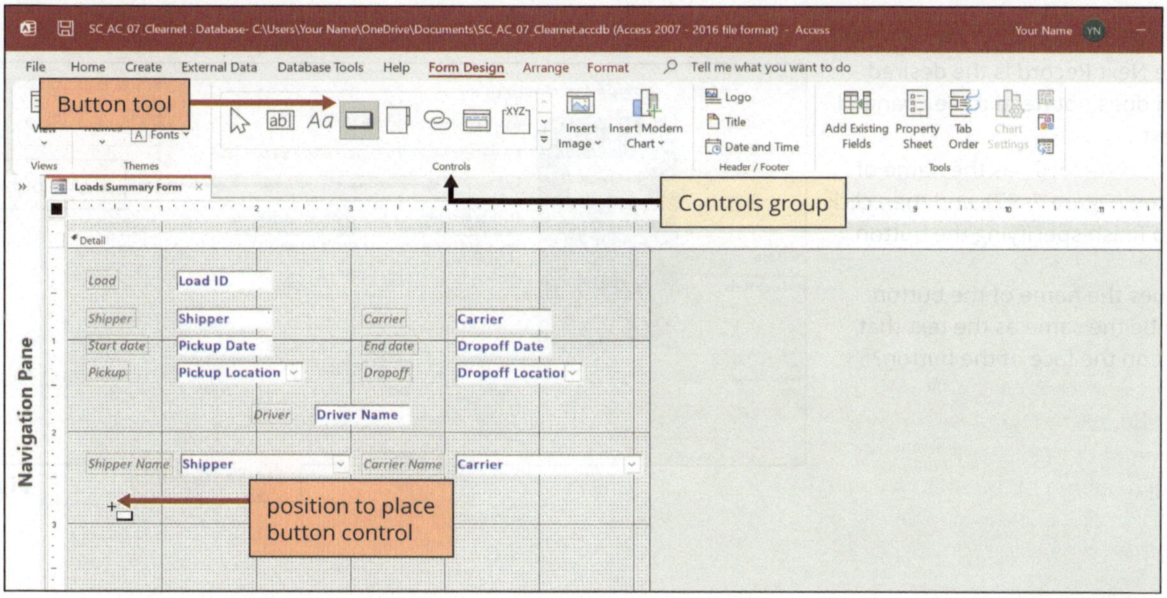

Figure 7–24

2

- Click the position shown in Figure 7–24 to display the Command Button Wizard dialog box.
- With Record Navigation selected in the Categories box, click Go To Next Record in the Actions box (Figure 7–25).

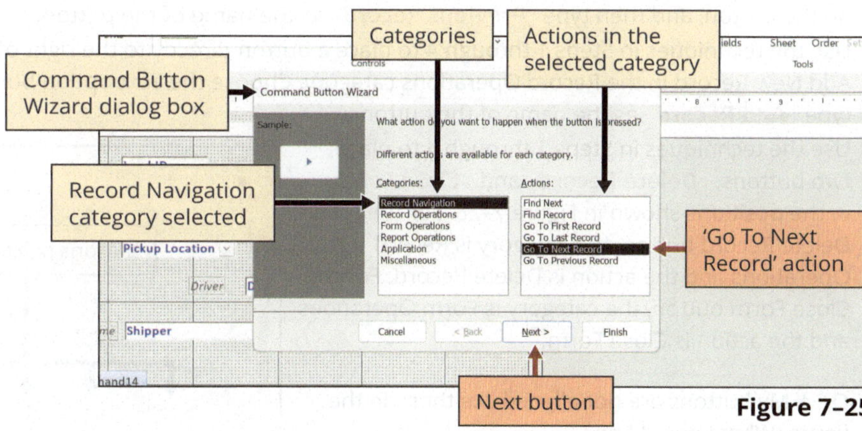

Figure 7–25

3

- Click Next to display the next Command Button Wizard screen.
- Click the Text option button (Figure 7–26).

Q&A What is the purpose of these option buttons?
Choose the first option button to place text on the button. You then can specify the text to be included or accept the default choice. Choose the second option button to place a picture on the button. You can then select a picture.

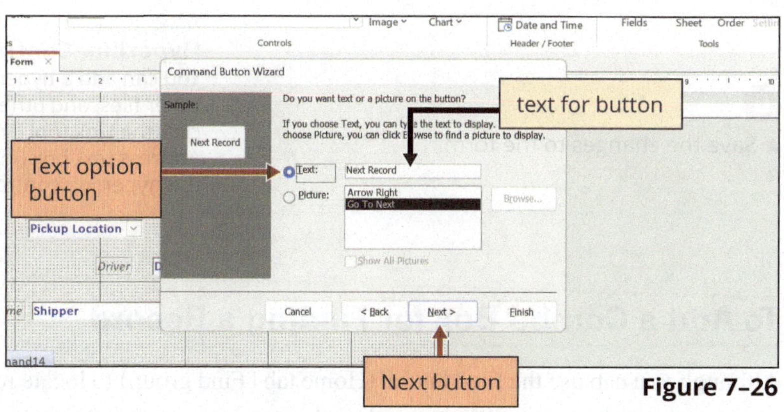

Figure 7–26

4

- Because Next Record is the desired text and does not need to be changed, click Next.
- Type **Next Record** as the name of the button (Figure 7–27), and then click Finish to finish specifying the button.

Q&A Does the name of the button have to be the same as the text that appears on the face of the button?
No. The text is what will appear on the screen. You use the name when you need to refer to the specific button. They can be different, but this can lead to confusion. Thus, many people will typically make them the same.

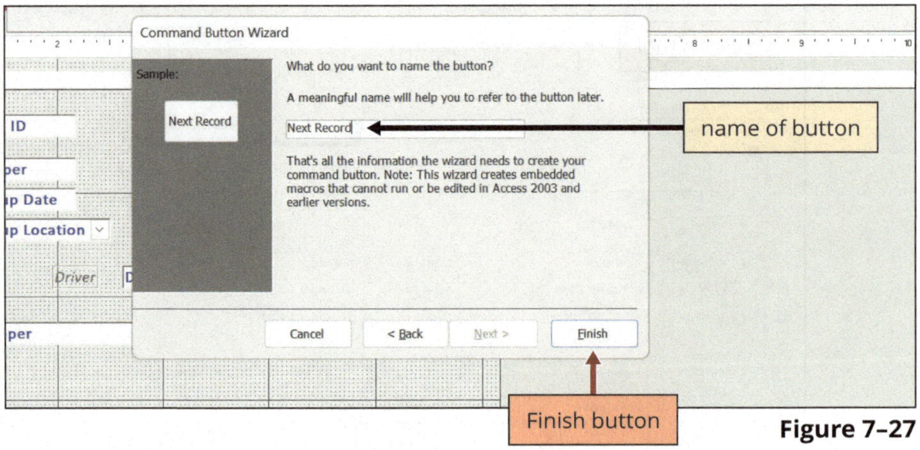

Figure 7–27

5

- Use the techniques in Steps 1 through 4 to place the Previous Record button directly to the right of the Next Record button. The action is Go To Previous Record in the Record Navigation category. Choose the Text option button and Previous Record on the button, and then type **Previous Record** as the name of the button.
- Use the techniques in Steps 1 through 4 to place a button directly to the right of the Previous Record button. The action is Add New Record in the Record Operations category. Choose the Text option button and Add Record on the button, and then type **Add Record** as the name of the button.
- Use the techniques in Steps 1 through 4 to place two buttons, **Delete Record** and **Close Form**, in the positions shown in Figure 7–28. For the Delete Record button, the category is Record Operations and the action is Delete Record. For the Close Form button, the category is Form Operations and the action is Close Form.

Q&A My buttons are not aligned like those in the figure. What should I do?
If your buttons are not aligned properly, you can drag them to the correct positions. You can also use the buttons in the Sizing & Ordering group on the Arrange tab.

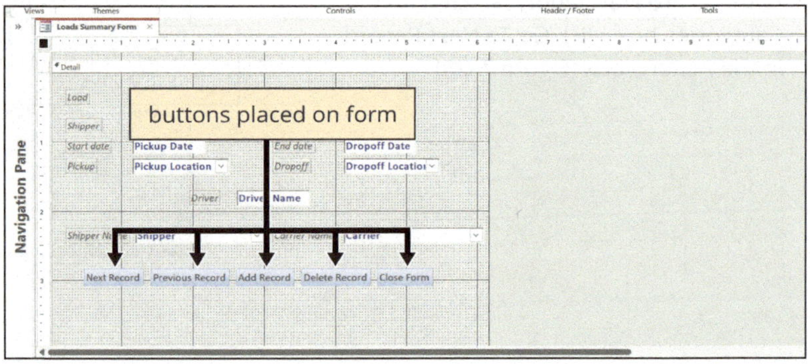

Figure 7–28

6

- Save the changes to the form.

BTW
Hyperlink Controls
You can add a hyperlink to forms, which can be used to navigate to web pages, other files, and other locations within the current database. To add a hyperlink, click the Link tool (Form Design tab | Controls group), enter the hyperlink in the Address text box (Insert Hyperlink dialog box), and click OK. If necessary, move the hyperlink control to the desired location on the form.

To Add a Combo Box for Finding a Record

Although you can use the Find button (Home tab | Find group) to locate records on a form or a report, it is often more convenient to use a combo box. *Why? You can click the combo box arrow to display a list and then select the desired entry from the list.*

To create a combo box, use the Combo Box tool in the Controls group on the Design tab. Before the Combo Box will find records, Microsoft Access requires the form to be bound to an existing table or query. In this case, you will bind the form to a saved query. Once that is accomplished, the Combo Box Wizard will guide you through the steps of adding the combo box. The following steps create the query and then place a combo box for names on the form.

1

- Click the form selector in the upper left corner.
- Open the Property Sheet pane and select the Data tab, and then confirm the selection type is form.
- Click the build button for the Record Source property (Figure 7–29) to create a query based on the Loads table and open the Loads Summary Form: Query Builder tab.

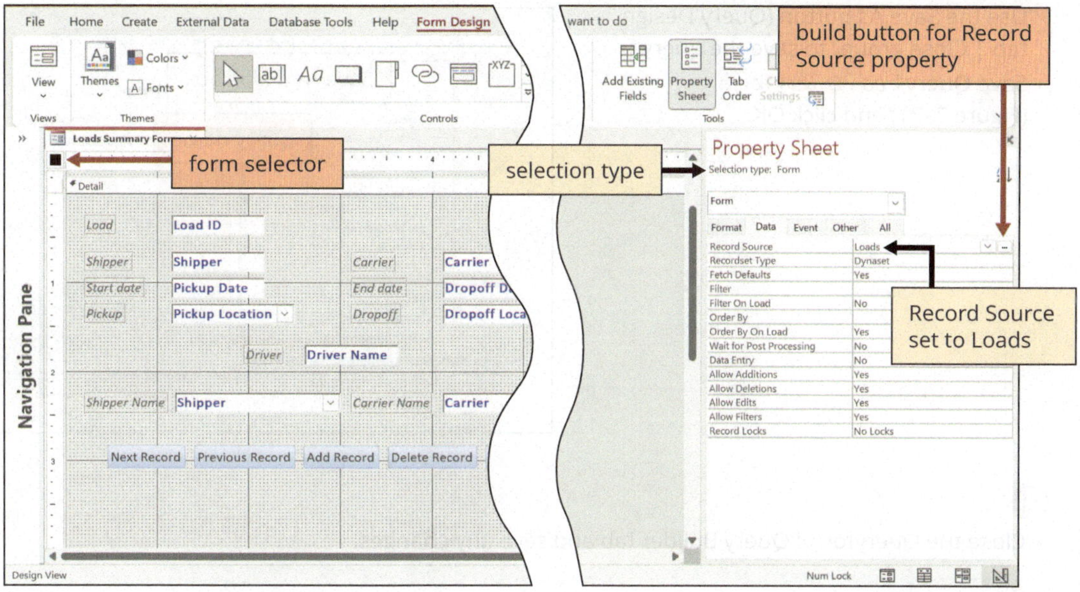

Figure 7–29

Q&A A warning dialog box opened. What should I do?
If you see a warning stating 'You invoked the Query Builder on a table. Do you want to create a query based on the table?' click Yes.

Why click the Data tab in the Property Sheet pane? Why not just use the All tab as we have before?
You can always use the All tab; however, if you know the category that contains the property in which you are interested, you can greatly reduce the number of properties that Access will display by clicking the tab for that category. This gives you fewer properties to search through to find the property you want. Whether you use the All tab or one of the other tabs is strictly a matter of personal preference.

2

- If necessary, close the Property Sheet pane.
- Create the query by adding the fields as shown in Figure 7–30.

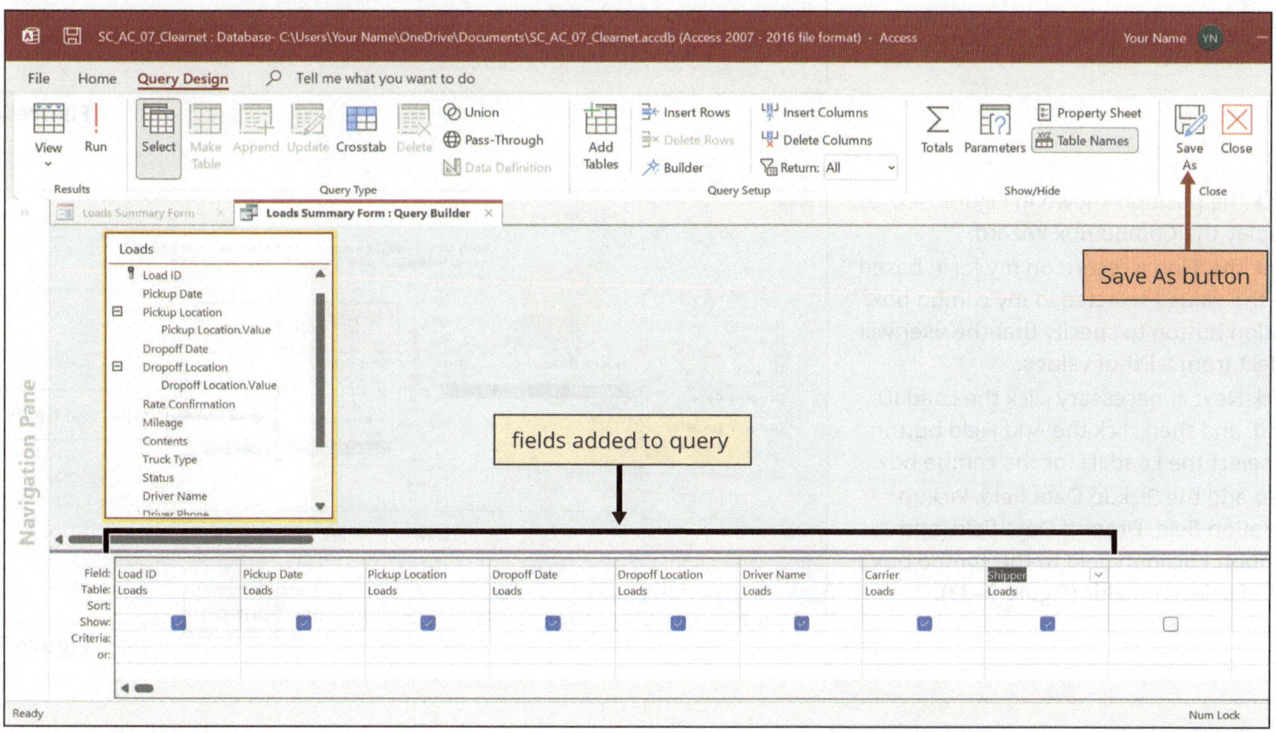

Figure 7–30

3

- Use the Save As button (Query Design tab | Close group) to save the query.
- Save Query1 as **Queryform** (Figure 7–31) and click OK.

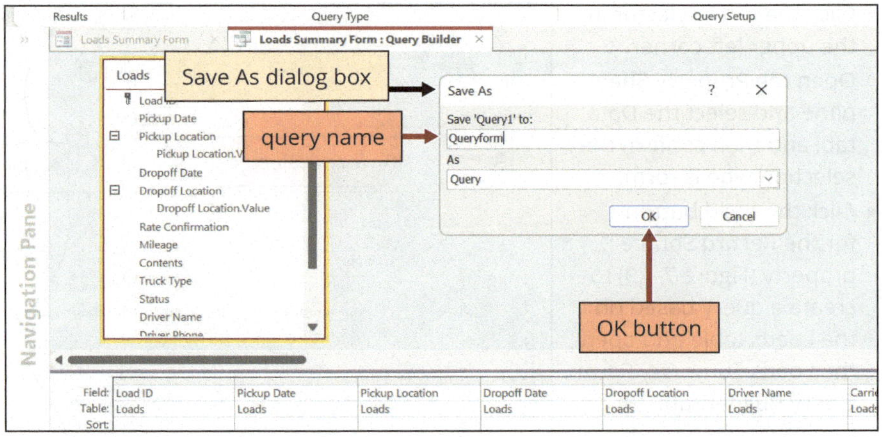

Figure 7–31

4

- Close the Queryform: Query Builder tab and save any changes.

5

- If necessary, display the Form Design tab.
- Click the More button (Form Design tab | Controls group) to display all the controls.
- With the 'Use Control Wizards' button selected, click the Combo Box tool (Form Design tab | Controls group), and then move the pointer, whose shape has changed to a small plus sign with a combo box, to the position shown in Figure 7–32.

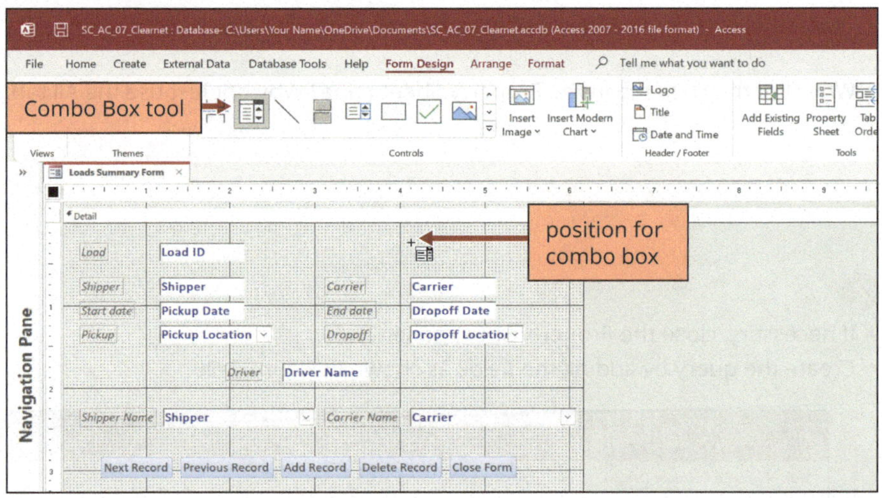

Figure 7–32

6

- Click the position shown in Figure 7–32 to display the Combo Box Wizard.
- Click the 'Find a record on my form based on the value I selected in my combo box.' option button to specify that the user will select from a list of values.
- Click Next, if necessary click the Load ID field, and then click the Add Field button to select the Load ID for the combo box.
- Also add the Pickup Date field, Pickup Location field, Dropoff Date field, and Dropoff Location field to the combo box's list of selected fields (Figure 7–33).

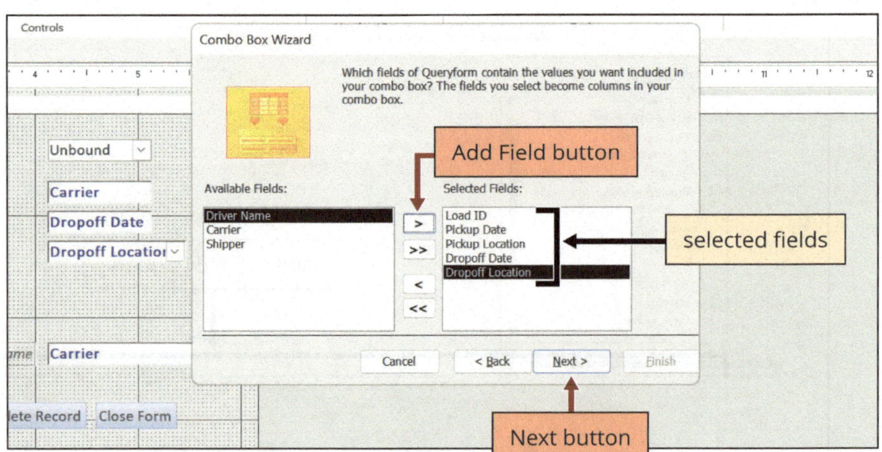

Figure 7–33

7

- Click Next.
- Adjust each column width for best fit (Figure 7–34).

Q&A What options do I have to resize each column to best fit the data?
You could either drag the right edge of each column to a position that allows all text in the column to be visible without using too much space, or you could double-click the right edge of each column so Access will choose the best fit for you.

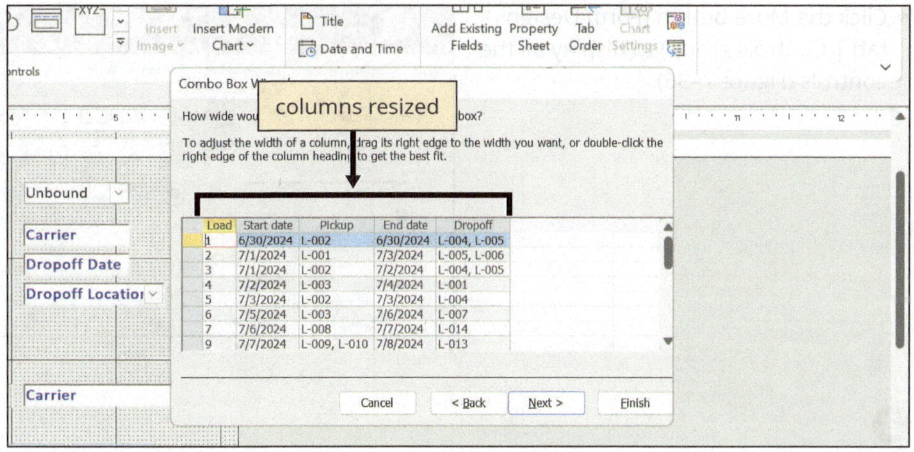

Figure 7–34

8

- Click Next, and then type **&Load to Find** as the label for the combo box.

Q&A What is the purpose of the ampersand in front of the letter, L?
The ampersand (&) in front of the letter, L, indicates that users can select the combo box by pressing ALT+L when using the form.

- Click Finish, and, as necessary, reposition and resize the control and label so your screen resembles Figure 7–35.

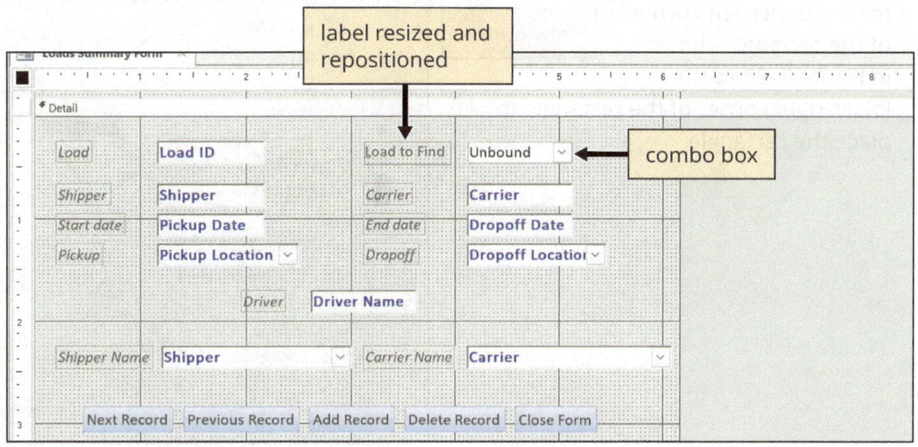

Figure 7–35

Q&A Why is the letter, L, underlined?
The underlined letter, L, in the word, Load, indicates that you can press ALT+L to select the combo box. It is underlined because you preceded the letter, L, with the ampersand.

Consider This

When would you include a combo box in your form?

A combo box is a combination of a text box, where users can type data, and a list box, where users can click an arrow to display a list. Would a combo box improve the functionality of the form? Is there a place where it would be convenient for users to enter data by selecting the data from a list, either a list of predefined items or a list of values from a related table? If users need to search for records, including a combo box can assist in the process.

To Place a Rectangle

The following steps use the Rectangle tool to place a rectangle around the combo box. **Why?** To emphasize an area of a form, you can place a rectangle around it as a visual cue.

1

- Click the More button (Form Design tab | Controls group) to display all the controls (Figure 7–36).

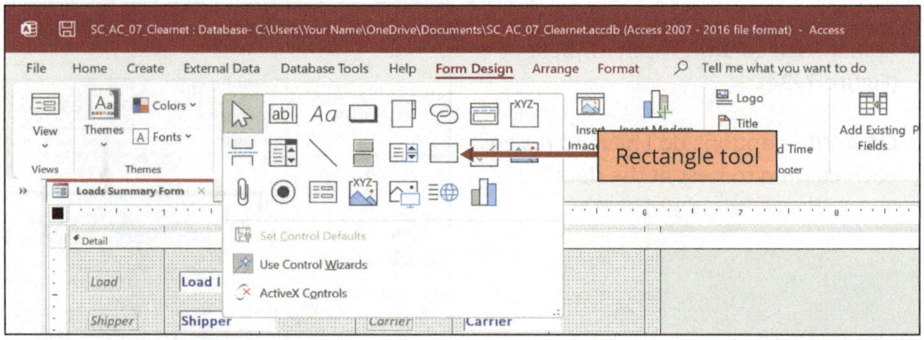

Figure 7–36

2

- Click the Rectangle tool, and then press and drag from the position for the upper-left corner of the rectangle shown in Figure 7–37 to the lower-right corner of the rectangle to place the rectangle.

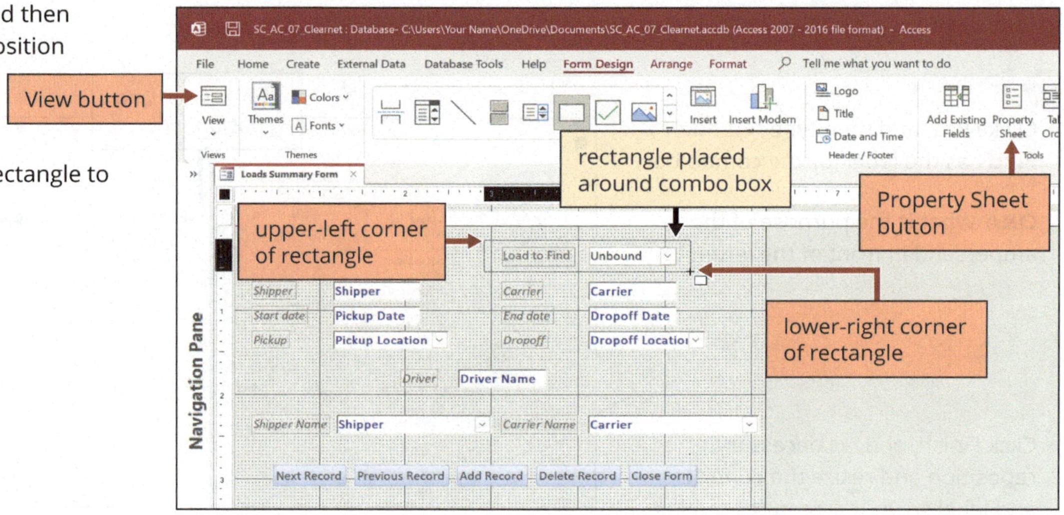

Figure 7–37

3

- Click the Property Sheet button (Form Design tab | Tools group) to display the property sheet for the rectangle, and click the All tab.
- If necessary, change the value of the Special Effect property to Etched.
- If necessary, change the value of the Back Style property to Transparent so the combo box will appear within the rectangle.
- Adjust any control widths to make all labels visible.
- Click the Pickup Date control (not the label) and change the Text Align property to Left (Property Sheet pane).
- Click the Dropoff Date control (not the label) and change the Text Align property to Left (Property Sheet pane).

Q&A What if the Back Style value is not Transparent ?
If the value is not Transparent, the rectangle will cover the combo box completely and the combo box will not be visible.

4

- Close the Property Sheet pane and save the form.
- Click the View button (Form Design tab | Views group) to switch to Form view (Figure 7–38). You will use this view to test the form.

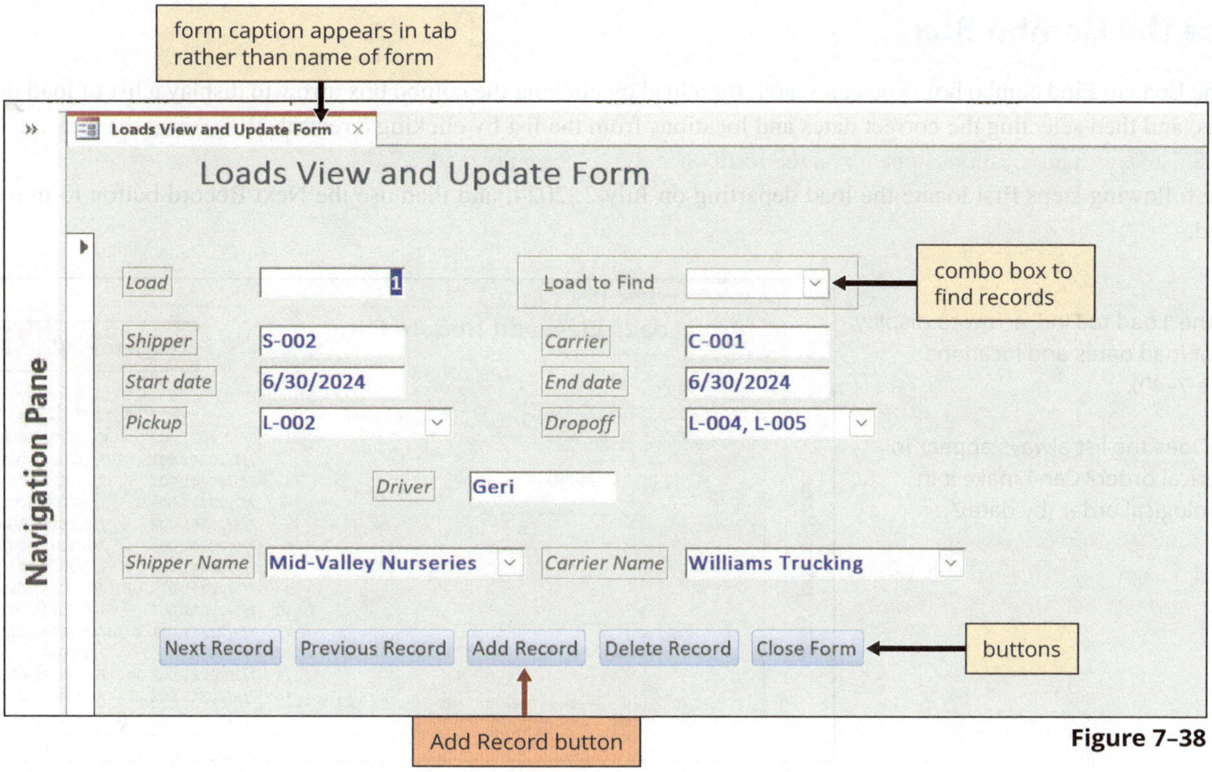

Figure 7–38

Using the Buttons

To move from record to record on the form, you can use the buttons to perform the actions you specify. To move forward to the next record, click the Next Record button. Click the Previous Record button to move back to the previous record. Clicking the Delete Record button would delete the record currently on the screen. Access will display a message requesting that you verify the deletion before the record is actually deleted. Clicking the Close Form button will remove the form from the screen.

To Test the Add Record Button

The following step uses the Add Record button. **Why?** Clicking the Add Record button will clear the contents of the form so you can add a new record.

1

- In Form view, click the Add Record button (Figure 7–39).
- **Experiment:** Try each of the other buttons to see their effects. Do not delete any records. After clicking the Close Form button, open the Navigation Pane if necessary, open the form once again, and then close the Navigation Pane.

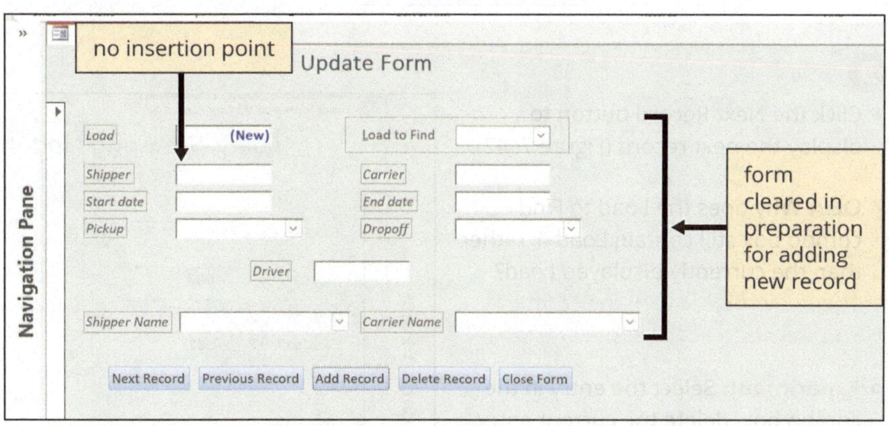

Figure 7–39

Q&A Why does the word, "(New)", appear in the Load field?

The value, (New), refers to the autonumber type field, which will automatically assign a new Load ID as you begin to fill in the form.

There is no insertion point in the Shipper field. How would I begin entering a new record?

To begin entering a record, you would have to click the Shipper field before you can start typing.

To Use the Combo Box

Using the Load to Find combo box, you can search for a load by clicking the combo box arrow to display a list of load dates and locations, and then selecting the correct dates and locations from the list by clicking a record. **Why?** The data for the selected load on those dates and locations appears on the form once the selection is made.

The following steps first locate the load departing on July 2, 2024, and then use the Next Record button to move to the next load.

1

- Click the 'Load to Find' arrow to display a list of load dates and locations (Figure 7–40).

Q&A Does the list always appear in numerical order? Can I make it in chronological order (by date)?

No, not always. You will change the combo box later so the records will always appear in chronological order.

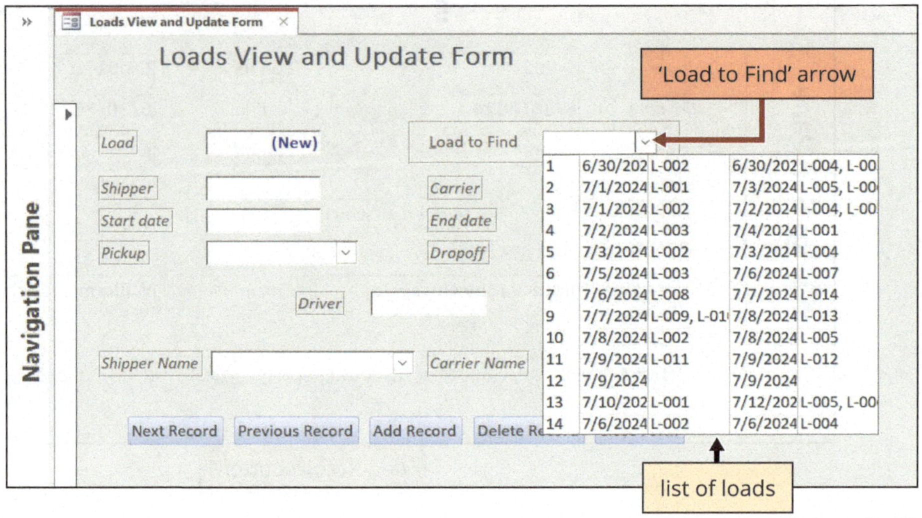

Figure 7–40

2

- Click 4 to display the data in the form for the load being picked up on 7/2/2024 (Figure 7–41).

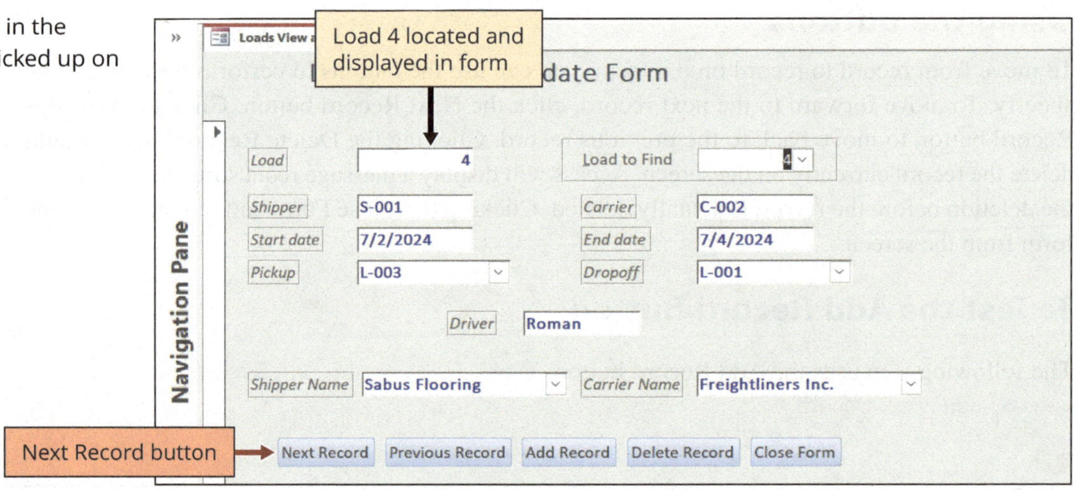

Figure 7–41

3

- Click the Next Record button to display the next record (Figure 7–42).

Q&A Why does the Load to Find combo box still contain Load 4, rather than the currently displayed Load?

This is a problem with the combo box. You will address this issue later.

- **Experiment:** Select the entry in the combo box, delete the current entry, enter the number, 7, and press TAB, to find the load departing on 7/6/2024.

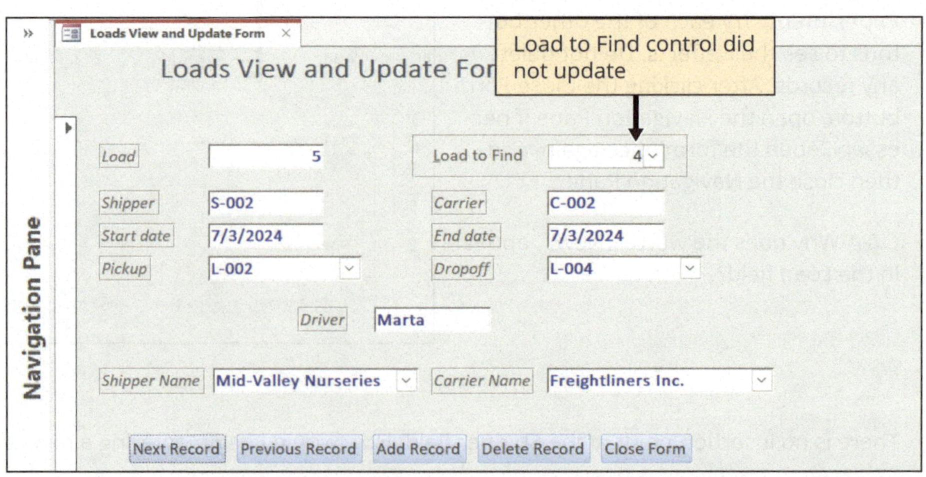

Figure 7–42

Issues with the Add Record Button

Although clicking the Add Record button does erase the contents of the form in preparation for adding a new record, there is a problem with it. After clicking the Add Record button, there should be an insertion point in the control for the first field you need to type into—the Shipper field—but there is not. To display an insertion point automatically when you click the Add Record button, you need to change the focus. A control is said to have the **focus** when it becomes active, that is, when it becomes able to receive user input through mouse, touch, or keyboard actions. At any point in time, only one item on the form has the focus. In addition to adding a new record, clicking the Add Record button needs to update the focus to the Shipper field.

BTW
Focus
Sometimes it is difficult to determine which object on the screen has the focus. If a field has the focus, an insertion point appears in the field. If a button has the focus, a small rectangle appears inside the button.

Macros

To correct the problem with the Add Record button not displaying an insertion point, you will update a **macro**, which is a series of actions that Access performs when a particular event occurs, in this case when the Add Record button is clicked. Access has already created the macro; you just need to add a single action to it.

Specifically, you need to add an action to the macro that will move the focus to the control for the Shipper field. The appropriate action is GoToControl. Like many actions, the GoToControl action requires additional information, called an argument or arguments. The argument for the GoToControl action is the name of the control, in this case, the Shipper control.

To Modify the Macro for the Add Record Button

The following steps modify the macro that is associated with the Add Record button. **Why?** Modifying the macro lets you add an action that changes the focus to the Shipper field. You will then complete an action that changes the focus to the control for the Shipper field.

1

- Click the View button arrow (Home tab | Views group), and then click Design View to return to Design view.

2

- Right-click the Add Record button to display a shortcut menu (Figure 7–43).

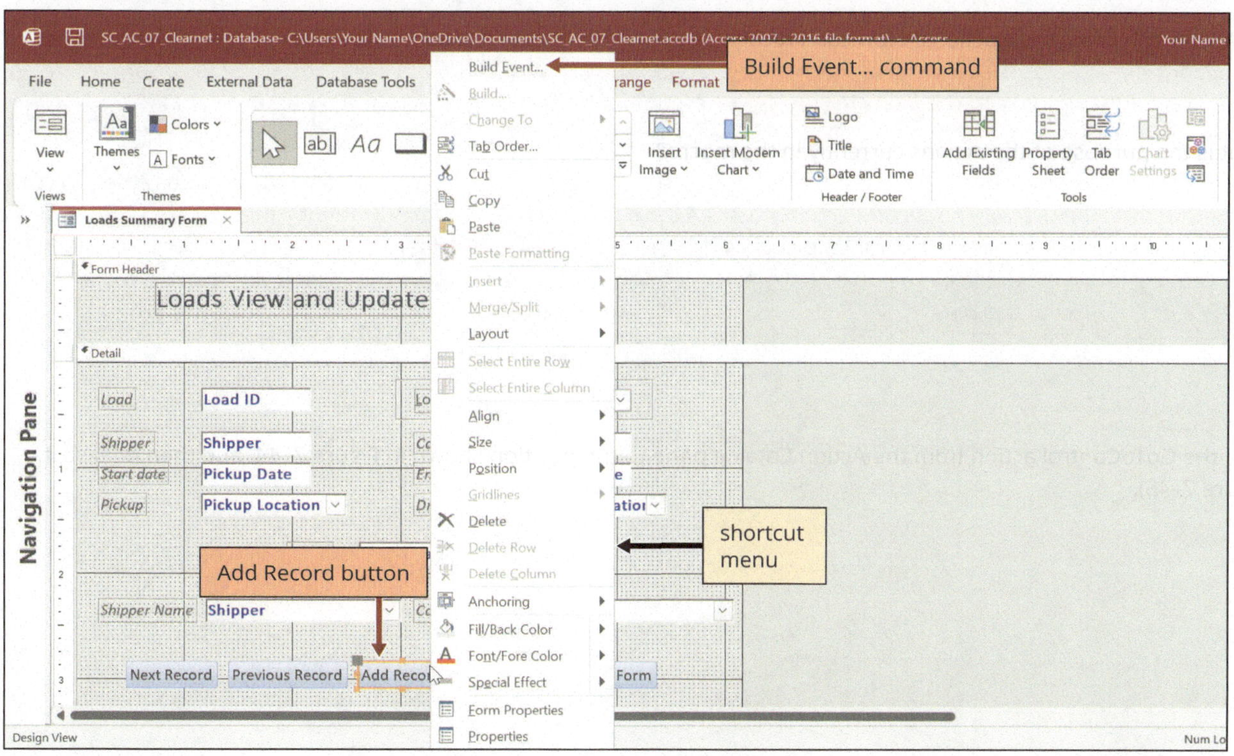

Figure 7–43

- Click Build Event... on the shortcut menu to display the macro associated with the On Click event that Access created automatically.
- If the Action Catalog pane, which lists all the available actions, does not appear, click the Action Catalog button (Macro Design tab | Show/Hide group) to display the Action Catalog pane.
- In the Action Catalog pane, if the expand indicator is an open triangle in front of Actions, click the triangle to display all actions.
- If the Database Objects expand indicator is an open triangle, click the expand indicator to display all actions associated with Database Objects (Figure 7–44).

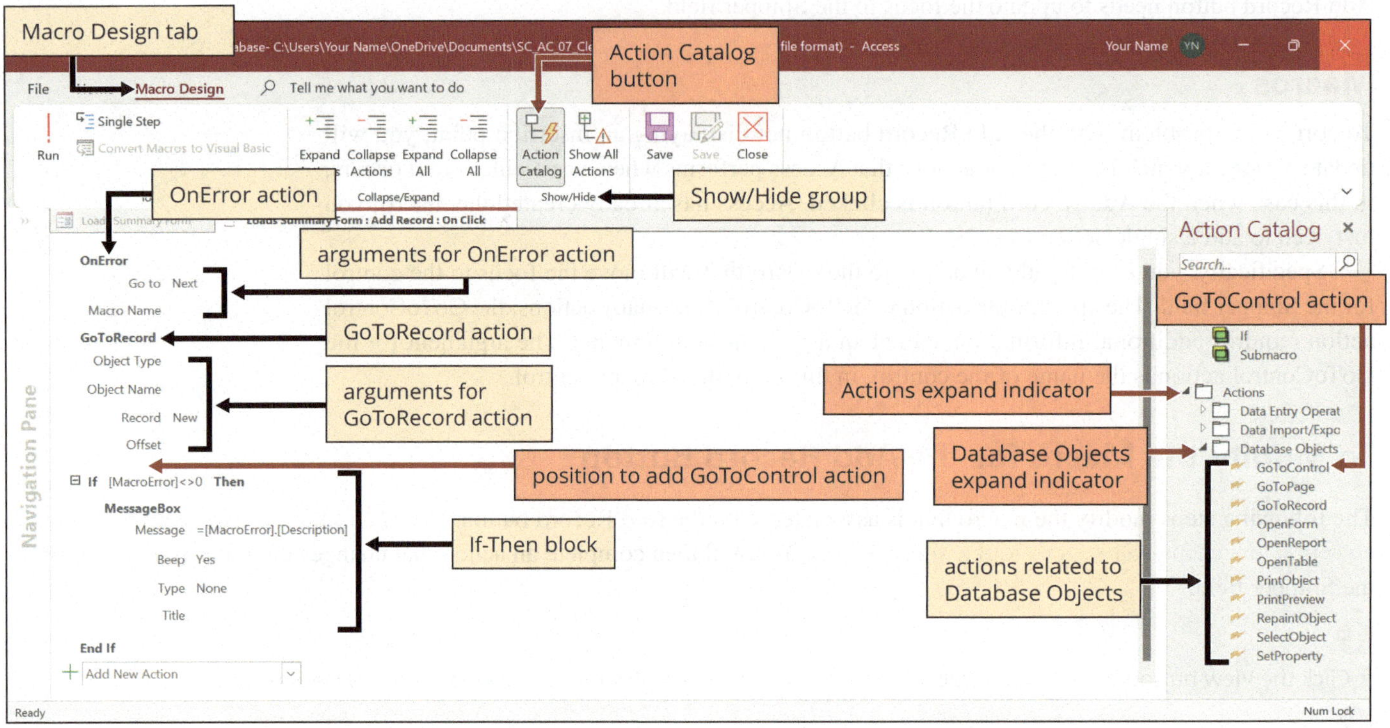

Figure 7–44

Q&A How can I recognize actions? How can I recognize the arguments of the actions?

The actions are in bold. The arguments for the action follow the action and are not bold. The value for an argument appears to the right of the argument. The value for the 'Go to' argument of the OnError action is Next, for example.

What is the purpose of the actions currently in the macro?

The first action indicates that, if there is an error, Access should proceed to the next action in the macro rather than immediately stopping the macro. The second action causes Access to go to the record indicated by the values in the arguments. The value, New, indicates that Access should go to a new record. Because the final action has a condition, the action will be executed only if the condition is true, that is, the error code contains a value other than 0. In that case, the MsgBox action will display a description of the error.

3

- Drag the GoToControl action from the Action Catalog pane to the position shown in Figure 7–44, and then release it (Figure 7–45).

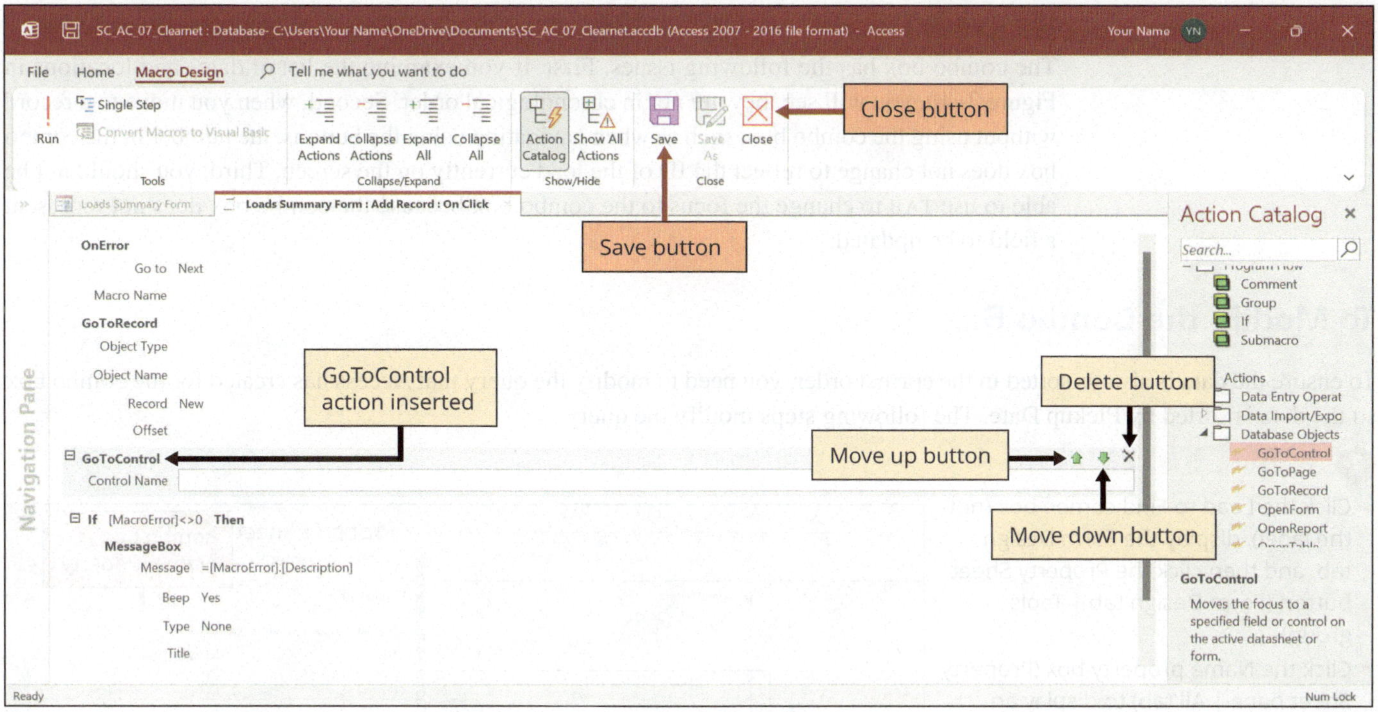

Figure 7–45

4

- Type **Shipper** as the Control Name argument (Figure 7–46).

Q&A What is the effect of the GoToControl action?

When Access executes this action, the focus will move to the control indicated in the Control Name argument, in this case, the Shipper control.

I added the GoToControl action to the wrong place in the macro. How do I move it?

To move it up in the list, click the Move up button. To move it down, click the Move down button.

I added the wrong action. What should I do?

Click the Delete button to delete the action you added, and then add the GoToControl action. If you decide you would rather start over instead, click Close (Macro Design tab | Close group) and then click the No button when asked if you want to save your changes. You can then begin again from Step 2.

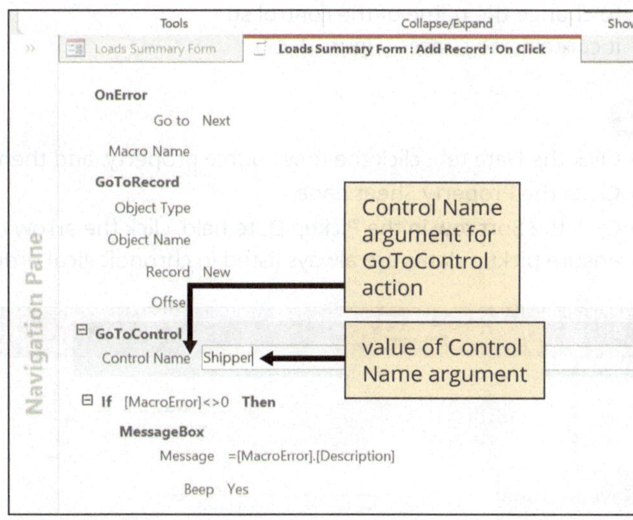

Figure 7–46

5

- Click the Save button (Macro Design tab | Close group) to save your changes.
- Click the Close button (Macro Design tab | Close group) to close the macro and return to the form design.

BTW
Events

Events are actions that have happened or are happening at the present time. An event can result from a user action. For example, one of the events associated with a button on a form is clicking the button. The corresponding event property is On Click. If you associate a macro with the On Click event property, the macro will execute any time you click the button. Using properties associated with events, you can instruct Access to run a macro, call a Visual Basic function, or run an event procedure in response to an event. You will learn more about Visual Basic later.

Issues with the Combo Box

The combo box has the following issues. First, if you examine the list of dates and locations in Figure 7–40, you will see they are not in chronological order. Second, when you move to a record without using the combo box, such as when navigating using the buttons, the number in the combo box does not change to reflect the ID of the load currently on the screen. Third, you should not be able to use TAB to change the focus to the combo box because the combo box does not represent a field to be updated.

To Modify the Combo Box

To ensure the data is always sorted in the correct order, you need to modify the query that Access has created for the combo box so the data is sorted by Pickup Date. The following steps modify the query.

1

- Click the Load to Find combo box (not the label), display the Form Design tab, and then click the Property Sheet button (Form Design tab | Tools group).
- Click the Name property box (Property Sheet pane | All tab) to display an insertion point, use DEL or BACKSPACE to remove the existing name, and then enter the new value, **Load_to_Find**, to change the name of the control so it contains no spaces (Figure 7–47).

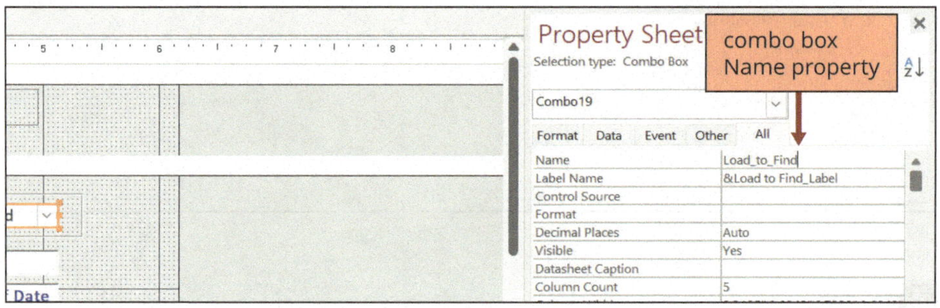

Figure 7–47

2

- Click the Data tab, click the Row Source property, and then click the Build button (the three dots) to display the Query Builder.
- Close the Property Sheet pane.
- Click the Sort row in the Pickup Date field, click the arrow that appears, and then click Ascending to change the order to ensure pickup dates are always listed in chronological order in the combo box (Figure 7–48).

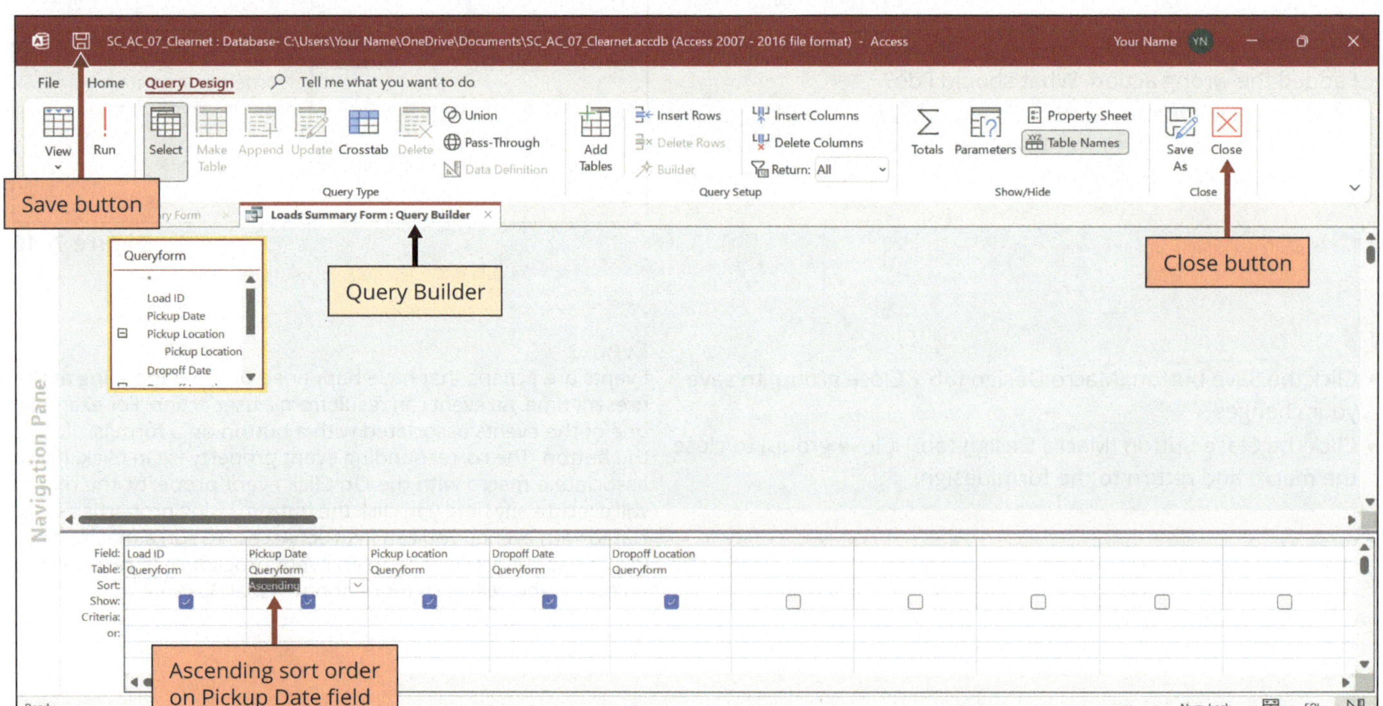

Figure 7–48

3

- Click Save on the Quick Access Toolbar to save your changes.
- Click the Close button (Query Design tab | Close group) to close the Query Builder tab.

To Correct Issues with the Combo Box

The form does not update the Load ID in the combo box to reflect the load currently on the screen unless the Load to Find box is used to find the load. The following steps first change the name of the Load ID control to remove the space, a requirement in VBA (Visual Basic for Applications), and then modify the query and the code associated with the On Current event property appropriately. **Why?** Modifying the VBA code lets you update the form actions appropriately. You can use different methods of changing control names so they do not contain spaces. One approach is to simply remove the space. This approach would change Load ID to LoadID, for example. The approach you will use is to insert an underscore (_) in place of the space. For example, you will change Load ID to Load_ID.

After changing the name of the Load ID control, the final step changes the Tab Stop property for the combo box from Yes to No.

BTW

VBA (Visual Basic for Applications)

Visual Basic for Applications (VBA) is a programming language that can be used with Access. As with other programming languages, programs in VBA consist of code, that is, a collection of statements, also called commands, which are instructions that will cause actions to take place when the program executes. VBA is included with all Microsoft Office apps.

1

- Click the control for the Load ID field (not the label).
- Open the Property Sheet pane.
- Click the All tab in the Property Sheet pane.
- In the Name property box, click the space immediately following the word, Load, press DEL to delete the space, and then type an underscore (_) to change the name to Load_ID (Figure 7–49).

Q&A Could I just erase the old name and type Load_ID?

Yes. Use whichever method you find most convenient.

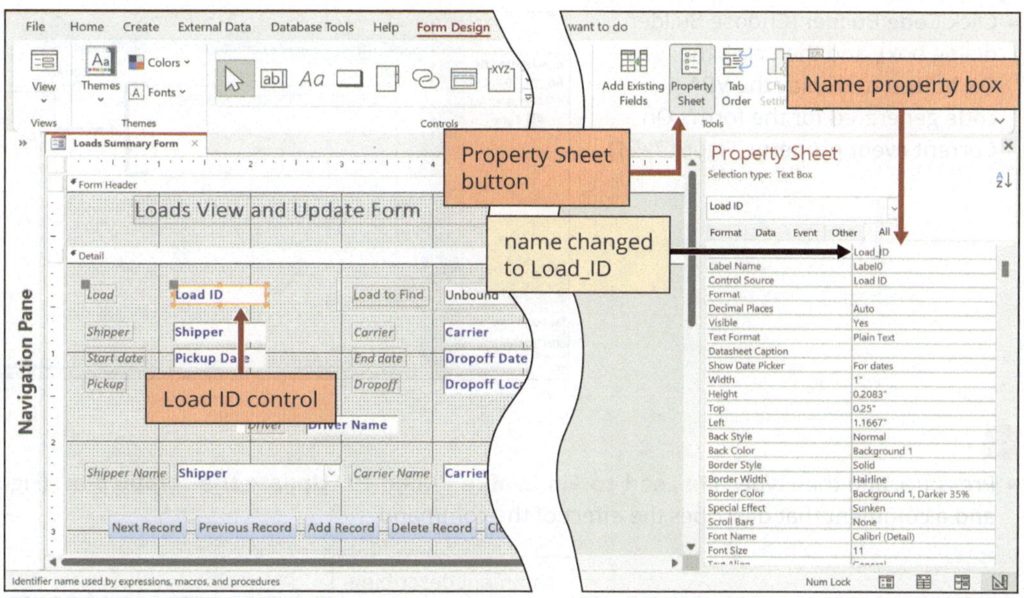

Figure 7–49

2

- Click the form selector (the box in the upper-left corner of the form) to select the form.
- In the Property Sheet pane, click the Event tab, and then click the On Current property box.
- Click the Build button (the three dots) to display the Choose Builder dialog box (Figure 7–50).

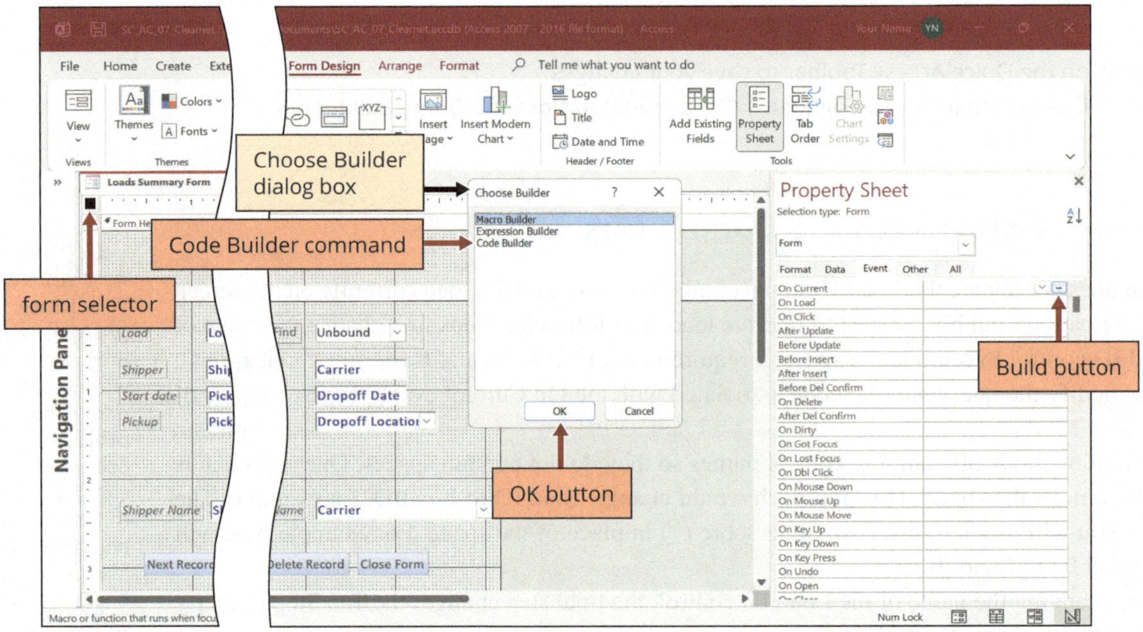

Figure 7–50

3

- Click Code Builder (Choose Builder dialog box), and then click the OK button to display the VBA code generated for the form's On Current event property (Figure 7–51).

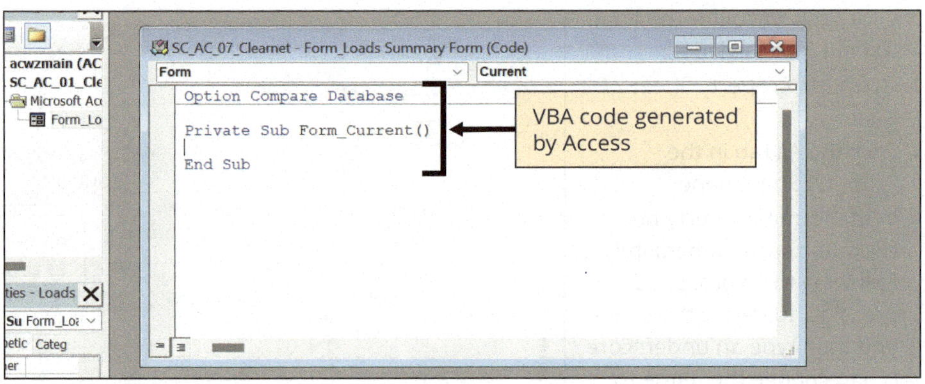

Figure 7–51

4

- Press TAB, and then type **Me.Load_to_Find.Value = Load_ID ' Update the combo box** (Figure 7–52) to create the command and a comment that describes the effect of the command.

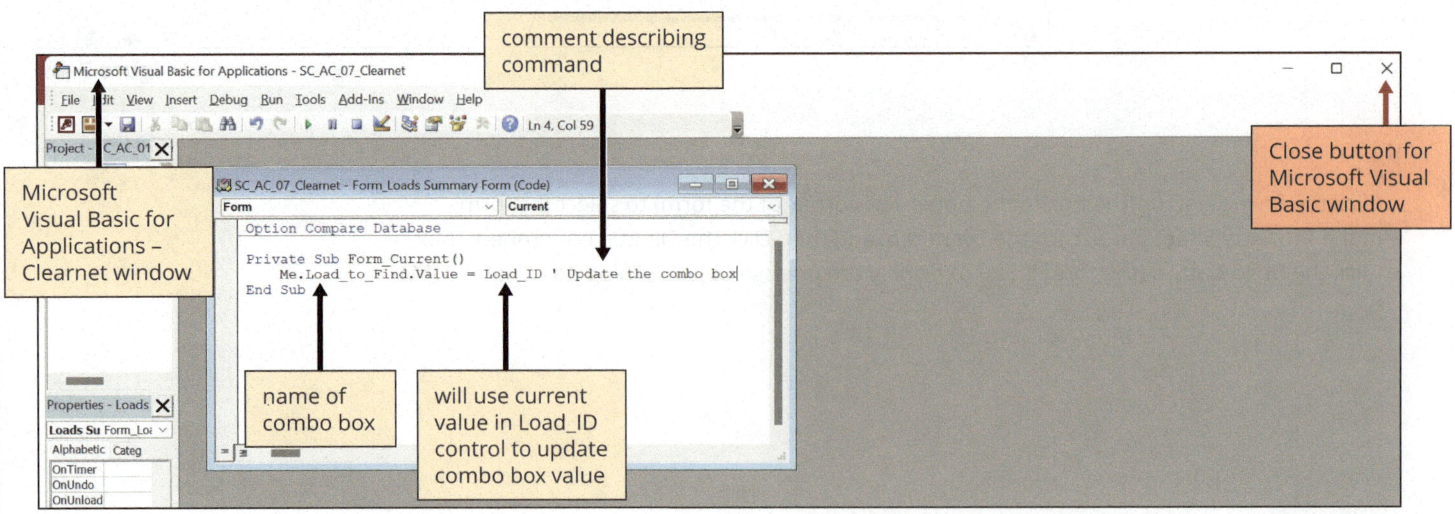

Figure 7–52

Q&A How would I construct a command like this in my own form?

Begin with the name you assigned to the combo box, followed by an equal sign, and then the name of the control containing the primary key of the table. The portion of the statement following the single quotation mark is a comment describing the purpose of the command. Comments are not read by the application and are provided by the programmer for future reference to help explain the purpose of the code; comments are helpful when troubleshooting or updating code later.

5

- Click Close for the Microsoft Visual Basic for Applications window.
- Click the Load to Find combo box (not the label).
- In the Property Sheet pane, click the Other tab, click the Tab Stop property box, and then click the Tab Stop property box arrow.
- Click No to change the value of the Tab Stop property, which skips over the combo box in the tab sequence.

BTW
Comments in Macros
You can use the Comment action in the Action Catalog to place comments in macros.

BTW
Converting Macros to VBA Code
You can convert macros that are attached to forms to VBA (Visual Basic for Applications) code. To do so, open the form in Design view and click the 'Convert Form's Macros to Visual Basic' button. You also can convert macros that are attached to reports.

To Adjust the Tab Stop Order

Currently, when pressing TAB to navigate through controls in the form, the focus skips from control to control in an illogical order. Setting the tab stop order can fix this problem. *Why? Pressing tab is a convenient way to move through fields in a form during data entry, and the tab stop order should be set for logical navigation through the form.* The following steps first provide descriptive names for the Shipper and Carrier combo boxes, and then they adjust the tab stop order.

1

- Click the Shipper Name combo box (not the label).
- In the Property Sheet pane, click the Name property box, and then change the Name value to **Shipper_Combo** (Figure 7–53).

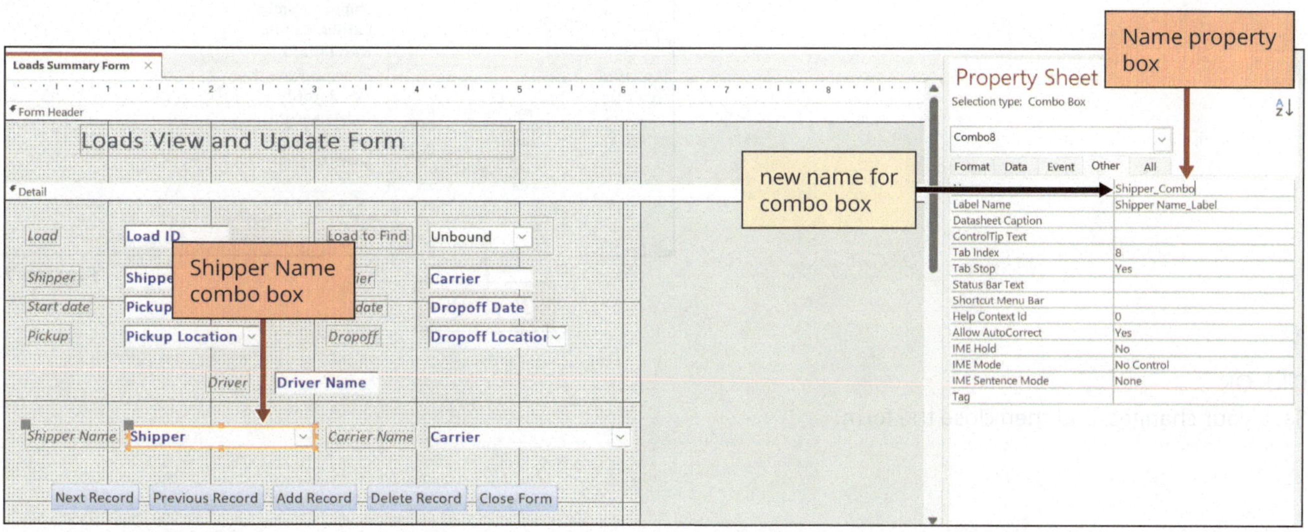

Figure 7–53

2

- Use the same technique to rename the Carrier combo box to **Carrier_Combo**, and then close the Property Sheet pane.

3

- Click the Tab Order button (Form Design tab | Tools group) to display the Tab Order dialog box.
- Click the box to the left of the Shipper row (Tab Order dialog box) to select Shipper, and then drag the left end of the row to move the Shipper row to just below the Load_ID row (Figure 7–54).

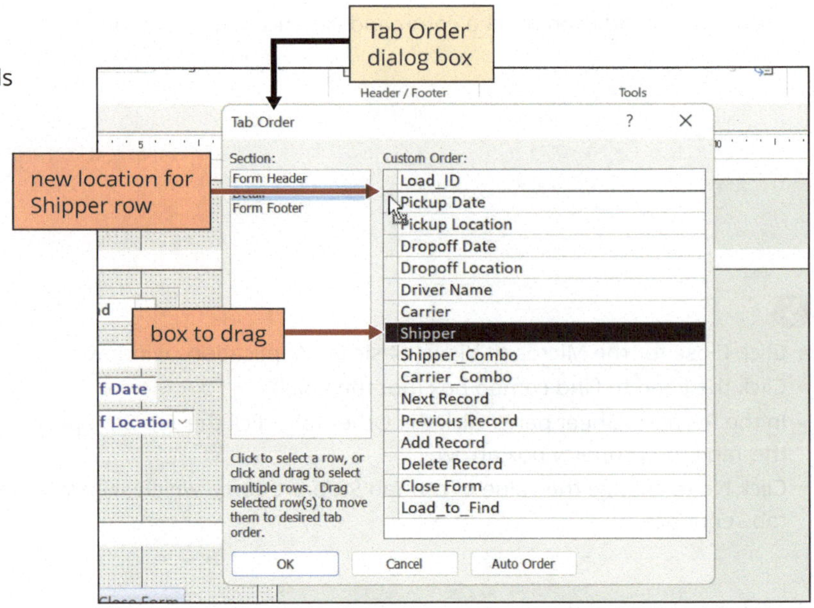

Figure 7–54

4

- Use the same technique to reorder all the rows to match the order shown in Figure 7–55.

Q&A I thought I removed the tab stop for the Load to Find combo box. Why is this control still listed in the Tab Stop dialog box?
The control is still listed simply because it exists in the form. However, it is disabled and will not receive focus as you tab through the form.

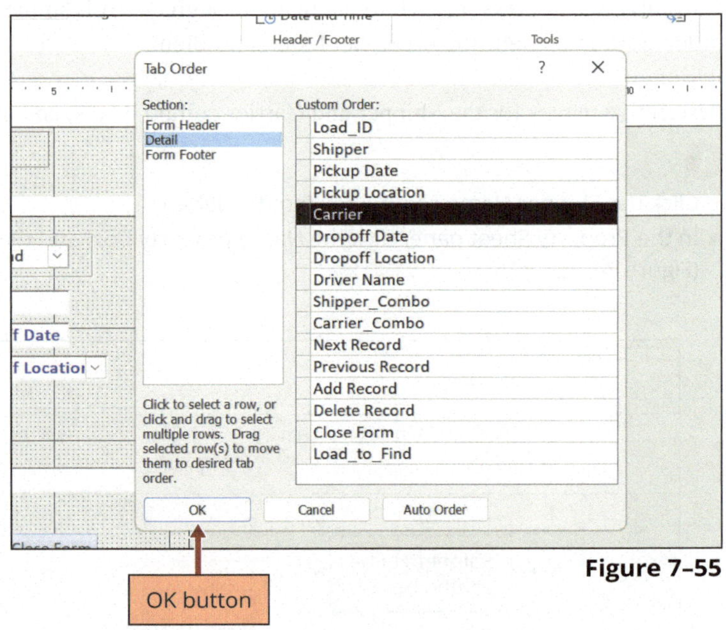

Figure 7–55

5

- Click OK.
- Save your changes, and then close the form.

Using the Modified Form

The problems with the Add Record button and the combo box are now corrected. When you click the Add Record button, an insertion point appears in the Shipper field (Figure 7–56a). When you click the Load to Find box arrow, the list of pickup dates is displayed in chronological order (Figure 7–56b). After using the Load to Find box to find a load (Figure 7–56c) and then clicking the Next Record button, the Load to Find box is updated with the correct Load ID (Figure 7–56d). When you press TAB while navigating through fields in the form, the tab stops occur in a logical order without including the Load to Find box.

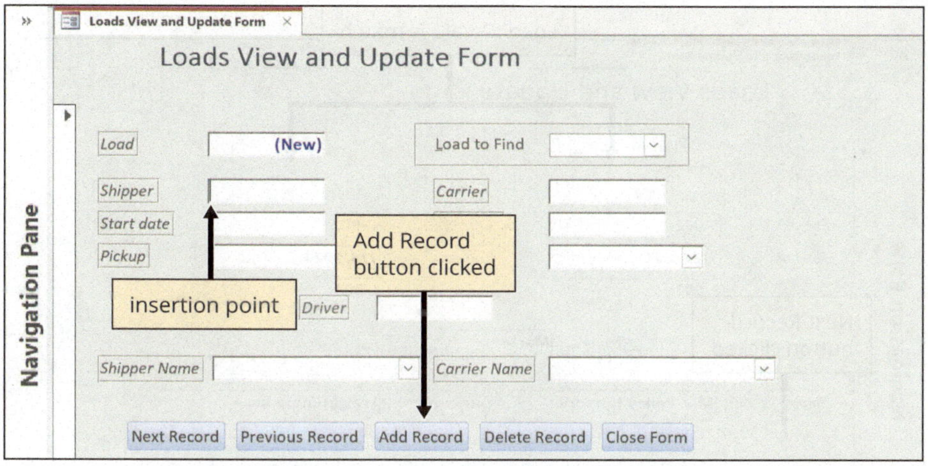

Figure 7–56a

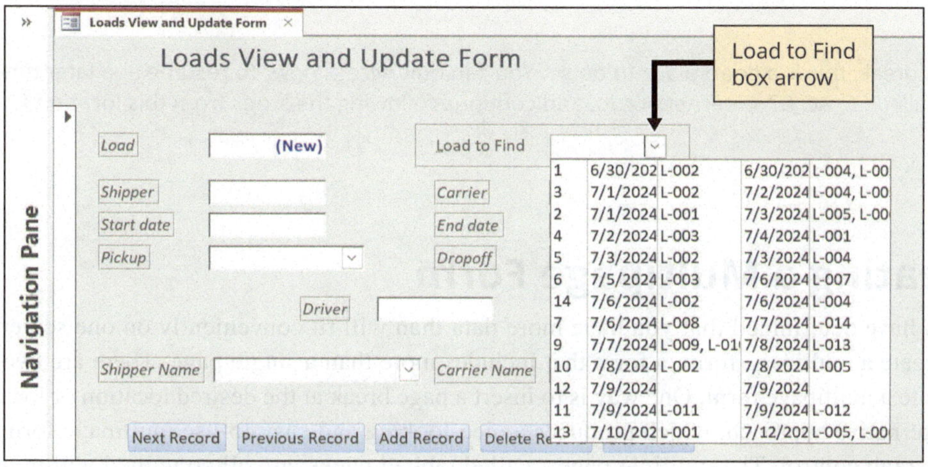

Figure 7–56b

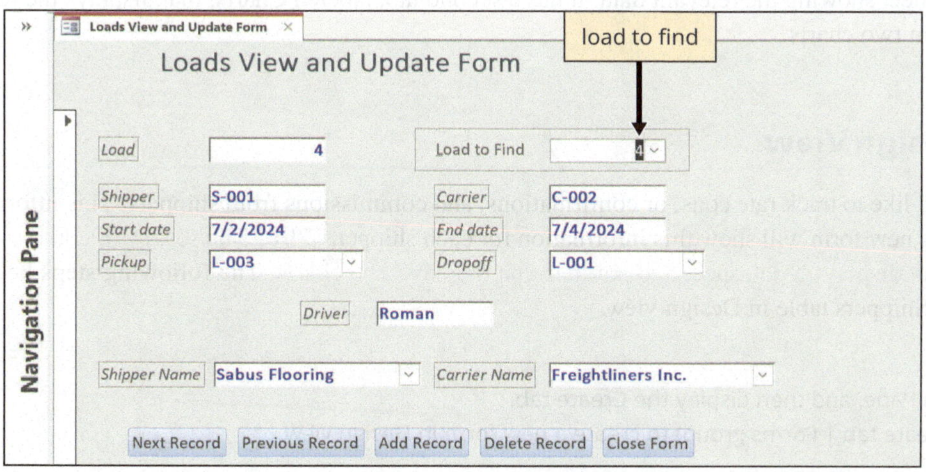

Figure 7–56c

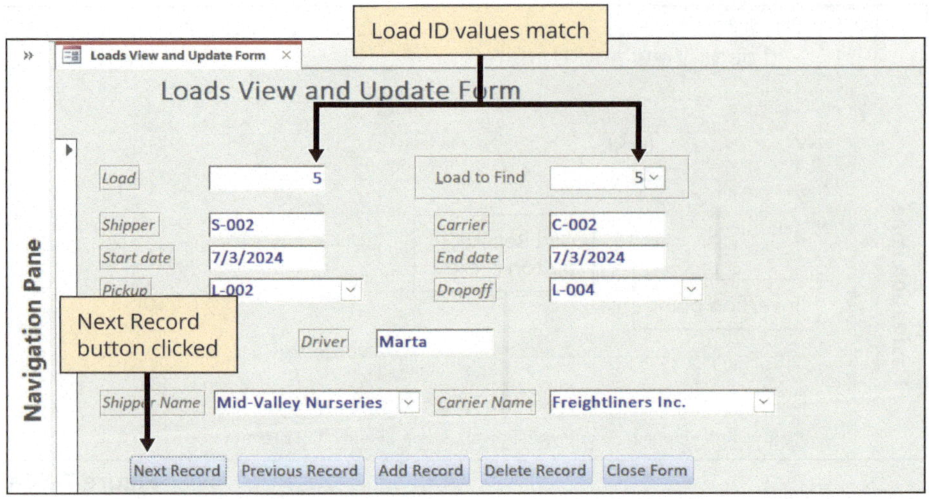

Figure 7–56d

Break Point: If you wish to take a break, this is a good place to do so. You can quit Access now. To resume at a later time, start Access, open the database called SC_AC_07_Clearnet.accdb, and continue following the steps from this location forward.

Creating a Multipage Form

If you have determined that you have more data than will fit conveniently on one screen, you can create a multipage form, a form that includes more than a single page. There are two ways to create a multipage form. One way is to insert a page break at the desired location or locations. An alternative approach, which produces a nice-looking and easy-to-use multipage form, is to insert a tab control. The multiple pages, called tabbed pages, are all contained within the tab control. To move from one page in the tab control to another, a user simply clicks the desired tab. The tab control shown in Figure 7–2, for example, has a tab labeled Datasheet that contains a datasheet showing the relevant data. It has a second tab, labeled Charts, that displays the relevant data in two charts.

To Create a Form in Design View

The management at Clearnet would like to track rate cons, or confirmations, and commissions from shippers. This information is stored in the Payments table. The new form will show this information for each shipper. **Why?** The form will contain the tab control including two tabs: one that displays a datasheet and another that displays two charts. The following steps begin the process by creating a form for the Shippers table in Design view.

1

- If necessary, close the Navigation Pane, and then display the Create tab.
- Click the Form Design button (Create tab | Forms group) to create a new form in Design view.

2

- Ensure the form selector — the box in the upper-left corner of the form — is selected.
- If necessary, click the Property Sheet button (Form Design tab | Tools group) to display the Property Sheet pane.
- Click the Data tab, click the Record Source property box arrow, and then click Shippers to select the Shippers table as the record source for the new form.
- Close the Property Sheet pane.

3

- Click the 'Add Existing Fields' button (Form Design tab | Tools group) to display the Field List pane, and then drag the Shipper ID field to the approximate position shown in Figure 7–57.

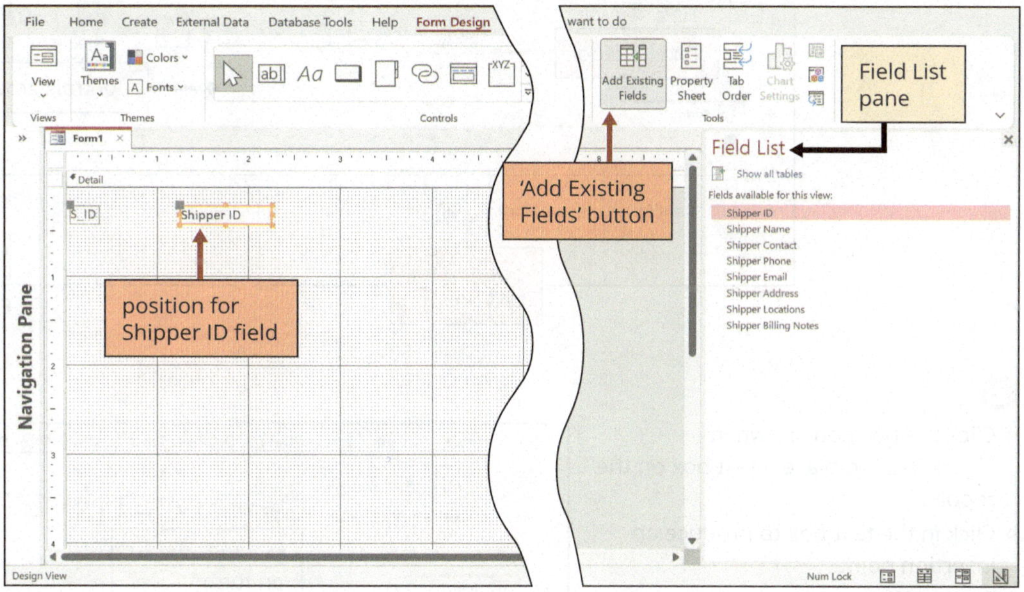

Figure 7–57

4

- Change the label for the Shipper ID field from S_ID to **Shipper Identification**.
- Resize and move the label and the Shipper ID control to match Figure 7–58.

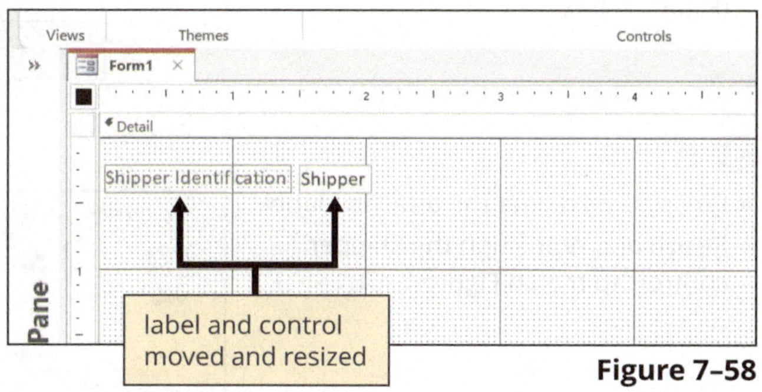

Figure 7–58

To Use the Text Box Tool with Concatenation

You can create a concatenated field by using the Text Box tool in the Controls group on the Design tab and then indicating the concatenation that is to be performed. **Why?** Concatenation means to combine objects in a series. The following steps add a concatenated field, involving two text fields, Shipper Name and Shipper Contact. Specifically, you will concatenate the shipper name, a colon, a single space, and the shipper's contact name.

1

- Click the Text Box tool (Form Design tab | Controls group), and then move the pointer, whose shape has changed to a small plus symbol (+) accompanied by a text box, to the position shown in Figure 7–59.

BTW

Concatenation

Concatenation is often used in computing to combine or merge two or more things. For example, if you have two separate fields, such as first name and last name, you can concatenate them to show a full name. You also can include punctuation between the fields, such as concatenating a city name, a comma, a space, and a state name.

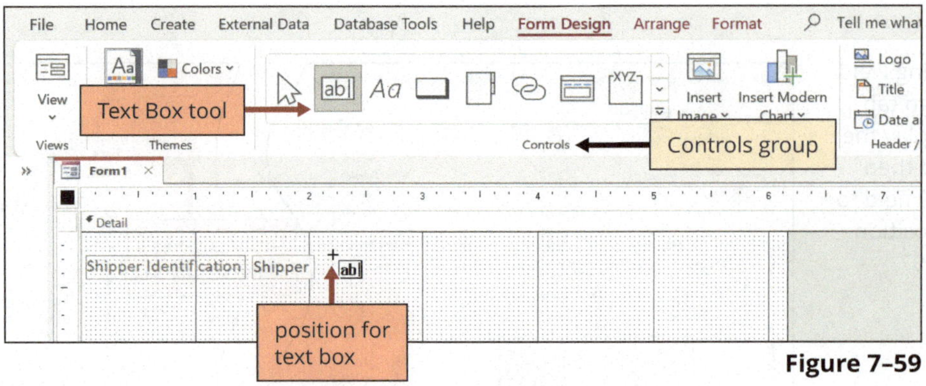

Figure 7–59

2

- Click the position shown in Figure 7–59 to place a text box on the report.
- Click in the text box to produce an insertion point.
- Type **=[Shipper Name] & ':' & ' ' & [Shipper Contact]** as the entry in the text box.
- Click the attached label to select it (Figure 7–60).

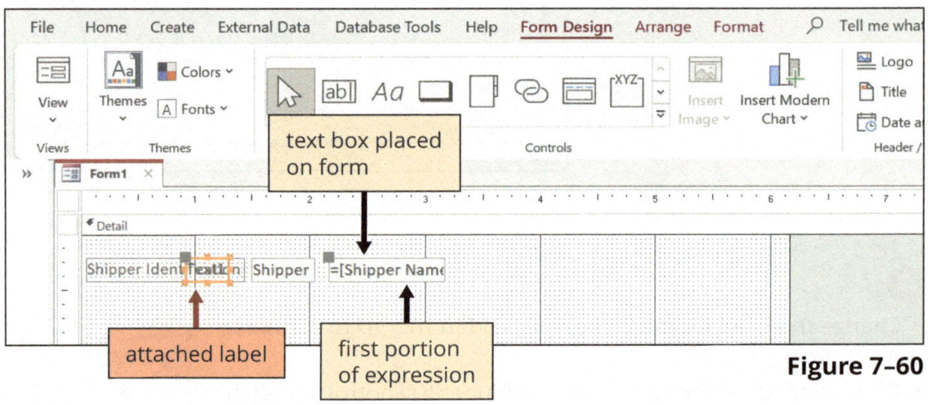

Figure 7–60

3

- Press DEL to delete the attached label.
- Resize and reposition the shipper controls to match Figure 7–61.

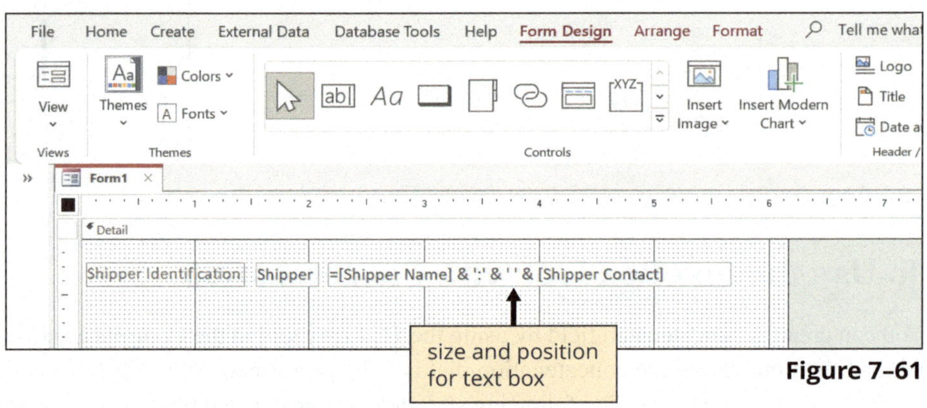

Figure 7–61

4

- Close the Field List pane.
- Save the form using the name, **Shipper Payments Form**.

To Use Tab Controls to Create a Multipage Form

To use tabs on a form, you need to insert a tab control. The following steps insert a tab control with two tabs: Datasheet and Charts. **Why?** Users will be able to click the Datasheet tab in the completed form to view rate confirmations and commissions in Datasheet view. Clicking the Charts tab will display two charts representing the similar data as in the Datasheet tab.

1

- Click the Tab Control tool (Form Design Tab | Controls group) and move the pointer to the approximate location shown in Figure 7–62.

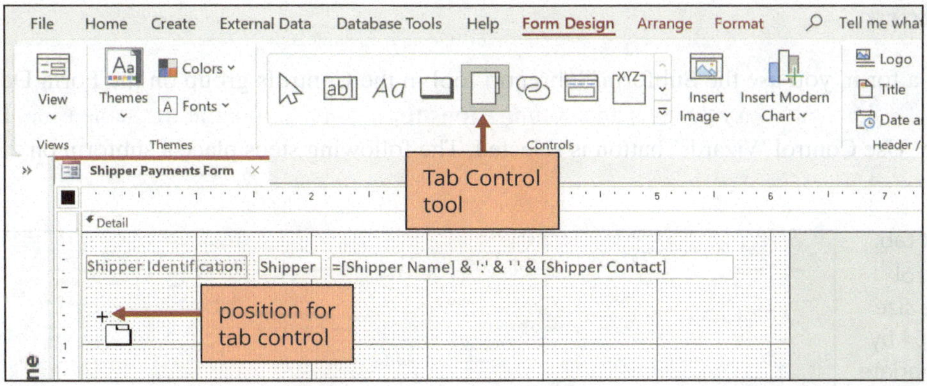

Figure 7–62

2

- Click the position shown in Figure 7–62 to place a tab control on the form.
- Click the left tab in the tab control, and then click the Property Sheet button (Form Design tab | Tools group) to display the Property Sheet pane.
- Click the Format tab.
- Set the value for the Caption property to **Datasheet** (Figure 7–63).

Q&A My property sheet looks different. What should I do?

Be sure you clicked the far-left tab before displaying the Property Sheet pane. The highlight should be within the border of the tab, as shown in the figure.

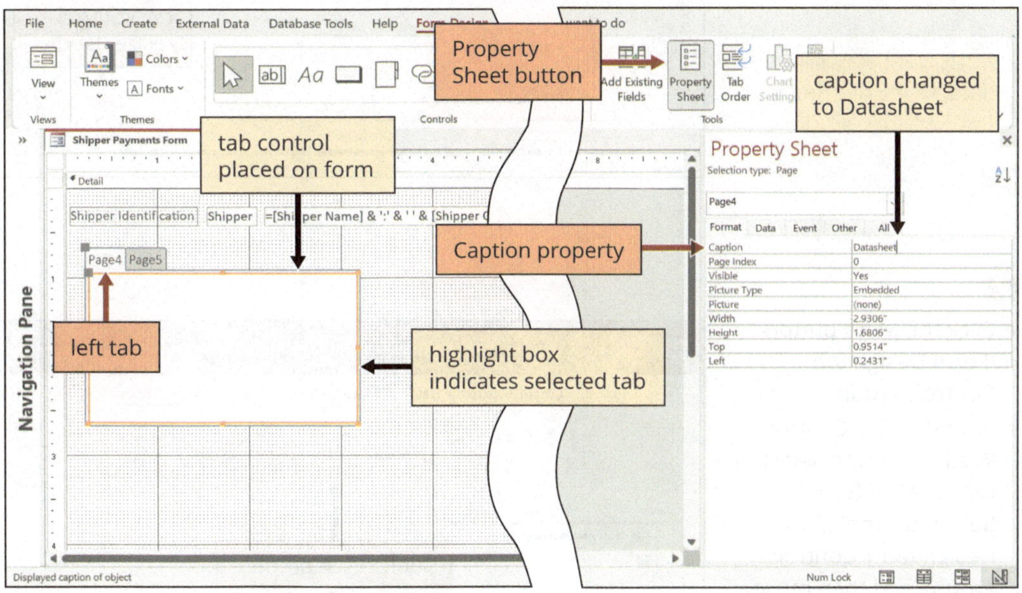

Figure 7–63

3

- Click the second tab in the tab control.
- Set the value for the Caption property to **Charts**, and then close the Property Sheet pane.

Consider This

When would you include a tab control in your form?

If the form contains more information than will conveniently fit on the screen at a time, consider adding a tab control. With a tab control, you can organize the information within a collection of tabbed pages. To access any of the tabbed pages, users need only click the corresponding tab.

BTW

Tab Control Order

You can change the order of tabs in a tab control. To do so, right-click any tab in the tab control and click Page Order on the shortcut menu. Use the Move Up and Move Down buttons to change to the desired order.

To Add a Subform

To add a subform to a form, you use the Subform/Subreport tool in the Controls group on the Form Design tab. **Why?** The subform enables you to show data for rate cons and commissions for a given shipper at the same time. Before doing so, you should make sure the 'Use Control Wizards' button is selected. The following steps place a subform on the Datasheet tab.

1

- Click the Datasheet tab.
- Resize the tab control to the approximate size shown in Figure 7–64 by dragging the appropriate sizing handles.

Q&A Why do I need to resize the tab control?
Because there needs to be enough room in the form to display all the datasheet columns and the two charts, you will need to make the tab control larger.

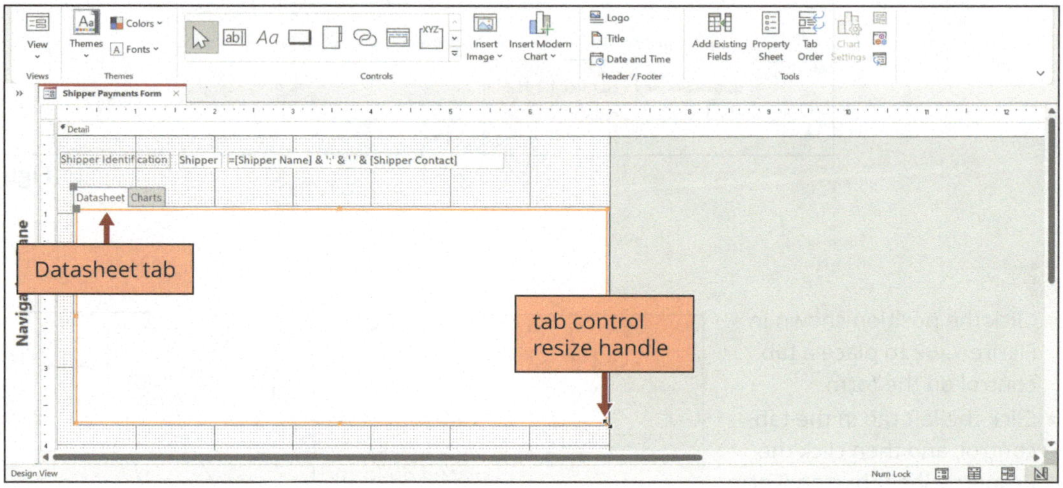

Figure 7–64

2

- Click the More button (Form Design tab | Controls group).
- With the 'Use Control Wizards' button selected, click the Subform/Subreport tool (Form Design tab | Controls group), and then move the pointer to the approximate position shown in Figure 7–65.

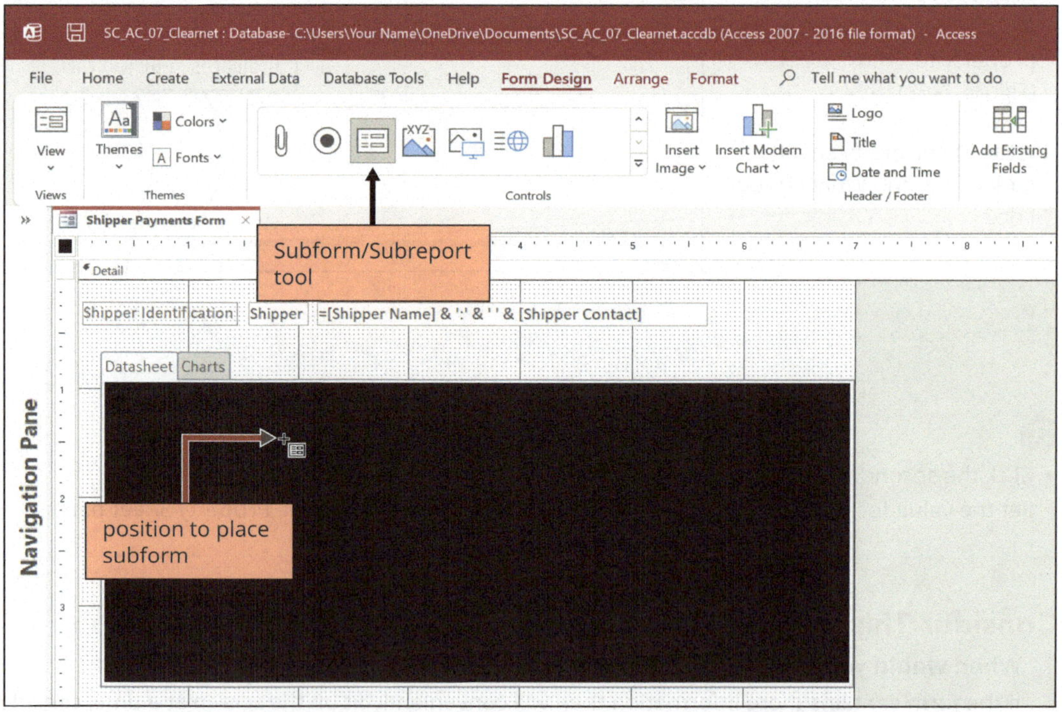

Figure 7–65

3

- Click the position shown in Figure 7–65 to open the SubForm Wizard dialog box.
- Be sure the 'Use existing Tables and Queries' option button is selected.
- Click Next to display the next SubForm Wizard screen.

- Click the Tables/Queries arrow, and then click the Payments table to indicate the fields for the subform will be selected from this table.
- If necessary, click the Payment ID field to select it, and then click the Add Field button.
- Use the same technique to add the Rate Confirmation field, Agent Commission field, Shipper Bill Status field, and Shipper ID field (Figure 7–66).

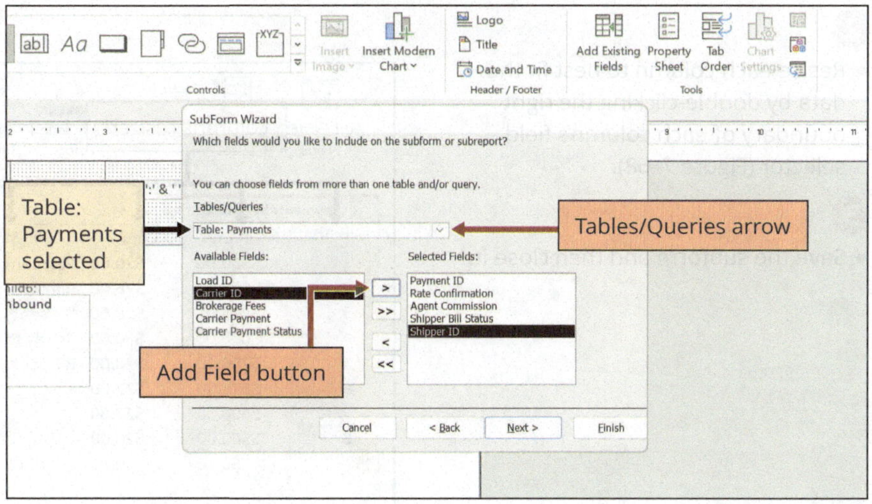

Figure 7–66

4

- Click Next.
- Be sure the 'Choose from a list' option button is selected.
- Click Next.
- Change the name of the subform to **Payments by Shipper**, and then click Finish to complete the creation of the subform (Figure 7–67).

5

- Save and close the Shipper Payments Form.

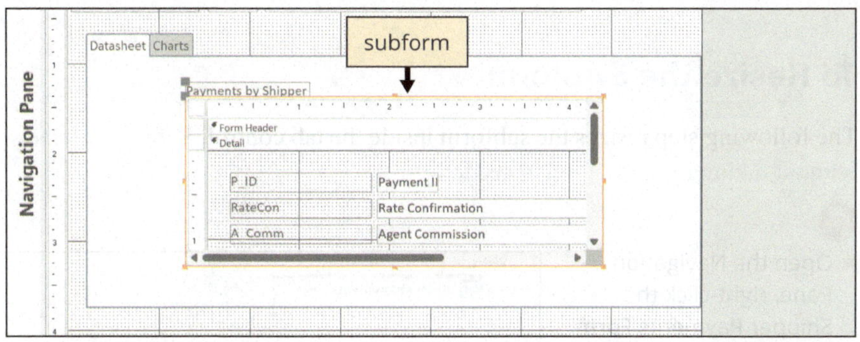

Figure 7–67

Consider This

When would you include a subform in your form?

If the fields for the form come from exactly two tables, a one-to-many relationship exists between the two tables, and the form is based on the "one" table, you will often place the data for the "many" table in a subform. If there are more than two tables involved, you might be able to create a query on which you can base the subform.

To Modify a Subform

The next task is to modify the subform. The first step is to remove the Shipper ID field from the subform. **Why?** The Shipper ID field needed to be included initially in the subform because it is the field that is used to link the data in the subform to the data in the main form. It is not supposed to appear in the form, however. In addition, the remaining columns need to be resized for best fit. The following step first removes the Shipper ID field. You then switch to Datasheet view to resize the remaining columns.

1

- Open the Navigation Pane, right-click the Payments by Shipper form, click Design View on the shortcut menu, and then close the Navigation Pane.
- Click the Shipper ID control, and then press DEL to delete the control.
- Switch to Datasheet view.

2

- Resize each column to best fit the data by double-clicking the right boundary of each column's field selector (Figure 7–68).

3

- Save the subform and then close it.

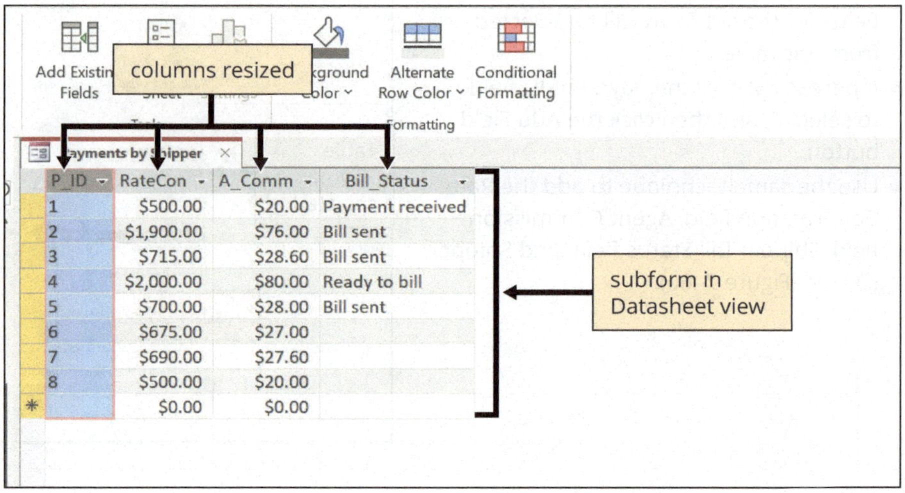

Figure 7–68

To Resize the Subform

The following step resizes the subform inside the tab control. **Why?** The size should enable the user to clearly view all the data without taking more room than needed.

1

- Open the Navigation Pane, right-click the Shipper Payments Form, and then click Design View on the shortcut menu.
- Close the Navigation Pane.
- Resize and reposition the subform to match Figure 7–69.

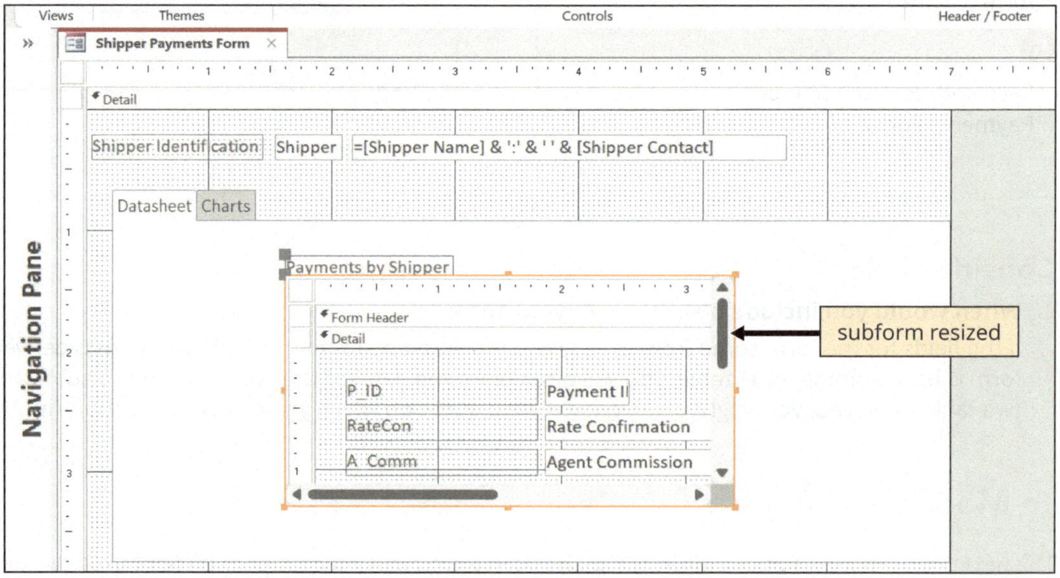

Figure 7–69

To Change the Background Color

The following steps change the background color of the form to a light gray.

1

- Click anywhere in the Detail section in the main form but outside all the controls to select the section.

2

- Display the Format tab.
- Click the Background Color button arrow (Format tab | Font group) to display a color palette (Figure 7–70).

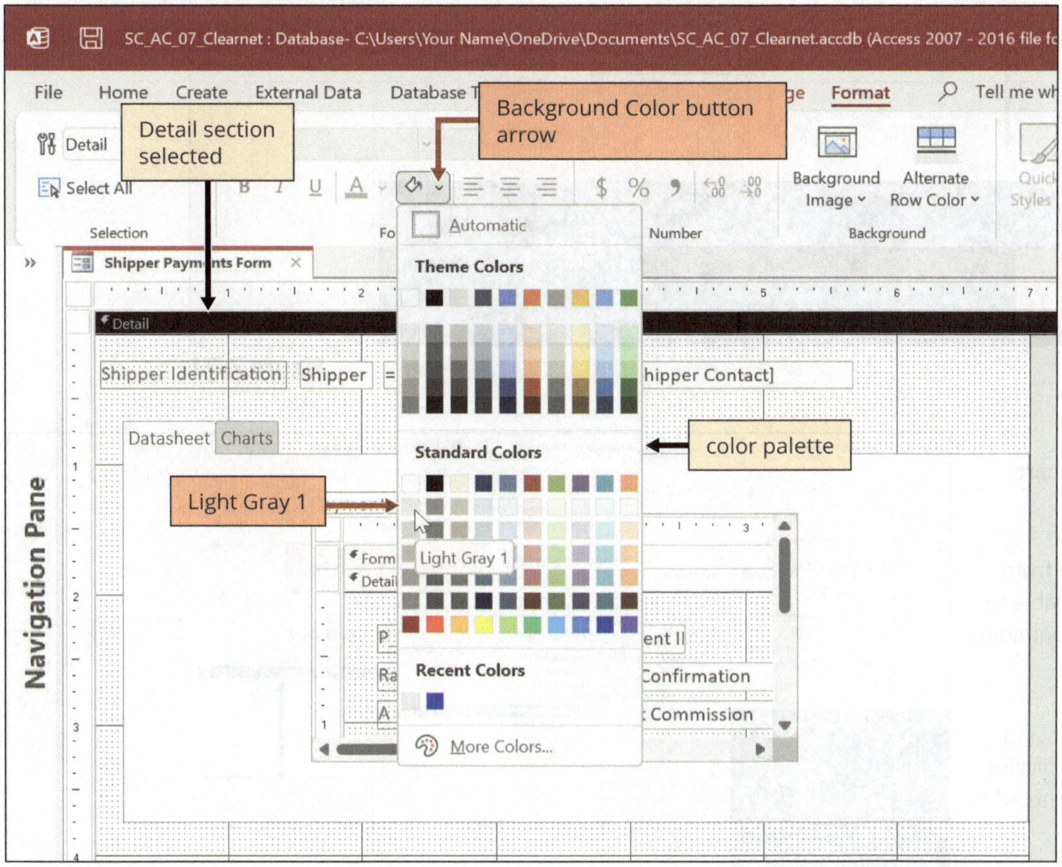

Figure 7–70

3

- Click Light Gray 1, the first color in the second row under Standard Colors, to change the background color.

To Insert Charts

Why? To visually represent data in a table or query, you can create a chart. To insert a chart, use the Chart tool on the Form Design tab. The Chart Wizard will then ask you to indicate the fields to be included on the chart and the type of chart you want to insert. The following steps insert a chart that visually represents the amount of payments from shippers.

1

- Display the Form Design tab.
- Click the Charts tab on the tab control to switch to that tab.
- Click the More button (Form Design tab | Controls group) to display the design tools.
- Click the Chart tool, and then move the pointer to the approximate position shown in Figure 7–71.

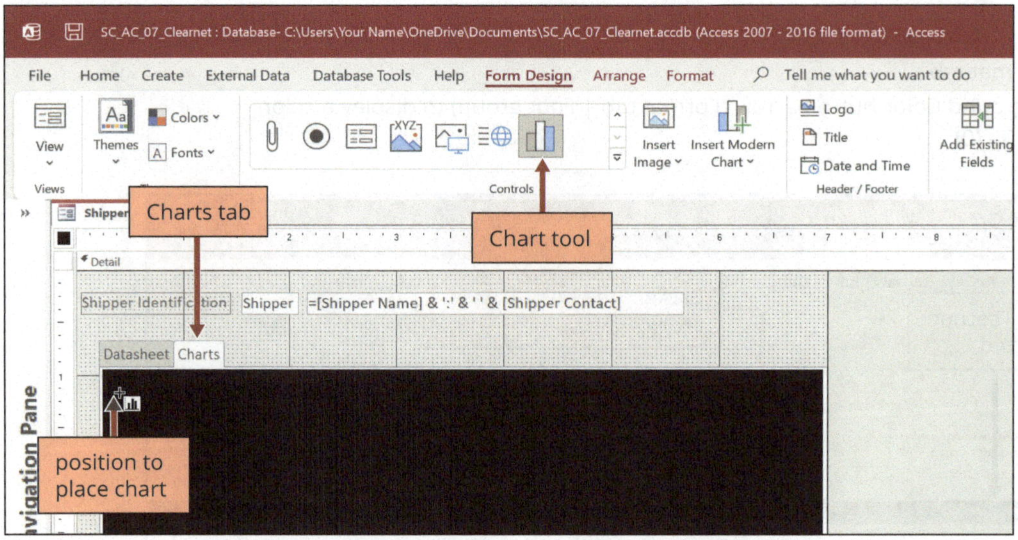

Figure 7–71

2

- Click the position shown in Figure 7–71 to display the Chart Wizard dialog box.
- The Chart Wizard dialog box indicates the data will come from a table; click the Payments table to indicate the specific table containing the desired fields.
- Click Next.
- Select the Rate Confirmation and Shipper Bill Status fields by clicking each one and then clicking the Add Field button (Figure 7–72).

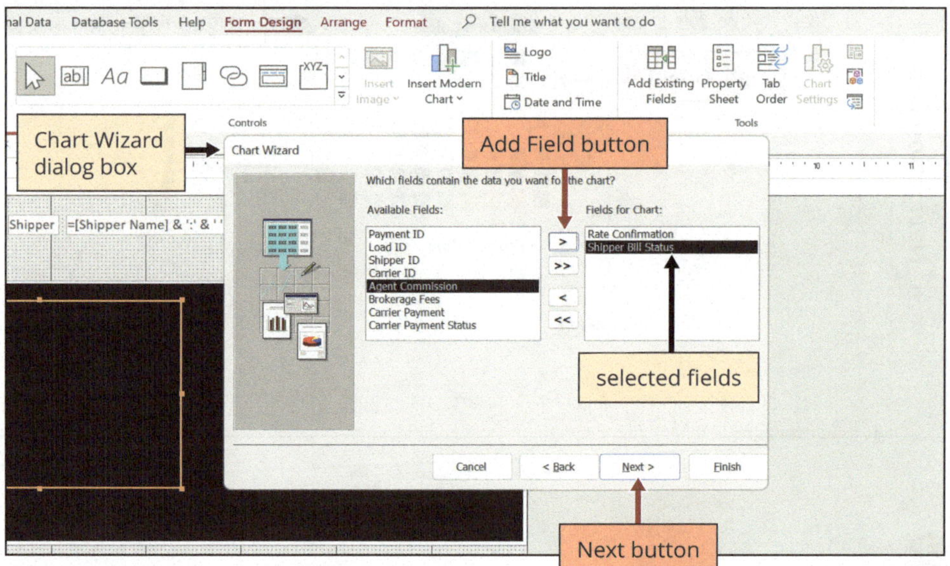

Figure 7–72

3

- Click Next.
- Click the Pie Chart type, the first chart in the bottom row (Chart Wizard dialog box) (Figure 7–73).
- **Experiment:** Click the other chart types and read the descriptions of chart types in the lower-right corner of the Chart Wizard dialog box. When finished, click the Pie Chart in the lower-left corner.

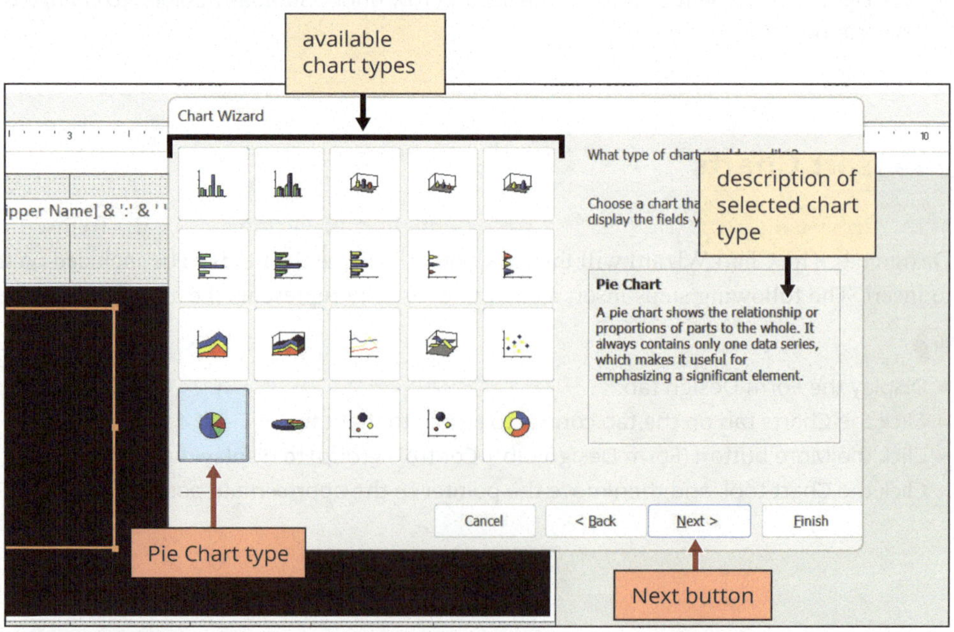

Figure 7–73

4

- Click Next to create the chart (Figure 7–74). Your screen might take several seconds to refresh.

Q&A What do the chart positions represent? Can I change them?
The field under the chart represents the data that will be summarized by slices of the pie. The other field is used to indicate the series. In this example, the field for the series is the shipper bill status, and the sizes of the slices of the pie will represent the sum of the rate confirmations for each bill status. You can change these by dragging the fields to the desired locations.

These positions make sense for a pie chart. What if I selected a different chart type?
The items on this screen will be relevant to the chart type you select. Just as with the pie chart, the correct fields will often be selected automatically. If not, you can drag the fields to the correct locations.

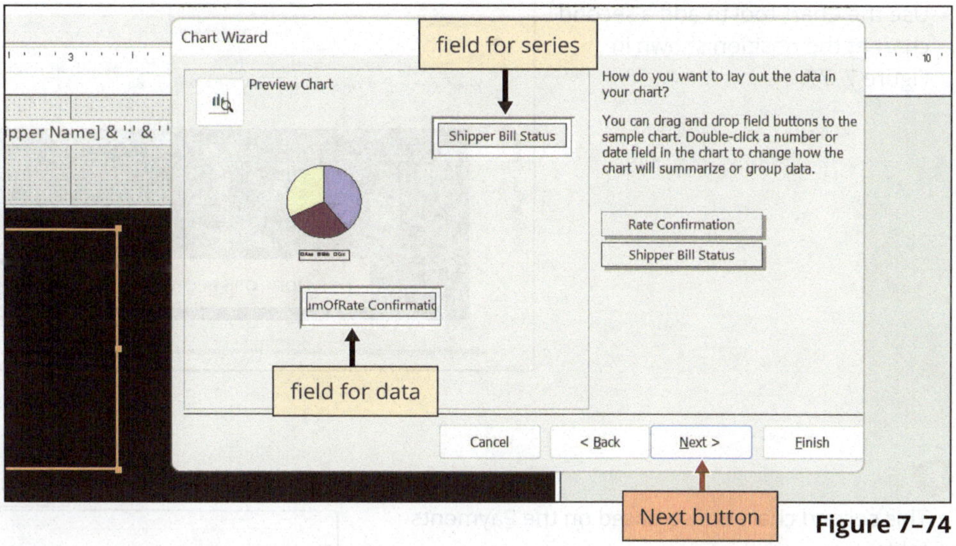

Figure 7–74

5

- Click Next to select the layout Access has proposed (Figure 7–75).

Q&A The Shipper ID field does not appear in my chart. Can I still use it to link the form and the chart?
Yes. Even though the Shipper ID does not appear, it is still included in the query on which the chart is based. In fact, it is essential that it is included so you can link the document (that is, the form) and the chart. Linking the document and the chart ensures the chart will accurately reflect the data for the correct shipper, that is, the shipper that currently appears in the form.

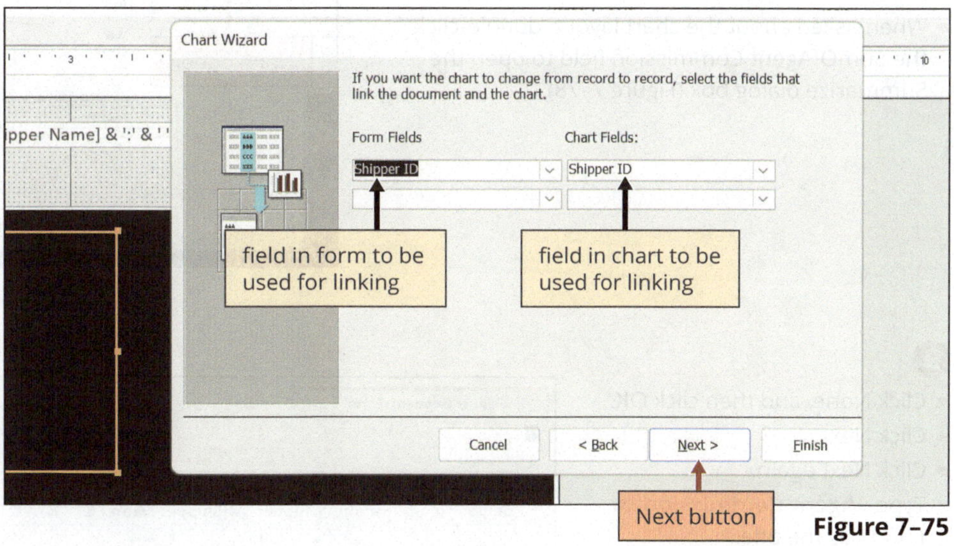

Figure 7–75

6

- Click Next, type **Rate Confirmation Statuses** as the title, and then click the Finish button (Figure 7–76).

Q&A The data does not look right. What is wrong and what do I need to do to fix it?
The data in your chart might be fictitious, as in Figure 7–76. In that case, the data simply represents the general way the chart will look. When you view the actual form, the data represented in the chart should be correct.

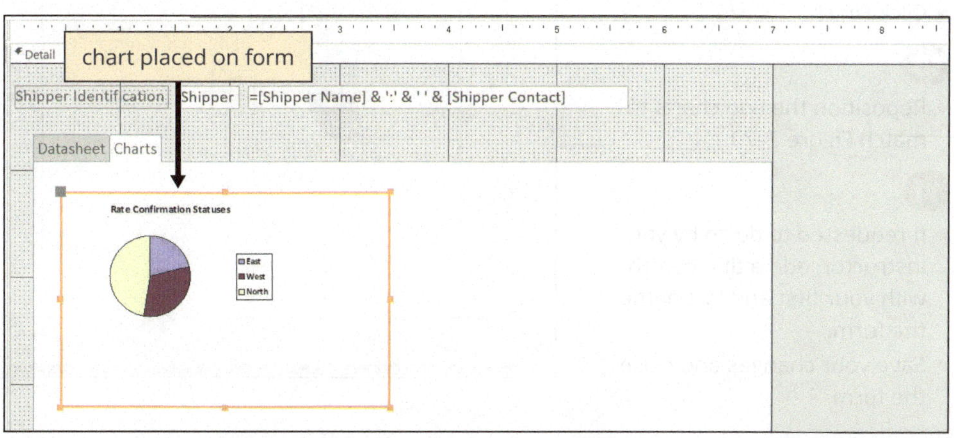

Figure 7–76

7

- Use the Chart tool to add a second chart at the position shown in Figure 7–77.

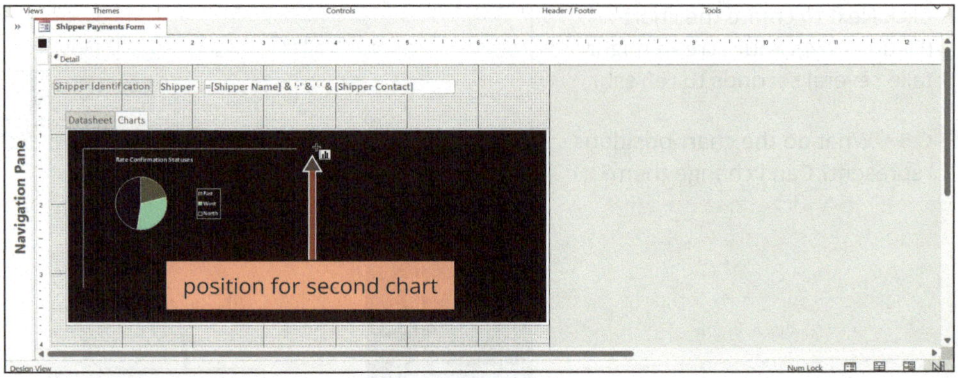

Figure 7–77

8

- This second chart is also based on the Payments table.
- Add the Load ID field and the Agent Commission field to the chart.
- Choose the Column Chart type, which is the default selection in the upper-left corner.
- When asked about the chart layout, double-click the SumOfAgent Commission field to open the Summarize dialog box (Figure 7–78).

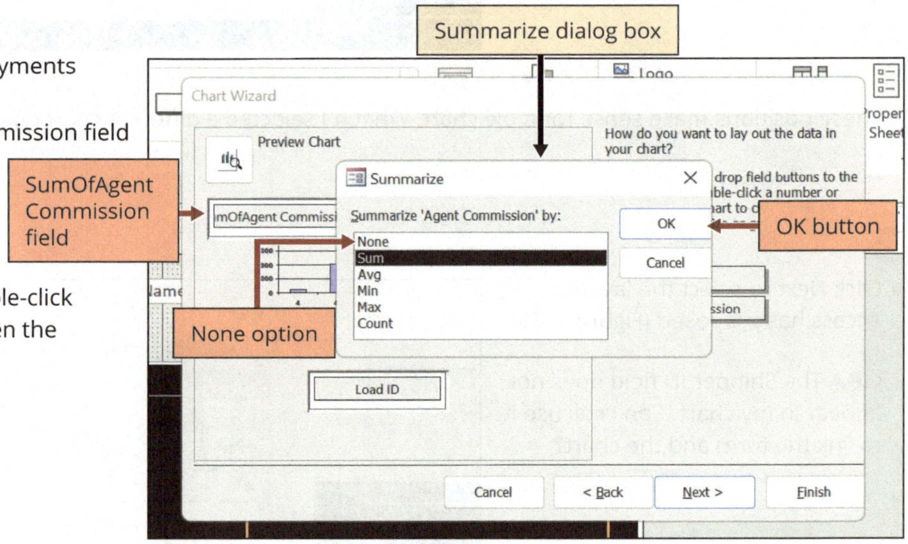

Figure 7–78

9

- Click None, and then click OK.
- Click Next.
- Click Next again.
- Type **Agent Commission by Load** as the title.
- Click the 'No, don't display a legend' option button.
- Click Finish.

10

- Reposition the two charts to match Figure 7–79.

11

- If requested to do so by your instructor, add a title control with your first and last name to the form.
- Save your changes and close the form.

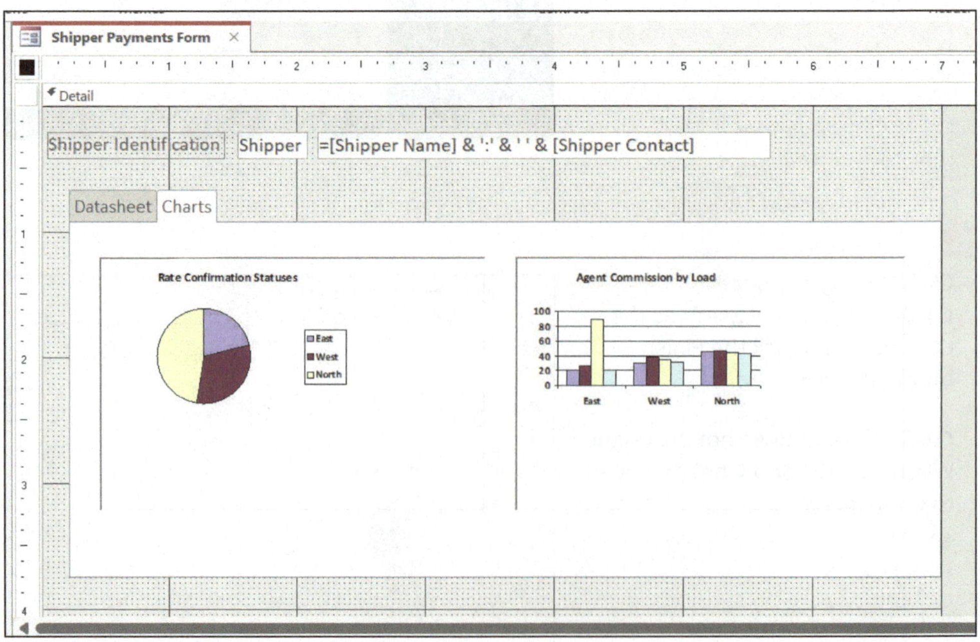

Figure 7–79

To Use the Form

You use this form just like the other forms you have created and used. When using the form, it is easy to move from one tabbed page to another. **Why?** Click each tab to navigate to the desired tabbed page. The following steps use the form to view the rate confirmation and agent commission data.

1

- Open the Navigation Pane, open the Shipper Payments Form in Form view, and then close the Navigation Pane (Figure 7–80). Ensure all headings are visible, and adjust any column widths if necessary.

Q&A What is the purpose of the navigation buttons in the subform?
These navigation buttons allow you to move within the records in the subform, that is, within the payment data for the shipper whose number and name appear at the top of the form.

2

- Click the Charts tab to display the charts.
- Click the Next record button to navigate through other shipper records to see different chart data.

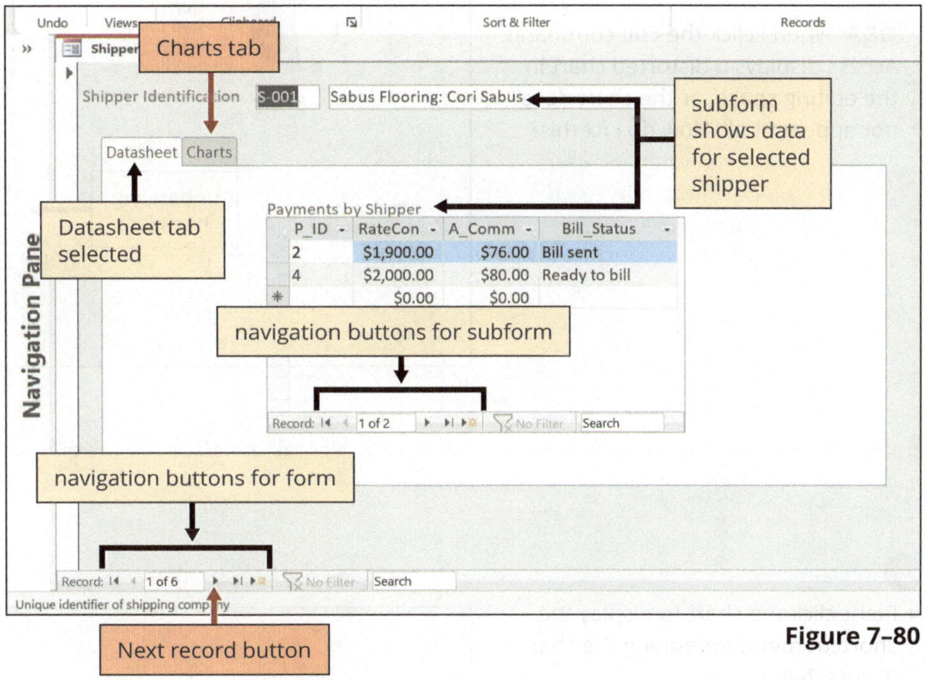

Figure 7–80

To Modify a Chart Type

When you first create a chart, you specify the chart type. You sometimes will later want to change the type. **Why?** You might find that a different chart type is a better way to represent the data. In addition, you have more options when you later change the chart type than when you first created the chart. You change the type by editing the chart and selecting the Chart Type command. The following steps change the chart type of the column chart by selecting a different style of column chart.

1

- Switch to Design view.
- Click the tab control, and then click the Charts tab to display the charts in Design view.
- Click the Agent Commission by Load chart to select it, and then right-click the chart to display a shortcut menu.
- Point to Chart Object on the shortcut menu to display the Chart Object submenu (Figure 7–81).

Q&A Does it matter where I right-click?
You should right-click within the rectangle but outside any of the items within the rectangle, in other words, in the white space.

My shortcut menu is very different. What should I do?
Click the View button arrow, then click Design View to ensure you are viewing the form in Design view, and then try again.

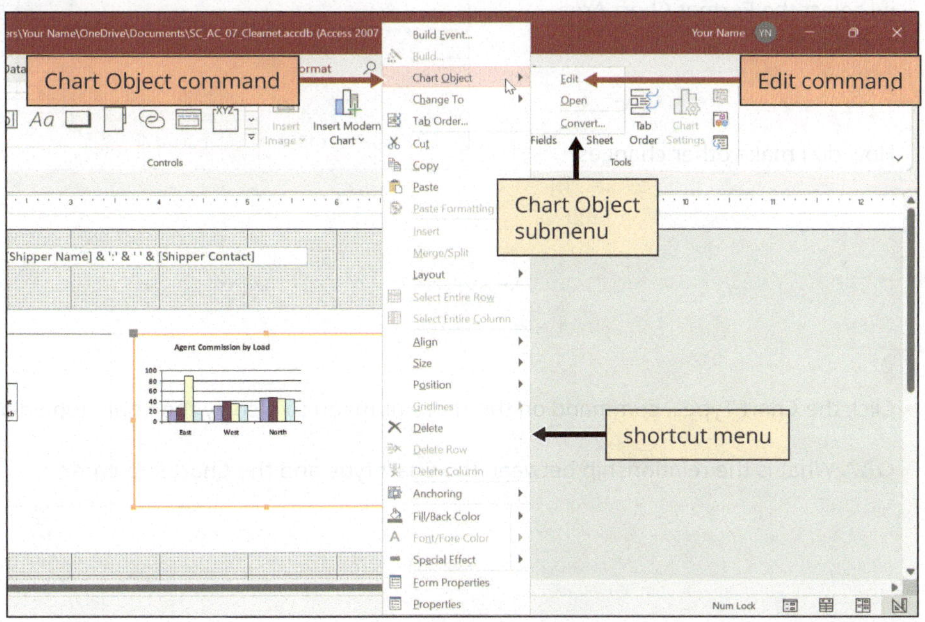

Figure 7–81

2

- Click Edit on the Chart Object submenu to edit the chart. Access will automatically display the underlying chart data in Datasheet view (Figure 7–82).

Q&A When I click the Edit command, Access displays a distorted chart in the editing space, or the chart does not appear at all. How do I fix this?
In some cases, you might need to use the Open command instead of the Edit command to get a usable interface for editing a chart. Click outside the chart editing space, again right-click the chart, point to Chart Object, and this time, click Open to display the Microsoft Graph window. The screen will look slightly different from the figures in this portion of the module; however, all the steps should work the same. When you are finished editing, you can close the Microsoft Graph window.

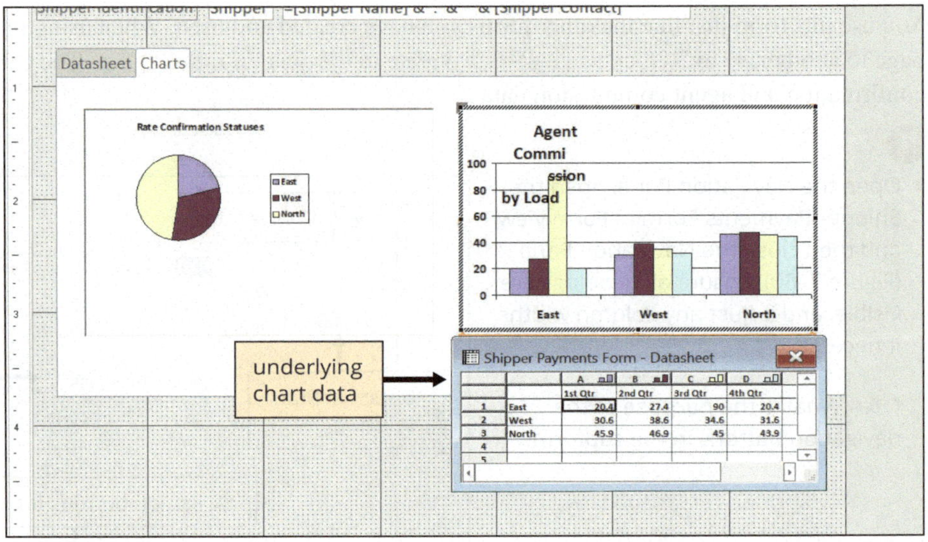

Figure 7–82

3

- Right-click the chart to display the shortcut menu for editing the chart (Figure 7–83).

Q&A Does it matter where I right-click?
You should right-click within the rectangle but outside any of the items within the rectangle, in other words, in the white space.

What types of changes can I make if I select the Format Chart Area... command?
You can change things such as border style, color, fill effects, and fonts.

How do I make other changes?
By clicking Chart Options... on the shortcut menu, you can change titles, legends, and labels. For 3-D charts, by clicking 3-D View... on the shortcut menu, you can change the elevation and rotation of the chart. You can also format specific items on the chart, as you will see in the next section.

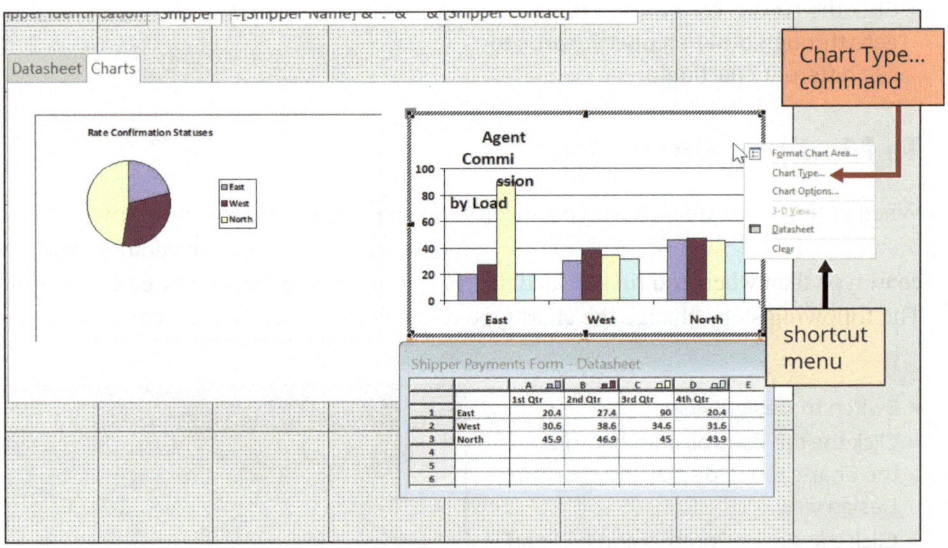

Figure 7–83

4

- Click the Chart Type... command on the shortcut menu to display the Chart Type dialog box (Figure 7–84).

Q&A What is the relationship between the Chart type and the Chart sub-type?
You can think of Chart types as categories of charts. There are column charts, bar charts, line charts, and so on. Once you have selected a category, the chart sub-types are charts in that category. If you have selected the Column chart category, for example, the charts within the category are the ones shown in the list of chart sub-types in Figure 7–85.

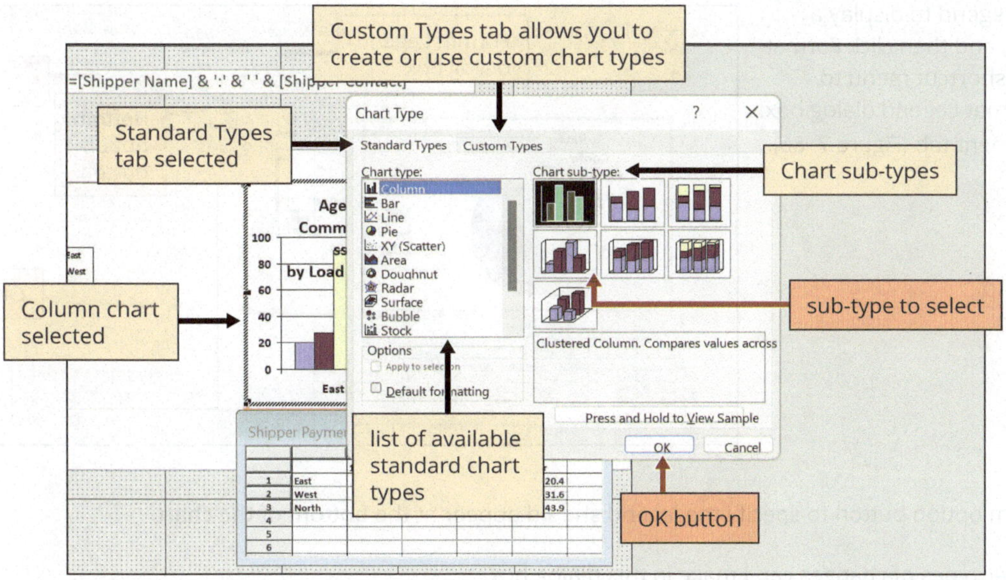

Figure 7–84

5

- Click the first chart sub-type in the second row of chart sub-types to select the 'Clustered column with a 3-D visual effect' chart sub-type.
- **Experiment:** Click each of the chart types and examine the chart sub-types associated with that chart type. When finished, select Column as the chart type and the first sub-type in the second row as the chart sub-type.
- Click the OK button to change the chart sub-type.
- Click outside the chart and the tab control to deselect the chart (Figure 7–85).

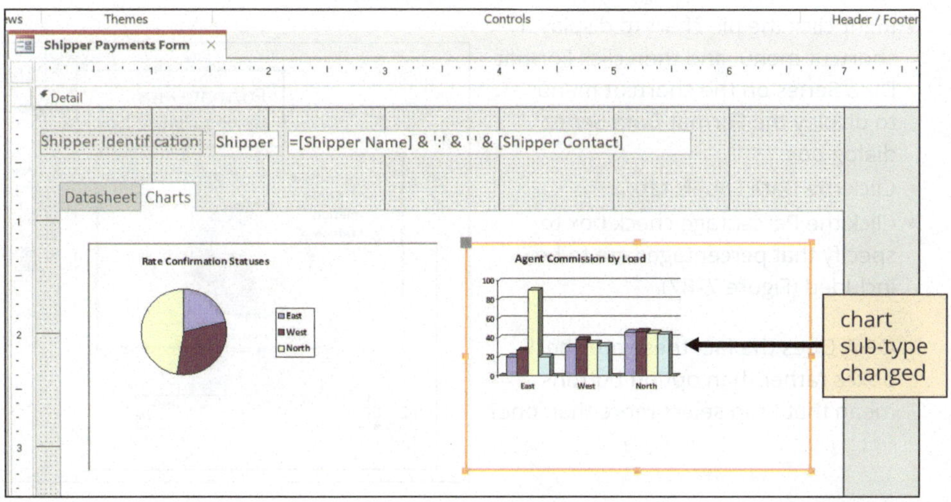

Figure 7–85

To Format a Chart

After right-clicking a chart, pointing to Chart Object, and then clicking Edit, you have many formatting options available. You can change the border style, color, fill effects, and fonts by using the Format Chart Area command. You can change titles, legends, and labels by using the Chart Options command. You can also format specific portions of a chart by right-clicking the portion you want to format and then clicking the appropriate command on the shortcut menu. The following steps use this technique to move the legend on the pie chart so it is at the bottom of the chart. They also include percentages in the chart. Why? Percentages provide valuable information in a pie chart.

1

- Right-click the Rate Confirmation Statuses chart to display a shortcut menu, point to Chart Object on the shortcut menu to display the Chart Object submenu, and then click Edit on the Chart Object submenu.

Q&A If the Edit command is not working well for me, will the Open command work here as before?

Yes, you can use the Open command here as an alternative to the Edit command, just as in the earlier steps. The Open command will open the Microsoft Graph window where you can make all the needed changes described in these steps. When you are finished editing, you can close the Microsoft Graph window.

- Right-click the legend to display a shortcut menu, and then click Format Legend on the shortcut menu to display the Format Legend dialog box.
- Click the Placement tab (Figure 7–86).

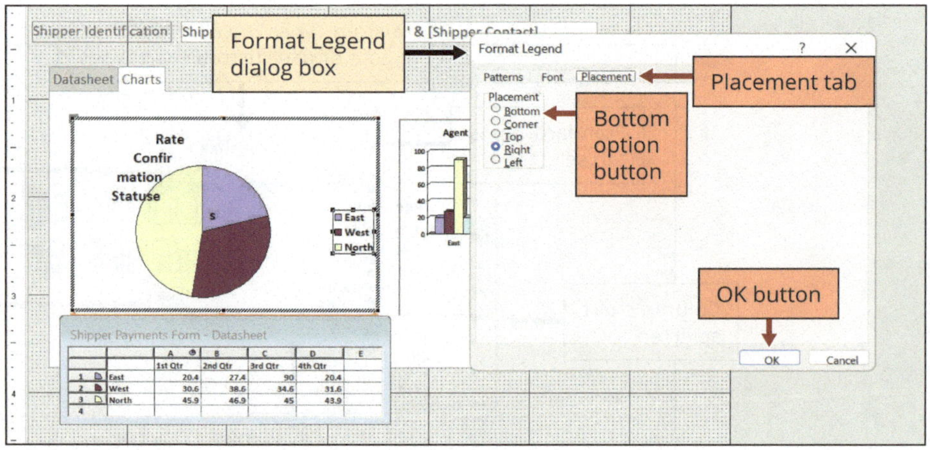

Figure 7–86

2

- Click the Bottom option button to specify the legend should appear at the bottom of the chart.

Q&A What other types of changes can I make in this dialog box?
Click the Patterns tab to change such things as border style, color, and fill effects. Click the Font tab to change the font and font characteristics.

- Click OK to place the legend at the location you selected.
- Right-click the pie chart to display a shortcut menu, and then click Format Data Series on the shortcut menu to display the Format Data Series dialog box.
- Click the Data Labels tab.
- Click the Percentage check box to specify that percentages are to be included (Figure 7–87).

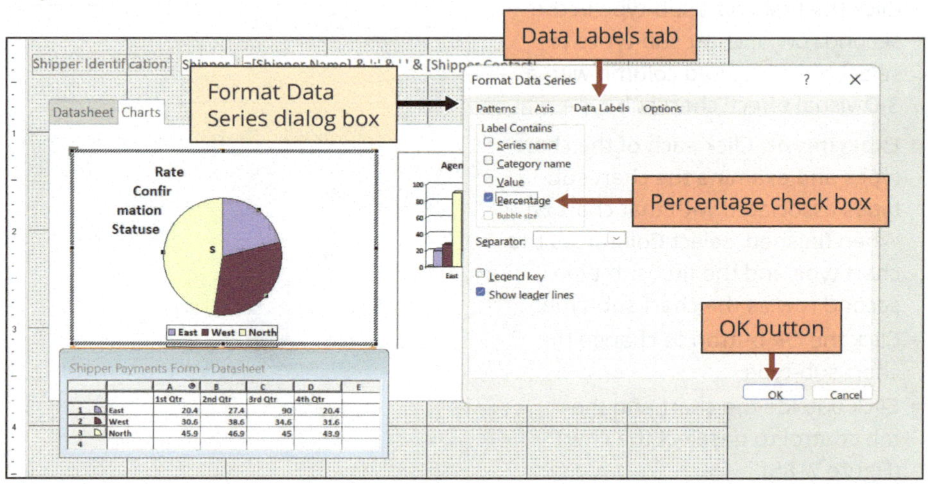

Figure 7–87

Q&A Does the fact these are check boxes rather than option buttons mean that I can select more than one?
Because these are check boxes, you can select as many as you want. Selecting too many can clutter the chart, however.

The tabs and options in the Format Data Series dialog box make sense for a pie chart, but what about other chart types?
The options you see will vary from one chart type to another. They will be relevant for the selected chart type.

3

- Click OK to include percentages on the chart.
- Click outside the chart and the tab control to deselect the chart.

4

- View the form in Form view to see the effect of your changes.
- Save and then close the form.
- If desired, sign out of your Microsoft account.
- sam Exit Access.

BTW

Distributing a Document

Instead of printing and distributing a hard copy of a document, you can distribute the document electronically. Options include sending the document via email; posting it on cloud storage (such as OneDrive) and sharing the file with others; posting it on a social networking site, blog, or other website; and sharing a link associated with an online location of the document. You also can create and share a PDF or XPS image of the document, so users can view the file in Acrobat Reader or XPS Viewer instead of in Access.

Consider This

What type of decisions should you make when considering whether to use a chart?

Do you want to represent data in a visual manner? If so, you can include a chart. If you decide to use a chart, you must determine which type of chart would best represent the data. If you want to represent total amounts, for example, a bar chart might be appropriate. If instead you want to represent portions of the whole, a pie chart might be better.

Summary

In this module you have learned how to create a form in Design view, add a combo box that displays information from a related table as well as a combo box that is used to find records on a form, format controls, add command buttons to a form, modify a button and a combo box, add a concatenated field to a form, use a tab control to create a multipage form, add and modify a subform, insert charts, change chart types, and format charts.

Consider This: Plan Ahead

What decisions will you need to make when creating your own forms?

Use these guidelines as you complete the assignments in this module and create your own forms outside of this class.

1. Determine the intended audience and the purpose of the form.
   a. Who will use the form?
   b. How will they use it?
   c. What data do they need?
   d. What level of detail do they need?
2. Determine the source of data for the form.
   a. Determine whether data comes from a single table or from multiple related tables.
   b. Which table or tables contain the data?
3. Determine the fields that belong on the form.
   a. What data items are needed by the user of the form?
4. Determine any calculations required for the form.
   a. Decide whether the form should contain any special calculations, such as adding two fields.
   b. Determine whether the form should contain any calculations involving text fields, such as concatenating (combining) the fields.
5. Determine the organization of the form.
   a. In what order should the fields appear?
   b. How should they be arranged?
   c. Does the form need multiple pages?
6. Determine any additional controls that should be on the form.
   a. Should the form contain a subform?
   b. Should the form contain a chart?
   c. Should the form contain command buttons to assist the user in performing various functions?
   d. Should the form contain a combo box to assist the user in searching for a record?
7. Determine the format and style of the form.
   a. What should be in the form heading?
   b. Do you want a title?
   c. Do you want an image?
   d. What should be in the body of the form?
   e. What visual characteristics, such as background color and special effects, should the various portions of the form have?

Consider This

How should you submit solutions to critical thinking questions in the assignments?

Every assignment in this course contains one or more critical thinking questions. These questions require you to think beyond the assigned database. Present your responses to the questions in the format required by your instructor. Possible formats might include one or more of these options: write the answer; create a document that contains the answer; present your answer to the class; discuss your answer in a group; record the answer as audio or video using a webcam, smartphone, or portable media player; or post answers on a blog, wiki, or website.

Student Assignments

Apply Your Knowledge

Reinforce the skills and apply the concepts you learned in this module.

Creating a Multipage Form for the Tutoring Services Database

Note: To complete this assignment, you will be required to use the Data Files. Please contact your instructor for information about accessing the Data Files.

Instructions: Start Access. Open the database, SC_AC_07-2.accdb, which is located in the Data Files folder. Enable the content.

Perform the following tasks:

1. Save the database using the file name, SC_AC_07_City-Tutoring. Enable the content.
2. Create the Amount Received and Current Due form shown in Figure 7–88. Concatenate the first and last name of the counselor, and change the control's background color to Light Gray 1 (the first color in row 2 of the Standard Colors). The Datasheet tab displays a subform listing information about payments from the counselor's students (Figure 7–88a). Data for the subform is based on the Accounting table. Data for the Chart tab is also based on the Accounting table and displays the amount received from each student for the specified counselor, in this case, the sum of amounts received by counselor Number 103, Enrique Estevez (Figure 7–88b).

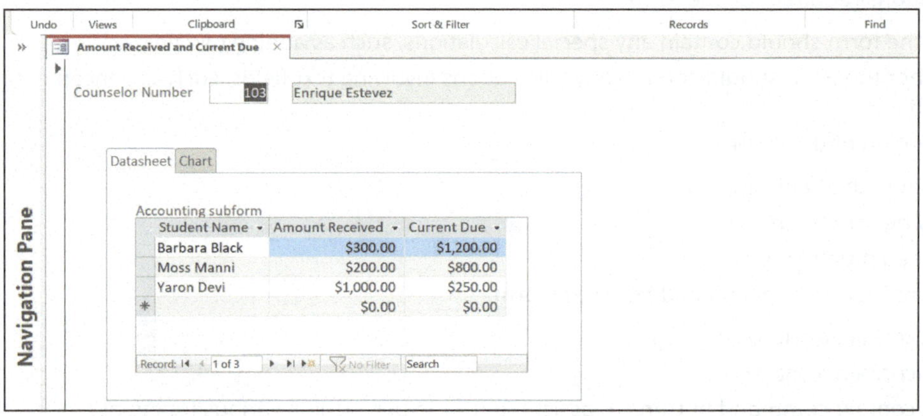

Figure 7–88a

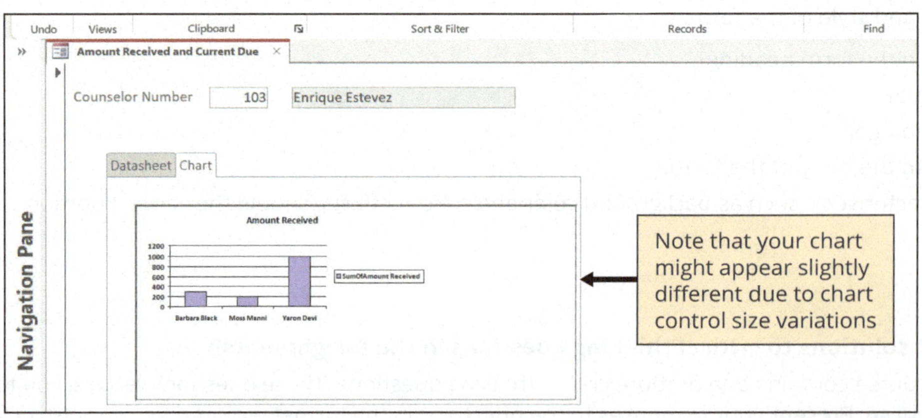

Figure 7–88b

3. If requested to do so by your instructor, rename the Amount Received and Current Due form as LastName Services Data where LastName is your last name.
4. Submit the revised database in the format specified by your instructor.
5. **Consider This:** How would you add a title to the Amount Received and Current Due form?

Extend Your Knowledge

Extend the skills you learned in this module and experiment with new skills. You may need to use Help to complete the assignment.

Modifying Forms

Note: To complete this assignment, you will be required to use the Data Files. Please contact your instructor for information about accessing the Data Files.

Instructions: Start Access. Open the database, SC_AC_07-3.accdb, which is located in the Data Files folder.

Perform the following tasks:

1. Save the database using the file name, SC_AC_07_Physical-Therapists. Enable the content.
2. Open the Technician Form in Design view. Insert the current date in the form header.
3. Bold the Technician Form title.
4. Change the font color of the title to Dark Red (Standard colors, first color in the last row).
5. Below the existing controls, add a tab control to the form (make room for the new control as needed). Change the caption for the first tab to Clients.
6. Add a subform to the Clients tab control. The Client table is the basis of the subform. Display the Client Name, Amount Paid, and Balance Due fields in a datasheet on the subform. Accept the default name for the subform and delete the label that appears above the datasheet. Resize the datasheet columns for best fit, and resize the datasheet control so all columns appear in the control.
7. Delete the other tab.
8. Add a command button to close the form and use the picture option to place the Exit Doorway picture on the button. Name the button Close Form.
9. Save the changes to the form.
10. If requested to do so by your instructor, open the Technician table in Datasheet view and change the first and last name of Technician 22 to your first and last name.
11. Submit the revised database in the format specified by your instructor.
12. **Consider This:** What chart would be appropriate to add to this form?

Expand Your World

Create a solution, which uses cloud and web technologies, by learning and investigating on your own from general guidance.

Note: To complete this assignment, you will be required to use the Data Files. Please contact your instructor for information about accessing the Data Files.

Instructions: Start Access. Open the database, SC_AC_07-4.accdb, which is located in the Data Files folder, and enable the content. Solutions IT Support needs a form to help them organize their technicians and clients. You will create a Summary Form to include a hyperlink. You will also include a combo box to find a field and link the box's code to the records displayed in the table by editing the VBA code.

Perform the following tasks:

1. Save the database using the file name, SC_AC_07_Solutions-IT-Support. Enable the content.
2. Create a form based on the Client table using Design view and save it as Summary Form.
3. At the top of the form, add the Client Number field and the Technician Number field.
4. Add any other fields you think are necessary from the Client table, such as the client's contact information.
5. Add a Client to Find combo box with an appropriate name of your choice for the subquery. Adjust the On Current VBA code so the client data changes to match the record when the records are advanced.

Continued on next page

6. Access any website containing royalty-free images, such as Unsplash.com or Pexels.com, and search for an image suitable to use as a background image to the form, and then add the background image to the Summary Form.
7. Add a hyperlink for a local computer repair website at the bottom of the form.
8. Access any website containing royalty-free images and search for an image suitable to use on a Close Form command button; for example, a Stop sign or a door. Save the image to a storage location of your choice.
9. Add a Close Form command button to the form using the image you downloaded. Note that if you found an image with a file extension other than .bmp, you will need to adjust settings in the Select Picture dialog box from Bitmaps (*.bmp) to All Files (*.*). The button might show only part of the image you chose; this is not a problem. Resize the button as needed.
10. Save your changes to the Summary Form.
11. Submit the revised database in the format specified by your instructor.
12. **Consider This:** What image did you choose as the background for your form? What image did you choose for the command button? Why did you make those choices?

In the Lab

Design and implement a solution using creative thinking and problem-solving skills.

Lab: Applying Advanced Form Techniques to the Great Outdoors Campground Database

Note: To complete this assignment, you will be required to use the Data Files. Please contact your instructor for information about accessing the Data Files.

Problem: The administrators at Great Outdoors Campground need a form to use to track staff members involved in each activity zone. They also need a form to track payments from campers for each camping event.

Perform the following tasks:

Part 1: Open the SC_AC_07-5.accdb database from the Data Files folder. Save the file with the name, SC_AC_07_Great-Outdoors, and enable the content. Use the concepts and techniques presented in this module to perform each of the following tasks.

1. Create a Staff Activities Summary Form that is similar in style and appearance to the form shown in Figure 7–1a. The form should include a combo box to search for activity zones by name, which should be listed in ascending order; give the subquery an appropriate name of your choice. Include command buttons to go to the next record, go to the previous record, add records, delete records, and close the form. The user should not be able to tab to the combo box. When the Add Record button is clicked, the focus should be the Activity Zone ID.
2. Create a query that joins the Campers, Enrollments, and Camper Payments tables. Include the Camper ID field from the Campers table, the Event field from the Enrollments table, and the Amount Paid and Balance Due fields from the Camper Payments table. Save the query using a name of your choice.
3. Create a form from the Campers table that is similar to the form shown in Figure 7–2a. The form should have two tabs, a Datasheet tab and a Charts tab. The Datasheet tab displays a subform listing the camper's event enrollments. Data for the subform is based on the query you created in Step 2; use an appropriate name of your choice for the subform. The Charts tab should include two charts that represent the amounts paid and balances due for each event. Data for the Charts tab is also based on the query created in Step 2.

Submit your assignment in the format specified by your instructor.

Part 2: **Consider This:** You made several decisions while creating these two forms. What was the rationale behind your decisions? What chart style did you choose for the two charts? Why? What other chart styles could you use to represent the data?

Macros, Navigation Forms, and Control Layouts

Objectives

After completing this module, you will be able to:

- Create a macro or a submacro
- Troubleshoot a macro
- Create a menu form containing command buttons
- Include an option group in a menu form
- Use an IF statement in a macro
- Set the value of a variable in a macro
- Create a datasheet form
- Create a UI (user interface) macro
- Create a navigation form
- Add a tab to a navigation form
- Create a data macro
- Describe options to manage cells in a form
- Explain how to modify a control layout in a form or report
- Explain how to modify Access application options

Introduction

Using built-in tools such as macros, you can design Access forms that provide an interactive user interface experience, complete with buttons and selection menus. In this module, you will learn how to create and test macros that open forms and that preview reports and export reports. You will create a menu form with command buttons as well as a menu form with an **option group**, which is an object that enables you to make a selection by choosing the option button corresponding to your choice. You will also create and use user interface (UI) macros in forms. You will learn about the use of data macros for ensuring that updates to the database are valid. Finally, you will learn how to use control layouts on forms and reports.

Project: Macros, Navigation Forms, and Control Layouts

Partners paralegals would like users to be able to access forms and reports simply by clicking tabs and buttons, rather than by using the Navigation Pane. A **navigation form**, like the one shown in Figure 8–1a, is a form that includes tabs that display other forms and reports. Partners paralegals plan to use the navigation form because they believe it will improve the user-friendliness of the database, thereby improving employee satisfaction and efficiency. This navigation form contains several useful features. With the Closings tab selected, you can click the Closing ID (or C-ID) in any row to view the data for the selected closing in a **pop-up form**, which is a form that stays on top of other open objects even when another object is active (Figure 8–1b).

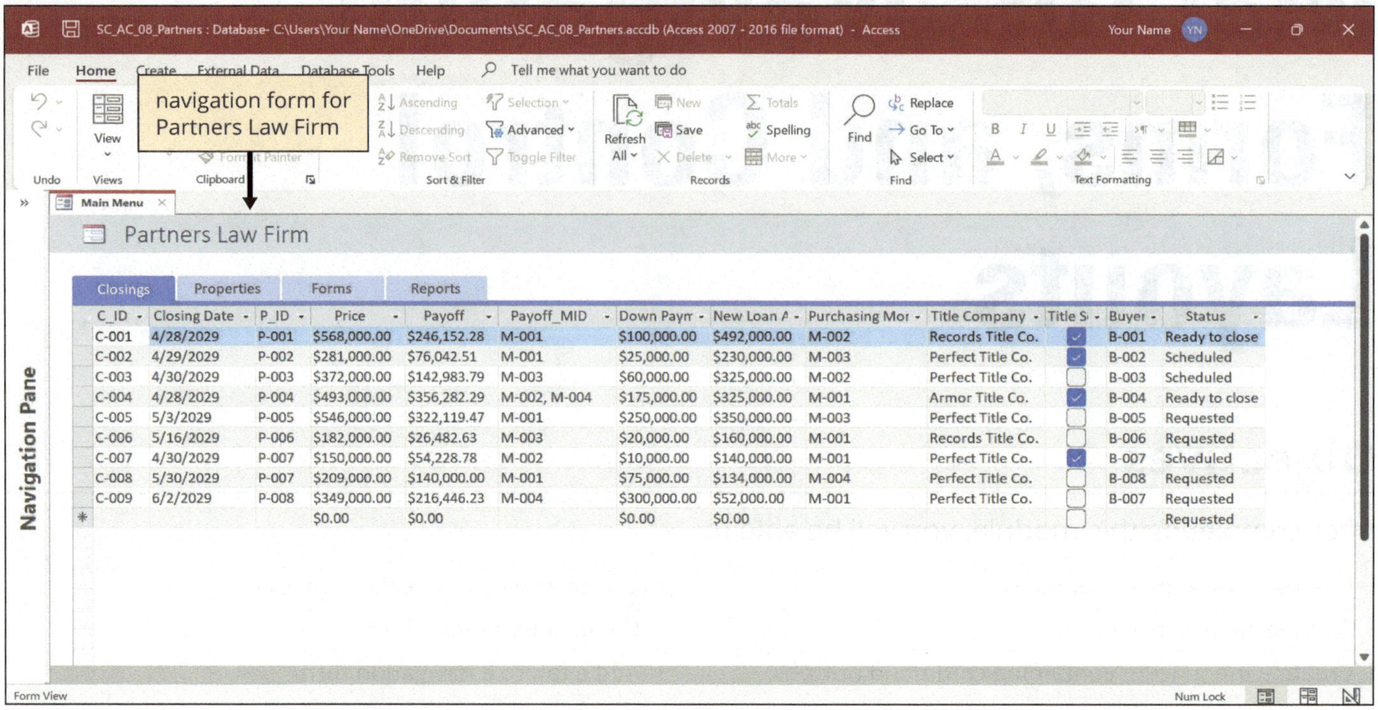

Figure 8–1a Navigation Form

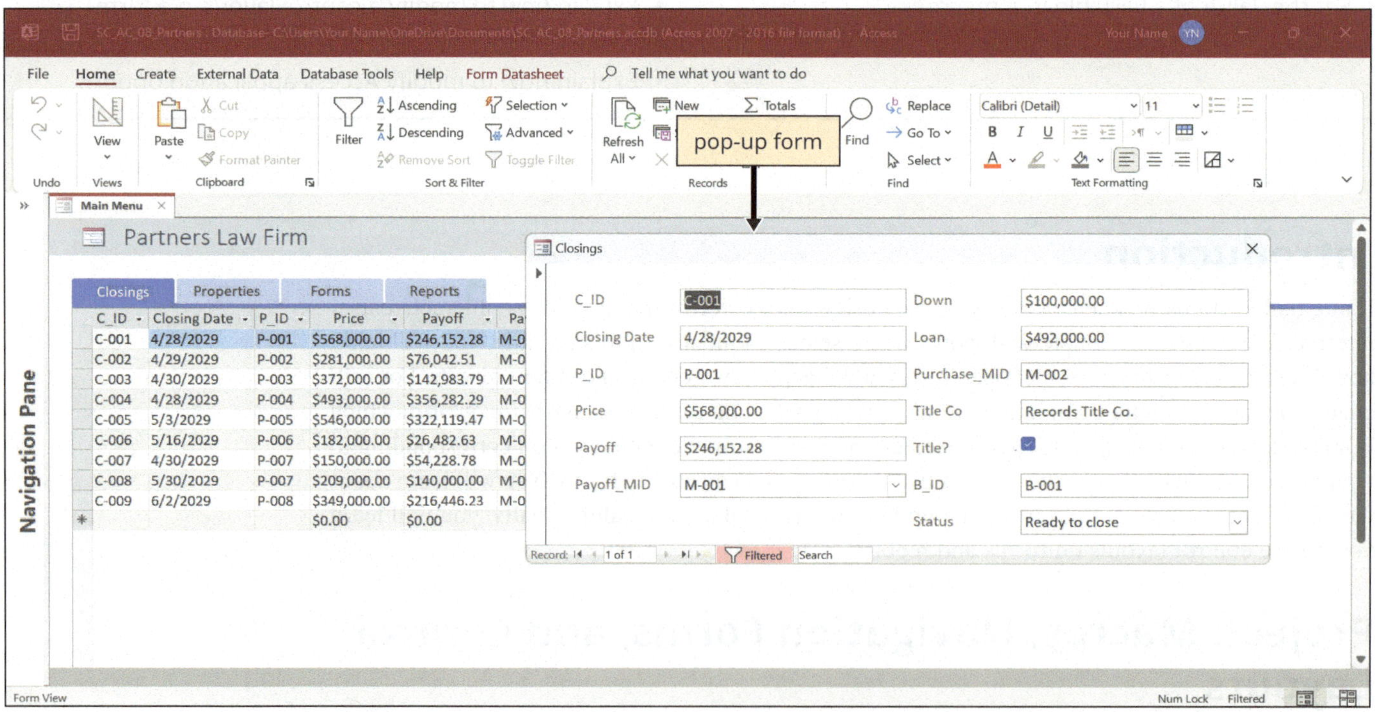

Figure 8–1b Pop-up Form Displaying Closing Data

Clicking the Properties tab of the navigation form displays a single property's data. As with closings, clicking the property number on any record displays data for that property in a pop-up form.

Clicking the Forms tab in the Partners navigation form displays a button for each of the available forms (Figure 8–1c). You can open the desired form by clicking the appropriate button.

Clicking the Reports tab displays an option group for previewing and exporting actions (Figure 8–1d). You can preview or export any of the reports one at a time by clicking the corresponding option button.

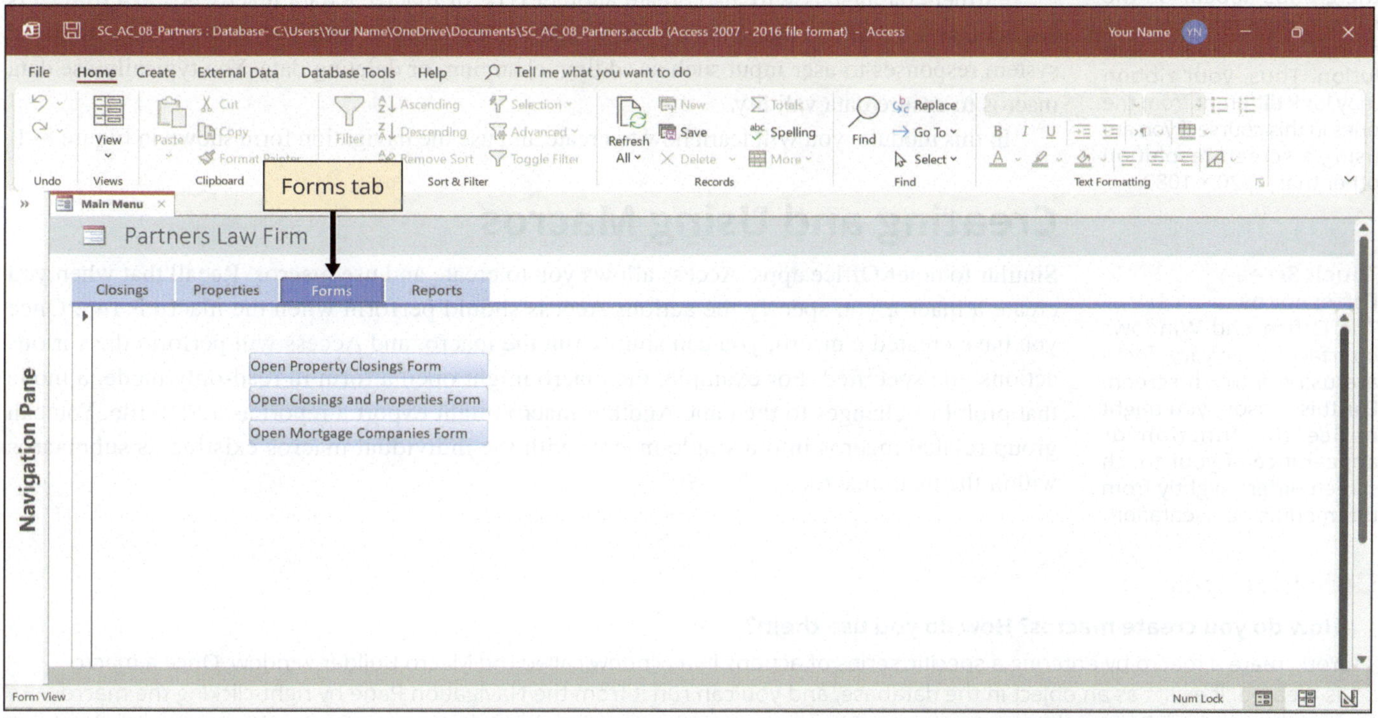

Figure 8–1c Buttons to Display Forms

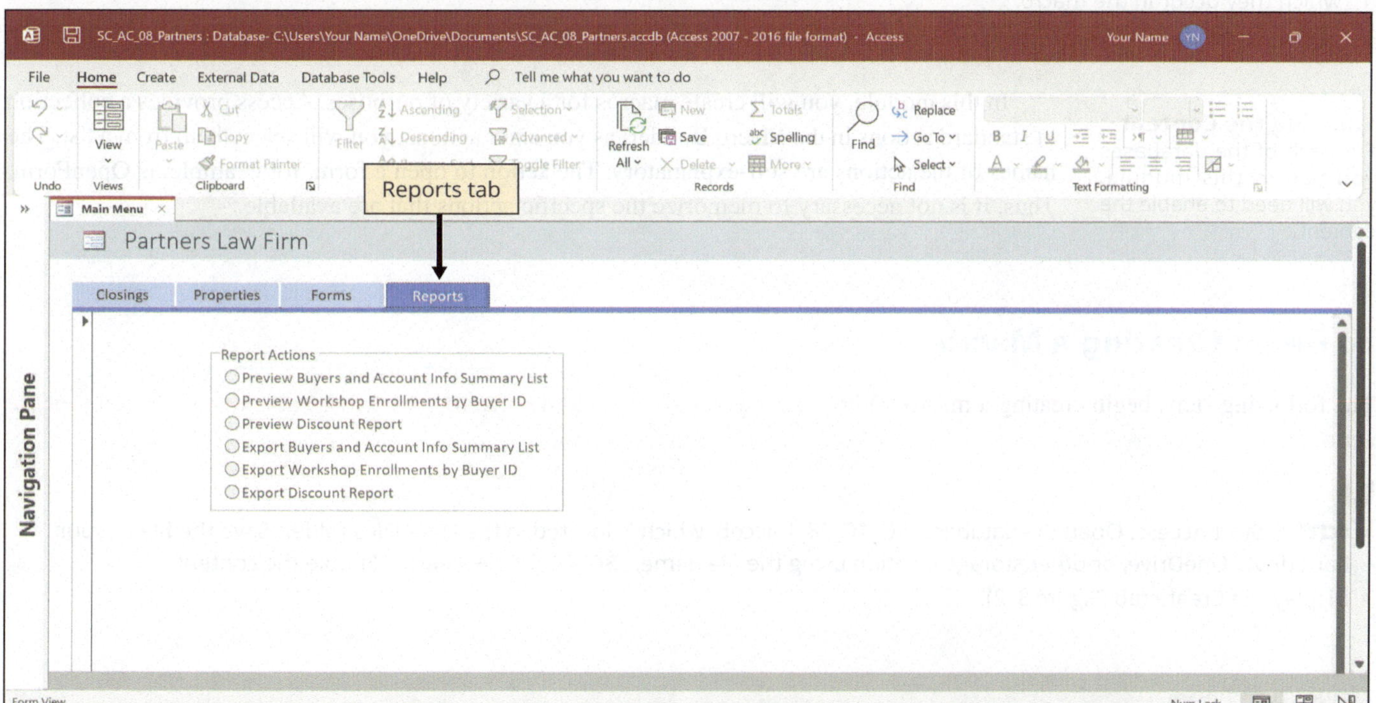

Figure 8–1d Option Group to Display or Export Reports

BTW
The Ribbon and Screen Resolution
Access may change how the groups and buttons within the groups appear on the ribbon, depending on the computer's screen resolution. Thus, your ribbon may look different from the ones in this course if you are using a screen resolution other than 1920 × 1080.

BTW
Touch Screen Differences
The Office and Windows interfaces may vary if you are using a touch screen. For this reason, you might notice the function or appearance of your touch screen differs slightly from this module's presentation.

Before creating the navigation form, Partners paralegals will create macros, collections of actions designed to carry out specific tasks. Recall that to perform the actions in a macro, you run the macro. When you run a macro, Access will execute the various steps, called **actions**, in the order indicated by the macro. You run the navigation form macros by clicking certain buttons in the form.

Partners paralegals will also create another type of macro, a data macro. A **data macro** is a special type of macro that enables you to add coding logic to table events—that is, automated system responses to user input such as adding, changing, or deleting data. You typically use data macros to ensure data validity.

In this module, you will learn how to create and use the navigation form shown in Figure 8–1.

Creating and Using Macros

Similar to other Office apps, Access allows you to create and use macros. Recall that when you create a macro, you specify the actions Access should perform when the macro is run. Once you have created a macro, you can simply run the macro, and Access will perform the various actions you specified. For example, the macro might open a form in read-only mode, a mode that prohibits changes to the data. Another macro might export a report as a PDF file. You can group related macros into a single macro, with the individual macros existing as submacros within the main macro.

Consider This

How do you create macros? How do you use them?

You create a macro by entering a specific series of actions in a window called the Macro Builder window. Once a macro is created, it exists as an object in the database, and you can run it from the Navigation Pane by right-clicking the macro and then clicking Run on the shortcut menu. Macros can also be associated with buttons on forms. When you click the corresponding button on the form, Access will run the macro and complete the corresponding action. Whether a macro is run from the Navigation Pane or from a form, the effect is the same: Access will execute the actions in the order in which they occur in the macro.

BTW
Enabling the Content
For each of the databases you use in this module, you will need to enable the content.

In this module, you will create macros for a variety of purposes. Access provides a collection of standard actions in the Macro Builder; as you enter actions, you will select them from a list. The names of the actions are self-explanatory. The action to open a form, for example, is OpenForm. Thus, it is not necessary to memorize the specific actions that are available.

To Begin Creating a Macro

The following steps begin creating a macro. **Why?** Once you have created the macro, you will be able to add the appropriate actions.

1

- sam Start Access. Open the database, SC_AC_08-1.accdb, which is located in the Data Files folder. Save the file to your hard drive, OneDrive, or other storage location using the file name, **SC_AC_08_Partners**. Enable the content.
- Display the Create tab (Figure 8–2).

BTW
Navigation Pane
As you work, you often need to open the Navigation Pane to view and select objects such as tables, forms, and reports. You may want to close the pane to make more room on the screen or to ensure your screen matches the figures in this course. Open the Navigation Pane as necessary to open an object when instructed, and then close or leave the pane open to suit your preferences.

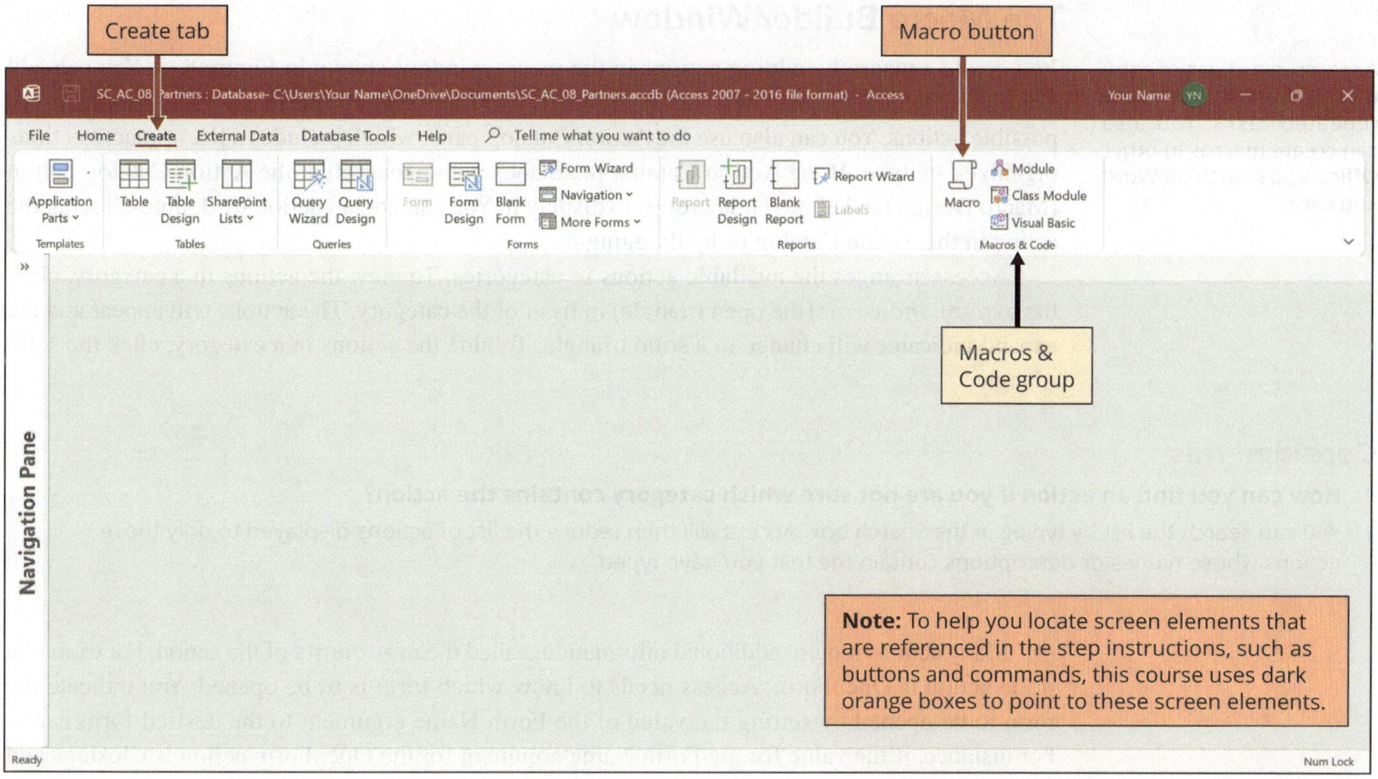

Figure 8–2

2

- Click the Macro button (Create tab | Macros & Code group) to create a new macro.
- If necessary, click the Action Catalog button (Macro Design tab | Show/Hide group) to display the Action Catalog pane (Figure 8–3).

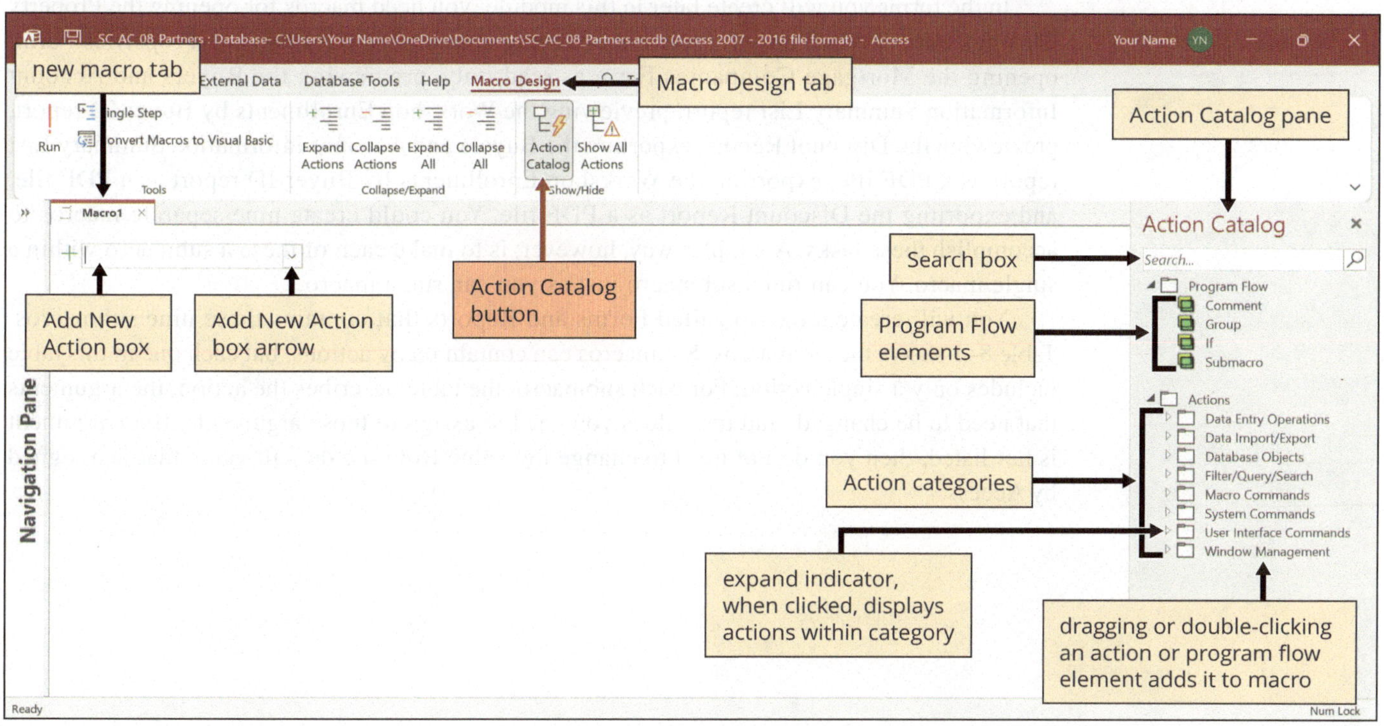

Figure 8–3

BTW
Macros
A macro is a series of commands used to automate repeated tasks. You also can create macros in other Office apps, such as Word and Excel.

The Macro Builder Window

You create a macro by adding actions in the macro window, shown in Figure 8–3. You can add actions by clicking the Add New Action box arrow and selecting the desired action from the list of possible actions. You can also use the Action Catalog pane, which includes a list of macro actions organized by type. If the Action Catalog pane does not appear, click the Action Catalog button (Macro Design tab | Show/Hide group) to display it. You can add an action by double-clicking the action in the Action Catalog or by dragging it.

Access arranges the available actions in categories. To view the actions in a category, click the **expand indicator** (the open triangle) in front of the category. The actions will appear and the expand indicator will change to a solid triangle. To hide the actions in a category, click the solid triangle.

Consider This

How can you find an action if you are not sure which category contains the action?

You can search the list by typing in the Search box. Access will then reduce the list of actions displayed to only those actions whose names or descriptions contain the text you have typed.

Many actions require additional information, called the **arguments** of the action. For example, if the action is OpenForm, Access needs to know which form is to be opened. You indicate the form to be opened by setting the value of the Form Name argument to the desired form name. For instance, if the value for the Form Name argument for the OpenForm action is Closings and Properties Form, then Access will open the Closings and Properties form when it executes this action.

Actions can have more than one argument. For example, in addition to the Form Name argument, the OpenForm action also has a Data Mode argument. If the value of the Data Mode argument is Read Only, then the form will be opened in read-only mode, which indicates users will be able to read, or view, data but not change it. When you select an action, the arguments will appear along with the action, and you can make any necessary changes to them.

In the forms you will create later in this module, you need macros for opening the Property Closings Form as read-only (to prevent updates), opening the Closings and Properties Form, opening the Mortgage Companies Form as read-only, previewing the Buyers and Account Information Summary List report, previewing the Workshop Enrollments by Buyer ID report, previewing the Discount Report, exporting the Buyers and Account Information Summary List report as a PDF file, exporting the Workshop Enrollments by Buyer ID report as a PDF file, and exporting the Discount Report as a PDF file. You could create nine separate macros to accomplish these tasks. A simpler way, however, is to make each of these a submacro within a single macro. You can run a submacro just as you can run a macro.

You will create a macro called Forms and Reports that contains these nine submacros. Table 8–1 shows the submacros. Submacros can contain many actions, but each one in this table includes only a single action. For each submacro, the table describes the action, the arguments that need to be changed, and the values you need to assign to those arguments. If an argument is not listed, then you do not need to change the value from the default value that is assigned by Access.

Table 8–1 Forms and Reports Macro

Submacro	Action	Arguments to Be Changed
Open Property Closings Form		
	OpenForm	Form Name: Property Closings Form Data Mode: Read Only
Open Closings and Properties Form		
	OpenForm	Form Name: Closings and Properties Form
Open Mortgage Companies Form		
	OpenForm	Form Name: Mortgage Companies Form Data Mode: Read Only
Preview Buyers and Account Information Summary List		
	OpenReport	Report Name: Buyers and Account Information Summary List View: Print Preview
Preview Workshop Enrollments by Buyer ID		
	OpenReport	Report Name: Workshop Enrollments by Buyer ID View: Print Preview
Preview Discount Report		
	OpenReport	Report Name: Discount Report View: Print Preview
Export Buyers and Account Information Summary List		
	ExportWithFormatting	Object Type: Report Object Name: Buyers and Account Information Summary List Output Format: PDF Format (*.pdf)
Export Workshop Enrollments by Buyer ID		
	ExportWithFormatting	Object Type: Report Object Name: Workshop Enrollments by Buyer ID Output Format: PDF Format (*.pdf)
Export Discount Report		
	ExportWithFormatting	Object Type: Report Object Name: Discount Report Output Format: PDF Format (*.pdf)

To Add an Action to a Macro

To continue creating the Forms and Reports macro, enter the actions on the Macro tab. In these steps, you will enter actions by double-clicking the action in the Action Catalog. **Why?** The actions in the Action Catalog are organized by function, making it easier to locate the action you want. Access will add the action to the Add New Action box. If more than one Add New Action box is displayed, you need to ensure the one where you want to add the action is selected before you double-click.

The following steps add the first action. They also make the necessary changes to any arguments. Finally, the steps save the macro.

1

- Double-click the Submacro element from the Program Flow section of the Action Catalog to add a submacro, and then type **Open Property Closings Form** as the name of the submacro (Figure 8–4).

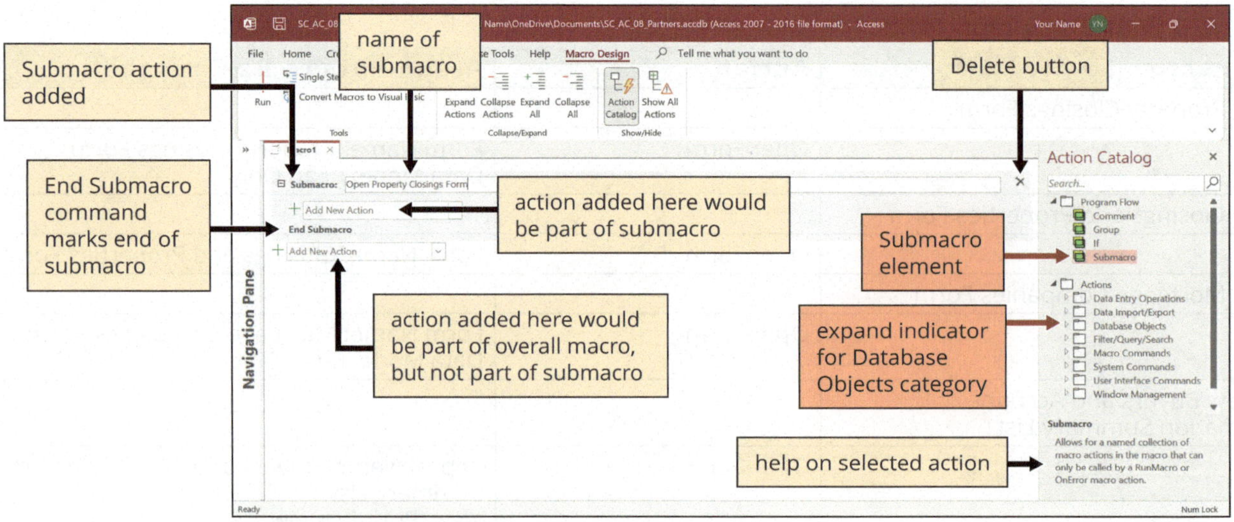

Figure 8–4

Q&A How can I tell the purpose of the various actions in the Action Catalog?

If necessary, expand the category containing the action so the action appears. Point to the action. An expanded ScreenTip will appear, giving you a description of the action.

2

- Click the expand indicator for the Database Objects category of actions to display the actions within the category.
- Double-click the OpenForm action to add it to the submacro (Figure 8–5).

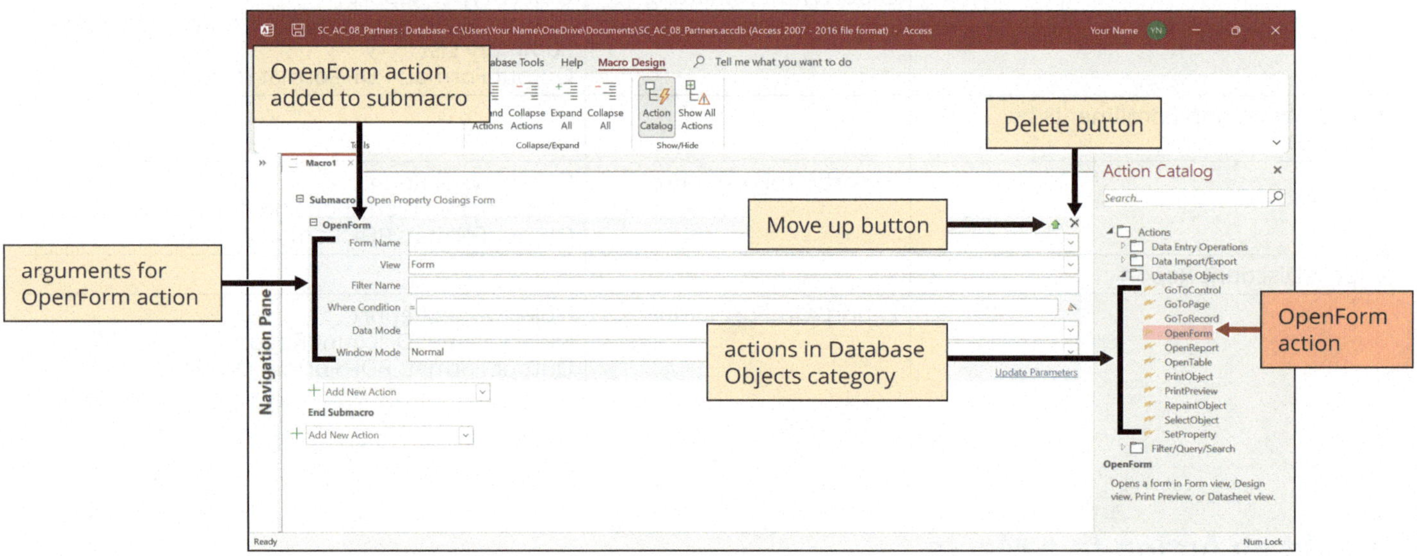

Figure 8–5

BTW

Program Flow Actions

Actions in the Program Flow category can change the order in which macro actions are executed or help structure a macro.

BTW

Touch and Pointers

Remember that if you are using your finger on a touch screen, the pointer or ScreenTips will not appear.

Q&A What should I do if I add an action in the wrong position? What should I do if I add the wrong action?

If you add an action in the wrong position, use the Move up or Move down buttons to move it to the correct position. If you add the wrong action, click the Delete button to delete the action, and then add the correct action.

3

- Click the drop-down arrow for the Form Name argument, and then select Property Closings Form as the name of the form to be opened.
- Click the drop-down arrow for the Data Mode argument, and then select Read Only to specify that users cannot change the data in the form (Figure 8–6).

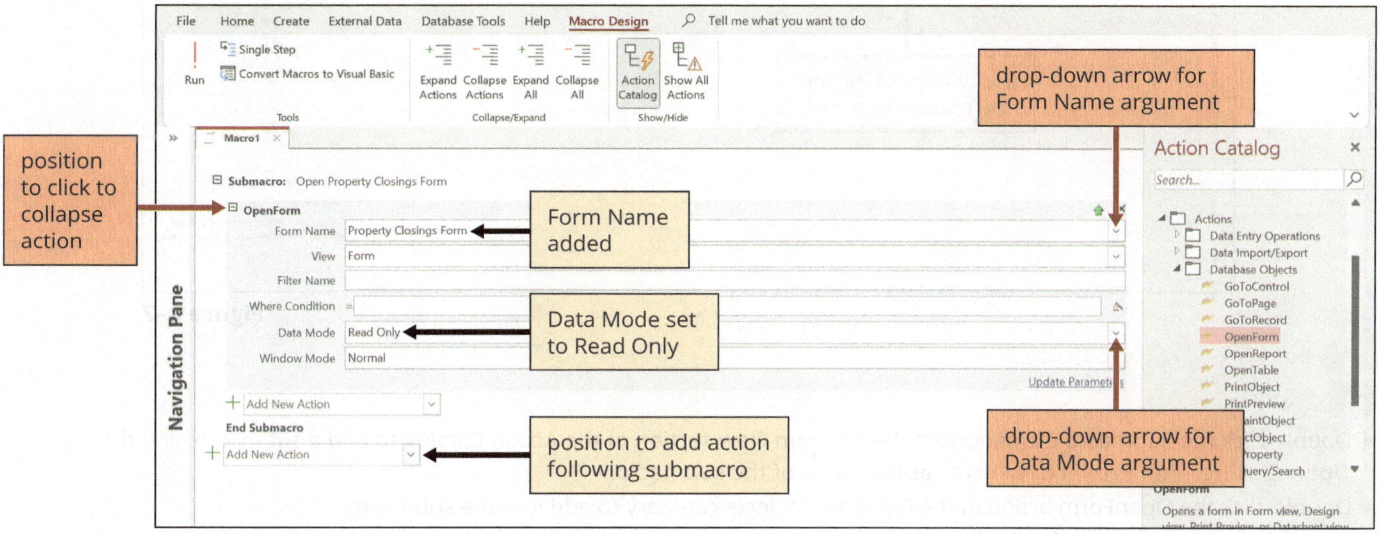

Figure 8–6

Q&A What is the effect of each of the other Data Mode options?
The Add option allows viewing records and adding new records, but not updating records. The Edit option allows viewing records, adding new records, and updating existing records.

4

- Click the Save button on the Quick Access Toolbar, type **Forms and Reports** as the name of the macro, and then click OK to save the macro.

To Add More Actions to a Macro

To complete the macro, you need to add the additional actions shown in Table 8–1. You add the additional actions just as you added the first action. Initially, Access displays all the actions you have added with their arguments clearly visible. After you have added several actions, you might want to collapse some or all of the actions. **Why?** Collapsing actions makes it easier to get an overall view of your macro. You can always expand any action later to view details concerning the arguments. The following steps add additional actions to a macro, collapsing existing actions when necessary to provide a better view of the overall macro structure.

1

- Click the minus sign (–) in front of the OpenForm action to collapse the action (Figure 8–7).

Q&A Could I also use the buttons on the ribbon?
Yes, you can use the buttons in the Collapse/Expand group on the Macro Design tab. Click the Expand Actions button to expand the selected action, or click the Collapse Actions button to collapse the selected action. You can expand all actions at once by clicking the Expand All button, or you can collapse all actions at once by clicking the Collapse All button.

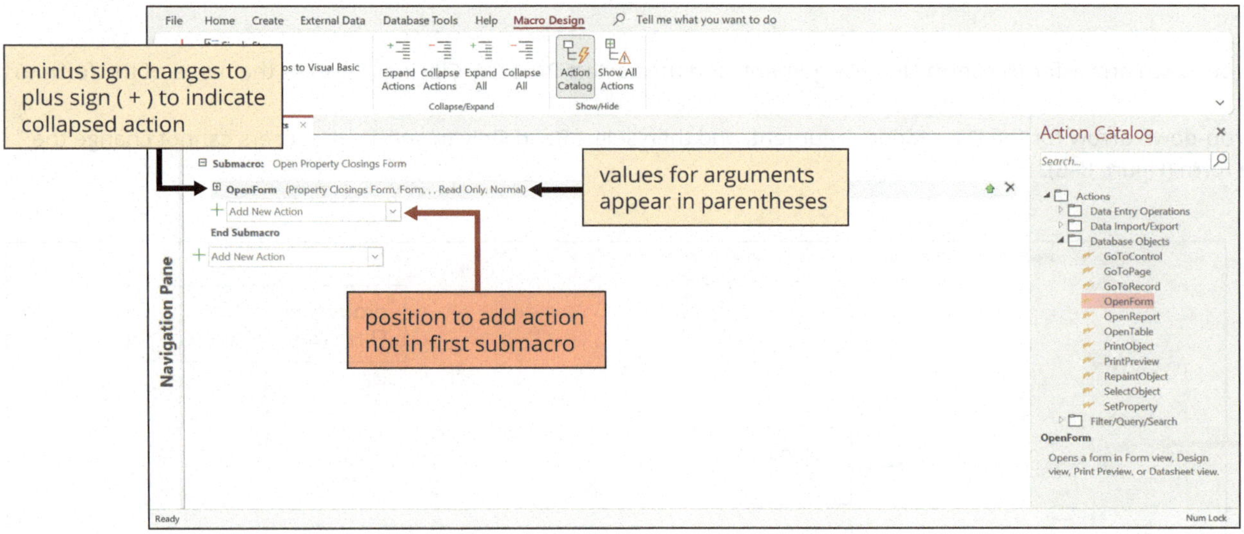

Figure 8–7

2

- Double-click the Submacro element from the Program Flow section of the Action Catalog to add a submacro, and then type **Open Closings and Properties Form** as the name of the submacro.
- Double-click the OpenForm action in the Database Objects category to add it to the submacro.
- Click the drop-down arrow for the Form Name argument, and then select Closings and Properties Form.
- Double-click the Submacro element again to create a third submacro, and then type **Open Mortgage Companies Form** as the name of the new submacro.
- Add the OpenForm action to the submacro.
- Select Mortgage Companies Form as the value for the Form Name argument.
- Set the Data Mode to Read Only and, if necessary, set Window Mode to Normal (Figure 8–8).

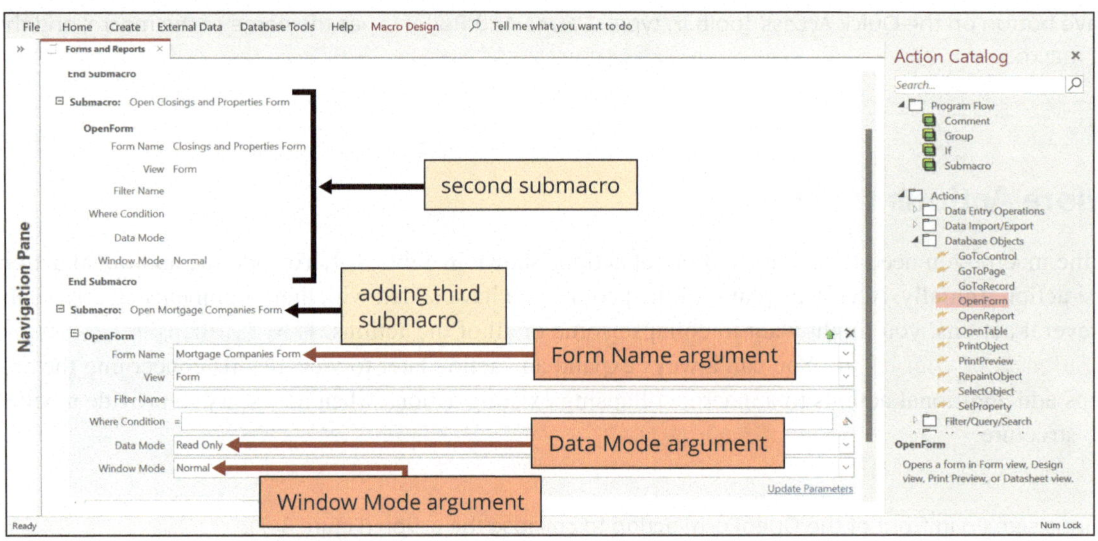

Figure 8–8

Q&A Do I have to change the values of any of the other arguments?
No. The default values that Access sets are appropriate.

3

- For each of the three new submacros, click the minus sign in front of it to collapse the submacro.
- Add a submacro named **Preview Buyers and Account Information Summary List**.

- Add the OpenReport action, which is located in the Database Objects category, to the submacro.
- Select Buyers and Account Information Summary List as the report name.
- Select Print Preview as the view (Figure 8–9).

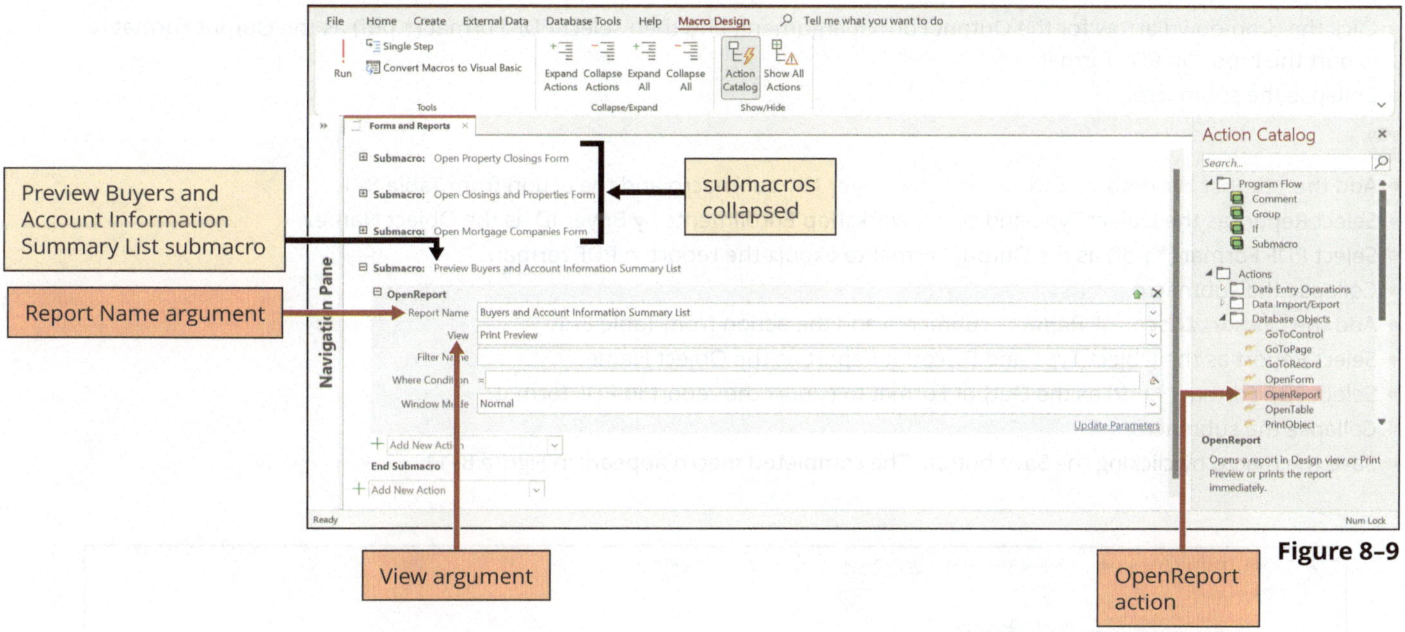

Figure 8–9

4

- Collapse the Preview Buyers and Account Information Summary List submacro.
- Add the **Preview Workshop Enrollments by Buyer ID** submacro. Include the action described in Table 8–1. The report name is Workshop Enrollments by Buyer ID and the view is Print Preview. Collapse the submacro.
- Add the **Preview Discount Report** submacro. Include the action described in Table 8–1. The report name is Discount Report and the view is Print Preview. Collapse the submacro.
- Click the triangle to the left of Database Objects in the Action Catalog to collapse the Database Objects category, and then click the expand indicator for the Data Import/Export category.
- Add a submacro called **Export Buyers and Account Information Summary List**.
- Add the ExportWithFormatting action, which will export and maintain any special formatting in the process.
- Click the drop-down arrow for the Object Type argument to display a list of possible object types (Figure 8–10).

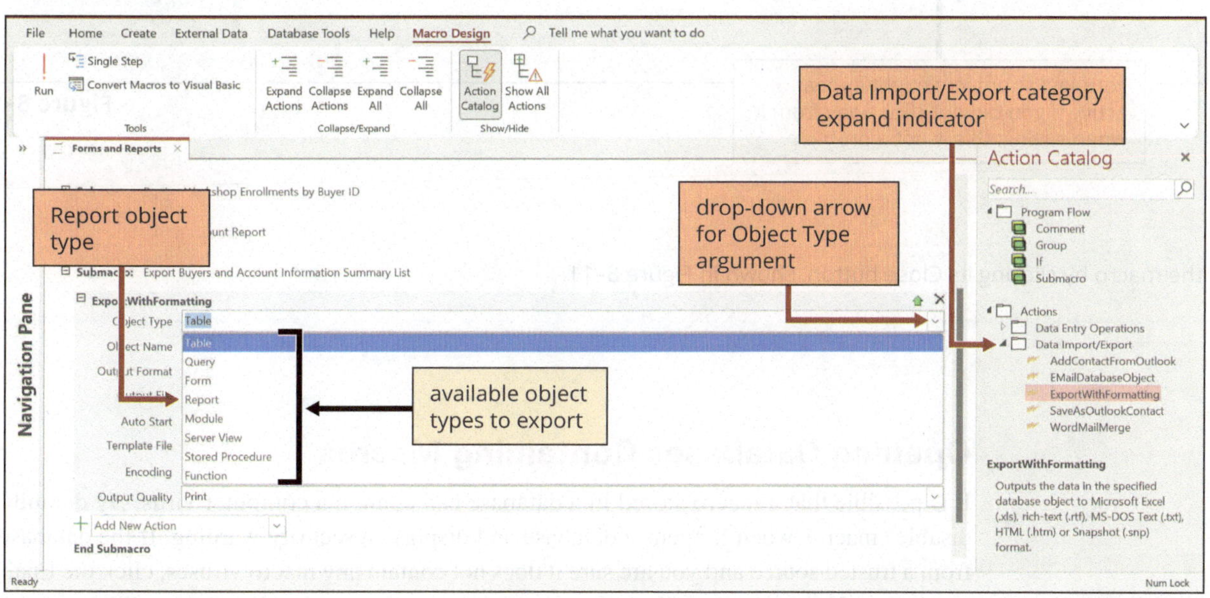

Figure 8–10

5

- Click Report in the list to indicate Access is to export a report.
- Click the drop-down arrow for the Object Name argument, and then select Buyers and Account Information Summary List as the object name.
- Click the drop-down arrow for the Output Format argument, and then select PDF Format (*.pdf) as the Output Format to export the report in PDF format.
- Collapse the submacro.

6

- Add the **Export Workshop Enrollments by Buyer ID** submacro and the action from Table 8–1.
- Select Report as the Object Type and select Workshop Enrollments by Buyer ID as the Object Name.
- Select PDF Format (*.pdf) as the Output Format to export the report in PDF format.
- Collapse the submacro.
- Add the **Export Discount Report** submacro and the action from Table 8–1.
- Select Report as the Object Type and Discount Report as the Object Name.
- Select PDF Format (*.pdf) as the Output Format to export the report in PDF format.
- Collapse the submacro.
- Save the macro by clicking the Save button. The completed macro appears in Figure 8–11.

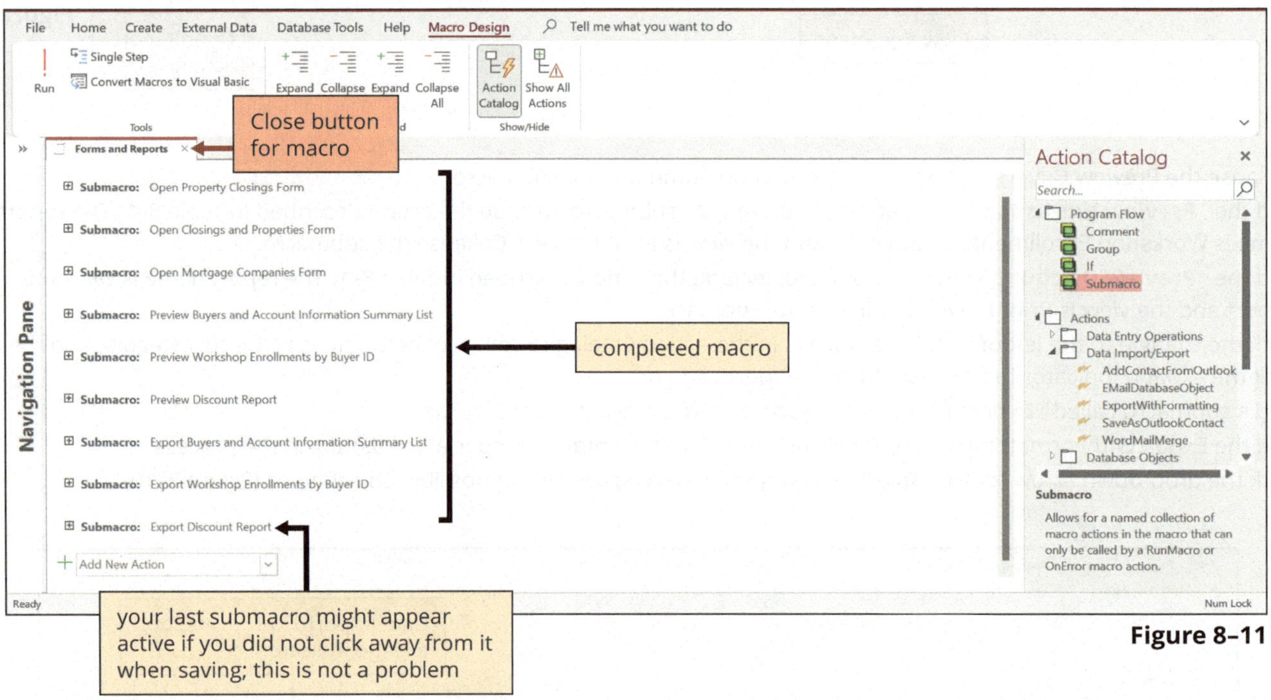

Figure 8–11

7

- Close the macro by clicking its Close button, shown in Figure 8–11.

Opening Databases Containing Macros

It is possible that a macro stored in a database can contain a computer virus. By default, Access disables macros when it opens a database and displays a security warning. If the database comes from a trusted source and you are sure it does not contain any macro viruses, click the Enable Content button. You can make adjustments to Access security settings by clicking File on the ribbon to open Backstage view, and then clicking Options to display the Access Options dialog box, clicking Trust Center, clicking Trust Center Settings, and then clicking Macro Settings.

Errors in Macros

Macros can contain errors. The macro might open the wrong table or produce a wrong message. If you have problems with a macro, you can **single-step the macro**, that is, proceed through a macro one step at a time in Design view.

Figure 8–12 shows a macro open in Design view. This macro first has an action to open the Closings table in Datasheet view in Read Only mode. It then changes the view to Print Preview. Next, it opens the Closings table in Datasheet view, this time in Edit mode. Finally, it opens the Properties Query in Datasheet view in Edit mode. The macro in the figure is a common type of macro that opens several objects at once. To open all these objects, the user only runs the macro. Unfortunately, this macro contains an error. The name of the Closings table is written as "Closing" in the second OpenTable action.

BTW

Converting a Macro to VBA Code

If you want to use many of the resources provided by Windows or communicate with another Windows app, you will need to convert any macros to VBA (Visual Basic for Applications) code. To convert a macro to VBA code, open the macro in Design view and click the 'Convert Macros to Visual Basic' button (Macro Design tab | Tools group). When the Convert Macro dialog box appears, select the appropriate options, and then click Convert.

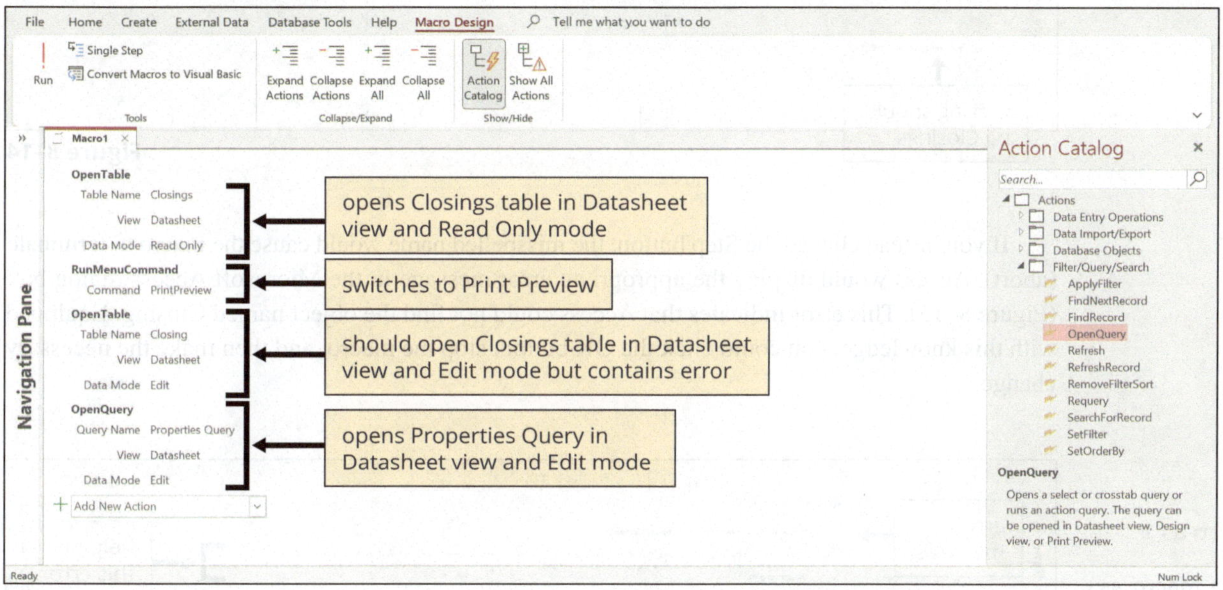

Figure 8–12

To run this macro in single-step mode, you would first save the macro and then click the Single Step button (Macro Design tab | Tools group). You would next click the Run button (Macro Design tab | Tools group) to run the macro. Because you clicked the Single Step button, Access would display the Macro Single Step dialog box (Figure 8–13). The dialog box shows the action

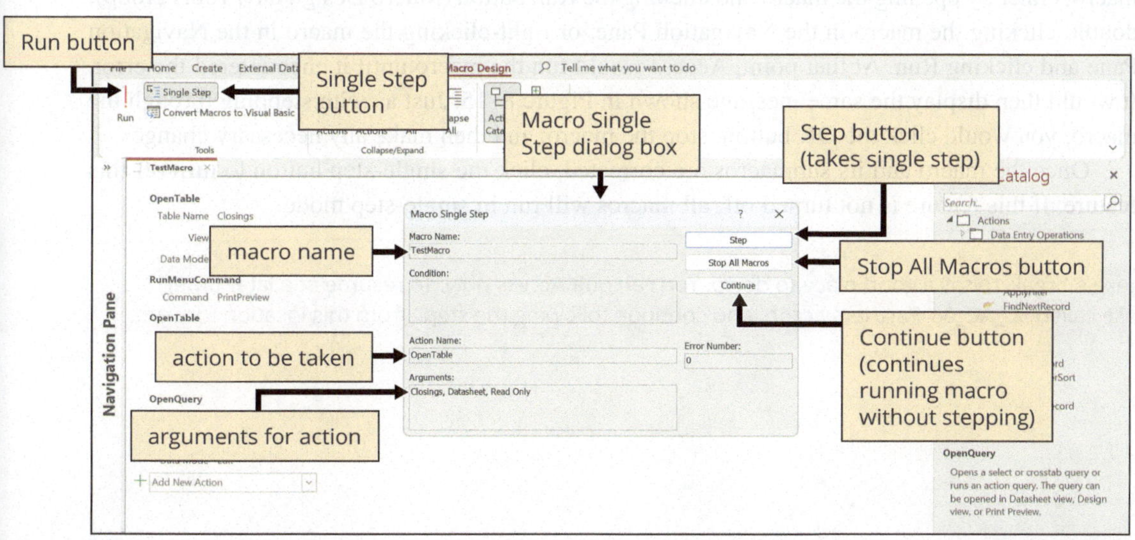

Figure 8–13

to be executed and the values of the various arguments. You can click the Step button to proceed to the next step.

With this macro, after you clicked the Step button twice, you would arrive at the screen shown in Figure 8–14. Access is about to execute the OpenTable command. The arguments are Closing, Datasheet, and Edit. At this point, you might spot the fact that "Closing" is misspelled. It should be "Closings" instead. If so, you could click the 'Stop All Macros' button and then correct the object name.

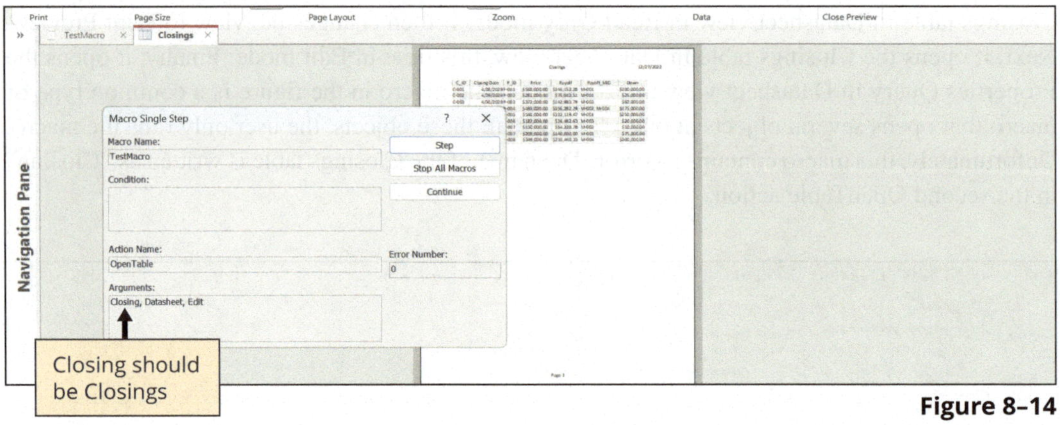

Figure 8–14

If you instead clicked the Step button, the misspelled name would cause the macro to terminate (abort). Access would display the appropriate error message in the Microsoft Access dialog box (Figure 8–15). This error indicates that Access could not find the object named Closing. Equipped with this knowledge, you could click the OK button, stop the macro, and then make the necessary change.

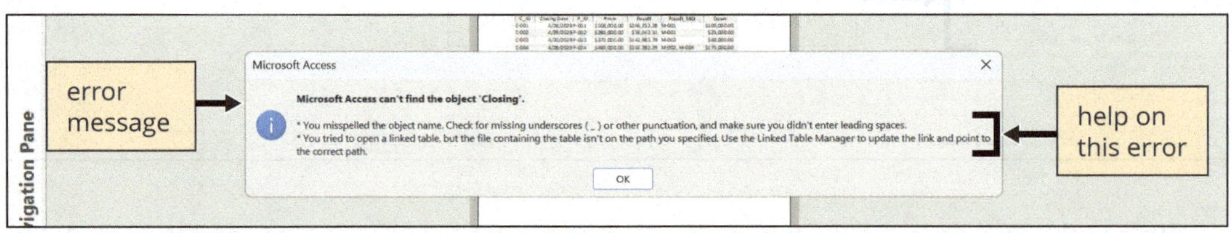

Figure 8–15

BTW

Saving a Macro as a VBA Module

You can save a macro as a VBA module using the Save Object As command in Backstage view. Open the macro in Design view, click File on the ribbon to open Backstage view, and then click Save As. When the Save As gallery appears, click 'Save Object As' in the File Types area, and then click the Save As button. When the Save As dialog box appears, click Module in the As text box, and then click the OK button.

You do not need to step through a macro to discover the error. You could simply run the macro, either by opening the macro and clicking the Run button (Macro Design tab | Tools group), double-clicking the macro in the Navigation Pane, or right-clicking the macro in the Navigation Pane and clicking Run. At that point, Access would run the macro until it encountered the error. It would then display the same message shown in Figure 8–15. Just as with stepping through the macro, you would click the OK button, stop the macro, and then make any necessary changes.

Once the macro and its submacros are corrected, click the single-step button to turn off this feature. If this feature is not turned off, all macros will run in single-step mode.

Break Point: If you wish to take a break, this is a good place to do so. You can quit Access now. To resume at a later time, start Access, open the database called SC_AC_08_Partners.accdb, and continue following the steps from this location forward.

Creating and Using a Navigation Form

Figure 8–1a showed a navigation form for Partners. A navigation form is a form that contains a **navigation control**, a control that can display a variety of forms and reports. Like the form in Figure 8–1, navigation controls contain tabs. Clicking a tab displays the corresponding form or report. The tabs can be arranged across the top and/or down the sides.

You can only include forms and reports on these tabs; you cannot include either tables or queries. The navigation form in Figure 8–1 appears to have a tab corresponding to the Closings table, but this is actually a datasheet form based on the Closings table, not the table itself. If you would find it desirable to display tables or queries on a navigation control tab, you can make it appear as though the navigation form contains these objects by creating a datasheet form based on the table or query.

Before creating the navigation form, you need to create some other forms. Partners Law Firm wants users to be able to click a tab in the navigation form and then choose from a list of forms or reports. Figure 8–16 shows a list of forms presented as buttons; these enable the user to simply click a button to open the desired form. Clicking the Open Property Closings Form button, for example, would display the Property Closings Form, as shown in Figure 8–17.

BTW
Navigation Forms
A navigation form often is used as a switchboard or main page for a database to reduce clutter and target the most commonly used database objects. A navigation form contains a navigation control and a subform control. After you create a navigation form, you can use the Navigation Where Clause property associated with a navigation control to automatically apply a filter.

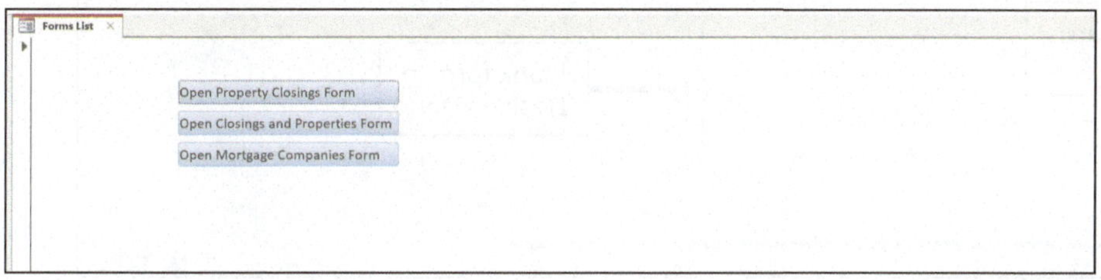

Figure 8–16

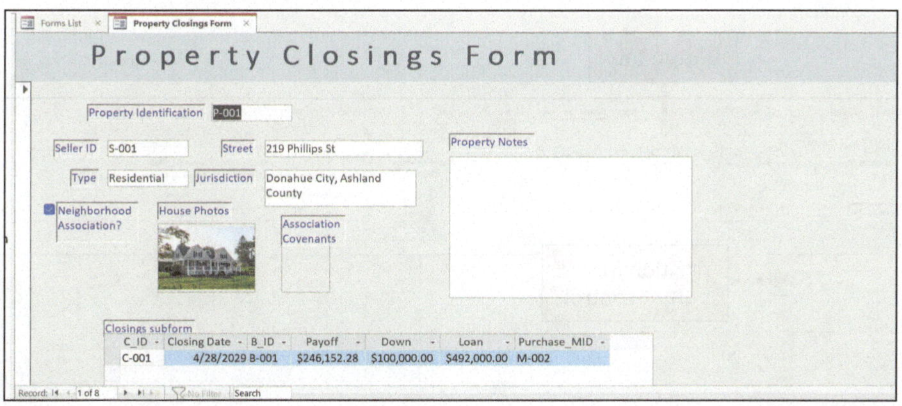

todd kent/Unsplash

Figure 8–17

To implement options like these, you create blank forms and add either command buttons or an option group. You then include the form you have created in the navigation form. When users click the corresponding tab, Access displays the form and users can then click the appropriate button.

To Create a Menu Form Containing Command Buttons

Why? A menu form in which you make a selection by clicking the appropriate command button provides a convenient way to select a desired option. You can create a menu form by adding command buttons to the form. The following steps use this technique to create a menu form with three buttons: Open Property Closings Form, Open Closings and Properties Form, and Open Mortgage Companies Form. The actions assigned to each button will run a macro that causes the desired action to occur. For example, the action for the Open Property Closings Form button will run the Open Property Closings Form submacro, which in turn will open the Property Closings Form.

The following steps create a form in Design view and then add the necessary buttons.

1

- Display the Create tab.
- Click the Form Design button (Create tab | Forms group) to create a blank form in Design view.
- If the Field List pane opens, click the 'Add Existing Fields' button (Form Design tab | Tools group) to close the Field List pane.
- If the Property Sheet pane opens, click the Property Sheet button (Form Design tab | Tools group) to close the Property Sheet pane.
- Confirm the 'Use Control Wizards' option is selected by clicking the More button located in the Controls group (Figure 8–18).

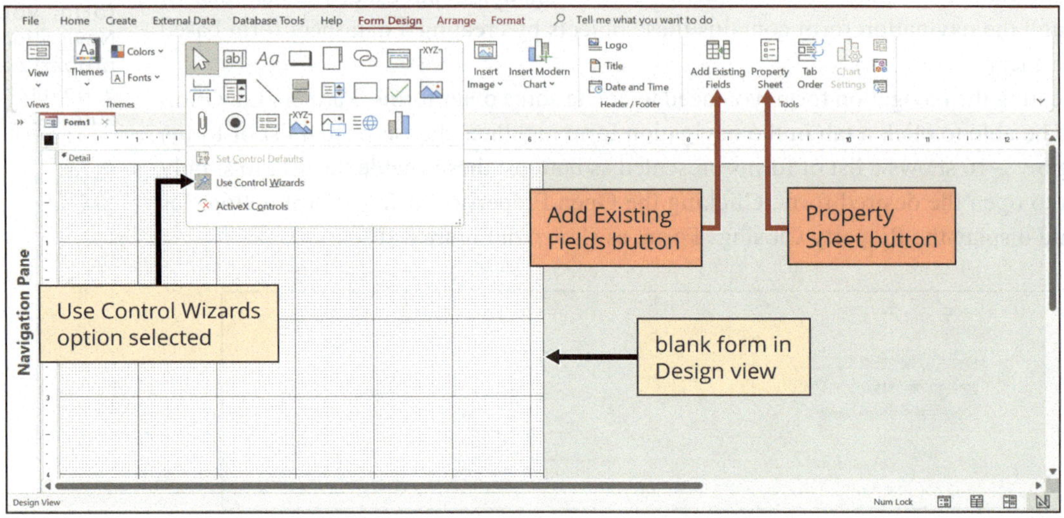

Figure 8–18

2

- Click the Button tool (Form Design tab | Controls group) and move the pointer to the approximate position shown in Figure 8–19.

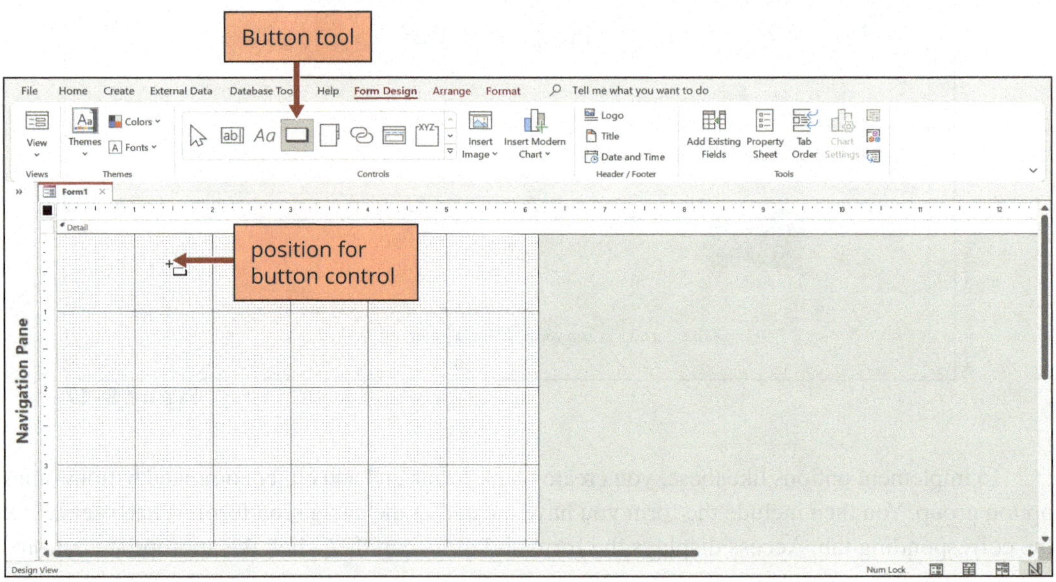

Figure 8–19

3

- Click the position shown in Figure 8–19 to display the Command Button Wizard dialog box.
- Click Miscellaneous in the Categories box, and then click Run Macro in the Actions box (Figure 8–20).

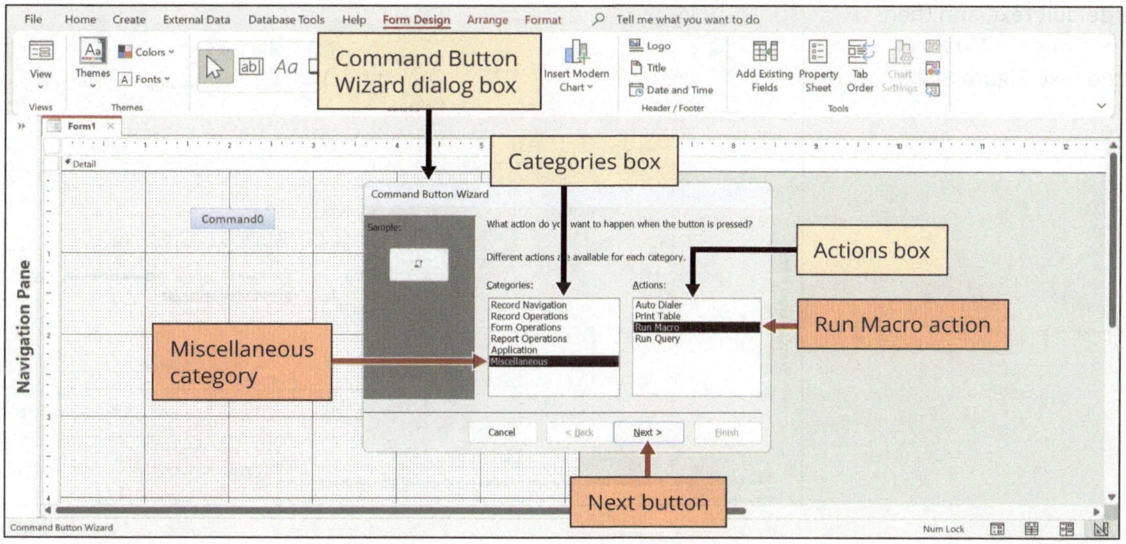

Figure 8–20

4

- Click Next to display the next Command Button Wizard screen.
- Click Forms and Reports. Open Property Closings Form to select the macro to be run (Figure 8–21).

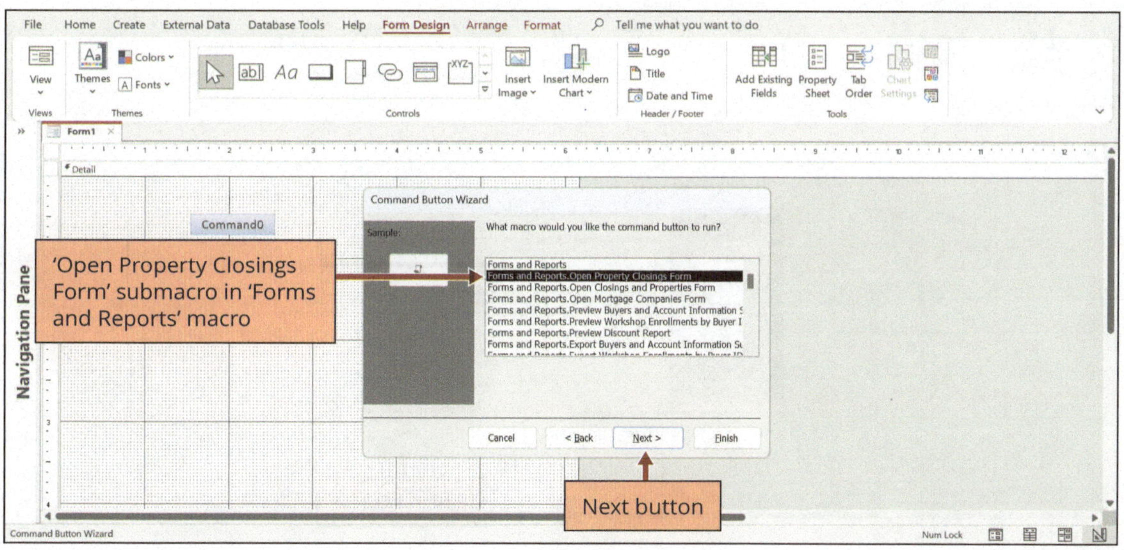

Figure 8–21

Q&A What does this notation mean?
The portion before the period is the macro and the portion after the period is the submacro. Thus, this notation refers to the Open Property Closings Form submacro within the Forms and Reports macro.

5

- Click Next to display the next Command Button Wizard screen.
- Click the Text option button to indicate the button should display explanatory text rather than an image.

Q&A What is the purpose of these option buttons?
Choose the first option button to place text on the button. You can then specify the text to be included or accept the default choice. Choose the second option button to place a picture on the button. You can then select a picture.

- Delete the default text, and then type **Open Property Closings Form** as the text (Figure 8–22).

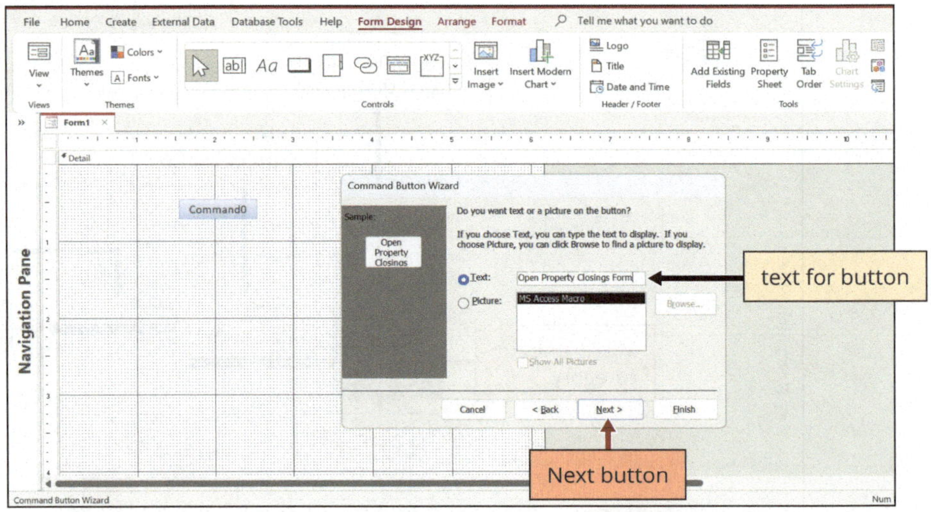

Figure 8–22

6

- Click Next.
- Type **Open_Property_Closings_Form** as the name of the button (Figure 8–23), and then click the Finish button to complete the button control's configuration.

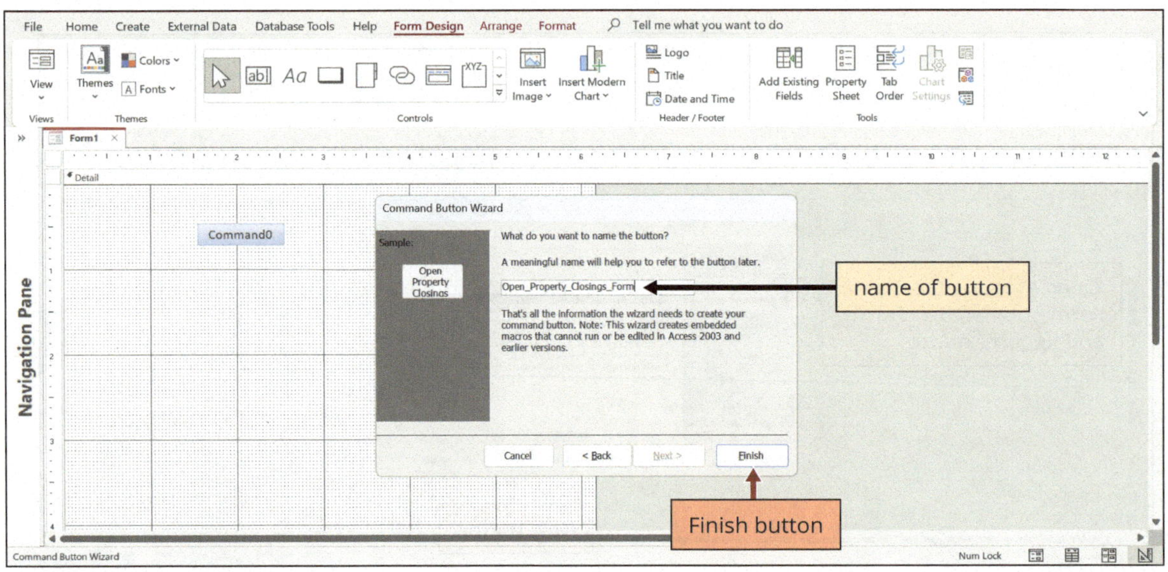

Figure 8–23

Q&A Why do I need to include the underscores in the name of the button?
If you are working with macros or VBA, you cannot have spaces in names. One way to avoid spaces and still make readable names is to include an underscore (_) where you would normally use a space. Thus, Open Property Closings Form becomes Open_Property_Closings_Form.

7

- Use the techniques in Steps 2 through 6 to place the Open Closings and Properties Form button below the Open Property Closings Form button. The only differences are that the macro to be run is the Open Closings and Properties Form submacro, the button text is **Open Closings and Properties Form**, and the name of the button is **Open_Closings_and_Properties_Form**.
- Use the techniques in Steps 2 through 6 to place the Open Mortgage Companies Form button below the Open Closings and Properties Form button. The only differences are that the macro to be run is the Open Mortgage Companies Form submacro, the text is **Open Mortgage Companies Form**, and the name of the button is **Open_Mortgage_Companies_Form**.

8

- Adjust the positions, sizing, and spacing of the buttons to approximately match those in Figure 8–24, using the tools on the Arrange tab. For equal spacing, select all the buttons, click the Size/Space button, and select the Equal Vertical option. To make the buttons the same width, select all the buttons, click the Size/Space button, and select the To Widest option.

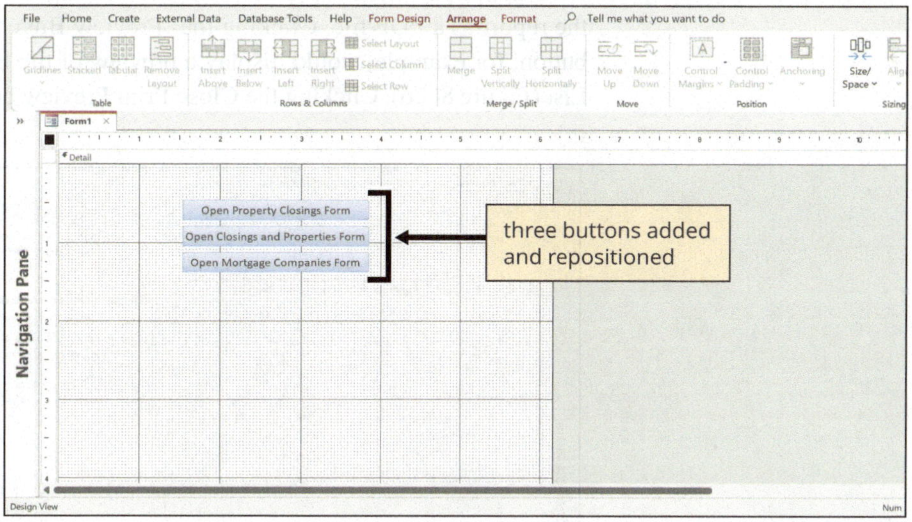

Figure 8–24

9

- Display the Form Design tab, click the Property Sheet button, and then, if necessary, click the Format tab.
- With all three buttons selected, click the Alignment property box (Property Sheet pane) to display an arrow, and then select Left from the list that appears.
- Close the Property Sheet pane.
- Save the form using the name, **Forms List**.
- **Experiment:** Use Form view to test each of the buttons on the form and ensure the correct form opens. If there are errors, correct the corresponding macro.

Q&A How can I test the buttons to make sure the macros work?
Switch to Form view. Click each of the buttons on the form. If there are errors in any of the macros, open the macro in Design view and correct the errors.

10

- Close the form.

Option Groups

You might find it useful to allow users to make a selection from some predefined options by including an option group, a rectangle containing a collection of option buttons. To perform an action, you simply click the corresponding option button. Figure 8–25 shows a list of reports presented

BTW
Viewing VBA Code
You can view VBA code that is attached to a form or report. To do so, open the form or report in Design view and click the View Code button (Report Design tab | Tools group) for reports or the View Code Button (Form Design tab | Tools group) for forms.

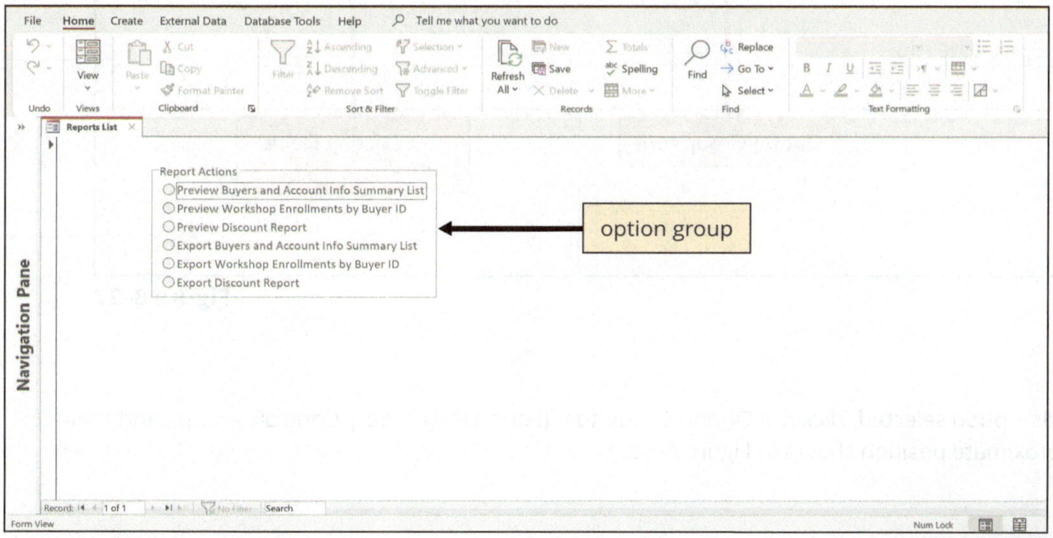

Figure 8–25

in an option group where the user would click the desired option button. Notice the user could click an option button to preview a report. The user could click a different option button to export the report as a PDF file. Clicking the 'Preview Buyers and Account Info Summary List' option button, for example, would display a preview of the Buyers and Account Information Summary List (Figure 8–26). Clicking the Close Print Preview button would return you to the option group.

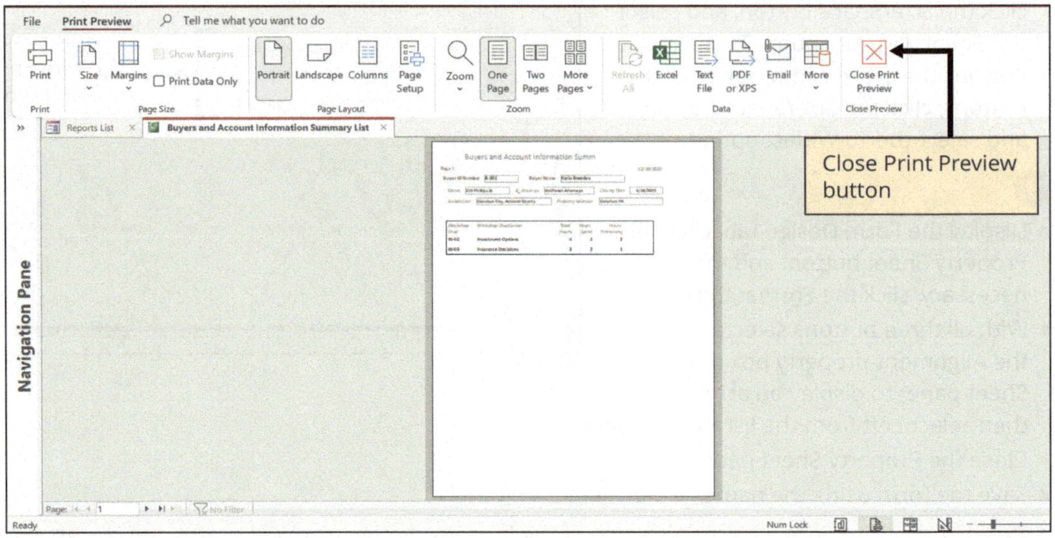

Figure 8–26

To Create a Menu Form Containing an Option Group

The form you are creating will contain an option group. **Why?** The option group allows users to select an option button to indicate either a report to preview or a report to export.

The following steps use the Option Group tool to create the option group named Report Actions.

1

- Display the Create tab.
- Click the Form Design button (Create tab | Forms group) to create a blank form in Design view.
- If a field list appears, click the 'Add Existing Fields' button (Form Design tab | Tools group) to remove the field list (Figure 8–27).

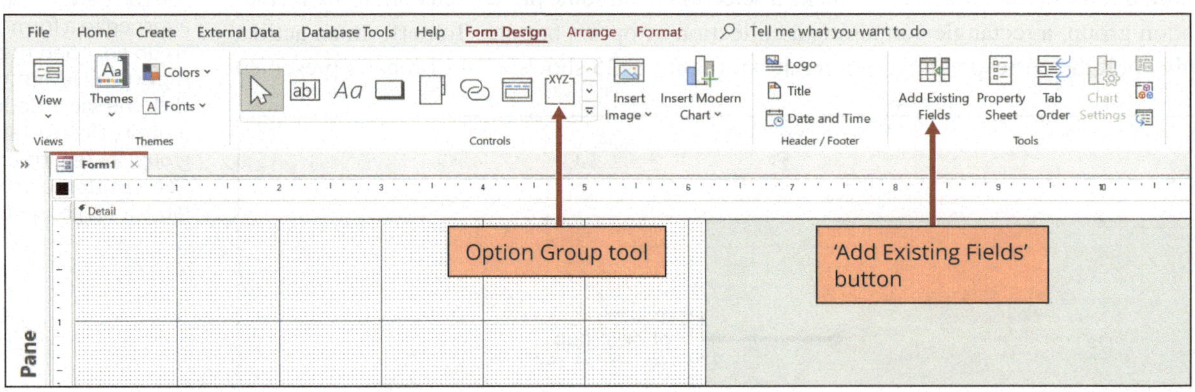

Figure 8–27

2

- With the 'Use Control Wizards' option selected, click the Option Group tool (Form Design tab | Controls group), and then move the pointer to the approximate position shown in Figure 8–28.

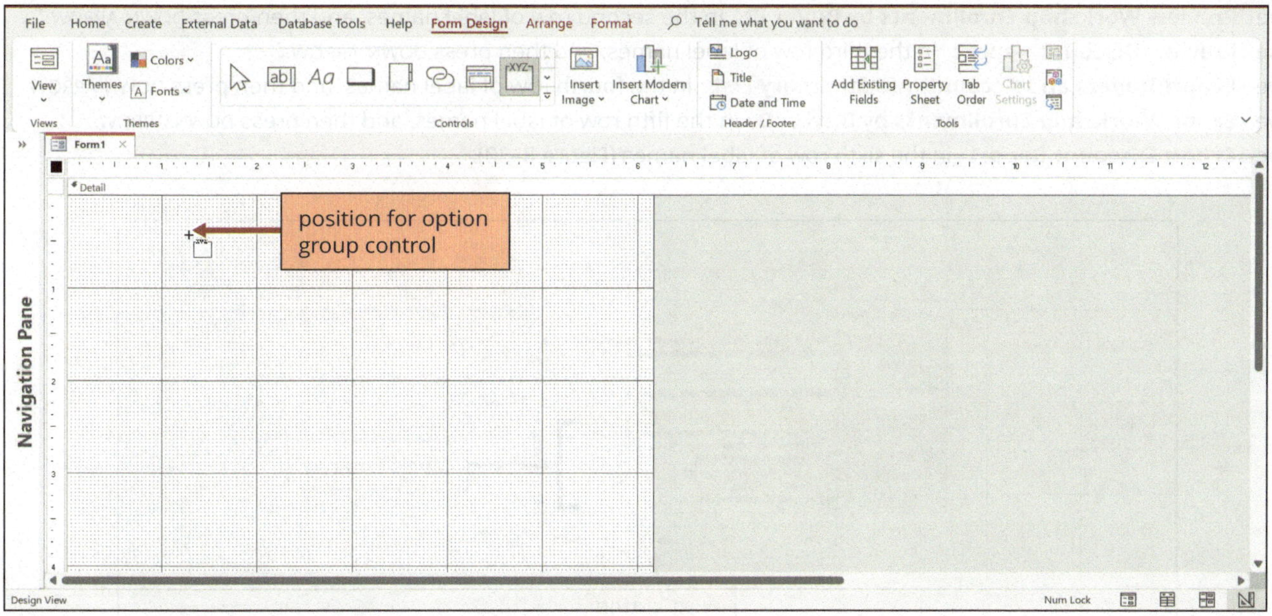

Figure 8–28

3

- Click the position shown in Figure 8–28 to place an option group and start the Option Group Wizard (Figure 8–29).

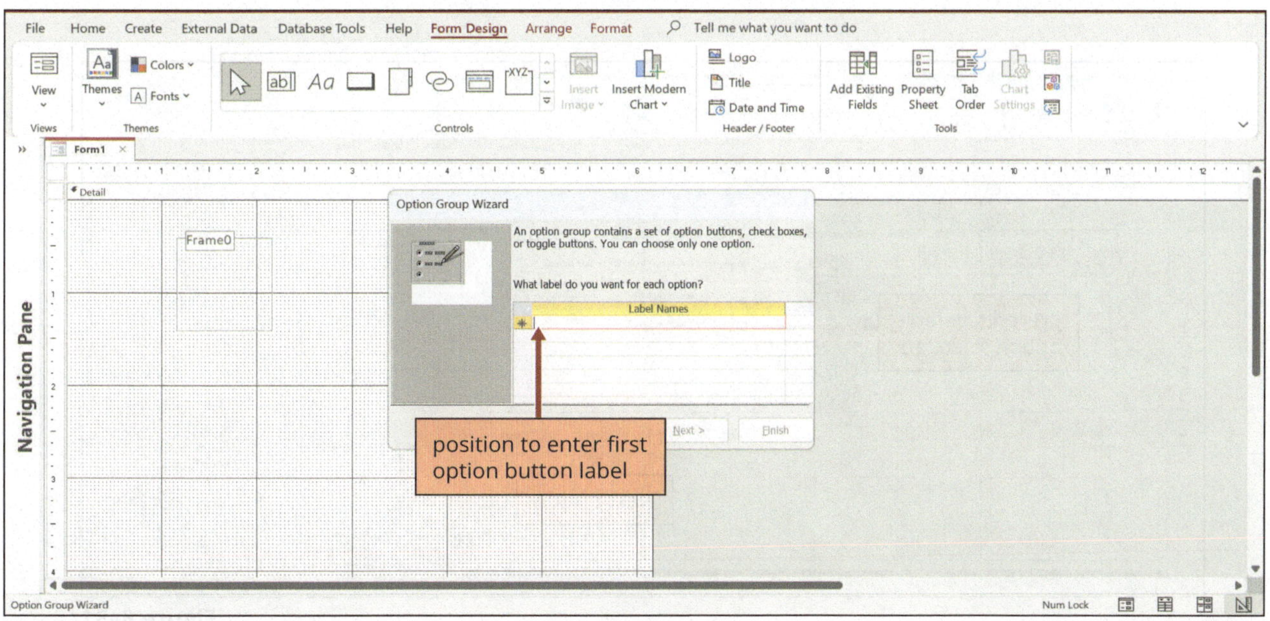

Figure 8–29

Q&A The Option Group Wizard did not start for me. What should I do?

You must not have had the 'Use Control Wizards' option selected. With the option group selected, press delete to delete the option group. Select the 'Use Control Wizards' button, and then add the option group a second time.

- Type **Preview Buyers and Account Info Summary List** in the first row of label names and press DOWN ARROW to specify the label for the first button in the group.

Q&A Why is the name of the form changed?

This form name is abbreviated from Information to Info here because there is not enough room for the entire name.

- Type **Preview Workshop Enrollments by Buyer ID** in the second row of label names, and then press DOWN ARROW.
- Type **Preview Discount Report** in the third row of label names, and then press DOWN ARROW.
- Type **Export Buyers and Account Info Summary List** in the fourth row of label names, and then press DOWN ARROW.
- Type **Export Workshop Enrollments by Buyer ID** in the fifth row of label names, and then press DOWN ARROW.
- Type **Export Discount Report** in the sixth row of label names (Figure 8–30).

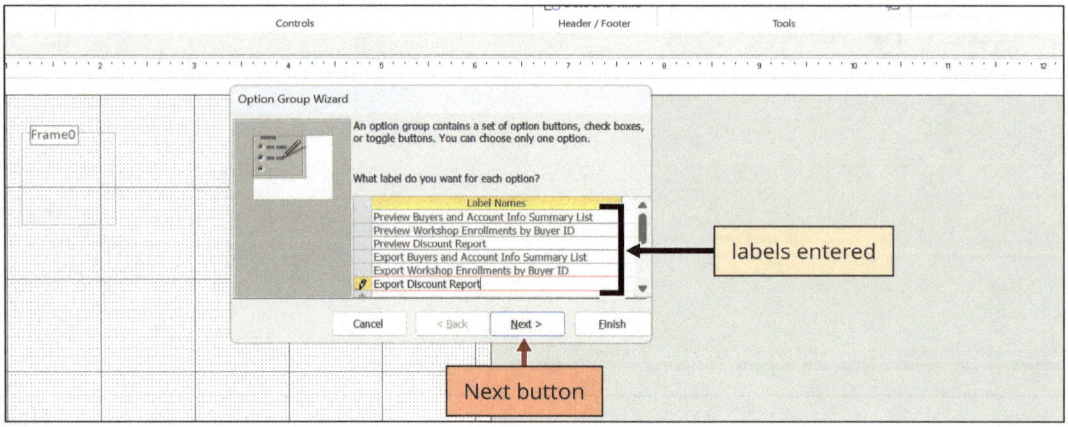

Figure 8–30

4

- Click the Next button to display the next Option Group Wizard screen.
- Click the 'No, I don't want a default.' option button to select it (Figure 8–31).

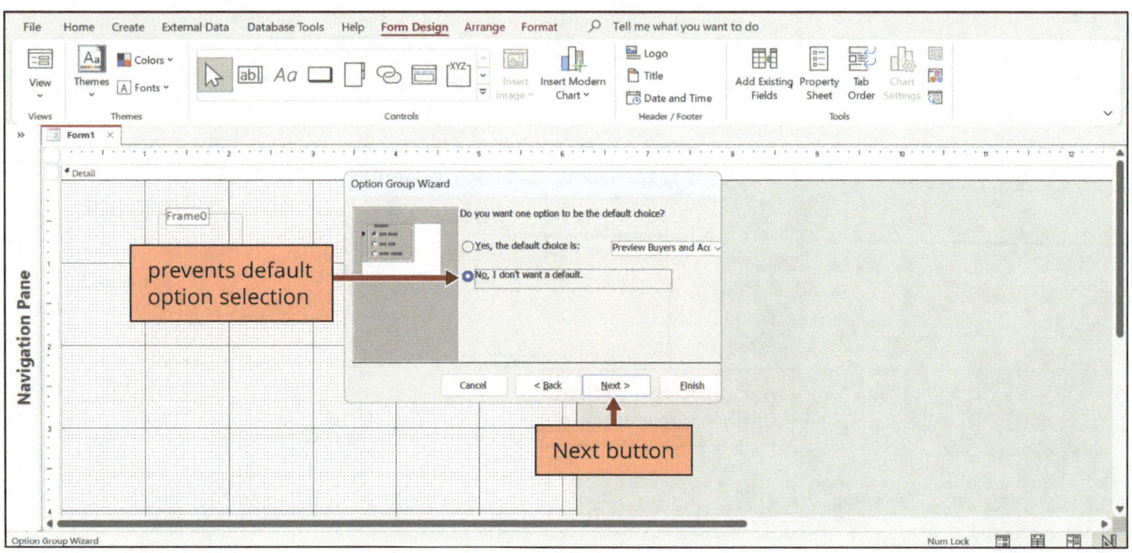

Figure 8–31

Q&A What is the effect of specifying one of the options as the default choice?

The default choice will initially be selected when you open the form. If there is no default choice, no option will be selected.

5

- Click Next to display the next Option Group Wizard screen, and then verify the values assigned to the labels match those shown in Figure 8–32.

Q&A What is the purpose of the values that appear for each option?

You can use the values in macros or VBA to refer to a specific option within the group. You will use them in a macro later in this module.

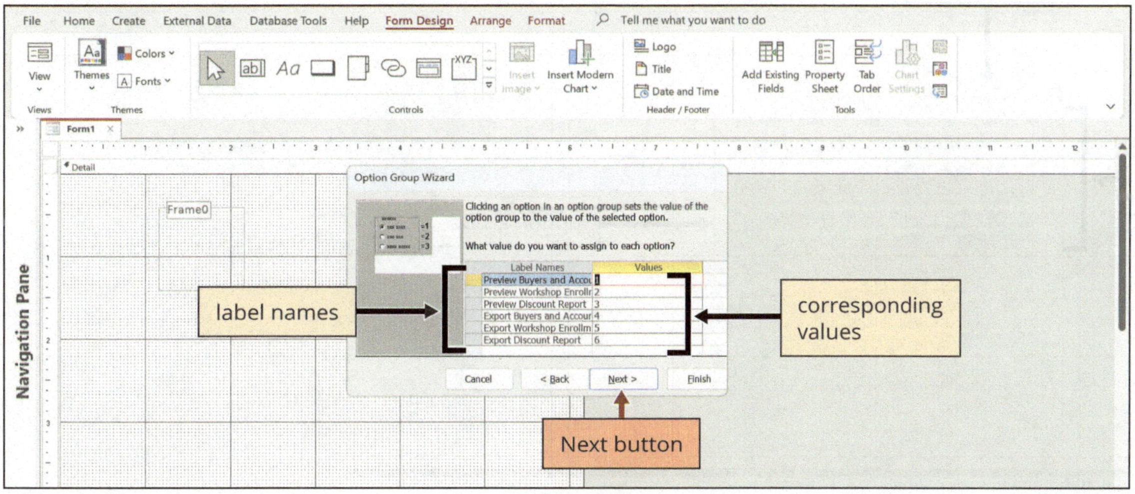

Figure 8–32

6

- Click Next to display the next Option Group Wizard screen, and then ensure Option buttons is selected as the type of control and Etched is selected as the style (Figure 8–33).
- **Experiment:** Click different combinations of types and styles to view the effects on the samples shown in the dialog box. When finished, select Option buttons as the type and Etched as the style.

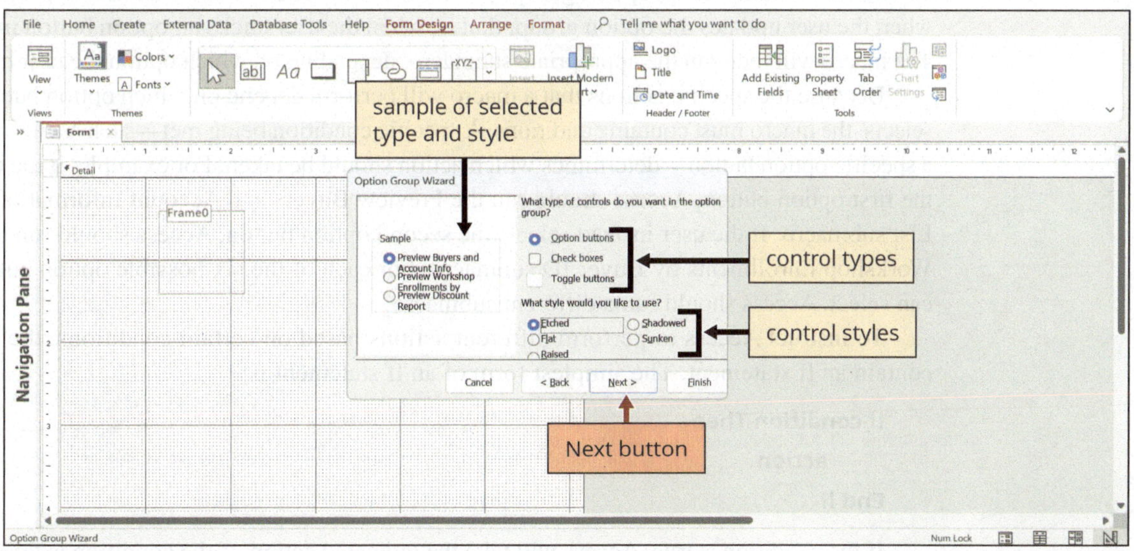

Figure 8–33

7

- Click Next to display the next Option Group Wizard screen, and then type **Report Actions** as the caption.
- Click Finish to complete the addition of the option group (Figure 8–34).

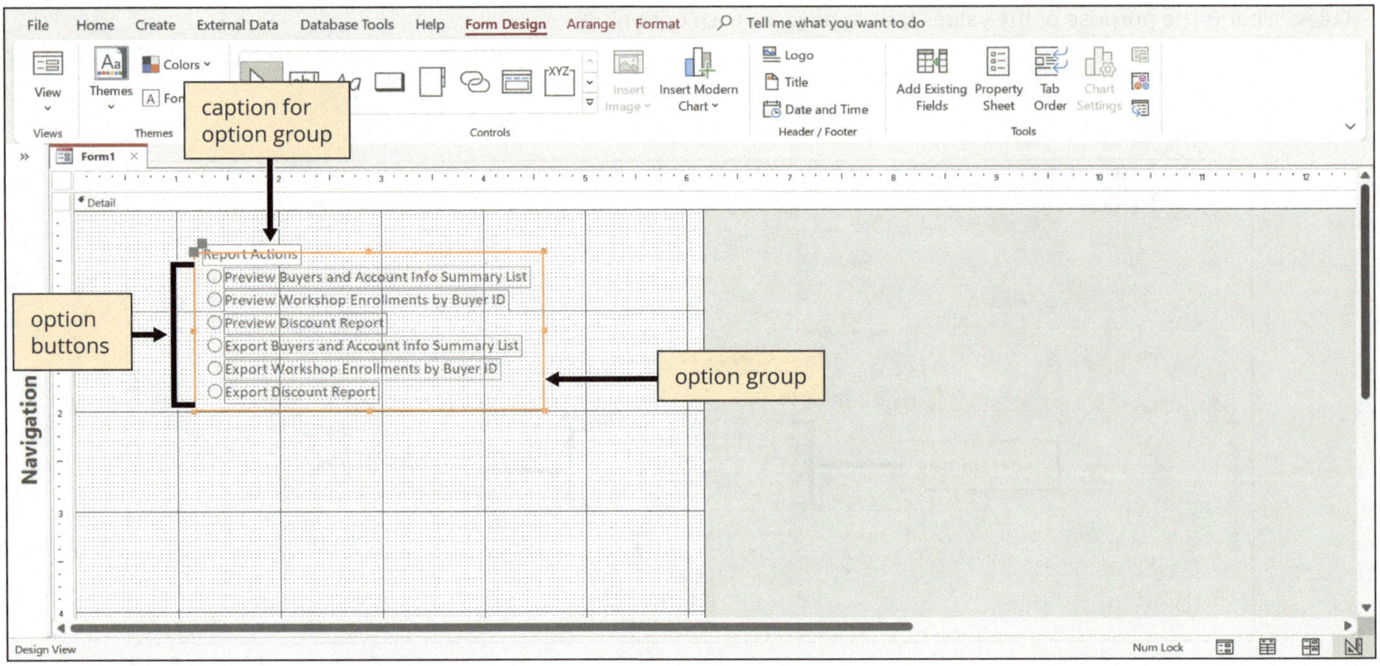

Figure 8–34

8

- Save the form using the name, **Reports List**.

Using an If Statement

To add functionality to an option group, you must create a macro that will take appropriate action when the user updates the option group, that is, when the user clicks an option button in the group. The macro will then run the appropriate submacro, depending on which option the user has selected.

Because the specific actions that a macro will perform depend on which option button the user selects, the macro must contain conditions. A specific condition being met—such as the user clicking a specific option button—determines which action should be taken. For example, if the user selects the first option button, Access should run the Preview Buyers and Account Information Summary List submacro. If the user instead selects the second option button, Access should run the Preview Workshop Enrollments by Buyer ID submacro. For each of the six possible option buttons a user can select, Access should run a different submacro.

To instruct Access to perform different actions based on certain conditions, the macro will contain an If statement. The simplest form of an If statement is:

If condition Then
    action
End If

If the condition is true, Access will take the indicated action. If the condition is false, no action will be taken. For example, the condition could be that the user selects the first option button, and the action could be to run the Buyers and Account Information Summary List submacro. No action would be taken if the user selects any other button.

Another form of the If statement contains an Else clause. This form is:

If condition Then
    first action
Else
    second action
End If

If the condition is true, the first action is taken; if the condition is false, the second action is taken. For example, the condition could be the user selects option button 1; the first action could be to run the Preview Buyers and Account Information Summary List submacro, and the second action could be to run the Preview Workshop Enrollments by Buyer ID submacro. If the user selects option button 1, Access would run the Preview Buyers and Account Information Summary List submacro. If the user selects any other option button, Access would run the Preview Workshop Enrollments by Buyer ID submacro.

Because there are six option buttons, the macro needs to use an If statement with multiple Else Ifs to account for all the options. This type of If statement has the form:

If first condition Then

first action

Else If second condition Then

second action

Else If third condition Then

third action

...

End If

The first condition could be the user selects the first option button; the second condition could be the user selects the second option button; the third condition could be the user selects the third option button, and so on. The first action could be that Access runs the first submacro, the second action could be that it runs the second submacro, and the third could be that it runs the third submacro. In this case, there are six option buttons and six submacros. For six conditions, as required in this macro, the If statement will contain five Else Ifs. The If statement along with the five Else Ifs will collectively contain six conditions: one to test if the user selected option 1, one for option 2, one for option 3, one for option 4, one for option 5, and one for option 6.

To Create a Macro with a Variable for the Option Group

The following steps begin creating the macro and add an action to set a variable to the desired value. The expression that contains the option number condition is [Forms]![Property Closings Form]![Form_Options]. The first portion of this expression, [Forms], refers to the Forms system object, which includes all the database's forms. A **system object** is a predefined object that contains a group of other objects. Referencing a system object helps Access choose the correct object even if multiple objects of different types have the same name (such as a form and a table both named Properties). If an object name has spaces, you must enclose it in square brackets. Thus, the name for the Property Closings Form is [Property Closings Form]. To reference a control that is part of any other form, the expression must include both the name of the form and the name of the control, separated by an exclamation point (!). Thus, the Form_Options control in the Property Closings Form would be [Forms]![Property Closings Form]![Form_Options].

Because this expression is fairly lengthy, the macro will begin by setting a temporary variable to this expression. A variable is a named location in computer memory. **Why?** You can use a variable to store a value that you can use later in the macro. You will assign the name Optno (short for option number) as the variable name for the expression. This location can contain a value, in this case, the option number on the form. In each of the conditions, you can then use Optno rather than the full expression.

1

- In Design view, select the option group if necessary.
- Click the Property Sheet button to display the Property Sheet pane. Ensure the selection type is Option Group.
- If necessary, click the All tab.
- Change the name of the option group to **Form_Options** (Figure 8–35).

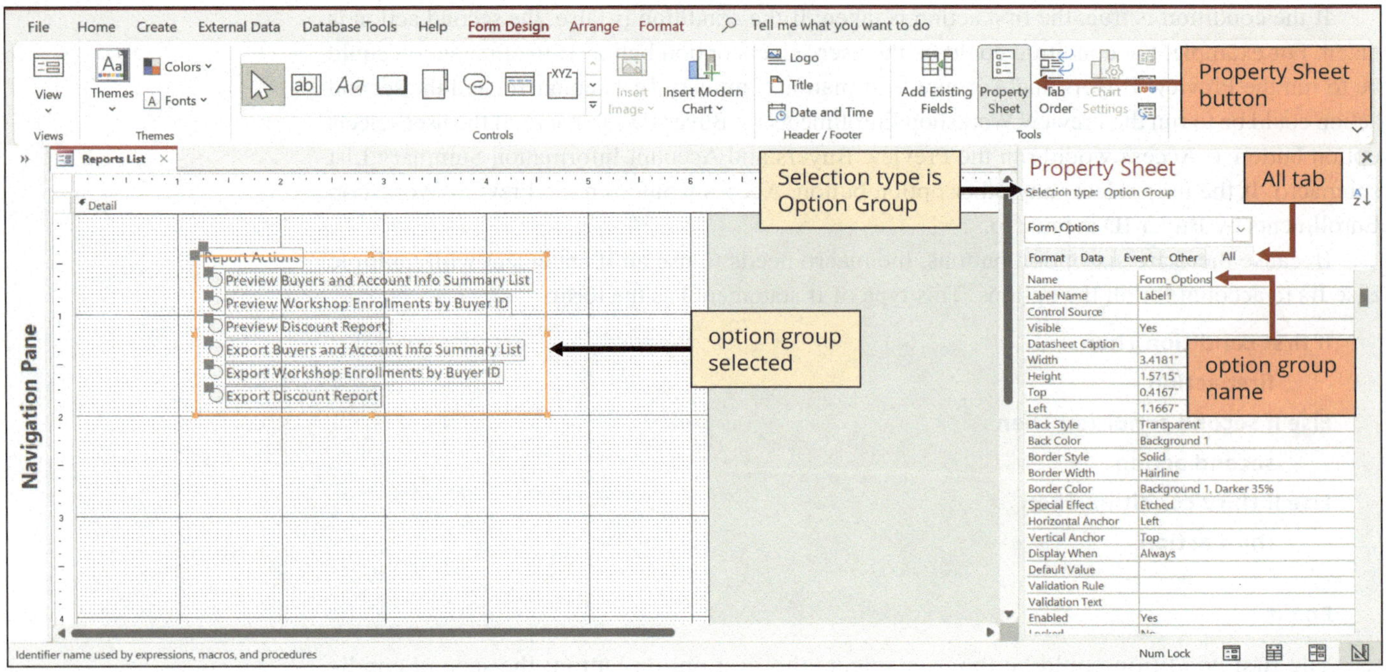

Figure 8–35

Q&A Why this name?

The name Form_Options reflects the fact that these options control the action that will be taken on this form. The underscore prevents the name from containing a space.

2

- Click the Event tab.
- Click the After Update property box.
- Click the Build button to display the Choose Builder dialog box (Figure 8–36).

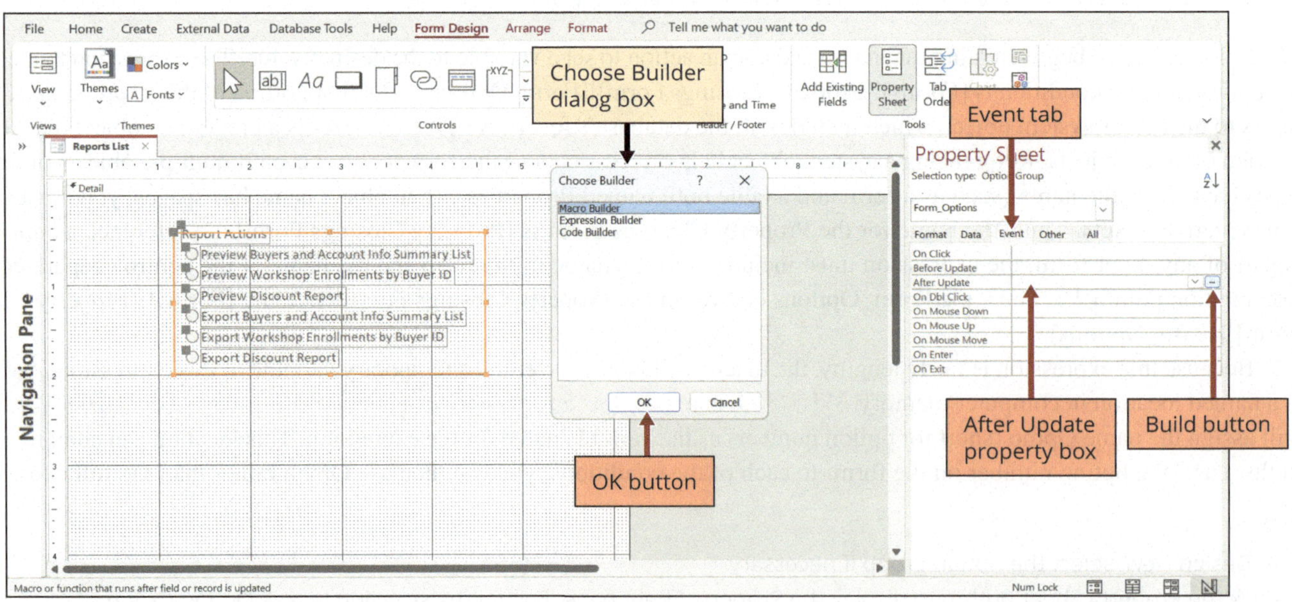

Figure 8–36

3

- With Macro Builder selected in the Choose Builder dialog box, click the OK button to create a macro.
- If necessary, click the Action Catalog button (Macro Design tab | Show/Hide group) to display the Action Catalog pane.

- If necessary, collapse any action category that is expanded.
- Expand the Macro Commands action category.
- Double-click the SetTempVar action in the Action Catalog to add the SetTempVar action to the macro.
- Type **Optno** as the value for the Name argument.
- Type **[Form_Options]** as the value for the Expression argument (Figure 8–37).

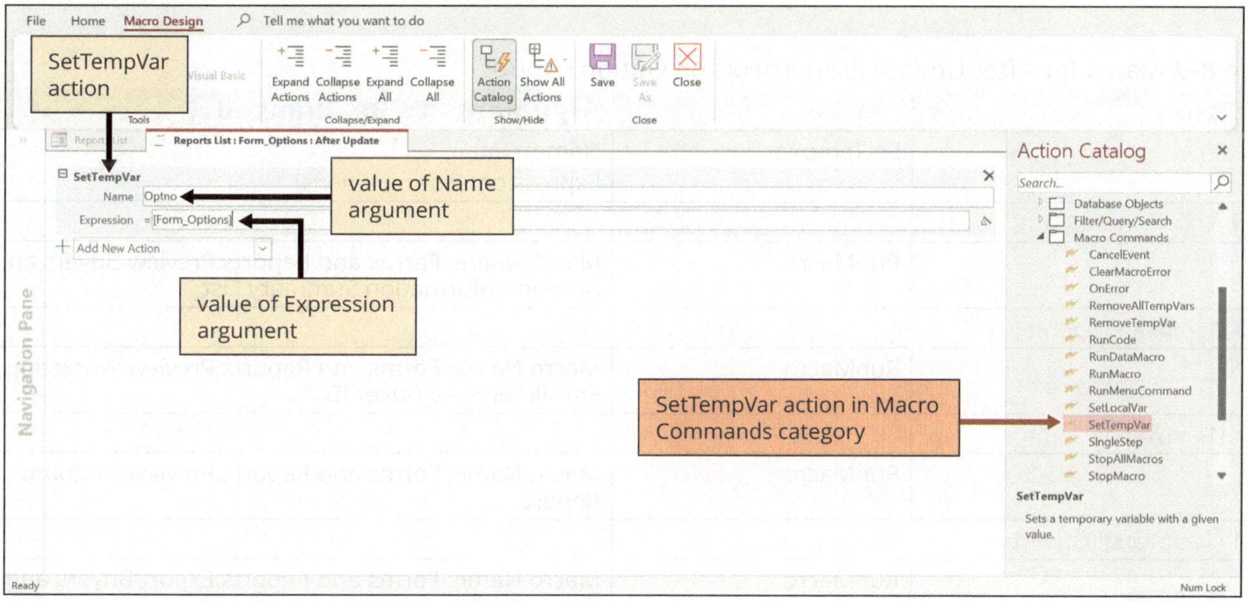

Figure 8–37

Consider This

How does Access make it easier to enter values for arguments?

Access helps you in three ways. First, if you point to the argument, Access displays a description of the argument. Second, many arguments feature a drop-down list, where you can display the list and then select the desired value. Finally, if you begin typing an expression, a feature called IntelliSense will suggest possible values that start with the letters you have already typed and that are appropriate in the context of what you are typing. If the value you want appears in the list, you can simply click it to select the value.

Macro Conditions for Option Group

As mentioned previously, the macro contains six conditions. The first is [TempVars]![Optno]=1, which simply means the value in the temporary variable Optno is equal to 1. In other words, this condition is met because the user selected the first option button. The action associated with this condition is RunMacro. The argument is the name of the macro. Because the macro to be run is a submacro, the name of the macro includes the name of the macro containing the submacro, a period, and then the name of the submacro. Because the submacro to be run is Preview Buyers and Account Information Summary List and is contained in the Forms and Reports macro, the value of the Macro Name argument is Forms and Reports.Preview Buyers and Account Info Summary List. (This name needs to be shortened to fit in the name space when creating the macro.)

The conditions and actions for options 2 through 6 are similar to the first submacro. The only difference is which submacro is associated with each option button. The conditions, actions, and arguments that you will change for the Form_Options macro are shown in Table 8–2. If the option number is 1, for example, the action is RunMacro. For the RunMacro action, you will change the Macro Name argument to Preview Buyers and Account Info Summary List submacro in the Forms and Reports macro. This name is shortened again to fit the space. On the other hand, if the option number is 2, for example, the action is again RunMacro. If the option number is 2, however, you will set the Macro Name argument to the Workshop Enrollments by Buyer ID submacro in the Forms and Reports macro. Similar actions take place for the other possible values for the Optno variable, that is, for option buttons 3 through 6. Because the temporary variable, Optno, is no longer needed at the end of the macro, the macro concludes with the RemoveTempVar command to remove this variable.

Table 8–2 Macro for After Update Property of the Option Group

Condition	Action	Arguments to Be Changed
	SetTempVar	Name: Optno Expression: [Form_Options]
If [TempVars]![Optno]=1		
	RunMacro	Macro Name: Forms and Reports.Preview Buyers and Account Information Summary List
Else If [TempVars]![Optno]=2		
	RunMacro	Macro Name: Forms and Reports.Preview Workshop Enrollments by Buyer ID
Else If [TempVars]![Optno]=3		
	RunMacro	Macro Name: Forms and Reports.Preview Discount Report
Else If [TempVars]![Optno]=4		
	RunMacro	Macro Name: Forms and Reports.Export Buyers and Account Information Summary List
Else If [TempVars]![Optno]=5		
	RunMacro	Macro Name: Forms and Reports.Export Workshop Enrollments by Buyer ID
Else If [TempVars]![Optno]=6		
	RunMacro	Macro Name: Forms and Reports.Export Discount Report
End If		
	RemoveTempVar	Name: Optno

To Add Actions to the Form_Options Macro

The following steps add the conditions and actions to the Form_Options macro. **Why?** Adding the conditions and actions will complete the macro.

1

- Double-click the If element from the Program Flow section of the Action Catalog to add an If statement to the submacro, and then type **[TempVars]![Optno]=1** as the condition in the If statement.
- With the Macro Commands category expanded, double-click RunMacro to add the RunMacro action.
- Click the drop-down arrow for the Macro Name argument and select the Preview Buyers and Account Information Summary List submacro within the Forms and Reports macro as the value for the argument (Figure 8–38).

Q&A What should I do if I add an action in the wrong position? What should I do if I add the wrong action?
If you add an action in the wrong position, use the Move up or Move down buttons to move it to the correct position. If you add the wrong action, click the Delete button to delete the action, and then add the correct action.

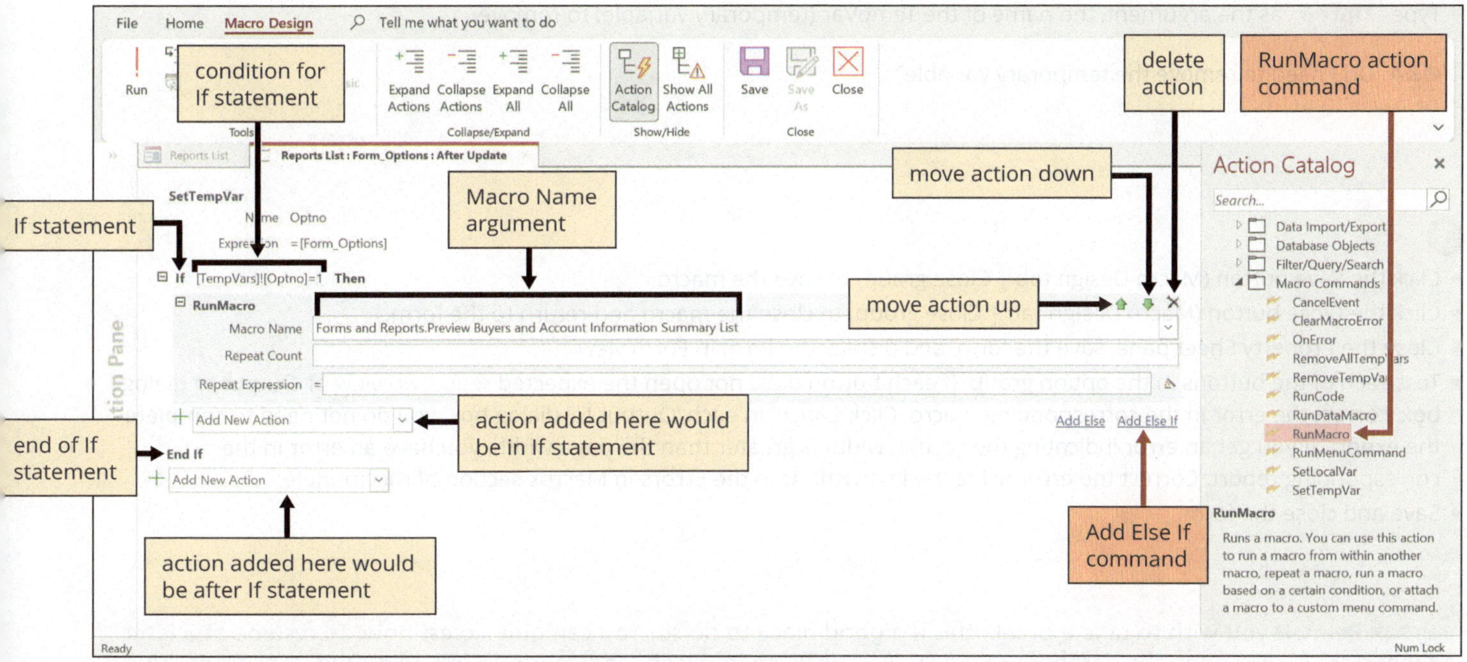

Figure 8–38

2

- Click 'Add Else If' to add an Else If clause to the If statement.
- Add the conditions and actions associated with options 2, 3, 4, 5, and 6 as described in Table 8–2, and specify the arguments for the actions. Click 'Add Else If' after adding each action except for the last one.

Q&A Do I have to enter all these actions? They seem to be very similar to the ones associated with option 1.
You can copy and paste the action for option 1. Right-click the action to select it and display a shortcut menu. Click Copy on the shortcut menu. Right-click the action just above where you want to insert the selected action and then click Paste. If the new action is not inserted in the correct position, select the new action and then click either the Move up or Move down buttons to move it to the correct location. Once the action is in the correct location, you can make any necessary changes to the arguments, such as changing the number 1 to the number 2.

- Click the Add New Action box below the End If statement, and then add the RemoveTempVar action and argument as shown in Figure 8–39.

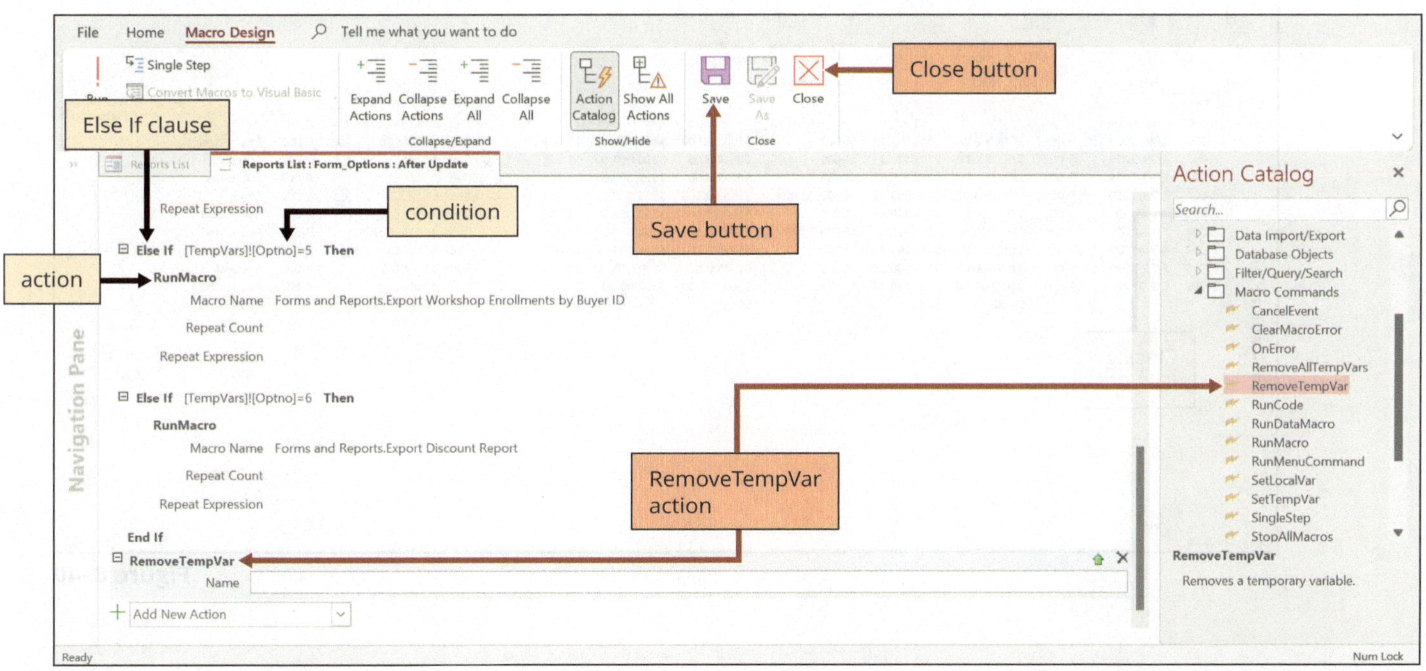

Figure 8–39

- Type **Optno** as the argument, the name of the TempVar (temporary variable) to remove.

Q&A Do I need to remove the temporary variable?
Technically, no. In fact, if you plan to use this temporary variable in another macro and want it to retain the value you assigned in this macro, you would definitely not remove it. However, if you do not plan to use it elsewhere, it is a good idea to remove it to maintain good database organization.

3

- Click the Save button (Macro Design tab | Close group) to save the macro.
- Click the Close button (Macro Design tab | Close group) to close the macro and return to the form.
- Close the Property Sheet pane, save the form, and display the form in Form view.
- Test each of the buttons in the option group. If each button does not open the expected report preview or Output to dialog box, correct the error in the corresponding macro. Click Cancel in each 'Output to' dialog box; you do not need to complete the export. If you get an error indicating the section width is greater than the page width, you have an error in the corresponding report. Correct the error using the instructions in the Errors in Macros section of this module.
- Save and close the form.

Break Point: If you wish to take a break, this is a good place to do so. You can quit Access now. To resume at a later time, start Access, open the database called SC_AC_08_Partners.accdb, and continue following the steps from this location forward.

User Interface (UI) Macros

A **user interface (UI) macro** is a macro that is attached to a user interface object, such as a command button, option group, or control on a form. The macro you just created for the option group is, therefore, a UI macro, as were the macros you attached to command buttons. A common use for UI macros is to associate actions with the clicking of a control on a form. In the Closings form shown in Figure 8–40, for example, if you click the Closing ID on the row in the datasheet where the Closing ID is C-005, Access displays the data for that account in a pop-up form (Figure 8–41), that is, a form that stays on top of other open objects, even when another object is active.

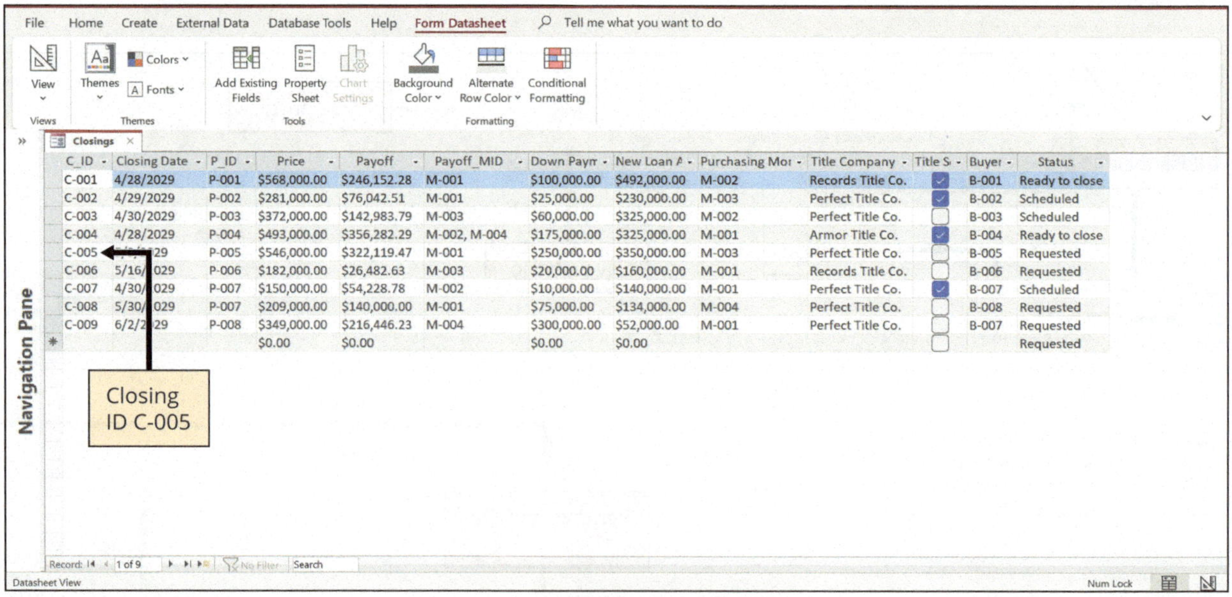

Figure 8–40

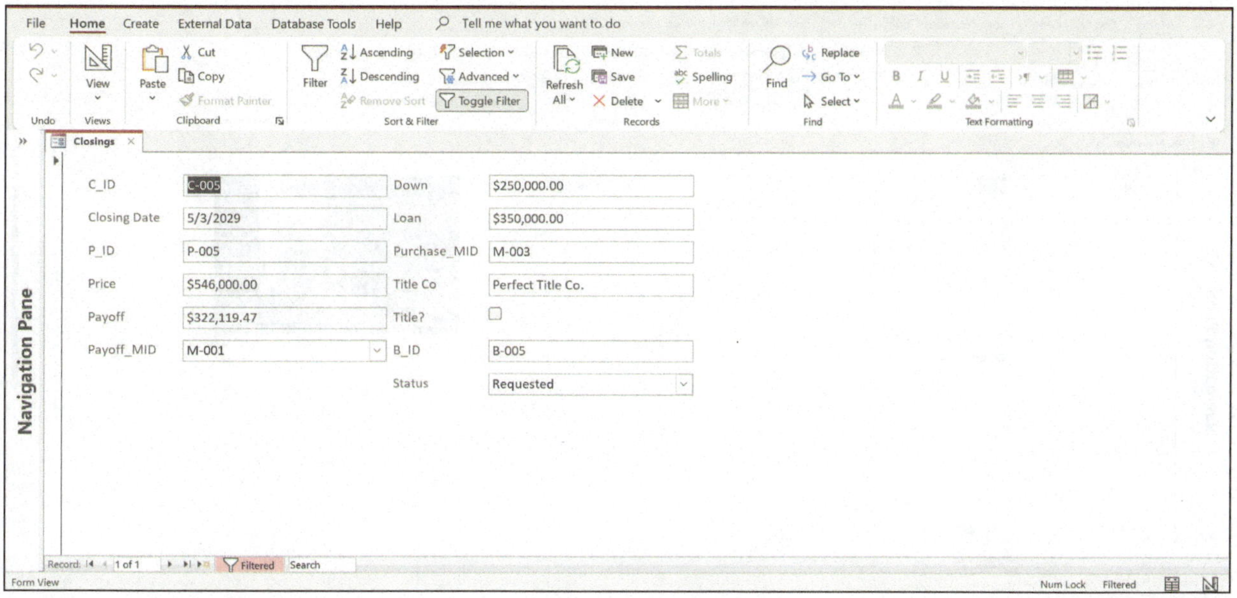

Figure 8–41

Similarly, in the Properties form shown in Figure 8–42, if you click the Property ID P-004, Access displays the data for that property in a pop-up form (Figure 8–43).

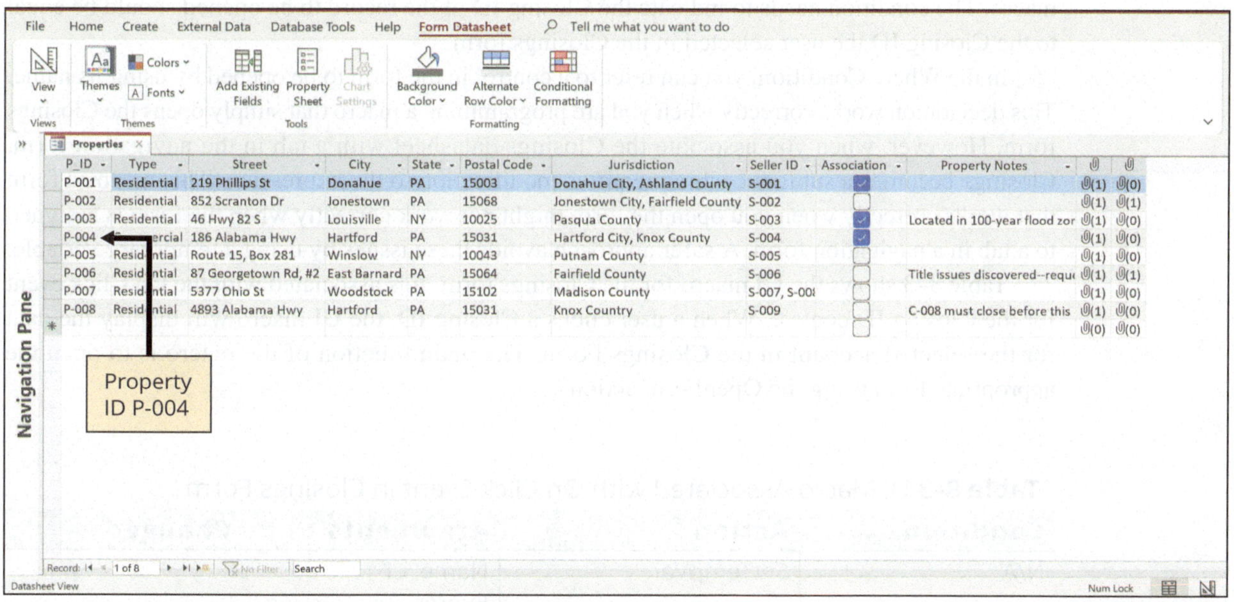

Figure 8–42

Recall that you can only use forms and reports for the tabs in a navigation form, yet the Closing ID tab appears to display the Closings table in Datasheet view. You can make it appear as though you are displaying the Closings table in Datasheet view by creating a datasheet form named Closings. You will create a UI macro in this Closings datasheet form. The UI macro that will be associated with clicking the Closing ID on some record in the Closings form will display the selected account in the Closings Form.

To display the Closings form, the UI macro will use the OpenForm action. You must set the Form Name argument of the OpenForm action to the actual name of the form to be opened, Closings. Partners wants to prevent the user from updating data using this form, so the Data Mode argument is set to Read Only. The form should appear as a pop-up, which you accomplish by setting the value of the Window Mode argument to Dialog.

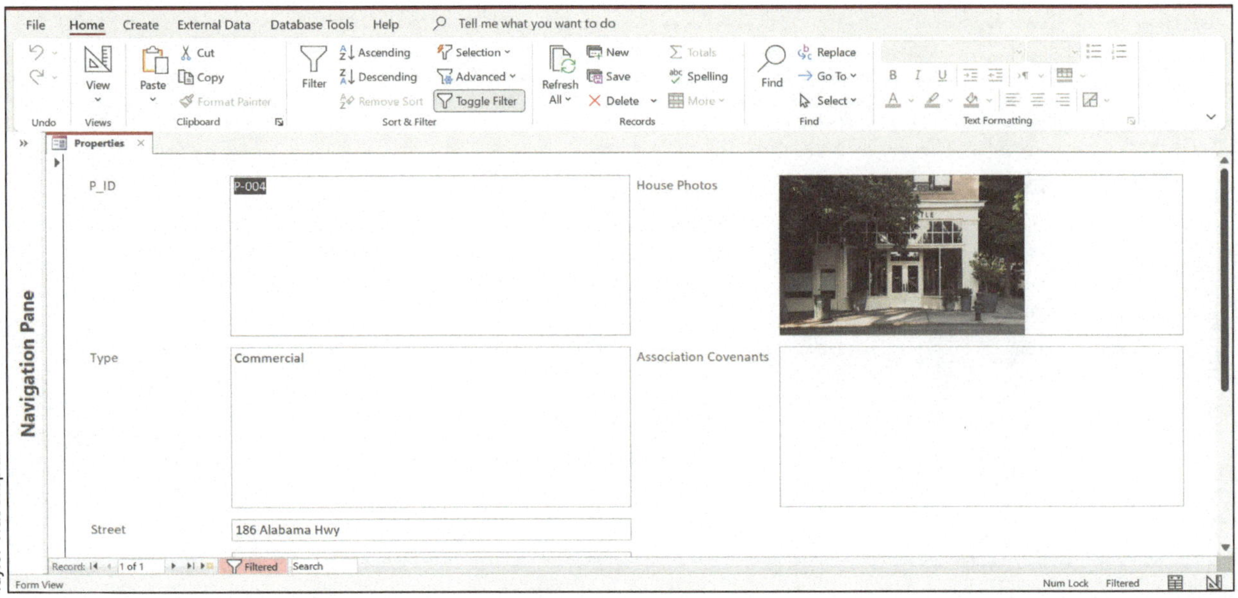

Taylor Vick/Unsplash

Figure 8–43

The form should display only the record the user selected. If the user clicks Closing ID C-005 in the Closings form, for example, the form should display only the data for record C-005. To restrict the record that appears in the form, you include the Where Condition argument in the UI macro. The condition needs to indicate the Closing ID of the record to be opened should be equal to the Closing ID the user selected in the Closings form.

In the Where Condition, you can refer to a control in the form to be opened by using its name. This declaration works correctly when you are programming a macro that simply opens the Closings form. However, when you associate the Closings datasheet with a tab in the navigation form, Closings becomes a subform, which requires modification to the expression. This means a form that works correctly when you open the form might not work correctly when the form is assigned to a tab in a navigation form. A safer approach avoids these issues by using a temporary variable.

Table 8–3 shows the UI macro for the Closings form. It is associated with the On Click event for the Closing ID control. When a user clicks a Closing ID, the UI macro will display the data for the selected account in the Closings Form. The main function of the macro is to open the appropriate form using the OpenForm action.

Table 8–3 UI Macro Associated with On Click Event in Closings Form

Condition	Action	Arguments to Be Changed
N/A	SetTempVar	Name: CI Expression: [Closing ID]
N/A	OpenForm	Form Name: Closings Where Condition: [Closing ID]=[TempVars]![CI] Data Mode: Read Only Window Mode: Dialog
N/A	RemoveTempVar	Name: CI

In the macro shown in Table 8–3, the first action, SetTempVar, assigns the temporary variable CI to the Closing ID. The two arguments are Name, which is set to CI, and Expression, which is set to [Closing ID]. The CI temporary variable refers to the Closing ID in the Closings form; recall that the completed macro will open the Closings form. You then can use this temporary variable in the Where Condition argument. The expression is thus [Closing ID]=[TempVars]![CI].

The [Closing ID] portion refers to the Closing ID in the Closings form. The [TempVars]![CI] portion is the temporary variable that has been set equal to the Closing ID in the Closings form. The macro ends by removing the temporary variable.

Table 8–4 shows the macro for the Properties form, which is very similar to the macro for the Closings form.

Table 8–4 UI Macro Associated with On Click Event in Properties Form

Condition	Action	Arguments to Be Changed
N/A	SetTempVar	Name: PI Expression: [Property ID]
N/A	OpenForm	Form Name: Properties Where Condition: [Property ID]=[TempVars]![PI] Data Mode: Read Only Window Mode: Dialog
N/A	RemoveTempVar	Name: PI

To Create Datasheet Forms

The following steps create two datasheet forms, one for the Closings table and one for the Properties table. **Why?** The datasheet forms enable the Closings and Properties tables to appear as if displayed in Datasheet view, despite the Access restriction that prevents tables from being used on tabs in a navigation form.

1

- In the Navigation Pane, select the Closings table.
- Display the Create tab, and then click the More Forms button (Create tab | Forms group) to display the More Forms gallery (Figure 8–44).

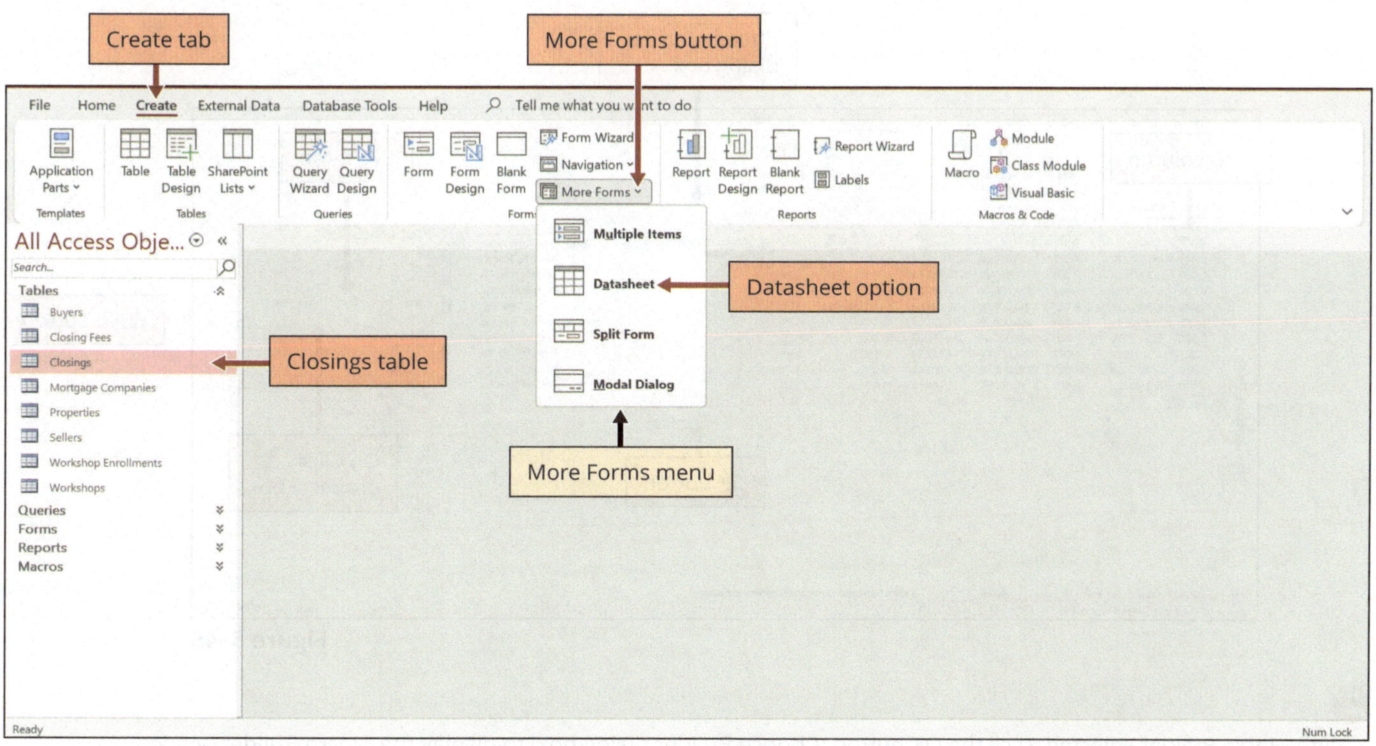

Figure 8–44

2

- Click Datasheet to create a datasheet form.
- Save the form using the name **Closings**.

Q&A Is it acceptable to use the same name for the form as for the table?

Yes. In this case, you want it to appear to the user that the Closings table is open in Datasheet view. One way to emphasize this fact is to use the same name as the table.

What is the difference between a datasheet form, such as this one, and a simple form, such as the Mortgage Companies Form?

The Mortgage Companies Form is a simple form that displays only one record at a time. The Closings form you just created displays all the closings records in a datasheet.

- Use the same technique to create a datasheet form named **Properties** for the Properties table.
- Close both forms.

To Create UI Macros for the Datasheet Forms

The following steps create the UI macro shown in Table 8–3 for the Closings datasheet form and the UI macro shown in Table 8–4 for the Properties datasheet form. **Why?** The UI macros will display the appropriate pop-up forms when a user clicks the appropriate position on the forms.

1

- Open the Closings form.
- Click the C_ID heading to select the C_ID column in the datasheet.
- If necessary, click the Property Sheet button (Form Datasheet tab | Tools group) to display the Property Sheet pane.
- If necessary, click the Event tab to display only event properties.
- Click the On Click property box, and then click the Build button (the three dots) to display the Choose Builder dialog box (Figure 8–45).

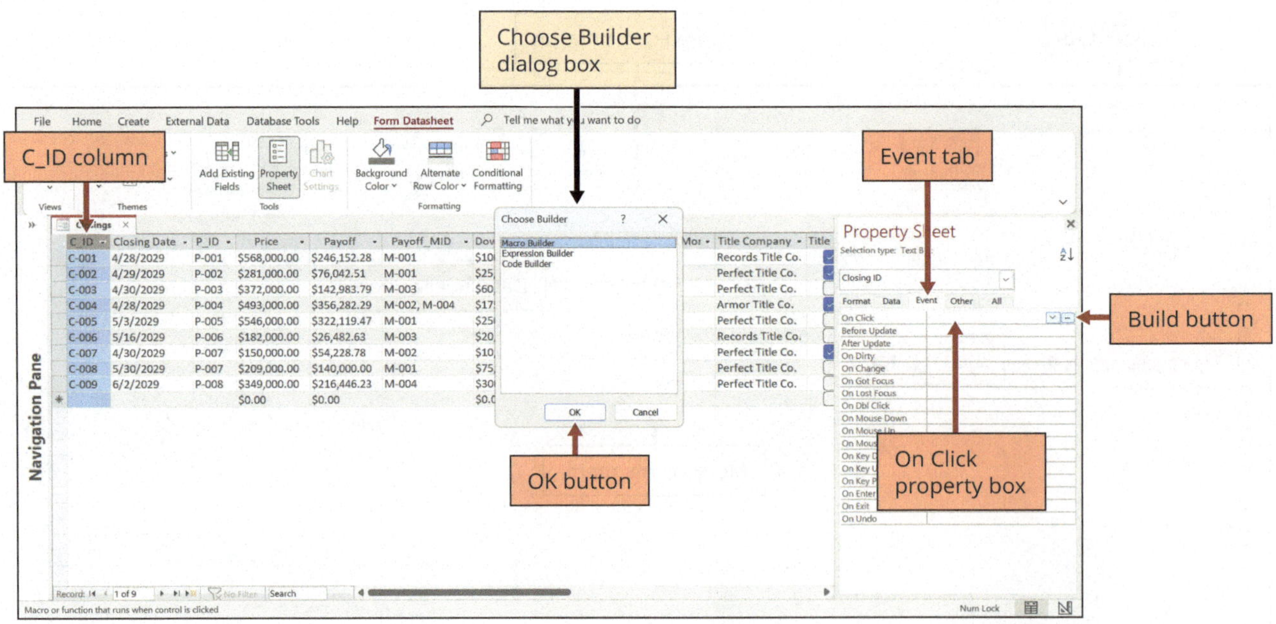

Figure 8–45

2

- With Macro Builder selected, click the OK button (Choose Builder dialog box) to display the Macro Builder window.
- Add the SetTempVar action to the macro, enter **CI** (be sure to use a capital i and not a number 1) as the value for the Name argument, and enter **[Closing ID]** as the value for the Expression argument.

- Expand the Database Objects category, add the OpenForm action to the macro, select Closings as the value for the Form Name argument, leave the value of the View argument set to Form, enter **[Closing ID]=[TempVars]![CI]** as the value for the Where Condition argument, select Read Only as the value for the Data Mode argument, and select Dialog as the value for the Window Mode argument.

Q&A Why am I setting a temporary value for the Closing ID field when the field in the datasheet form is called C_ID?
The Closing ID field has been given the caption, C_ID, to better fit the space in the table, and this caption also is what appears in the datasheet form. However, the actual name of the field is Closing ID.

What does the expression for the Where Condition value mean?
The portion before the equal sign, [Closing ID], refers to the Closing ID field in the form just opened, that is, in the Closings form. The portion to the right of the equal sign, [TempVars]![CI], is the temporary variable that was set equal to the Closing ID value on the selected record in the Closings form. This Where Condition guarantees the record displayed in the Closings form will be the record with the same Closing ID as the one selected in the Closings form.

- Add the RemoveTempVar action to the macro and enter **CI** as the value for the Name argument (Figure 8–46).

Q&A Why do I need to remove the temporary variable?
Technically, you do not. The temporary variable has fulfilled its function, however, so it makes sense to remove it at this point.

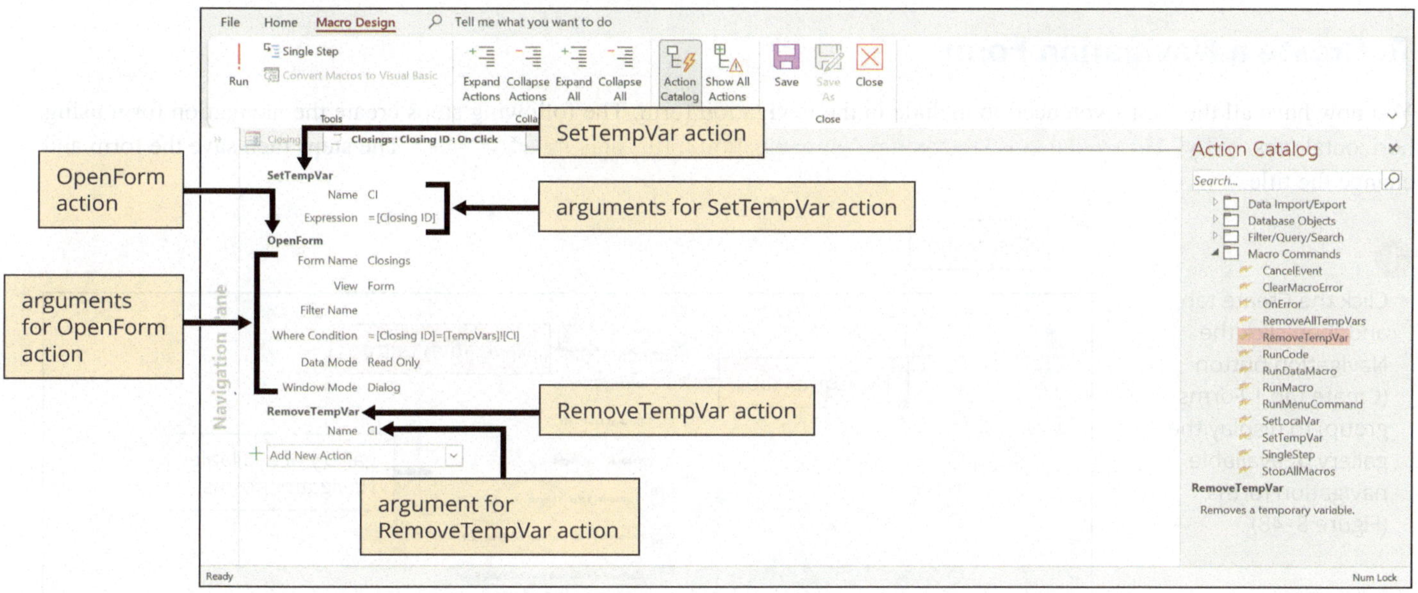

Figure 8–46

3

- Click the Save button (Macro Design tab | Close group) to save the macro.
- Click the Close button (Macro Design tab | Close group) to close the macro and return to the form.
- Close the Property Sheet pane.
- Save and close the form.

4

- Use the techniques in Steps 1 through 2 to create a UI macro for the Properties datasheet form called Properties, referring to Table 8–4 for the actions. Create the macro shown in Figure 8–47 associated with clicking the Property ID (P_ID) column.

5

- Click the Save button (Macro Design tab | Close group) to save the macro.
- Click the Close button (Macro Design tab | Close group) to close the macro and return to the datasheet form.
- Close the Property Sheet pane.
- Save and close the form.

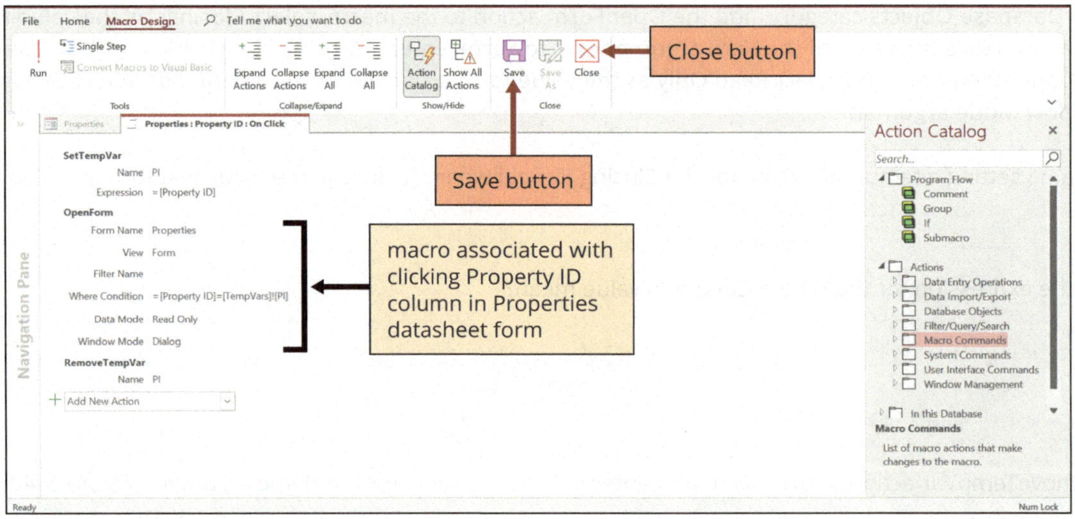

Figure 8–47

To Create a Navigation Form

You now have all the forms you need to include in the navigation form. The following steps create the navigation form using horizontal tabs. **Why?** Horizontal tabs are common on navigation forms and are easy to use. The steps then save the form and change the title.

1

- Click the Create tab, and then click the Navigation button (Create tab | Forms group) to display the gallery of available navigation forms (Figure 8–48).

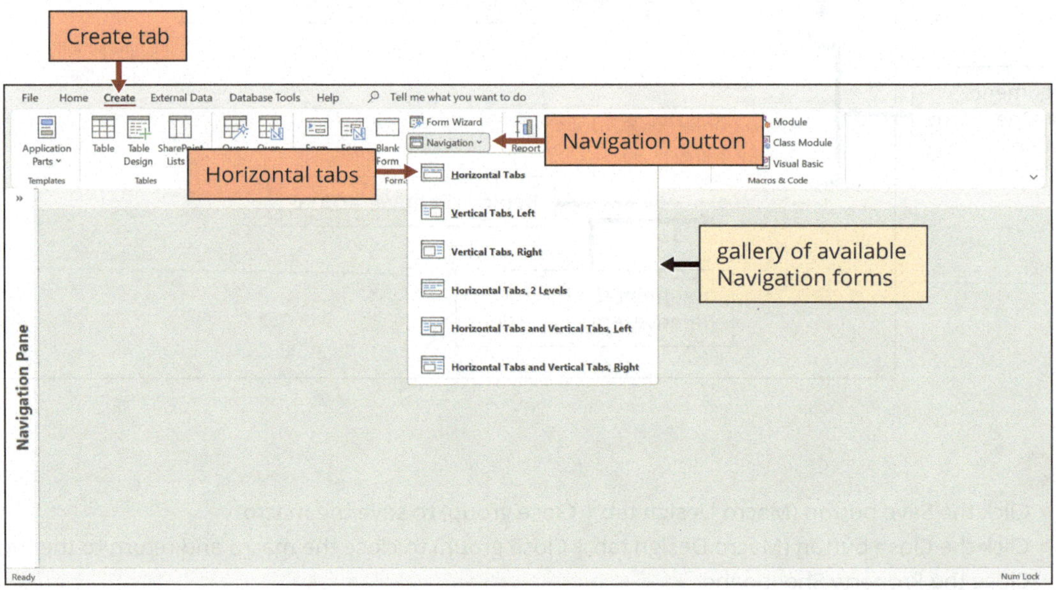

Figure 8–48

2

- Click Horizontal Tabs in the gallery to create a form with a navigation control in which the tabs are arranged horizontally in a single row.
- If necessary, click the 'Add Existing Fields' button (Form Layout Design tab | Tools group) to close the Field List pane (Figure 8–49).

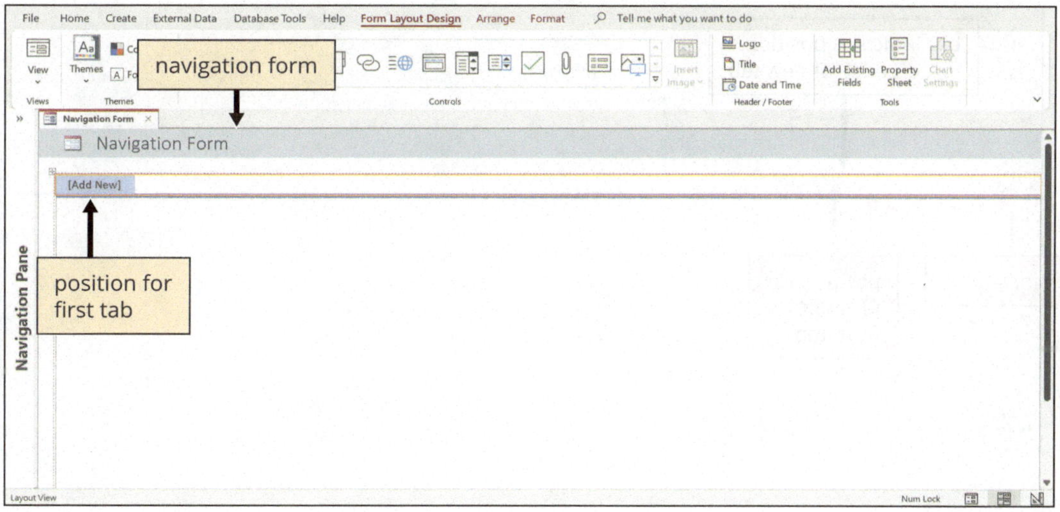

Figure 8–49

3

- Save the form using the name, **Main Menu**.
- Switch to Design view.
- Click the form title to produce an insertion point.
- Erase the current title, and then type **Partners Law Firm** as the new title (Figure 8–50).
- Save the form.

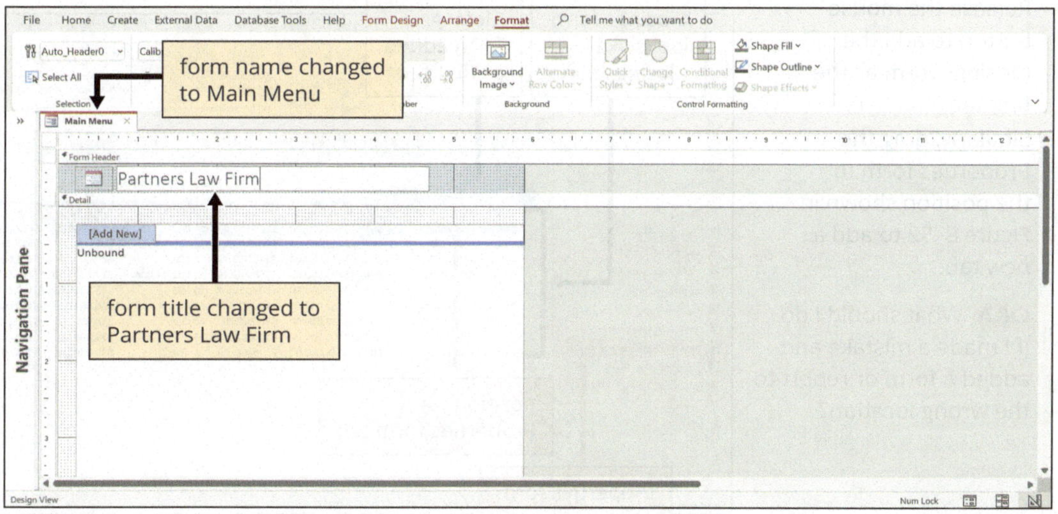

Figure 8–50

To Add Tabs to a Navigation Form

To add a form or report to a tab in a navigation form, be sure the Navigation Pane is open, and then drag the form or report to the desired tab. When using the navigation form, users can then display that form or report by clicking the tab. For the Partners Law Firm navigation form, you will drag four forms to the tabs. The first form is the Closings datasheet form that appears to display the Closings table open in Datasheet view. Similarly, the Properties form is a datasheet form that appears to display the Properties table open in Datasheet view. The Forms List form contains three buttons users can click to display the form of their choice. Finally, the Reports List form contains an option group where users can select a report to preview or export. The following steps add the tabs to the navigation form. They also change the name of the Forms List and Reports List tabs. **Why?** The names of the tabs do not have to be the same as the name of the corresponding forms. By changing them, you can often make tabs more readable.

1

- Return to Layout view (Home tab | Views group).
- In the Navigation Pane, scroll down so the form named Closings appears, and then drag the Closings form to the position shown in Figure 8–51 to add a new tab.

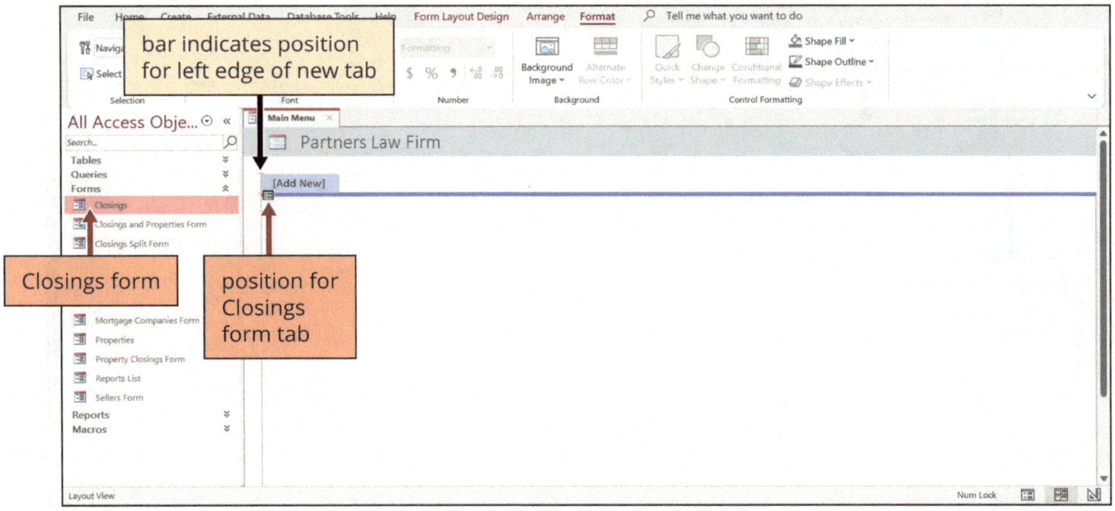

Figure 8–51

2

- Release the mouse button to add the Closings form as the first tab.
- Similarly, drag the Properties form to the position shown in Figure 8–52 to add a new tab.

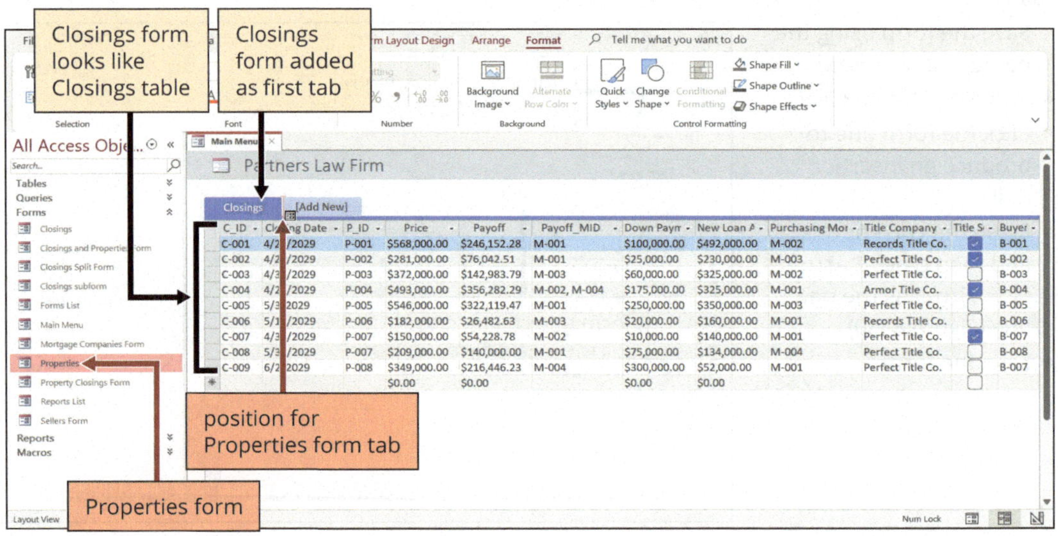

Figure 8–52

Q&A What should I do if I made a mistake and added a form or report to the wrong location?

You can rearrange the tabs by dragging them. Often, the simplest way to correct a mistake is to click the Undo button to reverse your most recent action, however. You can also choose to simply close the form without saving it and then start over.

3

- Release the mouse button to add the Properties form as the second tab.
- Using the techniques described in Steps 1 and 2, add the Forms List form as the third tab and the Reports List form as the fourth tab (Figure 8–53).

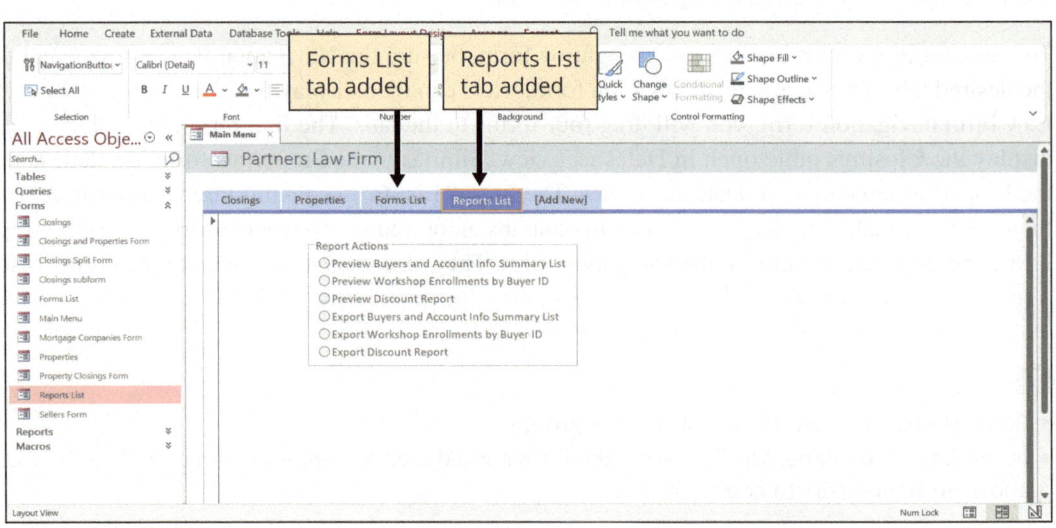

Figure 8–53

4

- Click the Forms List tab twice: once to select it and the second time to produce an insertion point.
- Change the name from Forms List to **Forms**.
- In a similar fashion, change the name of the Reports List tab from Reports List to **Reports** (Figure 8–54).

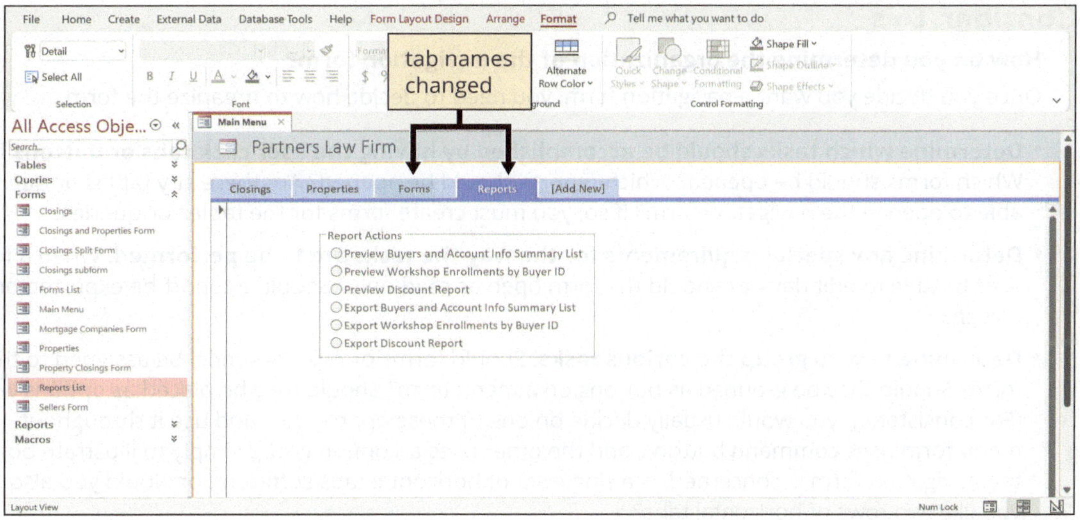

Figure 8–54

Q&A I created these two forms using the names Forms List and Reports List. Now I have changed the names to Forms and Reports. Why not call them Forms and Reports in the first place, so I would not have to rename the tabs?

Because the words, forms and reports, have specific meanings in Access, you cannot use these names when creating the forms. Thus, you needed to use other names, like Forms List and Reports List. Because tabs within forms are not database objects, you can rename them to be any name you want.

5

- Save the Main Menu form.
- Switch to Form view and click on each tab to test it for accuracy.
- If requested to do so by your instructor, rename the Main Menu form as LastName Main Menu where LastName is your last name.
- Close the form.

Using a Navigation Form

The Main Menu navigation form is complete and ready for use. To use the navigation form, double-click the form in the Navigation Pane. The Main Menu form then will appear with the first tabbed object (refer to Figure 8–1). To display the other forms, click the appropriate tab.

BTW
Quick Styles for Controls

To make a navigation form more visually appealing, you can change the style of command buttons or tabs. Quick styles change how the different colors, fonts, and effects are combined. To change the style of a command button or tab, open the navigation form in Layout view. Select the control(s) for which you want to change the style, and then click Quick Styles (Format tab | Control Formatting group). When the Quick Styles gallery appears, select the desired style. You also can change the style of a control in Design view.

BTW
Change the Shape of a Control

Command buttons and tabs have a default shape. For example, both command buttons and tabs have a rounded rectangle shape as the default shape. You can change the shape of a button or tab control on a navigation form. To do so, open the navigation form in Layout view. Select the control(s) for which you want to change the shape, and click Change Shape (Format tab | Control Formatting group). When the Change Shape gallery appears, select the desired shape. You also can change the shape of a command button or tab in Design view.

Consider This

How do you determine the organization of the navigation form?

Once you decide you want a navigation form, you need to decide how to organize the form.

- **Determine which tasks should be accomplished by having the user click tabs or buttons in the navigation form.** Which forms should be opened? Which reports should be opened? Are there any tables or queries that you need to be able to open in the navigation form? If so, you must create forms for the tables or queries.
- **Determine any special requirements for the way the tasks are to be performed.** When a form is opened, should a user be able to edit data, or should the form open as read-only? Should a report be exported or simply viewed on the screen?
- **Determine how to group the various tasks.** Should forms or reports simply be assigned to the tabs in the navigation form? Should they be grouped as buttons on a menu form? Should they be placed as options within an option group? (For consistency, you would usually decide on one of these approaches and use it throughout. In this module, one menu form uses command buttons, and the other uses an option group simply to illustrate both approaches.) As far as the navigation form is concerned, is a single set of horizontal tabs sufficient, or would you also like vertical tabs? Would you like two rows of horizontal tabs?

BTW
Distributing a Document
Instead of printing and distributing a hard copy of a document, you can distribute the document electronically. Options include sending the document via email; posting it on cloud storage (such as OneDrive) and sharing the file with others; posting it on a social networking site, blog, or other website; and sharing a link associated with an online location of the document. You also can create and share a PDF or XPS image of the document, so users can view the file in Acrobat Reader or XPS Viewer instead of in Access.

BTW
Data Macros
Data macros are similar to SQL (Structured Query Language) triggers. You attach logic to record or table events, and any forms and code that update those events inherit the logic. Data macros are stored with the table.

Data Macros

A data macro is a special type of macro that is associated with specific table-related events, such as updating a record in a table. The possible events are Before Change, Before Delete, After Insert, After Update, and After Delete. Data macros allow you to add logic to these events. For example, the data macro shown in Table 8–5 is associated with the Before Change event, an event that occurs after the user has changed the data but before the change is actually made in the database.

Table 8–5 Data Macro for Before Change Event

Condition	Action	Arguments to Be Changed
If [Hours Spent]>[Total Hours]		
	SetField	Name: [Hours Spent] Value: [Total Hours]
Else If [Hours Spent]<0		
	SetField	Name: [Hours Spent] Value: 0
End If		

This macro will examine the value in the Hours Spent field in the Workshop Enrollments table. If the user's update would cause the value in the Hours Spent field to be greater than the value in the Total Hours field, the macro will change the value in the Hours Spent field so it is equal to the value in the Total Hours field. Likewise, if the update would cause the value in the Hours Spent field to be less than zero, the macro will set the value in the Hours Spent field to 0. These changes take place after the user has made the change on the screen but before Access commits the change to the database, that is, before the data in the database is actually changed.

There are other events to which you can assign data macros. The actions in a data macro associated with the Before Delete event will take place after a user has given a delete command, but before the record is actually removed from the database. The actions in a macro associated with the After Insert event will take place immediately after a record physically is added to the database. The actions in a macro associated with the After Update event will take place immediately after a record is physically changed in the database. The actions in a macro associated with the After Delete event will take place immediately after a record is physically removed from the database.

To Create a Data Macro

The following steps create the data macro in Table 8–5, a macro that will be run after a user makes a change to a record in the Workshop Enrollments table, but before the record is updated in the database. **Why?** Partners paralegals want a way to prevent users from entering invalid data into the database.

1

- Open the Workshop Enrollments table in Datasheet view.
- Display the Table tab (Figure 8–55).

Q&A What is the meaning of the buttons in the Before Events and After Events groups?

Actions in macros associated with the Before Events group will occur after the user has taken action to change or delete a record, but before the change or deletion is made permanent in the database. Actions in macros associated with the After Events group will occur after the corresponding update has been made permanent in the database.

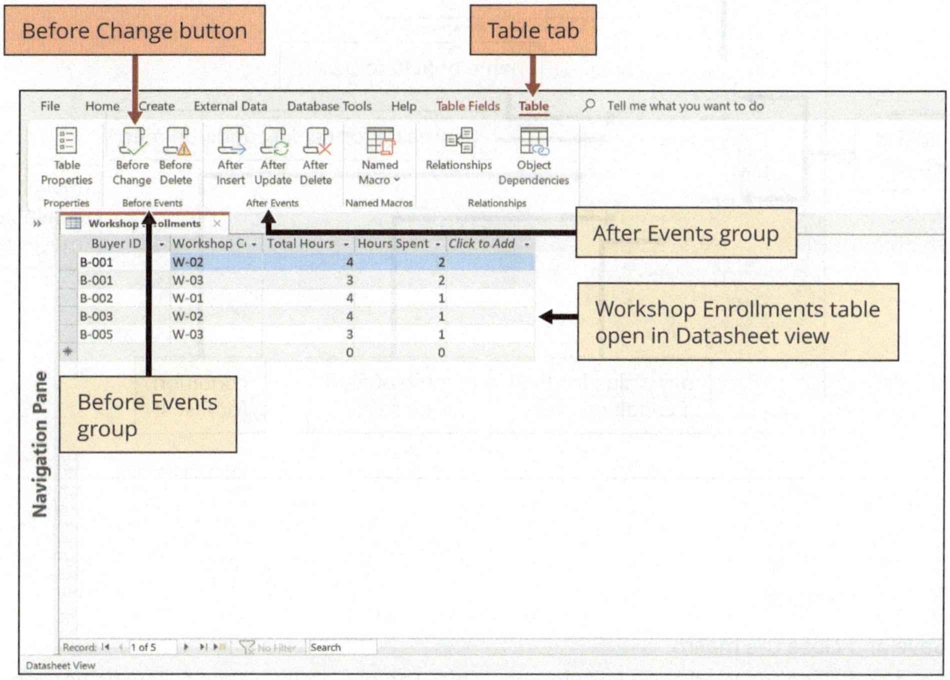

Figure 8–55

2

- Click the Before Change button (Table tab | Before Events group) to create a Before Change macro.
- Double-click the If element from the Program Flow section of the Action Catalog to add an If statement to the macro, and then type **[Hours Spent]>[Total Hours]** as the condition in the If statement.
- Add the SetField action to the macro.
- Enter **[Hours Spent]** in the Name field, and then enter **[Total Hours]** in the Value field.
- Add an Else If statement.
- Type **[Hours Spent]<0** for the Else If condition.
- Add the SetField action to the macro.
- Enter **[Hours Spent]** in the Name field, and then enter **0** (zero) in the Value field.
- Confirm that your macro looks like the one shown in Figure 8–56 and correct any errors if necessary.

Q&A What happened to all the actions that were in the list? In the previous macros I created, there were many more actions available.

There are only certain actions that make sense in data macros. Only those actions appear. Therefore, the list of actions that appears is much smaller in a data macro than in other macros.

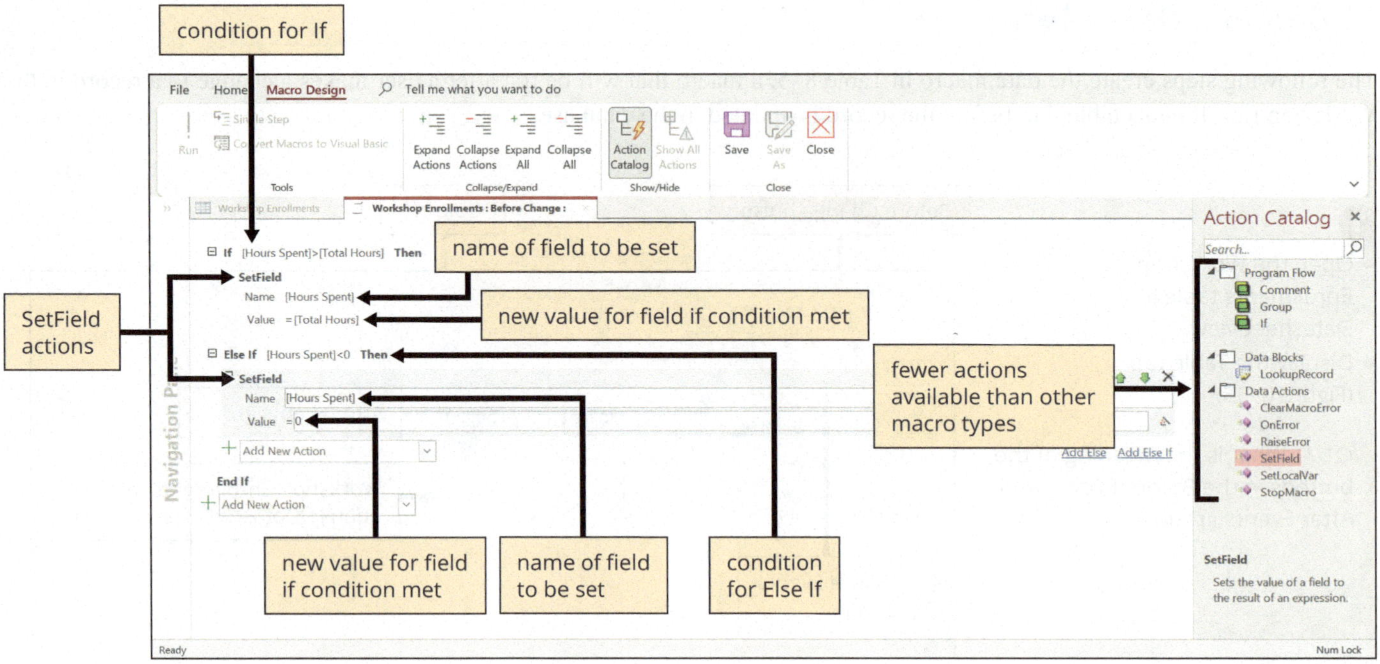

Figure 8–56

3

- Save and close the macro.
- Save and close the Workshop Enrollments table. The discussion in the following section will explore the effects of the new macro.
- If desired, sign out of your Microsoft account.
- **sam** Exit Access.

Note: Unless your instructor indicates otherwise, you are encouraged to simply read the material in this module from this point on for understanding without carrying out any operations.

Q&A What did I accomplish with these changes?

The preceding steps set parameters for data values in the Workshop Enrollments table. The following section will demonstrate the boundaries of these parameters and the actions the macro will take to prevent data from straying outside these limitations.

Using a Table That Contains a Data Macro

If you update a table that contains a data macro, the actions in the data macro will be executed whenever the corresponding event takes place. If the data macro corresponds to the Before Change event, the actions will be executed after the user has changed the data, but before the change is saved in the database. With the data macro you just created, for example, if a user attempts to change the data in such a way that the Hours Spent is greater than the Total Hours (Figure 8–57a), as soon as the user takes an action that would require saving the record, Access makes Hours Spent equal to Total Hours (Figure 8–57b). Likewise, if a user attempts to set Hours Spent to a negative number (Figure 8–58a), as soon as the user takes an action that would require saving the record, Access will set Hours Spent to 0 (Figure 8–58b). These changes will take place automatically, regardless of whether the user changes the values in Datasheet view, with a form, in an update query, or in any other fashion.

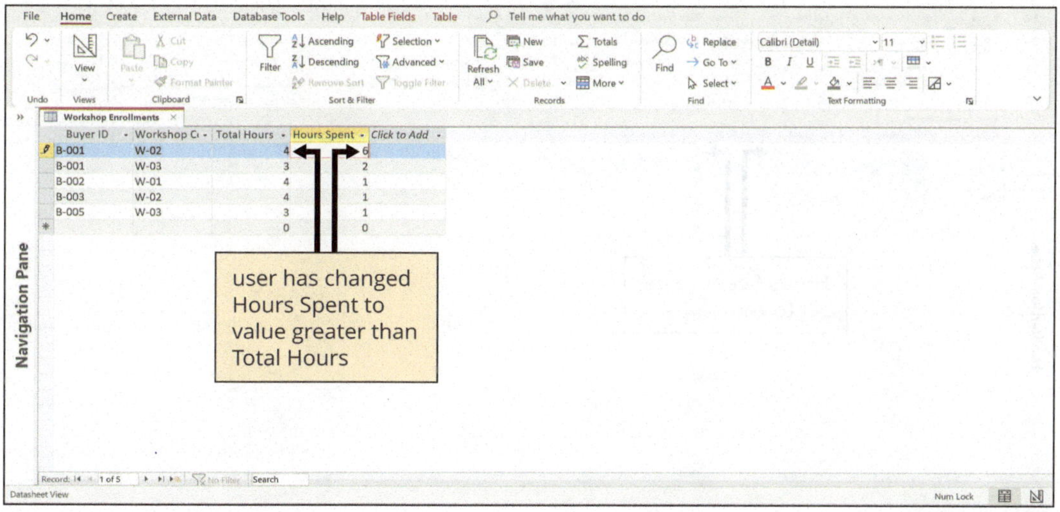

Figure 8–57a

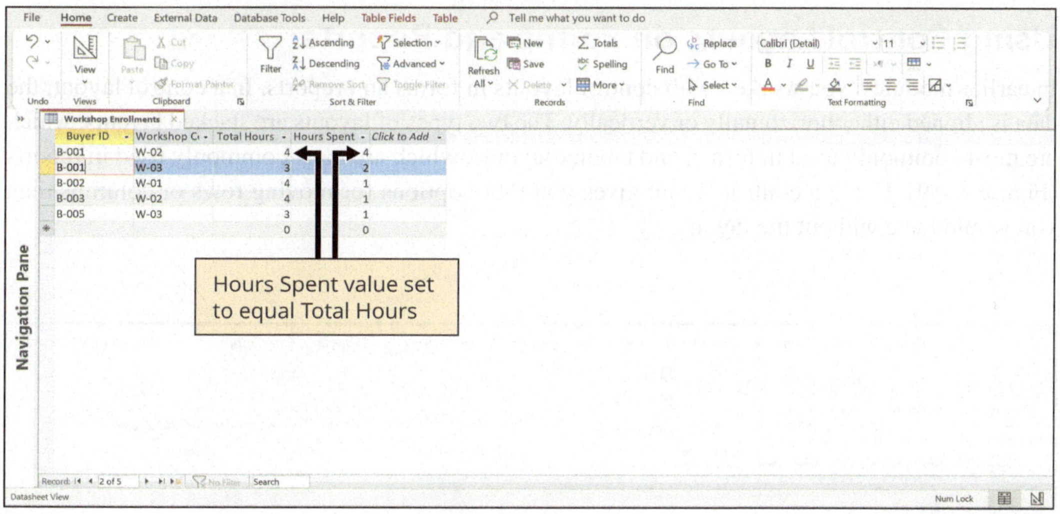

Figure 8–57b

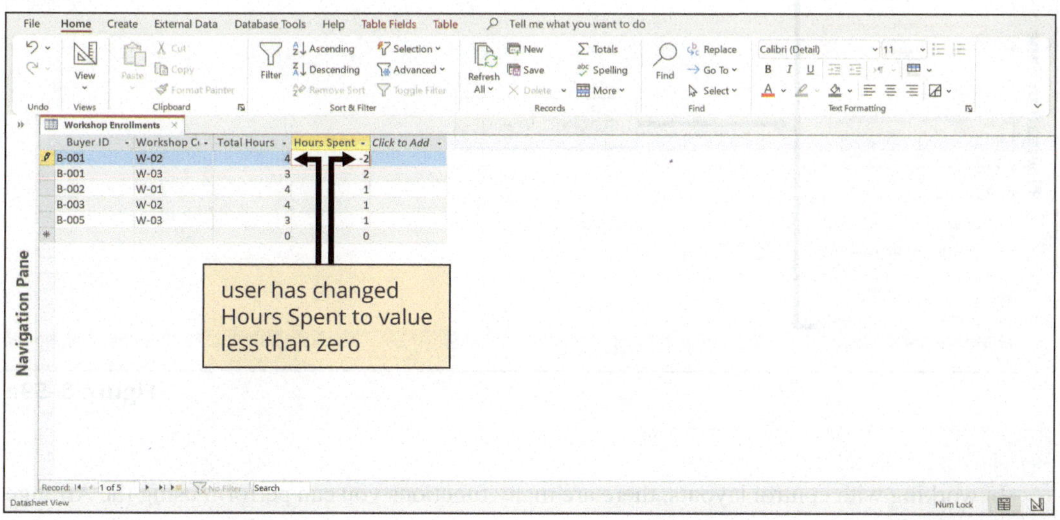

Figure 8–58a

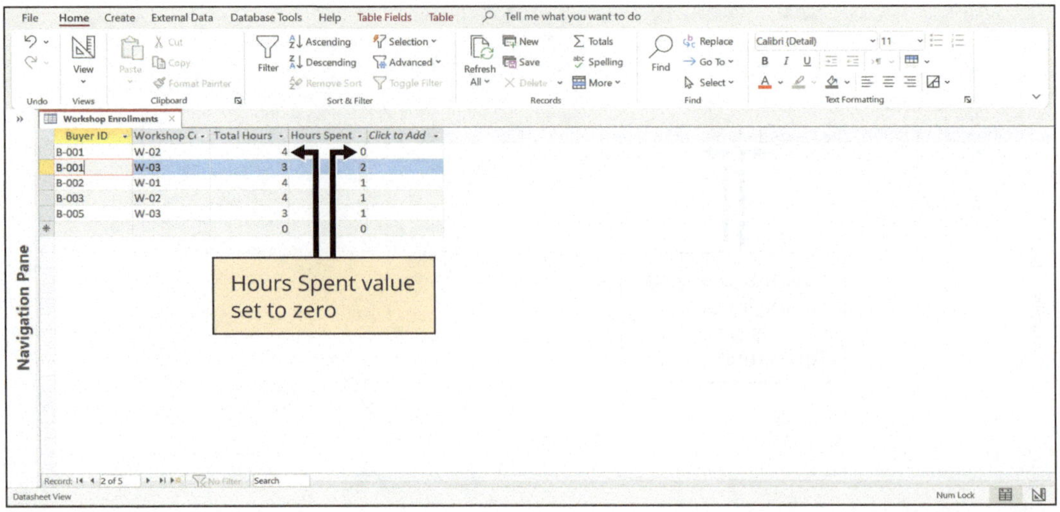

Figure 8–58b

Using Control Layouts on Forms and Reports

In earlier modules, you worked with control layouts in forms and reports. In a control layout, the data is aligned either horizontally or vertically. The two types of layouts are stacked layouts, which are most commonly used in forms, and tabular layouts, which are most commonly used in reports (Figure 8–59). Using a control layout gives you more options for moving rows or columns than you would have without the layout.

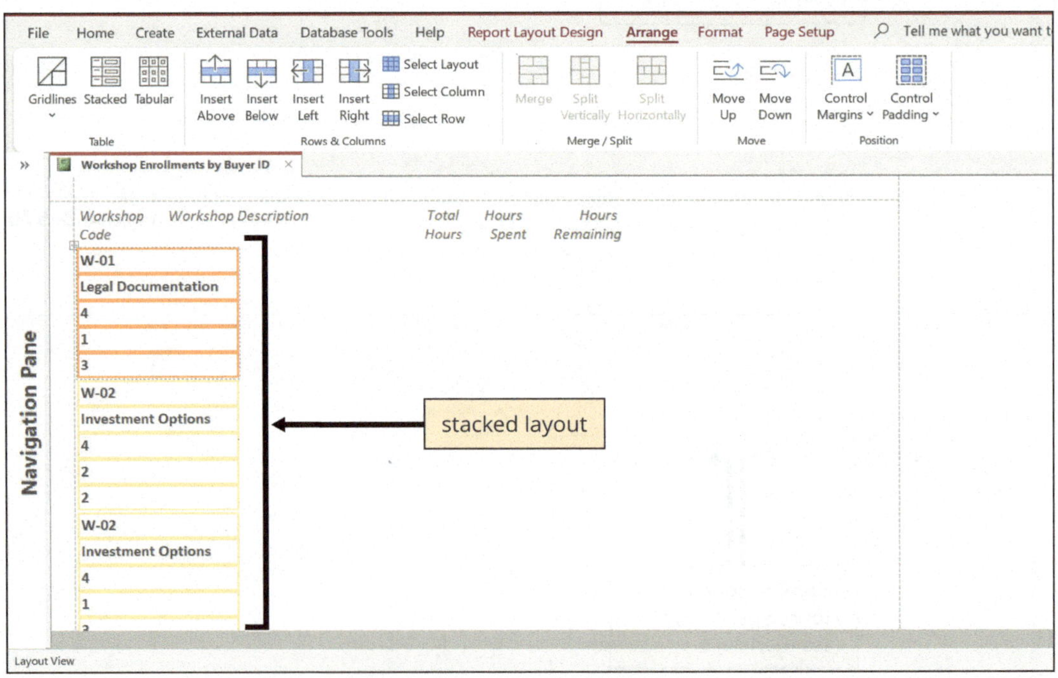

Figure 8–59a

In working with control layouts, there are many functions you can perform using the Arrange tab when the form is in Layout view. You can insert rows and columns, delete rows and columns, split and merge cells, and move rows. You can also change margins, which affects spacing within cells, and padding, which affects spacing between rows and columns. You can split a layout into

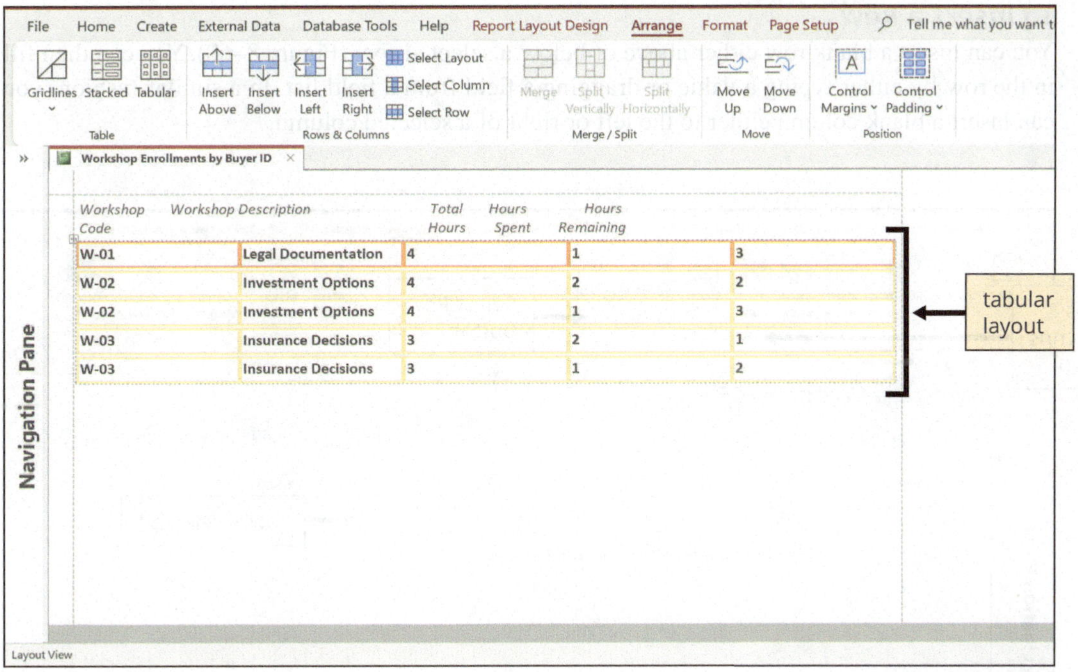

Figure 8–59b

two layouts and move layouts. Finally, you can anchor controls so they maintain the same distance between the control and the anchor position as the form or report is resized. Table 8–6 lists some of the functions available on the Arrange tab and the enhanced ScreenTip that explains their purpose.

Table 8–6 Arrange Tab

Button	Enhanced ScreenTip
Stacked	Create a layout similar to a paper form, with labels to the left of each field.
Tabular	Create a layout similar to a spreadsheet, with labels across the top and data in columns below the labels.
Split Vertically	Split the selected control into two rows.
Split Horizontally	Split the selected control into two columns.
Anchoring	Tie a control to a section or another control so that it moves or resizes in conjunction with movement or resizing of the parent.

To Create a Layout for a Form or Report

If you create a form using the Form button (Create tab | Forms group), Access automatically creates a stacked layout. If you create a report using the Report button (Create tab | Reports group), Access automatically creates a tabular layout. In other cases, you can create a layout using the Arrange tab. If you no longer want controls to be in a control layout, you can remove the layout.

To create a layout in either a form or report, you would use the following steps.

1. Select all the controls that you want to place in a layout.
2. Click the Stacked button (Arrange tab | Table group) to create a stacked layout or the Tabular button (Arrange tab | Table group) to create a tabular layout.

To Remove a Layout for a Form or Report

To remove a layout from either a form or report, you would use the following steps.

1. Right-click any control in the layout you want to remove to produce a shortcut menu.
2. Point to Layout on the shortcut menu, and then click Remove Layout on the submenu to remove the layout. Removing the layout does not reposition the controls.

To Insert a Row

You can insert a blank row either above or below a selected row (Figure 8–60). You can then fill in the row by either typing a value or dragging a field from a field list. In a similar fashion, you can insert a blank column either to the left or right of a selected column.

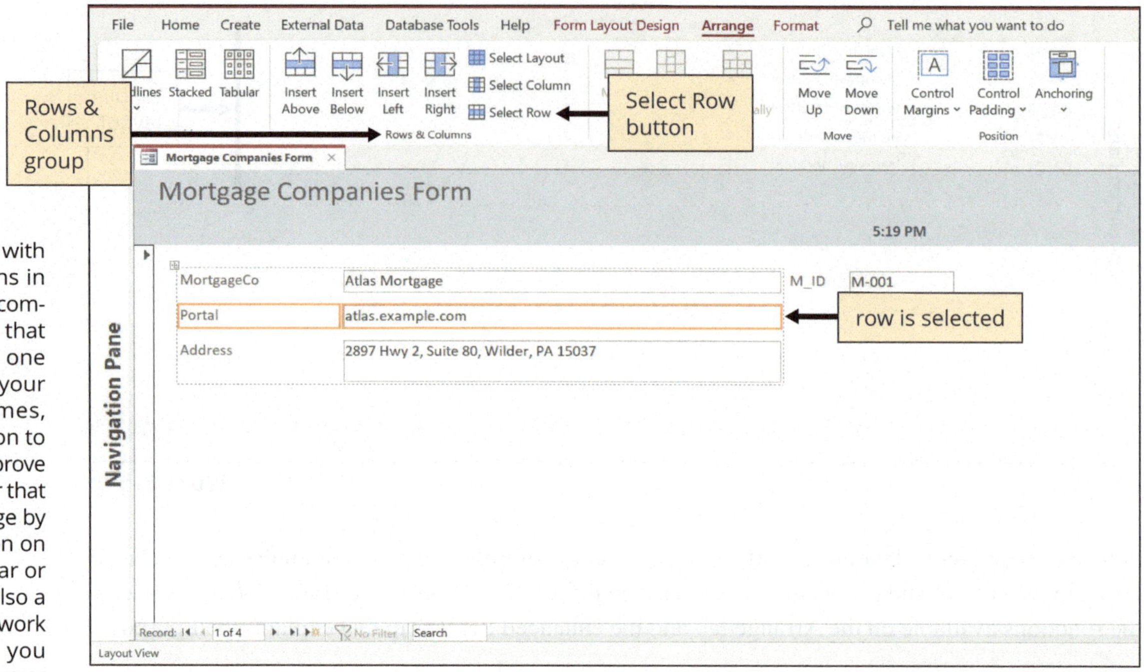

Figure 8–60a

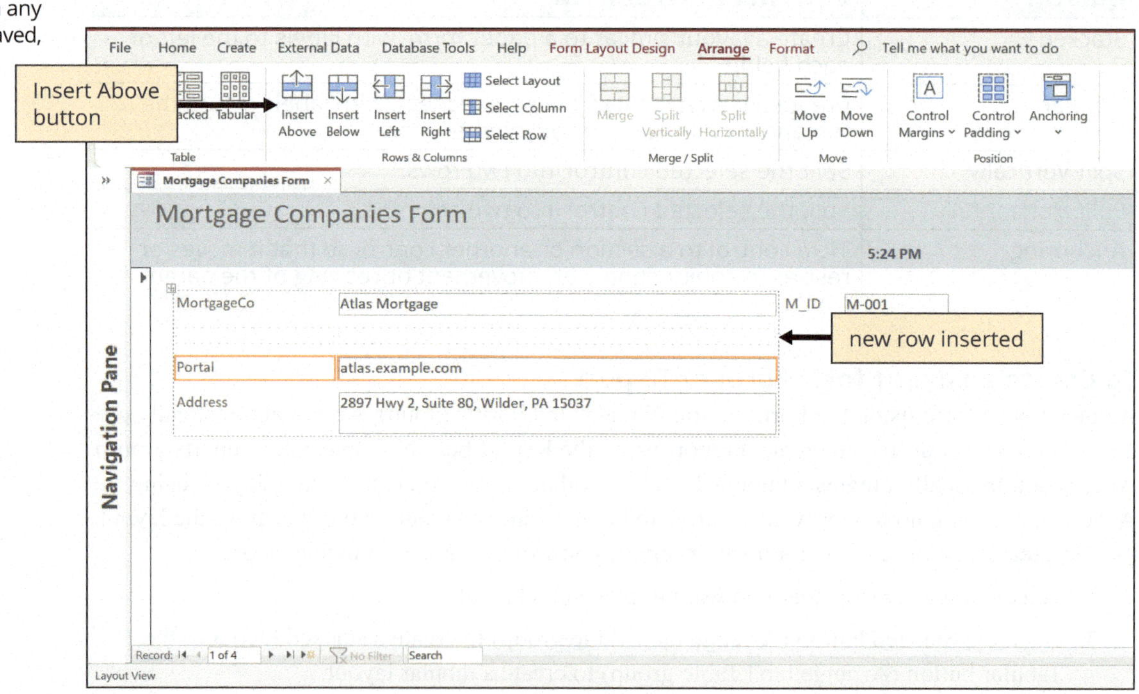

Figure 8–60b

BTW
The Undo Button
When making changes with the Arrange tab buttons in Layout view, it is not uncommon to make a change that you did not intend, or one that you later change your mind about. Sometimes, taking appropriate action to reverse the change can prove difficult. If so, remember that you can undo the change by clicking the Undo button on the Quick Access Toolbar or on the Home tab. It is also a good idea to save your work frequently. That way, you can always close the form or report without saving. Then, when you reopen the form or report, it will not contain any of your most recent, unsaved, changes.

You would use the following steps to insert a blank row.

1. Select any control in the row above or below where you want to insert a new row.
2. Click the Insert Above button (Arrange tab | Rows & Columns group) to insert a blank row above the selected row or the Insert Below button (Arrange tab | Rows & Columns group) to insert a blank row below the selected row.

As you learned earlier in the text, you also can insert a row containing a field by simply dragging the field from the field list to the desired location.

To Insert a Column

You would use the following steps to insert a new column.

1. Select any control in the column to the right or left of where you want to insert a new column.
2. Click the Insert Left button (Arrange tab | Rows & Columns group) to insert a blank column to the left of the selected column or the Insert Right button (Arrange tab | Rows & Columns group) to insert a blank column to the right of the selected column.

To Delete a Row

You can delete any unwanted row or column from a control layout. You would use the following steps to delete a row.

1. Click any control in the row you want to delete.
2. Click Select Row (Arrange tab | Rows & Columns group).
3. Press DEL to delete the row.

To Delete a Column

You would use the following steps to delete a column.

1. Click any control in the column you want to delete.
2. Click Select Column (Arrange tab | Rows & Columns group).
3. Press DEL to delete the column.

Splitting and Merging Cells

You can split a cell into two cells either horizontally, as shown in Figure 8–61, or vertically. You can then enter contents into the new cell. For example, in Figure 8–61, you could type text into the new cell that gives information about Property IDs or alternative contact information. You can also merge two cells into one.

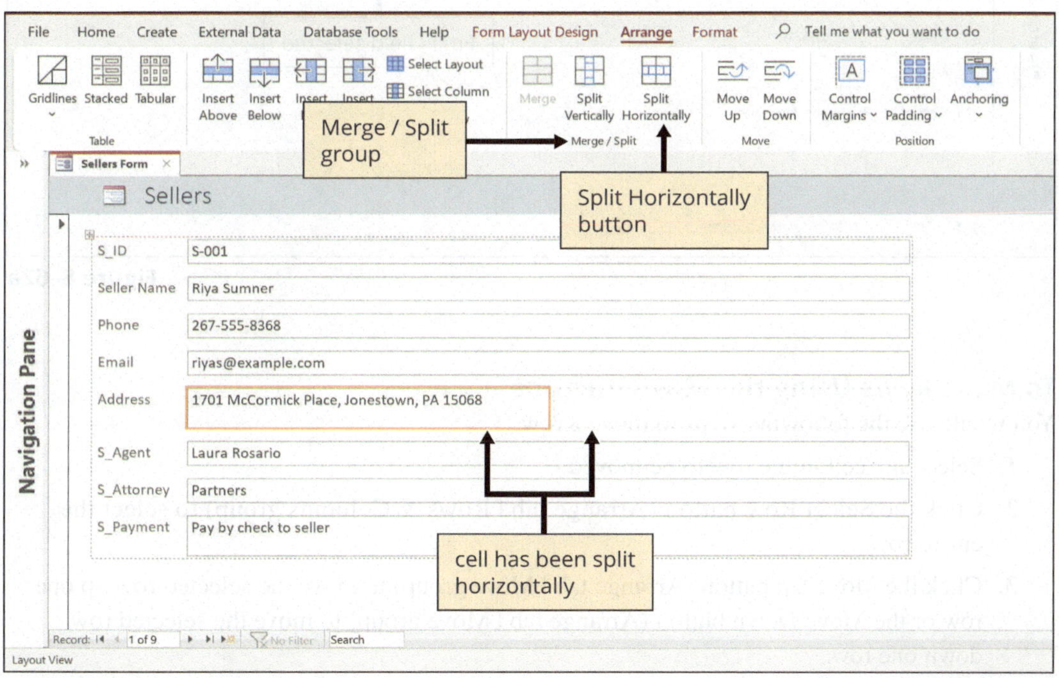

Figure 8–61

To Split a Cell

To split a cell, you would use the following steps.

1. Click the cell to be split.
2. Click the Split Vertically button (Arrange tab | Merge / Split group) to split the selected cell vertically or the Split Horizontally button (Arrange tab | Merge / Split group) to split the selected cell horizontally.

To Merge Cells

You would use the following steps to merge cells.

1. Select the first cell to be merged.
2. While holding down CTRL, click all the other cells to be merged.
3. Click the Merge button (Arrange tab | Merge / Split group) to merge the cells.

Moving Cells

You can move a cell in a layout by dragging it to its new position. Most often, however, you will not want to move individual cells, but rather whole rows (Figure 8–62). You can move a row by selecting the row and then dragging it to the new position, or you can use the Move buttons on the Arrange tab.

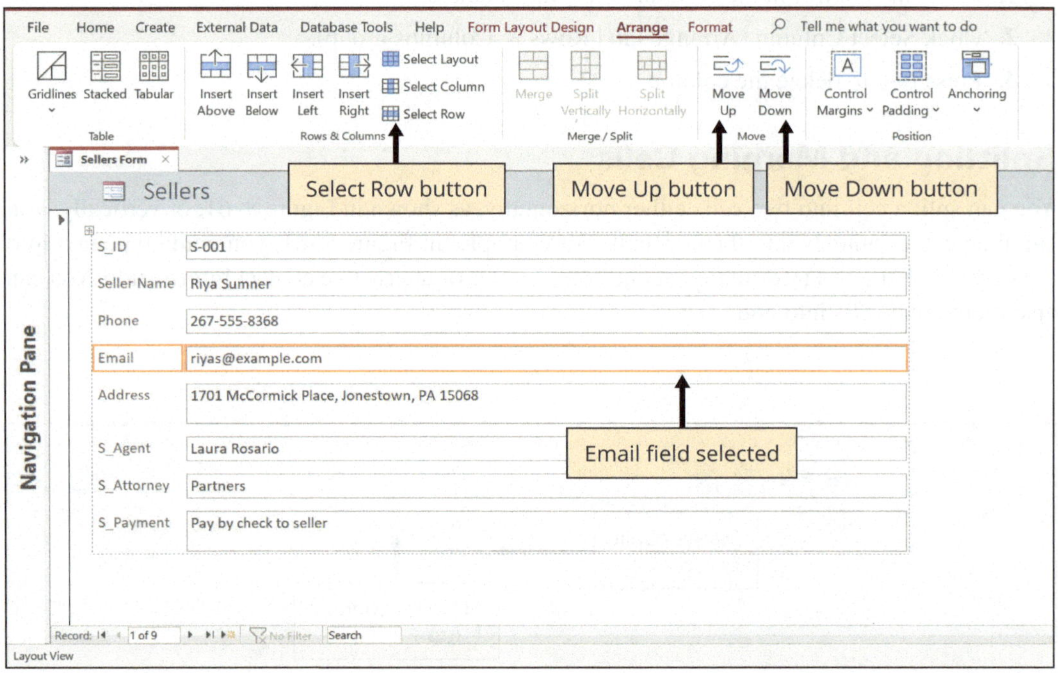

Figure 8–62a

To Move Rows Using the Move Buttons

You would use the following steps to move a row.

1. Select any cell in the row to be moved.
2. Click the Select Row button (Arrange tab | Rows & Columns group) to select the entire row.
3. Click the Move Up button (Arrange tab | Move group) to move the selected row up one row or the Move Down button (Arrange tab | Move group) to move the selected row down one row.

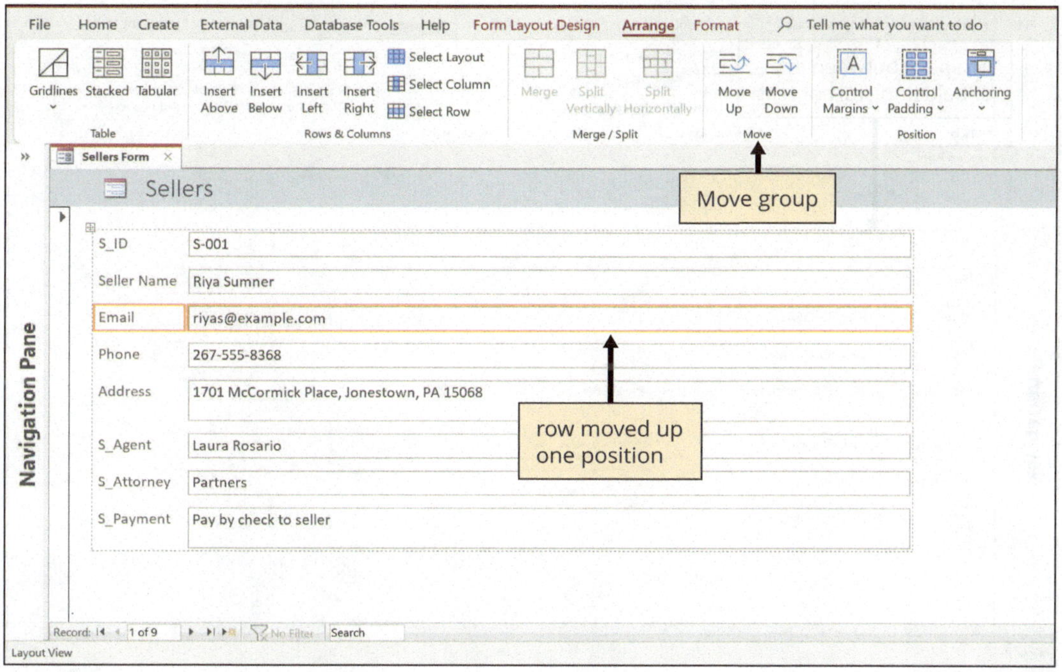

Figure 8–62b

Margins and Padding

You can change the spacing within a layout by changing the control margins and the control padding. The control margins, which you change with the Control Margins button, affect the spacing around the text inside a control. Figure 8–63 shows the various options as well as samples of two of the options.

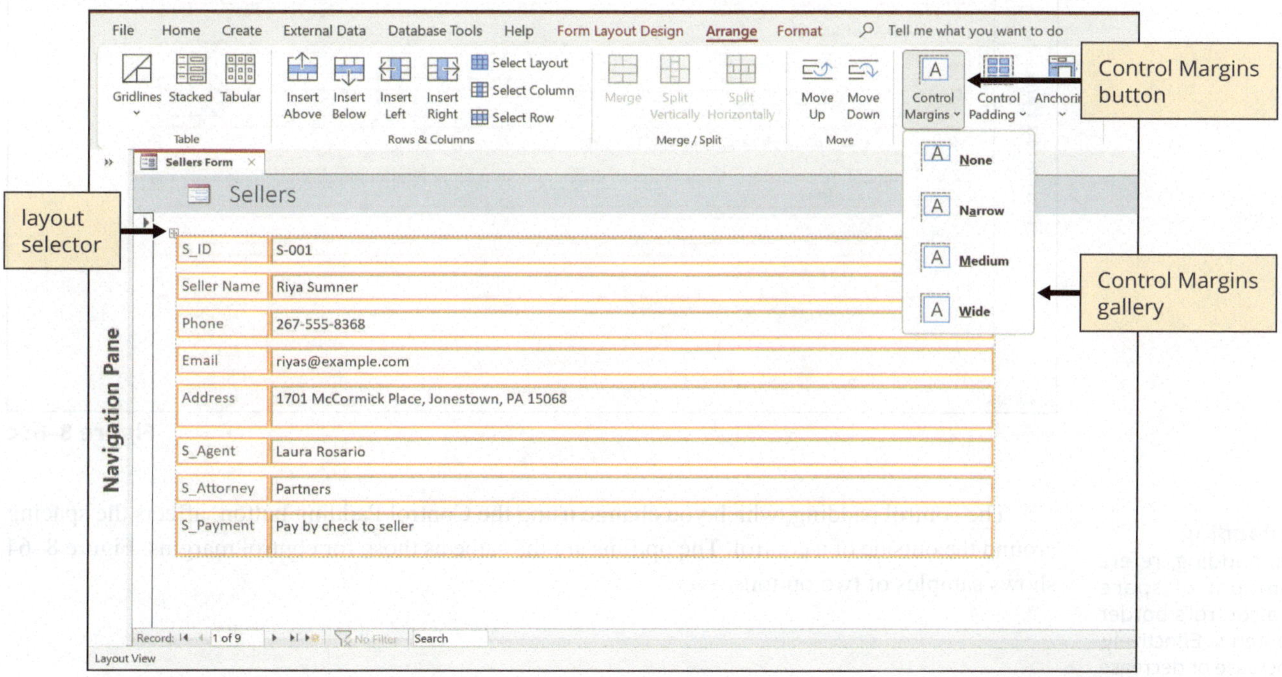

Figure 8–63a

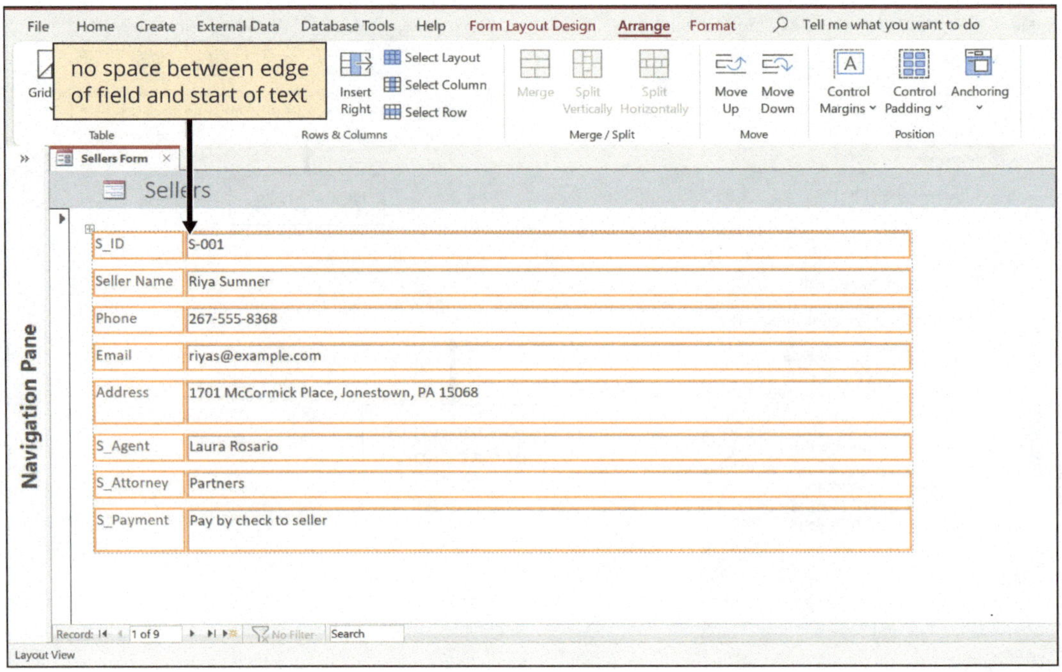

Figure 8–63b

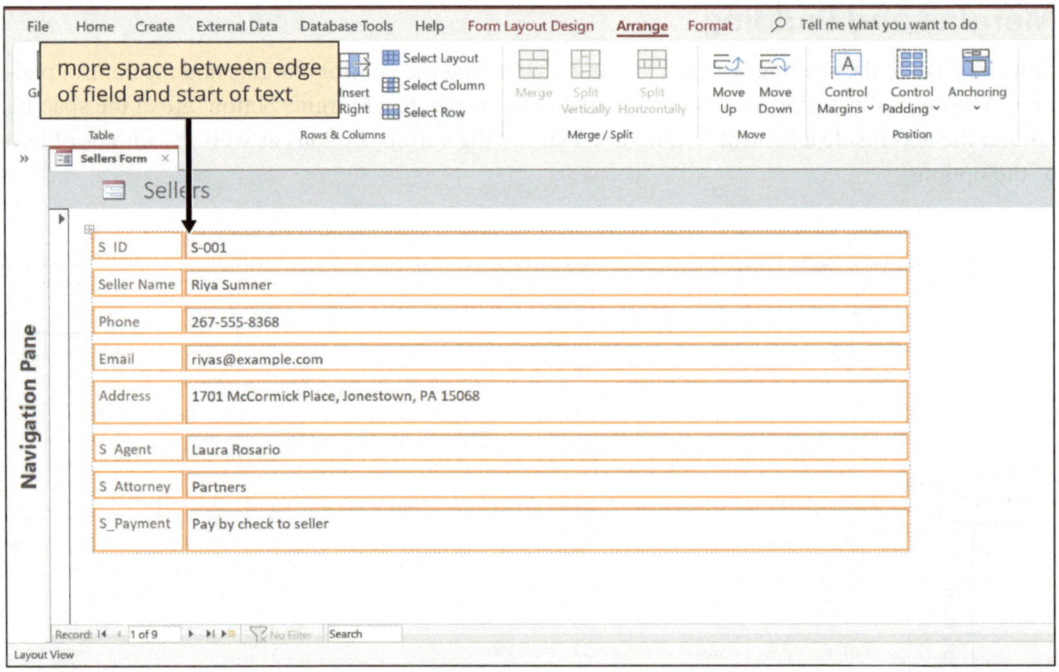

Figure 8–63c

BTW

Control Padding

The term, padding, refers to the amount of space between a control's border and its contents. Effectively, you can increase or decrease the amount of white space in a control.

The control padding, which you change using the Control Padding button, affects the spacing around the outside of a control. The options are the same as those for control margins. Figure 8–64 shows samples of two options.

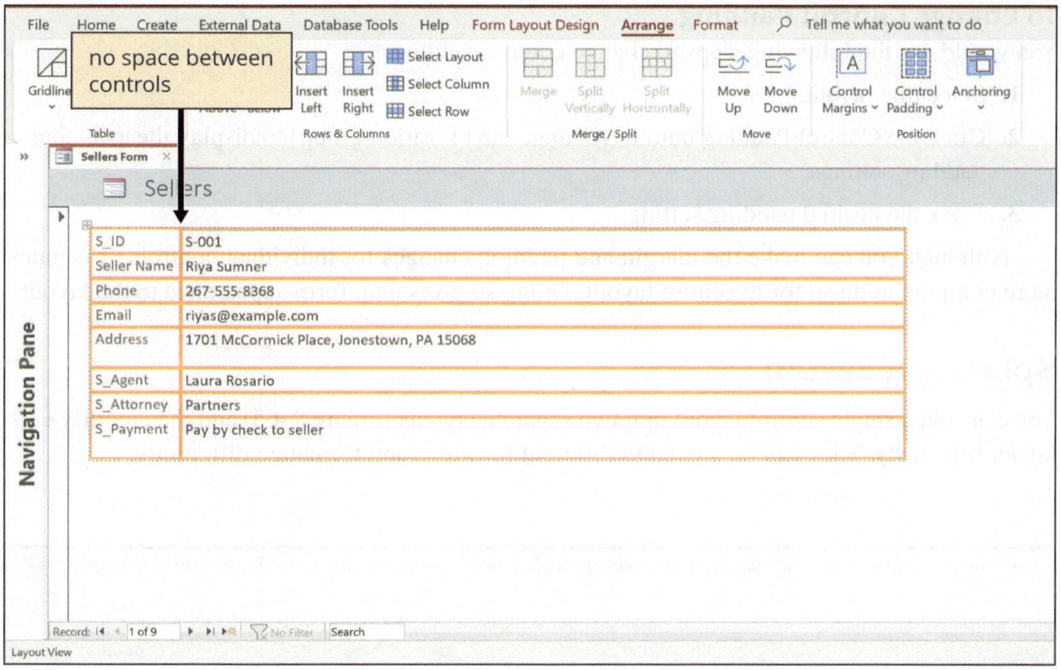

Figure 8–64a

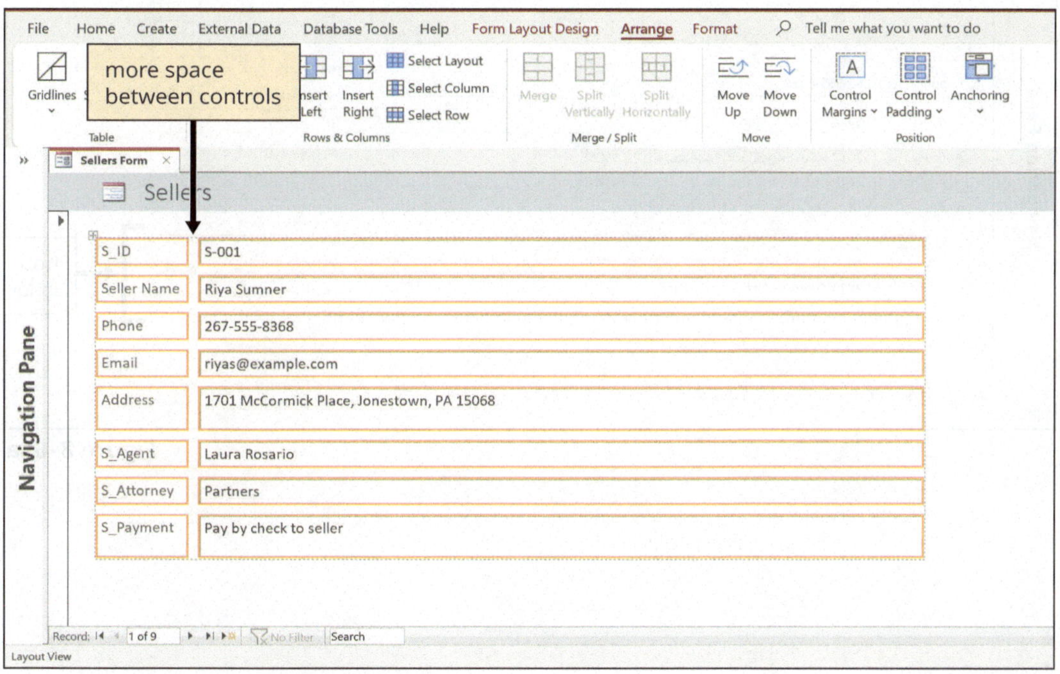

Figure 8–64b

To Change Control Margins

You would use the following steps to change a control's margins.

1. Select any cell in the layout.
2. Click the Select Layout button (Arrange tab | Rows & Columns group) to select the entire layout. (You also can select the layout by clicking the layout selector.)
3. Click the Control Margins button (Arrange tab | Position group) to display the available margin settings.
4. Click the desired margin setting.

To Change Control Padding

You would use the following steps to change control padding.

1. Select the layout.
2. Click the Control Padding button (Arrange tab | Position group) to display the available padding settings.
3. Click the desired padding setting.

Although you can make the margin and padding changes for individual controls, it is much more common to do so for the entire layout. Doing so gives a uniform appearance to the layout.

Splitting a Layout

You can split a single control layout into two separate layouts (Figure 8–65) and then modify each layout separately. They can be moved to different locations and formatted differently.

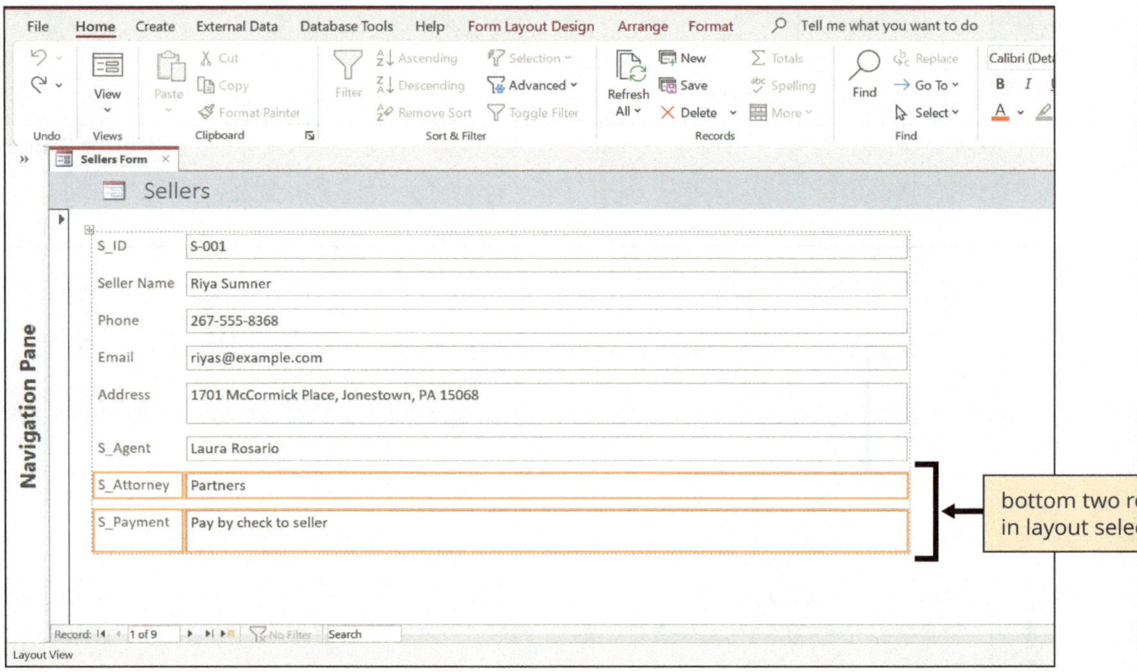

Figure 8–65a

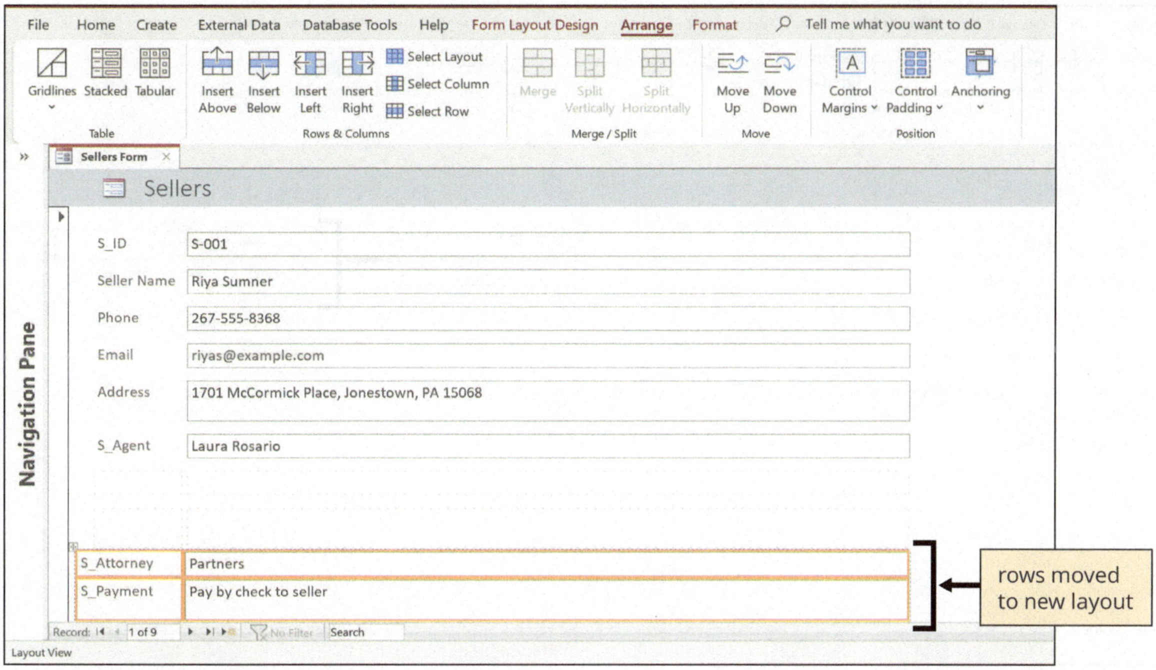

Figure 8–65b

To Split a Layout

To split a layout, you would use the following steps.

1. Select all the cells that you want to move to a new layout.
2. Click the Stacked button (Arrange tab | Table group) to place the cells in a stacked layout or the Tabular button (Arrange tab | Table group) to place the cells in a tabular layout.

BTW
Gridlines
You can add gridlines to a form. To do so, select the control(s) for which you want to add gridlines, then click the Gridlines button. When the Gridlines menu appears, select the desired option. You also can change the color, border, style, and width of gridlines using the Gridlines menu.

Moving a Layout

You can move a control layout to a different location on the form (Figure 8–66).

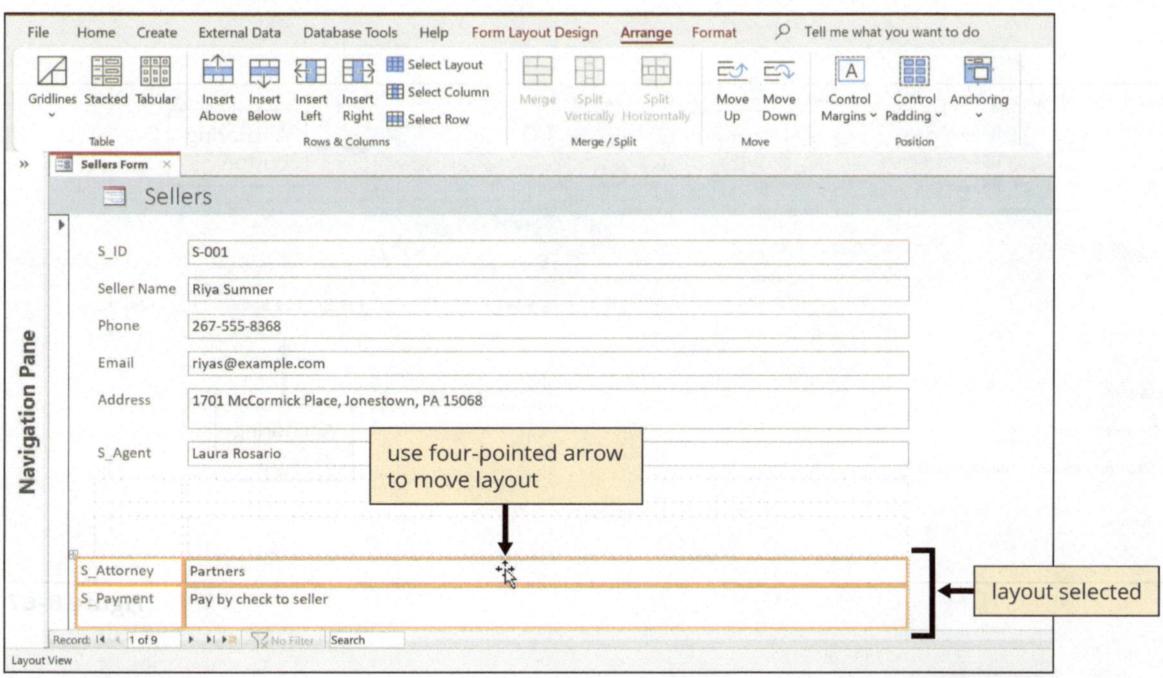

Figure 8–66a

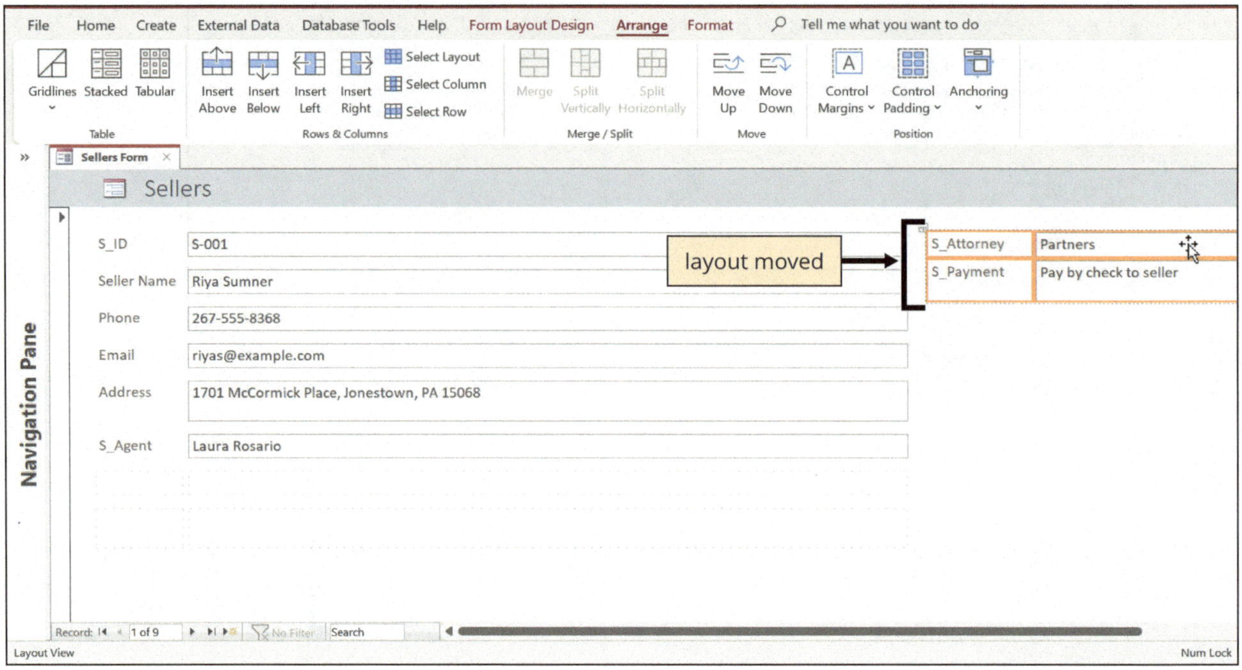

Figure 8–66b

To Move a Layout

You would use the following steps to move a layout.

1. Click any cell in the layout to be moved, and then click the Select Layout button (Arrange tab | Rows & Columns group) to select the layout.
2. Drag the layout to the new location.

Anchoring Controls

The Anchoring button allows you to tie (anchor) controls to a section or to other controls so they maintain the same distance between the control and the anchor position as the form is resized. To anchor the controls you have selected, you use the Anchoring gallery (Figure 8–67).

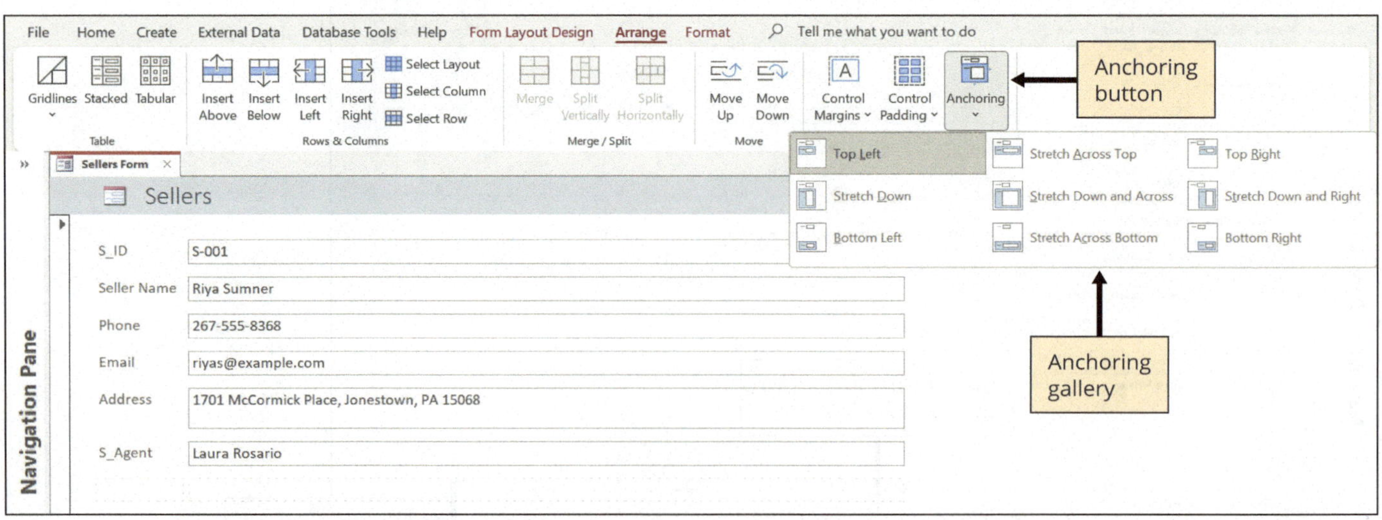

Figure 8–67

The Top Left, Top Right, Bottom Left, and Bottom Right options anchor the control in the indicated position on the form. The other five operations also stretch the controls in the indicated direction.

To Anchor Controls

You would use the following steps to anchor controls.

1. Select the control or controls to be anchored.
2. Click the Anchoring button (Arrange tab | Position group) to produce the Anchoring gallery.
3. Select the desired Anchoring option from the Anchoring gallery.

Overlapping Windows

To view the effect of anchoring, you need to display objects in overlapping windows rather than standard tabbed documents. With overlapping windows, you can resize the object by dragging the border of the object. Anchored objects keep their same relative position (Figure 8–68).

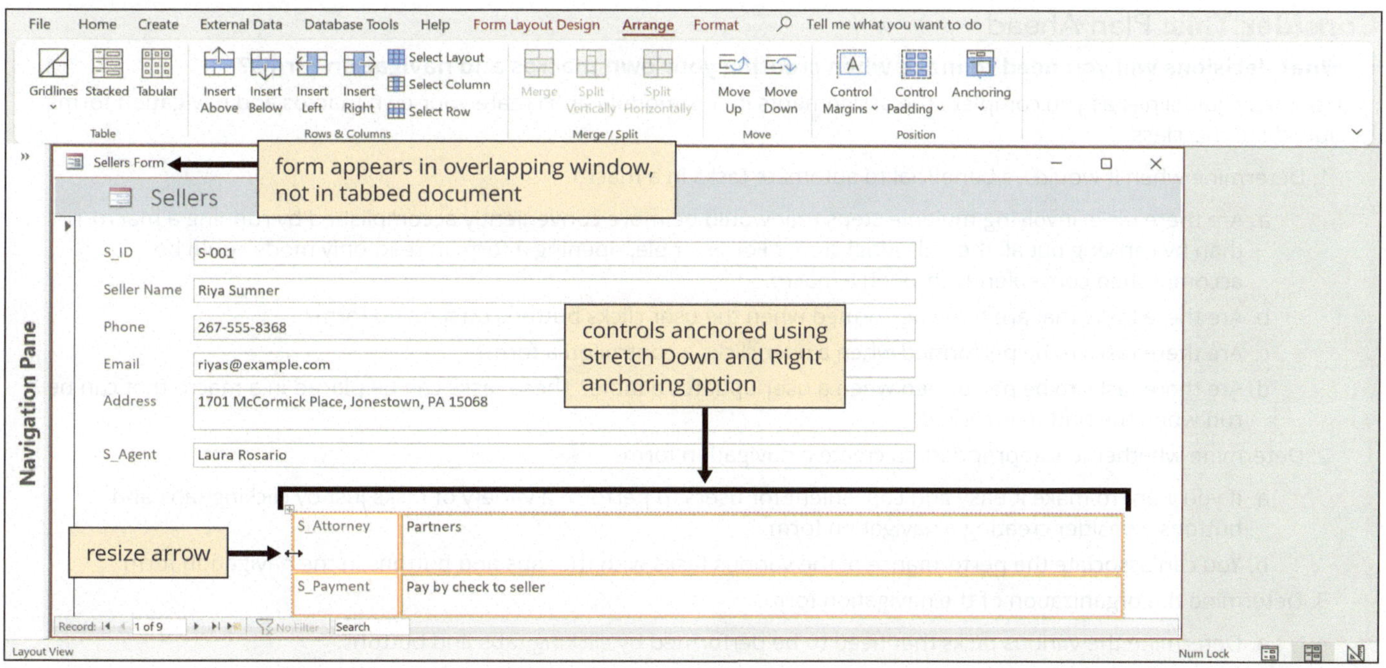

Figure 8–68

If you want to display objects in overlapping windows, you have to modify the appropriate Access option.

To Display Objects in Overlapping Windows

You would use the following steps to overlap windows.

1. Click File on the ribbon to open Backstage view.
2. Click Options to display the Access Options dialog box.
3. Click Current Database to display the Current Database options.
4. In the Application Options area, click the Overlapping Windows option button.
5. Click the OK button to close the Access Options dialog box.
6. For the changes to take effect, you will need to close and then reopen the database.

   You use a similar process to return to displaying objects in tabbed documents.

BTW

Overlapping Windows

When you display objects in overlapping windows, each database object appears in its own window. When multiple objects are open, these windows overlap each other. By default, Access displays database objects in a single pane separated by tabs.

To Display Objects in Tabbed Documents

You would use the following steps to display tabbed documents.

1. Click File on the ribbon to open Backstage view.
2. Click Options to display the Access Options dialog box.
3. Click Current Database to display the Current Database options.
4. In the Application Options area, click the Tabbed Documents option button.
5. Click the OK button to close the Access Options dialog box.
6. For the changes to take effect, you will need to close and then reopen the database.

Summary

In this module you have learned to create and use macros, create a menu form that uses command buttons for the choices, create a menu form that uses an option group for the choices, create a macro that implements the choices in the option group, create datasheet forms that utilize user interface macros, create a navigation form, add tabs to a navigation form, and create data macros. You also learned to modify control layouts.

Consider This: Plan Ahead

What decisions will you need to make when creating your own macros and navigation forms?

Use these guidelines as you complete the assignments in this module and create your own macros and navigation forms outside of this class.

1. Determine when it would be beneficial to automate tasks in a macro.
   a. Are there tasks involving multiple steps that would be more conveniently accomplished by running a macro than by carrying out all the individual steps? For example, opening a form in read-only mode could be accomplished conveniently through a macro.
   b. Are there tasks that are to be performed when the user clicks buttons on a menu form?
   c. Are there tasks to be performed when a user clicks a control on a form?
   d. Are there tasks to be performed when a user updates a table? These tasks can be placed in a macro that can be run when the button is clicked.
2. Determine whether it is appropriate to create a navigation form.
   a. If you want to make it easy and convenient for users to perform a variety of tasks just by clicking tabs and buttons, consider creating a navigation form.
   b. You can associate the performance of the various tasks with the tabs and buttons in the navigation form.
3. Determine the organization of the navigation form.
   a. Determine the various tasks that need to be performed by clicking tabs and buttons.
   b. Decide the logical grouping of the tabs and buttons.

Consider This

How should you submit solutions to critical thinking questions in the assignments?

Every assignment in this course contains one or more critical thinking questions. These questions require you to think beyond the assigned database. Present your responses to the questions in the format required by your instructor. Possible formats might include one or more of these options: write the answer; create a document that contains the answer; present your answer to the class; discuss your answer in a group; record the answer as audio or video using a webcam, smartphone, or portable media player; or post answers on a blog, wiki, or website.

Student Assignments

Apply Your Knowledge

Reinforce the skills and apply the concepts you learned in this module.

Creating UI Macros and a Navigation Form

Note: To complete this assignment, you will be required to use the Data Files. Please contact your instructor for information about accessing the Data Files.

Instructions: Start Access. Open the database, SC_AC_08-2.accdb, which is located in the Data Files folder. Enable the content.

Perform the following tasks:

1. Save the database using the file name, SC_AC_08_Construction. Enable the content.
2. Create a datasheet form for the Job Sites table and name the form Job Sites List.
3. Create a UI macro for the Job Sites List form. Use JS as the temporary variable name. When a user clicks a job site number on a row in the datasheet form, the Job Sites List form should appear in a dialog window in read-only mode. Remove the temporary variable.
4. Create a datasheet form for the Subcontractors table and save the form with the name Subcontractors. Create a UI macro for the Subcontractors form. Use SC as the temporary variable name. When a user clicks a subcontractor number on a row in the datasheet form, the Subcontractors form should appear in a dialog window in read-only mode. Remember to remove the temporary variable as part of good database management.
5. Create the navigation form shown in Figure 8–69. The purpose of the form is to display the two datasheet forms in the database as horizontal tabs. Name the form Main Menu and change the title to Build It Construction: Main Menu. Save and close the form.

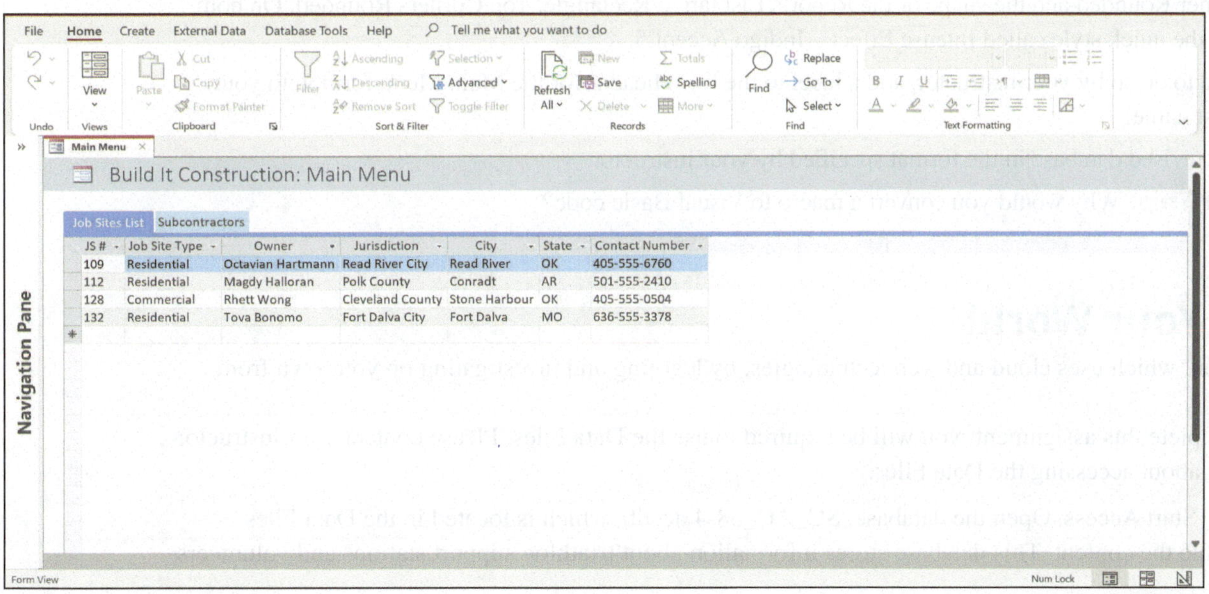

Figure 8–69

6. If requested to do so by your instructor, open the Subcontractors datasheet form and change the first and last names of subcontractor SC040 to your first and last name.
7. Submit the revised database in the format specified by your instructor.
8. **Consider This:** How could you add an Accounting datasheet form to the navigation form?

Extend Your Knowledge

Extend the skills you learned in this module and experiment with new skills. You may need to use Help to complete the assignment.

Creating and Modifying Navigation Forms

Note: To complete this assignment, you will be required to use the Data Files. Please contact your instructor for information about accessing the Data Files.

Instructions: Start Access. Open the database, SC_AC_08-3.accdb, which is located in the Data Files folder. PicsPlus is a photographers' cooperative that is applying for a grant. To complete the grant application, the PicsPlus database needs to be updated so it is compatible with the configurations required in the grant standards and so the files can be exported as required for grant consideration.

Perform the following tasks:

1. Save the database using the file name, SC_AC_08_PicsPlus. Enable the content.
2. Create a menu form named Forms List that contains command buttons that open the Clients by Photographer form and the Photographer Form in Edit mode.
3. Create a form named Reports List that contains a macro to open the Photographer Balances Summary Report.
4. Create a Main Menu form for forms and reports. The Forms List menu should include the command buttons for the Clients by Photographer form and the Photographer Form. The Reports List menu should include a command button for the summary report. Test the macros before closing the form.
5. Open the Forms List form in Design view. Select the button controls, and change the font weight to semi-bold. Use the Size/Space menu to adjust the controls to be the same width as the widest button. Change the buttons' back color and border color to colors of your choice. Change the buttons' hover color to Brown. Test the formatting changes in Form view.
6. Open the Reports List form in Design view and make the same changes that you made to the Forms List form.
7. Open the Main Menu navigation form in Layout view. Change the shape of the Forms List tab to Rectangle: Single Corner Rounded and the shape of the Reports List tab to Rectangle: Top Corners Rounded. On both tabs, apply the quick style called Intense Effect – Indigo Accent 5.
8. If requested to do so by your instructor, add a label to the form header for the Main Menu form with your first and last name.
9. Submit the revised database in the format specified by your instructor.
10. **Consider This:** Why would you convert a macro to Visual Basic code?

Expand Your World

Create a solution, which uses cloud and web technologies, by learning and investigating on your own from general guidance.

Note: To complete this assignment, you will be required to use the Data Files. Please contact your instructor for information about accessing the Data Files.

Instructions: Start Access. Open the database, SC_AC_08-4.accdb, which is located in the Data Files folder, and enable the content. This database stores information about triathlon support stations and volunteers at each station.

Perform the following tasks:

1. Save the database using the file name, SC_AC_08_Triathlon. Enable the content.
2. Open the Volunteer Station Form in Layout view. Split the existing control layout so the station information is listed to the right of the volunteer information, as shown in Figure 8–70. Be sure to remove any remaining blank rows.

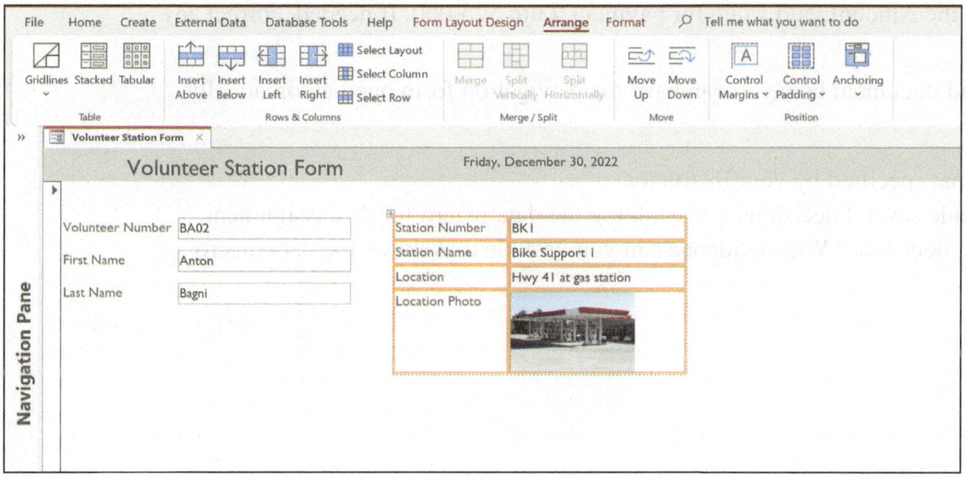

Mehluli Hikwa/Unsplash

Figure 8–70

3. Insert a new row below the Last Name field. Name the new row Email.
4. Create a menu form named Reports List containing an option group with the caption Report Actions. Include options to preview or export to PDF each of the two reports, and configure no default choice.
5. **Consider This:** Research online to determine the differences between importing a database object between Access databases and exporting a database object between Access databases. What are two, significant limitations of the export operation compared to the import operation between Access databases?
6. Submit your research response and the revised database in the format specified by your instructor.
7. **Consider This:** What macros did you create for this project? Why did you make those choices?

In the Lab

Design and implement a solution using creative thinking and problem-solving skills.

Lab: Adding a Navigation Form to the Homegrown Nursing Staff Agency Database

Note: To complete this assignment, you will be required to use the Data Files. Please contact your instructor for information about accessing the Data Files.

Problem: Homegrown Nursing Staff Agency would like you to create a main menu that allows easy access to forms and reports. They also need a way to ensure traveler payments do not exceed the amount due.

Perform the following tasks:

Part 1: Open the SC_AC_08-5.accdb database from the Data Files folder. Save the file with the name, SC_AC_08_Travel-Nurses, and enable the content. Use the concepts and techniques presented in this module to perform each of the following tasks.

1. Create a form with macro command buttons that open the Facility Assignments Form and the Traveler Assignments Form in Read Only mode. Name the form List of Available Forms.
2. Create a form with macro buttons that opens the Assignment Bill Rates report and the Travelers and Payments Summary List report. Name the form List of Available Reports.
3. Create a Main Menu navigation form that includes the List of Available Forms form and the List of Available Reports form. Test the navigation form and correct any errors.
4. Add a data macro to the Traveler Payments table that replaces any value entered into the Amount Paid field that is greater than the value in the Current Due field with the value of the Current Due field.

Continued on next page

5. To test the data macro, change the Amount Paid value for payment 23 to $25,000. If needed, correct any errors in the data macro.
6. **Consider This:** Research and document how you can have the Navigation form open automatically when the database is opened.

Submit your assignment in the format specified by your instructor.

Part 2: **Consider This:** You made several decisions while adding the data macro for this assignment. What was the rationale behind your decisions? What evidence can you provide that shows the data macro works as intended?

Administering a Database System

Objectives

After completing this module, you will be able to:

- Explain how to convert a database between versions of Access
- Use the Table Analyzer, Performance Analyzer, and Database Documenter
- Create custom categories and groups in the Navigation Pane
- Modify table, database, and field properties
- Create an index
- Enable automatic error checking
- Create a custom data type
- Create a database template
- Select a startup form
- Create an application part
- Use a database template
- Explain how to encrypt a database with a password
- Explain how to lock a database
- Explain how to split a database

Introduction

Administering a database system is an important activity that has many facets. Administrative activities are an important aspect of database management because they improve the usability, accessibility, security, and efficiency of the database. In this module, you will learn how to perform a variety of database administration tasks.

Project: Administering a Database System

Clearnet realizes the importance of database administration, that is, the importance of administering its database system responsibly and with the user experience in mind. An important activity in administering databases is the creation of custom templates, application parts, and data type parts. A **custom template** is a customized database application that can be used as a basis for additional databases. The template contains tables, forms, queries, and other objects that can be used by others to create a database based on that template. Application parts and data type parts are templates included in Access that you can add to your database to extend its functionality. Clicking an application part adds to your database a predetermined collection of objects such as tables, queries, forms, reports, and macros. Clicking a data type part adds a predetermined collection of fields to a table. Creating an understandable startup form gives database users easy access to the forms when the database is opened.

Clearnet has decided to create a streamlined version of its database that drivers can use to track their own loads. As drivers are contacted with offers of additional loads, it's helpful for them to have all relevant information in one place to help them decide which loads will be cost effective for them to take. The Clearnet staff organizing the driver database realize that some drivers might not be familiar with operating a database, and a startup menu would be extremely helpful. Figure 9–1 shows a startup form that is automatically opened when the database is opened.

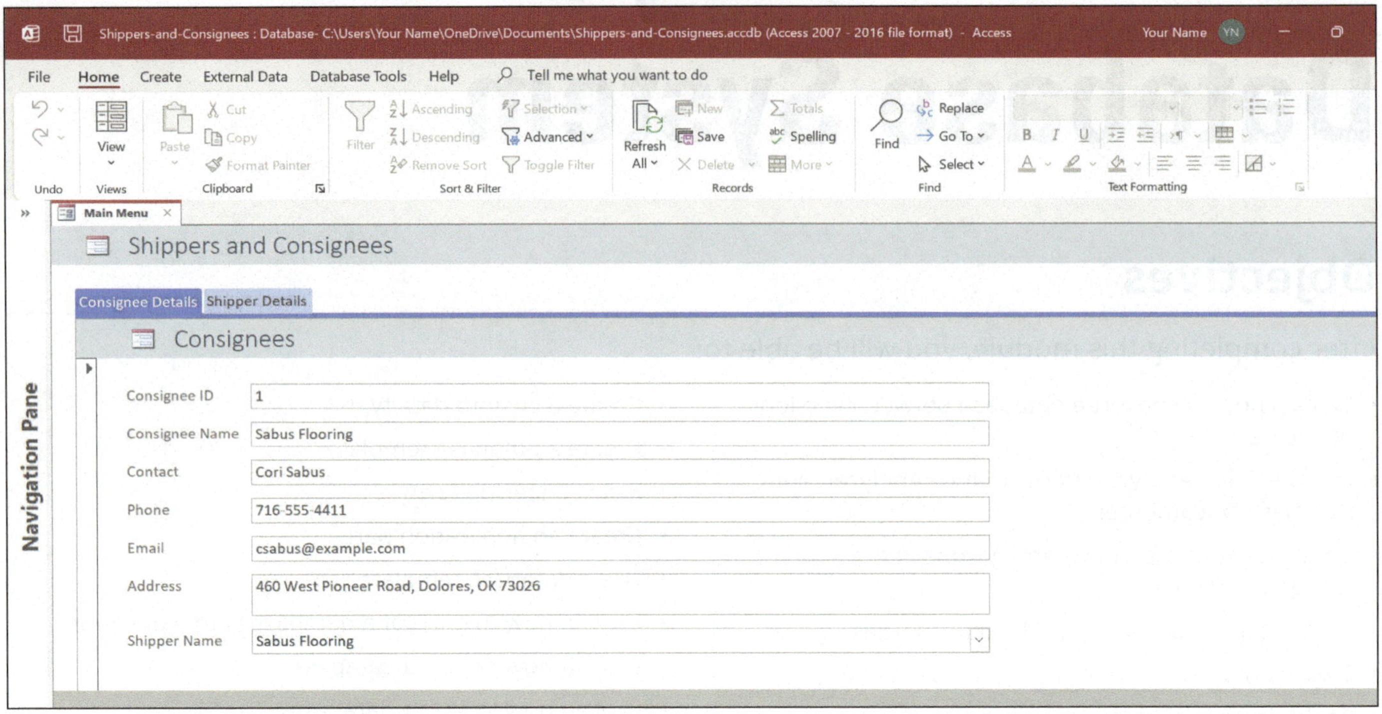

Figure 9–1

BTW
Enabling the Content
For each of the databases you use in this module, you will need to enable the content.

BTW
The Ribbon and Screen Resolution
Access may change how the groups and buttons within the groups appear on the ribbon, depending on the computer's screen resolution. Thus, your ribbon may look different from the ones in this book if you are using a screen resolution other than 1920 x 1080.

For Clearnet's own, internal database, performing administration tasks and reviewing database protection procedures will improve the Clearnet database system and enable all employees to use it more easily and securely. Figure 9–2 illustrates the range of activities involved in database administration, including the conversion of an Access database to an earlier version of Access. Database administration usually includes such activities as analyzing tables for potential problems, analyzing performance to see if changes could make the system perform more efficiently, and documenting the various objects in the database. It can include creating custom categories and groups in the Navigation Pane as well as changing table and database properties. It can also include the use of field properties in such tasks as creating a custom input mask and allowing zero-length strings. It can include the creation of indexes to speed up retrieval. The inclusion of automatic error checking is part of the administration of a database system. Understanding the purpose of the Trust Center is critical to the database administration function. Another important area of database administration is the protection of the database. This protection includes locking the database through the creation of an ACCDE file to prevent unauthorized changes from being made to the VBA source code or to the design of forms and reports. Splitting the database into a front-end and a back-end database is another way to protect the functionality and improve the efficiency of a database.

Figure 9–2

BTW

Converting Databases

If you try to convert a database that contains features specific to a later version of Access, Access displays an error message alerting you that you cannot save the database as an earlier version because it contains features that require the current file format.

Converting Databases

Access 2007, Access 2010, Access 2013, Access 2016, Access 2019, Access 2021, and Access in Microsoft 365 all use the same file format, the .accdb format. The format is usually referred to as the Access 2007 file format due to that being the version of first use. Thus, in current versions of Access, you can use any database created with Access 2007 or beyond. You should be aware of the following changes in Access 2013 and later versions (including Access 2021 and Microsoft 365) from the earlier versions.

1. Unlike previous versions, these later versions do not support PivotTables or PivotCharts.
2. The Text data type is now Short Text, and the Memo data type is now Long Text.
3. Smart Tags are no longer supported.
4. Replication is no longer available.

To convert an Access 2007 database to an earlier version, the database cannot contain any features that are specific to Access 2007 or later. These include attachments, multivalued fields, large integers, offline data, data macros, calculated columns, links to unsupported external files, newer sort orders, newer encryption types, or navigation controls. Provided the database does not contain such features, you can convert the database by clicking the Save As tab in Backstage view (Figure 9–3). You can then choose the appropriate format.

BTW

Maintaining Backward Compatibility

If you plan to share your database with users who may have an earlier version of Access, be sure to maintain backward compatibility. Do not include multivalued fields, attachment fields, or calculated fields in your database design. For example, if there is a calculation that is used frequently, create a query with the calculated field and use the query as the basis for forms and reports rather than adding the field to the table design.

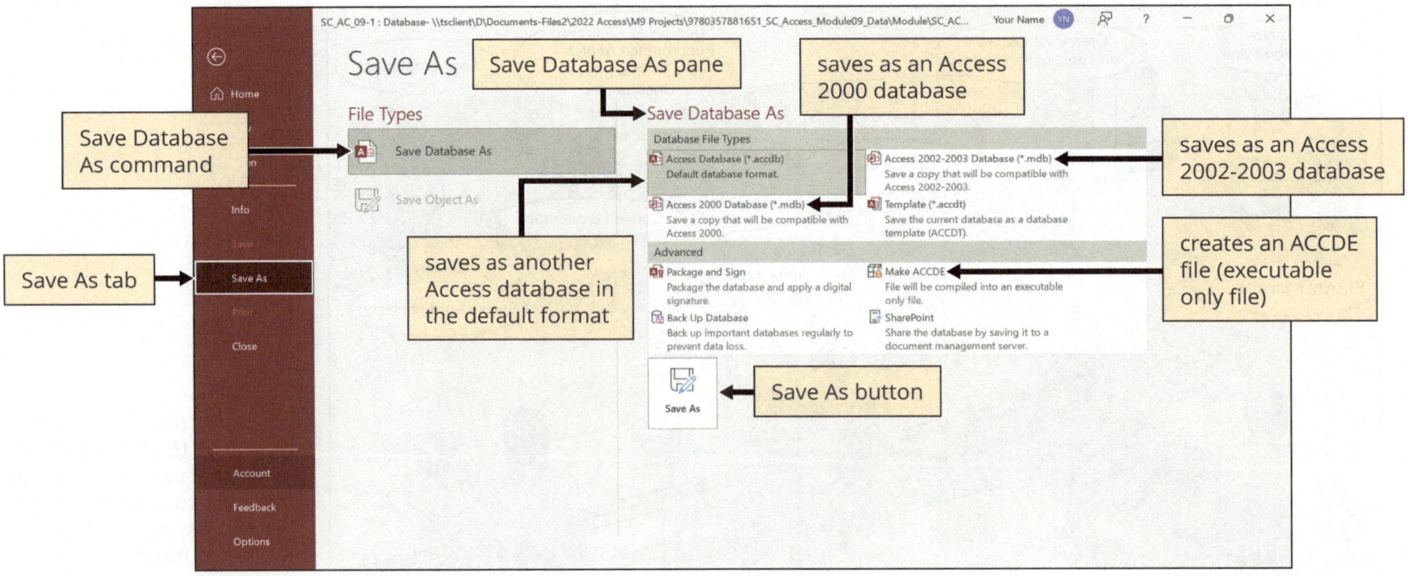

Figure 9–3

BTW
Saving Databases to External Locations
You also can save a database to an external location, such as OneDrive, and to any portable storage device, such as a USB flash drive. To do so, select the desired external location or portable storage device when you browse to specify a location for your database.

BTW
Exporting XML Data
Database administration also might include responsibility for exchanging data between dissimilar systems or apps. Extensible Markup Language (XML) is a data interchange standard for describing and delivering data on the web. With XML, you can describe both the data and the structure (schema) of the data. You can export tables, queries, forms, or reports. To export a database object, select the object, click the More button (External Data tab | Export group), and then click XML File. Select the appropriate options in the Export - XML File dialog box.

To Convert an Access 2007–2021 Database to an Earlier Version

Specifically, to convert an Access 2007–2021 database to an earlier version, you would use the following steps.

1. With the database to be converted open, click File on the ribbon to open Backstage view.
2. Click Save As.
3. With the 'Save Database As' command selected, click the desired format, and then click the Save As button.
4. Type the name you want for the converted database, select a location in which to save the converted database, and click the Save button.

To Convert an Access 2000 or 2002–2003 Database to an Access 2021 Database

To convert an Access 2000 or Access 2002–2003 database to the default database format for Access 2021, you open the database in Access 2021. Initially, the database is open in compatibility mode, where features that are new to the current version of Access and that cannot easily be displayed or converted are disabled. In this mode, the database remains in its original format. If you want to convert it so you can use it in Access 2021, you use the Access Database command in Backstage view. Once the database is converted, the disabled features will be enabled. You will no longer be able to share the database with users of Access 2000 or Access 2002–2003, however.

Specifically, to convert an Access 2000 or 2002–2003 database to the default database format for Access 2021, you would use the following steps.

1. With the database to be converted open, click File on the ribbon to open Backstage view.
2. Click Save As.
3. With the Save Database As command selected, click Access Database (*.accdb), and then click the Save As button.
4. Type the name you want for the converted database, select a location, and click the Save button.

Microsoft Access Analysis Tools

Microsoft Access has a variety of tools that are useful in analyzing databases. Analyzing a database gives information about how the database functions and identifies opportunities for improving functionality. You can use the Access analysis tools to analyze tables and database performance, and to create detailed documentation.

BTW
Creating Databases in Older Formats
To create a database in an older format, create a database and browse to select a location for creating the database, click the "Save as type" arrow in the File New Database dialog box, and select either the 2002–2003 format or the 2000 format.

To Use the Table Analyzer

Access contains a Table Analyzer tool that performs three separate functions. This tool can analyze tables while looking for potential redundancy (duplicated data). The Table Analyzer can also analyze performance and check for ways to make queries, reports, or forms more efficient. Then, the tool will make suggestions for possible changes. The final function of the analyzer is to produce detailed documentation describing the structure and content of the various tables, queries, forms, reports, and other objects in the database.

The following steps use the Table Analyzer to examine the Carriers table for **redundancy**, or duplicated data. **Why?** Redundancy is one of the biggest potential sources of problems in a database. If redundancy is found, the Table Analyzer will suggest ways to split the table to eliminate the redundancy.

1

- **sam** Start Access. Open the database, SC_AC_09-1.accdb, which is located in the Data Files folder. Save the file to your hard disk, OneDrive, or other storage location using the file name, **SC_AC_09_Clearnet**. Enable the content; or, if a message opens, stating that active content in the file is blocked, read the message and then click OK to close the dialog box. Then, enable the content.
- Display the Database Tools tab (Figure 9–4).

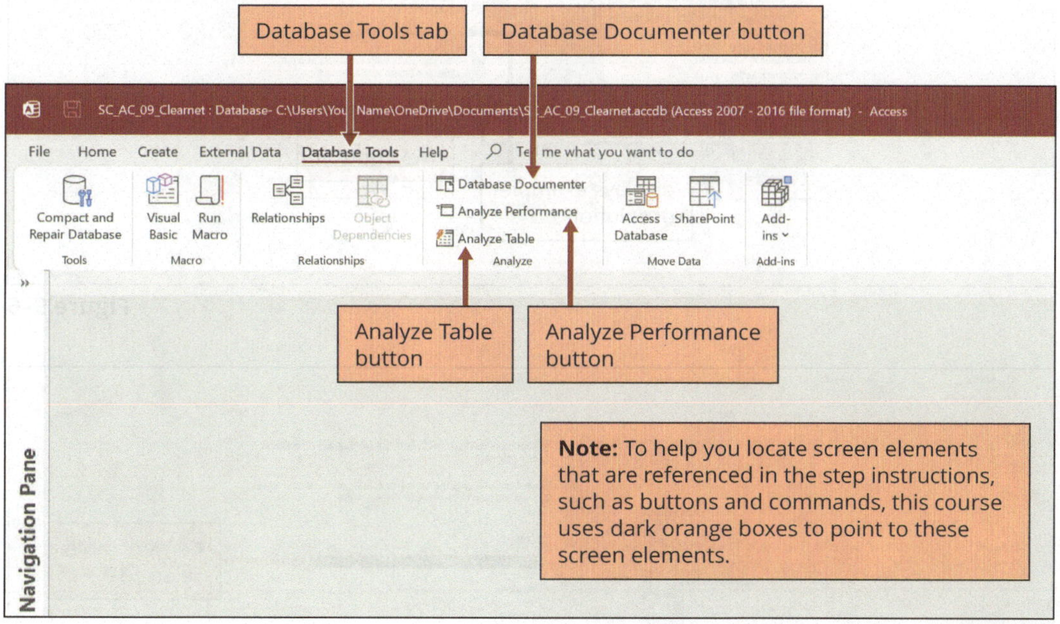

Figure 9–4

BTW
Navigation Pane
As you work, you often need to open the Navigation Pane to view and select objects such as tables, forms, and reports. You often need to close the pane to make more room on the screen or to ensure your screen matches the figures in this course. Open the Navigation Pane as necessary to open an object when instructed, and close the pane to suit your preferences.

BTW
Active Content
Depending on your Trust Settings, Access may initially block active content when it opens a database that contains macros. When you are opening content from a trusted source, such as databases included in this course, you can click OK in the dialog box and proceed with enabling the content.

2

- Click the Analyze Table button (Database Tools tab | Analyze group) to display the Table Analyzer Wizard dialog box (Figure 9–5).

Q&A Where did the data in the figure come from? It does not look like my data.

The data is fictitious. It is just intended to give you an idea of what the data might look like.

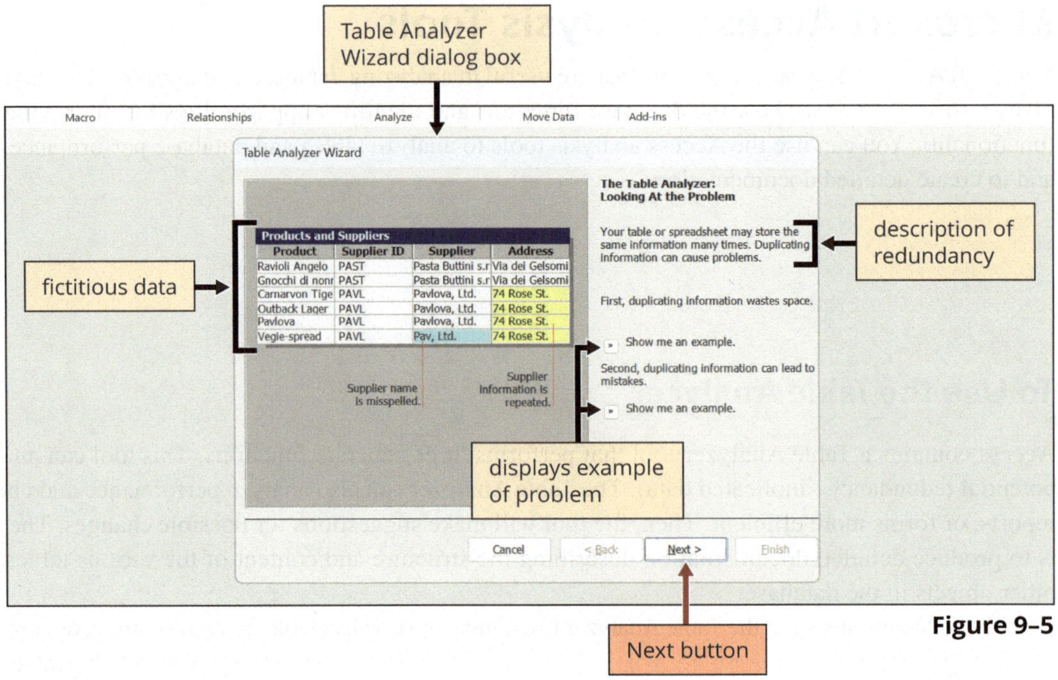

Figure 9–5

3

- Click Next to display the next Table Analyzer Wizard screen (Figure 9–6).

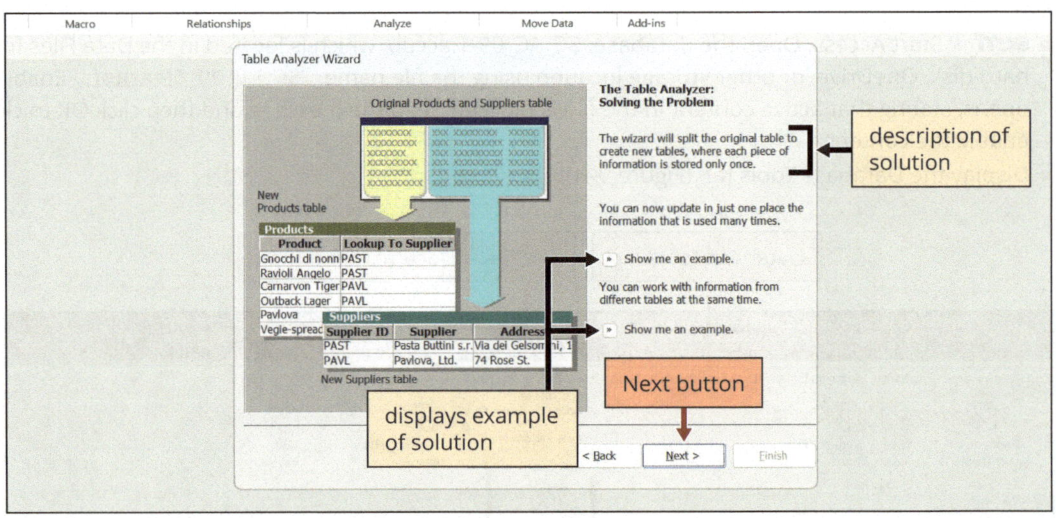

Figure 9–6

4

- Click Next to display the next Table Analyzer Wizard screen.
- If necessary, select the Carriers table (Figure 9–7).

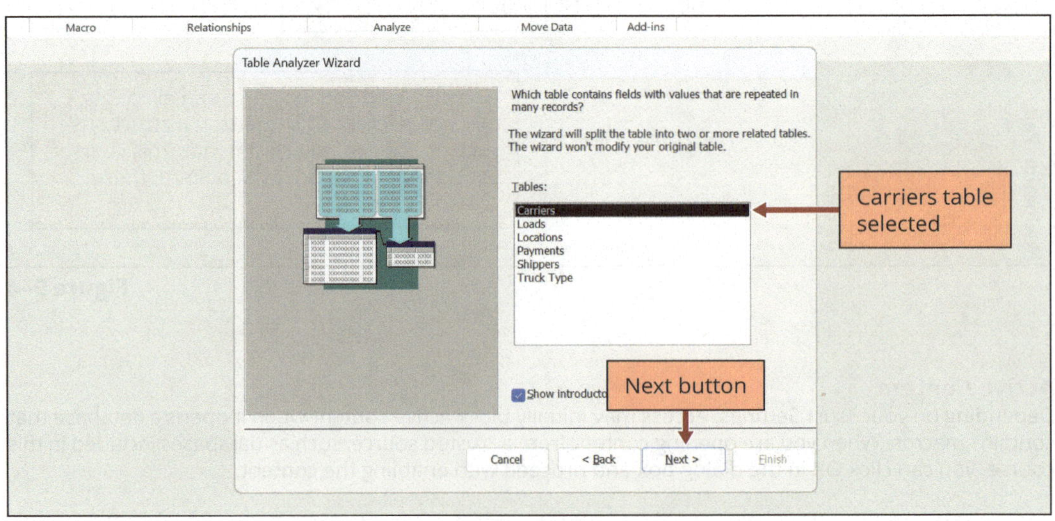

Figure 9–7

5

- Click Next.
- Be sure the 'Yes, let the wizard decide.' option button is selected (Figure 9–8) to let the wizard determine what action to take.

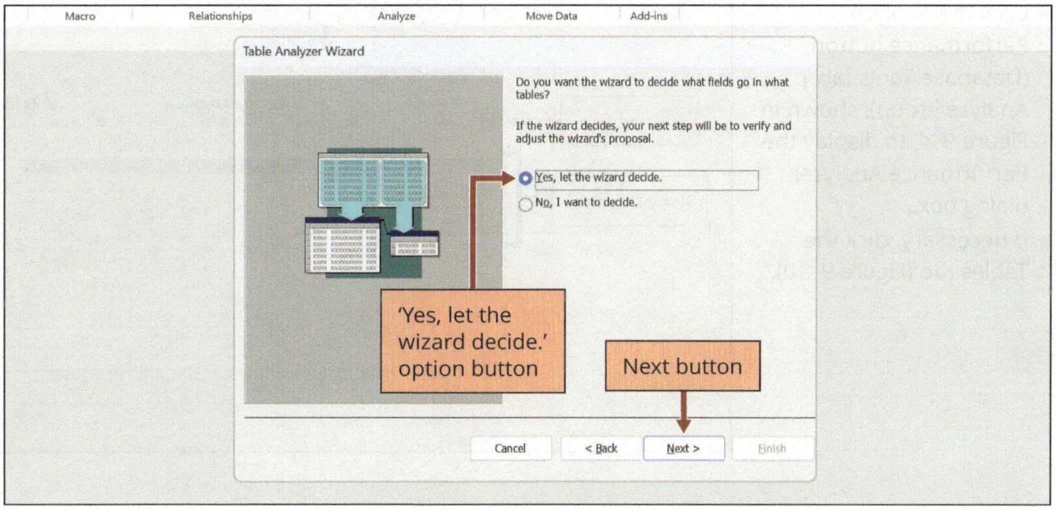

Figure 9–8

6

- Click Next to run the analysis, which indicates redundancy in the table.
- Reposition and resize the tables so you can see the field recommended to be split into a new table (Figure 9–9).

Q&A I do not really want to put the Carrier Payment Instructions field in a different table, even though I realize that this data does appear to be duplicated. Do I have to follow this advice?

Certainly not. This is only a suggestion.

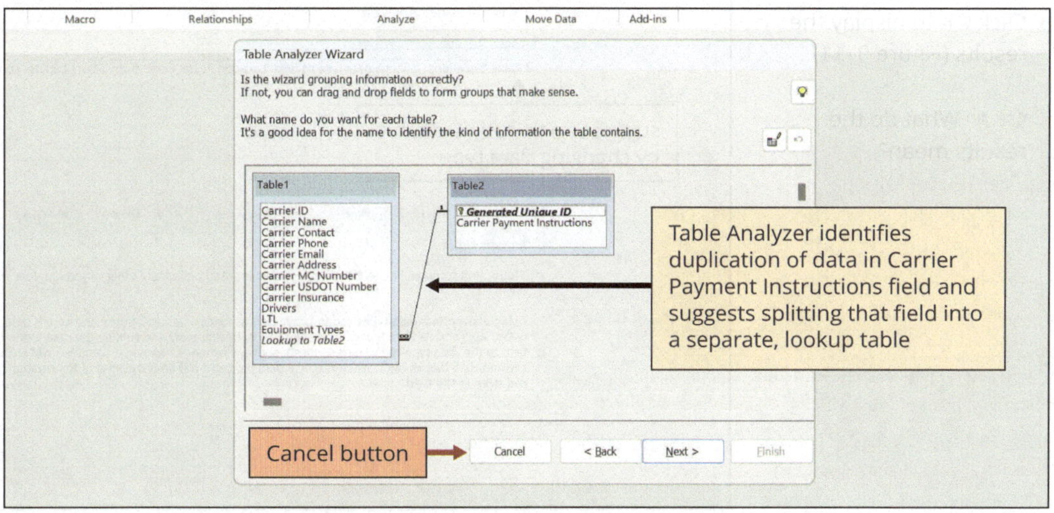

Figure 9–9

7

- Because the type of duplication identified by the analyzer does not pose a problem, click the Cancel button to close the analyzer.

To Use the Performance Analyzer

The Performance Analyzer examines the database's tables, queries, reports, forms, and other objects in your system, looking for ways to improve the efficiency of database operations. These improvements could include modifications to the way data is stored, as well as changes to the indexes created for the system. (You will learn about indexes later in this module.) The following steps use the Performance Analyzer. **Why?** The Performance Analyzer identifies possible areas for improvement in the Clearnet database. Users then can determine whether to implement the suggested changes.

1

- Click the Analyze Performance button (Database Tools tab | Analyze group), shown in Figure 9–4, to display the Performance Analyzer dialog box.
- If necessary, click the Tables tab (Figure 9–10).

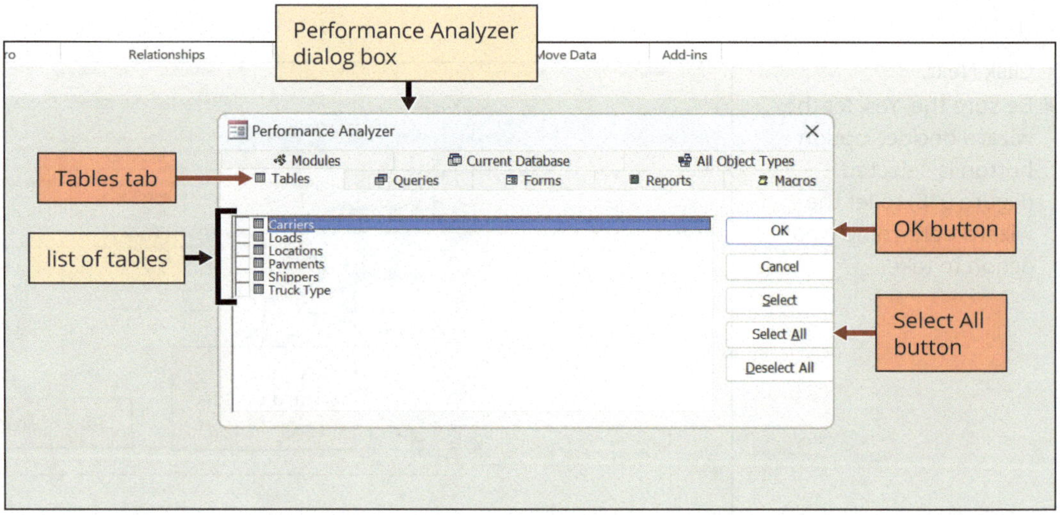

Figure 9–10

2

- Click the Select All button to select all tables.
- Click OK to display the results (Figure 9–11).

Q&A What do the results mean?
The Performance Analyzer suggests the Location Postal Code field would better be stored as a Long Integer data type. However, a postal code is better stored with Short Text data type because postal codes are never used in calculations.

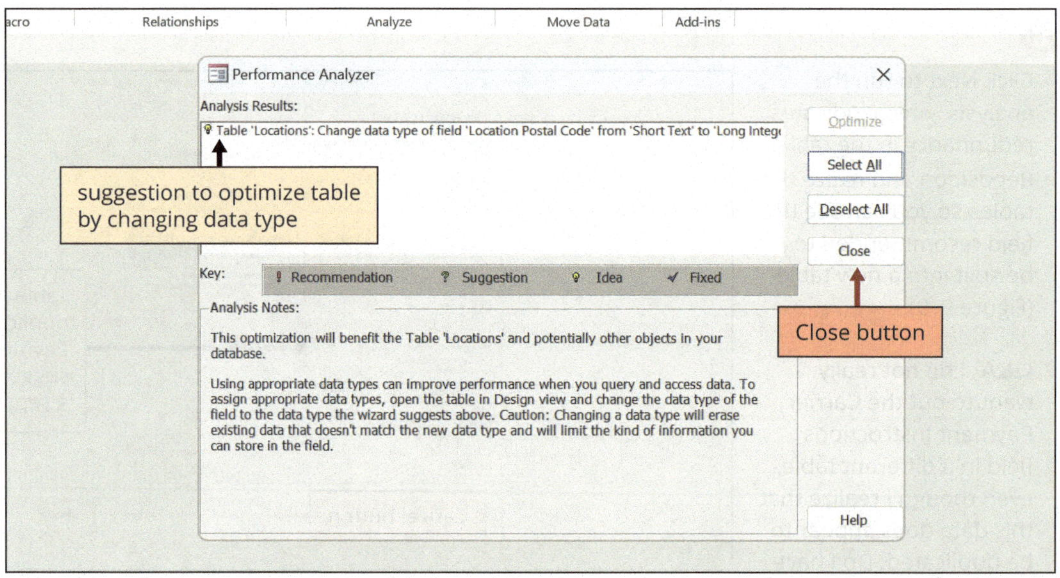

Figure 9–11

3

- Click Close to finish working with the Performance Analyzer.

To Use the Database Documenter

The Database Documenter allows you to produce detailed documentation of the various tables, queries, forms, reports, and other objects in your database. Documentation is required by many organizations. It is used for backup, disaster recovery, and planning for database enhancements. Figure 9–12 shows a portion of the documentation for the Loads table. The complete documentation is much lengthier than the one shown in the figure.

The following steps use the Database Documenter. **Why?** The Database Documenter is the easiest way to produce detailed documentation for the Loads table.

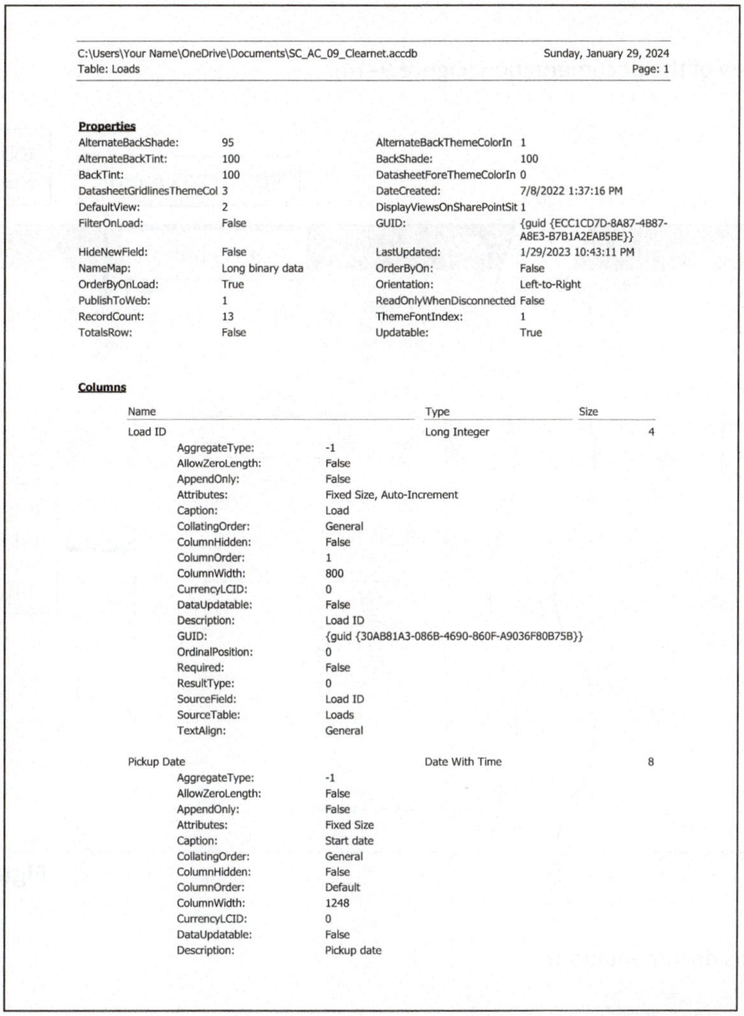
C:\Users\Your Name\OneDrive\Documents\SC_AC_09_Clearnet.accdb Sunday, January 29, 2024
Table: Loads Page: 1

Properties

AlternateBackShade:	95	AlternateBackThemeColorIn	1
AlternateBackTint:	100	BackShade:	100
BackTint:	100	DatasheetForeThemeColorIn	0
DatasheetGridlinesThemeCol	3	DateCreated:	7/8/2022 1:37:16 PM
DefaultView:	2	DisplayViewsOnSharePointSit	1
FilterOnLoad:	False	GUID:	{guid {ECC1CD7D-8A87-4B87-A8E3-B7B1A2EAB5BE}}
HideNewField:	False	LastUpdated:	1/29/2023 10:43:11 PM
NameMap:	Long binary data	OrderByOn:	False
OrderByOnLoad:	True	Orientation:	Left-to-Right
PublishToWeb:	1	ReadOnlyWhenDisconnected	False
RecordCount:	13	ThemeFontIndex:	1
TotalsRow:	False	Updatable:	True

Columns

Name	Type	Size
Load ID	Long Integer	4

AggregateType:	-1
AllowZeroLength:	False
AppendOnly:	False
Attributes:	Fixed Size, Auto-Increment
Caption:	Load
CollatingOrder:	General
ColumnHidden:	False
ColumnOrder:	1
ColumnWidth:	800
CurrencyLCID:	0
DataUpdatable:	False
Description:	Load ID
GUID:	{guid {30AB81A3-086B-4690-860F-A9036F80B75B}}
OrdinalPosition:	0
Required:	False
ResultType:	0
SourceField:	Load ID
SourceTable:	Loads
TextAlign:	General

Name	Type	Size
Pickup Date	Date With Time	8

AggregateType:	-1
AllowZeroLength:	False
AppendOnly:	False
Attributes:	Fixed Size
Caption:	Start date
CollatingOrder:	General
ColumnHidden:	False
ColumnOrder:	Default
ColumnWidth:	1248
CurrencyLCID:	0
DataUpdatable:	False
Description:	Pickup date

Figure 9–12

1

- Click the Database Documenter button, shown in Figure 9–4 (Database Tools tab | Analyze group), to display the Documenter dialog box.
- If necessary, click the Tables tab and then click the Loads check box to specify documentation for the Loads table (Figure 9–13).

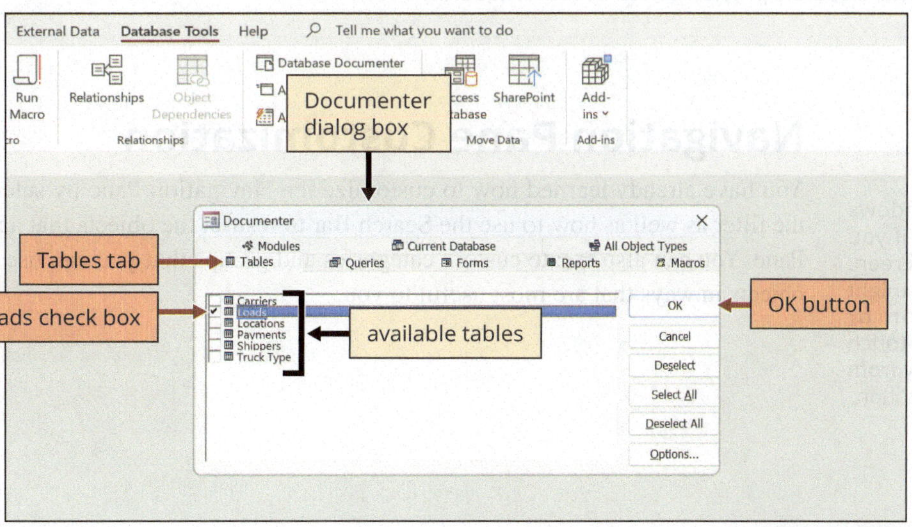

Figure 9–13

2

- Click OK to produce a preview of the documentation (Figure 9–14).

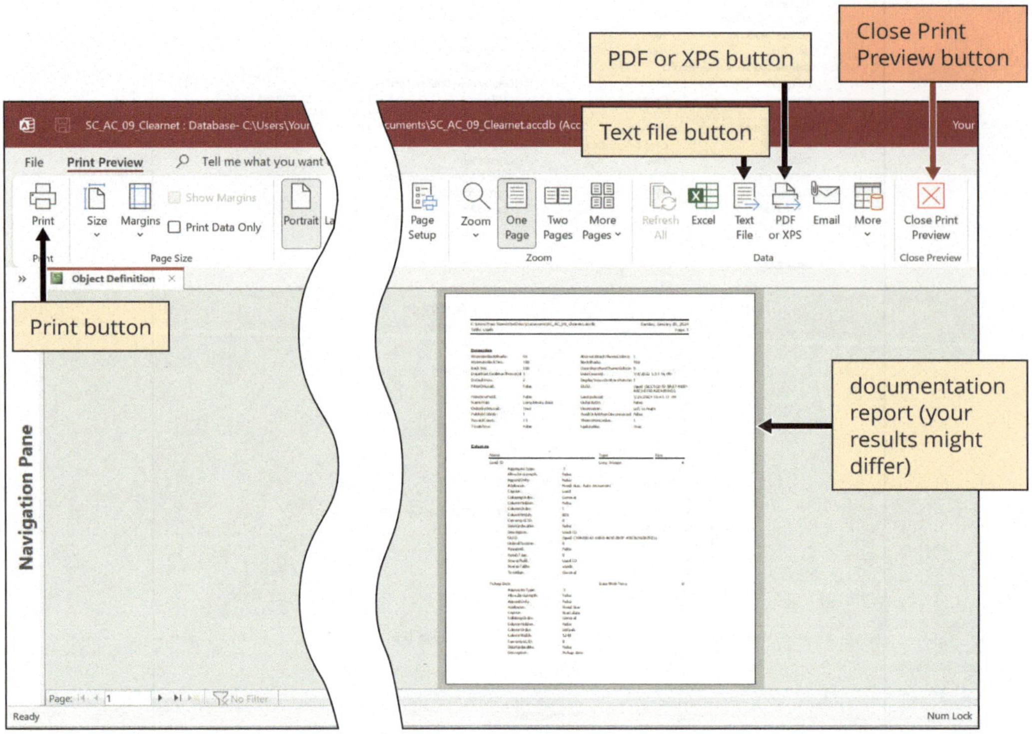

Figure 9–14

Q&A What can I do with this documentation?
You could print it by clicking the Print button (Print Preview tab | Print group). You could create a PDF or XPS file containing the documentation by clicking the PDF or XPS button (Print Preview tab | Data group) and following the directions. You could create a Word (RTF) file by clicking the More button (Print Preview tab | Data group), and then clicking Word and following the directions. Whatever option you choose, you might need to use this documentation later if you make changes to the database design.

- Click the 'Close Print Preview' button (Print Preview tab | Close Preview group) to close the preview of the documentation.
- **Experiment:** Try other options within the Database Documenter to see the effect of your choice on the documentation produced. Each time, close the preview of the documentation.

BTW
Touch Screen Differences
The Office and Windows interfaces may vary if you are using a touch screen. For this reason, you might notice the function or appearance of your touch screen differs slightly from this module's presentation.

Navigation Pane Customization

You have already learned how to customize the Navigation Pane by selecting the category and the filter as well as how to use the Search Bar to restrict the objects that appear in the Navigation Pane. You can also create custom categories and groups that you can use to categorize database objects in ways that are most useful to you.

To Create Custom Categories and Groups

You can create custom categories in the Navigation Pane. You can further refine the objects you place in a category by adding custom groups to the categories. **Why?** Custom categories and groups allow you to tailor the Navigation Pane for your specific needs. The following steps create a custom category called Loads Information. They then add two custom groups, Tracking and Accounting, to the Loads Information category.

1

- Display the Navigation Pane and resize it, if necessary, so you can read the full title of all listed objects.
- Right-click the Navigation Pane title bar to display a shortcut menu (Figure 9–15).

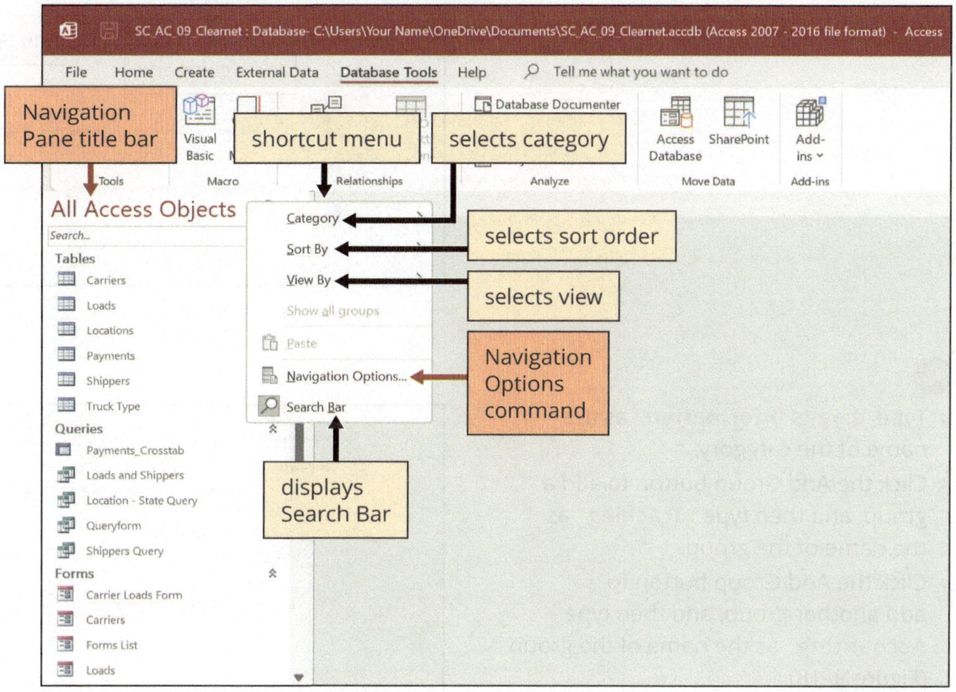

Figure 9–15

2

- Click the Navigation Options command on the shortcut menu to display the Navigation Options dialog box (Figure 9–16).

Q&A What else could I do with the shortcut menu?
You could select a category, select a sort order, or select how to view the items within the Navigation Pane.

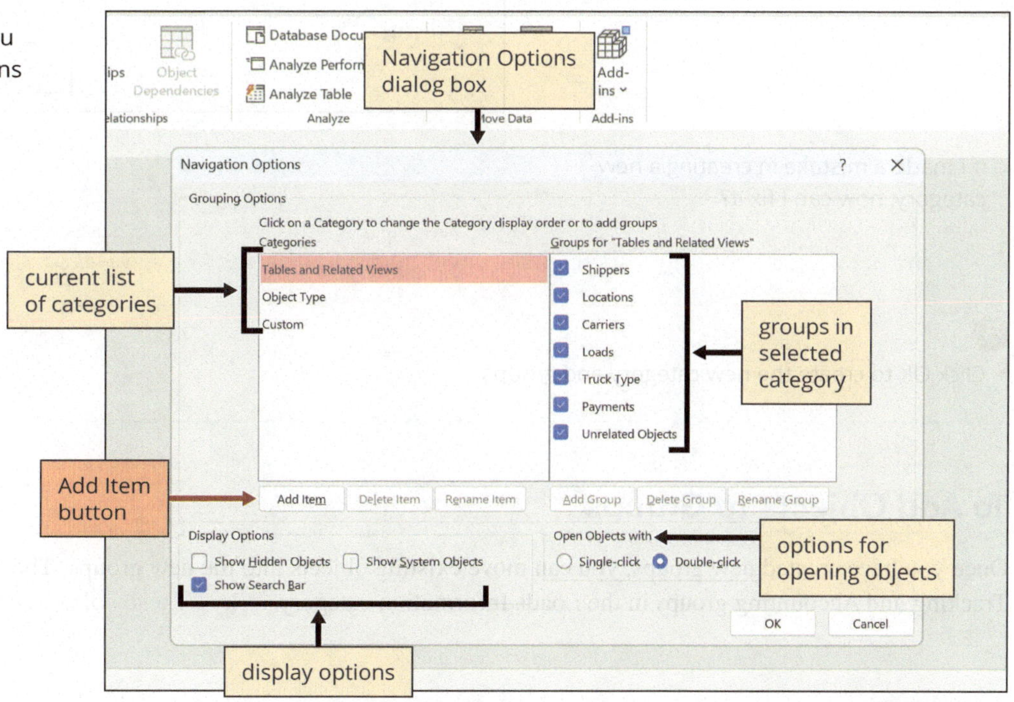

Figure 9–16

3

- Click the Add Item button to add a new category (Figure 9–17).

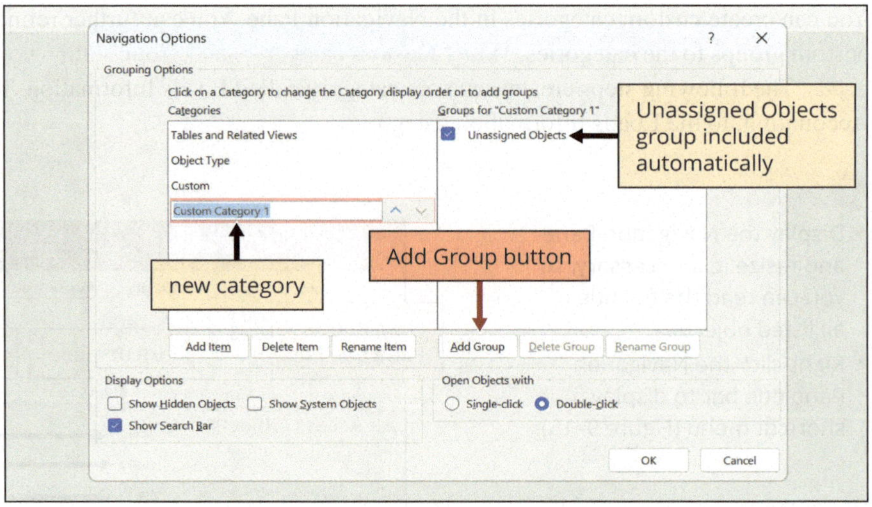

Figure 9–17

4

- Type **Loads Information** as the name of the category.
- Click the Add Group button to add a group, and then type **Tracking** as the name of the group.
- Click the Add Group button to add another group, and then type **Accounting** as the name of the group (Figure 9–18).

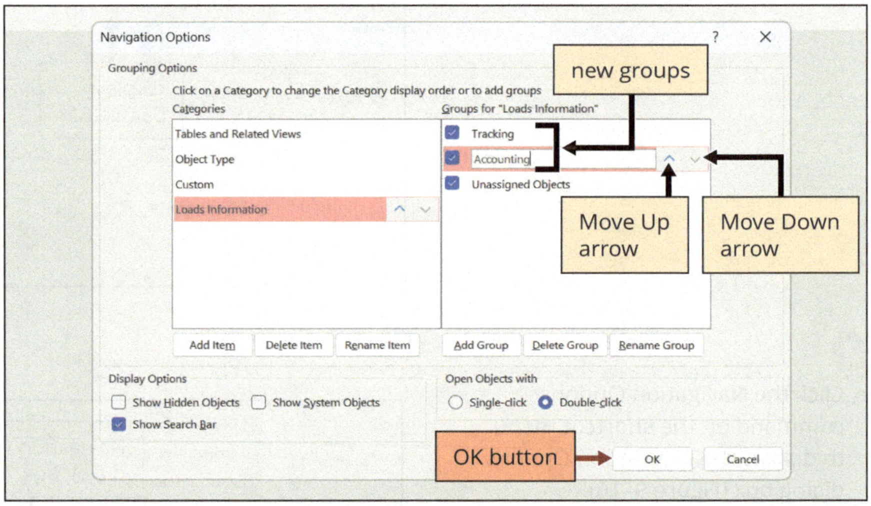

Figure 9–18

Q&A I added the groups in the wrong order. How can I change the order?
Select the group that is in the wrong position. Click the Move Up or Move Down arrow to move the group to the correct location.

If I made a mistake in creating a new category, how can I fix it?
Select the category that is incorrect. If the name is wrong, click the Rename Item button and change the name appropriately. If you do not want the category, click the Delete Item button to delete the category and then click OK.

5

- Click OK to create the new category and groups.

To Add Objects to Groups

Once you have created new groups, you can move existing objects into the new groups. The following steps add objects to the Tracking and Accounting groups in the Loads Information category. **Why?** These objects are all related to the loads.

1

- Click the Navigation Pane arrow to produce the Navigation Pane menu, and then scroll if necessary to display the Loads Information category (Figure 9–19).

Q&A Do I have to click the arrow?
No. If you prefer, you can click anywhere in the title bar for the Navigation Pane. Clicking arrows is a good habit, however, because there are many situations in which you must click the arrow.

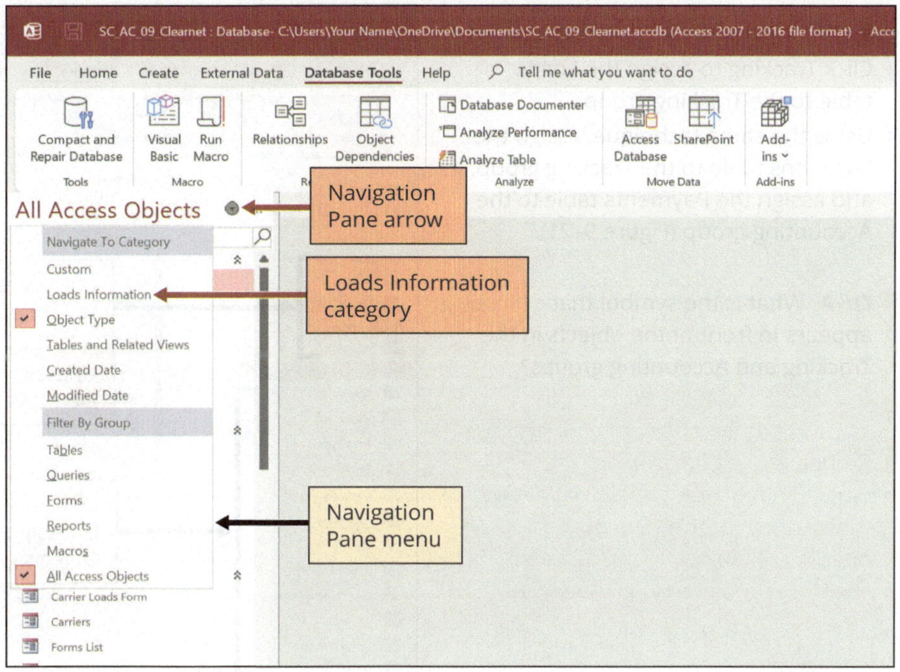

Figure 9–19

2

- Click the Loads Information category to display the groups within the category. Because you created the Tracking and Accounting groups but did not assign objects, the table objects all appear in the Unassigned Objects area of the Navigation Pane.
- Right-click the Loads table to display the shortcut menu.
- Point to the 'Add to group' command on the shortcut menu to display the list of available groups (Figure 9–20).

BTW
Touch and Pointers
Remember that if you are using your finger on a touch screen, you will not see the pointer.

Q&A I did not create an Unassigned Objects group. Where did it come from?
Access creates the Unassigned Objects group automatically. Until you add an object to one of the groups you created, it will be in the Unassigned Objects group.

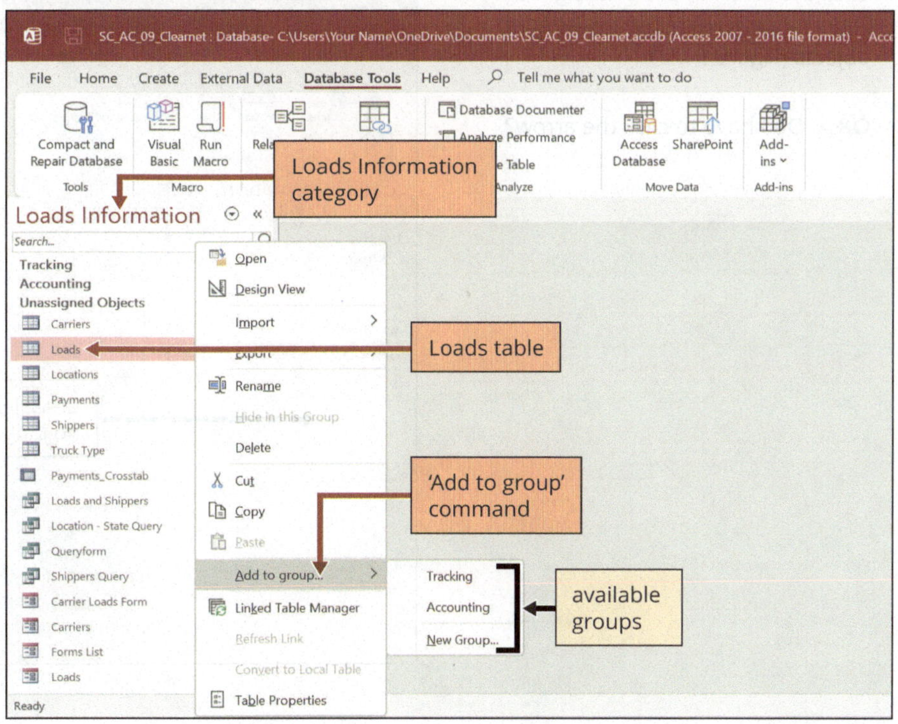

Figure 9–20

What is the purpose of the New Group command on the submenu?
You can create a new group using this submenu. This is an alternative to using the Navigation Options dialog box. Use whichever approach you find most convenient.

3

- Click Tracking to assign the Loads table to the Tracking group.
- Using the same technique, assign the Locations table to the Tracking group, and assign the Payments table to the Accounting group (Figure 9–21).

Q&A What is the symbol that appears in front of the objects in the Tracking and Accounting groups?
It is the link symbol. You do not actually add an object to your group. Rather, you create a link to the object. In practice, you do not have to worry about this. The process for opening an object in one of your custom groups remains the same.

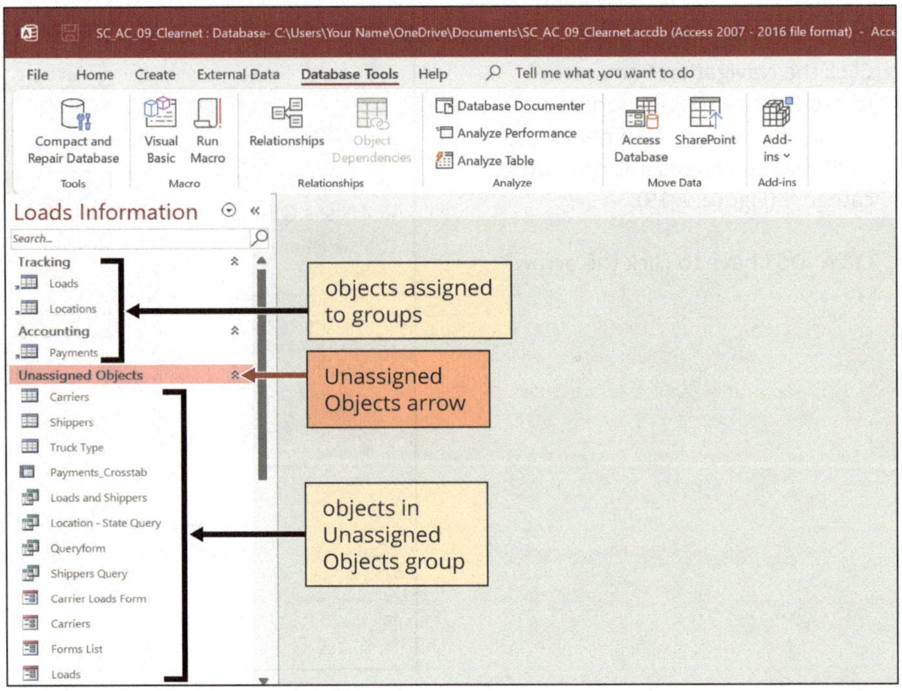

Figure 9–21

4

- Click the arrow in the Unassigned Objects bar to hide the unassigned objects (Figure 9–22).

Q&A Do I have to click the arrow?
No. Just as with the Navigation Pane, you can click anywhere in the Unassigned Objects bar.

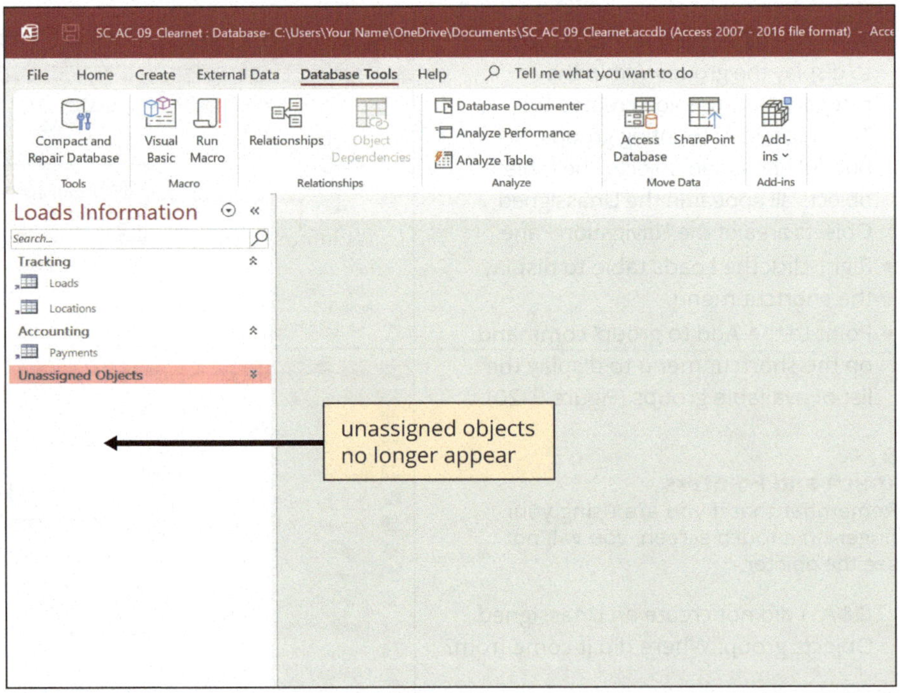

Figure 9–22

Consider This

What issues do you consider in determining the customization of the Navigation Pane?

The types of issues to consider include the following:

- Would a new category be useful?
- If so, are there new groups that would be useful to include in the new category?
- If you have created a new category and new groups, which objects should be included in the new groups, and which should be left uncategorized?

Break Point: If you wish to take a break, this is a good place to do so. You can quit Access now. To resume at a later time, start Access, open the database called SC_AC_09_Clearnet.accdb, and continue following the steps from this location forward.

Table and Database Properties

You can assign properties to tables. For example, you could assign a validation rule and validation text to an entire table. You can also assign properties to the database, typically for documentation purposes.

To Create a Validation Rule for a Table

Previously, you created validation rules that applied to individual fields within a table. Some, however, apply to more than one field. In the Workshop Enrollments table in the Partners database, you created a macro that would change the value of the Hours Spent field in such a way that it could never be greater than the Total Hours field. You can also create a validation rule that ensures this will never be the case; that is, the validation rule would require that the hours spent must be less than or equal to the total hours. In the Clearnet database's Payments table, you will create a validation rule that ensures, for every load, the agent commission value does not exceed four percent of the rate confirmation value. To create a validation rule that involves two or more fields, you need to create the rule for the table using the table's Validation Rule property. The following steps create a **table validation rule**. **Why?** This rule involves two fields: Agent Commission and Rate Confirmation.

1

- Open the Payments table in Design view.
- If necessary, click the Property Sheet button (Table Design tab | Show/Hide group) to display the table's property sheet.
- Click the Validation Rule property and type **[Agent Commission]<=[Rate Confirmation]*0.04** as the validation rule.
- Click the Validation Text property and type **Agent Commission cannot exceed 4% of Rate Con** as the validation text (Figure 9–23).

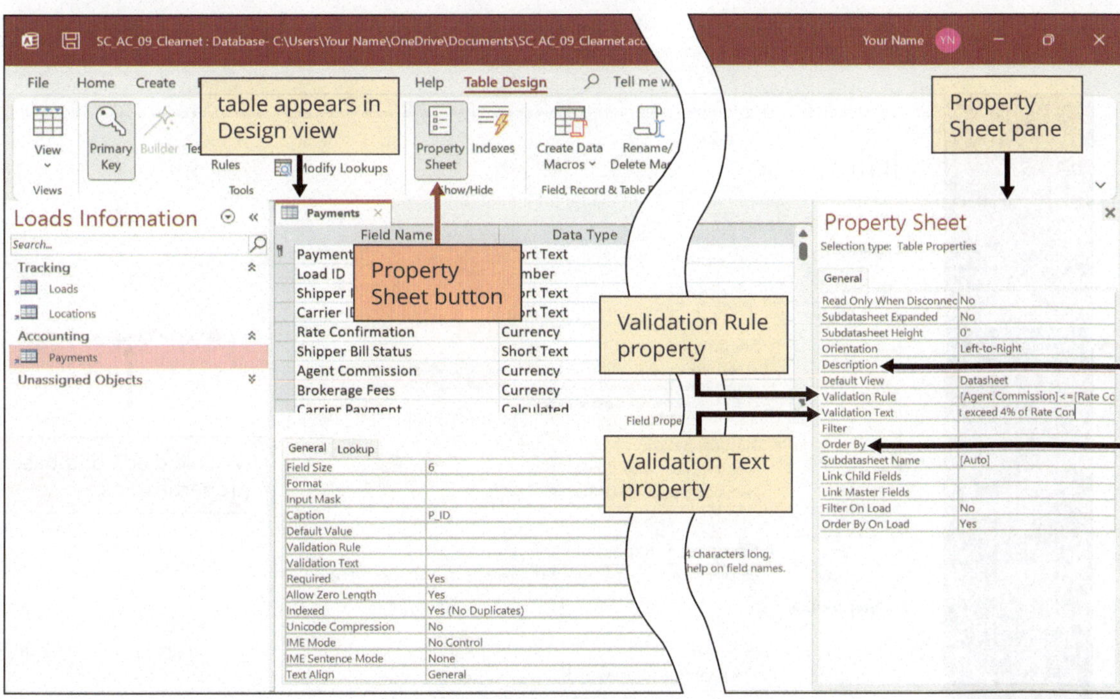

Figure 9–23

Q&A Why does the expression use 0.04 instead of 4%?

The value 4% needs to be converted to decimal form, which is 0.04.

Could I use the Expression Builder to create the validation rule?

Yes. Use whichever method you find most convenient.

2

- Close the Property Sheet pane.
- Click the Save button on the Quick Access Toolbar to save the validation rule and the validation text.
- When asked if you want to test existing data, click the No button.
- **Experiment:** Switch to Datasheet view and attempt to change the A_Comm value for P_ID 8 from $20.00 to $50.00 to confirm the validation rule and error message work correctly. When you attempt to move to a different record or close the datasheet, an error message appears. To fix the problem, reset P_ID 8's agent commission to $20.00.
- Close the Payments table.

BTW
Table Descriptions
To add a description for a table, right-click the table in the Navigation Pane and then click Table Properties on the shortcut menu. When the table's Properties dialog box appears, enter the description in the Description property and then click OK. To enter a description for a table in Design view, click the Property Sheet button, and then enter a description in the Description property on the Property Sheet pane (see Figure 9–23).

BTW
Changing Default Sort Order
To display the records in a table in an order other than the primary key (the default sort order), use the Order By property on the table's property sheet (see Figure 9–23).

To Create Custom Properties

In addition to the general database property categories, you can also use custom properties. **Why?** You can use custom properties to further document your database in a variety of ways. If you have needs that go beyond the custom properties, you can create your own original or unique properties. The following steps **populate** the Status custom property; that is, they set a value for the property. In this case, they set the Status property to Live Version, indicating this is the live version of the database. If the database were still in a test environment, the property would be set to Test Version. The steps also create and populate a new property, Production, which represents the date the database was placed into production.

1

- Click File on the ribbon to open Backstage view.
- Click Info (Figure 9–24).

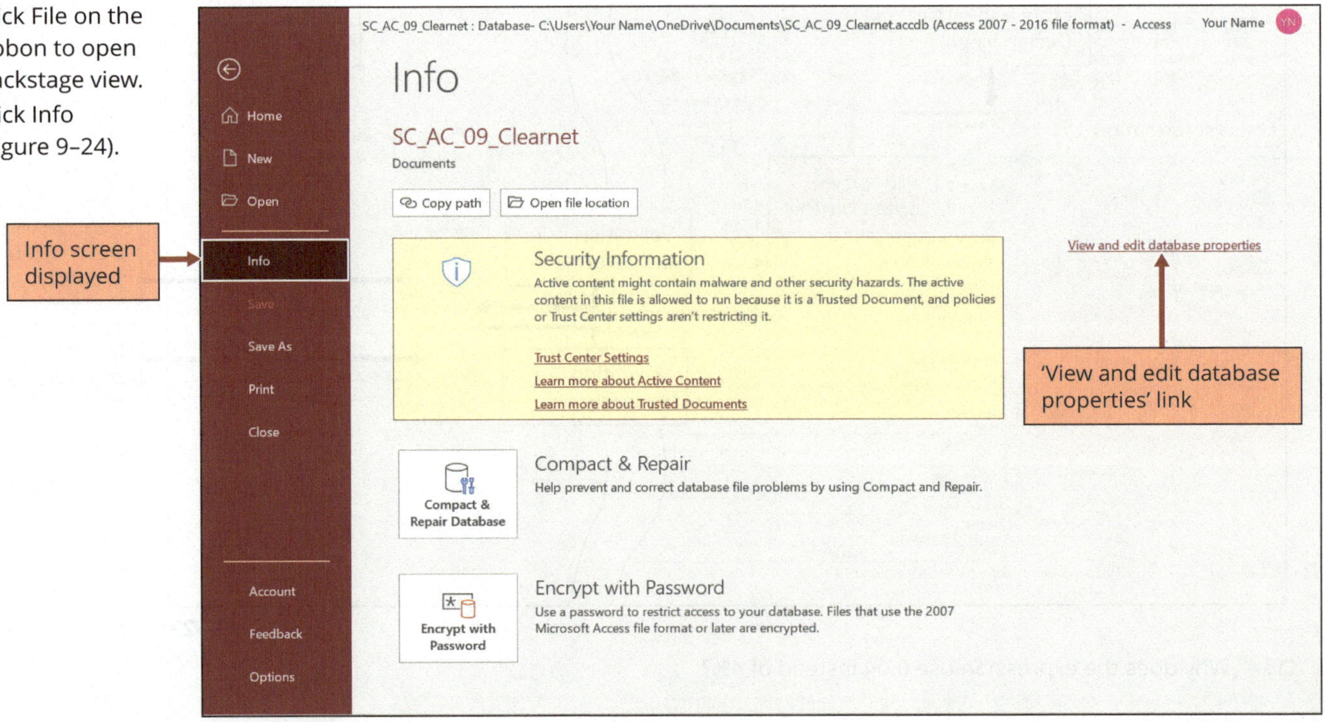

Figure 9–24

2

- Click the 'View and edit database properties' link to display the Clearnet database's Properties dialog box.
- Click the Custom tab.
- Scroll down in the Name list so Status appears, and then click Status.
- If necessary, click the Type arrow to set the data type to Text.
- Click the Value box, and type **Live Version** as the value to create the custom property (Figure 9–25).

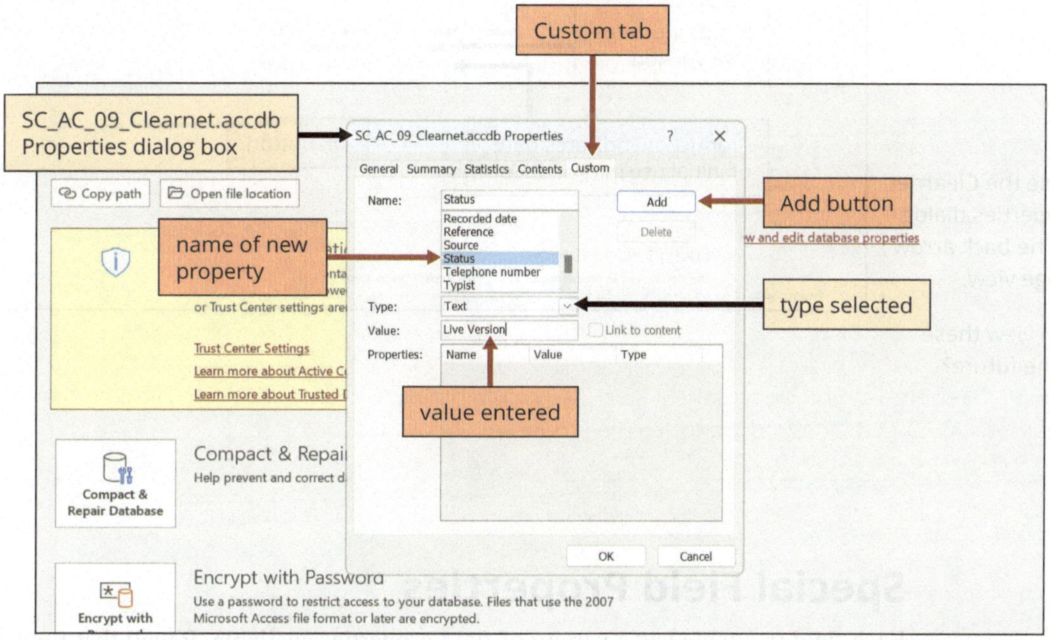

Figure 9–25

3

- Click the Add button to add the property.
- Type **Production** in the Name box to create a new property.
- If requested to do so by your instructor, type your first and last name in the Name box.
- Select Date as the Type.
- Type **6/25/2024** as the value (Figure 9–26) to indicate the database went into production on June 25, 2024.

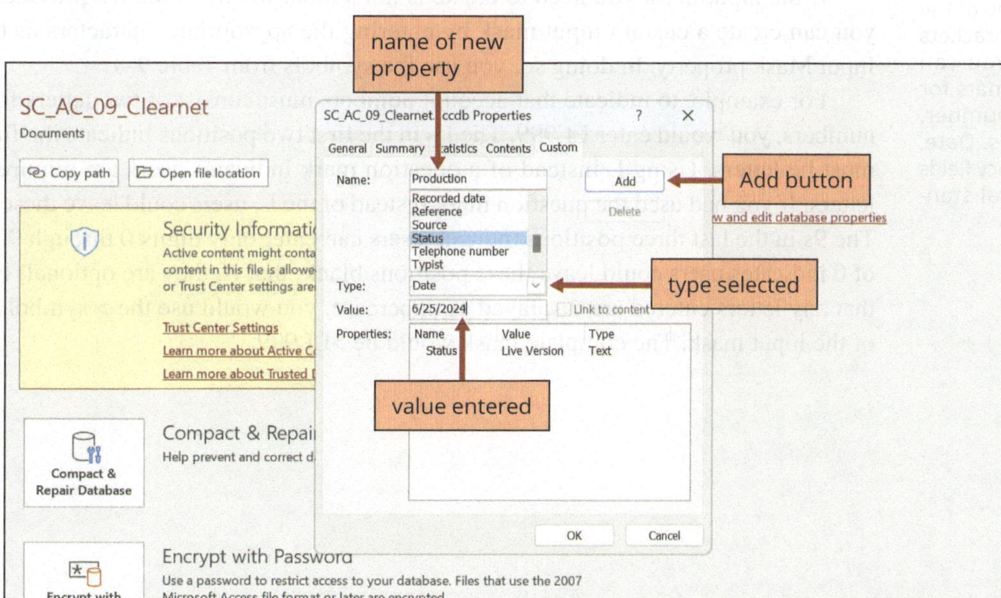

Figure 9–26

4

- Click the Add button to add the property (Figure 9–27).

Q&A What if I add a property that I decide I do not want?
You can delete it. To do so, click the property you no longer want and then click the Delete button.

5

- Click OK to close the Clearnet database's Properties dialog box, and click the back arrow to exit Backstage view.

Q&A How do I view these properties in the future?
You can view them the same way you created them. Click File on the ribbon, click Info, and then click the 'View and edit database properties' link. Click the desired tab to see the properties you want.

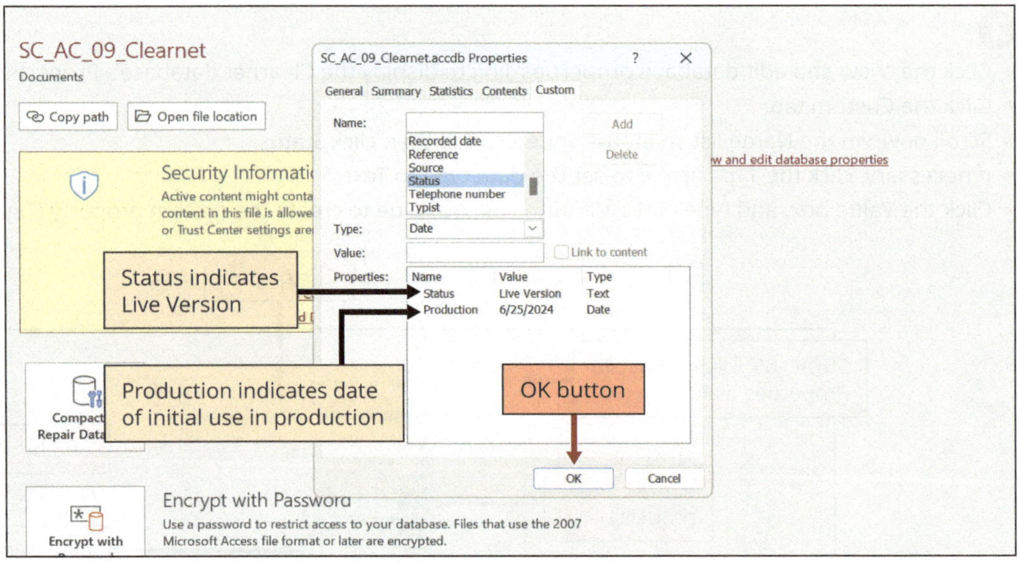

Figure 9–27

BTW
Changing Data Formats
To create custom data formats, enter the necessary characters in the Format property of a table field. The characters can be placeholders (such as 0 and #), separators (such as periods and commas), literal text with the required text enclosed in double quotation marks (such as "literal text"), and colors with the name of the color enclosed in brackets (such as [blue]). You can create custom formats for short text, date, number, and currency fields. Date, number, and currency fields also include several standard data formats.

Special Field Properties

Each field in a table has a variety of field properties available. Recall that field properties are characteristics of a field. Two special field properties, the Custom Input Mask property and the Allow Zero Length property, are described in this section.

Custom Input Masks

One way to help users enter data using a certain format is to use an input mask. You have already used the Input Mask Wizard to create an input mask. Using the wizard, you can select the input mask that meets your needs. This is often the best way to create the input mask.

If the input mask you need to create is not similar to any in the list provided by the wizard, you can create a custom input mask by entering the appropriate characters as the value for the Input Mask property. In doing so, you use the symbols from Table 9–1.

For example, to indicate that account numbers must consist of two letters followed by three numbers, you would enter LL999. The Ls in the first two positions indicate the first two positions must be letters. Using L instead of a question mark indicates users are required to enter these letters. If you had used the question mark instead of the L, users could leave these positions blank. The 9s in the last three positions indicate users can enter only digits 0 through 9. Using 9 instead of 0 indicates users could leave these positions blank; that is, they are optional. Finally, to ensure that any letters entered are displayed as uppercase, you would use the > symbol at the beginning of the input mask. The complete mask would be >LL999.

Table 9–1 Input Mask Symbols

Symbol	Type of Data Accepted	Data Entry
0	Digits 0 through 9 without plus (+) or minus (–) sign are accepted. Positions left blank appear as zeros.	Required
9	Digits 0 through 9 without plus (+) or minus (–) sign are accepted. Positions left blank appear as spaces.	Optional
#	Digits 0 through 9 with plus (+) or minus (–) sign are accepted. Positions left blank appear as spaces.	Optional
L	Letters A through Z are accepted.	Required
?	Letters A through Z are accepted.	Optional
A	Letters A through Z or digits 0 through 9 are accepted.	Required
a	Letters A through Z or digits 0 through 9 are accepted.	Optional
&	Any character or a space is accepted.	Required
C	Any character or a space is accepted.	Optional
<	Symbol converts any letter entered to lowercase.	N/A
>	Symbol converts any letter entered to uppercase.	N/A
!	Characters typed in the input mask fill it from left to right.	N/A
\	Character following the slash is treated as a literal in the input mask.	N/A

To Create a Custom Input Mask

The following steps create a custom input mask for the Location ID field in the Locations table. **Why?** None of the input masks in the list meet the specific needs for the Location ID field.

1

- Open the Locations table in Design view.
- With the Location ID field selected, click the Input Mask property, and then type **>L-999** as the value (Figure 9–28). Access will add a backslash to your custom input mask, like this, >L\-999, when you click outside the property box.

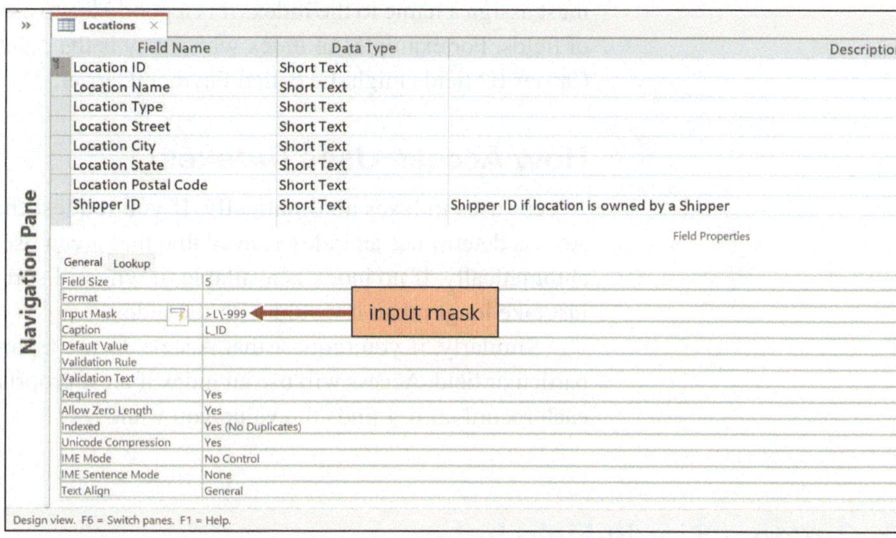

Figure 9–28

2

- Save the changes and close the table.

Q&A What is the difference between the Format property and the Input Mask property?

The Format property ensures that data is displayed consistently, for example, always in uppercase. The Input Mask property controls how data is entered by the user.

What is the effect of this input mask?

From this point on, anyone entering a location ID will be restricted to a letter in the first position, followed by a dash and numeric digits in the last three positions. Further, any letter entered in the first position will be displayed as uppercase.

Can you have a field that has both a custom input mask and a format requirement? Would this be a problem?

Technically, you do not need both. When the same field has both an input mask and a format, the format takes precedence. However, if the format specified for the field is the same as the input mask (uppercase), it will not affect the data.

Creating and Using Indexes

BTW
B-tree Indexes
The most common structure for high-performance indexes is called a B-tree. It is a highly efficient structure that supports very rapid access to records in the database as well as a rapid alternative to sorting records. Virtually all systems use some version of the B-tree structure.

You are already familiar with the concept of an index. The index in the back of a book contains important words or phrases along with a list of pages on which the given words or phrases can be found. An index for a table is similar. An **index** is a database object that is created based on a field or combination of fields. An index on the Carrier Name field, for example, would enable Access to rapidly locate a record that contains a particular carrier. In this case, the items of interest are carrier names instead of keywords or phrases, as is the case for the index in the back of most books. The field or fields on which the index is built is called the index key. Thus, in the index on account names, the Carrier Name field is the index key.

Each name occurs in the index along with the number of the record on which the corresponding account is located. Further, the names appear in the index in alphabetical order, so Access can use this index to rapidly produce a list of carriers alphabetized by account name.

Another benefit of indexes is that they provide an efficient way to order records. That is, if the records are to appear in a certain order in a database object, Access can use an index instead of physically having to rearrange the records in the database. Physically rearranging the records in a different order can be a very time-consuming process.

To gain the benefits of an index, you must first create one. Access automatically creates an index on some special fields. If, for example, a table contains a field called Postal Code, Access creates an index for this field automatically. You must create any other indexes you determine would improve database performance, indicating the field or fields on which the index is to be built.

Although the index key will usually be a single field, it can be a combination of fields. For example, you might want to sort records by carrier ID within payment status. In other words, the records are ordered by a combination of fields: Carrier Payment Status and Carrier ID. An index can be used for this purpose by using a combination of fields for the index key. In this case, you must assign a name to the index. It is a good idea to assign a name that represents the combination of fields. For example, an index whose key is the combination of the Carrier Payment Status and Carrier ID fields might be called PaymentCarrier.

How Access Uses Indexes

Access uses indexes automatically. If you request that data be sorted in a particular order and Access determines an index is available that it can use to make the process efficient, it will do so automatically. If no index is available, it will still sort the data in the order you requested; it will just take longer than it would with the index.

Similarly, if you request that Access locate a particular record that has a certain value in a particular field, Access will use an index if an appropriate one exists. If not, it will have to examine each record until it finds the value you want.

To Create a Single-Field Index

The following steps create a single-field index on the Carrier Name field in the Carriers table. **Why?** This index will make finding carriers based on their name more efficient than it would be without the index. It will also improve the efficiency of sorting by carrier name.

1

- Open the Carriers table in Design view. Note that you will need to unhide the unassigned objects in the Navigation Pane to do this. You can then hide the unassigned objects again if desired.
- Select the Carrier Name field.
- Click the Indexed property box in the Field Properties pane to select the property.
- Click the arrow that appears to display the Indexed list.

2

- Click Yes (Duplicates OK) in the list to specify that duplicates are to be allowed (Figure 9–29).

3

- Save your changes and close the table.

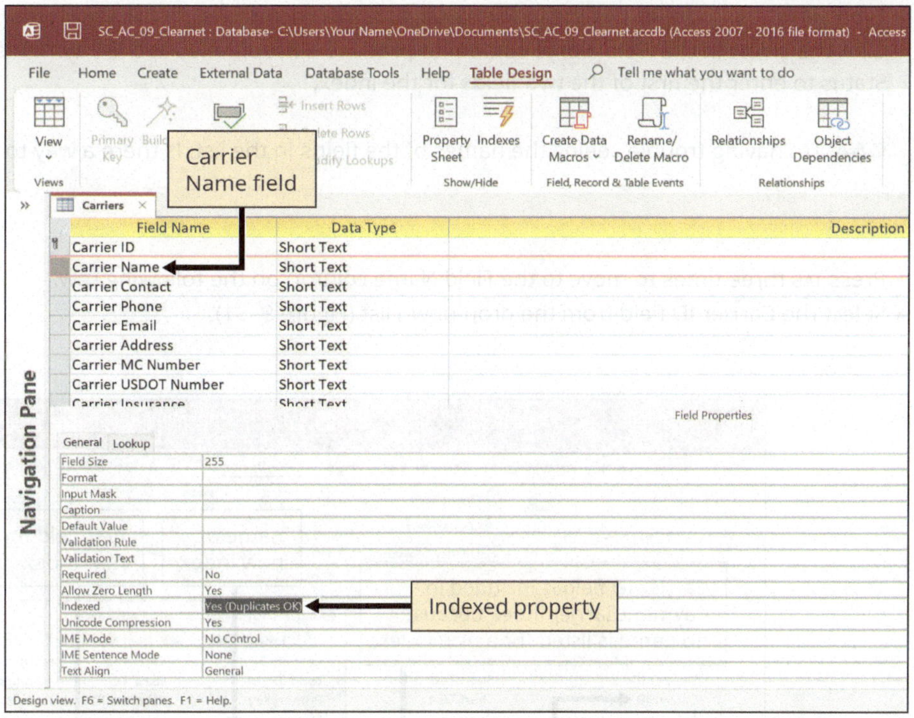

Figure 9–29

To Create a Multiple-Field Index

Creating a **multiple-field index** — that is, an index whose key is a combination of fields — involves a different process than creating a single-field index. To create a multiple-field index, you will use the Indexes button, enter a name for the index, and then enter the combination of fields that make up the index key. The following steps create a multiple-field index on the combination of Carrier Payment Status and Carrier ID. **Why?** Clearnet needs to sort records on the combination of Carrier Payment Status and Carrier ID and wants to improve the efficiency of this sort. The steps assign this index the name PaymentCarrier.

1

- Open the Payments table in Design view.
- Click the Indexes button (Table Design tab | Show/Hide group) to display the Indexes: Payments window, and then resize it as needed to see all the included data (Figure 9–30).

2

- Click in the blank row (the row below Shipper ID) in the Index Name column (Indexes: Payments window) to select the position to enter the name of the new index.

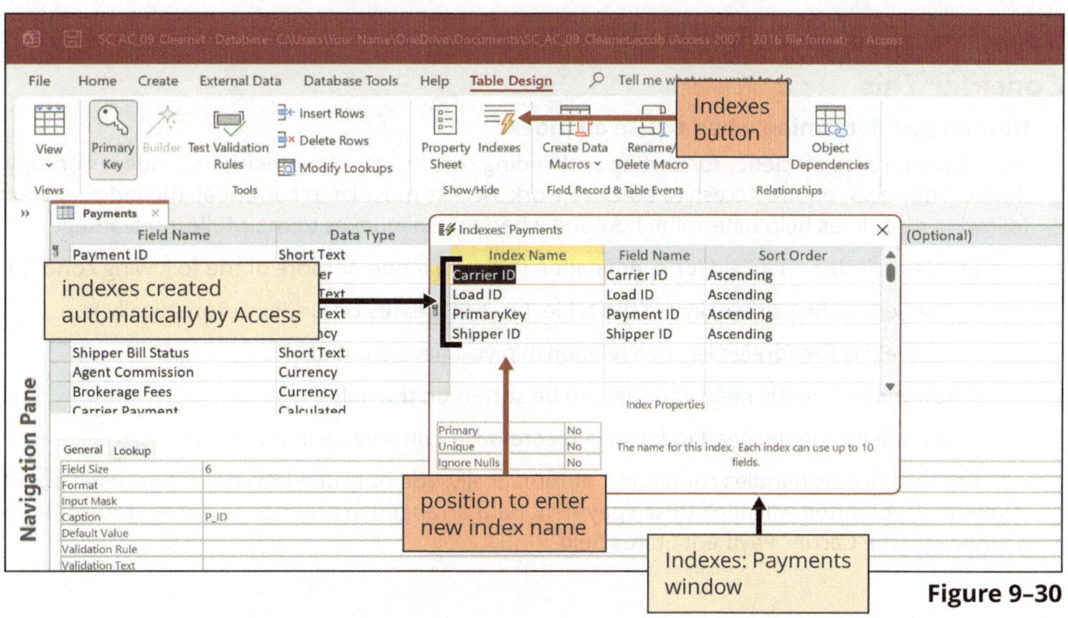

Figure 9–30

- Type **PaymentCarrier** as the index name, and then press TAB.
- Click the arrow in the Field Name column to produce a list of fields in the Payments table, and then click Carrier Payment Status to enter the first of the two fields for the index.

Q&A I'm having trouble seeing the names of the fields in the list. Is there a way to fix this?
Yes, you can drag the border of the Indexes: Payments window to widen it. Then, drag the border between the Field Name column and the Sort Order column to widen it.

- Press TAB three times to move to the Field Name column on the following row.
- Select the Carrier ID field from the drop-down list (Figure 9–31).

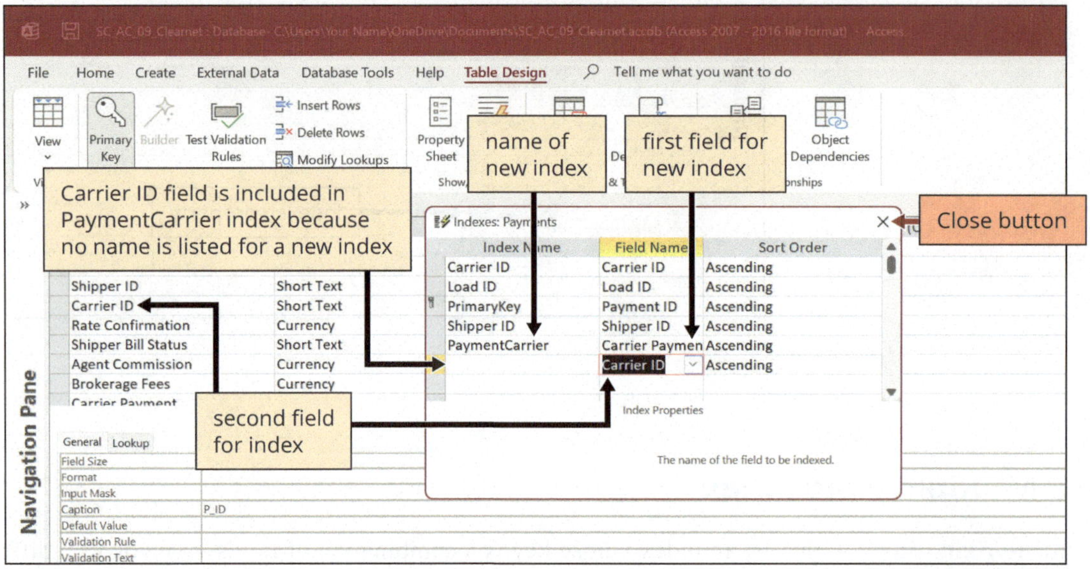

Figure 9–31

3

- Close the Indexes: Payments window by clicking its Close button.
- Save your changes and close the table.

Consider This

How do you determine when to use an index?

An index improves efficiency for sorting and finding records. On the other hand, indexes occupy space on your storage device. They also require Access to do extra work. Access must keep current all the indexes that have been created. The following guidelines help determine how and when to use indexes to their fullest advantage.

Create an index on a field (or combination of fields) if one or more of the following conditions are present:

1. The field is the primary key of the table. (Access creates this index automatically.)
2. The field is the foreign key in a relationship you have created.
3. You will frequently need your data to be sorted on the field.
4. You will frequently need to locate a record based on a value in this field.

Because Access handles condition 1 automatically, you only need to concern yourself about conditions 2, 3, and 4. If you think you often will need to see payment data arranged in order of payment status, for example, you should create an index on the Carrier Payment Status field.

Automatic Error Checking

Access can automatically check for several types of errors in forms and reports. When Access detects an error, it warns you about the existence of the error and provides you with options for correcting it. The types of errors that Access can detect and correct are shown in Table 9–2.

Table 9–2 Types of Errors

Error Type	Description
Unassociated label and control	A label and control are selected and are not associated with each other.
New unassociated labels	A newly added label is not associated with any other control.
Keyboard shortcut errors	A shortcut key is invalid. This can happen because an unassociated label has a shortcut key, there are duplicate shortcut keys assigned, or a blank space is assigned as a shortcut key.
Invalid control properties	A control property is invalid. For example, the property contains invalid characters.
Common report errors	The report has invalid sorting or grouping specifications, or the report is wider than the page size.

To Enable Error Checking

Why? For automatic error checking to take place, it must be enabled. The following steps ensure that error checking is enabled and that errors are found and reported.

1

- Click File on the ribbon and then click Options to display the Access Options dialog box.
- Click Object Designers to display the options for creating and modifying objects.
- Scroll down so the Error checking area appears.
- Ensure the 'Enable error checking' check box is checked (Figure 9–32).

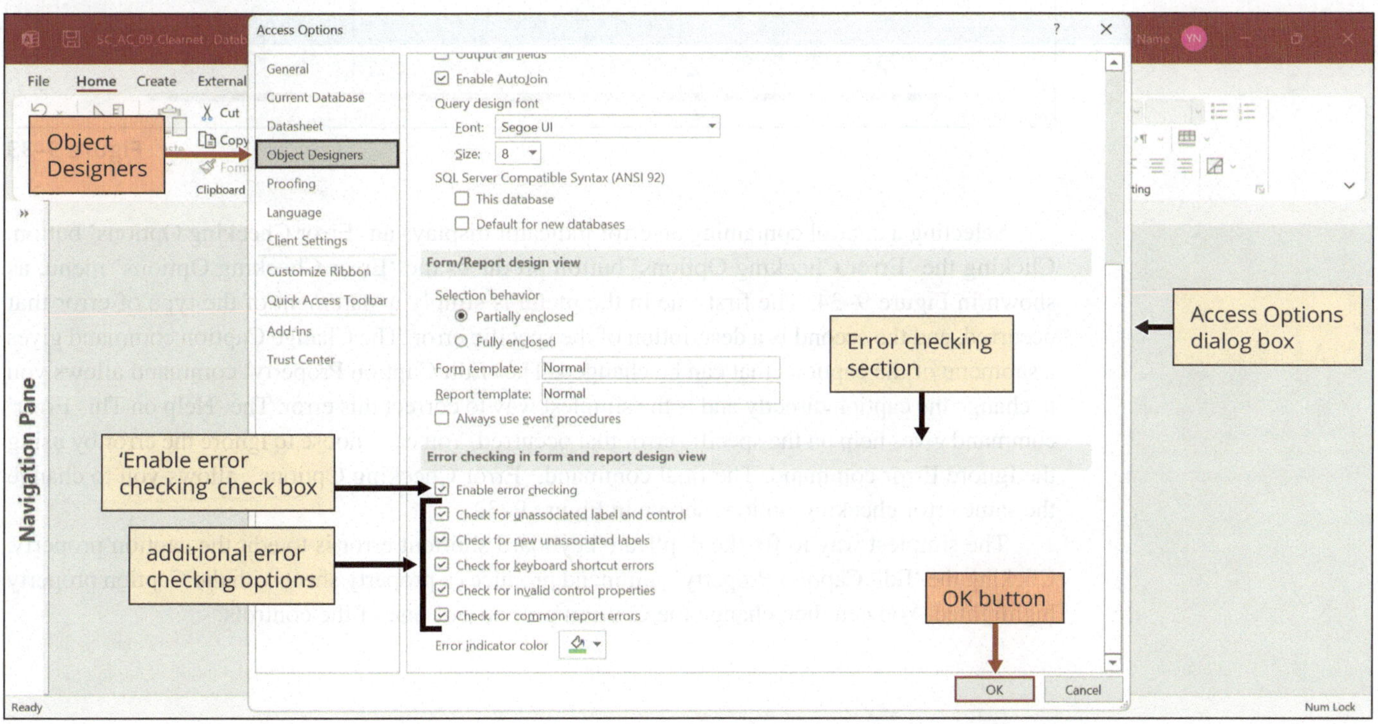

Figure 9–32

Q&A What is the purpose of the other check boxes in the section?

All the other check boxes are checked, indicating that Access will perform all the various types of automatic error checking that are possible. If there were a particular type of error checking that you would prefer to skip, you would remove its check mark before clicking OK.

2

- Click OK to close the Access Options dialog box.

Error Indication

With error checking enabled, if an error occurs, an error indicator appears in the appropriate field or control. For example, you could change the label for Load ID in the Loads Summary Form to include an ampersand (&) and the letter L, making it a keyboard shortcut for this control. This would be a problem because L is already a shortcut for Load to Find. If this happens, an error indicator appears in both controls in which L is the keyboard shortcut, as shown in Figure 9–33.

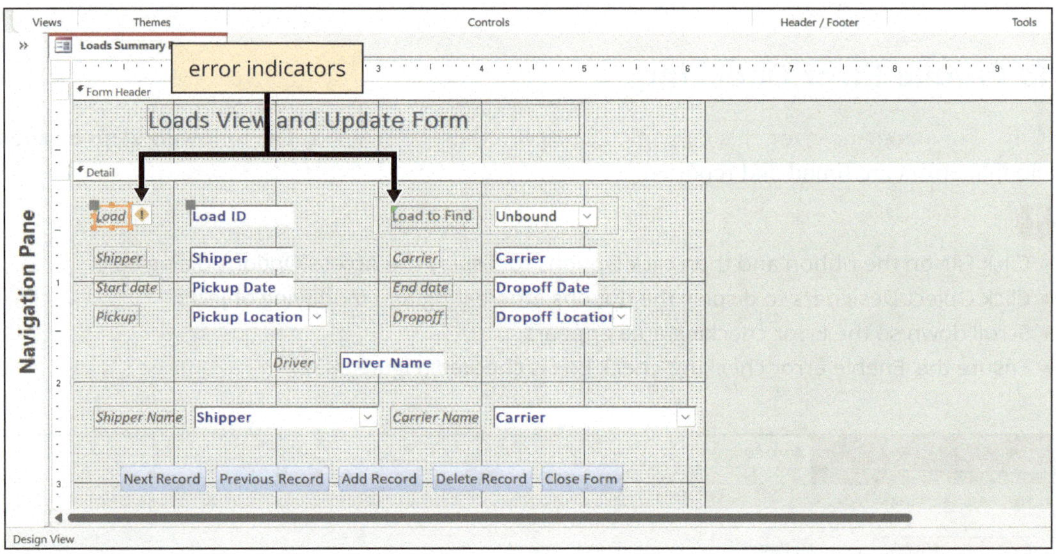

Figure 9–33

Selecting a control containing an error indicator displays an 'Error Checking Options' button. Clicking the 'Error Checking Options' button produces the 'Error Checking Options' menu, as shown in Figure 9–34. The first line in the menu is simply a statement of the type of error that occurred, and the second is a description of the specific error. The Change Caption command gives a submenu of the captions that can be changed. The 'Edit Caption Property' command allows you to change the caption directly and is the simplest way to correct this error. The 'Help on This Error' command gives help on the specific error that occurred. You can choose to ignore the error by using the Ignore Error command. The final command, 'Error Checking Options', allows you to change the same error checking options shown in Figure 9–32.

The simplest way to fix the duplicate keyboard shortcut error is to edit the caption property. Clicking the 'Edit Caption Property' command produces a property sheet with the Caption property highlighted. You can then change the Caption property of one of the controls.

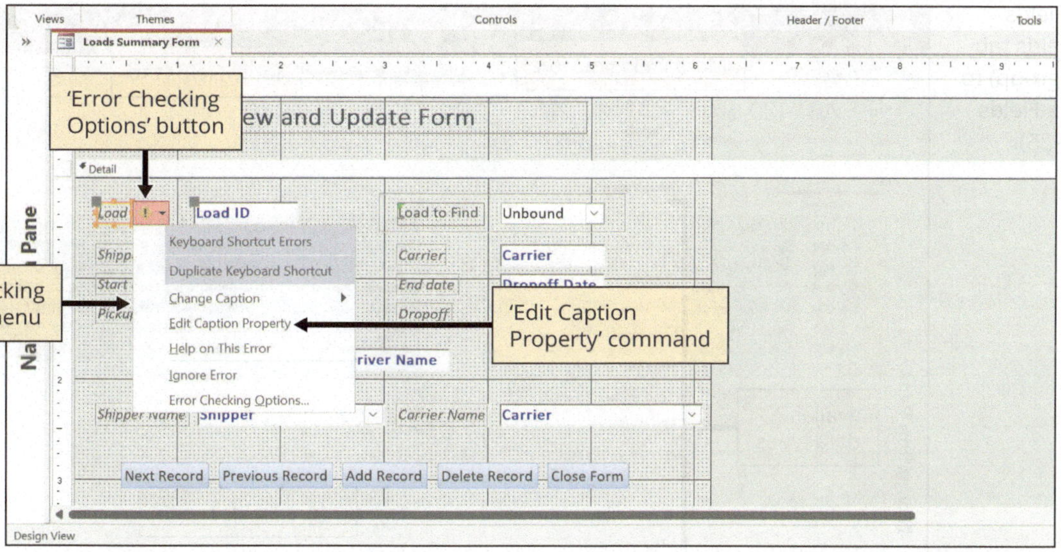

Figure 9–34

Data Type Parts

Access contains data type parts that are available on the More Fields gallery, which you might use when adding new fields to a table. Some data type parts, such as the Category part, consist of a single field. Others, such as the Address part, consist of multiple fields. In addition to the parts provided by Access, you can create your own parts. Quick Start fields act as a framework that lets you rapidly add several fields to a table in a single operation. For example, you could create a quick start field called Name-Address that consists of a Last Name field, a First Name field, a Street field, a City field, a State field, and a Postal Code field. Once you have created this quick start field, you can use it when creating tables in the future. Simply by selecting the Name-Address quick start field, you would immediately add the Last Name, First Name, Street, City, State, and Postal Code fields to a table.

To Create Custom Data Parts

Clearnet has decided that combining several address-related fields into a single data part would make future database updates easier. To create data parts in the Quick Start category from existing fields, you select the desired field or fields and then select the Save Selection as New Data Type command in the More Fields gallery. If you wish to select multiple fields, the fields must be adjacent.

The following steps create a Quick Start field consisting of the Shipper Name, Contact, Phone, Email, and Address fields from the Shippers table. **Why?** Once you have created this Quick Start field, users can add this collection of fields to a table by simply clicking the Quick Start field.

1

- Open the Shippers table in Datasheet view.
- Click the column heading for the Shipper Name field to select the field.
- Hold SHIFT and click the column heading for the Address field to select all the fields from the Shipper Name field to the Address field.
- Display the Table Fields tab.

- Click the More Fields button (Table Fields tab | Add & Delete group) to display the More Fields menu (Figure 9–35).

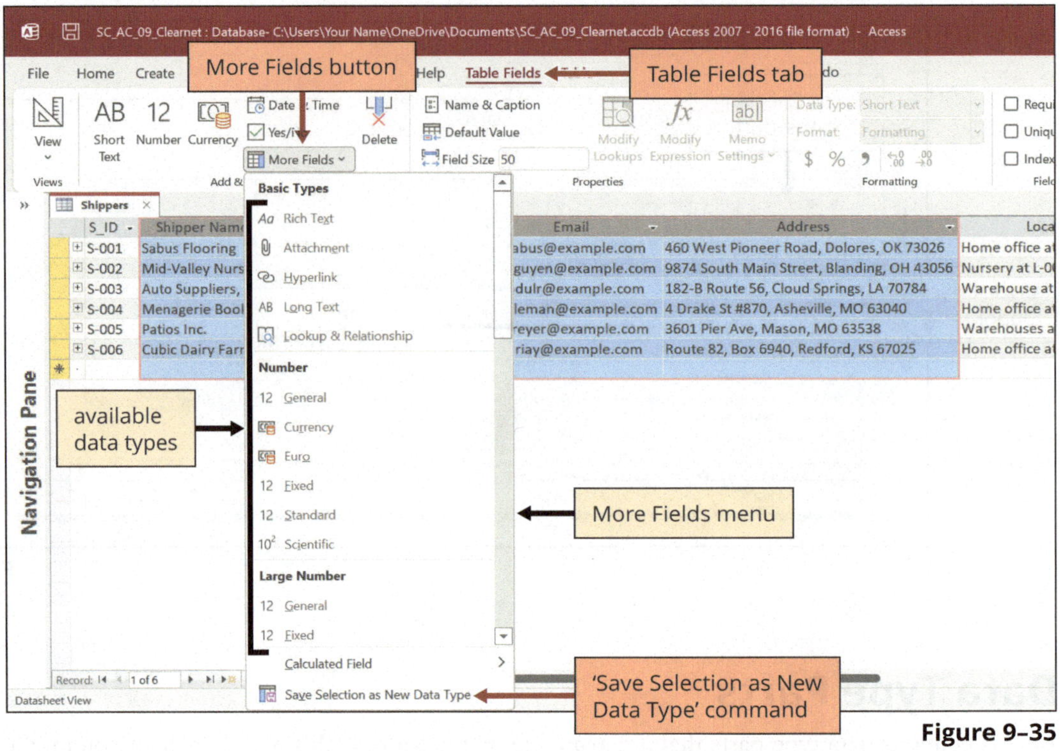

Figure 9–35

2

- Click 'Save Selection as New Data Type' to display the Create New Data Type from Fields dialog box.
- Enter **Name-Contact-Address** as the name.
- Enter **Name, Contact, Phone, Email, and Address fields** as the description.

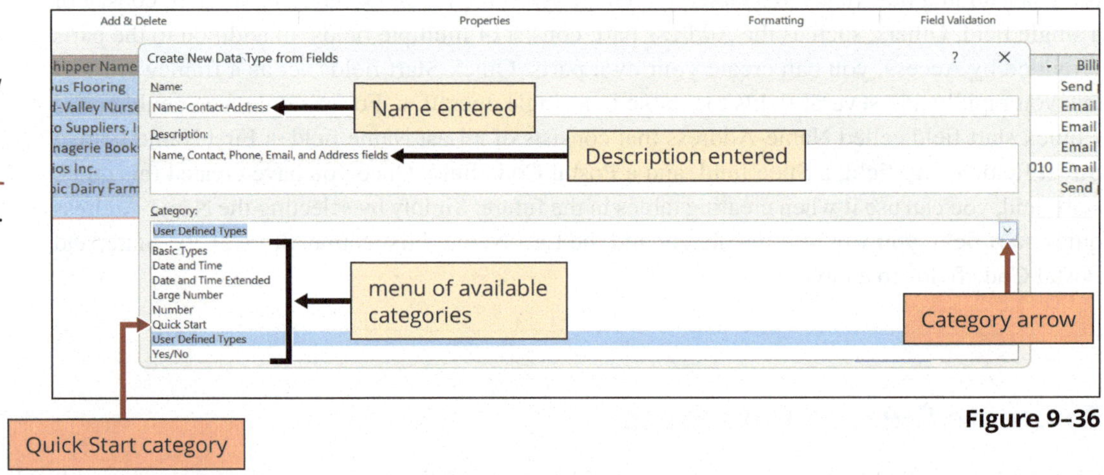

Figure 9–36

Q&A What is the purpose of the description?
When a user points to the Quick Start field you created, a ScreenTip will appear containing the description you entered.

- Click the Category arrow to display a list of available categories (Figure 9–36).

3

- Click Quick Start to indicate the new data type will be added to the Quick Start category.

Q&A What is the difference between the Quick Start and User Defined Types categories?
If you select the Quick Start category, the data type you create will be listed among the Quick Start data types that are part of Access. If you select the User Defined Types category, the data type you create will be in a separate category containing only those data types you create. In both cases, however, clicking the data type will produce the same result.

- Click OK (Create New Data Type from Fields dialog box) to save the data type.
- When Access indicates that your template (that is, your Quick Start field) has been saved, click OK (Microsoft Access dialog box).
- Close the table.
- If necessary, click No when asked if you want to save the changes to the layout of the table.
- sam Click File and then click Close to close the database without closing Access.

Consider This

How do you rearrange fields that are not adjacent?

When adding new data type fields, you can hide the fields that keep your fields from being adjacent. To hide a field, right-click the field to display a shortcut menu, and then click Hide Fields on the shortcut menu. To later unhide a field you have hidden, right-click any column heading and then click Unhide Fields on the shortcut menu. You will see a list of fields with a check box for each field. The hidden field will not have a check mark in the check box. To unhide the field, click the check box for the field.

Templates

Often, Access users find they create and use multiple databases containing the same objects. You can use a template to create a complete database application containing tables, forms, queries, and other objects. There are many templates available for Access.

You also can create your own template from an existing database. To do so, you must first ensure you have created a database with all the characteristics you want in your template. In this module, the database you create will have two tables, a query, two single-item forms, two datasheet forms that use macros, and a navigation form that will serve as the main menu. In addition, the navigation form will be set to appear automatically whenever you open the database. Once you have incorporated all these features, you will save the database as a template. From that point on, anyone can use your template to create a new database. The database that is created will incorporate all the same features as your original database.

BTW
Templates and Application Parts
By default, user-created templates and application parts are stored in the C:\Users*user name*\AppData\Roaming\Microsoft\Templates\Access folder using the .accft file type.

sam! **The following steps on pages 27–39 require completion in order to receive credit for this module's second SAM project.** Follow the instructions to create the desktop database you'll use to form the Shippers and Consignees template, and save it locally to your computer.

To Create a Desktop Database

The following steps create the Shippers and Consignees **desktop database**, that is, a database designed to run on a personal computer. **Why?** This database will become the basis for a template.

1

- With Access open, click File on the ribbon to open Backstage view.
- Click the 'Blank database' button.
- Type **Shippers-and-Consignees** as the name of the database file.
- Click the 'Browse for a location to put your database' button to display the File New Database dialog box, navigate to the desired save location (for example, the Access folder in the CIS 101 folder), and then click OK to return to Backstage view (Figure 9–37).

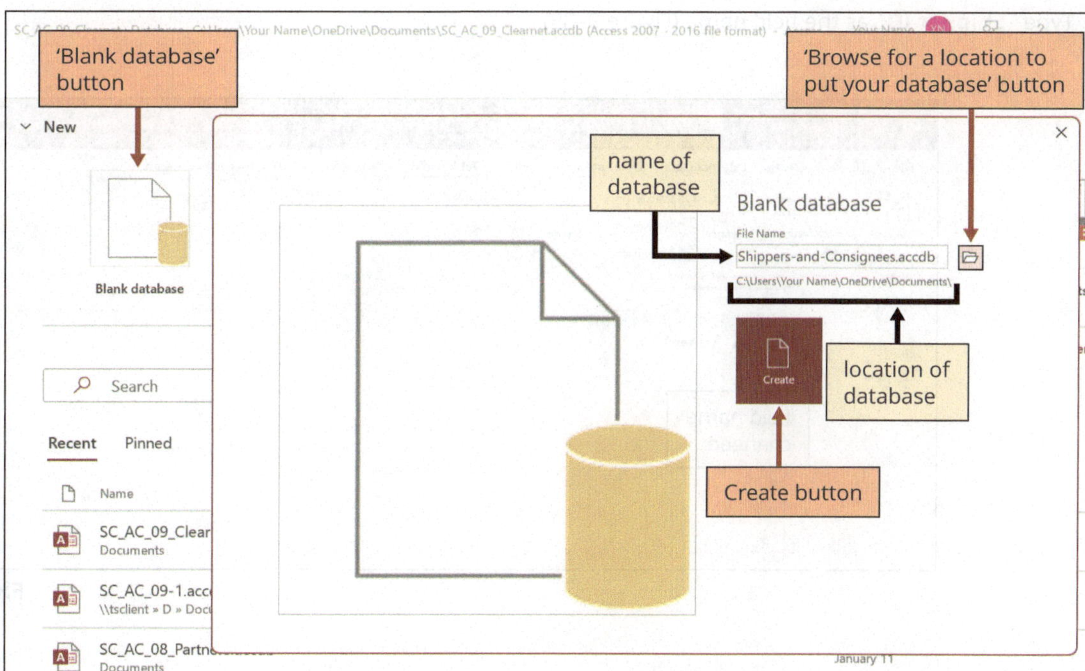

Figure 9–37

2

- Click the Create button to create the database (Figure 9–38).

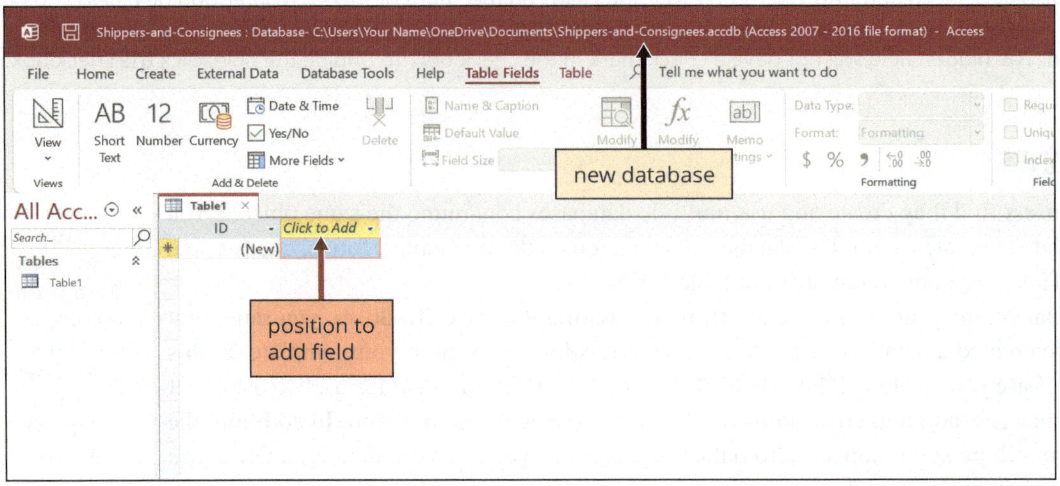

Figure 9–38

To Add Fields to the Table

The tables in the new database will each have an autonumber ID field as the primary key. The following steps add the Shipper ID, Shipper Name, Contact, Phone, Email, and Address fields to a table.

The steps rename the default ID field, which is the table's primary key and is an Autonumber data type, as the Shipper ID field. They add the Shipper Name, Contact, Phone, Email, and Address fields as a single operation by using the Quick Start field created earlier. After adding the fields, they save the table using the name, Shippers.

1

- Right-click the ID column heading and click Rename Field.
- Type **Shipper ID** as the field name (Figure 9–39).

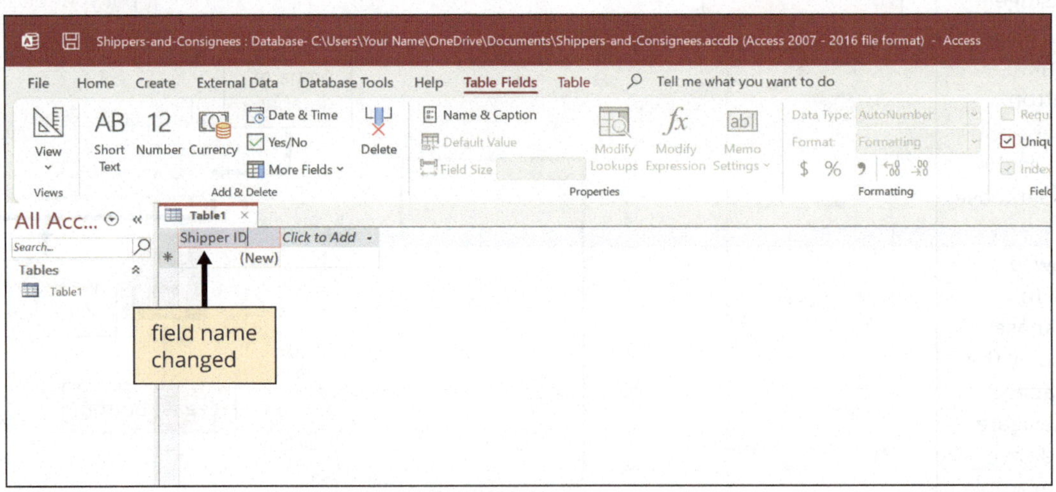

Figure 9–39

2

- Click under the 'Click to Add' column heading and then click it again to produce an insertion point in the next field.
- Click the More Fields button (Table Fields tab | Add & Delete group) to display the More Fields menu.
- Scroll as necessary to display the Name-Contact-Address Quick Start field you created earlier (Figure 9–40).

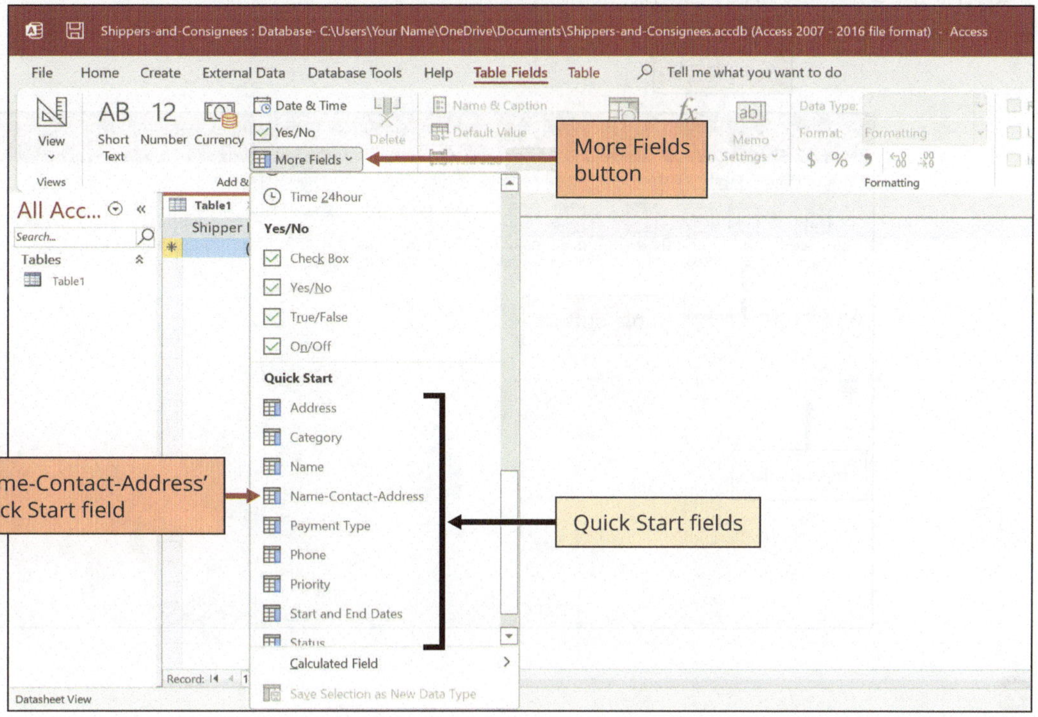

Figure 9–40

3

- Click the Name-Contact-Address Quick Start field to add the Shipper Name, Contact, Phone, Email, and Address fields (Figure 9–41).

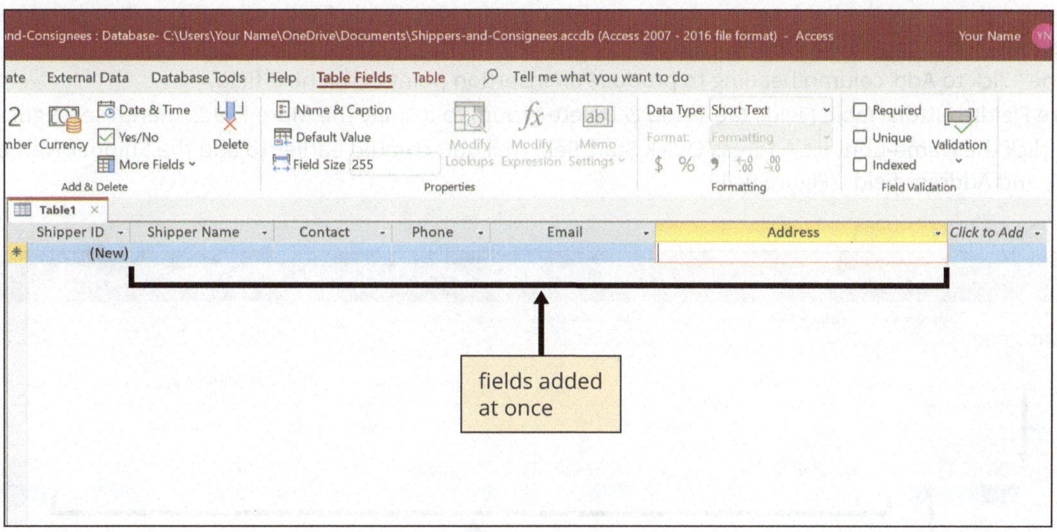

Figure 9–41

4

- Save the table, assigning **Shippers** as the table name.
- Close the table.

To Create a Second Table

The following steps create the Consignees table, which are companies that receive shipments transferred by carriers. The steps add a lookup field for Shipper Name to relate the two tables. **Why?** Because no existing field links the two tables, the relationship between the tables needs to be implemented using a lookup field.

1

- Display the Create tab (Figure 9–42).

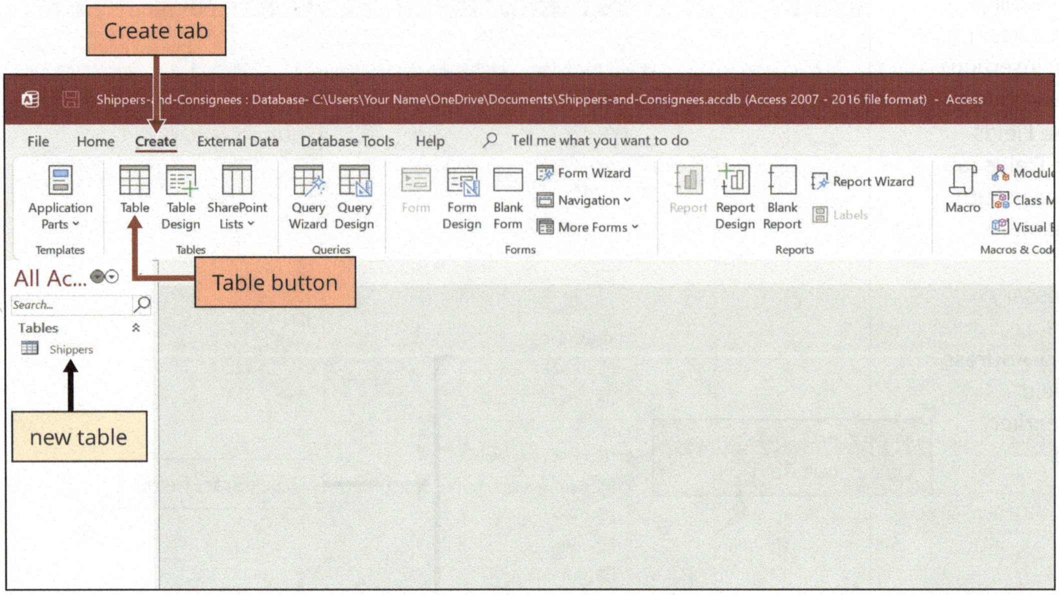

Figure 9–42

2

- Click the Table button (Create tab | Tables group) to create a new table.
- Right-click the ID column heading and click Rename Field.
- Type **Consignee ID** as the field name.
- Click the 'Click to Add' column heading and select Short Text as the data type.
- Type **Consignee Name** as the field name, change the field size to **50** (Table Fields tab | Properties group), and then click under the new field's heading to accept the changes.
- Click under the 'Click to Add' column heading to produce an insertion point in the next field.
- Click the More Fields button (Table Fields tab | Add & Delete group) to display the More Fields menu (see Figure 9–40).
- Scroll to and click the Name-Contact-Address Quick Start field that you created earlier to add the Shipper Name, Contact, Phone, Email, and Address fields (Figure 9–43).

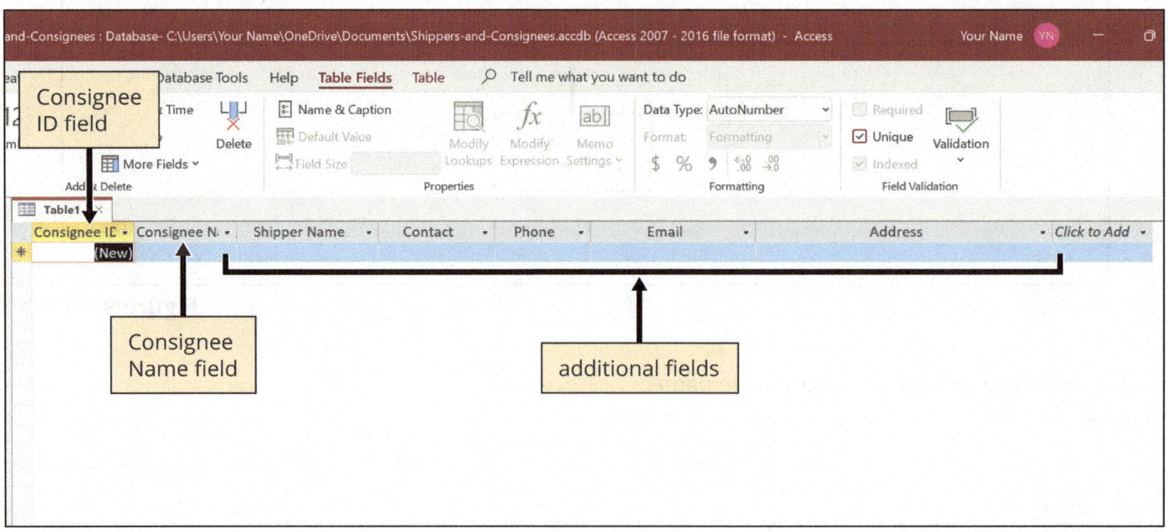

Figure 9–43

3

- Right-click the Shipper Name field to produce a shortcut menu, and then click Delete Field to delete the field.
- Save the table, assigning **Consignees** as the table name.

4

- Switch to Design view.
- Delete the word, Shipper, from the other fields (Figure 9–44).

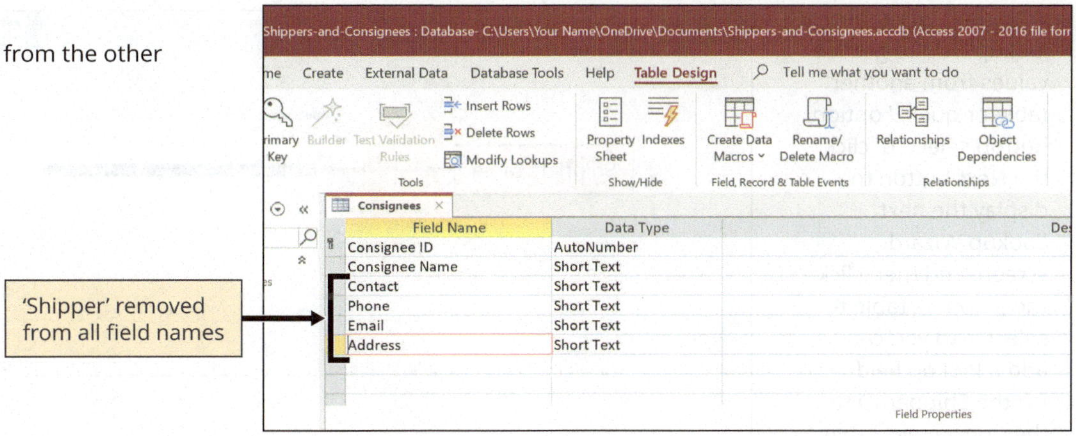

Figure 9–44

5

- Save the table, and switch to Datasheet view.
- Scroll if necessary so the 'Click to Add' column appears on your screen.
- Click the 'Click to Add' column heading to display a menu of available data types (Figure 9–45).

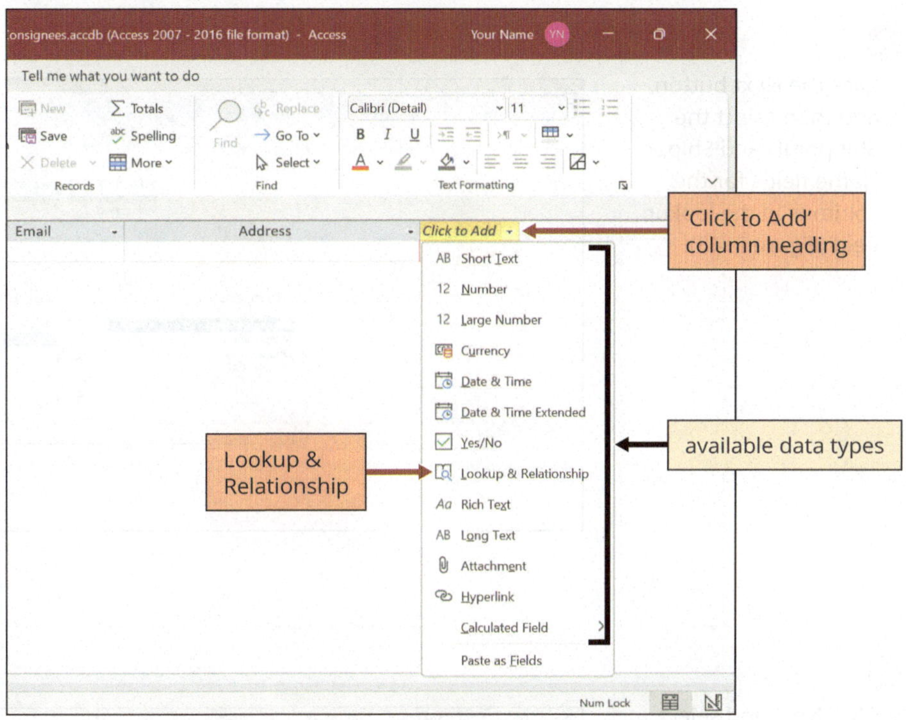

Figure 9–45

BTW

Freezing Fields

The Freeze Fields command allows you to place a column or columns in a table on the left side of the table. As you scroll to the right, the column or columns remain visible. To freeze a column or columns, select the column(s) in Datasheet view, right-click and click Freeze Fields on the shortcut menu. To unfreeze fields, click the `Unfreeze All Fields' command on the shortcut menu. When you freeze a column, Access considers it a change to the layout of the table. When you close the table, Access will ask you if you want to save the changes.

6

- Click Lookup & Relationship to display the Lookup Wizard dialog box (Figure 9–46).

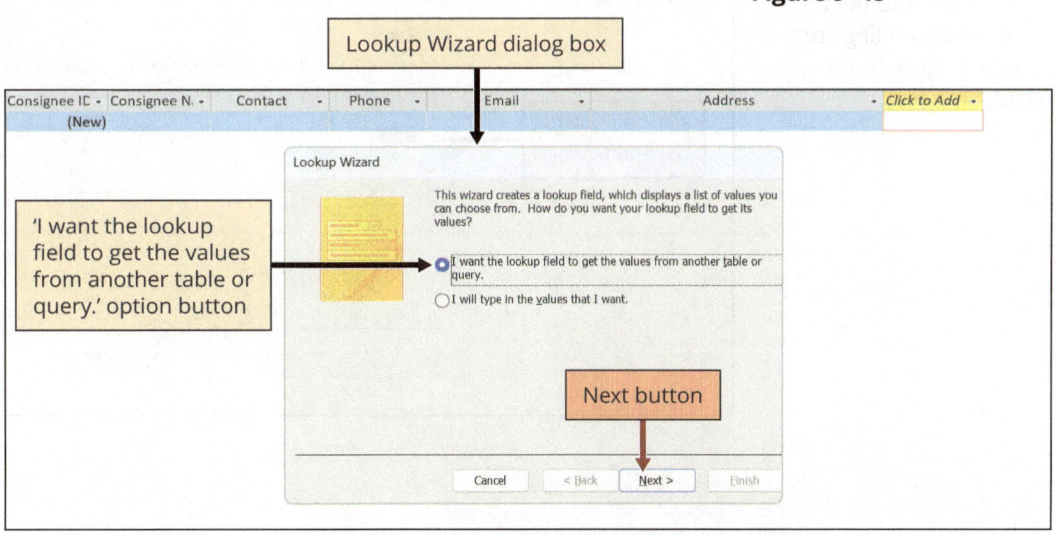

Figure 9–46

7

- With the 'I want the lookup field to get the values from another table or query.' option button selected, click the Next button to display the next Lookup Wizard screen, and then click the Shippers table to select it so you can add a lookup field for the Shipper ID to the Consignees table (Figure 9–47).

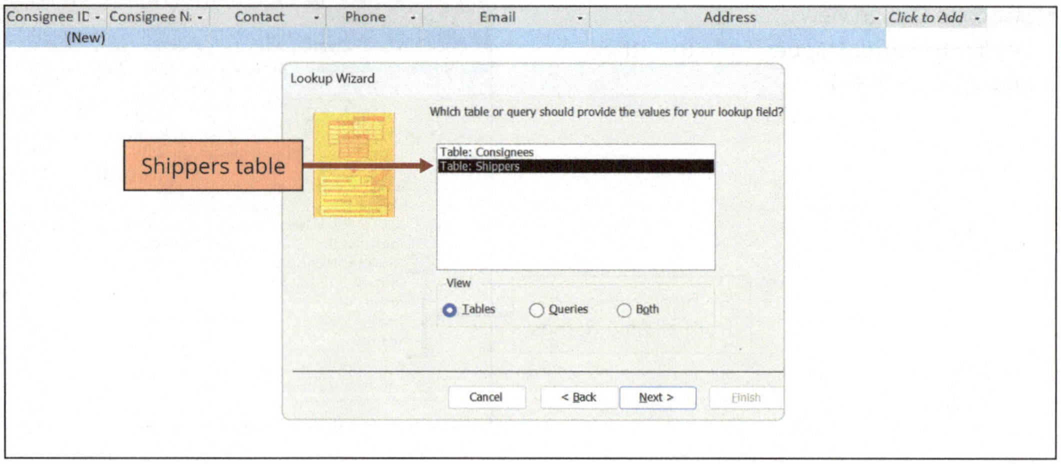

Figure 9–47

8

- Click the Next button, and then select the Shipper ID and Shipper Name fields for the columns in the lookup field (Figure 9–48).

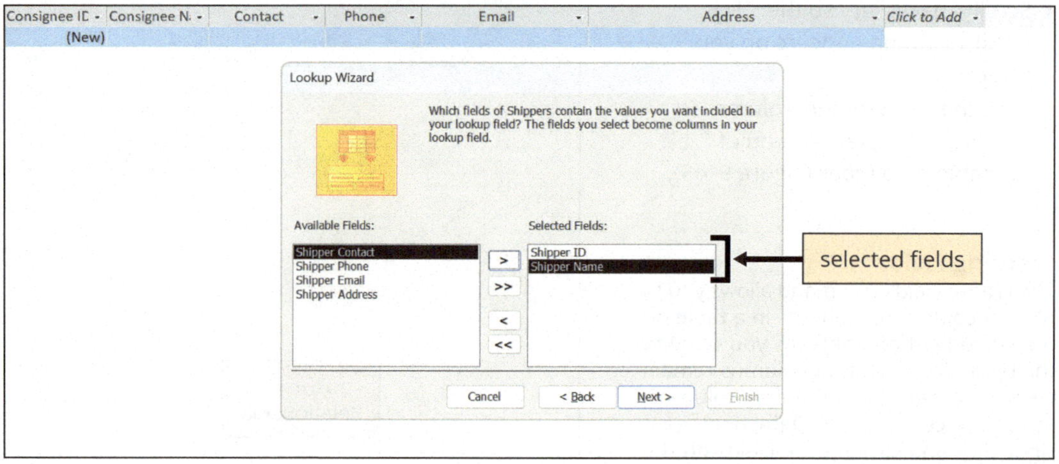

Figure 9–48

9

- Click Next and select the Shipper ID field for the ascending sort order (Figure 9–49).

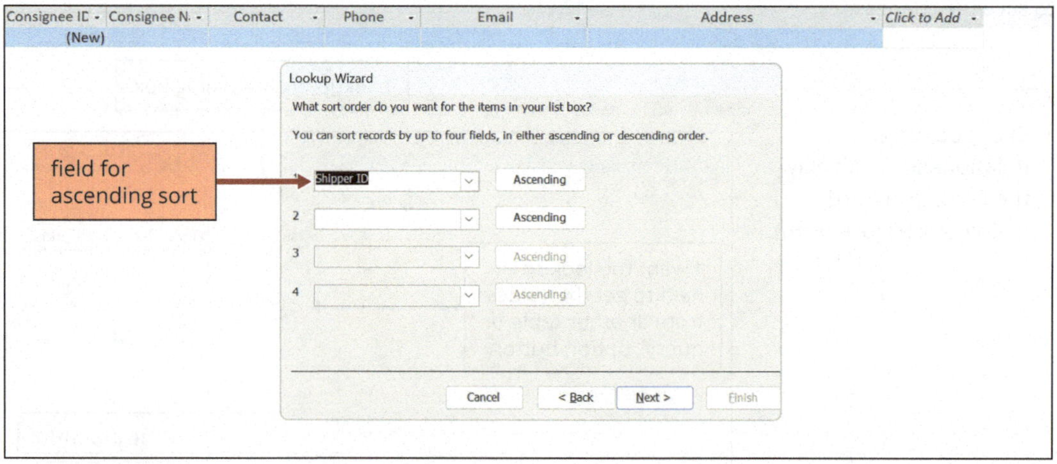

Figure 9–49

10

- Click Next.
- Ensure the 'Hide key column (recommended)' check box is selected, and then click Next.
- Type **Shipper ID** as the label for the lookup field.
- Click the 'Enable Data Integrity' check box to add a check mark (Figure 9–50).

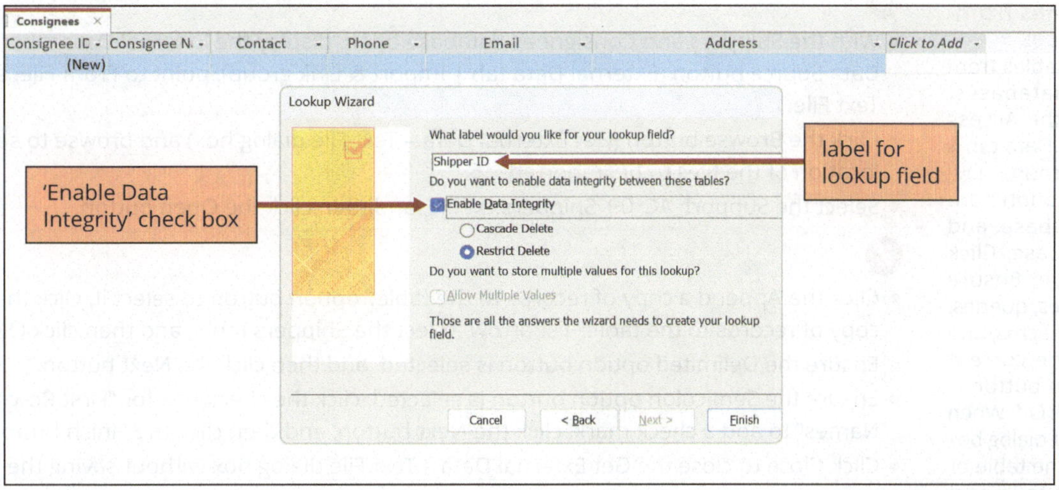

Figure 9–50

Q&A What is the effect of selecting Enable Data Integrity?
Access will enforce referential integrity for the Shipper ID field. That is, Access will not allow a Shipper ID in a consignee record that does not match a shipper in the Shippers table.

11

- Click Finish to add the lookup field.
- Switch to Design view.
- Select the Shipper ID field.
- Type **Shipper Name** in the Caption property box (Figure 9–51).

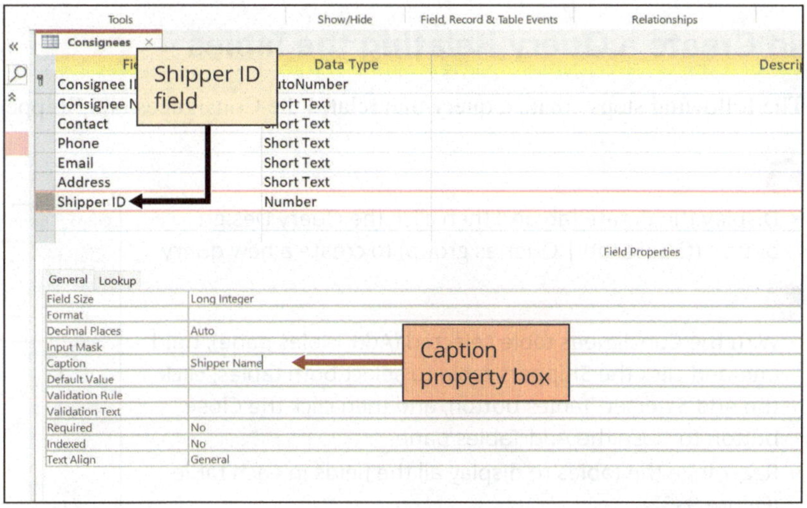

Figure 9–51

12

- Save the table and switch to Datasheet view.
- Resize the Consignee ID, Consignee Name, and Shipper Name fields for best fit.
- Save and close the table.

Q&A Why does the field's caption need to be Shipper Name if the field will look up the Shipper ID?
The lookup field will create a relationship in this table with the Shipper ID field in the Shippers table. However, you also added the Shipper Name field to the lookup, and the Shipper Name data is what will display in the Consignees table.

To Import the Data

Now that the tables have been created, you need to add data to them. You could enter the data, or if the data is already in electronic form, you could import the data. The data for the Shippers and Consignees tables is included in the Data Files as text files. The following steps import the data.

BTW

Importing Tables from Other Databases

You can import tables from other Access databases. To do so, click the Access button (External Data tab | Import & Link group), navigate to the location containing the database, and select the database. Click the Open button. Ensure the `Import tables, queries, forms, reports, macros, and modules into the current database' option button is selected and click OK. When the Import Object dialog box appears, select the table or tables you want to import and then click OK. You also can import other objects by clicking the appropriate object tabs.

1

- With the Shippers and Consignees database open, display the External Data tab, click the New Data Source button (External Data tab | Import & Link group), point to From File, and then click Text File.
- Click the Browse button (Get External Data – Text File dialog box) and browse to select the location of the files to be imported.
- Select the Support_AC_09_Shippers.txt file, and then click the Open button.

2

- Click the 'Append a copy of records to the table:' option button to select it, click the 'Append a copy of records to the table:' list arrow, select the Shippers table, and then click OK.
- Ensure the Delimited option button is selected, and then click the Next button.
- Ensure the Semicolon option button is selected, click the check box for "First Row Contains Field Names" to add a check mark, click the Next button, and then click the Finish button.
- Click Close to close the Get External Data – Text File dialog box without saving the import steps.
- Open the Shippers table to confirm the data imported correctly, troubleshoot any problems if necessary, resize all columns for best fit, and then save and close the table.

3

- Use the technique shown in Steps 1 and 2 to import the Support_AC_09_Consignees.txt file into the Consignees table.

To Create a Query Relating the Tables

The following steps create a query that relates the Consignees and Shippers tables.

1

- Display the Create tab and then click the Query Design button (Create tab | Queries group) to create a new query.

2

- With the Consignees table selected (Add Tables pane), hold CTRL and click the Shippers table to select both tables, click the Add Selected Tables button, and then click the Close button to close the Add Tables pane.
- Rearrange the tables to display all the fields in each table (Figure 9–52).

3

- Double-click the Consignee Name and Shipper ID fields from the Consignees table to add these fields to the design grid.
- Double-click the Shipper Contact field from the Shippers table to add this field to the design grid.

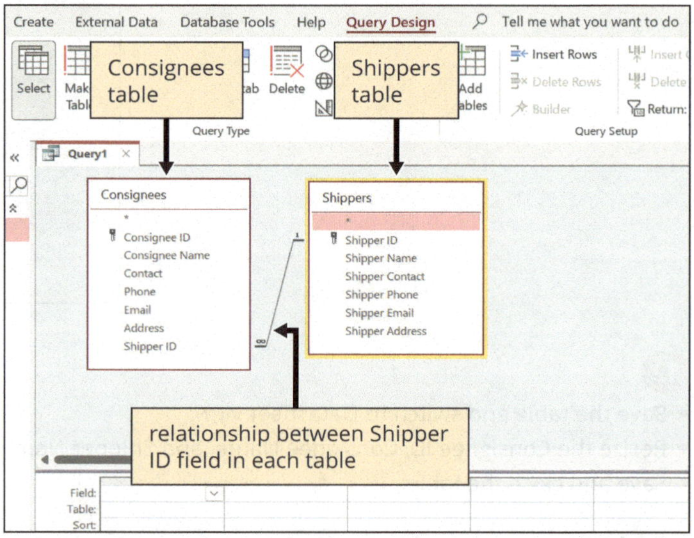

Figure 9–52

4

- Save the query with the name, **Consignee-Shipper Query**, and close the query.

Creating Forms

There are a few types of forms that need to be created for this database. The Consignee and Shipper detail forms each show a single record at a time. The Consignee, Shipper, and Consignee-Shipper Query forms are intended to look like the corresponding table or query in Datasheet view. Finally, the main menu is a navigation form.

BTW
Rearranging Fields in a Query
If you add fields to a query in the wrong order, you can select the field in the design grid, and drag it to the appropriate location.

To Create Single-Item Forms

The following steps create two single-item forms, that is, forms that display a single record at a time. The first form, called Consignee Details, is for the Consignees table. The second form is for the Shippers table and is called Shipper Details.

1

- Select the Consignees table in the Navigation Pane if necessary, and then display the Create tab.
- Click the Form button (Create tab | Forms group) to create a single-item form for the Consignees table.
- Save the form with the name, **Consignee Details**, and then close the form.

2

- Select the Shippers table in the Navigation Pane, display the Create tab, and then click the Form button (Create tab | Forms group) to create a form for the Shippers table that shows the consignees receiving loads from that particular shipper.

3

- Save the form with the name, **Shipper Details**, and then close the form.

To Create a Navigation Form

The following steps create a navigation form containing a single row of horizontal tabs. The steps save the form using the name, Main Menu. **Why?** This form is intended to function as a menu. The steps change the form title and add the appropriate tabs.

1

- Display the Create tab and then click the Navigation button (Create tab | Forms group) to display the menu of available navigation forms.
- Click Horizontal Tabs in the menu to create a form with a navigation control in which the tabs are arranged horizontally in a single row.
- If the Field List pane appears, click the 'Add Existing Fields' button (Form Layout Design tab | Tools group) to close the pane.
- Save the navigation form with the name, **Main Menu**, and do not close it yet.

2

- Click the form title twice, once to select it and the second time to produce an insertion point.
- Delete the current title and then type **Shippers and Consignees** as the new title (Figure 9–53).

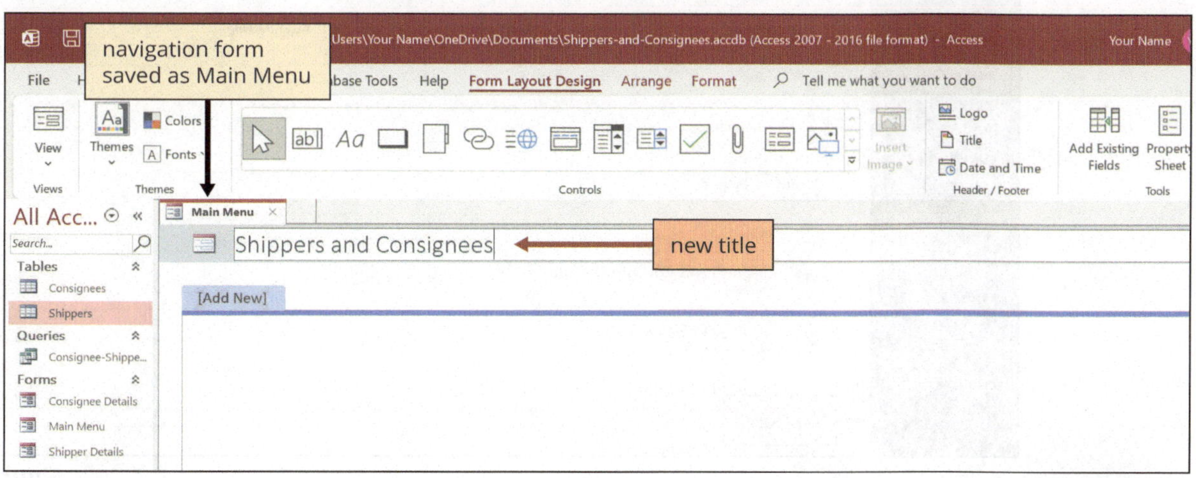

Figure 9–53

3

- One at a time, drag the Shipper Details form and the Consignee Details form to the positions shown in Figure 9–54.
- Save and close the form.

Q&A What should I do if I made a mistake and added a form to the wrong location?
You can rearrange the tabs by dragging. However, the simplest way to correct a mistake is to click the Undo button (Home tab | Undo group) to reverse your most recent action. You can also choose to simply close the form without saving it and then start over.

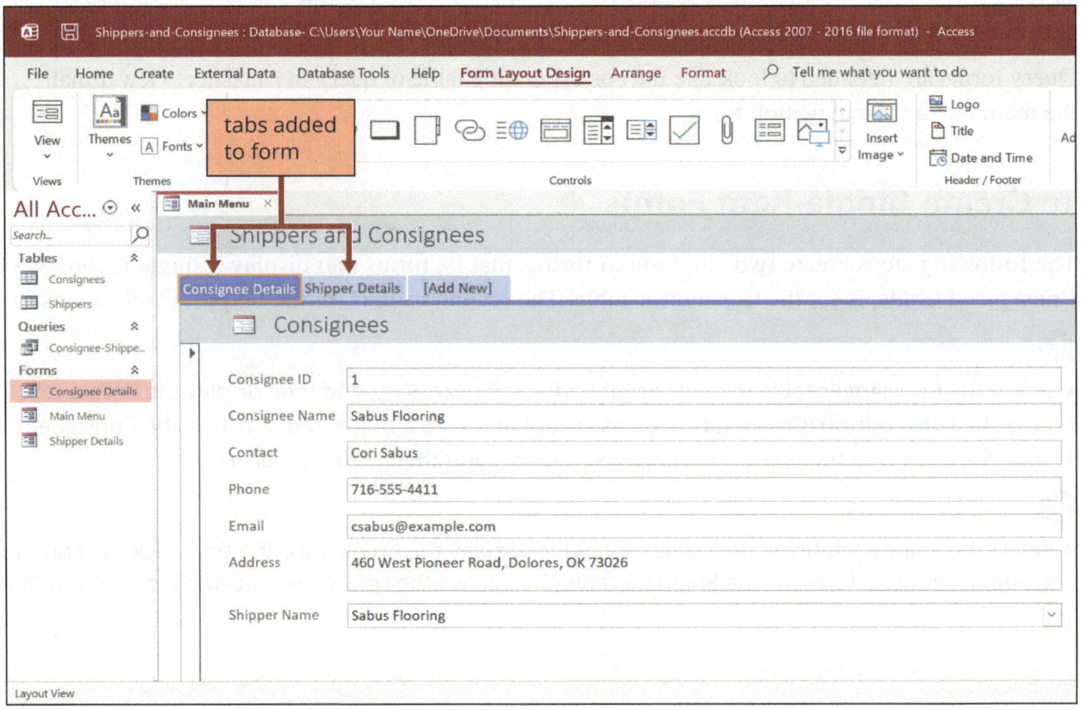

Figure 9–54

To Select a Startup Form

If the database includes a navigation form, it is common to select the navigation form as a **startup form**, which launches when the user opens the database. **Why?** Designating the navigation form as a startup form ensures the form will appear automatically when a user opens the database. The following steps designate the navigation form as a startup form.

1

- Click File on the ribbon to display Backstage view (Figure 9–55).

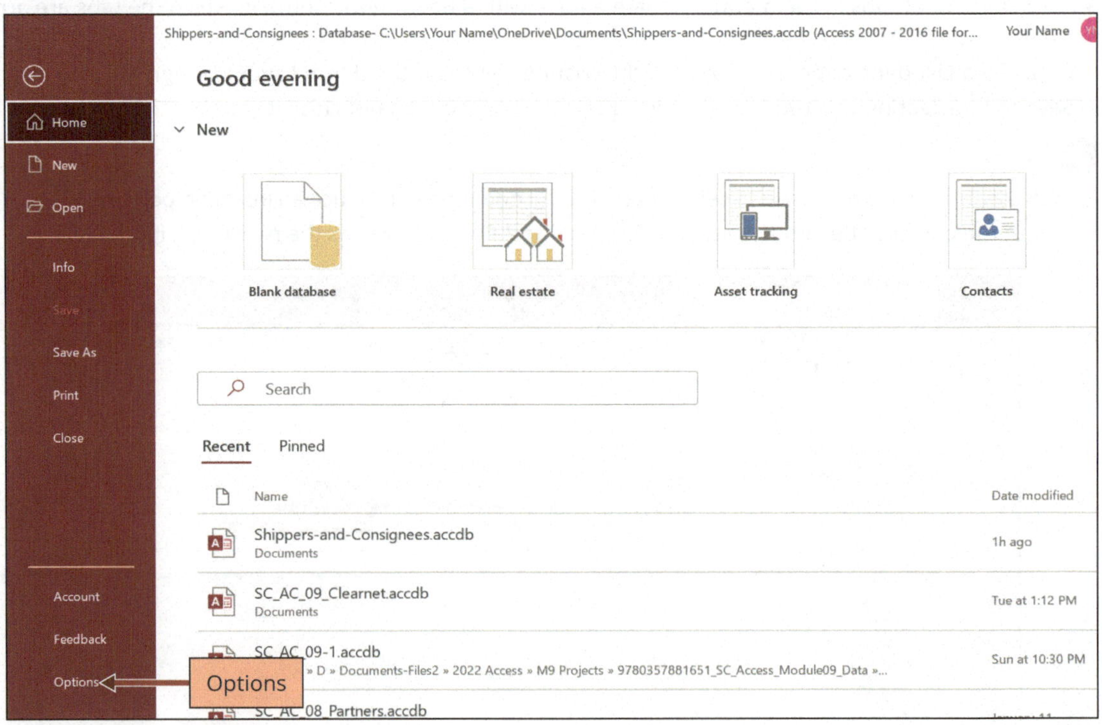

Figure 9–55

2

- Click Options to open the Access Options dialog box.
- Click Current Database (Access Options dialog box) to select the options for the current database.
- Click the Display Form arrow to display the list of available forms (Figure 9–56).

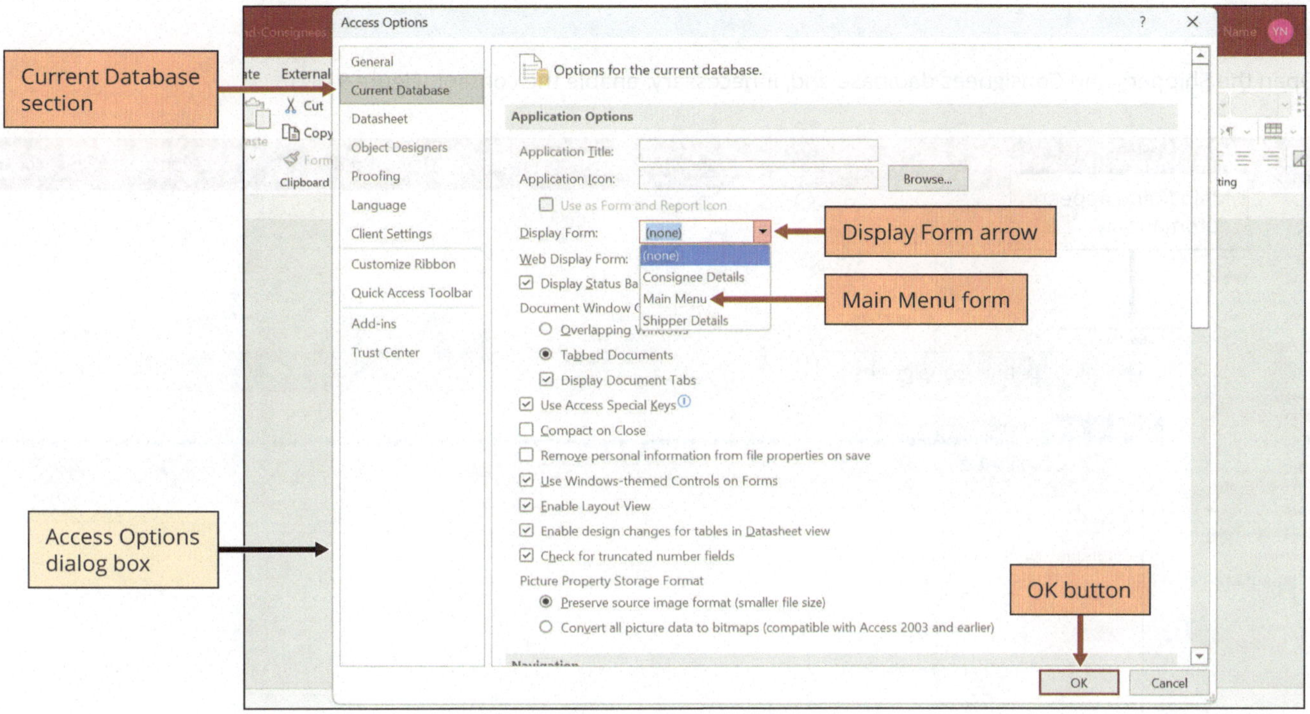

Figure 9–56

3

- Click Main Menu to select it as the form that will be automatically displayed whenever the database is opened.
- Click OK (Access Options dialog box) to save your changes.
- Click OK (Microsoft Access dialog box) when Access displays a message indicating that you must close and reopen the database for the change to take effect.
- Close the database without exiting Access.

Break Point: If you wish to take a break, this is a good place to do so. You can quit Access now. To resume at a later time, start Access and continue following the steps from this location forward.

Templates and Application Parts

An Access **template** is a file that contains the elements needed to produce a specific type of complete database. You can select a template when you create a database. The resulting database will contain all the tables, queries, forms, reports, and macros included in the template. In addition, with some templates, the resulting database might also contain data.

Some templates are also available as **application parts**. Application parts are a type of template, and selecting a single application part can also create tables, queries, forms, reports, and macros. Typically, application parts are used for adding one or a few objects, while larger templates are more often used to create a larger group of objects, even a complete database. Templates that are also saved as application parts can be accessed during database creation or after the database is created.

Access provides a number of templates representing a variety of types of databases. You can also create your own template from an existing database. When you create a template, you can choose to create an application part as well. When creating templates and application parts, you can also include data if desired.

To Create a Template and an Application Part

The following steps create a template from the Shippers and Consignees database. **Why?** The Shippers and Consignees database now contains all the tables, queries, and forms you want in the template. A template will create all the same objects when you want to create similar databases. The steps also create an application part from the database so you can reuse the parts in other databases.

1

- Open the Shippers and Consignees database and, if necessary, enable the content (Figure 9–57).

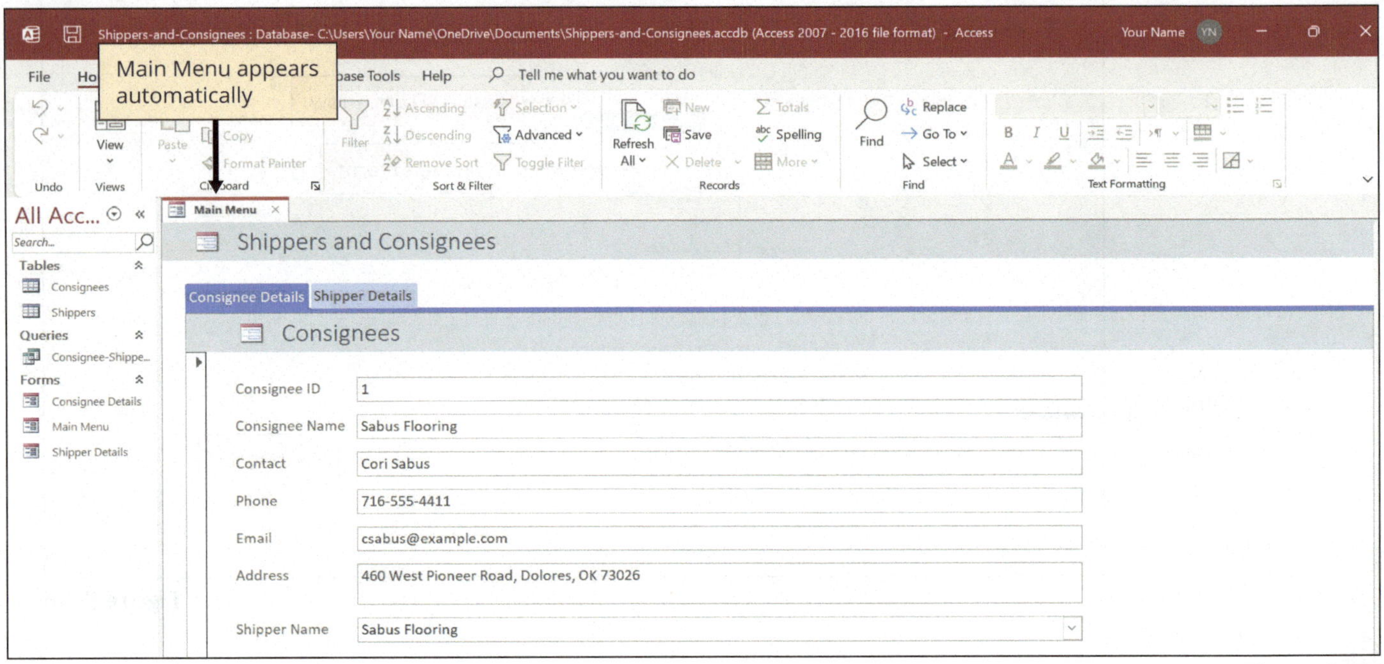

Figure 9–57

2

- Close the Main Menu form.
- Open Backstage view.
- Click Save As to open the Save As screen.
- Click the Template (*.accdt) button in the Save Database As area to indicate you are creating a template (Figure 9–58).

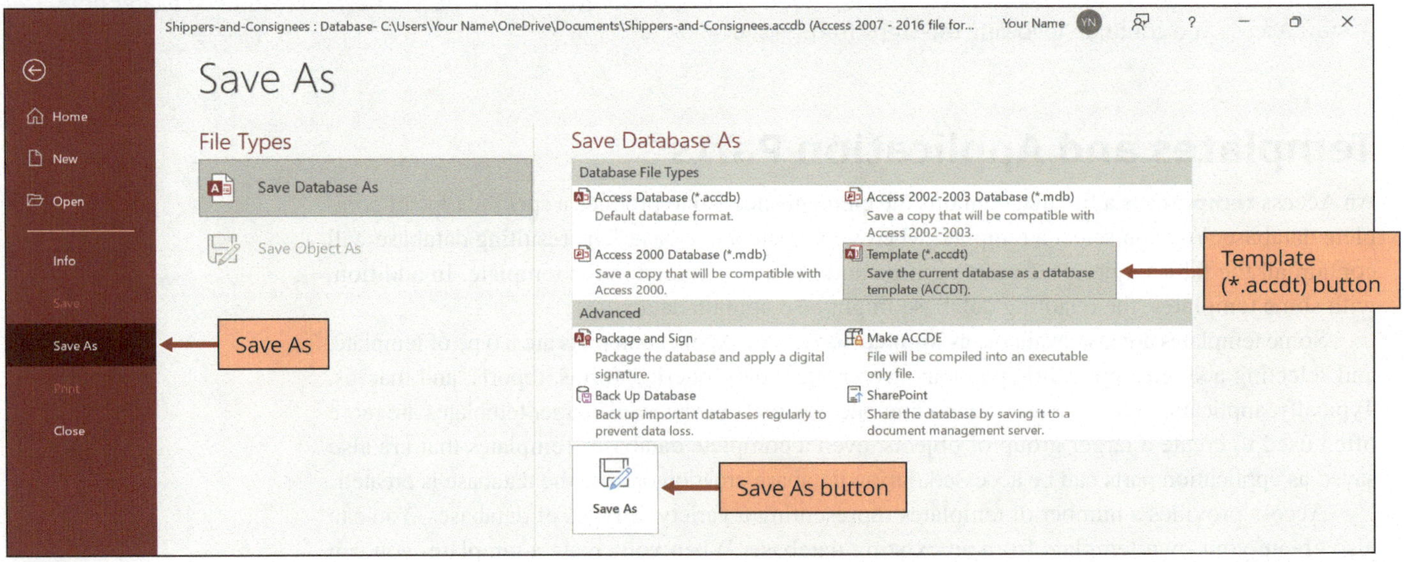

Figure 9–58

3

- Click the Save As button to display the Create New Template from This Database dialog box.
- Type **Shippers and Consignees** as the name for the new template.
- Type **Database of shippers and consignees with navigation form menu** as the description.
- Click the Application Part check box to indicate you also want to create an application part.
- Click the 'Include All Data in Package' check box to indicate you want to include the data in the database as part of the template (Figure 9–59).

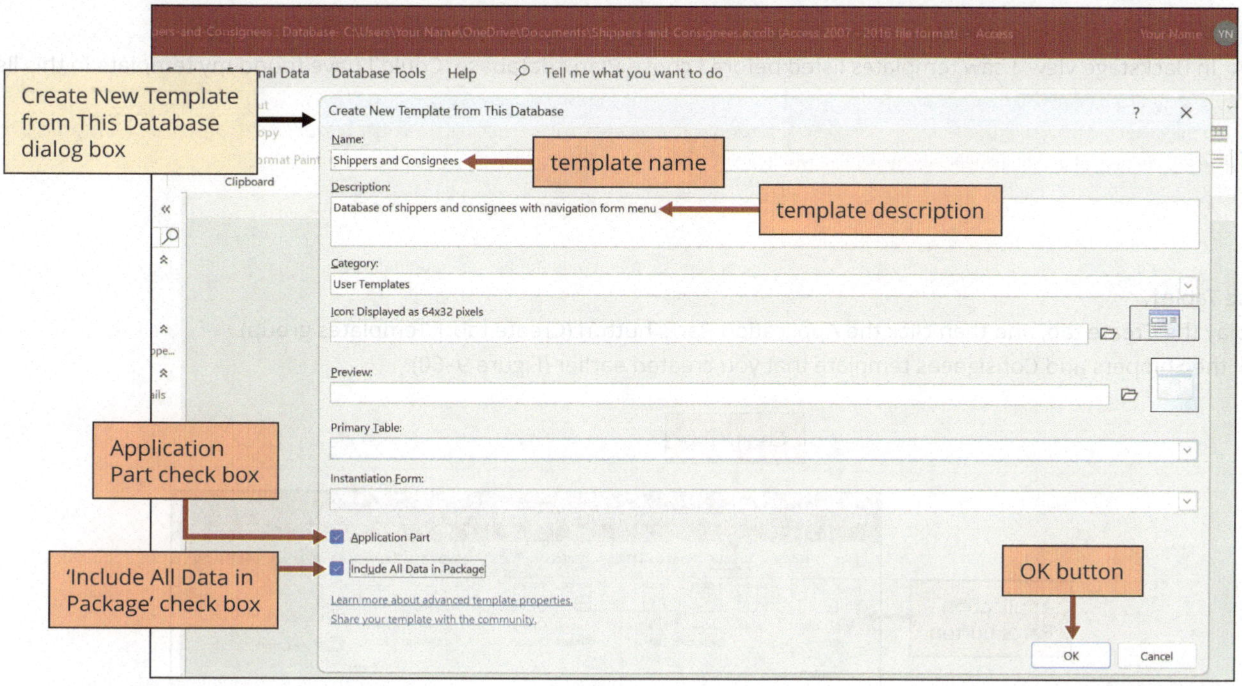

Figure 9–59

Q&A Why include data in the template?
Anytime a user creates a database using the template, the database will automatically include data. This enables the users to see what any reports, forms, or queries look like with data in them. Once the users have the reports, forms, and queries the way they want them, they can delete all this data. At that point, they can begin adding their own data to the database.

4

- Click OK (Create New Template from This Database dialog box) to create the template.
- When Access indicates the template has been successfully saved, click OK (Microsoft Access dialog box).

Q&A Access did not let me choose where to save my template. How can I find my template file?
By default, Access saves new templates to the following location:
C:\Users*user name*\AppData\Roaming\Microsoft\Templates\Access\
You can find your template at this location along with the quick start field you created earlier in this module. However, in the next section, you will access the template from within Access, which will know where your template is stored.

sam! **The following steps on pages 40–41 require the Shippers and Consignees template created in the previous section.** Credit will not be received unless the correct template is imported to the start file downloaded below. Please make sure you have completed the steps on pages 27–39 before starting the next section.

To Use a Template or Application Part

You can use the Shippers and Consignees template just as you would use any other template, such as the Blank database template you previously used. To do this, you click the Personal link in Backstage view to list any templates you have created and choose a template from that list. Alternatively, because you also created the template as an application part, you can apply the application part after creating a database. The only difference is that, after creating a blank database, you need to apply the template using the Application Parts button on the Create ribbon. **Why?** The application part contains the objects and data that should be created in the new database.

The following steps use the application part created earlier to create the Freightliners Customers database.

1

- sam With Access open, click File on the ribbon to open Backstage view.
- Click the 'Blank database' button.
- Type **SC_AC_09_Freightliners-Customers** as the name of the database, and then navigate to the location where you will store the new database.
- Click the Create button to create the database.

Q&A In Backstage view, I saw templates listed before I chose Blank database. Could I have found my template in this list?
Yes. Access lists a few templates on the Home tab in Backstage view. You can click the New tab for a longer list. On the New screen, scroll down and click Personal to list user-created templates stored on the local computer. Your Shippers and Consignees template would be included in this list.

2

- Close Table1.
- Display the Create tab, and then click the Application Parts button (Create tab | Templates group).
- Click the Shippers and Consignees template that you created earlier (Figure 9–60).

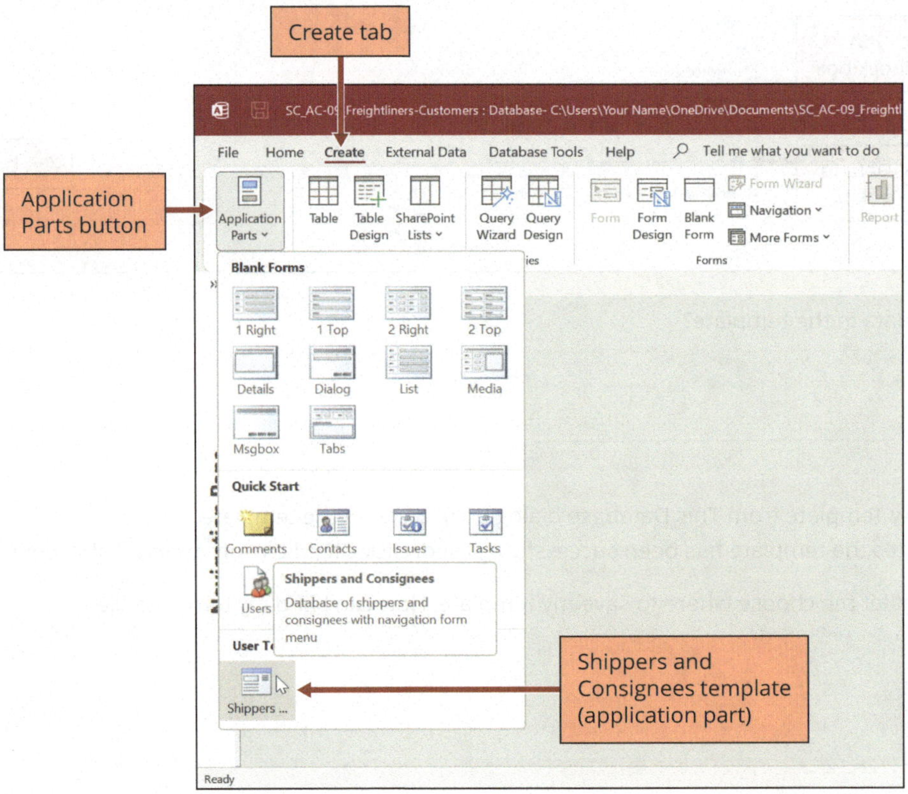

Figure 9–60

Q&A When I clicked my template, I got a message saying "All open objects must be closed before instantiating this application part." Is this a problem?
This is not a problem. You will receive this message if you did not first close the default Table1, and the message is offering to close all open objects. After you click the Yes button, Access will add all the objects in the application part to the database. If you had already created other objects in the database, they would still be included.

3

- Open the Navigation Pane and explore the database to confirm all the objects and data are included from the template (Figure 9–61). Make sure to open each table to confirm all data is included.
- Close the database.
- If desired, sign out of your Microsoft account.
- **sam** Exit Access.

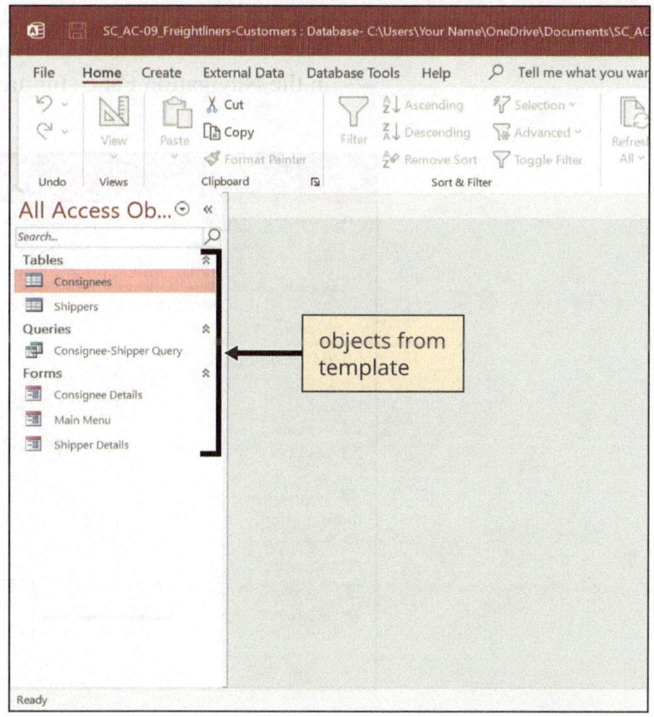

Figure 9–61

Note: Unless your instructor indicates otherwise, you are encouraged to simply read the material in this module from this point forward without carrying out any operations. If you decide to try these steps for yourself, it is important to make a backup copy of your database and store it in a secure location before performing the following operations. This way, if something damages your database or you can no longer access your database, you still can use the backup copy.

Blank Forms Application Parts

Blank Forms application parts (see Figure 9–62) represent a way to create certain types of forms. To do so, you click the Application Parts button to display the gallery of application part styles,

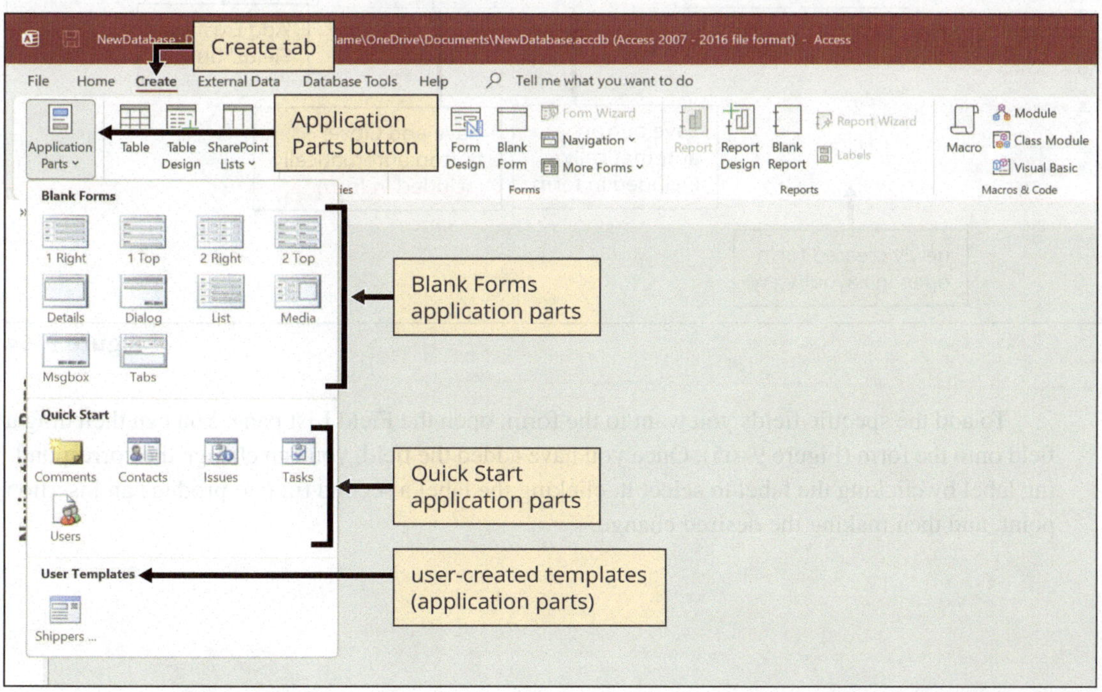

Figure 9–62

and then click the desired type of form, for example, 1 Right. Access then creates a form with the desired characteristics and assigns it a name. It does not open the form, but you can see the form in the Navigation Pane (Figure 9–63).

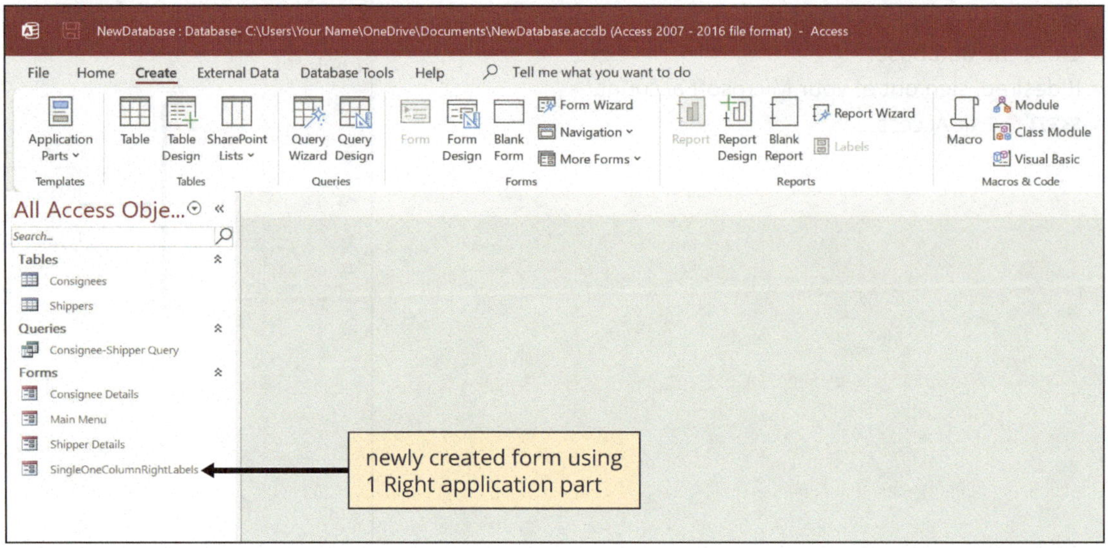

Figure 9–63

You can modify the form by opening the form in Layout or Design view (Figure 9–64). This particular form automatically creates a Save button. Clicking this button when you are using the form will save changes to the current record. The form also automatically includes a Save & Close button. Clicking this button will save changes to the current record and then close the form.

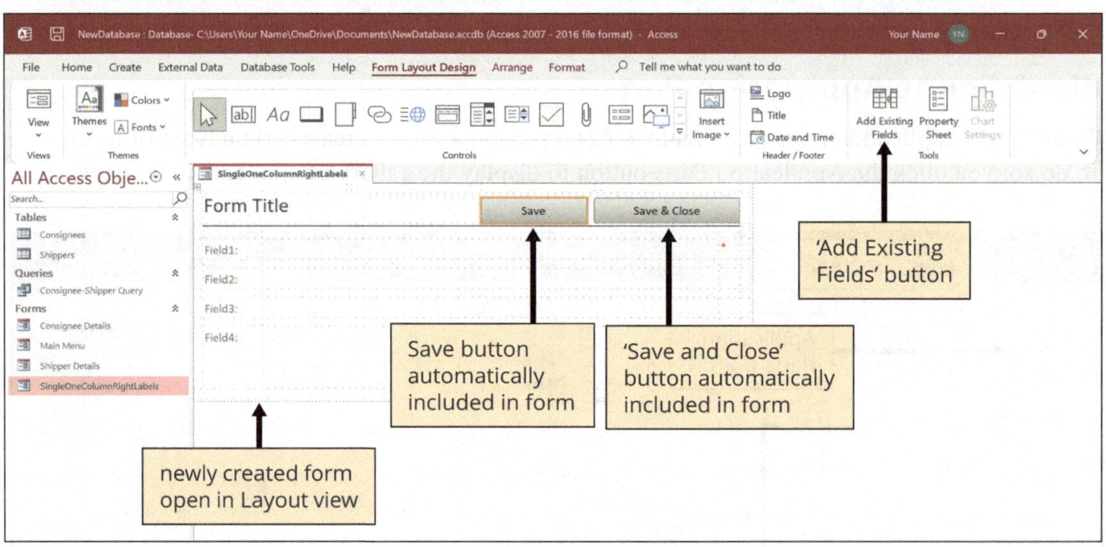

Figure 9–64

To add the specific fields you want to the form, open the Field List pane. You can then drag a field onto the form (Figure 9–65). Once you have added the field, you can change the corresponding label by clicking the label to select it, clicking the label a second time to produce an insertion point, and then making the desired change.

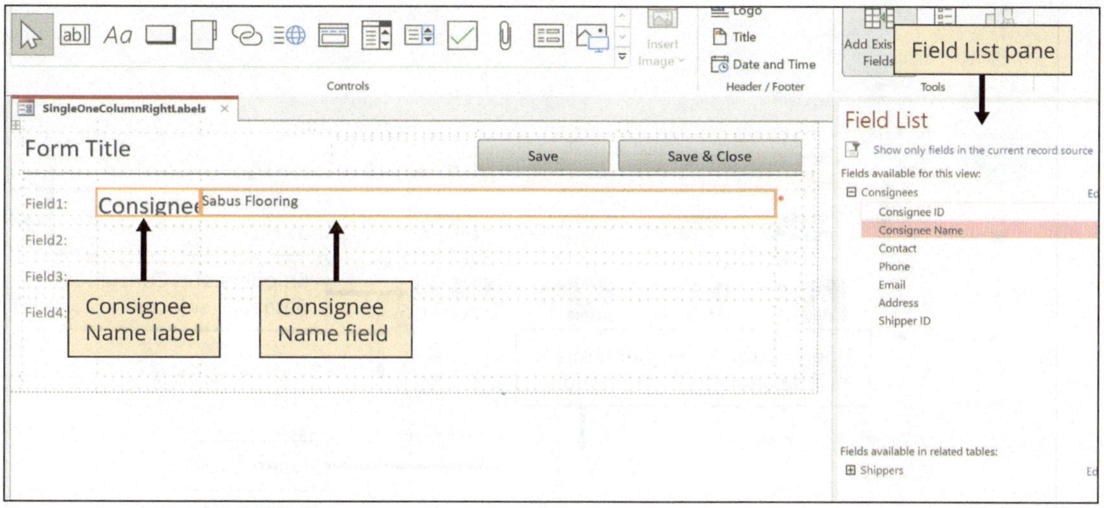

Figure 9–65

Q&A When adding fields to the form, can I add only the field itself and not the label?
Yes. If you want to add only the data within each field and not the label (such as "Consignee Name"), hold CTRL while dragging the field to the form from the Field List pane.

Database Encryption

Encryption refers to storing data in an encoded format that typically cannot be read without first decrypting it. Anytime a user stores or modifies data in the encrypted database, the database management system (DBMS) will encode the data before updating the database. When a legitimate user retrieves the data using the DBMS, the data is first decoded. The entire encryption process is transparent to legitimate users; that is, they are not even aware it is happening. If unauthorized users attempt to bypass all the controls of the DBMS and get to the database through a utility program or a word processor, however, they will only be able to see the encoded, and unreadable, version of the data. In Access, you encrypt a database and set a password as part of the same operation.

BTW
Encryption and Passwords
Encryption helps prevent unauthorized use of an Access database. Consider using encryption when the database contains sensitive data, such as medical records or employee records. Passwords should be 12 or more characters in length. The longer the length of the password and the more random the characters, the more difficult it is for someone to determine. Use a combination of uppercase and lowercase letters as well as numbers and special symbols when you create a password. Make sure that you remember your password. If you forget it, there is no method for retrieving it. You will be unable to open the encrypted database.

To Open a Database in Exclusive Mode

To encrypt a database and set a password, the database first must be open in exclusive mode, which prevents other users from accessing the database in any way. To open a database in exclusive mode, you use the Open arrow (Figure 9–66) rather than simply clicking the Open button.

To open a database in exclusive mode, you would use the following steps.

1. If necessary, close any open databases while keeping Access open.

   Q&A How can I close the database without closing Access?
   Click the File tab to open Backstage view, and then click Close.

2. Click Open to display the Open screen.
3. Click Browse on the Open screen to display the Open dialog box.
4. Navigate to the location of the database to be opened.
5. Click the name of the database to be opened.
6. Click the Open arrow to display the Open button menu.
7. Click Open Exclusive to open the database in exclusive mode.

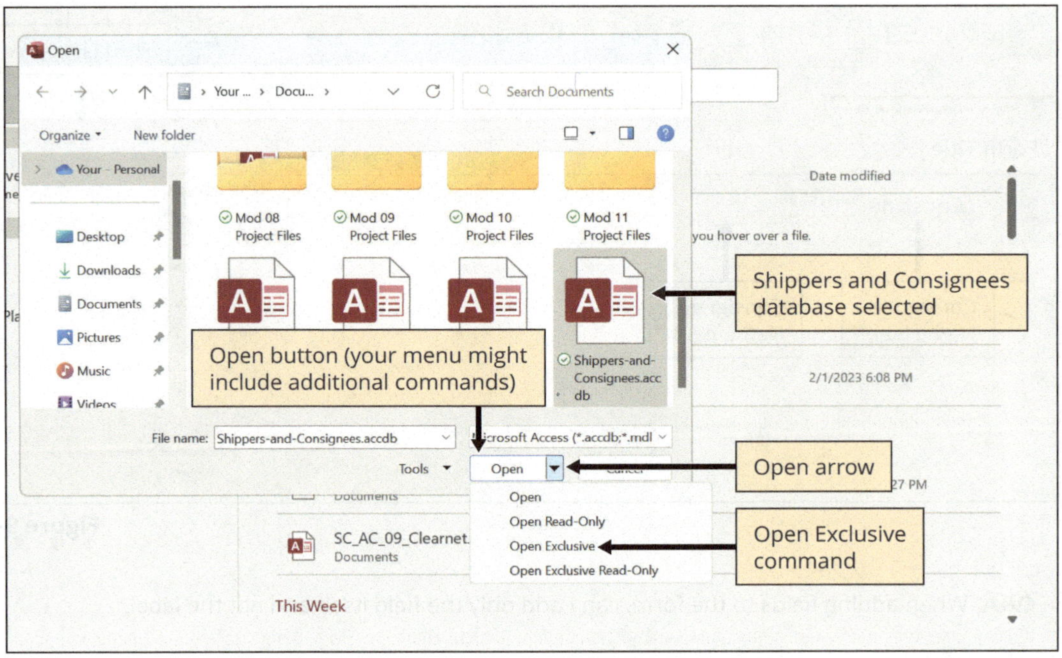

Figure 9–66

Consider This

What is the purpose of each of the other modes?

The Open option opens the database in a mode so it can be shared by other users. Open Read-Only allows you to read the data in the database, but not update the database.

Encrypting a Database with a Password

If you wanted to encrypt the database with a password, you first would open Backstage view and display the Info screen (Figure 9–67).

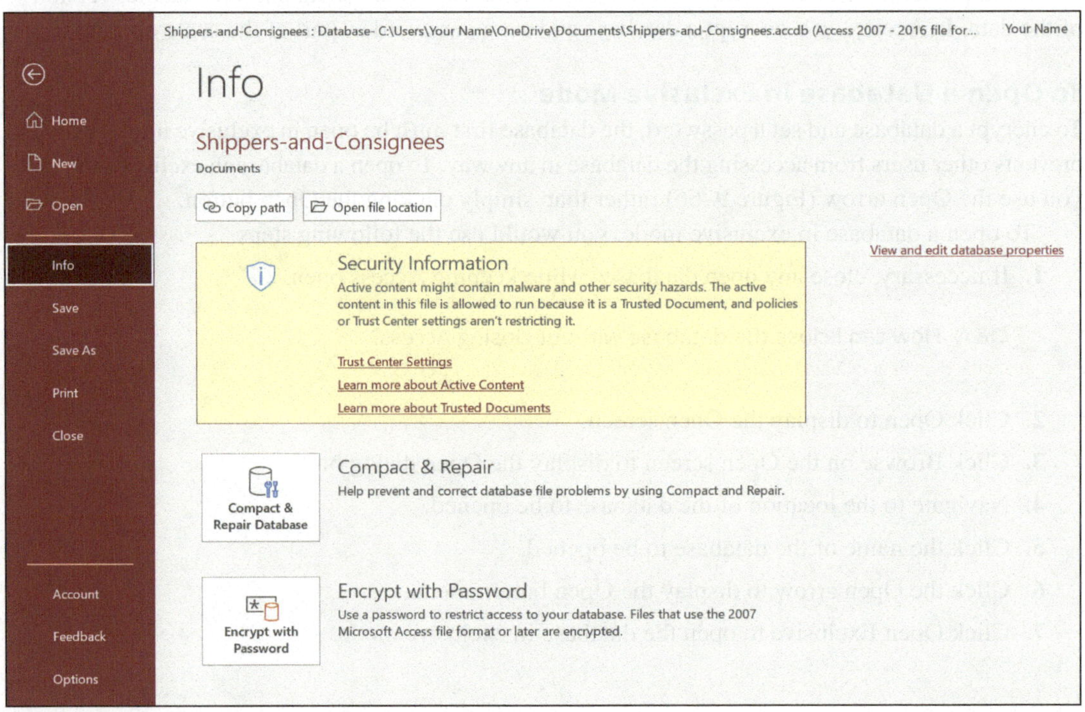

Figure 9–67

You would then click the 'Encrypt with Password' button to display the Set Database Password dialog box. Enter the password you have chosen in both the Password text box and the Verify text box (Figure 9–68).

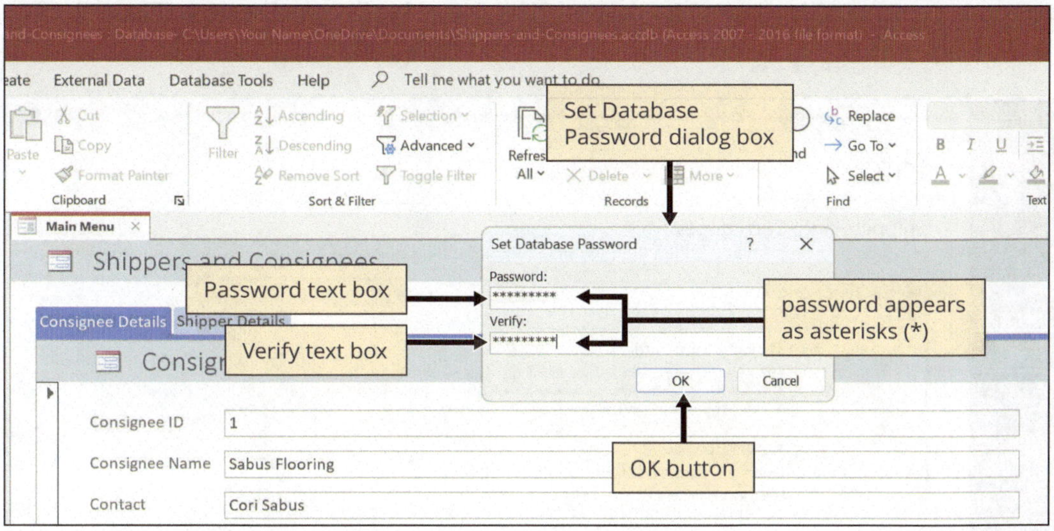

Figure 9–68

To Encrypt a Database with a Password

With the database open in exclusive mode, you would use the following steps to encrypt the database with a password.

1. Click File on the ribbon to open Backstage view and ensure that the Info screen is displayed.
2. Click the 'Encrypt with Password' button to display the Set Database Password dialog box.
3. Type the desired password in the Password text box (Set Database Password dialog box).
4. Press TAB and then type the password again in the Verify text box.
5. Click OK to encrypt the database and set the password.
6. If you get a message indicating that row level locking will be ignored, click OK.
7. Close the database.

Consider This

Is the password case sensitive?

Yes, you must enter the password using the same case you used when you created it.

Opening a Database with a Password

When you open a database that has a password, you will be prompted to enter your password in the Password Required dialog box. Once you have done so, click OK. Assuming you have entered your password correctly, Access will then open the database.

Decrypting a Database and Removing a Password

If the encryption and the password are no longer necessary, you can decrypt the database. The database will no longer have a password. If you later found you needed the database to be encrypted, you could repeat the steps to encrypt the database and add a password. On the Info screen in Backstage view, the button to encrypt a database with a password has changed to Decrypt Database (Figure 9–69).

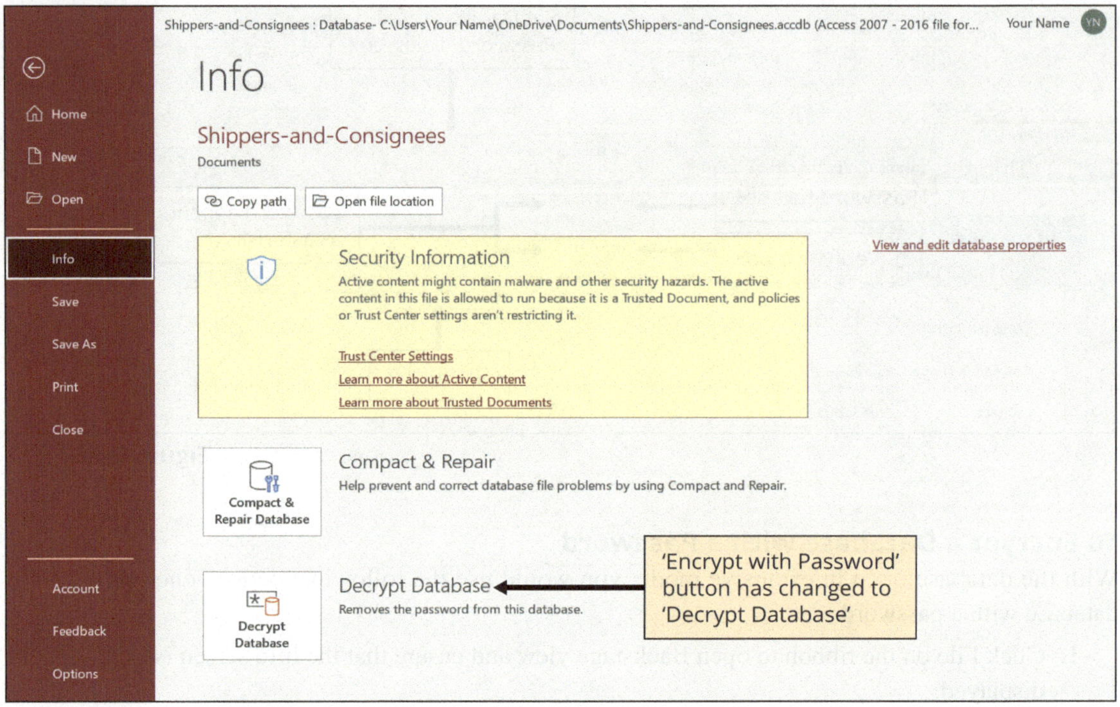

Figure 9–69

BTW
Security
One part of database security is the prevention of unauthorized access to a database. Within an organization, the database administrator determines the types of access individual users can have to the database. Various government rules and regulations, such as the Sarbanes-Oxley Act (SOX) and the Health Insurance Portability and Accountability Act (HIPAA), require database administrators to have strict security procedures in place to protect data from unauthorized users.

To Decrypt the Database and Remove the Password

To decrypt a database that you have previously encrypted and remove the password, you would use the following steps.

1. Open in exclusive mode the database to be decrypted, entering your password when requested.
2. Open Backstage view and then click Info.
3. Click the Decrypt Database button to display the Unset Database Password dialog box.
4. Type the password in the Password box.
5. Click OK to remove the password and decrypt the database.
6. Close the database.

The Trust Center

The Trust Center is a feature within Access where you can set security options and also find the latest information on technology related to privacy, safety, and security. To use the Trust Center, you click File on the ribbon and then click Options to display the Access Options dialog box. You then click Trust Center to display the Trust Center content (Figure 9–70). You then click the 'Trust Center Settings' button to display the Trust Center dialog box in which you can make changes in the following categories.

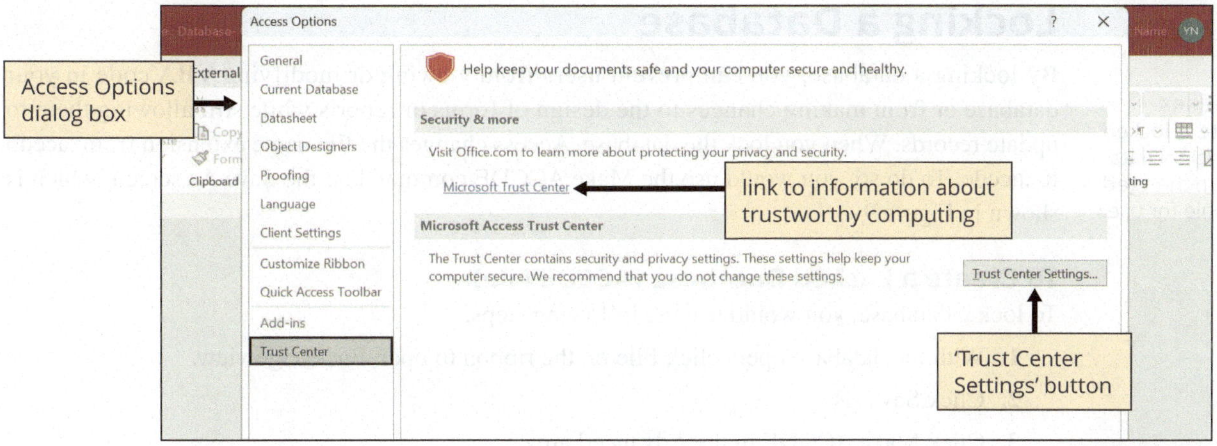

Figure 9–70

Trusted Publishers. Clicking Trusted Publishers in the Trust Center dialog box shows the list of trusted software publishers. To view details about a trusted publisher, click the publisher and then click the View button. To remove a trusted publisher from the list, click the publisher and then click the Remove button if it is available for that publisher. Users may also add trusted publishers.

Trusted Locations. Clicking Trusted Locations shows the list of trusted locations on the Internet or within a user's network. A trusted location is treated as a trusted source for opening a database stored in that location. To add a new location, click the 'Add new location…' button. To remove or modify an existing location, click the location and then click the Remove or Modify button.

Trusted Documents. You can designate certain documents, including database, Word, Excel, and other files, as trusted. When opening a trusted document, you will not be prompted to enable the content, even if the content of the document has changed. You should be very careful when designating a document as trusted and only do so when you are absolutely sure the document is from a trusted source.

Trusted Add-in Catalogs. Use this option to specify trusted catalogs of web add-ins. You can also indicate whether Access will allow web add-ins to start.

Add-ins. Add-ins are additional programs that you can install and use within Access. Some come with Access and are typically installed using the Access Setup program. Others can be purchased from other vendors. Clicking Add-ins gives you the opportunity to specify restrictions concerning Add-ins.

ActiveX Settings. When you use ActiveX controls within an Office app, Office prompts you to accept the controls. The ActiveX settings allow you to determine the level of prompting from Office.

Macro Settings. Macros written by other users have the potential to harm your computer; for example, a macro could spread a virus. The Trust Center uses special criteria, including valid digital signatures, reputable certificates, and trusted publishers, to determine whether a macro is safe. If the Trust Center discovers a macro that is potentially unsafe, it will take appropriate action. The action the Trust Center takes depends on the Macro Setting you have selected. Clicking Macro Settings enables you to select or change this setting.

Message Bar. Clicking Message Bar lets you choose whether the message bar should appear when content has been blocked.

Privacy Options. Clicking Privacy Options lets you set security settings to protect your personal privacy.

Form-based Sign-in. Clicking Form-based Sign-in lets you choose whether to allow sign-in prompts separate from an organizationally administered directory service (such as Active Directory). Because this setting introduces a security risk, the default setting blocks form-based authentication.

BTW
ActiveX controls
ActiveX controls are small programs that can run within an Office app. The calendar control is an example of an ActiveX control.

Locking a Database

BTW
Locked Databases
When you create a locked database, the original database remains unchanged and is still available for use.

By locking a database, you can prevent users from viewing or modifying VBA code in your database or from making changes to the design of forms or reports while still allowing them to update records. When you lock the database, Access changes the file name extension from .accdb to .accde. To do so, you would use the Make ACCDE command on the Save As screen, which is shown in Figure 9–3.

To Create a Locked Database (ACCDE File)

To lock a database, you would use the following steps.

1. With the database open, click File on the ribbon to open Backstage view.
2. Click Save As.
3. Click Make ACCDE in the Advanced area.
4. Click the Save As button.
5. In the Save As dialog box, indicate a location and name for the ACCDE file.
6. Click the Save button in the Save As dialog box to create the file.

Using a Locked Database

You would use an ACCDE file just as you use the databases with which you are now familiar, with two exceptions. First, you must select ACCDE files in the 'Files of type' box when opening the file. Second, be aware that you will not be able to modify any source code or change the design of any forms or reports. If you right-clicked the Consignee form, for example, you would find the Design View command on the shortcut menu is dimmed, as are many other commands (Figure 9–71).

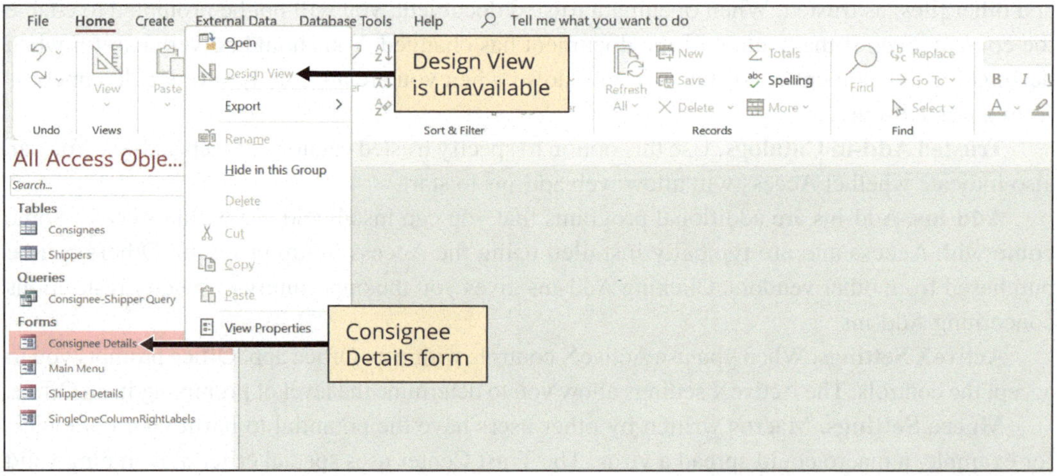

Figure 9–71

It is very important that you save your original database in case you ever need to make changes to VBA code or to the design of a form or report. You cannot use the ACCDE file to make such changes, nor can you convert the ACCDE file back to the ACCDB file format.

Record Locking

You can indicate how records are to be locked when multiple users are using a database at the same time. To do so, click File on the ribbon, click Options, and then click the Client Settings tab. Scroll down so the Advanced area appears on the screen (Figure 9–72).

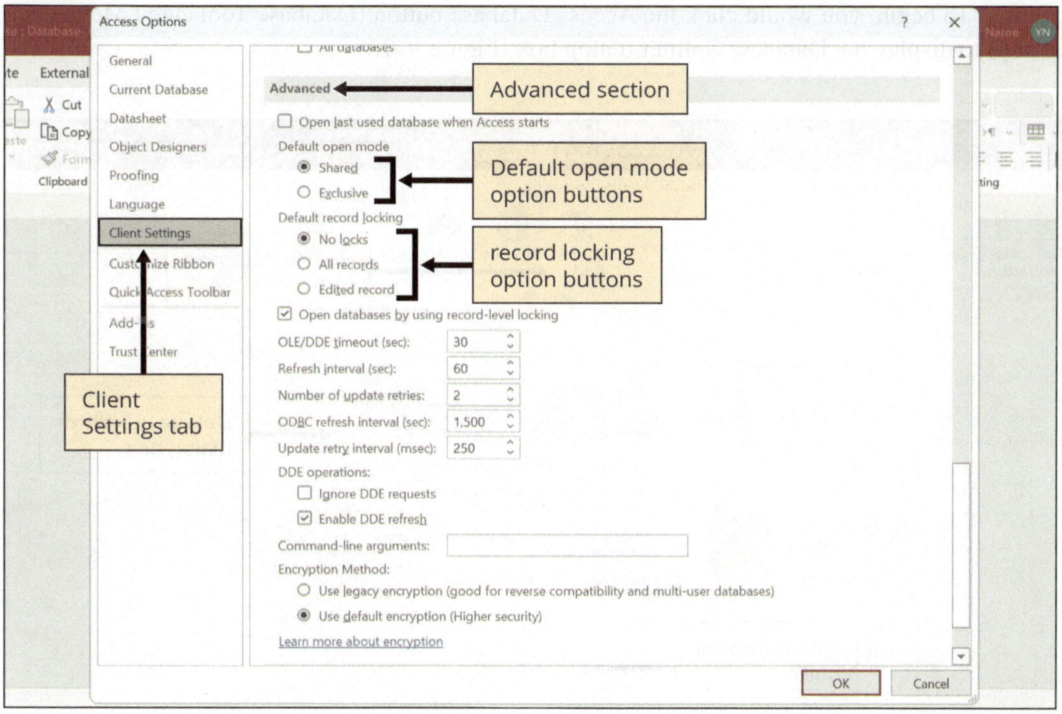

Figure 9–72

If you wanted the default open mode to be exclusive (only one user can use the database at a time) rather than shared (multiple users can simultaneously use the database), you could click the Exclusive option button. You can also select the approach you want for record locking by clicking the appropriate record locking option button. The possible approaches to record locking are shown in Table 9–3.

Table 9–3 Record Locking Approaches

Locking Type	Description
No locks	When you edit a record, Access will not lock the record. Thus, other users also could edit the same record at the same time. When you have finished your changes and attempt to save the record, Access will give you the option of overwriting the other user's changes (not recommended), copying your changes to the clipboard, or canceling your changes.
All records	All records will be locked as long as you have the database open. No other user can edit or lock the records during this time.
Edited record	When you edit a record, Access will lock the record. When other users attempt to edit the same record, they will not be able to do so. Instead, they will see the locked record indicator.

Database Splitting

You can split a database into two databases, one called the back-end database containing only table objects, and another database called the front-end database containing the other objects. Only a single copy of the back-end database can exist, but each user could have their own copy of the front-end database. Each user would create the desired custom reports, forms, and other objects in their own front-end database, thereby not interfering with any other user.

When splitting a database, the database to be split must be open. During the splitting process, you identify a name and location for the back-end database that will be created by the Access splitter. To begin, you would click the Access Database button (Database Tools tab | Move Data group) to display the Database Splitter dialog box (Figure 9–73).

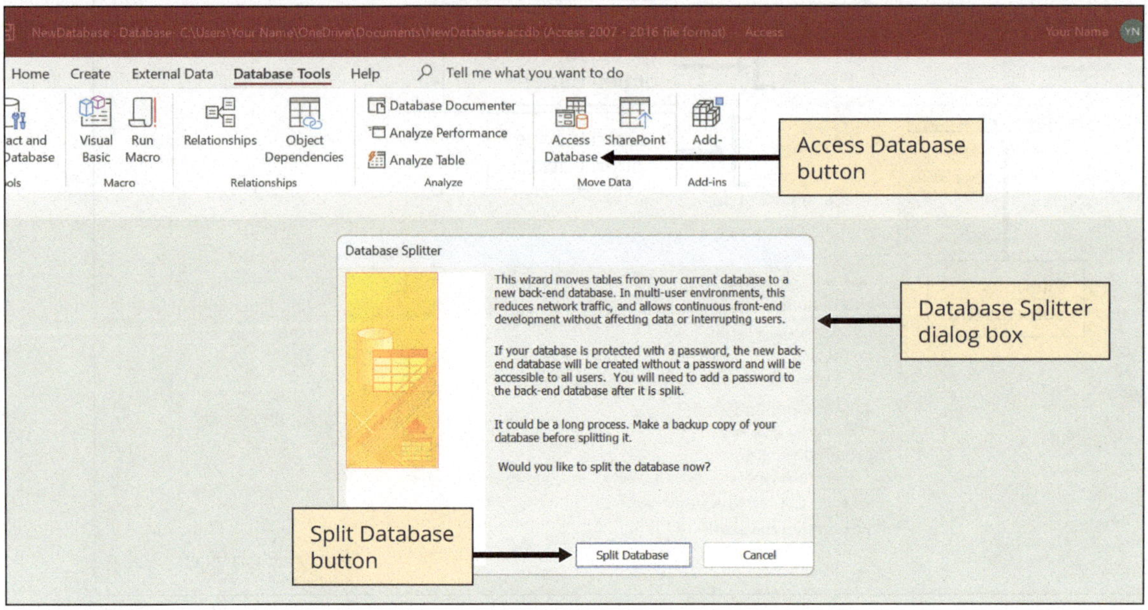

Figure 9–73

You would then select a location for the back-end database (Figure 9–74). Access assigns a name to the back-end database that ends with an underscore (_) and the letters, be. You can override this name if you prefer.

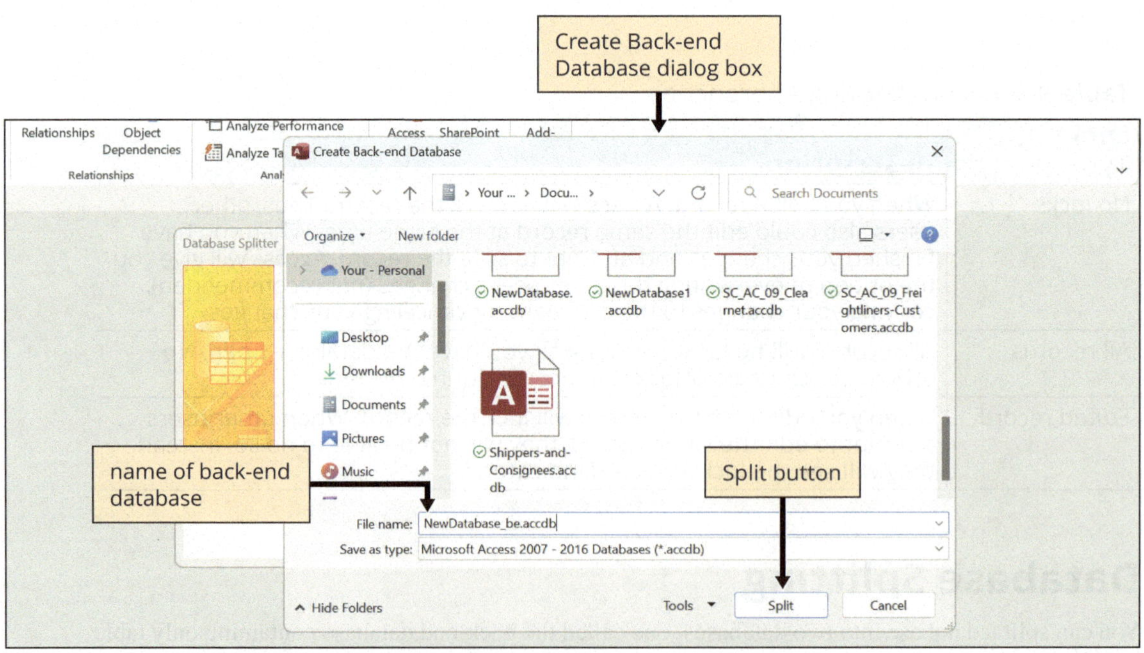

Figure 9–74

To Split a Database

To split a database, you would use the following steps.

1. Open the database to be split.
2. Display the Database Tools tab.

3. Click the Access Database button (Database Tools tab | Move Data group) to display the Database Splitter dialog box.
4. Click the Split Database button to display the Create Back-end Database dialog box.
5. Type a file name for the back-end database.
6. Select a location for the back-end database.
7. Click the Split button to split the database.
8. Click OK to close the dialog box reporting the split was successful.

The Front-End and Back-End Databases

The database has now been split into separate front-end and back-end databases. The front-end database is the one that you will use; it contains all the queries, reports, forms, and other components from the original database. The front-end database contains only links to the tables, however, instead of the tables themselves (Figure 9–75). The back-end database contains the actual tables but does not contain any other objects.

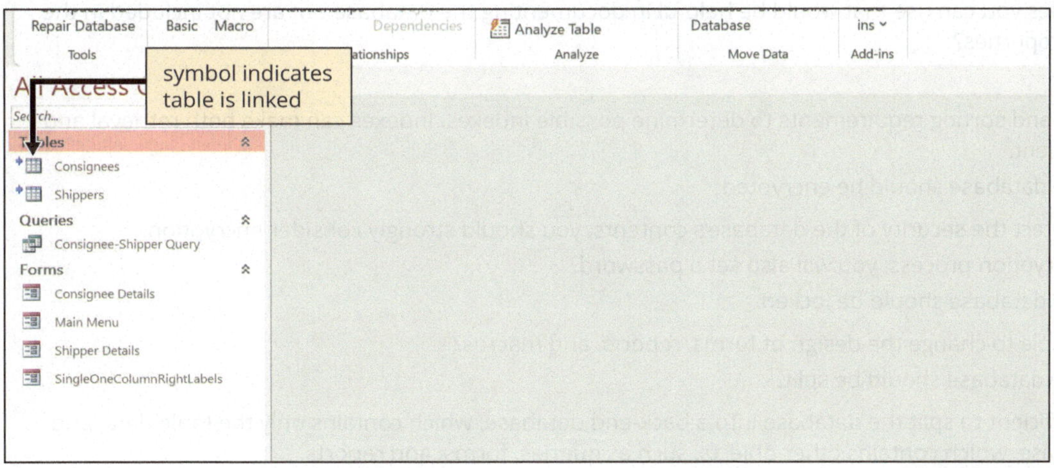

Figure 9–75

Summary

In this module you have learned to convert Access databases to and from earlier versions, use Microsoft Access tools to analyze and document an Access database, add custom categories and groups to the Navigation Pane, use table and database properties, use field properties to create a custom input mask, allow zero-length strings, create indexes, use automatic error checking, create custom data parts, create and use templates and application parts, encrypt a database and set a password, understand the Trust Center, lock a database, and split a database.

Consider This: Plan Ahead

What decisions will you need to make when administering your own databases?

Use these guidelines as you complete the assignments in this module and administer your own databases outside of this class.

1. Determine whether you should create any templates, application parts, or data type parts.
   a. Is there a particular combination of tables, queries, forms, reports, or macros you would like to enable users to easily include in their databases? If so, you could create a template and an application part containing the specific objects you want them to be able to include.
   b. Is there a particular collection of fields you would like to enable users to include in a table with a single click? If so, you could create a data type part containing those fields.

2. Determine whether a database needs to be converted to or from an earlier version.
   a. Do users of a previous version of Access need to be able to use the database? If so, you will need to be sure the database does not contain any features that would prevent it from being converted.
   b. Do you use a database that was created in an earlier version of Access that you would like to use in Access 2021 or Microsoft 365 Access? If so, you can convert the database for use in Access 2021 or Microsoft 365 Access.
3. Determine when to analyze or document the database.
   a. Once you create a database, you should use the table and performance analyzers to determine if any changes to the structure are warranted.
   b. You should also document the database.
4. Determine the most useful way to customize the Navigation Pane.
   a. Would it be helpful to have custom categories and groups?
   b. What objects should be in the groups?
   c. Would it be helpful to restrict the objects that appear to only those whose names contain certain characters?
5. Determine any table-wide validation rules.
   a. Are there any validation rules that involve more than a single field?
6. Determine any custom database properties.
   a. Are there properties you can use that would be helpful in documenting the database but are not included in the list of database properties?
7. Determine indexes.
   a. Examine retrieval and sorting requirements to determine possible indexes. Indexes can make both retrieval and sorting more efficient.
8. Determine whether the database should be encrypted.
   a. If you need to protect the security of the database's contents, you should strongly consider encryption.
   b. As part of the encryption process, you will also set a password.
9. Determine whether the database should be locked.
   a. Should users be able to change the design of forms, reports, and macros?
10. Determine whether the database should be split.
    a. It is often more efficient to split the database into a back-end database, which contains only the table data, and a front-end database, which contains other objects, such as queries, forms, and reports.

Consider This

How should you submit solutions to critical thinking questions in the assignments?

Every assignment in this course contains one or more critical thinking questions. These questions require you to think beyond the assigned database. Present your responses to the questions in the format required by your instructor. Possible formats might include one or more of these options: write the answer; create a document that contains the answer; present your answer to the class; discuss your answer in a group; record the answer as audio or video using a webcam, smartphone, or portable media player; or post answers on a blog, wiki, or website.

Student Assignments

Apply Your Knowledge

Reinforce the skills and apply the concepts you learned in this module.

Administering the City Tutoring Services Database

Note: To complete this assignment, you will be required to use the Data Files. Please contact your instructor for information about accessing the Data Files.

Instructions: Start Access. Open the database, SC_AC_09-2.accdb, which is located in the Data Files folder. Enable the content.

Perform the following tasks:

1. Save the database using the file name, SC_AC_09_City-Tutoring. Enable the content.
2. Open the Students table in Design view and create a custom input mask for the Student Number field. The first two characters of the student number must be uppercase letters and the last two characters must be numerical digits.
3. Create an index on the combination of Student Type and Counselor Number. Name the index TypeCnslr.
4. Save the changes to the Students table, and then close the table.
5. Use the Database Documenter to produce detailed documentation for the Accounting table. Export the documentation to a Word RTF file. Change the name of the file to LastName_Documentation where LastName is your last name.
6. Use the Table Analyzer to analyze the table structure of the Students table. Open the Word RTF file that you created in Step 5 and make a note at the end of the document describing the results of the table analysis.
7. Use the Performance Analyzer to analyze all the tables in the database. Describe the results of your analysis in your RTF file.
8. Populate the Status custom property for the database to Live Version.
9. Add a Production property with today's date.
10. Submit the revised database and the RTF file in the format specified by your instructor.
11. **Consider This:** Can you convert the City Tutoring database to an Access 2002–2003 database? Why or why not?

Extend Your Knowledge

Extend the skills you learned in this module and experiment with new skills. You may need to use Help to complete the assignment.

Administering the Physical Therapists Database

Note: To complete this assignment, you will be required to use the Data Files. Please contact your instructor for information about accessing the Data Files.

Instructions: Start Access. Open the database, SC_AC_09-3.accdb, which is located in the Data Files folder.

Perform the following tasks:

1. Save the database using the file name, SC_AC_09_Physical-Therapists. Enable the content.
2. Create a navigation form that is named and titled Clients and Technicians and that contains a single row with two horizontal tabs. Add two forms to the Navigation Form: Clients by Technician Form and Technician Form.

Continued on next page

3. Change the Current Database options to ensure the Main Menu opens automatically. Confirm your settings work as intended.
4. Currently, when you open the Potential Clients table in Datasheet view, the table is ordered by Client Number. Change the property for the table so the table is in order by Client Name.
5. Create an additional table called Potential Technicians. Add the Name-Contact-Address Quick Start fields to easily create the fields. For each field name, replace any instances of the word Shipper with the word Technician. Save the table and close it.
6. Customize the Navigation Pane by adding a custom category called Tracking. Then add two custom groups, Clients and Technicians, to the Tracking category.
7. Add the Client table, the Potential Clients table, and the Clients by Technician form to the Clients custom group under the Tracking category. Add the Technician table, the Technician Form, and the Technician Balances Summary Report to the Technicians custom group under the Tracking category.
8. Submit the revised database in the format specified by your instructor.
9. **Consider This:** What advantages are there to using a custom Navigation Pane as opposed to the standard Navigation Pane?

Expand Your World

Create a solution, which uses cloud and web technologies, by learning and investigating on your own from general guidance.

Instructions: There are many ways to share an Access database. Some ways require each user to have Microsoft Access installed on their computer, while others do not. The method you select depends on factors such as need and available resources.

Perform the following tasks:

1. Create a blog post, a Google document, or a Word document on OneDrive on which to store your findings for this project. Make sure the blog post or document is configured to share with other users when you provide them with a link.
2. Use the web to research different ways to share an Access database, such as Clearnet, with others. Be sure to note any specific resources needed, such as an Access database or a SharePoint server, explain any costs involved, and provide examples of different reasons for sharing a database such as Clearnet. Record your findings in your blog, Google document, or Word document, being sure to appropriately reference your sources.
3. Submit the blog or document's link in the format specified by your instructor.
4. **Consider This:** Based on your research, what method would you choose to share your Access databases?

In the Lab

Design and implement a solution using creative thinking and problem-solving skills.

Lab: Administering the Great Outdoors Campground Database

Note: To complete this assignment, you will be required to use the Data Files. Please contact your instructor for information about accessing the Data Files.

Problem: The staff at Great Outdoors Campground has asked you to perform a number of administrative tasks to help increase the functionality and efficiency of their database.

Perform the following tasks:

Part 1: Open the SC_AC_09-4.accdb database from the Data Files folder. Save the file with the name, SC_AC_09_Great-Outdoors, and enable the content. Use the concepts and techniques presented in this module to perform each of the following tasks.

1. Create a horizontal tabs navigation form that includes the Staff Activities Summary Form and the Filtered Staff WorkTeam form. Give the navigation form an appropriate form name and title that reflect its contents, such as Staff Forms. Whatever name you choose, make sure not to use a form name currently in use in the database.
2. Change the Current Database options to ensure that the Main Menu form opens automatically when the user opens the database.
3. Open the Counselors table in Design view and create an index for the LastName field that allows duplicates. Save the changes.
4. Open the Enrollments table in Design view and create an index named CamperIDEvent on the CamperID and the Event fields.
5. Open the Cabins table in Design view and create a validation rule to ensure the minimum campers value is always less than or equal to the maximum campers. Include validation text.
6. Create a new table called Vendors and add the Quick Start Name-Contact-Address field to the table. Replace the word Shipper with the word Vendor in all fields.
7. Create a template of the database as an application part and do not include the data. Name the template Campground-Template.
8. From that template, create a new database called SC_AC_09_YN-Campground, where YN is your own initials. Close the database.

Submit your assignment in the format specified by your instructor.

Part 2: **Consider This:** You made several decisions while completing this project, including creating a navigation form and a validation rule. What was the rationale behind your decisions? What other navigation forms or validation rules would you add to the Great Outdoors Campground database?

Using SQL

Objectives

After completing this module, you will be able to:

- Describe the background and purpose of SQL (Structured Query Language)
- Change the font or font size in a query
- Create a SQL query
- Include specific fields in a SQL query
- Apply criteria to a SQL query
- Include a computed field in a SQL query
- Sort the results of a SQL query
- Use a built-in, or aggregate, function in a SQL query
- Group the results of a SQL query
- Join tables in a SQL query
- Use a subquery
- Compare a SQL query with an Access query
- Use SQL commands to insert, update, and delete records
- Link external data to a table

Introduction

The language called **SQL (Structured Query Language)** is a very important language for querying and updating databases. It is the closest thing to a universal database language because the vast majority of database management systems, including Access, use it in some fashion. Although some users will be able to do all their queries through the query features of Access without ever using SQL, those in charge of administering and maintaining the database system should be familiar with this important language. You can also use Access as an interface to other database management systems, such as SQL Server. Using or interfacing with SQL Server requires knowledge of SQL. Nearly every relational DBMS supports SQL to some degree, as do many non-relational DBMSs.

Project: Using SQL

Partners Law Firm wants to be able to use the extended data management capabilities available through SQL. As part of becoming familiar with SQL, Partners would like to create a wide variety of SQL queries.

Similarly to creating queries in Design view, SQL provides a way of querying relational databases. In SQL, however, instead of making entries in the design grid, you type commands into SQL view to obtain the desired results, as shown in Figure 10–1a. You can then click the View button to view the results just as when you are creating queries in Design view. The results for the query in Figure 10–1a are shown in Figure 10–1b.

BTW
The Ribbon and Screen Resolution
Access may change how the groups and buttons within the groups appear on the ribbon, depending on the computer's screen resolution. Thus, your ribbon might look different from the ones in this course if you are using a screen resolution other than 1920 × 1080.

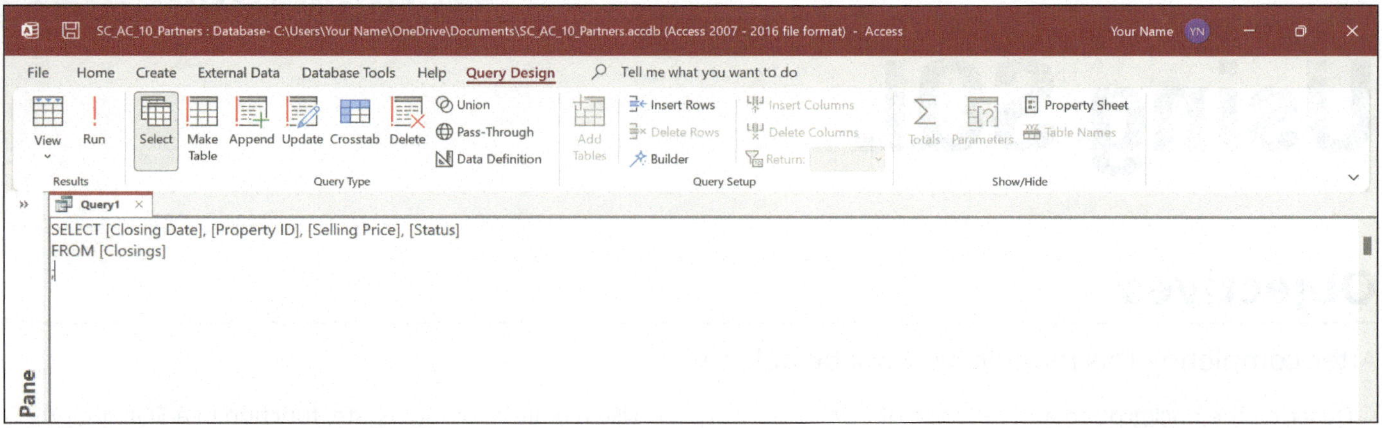

Figure 10–1(a): Query in SQL

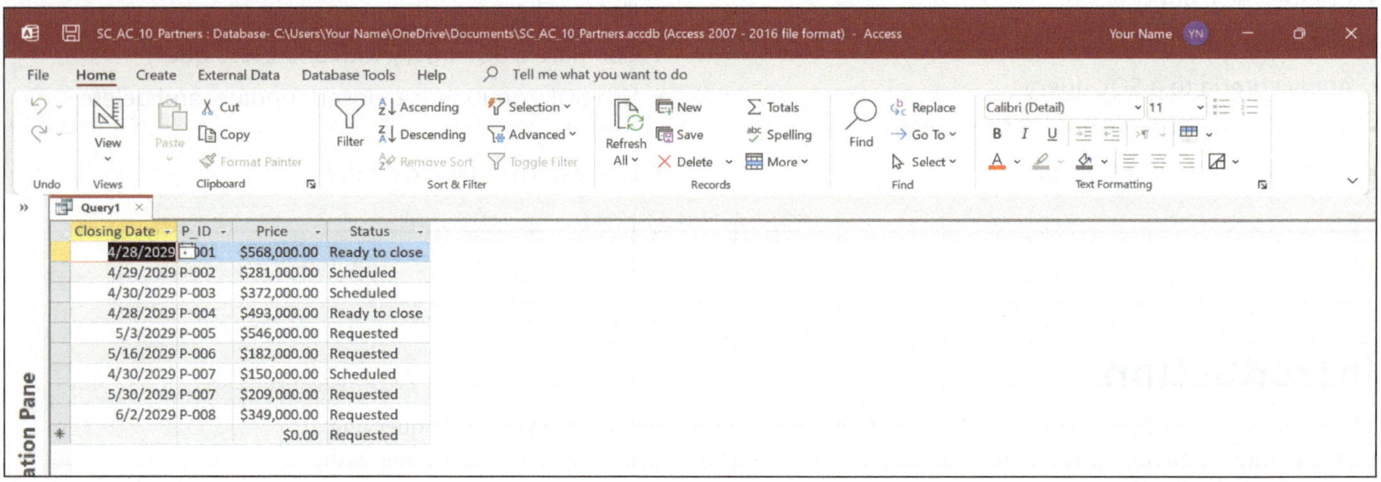

Figure 10–1(b): Query Results

In this module, you will learn how to create and use SQL queries like the one shown in Figure 10–1a.

BTW
Distributing a Document
Instead of printing and distributing a hard copy of a document, you can distribute the document electronically. Options include sending the document via email; posting it on cloud storage (such as OneDrive) and sharing the file with others; posting it on a social networking site, blog, or other website; and sharing a link associated with an online location of the document. You also can create and share a PDF or XPS image of the document, so that users can view the file in Acrobat Reader or XPS Viewer instead of in Access.

SQL Background

In this module, you query and update a database using the language called SQL (Structured Query Language). Similarly to using the design grid in the Access Query window, SQL provides users with the capability of querying a relational database. Because SQL is a language, however, you must enter **commands** to obtain the desired results, rather than completing entries in the design grid. SQL uses commands to update tables and to retrieve data from tables. The commands that are used to retrieve data are usually called queries.

SQL was developed under the name SEQUEL at the IBM San Jose research facilities as the data manipulation language for IBM's prototype relational model DBMS, System R, in the mid-1970s. In 1980, it was renamed SQL to avoid confusion with an unrelated hardware product called SEQUEL. Most relational DBMSs, including Microsoft Access and Microsoft SQL Server, use a version of SQL as a data manipulation language.

Some people pronounce SQL by pronouncing the three letters, that is, "ess-que-ell." It is very common, however, to pronounce it as the name under which it was developed originally, that is, "sequel." This course assumes the "sequel" pronunciation; for instance, it uses the wording "a SQL query" rather than "an SQL query."

To Change the Font Size

You can change the font and/or the font size for queries using the Options button in Backstage view and then the Object Designers section of the Access Options dialog box. There is not usually a compelling reason to change the font unless there is a strong preference for some other font. It often is worthwhile to change the font size, however. **Why?** Increasing the font size to 11 can make a big difference. The following steps change the font size for queries to 11.

1

- **sam** Start Access. Open the database, SC_AC_10-1.accdb, which is located in the Data Files folder. Save the file to your hard drive, OneDrive, or other storage location using the file name, **SC_AC_10_Partners**. Enable the content.
- Click File on the ribbon to open Backstage view.
- Click Options to display the Access Options dialog box.
- Click Object Designers to display the Object Designer section.
- In the Query design area, under Query design font, click the Size box arrow, and then click 11 in the list to change the size to 11 (Figure 10–2).

BTW
Active Content
Depending on your Trust Settings, Access may initially block active content when it opens a database that contains macros. When you are opening content from a trusted source, such as databases included in this course, you can click OK in the dialog box and proceed with enabling the content.

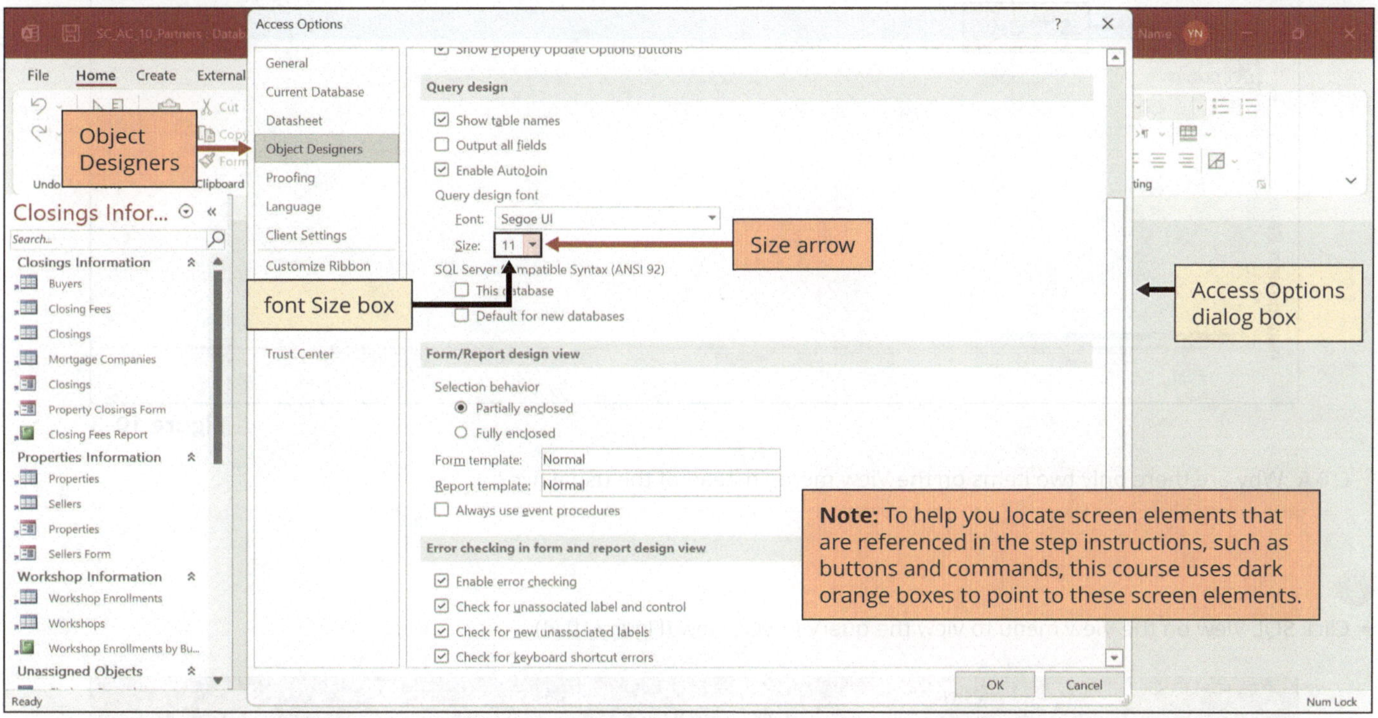

Figure 10–2

Q&A Can I choose a larger size if I need the font to be bigger?
Yes. Examples in this module will be given using the font size of 11. However, you can choose a larger size if that is helpful for you.

BTW
Enabling the Content
For each of the databases you use in this module, you will need to enable the content.

2

- Click OK to close the Access Options dialog box.

SQL Queries

When you query a database using SQL, you type commands in a blank window rather than filling in the design grid. When the command is complete, you can view your results just as you do with queries you create using the design grid.

BTW
Touch Screen Differences
The Office and Windows interfaces may vary if you are using a touch screen. For this reason, you might notice that the function or appearance of your touch screen differs slightly from this module's presentation.

To Create a New SQL Query

You begin the creation of a new **SQL query**, which is a query expressed using the SQL language, just as you begin the creation of any other query in Access. The only difference is that you will use SQL view instead of Design view. **Why?** SQL view enables you to type SQL commands rather than making entries in the design grid. The following steps create a new SQL query.

1

- Display the Create tab.
- Click the Query Design button (Create tab | Queries group) to create a query.
- Close the Add Tables pane without adding any tables.
- Click the View button arrow (Query Design tab | Results group) to display the View menu (Figure 10–3).

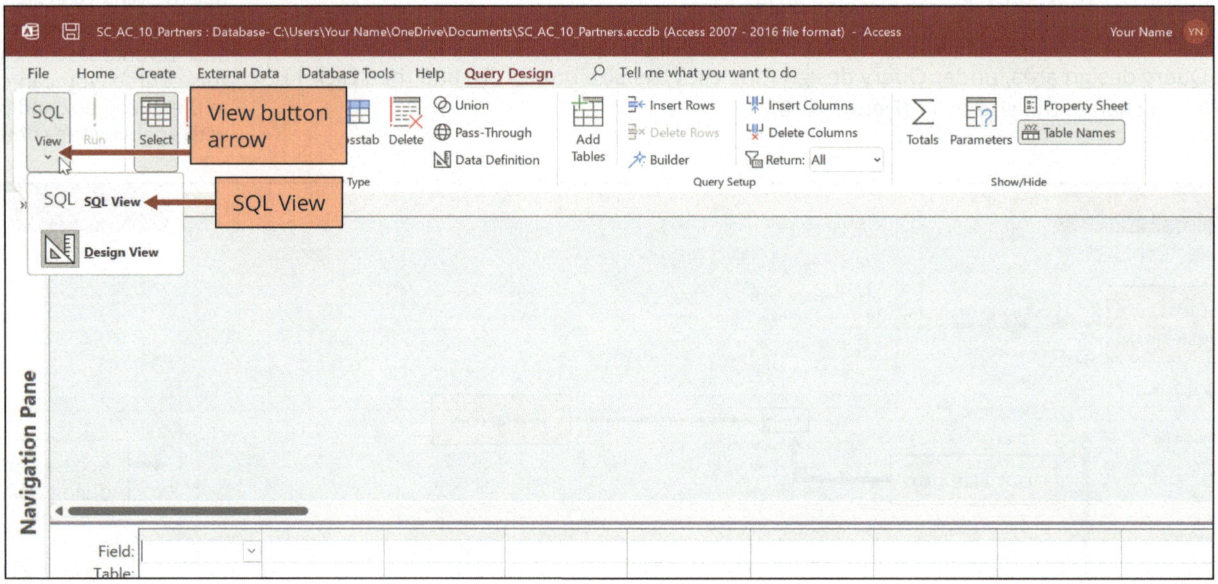

Figure 10–3

Q&A Why are there only two items on the View menu instead of the usual five?
Without any tables selected, you cannot view any results. You can only use the normal Design view or SQL view.

2

- Click SQL View on the View menu to view the query in SQL view (Figure 10–4).

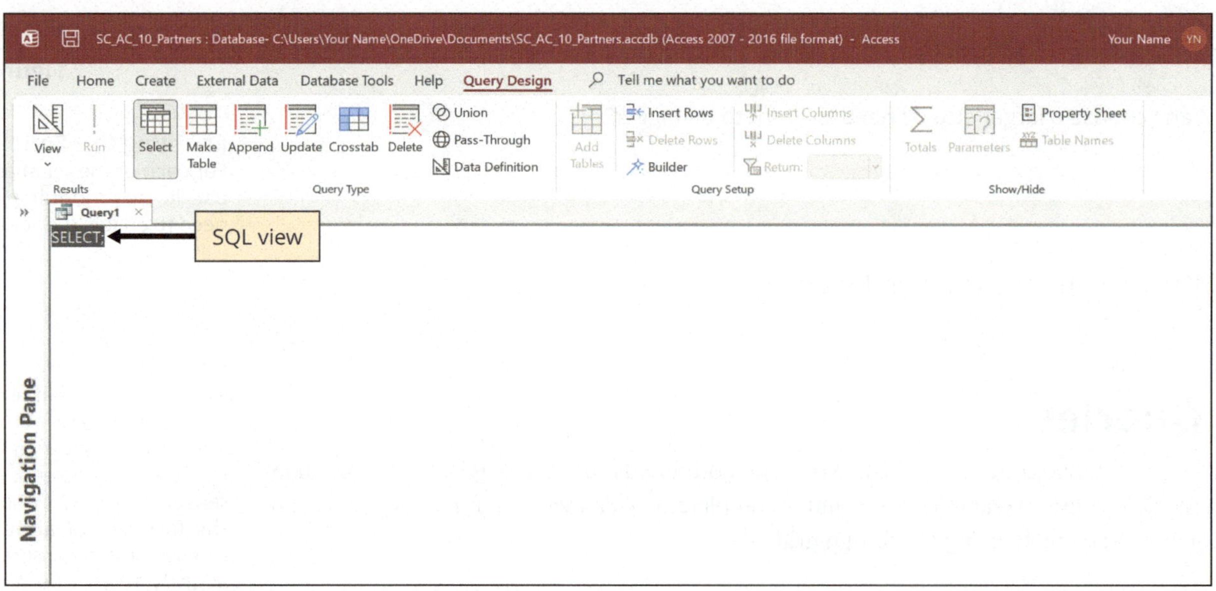

Figure 10–4

Q&A What happened to the design grid?
In SQL view, you specify the queries by typing SQL commands rather than making entries in the design grid.

BTW
Navigation Pane
As you work, you often need to open the Navigation Pane to view and select objects such as tables, forms, and reports. You often need to close the pane to make more room on the screen or to ensure your screen matches the figures in this course. Open the Navigation Pane as necessary to open an object when instructed, and close the pane to suit your preferences.

SQL Commands

The basic form of SQL expressions is quite simple: SELECT-FROM-WHERE. The command begins with a **SELECT clause**, which consists of the word, SELECT, followed by a list of those fields you want to include. The fields will appear in the results in the order in which they are listed in the expression. Next, the command contains a **FROM clause**, which consists of the word, FROM, followed by a list of the table or tables involved in the query. Finally, there is an optional **WHERE clause**, which consists of the word, WHERE, followed by any criteria that the data you want to retrieve must satisfy. The command ends with a semicolon (;), which in this text will appear on a separate line.

SQL has no special format rules for placement of terms, capitalization, and so on. One common style is to place the word, FROM, on a new line, and then place the word, WHERE (when it is used), on the next line. This style makes the commands easier to read. It is also common to show words that are part of the SQL language in uppercase and other words in a combination of uppercase and lowercase. This text formats SQL terms in uppercase letters. Because it is a common convention, and necessary in some versions of SQL, you will place a semicolon (;) at the end of each command.

Microsoft Access has its own version of SQL that, unlike some other versions of SQL, allows spaces within field names and table names. There is a restriction, however, to the way such names are used in SQL queries. When a name containing a space appears in SQL, it must be enclosed in square brackets. For example, a field named Closing Date must appear as [Closing Date] because the name includes a space. On the other hand, a field named Status does not need to be enclosed in square brackets because its name does not include a space. For consistency, all names in this text are enclosed in square brackets. Thus, the Status field would appear as [Status] even though the brackets are not technically required by SQL.

To Include Only Certain Fields

To include only certain fields in a query, list them after the word, SELECT. If you want to list all rows in the table, you do not include the word, WHERE. **Why?** If there is no WHERE clause, there is no criterion restricting which rows appear in the results. In that case, all rows will appear. The following steps create a query for Partners Law Firm that will list the closing date, property ID, selling price, and status for all closings.

1

- Click to the right of the word, SELECT, delete the semicolon (;), press SPACEBAR, type **[Closing Date], [Property ID], [Selling Price], [Status]** as the first line of the command, and then press ENTER.

Q&A What is the purpose of the SELECT clause?
The SELECT clause indicates the fields that are to be included in the query results. This SELECT clause, for example, indicates the Closing Date, Property ID, Selling Price, and Status fields are to be included.

- Type **FROM [Closings]** as the second line to specify the source table, press ENTER, and then type a semicolon (;) on the third line (Figure 10–5a).

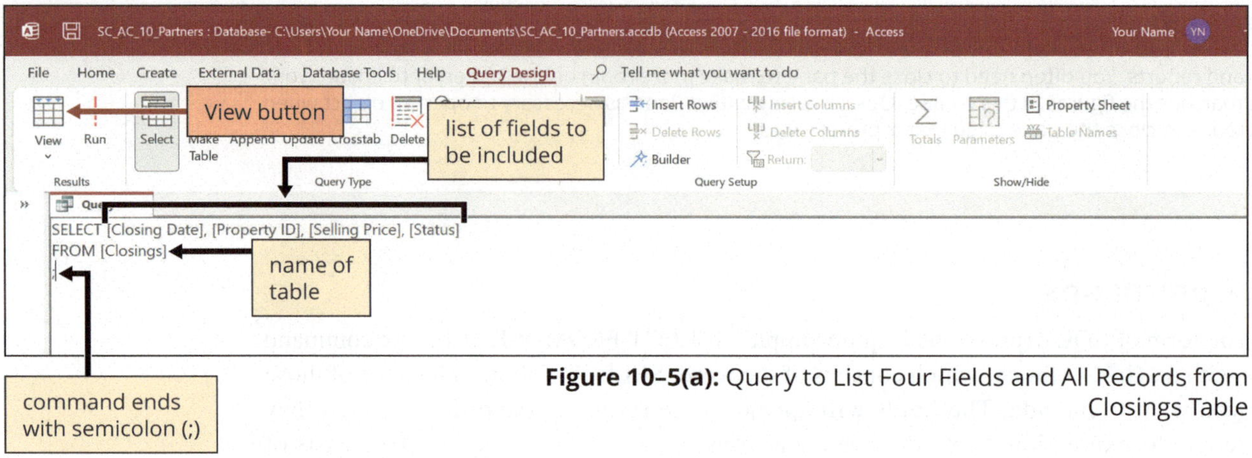

Figure 10–5(a): Query to List Four Fields and All Records from Closings Table

Q&A What is the purpose of the FROM clause?
The FROM clause indicates the table or tables that contain the fields used in the query. This FROM clause indicates that all the fields in this query come from the Closings table.

- Click the View button (Query Design tab | Results group) to view the results (Figure 10–5b).

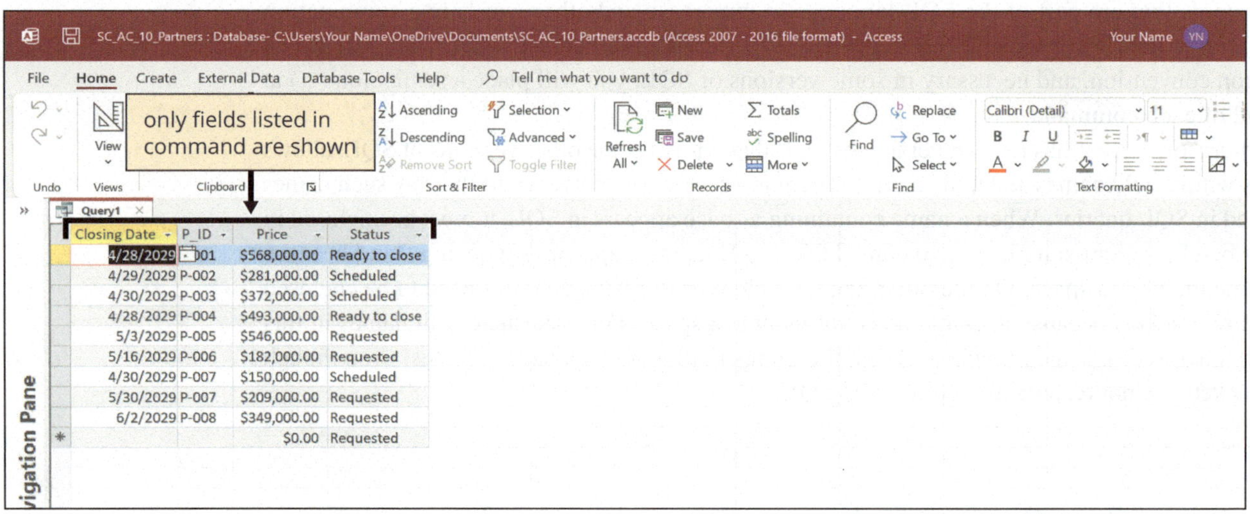

Closing Date	P_ID	Price	Status
4/28/2029	P-001	$568,000.00	Ready to close
4/29/2029	P-002	$281,000.00	Scheduled
4/30/2029	P-003	$372,000.00	Scheduled
4/28/2029	P-004	$493,000.00	Ready to close
5/3/2029	P-005	$546,000.00	Requested
5/16/2029	P-006	$182,000.00	Requested
4/30/2029	P-007	$150,000.00	Scheduled
5/30/2029	P-007	$209,000.00	Requested
6/2/2029	P-008	$349,000.00	Requested
		$0.00	Requested

Figure 10–5(b): Query Results

Q&A My screen displays a dialog box that asks me to enter a parameter value. What did I do wrong?
You typed a field name incorrectly. Click Cancel to close the dialog box, and then correct your SQL statement.

2

- Click the Save button on the Quick Access Toolbar, type **m10q01** as the query name in the Save As dialog box, and then click OK to save the query.

BTW
SELECT Clause
When you enter field names in a SELECT clause, you do not need to enter a space after the comma. Access inserts a space after the comma when you save the query and close it. When you reopen the query in SQL view, a space will appear after each comma that separates fields in the SELECT clause, even if you did not enter spaces initially.

To Prepare to Enter a New SQL Query

To enter a new SQL query, you could close the window, click the No button when asked if you want to save your changes, and then begin the process again from scratch. A quicker alternative is to use the View menu and then select SQL View. **Why?** You will be returned to SQL view with the current command appearing. At that point, you could erase the current command and then enter a new one. If the next command is similar to the previous one, however, it often is simpler to modify the current command instead of erasing it and starting over. The following step shows how to prepare to enter a new SQL query.

1

- Click the View button arrow (Home tab | Views group) to display the View menu (Figure 10–6).
- Click SQL View to return to SQL view.

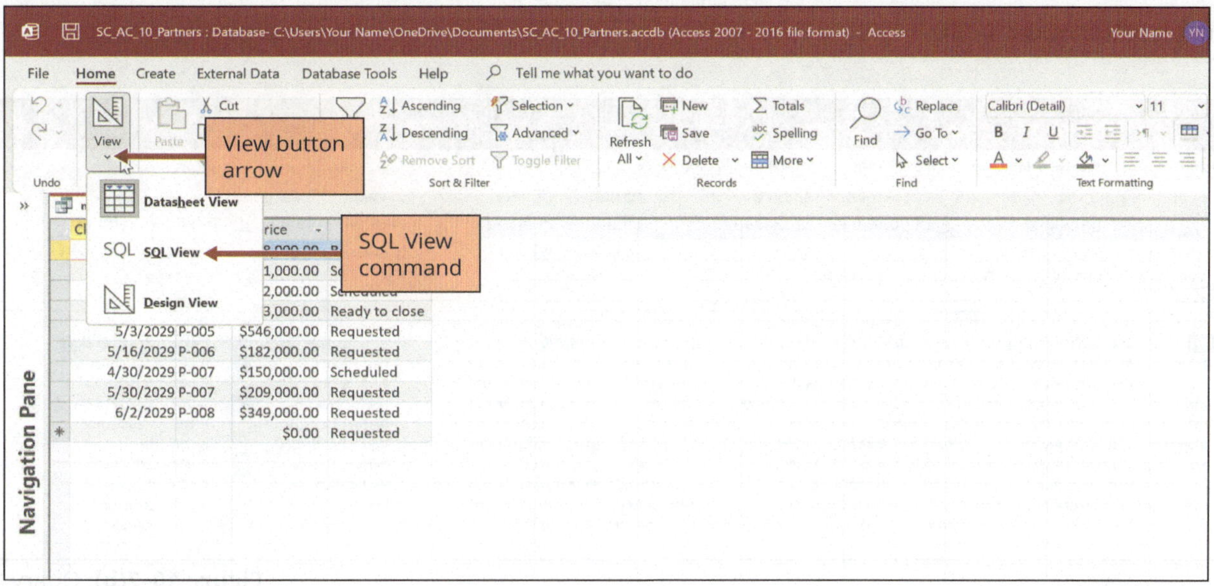

Figure 10–6

Q&A Could I just click the View button, or do I have to click the arrow?
Because the icon on the button is not the icon for SQL view, you must first click the arrow.

BTW
Editing or Replacing a Query
To ensure accuracy in the instructions, this module typically instructs you to delete an existing query's commands and type the new query's commands. However, you might find it more convenient instead to edit the previous query's commands to match a new query's commands. While either approach is acceptable, be careful to ensure you make all needed edits if you are changing existing text. It is easy to miss a small difference between the previous query and the new query that can have a significant effect on the query results.

To Include All Fields

To include all fields, you could use the same approach as in the previous steps, that is, list each field in the Closings table after the word SELECT. There is a shortcut, however. Instead of listing all the field names after SELECT, you can use the asterisk (*) symbol. **Why?** Just as when working in the design grid, the asterisk symbol represents all fields. This indicates that you want all fields listed in the order in which you described them to the system during data definition. The following steps list all fields and all records in the Closings table.

1

- Delete the current command, type **SELECT *** as the first line of the command, and then press ENTER.
- Type **FROM [Closings]** as the second line, press ENTER, and type a semicolon (**;**) on the third line (Figure 10–7a).

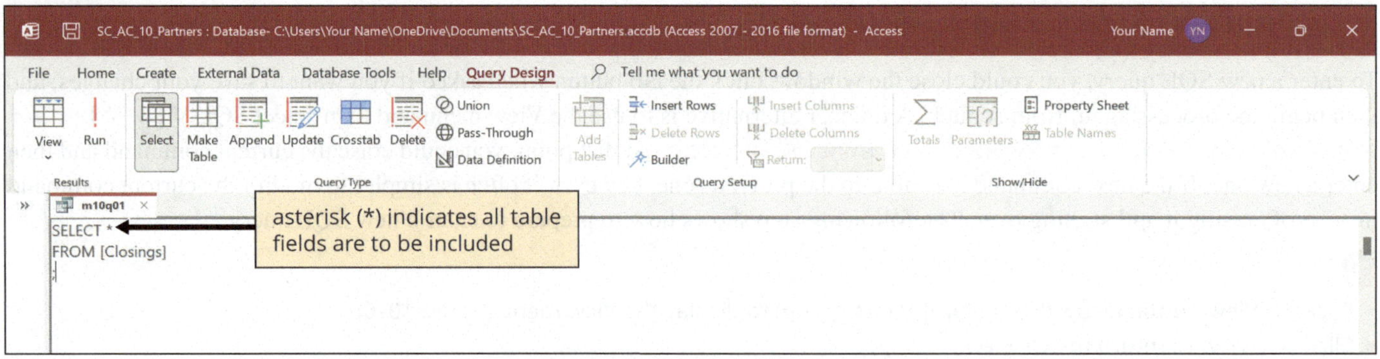

Figure 10–7(a): Query to List All Fields and All Records from Closings Table

- View the results (Figure 10–7b).

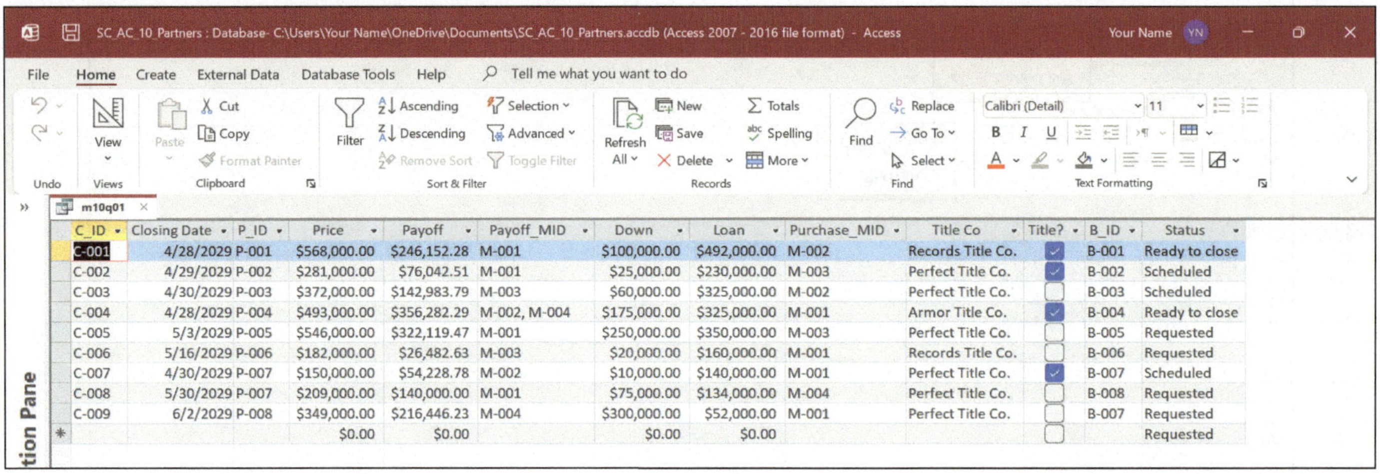

Figure 10–7(b): Query Results

Q&A Can I use copy and paste commands when I enter SQL commands?

Yes, you can use copy and paste as well as other editing techniques, such as replacing text. Throughout this module, directions are given to delete existing text from a SQL command and then type new text. However, you can keep text that will be reused and only replace text that is not needed for the new query. Be sure to check your new command carefully, as it is easy to miss minor changes in field names, punctuation, or clauses.

2

- Click File on the ribbon to open Backstage view, click Save As to display the Save As gallery, click Save Object As in the File Types area, click the Save As button to display the Save As dialog box, type **m10q02** as the name for the new query, and then click OK to save the new query and return to the query.

Q&A Can I just click the Save button on the Quick Access Toolbar as I did when I saved the previous query?

If you did, you would replace the previous query with the version you just created. Because you want to save both the previous query and the new one, you need to save the new version with a different name. To do so, you must use Save Object As, which is available through Backstage view.

To Use a Criterion Involving a Numeric Field

To restrict the records to be displayed, include the word, WHERE, followed by a criterion as part of the command. If the field involved is a numeric field, you simply type the value. In typing the number, you do not type commas or dollar signs. Why? If you enter a dollar sign, Access assumes you are entering text. If you enter a comma, Access considers the criterion invalid. The following steps create a query to list the property IDs of all closings where the selling price is equal to $150,000.

1

- Return to SQL view and delete the current command.
- Type **SELECT [Property ID], [Closing Date], [Selling Price]** as the first line of the command.
- Type **FROM [Closings]** as the second line.
- Type **WHERE [Selling Price]=150000** as the third line, and then type a semicolon (**;**) on the fourth line (Figure 10–8a).

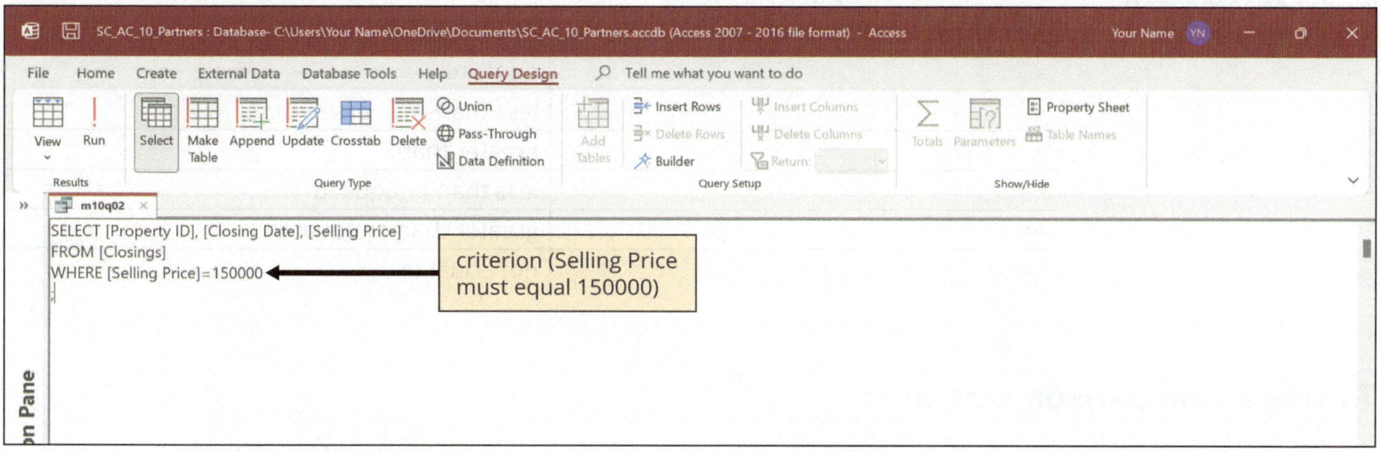

Figure 10–8(a): Query to List Property ID, Closing Date, and Selling Price for Closings Where Selling Price Is Equal to $150,000

Q&A What is the purpose of the WHERE clause?

The WHERE clause restricts the rows to be included in the results to only those that satisfy the criteria included in the clause. With this WHERE clause, for example, only those rows where the Selling Price is equal to $150,000 will be included.

- View the results (Figure 10–8b).

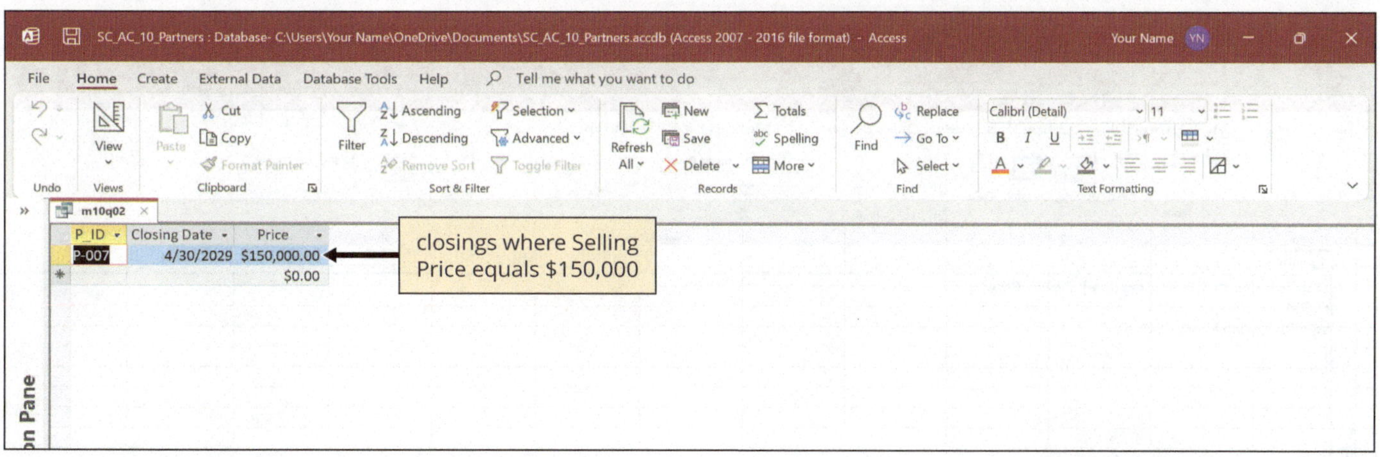

Figure 10–8(b): Query Results

2

- Save the query as **m10q03**.

BTW
Context-Sensitive Help in SQL
When you are working in SQL view, you can obtain context-sensitive help on any of the keywords in your query. To do so, click anywhere in the word about which you wish to obtain help and press F1.

Simple Criteria

The criterion following the word WHERE in the preceding query is called a simple criterion. A **simple criterion** has the form: field name, comparison operator, then either another field name or a value. The possible comparison operators are shown in Table 10–1.

Table 10–1 Comparison Operators

Comparison Operator	Meaning
=	equal to
<	less than
>	greater than
<=	less than or equal to
>=	greater than or equal to
<>	not equal to

To Use a Comparison Operator

In the following steps, you will use a comparison operator to list the property ID, closing date, and selling price for all vendors who have a selling price greater than $300,000. **Why?** A comparison operator allows you to compare the value in a field with a specific value or with the value in another field.

1

- Return to SQL view and delete the current command.
- Type **SELECT [Property ID], [Closing Date], [Selling Price]** as the first line of the command.
- Type **FROM [Closings]** as the second line.
- Type **WHERE [Selling Price]>300000** as the third line.
- Type a semicolon (**;**) on the fourth line (Figure 10–9a).

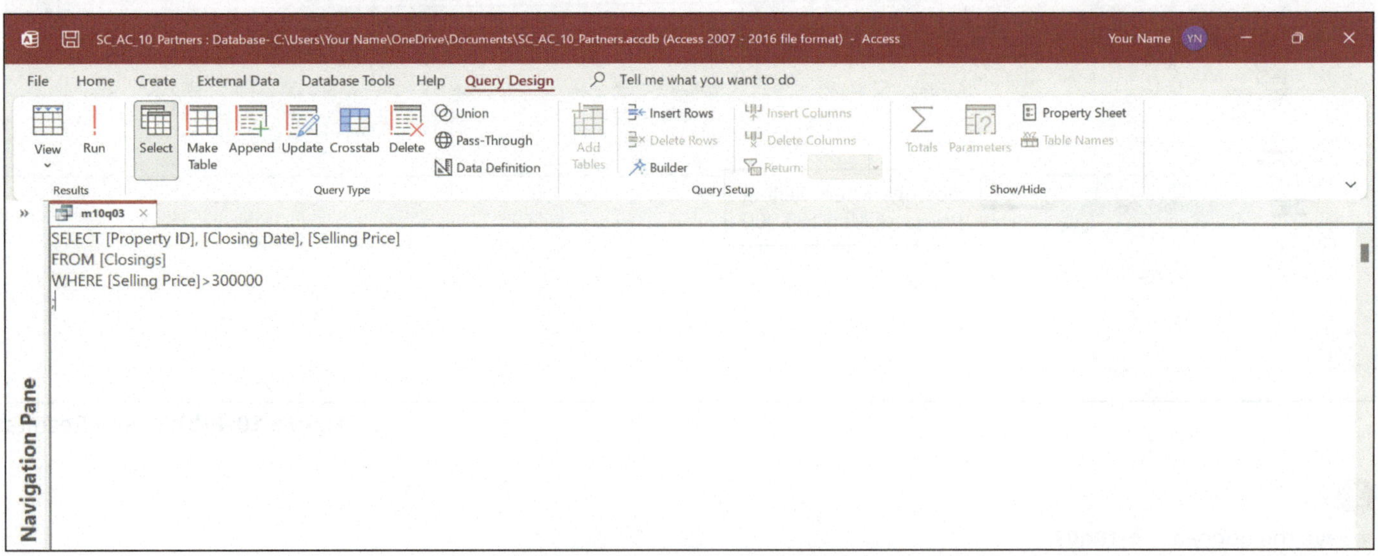

Figure 10–9(a): Query to List Property ID, Closing Date, and Selling Price for Closings Where Selling Price Is Greater Than $300,000

- View the results (Figure 10–9b).

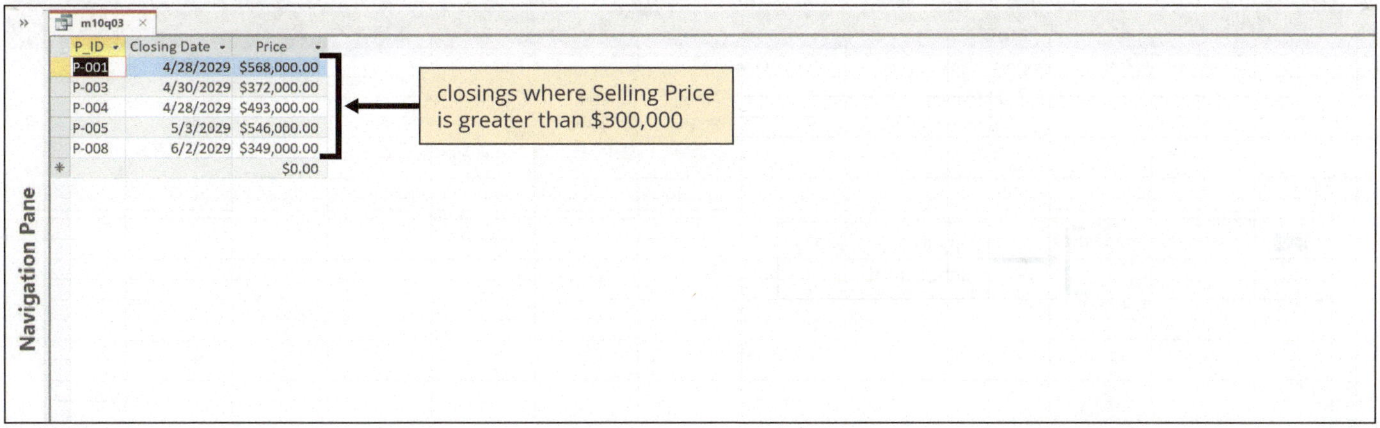

Figure 10–9(b): Query Results

2

- Save the query as **m10q04**.

To Use a Criterion Involving a Text Field

If the criterion involves a text field, the value must be enclosed in quotation marks. **Why?** Unlike when you work in the design grid, Access will not automatically insert in SQL view the quotation marks around text data. You need to include them yourself. The following steps create a query that lists the Property ID, Closing Date, and Status of all closings currently scheduled, that is, all closings where the value of the Status field is Scheduled.

1

- Return to SQL view, delete the current command, and then type **SELECT [Property ID], [Closing Date], [Status]** as the first line of the command.
- Type **FROM [Closings]** as the second line.
- Type **WHERE [Status]='Scheduled'** as the third line and type a semicolon (**;**) on the fourth line (Figure 10–10a).

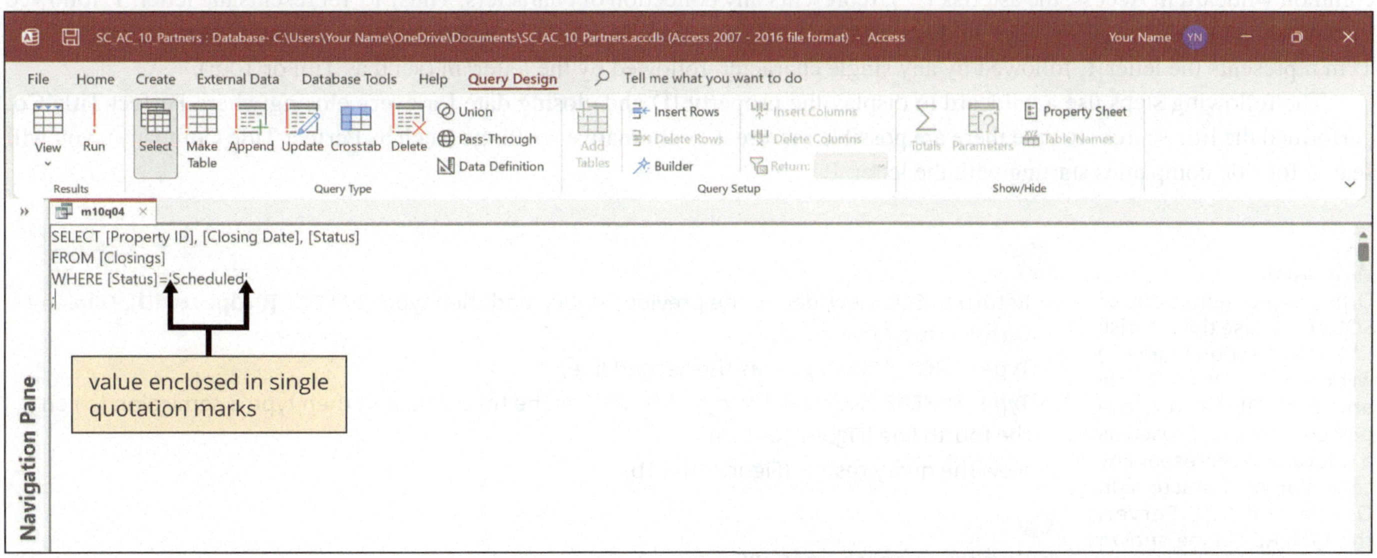

Figure 10–10(a): Query to List Currently Scheduled Closings

- View the results (Figure 10–10b).

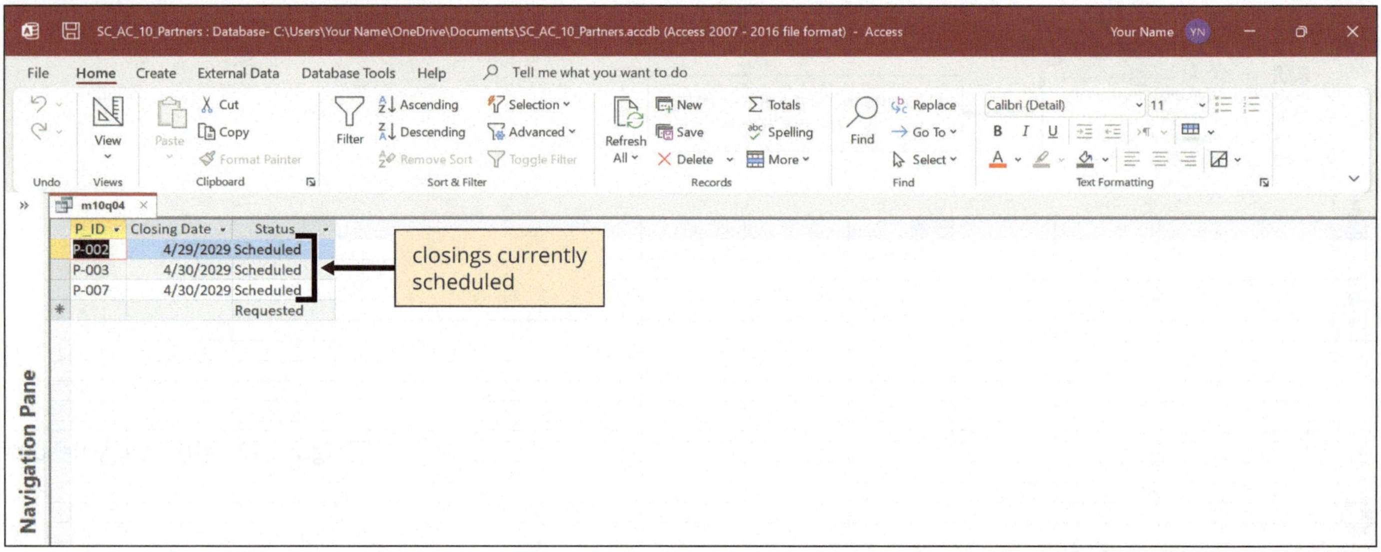

Figure 10–10(b): Query Results

Q&A Could I enclose the text field value in double quotation marks instead of single quotation marks?
Yes. It is usually easier, however, to use single quotes when entering SQL commands.

2

- Save the query as **m10q05**.

To Use a Wildcard

In most cases, the conditions in WHERE clauses involve exact matches, such as retrieving rows for each closing with a Scheduled status. In some cases, however, exact matches do not work. **Why?** You might only know that the desired value contains a certain collection of characters. In such cases, you use the LIKE operator with a wildcard symbol.

Rather than testing for equality, the LIKE operator uses one or more wildcard characters to test for a pattern match. One common wildcard in Access, the asterisk (*), represents any collection of characters. Thus, T* represents the letter, T, followed by any string of characters. Another wildcard symbol is the question mark (?), which represents any individual character. Thus, T?m represents the letter T, followed by any single character, followed by the letter, m (such as Tim or Tom).

The following steps use a wildcard to display the property ID and closing date for every closing where Perfect Title Co. performed the title search. In case there are possible incorrect or alternative spellings (such as Perfect Title Company), you will search for title companies starting with the letter, P.

BTW
Wildcards
Other implementations of SQL do not use the asterisk (*) and question mark (?) wildcards. In SQL for Oracle and for SQL Server, the percent sign (%) is used as a wildcard to represent any collection of characters. In Oracle and SQL Server, the WHERE clause shown in Figure 10–11a would be WHERE [Title Company] LIKE 'P%'.

1

- Return to SQL view, delete the previous query, and then type **SELECT [Property ID], [Closing Date], [Title Company]**.
- Type **FROM [Closings]** as the second line.
- Type **WHERE [Title Company] LIKE 'P*'** as the third line, and then type a semicolon (;) on the fourth line (Figure 10–11a).
- View the query results (Figure 10–11b).

2

- Save the query as **m10q06**.

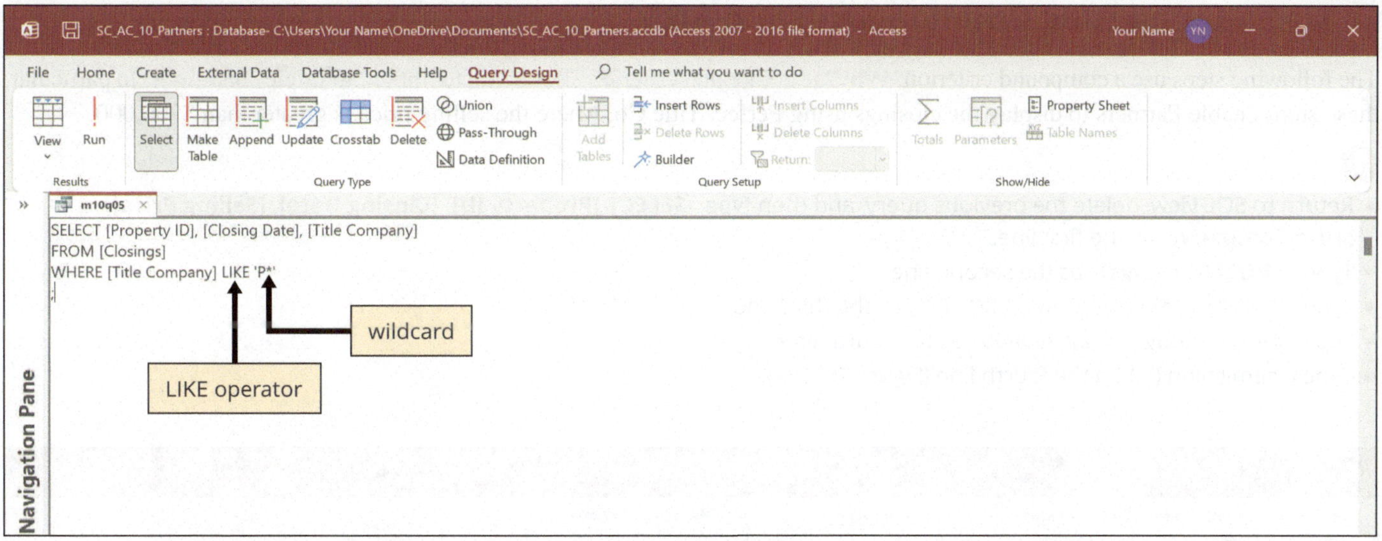

Figure 10–11(a): Query to List Property ID and Closing Date for Closings Where Title Company Starts with 'P'

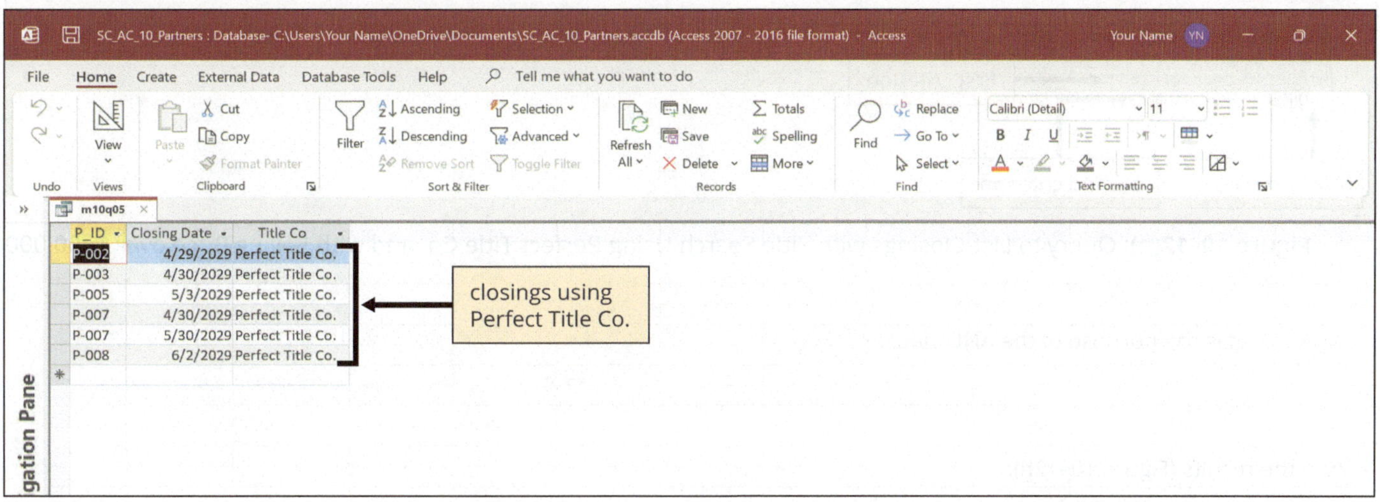

Figure 10–11(b): Query Results

Compound Criteria

You are not limited to simple criteria in SQL. You can also use compound criteria. Recall that compound criteria are formed by connecting two or more simple criteria using AND, OR, and NOT. When simple criteria are connected by the word, AND, all the simple criteria must be true for the compound criterion to be true. When simple criteria are connected by the word, OR, the compound criterion will be true when any one of the simple criteria is true. Preceding a criterion by the word, NOT, reverses the truth or falsity of the original criterion. That is, if the original criterion is true, the new criterion will be false; if the original criterion is false, the new one will be true.

BTW
SQL Standards
The International Organization for Standardization (ISO) and the American National Standards Institute (ANSI) recognize SQL as a standardized language. Different relational database management systems may support the entire set of standardized SQL commands or only a subset.

BTW
Entering Field Names
Be sure to enclose field names in square brackets. If you accidentally use parentheses or curly braces, Access will display a syntax error (missing operator) message.

To Use a Compound Criterion Involving AND

The following steps use a compound criterion. **Why?** A compound criterion allows you to impose multiple conditions. In particular, these steps enable Partners to display the closings using Perfect Title Co. where the selling price is greater than $300,000.

1

- Return to SQL view, delete the previous query, and then type **SELECT [Property ID], [Closing Date], [Selling Price], [Title Company]** as the first line.
- Type **FROM [Closings]** as the second line.
- Type **WHERE [Title Company] LIKE 'P*'** as the third line.
- Type **AND [Selling Price]>300000** as the fourth line.
- Type a semicolon (**;**) on the fourth line (Figure 10–12a).

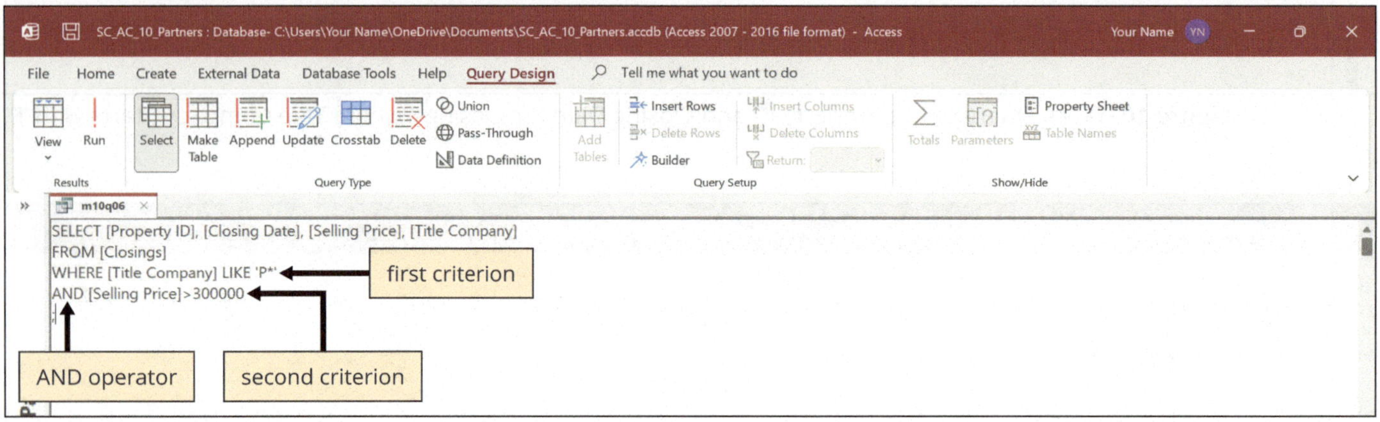

Figure 10–12(a): Query to List Closings with Title Search Using Perfect Title Co. and with Selling Price over $300,000

Q&A What is the purpose of the AND clause?

The AND clause indicates there are multiple criteria, all of which must be true. With this AND clause, only rows on which *both* Title Company starts with P (resulting in "Perfect Title Co.") *and* Selling Price is greater than $300,000 will be included.

- View the results (Figure 10–12b).

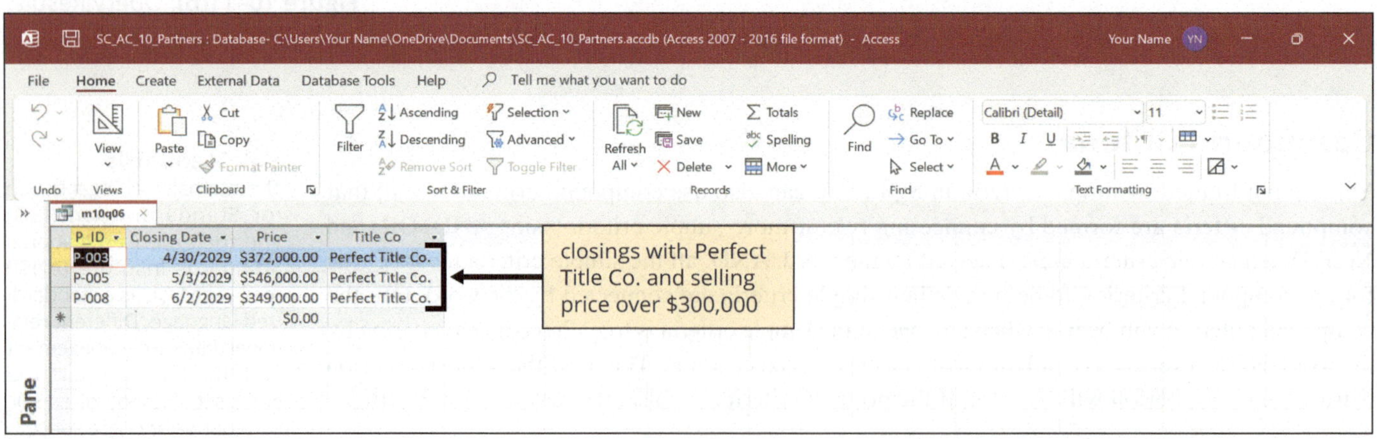

Figure 10–12(b): Query Results

2

- Save the query as **m10q07**.

To Use a Compound Criterion Involving OR

The following steps use a compound criterion involving OR to enable Partners to display closings with Perfect Title Co. *or* where the selling price is greater than $300,000. **Why?** In an OR criterion, only one of the individual criteria needs to be true for the record to be included in the results.

1

- Return to SQL view, delete the previous query, and type **SELECT [Property ID], [Closing Date], [Selling Price], [Title Company]** as the first line.
- Type **FROM [Closings]** as the second line.
- Type **WHERE [Title Company] LIKE 'P*'** as the third line.
- Type **OR [Selling Price]>300000** as the fourth line.
- Type a semicolon (**;**) on the fifth line (Figure 10–13a).

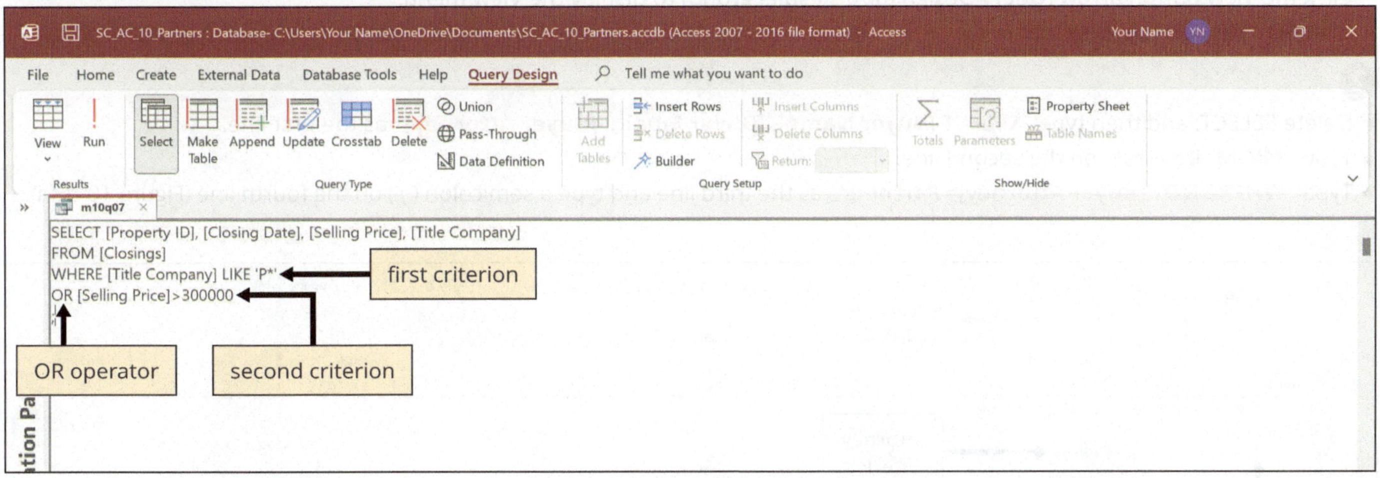

Figure 10–13(a): Query to List Closings Where Title Company Starts with 'P' or Selling Price Is over $300,000

Q&A What is the purpose of the OR clause?

The OR clause indicates there are multiple criteria, only one of which needs to be true. With this OR clause, those rows on which *either* Title Company is Perfect Title Co. *or* Selling Price is greater than $300,000 (or both) will be included.

- View the results (Figure 10–13b).

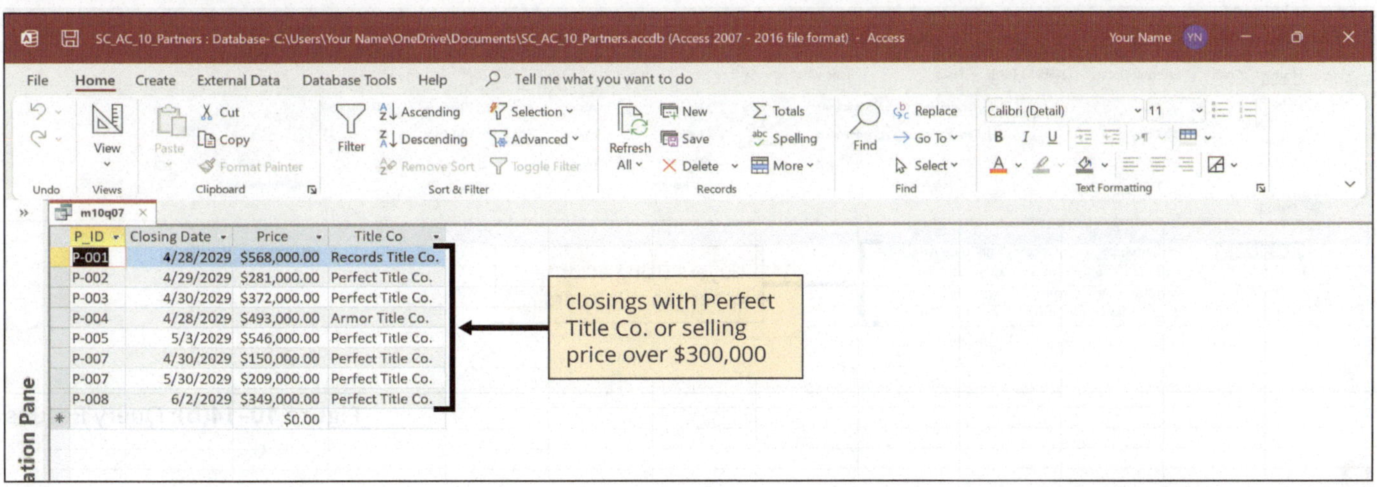

Figure 10–13(b): Query Results

2

- Save the query as **m10q08**.
- Close the query.

Break Point: If you wish to take a break, this is a good place to do so. You can quit Access now. To resume at a later time, start Access, open the database called SC_AC_10_Partners.accdb, and continue following the steps from this location forward.

To Use NOT in a Criterion

Why? You can negate any criterion by preceding the criterion with the word NOT. The following steps use NOT in a criterion to list the name, email, and attorney of buyers who are not represented by Partners Law Firm for their closing.

1

- Click the Create tab, and then click the Query Design button (Create tab | Queries group) to create a query.
- Close the Add Tables pane without adding any tables.
- Click the View button arrow (Query Design tab | Results group) to display the View menu.
- Click SQL View on the View menu.

2

- Delete SELECT; and then type **SELECT [Buyer Name], [Buyer Email], [Buyer Attorney]** as the first line.
- Type **FROM [Buyers]** on the second line.
- Type **WHERE NOT [Buyer Attorney]='Partners'** as the third line and type a semicolon (**;**) on the fourth line (Figure 10–14a).

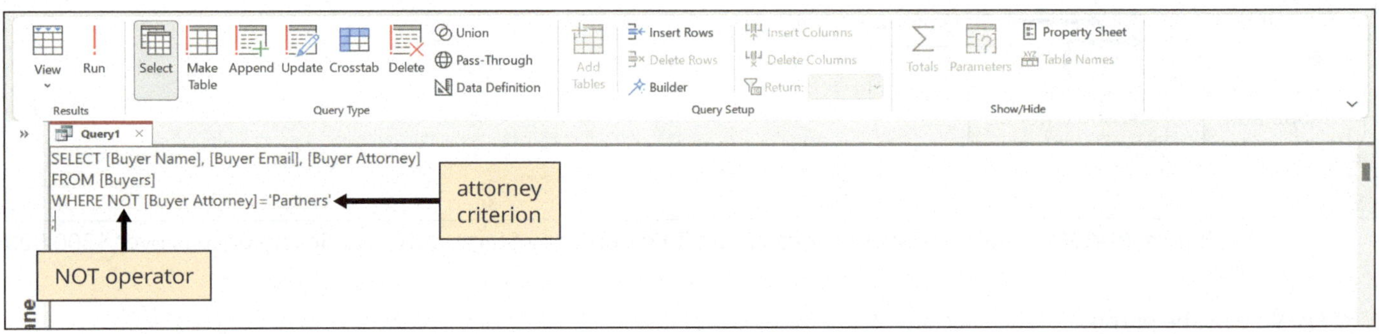

Figure 10–14(a): Query to List Buyer Name, Email, and Attorney for Buyers Not Represented by Partners Law Firm

- View the results (Figure 10–14b).

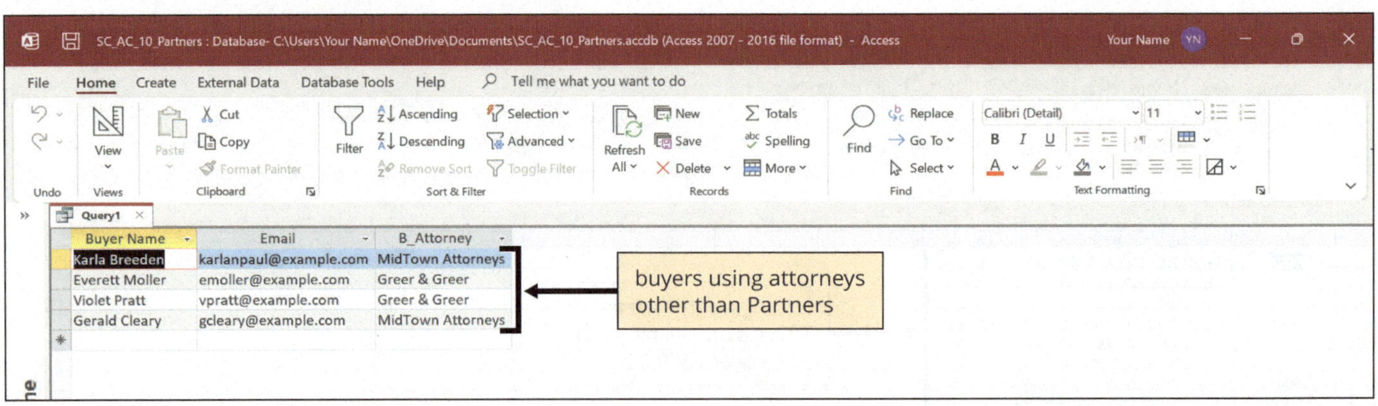

Figure 10–14(b): Query Results

3

- Save the query as **m10q09**.

To Use a Computed Field

Just as with queries created in Design view, you can include fields in queries that are not listed in the database but that can be computed from fields that are. Recall that such a field is called a computed or calculated field. Computations can involve addition (+), subtraction (–), multiplication (*), or division (/). The query in the following steps computes the workshop hours remaining, which is equal to the total hours minus the hours spent.

To indicate the contents of the new field (the computed field), you can name the field by following the computation with the word, AS, and then the name you want to assign the field. Why? Assigning the field a descriptive name makes the results much more readable. The following steps calculate the hours remaining for each workshop enrollment by subtracting the hours spent from the total hours and then assigning the name, Remaining, to the calculation. The steps also list the Buyer ID, Workshop Code, Total Hours, and Hours Spent for all workshop enrollments for which the number of hours spent is greater than 0.

1

- Return to SQL view and delete the previous query.
- Type **SELECT [Buyer ID], [Workshop Code], [Total Hours], [Hours Spent], [Total Hours]-[Hours Spent] AS Remaining** as the first line.
- Type **FROM [Workshop Enrollments]** as the second line.
- Type **WHERE [Hours Spent]>0** as the third line, and then type a semicolon (**;**) on the fourth line (Figure 10–15a).

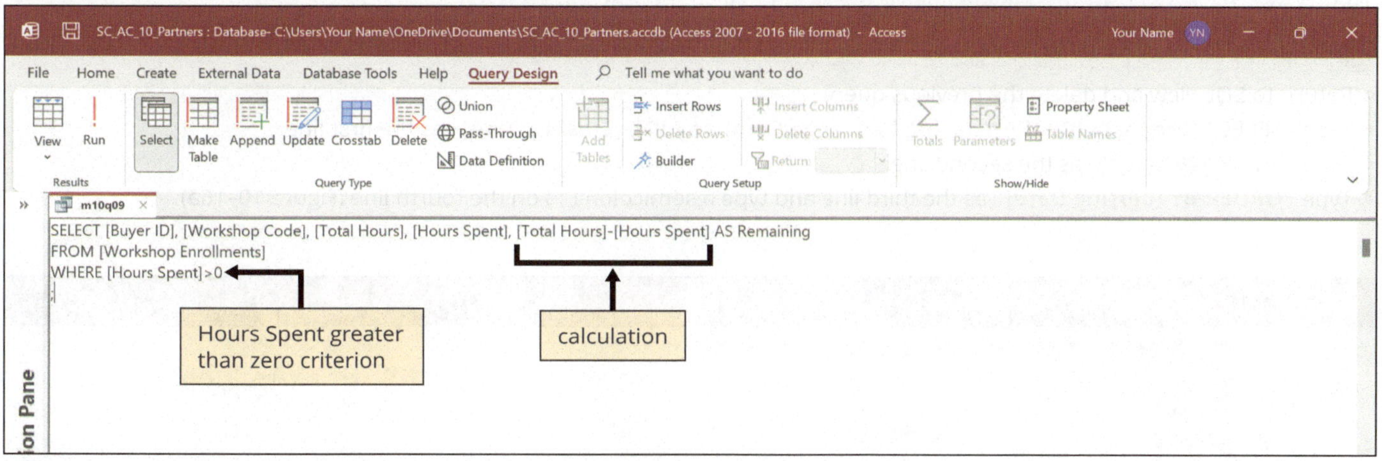

Figure 10–15(a): Query to List Total Hours and Remaining Hours for Each Workshop Enrollment Where Buyer Has Spent More Than 0 Hours

- View the results (Figure 10–15b).

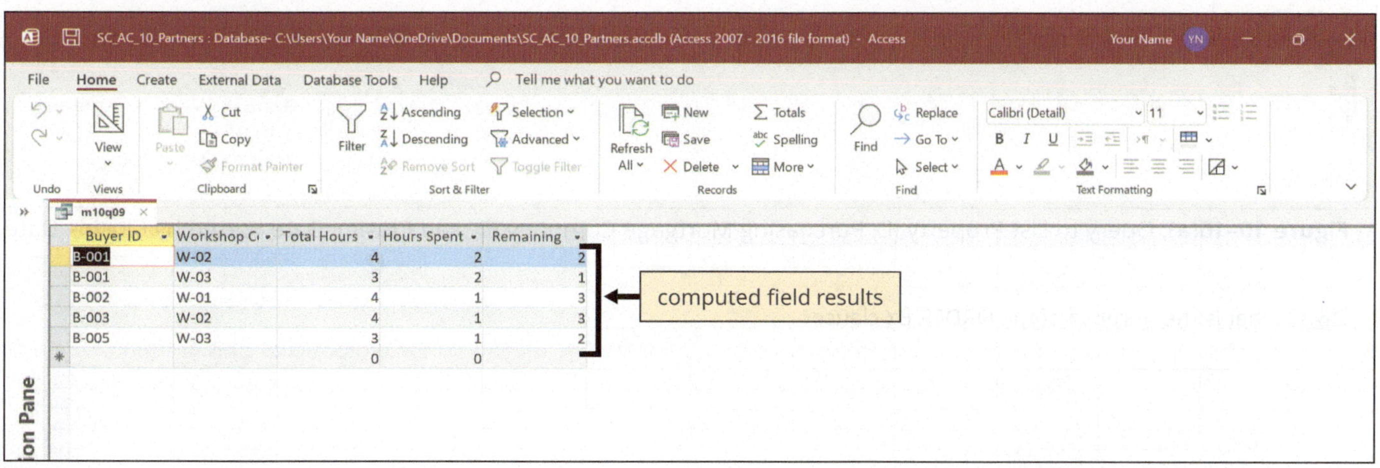

Figure 10–15(b): Query Results

2

- Save the query as **m10q10**.

Sorting

Sorting in SQL follows the same principles as when using Design view to specify sorted query results, employing a sort key as the field on which data is to be sorted. SQL uses major and minor sort keys when sorting on multiple fields. By following a sort key with the word, DESC, with no comma in between, you can specify descending sort order. If you do not specify DESC, the data will be sorted in ascending order.

To sort the output, you include an **ORDER BY clause**, which consists of the words, ORDER BY, followed by the sort key. If there are two sort keys, the major sort key is listed first. Queries that you construct in Design view require that the major sort key is positioned to the left of the minor sort key in the list of fields to be included. In SQL, there is no such restriction. The fields to be included in the query are listed in the SELECT clause, and the fields to be used for sorting are listed in the ORDER BY clause. The two clauses are independent of each other.

To Sort the Results on a Single Field

The following steps list the property ID, purchasing mortgage company ID, and closing date for all closings sorted by closing date. **Why?** Partners wants this data to appear in chronological order by closing date.

1

- Return to SQL view and delete the previous query.
- Type **SELECT [Property ID], [Purchasing Mortgage Company ID], [Closing Date]** as the first line.
- Type **FROM [Closings]** as the second line.
- Type **ORDER BY [Closing Date]** as the third line and type a semicolon (**;**) on the fourth line (Figure 10–16a).

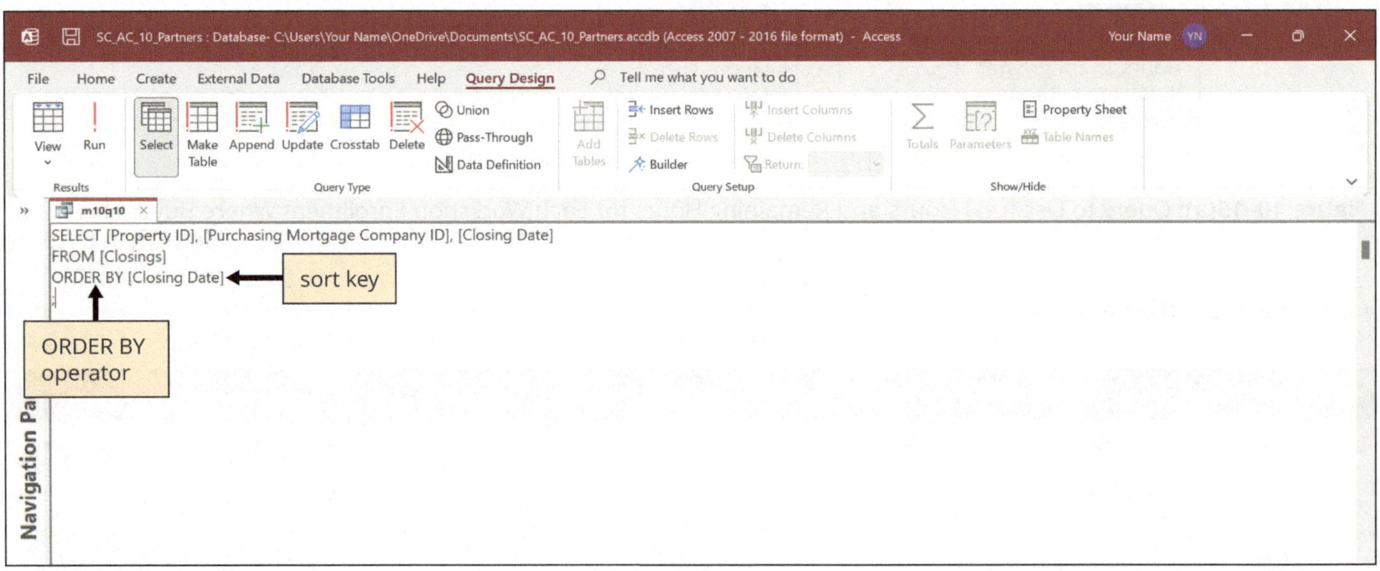

Figure 10–16(a): Query to List Property ID, Purchasing Mortgage Company ID, and Closing Date Sorted by Closing Date

Q&A What is the purpose of the ORDER BY clause?
The ORDER BY clause indicates the results of the query are to be sorted by the indicated field or fields. This ORDER BY clause, for example, would cause the results to be sorted by Closing Date.

- View the results (Figure 10–16b).

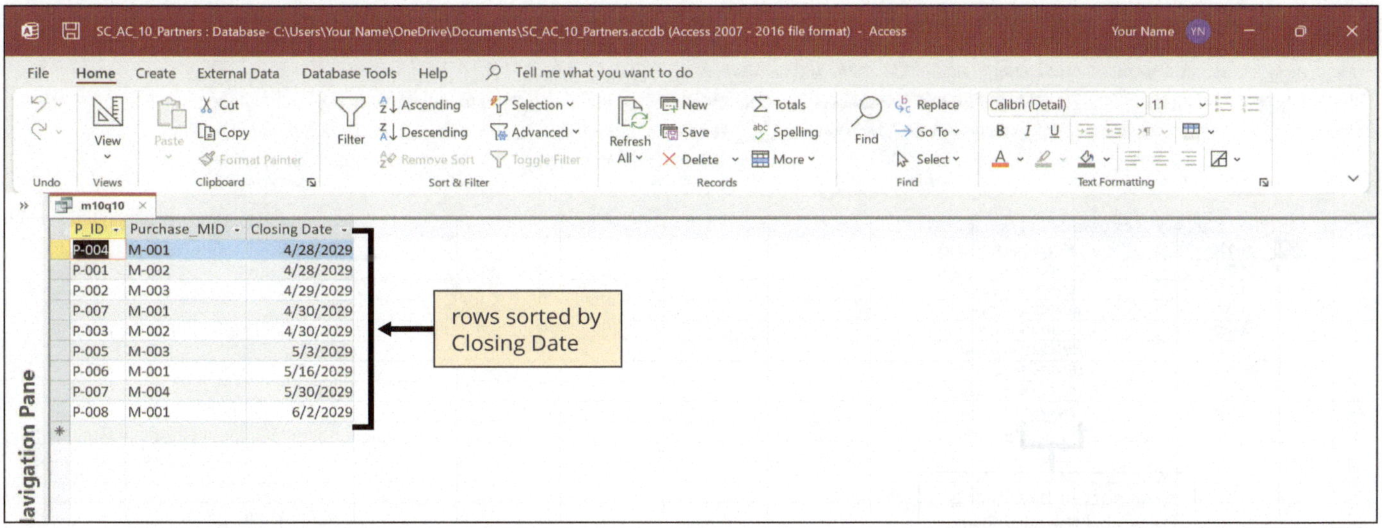

Figure 10–16(b): Query Results

2

- Save the query as **m10q11**.

To Sort the Results on Multiple Fields

The following steps list the property ID, purchasing mortgage company ID, closing date, and status for all closings. The data is to be sorted on multiple fields. **Why?** Partners wants the data to be sorted by status within closing date. That is, the data should be sorted by closing date. In addition, within the group of closings that have the same closing date, the data is to be sorted further by status. To accomplish this sort, the Closing Date field is the major (primary) sort key and the Status field is the minor (secondary) sort key. Remember that the major sort key must be listed first in the ORDER BY clause.

1

- Return to SQL view and delete the previous query.
- Type **SELECT [Property ID], [Purchasing Mortgage Company ID], [Closing Date], [Status]** as the first line.
- Type **FROM [Closings]** as the second line.
- Type **ORDER BY [Closing Date], [Status]** as the third line, and then type a semicolon (**;**) on the fourth line (Figure 10–17a).

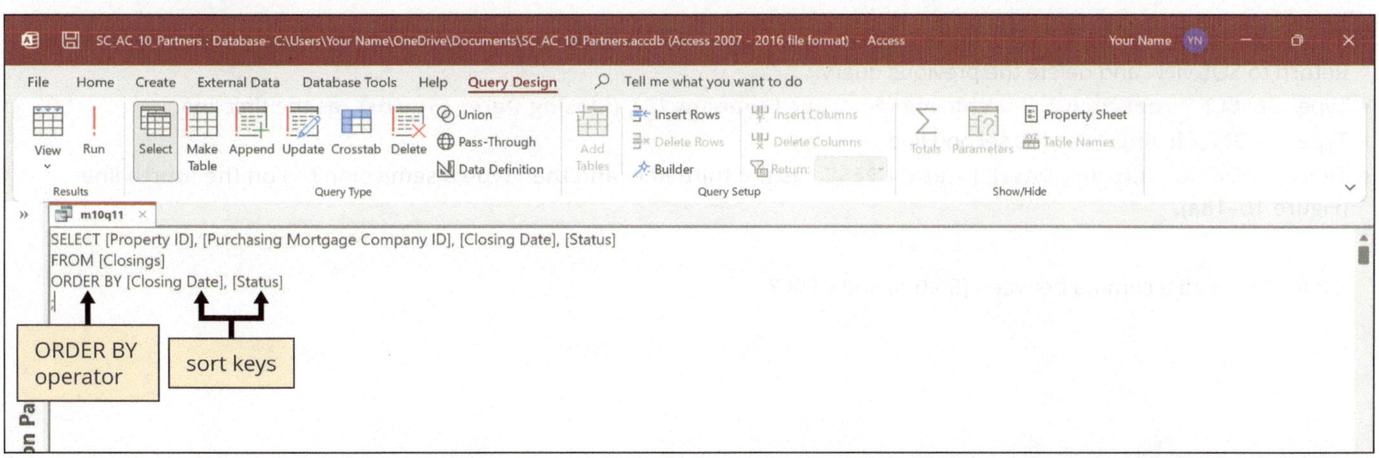

Figure 10–17(a): Query to List Property ID, Purchasing Mortgage Company ID, Closing Date, and Status Sorted by Closing Date and Status

- View the results (Figure 10–17b).

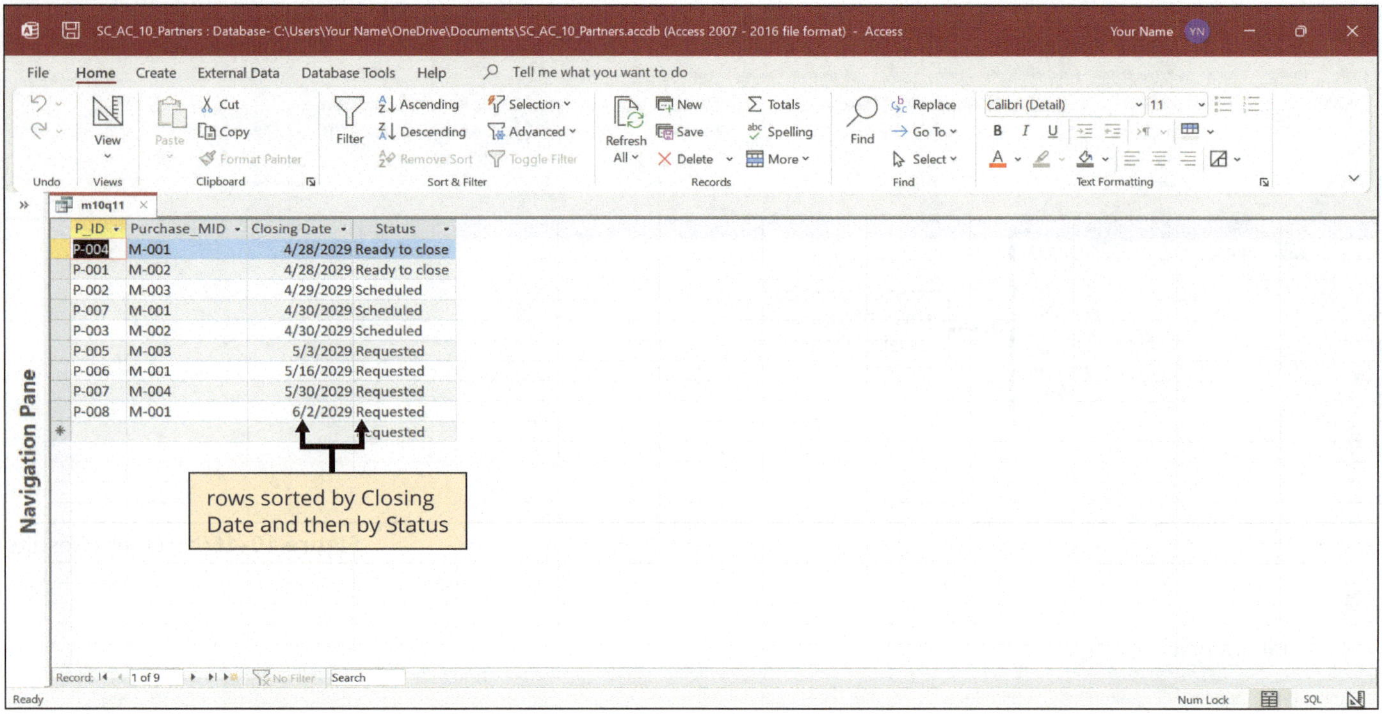

Figure 10–17(b): Query Results

- **Experiment:** Try reversing the order of the sort keys to see the effect. View the results to see the effect of your choice. When finished, return to the original sorting order for both fields.

2

- Save the query as **m10q12**.

To Sort the Results in Descending Order

Why? To show the results in high-to-low rather than low-to-high order, you sort in descending order. To sort in descending order, you follow the name of the sort key with the DESC operator. The following steps list the property ID, purchasing mortgage company ID, closing date, and status for all closings. Partners wants the data to be sorted by descending status within closing date. That is, within the closings having the same date, the data is to be sorted further by status in descending order.

1

- Return to SQL view and delete the previous query.
- Type **SELECT [Property ID], [Purchasing Mortgage Company ID], [Closing Date], [Status]** as the first line.
- Type **FROM [Closings]** as the second line.
- Type **ORDER BY [Closing Date], [Status] DESC** as the third line, and then type a semicolon (;) on the fourth line (Figure 10–18a).

Q&A Do I need a comma between [Status] and DESC?

No. In fact, you must not use a comma. If you did, SQL would assume that you want a field called DESC. Without the comma, SQL knows that the DESC operator indicates the sort on the Status field is to be in descending order.

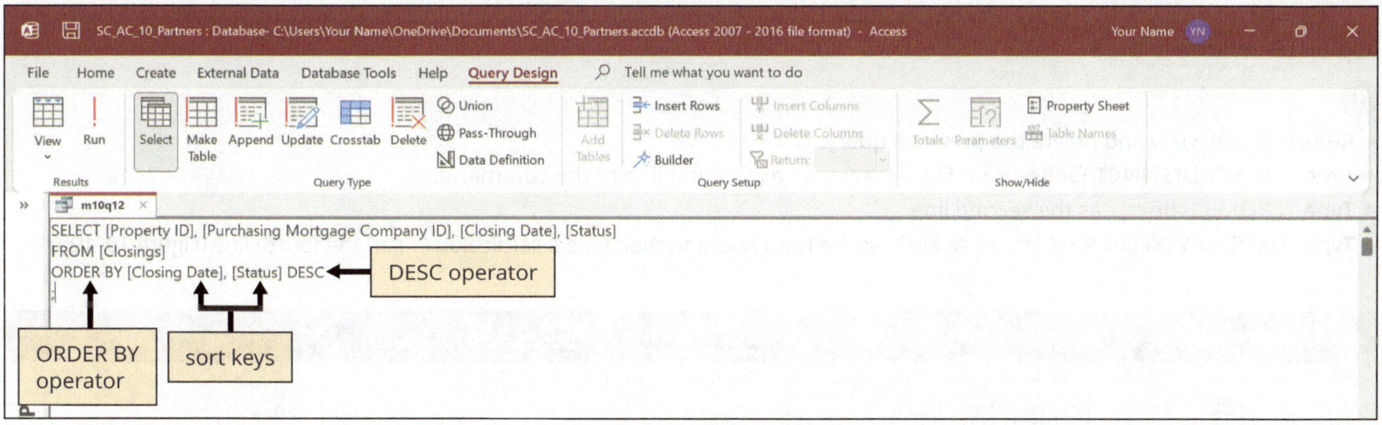

Figure 10–18(a): Query to List Property ID, Purchasing Mortgage Company ID, Closing Date, and Status with Results Sorted by Closing Date and Descending Status Order

- View the results (Figure 10–18b).

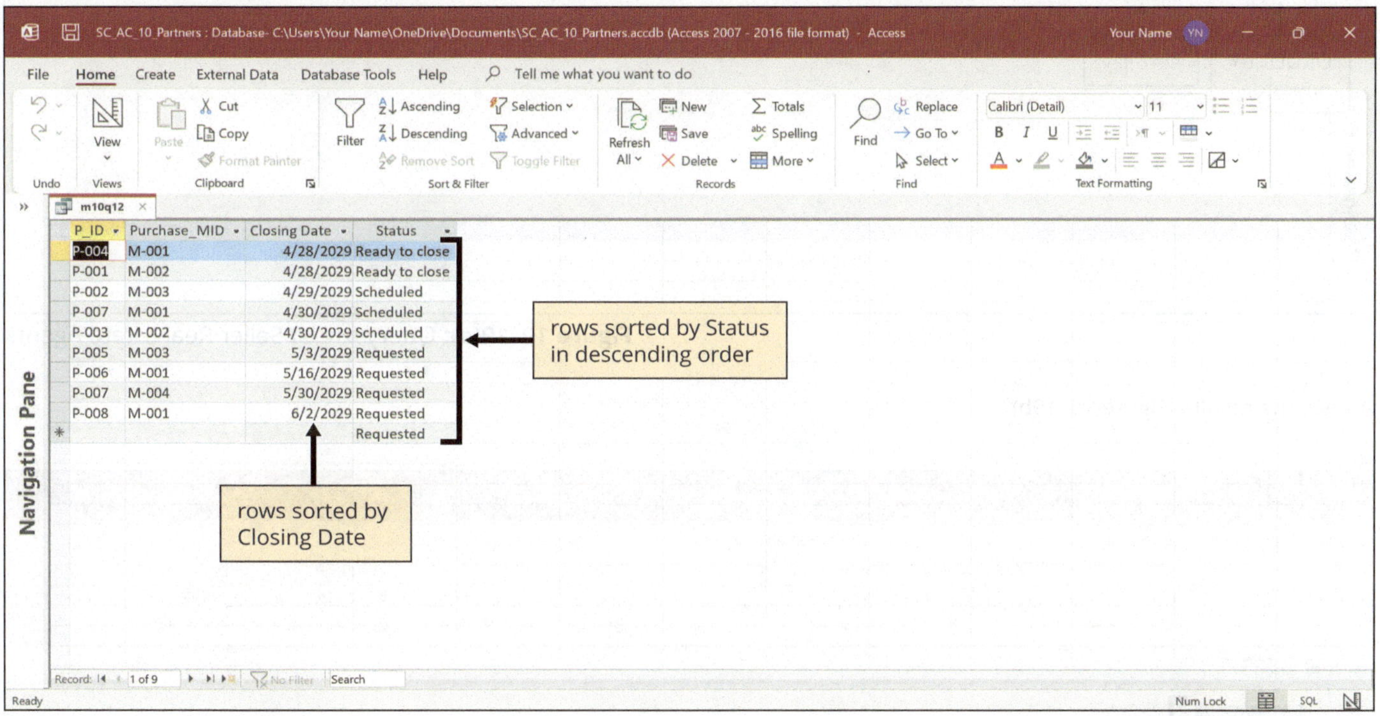

Figure 10–18(b): Query Results

2

- Save the query as **m10q13**.

To Omit Duplicates When Sorting

When you sort data, duplicates are normally included. For example, the query in Figure 10–19 sorts the Seller Real Estate Agents in the Sellers table. Because there are several real estate agents representing multiple sellers, Partners would like to eliminate duplicate agents in the list. To do so, use the DISTINCT operator in the query. **Why?** The DISTINCT operator eliminates duplicate values in the results of a query. To use the operator, you follow the word, DISTINCT, with the relevant field name in parentheses.

The following steps display the Seller Real Estate Agents from the Sellers table in alphabetical order, but with any duplicates removed.

1

- Return to SQL view and delete the previous query.
- Type **SELECT DISTINCT [Seller Real Estate Agent]** as the first line of the command.
- Type **FROM [Sellers]** as the second line.
- Type **ORDER BY [Seller Real Estate Agent]** as the third line, and then type a semicolon (**;**) on the fourth line (Figure 10–19a).

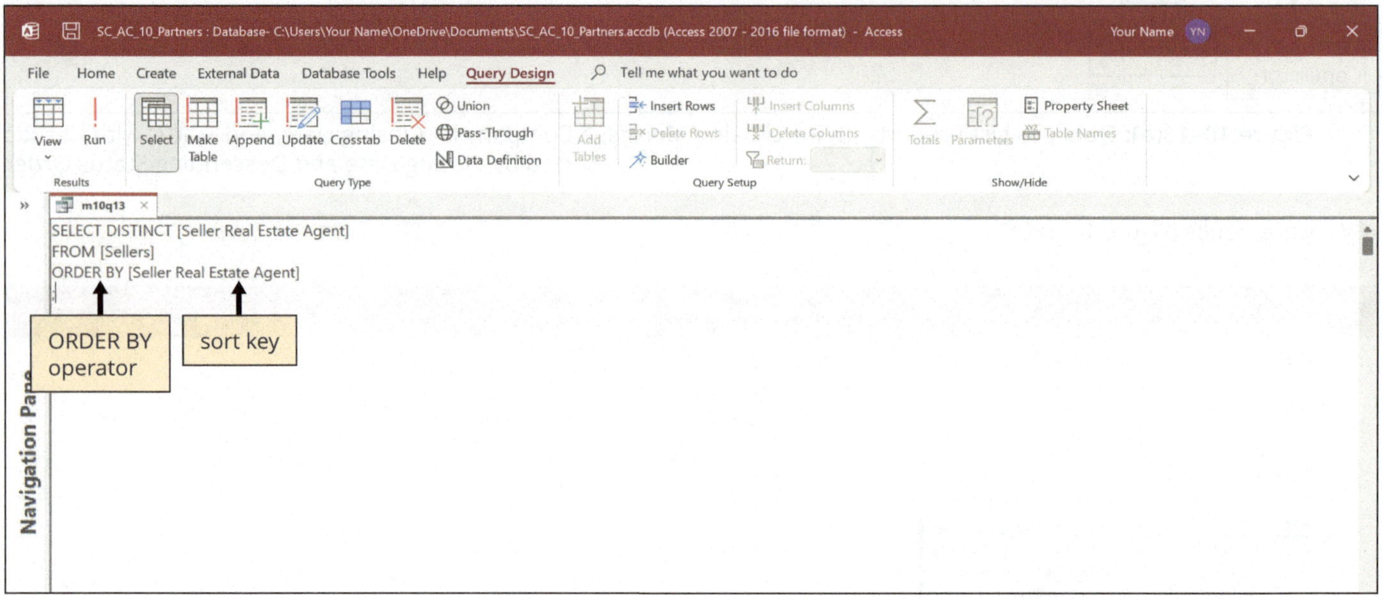

Figure 10–19(a): Query to List Seller Real Estate Agents

- View the results (Figure 10–19b).

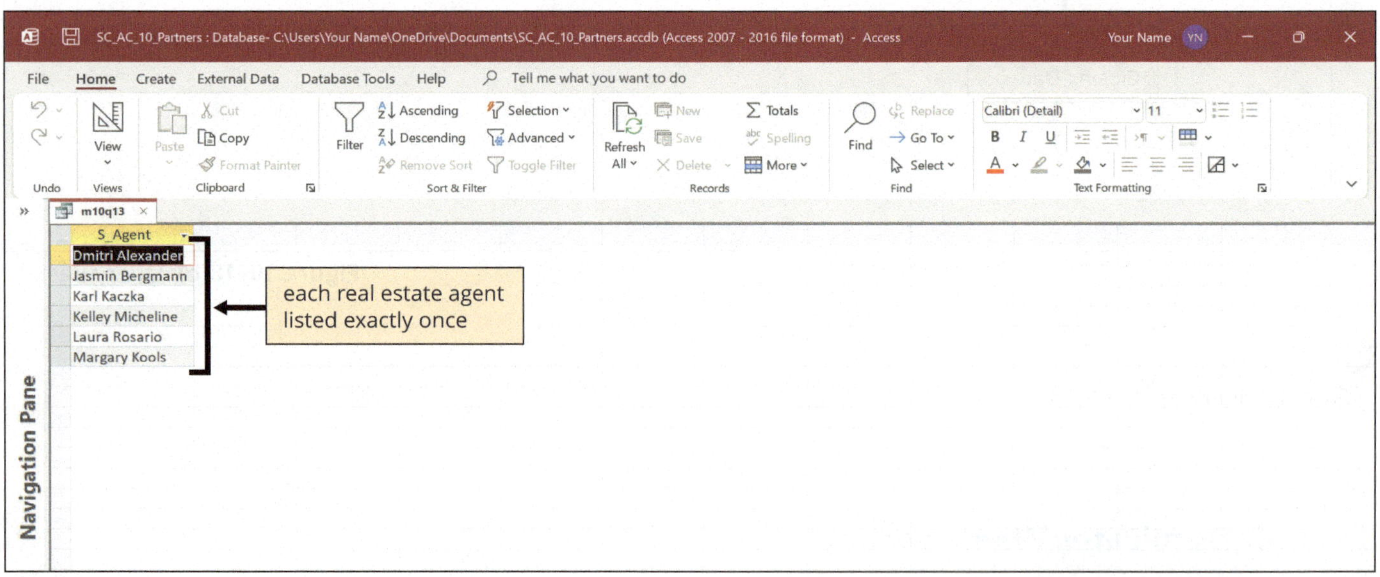

Figure 10–19(b): Query Results

2

- Save the query as **m10q14**.

Consider This

How do you determine sorting when creating a query?

Examine the query or request to see if it contains words such as *order* or *sort* that would imply the order of the query results is important. If so, you need to sort the query.

- **Determine whether data is to be sorted.** Examine the requirements for the query looking for words like *sorted by*, *ordered by*, *arranged by*, and so on.
- **Determine sort keys.** Look for the fields that follow sorted by, ordered by, or any other words that signify sorting. For example, if the requirements for the query include the phrase, ordered by real estate agent name, then real estate agent name is a sort key.
- **If there is more than one sort key, determine which one will be the major sort key and which will be the minor sort key.** Look for words that indicate which field is more important. For example, if the requirements indicate the results are to be ordered by status within closing date, then Closing Date is the more important sort key.

To Use a Built-In Function

SQL has built-in functions, also called aggregate functions, to perform various calculations. Similar to the functions you learned about in an earlier module, these functions in SQL are COUNT, SUM, AVG, MAX, and MIN, respectively. Partners uses the following steps to determine the number of property purchases closing with Atlas Mortgage (M-001) by using the COUNT function with an asterisk (*). **Why use an asterisk rather than a field name when using the COUNT function?** You could select a field name, but that would be cumbersome and imply that you were just counting that field. You are really counting records. It does not matter whether you are counting names or street addresses or anything else.

1

- Return to SQL view and delete the previous query.
- Type **SELECT COUNT(*)** as the first line of the command.
- Type **FROM [Closings]** as the second line.
- Type **WHERE [Purchasing Mortgage Company ID]='M-001'** as the third line, and then type a semicolon (;) on the fourth line (Figure 10–20a).

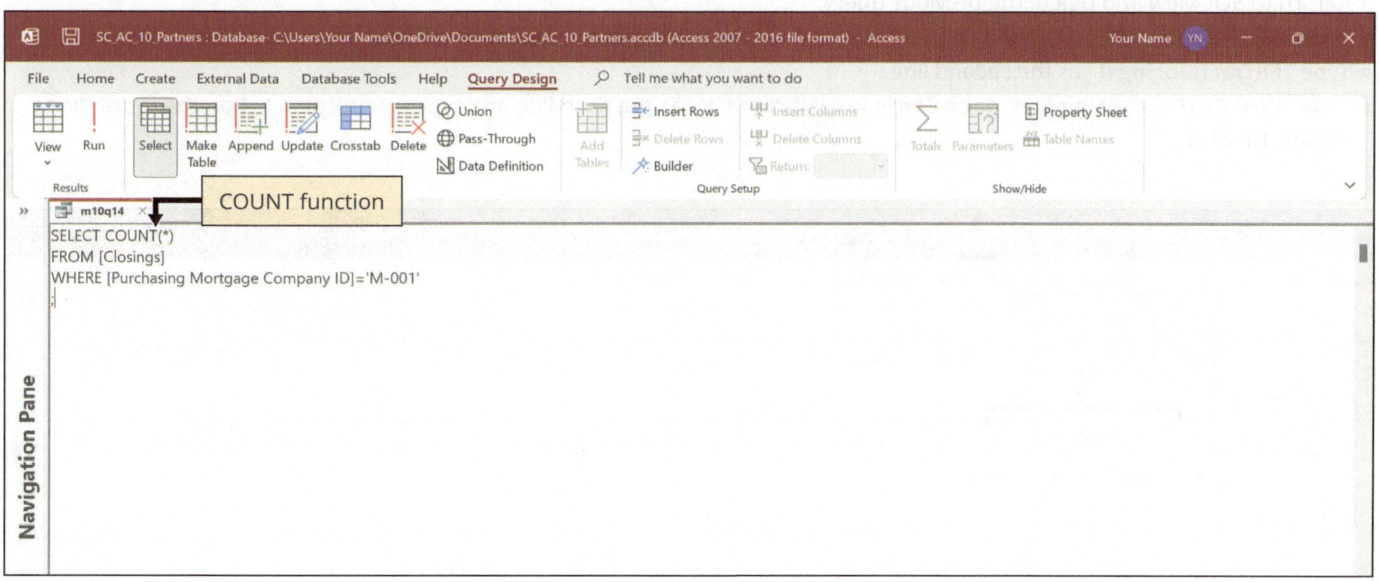

Figure 10–20(a): Query to Count Closings for Mortgage Company M-001

- View the results (Figure 10–20b).

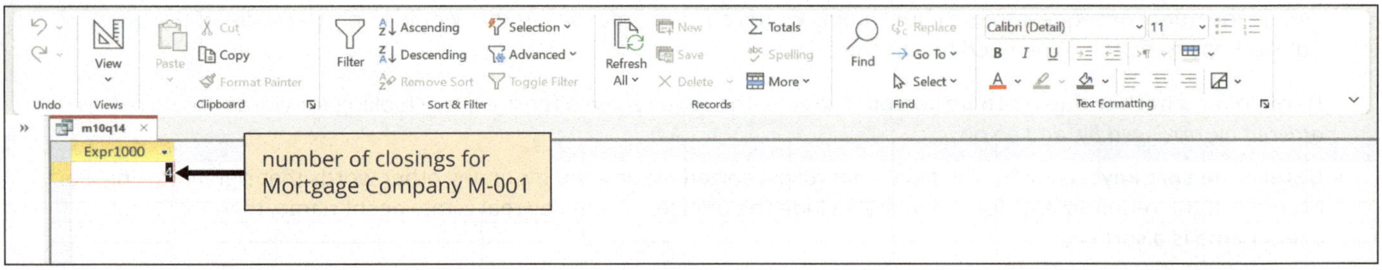

Figure 10–20(b): Query Results

Q&A Why does Expr1000 appear in the column heading of the results?

Because the field is a computed field, it does not have a name. Access assigns a generic expression name. You can assign a meaningful name for the field by including the AS clause in the query, and it is good practice to do so.

2

- Save the query as **m10q15**.

To Assign a Name to the Results of a Function

Partners would prefer to have a more meaningful name than Expr1000 for the results of counting closings. **Why?** The default name of Expr1000 does not describe the meaning of the calculation. Fortunately, just as you can assign a name to a calculation that includes two fields, you can assign a name to the results of a function. To do so, follow the expression for the function with the word, AS, and then the name to be assigned to the result. The following steps assign the name, Atlas Mortgage Purchases, to the expression in the previous query.

1

- Return to SQL view and delete the previous query.
- Type **SELECT COUNT(*) AS [Atlas Mortgage Purchases]** as the first line of the command.
- Type **FROM [Closings]** as the second line.
- Type **WHERE [Purchasing Mortgage Company ID]='M-001'** as the third line and type a semicolon (**;**) on the fourth line (Figure 10–21a).

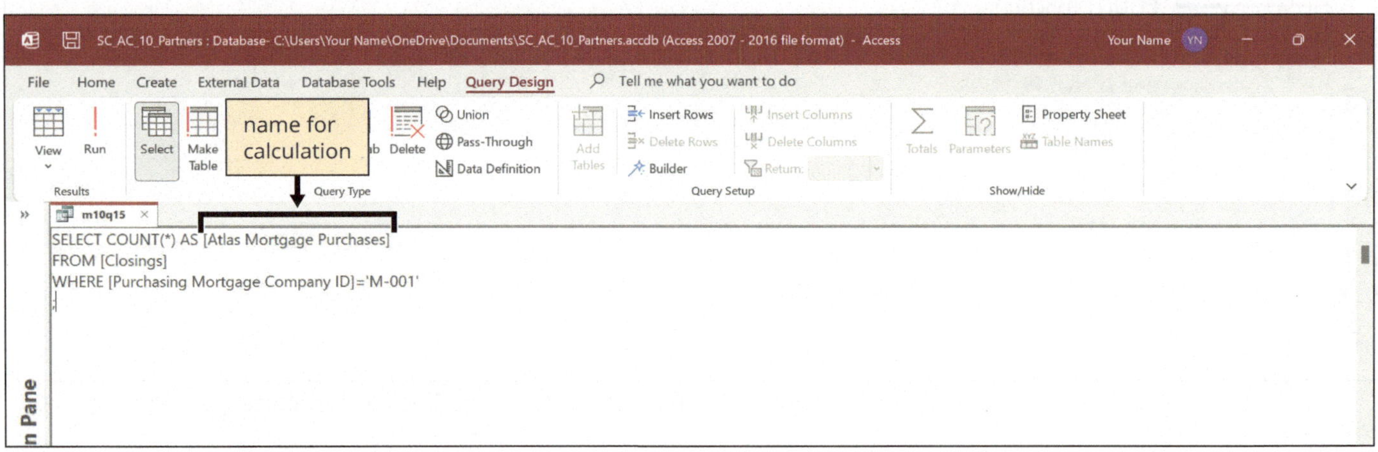

Figure 10–21(a): Query to Count Closings for Mortgage Company M-001 and to Name the Expression

- View the results. If necessary, increase the width of the Atlas Mortgage Purchases column to view the entire field name (Figure 10–21b).

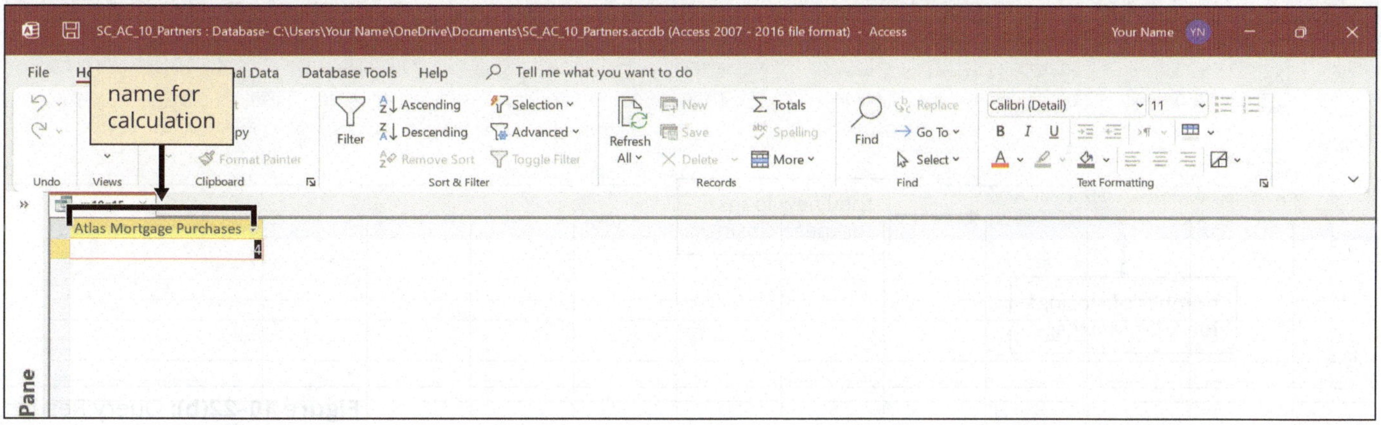

Figure 10–21(b): Query Results

2

- Save the query as **m10q16**.

To Use Multiple Functions in the Same Command

There are two differences between COUNT and SUM, other than the fact they are computing different statistics. First, in the case of SUM, you must specify the field for which you want a total, instead of using an asterisk (*); second, the field must be numeric. **Why?** If the field is not numeric, it does not make sense to calculate a sum. You could not calculate a sum of names or addresses, for example. The following steps use both the COUNT and SUM functions to count the number of closings whose purchasing mortgage company ID is M-001 and to calculate the sum (total) of the new loan amounts. The steps use the word, AS, to name COUNT(*) as Atlas Mortgage Purchases and to name SUM([New Loan Amount]) as Total New Loans.

1

- Return to SQL view and delete the previous query.
- Type **SELECT COUNT(*) AS [Atlas Mortgage Purchases], SUM([New Loan Amount]) AS [Total New Loans]** as the first line of the command.
- Type **FROM [Closings]** as the second line.
- Type **WHERE [Purchasing Mortgage Company ID]='M-001'** as the third line and type a semicolon (**;**) on the fourth line (Figure 10–22a).

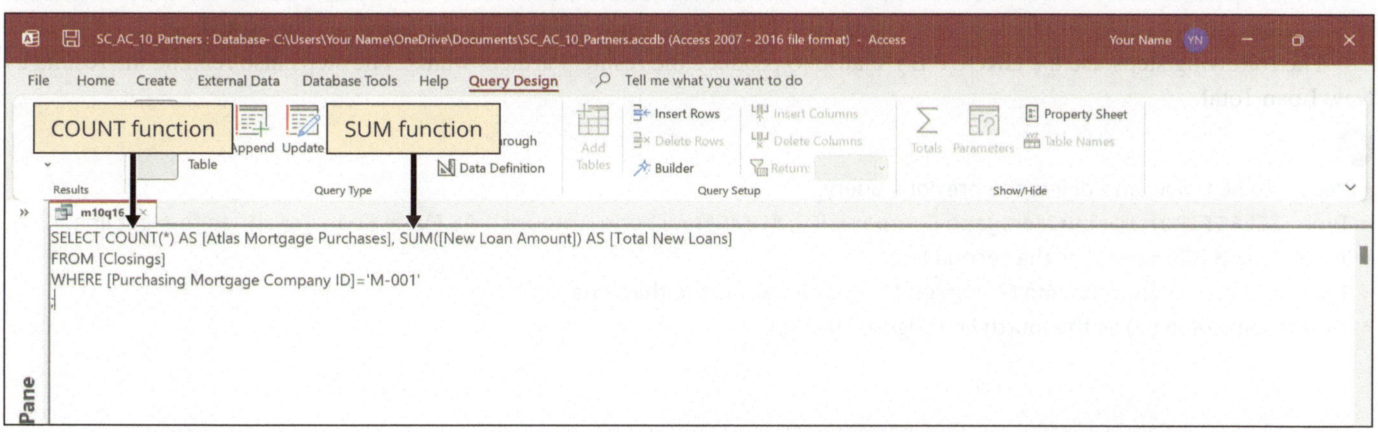

Figure 10–22(a): Query to Count Closings for Mortgage Company M-001 Using a Named Expression and to Calculate Sum of New Loan Amounts Using a Named Expression

- View the results. If necessary, increase the width of the Total New Loans column to view the entire field name (Figure 10–22b).

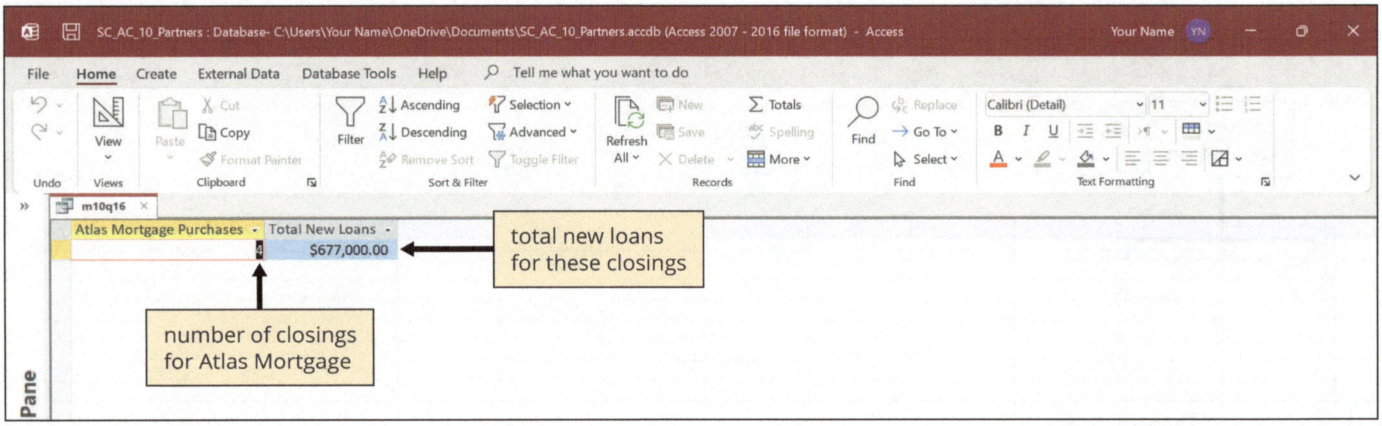

Figure 10–22(b): Query Results

- **Experiment:** Try using other functions in place of SUM. The use of AVG, MAX, and MIN is similar to SUM. The only difference is that a different statistic is calculated with each function. In each case, view the results to see the effect of your choice. When finished, once again select SUM.

2

- Save the query as **m10q17**.

Grouping

Recall that grouping means creating groups of records that share some common characteristic. When you group rows, any calculations indicated in the SELECT command are performed for the entire group.

To Use Grouping

Partners wants to calculate the totals of the New Loan Amount field for all Purchasing Mortgage Company IDs in the Closings table. To calculate the totals, the query will include the calculation, SUM([New Loan Amount]). To get totals for each mortgage company, the query will also include a **GROUP BY clause**, which consists of the words, GROUP BY, followed by the field used for grouping, in this case, Purchasing Mortgage Company ID. **Why?** Including GROUP BY Purchasing Mortgage Company ID will cause the new loan amounts for each mortgage company to be grouped together; that is, all new loan amounts with the same purchasing mortgage company will form a group. Any statistics, such as new loan totals, appearing after the word, SELECT, will be calculated for each of these groups. Using GROUP BY does not mean the information will be sorted.

The following steps use the GROUP BY clause to produce the results Partners wants. The steps also rename the results as New Loan Total.

1

- Return to SQL view and delete the previous query.
- Type **SELECT [Purchasing Mortgage Company ID], SUM([New Loan Amount]) AS [New Loan Total]** as the first line.
- Type **FROM [Closings]** as the second line.
- Type **GROUP BY [Purchasing Mortgage Company ID]** as the third line.
- Type a semicolon (**;**) as the fourth line (Figure 10–23a).

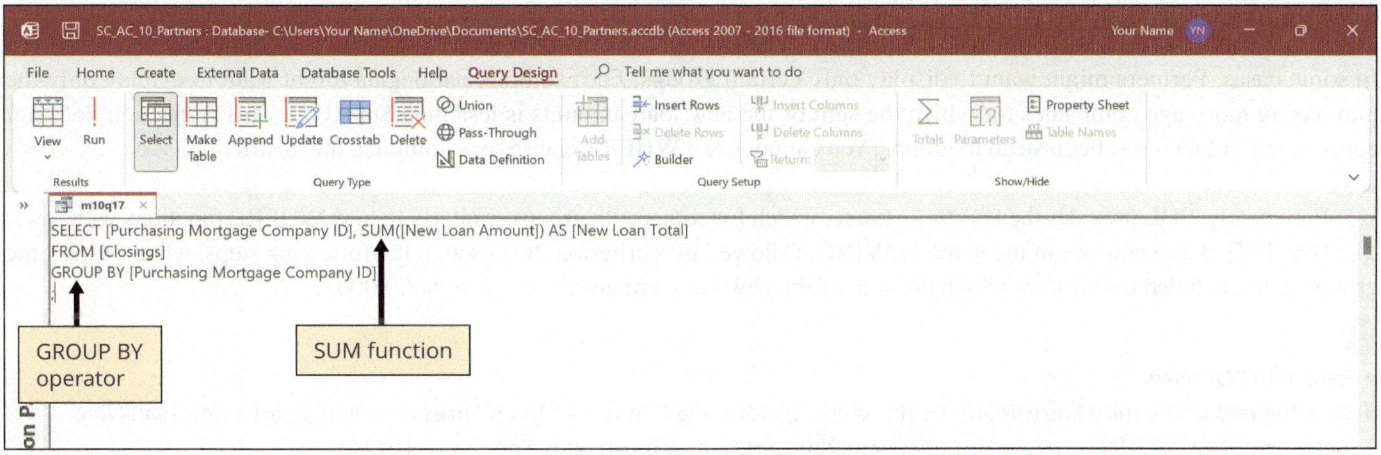

Figure 10–23(a): Query to Group By Purchasing Mortgage Company ID and Display New Loan Totals for Each Group

Q&A What is the purpose of the GROUP BY clause?
The GROUP BY clause causes the rows to be grouped by the indicated field. With this GROUP BY clause, the rows will be grouped by Purchasing Mortgage Company ID.

- View the results. If necessary, increase the widths of the columns to display their entire field names (Figure 10–23b).

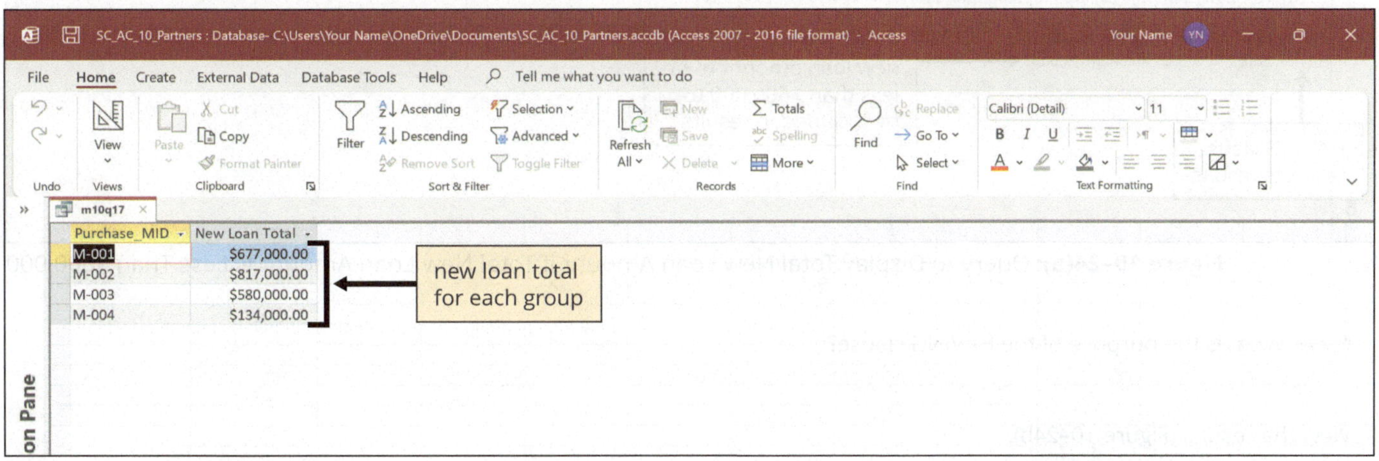

Figure 10–23(b): Query Results

2

- Save the query as **m10q18**.

Grouping Requirements

When rows are grouped, one line of output is produced for each group. The only output that SQL can display is statistics that are calculated for the group or fields whose values are the same for all rows in a group. For example, when grouping rows by purchasing mortgage company as in the previous query, it is appropriate to display the purchasing mortgage company ID, because the ID in one row in a group must be the same as the ID in any other row in the group. It is appropriate to display the sum of the new loan amounts because this is a statistic calculated for the group. It would not be appropriate to display a buyer ID, however, because the buyer varies on the rows in a group; the purchasing mortgage company ID is associated with many closings. SQL would not be able to determine which buyer ID to display for the group. SQL will display an error message if you attempt to display a field that is not appropriate for the query, such as the buyer ID.

To Restrict the Groups That Appear

In some cases, Partners might want to display only certain groups. For example, paralegals might want to display only the purchasing mortgage companies for which the sum of the new loan amounts is less than $600,000. This restriction does not apply to individual rows, but instead to groups. You cannot use a WHERE clause to accomplish this restriction. **Why?** WHERE applies only to rows, not groups.

Fortunately, SQL provides the **HAVING clause**, which functions with groups similarly to how WHERE functions with rows. The HAVING clause consists of the word, HAVING, followed by a criterion. It is used in the following steps, which restrict the groups to be included to those for which the sum of the new loan amounts is less than $600,000.

1

- Return to SQL view.
- Click the end of the third line (GROUP BY [Purchasing Mortgage Company ID]) and press ENTER to insert a new blank line.
- Type **HAVING SUM([New Loan Amount])<600000** as the new fourth line. See Figure 10–24a.

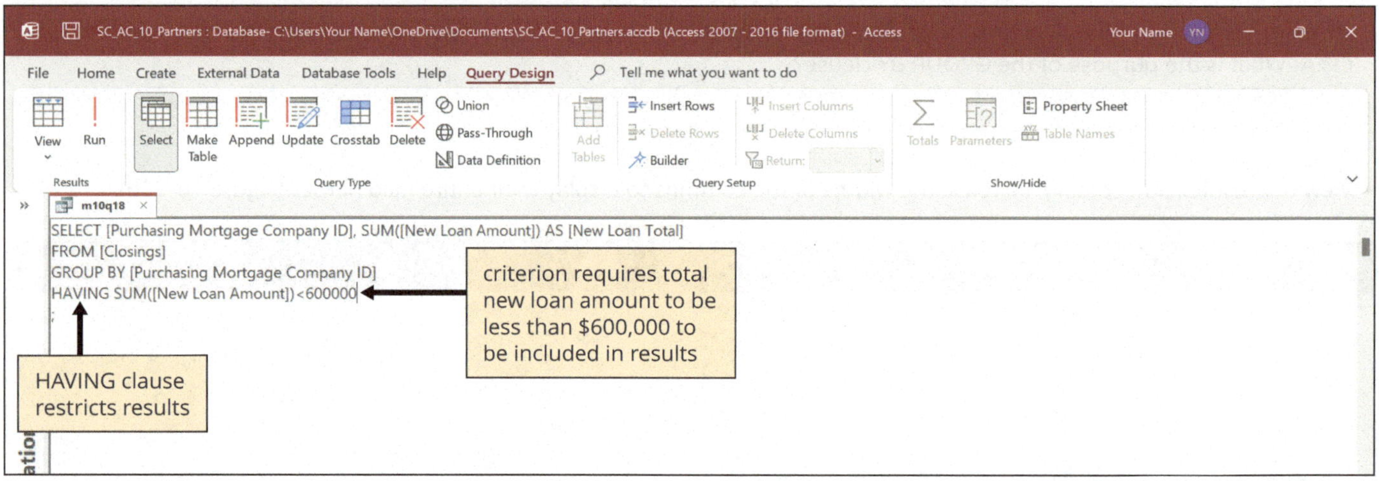

Figure 10–24(a): Query to Display Total New Loan Amount if Total New Loan Amount Is Less Than $600,000

Q&A What is the purpose of the HAVING clause?
The HAVING clause restricts the groups that will be included in the results to only those satisfying the indicated criteria.

- View the results (Figure 10–24b).

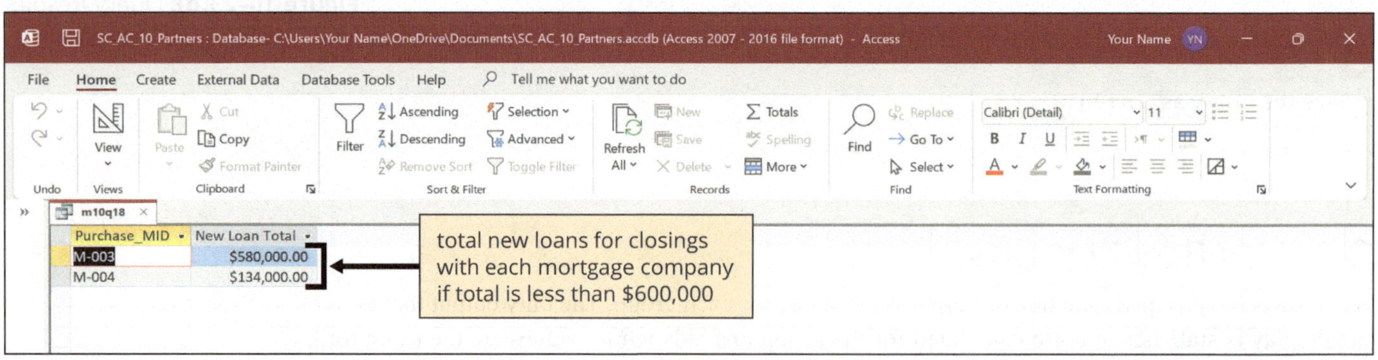

Figure 10–24(b): Query Results

2

- Save the query as **m10q19**.

BTW

BETWEEN Operator

The BETWEEN operator allows you to search for a range of values in one field. For example, to find all closings where the new loan amount is between $100,000 and $200,000, the WHERE clause would be WHERE [New Loan Amount] BETWEEN 100000 AND 200000.

Consider This

How do you determine grouping when creating a query?
Examine the question or request to determine whether records should be organized by some common characteristic.

- **Determine whether data is to be grouped in some fashion.** Examine the requirements for the query to see if they contain individual rows or information about groups of rows.
- **Determine the field or fields on which grouping is to take place.** By which field is the data to be grouped? Look to see if the requirements indicate a field along with several group calculations.
- **Determine which fields or calculations are appropriate to display.** When rows are grouped, one line of output is produced for each group. The only output that can appear are statistics that are calculated for the group or fields whose values are the same for all rows in a group. For example, it would make sense to display the mortgage company ID, because all the closings in the group have the same mortgage company ID. It would not make sense to display the Buyer ID, because the Buyer ID will vary from one row in a group to another. SQL could not determine which Buyer ID to display for the group.

Break Point: If you wish to take a break, this is a good place to do so. You can quit Access now. To resume at a later time, start Access, open the database called SC_AC_10_Partners.accdb, create a new query in SQL view, and continue following the steps from this location forward.

Joining Tables

Many queries require data from more than one table. Just as with creating queries in Design view, SQL should provide a way to join tables, that is, to find rows in two tables that have identical values in matching fields. In SQL, this is accomplished through appropriate criteria following the word, WHERE.

If you want to list the closing date, buyer ID, and name of the buyer for all closings, you need data from both the Closings and Buyers tables. The Buyer ID field is in both tables, the Closing Date field is only in the Closings table, and the Buyer Name field is only in the Buyers table. You need to access both tables in your SQL query, as follows:

1. In the SELECT clause, you indicate all fields you want to appear.
2. In the FROM clause, you list all tables involved in the query.
3. In the WHERE clause, you give the criterion that will restrict the data to be retrieved to only those rows included in both of the two tables, that is, to the rows that have common values in matching fields.

Qualifying Fields

If there is a problem with matching fields, such as a field named Buyer ID that exists in both tables, it is necessary to **qualify** Buyer ID, that is, to specify to which field in which table you are referring. You do this by preceding the name of the field with the name of the table, followed by a period. The Buyer ID field in the Buyers table, for example, is [Buyers].[Buyer ID]. The Buyer ID field in the Closings table would then be indicated as [Closings].[Buyer ID]. If the fields had slightly different names (such as Buyer ID and Buyer), it would not be necessary to qualify the fields; however, it is permissible to qualify fields even if there is no confusion. For example, instead of [Buyer Name], you could type [Buyers].[Buyer Name] to indicate the Buyer Name field in the Buyers table, even though no other table contains a field called Buyer Name. Some people prefer to qualify all fields, and this is not a bad approach. In this text, you will only qualify fields when it is necessary to do so and for learning purposes.

BTW
Qualifying Fields
There is no space on either side of the period that is used to separate the table name from the field name. Adding a space will result in an error message.

To Join Tables

Partners wants to list the closing date, buyer ID, and buyer name for all closings. The following steps create a query to join the tables using an INNER JOIN. **Why?** The data comes from two tables. The steps also order the results by closing date.

1

- If necessary, return to SQL view and delete the previous query.
- Type **SELECT [Closings].[Buyer ID], [Closings].[Closing Date], [Buyers].[Buyer ID], [Buyers].[Buyer Name]** as the first line of the command.
- Type **FROM [Closings] INNER JOIN [Buyers] ON [Closings].[Buyer ID] = [Buyers].[Buyer ID]** as the second line.

Q&A Why does the FROM clause contain more than one table?
The query involves fields from both tables.

- Type **ORDER BY [Closings].[Closing Date]** as the third line, and then type a semicolon (**;**) on the fourth line (Figure 10–25a).

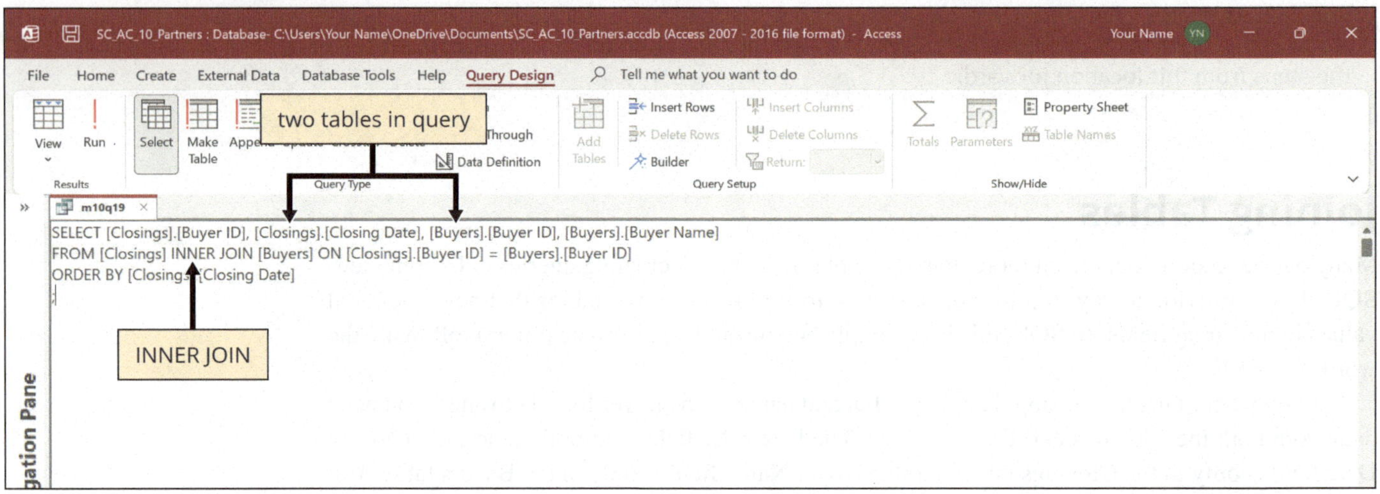

Figure 10–25(a): Query to Join Tables and Order by Closing Date

- View the results (Figure 10–25b).

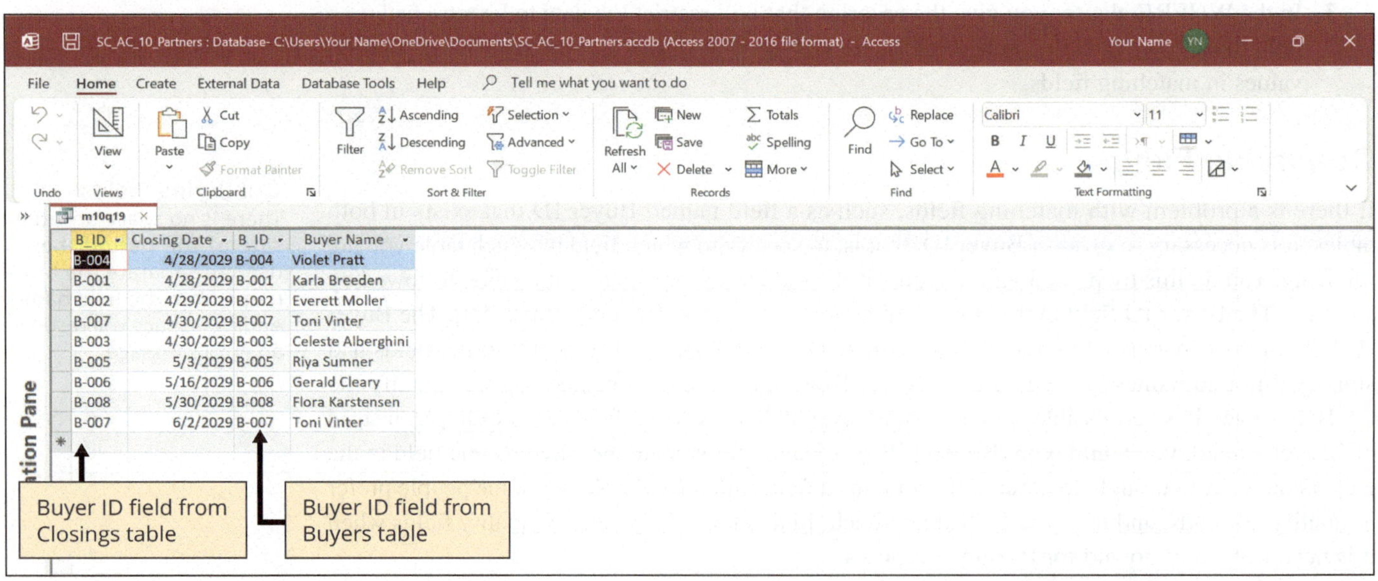

Figure 10–25(b): Query Results

2

- Save the query as **m10q20**.

To Restrict the Records in a Join

You can restrict the records to be included in a join by creating a compound criterion. The compound criterion will include the criterion necessary to join the tables along with a criterion to restrict the records. The criteria will be connected with AND. **Why?** Both the criterion that determines the records to be joined and the criterion to restrict the records must be true.

Partners would like to modify the previous query so that only closings whose start date is prior to May 1, 2029, are included. The following steps modify the previous query appropriately. The WHERE command is included as the join. The date is enclosed between hash signs (#), which is the date format used in the Access version of SQL.

1

- Return to SQL view and delete the previous query.
- Type **SELECT [Closings].[Buyer ID], [Closings].[Closing Date], [Buyers].[Buyer ID], [Buyers].[Buyer Name]** for the first line.
- Type **FROM [Closings], [Buyers]** for the second line.
- Type **WHERE [Closings].[Buyer ID] = [Buyers].[Buyer ID]** as the third line.
- Type **AND [Closing Date]<#5/1/2029#** for the fourth line.
- Type **ORDER BY [Closings].[Closing Date]** as the fifth line, and then type a semicolon (**;**) on the sixth line (Figure 10–26a).

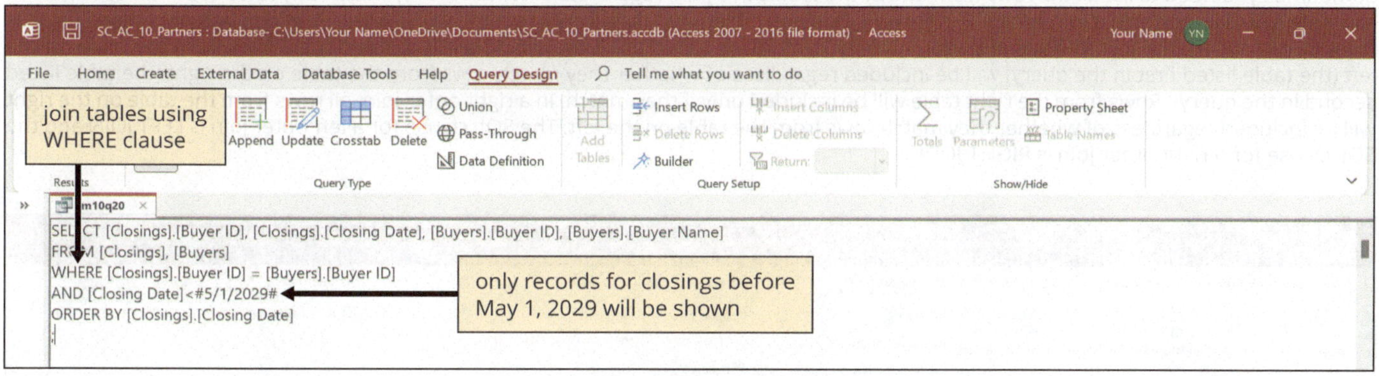

Figure 10–26(a): Query to Display Closings Before May 1, 2029

Q&A Could I use other formats for the date in the criterion?

Yes. You could type #May 1, 2029# or #1-May-2029#.

- View the results (Figure 10–26b).

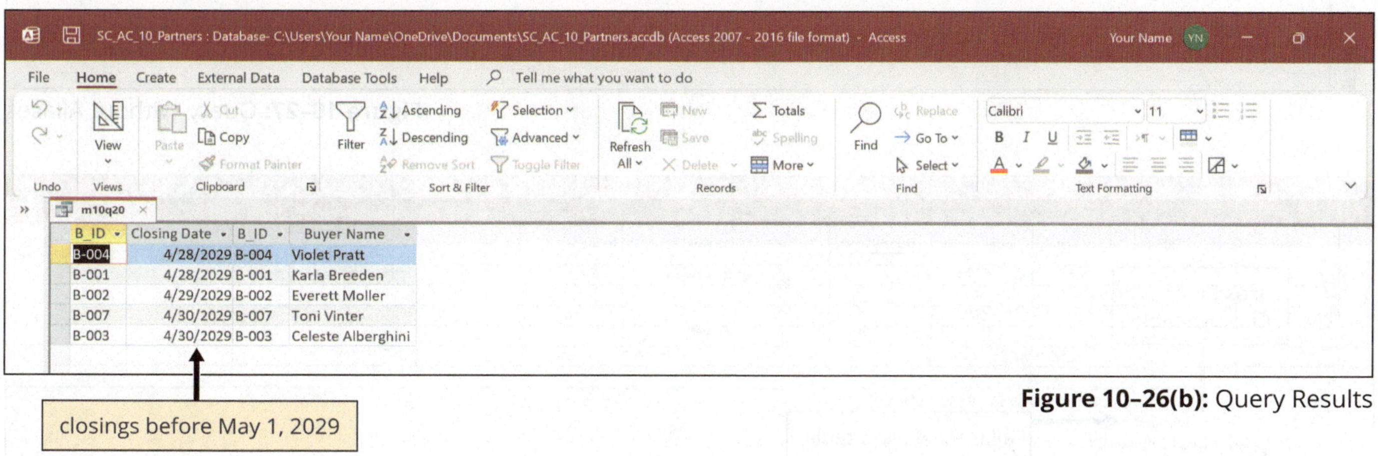

Figure 10–26(b): Query Results

2

- Save the query as **m10q21**.

BTW
Inner Joins
A join that compares the tables in the FROM clause and lists only those rows that satisfy the condition in the WHERE clause is called an inner join. As you saw earlier in this module, SQL has an INNER JOIN clause. You could replace the second line of the query shown in Figure 10–26a with FROM [Buyers] INNER JOIN [Closings] ON [Buyers].[Buyer ID] = [Closings].[Buyer ID] to get the same results as shown in Figure 10–26b.

Aliases

When tables appear in the FROM clause, you can give each table an **alias**, or an alternative name, that you can use in the rest of the statement. You create an alias by typing the name of the table, pressing SPACEBAR, and then typing the name of the alias. No commas or periods are necessary to separate the two names.

You can use an alias for two basic reasons: for simplicity or to join a table to itself. Figures 10–27 and 10–28 show the same query, but Figure 10–28 assigns the letter, C, as an alias for the Closings table and the letter, B, as an alias for the Buyers table. The query in Figure 10–28 is less complex. Whenever you need to qualify a field name, you can use the alias. Thus, you only need to type C.[Buyer ID] rather than [Closings].[Buyer ID].

BTW
Outer Joins
Sometimes you need to list all the rows from one of the tables in a join, regardless of whether they match any rows in the other table. For example, you can perform a join on the Buyers and Closings tables that displays all records in Closings—but displays only those records from Buyers where the joined fields are equal. This type of join is called an outer join. In a left outer join, all rows from the table on the left (the table listed first in the query) will be included regardless of whether they match rows from the table on the right (the table listed second in the query). Rows from the right table will be included only if they match. In a right outer join, all rows from the table on the right will be included regardless of whether they match rows from the table on the left. The SQL clause for a left outer join is LEFT JOIN and the SQL clause for a right outer join is RIGHT JOIN.

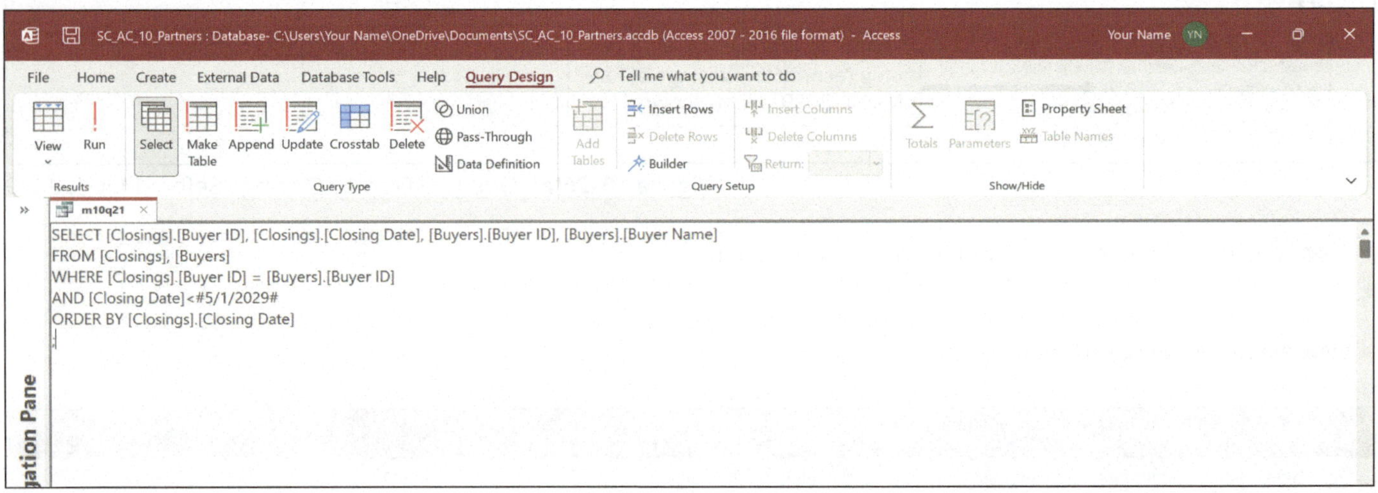

Figure 10–27: Query Without Aliases

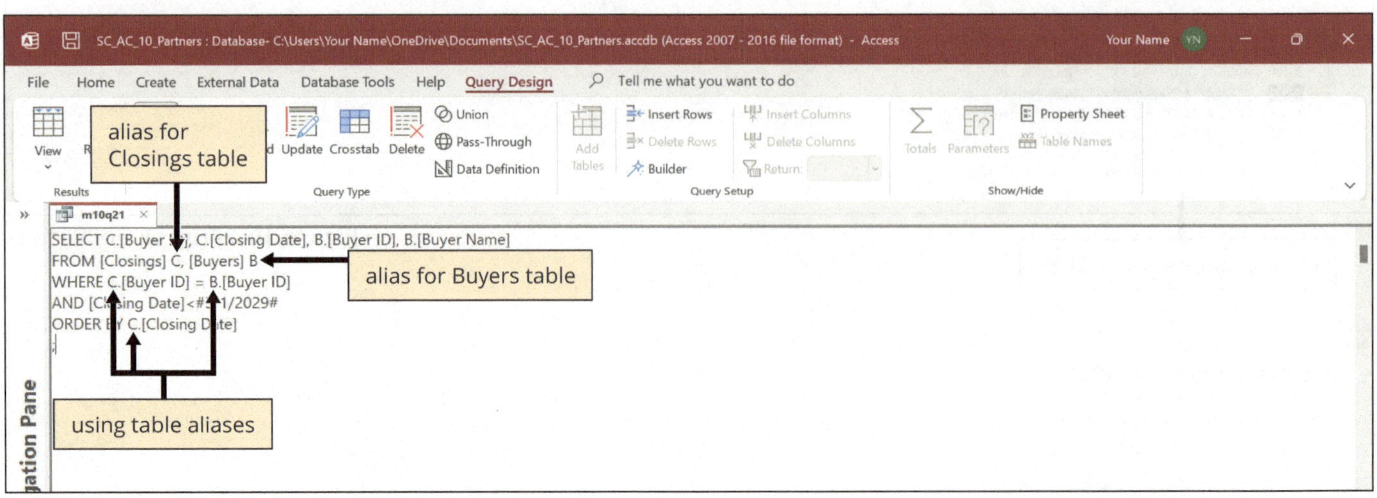

Figure 10–28: Query With Aliases

To Join a Table to Itself

The other use of aliases is in joining a table to itself. An example of this type of join would enable Partners to find buyer ID and names for every buyer using the same real estate agent. One such pair, for example, would be Buyer ID B-003 (Celeste Alberghini) and Buyer ID B-006 (Gerald Cleary) because both buyers are using the same real estate agent (Jeong-Ho Azzara). Because there are two buyers working with this agent, you will see the buyers for this agent appear on more than one line in the results.

If there were two Buyers tables in the database, Partners could obtain the results they want by simply joining the two Buyers tables and looking for rows where the buyer agent were the same. Even though there is only one Buyers table, you can actually treat the Buyers table as two tables in the query by creating two aliases. You would change the FROM clause to:

FROM [Buyers] A, [Buyers] B

SQL treats this clause as a query of two tables. The clause assigns the first Buyers table the letter, A, as an alias. It also assigns the letter, B, as an alias for the Buyers table. The fact that both tables are really the single Buyers table is not a problem. The following steps assign two aliases (A and B) to the Buyers table and list the Buyer ID and Buyer Name of both records using the same real estate agent. The steps also include a criterion to ensure A.[Buyer ID] < B.[Buyer ID]. **Why?** If you did not include this criterion, the query would contain four times as many results. On the first row in the results, for example, the first Buyer ID is B-003 and the second is B-006. Without this criterion, there would additionally be a row on which both the first and second Buyer IDs are B-003, a row on which both are B-006, and a row on which the first is B-006 and the second is B-003. This criterion only selects the one row on which the first Buyer ID (B-003) is less than the second Buyer ID (B-006).

1

- Return to SQL view and delete the previous query.
- Type **SELECT A.[Buyer ID], A.[Buyer Name], B.[Buyer ID], B.[Buyer Name], A.[Buyer Real Estate Agent]** as the first line of the command to select the fields to display in the query result.
- Type **FROM Buyers A, Buyers B** as the second line to create the aliases for the first and second Buyers tables.
- Type **WHERE A.[Buyer Real Estate Agent] = B.[Buyer Real Estate Agent]** as the third line to indicate that the agents in each table must match.
- Type **AND A.[Buyer ID] < B.[Buyer ID]** as the fourth line to indicate that the Buyer ID from the first table must be less than the Buyer ID from the second table.
- Type **ORDER BY A.[Buyer ID], B.[Buyer ID]** as the fifth line to ensure that the results are sorted by the Buyer ID from the first table and further sorted by the Buyer ID from the second table.
- Type a semicolon (**;**) on the sixth line (Figure 10–29a).

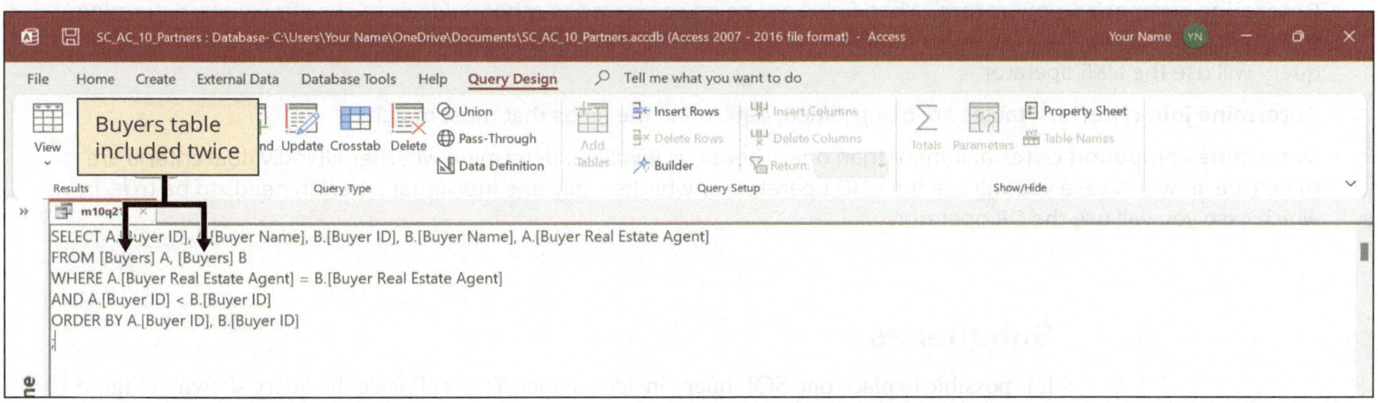

Figure 10–29(a): Query for Buyers Using the Same Agents

- View the results (Figure 10–29b).

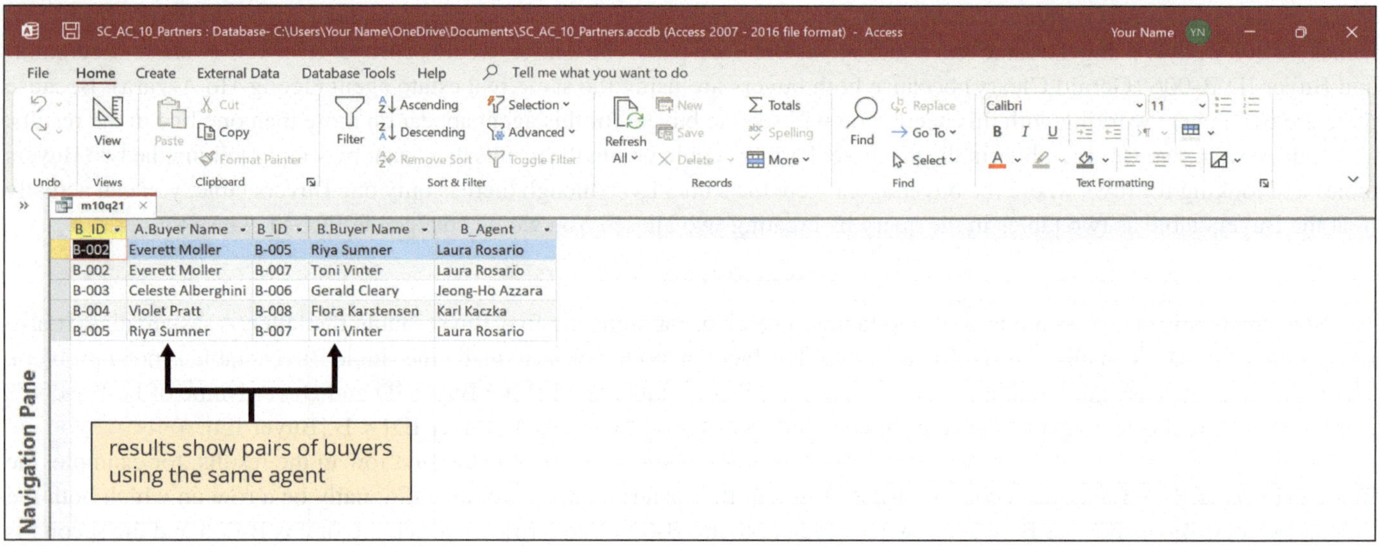

Figure 10–29(b): Query Results

2

- Save the query as **m10q22**.

Consider This

How do you determine criteria when creating a query?

Examine the query or request to determine any restrictions or conditions that records must satisfy to be included in the results.

- **Determine the fields involved in the criteria.** For any criterion, determine the fields that are included. Determine the data types for these fields. If the criterion uses a value that corresponds to a Text field, enclose the value in single quotation marks. If the criterion uses a date, enclose the value between hash signs (for example, #5/1/2029#).
- **Determine comparison operators.** When fields are being compared to other fields or to specific values, determine the appropriate comparison operator (equals, less than, greater than, and so on). If a wildcard is involved, then the query will use the LIKE operator.
- **Determine join criteria.** If tables are being joined, determine the fields that must match.
- **Determine compound criteria.** If more than one criterion is involved, determine whether all individual criteria are to be true, in which case you will use the AND operator, or whether only one individual criterion needs to be true, in which case you will use the OR operator.

Subqueries

It is possible to place one SQL query inside another. You will place the query shown in Figure 10–30 inside another query. When you have done so, it will be called a **subquery**, which is an inner query contained within parentheses that is evaluated first. Then the outer query can use the results of the subquery to find its results. In some cases, using a subquery can be the simplest way to produce the desired results.

To Use a Subquery

The following steps use the query shown in Figure 10–30 as a subquery. **Why?** Partners can use this query to select buyers who are being represented by Partners in their property purchases. After the subquery is evaluated, the outer query will select the buyer ID, closing date, purchasing mortgage company, and status for those closings where the Buyer ID is in the list produced by the subquery.

1

- Return to SQL view and delete the previous query.
- To first test the inner query, type **SELECT [Buyers].[Buyer ID]** as the first line of the command.
- Type **FROM [Buyers]** as the second line.
- Type **WHERE [Buyers].[Buyer Attorney] = 'Partners'** as the third line and type a semicolon (**;**) on the fourth line (Figure 10–30a).

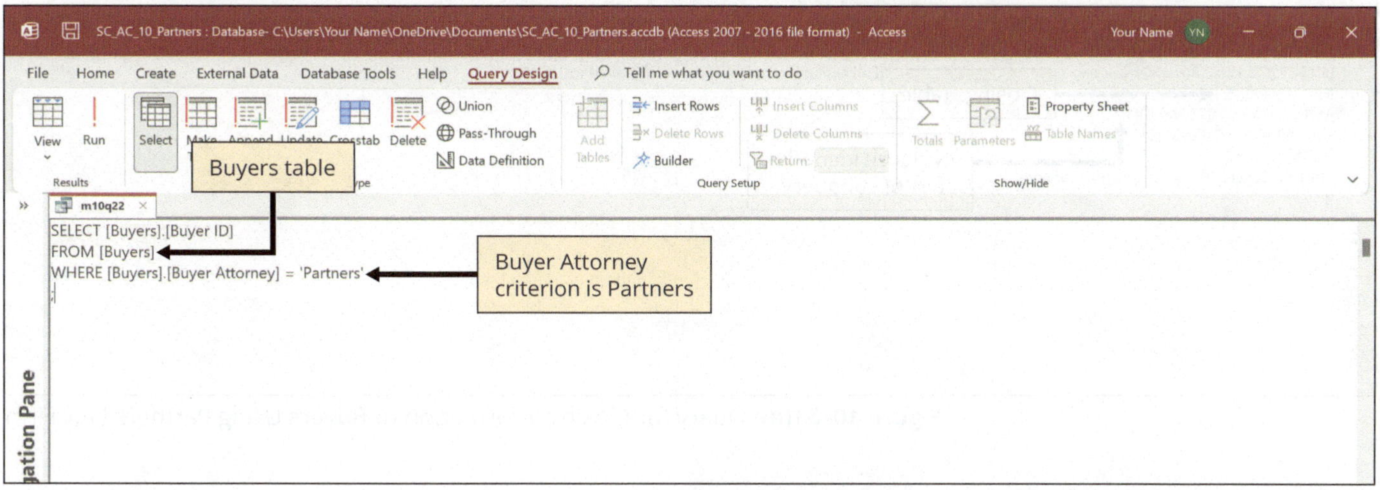

Figure 10–30(a): Test Query for Buyers Using Partners Law Firm

- View the results (Figure 10–30b). You will not save the current query. Now that you have confirmed that the subquery works, you will delete it and then place it in the correct location in the new query.

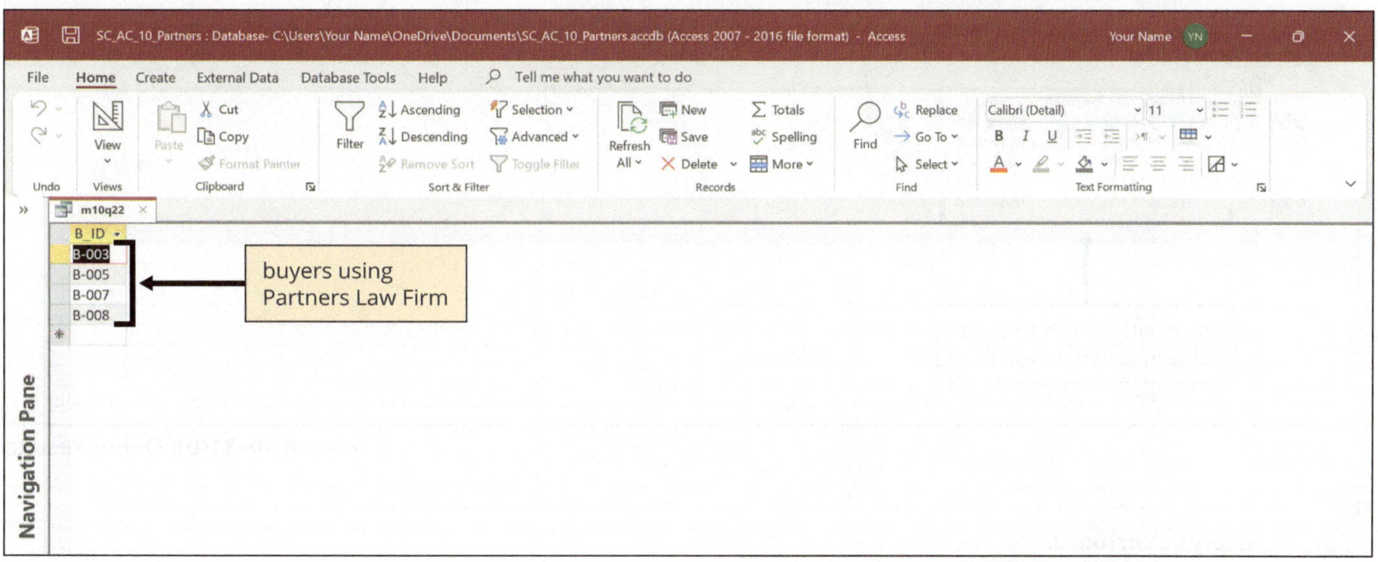

Figure 10–30(b): Test Query Results

2

- Return to SQL view and delete the previous query.
- To build the query and subquery, type **SELECT [Closings].[Buyer ID], [Closings].[Closing Date], [Closings].[Purchasing Mortgage Company ID], [Closings].[Status]** as the first line of the command.
- Type **FROM [Closings]** as the second line.
- Type **WHERE [Closings].[Buyer ID] IN** as the third line.

- Type **(SELECT [Buyers].[Buyer ID])** as the fourth line.
- Type **FROM [Buyers]** as the fifth line.
- Type **WHERE [Buyers].[Buyer Attorney] = 'Partners')** as the sixth line and type a semicolon (**;**) on the seventh line (Figure 10–31a).

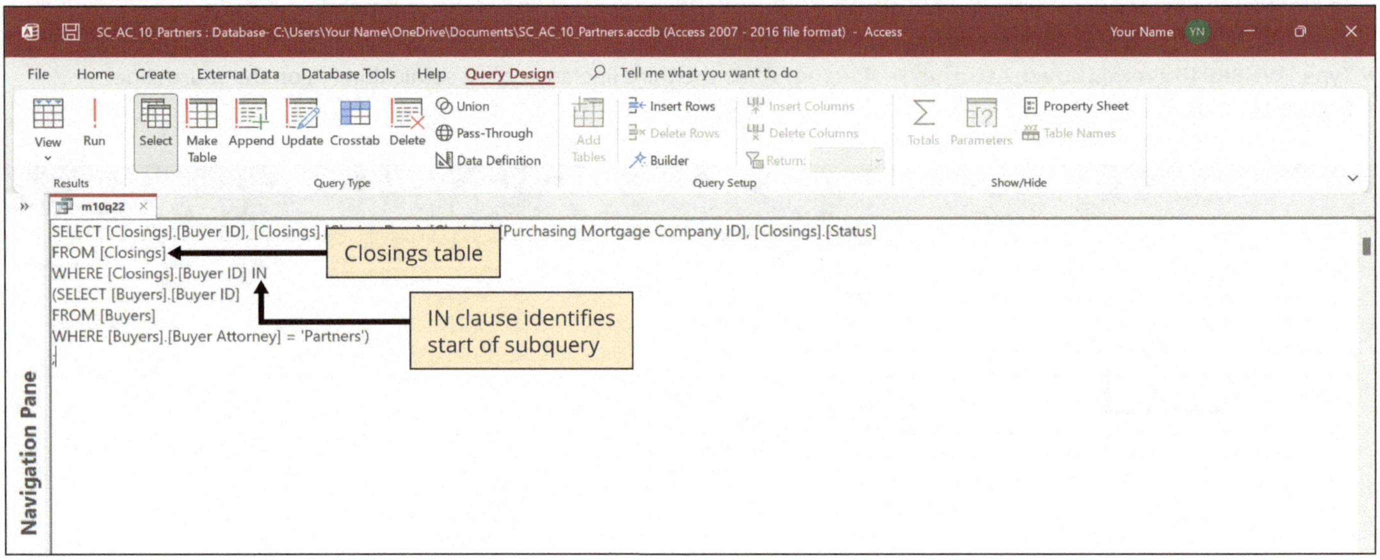

Figure 10–31(a): Query for Closing Information of Buyers Using Partners Law Firm

- View the results (Figure 10–31b).

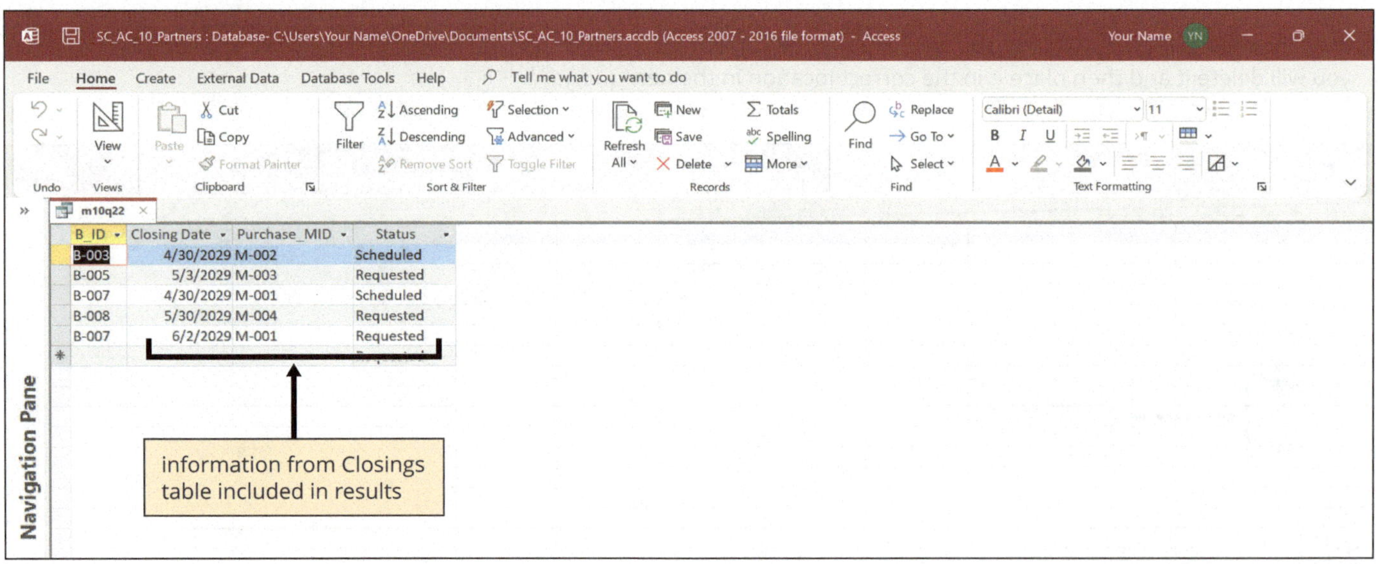

Figure 10–31(b): Query Results

3

- Save the query as **m10q23**.

Using an IN Clause

The query in Figure 10–31 uses an IN clause with a subquery. You can also use an IN clause with a list as an alternative to an OR criterion when the OR criterion involves a single field. For example, to find properties whose city is Donahue, Jonestown, Hartford, or Woodstock, the criterion using IN would be the following:

City IN ('Donahue', 'Jonestown', 'Hartford', 'Woodstock')

The corresponding OR criterion would be the following:

City='Donahue' OR City='Jonestown' OR City='Hartford' OR City='Woodstock'

The choice of whether to use an IN clause with a list or an OR criterion is a matter of personal preference.

You can also use this type of IN clause when creating queries in Design view. To use the criterion in the previous paragraph, for example, include the City field in the design grid and enter the criterion in the Criteria row.

Comparison with Access-Generated SQL

When you create a query in Design view, Access automatically creates a corresponding SQL query that is similar to the queries you have created in this module. The Access query shown in Figure 10–32, for example, was created in Design view and includes the Property ID, Association, Property Street, and Property City fields. The Property City field has a criterion (Hartford).

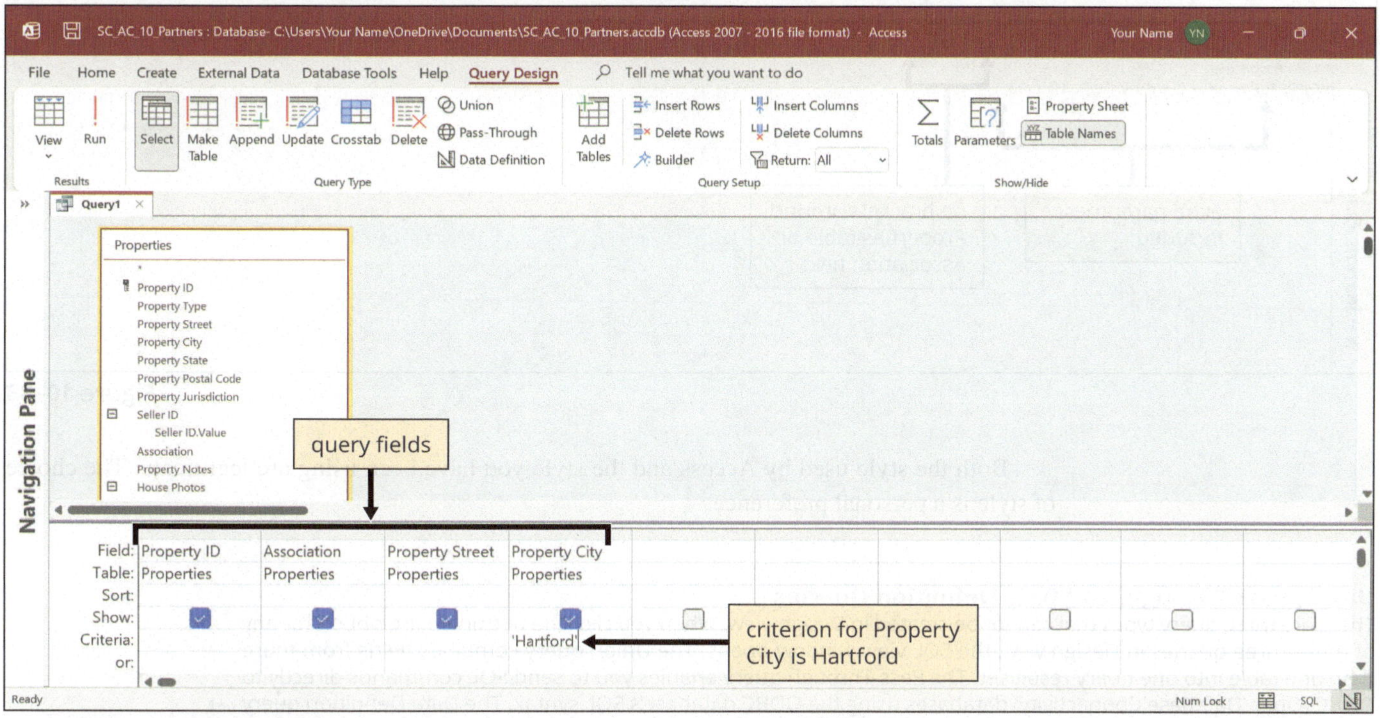

Figure 10–32(a): Query to List Property ID, Association, Property Street, and Property City for Properties in Hartford

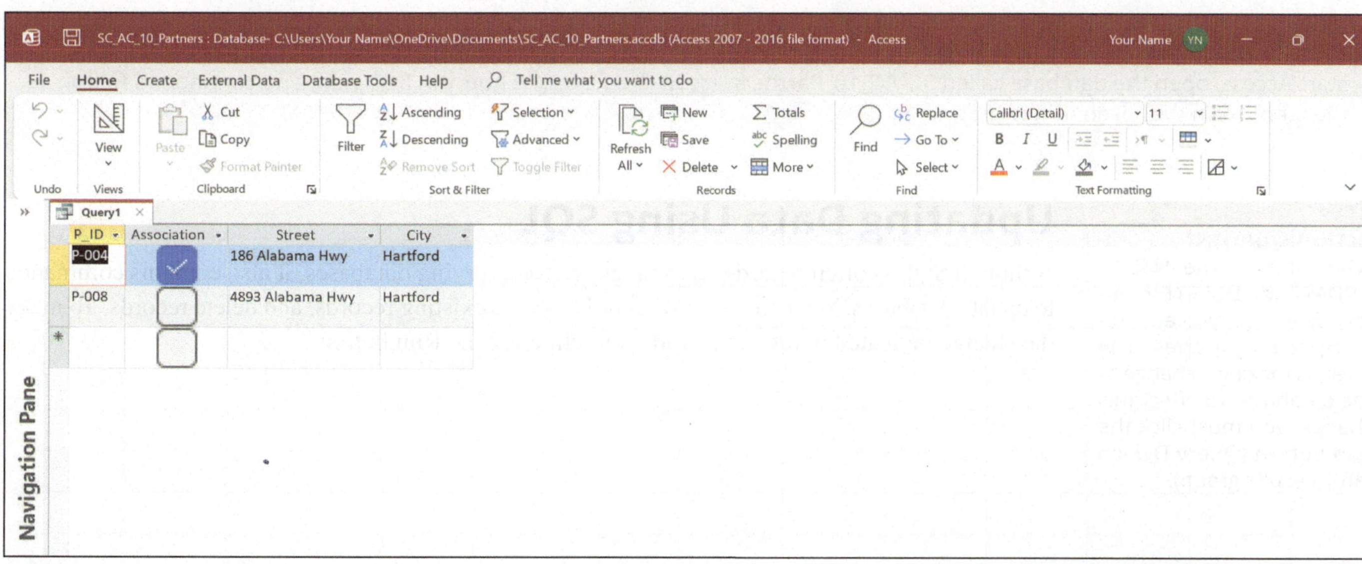

Figure 10–32(b): Query Results

The SQL query that Access generates in correspondence to the Design view query is shown in Figure 10–33. The query is very similar to the queries you have entered, but there are three slight differences. First, the Properties.[Property ID], Properties.[Association], Properties.[Property Street], and Properties.[Property City] fields are qualified, even though they do not need to be; only one table is involved in the query, so no qualification is necessary. Second, the Properties table and the Association field are not enclosed in square brackets. The table and field names are legitimately not enclosed in square brackets because there are no spaces or other special characters in each name. Finally, there are extra parentheses in the WHERE clause.

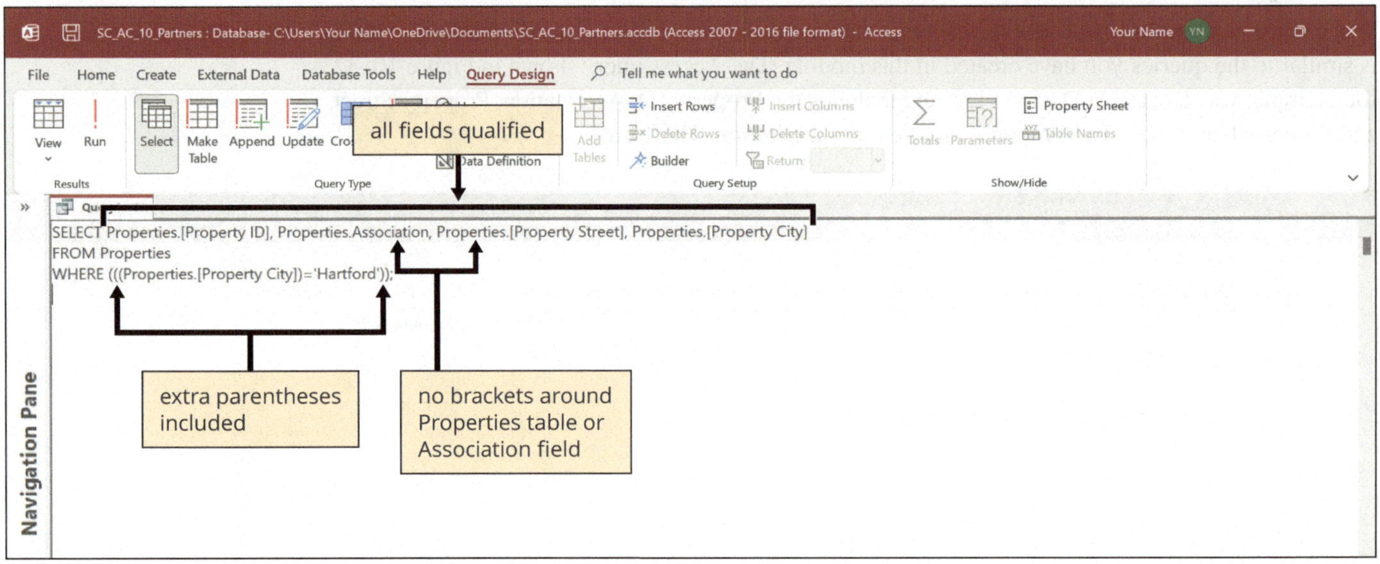

Figure 10–33

Both the style used by Access and the style you have been using are legitimate. The choice of style is a personal preference.

BTW

Union, Pass-Through, and Data Definition Queries

There are three query types that cannot be created in Design view. When you click the button on the ribbon for any of these three queries in Design view, the SQL view window opens. The Union query combines fields from more than one table into one query result set. The Pass-Through query enables you to send SQL commands directly to ODBC (Open Database Connectivity) databases using the ODBC database's SQL syntax. The Data Definition query allows you to create or alter database tables or create indexes in Access directly.

Break Point: If you wish to take a break, this is a good place to do so. You can quit Access now. To resume at a later time, start Access, open the database called SC_AC_10_Partners.accdb, create a new query in SQL view, and continue to follow the steps from this location forward.

BTW

Action Queries

When you use the INSERT, UPDATE, or DELETE commands in SQL, you are creating action queries. The query is making a change to the database. To effect this change, you must click the Run button (Query Design tab | Results group).

Updating Data Using SQL

Although SQL is often regarded as a language for querying databases, it also contains commands to update databases. You can add new records, update existing records, and delete records. To make the change indicated in the command, you will click the Run button.

To Use an INSERT Command

You can add records to a table using the SQL INSERT command. The command consists of the words, INSERT INTO, followed by the name of the table into which the record is to be inserted. Next is the word, VALUE, followed by the values for the fields in the record. Values for text fields must be enclosed within quotation marks. **Why?** Just as you needed to type the quotation marks when you used text data in a criterion, you need to do so when you use text values in an INSERT INTO command. The following steps add a record to the Workshop Enrollments table. The record is for Buyer ID B-007 and Workshop W-01, and it indicates the workshop will be offered for a total of 4 hours, of which 0 hours have already been spent.

1

- If necessary, return to SQL view and delete the existing query.
- Type **INSERT INTO [Workshop Enrollments]** as the first line of the command.
- Type **VALUES ('B-007', 'W-01', 4, 0)** as the second line.
- Type a semicolon (**;**) on the third line (Figure 10–34).

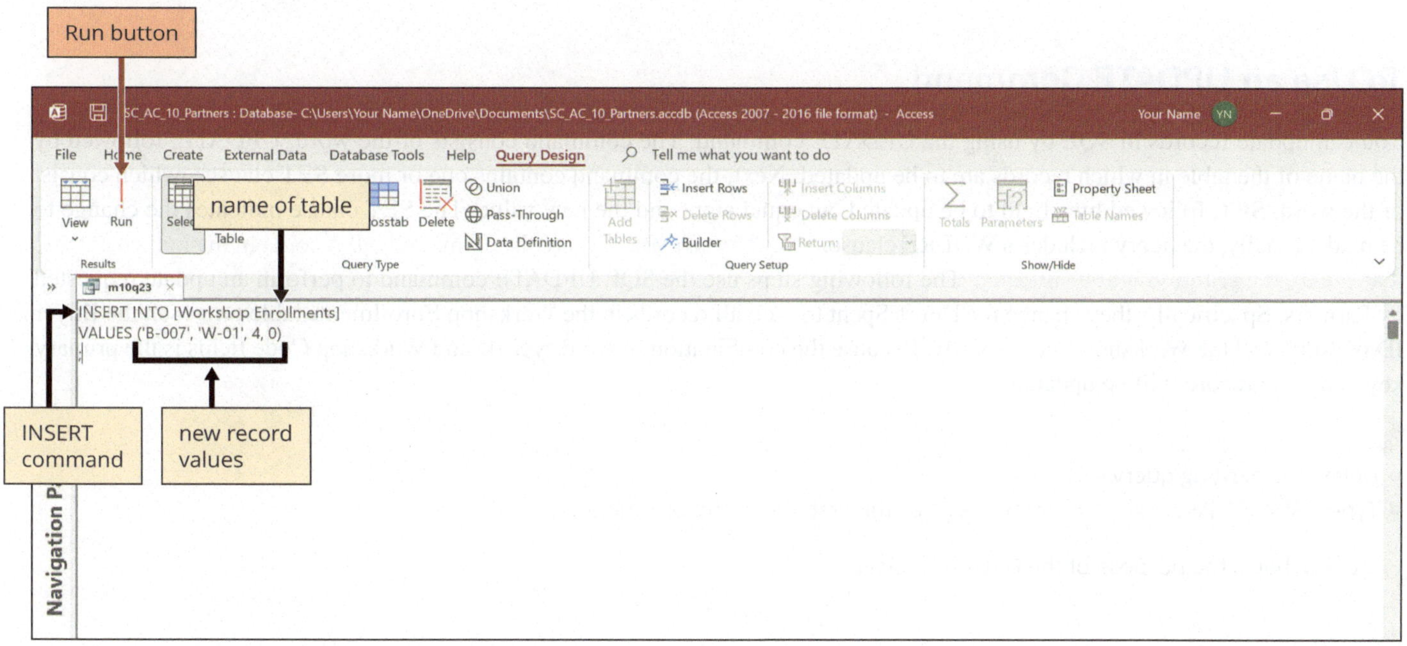

Figure 10–34

Q&A What is the purpose of the INSERT INTO clause?
The clause indicates the table into which data is to be inserted.

What is the purpose of the VALUES clause?
The VALUES clause, which typically extends over two lines, indicates the values that are to be inserted into a new record in the table. For readability, it is common to place the word, VALUES, on one line and the actual values on a separate line.

2

- Run the query by clicking the Run button (Query Design tab | Results group).
- When Access displays a message indicating one row is to be appended (inserted), click the Yes button to insert the row.

Q&A I clicked the View button and did not get the message. Do I need to click the Run button?
Yes. You are making a change to the database by adding a record to a table, so you must click the Run button, or the change will not be made.

How can I see if the record was actually inserted?
Use a SELECT query to view the records in the Workshop Enrollments table, or you can just open the table and view the records.

BTW
Touch and Pointers
Remember that if you are using your finger on a touch screen, you will not see the pointer.

3

- Save the query as **m10q24**.

Q&A Why does this query have a different icon in the Navigation Pane than the other queries do?
In the Navigation Pane, the query is saved in a separate location from the other queries and is marked with a different icon because this query is an append query, that is, it appends (or adds) data in a table when the query is run rather than simply displaying data gathered from one or more tables. If you point your cursor to the append query in the Navigation Pane, the ScreenTip shows not only the query name but also the table affected by the query. All this information helps users decide if or when to use a query that will make changes to data. Other query types with different icons include update queries and delete queries. Because all these queries make changes to data in one or more tables, you might choose to first open the query in Design view or SQL view to evaluate or edit the query before running it.

To Use an UPDATE Command

You can update records in SQL by using the UPDATE command. The command consists of the word, UPDATE, followed by the name of the table in which records are to be updated. Next, the command contains one or more SET clauses, which consist of the word, SET, followed by a field to be updated, an equal sign, and the new value. The SET clause indicates the change to be made. Finally, the query includes a WHERE clause. **Why?** When you execute the command, all records in the indicated table that satisfy the criterion will be updated. The following steps use the SQL UPDATE command to perform an update requested by Partners. Specifically, they change the Hours Spent to 4 on all records in the Workshop Enrollments table on which the Buyer ID is B-007 and the Workshop Code is W-01. Because the combination of the Buyer ID and Workshop Code fields is the primary key, only one record will be updated.

1

- Delete the existing query.
- Type **UPDATE [Workshop Enrollments]** as the first line of the command.

Q&A What is the purpose of the UPDATE clause?
The UPDATE clause indicates the table to be updated. This clause indicates that the update is to be applied to the Workshop Enrollments table.

- Type **SET [Hours Spent]=4** as the second line.

Q&A What is the purpose of the SET clause?
The SET clause indicates the field to be changed as well as the new value. This SET clause indicates the hours spent value is to be set to 4.

Why did I not have to type spaces on either side of the equals sign in the SET clause?
Spaces around comparative operators, such as equals (=) and greater than (>), are not required when typing statements in SQL. Whether or not you type the spaces around these operators is a matter of personal preference. In this course, spaces are included when they help improve readability of the statement in the instructions. For shorter statements such as this one, spaces do not contribute to readability.

- Type **WHERE [Buyer ID]='B-007'** as the third line.
- Type **AND [Workshop Code]='W-01'** as the fourth line, and then type a semicolon (;) on the fifth line (Figure 10–35).

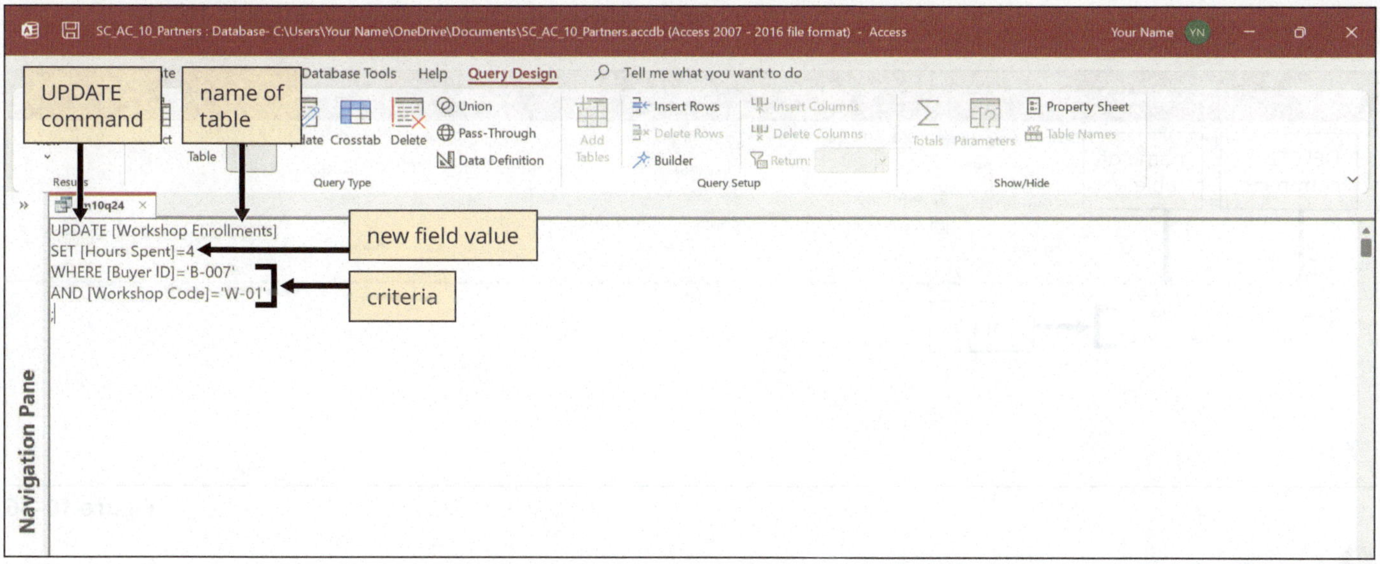

Figure 10–35

Q&A Do I need to change a field to a specific value such as 4?

No, you could use an expression. For example, to add $1,000 to the New Loan Amount in the Closings table, the SET clause would be SET [New Loan Amount] = [New Loan Amount]+100.

2

- Run the query.
- When Access displays a message indicating one row is to be updated, click the Yes button to update the row.

Q&A How can I see if the update actually occurred?

Use a SELECT query to view the records in the Workshop Enrollments table or open the table and view the results.

3

- Save the query as **m10q25**.

To Use a DELETE Command

You can delete records in SQL using the DELETE command. The command consists of DELETE FROM, followed by the name of the table from which records are to be deleted. Finally, you include a WHERE clause to specify the criteria. **Why?** When you execute the command, all records in the indicated table that satisfy the criteria will be deleted. The following steps use the SQL DELETE command to delete all records in the Workshop Enrollments table on which the Buyer ID is B-007, and the Workshop Code is W-01. Because the combination of the Buyer ID and Workshop Code fields is the primary key, only one record will be deleted.

1

- Delete the existing query.
- Type **DELETE FROM [Workshop Enrollments]** as the first line of the command.

Q&A What is the purpose of the DELETE clause?

The DELETE clause indicates the table from which records will be deleted. This DELETE clause indicates that records will be deleted from the Workshop Enrollments table.

- Type **WHERE [Buyer ID]='B-007'** as the second line.

- Type **AND [Workshop Code]='W-01'** as the third line and type a semicolon (;) on the fourth line (Figure 10–36).

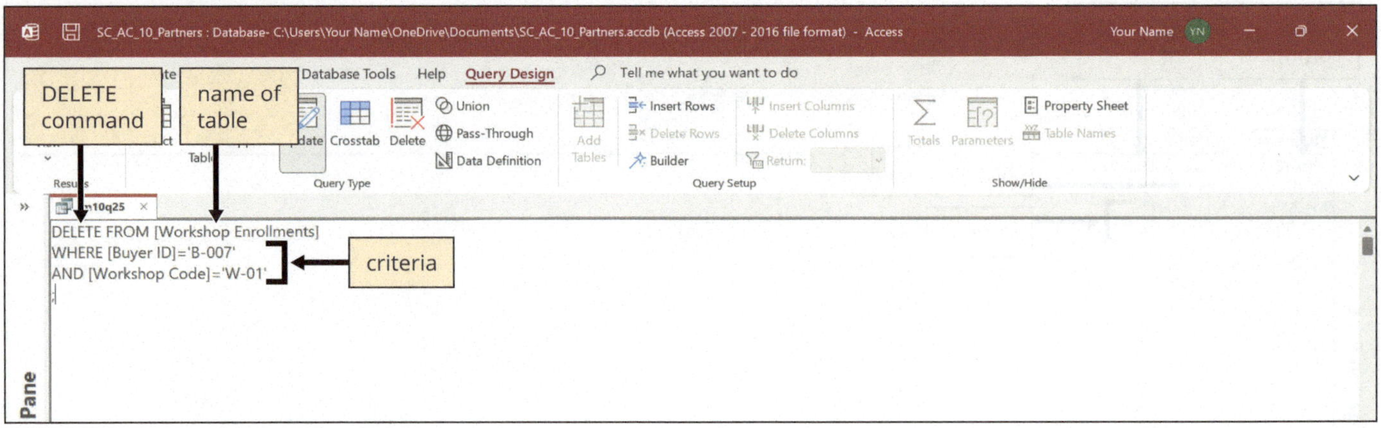

Figure 10–36

2

- Run the query.
- When Access displays a message indicating one row is to be deleted, click the Yes button to delete the row.

Q&A How can I see if the deletion actually occurred?
Use a SELECT query to view the records in the Workshop Enrollments table or open the table and view the results.

3

- Save the query as **m10q26**.
- Close the query.

Consider This

How do you determine any update operations to be performed?

Examine the database to determine if records must be added, updated, and/or deleted.

- **Determine INSERT operations.** Determine whether new records need to be added. Determine to which table they should be added.
- **Determine UPDATE operations.** Determine changes that need to be made to existing records. Which fields need to be changed? Which tables contain these fields? What criteria identify the rows that need to be changed?
- **Determine DELETE operations.** Determine which tables contain records that are to be deleted. What criteria identify the rows that need to be deleted?

Linking a Table to an Another File

Linking an Access database to data in other programs, such as an Excel worksheet, lets you work with this data in Access without having to maintain a copy of the Excel data in the database. When linking to an Excel workbook, or a named range in Excel, Access creates a new table in the database that is linked to the source cells. New records can be added, records edited, and records deleted in the Excel file, but only in Excel. You cannot make changes to the Excel data in the linked Access table.

To Link a Table to an Outside Data Source

Partners created a file containing information about real estate agents, allowing the practice to refer clients to agents who have worked well with Partners for past closings. You will link to the Excel file and then add a record to the file in Excel. **Why?** Linking to an external file allows you to store and access information in other file formats. When you link an Excel file in the database, an Excel icon appears next to the table name. The following steps first create a copy of the Partners Agents file so you can later make changes to it, and then create a link to the file in a database table.

1

- Open the spreadsheet, Support_AC_10_Agents.xlsx, which is located in the Data Files folder.
- Save the file to your hard drive, OneDrive, or other storage location using the file name, **SC_AC_10_Agents**. Saving the spreadsheet with a new name preserves the original support file in case you need to return to this project. Enable the content and then close the file.

2

- With the Partners database open, click the External Data tab.
- Click the New Data Source button arrow and point to From File (Figure 10–37), and then click Excel.

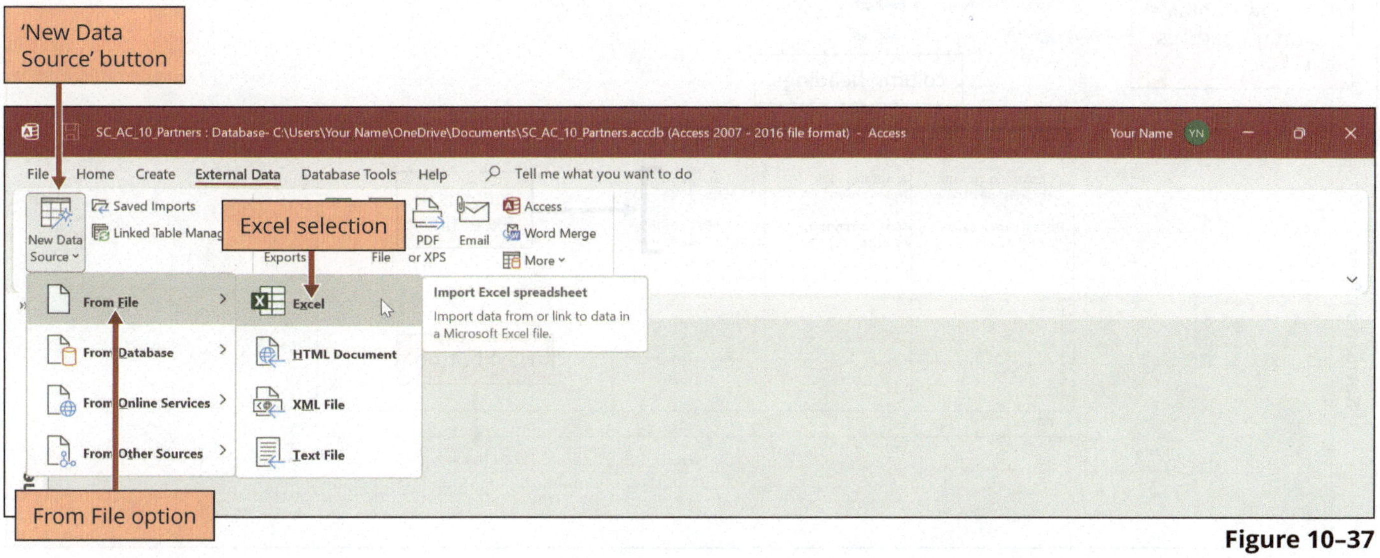

Figure 10–37

3

- Click the Browse button (Get External Data – Excel Spreadsheet dialog box), navigate to the file named SC_AC_10_Agents.xlsx, click to select it, and then click Open.
- Click the 'Link to the data source by creating a linked table.' option button (Figure 10–38).

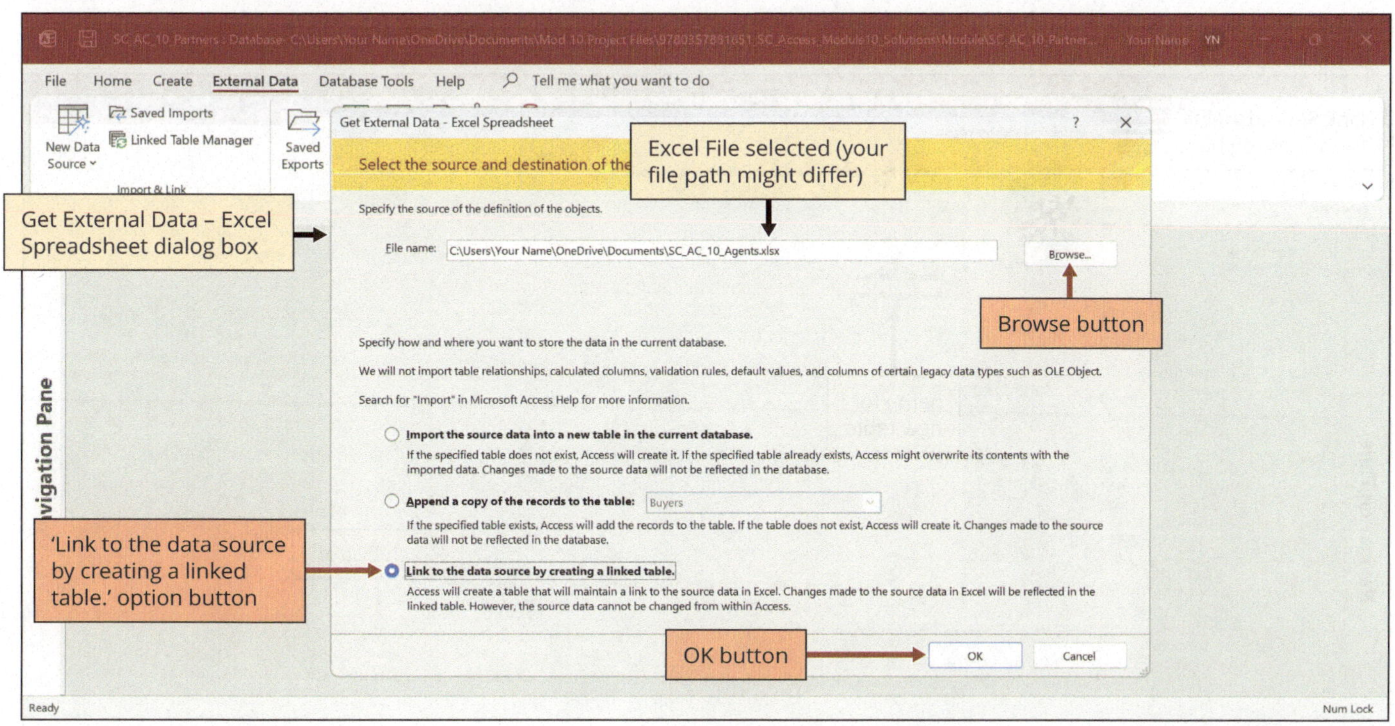

Figure 10–38

4

- Click OK.
- Check the First Row Contains Column Headings check box to select it (Figure 10–39), and then click Next.

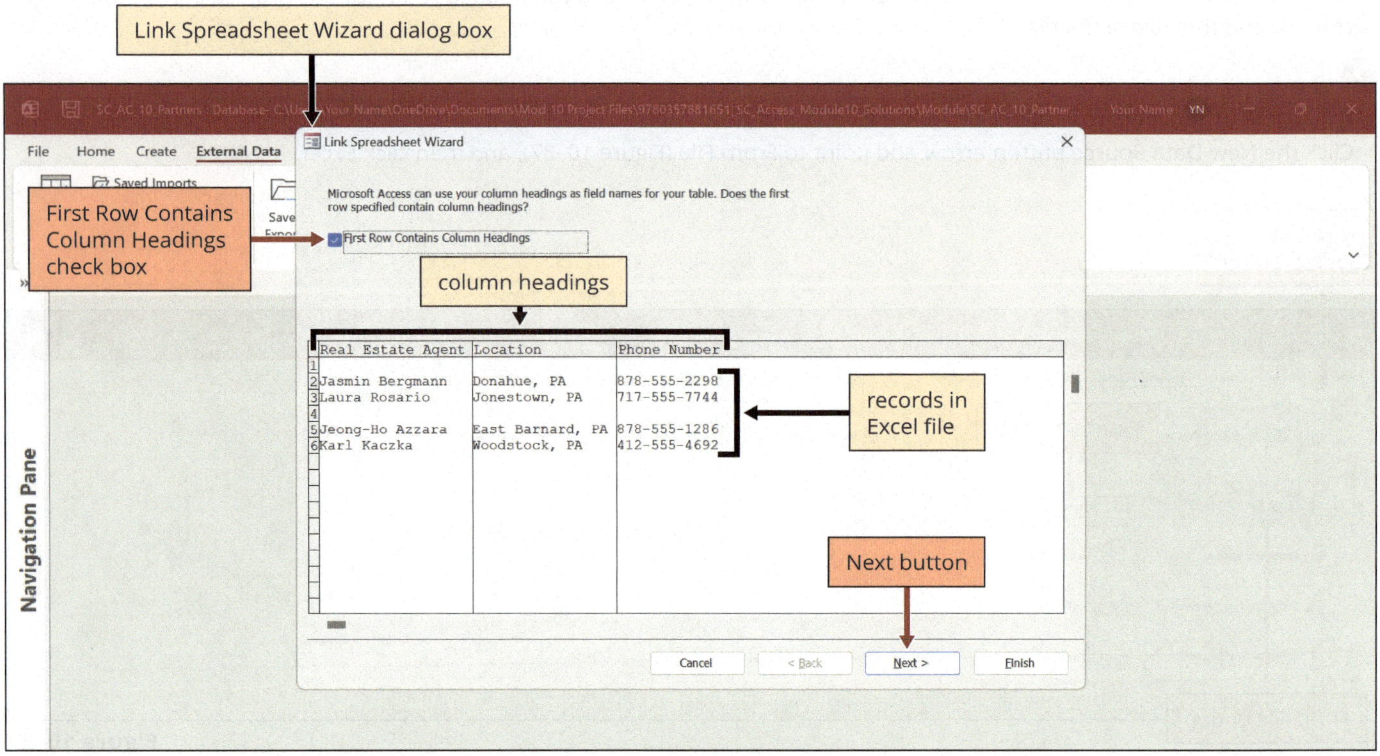

Figure 10–39

Q&A Why is there a blank row in the middle of the data being linked from Excel?
Later in these steps, you will add a new record to the Excel table in the blank line. Because this course is not designed to teach Excel, the data file already contains a blank row, and you will not have to insert a new row in the needed location.

5

- Type **Real Estate Agents** in the Linked Table Name box (Figure 10–40).

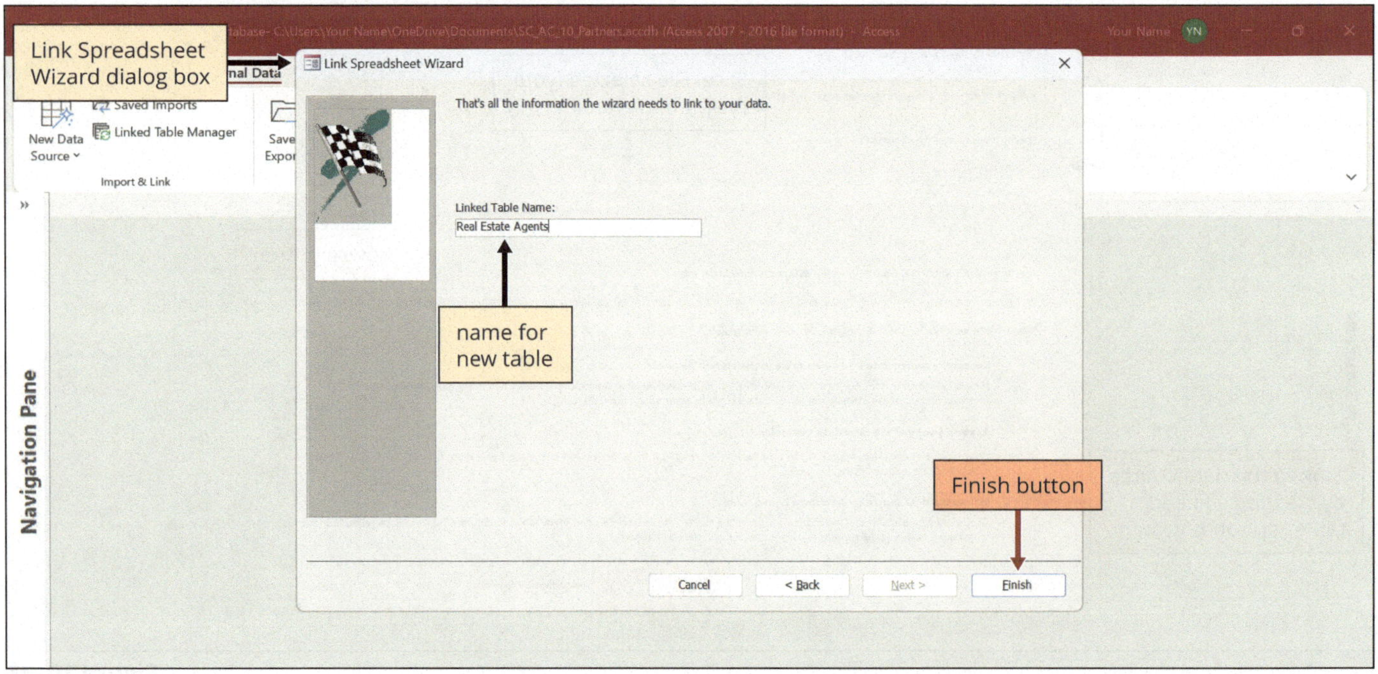

Figure 10–40

6

- Click Finish.
- Click OK in the Link Spreadsheet Wizard dialog box.
- Open the Navigation Pane, if necessary, to see the new linked Real Estate Agents table (Figure 10–41).

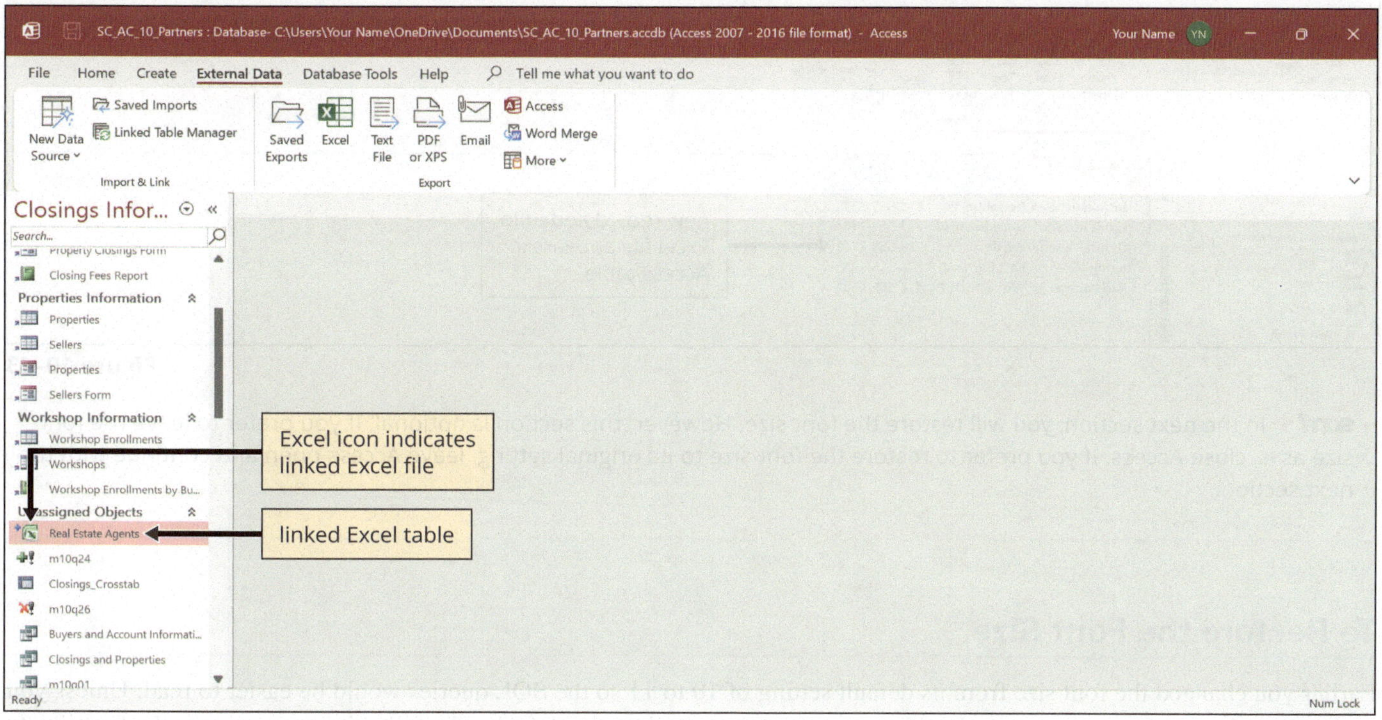

Figure 10–41

7

- Open the table to view the four records (Figure 10–42).

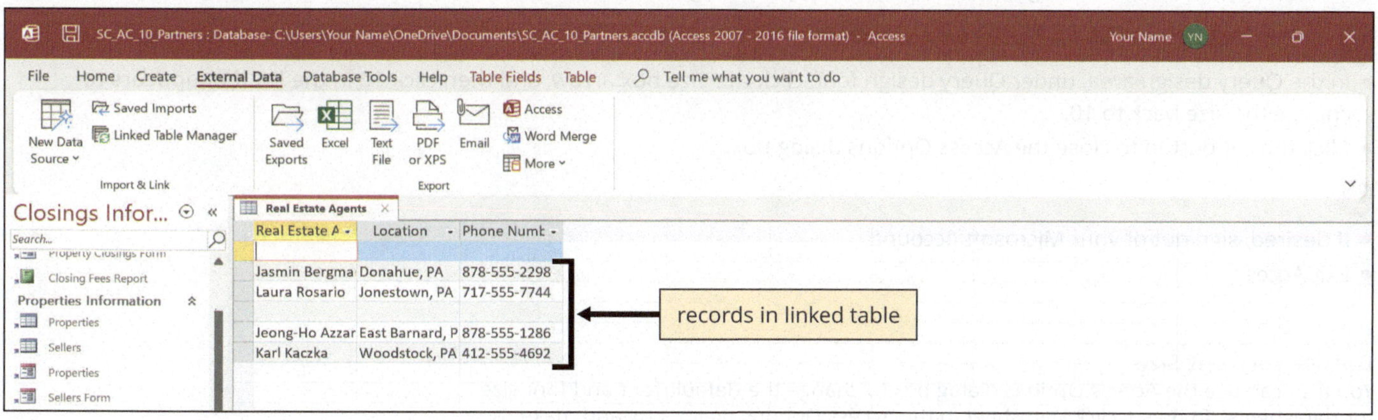

Figure 10–42

8

- Click in a cell with no data and try to add a record. Notice that Access prohibits you from entering data.
- Close the Real Estate Agents table.
- Open the SC_AC_10_Agents.xlsx spreadsheet in Excel, and add the following record to the worksheet as the fifth row:
  Dmitri Alexander   Hartford, PA   888-555-2713
- Save the Excel file and exit Excel.

9

- View the revised table in Access (Figure 10–43), and then close the table.

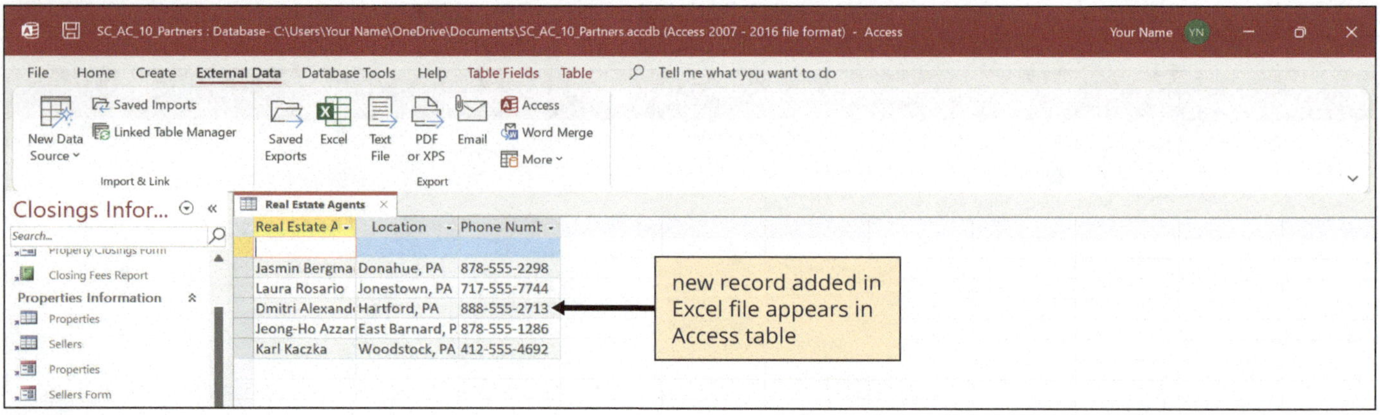

Figure 10–43

- **sam** In the next section, you will restore the font size. However, this section is optional. If you prefer to leave the font size as is, close Access. If you prefer to restore the font size to its original setting, leave Access open and continue with the next section.

To Restore the Font Size

Earlier you changed the font size from its default setting of 10 to 11 so the SQL queries would be easier to read. Unless you prefer to retain this new setting, you should change the setting back to the default. The following steps restore the font size to its default setting.

1

- Click File on the ribbon to open Backstage view.
- Click Options to display the Access Options dialog box.
- If necessary, click Object Designers to display the Object Designer section.

2

- In the Query design area, under Query design font, click the Size box arrow, and then click 10 in the list that appears to change the size back to 10.
- Click the OK button to close the Access Options dialog box.

3

- If desired, sign out of your Microsoft account.
- Exit Access.

BTW

Datasheet Font Size

You also can use the Access Options dialog box to change the default font and font size for datasheets. To do so, click Datasheet in the Access Options dialog box and make the desired changes in the Default font area.

Summary

In this module you have learned to create SQL queries, include fields in a query, use criteria involving both numeric and text fields as well as use compound criteria, use computed fields and rename the computation, sort the results of a query, use the built-in functions, group records in a query and also restrict the groups that appear in the results, join tables and restrict the records in a join, and use subqueries. You looked at a SQL query that was generated automatically by Access. Then, you used the INSERT, UPDATE, and DELETE commands to update data. Finally, you learned how to create a table in Access that is linked to an Excel spreadsheet.

Consider This: Plan Ahead

What decisions will you need to make when creating your own SQL queries?

Use these guidelines as you complete the assignments in this module and create your own queries outside of this class.

1. Select the fields for the query.
   a. Examine the requirements for the query you are constructing to determine which fields are to be included.
2. Determine which table or tables contain these fields.
   a. For each field, determine the table in which it is located.
3. Determine criteria.
   a. Determine any criteria that data must satisfy to be included in the results.
   b. If there are more than two tables in the query, determine the criteria to be used to ensure the data matches correctly.
4. Determine sort order.
   a. Is the data to be sorted in some way?
   b. If so, by what field or fields is it to be sorted?
5. Determine grouping.
   a. Is the data to be grouped in some way?
   b. If so, by what field is it to be grouped?
   c. Identify any calculations to be made for the group.
6. Determine any update operations to be performed.
   a. Determine whether rows need to be inserted, changed, or deleted.
   b. Determine the tables involved.

Consider This

How should you submit solutions to critical thinking questions in the assignments?

Every assignment in this course contains one or more critical thinking questions. These questions require you to think beyond the assigned database. Present your responses to the questions in the format required by your instructor. Possible formats might include one or more of these options: write the answer; create a document that contains the answer; present your answer to the class; discuss your answer in a group; record the answer as audio or video using a webcam, smartphone, or portable media player; or post answers on a blog, wiki, or website.

Student Assignments

Apply Your Knowledge

Reinforce the skills and apply the concepts you learned in this module.

Using Criteria, Joining Tables, and Sorting in SQL Queries in the Build It Construction Database

Note: To complete this assignment, you will be required to use the Data Files. Please contact your instructor for information about accessing the Data Files.

Instructions: Start Access. Open the database, SC_AC_10-2.accdb, which is located in the Data Files folder. Enable the content. Use SQL to query the Build It Construction database in the following steps. Note that for each new query, you can either edit the existing query and save a copy of it with the name indicated, or you can create a new query.

Perform the following tasks:

1. Save the database using the file name, SC_AC_10_Construction. Enable the content.
2. Find all subcontractors whose specialty is HVAC. Display all fields in the query results. Save the query as AYK Step 2 Query.
3. Find all subcontractors listed in the Accounting table whose current due is over $500.00. Display the fields SC #, Subcontractor Name, Amount Paid, and Current Due in the query results. Save this query as AYK Step 3 Query.
4. Find all job sites in the Job Sites table that are not located in OK. Display the fields Job Site Number, Owner, City, and State in the query results. Save the query as AYK Step 4 Query.
5. Display the fields Job Site Number, Subcontractor Number, Subcontractor Name, Mobile Phone, and Specialty for all subcontractors. Sort the records in ascending order by Job Site Number and Subcontractor Number. Save the query as AYK Step 5 Query.
6. Display the fields Subcontractor Number, Subcontractor Name, Specialty, and Employees for all subcontractors who are licensed. Save the query as AYK Step 6 Query.
7. If requested to do so by your instructor, rename the AYK Step 6 Query as Last Name Query where Last Name is your last name.
8. Submit the revised database in the format specified by your instructor.
9. **Consider This:** What WHERE clause would you use if you wanted to find all subcontractors whose specialty starts with the letter C? How might these query results be helpful in a real-world scenario?

Extend Your Knowledge

Extend the skills you learned in this module and experiment with new skills. You may need to use Help to complete the assignment.

Creating Queries to Find Specific Criteria

Note: To complete this assignment, you will be required to use the Data Files. Please contact your instructor for information about accessing the Data Files.

Instructions: Start Access. Open the database, SC_AC_10-3.accdb, which is located in the Data Files folder. The PicsPlus cooperative would like more information about some of the clients of its member photographers. Use SQL queries to find specific information.

Perform the following tasks:

1. Close the Main Menu, and then save the database using the file name, SC_AC_10_PicsPlus. Enable the content.
2. Find all clients where the Client Number begins with either R or S. Display the Client Number, Client Name, City, and State fields in the query results. Save the query as EYK Step 2 Query.
3. Find all clients who live in Kirkland or Medina. Use the IN operator. Display the Client Number, Client Name, City, and State fields in the query results. Save the query as EYK Step 3 Query.
4. Find all clients whose amount paid is greater than or equal to $500 and less than or equal to $1,000. Use the BETWEEN operator. Display the Client Number, Client Name, Photographer Number, and Amount Paid fields in the query results. Save the query as EYK Step 4 Query.
5. Use an INNER JOIN in a query to find all photographers who are located in Kirkland and whose clients are also located in Kirkland. Display the Client Name, Photographer Number, Photographer First Name, Photographer Last Name, and Photographer City fields in the query result. Save the query as EYK Step 5 Query.
6. If requested to do so by your instructor, rename the EYK Step 5 Query as First Name City Query where First Name is your first name and City is the city where you currently reside.
7. Submit the revised database in the format specified by your instructor.
8. **Consider This:** What WHERE clause would you use to find the answer to Step 3 without using the IN operator?

Expand Your World

Create a solution, which uses cloud and web technologies, by learning and investigating on your own from general guidance.

Instructions: Many SQL tutorials are available on the web. One site, www.w3schools.com/sql, has an online SQL editor that allows you to edit SQL commands and then run commands. You will use this editor to create and run queries in the following steps.

Perform the following tasks:

1. Create a blog, Google document, or Word document on OneDrive on which to store your SQL statements and the number of results obtained from the query. Include your name and the current date at the beginning of the blog or document.
2. Access the www.w3schools.com/sql website, and spend some time becoming familiar with the tutorial and how it works.
3. Using the website, explain how you would create a query to find records in a table where the CustomerName value begins with the letter P. Note the section of the website where you located the answer.
4. Submit the document containing your responses in the format specified by your instructor.
5. **Consider This:** In this module, you learned to use the asterisk (*) as a wildcard for an undetermined number of characters. However, in this exercise, you used a different symbol. Why is this different wildcard symbol required?

In the Lab

Design and implement a solution using creative thinking and problem-solving skills.

Lab: Using SQL in the Travel Nurses Database

Note: To complete this assignment, you will be required to use the Data Files. Please contact your instructor for information about accessing the Data Files.

Continued on next page

Problem: The administration at Homegrown Nurse Staffing Agency has asked you to perform a number of queries to collect information from their database.

Perform the following tasks:

Part 1: Open the SC_AC_10-4.accdb database from the Data Files folder. Close the Main Menu and save the file with the name, SC_AC_10_Travel-Nurses, and then enable the content. Use the concepts and techniques presented in this module to perform each of the following tasks. Create all queries using SQL view.

1. Find all the assignments where the bill rate is less than $25,000. Show all Assignments table fields in the results and save the query as ITL Step 1 Query.
2. Use the WHERE command to identify all hospital type facilities and showing all Facilities table fields. Save the query as ITL Step 2 Query.
3. Use the AND command to identify all travelers whose background check and drug screen have been completed. Show the Traveler ID field in the query. Save the query as ITL Step 3 Query.
4. Using the NOT command, find all facilities that are not a private practice. Show the Facility ID field in the query. Save the query as ITL Step 4 Query.
5. Using the ORDER BY command, sort the travelers by their license and then by their Traveler ID. Sort both fields in ascending order. Save the query as ITL Step 5 Query.
6. Use the AND command to find the housing ID for apartment type housing in location L-001, include contact name and phone number in the results, and sort the results in descending order by Housing ID. Save the query as ITL Step 6 Query.
7. Group the traveler payments by Traveler ID and count the number of payments with an amount paid greater than $1,000. Assign the name, Payments over $1,000, to the COUNT column, and autofit the column width in the query results to show the full column name. Save the query as ITL Step 7 Query.
8. Close the database.

Submit your assignment in the format specified by your instructor.

Part 2: **Consider This:** You made several decisions while creating these queries, including the decision of how to design the SELECT clause for the final query. What was the rationale behind your decisions for the last query's SELECT clause? What is another clause you could add to this query that you think would be relevant within the context of the Travel Nurses scenario?

Database Design

Objectives

After completing this module, you will be able to:

- Compare entities, attributes, and relationships
- Describe the characteristics of a relational database
- Identify functional dependence between fields
- Identify a table's primary key
- Explain the basic process of database design
- Explain how to convert an unnormalized relation to first normal form
- Explain how to convert a table from first normal form to second normal form
- Explain how to convert a table from second normal form to third normal form
- Describe information that can be obtained about a database from available documentation
- Describe how diagrams can represent a database's design

Introduction

This module presents a method for determining the tables and fields necessary to satisfy a set of requirements. **Database design** is the process of determining the particular tables and fields that will comprise a database. When designing a database, you must identify the tables that will be in the database, the fields in the tables, the primary keys of the tables, and the relationships between the tables.

This module begins by examining some important concepts concerning relational databases and then presents the design method. To illustrate the process, the module presents the requirements for the Clearnet Freight Brokers database. It then applies the design method to those requirements to produce the database design. The module applies the design method to a second set of requirements, which are requirements for a watersports company called Water Fun Rentals. It next examines normalization, which is a process that you can use to identify and fix potential problems in database designs. You will see normalization techniques applied to design requirements for the Partners Law Firm database. The module concludes by explaining how to use a company's policies and objectives—which are typically addressed in existing documentation—to plan and design a database. Finally, you will learn how to represent a database design with a diagram.

Project: Design a Database

BTW
Systems Analysis
The determination of database requirements is part of a process known as systems analysis. A systems analyst interviews users, examines existing and proposed documents, investigates current procedures, and reviews organizational policies to determine exactly the type of data needs the database must support.

This module expands on the database design guidelines presented earlier. Without a good understanding of database design, you cannot use a database management system such as Access effectively. In this module, you will learn database design principles by using the database design process shown in Figure 11–1.

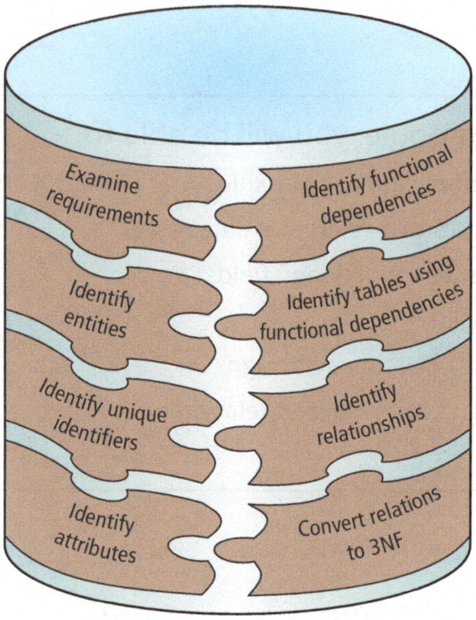

Database Design Process

Figure 11–1

You will design a database for Clearnet that is similar to the database you have used in previous modules. You will also design a new database for Water Fun Rentals, a watersport equipment rental company. You will then make normalization design improvements for the Partners database, based on the database you have used in previous modules, and for the Water Fun Rentals database.

Entities, Attributes, and Relationships

BTW
Entities
Clearnet could include many other entities in a database, such as entities for employees and hours the employees work. The decisions on which entities to include are part of the process of determining database requirements based on user needs.

Working in the database environment requires that you be familiar with some specific terms and concepts. The terms *entity*, *attribute*, and *relationship* are fundamental when discussing databases. An **entity** in a database is similar to a noun in grammar: it is a person, place, thing, or event. The entities of interest to Clearnet, for example, are such things as shippers, carriers, locations, and loads. The entities that are of interest to a college include students, faculty, and classes; a real estate agency is interested in buyers, sellers, properties, and agents; and a watersports company is interested in boats, rentals, customers, and boaters. When creating a database, an entity is represented as a table.

An **attribute** is a property of an entity. The term is used here exactly as it is used in everyday English. For the entity *company*, for example, the list of attributes might include such things as name and address. For Clearnet, the attributes of interest for the entity *carriers* are such things as name, contact person, address, insurance company, and so on. For the entity *faculty* at a school, the attributes would be such things as faculty number, name, office number, phone, department, and so on. For the entity *boat* at a watersports company, the attributes are such things as the hull identification number, brand, color, type of boat, and so on. In databases, attributes are represented as the fields in a table or tables.

A **relationship** is an association between entities. For example, there is an association between carriers and loads at Clearnet. A carrier is associated with all of its loads, and a load is associated with the one carrier to whom the load is assigned. Technically, you say that a carrier is *related* to all of its loads, and a load is *related* to a specific carrier.

The relationship between carriers and loads is an example of a one-to-many relationship because one carrier is associated with many loads, but each load is associated with only one carrier. Recall that in a one-to-many relationship, a table's record can be related to many records in another table. The other table's records are only related to one record in the first table. In this type of relationship, the word *many* is used in a way that is different from everyday English; it might not always mean a large number. In this context, for example, the term *many* means that a carrier might be associated with *any* number of loads. That is, one carrier can be associated with zero, one, or more loads.

There is also a relationship between shippers and carriers. Each shipper sends loads with many carriers, and each carrier can handle loads with many different shippers. This is an example of a **many-to-many relationship**.

How does a relational database handle entities, attributes of entities, and relationships between entities? Entities and attributes are fairly simple. Each entity has its own table; in the Clearnet database, there is one table for carriers, one table for loads, and so on. The attributes of an entity become the columns in the table. In the table for carriers, for example, there is a column for the carrier ID, a column for the carrier name, and so on.

What about relationships? Relationships are implemented through matching fields. One-to-many relationships, for example, are implemented by including matching fields in the related tables. Carriers and loads are related, for example, by including the Carrier ID field in both the Carriers table and the Loads table.

Many-to-many relationships are implemented through an additional table that contains matching fields for both related tables. Carriers and shippers are related, for example, through the Loads table. The Loads table contains the Shipper ID and the Carrier ID. This table links the two tables, Carriers and Shippers, together in the many-to-many relationship.

BTW
One-to-One Relationships
One-to-one relationships also can occur, but they are not common. To implement a one-to-one relationship, treat it as a one-to-many relationship. You must determine which table will be the "one" table and which table will be the "many" table. To do so, consider what may happen in the future. In the case of one project that has one employee assigned to it, more employees could possibly be added, even if that is not the current plan. Therefore, the project table would be the "one" table and the employee table would be the "many" table.

Relational Databases

A relational database is a collection of tables. Figure 11–2 shows portions of two of the tables from the Clearnet database. The Loads table contains information about the loads booked by Clearnet agents (Figure 11–2a).

Loads

Load ID	Pickup Date	Pickup Location	Rate	Mileage	Carrier	Shipper
1	6/30/2024	L-002	$500	159	C-001	S-002
2	7/1/2024	L-001	$1,900	687	C-003	S-001
3	7/1/2024	L-002	$715	218	C-001	S-002
4	7/2/2024	L-003	$2,000	694	C-002	S-001
5	7/3/2024	L-002	$700	159	C-002	S-002
6	7/5/2024	L-003	$675	243	C-001	S-003

Figure 11–2(a): Loads Table

Clearnet assigns each load to a specific carrier. The Carriers table contains information about the carriers to whom these loads are assigned (Figure 11–2b).

Carriers				
Carrier ID	**Carrier Name**	**Carrier Contact**	**Carrier Phone**	**Carrier Insurance**
C-001	Williams Trucking	Marco Bailey	220-555-6682	Shipping Insurance, Inc.
C-002	Freightliners Inc.	Teresa Gomez	435-555-4545	Overland Insurers
C-003	Spotters Freight	Lata Gaspar	617-555-9888	US Motor Group
C-004	Freight Mobile	Doris Cracchiolo	816-555-4933	Shipping Insurance, Inc.
C-005	Truck-n-Go Inc.	Filipa Martinez	816-555-2442	Overland Insurers

Figure 11–2(b): Carriers Table

The formal term for a table is *relation*. If you study the tables shown in Figure 11–2, you might see that there are certain restrictions you should place on relations. Each column in a table should have a unique name, and entries in each column should match this column name. For example, in the Pickup Date column, all entries should in fact *be* dates. In addition, each row should be unique. After all, if two rows in a table contain identical data, the second row does not provide any information that you do not already have. In addition, for maximum flexibility, the order in which columns and rows appear in a table should be immaterial. Finally, a table's design is less complex if you restrict each position in the table to a single entry, that is, you do not permit multiple entries, often called **repeating groups**, in the table. These restrictions lead to the following definition.

A **relation** is a two-dimensional table in which:

1. The entries in the table are single-valued; that is, each location in the table contains a single entry.
2. Each column has a distinct name, technically called the *attribute name*.
3. All values in a column are values of the same attribute; that is, all entries correspond to the column name.
4. Each row is distinct; that is, no two rows are identical.

Figure 11–3a shows a table with repeating groups, which violates Rule 1. Figure 11–3b shows a table in which two columns have the same name, which violates Rule 2. Figure 11–3c shows a table in which one of the entries in the Pickup Date column is not a date, which violates Rule 3. Figure 11–3d shows a table with two identical rows, which violates Rule 4.

repeating group (more than one entry in a single table row)

Loads						
Load ID	**Pickup Date**	**Pickup Location**	**Rate**	**Mileage**	**Carrier**	**Shipper**
1	6/30/2024	L-002 L-004 L-005	$500 $715 $675	159 218 243	C-001	S-002 S-004 S-001
2	7/1/2024	L-001	$1,900	687	C-003	S-001
3	7/1/2024	L-002	$715	218	C-001	S-002
4	7/2/2024	L-003	$2,000	694	C-002	S-001
5	7/3/2024	L-002	$700	159	C-002	S-002
6	7/5/2024	L-003	$675	243	C-001	S-003

Figure 11–3(a): Loads Table Violation of Rule 1—Table Contains Repeating Groups

two columns with same name

Carriers				
Carrier ID	**Carrier Name**	**Carrier Contact**	**Carrier Contact**	**Carrier Insurance**
C-001	Williams Trucking	Marco Bailey	220-555-6682	Shipping Insurance, Inc.
C-002	Freightliners Inc.	Teresa Gomez	435-555-4545	Overland Insurers
C-003	Spotters Freight	Lata Gaspar	617-555-9888	US Motor Group
C-004	Freight Mobile	Doris Cracchiolo	816-555-4933	Shipping Insurance, Inc.
C-005	Truck-n-Go Inc.	Filipa Martinez	816-555-2442	Overland Insurers

Figure 11–3(b): Carriers Table Violation of Rule 2—Each Column Should Have a Distinct Name

Loads						
Load ID	**Pickup Date**	**Pickup Location**	**Rate**	**Mileage**	**Carrier**	**Shipper**
1	6/30/2024	L-002	$500	159	C-001	S-002
2	Monday AM	L-001	$1,900	687	C-003	S-001
3	7/1/2024	L-002	$715	218	C-001	S-002
4	7/2/2024	L-003	$2,000	694	C-002	S-001
5	7/3/2024	L-002	$700	159	C-002	S-002
6	7/5/2024	L-003	$675	243	C-001	S-003

value does not correspond to column name; that is, it is not a Pickup Date

Figure 11–3(c): Loads Table Violation of Rule 3—All Entries in a Column Must Correspond to the Column Name

Carriers				
Carrier ID	**Carrier Name**	**Carrier Contact**	**Carrier Phone**	**Carrier Insurance**
C-001	Williams Trucking	Marco Bailey	220-555-6682	Shipping Insurance, Inc.
C-002	Freightliners Inc.	Teresa Gomez	435-555-4545	Overland Insurers
C-002	Freightliners Inc.	Teresa Gomez	435-555-4545	Overland Insurers
C-003	Spotters Freight	Lata Gaspar	617-555-9888	US Motor Group
C-004	Freight Mobile	Doris Cracchiolo	816-555-4933	Shipping Insurance, Inc.
C-005	Truck-n-Go Inc.	Filipa Martinez	816-555-2442	Overland Insurers

identical rows

Figure 11–3(d): Carriers Table Violation of Rule 4—Each Row Should Contain Distinct Data

In a relation, the order of columns is immaterial. The order of rows is also immaterial. You can view the columns or rows in any order you want. Rows in a table (relation) are often called records or **tuples**. Columns in a table (relation) are often called fields or attributes. Typically, the terms *record* and *field* are used in Access. A relational database is a collection of relations.

To depict the structure of a relational database, you can use a commonly accepted shorthand representation: you write the name of the table and then, within parentheses, list all the fields in the table. Each table should begin on a new line. If the entries in the table occupy more than one line, the entries that appear on the next line should be indented so it is clear that they do not constitute another table. Using this method, you would represent the Clearnet database as shown in Figure 11–4.

Loads (Load ID, Pickup Date, Pickup Location, Rate, Mileage, Carrier, Shipper)
Carriers (Carrier ID, Carrier Name, Carrier Contact, Carrier Phone, Carrier Insurance)

Figure 11–4

Duplicate field names in different tables can also cause problems. This is why the modules in this course often had you name a field with additional information referencing the table the field belonged to. For example, the Contact field in the Carriers table is named Carrier Contact. In the Shippers table, the Contact field is named Shipper Contact. Consider if the Clearnet database named the Contact field simply the word, Contact, in *both* the Carriers table *and* the Shippers table. This duplication of names can lead to possible confusion. If you write Contact, it is not clear to which Contact field you are referring.

When duplicate field names exist in different tables in a database, you need to indicate the field to which you are referring. You do so by writing both the table name and the field name, separated by a period. You would write the Contact field in the Carriers table as Carriers.Contact and the Contact field in the Shippers table as Shippers.Contact. As you learned previously, when you combine a field name with a table name, you say that you qualify the field names. It is *always* acceptable to qualify field names, even if there is no possibility of confusion. If confusion might arise, however, it is *essential* to qualify field names.

Functional Dependence

BTW
Functional Dependence
To help identify functional dependencies, ask yourself the following question. If you know a unique value for an attribute, do you know the specific values for other attributes? For example, when you have three attributes—Carrier ID, Carrier Name, and Carrier Insurance—and you know a unique value for Carrier ID, do you also know a specific value for Carrier Name and Carrier Insurance? If so, then Carrier Name and Carrier Insurance are functionally dependent on Carrier ID.

In the Clearnet database (Figure 11–2), a given carrier ID in the database will correspond to a single carrier because carrier ID numbers are unique. Thus, if you are given a carrier ID in the database, you could find a carrier name that corresponds to it. No ambiguity exists. The database terminology for this relationship between carrier ID numbers and carrier names is that Carrier ID determines Carrier Name, or, equivalently, that Carrier Name is functionally dependent on Carrier ID. Specifically, if you know that whenever you are given a value for one field, you will be able to determine a single value for a second field, the first field is said to **determine** the second field. In addition, the second field is said to be **functionally dependent** on the first.

There is a shorthand notation that represents functional dependencies using an arrow. To indicate that Carrier ID determines Carrier Name, or, equivalently, that Carrier Name is functionally dependent on Carrier ID, you would write Carrier ID → Carrier Name. The field that precedes the arrow determines the field that follows the arrow.

If you were given an insurance company name and asked to find a single carrier's name, you could not do it. Given Overland Insurers, for example, you would find two carrier names, Freightliners Inc. and Truck-n-Go Inc. (Figure 11–5). Formally, you would say the insurance company does *not* determine Carrier Name, or that Carrier Name is *not* functionally dependent on Carrier Insurance.

Carrier Insurance is Overland Insurers; Carrier Name is Freightliners Inc.

Carriers

Carrier ID	Carrier Name	Carrier Contact	Carrier Phone	Carrier Insurance
C-001	Williams Trucking	Marco Bailey	220-555-6682	Shipping Insurance, Inc.
C-002	Freightliners Inc.	Teresa Gomez	435-555-4545	Overland Insurers
C-003	Spotters Freight	Lata Gaspar	617-555-9888	US Motor Group
C-004	Freight Mobile	Doris Cracchiolo	816-555-4933	Shipping Insurance, Inc.
C-005	Truck-n-Go Inc.	Filipa Martinez	816-555-2442	Overland Insurers

Figure 11–5

Carrier Insurance is Overland Insurers, but Carrier Name is Truck-n-Go Inc. (same insurance company but different carrier name)

Consider This

In the Loads table, is Shipper ID functionally dependent on Load ID?

Yes. If you are given a value for Load ID, for example 4, you will always find a *single* Shipper ID, in this case S-001, associated with it.

In the Loads table in the Clearnet database, is Shipper ID functionally dependent on Carrier ID?

No. There is a row, for example, in which the Carrier ID is C-003 and the Shipper ID is S-001. There is another row in which the Carrier ID is C-002 and the Shipper ID is again S-001. A carrier can transport loads from multiple shippers. Thus, carriers are associated with more than one shipper.

On which fields is the Contents field functionally dependent?

To determine the Contents value, you need the Load ID.

Primary Key

The primary key of a table is the field or minimum collection of fields—the fewest number of fields possible—that uniquely identifies a given row in that table. In the Loads table, the Load ID uniquely identifies a given row. Any Load ID appears on only one row of the table. Thus, Load ID is the primary key. Similarly, Carrier ID is the primary key of the Carriers table.

Consider This

Is the Carrier Name another possibility for the key field in the Carriers table?

No. While unlikely in a list of businesses, it is possible there may be two carriers with the same name. This is even more likely in a list of people where multiple people can have the same name. A key field must be unique for each row.

Could the combination of the Carrier Name and the Carrier Phone fields be the primary key for the Carriers table?

Yes, the combination of the two fields, Carrier Name and Carrier Phone, make each row unique. This would be an alternative to using the current key field, Carrier ID.

Could the combination of the Carrier Name and the Pickup Date fields be the primary key for the Loads table?

The combination of the two fields, Carrier Name and Pickup Date, does make each row unique, assuming that each carrier has only one load each day. This could be an alternative to using the current key field, Load ID. However, many loads are entered in the database before a carrier is assigned. In these cases, you would either have to wait to enter the load until a carrier is assigned, or you would have to temporarily assign a placeholder carrier value (such as Unassigned) until a carrier is selected. Further, you could only have one unassigned load for each day at a time, which is unreasonable in this scenario.

What if some carriers have more than one load in any day?

In this case, you would need to use three fields as the combined primary key. Depending on the type of loads transported by the carriers Clearnet works with, Carrier ID, Pickup Date, and Pickup Location might work. These three fields would provide a unique combination for each row as long as a carrier would not ever need to send multiple trucks to a single location for multiple loads on the same day. If that scenario could happen, then Clearnet would need to use a different combination of fields, such as Carrier ID, Pickup Date, and Driver Name.

The primary key provides an important way of distinguishing one row in a table from another. In the shorthand representation, you underline the field or collection of fields that comprise the primary key for each table in the database. Thus, the complete shorthand representation for the Clearnet database is shown in Figure 11–6.

Loads (Load ID, Pickup Date, Pickup Location, Rate, Mileage, Carrier, Shipper)
Carriers (Carrier ID, Carrier Name, Carrier Contact, Carrier Phone, Carrier Insurance)

Figure 11–6

BTW
Candidate Keys
According to the definition of a candidate key, a Social Security number is a legitimate primary key. Many databases use a person's Social Security number as a primary key. However, many institutions and organizations are moving away from using Social Security numbers because of privacy issues. Instead, many institutions and organizations use unique student numbers or employee numbers as primary keys.

Occasionally, but not often, there might be more than one possibility for the primary key. For example, if the Clearnet database included an Employees table with employees' Social Security numbers, either the Employee ID or the Social Security number could serve as the primary key. In this case, both fields are referred to as candidate keys. Similar to a primary key, a **candidate key** is a field or combination of fields on which all fields in the table are functionally dependent. Thus, the definition for primary key really defines candidate key as well. There can be many candidate keys, although having more than one is very rare. By contrast, there is only one primary key. The remaining candidate keys are called **alternate keys**.

Database Design

This section presents a specific database design method, based on a set of requirements that the database must support. The section then presents a sample of such requirements and illustrates the design method by designing a database to satisfy these requirements.

Design Process

The following is a method for designing a database for a set of requirements.

1. Examine the requirements and identify the entities, or objects, involved. Assign names to the entities. The entities will become tables. If, for example, the design involves the entities departments and employees, you could assign the names, Departments and Employees. If the design involves the entities accounts, orders, and parts, you could assign the names, Accounts, Orders, and Parts.

BTW
Singular Vs. Plural Table Names
A common debate in database design is whether to use singular or plural table names when designing a database. Most experts agree this decision is a matter of personal opinion. However, the important thing is to be consistent—if you start with singular names, then continue to use singular names throughout, and vice versa. However, some singular names you might want to use are not allowed by Access. For example, the word, Order, has special meaning in SQL. If you use it for the name of a table, you will not be able to use SQL to query that table. A common approach to avoid this problem is to make the name plural. That is one reason for choosing Orders rather than Order as the name of the table. If you will need to use a name for a table that must be plural, such as Orders, you might prefer to use plural names for all your tables in the interest of consistency. Still, there are many other valid reasons why singular names might be preferred, such as lending more intuitive sense when a field is qualified by its table name in a SQL query, such as [Customer].[Customer Name]. Again, the important thing is to choose one approach, either singular or plural, and be consistent as much as possible.

2. Assign a unique identifier to each entity. For example, if one of the entities were "item," you would determine what it takes to uniquely identify each individual item. In other words, what enables the organization to distinguish one item from another? For an item entity, it might be Item Number. For an account entity, it might be Account Number. If there is no such unique identifier, it is a good idea to add one. Perhaps the previous system was a manual one where accounts were not assigned numbers, in which case this would be a good time to add Account Numbers to the system. If there is no natural candidate for a primary key, you can add an AutoNumber field, which is similar to the ID field that Access adds automatically when you create a new table.
3. Identify the attributes for all the entities. These attributes will become the fields in the tables. It is possible that more than one entity has the same attribute. At Clearnet, for example, carriers and shippers both have the attributes of contact, phone, email, and address. To handle this duplication, you can follow the name of the attribute with the corresponding entity in parentheses. Thus, Contact (Shippers) would be the contact person for a shipper, whereas Contact (Carriers) would be the contact person for a carrier.
4. Identify the functional dependencies that exist among the attributes.
5. Use the functional dependencies to identify the tables. You do this by placing each attribute with the attribute or minimum combination of attributes on which it is functionally dependent. The attribute or attributes on which all other attributes in the table are dependent will be the primary key of the table. The remaining attributes will be the other fields in the table. Once you have determined all the fields in the table, you can assign an appropriate name to the table.
6. Determine and implement relationships among the entities. The basic relationships are one-to-many and many-to-many.
   - **One-to-many.** You implement a one-to-many relationship by including the primary key of the "one" table as a foreign key in the "many" table. A foreign key is a field in one table whose values are required to match the primary key of another table. In the one-to-many relationship between loads and carriers, for example, you include the *primary key* of the Carriers table, which is Carrier ID, as a foreign key in the Loads table. You might have already included this field in the earlier steps. If so, you would simply designate it as a foreign key. If you had not already added it, you would need to add it at this point, designating it as a foreign key.
   - **Many-to-many.** A many-to-many relationship is implemented by creating a new table whose primary key is the combination of the keys of the original tables.

BTW

Line Items

A line item is a unit of information that appears on its own line. For example, when you purchase groceries, each grocery item appears on its own line. Line items also can be referred to as order line items or item detail lines.

You may have already identified such a table in the earlier steps, in which case, all you need to do is be sure you have designated each portion of the primary key as a foreign key that is required to match the primary key of the appropriate table. If you have not, you would add the table at this point. The primary key will consist of the primary keys from each of the tables to be related. If there are any attributes that depend on the combination of fields that make up the primary key, you need to include them in this table. (*Note:* There might not be any other fields that are dependent on this combination. In that case, there will be no fields besides the fields that make up the primary key.)

The following sections illustrate the design process by designing the database for Clearnet. The first section gives the requirements the database must support, and then the following section creates a database design based on those requirements.

Requirements for the Clearnet Database

Systems analysts have examined the needs and organizational policies at Clearnet and have determined that the Clearnet database must support the following requirements:

1. For a shipper, Clearnet needs to maintain the shipper's name, contact person and their information, locations, and billing notes.

2. For a carrier, Clearnet needs the carrier's name, contact person and their information, MC Number, USDOT Number, insurance and payment information, and information on the drivers and trucks.
3. For locations, Clearnet needs the location name, type, address, and related shipper if applicable.
4. Each load must be recorded as well. Information for loads indicates when and where the load is scheduled for pickup and dropoff, rate confirmation, mileage, contents, required truck type, current status, assigned driver with their contact information, and identification of the related carrier, shipper, and agent.
5. Any given carrier can have many loads, and any shipper can also have many loads.

Design of the Clearnet Database

The following represents the application of the design method for the Clearnet requirements.

1. There appear to be four entities: shippers, carriers, locations, and loads. Reasonable names for the corresponding tables are Shippers, Carriers, Locations, and Loads.
2. The unique identifier for shippers is the shipper ID. The unique identifier for carriers is the carrier ID. The unique identifier for locations is the location ID. The unique identifier of loads is the load ID. Reasonable names for the unique identifiers are Shipper ID, Carrier ID, Location ID, and Load ID, respectively.
3. The attributes are:

   Shipper ID

   Shipper Name

   Shipper Contact

   Shipper Phone

   Shipper Email

   Shipper Address

   Shipper Locations

   Shipper Billing Notes

   Carrier ID

   Carrier Name

   Carrier Contact

   Carrier Phone

   Carrier Email

   Carrier Address

   Carrier MC Number

   Carrier USDOT Number

   Carrier Insurance

   Carrier Payment Instructions

   Drivers

   LTL

   Equipment Types

   Driver Photos

   Carrier Documentation

Location ID
Location Name
Location Type
Location Street
Location City
Location State
Location Postal Code
Shipper ID
Load ID
Pickup Date
Pickup Location
Dropoff Date
Dropoff Location
Rate Confirmation
Mileage
Contents
Truck Type
Status
Driver Name
Driver Phone
Carrier
Shipper
Load Notes
Agent

Remember that, if two entities contain attributes with the same name, parentheses after an attribute indicate the entity to which the attribute corresponds. Thus, Address (Shippers) represents the address of a shipper in a way that distinguishes it from Address (Carriers), which represents the address of a carrier. In this case, however, each attribute is named with a built-in reference to the entity, such as Shipper Address and Carrier Address.

4. The functional dependencies among the attributes are:

Shipper ID → Shipper Name, Shipper Contact, Shipper Phone, Shipper Email, Shipper Address, Shipper Locations, Shipper Billing Notes

Carrier ID → Carrier Name, Carrier Contact, Carrier Phone, Carrier Email, Carrier Address, Carrier MC Number, Carrier USDOT Number, Carrier Insurance, Carrier Payment Instructions, Drivers, LTL, Equipment Types, Driver Photos, Carrier Documentation

Location ID → Location Name, Location Type, Location Street, Location City, Location State, Location Postal Code, Shipper ID

Load ID → Pickup Date, Pickup Location, Dropoff Date, Dropoff Location, Rate Confirmation, Mileage, Contents, Truck Type, Status, Driver Name, Driver Phone, Carrier, Shipper, Load Notes, Agent

The pickup and dropoff dates and locations are dependent only on load ID. Because a load has a single shipper and a single carrier, the shipper and carrier are dependent on load ID as well. The carrier's name, contact information, and documentation information are dependent only on the carrier ID. The shipper's name, contact information, locations, and billing notes are dependent only on the shipper ID. Similarly, the location name, type, and address are dependent only on the location ID. The shorthand representation for the tables is shown in Figure 11–7.

Loads (<u>Load ID</u>, Pickup Date, Pickup Location, Dropoff Date, Dropoff Location, Rate Confirmation, Mileage, Contents, Truck Type, Status, Driver Name, Driver Phone, Carrier, Shipper, Load Notes, Agent)

Carriers (<u>Carrier ID</u>, Carrier Name, Carrier Contact, Carrier Phone, Carrier Email, Carrier Address, Carrier MC Number, Carrier USDOT Number, Carrier Insurance, Carrier Payment Instructions, Drivers, LTL, Equipment Types, Driver Photos, Carrier Documentation)

Shippers (<u>Shipper ID</u>, Shipper Name, Shipper Contact, Shipper Phone, Shipper Email, Shipper Address, Shipper Locations, Shipper Billing Notes)

Locations (<u>Location ID</u>, Location Name, Location Type, Location Street, Location City, Location State, Location Postal Code, Shipper ID)

Figure 11–7

5. The following are the relationships between the tables:
   a. The Loads and Carriers tables are related using the Carrier ID fields, which is the primary key of the Carriers table. The Carrier field in the Loads table is a foreign key.
   b. The Loads and Shippers tables are related using the Shipper ID fields, which is the primary key of the Shippers table. The Shipper field in the Loads table is a foreign key.
   c. The Loads and Locations tables are related using either the Pickup Location field or the Dropoff Location field in the Loads table and the Location ID field, which is the primary key of the Locations table. This creates two relationships between the Loads table and the Locations table, one on each Location field in the Loads table. The Pickup Location and Dropoff Location fields in the Loads table are both foreign keys.

Note: In the shorthand representation for a table containing a foreign key, you would represent the foreign key by using the letters, FK, followed by an arrow, followed by the name of the table in which that field is the primary key. For example, to indicate that the Carrier ID in the Loads table is a foreign key that must match the primary key of the Carriers table, you would write FK Carrier ID → Carriers.

The shorthand representation for the tables and foreign keys is shown in Figure 11–8. It is common to list a table containing a foreign key after the table that contains the corresponding

Shippers (<u>Shipper ID</u>, Shipper Name, Shipper Contact, Shipper Phone, Shipper Email, Shipper Address, Shipper Locations, Shipper Billing Notes)

Carriers (<u>Carrier ID</u>, Carrier Name, Carrier Contact, Carrier Phone, Carrier Email, Carrier Address, Carrier MC Number, Carrier USDOT Number, Carrier Insurance, Carrier Payment Instructions, Drivers, LTL, Equipment Types, Driver Photos, Carrier Documentation)

FK Shipper ID → Shippers

Locations (<u>Location ID</u>, Location Name, Location Type, Location Street, Location City, Location State, Location Postal Code, Shipper ID)

Loads (<u>Load ID</u>, Pickup Date, Pickup Location, Dropoff Date, Dropoff Location, Rate Confirmation, Mileage, Contents, Truck Type, Status, Driver Name, Driver Phone, Carrier, Shipper, Load Notes, Agent)

FK Carrier ID → Carriers

FK Location ID → Locations

Figure 11–8

primary key, when possible. Thus, in the figure, the Loads table comes after the other tables because it contains foreign keys from the tables listed above it.

Water Fun Rentals

The management of Water Fun Rentals, a watersport equipment rental company, has determined that the company's rapid growth requires a database to maintain information about rentals, customers, and boating equipment such as kayaks and canoes. With the data stored in a database, management will be able to ensure that the data is current and more accurate. In addition, managers will be able to obtain answers to their questions concerning the data in the database quickly and easily, with the option of producing a variety of reports. Note that the cost of the rentals and the payments to the Water Fun Rentals company are handled by a third party and are not requirements of this database design.

Requirements for the Water Fun Rentals Database

A system analyst has interviewed users and examined documents at Water Fun Rentals and has determined that the company needs a database that will support the following requirements:

1. For a customer, store the customer's first name, last name, street address, city, state, postal code, telephone number, and email address.
2. For a paddler, store the paddler's first name, last name, street address, city, state, postal code, telephone number, and email address. (Note that there might be many paddlers under one customer. For example, a business customer could pay for all the rentals of a group of paddlers on a company outing.)
3. For rented boats, store the hull identification number, type, brand, and color. The database also should store the rental agreement number under which each boat is rented.
4. The paddler and boat must be associated; the database must include a table that links these two entities.
5. The analyst also obtained the following information concerning boat rentals:
   - **a.** A customer could rent more than one boat.
   - **b.** There could be multiple paddlers associated with one rental agreement.
   - **c.** A customer can rent boats many times.
   - **d.** Each rental is effective on a single day for a certain number of hours.

Design of the Water Fun Rentals Database

The following steps apply the design process to the requirements for Water Fun Rentals to produce the appropriate database design:

1. Assign entity names. There appear to be four entities: customers, paddlers, rentals, and boats. The names assigned to these entities are Customers, Paddlers, Rentals, and Boats, respectively.
2. Determine unique identifiers. From the collection of entities, review the data and determine the unique identifier for each entity. For the Customers, Paddlers, and Rentals entities, the unique identifiers are the customer ID, paddler ID, and rental number, respectively. These unique identifiers are named Customer ID, Paddler ID, and Rental Number, respectively. For the Boats, the unique identifier is the hull identification number, known as HIN, which is a unique number assigned to each boat by its manufacturer.
3. Assign attribute names. The attributes mentioned in the first requirement all refer to customers. The specific attributes mentioned in the requirement are the customer ID,

first name, last name, street address, city, state, postal code, telephone number, and email address. Assigning appropriate names to these attributes produces the following list:

Customer ID
First Name
Last Name
Street
City
State
Postal Code
Telephone
Email Address

Consider This

Do you need to include the rental associated with the customer in the list of attributes for the first requirement?

There is no need to include rental information in this list because that information will be determined with a relationship between tables later on.

The attributes mentioned in the second requirement refer to paddlers. The specific attributes are the paddler ID, first name, last name, street address, city, state, postal code, telephone number, and email address. Assigning appropriate names to these attributes produces the following list:

Paddler ID
First Name
Last Name
Street
City
State
Postal Code
Telephone
Email Address

There are attributes named Street, City, State, and Postal Code for customers as well as attributes identically named Street, City, State, and Postal Code for paddlers. To distinguish these attributes in the final collection, the name of the attribute is followed by the name of the corresponding entity. For example, the street address for a customer is Street (Customers) and the street address for a paddler is Street (Paddlers).

The attributes mentioned in the third requirement refer to rental agreements. The specific attributes are the rental number, effective date, expire time, and customer, who is the rental holder. Assigning appropriate names to these attributes produces the following list:

Rental Number
Effective Date
Expire Time
Customer ID

The attributes mentioned in the fourth requirement refer to rental boats. The specific attributes include the hull identification number, type, brand, color, and rental number associated with the boat. Assigning appropriate names to these attributes produces the following list:

HIN
Type

Brand

Color

Rental Number

The statement concerning the linkage of paddler to boat indicates there are specific attributes to be stored for each boat when it is rented. These attributes are the boat and paddler. Assigning appropriate names to these attributes produces the following list:

HIN

Paddler ID

The complete list grouped by entity is as follows:

Customers

- **Customer ID**
- **First Name**
- **Last Name**
- **Street**
- **City**
- **State**
- **Postal Code**
- **Telephone**
- **Email Address**

Paddlers

- **Paddler ID**
- **First Name**
- **Last Name**
- **Street**
- **City**
- **State**
- **Postal Code**
- **Telephone**
- **Email Address**

Rentals

- **Rental Number**
- **Effective Date**
- **Expire Time**
- **Customer ID**

Boats

- **HIN**
- **Type**
- **Brand**
- **Color**
- **Rental Number**

For paddlers of boats:

HIN

Paddler ID

4. Identify functional dependencies. The fact that the unique identifier for customers is Customer ID gives the following functional dependencies:

Customer ID → First Name (Customers), Last Name (Customers), Street (Customers), City (Customers), State (Customers), Postal Code (Customers), Telephone (Customers), Email Address (Customers)

The fact that the unique identifier for paddlers is Paddler ID gives the following preliminary list of functional dependencies:

Paddler ID → First Name (Paddlers), Last Name (Paddlers), Street (Paddlers), City (Paddlers), State (Paddlers), Postal Code (Paddlers), Telephone (Paddlers), Email Address (Paddlers)

The fact that the unique identifier for rentals is Rental Number gives the following functional dependencies:

Rental Number → Effective Date, Expire Time, Customer ID

The fact that the unique identifier for boats is HIN gives the following functional dependencies:

HIN → Type, Brand, Color, Rental Number

Consider This

Do you need to include the name of a customer in the list of attributes determined by the rental number?

There is no need to include the customer name in this list because you can determine that information from the customer ID, and names are already included in the list of attributes determined by customer ID.

The final attributes to be examined are those associated with the paddlers and boats: HIN, Paddler ID.

Consider This

Why is Paddler ID not included in the Boats table?

There could be multiple paddlers for each boat, so this requires an additional table.

The following shorthand representation indicates the combination of HIN and Paddler ID. There are no functionally dependent fields in this table.

HIN, Paddler ID →

The complete list of functional dependencies with appropriate revisions is as follows:

Customer ID → First Name (Customers), Last Name (Customers), Street (Customers), City (Customers), State (Customers), Postal Code (Customers), Telephone (Customers), Email Address (Customers)

Paddler ID → First Name (Paddlers), Last Name (Paddlers), Street (Paddlers), City (Paddlers), State (Paddlers), Postal Code (Paddlers), Telephone (Paddlers), Email Address (Paddlers)

Rental Number → Effective Date, Expire Time, Customer ID

HIN → Type, Brand, Color, Rental Number

HIN, Paddler ID →

5. Create the tables. Using the functional dependencies, you can create tables with the attribute(s) to the left of the arrow being the primary key and the items to the right of the arrow being the other fields. For tables corresponding to those entities identified in Step 1, you can simply use the name you already determined. Because you did not identify any entity that had a unique identifier that was the combination of HIN and Paddler ID, you need to assign a name to the table whose primary key consists of these two fields.

Because this table represents the individual paddlers for one boat, the name Boat Paddlers is a good choice. The final collection of tables for Water Fun Rentals is shown in Figure 11–9.

Customers (Customer ID, First Name, Last Name, Address, City, State, Postal Code, Telephone, Email Address)
Paddlers (Paddler ID, First Name, Last Name, Address, City, State, Postal Code, Telephone, Email Address)
Rentals (Rental Number, Effective Date, Expire Time, Customer ID)
Boats (HIN, Type, Brand, Color, Rental Number)
Boat Paddlers (HIN, Paddler ID)

Figure 11–9

6. Identify relationships.
   a. The Customers and Rentals tables are related using the Customer ID fields. The Customer ID field in the Customers table is the primary key. The Customer ID field in the Rentals table is a foreign key.
   b. The Rentals and Boats tables are related using the Rental Number fields. The Rental Number field in the Rentals table is the primary key. The Rental Number field in the Boats table is a foreign key.
   c. The Boats and Paddlers tables are related using the HIN and Paddler ID fields. Both the HIN and the Paddler ID are key fields together.

Consider This

Does a many-to-many relationship exist between boats and paddlers?

Yes. The Boat Paddlers table will implement a many-to-many relationship between boats and paddlers. You identified this table as Boat Paddlers in the database design process.

In the Boat Paddlers table, the primary key consists of two fields, HIN and Paddler ID. Do you need both fields to be key fields?

Yes, because this table implements the many-to-many relationship between boats and paddlers. It is perfectly legitimate for the table that implements a many-to-many relationship to contain only the two columns that constitute the primary key.

The shorthand representation for the tables and foreign keys is shown in Figure 11–10.

Customers (Customer ID, First Name, Last Name, Address, City, State, Postal Code, Telephone, Email Address)
Paddlers (Paddler ID, First Name, Last Name, Address, City, State, Postal Code, Telephone, Email Address)
Rentals (Rental Number, Effective Date, Expire Time, Customer ID)
FK Customer ID → Customers
Boats (HIN, Type, Brand, Color, Rental Number)
FK Rental Number → Rentals
Boat Paddlers (HIN, Paddler ID)
FK HIN → Boats
FK Paddler ID → Paddlers

Figure 11–10

Sample data for the Water Fun Rentals database is shown in Figure 11–11.

Customers

Customer ID	Customer First Name	Customer Last Name	Customer Street Address	Customer City	Customer State	Customer Postal Code	Customer Phone	Customer Email Address
C398	Tricia	Morris	460 West Longberg Rd	Gainesville	SC	29101	854-555-4411	tmorris@example.com
C416	Shinju	Niack	9874 South Main St	Gainesville	SC	29103	854-555-5670	sniack@example.com

Paddlers

Paddler ID	Paddler First Name	Paddler Last Name	Paddler Street Address	Paddler City	Paddler State	Paddler Postal Code	Paddler Phone	Paddler Email Address
P410	Steve	Chen	3 Hanover Park	Newberry	NC	27237	828-555-4234	schen@example.com
P434	Tiffanie	D'Vivo	14435 Keller Way	Gainesville	SC	29101	854-555-9135	tdvivo@example.com
P552	Cyrus	Killigan	784 Hilltop Cir	Gainesville	SC	29101	854-555-6547	ckilligan@example.com

Rentals

Rental Number	Effective Date	Expire Time	Customer ID
R-123	2/13/2029	14:00	C398
R-142	4/1/2029	19:30	C416

Boats

HIN	Type	Brand	Color	Rental Number
ALL7HA470011	1-person kayak	Water Systems	Green	R-123
ALS7DA761712	2-person kayak	SeaCruise	Blue	R-142
JMB4A1138112	Canoe	Water Systems	Yellow	R-142

Boat Paddlers

HIN	Paddler ID
ALL7HA470011	P410
ALS7DA761712	P552
ALS7DA761712	P434

Figure 11–11

Break Point: If you wish to take a break, this is a good place to do so. To resume at a later time, continue reading from this location forward.

Normalization

After you create your database design, you should analyze it using a process called **normalization** to make sure the design is free of potential update, redundancy, and consistency problems. This process also supplies methods for correcting these problems.

The normalization process involves converting tables into various types of **normal forms**. A table in a particular normal form possesses a certain desirable set of properties. Several normal forms exist, the most common being first normal form (1NF), second normal form (2NF), and third normal form (3NF). The forms create a progression in which a table that is in 1NF is better than a table that is not in 1NF, a table that is in 2NF is better than one that is in 1NF, and so on. The goal of normalization is to take a table or collection of tables and produce a new collection of tables that represents the same information but is free of problems.

First Normal Form

A table that contains a repeating group, or multiple entries for a single row, is called an **unnormalized table** and is, therefore, in **unnormalized form (UNF)**. An unnormalized table is one that does not meet the definition of a relation. Recall from earlier in this module that a relation is a two-dimensional table in which the entries in the table are single valued, each column has a distinct name, all values in a column are values of the same attribute (that is, all entries must correspond to the column name), and each row is distinct.

BTW
UNF
Some databases are intentionally designed to support unnormalized form. These databases are called nonrelational databases or NoSQL (Not-only SQL) databases.

The normalization process consists of multiple tests of the database's tables to ensure they meet certain rules. Removal of repeating groups is the starting point in the goal of having tables that are as free of problems as possible. In fact, in most database management systems, tables cannot contain repeating groups. A table (relation) is in **first normal form (1NF)** if it does not contain repeating groups.

In designing a database, you might have created a table with a repeating group. For example, you might have created a Closings Worked table in which the primary key is the Attorney ID and there is a repeating group consisting of Property ID and Attorney Fees. In the example, each attorney appears on a single row, and Property ID and Attorney Fees are repeated as many times as necessary for each attorney (Figure 11–12).

Closings Worked

Attorney ID	Property ID	Attorney Fees
A-001	P-003	350
A-002	P-008 P-005 P-006	350 350 250
A-003	P-002	1
A-004	P-001 P-007	250 250
A-005	P-004	250

repeating group (more than one entry in a single table location) indicates each of these attorneys is performing more than one closing

Figure 11–12

In the shorthand representation, you represent a repeating group by enclosing the repeating group within parentheses. The shorthand representation for the Closings Worked table from Figure 11–12 is shown in Figure 11–13.

Closings Worked (<u>Attorney ID</u>, Property ID, Attorney Fees)

Figure 11–13

Conversion to First Normal Form

Figure 11–14 shows the normalized version of the table. Note that the second row of the unnormalized table (Figure 11–12) indicates that attorney A-002 has closed properties P-008, P-005, and P-006. In the normalized table, this information is represented by *three* rows: the second, third, and fourth. The primary key for the unnormalized Closings Worked table was the Attorney ID only. The primary key for the normalized table is now the combination of Attorney ID and Property ID.

Closings Worked		
Attorney ID	**Property ID**	**Attorney Fees**
A-001	P-003	350
A-002	P-008	350
A-002	P-005	350
A-002	P-006	250
A-003	P-002	1
A-004	P-001	250
A-004	P-007	250
A-005	P-004	250

second, third, and fourth rows indicate Attorney A-002 has closed properties P-008, P-005, and P-006

sixth and seventh rows indicate Attorney A-004 has closed properties P-001 and P-007

Figure 11–14

In general, when converting a non-1NF table to 1NF, the primary key will typically include the original primary key concatenated with the key of the repeating group, that is, the field that distinguishes one occurrence of the repeating group from another within a given row in the table. In this case, Property ID is the key to the repeating group and thus becomes part of the primary key of the 1NF table.

To convert the table to 1NF, remove the parentheses enclosing the repeating group and expand the primary key to include the key to the repeating group. The shorthand representation for the resulting table is shown in Figure 11–15. Notice that the primary key is now the combination of the Attorney ID field and the Property ID field.

Closings Worked (Attorney ID, Property ID, Attorney Fees)

Figure 11–15

BTW

Primary Key for 1NF

Creating a compound primary key consisting of two fields is not the only way to convert an unnormalized table to 1NF. You could instead create a completely new field for the primary key. For example, for the Closings Worked table, you could add a new field called something like Assignment ID and make that field the table's primary key. Each assignment would then list the attorney ID, property ID, and attorney fees as functional dependencies.

Second Normal Form

Even though the following table is in 1NF, problems may exist that will cause you to want to restructure the table. In the database design process, for example, you might have created the Closings Worked table shown in Figure 11–16.

Closings Worked (Attorney ID, Attorney Last Name, Property ID, Property Street Address, Attorney Fees)

Figure 11–16

This table contains the following functional dependencies:

Attorney ID → Attorney Last Name

Property ID → Property Street Address

Attorney ID, Property ID → Attorney Fees

This notation indicates that Attorney ID alone determines Attorney Last Name, and Property ID alone determines Property Street Address, but it requires *both* an Attorney ID *and* a Property ID to determine Attorney Fees. Figure 11–17 shows a sample of this table.

Closings Worked

Attorney ID	Attorney Last Name	Property ID	Property Street Address	Attorney Fees
A-001	Hastings	P-003	46 Hwy 82 S	350
A-002	Black	P-008	4893 Alabama Hwy	350
A-002	Black	P-005	Route 15, Box 281	350
A-002	Black	P-006	87 Georgetown Rd, #2	250
A-003	Edwards	P-002	852 Scranton Dr	1
A-004	Konig	P-001	219 Phillips St	250
A-004	Konig	P-007	5377 Ohio St	250
A-005	Gomez	P-004	186 Alabama Hwy	250

same Attorney Last Name appears more than once

Figure 11–17

The name of a specific attorney, A-002 for example, occurs multiple times in the table. This redundancy causes several problems. It is certainly wasteful of space, but that is not nearly as serious as some of the other problems. These other problems are called **update anomalies**, and they fall into four categories:

1. **Update.** A change to the name of attorney A-002 requires not one change to the table, but several: you must change each row in which A-002 appears. This certainly makes the update process much more cumbersome; it is logically more complicated and takes longer to update.
2. **Inconsistent data.** There is nothing about the design that would prohibit attorney A-002 from having two or more different names in the database. The first row, for example, might have Black as the name, whereas the second row might have Blacks, a typo.
3. **Additions.** There is a real problem when you try to add a new property ID and its address to the database. Because the primary key for the table consists of both Attorney ID and Property ID, you need values for both these fields to add a new row. If you have a new property to add (that is, a purchase contract has been received by the office), but there is so far no attorney assigned to it, what do you use for an Attorney ID? The only solution would be to make up a placeholder Attorney ID and then replace it with a real Attorney ID once the attorney is assigned. This is certainly not an acceptable solution.
4. **Deletions.** In Figure 11–17, if you deleted Attorney A-003 from the database, you would need to delete all rows on which the Attorney is A-003. In the process, you would delete the only row on which property P-002 appears, so you would also lose all the information about property P-002. You would no longer know that the street address of property P-002 is 852 Scranton Dr.

These problems occur because there is a field, Attorney Last Name, that is dependent only on Attorney ID, which is just a portion of the primary key. There is a similar problem with Property Street Address, which depends only on the Property ID, not the complete primary key. This leads to the definition of second normal form. Second normal form represents an improvement over first normal form because it eliminates update anomalies in these situations. To understand second normal form, you need to understand the term, nonkey field.

A field is a **nonkey field**, also called a **nonkey attribute**, if it is not a part of the primary key. A table (that is, a relation) is in **second normal form (2NF)** if it is in first normal form and no nonkey field is dependent on only a portion of the primary key.

Note that if the primary key of a table contains only a single field, the table is automatically in second normal form. In that case, there could not be any field dependent on only a portion of the primary key.

Conversion to Second Normal Form

To correct the problems, convert the table to a collection of tables in second normal form, and then name the new tables. The following is a method for performing this conversion.

1. Take each subset of the set of fields that make up the primary key, and begin a new table with this subset as its primary key. The result of applying this step to the Closings Worked table is shown in Figure 11–18.

(Attorney ID,
(Property ID,
(Attorney ID, Property ID,

Figure 11–18

2. Place each of the other fields with the appropriate primary key; that is, place each one with the minimal collection of fields on which it depends. The result of applying this step to the Closings Worked table is shown in Figure 11–19.

(Attorney ID, Attorney Last Name
(Property ID, Property Street Address
(Attorney ID, Property ID, Attorney Fees

Figure 11–19

3. Give each of these new tables a name that is descriptive of the meaning of the table, such as Attorneys, Properties, and Closings Worked.

Attorneys

Attorney ID	Attorney Last Name
A-001	Hastings
A-002	Black
A-003	Edwards
A-004	Konig
A-005	Gomez

each attorney name appears only once

Properties

Property ID	Property Street Address
P-003	46 Hwy 82 S
P-008	4893 Alabama Hwy
P-005	Route 15, Box 281
P-006	87 Georgetown Rd, #2
P-002	852 Scranton Dr
P-001	219 Phillips St
P-007	5377 Ohio St
P-004	186 Alabama Hwy

Closings Worked		
Attorney ID	**Property ID**	**Attorney Fees**
A-001	P-003	350
A-002	P-008	350
A-002	P-005	350
A-002	P-006	250
A-003	P-002	1
A-004	P-001	250
A-004	P-007	250
A-005	P-004	250

Figure 11–20

The new design eliminates the update anomalies. An attorney's last name occurs only once for each attorney ID, so you do not have the redundancy that occurred in the earlier design. Changing an attorney's name is now a simple process involving a single change. Because the attorney's name occurs in a single place, it is not possible to have multiple versions of a name for the same attorney.

To add a new property, you create a new row in the Properties table, and thus there is no need to have an attorney already assigned to that property. In addition, deleting attorney A-003 has nothing to do with the Properties table and, consequently, does not cause property P-002 to be deleted. Thus, you still have the property's street address, 852 Scranton Dr, in the database. Finally, you have not lost any information in the normalization process.

Third Normal Form

Problems can still exist with tables that are in 2NF, as illustrated in the Closings table whose shorthand representation is shown in Figure 11–21.

Closings (Closing ID, Closing Date, Property ID, Purchase Price, Buyer ID, Buyer First Name, Buyer Last Name)

Figure 11–21

The functional dependencies in this table are:

Closing ID → Closing Date, Property ID, Purchase Price, Buyer ID, Buyer First Name, Buyer Last Name

Buyer ID → Buyer First Name, Buyer Last Name

As these dependencies indicate, Closing ID determines all the other fields. In addition, Buyer ID determines Buyer First Name and Buyer Last Name.

Because the primary key of the table is a single field, the table is automatically in second normal form. As the sample of the table shown in Figure 11–22 demonstrates, however, this table has problems similar to those encountered earlier, even though it is in 2NF. In this case, it is the first name and last name of a buyer that can occur many times in the table; see buyer B-007, Toni Vinter, for example.

Closings						
Closing ID	**Closing Date**	**Property ID**	**Purchase Price**	**Buyer ID**	**Buyer First Name**	**Buyer Last Name**
C-001	4/28/2029	P-001	568,000	B-001	Karla	Breeden
C-002	4/29/2029	P-002	281,000	B-002	Everett	Moller
C-003	4/30/2029	P-003	372,000	B-003	Celeste	Alberghini
C-004	4/28/2029	P-004	493,000	B-004	Violet	Pratt
C-005	5/3/2029	P-005	546,000	B-005	Riya	Sumner
C-006	5/16/2029	P-006	182,000	B-006	Gerald	Cleary
C-007	4/30/2029	P-007	150,000	B-007	Toni	Vinter
C-008	5/30/2029	P-007	209,000	B-008	Flora	Karstensen
C-009	6/2/2029	P-008	349,000	B-007	Toni	Vinter

buyer name appears more than once

Figure 11–22

This redundancy results in the same set of problems described previously with the Closings Worked table. In addition to the problem of wasted space, you have similar update anomalies, as follows:

1. **Updates.** A change to the name of a buyer requires not one change to the table but possibly several changes. Again, the update process becomes very cumbersome.
2. **Inconsistent data.** There is nothing about the design that would prohibit a buyer from having two different names in the database. Closing C-007, for example, shows the name of buyer B-007 as Toni Vinter, whereas in Closing C-009 (another closing with the same buyer B-007), the name might appear as Toni Winter (which contains a typo).
3. **Additions.** To add a new buyer to the database, they must have at least one closing (which most likely would be the case, but not always). For example, consider the situation in which Maryanne Webb, who has made an offer on a property, does not yet have a finalized purchase contract. She would like to register with Partners Law Firm now in order to schedule the closing soon, but you could not input her buyer information and schedule the closing without the property and closing information from the purchase contract. Perhaps you could create a fictitious property and closing for her while she waits for the sellers to sign the contract. Again, this is not a desirable solution to the problem.
4. **Deletions.** If a buyer, such as B-006, dies, you might delete or archive all the accounts of buyer B-006 from the database, and then you would also lose all information concerning each closing for that buyer. This could be problematic if your law firm needs to review information about that closing in the future.

These update anomalies are due to the fact that Buyer ID determines Buyer First Name and Buyer Last Name, but Buyer ID is not the primary key. As a result, the same Buyer ID, and consequently the same Buyer First Name and Buyer Last Name, can appear on many different rows.

You have seen that 2NF is an improvement over 1NF, but to eliminate 2NF problems, you need an even better strategy for creating tables in the database. Third normal form (3NF) provides that strategy.

Before looking at third normal form, you need to become familiar with the special name that is given to any field that determines another field, like Buyer ID in the Closings table. Any field or collection of fields that determines another field is called a **determinant**. Certainly the primary key in a table is a determinant. Any candidate key is a determinant as well. (Remember that a candidate key is a field or collection of fields that could function as the primary key.) In this case, Buyer ID is a determinant, but because several rows in the Closings table could have the same Buyer ID, that field is not a candidate key for the Closings table shown in Figure 11–22, and that is the problem.

A table is in **third normal form (3NF)** if it is in second normal form and if the only determinants it contains are candidate keys.

BTW
3NF
The definition given for third normal form is not the original definition. This more recent definition, which is preferable to the original, is often referred to as Boyce-Codd normal form (BCNF) when it is important to make a distinction between this definition and the original definition. This text does not make such a distinction but will take this to be the definition of third normal form.

Conversion to Third Normal Form

You have now identified the problem with the Closings table: it is not in 3NF. You need a way to correct the deficiency in the Closings table and in all tables having similar deficiencies. Such a method follows.

First, for each determinant that is not a candidate key, remove from the table the fields that depend on this determinant, but do not remove the determinant. Next, create a new table containing all the fields from the original table that depend on this determinant. Finally, make the determinant the primary key of this new table.

In the Closings table, for example, Buyer First Name and Buyer Last Name are removed because they depend on the determinant Buyer ID, which is not a candidate key. A new table is formed, consisting of Buyer ID as the primary key, Buyer First Name, and Buyer Last Name. Specifically, you would replace the Closings table in Figure 11–22 with the two tables shown in Figure 11–23.

Closings (Closing ID, Closing Date, Property ID, Purchase Price, Buyer ID)
Buyers (Buyer ID, Buyer First Name, Buyer Last Name)

Figure 11–23

Figure 11–24 shows samples of the tables.

Closings

Closing ID	Closing Date	Property ID	Purchase Price	Buyer ID
C-001	4/28/2029	P-001	568,000	B-001
C-002	4/29/2029	P-002	281,000	B-002
C-003	4/30/2029	P-003	372,000	B-003
C-004	4/28/2029	P-004	493,000	B-004
C-005	5/3/2029	P-005	546,000	B-005
C-006	5/16/2029	P-006	182,000	B-006
C-007	4/30/2029	P-007	150,000	B-007
C-008	5/30/2029	P-007	209,000	B-008
C-009	6/2/2029	P-008	349,000	B-007

Buyers

Buyer ID	Buyer First Name	Buyer Last Name
B-001	Karla	Breeden
B-002	Everett	Moller
B-003	Celeste	Alberghini
B-004	Violet	Pratt
B-005	Riya	Sumner
B-006	Gerald	Cleary
B-007	Toni	Vinter
B-008	Flora	Karstensen

buyer Toni Vinter appears only once

Figure 11–24

This design corrects the previously identified problems. Each buyer's name appears only once, thus avoiding redundancy and making the process of changing a buyer's name a very simple one. With this design, it is not possible for a buyer to have two different versions of their name in the database. To add a new buyer to the database, you add a row in the Buyers table; it is not necessary to have a preexisting property or closing for the buyer. Finally, deleting or archiving a buyer will not remove the closing records from the Closings table, so you will retain the closing and property information; all the data in the original table can be reconstructed from the data in the new collection of tables. All previously mentioned problems have indeed been solved.

Special Topics

In addition to knowing how to design a database and how to normalize tables, there are two other topics with which you should be familiar. First, you may be given a requirement for a database in the form of a document that contains data and business requirements for the database; for example, a rental agreement. In addition, you should know how to represent your design with a diagram.

BTW
Existing Documents
Other examples of existing documents could include purchase orders, procedure manuals, organizational policy manuals, inventory lists, insurance policies, and so on.

Obtaining Information from Existing Documents

Existing documents can often furnish helpful information concerning the database design. You need to know how to obtain information from a document that you will then use in the design process. An existing document, like the rental agreement for Water Fun Rentals shown in Figure 11–25, will often provide the details that determine the tables and fields required to produce the database.

Rental Agreement
Water Fun Rentals

1. Name: Tricia (First Name) Morris (Last Name) (Date of Birth (if Under 18))
2. Address: 460 West Longberg Rd (Street Address) Gainesville (City) SC (State) 29101 (Postal Code)

I understand that using kayaks and other boat types incurs risk. I release Water Fun Rentals from all responsibilities of liability, injury, or property damage.

3 Boat Rentals for Rental Number: R-123

Boat 1ALLDVAF7HA470011 (HIN) 1-person kayak, Water Systems, green (Type, Brand, Color)
Boat (HIN) (Type, Brand, Color)
Boat (HIN) (Type, Brand, Color)
Boat (HIN) (Type, Brand, Color)

Rental Date: 2/13/2029

Expiration Time
ATTN: This is the time your rentals are due to be returned to the dock. Missing this time will result in additional charges.
14:00

5. Signature Date of Signature (MM) (DD) (YY)

Figure 11–25

The first step in obtaining information from an existing document is to identify and list all fields and give them appropriate names. You also need to understand the business needs and policies of the organization. For example, in the rental agreement shown in Figure 11–25, the information on Water Fun Rentals is preprinted on the form, and it is not necessary to describe the company. The following is a list of the fields you can determine from the document shown in Figure 11–25.

Rental Number

Rental Effective Date

Rental Expire Time

Customer First Name

Customer Last Name

Address (Customers)

City (Customers)

State (Customers)

Postal Code (Customers)

Boat HIN

Boat Type

Boat Brand

Boat Color

Next, you need to identify functional dependencies. If the document you are examining is unfamiliar to you, you might have difficulty determining the dependencies and might need to get all the information directly from the user. On the other hand, you can often make intelligent guesses based on your general knowledge of the type of document you are studying. You might make mistakes, of course, and these should be corrected when you interact with the user. After initially determining the functional dependencies, you might discover additional information. The following are possible initial functional dependencies:

Customer ID → First Name (Customers), Last Name (Customers), Address (Customers), City (Customers), State (Customers), Postal Code (Customers)

Rental Number → Effective Date, Expire Time, Customer ID

HIN → Type, Brand, Color, Rental Number

You might realize that other attributes of the customer are required. For example, you might want to include the customer's telephone number and email address. If that is the case, then telephone number and email address are functionally dependent on the customer.

You might also realize that the rental agreement does not include any information about approved paddlers. For example, the customer shown in Figure 11–25 could be paying for a group of three friends who will be paddling together in their rented boats. In that case, you will need to add all information about the paddler entity and then also have an entity that combines the boat (HIN) with the paddlers who will operate each boat.

Given these corrections, a revised list of functional dependencies might look like the following:

Customer ID → First Name (Customers), Last Name (Customers), Address (Customers), City (Customers), State (Customers), Postal Code (Customers), Telephone (Customers), Email Address (Customers)

Paddler ID → First Name (Paddlers), Last Name (Paddlers), Address (Paddlers), City (Paddlers), State (Paddlers), Postal Code (Paddlers), Telephone (Paddlers), Email Address (Paddlers)

Rental Number → Effective Date, Expire Time, Customer ID

HIN → Type, Brand, Color, Rental Number

HIN, Paddler ID →

After you have determined the preliminary functional dependencies, you can begin determining the tables and assigning fields. You could create tables with the determinant—the field or fields to the left of the arrow—as the primary key and with the fields to the right of the arrow as the remaining fields. This would lead to the initial collection of tables shown in Figure 11–26.

Customers (<u>Customer ID</u>, First Name, Last Name, Address, City, State, Postal Code, Telephone, Email Address)
Paddlers (<u>Paddler ID</u>, First Name, Last Name, Address, City, State, Postal Code, Telephone, Email Address)
Rentals (<u>Rental Number</u>, Effective Date, Expire Time, Customer ID)
Boats (<u>HIN</u>, Type, Brand, Color, Rental Number)
Boat Paddlers (<u>HIN</u>, <u>Paddler ID</u>)

Figure 11–26

Adding the foreign key information produces the shorthand representation shown in Figure 11–27.

Customers (<u>Customer ID</u>, First Name, Last Name, Address, City, State, Postal Code, Telephone, Email Address)
Paddlers (<u>Paddler ID</u>, First Name, Last Name, Address, City, State, Postal Code, Telephone, Email Address)
Rentals (<u>Rental Number</u>, Effective Date, Expire Time, Customer ID)
FK Customer ID → Customers
Boats (<u>HIN</u>, Type, Brand, Color, Rental Number)
FK Rental Number → Rentals
Boat Paddlers (<u>HIN</u>, <u>Paddler ID</u>)
FK HIN → Boats
FK Paddler ID → Paddlers

Figure 11–27

At this point, you would need to verify that all the tables are in third normal form. If any are not in 3NF, you need to convert them. For example, if you had not determined the functional dependency of Effective Date and Expire Time on Rental Number earlier, you would have had Effective Date and Expire Time as fields in the Customers table. These fields are dependent on Rental Number, making Rental Number a determinant that is not a primary key, which would violate third normal form. Once you converted that table to 3NF, you would have the tables shown in Figure 11–27.

You might have already created some tables in your database design. For example, you might have obtained financial data on customers from the company's sales records following a recent social media campaign selling special event t-shirts. If so, you would need to merge the tables in Figure 11–27 with those tables you already created.

To merge tables, you combine tables that have the same primary key. The new table contains all the fields in either individual table and does not repeat fields that are present in both tables. Figure 11–28, for example, illustrates the merging of two tables that both have the Customer ID field as the primary key. In addition to the primary key, the result contains the City, State, and Postal Code fields, which are included in both the original tables; the Address, Telephone, and Email Address fields, which are only in the first table; and the Credit Card Number, Expiration Date, and CVV (Card Verification Value) fields, which are only in the second table. The order in which you decide to list the fields is immaterial.

BTW
Merging Entities
When you merge entities, do not assume that the merged entities will be in 3NF. Apply normalization techniques to convert all entities to 3NF.

Merging

Customers (<u>Customer ID</u>, First Name, Last Name, Address, City, State, Postal Code, Telephone, Email Address)

And

Customers (<u>Customer ID</u>, City, State, Postal Code, Credit Card Number, Expiration Date, CVV Code)

Gives

Customers (<u>Customer ID</u>, First Name, Last Name, Address, City, State, Postal Code, Telephone, Email Address, Credit Card Number, Expiration Date, CVV Code)

Figure 11–28

BTW

Storing Private Customer Data

Many types of data collected and stored about customers—such as customer names, addresses, and credit card numbers—are called personally identifiable information (PII). Most country and state governments require special protections for this data. Furthermore, some data requires additional layers of protection due to industry standards. For example, credit card information is protected by rules defined by the Payment Card Industry Data Security Standard (PCI DSS). Medical information in the United States is protected by the Health Insurance Portability and Accountability Act (HIPAA).

If you work with any of this protected information, you must understand the laws and regulations that apply, and be diligent to comply with these requirements. When hired by a company that handles this data, you should receive appropriate training relevant to the data you will encounter. If you start your own business, make sure to research the requirements for any data you will store. Many small business owners do not have the expertise on staff to establish secure payment systems and instead will contract with payment services to handle customer financial transactions. This arrangement provides small businesses with some protection from the liability of having access to legally protected customer data.

Diagrams for Database Design

You have now seen how to represent a database design as a list of tables, fields, primary keys, and foreign keys. It is often helpful to also be able to represent a database design with a diagram. If you have already created the database and relationships in Access, the Relationships window and Relationships report provide a helpful diagram of the design. Figure 11–29 shows the Access Relationship diagram and report for the Clearnet database. In these diagrams, rectangles represent tables. The fields in the table are listed in the corresponding rectangle with a key symbol appearing in front of the primary key. Relationships are represented by lines with the "one" end of the relationship represented by the number, 1, and the "many" end represented by the infinity symbol (∞).

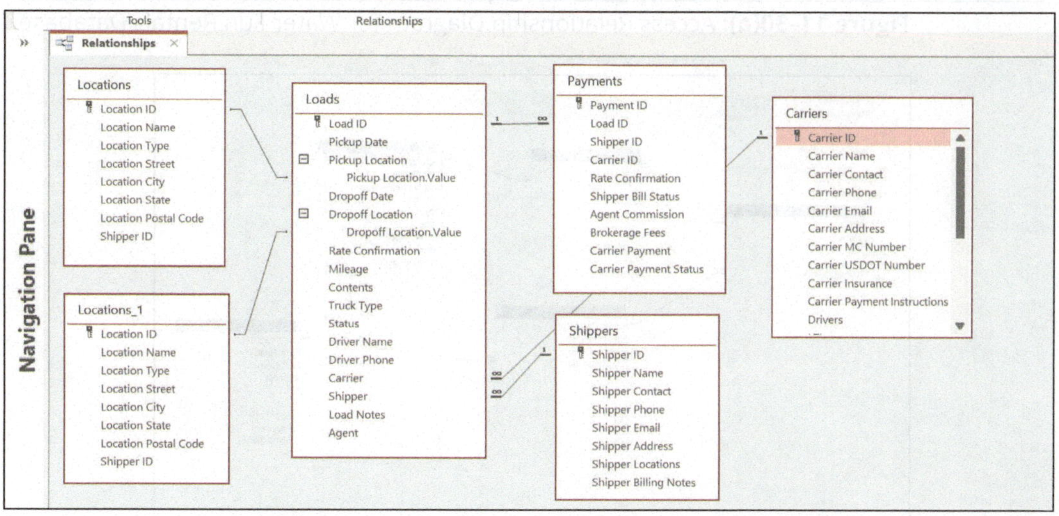

Figure 11–29(a): Access Relationship Diagram for Clearnet Database

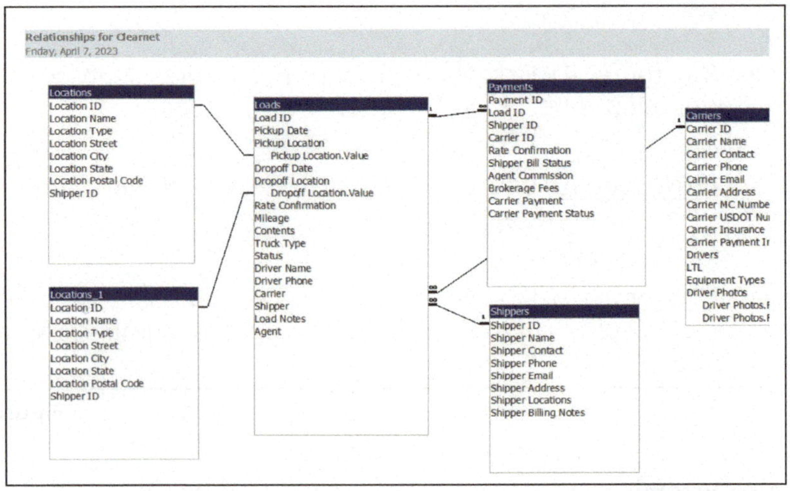

Figure 11–29(b): Access Relationship Report for Clearnet Database

Figure 11–30 shows the Access Relationship diagram and report for the Water Fun Rentals database.

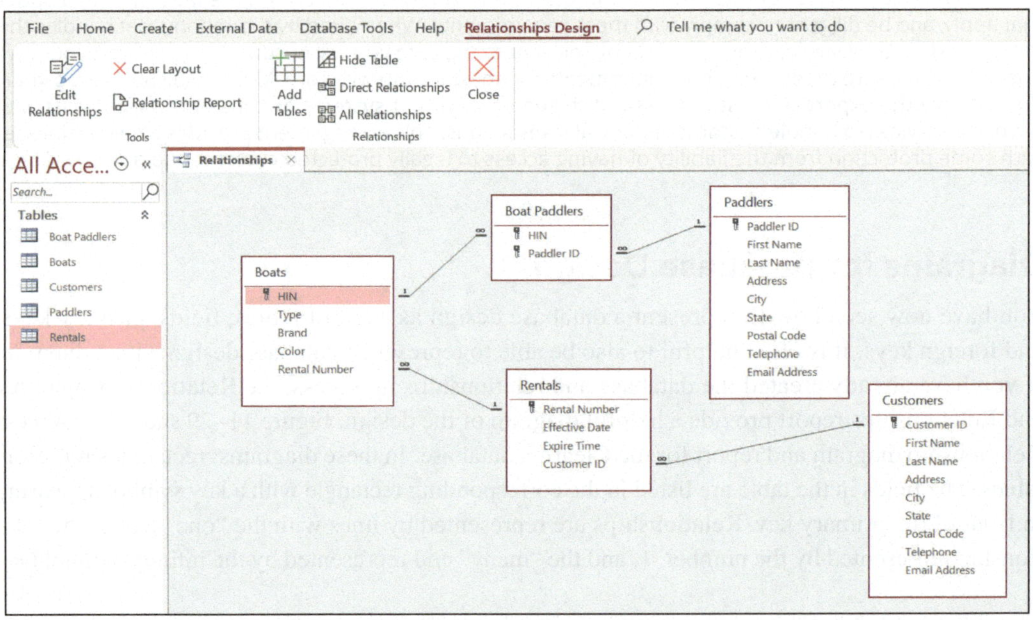

Figure 11–30(a): Access Relationship Diagram for Water Fun Rentals Database

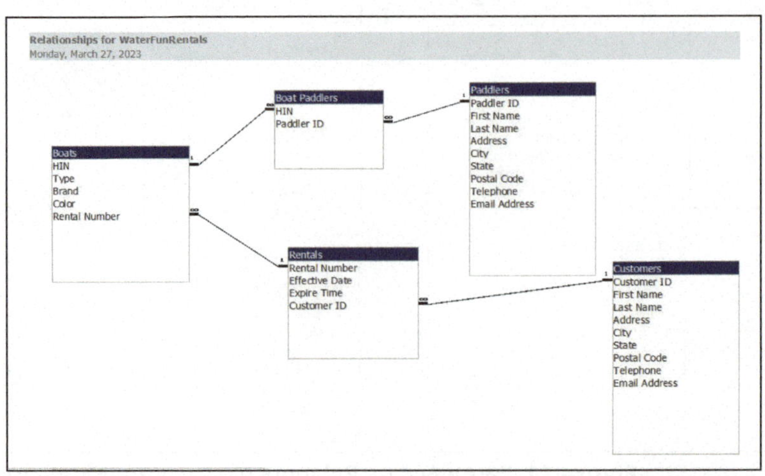

Figure 11–30(b): Access Relationship Report for Water Fun Rentals Database

Another popular option for diagramming a database design is the **entity-relationship diagram (ERD)**. Figure 11–31 shows a sample ERD for a portion of the Clearnet database. In this type of diagram, rectangles represent the tables. The primary key is listed within the table above a line. Below the line are the other fields in the table. The arrow goes from the rectangle that represents the "many" part of the relationship to the "one" part of the relationship.

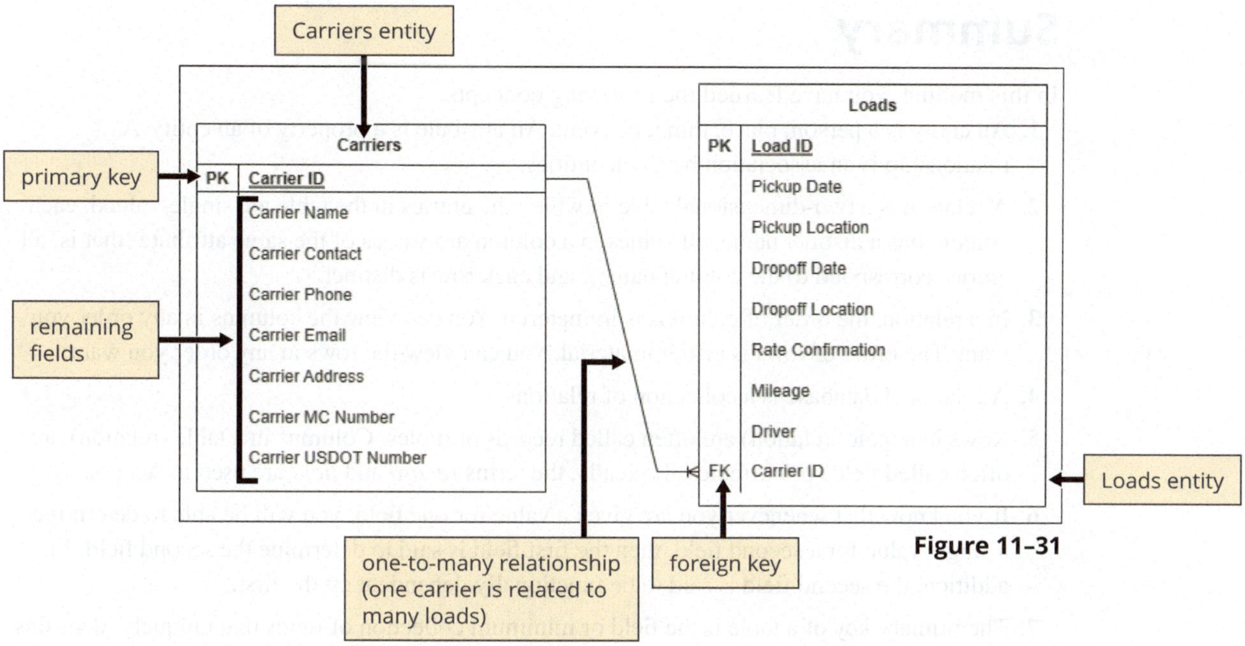

Figure 11–31

Figure 11–32 shows a similar diagram for the full Water Fun Rentals database.

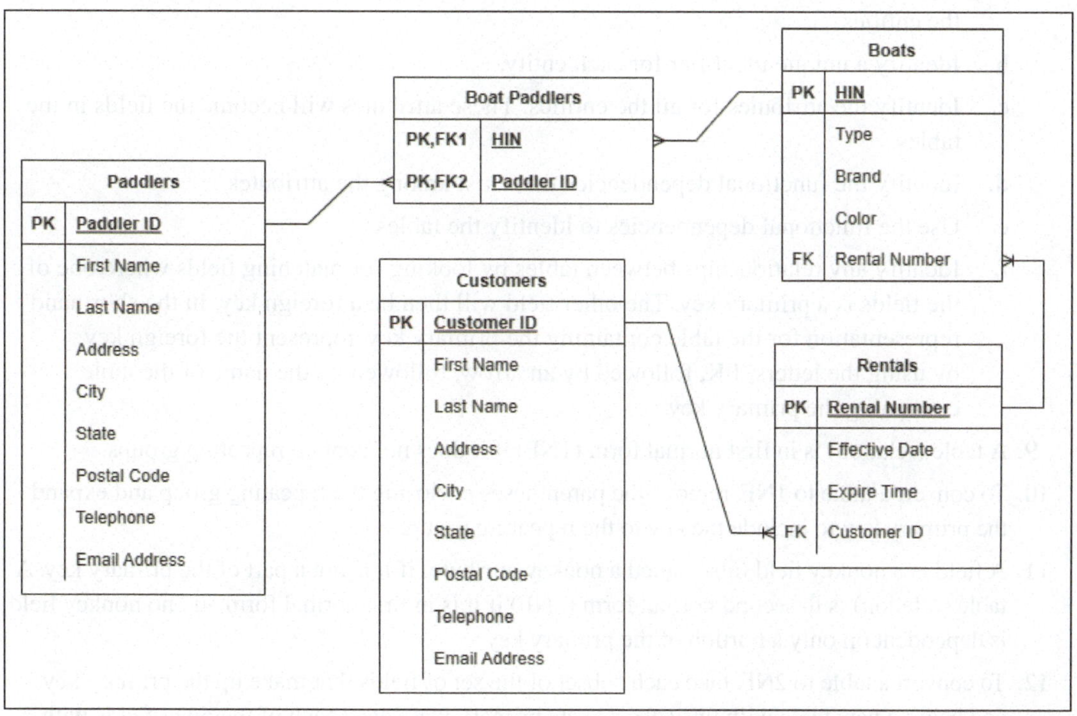

Figure 11–32

There are many options for such diagrams. Some options include more detail than shown in the figure. You can include, for example, such details as data types and indexes. Other options have less detail, showing only the name of the table in the rectangle, for example. There are also other options for the appearance of the lines representing relationships.

Summary

In this module, you have learned the following concepts.

1. An entity is a person, place, thing, or event. An attribute is a property of an entity. A relationship is an association between entities.
2. A relation is a two-dimensional table in which the entries in the table are single-valued, each column has a distinct name, all values in a column are values of the same attribute (that is, all entries correspond to the column name), and each row is distinct.
3. In a relation, the order of columns is immaterial. You can view the columns in any order you want. The order of rows is also immaterial. You can view the rows in any order you want.
4. A relational database is a collection of relations.
5. Rows in a table (relation) are often called records or tuples. Columns in a table (relation) are often called fields or attributes. Typically, the terms *record* and *field* are used in Access.
6. If you know that whenever you are given a value for one field, you will be able to determine a single value for a second field, then the first field is said to determine the second field. In addition, the second field is said to be functionally dependent on the first.
7. The primary key of a table is the field or minimum collection of fields that uniquely identifies a given row in that table.
8. The following is a method for designing a database for a set of requirements.
    a. Examine the requirements and identify the entities (objects) involved. Assign names to the entities.
    b. Identify a unique identifier for each entity.
    c. Identify the attributes for all the entities. These attributes will become the fields in the tables.
    d. Identify the functional dependencies that exist among the attributes.
    e. Use the functional dependencies to identify the tables.
    f. Identify any relationships between tables by looking for matching fields where one of the fields is a primary key. The other field will then be a foreign key. In the shorthand representation for the table containing the primary key, represent the foreign key by using the letters, FK, followed by an arrow, followed by the name of the table containing the primary key.
9. A table (relation) is in first normal form (1NF) if it does not contain repeating groups.
10. To convert a table to 1NF, remove the parentheses enclosing the repeating group and expand the primary key to include the key to the repeating group.
11. A field is a nonkey field (also called a nonkey attribute) if it is not a part of the primary key. A table (relation) is in second normal form (2NF) if it is in first normal form and no nonkey field is dependent on only a portion of the primary key.
12. To convert a table to 2NF, take each subset of the set of fields that make up the primary key and begin a new table with this subset as its primary key. Place each of the other fields with the appropriate primary key; that is, place each one with the minimal collection of fields on which it depends. Give each of these new tables a name that is descriptive of the meaning of the table.

13. Any field (or collection of fields) that determines another field is called a determinant. A table is in third normal form (3NF) if it is in second normal form and if the only determinants it contains are candidate keys.
14. To convert a table to 3NF, for each determinant that is not a candidate key, remove from the table the fields that depend on this determinant, but do not remove the determinant. Create a new table containing all the fields from the original table that depend on this determinant and make the determinant the primary key of this new table.
15. An entity-relationship diagram (ERD) is a diagram used to represent database designs. In ERDs, rectangles represent tables and lines between rectangles represent one-to-many relationships between the corresponding tables. You can also diagram a database design by using the Access relationship window.

Consider This: Plan Ahead

How should you submit solutions to critical thinking questions in the assignments?

Every assignment in this course contains one or more critical thinking questions. These questions require you to think beyond the assigned database. Present your responses to the questions in the format required by your instructor. Possible formats might include one or more of these options: write the answer; create a document that contains the answer; present your answer to the class; discuss your answer in a group; record the answer as audio or video using a webcam, smartphone, or portable media player; or post answers on a blog, wiki, or website.

Student Assignments

Apply Your Knowledge

Reinforce the skills and apply the concepts you learned in this module.

Understanding Keys and Normalization

Instructions: Answer the following questions in the format specified by your instructor.

1. Figure 11–33 contains sample data for a Competitors table in an art competition database. Use this figure to answer the following:

   a. Is the table in first normal form (1NF)? Why or why not?

   b. Is the table in second normal form (2NF)? Why or why not?

   c. Is the table in third normal form (3NF)? Why or why not?

   d. Identify candidate keys for the table.

Competitors				
CID	**FirstName**	**LastName**	**ContestID**	**ContestName**
23483	Nadra	Como	SA-1	Street Art
23423	Samuel	Oliver	PH-1	Photography
23480	Paulinha	Davies	DA-1	Digital Art
23468	Braden	Draper	SA-1	Street Art

Figure 11–33

2. Figure 11–34 contains sample data for tutors and clients who hire those tutors. In discussing the data with users, you find that tutor IDs—but not tutor names—uniquely identify tutors and their offered pay rate, and that client IDs uniquely identify clients. Multiple clients can use the same tutor and clients can use more than one tutor. For example, client Lizzy Haywood uses tutors Gena Romano and Sofie Roberts.

   a. Convert the data in Figure 11–34 into a relation in first normal form (1NF) using the shorthand representation used in this module. Recommend additional fields as needed to design a 1NF structure.

   b. Identify all functional dependencies using the notation demonstrated in the module.

Clients				
ClientID	**FirstName**	**LastName**	**TutorName**	**HourlyRate**
21	Felix	Coy	Sofie Roberts	$20
			Gena Romano	$25
			Stefan Tomczak	$20
24	Lizzy	Haywood	Gena Romano	$25
			Sofie Roberts	$20
27	Karoline	Janson	Karel Gott	$20
34	Conway	Ottosen	Stefan Tomczak	$20

Figure 11–34

3. **Consider This:** Using only the data in Figure 11–33, how could you identify the entities and attributes that would be the starting point for a database design? Include indications of the primary key for each table and any foreign keys.

Extend Your Knowledge

Extend the skills you learned in this module and experiment with new skills. You may need to use Help to complete the assignment.

Modifying a Database Design and Understanding Diagrams

Instructions: Answer the following questions in the format specified by your instructor.

1. Using the shorthand representation illustrated in this module, indicate the changes you would need to make to the Clearnet database design shown in Figure 11–8 so that a given load may be assigned to more than one carrier.
2. Using the shorthand representation illustrated in this module, indicate the changes you would need to make to the Water Fun Rentals database design shown in Figure 11–10 so that it supports the following requirements:
   a. Water Fun Rentals is expanding its business to rent rafts and large canoes for customers with children or others who will ride along as passengers but not as paddlers.
   b. Due to data security concerns related to minors, the company does not want to include data on individual children, only the number of passengers in each boat.
   c. In this expansion, the number of passengers must be recorded for each boat.
3. Use the Access Relationships Report for the Build It Construction database shown in Figure 11–35 to answer the following:
   a. What is the foreign key in the Subcontractors table?
   b. What is the primary key of the Job Sites table?
   c. What is the purpose of the Accounting table?

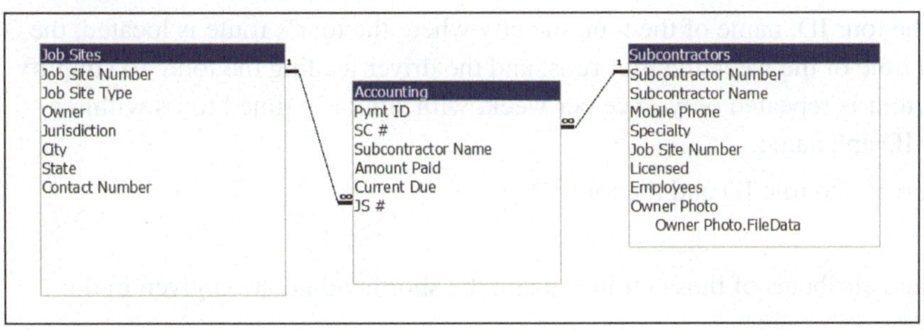

Figure 11–35

4. **Consider This:** Build It Construction has decided to add project managers to the database. One project manager can service many job sites, and job sites might use different project managers, depending on their needs. What changes would you need to make to the database design for Build It Construction?

Expand Your World

Create a solution, which uses cloud and web technologies, by learning and investigating on your own from general guidance.

Instructions: There are several websites that provide descriptions of various types of databases, including both relational and nonrelational databases. Comparing these database types helps clarify the purpose of each type and provides a good starting point for creating your own database design.

1. Create a blog, a Google document, or a Word document on OneDrive on which to store your assignment. Include your name and the current date at the beginning of the blog or document.
2. **Consider This:** Find a website of your choice that lists and describes different types of databases. For example, the MongoDB website provides a list and concise descriptions at mongodb.com/databases/types. What website did you choose and why?

Continued on next page

3. **Consider This:** Compare relational and nonrelational (also called NoSQL) databases in your own words. Other than Access for relational databases, give an example of each type.
4. Browse the different database types and select one (other than Access) in which you have an interest.
5. **Consider This:** In your own words, describe a scenario for which the database type would provide appropriate data storage and management. Why is the database type you chose better for this scenario than another database type would be?
6. **Consider This:** Why did you select the database type that you did? How easy was it to understand the elements of this database type? What design standards are required for this database type?

In the Lab

Design and implement a solution using creative thinking and problem-solving skills.

Lab: Designing a Database for Sunrise Bus Tours

Instructions: Sunrise Bus Tours is a downtown tour service with routes along area beaches and overlooks in three cities. You have been asked to create a database to keep track of the tourists, drivers, tours, and tour reservations. Use the concepts and techniques presented in this module to design a database to meet the following requirements, and record it using this module's shorthand notation style.

Part 1: The Sunrise Bus Tours database must support the following requirements:

1. For each bus driver, store their commercial driver's license (CDL) number, last name, first name, street address, city, state, postal code, telephone number, and date hired.
2. For each tourist, store their tourist ID, last name, first name, street address, city, state, postal code, telephone number, and email address.
3. For each tour offered, store the tour ID, name of the tour, the city where the tour's route is located, the price of the tour, the day and time of the week the tour runs, and the driver leading the tour. To simplify the design, assume that each tour is repeated only once per week, with similarly timed tours within a week being given a different ID and name.
4. For each tour reservation, store the tourist ID and the tour ID.

Based on these requirements:

5. Identify and list the entities and attributes of those entities using the shorthand notation given in this module.
6. Identify and list the functional dependencies using the shorthand notation given in this module.
7. Ensure that in both lists, the database is in third normal form (3NF). Identify all primary keys and foreign keys appropriately.

Submit your database design in the format specified by your instructor.

Part 2: **Consider This:** You made several decisions while designing this database. What was the rationale behind these decisions? Are there other requirements, such as specific business practices, that would have been helpful to you in the design process?

Index

Note: **Bold** page numbers refer to pages where key terms are defined.

A

E

F

Q

R

S

T

U

V

W

Y

9 780357 881668 90000